IL DUCE'S

Other Woman

IL DUCE'S

Other Woman

PHILIP V. CANNISTRARO
AND BRIAN R. SULLIVAN

William Morrow and Company, Inc.

New York

It is the policy of William Morrow and Company, Inc., and its imprints and affiliates, recognizing the importance of preserving what has been written, to print the books we publish on acid-free paper, and we exert our best efforts to that end.

Library of Congress Cataloging-in-Publication Data

Cannistraro, Philip V., 1942–
    Il Duce's other woman / by Philip Cannistraro and Brian Sullivan.
        p.   cm.
    Includes bibliographical references.
    ISBN 0-688-06299-7
    1. Sarfatti, Margherita, 1880–1961—Biography.   2. Authors,
Italian—20th century—Biography.   3. Jews—Italy—Biography.
4. Mussolini, Benito, 1883–1945—Friends and associates.
I. Sullivan, Brian R., 1945–   .   II. Title.
PQ4841.A78Z88   1992
945.091′092—dc20   92–7446
[B]   CIP

Printed in the United States of America

First Edition

1   2   3   4   5   6   7   8   9   10

BOOK DESIGN BY DOROTHY SCHMIDERER BAKER

To Renzo De Felice

$\mathcal{Preface}$

We began this book attempting to solve a mystery. One rainy afternoon in February 1984, Philip Cannistraro told Brian Sullivan that letters from Benito Mussolini to his lover and confidante, Margherita Sarfatti, might be in the United States. Renzo De Felice, the distinguished historian of Italian Fascism, had confided the story to Phil in Rome the previous year. It appeared that more than thirty-five years earlier, Sarfatti had sold these letters—some twelve hundred of them, written over the course of perhaps fifteen years—to an American plastic surgeon, Dr. I. Daniel Shorell. Mysteriously, however, they had never surfaced.

Following the clues provided by Professor De Felice, we began to search for the letters, which would surely contain not just the record of a love affair but a chronicle of the origins and development of the Fascist dictatorship. Sarfatti had been not only Mussolini's lover but his most trusted political adviser.

We located members of Dr. Shorell's family, who confirmed much of Professor De Felice's story and supplied us with copies of several of Mussolini's letters to Sarfatti. They could not, however, explain the fate of the originals. (What actually happened to the letters is explained in the last chapter of this book.)

While searching for the missing letters, we discovered Margherita Sarfatti. Like many women, she had been deliberately written out of history. Not only did Mussolini try to deny Sarfatti's part in the creation of Fascism, but after he had made his alliance with Hitler, he could not tolerate public knowledge that a woman and a Jew had done as much as she had to build the Fascist regime. In the final years of his dictatorship, Mussolini made Sarfatti a non-person. To save herself and her family, she cooperated. As a result, even before her death, Margherita Sarfatti faded into insignificance. For those who remembered her at all, she seemed no more than the object of Mussolini's longest love affair. Claretta Petacci, through the gruesome display of her corpse alongside his, gained perpetual notoriety as

Mussolini's most cherished mistress. Margherita Sarfatti acquired the status of just "the Duce's other woman." The horrors of World War II, the desire of most Italians to forget their Fascist past, the embarrassment of Sarfatti's relatives over her personal and political relationship with Mussolini, completed the burial of her memory.

Much to our astonishment, we eventually learned that Sarfatti had exercised a profound influence on Mussolini and that many of her ideas had shaped the nascent Fascist movement and its ideology. A brilliant woman of exceptional learning and culture, Sarfatti did much to attract prominent intellectuals and artists to the regime. Moreover, apart from Mussolini, she had been a major figure in Italian cultural life in her own right for almost half a century.

The worldly, sophisticated Sarfatti was born Margherita Grassini, the daughter of wealthy Jewish parents from Venice. Under the guidance of prominent private tutors, she developed a lifelong interest in art, literature, and languages, a taste for stimulating conversation, and a thirst for the clash of ideas. As a rebellious but idealistic teenager, she became a Socialist and a feminist. In 1898 she married Cesare Sarfatti, a somewhat older lawyer whom she converted to her Socialist faith. They had three children. During an intense, crowded professional life as a journalist and one of Italy's first women art critics, she managed to write two dozen books and thousands of newspaper articles. She knew and corresponded with many famous cultural and political figures, and presided over one of the most important salons of the era. Among her friends and acquaintances she counted Marconi, D'Annunzio, Boccioni, Colette, Toscanini, Matisse, Marinetti, Gide, Cocteau, Pirandello, Ezra Pound, Josephine Baker, even Fannie Hurst and Hermann Göring. Sarfatti had tea at the White House with Franklin and Eleanor Roosevelt, dined on the Nile with Crown Prince Umberto and Princess Maria Josè, spent the weekend with William Randolph Hearst at San Simeon, floated in a gondola with George Bernard Shaw, toured Mexico City with Diego Rivera, and received a bedside violin serenade from Albert Einstein.

But from the time their lives became linked in 1912, the most important person in Sarfatti's life was Benito Mussolini. He, too, was a Socialist then, although from the revolutionary wing of the movement, and had just been appointed editor of the party newspaper, *Avanti!*. A fiery but unpolished provincial, Mussolini stood in sharp contrast to Sarfatti. Yet their mutual attraction was intense and passionate. Together they confronted the political crisis produced by the outbreak of World War I, redefining their Socialist ideals with an intense nationalism and forging a new revolutionary force known as Fascism. Over the next four years, Sarfatti's ideas, wealth, and emotional support sustained Mussolini through a violent struggle for power. After Mussolini became the youngest prime minister in the country's history in 1922, Sarfatti helped guide him to full power and shaped his personal dictatorship as Italy's twentieth-century Caesar. As the biographer, trusted confidante, and intellectual mentor to the Duce, Sarfatti became one of the most influential women in interwar Europe.

But their intimacy, which was the basis for Sarfatti's significant but informal power, soon waned. Mussolini's personal isolation and megalomania grew at the same time that their physical relationship cooled. As the dictatorship hardened in the early 1930s, Mussolini increasingly insisted on blind obedience, ideological conformity, and a narrow chauvinism. These trends, together with a Fascist antipathy toward both foreign influences and women, seriously undermined Sarfatti's position within the regime. The fact that for twenty years she had been a vigorous champion of modern, international currents in cultural life now made her suspect. Moreover, Sarfatti's opposition to Mussolini's growing attachment to Hitler made her a target of attacks from those increasingly influential Fascist leaders who advocated anti-Semitism and an alliance with Nazi Germany. Her forced departure from Italy in 1938, the year Mussolini instituted his own anti-Semitic policies, proved her salvation. Sarfatti escaped the Holocaust by her exile in South America. When she returned home in 1947, Mussolini was dead and the Fascist regime destroyed.

After eight years of reading Sarfatti's prose, searching for insights into her mind and character, and writing about her life, we still feel ambivalent about our subject. As historians we felt the need to retain an objective attitude toward our subject. But interviews with her son, daughter, and grandchildren gave us a flattering vision of Sarfatti through the eyes of those who had loved her and granted us a sense of the powerful influence of her personality. Furthermore, Sarfatti's cultural sensitivity, her support for talented artists and writers, and her enormous intelligence, all render her an exceptionally interesting and compelling figure.

While we came to admire her intellectual accomplishments, Sarfatti does not seem to have been easy to like. She was often greedy, calculating, thirsty for power, arrogant, opinionated, and self-centered. More important, though, we recognized that Sarfatti deserved a great deal of responsibility for the imposition of a brutal tyranny on her country. The fact that she was the target of attacks from the most vicious elements in the Fascist movement stimulated only a small degree of sympathy for her. In the end, we found it impossible to characterize her as a victim, except to the extent that she was a victim of forces that she herself had done so much to create.

Acknowledgments

We wrote and rewrote this book over six years. Originally, each of us created chapters that reflected our individual expertise or interests. Philip Cannistraro dealt with those aspects of Margherita Sarfatti's life that touched on art, architecture, and culture. He also wrote the sections describing her early and late years. Brian Sullivan covered the parts of Sarfatti's life affected by politics, war, and diplomacy. However, our editor, Maria Guarnaschelli, wisely suggested that some sections of our manuscript be reorganized. Consequently, the three of us rearranged the text and created some composite chapters. As a result, the sections written solely by Philip Cannistraro are Chapters 1 through 6, 10, 19 through 21, 24, 30, and 31. Brian Sullivan wrote Chapters 7, 9, 11, 16, 17, 23, and 25 through 29. Chapters 8, 12 through 15, 18, and 22 are jointly authored. Each author also wrote short sections of the other's chapters.

This book would not have been possible without the support and active assistance of scores of people on four continents. We wish to express our sincere gratitude to all of them.

First and foremost, we wish to acknowledge the cooperation of those members of the Sarfatti family who shared with us their memories and documents. We are especially grateful to the late Amedeo Sarfatti (1902–1989) and the late Countess Fiammetta Sarfatti Gaetani (1909–1990), son and daughter, respectively, of Margherita Sarfatti. Their interest in our efforts to write a biography of their mother, and their willingness to allow us to pry into family matters in order to reconstruct historical events, were important to our work. Both also provided us with photographs.

Amedeo Sarfatti, a tall, gentle, and engagingly shy man, not only answered our endless questions with openness and sincerity, but also put at our disposition those of his mother's letters and documents in his possession. His wife, Pierangela Daclon Sarfatti, also liberally shared her recollections with us and allowed us access to the unpublished memoir written by her late husband. Their daughter, Professor Magalì Sarfatti-Larson of Philadelphia, supported our work with the intellectual sympathies of a scholar, the fond memories of a granddaughter, and the unquestioning generosity of a friend. Thanks also to her husband, Charles Larson, and her brother Roberto Sarfatti of Milan.

Countess Fiammetta Gaetani, who in her seventies was still an attractive, graceful woman of sharp intelligence, answered our numerous queries with alacrity, showed us some of the documents in her possession, and never hesitated to disagree with our assessments. Her daughters Margherita Manili, Ippolita Gaetani, and Sancia Gaetani also provided assistance.

Professor Renzo De Felice, the premier scholar of Italian Fascism, not only suggested the topic but repeatedly demonstrated his support and generosity by providing us with valuable documents, sources, and leads, and using his extensive contacts to gain us entry to private and public archives. Our debt to him is enormous.

A large number of research institutions in Italy, Great Britain, Belgium, France, Switzerland, Israel, and the United States put their resources at our disposal. These include the libraries and repositories of the following institutions: the Archivio Centrale dello Stato, Rome, the Archivio Storico d'Arte Contemporanea della Biennale, Venice, the Archivio Storico del Ministero degli Affari Esteri, Rome, Balliol College, Oxford, the Biblioteca Comunale di Imola, the Biblioteca Nazionale Centrale in Florence and its counterparts in Rome and Venice, the Biblioteca di Storia Moderna e Contemporanea in Rome, the Bibliotèque Nationale, Paris, the Boston Public Library, Boston University, Brandeis University, University of California at Berkeley, University of California at Los Angeles, the Central Zionist Archives, Jerusalem, Chicago Public Library, Columbia University, Dartmouth College, Drexel University, the Fondazione Primo Conti, Fiesole, Georgetown University, Harvard University, the Hoover Institution, the Hollywood Academy of Motion Picture Arts and Sciences, the University of Indiana at Bloomington, the University of Iowa, the Library of Congress, the Long Island Historical Society, Marymount College, the National Archives, the New Hope Free Library, the New York Public Library, New York University, the University of Pennsylvania, Princeton University, the Public Record Office, London, Radcliffe College, the University of South Carolina, Columbia, Stanford University, Syracuse University, the University of Texas, Austin, Trinity College, Washington, D.C., and Yale University.

In Italy, Dott. Mario Missori of the Archivio Centrale dello Stato was, as always, anxious to help by putting his unparalleled knowledge of the Fascist archives at our disposal. Nicoletta Alegi provided us with a number of skillful translations. Gregory Alegi tracked down documents and located books and articles for us with great enthusiasm and skill. Our thanks also to Paolo Balbo, Rossana Bossaglia, Viviana Bottai, Massimo Carrà and Luca Carrà, Gherardo Casini, Lanfredo Castelletti of Como, Lucio and Rosa Ceva, Ester Coen, Caterina Del Vivo of the Gabinetto G. P. Vieusseux, Francesco Lefebvre D'Ovidio, Nelda Ferace and Fiorella Superbi of the Berenson Archives at the Villa I Tatti, Emilio Gentile, Elisabeth Giansiracusa, Leonardo Gori and Signora Gori, Giordano Bruno Guerri, Giuseppe Longo of the Vittoriale, Luce Marinetti, Sergio Marzorati, Lamberto Mercuri, Pietro Pastorelli, Jens Petersen, Luca Picchi, John J. Reich, Gianfausto Rosoli of the Centro Studi Emigrazione, Michele Sarfatti of the Centro di Documentazione Ebraica Contemporanea, Gianguido Scalfi, Aglae Sironi and Andrea Sironi, Riccardo Terzoli of the Biblioteca Comunale di Como, and Niccolò Zapponi. We also express our thanks to the following: in Canada, Robert J. Young; in England, John Gooch, Sir Anthony Havelock-Allan, W.N.M. Lawrence, Denis Mack Smith, Meg Sweet, and Shirley Zangwill; in France, Edmonde Charles-Roux, Stéphane Dujarric, and Mme. Salome Chalandon; in Israel, Dr. Renato Spiegel of the Central Archives for the History of the Jewish People, and Simonetta Della Seta of Jerusalem; in Switzerland, Dr. Diana Ruesch of the Prezzolini Archives in the Biblioteca Cantonale, Lugano. Robert Dujarric offered unstintingly of his time over many years to do research for us in England, France, Belgium, and Japan.

In the United States, several people were especially generous in giving of their time and expertise. Emily Braun, whose important work on Mario Sironi and Fascist cultural policy has been an inspiration, shared unselfishly of her research, knowledge, and her critical insights. Terry M. Simpson of Washington, D.C., tracked down materials from libraries and archives and made the research process easier. Kathleen Hill offered greatly appreciated support at a very difficult moment during the initiation of this project. Doris Ranck Rend generously offered us complete access to the papers of her father, T. V. Ranck, and later donated them to Yale University.

Dr. Alvin Bernstein, former head of the Strategy Department of the Naval War College, and Captain Bob Watts of the Naval War College Foundation arranged major financial support for an investigation into questions concerning the Mussolini diaries. At Drexel University, Dean Thomas L. Canavan and Vice-President Richard W. Schneider also provided valuable support at various points in the work.

We are grateful for the assistance of the following individuals: Jacques Barzun, Joel Blatt, Michael Blim, Sandra Buchman, Art Buchwald, Tita Brown-Castellanos, H. James Burgwyn, Taylor Coffman, Richard Oliver Collin, Natalie Zemon Davis, Alexander J. De Grand, Eleanor Lansing Dulles, Richard Dunlop, Monte S. Finkelstein, Piero Foà, Richard and Judy Greaves, Stephen Neil Greengard, Michael Hembree, the Hill family,

H. Stuart Hughes, the late Frank Gervasi, Mac Knox, Dan H. Laurence, Mr. and Mrs. Harold Lightman, Anne Child Lindsley, the late Clare Boothe Luce, Elizabeth MacIntosh, the late Lydia W. Malbin, Aldo Marchini, Jay Massey, Chris N. Nacci, Robert O. Paxton, Frances W. Roosevelt, Carol Ann Rusche, Thomas L. Schumacher, Irene Mayer Selznick, Ellen R. Shapiro, Joel Sorkin, Fritz Stern, Marcia E. Vetrocq, Adam Vital, Mrs. Christine Willcox, and Sasha Zeif.

Our thanks to Richard Binder, Eric Dorn Brose, Patricia A. Cooper, Julie Mostov, Nunzio Pernicone, Ellen C. Rose, Cecil O. Smith, Julia Southard, Donald F. Stevens, and Vivien Thweatt of Drexel University, and to the late Roberto Lopez, Steve Gillon, Paul Kennedy, Jonathan Spence, and Henry Turner of Yale University. Daniel James of Duke University obtained microfilm copies of *Mussolini: Como lo Conocí* from Buenos Aires. Peter Groesbeck of Drexel skillfully reproduced numerous photographs and drew the maps that appear in this book.

Laura K. Fleming deserves special mention for uncovering the papers of I. Daniel Shorell, Gianguido Scalfi, Guido Orlando, and especially, T. V. Ranck. Her uncounted hours of research and editing helped create this book.

Our agent, Charlotte Sheedy, and our editor, Maria Guarnaschelli, both believed in this book, showed uncommon patience in the face of our uncertainties and delays, and brought their considerable professional skills to bear in making this a far better book. Maria Guarnaschelli also chose the title of our biography. Our appreciation also to Katharina Buck and Chas Edwards.

Brian Sullivan is required to state that nothing in this book reflects the policies or positions of the United States government, the National Defense University, or the Institute for National Strategic Studies.

One last and particularly pleasant duty remains: to acknowledge the two people whose support and assistance throughout the project cannot be adequately expressed—Robert S. Browning and Laura K. Fleming. They shared with us at every step of the way the highs and lows of the research and the writing of this book, and for eight years allowed too much of their lives to be consumed with the search for Margherita Sarfatti.

Contents

Part Four THE FALL

Part One

THE RED VIRGIN

MODERN ITALY

1

In the Garden

At age seventy-two, Margherita Sarfatti began her memoirs with nostalgic impressions of the garden she played in as a child. Scented by cherry blossoms and the damp fragrance of a canal along the Fondamenta della Misericordia, the garden seemed to her to be a biblical paradise. "I have already looked into heaven," runs one of her lyric poems: "at the age of five I stood at the threshold of contested Eden."

For Margherita, the Garden of Eden was an apt image, since she regarded her life as a process of casting off the restraints of innocence. She grew up in a realm of protection and dependency, and as a child she clung fiercely to it. Only upon reaching adolescence did she begin consciously and deliberately to make the choices that tore down the protective walls of her childhood. She continued making those rebellious choices for the rest of her life.

She was born Margherita Grassini on April 8, 1880, in a fifteenth-century *palazzo* located in that section of Venice known as the Old Ghetto. She was the fourth and last child of Emma and Amedeo Grassini, rich and cultured members of Venetian Jewish society.

When Amedeo Grassini entered his daughter's name in the city registry, it was one of the few times that her date of birth was recorded accurately. One day a half century later, when Margherita took out her passport in order to have it renewed, she suddenly realized that it gave away her age. Taking an eraser and a pen, she carefully altered the zero in 1880 to a three—a small but psychologically important advantage, for the prospect of turning fifty unsettled her. Perhaps she chose 1883 because it was the year Mussolini was born.

The Grassini *palazzo* stood at the edge of the Old Ghetto, where a handful of wealthy families still lived among the many poor Venetian Jews. Community life centered around the five historic synagogues of the district, which were dominated by a number of long-established families. The Grassinis were relative newcomers, having moved to Venice barely a generation earlier. Nevertheless, Amedeo's wealth made him one of the respected Jewish *signori*.[1]

Margherita's memoirs contain only a few passing, though tender, references to her mother, who perhaps exercised little impact on her early development. An urbane woman, Emma Grassini read English novels and had her dresses made by a Parisian designer, but her attitudes were those of an upper-middle-class leisured *signora*. Servants and cooks abounded in the Grassini household, and Margherita had her own governess, a young Swiss woman who tutored her and shared her confidences. She was deeply attached to her governess, whose kind affection she easily manipulated.

Margherita wanted for nothing that money could buy. Her childhood passed as an idyll of games and adventure in her garden. The Grassinis, true to their upper-middle-class status, tried hard to shelter their daughter from life beyond the confines of home. She was not allowed to play with other children in the neighborhood or to leave the garden unattended. Yet the denizens of the narrow streets of the Old Ghetto inevitably intruded on Margherita's sanctuary. Each Saturday evening, the poor of the neighborhood came to the front door of the *palazzo* to receive alms from her father. She could see for herself that others were less fortunate, and that this imposed certain charitable responsibilities on the rich. On walks with her governess, she passed dank, crumbling working-class homes, populated by swarms of soiled children and their invariably pregnant mothers. She never forgot the pinched face of one small, squalid boy who peered at her "wide-eyed" through the garden gates, "hungry for my paradise." As Margherita gradually became aware of her advantages, stirrings of conscience and uncertainty began to trouble her.

Even as a young girl Margherita claimed to sense the precarious nature of her happiness. Each night, before going to bed, she repeated a prayer asking God that she might know how to be grateful for all the beautiful and good things she had. She would often ask her governess for reassurance that "nothing would happen" to her. Though her mother always woke her on birthday mornings with kisses and a doll, birthdays brought with them a combination of joy and sadness. She remembered guessing that adulthood would mean "expulsion" from the joys and safety of her garden.

The large, dark rooms of the Grassini *palazzo*, illuminated only by candlelight, frightened her and riddled her dreams with nightmare visions of witches, savage beasts, and death. She knew that ferocious creatures lurked inside closets and behind drapes, but despite the derisive taunts of her older sisters, she forced herself to confront the monsters. "How my heart beat," she later wrote, "as I pulled the curtains aside!"[2]

A studio photograph, taken when Margherita was about ten, shows another side of her nature, one that was willful and spoiled: She is sitting in a white lace dress belted with a tartan scarf, crowned by a feathered bonnet; the fingers of her plump young hands touch each other demurely, yet the right foot is pushed forward and sits on its heel just pertly enough to suggest her self-assurance. Her rather large head is tilted slightly to the right, her long curls fall to her shoulder, and her dark, deeply set eyes look directly at the camera. It is the frown of the sensuous mouth and the slightly protruding lower lip, however, that give away the personality and complete the picture—intelligent, serious, and determined. The photograph reveals the precociously mature face of a beautiful young girl.

As she matured into adolescence, Margherita grew more sensitive to the beauty of her surroundings. Venice offered an enchanted setting in which to grow up, especially for a young girl with her advantages. Steeped in its history since youth, she credited the old city with shaping much of her own experience and character.[3]

In the 1890s, when Margherita grew into her teens, Venice was still a high point of the European grand tour. Foreigners were charmed by the romance of a world frozen in the past: "a refined civilization," as she explained to Mussolini many years later, "heading toward sunset like the post-Periclean Athens of Alexander the Great." The vast wealth accumulated by the Venetians had enabled them to build a city unmatched for opulence and artistic splendor. Margherita explored the city with her governess, visiting the countless churches, museums, and public buildings that displayed voluptuous masterpieces of Venetian Renaissance art. A lifetime later, she remembered the glittering fantasies of Byzantine mosaics, the richly colored marbles and tiled roofs of the city's palaces, the sun reflecting off its canals, all blazing vividly against the airy blues of its sky and the roseate tints of its clouds, just as in the vibrant paintings of Giorgione and Tintoretto. These paintings and the Venice they represented taught her to see the world with a keen sense of line and color. In later years, her admirers often noted that the stylish dresses and jewelry she chose set off her full body, deep gray-green eyes, and reddish-blond hair, as if in deliberate imitation of Titian.[4]

The charmed Venetian environment nurtured a delicate tension between her mind and body. Tradition has it that the sultry Venetian air, combined with the impermanence of a city built on water, inclines its inhabitants to a romantic sensibility and the pursuit of sensuous pleasures. But Margherita believed that the seductive Venetian manner also hid a core of "vulgar and brutal lust." Only a shrewd sense of commerce offset the romantic passions of her fellow Venetians, and she frankly applauded her own temperament as being a harmonious blend of the sensuous and the intellectual. She concluded that "ideas untouched by the senses are useless, if not actually harmful. They do not lead us to truth."[5]

Despite the city's beauty and romance, there were repressive aspects of Venice. Its decaying buildings wore heavily on the soul, and its countless small canals and narrow, dead-end streets created a sense of claustrophobia. For Margherita welcome relief came each summer when the Grassini family left for Conegliano. She spent her days hiking through forests and climbing hills in the rugged countryside of the Veneto or swimming off the Adriatic coast. Most important, the summer months offered her precious hours with her maternal grandparents, Dolcetta and Giuseppe Levi.[6]

Dolcetta Levi was "Nonna Dolcetta" to her grandchildren, and was described by one of them as "short and fat, like a ball . . . she always had indigestion because she ate too much." Margherita remembered her "tottering on short legs and tiny feet that could hardly sustain her weight." Nonna's strong personality deeply affected Margherita. She tolerated neither laziness nor inactivity. She arose before sunrise, ordering her family and servants about with the air of a drill sergeant and keeping a careful eye on her son-in-law's administration of her estates. Despite the family's wealth, she acted as frugal as a peasant, watching her money carefully, although always giving food to the panhandlers who begged at her door. Her brother, a famous physician, had taught her the importance of fresh air and exercise, and every morning she made sure the mattresses were aired and the children chased out of doors for walks.

In addition to running a large household, Dolcetta found time to read and educate herself. The Levi home was filled with books, and at sixty she was taking French, German, and English lessons along with her grandchildren. From her they learned that women could be strong and determined in mind as well as in character.

Dolcetta was nevertheless a complicated woman. The intricacies of her life taught Margherita a valuable lesson about their male-dominated Italian culture. Dolcetta knew that her husband had an illegitimate family, but still looked after his needs with solicitous care. She pretended to ignore her husband's infidelity without sacrificing her own strong and independent personality. "Morally," Margherita later wrote, "Dolcetta was an eighteenth-century rationalist," unaffected by notions of romantic love, whose sighs and regrets she rejected as "futile sentimentalism, as useless baggage and weakness." Margherita understood that Dolcetta's philosophy provided a self-protective device.

Dolcetta's death presented the first real tragedy in her teenage granddaughter's life. Margherita tried to console herself with Nonna's admonition "to live without looking back." But the lessons offered by her grandmother's life were painfully mixed.[7]

The Grassinis habitually left Conegliano in August for Bagni della Porretta, a fashionable mountain spa in the Apennines, where Margherita's asthmatic father took the cure. Their particular friends there were the Marconis, whose son Guglielmo developed an infatuation for Margherita. She never forgot their warm summer nights together in the hills, where he taught her to identify the constellations. The two remained friends long after the boy had become world famous as the inventor of wireless radio.[8]

Margherita's father also represented an important focus of her early life. Amedeo Grassini was the center of family power, the keeper of its Judaic traditions, and a highly respected Venetian. He set the values by which he wished his family to live—political conservatism, a sense of responsibility, belief in authority and religion, and social respectability. As the patriarch of a prominent and wealthy family, he was greatly concerned with status. He felt pride that his first two daughters had brought him marriage alliances with two old and prominent Jewish clans. But Margherita was clearly his favorite, and with her he acted hopelessly indulgent. She readily handled his occasional bouts of bluster, knowing in the end she would have her way.

He was descended from Jews who had settled on the Adriatic coast. His grandparents, Laudadio and Sarina Gentilomo, came from Pesaro, where exiled Spanish and Portuguese Jews had built a thriving community after their expulsion from the Iberian peninsula in the fifteenth century. One of Pesaro's most prominent Jewish families, the Gentilomos ran the city's import trade from Turkey and the Middle East. Laudadio himself was a loan banker and shipowner.[9]

Because Pesaro belonged to the papacy, its Jewish subjects were often the target of oppression. The Gentilomo family was prevented from owning land, attending universities, and working in the papal administration, and was forced to pay heavy financial levies. This injustice was temporarily ended in 1797 when Napoleon Bonaparte seized Pesaro. As the French army conquered city after city, Bonaparte proclaimed the emancipation of the Jews, earning the support of Laudadio and the other leaders of the Jewish community.

But after the fall of Napoleon's short-lived Kingdom of Italy in 1814, the papacy reestablished its control over Pesaro. A grand inquisitor stamped out heresy and reimposed the old restrictions on the Jews. In 1828, the Jews were ordered to sell all real property within five years. Three years later, when a local revolt broke out and Pope Gregory XVI unleashed a new wave of violence against his rebellious subjects, Laudadio, Sarina, and their three daughters fled Pesaro for Venice.

There the Gentilomos found relief from persecution, for the city boasted a long tradition of tolerance. Since the early Middle Ages, the stubborn independence and vast wealth of a merchant aristocracy had enabled the Venetians to resist the uncongenial policies of the Roman

Church, so that even Jews found a remarkable degree of freedom. Large numbers of Sephardic Jews had come to Venice after 1492, when Ferdinand and Isabella expelled them from Spain and southern Italy. In 1516, city fathers rejected a papal demand to expel the Jews, deciding instead to segregate them in a restricted community called the *ghetto* after the Venetian word for the metal foundry located in the newly established Jewish quarter.

Life for Jews was better there than in most other Italian states. They were permitted to engage in commerce, own shops, and interact socially with Christians. The government did extract onerous financial tribute from them, but in return gave them centuries of relative security.[10]

After the fall of Napoleon's empire, Venice and its surrounding hinterland were ceded to the Austrian Empire, a fortunate circumstance because Emperor Joseph II had decreed Jewish emancipation in Austrian territories: Jews could own land, attend schools and universities, and even hold posts in the state administration and the army.

Laudadio Gentilomo was said to have arrived in Venice with "a ship full of money." Laudadio prospered once again as a moneylender—in 1985, his great-great-grandson, Amedeo Sarfatti, himself a banker, still joked about Laudadio's "usurious" business. Once established in Venetian Jewish society, the Gentilomos commissioned a noted artist to paint their portraits. More than a half century later, Margherita rediscovered these portraits, long forgotten in the attic of her family home. She was delighted both by the skillful hand of Michelangelo Grigoletti, whom she likened to Goya, and by the likeness of Sarina, known in family lore for her beauty as "la bella Sarina."[11]

In 1842, one of the Gentilomo daughters married Marco Grassini.[12] Margherita was their granddaughter.

The Grassinis traced their family back to 1518, when a Caliman Grassini lived in Venice. Caliman's descendants later moved to Conegliano, where they prospered in the agricultural market and in silk manufacturing. Marco was born there in 1816. Although educated as a lawyer at the University of Padua, he devoted much of his energy to introducing modern farming techniques to the extensive lands he had inherited in the Conegliano area.[13]

Marco Grassini married Colomba Gentilomo at a time when Italian patriots still dreamed of the united and free Italy Napoleon had promised to establish. In Marco's teens in the early 1830s, revolutionaries had made repeated attempts to overthrow Italy's repressive monarchs and free its territory from the Austrians. Once he had come of age, the goal of a single Italian state fired the enthusiasm of Marco, who foresaw like other liberal middle-class landowners that unification would bring the advantages of free trade.

In 1848, Colomba gave birth to a son, Amedeo. Margherita's future father was the first of three children. Margherita never knew Colomba Grassini, who died before she was born. And though she hardly remembered her grandfather, she affectionately described him as "a moderate conservative in politics and a moderately religious Jew"—a remark occasioned by Marco's unusual choice of a Christian for a second wife. Though he continued to practice Judaism and raise his children as Jews, Marco was married in a Catholic ceremony performed by the cardinal patriarch of Venice. His marital alliance proved to be of great advantage to his son Amedeo.[14]

Amedeo was raised in an era of unrest and revolution, in which his father took an active part. Marco joined the efforts of his fellow Venetians in 1848 and 1849 to win freedom from their Austrian rulers, and went unpunished when those efforts failed. This period in Italian history is called the Risorgimento, or "resurgence"—suggestive of the rebirth of the Italian spirit after centuries of subjugation to foreign princes and local tyrants. Italy's poets and heroes had long dreamed of unity and independence, but the upheavals provoked by the French Revolution and Napoleon's invasions spread these ideas throughout the Italian middle class.

Some followed the indefatigable conspirator Giuseppe Mazzini, who argued for a democratic republic created by popular revolution. Others supported Piedmont's ruler, Vittorio Emanuele II, and his brilliant, devious prime minister Count Cavour. Their supporters were willing to forgo a democratic republic for a Kingdom of Italy under Vittorio Emanuele as the price for unity and national freedom. After Cavour in 1858 enlisted the assistance of Emperor Napoleon III of France for a war against the Austrians, Italian patriots separately instigated revolutions in central Italy and an invasion of the south under the daring leadership of Giuseppe Garibaldi. In the end Garibaldi joined forces with Cavour to avoid civil war, and in 1861 Cavour proclaimed a new Kingdom of Italy, though the territories of Venice, Trento, and Trieste remained under the Austrian yoke and Rome still languished under papal domination.

In 1866 King Vittorio Emanuele II joined the Prussians in another war against Austria and took Venice as his prize. That August, a royal decree proclaimed all citizens—including Jews—equal before the law. Marco's prominence in the unification movement won him election in 1866 to the municipal council of Conegliano. His fellow councilmen then overwhelmingly chose him as mayor, a position he held for eleven years. He was probably the first Jewish mayor elected in the Kingdom of Italy. Marco spent the town's budget conservatively, but his administration built a hospital and a theater, and the first school of viniculture and wine production in the country. In 1868, Vittorio Emanuele made Marco a Knight of the Crown of Italy. Later on, Marco also served as mayor of San Fiore, a small town near Conegliano, and as a member of the provincial council in the district capital of Treviso.[15]

Late in 1870, Marco moved his family to Venice, settling near the Old Ghetto district to the north of the Grand Canal, where most Venetian Jews still lived. They bought the lovely fifteenth-century gothic *palazzo* on the Fondamenta della Misericordia, whose garden Margherita so loved. In May 1885, when Margherita was five, Marco became ill and died, his family at his bedside. His funeral was attended by many prominent Venetians and city officials.[16]

Amedeo Grassini made the most of the new opportunities that unification offered. Many of Italy's Jews had, like his father, been in the forefront of the national struggle. Unification meant opportunity, and Jews entered into the universities, public administration, and politics. Because Italian Jews were recognized as particularly loyal citizens of the new state, a surprising number became generals and admirals, a situation unique among Europe's military establishments.

Amedeo Grassini provided a model of the new Italian Jew. Heir to a large fortune, scion of a well-connected family, he combined the new Italian civic consciousness with a sharp eye for the business opportunities that came with public office. Like Marco, Amedeo was trained as a lawyer at the University of Padua, but sometime in the 1870s he abandoned private practice to become a fiscal attorney for the Venetian city government. He also succeeded his father as mayor of the village of San Fiore and served as president of the Monte di Pietà, an important charitable organization, as well as head of the Talmud Torah Hebrew School. Amedeo managed the family's country properties while holding municipal office, but he was also sensitive to the growing entrepreneurial spirit of the times. With great foresight, he invested in a number of urban business enterprises that increased both his fortune and his status.[17] His first public recognition came in 1890, when King Umberto I made him, as his father had been before him, a Knight of the Crown of Italy.[18]

Intensely religious, Amedeo Grassini regularly attended the Scuola Grande Tedesca (the Ashkenazi synagogue), strictly observed shabbat, and was active in the Jewish community. But his father's second marriage also gave him entrée to Catholic circles and an appreciation for the advantages of good relations with the Church.

In Treviso, Amedeo met Giuseppe Sarto, a parish priest of peasant origins. Sarto was poor and full of folksy common sense, but his piety and shrewd intelligence impressed Amedeo. The two became fast friends, and as Sarto rose in the Church hierarchy over the years, he relied increasingly on Amedeo's advice and financial generosity.[19]

A most eligible bachelor, Amedeo in about 1870 met and married Emma Levi, the daughter of a family from Trieste. The Levis also owned property in Conegliano and knew the Grassinis. Emma's mother, Margherita's treasured Dolcetta, had left Conegliano at the age of sixteen to marry Giuseppe Levi, a prosperous banker from Trieste. The Levi household was much given to intellectual pursuits and produced several generations of eminent personalities. Emma's uncle, the famous Dr. Giacinto Namias, had been court physician in Vienna; one of her nephews, Cesare, was a theater critic, and another, Giuseppe, a biologist. Giuseppe's daughter, Natalia—Margherita's cousin—became a distinguished writer and the wife of the anti-Fascist literary critic Leone Ginzburg. The strong cultural traditions of the Levi family complemented the entrepreneurial energies of Amedeo Grassini.[20]

There was no better indication of his breadth of vision than his alliance with Giuseppe Sarto. Amedeo's influence and status increased markedly after 1893, when Sarto rose to the exalted position of cardinal patriarch of Venice. Although the broad-minded Sarto was more than willing to accept other Jewish business leaders into the circle of his associates, none was as close to him as Grassini, and few could claim the patriarch as a frequent dinner guest.

The two men shared the same cautious views in matters of politics. In 1890, after years of political power wielded by a conservative faction, a new municipal administration had come into office in Venice. The recently widened franchise resulted in the election of a progressive city council and a dynamic, liberal mayor, Riccardo Selvatico. Sarto and Grassini considered Selvatico a political disaster. His strong anti-clerical views had led him to oppose religious instruction in schools, while his liberalism had resulted in official support for Socialist efforts to organize the city's workers into unions. Selvatico had replaced a long-standing policy of fiscal restraint with what seemed to be wildly uncontrolled public spending, going so far as to authorize the creation of an expensive, biennial art exhibition under municipal auspices—the now famous Venice Biennale.

Determined to oppose Selvatico's threat to the status quo, the wily Cardinal Sarto organized an effective opposition to the new administration. In doing so, he broke with a long-standing papal policy forbidding Catholics to take part in the political life of the "Godless" Italian state, which had seized Rome from the papacy in 1870. Sarto was nonetheless convinced that Catholics had an obligation to oppose the election of dangerous radicals and atheistic Socialists, and concluded a political pact in 1895 between moderate and conservative pro-clerical leaders to support a common list of candidates.[21]

The pro-clerical candidates swept the elections for the city council, thus ousting the progressive Selvatico government. Sarto's success at once opened new avenues for profit to Grassini and his friends, who set up private investment groups to exploit the growing need for municipal services and urban development. Along with Giuseppe Musatti, the head of the city's Jewish community, Amedeo Grassini formed a consortium to establish the city's public boat transportation system of steam-powered *vaporetti*. Another of his groups developed the Venetian beach known as the Lido, building a series of luxurious hotels along the fashionable resort strip, including the Hôtel des Bains later made famous by Thomas Mann's novella *Death in Venice*.

Early in their marriage, Amedeo and Emma Grassini had two daughters, Nella and Lina, and a son, Marco. Because Margherita was born six years after the last of the others, she grew up enjoying the kind of affection that parents, servants, and older siblings often lavish on the youngest child. That she was also beautiful only enhanced her special status as family favorite. Margherita soon became—and remained—a very spoiled little girl.[22]

In 1894, Amedeo Grassini decided to move his family out of the Old Ghetto district, as many successful Jewish businessmen were doing, and into a home that better reflected his growing stature. The new Grassini residence was a Gothic palace known as Palazzo Bembo, named after Cardinal Pietro Bembo, an illustrious historian and poet who was born there in 1470. Palazzo Bembo was an imposing, massive structure that faced the Grand Canal, just south of the Rialto Bridge, along the Fondamenta del Carbon. When John Ruskin, the distinguished English art theorist, first saw the building in 1849, it had fallen into sad disrepair, its bottom stories having been converted into a coal warehouse. Yet Margherita's father knew, as Ruskin did, that at one time Palazzo Bembo was "among the most noble in effect on the whole Grand Canal," and he proceeded to restore it to its former grandeur. As an added mark of distinction, he installed the first elevator in Venice to help him ascend its five high floors.

The huge, stately rooms of the *palazzo* served as impressive reception areas for the many distinguished guests from the world of politics, culture, business, and the Church whom the Grassinis entertained with increasing frequency. In 1898, King Umberto raised Amedeo's social standing further by awarding him the insignia of the prestigious Order of Saints Maurizio and Lazzaro. Basking in what Margherita chidingly called their "ultra bourgeois" status, the Grassini family had reached the pinnacle of status and success. Margherita, just turned fifteen, was never again to see her garden.[23]

2

Wide Vistas of Thought

Margherita blossomed into a strikingly pretty teenager with long reddish-blond hair and deep gray-green eyes. Intellect dominated her personality. Her inquiring and highly retentive mind enabled her to engage adults with a self-assurance startling in a girl of her age. She was often the center of attention, and she reveled in it. Her obvious brilliance was cultivated by her parents, but not through a conventional education.

As Margherita described it, "I have always been a student, but I never went to school." Her intellectual training was initiated by her mother and her Swiss governess, who between them taught her the rudiments of reading, writing, and mathematics, as well as a basic knowledge of French, German, and English.[1] The cultural life the Grassinis led also contributed to her development. Amedeo kept a permanent box at Venice's famous La Fenice Theater where Margherita regularly attended operas and concerts. Emma Grassini was an enthusiastic reader of novels in several languages. When Margherita began reading, her mother was happy to feed her hunger for books, and after "tantrum and cajolery" even allowed her to attend a lecture by the scandalous writer Gabriele D'Annunzio.[2]

Margherita later confessed to possessing "an insatiable appetite for beautiful things." The stirrings of social conscience she experienced as a child did not mitigate her desire to possess the things she admired. At age twelve, she was allowed to bid on a lovely but unsigned portrait of Mary Magdalene at an art sale. None of the other buyers could bring themselves to deprive the self-assured young girl of the prize—which experts subsequently identified as a painting from the school of the Baroque master Guido Reni. The portrait was the first acquisition in what was to become one of the most important private art collections in Italy.[3]

Margherita could not have enjoyed a more stimulating environment at home. Her father cultivated the company of intelligent and refined people to grace his dinner table. Margherita's exposure to prominent intellectuals and artists soon taught her the art of the salon—she later admitted that the experience made her a lifelong "collector of celebrities."[4]

Legal restraints and social convention severely limited opportunities for women everywhere in Europe in the late nineteenth century. Italy was a predominantly agricultural society where traditional mores hardly had been affected by industrialization and urban life. Religion and a deeply entrenched patriarchal culture kept women in a status subordinate to men. The only respectable paying work available to women was in the fields, in the burgeoning textile mills in the north, or in the case of the lower middle class, in careers as servants, teachers, governesses, and nurses.

A tiny fraction of Italian women enjoyed Margherita's leisured status, but even they were scarcely liberated. Laws passed in the 1870s enabled women to own land, but control of the property generally passed to the husband. Men could sue for divorce on the basis of adultery, but women could not. Girls from prominent families were not encouraged to pursue formal education—convention dictated the development of social graces, not intellects. Professional careers remained closed to women. Volunteer charity work provided the only outlet for women of Margherita's class.[5]

Margherita rebelled against all such restrictions. She took no interest in domestic affairs. Fortunately her parents condoned her thirst for knowledge; when she turned fourteen the Grassinis hired private tutors for their precocious daughter.

Three men—Pietro Orsi, Pompeo Molmenti, and Antonio Fradeletto—gave Margherita an education of extraordinary quality, rigor, and breadth. All three men combined academic careers with an active public life. Margherita gained the unforeseen advantage of a close acquaintance with three influential men, each one of whom would serve, over the course of the next twenty-five years, as a deputy and then as a senator in Parliament.

Orsi was a historian in his early thirties. He had written extensively about the Middle Ages, but had begun to focus on contemporary Italian history. Orsi taught Margherita the history of Italy's long struggle for unification, which he traced for her back to the Renaissance. Together they studied the efforts of Mazzini, Garibaldi, and Cavour in forging disparate Italian states into a nation. Orsi argued that a nation's history was reflected in its cultural and intellectual progress as much as in wars and politics. This lesson she never forgot.[6]

The forty-two-year-old Molmenti was an acknowledged expert on Venetian life and culture. His works included an elegant three-volume social history of Venice, and several important volumes on Venetian Renaissance painting. His monographs on Carpaccio argued that the cycles of huge paintings executed by that fifteenth-century painter—whose canvases Margherita saw first hand in the Accademia—were efforts to achieve a symbolic integration of the Venetian social classes, from the privileged aristocracy to the gondoliers and workers. With him Margherita surveyed the history of art, her education structured around the idea that painting and sculpture reinforced civic values.

Fradeletto influenced Margherita's values more than her other two tutors. A native of Venice, Fradeletto had in 1894 already won a degree in literature, worked as a drama critic, written a successful comedy, and become a popular and provocative lecturer on art, literature, and music. Fradeletto had supported Selvatico, and it was he who persuaded the radical mayor to sponsor the Biennale. Thus it might seem surprising that Amedeo Grassini chose Fradeletto to tutor his daughter. But when Cardinal Sarto unseated Selvatico, Fradeletto adroitly switched allegiance to the Sarto camp, ensuring his biennial art exhibition was not canceled. He argued, and the new city council agreed, that municipal sponsorship of the exhibit would bring Venice international attention—and that, in turn, would mean a substantial increase in tourism and commerce. The council appointed Fradeletto secretary-general of the Biennale, a position he held for almost twenty years. Amedeo Grassini admired Fradeletto's political realism, and appreciated the fact that the younger man's interest in reform had never included support for Socialism. He and Fradeletto actually shared conservative social views and a deep sense of patriotism. Moreover, Fradeletto's prominence as a man of deep artistic and literary erudition made him the obvious choice as a tutor for a pupil with Margherita's cultural interests.[7]

Fradeletto imbued Margherita with his belief that the cooperative spirit of traditional society had broken down under the impact of the selfish class interests and excessive devotion to individualism that characterized modern capitalism. Influenced by Schopenhauer and Nietzsche, whose works Margherita now read, Fradeletto preached the need for a collective national will that would inspire all Italians to work together for their country's greatness. He did not believe in democracy. Because, in his view, the ignorant working class responded only to emotional appeals rather than to ideas, it was the moral responsibility of an educated elite to rule the masses.

Fradeletto enjoyed a tense, high-spirited relationship with his young pupil. He soon found her to be too independent and sharp-witted to accept blindly all his views. He was able to fire Margherita's imagination with a love of art and literature, and she faithfully read the books he gave her. She also enjoyed discussing provocative unassigned books, and scandalizing him with her modern views. And though she absorbed some of his political and social theories, she rejected others as old-fashioned nonsense.

Fradeletto interpreted art and literature in the light of his political philosophy. Looking to ancient Rome for his model, he convinced Margherita that all truly creative art arose from a unified culture—where beliefs, customs, and aspirations were not divided by dissension or conflict. Margherita accepted this view, and agreed that all great literature and art had come from societies that followed the ancient Roman example. Certainly this teaching was bolstered by the views Orsi and Molmenti held concerning the relationship between a society and its culture. She found similar views expounded by her favorite modern poet, Giosuè Carducci, whose masterpiece, *Barbarian Odes,* exalted a new pagan consciousness and the inspirational example of Imperial Rome.[8]

Fradeletto introduced Margherita to the works of John Ruskin. Margherita was fascinated by the elaborate principles Ruskin set forth in *The Seven Lamps of Architecture,* where he argued that churches, palaces, and houses were like books in which a people wrote their national character. *The Stones of Venice* influenced her even more. Ruskin believed that the medieval Gothic architecture of Venice reflected the social vitality and civic virtue of the city during its heyday, whereas the less original Renaissance architecture showed that the city later rejected things of the spirit in favor of materialism and pleasure. "John Ruskin helped me to understand Venice," Margherita later wrote. "[I]ts dreaming palaces, canals and lagoons, its gorgeous churches, monuments and museums and its mystic islands . . . taught me the love of art." When she herself chose art criticism as a profession, Ruskin's theories continued to guide her.

Margherita learned more from Ruskin than Fradeletto intended to teach her. She linked Ruskin's argument concerning the moral function of art to Fradeletto's ideas about social unity, and concluded that art could both reveal and *reform* a people's spirit, morality, and politics. Her study of Italian history under Orsi reinforced the idea that art was much more than a private affair reserved for an educated elite. She learned how past rulers had deliberately used painting, sculpture, and architecture to create particular political attitudes among their subjects. She came to believe that government had a duty to sponsor artistic creativity and to control the values expressed through art.[9]

Ruskin's writings taught Margherita to reject the notion of art for art's sake, because art must express values. The most important aspect of a painting or a building was its "ethical" meaning—that is, the social concept of morality that inspired the artist. Great art reflected the highest ideals of the human spirit. Ruskin's eloquent arguments convinced her that the real function of a critic was to explain an artist's ideals rather than his or her style or technique.

So deep was Ruskin's influence on Margherita that more than half a century later she explained her dislike of Caravaggio to fellow art critic Bernard Berenson in these terms:

> Well, frankly, the more I see of him [Caravaggio], the less I love him. Of course he is a very great painter & a master of his craft. But such a nasty spirit, so, may I say, <u>vulgar</u>? Low, rather. Rembrandt touches mud & by his magic it becomes a spiritual hymn to mystery, love & beauty. Caravaggio handles beautiful creatures, gold & brocades or young beautiful bodies & faces, & they turn to fiendish mud. Am I old-fashioned, to still set such value on soul & loftiness? Maybe my Ruskin years have left me since my fifteenth, or tenth, birthday marked to old-fashioned ideas and, yes, why not?, ideals.

Within a year of beginning lessons with Fradeletto, Margherita was able to see her tutor put into action his conception of art as an agent of civic pedagogy. King Umberto inaugurated the first Venice Biennale exhibit in 1895, when she was fifteen years old. Paintings from more than a dozen countries were exhibited, and most in attendance judged it to be a resounding success—except for Margherita Grassini.

The Biennale proved to be a major point of contention between Margherita and her tutor. He had no patience for modern currents of art, especially those that tended toward abstraction, which he called "aesthetic atomism," or the breaking down of realistic objects into unrecognizable parts. Fradeletto therefore influenced the exhibit's selection committee in favor of the stodgy representational art then in vogue, known as "academic" painting.[10]

His young student was impressed with what she knew of the bold new work of the French Post-Impressionists, as well as the Art Nouveau and Symbolist currents just then emerging, and she objected to Fradeletto's prejudice. She was able to use her master's Ruskin against him. In *Modern Painters* Ruskin had extolled the genius and power of J.M.W. Turner against the Victorian artistic establishment of his day. At fifteen Margherita was also beginning to champion artistic modernism.

Fradeletto guided Margherita's reading in the great masterpieces of Western literature. She showed scant interest in classical authors, but later recalled how her introduction to Dante "opened up wide vistas of thought and vision." The poet's epic journey into hell, purgatory, and heaven led her to reflect on the relationship between the visible world and the world of the spirit. His depiction of Lucifer, and of sin, punishment, and damnation, left an especially deep mark on her. Margherita saw *The Divine Comedy* not only as a grand allegory but as a literal guide for human life.

Dante was to be in some ways as profound an influence as Ruskin, for in the 1920s Margherita began using a heavily annotated copy of the book as an oracle, consulting it concerning the important events in her life.[11] Because of Fradeletto she read deeply also in Petrarch and Machiavelli. Shakespeare was perhaps the only Renaissance writer from outside Italy with whom she became familiar, but she virtually memorized his *Hamlet*.

Her preference, to Fradeletto's distaste, was for modern works, and she devoured novels and poetry in Italian, English, German, and French. Her adolescent process of self-discovery led her naturally to the romantic poets, and especially to Percy Bysshe Shelley. She recalled "weeping with joy at the overwhelming beauty of some lines of *Prometheus Unbound*." Shelley's romantic idealism and his defiance of sexual and religious convention fed her growing distaste for her family's bourgeois gentility. Alessandro Manzoni's *I promessi sposi* (*The Betrothed*), a romantic tale of two lovers kept apart by human cowardice and tumultuous political events, kept her in the house "even on the finest day at the Lido." Realist novelists such as Balzac and Hugo broadened her awareness of injustice, poverty, economic exploitation, and the oppression of women. *A Doll's House*, Henrik Ibsen's play about a middle-class wife who walks out of a confining, conventional marriage, strongly impressed her. When Margherita first encountered Marxism in her mid-teens, literature had already provided an imaginative basis for her advocacy of feminism and political Socialism. Her discovery a few years later of George Bernard Shaw's works reinforced her convictions.

Rebellion was stirring post-unification Italy. Writers, poets, dramatists, and artists were exposing the shortcomings of Italian society in an effort to upset the staid, unheroic conventions of late-nineteenth-century Italian life. The lyrical works of Mario Rapisardi, a Sicilian poet, appealed to Margherita. She was familiar with his translation of Shelley's *Prometheus Unbound*, and his epic *Lucifer*. His appeal to her and to the nascent Socialist movement was strengthened by his defense of the poverty-ridden southern peasantry. Giovanni Pascoli, the introspective poet whose mystical-symbolist works also reflected Socialist ideas, was another favorite.

Margherita was attracted too to the irreverent Bohemian writers whose lives were as scandalous as their works. Gabriele D'Annunzio's plays and novels, as well as his outrageous personal life, reflected the "decadent" vogue of the period. She found him entrancing. She also admired Oscar Wilde, whose trial and imprisonment as a result of his affair with Lord Alfred Douglas caused an international scandal in 1895. She saw D'Annunzio and Wilde as being part of the process by which "the naughty nineties broke the stays of Queen Victoria's prudish stiffness."[12]

Many aspects of Margherita's daily life and orthodox classical education

naturally collided with the controversial ideas she found in modern literature. She was personally and aesthetically drawn both to resurrecting past
tradition and to the most modern ideas she could find, and she struggled
all her life to resolve the conflicts this created. The ambiguous religious
environment of the Grassini household made her dilemma all the more
poignant.

Margherita grew up in a Jewish family, but a Catholic society. She read
the Bible but received no instruction in Hebrew or in Judaism. Amedeo
Grassini's ties to the Catholic hierarchy had exposed her to Catholic traditions and contradictions. She and her father had visited the Vatican and had
been accorded an audience by Pope Leo XIII. She liked and respected her
father's friend, the affable Cardinal Sarto, until he attempted to have a
painting removed from the first Biennale.[13] This was Giacomo Grosso's
The Last Meeting, which depicted female nudes draped across a coffin.
Cardinal Sarto denounced the picture as offensive to public morals. Its
showing was saved only by the intervention of Antonio Fogazzaro, one of
Italy's premier novelists and another friend of the family. Margherita remembered reciting as a young girl the lines of his "The Madonnina del
Faggio," a sentimental poem about a child for which she herself provided
the inspiration.

Margherita encountered her Jewish heritage in the person of the brilliant British writer Israel Zangwill. Born in Whitechapel, then the poor
Jewish district in London, Zangwill—the "Jewish Dickens"—achieved
literary fame in 1893 with *The Children of the Ghetto.* He gave zealous
support to establishing a Jewish homeland. In his work, Zangwill explored
the saga of the Jews after their emancipation from the ghettos and preached
against the loss of Jewish identity through assimilation. Zangwill passed
through Venice in the mid-1890s, and Margherita insisted that her father
invite him to attend Passover seder at Palazzo Bembo. He was among the
first in her "collection" of celebrities, one that would prove to be as
extensive and remarkable as her collection of art. Zangwill's large, unattractive face reminded her of an anti-Semitic caricature, but his charming
manner, his strong advocacy of women's suffrage, and his view that art
should have social and moral content soon captivated her.

She disagreed with Zangwill over the importance of Judaism. She had
already proclaimed herself an atheist, much to her father's chagrin. Zangwill joked with her that he, too, could not be religious because his father
was intensely so, "and one person in a family is enough." He was saddened,
however, to find that the Grassini household was typical of the modern
Jewish experience, for both Margherita and her older brother, Marco, had
moved away from their father's observance of Judaic tradition.[14]

Zangwill immortalized his visit to Palazzo Bembo in the short story

"Chad Gadya," a literary masterpiece published in 1898. He was struck by the irony of Amedeo Grassini's status: "Well, the Doges were done with, Venice was a melancholy ruin, and the Jew—the Jew lived sumptuously in the palaces of her proud nobles. He looked around the magnificent long-stretching dining-room, with its rugs, oil-paintings, frescoed ceiling, palms . . . and thought of the old Latin statute forbidding the Jews to keep schools of any kind in Venice. . . . Well, the Jews had taught the Venetians something after all—that the only abiding wealth is human energy." Zangwill based his chief character on Margherita's brother, Marco. The story follows an "emancipated" son, who arrives toward the end of the family seder, "as homely and as piously simple as in the past when the Ghetto Vecchio, and not this palace on the Grand Canal, had meant home." Listening to his father chant the prayers, the son is torn by the conflict between his modern, secular life and the pull of Jewish tradition. He realizes in despair that emancipation has forced him to abandon his faith, and he drowns himself in the canal. Zangwill's story would one day be a poignant reminder to Margherita that no matter how far she removed herself from her father's world, it would prove impossible to escape her heritage.[15]

3

The Red Virgin

"**M**y dear," Nonna Dolcetta once told her granddaughter, "it's a good thing you are so beautiful. Else what man would look at you twice?" She worried that Margherita loved books so much that she was likely to intimidate prospective husbands. Such apprehensions proved misplaced, for Margherita Grassini was growing into a striking young woman. In the summer months she was often seen at the Lido, riding a horse along the beach with her hair flowing in the wind. Already in her mid-teens she was capturing many admirers.[1]

Her first serious courtship occurred at this time. While vacationing at an Adriatic resort with her governess, she met a middle-aged professor who fell passionately in love with her—she called him the "fatal man" of her adolescence.

The affair, though it was entirely innocent (according to Margherita), nevertheless changed her sociopolitical outlook profoundly—for her suitor was a Socialist, and he taught Margherita the basic tenets of Marxism. She never revealed his name, describing him in her memoirs only as a forty-year-old anthropologist from Florence, with a flaming red beard, ascetic profile, and deep voice, a widower once married to a Russian woman.[2]

Margherita corresponded secretly with her new admirer, hiding his letters and gifts from her parents.[3] She deflected the professor's amorous pursuit and kept the relationship on an intellectual level. When her frustrated suitor begged for her photograph, she sent instead an inscribed picture of Shelley: "My favorite poet, to the friend that I most admire." He reciprocated with photographs of Marx and Achille Loria, a Socialist economist, and began showering her with books, pamphlets, and newspapers, including Marx's *Capital* and the works of the Russian anarchist Peter Kropotkin. When she finally sent him her photo, she placed it between the pages of Shelley's "Epipsychidion," an allegorical poem depicting a female protagonist imprisoned in a convent and sought by a spiritual lover.

As she read through his gifts, Margherita now began to understand more clearly the social criticism that inspired her favorite literature. The Socialists saw human history as the result of a ceaseless struggle between those who controlled property and power and the exploited classes of peasants and workers. If the latter developed a class consciousness, the argument went, they could organize to overthrow their masters and create a world free of hunger and poverty, with all people sharing equally in the wealth and benefits of a free society.

Margherita found it easier to spurn the professor's advances than to reject his heady ideas. The seductive, exhilarating Socialism he preached filled a void in Margherita's soul. Judaism had failed to satisfy that emptiness and Catholicism offered her little spiritual attraction. His arguments supplied a philosophical justification for her adolescent rebellion, and a vocabulary for the guilt and indignation—Marx called it the "revolt of shame"—she felt about her family's wealth and privilege in the midst of so much deprivation. Besides, she was only fifteen, and her secret liaison offered an exciting chance to flirt with an older man.

Her parents soon discovered her secret. Amedeo Grassini "flew into a terrible rage," warning his daughter that if she continued her "subversive" activities, he, as a state official, would probably be exiled to some wretched backwater like Sardinia and would have to give up the *palazzo* on the Grand Canal! This was poor psychology, she later wrote, which only reinforced her allegiance to the Socialist cause.

She did become more discreet, greeting the postman each morning and removing the professor's letters from the rest of the mail, and persuading her Swiss governess to accompany her on walks to a small back-street newsstand where she could buy copies of the proscribed Socialist newspapers. The serialized stories of working-class rebellion enthralled her. She read with indignant fascination about two young women so inflamed by the injustice of a bloody despot that they abandoned their privileged status to work among the poor. The story inspired her to visit a poor peasant girl paralyzed from birth. The child, lying in a crude hut and unable to move or speak, filled her with a profound pity and outrage she expressed in an article published by a Socialist literary paper in Turin. She used the pseudonym "Marta Grani," coined from the first and last syllables of her names.[4]

The professor in Florence acknowledged the article with a huge bouquet of red roses. When her stunned parents seized the accompanying impassioned letter and confronted her, she confessed what she had done. Her father drove her to tears as he raged again about scandal and family disgrace. But in her mother's muted disapproval, Margherita detected a secret note of pride and respect. Emma's silent affirmation was perhaps her most important gift to her teenage daughter, for the newspaper was the first of many to publish Margherita. She never forgot the pungent fragrance of the professor's blood-red roses, which she pressed into her copies of Dante, Pascoli, and Carducci.

News soon spread among local Socialists that the young daughter of the prosperous and respected Amedeo Grassini had been converted to the cause. Before long they began to call her the "Red Virgin," after Louise Michel, a famous feminist leader of the 1871 uprising of the Paris Commune, a brief experiment in radical government that many had hailed as the first working example of Socialist ideas. The Commune had controlled the French capital for three months, until routed in May 1871. Margherita recalled that her nickname stuck "even after it was no longer appropriate."[5]

In Italy in 1895, most Socialists traced their roots to Giuseppe Mazzini's radical program with its emphasis on the rights of the common people and insurrection from below. But Mazzini was not a Marxist, and in fact had disavowed the Paris Commune. He believed Socialism was antithetical to his vision of a European brotherhood of republican nation states. Mazzini's disgruntled radical followers turned to the anarchist Mikhail Bakunin, a Russian exile working in Italy. Bakunin's revolutionary rhetoric and millenarian ideals sparked a series of unsuccessful uprisings in the 1870s that were brutally suppressed by the Italian government.

It was only in the early 1880s that the Socialist movement was able to establish a real presence in Italy, when large northern cities such as Milan and Turin started to industrialize, attracting tens of thousands of workers to new factories. But unlike the long-established Socialist parties of their European neighbors, the Italian party did not adhere to a strict Marxist orthodoxy. Quite different currents of Socialist thought developed in Italy, often reflecting the personal style and ideas of individual leaders.

Andrea Costa was already something of a legendary figure by the time Margherita encountered Socialism, but he had been the first Italian radical to make the transition from anarchism to Socialism. Costa came from the volatile Romagna region south of Venice, the home of perpetual rebellion and intense hatred of the Church born out of centuries of papal misrule. Costa's fiery ardor and thirst for action attracted him to Bakunin's anarchist philosophy. After years of tireless organizing interspersed with several prison sentences, Costa concluded that the Italians lacked a genuine revolutionary spirit, and he began to argue the need for education and propaganda within a framework of legal political activity. This soon led to a break with Bakunin, who was bitterly opposed to peaceful participation in parliamentary politics.

In 1877, while in exile in Switzerland, the handsome young Costa met Anna Kuliscioff, a brilliant and beautiful revolutionary. Anna came from a wealthy Russian Jewish family, and had worked for many years in the anti-tsarist underground before leaving Russia to study medicine in Switzerland. She had been an anarchist in her younger days, but by the time she met Costa she had abandoned Bakunin for Marx. Kuliscioff and Costa became lovers, and Anna bore an illegitimate daughter, Andreanna. They worked together in the nascent Italian Socialist movement until they separated. In 1882, Costa was elected to Parliament as the first self-declared Socialist candidate.[6]

The formation of the Second International in 1889, together with the rapid development of Italian industry, gave the Socialist movement the impetus it needed. In August 1892, the Italian Laborers' party (PLI) was founded in Milan and within a year claimed some 120,000 members. By the time Margherita met her professor in 1895, the PLI had renamed itself the Italian Socialist party.[7]

Socialism spread quickly, especially among educated middle-class Italians, as well as academics and students, for whom it became a new, exciting intellectual gospel. Costa's mantle fell to Filippo Turati, one of the founders of the PLI. A lawyer by training, Turati proved skillful at the political compromise necessary to hold the party together under the strain of severe ideological disputes. Although arrested numerous times for his political activism, he detested violence and masterminded the Socialist party's program of peaceful social and economic reforms.

Turati and Kuliscioff became lovers in 1885 and lived together for the next forty years. Unlike Costa, Turati possessed a cautious, somewhat neurotic personality, and he soon fell under the influence of Kuliscioff's sharper mind and stronger character. Together they edited *Critica Sociale,* an important Socialist journal Turati had founded in 1891. Their apartment in Milan became the nerve center of the Socialist party. Kuliscioff led the fight for women's rights, inspiring the many young Italian women who followed the Socialists—including Margherita Grassini.[8]

Italian government authorities believed Socialism to be dangerously subversive. After discovering an anarchist plot to assassinate him, Prime Minister Francesco Crispi led Parliament to pass a series of special laws. These allowed the arrest of anyone deemed potentially dangerous and the deportation of those considered subversive. Parliament also struck nearly one million leftists from the voting rolls. Crispi was desperate to eradicate anarchists and Socialists and he strained the Italian constitution to its limits. In 1894–1895 he used troops, martial law, censorship, and mass arrests to crush the Socialist movement. Amedeo Grassini had good reason to react so strongly to what he thought was his daughter's flirtation with Socialism.[9]

But for Margherita Socialism was not a mere flirtation. It was "real life: ardent and feverish spiritual life." She rapaciously devoured material on economics, Socialist theory, and women's issues, and tried to engage her unwilling tutors in serious discussion of the new ideas. Not surprisingly, Orsi and Fradeletto were disturbed, partly because of conservative political values, but primarily because they found abhorrent a philosophy that reduced human life to a struggle for material gain. Books on political economy, she observed with amusement, "made the heads of my humanist professors boil."[10]

Again Margherita found inspiration in the works of John Ruskin. She came to see the English writer as a profound social reformer whose artistic principles derived from a deep criticism of industrial capitalism. From Ruskin Margherita drew "a contempt of the idle joys of mere aesthetics, of the illusion of finding harmony only in art and closing one's eyes to the beauty of life." In a famous chapter from *The Stones of Venice,* Ruskin described the essence of his social criticism as the link between art and "the right kind of labour." How maddeningly ironic for Fradeletto to hear his pupil use Ruskin's arguments to support her Socialist views.

Margherita had already learned from Ruskin that if the artist's function is to reveal truth, then the moral corruption of the artist also causes a corruption of the artistic truth. Now she made the most of those passages where Ruskin claimed that industrial civilization, based on laws of supply and demand instead of on human values, corrupted the artist by making money more important than the search for perfection. Industrial capitalism turned both worker and artist into mindless machines. Factory production and the division of labor robbed all workers of their humanity and their creativity. "Go forth again," Ruskin urged, "to gaze upon the old cathedral front, where you have smiled so often at the fantastic ignorance of the old sculptors: examine once more those ugly goblins, and formless monsters, and stern statues, anatomiless and rigid; but do not mock them, for they are signs of the life and liberty of every workman who struck the stone."[11]

Most Marxists grounded their sympathies in eighteenth-century rationalism and its offshoot: Positivism. Positivists had extended the ideas of the Enlightenment by arguing that discoverable and precise scientific phenomena underlay everything, including human behavior. This belief had gained new support in the nineteenth century, especially in light of the evolutionary theories of Charles Darwin. Marx embraced this philosophic attitude about the material basis of life and the power of human reason to explain human existence. His "Scientific Socialism," commonly known as Marxism, represented an attempt to understand human history as an evolving set of responses to different economic laws.

Margherita was not greatly interested in the intellectual aspects of Scientific Socialism, nor did she find other Marxist theory satisfactory.

While she had read Descartes, Voltaire, and the Positivists, her understanding of Socialism stemmed from more unusual sources. She was not initially familiar with the anarchist tradition most Italian Socialists had begun with, nor did she respond much to the brand of Marxism to which Turati and Kuliscioff gave their allegiance. Rather, as Margherita described it, she had come to her new Socialist faith through a "combination of idealistic, ethical, philosophical, and sentimental movements" that regarded Socialism as a kind of "religious humanitarianism."

Steeped in the emotive power of Romanticism and in the idealism of Ruskin, a young woman of her character could not help but repudiate a Socialism that offered only a materialist and purely scientific definition of human nature. Fradeletto, although no enemy of capitalism himself, had instilled in Margherita the notion that a healthy society required a "collective will" that would replace selfish individualism, as in the days of ancient Rome or Dante's medieval Christendom. She found in Ruskin a confluence of these separate threads of her intellectual experience, allowing her to see in Socialism a way to make sense out of history, artistic creation, and her own perception of the injustice of life. Once she discovered aesthetic possibilities in Socialism, Margherita dedicated herself to a life in its service.[12]

4

A Socialist Marriage

One evening in 1895, while leaving the Teatro La Fenice after the opera, the Grassinis encountered Cesare Sarfatti, a young man distantly related but known only slightly to them. Cesare soon turned his attention to Margherita, and with the studied affectation of an adult flattering a teenager, kissed her hand. The two were immediately charmed by each other. After what seemed to the elder Grassinis to be an overly lengthy conversation, Sarfatti bade the family good evening and promised to call soon at their home.[1]

Cesare was born in Venice on November 21, 1866, one of thirteen children. His father's surname derived from "Zarfatti," the name given to all Jews of French descent who fled to Italy early in the fourteenth century to escape persecution at the hands of King Philippe IV. The family prospered in the following centuries; many became rabbis. Joseph Ben Samuel Zarfatti, who died in 1527, was such a notable physician that he was exempted by the Venetian senate from wearing the humiliating yellow hat required of Jews. Cesare's father was a lawyer who represented English business firms in Venice, and his mother also came from a distinguished Jewish family.[2]

Cesare graduated from the University of Padua with a degree in law, and performed his required military service as an army officer. He was twenty-eight when Margherita met him and had just begun to practice as an attorney. He had thick, jet-black hair and an imposing curled mustache; his large, square features and dark eyes gave his face a kind and expressive appearance. While well-built, he was already tending toward a stoutness compatible with his robust personality and hearty sense of humor. He also possessed a serious side. His eloquence, combined with a deeply resonant voice, made him a superb public speaker.

Margherita was only fifteen when they met. She recalled that Cesare's words of affection had brought a blush to her face, stimulating both disdain and a secret fascination that she did not fully comprehend. Margherita's interest in Cesare grew over the next few years. He cut a handsome figure and she enjoyed his self-confident vigor, besides being flattered by his obvious interest in her. But most important, with Cesare Margherita was able to reverse the roles she and her professors had played. Cesare was the first Italian male she had met who treated her as an equal, listened seriously to her opinions, and even changed his own thinking in response. Cesare found her maturing intellect as fascinating as he found her beauty irresistible. With him, she was comfortably able to develop her own emerging identity, unencumbered by social expectations. She began to view Cesare as an avenue of escape from the confining world of her family.

Cesare had always taken an active interest in politics. During his army days he had been a right-wing monarchist, but afterward he supported the Radical party, which advocated social and parliamentary reform in opposition to Crispi's repressive government. By the time he met Margherita, Cesare had moved farther to the left and joined the Republican party, which upheld Mazzini's democratic, anti-monarchist ideals. Margherita persuaded him to join the Socialists—partly by declaring she would never marry a man who was not in the Party.[3]

Cesare's willingness to adopt Socialism gave Margherita an important advantage in her search for personal freedom. Socialism promised to reorder all aspects of society. A major goal was the emancipation of women. If he was a compliant Socialist, Margherita knew Cesare would support her yearning for independence and desire for power. But she also knew that she could not easily achieve her goals, even if Cesare treated her as a full partner in the marriage. Turn-of-the-century Italian mores prevented women from directly exercising power, even in Socialist circles. Margherita wanted to change this in the years ahead, but she had already begun to understand that the influence she exercised through the men in her life would both define and limit her identity as a woman.[4]

Amedeo Grassini, intuiting his daughter's aims, was opposed to her marrying Cesare Sarfatti. He felt she was much too young, the age difference was socially unacceptable, and Cesare's prospects were too limited for the husband of a Grassini. Once he learned Cesare was leaning toward Socialism, he refused even to allow his daughter's suitor in the house. Cesare and Margherita then arranged to meet at the home of Margherita's older sister, Nella Errera, who was already married and therefore an appropriate chaperon.

This awkward state of affairs persisted for several years. Once Margherita turned eighteen she was legally free to marry, and she defiantly announced that she would marry Cesare with or without the family's permission. Amedeo continued to resist what he was sure would be a misalliance but finally gave his grudging consent and a generous dowry. He admonished the couple to "make sure you circumcise the children!"[5] But Margherita rejected a religious wedding. Her father found consolation only in her agreement to marry Cesare formally, for most Socialist couples regarded the concept of marriage as enslavement both to organized religion and to the bourgeois state that sanctioned it. Margherita and Cesare were married at Palazzo Bembo in a civil ceremony on May 29, 1898.

They honeymooned in Switzerland and France. Margherita, who loved vigorous hiking, led the way along steep Alpine paths and teased her less athletic husband into keeping up. In Paris she climbed the Eiffel Tower on foot while Cesare rode the elevator. They shopped in the galleries of Montmartre, the Parisian district made famous by the Bohemian artists who lived there. Art dealers along the rue La Fitte, such as Ambroise Vollard, who held a salon in the basement kitchen of his shop, and Clovis Sagot, a former circus clown, displayed the newest Post-Impressionist works. Margherita knew of these developments through journals, but was delighted to see the actual canvases. Vollard, whom Margherita came to know and admire, was a champion of Paul Cézanne and was then hosting a one-man exhibit of the controversial artist.[6]

At Sagot's modest shop, where Gertrude Stein bought her first Picasso, Margherita discovered the vibrant lithographs of Toulouse-Lautrec. The disabled artist had first exhibited his *Elles* series, depicting the intimate lives of Parisian prostitutes in the elegant brothels of the rue Joubert and the rue d'Amboise, in 1896. The Sarfattis bought a complete set—Toulouse-Lautrec's brilliant command of line and form epitomized Margherita's sense of the essence of pictorial art. They also acquired posters advertising the dancer Jane Avril and her mysterious friend, May Milton. Margherita cherished Toulouse-Lautrec's lithographs all her life. "I was the first in Italy," she proudly told Bernard Berenson a half century later, "to appreciate the French painter."[7]

Back home, the newlyweds moved into the small apartment Amedeo had given them along the Fondamenta San Lorenzo, a quiet canal not far from St. Mark's Basilica. Cesare worked hard at his law practice and his sharp legal mind and rhetorical flair in the courtroom soon gained him an impressive reputation. He won great notoriety in 1901 for his defense of Mario Todeschini, a Socialist deputy who had accused a cavalry officer of hacking to pieces a young working-class girl. The officer sued Todeschini for slander, and despite Cesare's vigorous courtroom performance, the magistrates found him guilty. Cesare's activities prompted the Italian government to open a surveillance file on him. Because the local authorities considered him "one of the best criminal lawyers in Venice," they thought him dangerous. They also considered him an opportunist, "without any real convictions of his own" but "dominated by an intense ambition" for political office.

Cesare and Margherita lived well on his income and the 200,000-lire dowry. At the turn of the century an average Italian earned less than a thousand lire a year, a good theater ticket cost only one lira, food was plentiful and cheap, and servants cost next to nothing. Their income enabled Cesare to accept a good number of clients—generally Socialists or workers—who could pay him little or nothing.[8]

Cesare hoped that by working hard for Socialism in Venice, he would one day win the Party's endorsement to run for Parliament. He quickly found that Venice provided an inhospitable arena for Socialist militancy. Unlike those areas of Italy where hostility to the Church ran deep, Venice nurtured a highly religious Catholic population. Cardinal Sarto's coalition of priests and conservative politicians continued their crusade against atheistic Socialism. Amedeo Grassini himself held a leading position in Sarto's Catholic-conservative alliance, contributing significant amounts of his time and money to the fight against the Socialists.[9]

Other factors hampered the Socialist movement. Venice lacked heavy industry, so there was no large, compact working class to organize. Disparate groups of Venetian workers included fishermen, dock workers, porters, cigar rollers, artisans engaged in glassmaking and other handicrafts, and those who serviced the great hotels and restaurants catering to the tourist trade. Enormous differences in income separated these workers from the prosperous middle class, but differences in outlook separated them from each other. Venetian Socialists were nonetheless determined to organize them, and to that end Margherita and Cesare joined a small but dedicated cadre of local leaders.

Cesare's political ambitions were encouraged by a disastrous political crisis that threatened the Socialist party throughout Italy. Prime Minister Francesco Crispi in 1895 had sought to relieve Italy's economic problems and bolster her international prestige by ordering an invasion of the independent African country of Ethiopia. He hoped to settle poor and landless Italian peasants there. But the invading Italian army suffered a catastrophic defeat at Adua in March 1896, which led to peace on Ethiopian terms and Crispi's disgraced exit from office.[10]

Two years of widespread social unrest followed. In May of 1898, shortly before Margherita's marriage, a series of violent demonstrations and a general strike erupted in Milan. King Umberto and his new prime minister Antonio di Rudinì panicked, declaring martial law and calling out the army. Commanding thousands of troops, General Bava-Beccaris broke the riots with gunfire. His artillerymen bombarded what was thought to be a revolutionary stronghold, only to discover they had destroyed a monastery. Officials later admitted to 80 dead and 450 wounded, but many more had actually been slaughtered.

The government blamed the Socialists and unleashed a reign of suppression unknown even in the harsh days of Crispi. Police indiscriminately arrested thousands of radicals, shut down more than a hundred newspapers, broke up unions and cooperatives, and disbanded Socialist groups all over the country, including the Venetian branch. Even moderates protested such severe methods, and the government soon fell. General Luigi Pelloux became prime minister.[11]

After returning from their honeymoon Cesare joined with a close friend, Elia Musatti, to rebuild the local Socialist organization. Both came from Jewish families, had been trained as lawyers, and shared former Republican backgrounds. Elia's father, Giuseppe Musatti, and Margherita's father were business associates; Giuseppe had disowned his Socialist son. By the turn of the century Cesare and Elia had reconstructed the Venetian branch of the defunct Socialist party, and Elia had started a weekly newspaper, *Il Secolo Nuovo* (*The New Century*), for which Cesare and Margherita wrote.[12]

Venetian authorities reported to Rome that local Socialists considered Cesare "their respected leader," and a fiery political orator, "much admired for his violent style and exaggerated ideas against every principle of authority." Cesare's prominence in the Party was attributed to his recently enhanced "economic condition" and the valuable help received from his "young, beautiful, and wealthy wife, herself a fanatical Socialist bent on making both of them proselytes."[13]

Margherita campaigned for Cesare during his first bid for political office in the spring of 1900. Cesare ran as the Socialist candidate for Parliament from Lonigo, a mainland town not far from Venice. He spoke out for the elimination of the tariff on food imports, an important issue among the workers, but since Italian workers had not yet gained the right to vote, Cesare was easily defeated by his moderate Liberal opponent. To the sting of defeat was added a 100-lire fine. The police charged that one of his speeches had incited workers against their employers and therefore violated the public-security provisions of the penal code.[14]

With Cesare's electoral disappointment came a personal tragedy when Margherita's mother died suddenly at age fifty. Her coffin was met at the Venice train station by the mayor, the police chief, all the city's rabbis, and many of Amedeo Grassini's business associates. An impressive fleet of gondolas and *vaporetti* accompanied the funeral barge to the Jewish cemetary at the Lido, where a large crowd of mourners met the family. An obituary published by a Jewish newspaper expressed its sympathy publicly to Amedeo Grassini, his children, and to two of his sons-in-law. It failed to mention Cesare, whose Socialist activities made him persona non grata in the family.[15]

At first, neither Cesare nor Margherita took sides in Party doctrinal divisions between those advocating reform through electoral politics and those calling for violent revolution. The same arguments raged within all European Socialist parties but in Italy the two sides enjoyed nearly equal strength, which caused constant Party turmoil.

Filippo Turati, a member of Parliament since 1896, led the reformist wing of the Party from Milan. He pushed for pragmatic cooperation with the existing government in order to secure social and economic reforms leading to bread-and-butter benefits for the workers. His gradual approach depended upon the election of other Socialist deputies to Parliament, the defense and widening of democratic freedoms, and propaganda designed to arouse class consciousness among the workers. Turati and his reformists revised Marxist dogma by denying the necessity of revolution, though they continued to insist that the triumph of Socialism was inevitable.

Other Socialists were unwilling to abandon their dream of violent revolution. They insisted on the destruction of capitalism and the overthrow of a state controlled by the rich. These repressive systems were to be replaced by a dictatorship of the proletariat. The revolutionary Socialists hoped to achieve a new social and political order by organizing workers into a syndicate of powerful trade unions with political goals, rather than into a conventional political party. Uncompromising, violent rhetoric was to keep the workers in a perpetual state of excitement and lead to a crippling general strike. As the reformists increasingly cooperated with the government, the revolutionaries grew ever more militant, denouncing the moderates as traitors to the working class. Control of the party shifted back and forth between reformists and revolutionaries during constant, bitter battles over ideas and strategy.[16]

Cesare's opportunism and ambition eventually drew him toward the reformists, who seemed more likely to control the Party. In September 1900, Cesare and Elia Musatti went to Rome to attend the Sixth Socialist Party Congress as official representatives of the Venetian federation. Party factionalism led Musatti to back the revolutionaries and Cesare the reformists. Cesare supported a vote of confidence in favor of Turati's ally, Leonida Bissolati, the editor of the official Party newspaper, *Avanti! (Forward!)*. The congress ended in triumph for the reformists and confirmed Turati's leadership.[17]

The Rome congress was the first in which Anna Kuliscioff was able to force an in-depth discussion of women's issues. Margherita was not present. She was still in mourning for her mother, and her first child, Roberto, had recently been born. Cesare remembered her by co-sponsoring a motion to publish a special newspaper aimed at Socialist women and their special concerns.

Since the translation in 1891 of August Bebel's influential *Women and Socialism,* most Socialist women believed that their emancipation would have to wait until after the broader triumph over capitalism and the bourgeois state. But others sought more immediate liberation. Even Margherita's conservative intellectual mentors, such as Fradeletto, Fogazzaro, and Zangwill, believed women deserved full equality with men, including the right to vote and hold public office. A variety of feminist leagues, organizations, and newspapers advocating similar views appeared throughout Italy in the 1890s, and Margherita began an active involvement in the movement soon after her marriage. The Milan Feminist League, founded by a group of Socialist women that included the poet Ada Negri, in 1901 brought out a journal, *Unione Femminile,* for which Margherita wrote a number of articles. The following year she attended a meeting in Venice on equal pay for equal work, and soon became a contributor to feminist newspapers.[18]

But art remained the center of her intellectual interests. The four Venetian Biennale art exhibits held between 1895 and 1901 inspired her to make a career of art criticism, something virtually unheard of for a well-off married woman. In the spring of 1901 she began writing a series of ten articles on the exhibits of the Fourth Biennale, which Elia Musatti published in *Il Secolo Nuovo.* The first piece, "For Art and for the Public," called for the spread of art appreciation from the select sphere of the upper classes to the general public, especially the working classes. Subsequent articles treated the works on exhibit in thematic categories—"The Art of Force" and "The Art of Pain and Pity"—revealing her psychological interpretation of art and a remarkably detailed historical and technical knowledge of painting.[19]

At the same time a young Socialist journalist named Ugo Ojetti published an article on the 1901 Biennale that had a profound influence on Italian art criticism. His views were close to Margherita's own. Because Ojetti had won a prize two years earlier for his coverage of the Third Biennale, he already had established an audience for his articles. Ojetti rejected the isolated world of aesthetics that held most critics captive, and insisted on a critic's responsibility to act as an educational link between artists and their public. Margherita and Ojetti both believed that the Socialist party should stimulate worker consciousness through art; her husband joined forces with Ojetti at the 1902 Socialist Party Congress to interest the leadership in the plight of the exploited "artistic proletariat."[20]

Margherita and Cesare Sarfatti enjoyed their lives as political renegades, rejecting their staid Victorian culture in favor of values and attitudes they believed to be more compatible with the new century. They led the intense, hopeful, and stylishly disreputable lives of young radicals, secure in the knowledge that their family connections gave them access to Italy's social elite when this was desirable. Their numerous friends included Cesare's law and business associates, Socialist comrades, and a wide range of intellectuals, writers, and artists. Gabriele D'Annunzio, Cesare's childhood friend, was the kind of stimulating, iconoclastic figure Margherita cultivated. A very young Margherita had heard the decadent aesthete lecture, but she first met him around 1900, when he visited Venice. In 1908, D'Annunzio would invite the Sarfattis to the Venice premiere of his play, La Nave, after which he would present a glorious bouquet of roses to Margherita. D'Annunzio's controversial reputation stemmed from unbridled love affairs with famous actresses, and literary works seething with shockingly explicit sexual allusions. At the time, however, Margherita was struck by his tender kindness.[21]

Margherita and Cesare's family life began when Roberto was born in May of 1900. He was a beautiful boy with gray-green eyes and copper-colored hair. Their dark-haired second son, Amedeo Giovanni Giosuè Percy Sarfatti, was born two years later, on June 24, 1902, and named in commemoration of Margherita's father and her favorite poets—Pascoli, Carducci, and Shelley.[22]

Motherhood scarcely curbed Margherita's public or professional activities. She continued to write art criticism and to campaign for Socialist and women's causes. One observer remembered Margherita standing on a table outside a fashionable café in St. Mark's Square, haranguing a crowd while Roberto nodded in a carriage by her feet.[23]

The new century brought Italy its best times since the heady days of the Risorgimento. The political violence of 1898 had left both government and Socialists exhausted. Both sides drew back from confrontation while the Italian economy, propelled by a wave of industrial expansion, began a period of sustained growth. But Prime Minister Pelloux rejected the chance to reach an accommodation with the Socialists and proposed laws that would have turned Italy into a thinly disguised dictatorship ruled by army and king. These measures, he told Parliament, would destroy the Socialist menace forever.

Parliament refused to halt Italy's slow movement toward democracy and resisted Pelloux's proposals. In June 1900, Pelloux resigned. A month later, King Umberto was shot to death by an Italian anarchist who had returned from New Jersey to take revenge for the bloodshed in Milan two years earlier. As news of the murder spread, the nation braced for another brutal government crackdown.

However, common sense and a weariness with constant turmoil prevailed, and the government did not order repressive measures. Almost the entire country mourned the fallen king despite his harsh and authoritarian rule. The new king, thirty-year-old Vittorio Emanuele III, thrilled the nation when he dedicated the Crown to uphold the political rights of all Italians and to defend their liberty. It seemed that reactionary times had ended in favor of a hopeful era of more liberal politics.[24]

Margherita and Cesare shared in the joy that the country had escaped fresh disaster. Now they looked forward to a future more bright with promise. Although Venice throbbed with beauty and romance, the old city seemed out of step with the times, ever more provincial and backward, a hindrance to Cesare's political aspirations and to Margherita's professional career. Intellect, ambition, and a thirst to live at the center of modern life pulled them from the canals of Venice to the crowded, bustling streets of Milan.

5

Three or Four Prime Donne

The Sarfattis arrived in Milan on October 15, 1902, settling in a modest apartment at Via Brera, 19, in the heart of the city's art district. Milan was a different world to them, the "most technological city in Italy," according to the flamboyant poet Filippo Tommaso Marinetti; to the young painter Umberto Boccioni it was "the only Italian city where anything ever happens." A booming, commercial metropolis of some half million inhabitants, Milan was one of the fastest growing cities in the country, and while it lacked charm, it was an exciting and cosmopolitan place to live. Thousands of workers arrived each year for jobs in the manufacture of textiles, machinery, and metals. Its expanding labor force made Milan the natural headquarters of the Socialist party, and its energy and diversity attracted the intellectuals and artists of the avant-garde.[1]

A requisite visit to the apartment Filippo Turati and Anna Kuliscioff shared was the first item on the itinerary of Socialists arriving in Milan. Margherita soon made her appearance at their fourth-floor home with an unobstructed view of the square in front of the Milan Cathedral, the Piazza del Duomo. She was excited, but felt awkward and shy at the thought of meeting the two Party leaders.[2]

Margherita found the dark, bearded Turati unimpressive, but not so the forty-eight-year-old Kuliscioff. Kuliscioff seemed to Margherita to be the more intelligent of the two, the *éminence grise* behind Turati's red cardinal. "I believe that she had been beautiful in her youth," Margherita recalled, "and she still remained interesting when I knew her. Always impeccable, dressed in black with the whitest of blouses, she was a *signora* and grande dame beneath that halo of fine hair of a faded gold color, not grey but shaded to an old vermeil." She was also rather cold, "a great woman, with the hard brilliance and many-sidedness of a diamond."

Margherita's subsequent relationship with Kuliscioff proved tense and ambivalent. She respected Kuliscioff but she chafed under the older woman's domineering personality and sharp tongue. With deep bitterness

Margherita remembered when Kulis012347, feigning a protective concern for Margherita, publicly berated Cesare for looking at other women when he had such a beautiful and solicitous wife. Kuliscioff resented Margherita's independence and wealth. Once when Margherita was proudly showing Kuliscioff's daughter a new jeweled brooch, Kuliscioff condescendingly interrupted: "Yes, dear, certainly . . . it justifies the wages of the workers . . . truly very beautiful. . . ." The ideological snub was all the more grating because Margherita knew that Kuliscioff was anxious to secure a good bourgeois husband for her daughter![3]

But Margherita in large part opened herself up to criticism from Kuliscioff. Neither she nor Cesare made any effort to hide either their wealth or their love of bourgeois comforts. Margherita's father, whose alliance with the anti-Socialist Cardinal Sarto was widely known, represented another awkward liability. Kuliscioff may also have been jealous of Margherita's beauty, and the great care she took with her appearance. She cultivated a richly elegant look that belied her Socialist politics. Her wealth allowed her to wear stylish clothes, expensive perfumes, and fine jewelry. She never adopted the deliberately drab proletarian manner affected by most of her women comrades or the masculine garb worn by many of her feminist friends. She stood out among her colleagues and knew it, having once described a feminist convention she attended as "a congress of the ugly and the old." One of her associates claimed that Margherita regarded Socialism "more as a sport, in which she never risked anything, than a militancy."[4]

Cesare and Margherita dulled the edge of criticism by paying homage to the revered Socialist leaders, acknowledging Kuliscioff as the doyenne of Socialist women and Turati as their political mentor. The Turati-Kuliscioff apartment housed the editorial office for *Critica Sociale* and supported one of the most vibrant salons in Italy. Visitors perched on the leather sofas in the parlor surrounded by huge arched windows overlooking the busy trams in the piazza, and the crowds shopping in the glass-covered Galleria Vittorio Emanuele II. Margherita and Cesare attended at least twice a week "to breathe that elevated, though down-to-earth, air." While the guests engaged in intellectual jousts over politics and social issues, "Anna smoked and listened, her steely eyes intense, suddenly hurling an incisive objection or a flash of invective." Although largely a forum for Socialist issues, Kuliscioff's salon occasionally attracted dissident intellectuals or artists, such as F. T. Marinetti. Margherita relished these encounters with the most vibrant personalities of the day. Kuliscioff set a standard that Margherita later sought to surpass in her own salon.[5]

Margherita also associated with a wide range of activist women. Some, led by Anna Maria Mozzoni, advocated an independent feminist position outside the Party. But while ideological disputes divided the women, as they did all Socialists, most looked to Anna Kuliscioff for leadership. Kuliscioff conceived of women's liberation within the broader context of the social question. Class struggle was the means by which working women would achieve economic emancipation from the tyranny of men as well as from the chains of capitalism. She demanded for Italian women the right to vote, an eight-hour workday, equal pay for equal work, and complete control over their own bodies. Kuliscioff was supported by a group of women mostly a generation older than Margherita, including Ersilia Maino, Alessandrina Ravizza, and Maria Giudice, each of whom had years of feminist-Socialist activism behind them.[6]

Ersilia Maino and her husband, Luigi, were the Sarfattis' first really close friends in Milan. As president of the Milan Feminist League, Ersilia had worked for years with philanthropic and women's organizations, taking a moderate position both in the feminist movement and in the Socialist party. In 1901 she had founded a paper for the League, the *Unione Femminile,* to which Margherita had begun contributing while still in Venice. On Saturday evenings the Sarfattis were drawn to the Mainos for a variety of reasons. Ersilia entertained a number of newly prominent artists and literary figures. She was also close to women Margherita was anxious to know, such as Alessandrina Ravizza and Ada Negri. The genial and immensely popular Luigi, a prominent attorney and the head of the Milan lawyers' association, had repeatedly defended Turati, Kuliscioff, and other Socialists in court.[7]

Margherita contributed to several other feminist and Socialist newspapers. *La Rassegna Femminile (The Women's Review)* of Florence appeared as "the free tribune of women" for only ten months in 1902. It called for better economic conditions for women workers and teachers as well as for female suffrage. More important to her was *Avanti della Domenica (Sunday Forward)*, a lively four-page weekly published first in Florence and then in Rome between 1903 and 1907. The literary emphasis of this paper reflected Margherita's interests more clearly, and she began writing for it in 1904 after it was taken over by the Socialist party's official publishing house. To make culture accessible to poorly educated workers, the paper presented simply written articles on art, literature, science, and politics. Its many contributors were among the most eminent Socialists and left-wing intellectuals of the period—Gabriele D'Annunzio, Ugo Ojetti, and Filippo Turati, to name a few. In 1906 Margherita began contributing also to *Il Tempo*, a daily paper edited by Claudio Treves, for which Turati and other reformist Socialists wrote and on whose managerial board Cesare served.[8]

Margherita's reviews in these papers established her reputation as an art critic, but the controversial trial of the writer Umberto Notari in the summer of 1906 really opened avant-garde intellectual circles to her. Notari, the publisher of a number of literary reviews, faced government prosecution for "immorality" because of his novel *Quelle signore* (*Those Women*), which described in explicit terms the life of a young country girl forced into prostitution in the big city. Notari's friends, led by Marinetti, organized a campaign in his support. Margherita had become a frequent visitor to Marinetti's home, and was a determined foe of artistic censorship; she induced Cesare to volunteer to serve as one of Notari's five defense attorneys. Notari, found innocent of all charges, became a close friend of the Sarfattis' and later expressed his gratitude by publishing some of Margherita's art criticism.[9]

The Notari trial won Cesare a reputation as a skillful defender of radical causes and established his credentials among the Milanese Socialists. To advance his political career he had aligned himself with the reformist wing of the Party under Turati's leadership. When Milanese revolutionaries seized control of the Party in 1903, Turati created a separate reformist coalition, the Autonomous Socialist Groups, in which Cesare served as one of Turati's lieutenants. At the 1904 national Party congress, revolutionaries outvoted reformists and seized control of the Party apparatus. One result was a disastrous general strike called by the new Socialist leaders, during which period Cesare worked hard to hold the Turati coalition together.[10]

Cesare's loyalty to Turati eventually paid off. At the 1906 Rome congress the reformists recaptured the Party's leadership and Cesare was appointed to the board of the Popular University of Milan, a free Socialist school for workers. A year later the reformists backed him in provincial council elections, but he lost. He ran for the Milan city council in 1908, and was elected; he held the seat until 1914.

Margherita's own ambitious efforts met with mixed success. In 1907 she met Angelica Balabanoff, a Russian who had arrived in Italy in 1900, the same year that Kuliscioff had introduced the women's question at the Rome party congress. Like Kuliscioff, Balabanoff was from a wealthy Jewish family. Born near Kiev in 1869, the youngest of sixteen children, she had a privileged, multilingual education enhanced by extensive travel. She completed her education at universities in Brussels, Leipzig, and Rome, where she was indoctrinated in Marxism. In 1902, she joined the Italian Socialist party at the invitation of Turati and Kuliscioff, and almost immediately went to Switzerland to organize emigrant Italian women textile workers.

Margherita described her as "[s]mall, misshapen, hunch-backed. . . . Comrade Balabanoff was extraordinarily intelligent—a strange hysterical creature with a flashing mind. . . . I saw her delivering a speech in such a fashion that she became transformed. . . . Her cracked voice took on strange hoarse and guttural intonations that seized hold of you with that hypnotic spell which belongs to the hysterical and to saints. When she had finished her invocation . . . she fell back suddenly on her seat, weeping, and as pallid as death, and the rest of us, sitting round the small table, close by her, went pale to the lips also, and wept in sympathy." Margherita found Balabanoff much too fanatical for her taste, without any sense of humor, and worst of all, "lacking a sense of beauty."[11]

Balabanoff's arrival exacerbated an already tense situation among the women with whom Margherita associated. Margherita was not the only woman to chafe at Kuliscioff's imperious behavior. She later noted, "There took place in Milan the dramatic and comic cold war among three or four *prime donne*. . . . They each hated each other, no less than had they been men. Did they, like men, plead ideological reasons when their real motives, as in every war, were pretexts for hating each other?" Margherita eventually declared her independence from both Balabanoff and Kuliscioff, building an independent network of friends as she moved more and more into the world of art.[12]

Cesare's rising stature in the Party helped Margherita win an appointment as art critic for *Avanti!*. She had written a few free-lance articles for the Roman edition of the paper, but began a regular collaboration with the principal edition published in Milan in early 1908. These early articles appeared in the column "The Fortnight Hour" under the mysterious pseudonym "El Sereno," the Spanish word for night watchman.[13]

Less than a year after the Sarfattis arrived in Milan, Pope Leo XIII died and the College of Cardinals hurried to Rome to elect a new pontiff. The impoverished Sarto lacked the funds for the trip to Rome but was unwilling to place himself in the debt of Venetian bankers. He turned instead to Amedeo Grassini, who lent Sarto money for the round-trip train tickets to Rome and the necessary accoutrements. Most expected the election of Cardinal Mariano Rampolla, the papal secretary of state, but his candidacy collapsed when Emperor Franz Josef of Austria exercised his traditional veto. Rampolla favored Austria's enemies, France and Russia. Cardinal Sarto emerged as a compromise candidate. After several ballots, the Venetian prelate appeared on the balcony of St. Peter's Basilica as the new pope.

Taking the name of Pius X, Sarto displayed unexpected strength and imagination. In January 1904, he forbade any future attempt by outsiders to interfere in papal elections. Later that year, he lifted the restrictions that had prohibited Catholics from taking part in Italian politics, extending nationwide the Catholic-conservative alliance he had developed in Venice. In 1905, he nominated Amedeo Grassini—who, in Margherita's words, was "a bit of a clerical"—for a post on the Venetian city council. To those who questioned his nomination of a Jew, the new pope appropriated a remark of Pius IX to say that he saw "only one Christian among us, and he is a Jew." Amedeo won the city-council seat, a position that, according to Margherita, "crowned the aspirations of his entire life." Margherita's father now became a frequent visitor to the Vatican, and a formidable foe to the Socialists.

Margherita had a deep respect for the peasant priest who had become Pope Pius X. She also appreciated the beauty of Catholic ritual and its commissioned art. Yet she had a strong antipathy for organized religion, especially one that had persecuted her ancestors. In a propaganda pamphlet, *Christianity and Socialism,* she argued that Marx was one of the last prophets of a new age. The Catholics she preferred were renegades, like Don Brizio Casciola, a priest and a confidant of novelist Antonio Fogazzaro. Fogazzaro made Don Brizio the protagonist of *The Saint,* a man who questioned whether Christ had ever existed as a human being. When the novel appeared, Pius X placed it on the papal Index of Prohibited Books.[14] Don Brizio gave formal lectures on philosophy at the Sarfatti apartment until he too was silenced by the pontiff. Despite Margherita's politics, however, Pius X remained fond of his old friend's daughter and granted her at least one private audience.[15]

Margherita appreciated the importance of Catholic tradition in Italian culture, but Judaism had little meaning or importance for her. Nonetheless, she could see how much it meant to Cesare. He remained deeply attached to his Jewish roots and took an active interest in the Zionist movement. Jewish consciousness, not religious faith, mattered to him. He insisted on a strict separation of religious and cultural issues.[16] Cesare joined the Milanese Zionist Group soon after his arrival in the city. A year later, in December 1903, he presided over its general assembly and got himself elected to its executive council. By then, the Milanese Group had grown to more than 150 members, making it the largest group in the fledgling Italian Zionist Federation.[17]

At the fourth national Italian Zionist Congress, held in Milan in the spring of 1904, he spoke against "those vile Jews who forget that they're Jews." When a delegate proposed a committee to study the admission of non-Jews into the movement, Cesare rejected the idea passionately, attacking the delegate as a reactionary and pointing out that as Zionists their goal was to heighten a sense of Jewish nationalism.[18]

In 1906, Cesare served as a delegate of the Milanese Zionist Group to an international conference in Brussels dealing with the tsar's persecution of Russian Jews. Margherita may have encouraged Cesare to attend, for her old friend Israel Zangwill was going to be there. That winter, she accompanied Cesare to Brussels, where she took the opportunity to interview the Belgian painter Fernand Khnopff. At the conference, Cesare signed Zangwill's petition calling for the creation of an autonomous Jewish colony under British auspices. Sometime after their return to Milan, Cesare became the president of the Milanese Zionist Group.[19]

Margherita's father, the cause of some embarrassment to the Sarfattis among their Socialist friends, also made Cesare's life difficult in Jewish circles. Late in 1906, Grassini commissioned a painting as a gift for a hospital in the town of Mirano, where his son-in-law, Paolo Errera, served as mayor. Three facts soon scandalized the Jews of Venice: that the hospital was a Catholic institution, that Grassini was its president, and that the painting, intended for the altar of the hospital chapel, portrayed both a church and the Virgin Mary. When the Fraterna Israelitica, the principal Jewish charity of Venice, convened in December, irate members accused Grassini of "open and exaggerated clericalism." Despite a speech in his defense by his friend Giuseppe Musatti, the Fraterna refused to reelect Grassini to its board. Musatti and Edoardo Vivanti, Grassini's other son-in-law, resigned in protest.[20]

Squabbles of this kind indicated that Cesare and Margherita had made the correct decision in moving to Milan. Now they were directly involved in the most important political and cultural developments in Italy. Both were building rewarding but deeply divergent careers, Cesare as lawyer, politician, and Zionist; Margherita as writer and art critic. Their circle of acquaintances now included a number of major figures in the arts and the world of Italian Socialism. Their wealth allowed them a life of comfort, and travel to Socialist conferences, art exhibits, and the capitals of Europe. The Sarfattis seemed happy, outwardly, at least.

Their intimate relationship is a matter of some speculation; certainly their marriage reflected the egalitarian ethos of Socialist culture. Cesare was remarkably free from the attitudes of male supremacy typical among his peers. Margherita held strong feminist views, believing in total equality between wife and husband and rejecting all notions of traditional gender roles in family or public life. When a series of family laws concerning civil marriage, divorce, and the obligations of unwed fathers was introduced in the Italian Parliament, she campaigned hard for their adoption, railing against the fact that the all-male deputies discussed these issues without listening to women's views. She demanded an end to the idea that women needed "protection." Government, she insisted, should intervene in the realm of sexual relations only to protect the rights of children. She advocated a law to make fathers financially and legally liable for their illegitimate children and to establish the "sexual responsibility of men."

Margherita endorsed the libertarian mores that governed love affairs in her Bohemian world. She found bourgeois sexual morality stifling and psychologically destructive. (There is some evidence that she had affairs with women as well as with men.) She advised parents to deal openly with their children's sexual questions, and advocated formal sex education in schools as a natural "right" because "sex is such a large part of life." She believed explicit information about sex was especially important for young girls, who should be brought up to understand that a woman's life consists of much more than marriage and childbearing. Parents, she believed, must disabuse their daughters of the concept of love as romantic fantasy and teach them that "true, serious, and lasting love consists of the same precious and familiar elements that make up everyday life—respect, trust, affection, and friendship."[21]

Unusually for the time, Margherita to continued to sign her name "Margherita Grassini Sarfatti." She and Cesare often traveled alone to the innumerable conferences and meetings away from home. Clearly their feelings concerning Judaism were sharply divergent. While Cesare attended to his Zionist and Socialist affairs, Margherita spent evenings filled with intellectual discussion between the young men and women of Milan's cultural avant-garde. The physical differences between Margherita and her husband had become marked. A portrait by Lino Selvatico executed in 1901 shows Cesare looking considerably older than his thirty-five years. By 1914, Cesare was graying and almost obese, while the writer Nino Podenzani described Margherita as "tall, blond, and of triumphant beauty." Podenzani's admiration may have led to exaggeration, but Margherita did exude an extraordinary sensuousness that reflected the fashion of the day—a youthful but full-figured body, a soft, rounded face, and large, deeply set luminous eyes. To what extent her self-admitted physical appetite was satisfied must remain a matter of conjecture.[22]

The Sarfattis raised their children in a mixed atmosphere of Socialist theory and upper-middle-class comfort. Margherita paid scant attention to the tiresome details of housekeeping, and left her servants to feed, bathe, and train her children. Yet despite her frequent absences from home, the idea of motherhood was important to Margherita and she felt a deep attachment to her children. Cesare offered the little boys stability and conventional parenting, while Margherita added a nervous intensity and a sense of energetic activity to the family circle. She thought it amusing to buy them clothes that others thought outlandish or shocking but which she found stylish or whimsical. In any event Roberto and Amedeo were growing into intelligent, handsome boys, the delight of visitors and friends. In a lyric poem, "Germogli" ("Sprouts"), Margherita described Roberto as "an anxious, tormented ephebe," but Amedeo as "already wise and serene," for whom life appeared "serious."[23]

Margherita's happiness was abruptly shattered in 1907 by the tragic death of one of her older sisters, Lina Vivanti. Widowed at a young age, Lina became passionately obsessed with her son-in-law, and killed herself when he failed to respond. She left a younger daughter, Elena, of whom the Sarfattis were particularly fond; they encouraged her to spend a great deal of time with their sons. But Margherita's other sister, Nella, a proper woman of traditional views, raised the girl, and Nella disapproved of the stylish dresses Margherita encouraged Elena to wear.[24]

Amedeo Grassini's premature death in 1908 again sent the Sarfattis into mourning. His old friend Pius X sent a last blessing to the Jew "who was more Christian than the Christians."[25] In his memory, Marco and the families of Lina and Nella donated large sums of money to local civic charities and business-sponsored causes. Margherita and Cesare gave, instead, to Milanese Socialist groups.[26] Their family grieving ended at last on January 22, 1909, when Margherita gave birth to the daughter she had always wanted. She named her child Fiammetta, or "Little Flame," to which she added Emma and Chiara, after her grandmothers, and ambitiously perhaps, Anna, in honor of Kuliscioff.[27]

In the months following Amedeo Grassini's death, Cesare began a difficult, three-way electoral campaign for Parliament. Two anti-Socialist candidates opposed him. In the balloting on March 7, Cesare won 2,870 votes, only 51 votes more than his nearest rival, and too few to be declared the winner. The run-off proved a bitter disappointment for Cesare, who came in second. "Poor old Sarfatti," mocked Kuliscioff, "blocked at every turn from all positions."[28]

The settlement of her father's estate brought Margherita and Cesare some compensation, for the property they inherited yielded an additional annual income of some 40,000 lire. They enrolled Roberto in the Collegio Ravà in Venice, hoping that a disciplined life away from home would quiet his rebellious spirit. That same year they moved to a larger, more fashionable apartment on the Corso Venezia that overlooked the public gardens. The Corso Venezia, so named for its junction with the old post road running east to Venice, enjoyed great literary and historical fame. Through the East Gate Manzoni's protagonist, Renzo Tramoglino, had entered Milan in the pages of I promessi sposi. Napoleon had resided in the Palazzo Serbellini at number 16 after taking the city from the Austrians in 1796. The same mansion housed Italy's future king Vittorio Emanuele II in 1848, and fifty years after that, workers raised barricades across the street against government troops.

The Corso in 1909 was a wide, elegant avenue, lined with notable buildings and busy with traffic. The new apartment was spacious, with three bedrooms, a formal dining room, a study for the children, a guest room, and a large living room. It was ten minutes by cab to Kuliscioff's apartment and Cesare's new law offices in Milan's central piazza, and not far from Marinetti's home, the "Casa Rossa," where he lived amid "Persian carpets, Turkish tents, and Egyptian furniture."[29]

The Sarfattis also acquired a country refuge in Cavallasca, a few miles from Lake Como and the Swiss border. The farmhouse, which Margherita dubbed Il Soldo (The Penny), was a rustic two-story structure decorated with green shutters and a red stucco exterior. Perched on the edge of a hillside, Il Soldo commanded a magnificent view of the valley below and the Alpine foothills beyond. A garden of flowers, shrubs, and fruit trees surrounded the front courtyard, a large cypress towered over the property, and a giant laurel shaded the well. Margherita loved the simple interior of whitewashed walls, rough-beamed ceilings, and sparse wood furniture— "plain and devoid of luxuries but large, comfortable and peaceful." In the tumult of the coming years, Il Soldo would become the only place where Margherita truly felt at home.[30]

6

Primitives of a New Sensibility

One morning in April 1909, Margherita entered the Società Permanente, a Milanese art gallery, to cover an exhibit for her new column in *Avanti!*. She noticed a group of young artists huddled in conversation. "One among them," she later recalled, was "tall, with long hair, animated, without tie, collar, or coat, encased as in armour in a black, Mouzik-like sweater." An etching of an old woman sewing caught Margherita's attention—"I came close to decipher the signature and was repeating to myself 'Boccioni, Umberto' . . . when a voice behind me asked, 'Do you like it, signorina?'" It was the young man in black. The etching was his.

Margherita realized that she had noticed Boccioni's illustrations before, in the pages of *Avanti della Domenica* when she had written for that paper. Fascinated by his tense energy and his brooding, explosive personality, she invited him to lunch, and the quick pencil portrait he sketched of her was probably done at that first meeting. It was the beginning of a close and important friendship that may have included a love affair.[1]

In December, Margherita wrote a letter of introduction for Boccioni to Antonio Fradeletto, hoping that her former tutor would invite the young artist—"full of talent and the will to work"—to participate in the next Venice Biennale. Fradeletto did visit Boccioni's studio and, though impressed by his artistic ability, found his work too radical and refused him an invitation.[2]

Boccioni introduced Margherita to an exhilarating community of young Milanese artists and intellectuals who made their headquarters at the Caffè Savini, in the same *galleria* the Kuliscioff and Turati apartment overlooked. Most painted in cheap studios in working-class neighborhoods during the day and gathered in loud, exuberant groups in the evenings at the Savini. They showed their work at small exhibit halls, such as the Famiglia Artistica, and occasionally the Società Permanente. Margherita soon joined them, thrilled by their angry clamor for change and their intellectual rebellion against the snobbish bourgeois order.

By 1903 Margherita had established her reputation as an art critic. Her coverage of the Fifth Venice Biennale, written for the *Gazzetta degli Artisti* of Venice and *La Patria* of Rome, reflected her strong interest in modern painting, especially in the new Symbolist movement coming from Vienna. That year the Biennale awarded her third prize for the best critical reviews of the exhibit. Ugo Ojetti, who wrote the award decision on behalf of his fellow jurists, objected that Margherita's articles were addressed more to the artists she reviewed than the public. He also criticized her for lacking an overall critical approach, so that her comments too often read like notations in an exhibit catalog. On the other hand, Ojetti praised her for basing her criticism on a wide cultural background and for her fearlessness in making judgments that often contravened public taste and the opinions of her colleagues.[3]

The 1903 Biennale prize identified her as a serious art critic—one of the first women in Italy to pursue such a career—and created a demand for her writing. Between 1903 and 1908 she produced an average of two articles a month for such papers as *Avanti!*, *Avanti della Domenica*, *L'Adriatico* (Ancona), *Varietas* (Milan), the *Gazzetta di Venezia,* and *Il Tempo.*[4]

Margherita's enthusiasm for Boccioni and his friends reflected her deep commitment to transforming Italian culture. Italians had long seen themselves as the caretakers of their Roman and Renaissance past, but around the turn of the century a powerful intellectual ferment seized the country. Intellectuals and artists deliberately broke with their heritage, rebelling against established traditions of thought and taste. This upheaval was in part Italy's response to a general European movement known as the "revolt against Positivism." The movement rejected the belief that people were fundamentally rational and denied the idea that applying scientific methods to human problems would result in progress. As a result, the rejection of Positivism sometimes assumed anti-democratic and anti-Socialist aspects. If people were irrational, they were not fit to govern themselves. If human behavior could not be improved by scientific methods, then Scientific Socialism was a fraudulent notion. Instead, the rebellious anti-Positivists gave rise to irrational and sometimes mystical currents of thought. Thus Henri Bergson developed his philosophy of intuition as superior to rationality, and Georges Sorel presented his vision of a violent general strike as the only means by which society could be seized and transformed.[5]

Two Italians contributed to the anti-Positivist movement with serious, original, and coherent thinking. The brilliant Neapolitan scholar, Benedetto Croce, assisted by his Sicilian colleague, Giovanni Gentile, developed a neo-idealist philosophy, based on the ideas of Hegel and other German philosophers. Croce and Gentile argued that the mind and spiritual values are more important in shaping human society than nature and material objects. In particular, Croce and Gentile stressed the value of art and literature over science in expressing the highest form of truth. Croce went so far as to suggest that art, rather than politics or science, offered the primary means by which men could transform human life.

Croce and Gentile had a profound effect on Italian intellectual life, throwing it open to the influence of nineteenth-century northern European thought. However, a sophisticated understanding of their work went no further than a select circle of scholars. For the majority of her countrymen, as Margherita wrote, "[t]hese new ideas were presented to Italy only half assimilated and in quick succession." Less intellectually rigorous critiques of rationality and the scientific method were more generally appealing, serving only to weaken the attraction democracy held for many young Italians and offering them excuses to indulge in violent and irrational behavior.

Gabriele D'Annunzio's body of work was the most important source of anti-Positivist ideas for the wider Italian reading public. Like Croce and Gentile, D'Annunzio channeled northern European currents of thought into Italian life, but he did it in a far more accessible manner. D'Annunzio introduced into Italian culture the figure of the "superman," whose superiority allows him to move beyond conventional notions of good and evil. In Nietzschean terms, D'Annunzio began to create characters who relied on violent action and the sheer force of their will to overcome obstacles to their happiness. Margherita thoroughly approved. "At the end of the nineteenth century," she noted, "Italy appeared to be an isolated and forgotten province when Gabriele D'Annunzio brought it up to date and gave it the right to citizenship *ex aequo* in the literature of the modern world."[6]

Among those affected by D'Annunzio was a group of iconoclastic young writers who spearheaded provocative new literary journals in Florence such as *Il Leonardo,* founded in 1903 by Giuseppe Prezzolini and Giovanni Papini. Heavily influenced by William James's pragmatism and by the revolt against rationalism, *Il Leonardo* conducted a violent campaign against Positivism, democracy, and Socialism while advocating an elitist authoritarian form of government. *Il Regno* (*The Kingdom*), founded in the same year by Enrico Corradini, an unsuccessful novelist who would become the leading proponent of Italian nationalism, argued a similar position. These writers advocated the political and social theories of Gaetano Mosca and Vilfredo Pareto, both of whom held that elites, not the masses, were the real shaping forces of history.

Both magazines were short-lived, but in 1908 Prezzolini, again in collaboration with Papini, established *La Voce* (*The Voice*). Prezzolini was bent on reinvigorating Italian civilization by opening it to the disturbing winds of change sweeping across other European countries, especially France. The staff of *La Voce* held strongly conflicting opinions and often quarreled, but they did agree that Italy's prevailing separation of culture from politics needed to be broken down. In fact, Prezzolini, Papini, and their collaborators hoped to combat the influence of Positivism by reintroducing myth, religious symbolism, and ritual into modern intellectual life. *La Voce* explored a wide range of topics in these terms, from literature to parliamentary politics, from feminism to art; its iconoclastic approach attracted young Italian intellectuals committed to the modernization of their society—so long as modernization did not cut them off from the emotional, poetic, and spiritual side of life. Papini's editorial policy also advocated a cultural nationalism aimed at "restoring the historical awareness of [Italy's] own culture. . . . Nationalists no, but Italians yes."[7]

The anti-Positivist and anti-Socialist views expressed in *La Voce* did not repel Margherita. Her cultural and humanistic interests always extended beyond the confines of orthodox Socialism, and she had never hesitated to collaborate with other talented intellectuals. She had already offered to collaborate with Angiolo and Adolfo Orvieto, the two brothers who ran the Florentine literary journal *Il Marzocco,* noted for its anti-Positivist bias.[8] Margherita wrote to Giuseppe Prezzolini a few months after *La Voce* appeared that she found his review "alive and vibrant. . . . I cannot tell you with what enthusiasm I follow the open and magnificent road that your *Voce* is taking . . . it is truly the voice of all high and vigorous ideals, the only really Italian voice that is worthy of being supported and defended by people of serious culture."

She did take Prezzolini to task for publishing attacks against Socialism while allowing wildly nationalistic articles to appear. But on women's issues and literature they agreed, and their correspondence developed into an open and frank expression of views. Her first contribution, "A Mother's Thoughts on Sexual Instruction," appeared in a special issue devoted to sexuality. By 1911 she was translating "Chad Gadya," "The Promised Land," and other works by Israel Zangwill for *La Voce*'s publishing house, and she enlisted Cesare's help in securing financial support for Prezzolini. She did not subsequently publish much in *La Voce,* but she and Prezzolini formed an intellectual relationship that would last more than thirty years.[9]

La Voce jolted Florence out of its provincialism and fixation on the past, but Milan still generated the most revolutionary currents in modern Italian culture, especially in the plastic arts. Milanese artists of the 1860s had spearheaded the *Scapigliatura* ("disheveledness") movement, which experimented with new aesthetic principles and brought Italian art into contact with wider European developments. The dreamy, loosely brushed style of the *Scapigliati* resembled the techniques of the French Impressionists.

Among its exponents, Margherita most admired Daniele Ranzoni, a thoughtful, unappreciated painter whom she considered a precursor of modernism.[10]

By the late 1880s, when the influence of modern French and Dutch painting reached Milan, Divisionism replaced the *Scapigliatura* movement. The Divisionists drew from an assortment of foreign styles: Their use of basic color from the Post-Impressionists, their mystical concerns from the Pre-Raphaelites and German naturalists, and their symbolism from Art Nouveau. Margherita was struck by their use of optical blending and pointillist techniques. She most admired the expressive designs of Gaetano Previati, whose Divisionism maintained the three-dimensional "plastic" values of body and weight to which she remained attached. She also admired Medardo Rosso, the Italian Impressionist sculptor who lived in Paris, whose work had been generally ignored by Italian critics. She at once recognized a Divisionist approach in Boccioni's early work, but also sensed that he was moving beyond it.

Before 1909, her critical enthusiasm focused on these and other vital but neglected leaders of the late nineteenth-century avant-garde. Socialist-inspired "realist" painters she generally found uninteresting. Her keen eye for talent led her to praise the modern style of young artists such as Umberto Boccioni and Alberto Martini, regardless of their themes or politics. She considered the Divisionist style, together with Symbolism, the Vienna Secession, and "Liberty"—the Italian variety of Art Nouveau—to be the only true currents of modern art.[11]

Margherita practiced a distinctive literary and critical technique. Her sensitive and perceptive reviews were framed in an elegant, highly subjective style. She conveyed authoritative knowledge in an easy, almost colloquial manner, employing her command of the formal language of art without obscuring her meaning. Her criticism examined artists as well as their paintings, often probing the psychological and biographical sources of inspiration. She studded her articles with pertinent literary quotations from several languages. Margherita generally avoided detailed analysis of technique in favor of assessing intellectual and visual achievement. "When everything is said," she once explained to Bernard Berenson, "art is feeling, and so much the worse for those who place the handmaiden, technique, above the queen. Technique is important because of expression, but what do you have to express? . . . I prefer a clumsy expression to a beautified, clever void."[12]

The profile she did in Brussels of Symbolist painter Fernand Khnopff is illustrative. Margherita interviewed Khnopff at his home, and her article reveals a deep familiarity with Khnopff's iconography and intellectual background, placing his work within the broad context of European cultural developments ranging from Edward Burne-Jones and Dante Gabriel Rossetti to Baudelaire, Balzac, and Spenser. Her account of the Italian exhibits in which Khnopff showed his paintings unfolds as a personal memoir, and the portrait is an intellectual tour de force.[13]

Margherita's concept of art as primarily an expression of feeling drew her toward the new movement known as Futurism. Marinetti founded the Futurist movement with a literary manifesto, published in Paris on February 20, 1909. Marinetti declared war against those who looked only to the culture of the past: "We want to destroy museums, libraries, the academies . . . we want to liberate this country from its fetid cancer of professors, archaeologists, tourist guides and antiquaries. . . . To admire an old picture is to pour our sensibility into a funeral urn instead of hurling it forward with violent spurts of creation and action. Do you want to waste your best efforts in an eternal and useless admiration of the past . . . ? Let the happy incendiaries with charred fingers come! Here they are! Burn the library shelves! Divert the canals to flood the museums!"

The Futurists believed Italy's legacy of humanistic values burdened it, preventing Italy from embracing the modern world of technology. Marinetti and his followers therefore rejected the "moribund past" in favor of a "dynamic future." To spread their ideas, the Futurists deliberately set out to shock the public, adopting exaggerated postures against morality and in praise of violence and war. They did genuinely believe armed conflict was the means to cleanse Italians of their antiquated attitudes and to smash their monuments to the past. Afterward, a modern Italy could be constructed on the ruins of the old order. The Futurists also saw war as the quickest way to create a new society, and above all they worshiped speed. "We want to sing the love of danger, the habit of energy and rashness," Marinetti screamed, "to exalt movements of aggression, feverish sleepishness, the quick march, the perilous leap, the slap and the blow of the fist. We declare that the splendor of the world has been enriched by a new beauty: the beauty of speed. A racing automobile . . . is more beautiful than the Victory of Samothrace."

Futurists exalted machines, and the industrial civilization they brought about. They loved the noise and muscularity of the metal behemoths at work in the new factories of their city. Their credo of destruction and rebirth was a calculated attack on everything Italians held most sacred. A favorite tactic was to hold *serate,* scandalous Futurist "evening performances," the second of which took place at the Teatro Lirico in Milan on February 15, 1910. Marinetti and his cohorts rented theaters in order to recite Futurist works and outrage their audiences. The *serate* would invariably break up in fighting and confusion. Before one of the most famous of these events, held in the Teatro La Fenice in Venice, Marinetti flung tens

of thousands of insulting leaflets entitled "Against Backward-Looking Venice" from the city's clock tower. Margherita recalled that in Milan "Marinetti would leave from the Caffè Savini for his Futurist *serate* smartly
dressed, perfumed, and trimly elegant," only to return in total disarray,
with his clothes in tatters. His poorer followers objected to ruining their
few decent shirts and jackets, and resented the fact that Marinetti was
wealthy enough simply to buy a new suit. But they all enjoyed the action.[14]

Italian Futurism was self-consciously nationalistic. The Futurists appealed to the sense of cultural inferiority felt by many young Italian intellectuals, and the frustrated patriotism of critics who bemoaned the lack of
national grandeur and courage in united Italy. Marinetti preached a new,
dynamic Italy that would embark on virile campaigns of conquest and war
to build a new Roman Empire—war was "the world's only hygiene." "In
politics," he said during the March 1909 elections, "we are as far removed
from international and anti-patriotic socialism—that ignoble exaltation of
the rights of the belly—as we are from timid clerical conservatism." Marinetti was also openly contemptuous of feminism, insisting that women
should subordinate themselves to men's sexual dominance.[15]

All of this should have repelled Margherita. Instead it excited her. She
was intelligent enough to see through the Futurist cant to their vital call for
artistic change. She later wrote, "Next to that created by Gabriele D'Annunzio, the most lively and far-reaching intellectual movement of the
pre-war period in Italy was the Futurist movement . . . which brought a
fresh wind, young and new, to the stale atmosphere that had been mil-
dewed by archaeology and the love of the past." The Futurist call for
imperial greatness was anathema to most Socialists, but the degree of
cultural nationalism in Margherita's reviews of Italian artists at the Biennale
as well as in her correspondence with Prezzolini betrayed her own sympathy for the idea.[16]

Margherita's friends among the artistic avant-garde had enthusiastically
cheered Prezzolini's modernizing campaign in the pages of *La Voce,* and
many now saw Futurism as an even more radical alternative. Margherita's
political circle overlapped with the artistic community. Many of her Futurist friends were active in subversive politics. The young painter Carlo Carrà
had ties to anarcho-syndicalist circles in London and Paris. He was caught
up in Milan's tumultuous political upheavals, from demonstrations against
the Italian invasion of Ethiopia in 1895–1896 to the bloody repression of
the "Events of May" in 1898. Umberto Boccioni illustrated *Il Lavoro
Italiano,* and both he and Gino Severini did cover designs for *Avanti della
Domenica.*[17]

Margherita became actively involved in critiquing Futurism after five
artists whom she knew—Umberto Boccioni, Carlo Carrà, Luigi Russolo,

Giacomo Balla, and Gino Severini—joined Marinetti's movement in February 1910 with their own manifesto of Futurist painting. Claiming the Divisionists as their predecessors, they called for a new art that eliminated traditional forms and objects and emphasized the "universal dynamism" of life. A Futurist artist should not only use the subject matter of industry and urban life but also capture the feeling of an object in motion and depict moving, interpenetrating surfaces. The viewer would then experience a sense of being pulled into the painting rather than remaining a separate, passive onlooker.

The Futurists joined these new technical theories to philosophical and political ideas that Margherita also found congenial. Carrà's *Funeral of the Anarchist Galli* (1910–1911), one of the great paintings of the period, was inspired by the 1904 general strike. Russolo's *Nietzsche* (1909–1910) and *The Revolt* (1911), and Boccioni's better-known *Riot in the Galleria* (1910–1911), all testify to the Futurist preoccupation with action, violence, and revolution. "We are," Boccioni explained to Margherita, "the primitives of a new sensibility."[18]

The turning point in Margherita's relationship with the Futurists came during the government's prosecution of Marinetti for his novel *Mafarka il futurista,* originally published in Paris in 1909. The authorities seized the Italian translation and charged Marinetti with violating obscenity laws. In the novel, Mafarka, a desert warrior who becomes king of Africa, seeks liberation from all earthly pleasures and the corruption of the flesh. What particularly offended the state prosecutor was Mafarka's thirty-foot penis and his giving birth to a son without benefit of a woman.

Marinetti's prosecution naturally aroused the ire of the Italian cultural community. Not only was artistic freedom endangered, but the whole Futurist movement found itself on the defensive and the trial became a tumultuous *cause célèbre.* Luigi Freddi, who would become Mussolini's film censor in the 1930s, was fifteen years old at the time and recalled that for young Italians the state prosecutor represented everything wrong with their country, while Marinetti offered a symbol of rebellion and change. The distinguished author Luigi Capuana traveled from Sicily to testify on Marinetti's behalf. He was defended by three lawyers: Innocenzo Cappa, Salvatore Barzilai, both deputies in Parliament, and Cesare Sarfatti.[19]

The trial opened on October 8, 1910, before the Milan Tribunal, in a courtroom packed with Futurists and their sympathizers, including Margherita. Marinetti's testimony unleashed such rowdy cheers and applause from his supporters that the prosecution's case had to be made in a cleared courtroom. The next day, Cesare made the final arguments. In his now-famous aggressive style, Cesare assaulted the prosecution with a combination of irony, humor, and legal expertise. His summation, filled with allusions to classical art and sculpture, clearly revealed Margherita's influence. Cesare suggested that if Marinetti was condemned for pornography, the court would also have to judge Michelangelo guilty for his *David* and Canova for his *Venus*. He also cited the famous obscenity cases involving Flaubert, Baudelaire, and Swinburne. Cesare's concluding remarks created a sensation: "Marinetti is here," he concluded, "because at a certain point in his life he realized that it is not enough for literary figures to close themselves in their studies . . . rather, they must feel the impulses and the tempo of life around them. On that day, he became the head of Futurism. Innocenzo Cappa is partly a Futurist; Salvatore Barzilai not at all. This has no importance for the members of the Tribunal, but I am one completely . . . because they want to destroy that cult of the past that constitutes a disease in the artistic, literary, scientific, and political life of Italy." The tribunal deliberated only half an hour before returning a verdict of not guilty. Marinetti embraced his friends and was carried off amid triumphant applause and shouts of *"Viva Marinetti! Viva il Futurismo!"*[20]

Margherita later claimed partial credit for having "discovered" the Futurist painters, but she had mixed reactions to the movement. She agreed with Ardengo Soffici, who attacked the deliberately sensational methods of the Futurist *serate,* but she still appreciated their talent. Early Futurist paintings of 1909–1910 won her admiration, but not the later work. When the Futurist painters visited Paris in the fall of 1911, they found that the Cubists were grappling with similar aesthetic problems. Boccioni, Carrà, and others then incorporated some Cubist techniques in their own work, trying to capture a sense of space, time, form, and color into visual "states of mind" that would convey smells and noises as well as motion. These experiments projected art far beyond the confines of traditional painting, to the point of abandoning the representation of identifiable objects.[21]

Though a champion of cultural modernism, Margherita could never accept abstract art, and she voiced her critical opinions of the Futurist experiment with Cubism in the columns of *Avanti!* In 1912 Margherita and Boccioni actually broke off communication because they disagreed over artistic abstraction. In March of that year she suffered a fall, badly injuring her knee. Before it had healed properly, she went on a tour of central Italy and, while visiting the cathedral of Orvieto, slipped and fell again. This time the knee was severely fractured and required surgery. While recovering from the operation she had to stay off her feet for months. Boccioni reacted to her peace offer by unkindly comparing her art criticism to the injury: "Signora Sarfatti has started writing again, but her attempts to be nice irritate me. . . . It is odd how Signora Sarfatti seems destined to slip and hobble about in life just as she does when talking about art. . . . Fortunately, her falls down the stairs are not as serious as her screeching protests against abstractions . . . otherwise we'd have to put her neck back together!"[22]

Boccioni's caustic remarks may have been the reaction of a wounded lover. Mutual friends were convinced that they had been having an affair. He had long been a frequent guest at the Sarfatti apartment and at Il Soldo, but if Cesare noticed anything unseemly about his wife's behavior toward the artist, he kept it to himself. Boccioni's artistic creations at Margherita's country retreat remain part of the Sarfatti family legacy. In the summer of 1910, he painted Fiammetta toddling amid the flowers of a sunlit garden. Boccioni gave this remarkable portrait to Margherita with the words, "It is a masterpiece, and whoever denies it is a beast." He also began a portrait of Margherita but disliked it and ripped it with his palette knife. Margherita retrieved it from the trash and it remains a prized possession of the Sarfatti family. Boccioni's presence can still be seen on a wall stone of the villa on which he inscribed his initials in white paint.[23]

Boccioni's snide comments about Margherita were representative of the mixed feelings many Futurists had about her. No one could deny her valuable service in introducing the new movement in intelligent critical terms, especially after all the bad press Marinetti's antics had brought them. As Carrà had said, other Italian critics were so incompetent as to be incapable of "distinguishing a Cézanne from an Ettore Tito." But when she assumed for herself the role of patron of the Futurists, the artists were less pleased. In the spring of 1910, the Famiglia Artistica faced a financial crisis. Margherita interceded with the landlord, got the electricity restored, and raised funds to keep the gallery open. She also secured private commissions for the Futurists from such wealthy art buyers as Samuel and Betsy Baer, a German couple who owned a candy factory in Milan. A close friend of Betsy Baer, Margherita persuaded her to have Boccioni paint her portrait—the result was the famous painting *Le due amiche* (*The Two Friends*), which shows Betsy as a seated figure and her friend Luisa Ruberl standing.[24]

The Futurists acknowledged Margherita's work on their behalf, but resented her patronizing attitude. Young artists and writers chafed at the haughty self-aggrandizement that accompanied her role as protector as well as the self-assuredness with which she tossed off pronouncements about their work.[25] They nevertheless continued to court her, flocking to her salon on the Corso Venezia, now an important center of Milanese cultural life.

Margherita held court every Wednesday evening after dinner, except in the summer months when she was at Il Soldo. An assortment of painters, sculptors, writers, poets, architects, political figures, and personal friends sat around a table in the large living room. Cesare generally attended, but Margherita presided, smoking occasionally as she listened intently, asking questions in her deep, velvety voice. If bored or in disagreement with something, she tapped her nails impatiently on the table. One guest recalled that while Margherita remained at the center of the intense discussions, Cesare played with the children, and Boccioni, always the courtier, flirted with Margherita's orphaned niece, Elena. The food that usually followed the discussion was simple fare, such as fried polenta and beans, touted as "peasant" dishes.[26]

Boccioni and Russolo were regulars at the Wednesday sessions. Carrà came less often, especially after Margherita adversely criticized his more abstract work. Marinetti was often the center of attention, reciting the poems of Baudelaire, Mallarmé, or the Futurists. "I can still see him now," she wrote half a century later, "pounding his feet and screaming, his face enflamed." Ersilia and Luigi Maino frequently showed up, as did Betsy and Samuel Baer, the talented sculptor Adolfo Wildt, and Cesare Tallone, who taught painting at the Brera. Younger artists included the precocious architectural genius Antonio Sant'Elia, and the painters Mario Sironi, Enrico Prampolini, Aldo Carpi, Achille Funi, Arturo Tosi, Alberto Martini, and Libero Andreotti. Among the writers were novelists Aldo Palazzeschi and Alfredo Panzini, dramatist Sem Benelli, journalist Mario Missiroli, and the poet Ada Negri.[27]

The salon setting suited Margherita, for it satisfied her collector's instinct as well as stimulating her cultural interests. Certainly she liked being the center of attention. She had attended the salons held by Kuliscioff, Marinetti, and Maino. By the end of 1912, however, she had all but stopped going to Kuliscioff's and both Marinetti and Maino now came to the Sarfatti salon. Margherita realized Kuliscioff used her salon as a vehicle for exercising her influence in the Italian Socialist party. She criticized Kuliscioff's willingness "to influence events from behind the scenes"— "though she dominated men she was content to leave to them the show and trappings of power." But the same was true of Margherita; her own influence was exercised only through personal attentions, which were largely focused on male artists. Margherita wanted to be a participant, not an observer of life, but in prewar Italian society she had seized on the only real possibility available to a woman of ambition.[28]

Few of the people who passed through the Sarfatti salon meant more to Margherita than Ada Negri, a small but striking woman with a square face, dark hair parted in the middle, and large, pensive eyes. Negri had joined the Milanese radical-feminist network before the turn of the century and Margherita had first met her at one of Ersilia Maino's Saturday night receptions in her early days in Milan. Of working-class origins, Negri was teaching in a provincial school in 1892 when the publication of her first volume of poems, *Fatalità* (*Destiny*), won her national fame, an honorary teaching post in Milan, and a small stipend that allowed her to devote herself to writing.

Despite a ten-year age difference and fundamentally dissimilar personalities, Ada and Margherita became intimate friends. While Margherita exuded optimism and self-confidence, Ada was moody and pessimistic, consumed by loneliness and self-doubt, and constantly torn by personal crises. Indeed, most of Negri's literary works chronicled the spiritual and private traumas of her own life. Both women were attached to a humanistic rather than to a scientific view of Socialism and each was preoccupied with money, Margherita because of an avaricious streak that convinced her that she needed as much as possible, Negri because she had too little. Both were ambitious, Negri for achievement and recognition and Margherita for influence and power.[29]

Margherita's friendship with Ada Negri solidified following the collapse of the latter's marriage. Negri drew strength from Margherita's tougher, more resilient character and received much-needed familial affection from Cesare and the Sarfatti children, for whom she became "Aunt Ada." Margherita spent hours with Ada in private conversation, and found her the only person with whom she could share intimate confidences and the details of her own inner life. Ada, who lived in a small apartment with her aged mother and her daughter, was a constant guest in the Sarfatti household. She also stayed for long periods at Il Soldo, where she wrote portions of *Esilio* (*Exile*) and *Le solitarie* (*Solitary Women*), and poems about Margherita's children.

Margherita's belief in Negri's genius as a writer helped to bolster the poet in times of creative self-doubt. In the fall of 1916 Negri wanted to destroy the manuscript of *Le solitarie*—a series of stories about women who, despite family and love affairs, were essentially alone—but Margherita convinced her of their importance. When they were published during World War I, in the traumatic spring of 1917, Negri added a nostalgic dedication to Margherita evoking "those peaceful days, now gone, when we shared such complete interior harmony":

Days of a magical September at Il Soldo, that green haven of freshness, of beautiful field grasses and flowers that reached to our knees. The natural forest guarded by a black, fork-topped cypress. The sugary scent of the vines, the songs of women harvesting grapes, the festive bells ringing solemn vespers that filled the skies. And the giant bay tree shading the well, on whose branches our three mirthful adolescents recounted in the sun and the morning mist tales of the poets, from the *Odyssey* to the works of Pascoli, stealing between verses the barely ripened but succulent blood-red figs; and Fiammetta crowned in a golden halo, dressed in green, the

joy of life for having been born, Fiammetta winged and resplendent like
a little genie! . . .

And you with your own golden halo, a woman of beauty and of joy, who
found in every blade of grass and every ray of the sun reason for song and
smile, who took me by hand into your peaceful kingdom: so that even
I believed, for a moment, that the peace of God had entered my heart and
my life! . . .

Over the course of the next thirty years, Margherita and Ada's relationship proved to be as turbulent and acrimonious as one between two
passionate lovers. The memory of the days at Il Soldo remained like a sweet
dream, innocent and safe.[30]

Part Two

TWO LIVES

7

A Wonderful Lean Young Man

On the evening of September 29, 1911, Margherita joined a momentous debate between Socialist party leaders at the Kuliscioff-Turati apartment. The Italian government had that day declared war on Turkey as a prelude to invading its North African territories of Tripolitania and Cyrenaica, as Libya was then called. Everyone present agreed the war was an act of naked imperialist aggression, but Claudio Treves urged the Party to continue to support the government in order to protect working-class interests. Filippo Turati expressed acute discomfort in abandoning the Party's pacifist ideals, but yielded to Treves's eloquent arguments.

Anna Kuliscioff fixed Treves with her steely gaze and tore his argument to shreds. As for Turati: "Really, Filippino, even you don't understand anything!" According to Socialist theory, war merely pitted one country's proletariat against another's, and so could not possibly be advantageous to the workers. She forced both men to admit that the Party could not survive unless it condemned the unprovoked war with Turkey. The headlines in the next morning's *Avanti!* accordingly denounced Italian imperialism.[1]

The Socialists were not alone in their uncertain reactions to the war. Even Margherita's nationalist friend, Giuseppe Prezzolini, had changed his position. In mid-August, *La Voce* had carried an uncompromising article titled "Why We Must Not Go to Tripoli." Since the spring, Prezzolini's weekly review had argued against war with Turkey over Tripolitania and Cyrenaica. By the late summer, however, it was clear that Prime Minister Giovanni Giolitti was close to ordering the conquest of the Turkish colony.

In the fifteen years since Italy's humiliating defeat by the Ethiopians in 1896, the economic and military strength of the nation had surged. Now, in 1911, the government had decided to seize one of the last chunks of African territory that had escaped European domination. Such an act was no more than robbery but it hardly differed from what the other European powers had been doing in Africa for decades.

No doubt, Italy would emerge victorious. But, as Prezzolini had already warned his readers, such a conflict would force the total collapse of the decrepit Turkish Empire. Austria-Hungary, Italy's formal ally but actual rival, would be free to advance farther into the Balkans. As a result, Italy would lose access to markets and resources that were essential for her economic development. In contrast, what could the Italians gain in North Africa? Luigi Albertini, the conservative editor of Milan's highly influential *Corriere della Sera,* was running a series of articles on the question. These stressed the political and, above all, the economic advantages Italy could gain in Libya. Even more loudly, the fiery members of the new, radical right-wing Italian Nationalist Association were proclaiming Libya to be a paradise of fertility. Margherita had already questioned Israel Zangwill on the matter for *La Voce.* In 1907, Zangwill had studied the possibility of the Jewish colonization of Cyrenaica as an alternative to Palestine for the Jewish Territorial Organization. In a recent letter to Margherita, Zangwill had reported his pessimistic conclusions that the area could not be redeemed. It was and would remain a wasteland of sand and rock.[2]

Patriotic pride, however, overcame such practical considerations. Indeed, Prezzolini himself had founded *La Voce* in order to give expression to the growing sense of nationalism and self-confidence among many in the Italian cultural elite. In early October, therefore, a week after Italy declared war on Turkey, *La Voce* announced its grudging support for the invasion of Libya.[3]

The war provoked even greater conflict within the Socialist party. Giolitti, the "cunning old fox," as Margherita called him, whom the Party leadership had come to view with some benevolence, had clearly made Italy an imperialist aggressor. Yet, since Giolitti had come to dominate the Italian political system in 1901, he had shown considerable willingness to cooperate with the reformists. He had even tried to persuade the Socialists to abandon any pretense at revolution and to take part in his coalition government.

In March 1911, at Giolitti's request, King Vittorio Emanuele III had invited Leonida Bissolati to the Quirinal Palace to encourage him to join the prime minister's cabinet. Along with Ivanoe Bonomi, Bissolati led the right-wing reformists, the most moderate group within the Socialists in the Chamber of Deputies. Bissolati outraged even some of his own followers by accepting the invitation from a monarch who symbolized everything the Socialists were supposed to hate. Bissolati ostentatiously wore a fedora and gray suit, rather than the top hat and morning coat required by court etiquette. Nevertheless, he only reluctantly accepted Turati's argument that he must decline a Cabinet post to preserve Party unity.

Despite his failure to entice the Socialists into cooperation with him, Giolitti enfranchised the Party's working-class supporters anyway. In June

1911, his parliamentary forces introduced a bill that gave the vote to every literate male at age twenty-one and all illiterates who had done military service or reached the age of thirty. But Giolitti's style of consensus politics required concessions to the right as well, and in late September, he gave the conservatives in his coalition, as well as the Nationalists, the war they wanted.[4]

On October 5, 1911, Italian warships bombarded Tripoli and landed marines in the port city. By then, a widening split had opened within the Socialist party. Kuliscioff had persuaded Turati and Treves to condemn Giolitti, but Bissolati and other moderate Socialists did not agree. As the days passed and Bissolati refused to break with Giolitti, Kuliscioff insisted that he be driven from the ranks of Socialism. She came to this decision with great reluctance, for she cherished Bissolati. In fact, she cried in pain over the matter. As Turati later told Margherita, it was the first time he had ever seen her weep. Better than most, Kuliscioff understood what would happen to the Party.[5]

Margherita and Cesare soon came to the same difficult realization. For Margherita, in particular, any Socialist support for the Libyan War became intolerable. As the mother of two young boys, she experienced a special horror over the death and mutilation of so many young men. The depiction by the Nationalists of such suffering as glorious filled her with bitter rage. On a less emotional level, she saw the war provoking a narrow xenophobic jingoism among the Italians, aimed not only at the Turks and Arabs but at the Germans.

The German government displayed little sympathy when its Italian ally embarked on its imperial venture in North Africa. At the same time, by 1911 Germany was frightening many Europeans with its own threats of expansion and its claims to racial superiority. Under these circumstances, Italian resentment toward Germany was understandable. Yet it disgusted Margherita that any Socialist, such as Bissolati, would help worsen the general European climate of distrust and militarism by tolerating or even condoning a colonial war.[6]

What positions to take on the war, toward Giolitti, and over Bissolati's flirtation with the ruling class framed the debate when the Socialist party began its Twelfth Congress in Modena that October. To be sure, a pro forma condemnation of the attack on Tripoli received heavy applause but the speeches that followed revealed a deep fissure among the reformists.

Treves circulated a petition calling for an end to parliamentary cooperation with Giolitti. In contrast, Bissolati insisted that opposition to the Libyan War must not drive the Socialists into parliamentary opposition against Giolitti. All that would accomplish, he argued, would be the defeat of the universal male suffrage bill and the end to Socialist hopes to gain power through elections. Bonomi suggested that if the Socialists maintained their support for the prime minister, the Party could ensure that future Italian policies in Libya would promote the welfare of the Arabs. Socialist labor leader Angiolo Cabrini revealed himself to be even more influenced by nationalism when he described the expansion of Italian power in the world as a victory for the Italian working class. His speech prompted such violent attacks from the floor that twice the presiding officer had to suspend the session.[7]

Turati succeeded in holding the Party together only with great difficulty. At the conclusion of the congress, he eventually gained approval for a motion that called for an end to cooperation with Giolitti. But the wording rebuked Bissolati and his group only in the gentlest terms and suggested that when it benefited the Socialists, they could offer their parliamentary support to Giolitti on a case-by-case basis.[8]

Turati's carefully chosen words did little to resolve the truly serious problems of the Party. While the reformists argued over their degree of moral opposition to the war, more radical members of the Party protested by fighting in the streets. For such revolutionaries, moderates like Bissolati did not even deserve the name of "Socialist." These intransigents had resolved either to seize control of the Party from the reformists or, failing that, to break away and form their own revolutionary organization. Prominent among them was Benito Mussolini.

Three years younger than Margherita, Benito Mussolini had been born on the afternoon of July 29, 1883, in the tiny hamlet of Varano di Costa. His home region was in the commune of Predappio, situated in the Apennines of the Romagna, an area famous for its republican revolutionary politics. Centuries of subjugation to the popes, who had misruled the Romagna, had turned its people into enemies of the Church and of all forms of authority. After the province was annexed by the new Kingdom of Italy in 1860, the Romagna remained a stronghold of radicalism and rebellion. Mussolini grew up among these influences, for they had shaped his own family life.

His father, Alessandro, was a blacksmith and later an innkeeper. A generous and compassionate man, Alessandro was an early follower of the anarchist Bakunin, fiercely devoted to the Socialist cause and bitterly antagonistic to Church and monarchy. Mussolini's mother, Rosa Maltoni, came from better circumstances than her husband and was an elementary-school teacher. She was a sensitive, religious woman who was determined to raise her children above the precarious lower-middle-class existence she shared with her husband.

They named their first child Benito Amilcare Andrea, after Benito Juarez, the Mexican Indian who led the struggle against the French invaders of his country in the 1860s, Amilcare Cipriani, one of the few surviving leaders of the Paris Commune, and Andrea Costa. Benito Mussolini had a brother Arnaldo (named for Arnaldo da Brescia, a twelfth-century rebel priest), and a sister with the gentler name of Edvige.[9]

Mussolini developed into a moody, violent, and solitary young man, who displayed unusual intelligence and curiosity. He seems to have had no real friends among his male companions but, by his adolescence, had already revealed an extraordinary ability to attract the affections of women. As a student, Mussolini excelled in history, music, and Italian literature. He spent seven years in a private school run by Giosuè Carducci's brother, Valfredo, and was deeply influenced by the poet's calls for a revolutionary form of nationalism. But his family's lack of means prevented him from continuing his formal education, and after he finished his schooling in July 1901, Mussolini acquired a license to teach in elementary school.

With considerable difficulty, Mussolini found employment, a teaching job in the Po Valley town of Gualtieri. But he soon came to despise the region's reformist Socialists for their lack of revolutionary fervor. After five months' teaching at the wretched salary paid to primary-school instructors, and a physical confrontation with the mayor, Mussolini left Italy for the more prosperous countries to the north. He may also have been seeking to evade military service for a government he loathed; certainly, his departure made him a deserter under Italian law. He began a decade of wandering that Margherita described as having "driven him here and there without giving him peace, without, indeed, his giving peace to himself."[10]

Mussolini drifted for two years: to Switzerland, to France as far as Paris, to Germany and Austria, and back to Switzerland, working as a manual laborer where possible, often living the hand-to-mouth life of a tramp. He was in frequent trouble with the police and was jailed at least once, but this was as much for his Socialist activities as for his vagabondage.

The Socialist party was particularly active in Switzerland, trying to organize the large numbers of Italian emigrant laborers. Mussolini's talents for writing and speaking came to the attention of local Party officials. He soon found work as a labor-union secretary, speaker, and contributor to several Socialist newspapers. With his improved circumstances he was able to satisfy some of his craving for knowledge. He learned French, rudimentary German, even a little Spanish and English. He audited courses at the University of Lausanne, and read widely, if unsystematically, in the usual pattern of the autodidact. He was careful to test his new ideas on others in long conversations with Socialist comrades.[11]

While speaking in Lausanne in August or September 1902, Angelica

Balabanoff noticed a young man in the audience, "a face that I had never seen, contorted by extreme nervousness and . . . by hunger. His restless eyes, his troubled gaze, his hands in constant movement, his more than shabby clothes, all made me assume that this was a case of one of the poorest of the poor, of an outcast, of someone who was starving." After she finished speaking, Balabanoff discovered his name was Benito Mussolini.[12]

She approached him, discovered his plight—perhaps more psychological than physical at that point—and offered her assistance. While suspicious and proud, Mussolini reluctantly accepted her offer to share the work of a translation for a Milan publisher in return for fifty francs. From this collaboration there grew, as Margherita later delicately put it, "a very cordial relationship."

The differences between the two in age, education, and family background provoked an attraction of opposites. Balabanoff was no beauty, but she possessed a sensuous and compassionate nature. She provided the warmth and intimate companionship Mussolini craved in his lonely penury. Equally important, Balabanoff represented the intellectual and social status to which Mussolini aspired. Balabanoff soon discovered that her lover suffered from an agonizing sense of inferiority coupled to a ferocious ambition for prestige and power. He believed Socialism represented his only hope of escape from the miserable confines of his existence. Though Mussolini's father had taught him the skills of a blacksmith, he wanted to escape such a hard life through teaching. In Switzerland, he felt humiliated by his need to engage in manual labor and live among workers. Mussolini insisted proudly that he was an intellectual.

Mussolini shocked Balabanoff by his vision of the Party as a means of self-gratification. But his allegiance to political violence complemented her own conviction that Socialism could be achieved only by revolution. His powerful, if unformed, intellect and his explosive energy intrigued her. His willingness to voice his insecurities and fears appealed to her kindly nature, and she was drawn by his great physical magnetism.[13]

His harsh life had accentuated his strong jaw, hollowed his cheeks, and tightened the skin over his prominent cheekbones, emphasizing his truly remarkable eyes. They impressed everyone who met him. Sunk into deep sockets under his black brows, they seemed to shine from the center of his dark face. The whites of Mussolini's eyes glowed like unblemished porcelain and were so large that they completely encircled his irises of deep luminous brown. When they opened wide in surprise or rage, his eyes projected a mesmerizing force, like those of a bird of prey. "Eagle eyes," Margherita called them.[14]

Mussolini's voice complemented the attraction of his eyes. When he spoke, he displayed a remarkable range of tones from the shrill to the cavernous, almost as if he sang his words. Even silent, Mussolini dominated his surroundings. His body, while of average height and even short by today's standards, revealed such pent-up energy as to make him seem much taller than he was. He seemed to fill any space in which he stood.

Still, it is difficult to understand how a woman of Balabanoff's sensibilities could befriend a man who generally treated women with supreme contempt. Perhaps her progressive concepts about male-female relations played a role. She espoused a highly idealistic concept of sexual love: that it should be unrestrained by any rules save honesty and freedom. In her eyes, marriage perverted emotional relationships by the introduction of bourgeois property values. She rejected standard feminism because it defined men, rather than private property, class differences, and organized religion, as the cause of women's oppression. Balabanoff saw Socialism as the only road toward the liberation of women, in the context of the liberation of all humanity. Such ideas suggested a noble vision of human nature but they also could be taken advantage of by a man like Mussolini.[15]

Balabanoff later claimed that despite Mussolini's professed Marxism, he had read only *The Communist Manifesto*. She lent him numerous books, but soon realized that she could not alter Mussolini's preconceptions—all she could do was supply him with more sophisticated arguments for his theories.[16] Mussolini found the ideas of Nietzsche, Schopenhauer, Sorel, and Pareto particularly congenial. They reinforced his own tendency to reject any notion of human rationality. These thinkers also helped Mussolini abandon the Scientific Socialism of Marx and Engels. He could not agree with the stress laid by Marxists on the immutable laws of history and the insignificance of the individual.

Pareto made a particular impression. Mussolini managed to audit two of his courses at the University of Lausanne. Pareto argued that emotion and intuition swayed people more than economic self-interest or cold facts—he found a ready disciple in Mussolini. The young Italian even adopted Pareto's debating style, as he later admitted to Margherita.

Mussolini's reading supported his conviction that the exceptional man could alter history by imposing his will and projecting his beliefs on the mass of ordinary men. Emotions, myths, and force were far more effective in gaining and holding power than ideas. Action and violence held primacy over logic and thought. Democracy was a sham, for even in democracies elites controlled the sources of power. It would be far more honest to erect a government based upon this reality. A really great man could recognize the truth that life was brutal and uncertain, then heroically confront the odds and struggle to achieve success. But heroic failure was immensely preferable to the resignation of the masses.[17]

Balabanoff worked hard to improve her lover's German, and taught him to write simply and clearly without flaunting his learning. The point, she reminded him, was to educate and convince workers, not alienate or write down to them. She had no success convincing Mussolini to tone down his demagogic speaking style. She found his harangues vulgar and dishonest but had to admit that he was a powerfully persuasive speaker.

On one occasion, in late June 1904, Mussolini even had the temerity to debate the renowned Belgian Socialist, Émile Vandervelde. The Belgian had come to Lausanne to deliver a series of lectures, the last of which was on "Religion, a Private Affair." After Vandervelde insisted that Socialists had no special hostility to Christianity per se, the anti-clerical Mussolini leaped to his feet and loudly objected. But despite the violence of Mussolini's attack, Vandervelde won over the audience by arguing that Jesus had been the first Socialist, as demonstrated by his driving out the money changers from the Temple. Nonetheless, Mussolini had drawn a great deal of attention to himself, which may have been his main purpose all along.[18]

The Balabanoff-Mussolini relationship ended when in September 1904 King Vittorio Emanuele III celebrated the birth of a son with a general amnesty, one that included deserters. Mussolini returned home in November to fulfill his military obligation. Before departing, he spent a few final days with Balabanoff in Lugano. While Mussolini's ardor for her cooled in the months that followed, Balabanoff continued to harbor tender feelings for her young lover.

In January 1905, a month after his mother died, he began a period of service with the elite riflemen of the 10th Bersaglieri Regiment in Verona.[19] After his release in late 1906 he took another teaching post in a small village near the Austrian border. He found his job unpleasant, while his coarse language and insults to the Church offended the pious parents of his young students. Mussolini's contract was not renewed and he returned home in mid-1907. After studying for several months, he passed a state examination in French, enabling him to teach at the secondary-school level. He failed a similar German examination.

Giacinto M. Serrati, whom Mussolini had met in Switzerland, helped him find a job in a private school in Oneglia, on the Italian Riviera. Serrati's brother ran the local Socialist newspaper and soon Mussolini was dividing his time between teaching and writing newspaper articles. His violent attacks on the Church outraged local Catholics and his politics infuriated the local police. The authorities ordered him to leave town in June 1908 after just three months.

Mussolini joined his widowed father, who had moved to Forlì and opened an inn. Soon after his arrival, Mussolini helped organize a strike by regional farm workers and was arrested for advocating violence. He escaped a prison sentence on an appeal but was fined 100 lire two months later for a seditious speech. Mussolini had few outlets for his restless energy. He was clearly discontent and strengthened his reputation for eccentricity by his hostile, unruly behavior. When his growing political celebrity brought him an offer from the Socialists of Trento to become their local secretary and newspaper editor, Mussolini immediately accepted.[20]

Trento lay in Austria, in the Italian-speaking Alpine area known as the Trentino. For most Italians it was part of the *terra irredenta,* the "un-redeemed land" that was rightfully Italian on the basis of language and the desire of its people for union with Italy. Since 1882, however, Italy and Austria-Hungary had been allies, along with Germany, in the diplomatic-military union dubbed the Triple Alliance. This partnership was troubled by the Italian claims on Austrian territory and by rivalries between Italy and Austria-Hungary over influence in the Balkans. But the alliance calmed Italian fears of attack by its powerful French neighbor. It also reassured Italy's conservative rulers regarding their fears of Socialist revolution, for it placed the Italian social order under the implicit protection of the authoritarian monarchical systems that controlled Germany and Austria-Hungary.

But the attractions of the Triple Alliance for Italy declined during the political ascendancy of Giolitti. The shrewd prime minister engineered diplomatic understandings with France that greatly reduced the economic and colonial antagonisms that had divided Paris and Rome. After 1900, the Italian economy boomed, creating wealth that allowed some prosperity to trickle down to workers and farm laborers. When the working class demanded more, Giolitti forbade the police to intervene on the side of management during labor disputes, as had always been the case previously. Instead, he used the government in more of a mediating role, preparing the way for his strategy of wooing the Socialists into the political system. As a result of these policies, the defense that the Triple Alliance offered the Italian government against both foreign and domestic enemies decreased markedly in value.

During 1908–1909, Italy suffered a brief depression. In the midst of Italian troubles, the Austro-Hungarian government formally annexed the Balkan province of Bosnia-Herzogovina, which it had long occupied. The Italians protested this unilateral alteration of the status quo in an area of vital economic interest to both allies. The depression had underscored the needs of Italian industrialists for outlets beyond their own borders. Furthermore, Italy lacked virtually any iron, coal, or petroleum. All three minerals were available in the Balkans, to which Italian industry had to have access if it hoped for future expansion. But the Austro-Hungarians rejected Italian requests for compensation or guarantees. Germany supported Austria-Hungary.

Giolitti realized Italy had to back down. The only alternative was war against Austria, for which Italy was unprepared. Once the Italian economy had recovered, however, Giolitti began a massive armaments buildup in the spring of 1909. Italy would not be humiliated again.

One result of this crisis was the revival of Irredentism, as political commitment to the recovery of the *terra irredenta* was called. Giolitti could not espouse it so long as Italy remained too weak to defend its interests. But Giolitti's enemies seized Irredentism as an issue to use against the prime minister. It was a natural cause for the belligerently patriotic Nationalists, who could accuse Giolitti of cowardice. Most Socialists, of course, denounced nationalism as the cause of war and an excuse for the capitalists to make fat profits from arms production. But some Italian Socialists considered Irredentism in a different light. One of these was Cesare Battisti, the Socialist leader of Trento, the capital of one of the Italian-speaking areas of the Austro-Hungarian Empire.

Although Battisti had been converted to Socialism during his student days in Italy in the 1890s, he had devoted his life to the union of his native Trentino with Italy. Battisti was not so much a doctrinaire Marxist as an Italian patriot who saw in Socialism the fulfillment of the unrealized hopes of the Risorgimento. Like Mazzini, he dreamed of an Italy of the People, not one of kings or popes. In any case, even Socialists believed that national independence was a legitimate aim, as an intermediate step toward universal liberation. As Margherita described Battisti's beliefs: "First [the Italians] must achieve the triumphs of the principle of the nineteenth century, the principle of nationality, and [then], when the Italian race should have been reunited, the majority of the people should wring from the hands of the selfish minority its rights to life and welfare."[21]

For a while, Battisti based his hopes on the reformist Socialists of Austria. He had expected Austria-Hungary to evolve peacefully to Socialism and democracy, whereupon the Trentino would be granted self-determination and opt for inclusion into Italy. But Battisti had been severely disillusioned by the unwillingness of the Austrian Socialists to concede the loss of any of their national territory. The Austrian Socialist leaders feared losing support among the staunchly nationalist Austrian working class. At the same time, the Austrian Socialists were so wedded to reformism that they were clearly incapable of a revolutionary resolution of the Irredentism problem. Most distressing to Battisti were the private admissions of the Austrian Socialists about the attitudes of Austrian workers.

For years, European Socialists had intended to prevent a war among their countries by calling a general strike of all European workers in case of hostilities. At best, this might lead to the long-awaited triumph of Socialism. If not, it would at least hinder military operations and force a diplomatic settlement. But the Austrian comrades knew that their working class was riddled with patriotic sentiment. Not only would the workers not oppose the Austrian government in case of war, they probably would enthusiastically support it.

Ironically, these discoveries led Battisti himself into nationalist heresy. Thereafter, he saw war between Italy and Austria-Hungary as the only means to free Trento. Disarmament, one of the major goals of the Italian Socialists, made no sense in the face of unrestrained Austrian militarism. Battisti's thinking evolved into a strange mixture of nationalism and social- ism. Soon after Mussolini arrived in Trento in early February 1909, he met Battisti and discovered his ideas.[22]

Mussolini found life in Trento hard and lonely. In addition to his work as secretary of the Chamber of Labor, he put out the weekly Socialist newspaper virtually single-handed. He also contributed articles to Battisti's daily, *Il Popolo,* and continued to study French and German and to read extensively in the excellent public library. His numerous love affairs in Trento seem to have produced a number of offspring—as Margherita expressed it in her 1925 biography of Mussolini, "There are today in that region . . . one or two young men about twenty years old who do not have the usual physical appearance" of people of the area.

Mussolini devoted the bulk of his abundant energy to his work. While his journalistic attacks on the Church continued unabated, he found a new enemy: the Austrian government. He had not yet adopted Battisti's nation- alistic Socialism but he recognized that Irredentism and the struggle to defend Italian culture in the Trentino were powerful weapons to use to promote revolutionary sentiment. His assaults against the Austrian Church and State led to six stays in jail during his eight months in the Trentino; on three occasions he was heavily fined, and eleven issues of the newspaper were seized. Finally, in late September 1909, the police expelled Mussolini from Austrian territory.[23]

Mussolini's expulsion from the Trentino brought him a small measure of celebrity. Sympathetic Socialists raised the issue in Vienna and in Rome, but this did him little good. In early October, Mussolini returned to Forlì, where he faced a rather bleak future in his poor native region. The only work he could find was with his aging father at the inn.

Despite his lack of any apparent prospects, Mussolini married Rachele Guidi, the eighteen-year-old daughter of his father's companion. Mussolini had known her for years, for she had been a student in his mother's school. Only in late 1908, however, when Rachele Guidi turned seventeen, did Mussolini take any serious interest in her. She reciprocated his interest and agreed to move in with Mussolini in January 1910. It was a true Socialist union, unsanctioned by either civil or religious ceremony. Benito and

Rachele had their first child in September, a girl they named Edda. Two months later, Mussolini's father died.[24]

Radicals dominated political life in Forlì, but not the Socialist variety. Republicans held sway, invigorated by the leadership of the young and audacious Pietro Nenni. The Republican vision was that of the great Risorgimento hero, Giuseppe Mazzini: an egalitarian democratic Italy, free of the reactionary burden of monarchy, aristocracy, and papacy. Unlike the Socialists, the Republicans embraced Mazzini's unabashed nationalism and his dreams of Italian expansion. They believed that Italy, as a republic, would achieve greatness for the third time, ultimately commanding many nations and mastering the Mediterranean.

In late 1909 the Socialists of Forlì sought to restore their own fortunes by reviving their defunct local weekly. Mussolini alone was available to edit the paper and serve as Party secretary. He brought out the first issue of *La Lotta di Classe* (*The Class Struggle*) in January 1910. A month later, Mussolini became the Forlì correspondent for *Avanti!*. All this brought him the barely adequate salary of 120 lire a month.

His articles in *La Lotta di Classe* reflected his theoretical heresies, which were obscured only by the remarkable confusion of thinking within the Italian Socialist party. An elite group of intellectuals, Mussolini believed, could mobilize the masses, seize control over events, and bring about revolution by sheer force of willpower. Mussolini advanced a concept inimical to Socialism—that the true genius, armed with unbreakable idealism, unflinching courage, and deep learning, could discern opportunities for successful action and launch a victorious assault against the seat of power. His ideas were essentially similar to those of Lenin and his small band of Bolsheviks.[25]

Mussolini's views brought him into contact with Prezzolini and *La Voce*. Mussolini had discovered the journal during his days in Trento, in the spring of 1909. Mussolini responded positively to Prezzolini's call for a new generation of activists to lead Italy into a third historical cycle of national greatness. Encouraged by Prezzolini, Mussolini had begun to write a series of articles for *La Voce* on conditions in the Trentino. But Mussolini's expulsion from Austrian territory had interrupted his writing and, when he resumed work in Forlì, he expanded his project into a small book. *La Voce* published two excerpts in 1910, while Prezzolini published the completed manuscript as *Il Trentino veduto da un socialista* (*The Trentino Seen by a Socialist*) in May 1911.

Battisti's influence on Mussolini's conclusions seemed clear. Mussolini argued that German culture and language had assumed a racist and imperialist character, particularly toward the Italians. Even the German and Austrian working class had been infected with nationalism and militarism. But

Mussolini stopped short of advocating the war Battisti thought would free the *terra irredenta*. No Socialist could theoretically favor war, for war merely pitted the working class of one country against another.[26]

Despite its somewhat daunting political subject, Mussolini hoped to earn some money from *Il Trentino*. His only published novel, *Claudia Particella l'amante del cardinale,* which later appeared in English as *The Cardinal's Mistress,* had also been conceived as a money-maker, as well as an effective means of anti-clerical propaganda. Battisti brought the novel out in installments in his newspaper between January and May 1910. Mussolini earned disappointingly little from his scurrilous love story.[27] This was particularly unfortunate since he was far too generous with his meager earnings, spending or lending what he had to friends and associates despite the family he now had to support.

Mussolini's political work met with more success. His leadership brought many new recruits into the Forlì section of the Party, which almost doubled its membership in little more than a year. At a time when overall Socialist strength was declining, the appeal of Mussolini's violent, revolutionary rhetoric was a noticeable challenge to the Party's reformist leadership. Throughout 1910, while the Socialists planned for their national Party congress in Milan, Mussolini exhibited increasing contempt for the reformists. By October, when the Congress met, Mussolini was urging the revolutionaries to break completely with the reformists and to form their own political party; he saw himself as the natural leader of such a radical group.[28]

Mussolini presented a bizarre appearance when he made his speaking debut before the 1910 Socialist Party Congress. He wore slovenly, eccentric clothing and a heavy black beard; with his rolling eyes and wild gestures, he reminded one onlooker of a scarecrow. Even Party radicals found Mussolini an embarrassment, though they respected the hundreds of votes he commanded. Their attempt to take over the Party, however, met with overwhelming defeat. A few days later, at a separate meeting, the revolutionaries also rejected Mussolini's proposal to abandon the Party. But they did agree to create their own organization and appointed Mussolini its head in the Romagna.[29]

Margherita Sarfatti may have met Benito Mussolini for the first time at the Milan congress. If so, she kept the details of their first encounter to herself. The elegant figure she cut would have been striking to him, in contrast to the austere Socialists around her. And his shabby Bohemian appearance, offset by a burning, undisciplined vitality, would have made a strong impression on her.[30]

Mussolini now resolved to expand his role in Party politics. The compromise solution adopted by his faction left him completely dissatisfied.

Since they seemed to have no possibility of unseating the reformist Party leadership, he decided to renew his attempt to create an independent revolutionary Socialist party. He only awaited the appropriate opportunity to act.

This came in March 1911, when Bissolati paid his visit to the king. Mussolini demanded Bissolati's expulsion from the Party. When the leadership refused, Mussolini engineered a declaration by the Forlì Socialists of their "autonomy" from the Party, hoping that the other revolutionary sections would follow his group's example and accept him as leader. This they refused to do, however, leaving the matter to be decided at the next Party congress to be held in Modena in the fall of 1911.

Clearly, Mussolini had blundered. He had overestimated his strength and now found himself quite isolated. At Modena he would have to either recant, thus confessing his lack of real leadership abilities, or take his followers out of the Party altogether. He was not confident that many would go into political exile with him, and feared he might end up leading a party of one.

The Libyan War rescued Mussolini from this dismal situation. While Party leaders were debating at Modena, Mussolini and his Republican comrade Pietro Nenni were in jail in Forlì for inciting a crowd to insurrection. In late September, Mussolini and Nenni had tried to organize a regional strike to oppose the impending invasion of Tripoli. The strike grew violent and the local authorities arrested Mussolini and Nenni on October 14. Mussolini received a sentence of one year in prison for directing attacks on public officials, destroying state property, and leading armed resistance to the Libyan War.[31]

Bissolati's cooperation with Giolitti appeared in a very different light once the prime minister's war had begun. Mussolini's impetuous antiwar demonstrations of 1911 now seemed quite heroic. By the time Mussolini was sentenced, the Modena Party congress had revealed the resurgent strength of the Socialist radicals. As Mussolini noted in one of his last articles in La Lotta di Classe before his arrest: "We look forward to events with confidence. Almost always war leads to revolution."[32]

Events did unfold in Mussolini's favor. After an appeal, the court reduced his and Nenni's sentence and the two left prison on March 12, 1912. Two days later, while Mussolini was still celebrating his release, Bissolati paid another visit to Vittorio Emanuele III, this time accompanied by Bonomi and Cabrini. The three Socialist deputies had joined a parliamentary delegation to congratulate the king on his escape from an assassination attempt. Everyone in the Party was shocked to find its leaders paying court to the king while his royal army was slaughtering Arab civilians in Libya. With the reformists now deeply divided, control of the Party seemed to lie within the grasp of the revolutionaries. Mussolini concentrated his energies on uniting the Socialists of the Romagna under his leadership, in preparation for the next Party congress, scheduled for July in Reggio Emilia. There he would strive for his real goals: the editorship of *Avanti!* and the transformation of the Party from a political organization into "an aristocracy of intelligence and willpower."[33]

Margherita had meanwhile been trying to enlarge her role as a Party activist, but she remained at the fringes of power, frustrated by the impediments placed on her sex. The Party leadership allowed women some voice within its own councils, but Italian law forbade even the wealthiest and best-educated woman to hold public office or vote. The redoubtable Kuliscioff owed her political influence largely to her successive relationships with Andrea Costa and Filippo Turati. Margherita's own association with Kuliscioff was twice removed from real power within the Party. Margherita could satisfy her own ambitions only by an unlikely legal reform, or by a close connection with a man of real substance.

For now Margherita concentrated on the former. Her early work for *La Rassegna Femminile* and *Unione Femminile* had been for the cause of women's voting rights. By 1910, as universal male suffrage came under serious discussion in Parliament, the Party began debating the question. Turati and Kuliscioff split over the issue of demanding votes for women as well. Margherita helped form Pro-Suffrage Committees for women of all political persuasions, and she joined Kuliscioff in her fight. As usual in her disputes with Turati, Kuliscioff won. The Milan Party congress endorsed the idea of universal suffrage for both sexes.[34]

Kuliscioff pressed the struggle for women's rights following the introduction of Giolitti's male-suffrage bill in Parliament in June 1911. At the end of the year, she founded *La Difesa delle Lavoratrici* (*The Defense of Women Workers*) as the voice of Socialist feminism, with a special emphasis on the voting-rights question. The first issue appeared on January 7, 1912, thanks to considerable help from Margherita. Kuliscioff accepted Pietro Nenni as co-editor, following his and Mussolini's release from prison, to broaden the paper's political appeal.

Margherita devoted most of her initial articles for the new paper to condemnations of the Libyan war. She stressed issues particularly relevant to women, such as the plight of war widows struggling to survive on meager pensions, and increases in food costs brought on by war taxes. Her journalistic activities were interrupted in March 1912 by her knee injury; recuperation from the subsequent surgery prevented her attendance at the crucial Party congress that July.[35]

When the Reggio Emilia congress opened, most delegates already were convinced that advocates of cooperation with Giolitti must go. Even

Cesare Sarfatti, a moderate, had been openly condemning Bissolati since February. The revolutionaries were determined to drive Bissolati and his allies from the Party altogether. They chose Mussolini to present their indictment.[36]

Mussolini worked hard to prepare for this task. His speech that year was a striking feat of physical strength and endurance. His savage gestures and unrestrained emotion made more of an impact than his words. Mussolini assaulted the reformists with sarcasm, rage, and contempt. His ferocious delivery provoked excited cries of encouragement from the revolutionaries on the floor. The assembled Socialist party witnessed the exciting emergence of an oratorical wizard, but wiser heads noticed he seemed drunk with the adulation of the crowd. Mussolini concluded with a scathing rejection of collaboration with the ruling class: "Bissolati, Cabrini, Bonomi and the others awaiting our judgement can go to the Quirinal, even to the Vatican, if they want, but the Socialist Party declares that it is not prepared to follow them, not today, nor tomorrow nor ever!"[37]

Thunderous applause and shouts of congratulation followed. Mussolini descended from the podium pale and shaken. His revolutionary spirit had set the congress on fire. Even Cesare was carried away by the enthusiasm of the moment. When Bonomi attempted to defend himself, Cesare shouted crude insults from the floor. Afterward, Cesare described Mussolini to his convalescing wife: "a wonderful lean young man, with explosive eloquence, blunt, fiery, original; a man with a great future, we will hear more of him, he will be the future ruler of the Party."[38]

Mussolini surpassed his oratory with skillful political maneuvering. His motion for the expulsion of Bissolati, Bonomi, and Cabrini received nearly two and a half times as many votes as any of the various compromises offered. Mussolini was elected to a new Party directorate, along with twelve other revolutionaries, including Angelica Balabanoff. To Kuliscioff's fury, Turati was removed from his post on the directorate. Treves lost his position as editor of *Avanti!*.

Mussolini returned home to Forlì in triumph. His horizons had expanded far beyond the Romagna. During the next four months, he conducted a highly effective press campaign advancing his own candidacy for editorship of *Avanti!*. When the Party directors met in Milan in early November, they offered him the position. Mussolini responded negatively, stressing his inadequacies. Perhaps this was feigned, to encourage his comrades to beg him to accept, as they proceeded to do. But Mussolini had honestly pointed out his lack of education and culture. It may be that the enormity of the task had resurrected his deep-seated sense of insecurity. In the end, Mussolini did accept responsibility for the Party newspaper, on one condition: that Balabanoff serve as his assistant. The Party directors agreed. Mussolini moved to Milan that fall. He settled into an apartment on the Via Castel Morrone, just a few doors down from Balabanoff's flat. The two resumed their affair. A few months later, Rachele and Edda joined Mussolini, arriving on his doorstep quite unexpectedly.[39]

On December 1, 1912, Mussolini formally assumed the direction of *Avanti!*. He kept his true agenda to himself. His was apparently the triumph of an orthodox Socialist over those who had attempted to revise the Party's ideology. His close association with Balabanoff seemed to attest to that, for she was a particularly rigid Marxist.

Mussolini reinforced his revolutionary credentials by driving the reformist Treves off the staff of *Avanti!* altogether. He also accepted only 500 of the 700 lire per month salary Treves had received. Only Kuliscioff's personal intervention stopped Mussolini from publicly accusing Treves of corruption. For Treves and his mentors, Turati and Kuliscioff, the humiliation was profound.[40]

The Sarfattis suddenly found that the political alliance they had painstakingly constructed with Turati and Kuliscioff was virtually useless now that the revolutionaries controlled the Party. They hoped Mussolini might remember Cesare's vociferous support at the Reggio Emilia Party congress. Margherita's disappointment was mitigated by a sense of personal satisfaction in witnessing her feminist comrade's eclipse.

By September 1912, she had recovered from surgery sufficiently to return to active work on *La Difesa delle Lavoratrici*. She began a short-lived column in which she intended to describe the experiences of working women in Milan. One of her first articles described her visit the previous spring to the Agro di Roma, the vast agricultural region around the Italian capital. Margherita alluded to the wretched lives of the migrant farm workers of the area, but her column emphasized the work of a dedicated group of bourgeois intellectuals who had created schools for the laborers. She admired particularly the artist Duilio Cambelotti, who had decorated the walls of one school building with a colorful mural depicting shepherds with their flocks under a night sky luminous with stars.

The article infuriated Kuliscioff. It was the people, she argued, not their condescending "betters," who would lead Italy to Socialism. Margherita's column stressed art as a liberating force, and its distinct air of snobbery touched a chord of real fury in Kuliscioff. She castigated Sarfatti in front of an embarrassed editorial staff, and Margherita stormed out. Kuliscioff shrugged off the incident quickly but Margherita remembered her upbraiding for the rest of her life. She felt like a Russian peasant writhing under the lash of her mistress's knout. Though Kuliscioff eventually apologized, and Margherita returned briefly to the paper, their relationship never fully recovered. And Margherita thereafter was in need of a new political sponsor.[41]

Margherita and Mussolini encountered one another for the first time after the Reggio Emilia congress during one of his few appearances at Kuliscioff's salon. He had shaved off his unruly beard in favor of a mustache and was dressing better, now that he could afford it. Still, one can imagine his discomfort among the Party intellectuals, as those elegant sophisticates simultaneously excited his envy and disdain.

He knew that he was not welcome but he admired his hostess anyway. "Kuliscioff is worth more than even a good man," he once remarked, an extraordinary admission for Mussolini. Kuliscioff had more scathing words for Mussolini. As she angrily complained to Margherita, "In fact, he's really not a Marxist at all, nor even a Socialist. He's not even a politician. What he really is, is a little dreamer, a cheap poet who has read a bit of Nietzsche."[42]

Given the victory of Mussolini and the revolutionaries, Margherita's future as art critic for *Avanti!* had become uncertain. Whether out of discretion or guile, she visited Mussolini at his newspaper office soon after his arrival in Milan, to offer her resignation. Art, she suspected, would not rank high on a revolutionary's list of priorities.

But after Mussolini had admitted her to his office, Margherita quickly sensed that he was physically attracted to her. As Mussolini later confessed, he found full-figured, blond women like Margherita almost irresistible. In turn, Margherita felt herself drawn to him. Mussolini's eyes, the cruel line of his mouth, and most of all, the coiled energy that he radiated made a compelling impression on her.

They talked for a while about Margherita's work and then their conversation shifted to a discussion of Nietzsche. She soon realized that Mussolini did not have as firm a grasp of the German philosopher's ideas as he pretended, but she wisely said nothing to contradict him. Finally, to her delight, Mussolini begged her to remain with the paper. Nonetheless, he rejected art as a fit subject for Socialists and insisted that she write on other subjects. No signed articles by Margherita appeared in *Avanti!* for the rest of the year nor all of the next. It would take time for Margherita to convince Mussolini about the political power of art.

She saw him a few nights later at a concert, where she caught him staring brazenly at her. To Margherita, Mussolini's eyes seemed to be burning. It was clear that their disagreements about art would not keep them apart.[43]

Soon, Kuliscioff noticed a striking change in Margherita's behavior. Not only had she stopped telephoning and attending Kuliscioff's salon, but she had ceased to appear at Party functions. Kuliscioff wondered if she had wounded Margherita in some particularly serious way. Other comrades expressed more annoyance. They had long resented the Sarfattis' substantial income and their efforts to increase it still more. Now they gossiped that Margherita was dismissing the Party from her life altogether. In fact, Margherita had become fascinated by Mussolini. During frequent visits to his office they had begun engaging in lively arguments over a broad range of political and philosophical topics.[44]

But when Turati met Margherita at an educational conference in Rome in early December, she explained her disappearance by saying that she had not been herself lately. Her long convalescence after her knee injury seemed to support that. Turati indulged her, allowing Margherita to run far overtime when she delivered a report on Party efforts to bring theater to the people, until even he grew annoyed and cut her off.

This paper seems to have been the last written work that Margherita devoted to the arts for over a year to come. It seems that Mussolini's political attitudes had affected her deeply. Certainly, she was drawn to his tough, virile looks and his violently aggressive personality. Previously, Margherita had begun to find Party functions boring or irrelevant. But she started to attend again when she knew that Mussolini would be there.[45]

Eventually, she began spending time with him away from the *Avanti!* office or Party meetings. But on one of his first visits to her home, she was with friends and kept him waiting for hours. He responded with uncharacteristic patience and occupied himself reading newspapers in her drawing room. Margherita's friends, of course, could not contain their curiosity. What was he like? How did he dress? Finally, one of them blurted out: "But what's your impression of him, really, truly?" Margherita thought for a moment. Then she murmured, "He's a hoodlum."[46]

8

The Negation of Socialism

For a time Mussolini's reckless bravado captivated Margherita. His appearance at first "set me thinking rather of those legendary heroes who would make their way in rusty armour and wearing unknown devices into some great royal tournament and, in joust after joust, unhorse the proudest knights and, without ever raising their visor, accept the coveted prize of shield or coat of mail or splendid charger, and then, their identity still unguessed, spur back into the unknown." But once she knew him better she "could discern nothing about him either of the jousting knight or of the poet. He put me in mind rather of Savonarola, by reason of the strange fanatical gleam in his eyes and by the imperious curve of his nose!"

As Margherita discovered, the source of the fanaticism reflected in Mussolini's face sprang from ferocious rage and resentment. Despite the relative advantages he had enjoyed, Mussolini described his early years as stunted by deprivation and humiliation. He openly admitted that he longed for power primarily to take vengeance on the ruling class, which he blamed for his suffering.

Yet Mussolini revealed an underlying guilt over these feelings to Margherita. Despite his atheism, once, soon after they met, he confessed to her that he secretly believed that he had been tempted by Satan to sell his soul in return for earthly power. Loneliness also tortured him. While he had many companions, he enjoyed no real friendships—at least with men. Margherita came to understand that he had sublimated these urges and fears into a determination to overturn society by violent revolution.[1]

In early 1913 Milanese Socialists had their first taste of Mussolini's propensity for extremism. On January 6, the Carabinieri shot to death seven farm workers and wounded forty-nine others during a protest at Rocca Gorga, some forty miles southeast of Rome. The town lay on the slopes of the Apennines overlooking the Agro di Roma. Though Margherita's 1912 article concerning the area had been too focused on intellectual activists, the deprivation suffered by the workers there had shocked her profoundly.

Mussolini responded to the killings with inflammatory articles and speeches. He compared the actions of the police to the widespread shooting and hanging of Arabs by the army in Libya. At the end of a harangue to a group of workers in Milan on January 9, Mussolini shouted: "Death to those who massacre the people! Long live the Revolution!" His *Avanti!* article a week later stated: "Ours is a war cry. Those who massacre know that they can be, in their turn, massacred." These words constituted a felony under Italian law. Mussolini was indicted for incitement to violence and defending crimes against the State, although he did not stand trial until March 1914.[2]

Mussolini's actions gravely alarmed Turati and Kuliscioff, who found his rhetoric "insane." Both were convinced that he intended to provoke some kind of uprising in Milan. Indeed, in a February 5 article in *Avanti!*, Mussolini encouraged Socialists to hurl themselves against the bourgeoisie in a revolutionary assault. Turati raised the issue with the Party directors. With Balabanoff's support, after a five-day meeting of the Socialist leadership in Rome in early March, Mussolini emerged triumphant. The directorate authorized plans for a general strike to paralyze the country in case of new government attacks on the working class.

After having his appointment reconfirmed, Mussolini was secure enough to reveal his craving for adventure, confrontation, and even destruction. Writing in early April as "L'homme qui cherche" (his well-known pseudonym), Mussolini boasted of the direction in which he intended to lead Italian Socialism: "Now men must cross the frontier of their physical and moral possibilities, and challenge the unknown. To perish, if need be. . . . I want to hunt down common sense; I want to kill it." It would be better for the Party to set an example for future generations with a failed revolution, Mussolini argued, than to lose its soul in timid parliamentary politics.[3]

Margherita's interest in a man of such violent and impulsive character may have seemed odd to her friends but there is no doubt that she and Mussolini had become lovers by early 1913. Yet each found the other repellent as well as attractive. Margherita enjoyed a life of sexual freedom but she still felt upset at Mussolini's casual attitude toward the many other women in his life. He had recently had a baby with Fernanda Ostrovski, a Russian Jew he had met sometime before the birth of his daughter Edda. Yet he showed no responsibility toward his second child. In Milan, Mussolini made no secret of his relationship with Balabanoff. As a result, many of Mussolini's comrades thought that Edda was Balabanoff's daughter, not Rachele's. Margherita herself always remained unsure. Such matters complicated her relationship with Mussolini. By the early spring of 1913, they were having frequent jealous quarrels.

He met Leda Rafanelli in March. Her exotic nature greatly attracted him. In Egypt she had converted to Islam and Anarchism. Rafanelli had been Carlo Carrà's lover a few years before when he was painting his Futurist masterpiece, *The Funeral of the Anarchist Galli*. Mussolini began courting Rafanelli insistently but without success. He stoutly denied that he was married, but in a puerile attempt to win Rafanelli's admiration or to provoke her jealousy, he boasted of other conquests. "There are two women who love me madly but I do not love them. . . . One is rather plain but she has a noble and generous soul. The other is beautiful but she has a sly and greedy nature, she's stingy, in fact. Of course, that one is a Jew. . . ."

Rafanelli was torn between disbelief and compassion when Mussolini announced that the first of his lovers was Balabanoff. How, she wondered, could that tough, courageous revolutionary have fallen so low? Rafanelli asked about the other.

"The second, the beautiful but greedy one, as cunning as the first is pure of heart, is the writer Margherita Sarfatti."

"The wife of the lawyer?"

"Yes . . . She pursues me with her love, but I could never love her. Her stinginess disgusts me! Look! She's rich and lives in a big *palazzo* on the Corso Venezia. Then, when one of her articles is published, she sends her maid to *Avanti!* to get three free copies . . . to save a few cents . . . and she has a newsstand right next to her house!"

Mussolini explained all this by reiterating one fact: Margherita was a Jew. Outraged by his crude anti-Semitism, Rafanelli eventually forced Mussolini to admit that not all Jews were consumed by a love of money. After all, Balabanoff and Kuliscioff were Jewish too. Rafanelli did not think she really convinced him.[4]

In April 1913, a few weeks after this conversation, Margherita left for an extended trip to England and France. Either Mussolini had exaggerated the strength of her passion for him, or she had decided to flee a highly stressful relationship. Mussolini's worship of violence, his ignorant notions about Jews, his contempt for art, his abusive manipulation of women—indeed, his outright rejection of feminism—all ran counter to Margherita's deepest sensibilities. And she was interested in studying firsthand the English suffragist movement. After completing another article on the Agro di Roma, this time for *La Voce*, Margherita took the train to Paris, and then to London.

Margherita's visit to England coincided with a series of crises in the suffragist movement led by the Women's Social and Political Union

(WSPU). Over the previous six years, British public opinion had moved toward granting at least wealthier women the vote. But some militant feminists had grown impatient of further delay. In late 1912, they had started a campaign to destroy property in order to protest their continued exclusion from political equality. Arrests of suffragists followed, to which they responded with hunger strikes.

In response, groups of angry men began attacking suffragist demonstrations. Despite the support of such prominent men as Israel Zangwill and George Bernard Shaw, the WSPU moved toward barring male affiliation and adopting an anti-male, anti-marriage ideology.

The leaders of the WSPU, Emmeline Pankhurst and her two daughters, Christabel and Sylvia, had split over a different issue. While Sylvia Pankhurst urged the movement to concentrate on organizing working-class women, the other Pankhursts joined with Millicent Garrett Fawcett in adopting the limited goal of gaining the vote for propertied women. In May 1913 the House of Commons narrowly rejected a bill to enfranchise the wives of homeowners. Militant suffragist violence was answered by such severe government measures, by British standards, that many considered constitutional guarantees of individual rights to have been transgressed.[5]

All this was heady stuff for Margherita. In Italy the suffragist movement was humorously dismissed in the mainstream press. Italian women enjoyed few serious hopes of political rights in the immediate future. Italian juries routinely acquitted jealous husbands who had murdered their wives. Crude sexist attitudes dominated relations between most Italian men and women. But after discussions with Israel and Edith Zangwill, the Pankhursts, and Fawcett, Margherita saw new possibilities of action for Italian women.

Margherita concluded that English culture, with its emphasis on standards of decency and fair play, had aided the women's rights movement, but the effects of industrialization had been more important. A need for labor brought women into factories and some professions. Employed alongside men, women's eyes were opened to their oppression. A degree of financial autonomy weakened the idea that women were merely men's property, and strengthened the concept of marriage as a voluntary union of equals. Having gained a measure of economic and social status, English women had begun the struggle for political power.

Margherita took heart from the social pressures stimulated by the industrial process. England's present, in effect, represented Italy's future. The timing of her visit had allowed Margherita to observe the use of violence as a means for gaining women's rights. Previously she had denounced the use of force, but now she came to recognize its power to sharpen political consciousness. She had seen how a disciplined and determined cadre could, through violence, thoroughly disrupt the functioning of a constitutional system. Her discussions with Mussolini may have initiated the process, but it was her exposure to the ideas of militant suffragists that definitely changed her thinking.[6]

Margherita also found time to visit an exhibit Boccioni had encouraged her to see. By the time she arrived at Gino Severini's Marlborough Gallery show, the artist had already crated his paintings for shipment to Paris, where he lived. Margherita insisted he unpack everything. Certain of a sale, Severini complied; to his disgust, Margherita bought nothing. The painter complained bitterly to Boccioni, who eventually prevailed on Margherita to buy one of Severini's drawings.[7]

Margherita visited Paris on her way to England and she stayed there again on her return trip to Italy. She visited the galleries to see the latest examples of modern painting and sculpture; but her most memorable experiences in Paris were conversations with the poet and philosopher Charles Péguy, and encounters with expatriate Italians.

Péguy's journal, *Cahiers de la Quinzaine* (*Fortnightly Journal*), occupied roughly the same influential place in the cultural life of France that Prezzolini's *La Voce* did in Italy. Though they did not always agree, Péguy and Prezzolini admired each other's intellectual nationalism and had become friends in Paris. Péguy now sent his regards to the editor through Margherita.

One of the stoutest defenders of Dreyfus and an outspoken opponent of anti-Semitism, Péguy had already earned Margherita's admiration. His appreciation of Zangwill's writing, "Chad Gadya" in particular, also formed a bond between them. But Péguy had broken with the French Socialist party for the same reasons that he had rejected the Catholic Church: his hatred of any form of conformity or control over thought. Now he embraced a highly idiosyncratic blend of personal Catholicism, non-Marxist Socialism, and above all, fierce French nationalism.

Péguy had devoted much energy to popularizing the philosophical concepts of Henri Bergson. Bergson's stress on the primacy of feeling and action over thought and practical considerations helped Péguy justify his own constant attacks on authority. Bergson argued that true freedom lay in acting spontaneously on inspiration from one's inner being, and that human progress depended on directing such actions in assaults on the established, conservative order. Unfortunately, Péguy enlisted Bergson's ideas to support the notion that war could benefit mankind, specifically in the liberation of France from the German threat.

Péguy nourished an almost pathological hatred for Germany. He longed for a war of revenge to recover the provinces of Alsace and Lorraine, lost to the Germans in the war of 1870–1871. Péguy viewed any efforts to avert such a conflict as treason. At the time of his talks with Margherita, he had begun advocating the assassination of Jean Jaurès, the head of the French Socialist party. Once his close friend, Péguy now considered Jaurès's efforts to foster Franco-German understanding and prevent a war a vile betrayal of French interests. Péguy had come to see bloodshed as a heroic liberation from the timid and corrupt compromises of ordinary life. Once again, Margherita heard violence advocated by someone she admired.[8]

Margherita also saw a number of Italian expatriates, including Gabriele D'Annunzio, who had fled to Paris to escape creditors back home. She met the handsome but often drunk master painter Amedeo Modigliani, the Francophile Ricciotto Canudo, a dandified aesthete who wore an ivy leaf in his lapel and advocated the cinema as a new art form, and the Garibaldi brothers, grandsons of the Risorgimento hero, who were often enmeshed in political intrigues and outlandish adventures.

During past visits to Paris, Margherita had frequented the Montparnasse quarter with D'Annunzio and others. Diego Rivera, the brilliant, hulking Mexican painter, remembered her at their first meeting: "An exotic and beautiful figure, of such ability and distinction that, in the midst of a group of men without other women present, she only succeeded in passing unnoticed by downplaying her physical beauty and personal charm."[9]

Now, in the spring of 1913, Rivera encountered Margherita again, but this time in the company of Canudo and his bizarre mistress, Valentine de Saint Point. In one version of his memoirs, Rivera, who was famous for deliberate exaggerations, described Saint Point as "Margherita's lover"; in another version, he suggested a liaison between Canudo and Margherita.[10] Rivera's statements about Margherita's love affairs may have been sheer invention, but it is entirely possible that he based them on direct observation. Her involvement with Ada Negri depended on deep emotional intimacy, and she and Colette, an unabashed bisexual who dressed in male clothes, were close friends. Unlike many of her Socialist comrades, for whom homosexuality did not conform to Marxist orthodoxy, Margherita was comfortable with people of diverse sexual orientation. Margherita's granddaughter today points out that in later life many of her grandmother's closest friends were homosexual.[11]

Saint Point's personality would certainly have attracted Margherita. The great-granddaughter of the poet Lamartine, she was born in Lyons in 1875, five years before Margherita. She studied painting under the famous Art Nouveau poster artist Alphonse Mucha, and published volumes of poems, books on aesthetics, and a trilogy of novels titled *A Love, An Incest,* and *A Woman and Desire*. Saint Point's "Manifesto of Futurist Women," issued in 1912 in response to Marinetti's proclaimed contempt for women, revealed Nietzsche's influence in a call for brutal and harsh superwomen capable of violence, cruelty, and lust. Rejecting feminism, she advocated instead the principle of "virility" and the abandonment of rigid gender distinctions between men and women. *"It is absurd,"* she wrote, *"to divide humanity into women and men.* Every superman, every hero . . . is composed simultaneously of feminine and masculine elements of femininity and masculinity—he is a complete being. An exclusively male individual is nothing but a brute; an exclusively female individual is nothing but weakness. *What is most lacking in women and men alike is masculinity."*

In January 1913, a few months before Rivera saw her with Margherita, Saint Point launched her "Futurist Manifesto of Lust." Here she supported Futurism's sexual system, which saw the pleasures of the flesh as "the weapon of the conqueror," justifying rape and war as the means for annihilating the weak and fertilizing the world with creativity. Saint Point proclaimed lust as the dynamic force that drives civilization—"lust, under whatever aspects it shows itself, whether they are considered normal or abnormal, is always the supreme spur. . . . *We must stop despising Desire,* this attraction at once delicate and brutal between two bodies, of whatever sex, two bodies that want each other, striving for unity."[12]

A poised, beautiful woman, Saint Point had already achieved notoriety when Margherita met her. Besides her books, she had invented *La Metachorie,* an abstract dance performance that combined poetry, drama, light, and music—which Claude Debussy and others had composed for her—to render ideas rather than emotions. Margherita was in Paris when *La Metachorie* premiered at the Théâtre des Champs-Élysées. Saint Point and Canudo also co-founded *Montjoie!,* a short-lived journal dedicated to an intellectual elite, intent on celebrating the primacy of modern French and Italian culture. It enjoyed the collaboration of avant-garde writers such as Apollinaire and Raynal, and was illustrated with the work of Monet, Léger, and Cézanne.[13]

Margherita did not hurry back to Milan. Following her return to Italy, she underwent mudpack treatments for her leg at Acqui Termi, a health spa some sixty miles southwest of Milan. All July she enjoyed the seashore at the Venetian Lido, and in August and September she escaped the summer heat at Il Soldo. There she checked the proofs of her article on the Agro di Roma for *La Voce* and wrote another on the English suffragists. She also translated Zangwill's booklet on the militant feminists for Prezzolini's press. When subjects for other pieces occurred to her, ranging from art to alcoholism, she offered them to Prezzolini as well.

But her writing and her beautiful surroundings did not bring Margherita much happiness. Recent exposure to the English struggle for women's rights made the inferior status of Italian women all the more painful for her. Although she escaped the brutality suffered by less fortunate women, she still faced the sneers and condescension of Italian men, even among the educated classes. Margherita's passionate advocacy of modern art, her acquaintance with its creators, and her critical appraisal of their works provided much of the meaning of her life. But her commitment to controversial modern movements also exposed her to the hostility and ignorant derision of threatened intellectual conformists.[14]

The deterioration of Italian politics was even more upsetting to Margherita. The conclusion of the Libyan War by treaty in October 1912 left Italy in possession of the North African colony, but hardly ended the deleterious effects of the conflict. Encouraged by Turkey's defeat, Serbia, Montenegro, Bulgaria, and Greece invaded the remnants of the Turkish Empire's territory in the Balkans that same week. By the spring of 1913, the Turks had been driven back to the walls of Istanbul. This drastic alteration of the status quo threatened to involve Italy in new wars. Many Socialists feared the government would be tempted to seize new pieces of Turkey's shrinking domain. More threatening was the possibility of an Italian-Austrian clash over conflicting interests in the newly fragmented Balkans. The Nationalists began demanding that Italy assert itself.

The Libyan and Balkan wars, combined with the introduction of near-universal male suffrage, had exacerbated the political struggle between the extreme right and left. All parties viewed the next election, the first under the new voting law, as crucial. Despite the recent split in their ranks, many Socialists hoped the new working-class voters would substantially increase the Party's seats in the Chamber of Deputies. A large Socialist bloc in Parliament would fight for peace and concentrate Italian resources on domestic reforms. The Nationalists warned voters what too many Socialists in Parliament would mean, arguing that their own deputies would counterbalance the left and create pressure for an assertive Italian foreign policy. Realizing that Giolitti would call elections once passions generated by the Libyan War cooled, the Socialists prepared for the campaign.

Mussolini scoffed at parliamentary politics as a bourgeois tool to defuse revolutionary tendencies. He saw an electoral campaign only as an effective means of spreading revolutionary propaganda among the newly enfranchised workers and peasants. While Margherita was abroad, he had searched for some issue or incident to kindle revolutionary zeal in the new voters. A failed attempt at a general strike by workers in Milan seemed to offer the right opportunity. Led by a syndicalist, Filippo Corridoni, the strike was a failure partly because of the opposition of Turati and other Socialist labor leaders. Mussolini blasted them both for cowardice in the pages of *Avanti!*

In June, when Corridoni and his associates received severe prison sentences, the Milanese workers organized a successful general strike in protest. Although it paralyzed the city, the strike ended in a few days. Mussolini, however, proclaimed the labor action a triumph—not because it had accomplished anything concrete but because it had sent a warning to the ruling class and inspired the workers with a sense of their power.

This time, Mussolini provoked serious dismay within the Party leadership, and not only from the moderates. He appeared to act on vulgar misconceptions crudely drawn from Nietzsche and Bergson, stressing spontaneous actions based on rage and resentment, rather than from a clear understanding of the ideas of Marx and Engels. Turati wondered whether Mussolini considered a strike to be some kind of mystical act, and just what his politics were: "Religion? Magic? Utopia? Sport? Literature? Romance? Neurosis? Certainly it is not Socialism—because it is the negation of Socialism."[15]

Before the most important election in Party history, Mussolini's policies had sharply divided the Socialist leadership. He had acquired considerable support from the Party's followers. The circulation of *Avanti!* had climbed sharply and Socialist membership was on the rise. Still, Mussolini threatened to lead his followers in a wild new direction. A divided Party could only aid the forces of conservatism and reaction, as well as the new radical right. "It is," observed Margherita, "a sad time for public life in Italy."[16]

Party directors met in Rome on July 13 to discuss again Mussolini's control of *Avanti!*. This time he was harshly criticized, and the next day a vote was taken to determine his future. Mussolini and Balabanoff abstained as interested parties. Seven directors voted in his favor, three against. When Mussolini called their bluff and offered his resignation, the directors held a second vote, giving him their unanimous approval.

Still Mussolini knew he had received a warning. He returned to Milan determined to change course, at least for the moment, and find a scapegoat for his recent mistakes. Before the end of the month, Balabanoff resigned from *Avanti!*. Ostensibly her departure was triggered by her anger over Mussolini's broken promise to aid a woman friend, an incident he probably engineered deliberately. But their relationship had been stormy from the beginning. He had never been enough of a Marxist for her, and he knew he would be unable to moderate his editorial policy unless he broke with Balabanoff.

Pressure from Rachele appears to have been another motive for his break with Balabanoff. Mussolini's common-law wife finally had learned about his affair and had begun to plague him over it. Mussolini vehemently denied Rachele's accusations, stressing the Russian's homeliness. "If I found myself in a desert and Angelica was the only woman, I would prefer

to court an ape," he insisted. But Mussolini had never placed much emphasis on facial beauty in his lovers and Rachele knew it.[17]

In early August, Corridoni ignited a new general strike in Milan, which
he hoped would spread throughout Italy. This time Mussolini displayed a
critical tone in *Avanti!*. When the strike collapsed, he condemned Corridoni for leading the workers down a false path to revolution. The forthcoming election now received all Mussolini's attention. On September 7,
the Party launched its campaign across Italy. When Giolitti officially dissolved Parliament three weeks later and called elections for October 26, the
Socialists were well prepared. Mussolini ran as a Socialist candidate from
Forlì, knowing in advance he would lose to his Republican opponent.

In newspaper articles and election speeches, Mussolini reversed his
stand on the value of universal suffrage. He now spoke of it as a valuable
test of Party strength, and an opportunity to create an honest government.
Through the pages of *Avanti!*, Mussolini orchestrated the most effective
electoral campaign in Party history. He described the election as a referendum on the Libyan War, as a contest between warmongering nationalism
and peace-loving internationalism.

Fearing a triumph by the atheistic, revolutionary party, the Vatican
entered the election campaign on a massive scale. Pius X ended the ban on
Catholic voting in districts where a Socialist victory seemed possible, and
instructed the faithful to support Giolitti's candidates. In return, Giolitti
promised to fight any attempt to legalize divorce, to protect aid to Catholic
schools, and to defend religious instruction in public schools. Nonetheless,
after the voting in late October and the runoffs on November 2, the
Socialists emerged with major gains.

The expulsion of Bissolati and his followers, and the defection of others
as independents, had reduced Party representation in Parliament from 42
to 25. Now they won 53 seats, out of the 508 available. Eight more
independent Socialists and Revolutionary Syndicalists also won seats. Giolitti's supporters dropped in number from 382 to 310. For this, Mussolini
deserved much of the credit. On the other hand, Bissolati's Social Reform-
ers gained 6 places, giving them 19 in total. More ominously, the Nationalist party entered the Chamber of Deputies for the first time with 6 deputies.
The extreme left and right had been strengthened. One third of the
deputies had never served before. The result was a Parliament far less able
than its predecessor to compromise and to legislate effectively.[18]

In the early fall, Margherita returned to Milan, and to Mussolini. The
circumstances of their reconciliation are as unclear as their reasons for
parting, but now each wanted what the other could offer. Without Balabanoff, Mussolini lacked an intellectual mentor to whom he could turn in
his frequent crises of self-confidence. His inability to reveal his weaknesses

to another man, his need for someone he could trust in candid discussions of politics, and his desire for a spiritual intimacy that Rachele could not provide, all formed part of his interest in Margherita. Besides, his relationship with a member of the Kuliscioff salon was for him a "conquest" of the very group that had spurned him and derided his lack of intellectual polish. Knowing that he had won Margherita away from them gave Mussolini considerable pleasure.

For Margherita, the situation was more complicated. Months of rest, work, and absence from Milan had restored her sense of well-being. When she returned home, she was estranged from both power centers within the Party. But Socialism was more than politics for Margherita. It was a way of life, more like a religion than a set of political attitudes. Margherita's letters to Prezzolini over the spring and summer of 1913 had an importunate air, as if she sought something to fill an emptiness, and somewhere to pour out her ideas and energies.

In late August, La Voce printed Margherita's second article on the Agro di Roma. This time she stressed the filth, malaria, neglect, and despair that afflicted the laborers of the region as they struggled to survive on less than one lira a day. She believed these were people for whom the vote would mean nothing since they lived, suffered, and died outside any political system whatsoever. Six weeks later, Margherita's article on the English suffragists appeared in La Voce. It reaffirmed her determination to win the vote for Italian women, as well as her recent conversion to the need for political violence. Thus she managed to send expiatory signals to both Mussolini and Kuliscioff.[19]

Margherita accepted Kuliscioff's plea to rejoin the staff of La Difesa delle Lavoratrici. But after their dispute of the previous fall, she was not able to work comfortably with Kuliscioff. Mussolini offered an alluring combination of vulnerability and power, attractiveness and brutality, loneliness and celebrity, idealism and success. Within the sphere of Italian Socialism, he had made a spectacular rise from obscurity to unrivaled prominence in less than two years. She decided to make a future with him.[20]

9

Red Week

Margherita's sudden move from her reformist friends to Mussolini's revolutionary camp was politically opportunistic. She also knew Mussolini could offer a political future to Cesare, who was now almost fifty. Cesare's alternatives were few, and distinctly unpromising, as he discovered for himself in the 1913 elections, when he ran for Parliament for the third time.

Cesare entered the race as one of five candidates in the Oleggio district, twenty-five miles northwest of Milan. Margherita campaigned actively for him, canvassing the countryside by car, making as many as ten or twelve speeches a day. In the preliminary vote on October 26, Cesare came in second behind Ercole Varzi, a local industrialist. Once again Cesare faced a runoff for neither candidate had received enough votes for election.

Varzi had overstepped the understood limits of electoral corruption, buying votes and brutally pressuring the workers in his own factories to vote for him. These tactics so enraged the losing candidates that two agreed to support Cesare in the runoff. But they had no desire to have a Socialist represent Oleggio in parliament. Cesare promised that if he won with their help, he would immediately resign.

The runoff was close. Cesare won 6,718 votes to Varzi's 6,160. News of Cesare's deal became common knowledge, and on November 4, Albertini's *Corriere della Sera* published an interview to clear up the matter. Cesare claimed he had won by his own efforts, thanks to "the intense publicity campaign made by me and my comrades," and so would not resign. His insistence that he had not needed help from the losing candidates was the point on which both his election and his position in the Party turned, because Mussolini sometime earlier had secured a Party ruling against electoral alliances with other parties.

Cesare reiterated his statement for *Avanti!*, and Mussolini appended an unsigned comment. Mussolini asserted his faith in Cesare's good word and his certainty that the Party directors would approve Cesare's conduct. Twelve days later, Mussolini published another anonymous comment in which he denied Cesare's need to resign, although he applauded the nobility of his original promise to do so. There the matter rested for several months, while both the Party and Parliament conducted separate investigations into the dispute.[1]

Mussolini's support for a wealthy, last-minute convert from reform Socialism is inexplicable except in light of his relationship with Margherita. The two tried to be discreet. Cesare's hearty manner disguised an unusually sensitive personality, and neither Margherita nor her lover wanted to wound the dignity of a proud and fundamentally decent man. Before their temporary breach, Mussolini had made occasional appearances at Margherita's salon. After her return to Milan, to avoid provoking unnecessary gossip, Mussolini stopped coming for a while. But in the small world of the Party leadership, there were few secrets. Soon Balabanoff knew that Margherita had replaced her. Though Balabanoff had left *Avanti!*, the two women were both on the staff of *La Difesa delle Lavoratrici*. They developed a lifelong mutual hatred.[2]

For Mussolini, Margherita represented what previously had been unobtainable. As intelligent as Balabanoff, Margherita was far more attractive, elegant, and cultured. She also exuded an aura of warmth and good humor that offered a highly attractive alternative to Balabanoff's single-minded devotion to Marxism.

These qualities in Margherita held a special value for Mussolini at that time. In September or October 1913, a jealous lover had forced Rafanelli to break off her friendship with Mussolini. Although she soon began seeing him again, for the moment the rupture left him emotionally isolated. Mussolini was also preparing to launch his own ideological journal, one that would express his own point of view, rather than the Party's. He placed great hopes in his new venture, which he wanted to reflect both his revolutionary politics and the most exciting new intellectual trends from across Europe. But he feared that Italy would not provide enough of an audience for such a daring publication. Mussolini needed trusted and well-informed assistants to increase the journal's chances for success. The politically unorthodox enterprise was one in which Balabanoff hardly would have joined.

When the first issue appeared on November 22, it bore the title *Utopia*. This represented both homage to the precursor of Socialism, Thomas More, and an ironic reference to Turati's mockery of Mussolini's style of politics. *Utopia* was subtitled *A Biweekly Review of Italian Revolutionary Socialism*. Margherita was one of Mussolini's chief collaborators. Nothing else could have illustrated so dramatically her rupture with Kuliscioff and Turati and her adherence to Mussolini.

On New Year's Day of 1914, the first of a new series of articles by

Margherita appeared in *Avanti!*, her first since the fall of 1912. Others followed in *Utopia*. Like those that continued to be published in *La Difesa delle Lavoratrici*, Margherita's new pieces for Mussolini advocated women's issues or were devoted to art criticism. Mussolini himself now displayed a far more favorable public attitude toward women's rights, although his personal anti-feminist views had not really changed.[3]

An absurd example of this occurred when Maria Giudice, another member of the staff of *La Difesa delle Lavoratrici*, introduced a timid and adoring Socialist schoolmistress to Mussolini at the *Avanti!* offices. Glowering at his visitor, Mussolini pounded his fists on his desk and shouted: "Do you know what I think of women? That they must stay home to do their housework, that they must serve their man, and that sometimes their man must also beat them!"[4]

The year 1914 brought many surprises for the Italian Socialists. The 1913 elections had weakened Giolitti's strength in Parliament. In February 1914, the revelation of the high costs of the Libyan War provoked new defections from the prime minister's coalition. The left raged over profligate militarism and Giolitti's reactionary alliance with the Church, while the right accused him of dishonesty and of failure to restore the heavy losses of arms and ammunition. In early March, Giolitti resigned, fully expecting to be recalled by the king in a few months. King Vittorio Emanuele instead asked Antonio Salandra to form a new government. The new cabinet was considerably more conservative than Giolitti's had been. Salandra proved to be inflexible, authoritarian, and nationalistic.[5]

Soon after Salandra's appointment, Mussolini and five of his *Avanti!* staff members stood trial for their part in the January 1913 Rocca Gorga insurrection. Mussolini was defended by an old comrade from Forlì, Francesco Bonavita. Cesare Sarfatti represented Giuseppe Scalarini, the paper's political cartoonist, famous for his caustic anti-military drawings.

Cesare's advocacy was in part an effort to strengthen his new political friendship with Mussolini. Cesare had already annoyed the Party leadership with his electoral campaign behavior, and though the directors accepted his explanations, they insisted on his resignation as a newly-elected deputy. The parliamentary investigation proceeded independently of this internal Party matter. In March, just before the Rocca Gorga trial, Cesare defended his case before the electoral committee in Rome, but had yet to hear the committee's decision.[6]

At the trial, as Margherita looked on, Cesare produced a parade of forlorn witnesses on behalf of the Rocca Gorga defendants. All testified to the unnecessarily vicious behavior of the Carabinieri. Following Cesare's summation, Mussolini delivered an impassioned speech in favor of freedom of the press. Completely undaunted, he warned that the next time government forces fired on the people, his response would not be in ink but in blood. On April 1, 1914, the court acquitted the accused of all charges. Cesare's eloquence had been an essential factor in the victory, as Mussolini acknowledged, but Margherita found Mussolini's rhetoric far more stirring.[7]

Mussolini's bravado veiled a growing sense of frustration. His defiant posture at the trial was consistent with his unyielding commitment to the violent overthrow of the existing order; the young and the adventurous had swollen Socialist ranks as a result. Still, his impressive successes had not brought Italy any closer to revolution. Mussolini had advanced in the Party by leading the fight against reformism, but he needed a new approach if he was to gain further power and galvanize the Socialists into an organization capable of seizing control over Italy.

Prezzolini delineated Mussolini's dilemma when he hailed the appearance of *Utopia:*

> Directed by Benito Mussolini, therefore by the young. He attempts a desperate enterprise: to revive the theoretical consciousness of Socialism, an enterprise which seems even greater than the powers of Benito Mussolini, however great those are. This man is a *man* and he stands out all the more in a world of weaklings and of consciences frayed like rubber that has been stretched too much. . . .[8]

Rather than encouraging Mussolini, Socialist successes in the 1913 elections pushed him to the edge of despair. The Party's gains only reinforced enthusiasm for electoral politics over revolution. Opportunistic members like Cesare were willing to drum the reformists out of the movement, and yet remained eager to win office. Even when Cesare's election was revealed as "paper games," as Margherita described it, he fought desperately to retain his empty victory. Against such a mentality, Mussolini realized that "everything was useless."[9]

Even if he were to overcome such attitudes, the actual prospects for revolution were dismal. True, the Party had risen to 47,000 members by the spring of 1914 and had received 961,000 votes in the recent elections. But these figures represented only slightly more than 11 percent of the total ballots in a country of some thirty-five million. But two million members of the Italian working class had abandoned the country, emigrating to the United States, Argentina, Brazil, and other more hopeful lands.

Any revolution faced great physical odds. The government deployed a highly effective force of 25,000 Carabinieri, backed by an equal number of municipal police and Public Security agents. Their surveillance of subversives, based on a vast network of informers, postal inspection, and wire tapping, meant that a conspiracy on any scale would be an impossible secret to keep. A revolt of the masses, if one could be organized, would face a mobilized army of 725,000, backed by a militia of 680,000. These forces never hesitated to shoot, as recent events clearly demonstrated. The artillery pieces and machine guns at the disposal of the military left little doubt about the outcome of such a confrontation.[10]

Under these circumstances, events at the tranquil April 1914 Party congress at Ancona bore little relation to political reality. Mussolini and his revolutionaries retained their firm control over the Party and his policies met with general approval. "He's put the Party back on track!" someone shouted from the floor, as Mussolini mounted the podium and the congress thundered its applause. Mussolini's followers, among them Cesare, controlled the committee that nominated a new Party directorate. His appointment was renewed, along with Balabanoff's.

Mussolini chose a fairly insignificant controversy to test his control over the Party. He argued that Freemasons should be expelled from the Party, because they could form a secret clique within Socialist ranks. He introduced a resolution urging the Party locals to drive out their Masonic members. During an angry debate over individual rights, the Sarfattis supported his resolution enthusiastically. Giacomo Matteotti, a young protégé of Turati, proposed a less drastic measure but Mussolini's measure passed by an overwhelming majority.

With Mussolini's full approval, the congress condemned Salandra's increased spending on the armed forces. In August, the congress agreed, the Italian Socialists would send delegates to an international meeting in Vienna to promote European peace and disarmament.[11] However, nothing of substance was said about how to advance the cause of Socialist revolution. Violent events, beginning in the same city of Ancona, soon forced Mussolini to face the perplexing issue.

Anti-militarism was the one issue on which the entire Italian left—including the Anarchist, Revolutionary Syndicalist, Socialist, Republican, and Radical parties—agreed. On June 7 anti-military demonstrators in Ancona, organized by Anarchists and Republicans (among them Pietro Nenni), were fired upon by the Carabinieri. Three were killed and four wounded.

Taken by surprise, Socialist leaders hurriedly assembled in Rome. Mussolini was unable to attend the emergency session but agreed to the general strike they ordered to begin on June 9. The explosion of anarchic rebellion that followed, afterward known as "Red Week," turned out to be beyond the power of any political organization to direct or control.

The strike itself lasted for only two days. A broad leftist coalition brought economic life to a halt in most of the major towns and cities of

northern and central Italy and, to a lesser degree, in the south and the
islands. Some demonstrations turned violent and barricades were thrown
up in a number of municipalities. In Milan, Filippo Corridoni was arrested
in front of the cathedral while urging a group of workers to attack the
police. A few yards away, a Public Security agent cracked Mussolini across
the head with his nightstick, knocking him senseless to the ground.

The next evening, the Milan Nationalists launched a counterattack on
the *Avanti!* offices. They were led by the fashionably dressed young lawyer
Dino Alfieri, who had served under Cesare as an attorney for the city
council. Word of the impending Nationalist assault reached the *Avanti!*
staff. Mussolini, still groggy from his recent manhandling by the police,
ordered his men to arm themselves.

In the midst of the excitement, an assistant noticed that no one had
even a pistol. Margherita calmly ordered the staff to split their editorial
shears in half to make crude daggers, and engage the Nationalists hand-to-
hand. Mussolini took more fright than courage from Margherita's wild
suggestion, especially when only three pairs of shears could be found. He
was prepared to sneak away from the newspaper offices until news arrived
that Alfieri had called off his attack.

Elsewhere in Italy, Red Week took on a less comic aspect. In Rome,
mounted Carabinieri attacked a crowd erecting a barricade and fired a
volley of rifle fire to disperse them. In Florence, thousands of strikers and
hundreds of police traded blows in the streets. In Turin, a crowd of 30,000
marched through the city, smashing the windows of factories. Two hours
of gunfire and cavalry charges left three dead and five badly wounded
before the avenues were cleared.

Despite these examples of political violence, most of Italy witnessed
little serious bloodshed. The exception was in Mussolini's native region of
the Romagna. When the general strike was called off elsewhere, the
violence escalated there. *Avanti!* had been calling for class struggle in the
most unequivocal terms for eighteen months. The Party directorate had set
no limit, initially, to the duration of the protests. Mussolini felt real hope
and hailed the strike with the cry, "Long live the revolution!" In the
Romagna, with its ancient traditions of rebellion, these seeds had fallen
upon fertile ground. When news arrived of the cessation of the strike
elsewhere, it was taken as either betrayal or lies spread by the government.

For three more days insurrection raged across the region while, in the
pages of *Avanti!,* Mussolini praised the violence. The rebels seized government offices, raised the red flag and proclaimed the republic. They burned
tax records, sacked churches, tore up the railroads, ripped down telegraph
and telephone wires, looted the houses of the rich, all while conducting a
running fight with the army and the police. Another week passed before

Salandra could restore order with the aid of 10,000 troops rushed into the area. When it was over, Red Week had cost at least seventeen lives and well over one thousand seriously wounded.[12]

In public, Mussolini proudly compared Red Week to the Paris Commune and gloried in the name of "hoodlum" thrown at those who had conducted the uprising. But the implications of his encouragement of a week of senseless violence were all too clear. Turati and Treves again questioned the nature of Mussolini's Socialism and the meaning of his ideas about revolution. To urge attacks upon the government with no chance of success seemed both criminal and childish. These criticisms forced Mussolini to defend himself before the Party directorate again. He emerged exonerated but hardly comforted in his own mind.

Red Week only emphasized the seeming impasse in which Mussolini found himself. He had no horror of violence. Even Prezzolini had pointed out that it was absurd to label Red Week a criminal outrage and thus try to distinguish it from revolution, as Turati and Treves had done. Any revolution would necessarily contain elements of hooliganism and even crime. Instead, the problem was that Socialist revolution now appeared impossible in Italy.

Neither Mussolini nor the Party had planned Red Week. But when it happened, the Socialists proved incapable of directing or exploiting it. The Party had no communications system independent of that under government control. Neither did it possess an arsenal, a command organization, or a party militia. In reality, the Salandra government had exercised considerable restraint in its use of force. Even so, it had overcome even the insurrection in the Romagna with only a tiny fraction of its military power. Ultimately, Socialist revolution meant a confrontation between the Party and the army, but Red Week demonstrated that the Socialists lacked the will and the means to win such a struggle.[13]

Despite the expectations raised by the theories of Marx and Engels, the Italian bourgeoisie was hardly collapsing. During Red Week, well-dressed vigilantes had helped the police patrol their neighborhoods, and Nationalists had fought it out with "revolutionaries" in the streets. As Prezzolini had already warned, "The present bourgeoisie, however low it has sunk and however discouraged it may be, still has the energy and will to exercise its powers and continue to leave its forceful mark on the face of the world."[14]

Cesare discovered this while Red Week was still raging. On June 6, the parliamentary committee examining Cesare's disputed election unanimously declared him the winner. But things looked rather different in the Chamber of Deputies a week later. With the red flag still waving over parts of the Romagna, the full chamber was not about to admit into its ranks a revolutionary Socialist, a close ally of Mussolini and a class traitor. Cesare was humiliated by Guglielmo Gambarotta, the deputy who introduced the motion to invalidate his election. Gambarotta reminded the chamber that Cesare had voted for a city meat tax while a member of the Milan munici-pal council, only to be accused of smuggling three kilos of beef into the city. Parliament voted 166 to 45, the 30 Socialists present abstaining, to overturn Cesare's victory and ordered a by-election.[15]

Cesare's hopes were buoyed by the results of the local elections held across Italy in mid-June. The Socialists swept to big victories in a number of cities. In Milan, they won control of the city council. Mussolini himself became a member. It was his first elective office. He soon began talking of converting Milan into a revolutionary stronghold, even another Paris Commune. Cesare moved up to a place on the provincial council. He even had the satisfaction of winning a lawsuit over the old accusation of meat smuggling. On July 1, a Milan court cleared his name in a libel case. But eighteen days later, Cesare failed to gain the seat in Parliament for which he had endured so much. In his one-on-one rematch with Varzi, he lost by a mere thousand votes.[16]

Margherita must have blamed Mussolini's politics for Cesare's defeat. While she had admired Mussolini's physical courage during the battles of Red Week, she surely resented the fact that the anti-Socialist backlash that followed had affected Cesare's chances at the polls. She had, after all, put a great deal of work into her husband's campaign. Her old doubts about Mussolini's love of violence certainly must have resurfaced, if only tempo-rarily. In his last letter to Rafanelli, written at this time, Mussolini com-plained, rather plaintively, "You are perhaps the first woman who has understood something about me."[17]

Despite Cesare's defeat and any resentment that it might have caused, Margherita and Mussolini remained closely attuned during this time. And it was during these months that he made the fateful decision to renew his attempts to transform Italian Socialism into a truly dynamic force for revolution, whatever the costs to himself or the Party. Since late 1913, her political articles increasingly had stressed Mussolini's particular viewpoints: the obstacles to human progress presented by Christianity and the Church, fierce indignation over the privileges of the rich, a rejection of Marxist economic determinism, and most significant, a growing acceptance of violence. True, Margherita had expressed these attitudes before Red Week and Cesare's rejection at the polls might have given her second thoughts about the efficacy of violent action in politics. But she had gone so far as to justify the destruction of artistic masterworks for political purposes. Defending the Suffragist May Richardson's slashing of a Velásquez paint-ing—the *Rokeby Venus*—in the National Gallery in London, Margherita had written: "If . . . the loss of one or ten masterpieces could hasten the advent of a society . . . more favorable to the creation of new masterpieces, the gain, even for aesthetics, would be undeniable."[18]

Mussolini, too, had come to see destruction as the way to create a new civilization. Neither electoral politics nor insurrection would bring the triumph of Socialism. It could be achieved only by a catastrophic war that first would reduce European society to rubble. Out of the postwar ruins of the bourgeois order the revolution would arise like a phoenix.

But even in *Utopia,* which he edited with Margherita in complete independence from the Party, Mussolini himself did not yet dare express his heretical and shocking theory of revolution brought about by a war of unprecedented destruction. Nonetheless, he was determined to lead the Party in this direction. In May, he published an article by his friend Sergio Panunzio, a disillusioned revolutionary syndicalist. In an analysis of the problems confronting Italian Socialism, Panunzio drew this conclusion:

> "Down with war!" Who shouts that is the most ferocious conservative. From this point of view it seems that nobody is more desperately attached to the present system than the Socialist Party, which, instead of preparing a "revolutionary situation" at the cost of blood and battles that would would serve as "midwife" to the new society, shudders with senility . . . at the horrors of war and massacres.[19]

Panunzio's words proved prophetic. Less than a month after his article appeared in *Utopia,* the Archduke Franz Ferdinand, heir to the throne of Austria-Hungary, was assassinated. From this single murder followed that homicidal cataclysm known as the First World War. By the time the conflict ended, no one left alive in Europe would be the same, least of all Benito Mussolini and Margherita Sarfatti.

10

Neutralists or Not?

By the spring of 1914, Margherita Sarfatti had forged for herself a position of consequence and prestige rare for a man of the period, and truly remarkable for a woman. She was one of Italy's foremost art critics. When her tutor's tastes had proved too narrow for her, she had become modernism's champion. Now the artists of the avant-garde were intimate friends. No critic was more familiar with the brightest new Italian artists, and the movements they had created.

These new talents helped to make hers the most brilliant salon in Milan. The receptions she had begun in order to escape Kuliscioff's overbearing behavior now attracted an ever-widening circle of the gifted, the ambitious, and the rich. Her relationship with Mussolini was also part of her break with Kuliscioff, and this young man seemed poised to take Margherita with him to the pinnacle of Socialist power. Mussolini needed her intellectual skills for his *Utopia* as much as she wanted to be part of his career. She could expect no more from the politics of her time.

In the twelve years since moving to Milan, she had established her independence as critic, intellectual, and feminist. And whether or not by arrangement with her husband, she was clearly independent of him. Fortified by her alliance with Mussolini, she aspired to become the cultural arbiter for a generation.

Young artists hoped to be noticed by *la Sarfatti* and invited to her salon. A favorable review in one of her columns might follow. One group of promising, largely unknown artists invited Margherita to the debut in May 1914 of their exhibit entitled "New Tendencies." The participants included the architectural visionary Antonio Sant'Elia, and the painters Carlo Erba, Achille Funi, and Leonardo Dudreville.

The New Tendencies exhibit revealed the first signs of an aesthetic crisis in the world of Italian art. The artists in the show were themselves only partially aware of the significance of their innovations, but Margherita recognized what was new and experimental in the work. The New Tendencies artists claimed to be spiritual descendants of the Futurists, honestly admiring the bravura of the older group's eye-dazzling canvases. Still uncertain of their own ideas, their introductory catalog timidly expressed their desire to explore the possibilities offered by a more literal "artistic reality."[1]

Their expression of "filial loyalty" was sincere, but the works on display simply did not fit into the Futurist style. The New Tendencies paintings seemed infinitely calmer and more representational. One critic called this less artistically subversive group "the right wing of Futurism," but for Margherita these artists were not Futurists at all. In fact, the young men in the New Tendencies exhibit actually challenged the primacy of the Futurists.[2] The older artists had been notorious for so long that they took it for granted that they would always be in the avant-garde. In May 1914, as Margherita pointed out, the younger artists "gave the Futurists the unexpected surprise of finding themselves—they of all people!—already cast in the role of founding fathers."[3]

Margherita liked much of what she saw. Though the eclectic New Tendencies artists did not paint in a single, cohesive style, they shared a concern for restoring a measure of realism to art. The artists were starting to back away from the decomposition of reality so favored by the Futurists, but they did not embrace pure realism. Most artists of the time felt the invention of photography made literalistic painting totally useless. Margherita agreed: For her, style was the very essence of art—the careful selection of those elements that allow for the "reproduction and expression of a state of mind inspired by a given aspect of reality: not the reproduction of that exact reality."[4]

Margherita focused her review on the style of Dudreville, a fellow Venetian. In *The Seasons,* his four-panel landscape, she saw the result of a careful observation of nature, but nature as recollected by the artist with his "mind's eye." Dudreville overlaid landscapes with decorative surface painting, much in the manner of Klimt. The resulting landscape still appeared abstract, but she saw in his work an effort to achieve a classical balance of color, form, and movement, rather than to take them apart as a Futurist would have done. Margherita noted that Funi seemed to follow along the same path. This was the first occasion Margherita wrote about Funi, who became one of her personal favorites.

By mid-June, Margherita had turned in her final art review of the season. Now she looked forward to a pleasant summer divided between her country home and the beaches of Venice.[5] A sunset after a warm summer day lured Margherita and her family out of doors on June 28, 1914. "I think back, now, to that June twilight as the end of an era," she recalled. "How carefree and happy life was!" The Sarfattis were in the midst of dinner in a Milan restaurant when they heard newspaper criers announcing the murder of Archduke Franz Ferdinand. The Austro-Hungarian Emperor Franz Josef's nephew and heir had been shot by a Serbian nationalist in the town of Sarajevo.

Margherita smiled at the news of the murder. "Now, once Franz Josef dies, Austria will collapse." If the Austro-Hungarian Empire fell apart, Italy could hope to annex the *terre irredente* of the Trentino and Trieste. Socialists were supposed to promote harmony among the workers of all nations, but her patriotism in this instance proved stronger than her Socialist pacifism.

Franz Ferdinand's assassination convinced the Austro-Hungarian and German governments that the time had come to crush Serbia. Neither informed their Italian ally of the decision. If Russia were to try to defend its Serbian protégé, Europe's two alliance systems—Russia and France on one side, Austria-Hungary, Germany, and Italy on the other—would be dragged into conflict.[6]

Margherita, like most Europeans, hardly imagined that war was imminent. She left for Venice, and spent the twenty-second of July tending her five-year-old daughter, Fiammetta, in bed with measles. Margherita had not gone out or read the papers. When the physician arrived he brought with him news that the Austro-Hungarians had presented Serbia with an ultimatum.

Four days later it became clear that Serbia would reject some of the demands. Mussolini responded to the mounting crisis with an article in *Avanti!* titled "Down with War!" Demanding that Italy follow a policy of absolute neutrality, he threatened to arouse the workers against the government should it bring the country into war. "Either the government accepts this necessity," he wrote, "or the proletariat will impose it with all the means at its disposal—at any cost!"

Mussolini acted swiftly in order to prevent events from overtaking either him or the Party. On July 27, he called a meeting of Socialist deputies at the *Avanti!* offices. They issued two statements. One called for an emergency session of the Chamber of Deputies to demand neutrality. The other proposed an international Socialist congress to prevent a European war. Mussolini also suggested a general strike designed to topple the government if it attempted to lead Italy into war.

Although Mussolini had privately concluded that war was a necessary prelude to revolution in Italy, he was well aware of the contradiction between his conviction and the Party's unflinching pacifism. Beset with self-doubt, he characteristically took an inflexible position, which he believed would allow him to seize the initiative and gain control over the rank and file.

Margherita was unaware of the depth of Mussolini's turmoil. In the dreamlike world of Venice in high season, amid flashing jewels and carnival masks, she was far removed from reality. When the Austro-Hungarian ultimatum expired at midnight, July 28, she stood in the grand ballroom of the Excelsior Hotel on the Lido, watching the revelers dance the tango. It reminded her of the sinking of the *Titanic*—but this time, an entire civilization was going under. She telephoned Mussolini at *Avanti!* for news, but there was none. The next morning, Austria-Hungary declared war on Serbia.[7]

Margherita hurried back to Milan to find the city, as Carlo Carrà noted, like "a boiling cauldron." On August 1, Germany declared war on Russia and sent ultimatums simultaneously to France and Belgium. When the German Army invaded Belgium two days later, Britain declared war on Germany.

Following the German attack, Émile Vandervelde, now the leading Belgian Socialist and a friend of the Sarfattis', announced that his party supported resistance against German aggression. That decision stunned her, as it did Socialists everywhere. Within days, the Socialists of Germany, Austria-Hungary, France, and Britain followed the Belgian example, each abandoning the antiwar principles of the Second International in a wave of nationalist frenzy.

Italian Socialists were for the moment spared a decision. The government refused to join its allies in the war. The Austro-Hungarians had violated the terms of the Triple Alliance by not consulting the Italians over the Serbian crisis. Furthermore, they refused to guarantee Italy compensation for any annexation of Serbian territory. To fight a war simply to help the Austro-Hungarians made no sense to Prime Minister Antonio Salandra. On August 2, he announced Italian neutrality.

The Sarfattis shared the relief that Italy had escaped the bloodshed. But sorrow shattered their satisfaction, for on July 31, a French ultranationalist murdered Jean Jaurès, the leader of the French Socialist Party. Charles Péguy had called for Jaurès's death when the latter made efforts to prevent the conflict in the Balkans from spreading across Europe. A fanatic acted on Péguy's suggestion and gunned down Jaurès in a Paris café.

On August 5, Mussolini mourned the loss in a public address. At a meeting of the Milan provincial council, Cesare delivered an emotional eulogy for Jaurès, who had "consecrated the noblest efforts to secure peace for his country even as the bloody dawn was rising to dishonor Europe and civilization itself."

With the immediate question of Italy's neutrality resolved, Margherita spent the first weeks of August at Il Soldo. Even in the bucolic countryside surrounding Cavallasca, she found it impossible to escape the war. At the frontier railway station in nearby Chiasso, she saw the first Italian refugees.

"Every train that arrived, day and night, brought hungry, tired crowds of men, women, and children from Germany, already at war, crammed together for eight, ten, fifteen hours in locked box-cars." She and Cesare joined with the local Socialists in assisting the returning Italian workers, and they began to conceive a plan to provide the refugees with land on which to grow food for their families. But events drew her back to Milan.[8]

Salandra's decision to keep Italy neutral deeply divided his countrymen. The king and the prime minister authorized a series of secret diplomatic talks, first with the Austro-Hungarians and the Germans, then with the Allies. They wanted to know which side would offer the best terms for their intervention. But Giolitti still influenced most of the Liberals in Parliament, and he was decidedly against war. He realized, like Mussolini, that the strain of war might lead to revolution.

Many republicans and democrats wanted intervention against Austria in order to gain control of the Trentino and Trieste. Some radicals saw the war as a democratic struggle against Austro-Hungarian authoritarianism and militarism. The Nationalists, however, admired German technical and military efficiency and in July demanded that Italy join the German Empire in a war of conquest. By September, however, they joined the Futurists in calling for war for its own sake.

The war created a wrenching dilemma for the Socialists, pitting old comrades against each other in an emotional battle over fundamental principles. If war, as ideology taught, was a capitalist battle for markets and resources, the working class stood to gain nothing but death at the hands of other workers. Socialists had to do everything in their power to prevent war. But some Socialists, especially the reformists, supported a crusade against the oppressive German and Austro-Hungarian tyrannies. Even Anna Kuliscioff, increasingly sympathetic to the cause of France and Belgium, predicted an eventual Italian entry into the war on the side of the Allies.[9]

With the collapse of international Socialist solidarity in the first days of the war, the Italian Socialist party suddenly found itself isolated. On August 3, the Party's executive committee confirmed Mussolini's "absolute neutrality" formula. But elements of the Italian left began to break away. Some Anarchists declared themselves for intervention against Germany and Austria-Hungary. Cesare Battisti, Mussolini's friend from the Trentino, crossed into Italy from Austria-Hungary and began an anti-Austrian campaign for the *terre irredente*. Prominent Revolutionary Syndicalist leaders, including Filippo Corridoni, also came out in favor of fighting against Germany and Austria-Hungary.

The pro-war sentiments of Battisti, the renegade Syndicalists, and other leftists confirmed Mussolini's private belief that an insurrectionary general strike was no longer a viable option.[10] War seemed the only way to create conditions for revolution. In early August he and Margherita authored an article for publication in *Utopia* under his pseudonym. The piece recounted her experience at the Lido a few weeks earlier: "The Europe of 1914 danced the Argentine *Tango* while prostrating itself before the mystical Parsifal. (Tango and Parsifal are not so far apart as it may seem: each embodies a kind of transcendental *sexuality*.)" They mentioned also the millions of mothers condemned to weep as their sons poured out their blood on the battlefields.

Associations between love and death, sexual sublimation and violence, the Teutonic warrior Parsifal (whom Wagner depicted as torn between sacred and profane love) and the wild rhythm of the tango, all were typical of her baroque imagination. The political conclusions of the piece more obviously mirrored Mussolini's thinking. The article proclaimed the Socialist dream of working-class unity a foolish ideal. The hope that workers would revolt against their own governments before fighting their foreign brothers had been dashed. Even if an antiwar insurrection succeeded, would enemy soldiers refuse to attack a nation crippled by "pacifist" violence? Might not such a revolution compound the disaster of invasion? Mussolini insisted that nationalism was not about to disappear, regardless of the outcome of the war. While not drawing the lesson explicitly, his logic was obvious: Socialism's future was within the nation state, not on an idealistic international plane. No wonder they published under a pseudonym. They had suggested the abandonment of orthodox Marxism in favor of a kind of national Socialism.[11]

The article appeared in the form of diary entries. While there is no evidence that Mussolini kept a diary at this time, he did so beginning in late 1915, with Margherita's encouragement and collaboration. This article may have engendered that project.[12] The article indicated that Margherita's views had begun to shift, but she did not follow Mussolini blindly. For the next fifteen months, she underwent a tormented moral crisis. The unfolding war on the Western Front created a conflict of loyalties between her cultural sympathies for France and Belgium and her inconsistent pacifism.

During the Libyan War, Margherita had condemned war in classic Marxist terms as "the logical capstone of the entire modern social edifice." She argued then that "we cannot conceive of the bourgeois industrial-capitalist system, which is founded on the rights of the richest, and therefore of the strongest, without the expedient of war." She also had aimed some of her antiwar articles expressly at women whose sons were maimed and killed in Libya. Margherita's elder son, Roberto, was now almost fifteen, and showing his fascination with war and the military. The article in *Utopia* reflected her fear that she too might soon be a mother weeping for a son.[13]

She nevertheless saw this new war in a different light. The destruction unleashed by the Germans deeply angered her, as it did many other Italians. "In reality," she wrote, "on the day when Belgium was invaded the die was cast in favour of Italian intervention." As German armies pushed through the Belgian countryside in August, Italian papers reported the wanton destruction of defenseless villages and cities, the execution of civilian hostages in reprisal for partisan attacks, and the burning of Louvain. There the Germans destroyed the fourteenth-century Clothworkers' Hall, which contained a world-famous library of some 230,000 volumes, including priceless medieval manuscripts.

On August 28, *La Voce* carried a lead article by Prezzolini titled "Let Us Make War." The following night, Margherita found her friends at the Caffè Savini, where they mourned the Louvain tragedy. As Margherita wrote later, Belgium was "an open wound in the bloodied body of Europe."[14]

The German advance against Paris came to a halt at the Marne River in early September. Finding a gap between two of the advancing German armies, the French and English counterattacked and forced a German withdrawal. Paris had been saved. The French suffered heavy losses, among them Charles Péguy, who fell on the first day of the battle.[15]

The Battle of the Marne surprised pro-Allied supporters. Mussolini had expected a German victory, but now began to consider the possibility of Italian military intervention on the side of the Allies. He asked *Avanti!* readers to debate the question "Are you for or against the war?" The question is evidence of his increasingly uncertain state of mind.

On the evening of September 9, Cesare presided over a debate on Italian neutrality at a meeting of the local Milanese Socialist group. Mussolini and Enzo Ferrari, a reformist member of the provincial council, argued their positions. Margherita watched Mussolini visibly struggling with "the anguish of mind" that had been plaguing him. "He was," she remarked candidly, "seized with mistrust of himself, afraid of his own inability to resist the fascination, [of his] inability to keep his mind cool and well-balanced." By the end of the debate, Mussolini had admitted his sympathy for France and confessed that if the western nations were in serious danger, he could well change his mind about Italian participation in the war.

Ten days later, Mussolini debated the neutrality question again, coming to similar conclusions. In the early hours of the morning, as he and Margherita left the meeting hall together, he was distraught with emotion but strangely clearheaded about the issue. "His state of mind was in truth a complex one. It was not the Socialist in him that was for neutrality and the Italian in him for war. Rather it was the contrary." Supporters and opponents began to wonder out loud which urge would win out.[16]

Margherita saw many more join the interventionist cause over the next several weeks. Her friends among the Futurists had always glorified violence, and now they called for war for its own sake. On September 11, the painter Giacomo Balla published a ringing manifesto against neutrality, and four days later Marinetti and Umberto Boccioni staged a pro-war demonstration in the Teatro dal Verme in Milan. They burned Hapsburg flags to cries of "Down with Austria!" The next day they led another demonstration in the Piazza del Duomo, under the windows of the Turati-Kuliscioff apartment, and were arrested by the police. From jail they issued a manifesto titled "Futurist Synthesis of the War." Marinetti addressed two emotional appeals to Italian students that denounced neutralists as the enemies of Futurism. War—"the most beautiful Futurist poem"—would combat "Germanic culture." Eventually all the leading Futurists joined the interventionist movement.[17]

Faced with mounting sentiment for intervention, Mussolini summoned a joint meeting of the Party's directors and the Socialist parliamentary deputies. They met in Rome on September 21–22, and he drafted, together with Turati, an appeal to the working classes, reasserting his apparently implacable opposition to the war. They also arranged a meeting in Switzerland between Italian and Swiss militants to reinvigorate the Socialist International. But instead of attending the Swiss conference, Mussolini published a call for a referendum, designed to register a collective working-class opinion about the war. The results favored Italian neutrality.

On September 27, Cesare Battisti published a signed letter in Turin's *La Stampa* condemning the suppression of Italian nationals in the Trentino. He claimed that Italians of the Trentino would spearhead a revolution of all oppressed national groups held captive within the Austro-Hungarian Empire. On October 7, the Anarchist Libero Tancredi scornfully attacked Mussolini's indecision and demanded that "the man of straw" unmask himself.

Leda Rafanelli dropped by Mussolini's office that same evening. She found him enraged over Tancredi's article. After he scrawled an angry reply, they left the office sometime after midnight and parted at the tram stop. Feeling uneasy, Rafanelli retraced her steps and discovered Mussolini collapsed against a building. "What's wrong?" she asked. Mussolini grabbed her wrists with a sudden violence that made her cry out. "Promise me," he begged over and over, "promise me that you won't turn against me . . . that you won't be one of those who will attack me." She tried in vain to get him to explain, but all he would tell her was that "within days the press will make a great deal of noise over my name." They never saw each other again.[18]

On the morning of October 18, amazed Party comrades read a lengthy front-page article in *Avanti!* titled "From Absolute Neutrality to an Active and Working Neutrality." Mussolini had completely reversed his stand on the war. He rejected the formula of "absolute" neutrality that had left the Party paralyzed. Could the Italian Socialists remain passive while earth-shattering events unfolded? This could not be the position of a Party intent on "making history." In the light of German aggression, the patriotism of French and Belgian Socialists was entirely legitimate. The Italian Socialist party response had prevented members from "distinguishing between one war and another"—that is, between the defensive war waged by France and Belgium and the aggressive war launched by Germany and Austria-Hungary.

Mussolini insisted that Socialists who denied the crucial importance of "national" problems were blind and dogmatic. Just as Belgian and French Socialists had supported national defense, Italian Socialists could support the liberation of their comrades in the Trentino and Trieste. "Reality moves at an increasingly faster pace," he warned. "We have had the unique privilege of living in the most tragic hour of world history. Do we . . . want to be helpless spectators of this grand drama? Or do we not wish to be, in some way, its protagonists?"[19]

Mussolini had consulted no one before making this ringing call for Italian intervention. He had made an irrevocable decision. The Party was faced with a stark alternative: either choose to follow Mussolini or risk losing their most effective young leader.

The next day, the Party executive committee met with Mussolini in Bologna over the crisis he had precipitated. His fellow directors, especially Angelica Balabanoff, angrily denounced his action. Mussolini threatened to resign if they did not support his position. With only his own vote to the contrary, the executive committee reaffirmed its position of absolute neutrality.

Margherita was attending a special session of the Milan city council. After witnessing the plight of Italian refugees returning from Germany, she mobilized a group of agricultural experts and social workers behind a plan to allow unemployed workers to grow vegetables on parcels of unused land. Margherita urged the council to reserve the squalid industrial fields on the edge of Milan—areas she knew from Boccioni's landscapes—for cultivation by families who lacked the means to feed themselves. The council approved the plan and the Socialist mayor, Emilio Caldara, appointed Margherita head of a committee to put the plan into action.

During the meeting an aide brought in a telegram to Caldara. The mayor turned pale as he read the message. Muttering, "The damned fellow—I'm sorry," he passed it under the table to Margherita. The words stunned her: "Have irrevocably resigned editorship of *Avanti!* Free at last. Greetings. Mussolini."[20]

Margherita's reaction to Mussolini's resignation was tinged with resentment. Even the guarded description of the event she wrote years later revealed some anger. Only three years before, she and Cesare had abandoned the Turati-Kuliscioff reformists to support Mussolini's rising star. Now, instead of working to convert his fellow Socialists to his viewpoint, he simply repudiated his prominent post.

Despite their awkward position, the Sarfattis did not abandon Mussolini. The next night Cesare presided at a rally in honor of Mussolini's return to Milan. To the wild cheers of his friends, Mussolini proclaimed his Socialist faith "unchanged"—"I am still the same man I was yesterday evening." His statement prompted a debate over the conduct of other Socialists who had opted for intervention. To help Mussolini—and probably himself—Cesare offered a motion supporting the right of every Socialist, regardless of official position, to act "according to his own conscience."[21]

Mussolini's rash action nevertheless left him emotionally isolated. Leda Rafanelli severed all ties with him. Margherita maintained her friendship at a distance. In late October, Mussolini by chance ran into Ida Dalser, with whom he had had an affair in the Trentino in 1909. The impetuous and unbalanced Dalser had moved to Milan a year before the war and was operating a massage and beauty parlor. They renewed their intense and stormy relationship. She seemed to provide Mussolini with the kind of solace he could not find elsewhere.[22]

Mussolini aroused even more political controversy by publishing an interventionist newspaper, *Il Popolo d'Italia* (*The People of Italy*). A handful of leftist pro-war advocates put out the first issue of the paper on November 15. The sudden appearance of *Il Popolo d'Italia* immediately provoked accusations from neutralist Socialists that Mussolini had accepted money from the French government and from Italian capitalists. He in fact had been bankrolled by Filippo Naldi, a wealthy publisher, and by the industrial firms of FIAT and Ansaldo. He did not turn to France until Naldi's money was cut off in March 1915. Ida Dalser told a police informant she had sold her beauty shop in order to help finance the paper. Margherita most likely also contributed money to the enterprise. But none of these sources controlled what Mussolini printed.

Margherita soon sought out Mussolini's new office, located in a squalid working-class neighborhood. There she found Sandro Giuliani, who had left *Avanti!* with Mussolini, in "two tiny rooms furnished with only four tumble-down chairs and a rickety table." Giuliani showed her a modest advertising contract, which, she said, satisfied her that accusations of Mussolini's "French gold" were unfounded. Giuliani told her that if she was not "animated by the fires of enthusiasm," she should stay away. She did not stay away for long, instead becoming a frequent visitor. But her own unresolved attitudes toward the war prevented her from joining his staff.[23]

The founding of *Il Popolo d'Italia* forced the Party to decide on Mussolini's continued membership. On the night of November 24, the Milan Socialist group met to sit in judgment on Mussolini. Ida Dalser sat in the packed gallery and during the course of the evening slapped a man who was hurling invectives at Mussolini. The assembly spontaneously chose Cesare to preside, only to find that he was absent. The audience was overwhelmingly hostile, agreeing that Mussolini had violated the political and moral principles of Socialism and voting to expel him.

When Mussolini rose to speak, his staccato comments were constantly interrupted by angry screams of "Traitor!" and jeering hisses. Trembling and pale, he shouted over the din, "You think you have lost me. But you are fooling yourselves. You hate me because you still love me! I am and will remain a Socialist. . . . But I tell you that from this moment on I will have no pity or forgiveness for all who are reticent hypocrites and cowards. . . . Long live Socialism! Long live the revolution!" Then he stalked out of the room in a fury, followed by curses and derisive screams.

A young Socialist stood by the door as Mussolini burst from the tumultuous meeting. The young man had not dared to enter, for he was in uniform and feared the antimilitary reactions of those within. As Mussolini stormed by, the soldier heard him muttering to himself in his Romagnol dialect, "They will pay for this!"

Margherita later claimed she had stayed away from the meeting because, although she enjoyed bullfights and boxing matches, she took no pleasure in watching the "butchery" of a manhunt. But she and Cesare also avoided the pro-Mussolini rally the following day. They were not willing to risk their own membership in the Party.[24]

Throughout the rest of 1914, Margherita and Cesare attended a number of meetings about Socialist responses to the war. While Cesare tried especially hard to avoid revealing his own views, his pro-interventionist sentiments gradually became more obvious. Margherita's friendships with the Belgian Vandervelde and pro-war French Socialists made her position clearer.[25] Finally, in late December, Margherita expressed herself more openly in an article in *Avanti!,* "Proletariat and Patria."

Margherita's dilemma sprang from her new sense of nationalism. How could she reconcile it with her Socialist beliefs? While granting that all governments oppress and exploit workers, she rejected the "narrow-minded materialism" of those Socialists opposed on principle to the notion of homeland. She declared herself to be an "idealist" who saw Socialism as something akin to "religious humanitarianism." She believed that society must be inspired by ideals, not just material concerns. Even if workers could not take advantage of higher education, art, and culture, nevertheless those things were of vital importance.

Margherita conceived of the *patria* as a step toward the ultimate Socialist ideal of universal brotherhood. For her, the homeland was a "conglomer-ate" of individuals and social groups that, when unified into a political structure, give rise to the still broader solidarity of a "nation." Germany's invasion of Belgium emphasized the importance of nationality by exposing the crucial difference between internal capitalist oppression and foreign oppression. Every human entity—whether an individual, a family, or a nation—must evolve according to its own laws and needs, "in complete and balanced harmony with its organic structure," and not by foreign imposition. Thus even if another civilization were more advanced than Italian culture, "it would not correspond to the needs of our character, to the nature or the state of evolution, or to the physical and moral atmo-sphere, of our country, or to the spirit of our race."

The war convinced Margherita that the Italian middle class, despite its faults, knew these truths better than her fellow Socialists. All of Italy's classes had a common interest in preserving the nation from foreign domi-nation. "I am not," she concluded, "in favor of intervention. I am, rather, for an intelligently active and loyally operative neutrality . . . let's not equivocate . . . *neutrality* means to bear witness to, but not to take part in, the battles of others. But it cannot mean, and has never meant, not resisting and not defending ourselves if we are attacked."[26]

Margherita's statement of principles was something of an exercise in intellectual autobiography. The enduring principles of Fradeletto's tutelage led Margherita to an idealistic interpretation of human life, and a vision of national culture as the cohesive support for a modern society. Under the impact of the war, these ideas reconciled her to Mussolini's position. Her one qualification—and it was an important one—was that war would be justified only as an act of national defense. And more than Mussolini's declaration, hers revealed a clearer sense of the fusion of nationalism and Socialism that the two of them would soon create.

Margherita anticipated by only a few weeks the decision of other prominent Socialists, including Turati, to speak against absolute neutrality in the event of foreign invasion. But to Mussolini, Margherita had said too little. He was true to his word that he would "have no pity" for those he saw as "reticent hypocrites or cowards," and he dismissed Margherita's arguments as "academic discussion." Margherita had published her views at some personal risk—after all, her article proved to be her last for the Party's organ—but Mussolini was not satisfied with less than complete adherence to his position. He was vulnerable and isolated, and he wanted supporters. The incident with Rafanelli at the tram stop proved as much.

Cesare soon verified his own friendship with Mussolini. Cesare took over a commission appointed by Socialists on the city council to investigate the sources of Mussolini's funds for *Il Popolo d'Italia*. He helped absolve Mussolini of all charges of political or moral treachery.[27]

Margherita did not have a similar opportunity to reassure Mussolini of her support, and she was still not prepared to publish a wholehearted endorsement of his cause. Such an act would have provoked her expulsion from the Party. Torn by her political and emotional dilemmas, Margherita decided to see the war for herself. As with her previous trip to Paris and London, Margherita managed to combine leaving a difficult personal situation behind with studying at first hand a situation crucial to her political philosophy.

She arrived in Paris in January 1915. The French capital was virtually under siege. The front lines were less than fifty miles away. Troop columns and military convoys rumbled through the streets while ambulances and hospital trains brought a constant stream of wounded soldiers to badly overcrowded medical facilities. The sumptuous restaurants and theater night spots she had known now held hospital beds. She was impressed by the Parisians' grim but determined spirit.[28]

Her immediate purpose was to see what response Frenchwomen had to the war. Her friends Colette and Valentine Saint Point were already engaged in war work. For two months, Margherita visited Red Cross units, schools, and shelters. She interviewed all kinds of volunteers, from teachers, entertainers, and journalists to bandage makers, orderlies, and nurses. She was struck by the courage and calm efficiency of the women she met, "a female army, a militia standing alongside the other army: the militia of life beside the army of death." She toured facilities where clothing and gifts were being collected for soldiers at the front, free kitchens for the unemployed and the destitute, and military hospitals. In the provinces she saw private châteaux that had been converted into makeshift hospitals. She stayed for a time with her friend Louise Cruppi, an artist and writer who was organizing housing for civilian refugees from the war zones. The real heroines she met were the nurses, especially those working near or at the front, many of whom were killed or captured by the Germans.[29]

The hospitals made the deepest impression on her. She was shocked by the wounded soldiers piled into cramped rooms and hallways, awaiting attention from overworked doctors and nurses. While she was close to the front in Dunkerque, the hospital she was touring was bombed by a German plane. She escaped harm. After returning to Italy, the account she published of her experiences told of how shaken she had been by the ghastly scenes of mutilated men and the putrid smell of unwashed wounds and dirty dressings. Personal encounters with wounded soldiers continued to haunt her: a young man with much of his face blown off, who still managed to laugh; the echo of the canes of blinded soldiers reverberating in a hospital corridor; most of all, a severely injured seventeen-year-old boy from Bergamo who had gone to France against his parents' wishes to fight in an Italian volunteer legion.[30]

Margherita took time out in Paris to visit galleries and artists. Diego Rivera was still there, along with Gino Severini and Gabriele D'Annunzio. One day she stopped by Severini's apartment. His wife, Jeanne, had just given birth to their first child. Margherita brought greetings from Boccioni and asked to see Severini's latest work. The destitute artist showed Margherita a number of drawings and pastels, but she behaved just as she had in London two years earlier. "Signora Sarfatti examined and reexamined the work with great attention and lively interest," recalled Severini with some bitterness, "while Jeanne and I awaited her decision with our hearts beating, but it was not what we hoped: after many compliments to my wife, to the baby, and to me, again she left without buying anything."[31]

Margherita returned to Italy in March to find Cesare under attack for not clarifying his position on the war. He had sent a statement to the city's newspapers declaring that he was neither a neutralist nor an interventionist but "simply a socialist." *Il Popolo d'Italia* responded with scathing criticism on March 26. "For some time now," lamented Arturo Rossato, one of Mussolini's staff writers, "a tragic and anguished problem has weighed on the innocent heads of the Sarfatti couple: family discord. Are we interventionists or not? Neutralists or not?" Rossato was cruelly ironic in his reference to "Adam Sarfatti and hesitant Eve Margherita, who want to and do not want to bite the atrocious apple. . . . Come on, folks, a little courage! Just a little." The article certainly had Mussolini's approval.[32]

A week later, Margherita agreed to talk with a reporter from a pro-war Syndicalist paper about her trip to France. Late in the interview, she contrasted the title of the French Socialist organ *L'Humanité* with the "guttural war cry of *Vorwaerts*," the German Socialist paper. When the reporter asked whether she sympathized with one side over the other, she caustically replied that Germany was experiencing the consequences of "having fewer centuries of history in world civilization." She added that if German intellectuals had their way, even Italy would become a "Prussian barracks." The reporter concluded that "without explicitly declaring her-self an interventionist," Margherita clearly recognized why his paper sup-ported the war against Germany.[33]

A few days later Claudio Treves began a violent polemic with Mus-solini over interventionism. Their debate quickly degenerated, and after insulting each other, the two men fought a violent saber duel in which neither was seriously injured.[34]

On the evening of April 1, Margherita gave a speech on "Women and the War" before a large gathering in Milan. With deliberately provocative intent, she described the courage of French and Belgian nurses struggling against German barbarism, and ended her hour-long tirade with an emo-tionally charged account of women raped and made pregnant by German soldiers. Mussolini's paper commented that the visibly moved audience "had perhaps expected something different from the speaker."[35]

On April 26, Salandra's government concluded a secret treaty with Britain, France, and Russia that promised Italy significant territorial gains in return for intervention. Italy was to receive the Trentino, Trieste, central Dalmatia, part of Albania, and less specific areas in Turkey and Africa, provided the government entered the war within a month.

In early May, after rumors of the Treaty of London spread, demonstra-tions and violent street clashes between interventionists and neutralists broke out all across Italy. On May 5, D'Annunzio delivered a rousing pro-war speech in Quarto (outside Genoa) to 20,000 cheering Italians, and a week later repeated his war cry before a gathering of 100,000 interven-tionists in Rome. In Milan, Mussolini and Corridoni organized similar demonstrations and demanded that the king bow to the people or lose his throne.

Most Italians still opposed war. They turned to Giolitti to lead the fight to preserve neutrality. The pro-war street demonstrations helped create the false impression of widespread popular support for war, but Giolitti ably mobilized his political forces against intervention. With the expiration date on the Treaty of London close at hand, Salandra resigned on May 13. King Vittorio Emanuele rejected the resignation. In private, he threatened abdi-cation unless Parliament voted for war. Giolitti caved in. Mussolini and the other interventionists rejoiced, and a crowd of 300,000 marched through Rome calling for war.

Cesare finally sent a letter to *Avanti!* on May 18 declaring that he had abandoned neutralism in favor of war. *Il Popolo d'Italia* was gracious—"At last there is one among the hundreds of interventionist Socialists . . . who has had the moral courage to speak his mind."[36]

On May 20 Parliament reconvened to debate Salandra's request for emergency powers. Filippo Turati alone spoke against war in the Chamber, which voted 407 to 74 to support the government. Four days later, Italy went to war against Austria-Hungary.[37]

The Italian Socialist party shifted ground by adopting a policy of neutrality toward the Italian war effort. "Neither support nor sabotage" became the Party slogan. This left Margherita in a peculiar position. Both her husband and Mussolini now openly supported the war. Even Turati expressed quiet sympathy for the French and Belgians, and feared the consequences of a German and Austro-Hungarian victory. But Margherita still hesitated to make an open break with the Party.[38]

Nonetheless her activities clearly revealed her attitudes. Over the spring and summer of 1915, she worked feverishly on the account of her tour, which she called *La Milizia Femminile in Francia* (*The Female Militia in France*). If there was any doubt before as to her sympathies, the book put them to rest, for it was a powerful anti-German tract that concluded with a paean to the women of France, whose "love for their land and their civilization" had made them heroines.[39]

She spent much of her time in the company of old friends who were visiting Milan on behalf of the French or Belgian governments: Colette, who came to Italy to do propaganda work; Julien Luchaire, a noted Italophile, who opened a French war-information office in Milan; Louis Barthou, the cultured former French premier, who passed through the city on a lecture tour; and Émile Vandervelde, the Belgian Socialist leader, now a minister in the Belgian Cabinet, who visited the Sarfattis on his way to Rome for consultations with the Italian government.[40]

Margherita greeted Vandervelde at the Milan railroad station on July 20. Jules Destrée and a number of other Belgian deputies accompanied Vandervelde. Destrée noted how Margherita immediately monopolized Vandervelde's attention with a constant flurry of "irritating courtesies" from the moment that he stepped down from the train until the end of a lengthy luncheon in his honor. "It is curious," Destrée observed maliciously in his diary that night, "that everywhere Vandervelde goes, he is courted by Jews." That afternoon, Cesare and Margherita listened to Vandervelde address a huge patriotic rally in the dal Verme theater.[41]

Margherita arranged for Vandervelde and his companions to visit Turati, Kuliscioff, and Treves. After the usual sparring, Vandervelde addressed the main issue. With a sly smile on his face he demanded: "Well, Comrade Turati, Comrade Treves, in our place, with your country invaded, what would you have done?"

Treves replied without hesitation: "But I would have acted like you, my friend! Absolutely, I would have acted in the same way!" Turati sat without saying a word, stroking his beard in indecision.

Vandervelde pressed on: "But then why do you not want to help us, in an international manner? There will be socialist activity to carry on in the defense of the working class, even the German workers, after the war; in defense of Germany itself, if necessary. How would we be able to do it, if we stood aside or ran away, when the time came to defend our own country's rights? Internationalists for justice, yes; but not anti-nationalists to defend injustice."

Anna Kuliscioff had been smoking and listening in silence. Suddenly, she sprang up. She wasn't sure how the war would end, she said. But of one thing she was certain; the conflict could lead to consequences of revolutionary proportions, "especially for Russia." Even she feared a victory by reactionary German militarism if it left her motherland, *"la mia Russia,* chained to czarism forever." After years of bitter exile, what mattered most to Kuliscioff was her beloved nation.[42]

Despite their estrangement, Margherita harbored the greatest respect for Kuliscioff.[43] If the implacably internationalist Anna felt such concern for her native land, should Margherita feel ashamed of openly proclaiming her Italian patriotism? Over the summer and fall of 1915, the conviction gathered force within her that she should not.

11

Order, Counterorder, Disorder

Mussolini expected a "short and victorious" war. The day Italy declared war on Austria-Hungary he contemptuously dismissed warnings in *Avanti!* about the suffering in store for the Italian people. He predicted the Italian Army would soon parade in victory through the streets of Vienna.[1]

Mussolini longed to participate in the triumph. Nearly thirty-two, he was a bit old for combat but eager to get into the fighting before the war ended. His taste for adventure, his sense of personal honor, and his role as a leading interventionist all pushed him toward enrolling. Comrades like Filippo Corridoni, Cesare Battisti, Giuseppe Prezzolini and the fifty-two-year-old Gabriele D'Annunzio had already enlisted, as had old adversaries like Ivanoe Bonomi and Leonida Bissolati.[2]

Even Margherita's artist friends were leaving. Marinetti and most of the other Futurist and New Tendencies artists, among them Umberto Boccioni, Anselmo Bucci, Carlo Erba, Achille Funi, Luigi Russolo, Antonio Sant'Elia, and Mario Sironi, enrolled together in the Lombard Volunteer Cyclist Battalion. The battalion trained as a reconnaissance unit in Gallarate on the outskirts of Milan, whence the artists sent Margherita a playful postcard.[3]

Mussolini's own attempts to volunteer were thwarted. He was one man the War Ministry was not eager to have spreading his politics in the ranks. He was told to wait until his reserve class was called up.[4] His enemies' insults intensified his discomfort. By July, Socialist and neutralist presses were showering him with taunts. Why was the great warmonger still safely holed up in his newspaper office in Milan? At one point Mussolini even thought of going to France and enrolling in the Foreign Legion, although this would have been considered desertion from the Italian Army. Finally a friendly member of Parliament made inquiries for him in Rome, and assured Mussolini that he would be called up no later than the fall. Mussolini got his orders to report for duty on August 31 as a rifleman in his old corps, the Bersaglieri.[5]

After two weeks of refresher training at Brescia, Mussolini departed with a replacement unit. They traversed the old frontier on September 15, passed through the recently captured town of Caporetto, then traveled across the Isonzo River and up the slopes of Monte Nero, where they reached the front a few miles northeast of the town. There Mussolini was assigned to the 33rd Battalion of the 11th Bersaglieri Regiment, and immediately sent forward to a frontline company.

The Italian trench line was some 6,200 feet up the mountainside. About ten o'clock on his first night, September 18, 1915, the Bersaglieri began an exchange of rifle fire with the Austrians. Soon the two sides joined in with machine guns and hand grenades. A little after midnight, the Austrians exploded a mine under a section of the trench occupied by Mussolini's company, causing heavy casualties. At dawn the firing ceased, only to be quickly replaced by a brief retaliatory Italian artillery bombardment of the Austrian positions. Then quiet returned to the mountains. Mussolini had had his first sobering taste of war.[6]

The campaign was not going well. Luigi Cadorna, the Italian Chief of Staff, had planned to smash through Austrian mountain defenses along Italy's eastern borders and capture Trieste. From there he wanted to debouch onto the Hungarian plain and fight a great battle in the open field, bringing Italy victory before the snows fell. But Cadorna had ignored the lessons of 1914, when German attempts to seize Paris in a lightning campaign had foundered, like subsequent French and British efforts to drive the Germans out of France, in the face of accurate rifle and machine-gun fire, long-range artillery, and barbed wire. Modern industrial warfare had transformed battles into catastrophic slaughters costing hundreds of thousands of lives.

Cadorna's first offensive collapsed due to the deficiencies of the Italian Army and its weak industrial base. He proved initially inept at inspiring his commanders with the need for vigorous attack. Cadorna's incompetent generals forfeited their initial advantages of surprise and numbers by advancing hesitantly into Austrian territory, allowing the Austrians to fall back to high ground, rush reinforcements to the front, and dig in on critical terrain. Key positions the Italians could have seized easily in the first days of the war were soon heavily defended. Cadorna's first general offensive in late June was stopped by a wall of Austrian fire and steel.

Italy, the poorest and weakest of the great powers, fielded a badly equipped army at best, but the recent Libyan War had made a bad situation worse. Without sufficient artillery, machine guns, or ammunition, the Italian Army was stalled along the west bank of the Isonzo River. They also lacked medical supplies, blankets, tents, uniforms, and rations. Within sight were the granite hills of the Carso (Karst) plateau—formidable obstacles that stood between the Italian positions and Trieste. Suddenly a goal that had seemed immediate became a mirage shimmering out of reach.

Cadorna regrouped his forces and ordered a second offensive in mid-July. This too proved a disaster. What the far better equipped armies of Germany, France, and Britain could not accomplish on the Western Front, the Italians could hardly hope to do in the foothills of the Alps. They had to claw their way up rock-strewn mountains where every bursting artillery shell added hundreds of stone fragments to its deadly shrapnel. And now epidemics of cholera and typhus swept through the ranks. Already strained beyond capacity by the unimagined horrors of the battlefield, Italian medical services collapsed. Thousands of Italian soldiers died of disease in squalid field hospitals. Cadorna's second offensive ground to a bloody halt in early August. When Mussolini reached the front six weeks later, the army lay low in stunned exhaustion. The Italians had suffered over 130,000 casualties in return for gains measured only in yards. Even the determined Cadorna realized that the war would last at least until 1916 and began preparations for a third offensive in mid-October.[7]

Mussolini's first night in the trenches exposed him to mortal danger even during a quiet period at the front. But Mussolini had arrived with the other replacements in anticipation of renewed heavy combat. Two days after he arrived his colonel summoned him to regimental headquarters; perhaps hoping to spare a useful man, he offered Mussolini the chance to become a clerk at headquarters and keep the regimental diary. He refused—"I prefer to remain with my comrades in the trenches." When others marveled at his foolhardiness, he retorted angrily, "I came to war to fight, not to write!" In fact, Mussolini did both. He had started to keep two diaries of his own in early September. One he intended to publish in *Il Popolo d'Italia*. In the other he kept a more personal account of his war experiences.[8]

Transferred to another company, Mussolini was sent up the slopes of Monte Vrsig. Two weeks later, his unit shifted another few miles onto Monte Jaworcek. While they avoided heavy combat, they suffered continuous casualties from sniper fire and the erratic fall of mortar and artillery shells.

Mussolini graphically recorded the monotonous misery of trench warfare: the drudgery of work details by day and guard duty by night; the wretched rations fed to enlisted men; the bone-chilling damp and cold in winter, and the summer's clinging mud and excrement; the clouds of tormenting flies; the inescapable infestations of vermin; worst of all, the stomach-wrenching stench of rotting corpses. All this was borne against a constant background roar and rattle of projectiles.

Even in the published diary, in which Mussolini tried to demonstrate optimism and stoic fortitude, his horror at the sight and stink of putrefying flesh stands out. The unburied dead attracted huge swarms of rats that constantly forced Mussolini to acknowledge the inferno into which he had helped plunge himself, his companions, and his country.[9] On November 1, as Mussolini was returning to his company after a work detail, he received a stinging reminder of how much his politics were hated by some of his fellows. As he trudged uphill, he paused to rest. Another soldier approached him.

"Are you Mussolini?"

"Yes."

"Excellent. I have good news for you. They have killed Corridoni. They did well, it pleases me. Damn them all, these interventionists."

Mussolini turned pale, then rage overcame him. He leaped to his feet and pointed his rifle at the soldier's chest. A sergeant suddenly appeared. Mussolini managed to recover his self-control, shoulder his weapon, and resume his march up the mountain. Corridoni had been only one of the 67,000 Italian casualties in Cadorna's third offensive.[10]

Mussolini also recorded the simple pleasures of their few diversions—a bath perhaps once a month, an occasional canteen cup of wine. He wrote letters for his many illiterate comrades. He devoured the copies of *Il Popolo d'Italia* that reached him, his one source of contact with the outside world. But boredom and a sense of imprisonment under constant enemy shelling wore down his morale. Twice in the course of a single week in October, an Austrian artillery round exploded within a few yards of him, killing and wounding other members of his platoon. Mussolini began to long for some escape, even for involvement in a major action.

Mussolini's capabilities were appreciated by his officers. He was made an acting corporal and decided to apply for admission to officer-candidate school.[11] He received orders for the school but, less than a week after his arrival there, was sent back to his regiment. He did not ask why, but he must have realized that his political past had caught up with him. When the Army General Staff learned of Mussolini's admission, appeals were made directly to Prime Minister Salandra. While all agreed that Mussolini had been an exemplary soldier, the High Command stressed his "deplorable background" and pointed out that Mussolini had vowed to resume his revolutionary activities after the war. Salandra shared the General Staff's concern and agreed to Mussolini's dismissal from the school. The prime minister ordered the case kept confidential, to avoid political controversy.

On his way back to the trenches, Mussolini stopped in Caporetto for a few hours of rest. It was the afternoon of November 15, a year to the day since he had brought out the first issue of *Il Popolo d'Italia*. Mussolini joined a crowd of soldiers filing into the town church. He had not attended a religious service for over twenty years, but the deep notes of the organ and the plaintive singing of the soldier congregation brought him a melancholy pleasure. The next day he rejoined his unit during a heavy snowfall and suffered a night of almost unbearable cold.[12]

A few days before, Ida Dalser had given birth to a boy, whom she named Benito Albino. Mussolini seems to have made promises of matrimony which he had no intention of keeping. He did not reply to the letter Ida wrote him concerning the birth of their son. After a week or so, Ida obtained a court order allowing her to seize Mussolini's furniture. In a rage, she set fire to the furniture in her hotel room and fled. Rachele returned home to discover the furnishings missing. Before she could react, the police arrived to arrest her for arson. At the police station, Rachele was able to persuade the police that the culprit was the other "Signora Mussolini." Soon thereafter, Rachele received news that Mussolini had fallen gravely ill with typhus.

He was evacuated to the military hospital at Cividale. King Vittorio Emanuele happened to visit the hospital, and for the first time, he and Mussolini exchanged a few words. After two weeks, Mussolini was transferred to a convalescent center near Milan.[13] Since their son's birth, Ida had made increasingly desperate attempts to find Mussolini. But Rachele managed to get to his side first, with Edda. They had made the journey from Milan in a boxcar filled with army mules.

Mussolini faced some difficult choices. He now had two families but remained legally single. As a soldier under military discipline, he could not escape his paternal responsibilities. Margherita intervened, urging Mussolini to marry Rachele. She considered Rachele "an ignorant and brutal peasant," but this may have been the key to her advice to Mussolini. Despite a troubled mind, Ida cut a far more attractive figure than Rachele, and hence was more of a threat to Margherita.

Margherita reminded Mussolini of the danger he faced. Since Mussolini's bout with typhus had begun, Cadorna's fourth offensive had sputtered to a halt at the cost another 49,000 Italian casualties. "If anything should happen to you," she warned Mussolini, "[Rachele] will be left without a cent." On December 16, Mussolini overcame his Socialist principles and wed Rachele in a civil ceremony at the hospital. She stood by his bed while Mussolini uttered his vows in a clear, strong voice. Rachele was considerably more nervous. "You were afraid, eh?" he asked her with some amusement.[14]

Two days later, Ida arrived at the hospital with little Benito Albino. Mussolini soothed her with some vague assurances of financial security and affection. Mussolini soon arrived back in Milan on convalescent leave. Ida discovered that Mussolini's promises were worthless, that he had already married Rachele. Infuriated, Ida brought a paternity suit against her former lover. Margherita came to his rescue and arranged for a lawyer to represent him. Regina Terruzzi served as intermediary between Mussolini and Ida. On January 11, 1916, Mussolini formally recognized Benito Albino as his son and agreed to pay support for mother and child. Considering his poverty, the money Mussolini offered must have been pledged by the Sarfattis.[15]

During his leave, Mussolini returned to the direction of *Il Popolo d'Italia*. He mounted Corridoni's portrait on his office wall as a symbol of his commitment to total victory. He began publishing extracts from his war diary on December 28. In other articles, he gave vent to his deep resentment at the Socialist party and the Catholic Church for their pacifism and support for a compromise peace. He urged the Italian government to declare war on Germany, reminding his readers of German war crimes in Belgium, and the torpedoing of the *Lusitania*.[16]

The incident with Ida Dalser drew Margherita and Mussolini close again, and she felt reluctant to let him return to the front without some clear sign of her support. She soon found her opportunity. On December 17, news reached Milan that the Germans had executed Edith Cavell, a British nurse captured in Belgium and accused of harboring enemy soldiers. During her imprisonment and trial, Cavell had become an international *cause célèbre*. Her death made her an Allied martyr. Margherita, whose visit to France had made her a zealous admirer of war nurses, was outraged. All that winter, the Italian press ran stories on Cavell's life and death, while patriotic women's organizations organized rallies in her memory. Even Ada Negri paid public homage to her.[17]

Margherita agreed to be the principal speaker at a commemoration of Cavell, to be held while Mussolini was still in Milan. The speech proved to be Margherita's most important performance as a public figure. On the evening of December 29, 1915, Margherita entered the crowded auditorium of the Milan Conservatory. Nationalist and women's groups, city officials, military officers, and diplomats packed the hall. A huge portrait of Cavell had been hung across a stage draped with the Red Cross banner and the flags of the Allied nations. Margherita used every rhetorical device she could muster to dramatize the moment, lifting phrases from her book *La Milizia Femminile in Francia,* and conjuring images of a "fragile" nurse brutalized by cruel German soldiers. Calling her a "victim of infamy," Margherita recounted Cavell's life of humanitarian service, dwelling in detail on her last, dignified days before execution, awaiting a reprieve that never came. "History," she railed, "will never forgive the Hohenzollerns":

In this war that has been willed by Germany, in this monstrous tragedy that is without individual protagonists, the figure of Miss Cavell is resplendent with its own light. . . . Her blood will be the holy oil that will anoint the prison in memory of her sacrifice. We must not lament Cavell, we must envy her. In this war that we did not want, but which we must now fight to the last man, she is the purest and most radiant example of a martyr.

When she had finished, Margherita plucked a handful of flowers from a basket and posed under the portrait of Cavell. The audience rose to its feet in wild applause. The next day Mussolini's newspaper gave her performance a glowing review.[18] The Cavell speech was Margherita's personal declaration of war. The Socialist leadership clearly understood the symbolism of her actions, for within a few days they expelled her from the Party. When asked whether it was true that she had broken with the Party, she curtly replied "they broke from me."[19]

A week after Margherita's speech in honor of Cavell, Mussolini's sick leave expired and he left Milan for the front. After eight hours of hard marching, he stopped for the night in a crowded shelter by the side of the mountain road. Outside it was raining heavily, but the wind brought close the sound of rifle fire from the trench line on the mountainsides above them. The troops began speaking of the dead and of homes far distant, until they fell into sullen silence. Finally one said vehemently, "Dirty war!" From out of the darkness, Mussolini rebuked him. He spoke of the meaning of the war, of the need for duty and sacrifice, of the inevitability of death. One of those present, the artist Ardengo Soffici, never forgot the scene.[20]

In February 1916 Mussolini resumed life in the trenches in deep snow, cutting wind, and bitter cold. On March 1, he received official promotion to corporal for exemplary service. Soon he accompanied his regiment to the Carnic Alps. Along with some comrades, Mussolini arrived in Tolmezzo on March 24, searching for the location of their unit in the slopes to the north. There he encountered an old lover, who invited him to spend the night with her in the room they had once shared. The offer was tempting, but his sense of solidarity with his companions got the better of him. "No," Mussolini told her, "I am a soldier like the others. But give me that tricolored ribbon you wear on your breast as a memento. Addio!"

Three days later, Mussolini trudged to his company position along the torrent of Bordaglia, some eighteen miles northwest of Tolmezzo. His platoon had dug in at 5,200 feet above sea level, with company headquarters higher still.[21] His spirits lifted amid the jagged peaks of the Alps. The brilliant sunshine of early spring, reflecting off the snow and the dark green pine forests, induced a sense of purity and renewal in him. But the slopes could be treacherous, with sudden snowstorms and frequent avalanches.

Dangerous, too, were the constant exchanges of artillery fire and the necessity of reconnaissance patrols past the barbed wire separating the two lines. As a trusted veteran, Mussolini often led such forays, and he commanded a forward blockhouse as well. Mussolini kept himself and his men busy stringing new wire and improving the defenses of their primitive bunker. But he still found time to record in his diary the political observations that his war experiences had provoked.[22]

Mussolini had come to believe that victory would not be won by material superiority but by faith and determination. "He will conquer who wishes to conquer!" Mussolini noted in a Nietzschean entry early in April 1916. "He will conquer who controls the greater reserves of psychic willpower. 100,000 cannon will not bring victory if the soldiers are not capable of moving into the assault, if they do not have the courage, at a given moment, to confront their fears and to face death." But even among the select Bersaglieri, he saw only a small group of men in each company with the strength of character and the intuition necessary to inspire others. Most infantrymen carried out their assigned roles from fear of court-martial. Such men required stern discipline to do their duty. Nor were officers necessarily superior to their men in that regard. Victory depended on the minority of all ranks who composed a natural warrior elite. And what was true in wartime, could also apply in a time of peace.[23]

At the end of April, Mussolini's battalion shifted some thirty miles to the southeast, to face the Austrian lines on the ridges of Mount Montasio. As they approached their new position, Mussolini's unit encountered an engineer company constructing a road. One of them recognized Mussolini and pressed a volume of Mazzini's writings into his hands. Two days later, as Mussolini lay in his tent, he opened the book. The words of the Risorgimento's prophet amplified his own thoughts, and he copied the phrases that struck him into his diary:

> Great deeds are not accomplished with established procedures. . . . The secret of power is in the will. . . . There are lacking the leaders, there are lacking the few to lead the many, there are lacking the men fortified by faith and self-sacrifice, who comprehend the burning notions of the multitude . . . who write on their banner "to conquer or to die," and who keep that promise.

Then Mussolini wrote, "Is there not in these passages an intuition of present events? . . . But who among my 250 fellow soldiers knows it?"[24]

In early March, with the return of spring weather, Cadorna ordered his fifth offensive of the war. It achieved little, but that attack and other local actions cost nearly 18,000 casualties by mid-May. The Austro-Hungarians were meanwhile preparing a master stroke to knock Italy out of the war.

From the Swiss frontier in the northwest to the Carso in the southeast, the Italian Front formed a huge "S." Each side held a bulge of territory which was surrounded by enemy terrain on three sides. The area held by Austria was the Trentino, and facing Italian defenses were weak. There, in the spring of 1916, the Austro-Hungarians concentrated their reserves: The plan was to smash downward to the Po Valley below the mountains, cut the railroad lines that supplied Cadorna's forces, and trap the bulk of the Italian army in a box, leaving the rest of the peninsula open to invasion. Italy would then have little choice but to ask for surrender terms.[25]

Cadorna dismissed Austro-Hungarian movements in the Trentino as a ruse. Thus, when they attacked from the Trentino bulge on May 15, the force of their offensive took him by surprise. In the face of overwhelming enemy superiority, the Italians fell back. Cadorna rushed reinforcements across Venetia. By the barest of margins, the Italians held until fresh forces slowed the Austrian offensive to a halt. By the second week in June, the crisis had passed, but not before it brought down Salandra's government.

Salandra was replaced by a feeble seventy-eight-year-old, Paolo Boselli. He was a man above party politics, so interventionists hoped he would rally the nation and continue the war. His broad coalition government included Cabinet posts for Leonida Bissolati and Ivanoe Bonomi, who were summoned from the trenches to become ministers representing left-wing interventionists in the new government. Mussolini sent a private note of congratulations to Bissolati, which he followed with a commendatory letter in *Il Popolo d'Italia*. Though he had been instrumental in obtaining Bissolati's expulsion from the Socialist party, they had become kindred spirits, two Party exiles who supported the war. Now, Mussolini hoped, the war would be waged with a new intensity. After victory would come the time to settle accounts with the traitors in the Socialist party who had sabotaged the war effort with calls for peace before the *terre irredente* were taken.[26]

Mussolini's sector had remained quiet throughout the first days of the great struggle to the southwest. But, as he wrote to Prezzolini, he was determined to take part and had adopted a fatalistic attitude about his chances of survival. Once it grew clear that his area would not come under attack, he led the noncommissioned officers of his battalion to volunteer for assignment to the battle zone. When their offer was not accepted, Mussolini grew restless. He had decided that the hour of his death was fast approaching. He wished to get it over with as quickly as possible.[27]

Meanwhile, Cadorna had decided to launch a counterattack against the entire eastern flank of the Austrian penetration. Mussolini's company received orders to march some miles to the north to reinforce the 8th Alpini Regiment. In late June, both units went over to the attack.

The campaign achieved little. The Austrians fell back to prepared positions, and resisted the Italian attacks from behind multiple lines of field fortifications. Cadorna continued to fling his men against the enemy wire. As casualties mounted, cases of indiscipline multiplied. General Carlo Giordano, hated for his sadism, died from an Italian bullet. On July 1, soldiers of the Salerno Brigade attempted to surrender to the Austrians after a series of hopeless assaults. The Italian general commanding the sector ordered his artillery to bombard the deserters. Those who fled back to Italian lines were executed by firing squads.[28]

Others proved more stalwart but paid an equally heavy price. Cesare Battisti, leading his Alpini company in a night attack, found his unit cut off and surrounded. Battisti directed his men in a ferocious all-night battle, desperately seeking to escape the encirclement. Some Alpini managed to break free and return to Italian lines, but not Battisti. The next morning, he was forced to surrender. On July 12, after a perfunctory trial for treason, the Austrians hanged him. When news of the execution reached Mussolini, he vowed to avenge his friend.[29]

On July 15, Mussolini was engaged in particularly fierce fighting to capture the Austrian positions dominated by Fort Malborghetto, and he volunteered to lead a small reconnaissance unit up to the Austrian lines. For thirty-six hours, Mussolini led his men back and forth between the two lines under almost constant artillery, mortar, and machine-gun fire. Shrapnel riddled his helmet and he narrowly escaped death as shells burst around him. The bombardment set ablaze the woods through which he and his men crawled but they survived unscathed. Finally, on July 19, Cadorna called off his costly counteroffensive. The Italians had suffered another 148,000 casualties.[30]

Despite these terrible losses, Cadorna now saw an opportunity to gain the first real Italian victory of the war. Both sides had stripped the Isonzo River valley of forces in order to wage their struggle in the Trentino. But the Italians could switch reinforcements back across the Venetian plain, whereas the Austro-Hungarians had to bring their divisions back up the narrow Alpine valleys of the Trentino. The two armies raced to reinforce the Isonzo, but the Italians won, fighting their way across the Isonzo and seizing the city of Gorizia. In Cadorna's sixth offensive, the Italians had finally gained an important objective after breaching one of their enemy's main lines of defense. The victory gave the Boselli government the confidence to declare war on Germany on August 28. Until then, the Italian government had feared the consequences of conflict with the most powerful state in Europe, despite Italy's fifteen months of war with Germany's closest ally.

Italian optimism belied reality. Cadorna ordered a seventh offensive in September, an eighth in October, and a ninth in November—bloody actions that achieved nothing significant. Cadorna had underestimated his enemy's ability to recover and create still more defensive barriers across the rocky ground of the Carso. The onset of the heavy rains of autumn forced Cadorna to abandon any more major attacks for the year. The four offensives had cost over 128,000 Italian casualties. Italian losses from major and minor actions in 1916 numbered an appalling 118,000 dead and 285,000 wounded, with tens of thousands captured.[31]

Among the year's casualties were two of Margherita's closest friends. Back in November 1915, the army disbanded the Futurists' Volunteer Cyclist Battalion after fewer than five months of active service. The battalion was simply unfit for mountain warfare; at the time it was formed, Cadorna had planned to do most of the fighting on the plains of Hungary. Some of its men were scattered throughout other units. Umberto Boccioni, Luigi Russolo, and Mario Sironi were among older members granted extended leave. Already the harsh reality of combat had radically altered their Futurist fantasies of the regenerative value of violence. Boccioni returned to Milan, shaken by what he had seen.[32]

Boccioni was yearning to get down on canvas new artistic ideas he had been unable to paint while on active duty. After several months in the city, where he saw the Sarfattis frequently, Boccioni accepted an invitation to stay at a villa on the shores of Lake Maggiore. As spring moved toward summer, he began painting at a frantic pace.[33] He felt overwhelmed, as if he were working out "an entire century of painting" by himself. While in the midst of a portrait of the composer Ferruccio Busoni, he wrote to Margherita: "The portrait of M[aestr]o Busoni is coming along well but it is difficult to apply new things to it. . . . I want to experiment with the landscape by applying to the light and atmosphere a solid stylization. It is difficult. We'll see."[34]

When Margherita, together with Sironi and Russolo, visited Boccioni's Milan studio in July of 1916, she saw the completed Busoni portrait and a dozen other works. All had been turned out in a concentrated burst of creative energy. The new canvases emphasized the modeling of form in a way suggestive of Cézanne; Boccioni's masterful departure from his previous style astonished his friends.[35]

The path taken by Boccioni while he worked at Lake Maggiore that summer had been anticipated by Pablo Picasso in the summer of 1914, when he abandoned Cubist abstraction in favor of neoclassical portraits. Gino Severini made an equally drastic change shortly after Margherita visited his Paris apartment in January of 1915. The longtime expatriate painted an extraordinarily realistic, classically serene portrait of his wife suckling their infant son. The canvas, titled *Motherhood,* revealed Severini's abandonment of Futurism and his deliberate search for older artistic values. He called his new style "imagined realism."[36]

In April 1916, Marinetti complained bitterly when Carlo Carrà retreated from the Futurist attack against convention by "returning to forms." A few months later, Carrà confessed to his friend Ardengo Soffici that he had abandoned Futurist dynamism for more realistic studies of the human figure with a new concern for simplicity of tone and line. "For some time," Soffici replied from the front, "I, too, have been tormented by a frenzied desire to paint. I dream of an infinitely simple, fine, and exquisite art." When Carrà sent him a photograph of a recent painting, Soffici admitted that extreme modernism could lead back to ancient forms but expressed shock that Carrà had made the switch without a gradual transition.[37]

The stylistic changes adopted by all these modernists formed part of a general shift away from abstraction to more classic forms and a traditional pictorial language. Margherita understood that the war had played a major role in this transformation. The trenches, she said, had proved to be "a school of truth" that traumatized Italy's artists, bringing them face-to-face with the horrible reality of the destruction they had once gleefully demanded.

Heavy casualties from the fighting of 1916 left the Italian Army desperate for men, and Boccioni, Russolo, and Sironi were recalled to military service. In early August, Boccioni reported to the 29th Field Artillery Regiment and Russolo to the 80th Infantry Regiment, both outside Verona.

They found their return to army life difficult. The rigid discipline, the constant drilling, the bad food, the ignorant peasants with whom they served, all presented an unpleasant contrast with the months of painting on Lake Maggiore and the pleasures of Milan. Besides, the two friends were in different units; Russolo was leaving for the front and there was no telling what might happen.

Boccioni was deeply frustrated that military service interfered with his art. To one friend, he complained, "From this existence I will emerge with a contempt for everything except art. Nothing is more terrible than art. Everything I see is a mere game compared to a good stroke of the brush, a well-proportioned line, or a correct balance. . . . There is only art."[38] He spoke of his privations more gallantly to Margherita. "My superiors have been very kind to me," he wrote on August 16. "Thanks to them, I am always on horseback, and that relaxes me a little."

Boccioni went riding the same day he wrote to Margherita. His horse threw him; he struck his head on a rock, fractured his skull, and was trampled by the frightened animal. He died the next day. The story spread that the painter had died on a training exercise. Margherita revealed years later that he had been riding into Verona to court a woman.[39]

Margherita and Ada Negri both wrote to comfort Russolo, who grieved over the death of his friend and Italy's greatest artist. "Oh why create this force and then destroy him when he was at the height of his development?" Russolo asked Margherita. What answer could she give? The power of Boccioni's personality, his courageous honesty, his startling creativity as a painter and sculptor had made him an emotional and professional anchor in Margherita's life. Despite Boccioni's adherence to the precepts of the Futurist movement, she had recognized that his artistic genius overflowed any prescribed channels, always surging forward in unexpected directions. His death left an emptiness in her life, and ended the new possibilities he had begun to explore in his recent paintings.[40]

There was another tragedy still to come. On October 10, the first day of Cadorna's unsuccessful eighth offensive on the Carso plateau, an Austrian bullet cut down red-haired Antonio Sant'Elia. He died at the head of his troops, a cigarette in his mouth. Sant'Elia was buried in a military cemetery at Monfalcone that he had laid out himself at his commanding general's request. The cemetery was the only architectural work that Sant'Elia realized in his short lifetime. He was its first occupant. "Offspring of Prometheus," Margherita called him in a poem written after his death, "of sharp profile and biting words, of brown eye and flaming hair, sprinkled sparkling across your brow."[41]

Sant'Elia and Boccioni had made of Futurism something far more than a publicity vehicle for Marinetti's frequently incoherent concepts. In his architectural drawings, Sant'Elia had produced a concrete vision of aesthetics transformed by technology and the machine. Sant'Elia's imaginary "Cyclopean constructions," as Margherita described them, dwarfed even the existing skyscrapers of Manhattan in size and far surpassed them in their pure functionality of line. Margherita compared Sant'Elia to Nimrod, raising great towers to heaven in defiance even of God. But now the young designer would never see his buildings realized. His dream of a "supercity for supermen who seek no repose" was left for others to construct. Margherita could only cherish the architectural drawings Sant'Elia had given her. She sought to memorialize Boccioni and Sant'Elia in her prose, and she organized, with Marinetti's help, a retrospective exhibit of Boccioni's paintings that December in Milan.[42]

* * *

Mussolini's unit remained north of Cadorna's offensives in the Carso throughout the summer and the fall of 1916. Nonetheless, he did not escape danger completely. In early August, an Austrian shell scored a direct hit on Mussolini's dugout, burying him alive. He managed to claw his way out, his tunic torn to shreds, his face blackened but still without a scratch. "Well," he exclaimed with a big grin, as he dusted off the remnants of his uniform, "I've been lucky even this time!"[43]

Incidents like these frightened his friends and supporters. It seemed only a matter of time until some Austrian shell cut him down. While the junior officers who commanded Mussolini admired his outstanding performance, more-senior officers regarded him as a dangerous subversive. Many of Mussolini's fellow Bersaglieri considered him responsible for the war. Even if Mussolini escaped annihilation from a stray projectile, sooner or later he might receive a well-aimed bullet through the back.

In October, supporters who thought that Mussolini could do more useful war service directing *Il Popolo d'Italia* tried to get him removed from combat. But they gave up, as Bissolati noted, thinking Mussolini would never accept such favoritism. Bissolati knew better. Mussolini had written to the minister asking for his help to get him out of the fighting. Apparently Bissolati could do nothing and Mussolini remained in the trenches. The minister kept Mussolini's desperate letter to himself.[44]

Autumn 1916 brought other troubles to Mussolini. He had not sent the money he had promised to Ida Dalser and their child, despite an exchange of angry letters. In May she brought new charges against him, and in late July, a Milan court decided in her favor. With Mussolini in the trenches, there was little she could do to collect. In the eyes of the military authorities, Mussolini was responsible only for children by his spouse, Rachele. In late October she worked instead to obtain a subsidy from the Milan city government as Mussolini's wife, cutting Rachele off from the same benefits.[45]

Rachele had meanwhile given birth to their first son on September 21. Mussolini named him Vittorio Alessandro, as a sign of his faith in victory and in honor of his father. With the end of Cadorna's ninth offensive on November 4, Mussolini obtained leave to visit his new child. He returned home unannounced on the evening of November 12. The depths of his exhaustion frightened Rachele. His voice had grown so harsh that she did not recognize it when he called for her to unlock their apartment door. Mussolini had succumbed to the bleak state of spiritual isolation and emotional fatigue often experienced by veterans of heavy combat. Excerpts from his diary, covering February to May 1916, were published in *Il Popolo d'Italia,* but no sections from the late spring, summer, and fall of 1916 appeared in print. He refused to reveal his bitter feelings about the futile campaigns of 1916, when he had begged Bissolati to get him out of combat.[46]

Mussolini found it difficult to explain his experiences to anyone. He had never expected much understanding from Rachele, even under ordinary circumstances. Instead, he turned to Margherita. She could offer him the intelligent sympathy and sexual passion that Rachele could not. From this time onward, Margherita and Mussolini's relationship took on a new fervor, although he appears to have been more smitten than she. After all, he had desperate need for comfort. But even Margherita seemed to have been unable fully to comprehend Mussolini's nightmarish experiences at the front.[47] At any rate, a month after Mussolini left Milan, he noted in his diary:

> Feminine psychology only touches the superficial aspects of war and is absolutely incapable of penetrating into its intimate tragic essence. For a woman, a man who comes back from the war presents the same exotic attraction of a man returning from California and nothing more.[48]

One of Mussolini's surviving letters from the period reveals his fury and resentment. Twelve months of continual danger, exposure to the elements, and endless work details, among men of little education and less patriotism, had worn him down. Mussolini even raged against his recent promotion to sergeant. It was not that he felt undeserving, but it infuriated him that his new stripes had been awarded solely on the basis of seniority. Under that standard Italian Army policy, he reasoned, it was usually the shirkers and cowards who advanced to higher ranks. The bravest had for the most part already fallen on the battlefield. Even worse, the officer corps was filled with men granted commissions purely on the basis of their social status. No attention seemed to be paid to ability or motivation. His own battalion commander was a pro-German neutralist. A few men were commissioned for reasons of "exceptional merit," but Mussolini knew he would never be one of them. The Italian Army offered one more example of why Italy would benefit from a revolution.[49]

Mussolini had grown disillusioned by the political and military conduct of the war. The government had not revealed its war aims, ignoring the right of the Italian people to know why they were involved in a conflict that affected every aspect of their lives. The High Command seemed indifferent to the morale of the soldiers and incompetent in its conduct of operations.

During his leave that fall his presentiment of death in combat returned.

He spent most of his time at the offices of *Il Popolo d'Italia,* preparing the paper for his disappearance. He and his lawyer also worked out a settlement with Ida Dalser, providing her with a guaranteed monthly stipend. In return, Ida promised to leave him and Rachele in peace. Margherita was the likely source of the funds involved. With these matters settled, Mussolini returned to the front in late November.[50]

On December 1, he rejoined his company on Hill 144 on the Carso plateau, just a few miles northeast of Monfalcone and some three miles north of the Adriatic shoreline. The Italians had secured control over the hill after terrible fighting, and now thousands of moldering corpses scattered about the area produced an unbearable stench. The constant rain and the continuous fall of Austrian shells added to the misery. Mussolini's morale plummeted.[51]

Christmas Day of 1916 proved particularly grim. It marked the twentieth month of the seemingly endless war. Mussolini received a few cards, which only compounded his sense of utter abandonment. He drifted into a daydream about a boyhood Christmas back in the Romagna. He had followed his devout mother to the church, bright with hundreds of candles, decorated with a Nativity scene and filled with clouds of incense. After mass, his mother prepared the traditional Christmas feast, crowned by a smoking capon. The jarring explosion of an Austrian shell yanked Mussolini back from his reverie. As the sun went down on the dismal day, his misery grew profound. There was nothing to look forward to but a wretched army holiday meal of fish and potatoes.

Then the unexpected face of an old friend appeared out of the gloom, one of his staff from *Il Popolo d'Italia.* The man, now a captain, had trudged for miles through the muddy trenches to bring his old chief a Christmas greeting. He had more than friendly words for Mussolini—there was a delicious roast chicken under his officer's cape. Even years later, when Mussolini told Margherita the story, his voice quavered with emotion.[52]

The days following Christmas dragged by. Heavy exchanges of artillery fire shook Hill 144 day and night, showering the Bersaglieri with mud, excrement, and human remains. Clouds, fog, and rain alternated with dreary regularity. The unburied corpses contaminated the water, leading to another outbreak of cholera. Mussolini refused to bathe. He preferred living in filth to risking disease and dying in some wretched quarantine ward. Mussolini's company was finally relieved on New Year's Eve, and they spent ten days in what Mussolini called a "desert of mud," enjoying blissful boredom, hot baths, clean barracks, and plentiful brandy. Next they were marched a few miles farther back, to the outskirts of Aquileia, to dig trenches near the old Roman walls of the town. As they worked, the

Bersaglieri uncovered ruins of their ancient ancestors. The relics provoked Mussolini's curiosity.

During his hours of liberty Mussolini visited the Roman museum in Aquileia. The diggings awakened a sense of historical connection. As his company crossed the river on its way back to the front, he thought, "On the banks of the Tiber, Italy was born, on the banks of the Isonzo it is reborn." These were strange thoughts for a Socialist, to see Italy born not in the struggles of its people in the Risorgimento but in the inexorable march of the legions of Rome.[53]

Mussolini's war experiences strengthened his sense of nationalism. An individual's fate, he decided, does not matter. His death is insignificant, so long as the nation survives and grows stronger from his sacrifice. The war, Mussolini realized, would have meaning for him only if Italy emerged with a powerful new standing among the nations.[54]

Mussolini returned to the trenches under a bitter wind whipping in from the Adriatic. The troops shivered and froze. They dug new trench lines, uncovering bits and pieces of men in the process. Drudgery weighed heavily, day after day. As Mussolini noted: "Snow, cold, infinite boredom. Order, counterorder, disorder."[55]

In early February, his platoon was sent to the rear, to help form a new Bersaglieri battalion. Mussolini was offered the command of a trench mortar section instead, and he grabbed the opportunity. Anything, however dangerous, was preferable to the monotonous life of the barracks.[56]

The steep trajectories of the mortar shells made them ideal front-line trench weapons. Mussolini enjoyed the work. He kept busy day and night, as his section lobbed their bombs into the Austrian lines and endured the inevitable reply of enemy fire. Mussolini had become convinced that the only way out of the trenches and back home was to destroy as many of the enemy as he could.[57] As Mussolini later told Margherita:

> My speciality was to throw back hand grenades before they could explode, a dangerous game, but if you did it quickly you could hurl it back in time to go off in their trenches. And then, I taught my troops how to handle our own grenades. Often you had to light the fuse close to your face with a cigarette, because matches didn't burn long enough to do it, and then hold the grenade lit in your hand for a few moments. If you didn't, they would land in time to be thrown back at you. My poor little soldiers! They were all shaking, their teeth chattering, while I counted out loud, marking off the seconds, from one to sixty, for them and for me. But I kept a sharp eye on it: I didn't budge, you know! When I threw it, then we all ducked down together!

One night I remember, I saw the glow of two cigarettes on the other side in the dark. I took aim with the grenade, there was a big blast and no more lights. The day after, some prisoners said there had been four, five killed or wounded.

The captain asked me, "Why did you do that? They were relaxing, having a smoke, maybe talking of their girlfriends!"

"*Signor Capitano,* because then we can all go for a walk in the Galleria in Milan, which is a lot better!"[58]

In years to come, during evening walks with Margherita, sometimes he would see the glow of a cigarette in the dark and become moody. He would recount the incident with remorse, his voice shaking a bit. He would try to justify what he had done, telling her about fallen comrades who had died in his arms.[59]

On February 23, 1917, Mussolini spent the early afternoon on Hill 144, instructing a group of soldiers in the use of the mortar by firing shells onto the Austrian lines. "Lieutenant," Mussolini warned the officer in charge, "that's enough, the second box of ammunition is already empty. The metal is red hot, we're going to have trouble." "Well," the lieutenant replied, "one more round." Mussolini dropped the final bomb down the tube. It exploded immediately, scattering deadly shards of metal in all directions. Five soldiers died instantly, many others dropped wounded. Among them fell Mussolini.

The concussion knocked him unconscious. A friend who had witnessed the explosion ran up, calling to two other soldiers to help carry the wounded sergeant to an aid station. Both refused, cursing an interventionist who had got what he deserved. Mussolini's friend hoisted him onto his back and staggered back to the tent. After his wounds were bandaged, he was placed in an ambulance and driven to the sector hospital at Ronchi. There he remained for five weeks, too badly injured to be moved.

Mussolini had suffered scores of fragmentation wounds, a smashed right collarbone, a temporarily paralyzed left arm, dozens of punctures in his legs, and a severe laceration of his right thigh. The wounds required a series of painful operations. Infections set in and Mussolini ran a high fever for days, passing in and out of delirium. But he withstood his suffering manfully, enduring shrapnel extractions without anesthetic when his doctors required it.[60]

At first, Margherita heard in Milan that he was dead or dying, but when she learned his real condition, she and Cesare sent him a telegram. "We greet our dear friend, the heroic soldier, admiring, worrying, hoping for the best."[61] Among his visitors was King Vittorio Emanuele, making his usual rounds in the front-line hospitals, who asked Mussolini how he felt.

"Not too well, Your Majesty," Mussolini answered. "You must suffer a lot, in this painful confinement," the King remarked. "The other day, on Debeli, General M. spoke very well of you." The incident was the second encounter between the two men.[62]

By mid-March, Mussolini had begun to heal, although he remained in a very weakened condition. When Austrian aircraft attacked the hospital on March 18, Mussolini's doctors decided that he was too sick to be moved. He had to endure the bombardment helplessly in his bed. Fortunately, he escaped new injury. Later he embellished the story, telling Margherita that the Austrians had been attempting to assassinate him with an air raid.[63]

By early April, he had recovered sufficiently to be transferred to a military hospital in Milan. He remained in a very weak condition. An infection in his right leg required an agonizing scraping procedure, down to the marrow of his shinbone. Other wounds received frequent cauterizations and the application of searing antiseptics. Rachele remained at his side throughout, living at the hospital as a Red Cross volunteer. Mussolini's ordeal wore her down, until her weight dropped to a pitiful eighty-three pounds. Unable to endure the sight of her suffering, Mussolini sent Rachele away with their children for a rest in the country.[64]

Rachele's departure allowed Margherita to make her first visit, along with some of the staff from *Il Popolo d'Italia*. "I shall never forget going to see him," she later wrote. "He smiled out at us from his pale face, his eyes sunken in great hollows. His lips scarcely moved, one could see how horribly he had suffered." At her next visit, he was even worse. But the third time she came, in mid-May, he was able to sit up in bed and trace on a map of the Carso the progress of Cadorna's tenth offensive.[65]

A month after that, Mussolini was strong enough to resume writing for his newspaper from his hospital bed. On August 1 he left the hospital hobbling on crutches, on indefinite convalescent leave. His wounds healed very slowly and continued to drain even after he was discharged from the hospital. In the meantime, the Russians had overthrown the czar and begun their revolution, while the Americans had declared war against Germany and Austria-Hungary. The war dragged on.[66]

12

Roberto Sarfatti, Alpino

At two o'clock in the morning of May 23, 1915, fifteen-year-old Roberto Sarfatti composed a letter to his father. The news that the King had ordered mobilization left him too excited to sleep.

Dear Papa,

what a moment, what joy, what an aroused fervor of patriotism in this Italy of ours . . . !

I see it stirred up like a thoroughbred horse lashed with a whip. . . .

Italy has found its dignity as a nation, and woe to anyone who tries to soil its honor. Only now have I learned to love, if not Italy, at least the Italian people. I have seen old men weeping with emotion and young men embracing each other. From everyone comes the same shout: Viva l'Italia; the same hope: victory; the same resolve: to do one's duty. And I, too, have had only one duty, not just now, in this moment of excitement, but for some time: to enlist. . . .

Papa, my good papa, and you mamma, who understands my soul at this moment, give me your permission and your blessing, give them to me because I feel that with them I will go armored against the enemy bullets.

Believe me, papa, I do not go to war out of a stupid desire for destruction or adventure, I go because my conscience, my soul, and my convictions demand it. . . .

I don't know if I will die, but what would it mean anyway? Death encountered fighting for one's ideals is not death. And then, how terrible is death that one should fear and hate it like an enemy?[1]

Roberto's plea was not a complete surprise to Cesare and Margherita. Since childhood he had been adventurous, rebellious, and fascinated with the darker side of human nature: all the characteristics he denied in his letter. Margherita remembered a particularly telling episode from March 1908, when he was only eight years old. He came down with scarlet fever, which forced him to remain in his bed for weeks. During his confinement his mother read him stories about the medieval kings of France. One evening after she had finished, Roberto looked silently out the windows at the pedestrians walking below. Suddenly he said: "Back then it was really worth coming into the world! . . . In those days you didn't go to school, you went into combat. But now! . . . What good's life now? . . . Nothing but a boring walk along comfortable streets."[2]

Like his mother in her childhood, Roberto held the center of his family's attention. He was an unusually handsome boy, with silky, copper-colored hair, a high forehead, gray-green eyes accented by long dark lashes, and full, pouting lips. Ada Negri recalled that whenever Margherita took Roberto for a walk, people stared in admiration at the dazzling mother and her beautiful child—"a woman out of Veronese, a cherub from Tintoretto strolling through Milan."[3]

Roberto was restless and filled with destructive energy. Once, when the sculptor Libero Andreotti had just completed a medallion of Margherita and her two boys, Roberto cut mustaches in it for himself and Amedeo while the plaster was still wet. The furious Andreotti smashed the work. Roberto was a "storm center," as one family friend used to say, constantly causing a commotion. Alfredo Panzini called him a "little beast" and Ada Negri, who knew him best, a "wild lion." Both spoke of a sensuous quality that he projected even as a young boy.[4]

His wildness was combined with a peculiar inner tenacity. When adults spoke to him, he met their eyes with a gaze that was always uncannily confident, and at times defiant. He could be fiercely obstinate. One Christmas evening at the Sarfatti apartment, when he was twelve, Cesare teased him with a box of sweets, making him jump for pieces of candy. When Cesare thought the boy had grabbed enough sweets, he ended the game. But Roberto wanted more and became "transformed," Panzini recalled, "almost to the point of becoming ferocious," overturning chairs and scattering piles of books across the floor.[5]

Margherita and Cesare indulged Roberto, their clear favorite. Cesare spent more time with the boy than with his other children. Margherita enjoyed her son when he was old enough to respond to her intellectually, but Roberto bridled at her aggressive emotions and domineering personality. Indeed, he rebelled against all forms of authority, and appears to have interpreted discipline as mistreatment.[6]

Like Amedeo and Fiammetta, Roberto learned fluent French and German as well as Italian, and became accustomed to his parents' brilliant intellectual and artistic friends. His sharp mind allowed him to absorb information quickly and without effort. Negri recalled that although "[h]e seemed never to study . . . he knew everything." As Roberto grew older, his exposure to flamboyant Futurists like Marinetti and Boccioni helped him rationalize his own aggressive tendencies.[7] Roberto's precocity allowed him to speak with a remarkable assurance that bordered on arrogance, combined with an unsentimental outlook on reality. As Panzini put it, "[y]ou could see a maturity and an awareness of his own actions that was almost cold and unyielding."[8]

When he turned nine years old, the Sarfattis sent Roberto to study at the Collegio Rava, a private school in Venice. They hoped the school would teach him discipline, but the regimen at the Collegio only enhanced his rebelliousness. In November, all the students were instructed to write an essay celebrating the king's birthday. Roberto refused to comply. When he was punished, he went on a hunger strike, refusing to eat until Margherita brought him home.[9]

Roberto suffered expulsion from a variety of schools over the next few years. When Germany invaded Belgium in 1914, he was at a high school in Imola, south of Bologna. By then he had rejected the Socialist politics of his parents, and he experienced none of their hesitations about the war. He plunged enthusiastically into the interventionist movement, abandoning his studies altogether to organize pro-war demonstrations among his fellow students. The idea of fighting obsessed him. Margherita's anti-German views no doubt made an impact on him, for by the time Italy mobilized, he had come to see the war as a mythic struggle between the Latin and Teutonic peoples.[10]

The letter Roberto wrote to his father in May of 1915 was shrewdly calculated to elicit the parental consent he needed to enlist in the army—"if not, I feel that, with great pain, I will go without it, and will get myself killed perhaps without my parents having given me their permission and their blessing." Hoping that Mussolini would support his case, he added a postscript: "Write me immediately with your permission (of which I have no doubt) and give me especially news of B[enito] and have him write me. Let B. read this."[11]

Cesare and Margherita told Roberto that they approved his sentiments in principle but pointed out the foolishness of his trying to join the army by lying about his age. They insisted that he wait until he became eighteen, the legal age for enlistment.

That summer, Margherita was busy with the proofs of *La Milizia Femminile in Francia* and had little time for Roberto, who was back in Milan after the end of his school year. Margherita paid little attention to the influence friends like Colette and Émile Vandervelde, on their propaganda visits to Italy, had on the thinking of her oldest child. The possibility that the war could be over before he reached eighteen proved excruciating to him. Unbeknowst to his parents, he appealed to Filippo Corridoni, who had been inciting patriotic demonstrations in Milan. Corridoni agreed to help, securing for him the doctored birth certificate of an eighteen-year-old boy named Alfonso Allasia. Soon afterward, on July 2, Corridoni left Milan for the war.

On July 21, Roberto watched as the Volunteer Cyclist Battalion paraded through the city to mark their departure for the front. A huge crowd lined the streets, waving flags and pelting the Futurists with flowers. Three airplanes flew low overhead and one dived to bombard the cyclists with still more bouquets. In response to cheers from the onlookers, the battalion repeatedly shouted, *"Viva l'Italia!"* The parade passed under the Sarfattis' windows on the Corso Venezia, then wound its way out of the city. From there the battalion deployed to the Trentino, to serve alongside the Alpini.[12]

Seeing family friends march off to war fired young Roberto's determination to enlist. About this time, he went to see Mussolini, who sensed the boy's anxiety and restlessness. "He was still a child, tall, curly-haired, with regular features," Mussolini later recalled. "He hardly spoke. Even then, he was filled with fiery ardor and wanted to go to war. But regulations crushed his dream. It was more than a dream: it was an unbreakable desire, an irrevocable decision."[13]

In late July, Roberto ran away from home. He wrote to Margherita and Cesare that he would send them his false name and location on the promise that they would not betray his true identity. Having no recourse, they agreed, and Roberto signed up with the 35th "Pistoia" Infantry Regiment in Bologna. Cesare visited him secretly.

After a month, Roberto was recognized, and his regimental commander had no choice but to discharge him. But the colonel dismissed him with high praise for his patriotism. Cesare rushed to Bologna again, consoling Roberto with the promise that he could enlist when he reached legal age. Roberto agreed to enroll in the fall in the Nautical Institute of Venice, whose merchant-marine training Cesare hoped might satisfy his son's thirst for military adventure. Once back home, Roberto gave Cesare a small photo of himself dressed in his infantry uniform, with an inscription below: "To papa, in memory of an unsuccessful first effort that won't fail the second time—Roberto."[14]

Roberto found the Nautical Institute confining. His professors judged him insubordinate, while fellow students feared his violent nature. Unless he received some outlet for his exuberant energies, the Sarfattis knew Roberto would find a way to rejoin the army. After the heavy casualties the Italian Army had suffered in 1915, the military authorities needed recruits desperately. If he ran off to war again, this time his parents might not get him back.[15]

Cesare found a solution: Roberto would embark on a long ocean

voyage as an officer candidate in the merchant marine. Surely the chance
to see some of the more exotic ports of call would be tempting. The idea
of such a trip ordinarily would have delighted him, Roberto assured his
father. But now the country needed him. Surely his father understood and
would let him volunteer. In the end, however, Roberto accepted his
father's idea. In late June 1916, he sailed from Genoa on the Italian Lloyd
steamer *Luisiana,* bound for Rio de Janeiro and Buenos Aires via West
Africa.[16]

Roberto enjoyed a splendid time in the months that followed. He
encountered endless expanses of sea, scorching tropical heat, and entirely
different lands and peoples. His only disappointment seemed to be the
failure of the *Luisiana* to encounter any German submarines. When the
Luisiana left South America for Europe, the ship had lost its second mate
and gained an overflow passenger list of fifteen hundred emigrants returning to Italy. The captain promoted Roberto, barely sixteen, to the rank of
second officer.

The trust proved warranted. When two male passengers, crowded
together in the confinement of the steerage, drew pistols over a woman,
Roberto managed to disarm them. He brought the pistols home as trophies, proudly displaying them to his parents when he returned in September 1916, a month after Boccioni's untimely death.[17]

His adventures at sea had done nothing to curb Roberto's restlessness.
He practiced knife throwing in his parent's elegant apartment on the Corso
Venezia—with predictably destructive results. His second year at the Nautical Institute proved even more difficult for him. The government provided his escape by lowering the enlistment age to seventeen. He agreed
to continue school until the end of the academic year, but as soon as he
finished classes in July 1917, he enlisted in the elite mountain troops, the
Alpini. Roberto had turned seventeen just two months earlier.[18]

Along with the Bersaglieri and the marines of the San Marco Regiment, the General Staff deployed the Alpini in sectors requiring special
combat skills and the highest courage. Italy's Alpini troops served as the
spearheads of assaults in mountainous terrain, and braved the dangers of
rock climbing, avalanches, and winter at high altitudes as well.

As a rule, the army recruited Alpini exclusively from the population of
Italy's northern mountains. Each Alpine valley furnished recruits for its
own company. Adjacent companies were grouped into regionally recruited
battalions, which were named accordingly. This created a special sense of
cohesion, with relatives, friends and neighbors serving shoulder to shoulder
in units bearing the name of their birthplace.[19] But the Battle of Monte
Ortigara in June 1917 had left thousands of Alpini dead, virtually wiping

out some battalions, with average casualties ranging between 40 and 50 percent.[20]

After this disaster, the Alpini needed all the recruits they could find. Roberto had no illusions about what service in the mountain troops entailed. He reported to the 6th Alpini Regiment in July 1917. In a uniform several sizes too large for his slender frame, Roberto was sent for training to Caprino Veronese, a few miles east of Lake Garda. Despite his boyish appearance, Roberto proved more than equal to the rigorous training and gloried in his prowess among the rocks. Apparently to please Cesare, Roberto applied for an officers' training course, but made it clear to his parents that he really desired to get into combat as soon as possible.[21]

That summer the Sarfattis passed a peaceful time at Il Soldo with Fiammetta, Ada Negri, her daughter, Bianca, and guests including Mario Sironi, on leave from the army, and the writer Massimo Bontempelli. Amedeo had been sent to stay with Charles and Louise Cruppi at their château in the foothills of the Pyrenees. During his stay, Sironi etched two pensive studies of Margherita, and one each of Cesare, Bontempelli, and Negri. He also executed a more formal portrait of Margherita in pastel.[22]

Meanwhile many Italians had registered their growing impatience with the war. On August 1, Pope Benedict XV issued a peace note to all the warring states. Fearing that Cadorna's bloody offensives would pound a weakened Austria-Hungary into submission, thus losing the major Catholic power upon which the Holy See had so long depended for protection, the pontiff called for "a just and lasting peace" with neither victors nor vanquished. He denounced the ongoing conflict as "useless slaughter." *Avanti!* hailed Benedict's call. The Socialists stepped up denunciations of the "imperialist war," urging workers to resume the class struggle. The March 1917 revolution in Russia raised Italian Socialist hopes for a similar uprising. By July, even the moderate Treves demanded, "Out of the trenches before next winter."

Encouraged by the response to the Pope's call for peace, Giolitti suggested that the government respond to the nation's war weariness. Many dismissed this as Giolitti's bid to regain power. But even Salandra felt that secret peace talks would be a good idea.[23]

Mussolini was back at the offices of *Il Popolo d'Italia* and denounced Giolitti, the Socialists, and the papacy for their defeatism and treason. He also hailed the start of Cadorna's eleventh offensive across the Bainsizza plateau, to the north of the Carso, on August 1917. The first few days of the attack did bring the Italians notable successes. Cadorna unfortunately kept his grand assault going too long, and with forces dispersed across too broad a front and insufficient supplies of fresh water, the troops soon were brought to a halt under the blazing summer sun. The Italians had lost another 182,000 casualties.[24]

But even with Russia's collapse, the balance of forces was tipping inexorably in favor of the Allies. The United States was marshaling immense resources for the fight; the Austrians begged the Germans for reinforcements, hoping to defeat the Italians before the Americans reached Europe. The Germans were transferring forces from east to west, now that they had effectively defeated the Russians. They agreed to loan the Austro-Hungarians seven crack divisions of storm troops. By October, these German divisions lay in readiness on the Italian Front.

Cadorna failed to prepare adequately for the Austro-German onslaught. On the morning of October 24, the Germans swept forward, after saturating the Italian positions with a lightning artillery barrage of poison gas and high explosives. The troops were armed with flamethrowers, a terrifying new weapon, and sacks of hand grenades; they blasted and burned their way across the Italian trenches, bypassed strongpoints, and infiltrated into the rear. Once behind the Italian lines, the Germans burst across the Isonzo River at Caporetto.

Cadorna's demoralized armies fell back first to the Tagliamento River, then to the Piave River. His gains of two and a half years vanished in a few days. Units disintegrated as soldiers threw away their arms or surrendered to the advancing enemy. Calls for peace made by Benedict XV, Giolitti, and the Socialists suddenly made sense. As Cadorna and the king drove through the dispirited throngs of soldiers and civilian refugees streaming toward the west, they heard cries of *"Viva la pace!,"* *"Viva il papa!,"* or *"Viva Giolitti!"* By the time surviving divisions reached the Piave, the army had suffered immense losses—40,000 were dead or wounded, 280,000 taken prisoner, and 350,000 had deserted or been separated from their units. The army had left behind enormous caches of weapons, ammunition, and supplies. For many, further resistance seemed futile.[25]

After these calls for peace, Mussolini had joined other interventionists in demanding a government crackdown on "defeatists." Prime Minister Boselli's feeble response spread discontent through Parliament. On October 25, amid the first reports of the disaster at Caporetto, the Boselli government collapsed. Five days later, while Cadorna's forces fell back across the Tagliamento, Vittorio Emanuele Orlando took up the burden of leading the government.[26]

Cadorna refused to take the blame for the defeat, accusing the "defeatists" of undermining the morale of his troops. But he also heaped opprobrium on his own men, who, he claimed, "cravenly withdrew without fighting or ignominiously surrendered to the enemy. . . ."[27] In fact, his merciless discipline, his battering-ram tactics, and his lofty indifference to the morale of his troops were as much responsible for Caporetto as the brilliant battlefield innovations of the Germans. Yet even after this shattering defeat, many men under his command maintained order, even in cases where their officers abandoned them and fled to safety. Though Italy now lay at their mercy, Cadorna's soldiers did not revolt, as their counterparts in Russia had recently done. The war finally made sense to them. They were patriots fighting in defense of their homes against their traditional and hated enemies from beyond the Alps.

This realization spread from the front to the civilian population and to the politicians in Rome. A true sense of national unity took hold for the first time in united Italy's brief history. As Mussolini noted on November 1: "Today, from the head of the government to the lowliest citizen, a single preoccupation, a single thought, a single will, precise and implacable, must dominate: to exterminate the barbarians who profane the territory of the Fatherland."[28]

After a period of bewilderment and despair, Cadorna set about organizing an effective defense. By November 9, he had reassembled the remnants of his army along the west bank of the Piave. Cadorna anchored his new defensive position on the massif of Monte Grappa in the north, while the Adriatic formed his southern flank, less than thirty miles from Venice. The same day, the king and Orlando replaced Cadorna as Chief of Staff with the younger and more politically astute General Armando Diaz. The following morning, the Germans and Austro-Hungarians launched a furious attack against the Italians' hastily constructed line of resistance.[29]

The German and Austrian commanders recognized Monte Grappa as the key to the Italian defenses. If they could seize the mountain, they could descend its slopes behind the Italians dug in along the Piave. Then Venice would fall into their hands, and the rich Po Valley would lie open to invasion. The threat to her beloved Venice provoked both fear and determination in Margherita. As she wrote to Alfredo Panzini in mid-November, she had decided to drive the very idea of the capture of her birthplace out of her mind: "As long as the line of the Piave holds . . . there is no need, *one must not* be afraid: one must control oneself—it's a duty."

For sixteen days, the enemy battered the Italian lines. The Germans and Austro-Hungarians managed to throw two bridgeheads across the Piave. But they concentrated their might against the defenders of Monte Grappa. The struggle swung back and forth as Diaz desperately regrouped units shattered in the retreat from Caporetto, and threw them back into battle. After several appeals, the British and French also gave Diaz six of their divisions as reinforcements. By November 27, the Austro-German assaults had been beaten off. For the time being, the Italians held.[30]

In the meantime, the news of Caporetto had transformed Roberto's eagerness to reach the front into real desperation. Until now, his youth had prevented both his assignment to officers' training or to combat. But his intelligence and education had brought him a choice assignment as a telegraph operator. Caporetto changed all that. Roberto demanded and received reclassification as a regular infantryman. On October 30, his training battalion received orders to prepare for assignment to the war zone. Roberto exulted at the prospect of joining the fighting. "It's more than a battle," he wrote to his mother, "it's the collision of two races: Cimbri and Teutons against the Latins."[31]

Margherita decided that she must see her son before he departed and Roberto arranged a hotel room for her in a nearby town. She arrived in early November. Both rejoiced at being with each other again. They laughed at how much taller he had grown, towering now over his mother. But he was still her child, though very much a man in his deportment. Margherita discovered that Roberto was courting the two pretty daughters of the widow who owned the inn. He had ingratiated himself with mother and daughters by supplementing their meager wartime rations with delicacies obtained with money from home.

Mother and son walked together in the magnificent countryside overlooking Lake Garda. A heavy pall of foreboding weighed upon them, and they spoke very little. As the two of them strolled along the hillsides, they noticed below them the dejected columns of refugees trudging westward. Truck convoys laden with French and British troops bumped down the rutted dirt roads in the opposite direction. Each felt keenly the humiliation of having their country once again invaded, and once again rescued by foreigners.

That night, before heading back to the hotel, they sat in a field and watched the brilliant stars in the clear autumn sky. Roberto returned with his mother to the inn before his long walk back to camp. Margherita exhorted him to be a good soldier, to curb his rebelliousness and to make himself useful. "Useful?" he responded with a smile. "Why do you want me to be useful? What do you want me to be, one more rifle among a million rifles? I don't do anything for Italy; I do it for myself! For *my* duty, for my conscience. For the honor of dying."

Roberto's outburst made his mother shake uncontrollably. Roberto stopped and looked at her. "Mamma, how many at this moment in Europe do you think feel the honor of dying?" Margherita replied sadly, "A few, my son, but there is also the honor of living!" "Oh no, in other times perhaps they sensed the honor in dying: today they no longer feel it!" With those words, he left her and strode back to his barracks.[32]

On November 21, Roberto and his comrades joined the Monte Baldo Battalion, dug in on the slopes of Monte Fior, a few miles to the west of

Monte Grappa, across the Brenta Valley.[33] Roberto felt fortunate to have received over four months of training; he served beside men old enough to be his father, and eighteen-year-old conscripts thrown into combat after only a few weeks of hurried instruction. The tremendous casualties suffered by the Italian Army over the previous month had necessitated the most dire measures to replenish its ranks.

No sooner had Roberto arrived than the Austro-Hungarians unleashed a violent bombardment of high explosive and poison gas across his sector of the front. The next day the enemy attacked half drunk on the wine they received as fortification, shouting their traditional battle cry of "Hurrah, hurrah!" The Alpini responded with the traditional monarchist war cry of "Savoia!" and drove them back. The next day, the Monte Baldo Battalion joined in a general counterattack, recovering terrain previously lost to the enemy and capturing a fair number of prisoners as well. Roberto had survived without the slightest wound, though he had displayed exemplary valor.[34]

For the next seven weeks, Roberto experienced the life of stark essentials that separates combat infantrymen from all other soldiers. On December 4, the Austro-Hungarian High Command resumed the attacks aimed at the conquest of Monte Grappa and the outflanking of the Italian defenses along the Piave. Throughout the morning and into the afternoon, the Austro-Hungarians smashed against the Alpini dug in along the western slopes of the Brenta Valley. At 1:30, the Monte Baldo Battalion left its reserve position to reinforce the line. By evening, Roberto's company had reached the heights of the Sasso Rosso.

The day's fighting had ended in confusion, with units of both sides chaotically intermingled. Nonetheless, all that frigid night on the mountain slopes, the Austrian artillery kept up a steady bombardment of gas shells. As dawn broke, the Italian situation seemed hopeless. The Austrians renewed their attacks with a seemingly endless supply of fresh units, while no reinforcements reached the Alpini. True to their proud traditions, the Monte Baldo refused to yield and counterattacked with bayonets fixed.

This desperate action brought Roberto's battalion only a brief respite. About noon, a violent barrage hit the Monte Baldo position. Roberto later wrote to his father: "I had a knee a little bruised by a chunk of shrapnel, and my helmet dented by a little shell splinter which fortunately bounced off my helmet without touching me. I have been very lucky, as you can see." But many of his comrades had died under the terrible shellfire.[35]

On the late afternoon of December 5, the senior Alpini battalion commander ordered a retreat. Roberto volunteered to join the Arditi platoon of the Monte Baldo, which formed a rear-guard force of 150 men and two mountain artillery batteries on the peak of the Sasso Rosso.[36]

Service with the Arditi (the "Daring Ones") represented the most dangerous of all combat duty. These select troops had first been formed in the summer of 1917. The High Command had originally created company- and battalion-sized units of Arditi for attachment to regiments and divisions as the spearheads of offensives, for trench raids and for reconnaisance. The Arditi had proved successful but had suffered very heavy casualties in the battles during the second half of 1917. In the retreat from Caporetto, the Arditi had also served to fight desperate rear-guard actions, allowing their parent units to escape. By late 1917, many battalions had created their own Arditi platoons.[37]

As Roberto and his companions on the peak of Sasso Rosso observed the retreat of the other Alpini, few could have expected to survive. But if the Sasso Rosso and the surrounding peaks fell to the Austro-Hungarians, the way around Monte Grappa and down to the Po Valley would lie open. The men on the Sasso Rosso came under concentrated artillery fire. One by one, Austrian shells smashed the Italian mountain guns, leaving the Alpini gunners to pick up the rifles of their fallen comrades and fight as infantrymen. Eventually further resistance seemed pointless. Under orders, Roberto and his surviving comrades fell back, leaving the Sasso Rosso and the nearby heights to the enemy.

The Monte Baldo and the other Alpini battalions had retreated down the winding mountain road that led to safety. On the way down they encountered the formidable General Andrea Graziani, accompanied by his staff and Alpini Captain Dino Grandi. Known for his courage, as well as his cruelty, Graziani ordered his bugler to sound attention. "Everyone halt!" he bellowed. "Face front! Drive back the enemy! It's here that we save the fatherland!"

Surprisingly his measures bolstered the spirits of the dejected troops. After reassembling the disorganized soldiers, Graziani led them back up the mountainside. At the top, they encountered the advancing Austro-Hungarians. But Graziani's exhortations inspired the Monte Baldo Battalion to fight their enemy to a standstill. Though they failed to recapture the Sasso Rosso, the Alpini did throw an impenetrable barrier across the Austro-Hungarian path. Clinging to the very edge of the valleys, the mountain troops had redeemed their honor. The next day, Roberto rejoined his exhausted company.[38]

The fighting continued day and night, while Roberto remained a mile high on the freezing mountainside. He held on with little sleep, food, or drink, under constant enemy sniper and machine-gun fire, dressed in the same filthy uniform he had been wearing for over three weeks. But he had survived. He experienced a simple joy in his continued existence and a great pride in what he had done. By mid-December, the enemy offensive was stalled and Roberto was able to send and receive letters. He wrote his family and Ada Negri of his part in the action they had been reading about in the newspapers.

He assured "Aunt Ada" that he had acquired "the conviction of being absolutely invincible." To his mother, he described the sounds of battle in Futurist terms: the "Ssii . . . sssii" of a shell from a mountain gun rushing by, the "Ta-ta-ta-ta-ta" of a machine gun, the "Vvuuvvuff" of a 305-mm projectile. He asked his family to send him some decent boots (the army issue were wretched), food, money, and other useful items. He had been recommended for promotion to corporal for his heroism, which he hoped would earn him a leave soon.[39] On New Year's Day, 1918, he wrote to his mother:

> Oh year which is born in slaughter and from slaughter, may you be able to end in peace. . . . But peace can only signify victory for us; a Europe subjugated by Germany would be something so impossible and irrational—after 20 centuries in which the two races, Latin and Teuton, have found themselves face-to-face, sometimes in truce, but never at peace—that the mind refuses to think of it![40]

The new year found him in good spirits. He looked forward to leave and hoped that he would not find Milan gloomy, with wartime shortages and the sadness of so many deaths hanging over the city. On January 5, he wrote to Alfredo Panzini describing how the glorious sun reflecting off the snow made it seem like springtime in the mountains. Five days later, he received his corporal's stripes and the reward of fifteen days' leave. He left immediately for Milan and his family.[41]

Roberto's appearance shocked them. His uniform was reduced to tatters, his face hidden by a filthy beard, his hands encrusted with dirt, his body lice-ridden. One boot was half torn away, the other riddled by shrapnel. But once bathed, disinfected, shaved, and clothed, he seemed transformed. For two weeks, he gorged himself on every delicacy the family cook could provide.

Roberto told his family of the adventures and horrors he had experienced. His war stories were like nothing his mother and father had read in the censored press. He was emotionally exhausted, huddling close to the stove as if he could never get warm, and haunted by the killing he had seen close at hand. He had tried to discover some inner peace in the moral chaos of war. One day he asked Margherita, "Why was I born? Why, mamma? What cursed nature is mine that I must always cause suffering for those to whom I wish well?"[42]

Before he left Milan, Margherita took him to see Mussolini in his office at *Il Popolo d'Italia*. The two veterans exchanged a few words while Mussolini sat at his desk. Roberto had always been shy in his presence but Mussolini pressed Roberto about the condition of the troops in the aftermath of Caporetto. In December and January, rumors of mutiny plots and defeatist sentiment among the troops had caused the government alarm. "How is the spirit of the soldiers?" Mussolini demanded. "Morale is high?" Mussolini was satisfied when Roberto insisted with some heat that the army would hold together.[43]

The whole family insisted on walking with Roberto to the station when he left late on January 26. A thick fog blanketed Milan that chilly winter day. Roberto carried his pack the whole way. At the train, the little group seemed lost among the huge crowd of departing soldiers, surrounded by mothers, wives, and girlfriends. Everyone but little Fiammetta bravely suppressed their tears. All the fear and sorrow the eight-year-old had been hiding for two months appeared. She wailed piteously and flung her arms around Roberto's neck. Margherita tried to comfort her. "Roberto will return, don't cry," she soothed. "You will see, he will return. He'll return soon." Roberto hugged his little sister and put her down. Then he kissed everyone, smiled, waved good-bye, got onto the train, and was gone.[44]

Roberto rode back to the battle zone in a cattle car. Before reporting to his unit, he wrote to his father to tell him all was well. After returning to the Monte Baldo, he learned that the battalion had orders for an attack in the morning. He immediately rejoined his company in the front line, where his comrades were preparing for their assault.[45]

The Austro-Hungarian capture of the Sasso Rosso and other nearby peaks in early December left General Diaz profoundly worried. While the Alpini counterattack of December 5 had halted an actual breakthrough by the enemy, a new attack from the peaks might enable the Austro-Hungarians to sweep down the Brenta Valley and into the Venetian plain below. Therefore Diaz ordered an operation to recapture the Sasso Rosso, along with the Col del Rosso and the Col d'Echele slightly to the southwest. In addition to the purely military advantages of such an operation, he wished to impress on both the army and the nation that his troops had returned to the offensive.

Because of the narrow mountain paths, the plan assigned individual axes of advance to single battalions and companies. Roberto's company received instructions to attack up the eastern slope of the Col d'Echele and seize Quota 1039, some two miles to the southwest of the Sasso Rosso. After an intense artillery preparation, the attack began on the night of January 27, but the Austro-Hungarians' superior positions enabled them to beat off the Italian assaults all along the line.

Roberto's company, which had been held in reserve, advanced to the line of departure early on January 28. The Italian artillery fired on the enemy barbed wire, attempting to blast a path through the barrier. At 9:30, the Italian bombardment shifted to the Austrian positions and Roberto's company moved forward to the enemy wire. But despite the heavy artillery fire, the wire was still intact. As their advance stalled before the barbed-wire barricade, they came under murderous machine-gun fire. After suffering serious casualties, the company fell back to shelter in the ruins of a nearby village. The Italian artillery renewed its barrage on the wire and Roberto's company rushed forward again. As before, Roberto's comrades discovered the thick tangles of barbed wire still in place, while the enemy renewed their withering automatic-weapons fire.

Roberto crawled up to the wire and began battering at it with the butt of his rifle. Finally he forced open a passage and wriggled through. The top of Quota 1039 stood perhaps one hundred feet above him. From their trench, dug in below the summit, the enemy concentrated their fire on the young Alpini corporal. But Roberto leaped to his feet and rushed up the hill. Fired by his example, his comrades pushed through the wire and followed behind him. This daring attack proved too much for the Austrians. While some continued to resist, others fled. Roberto jumped down into the trench and charged its defenders. At the point of his bayonet, thirty terrified Austrians threw down their rifles and surrendered. Roberto also seized an enemy machine gun. Then he shouted to his advancing comrades to pursue the fleeing Austrian survivors.

Meanwhile, the Alpini battalion to the left of Roberto's company had seized the peak of the Col d'Echele, forcing the Austro-Hungarians to fall back to their next trench line. By now it was early afternoon. The weary Alpini had climbed and fought for many hours. But the enemy still held their defenses on the reverse slope and had to be dislodged. The Italians regrouped hastily for another attack. The Arditi advanced first and Roberto attached himself to his battalion's assault platoon.

Roberto's belief in his invulnerability fired his valor. The Austrians put up a ferocious resistance as the Arditi rushed their defense line. A machine gun firing from a bunker brought the assault to a halt. Shouting for the Arditi to follow him, Roberto jumped up and lunged toward the machine-gun nest. A bullet hit him square in the face. He fell dead into the arms of a wounded comrade who had dropped by his side.

The Italians went on to drive their enemies off the hill and repulsed the Austro-Hungarian counterattacks that followed. Hundreds of prisoners fell into Italian hands. Diaz commended Roberto's battalion "for heroic conduct." The next morning, the Alpini of the Monte Baldo gathered their dead and buried them in a common grave on the slopes of the Col d'Echele. Before they lowered Roberto's body into the pit, one of his

companions cut a lock of hair from his bloody head and sent it to Margherita.[46]

Roberto's commander recommended him for Italy's highest award for
heroism, the *medaglia d'oro per valore militare* (the Gold Medal for Military
Valor). But that honor gave Margherita little comfort. The news of
Roberto's death devastated her. "It's not true! It's not true!" she cried out.
Then she wept bitterly, unable to bear the thought of her seventeen-year-
old's broken body cast down into a hole. Later, she wrote:

> With all the bloody roots
> Twisting around you,
> Chaining you to life.
> Pregnant still, I feel you,
> I have you, within me,
> I cannot give you up to a grave.[47]

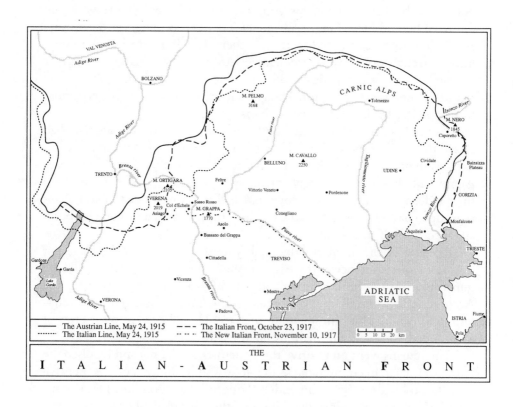

THE
I T A L I A N - A U S T R I A N   F R O N T

13

Italy and Victory

Mussolini and a few of his staff visited the Sarfattis' grim and silent household several days after Roberto's death. Margherita and Cesare tried valiantly to be stoic, but Mussolini sensed their agony—shock and grief were deeply etched into their faces. The visitors stayed some time, trying to console the parents with praise for a son who had laid down his life for his country. The next day, *Il Popolo d'Italia* carried a lengthy story about Roberto, together with a moving portrait by Mussolini.

Though Mussolini's sorrow was genuine, his deification of the young man in *Il Popolo d'Italia* was self-serving. He knew that from Roberto's short heroic life a powerful myth could be constructed—of duty, dedication, and patriotic fervor—which could animate his own political resurrection. Roberto, Mussolini proclaimed, had "immolated himself serenely and heroically for the well-being of our beloved Italy. . . . His offering to the Fatherland was complete, his devotion total. . . . There is, there must be in him that will to give of oneself that is the secret and the privilege of a great love."

Mussolini wanted Roberto's memory to inspire resistance and revenge against those who opposed the war and sought to rob Italy of the rewards of victory. Roberto's blood, "with which we take communion together as Italian brothers, is a sure guarantee that the peace of tomorrow will not be the peace of our shame." Mussolini had a special message for the devastated parents: "These are not hollow consolations. Margherita and Cesare Sarfatti have no need for them. They knew what war is, yet they did not stop their son from going toward his destiny of sacrifice and glory. In the name of friendship and for the memory of Roberto, I kneel before their anguished pride and ask to suffer some of their sacred pain."[1]

Their pain was paralyzing. Ada Negri stepped in to send out the notices of Roberto's death on their behalf. Condolences poured in. For Antonio Fradeletto, Margherita's old tutor, Roberto's death in battle personalized the "holocaust" that was blighting Italy's future. Even Kuliscioff grieved:

"He was still a child," she told Turati, "remember him? Yet the death of an adolescent—hardly 17—who renounces his life for an ideal, fighting heroically, is admirable. It is a great, noble, generous offering and the Sarfattis, once the first moment of the blow has passed, will find comfort in their pride for a son capable of sacrificing himself for an ideal so little felt by most Italians. By now, death triumphs everywhere."[2]

Margherita did draw some solace from the heroism her son had shown. She managed to write Mussolini a letter of appreciation, which he published in *Il Popolo d'Italia*. She also sent him the four war bonds into which the Sarfattis had put Roberto's savings, along with another donated by a friend in his memory, as gifts for Alpini in the Monte Baldo Battalion. "We draw tight around you, Mussolini: make sure, you who can, that so much sacrifice bears its precious fruit."[3]

But the consolations of Roberto's heroic death were limited. Margherita reached out to others who could appreciate her anguish, seeking some empathy for her grief. She wrote to D'Annunzio, sending him two pictures of Roberto in uniform and the issue of *Il Popolo d'Italia* that commemorated him. "My friend," she wrote, "do you remember the fragrant red roses that you gave me at the first production of *La Nave?* Then I did not know that I would have to pour out all my blood. God be with you for the vengeance and the glory of Italy."

After D'Annunzio sent his condolences, Margherita begged him to visit her. "If you would have even a minute of time to help me to battle with my sorrow, as with an evil beast, which *must* be lifted to another, higher plane." From this exchange of letters a still closer friendship developed between the two.[4] More often her grief cut her off from others. In a poem she titled "Buried Alive," Margherita described her sensation of being crushed under a terrible vault. "It weighs too heavily upon me/I feel no human pity/my heart is dried out."[5]

Part of the pain stemmed from guilt. She could not help but feel that her friendship with so many interventionists, and her decision to break with the Party and support the war, had led Roberto to seek his death on the Col d'Echele. She should have died, not he. "This thirst for ardor and sacrifice," she lamented to D'Annunzio, "brought him to his death just when he had begun to experience life. How unjust that I still breathe and he does not!"[6]

Her great suffering was partly a consequence of the sheltered life she had led. She had known some sorrow, after her sister's suicide, for example. But before World War I, Margherita had encountered few of the hardships other people routinely experienced. Margherita herself admitted as much, asking: "What did I know then of the dark abyss of pain?" The war taught her that wealth and position offered no protection for her friends or even her children. The anguish she suffered over Roberto's death left her a stronger—and a harder—woman.[7]

In an effort to purge her pain, Margherita wrote poetry, eventually creating an autobiography of her interior life called *I vivi e l'ombra* (*The Living and the Dead*). But she could never recover what she had lost. "I still live, still laugh and breathe, but the seed of my youth has been rent from me."[8]

Throughout 1918 death continued to strike close to home. Umberto Notari's son also fell that year and Ada Negri's lover, a simple worker, died in the terrible influenza epidemic. Negri mourned with the Sarfattis for the countless other young men whose bodies filled mass graves throughout Europe. She urged Margherita to "stand tall and proud" in the face of her suffering. Negri spent that spring and summer alone in her Milan apartment with a photograph of Roberto on her bedroom wall, writing poems in his memory and crafting a volume of prose orations dedicated to those who had fallen in battle.[9]

The same sense of loss that Ada and Margherita suffered had influenced Boccioni's return to aesthetic tradition in his last paintings. Ironically, an artist who had once been so violently anarchic embraced in the end a "return to order," a term first used in 1917 by the French poet Jean Cocteau.[10] Boccioni had pioneered the Italian return to a traditional illusion of space, an emphasis on solidity and volume, and an "architectonic" composition that served as a framework for the scene depicted on the canvas. The Futurists had always wanted to draw the viewer into the space and action of a painting. Now Boccioni kept the spectator outside the work, the passive observer of a world totally controlled by the artist.[11]

Some six months after Boccioni's death, a most unusual letter triggered Margherita's response to some of the aesthetic issues raised by his final paintings. The writer, a young army officer, refused to reveal his name or address, but he impressed her with his intelligence and sensitivity. Margherita made inquiries among her well-connected friends and discovered the officer's identity: Ferruccio Parri. Then a captain, Parri would soon be assigned to the Army General Staff.[12]

Parri had read a new Futurist magazine called *Gli Avvenimenti* (*Events*), founded by Umberto Notari. Margherita had taken over Boccioni's art column in the journal after his death. She began with a series of articles on the psychological, moral, and spiritual underpinnings of art. Parri took issue with her views, arguing that art consists not of morality or history but solely of plastic values and figurative elements, such as line, spatial relations, volume, color, and movement. Parri derived his ideas from a theory known as "pure visibility," disseminated in part by Bernard Berenson and other art experts.[13] Many supporters of the theory advocated abstraction as the purest method of dealing with these visible elements, because in an abstract work the elements could be appreciated on their own, and not merely in the context of their subject.

Margherita agreed with Parri's basic premise, but insisted that a work of art *had* to be more than the sum total of its formal values. In line with Ruskin, she insisted that as a product of human creativity, art must convey human values. "Art separate from life," she replied, "cannot exist. It is a contradiction in terms." She maintained that the technical elements of a painting serve as a language for the expression of emotions. She agreed that pure abstraction could express emotion, but only if it used lines and symbols as deliberate suggestions of concepts. For Margherita art was not accidental or arbitrary. It sought to discover truth rather than invent novelties prized for their own sake.

While Margherita accepted Parri's view that the subject of a painting in itself possesses no importance, she admonished him that great artists could imbue otherwise mundane objects with spiritual values. As proof, she reminded the young officer of the glowing and tactile apples in Cézanne's still lifes and his advice to a young artist to copy his stovepipe: "There is more genuine religiosity and more lyrical ardour in four apples or in the famous stove pipe as painted by Cézanne than in an entire gallery of Christs on the cross."[14]

She had in mind Boccioni's last efforts to build a new artistic language inspired by and surpassing the French master. Boccioni himself had praised the young Funi for following Cézanne's lead, while Margherita claimed Boccioni as the French painter's direct descendant. Cézanne, who called his own paintings "constructions after nature," had sought to reduce objects to their most simplified forms. Unlike the Impressionists, who had tried to capture the effects of sensory perception, Cézanne restored the dimensional quality of objects. He favored an ideal order informed by the mind.[15]

In assessing Cézanne's influence, Margherita contrasted the work of Picasso and Boccioni. Presumably she was unaware that Picasso's wartime neoclassical portraiture anticipated by two years Boccioni's own return to order. She argued that Picasso had betrayed the quest for order and harmony by overanalysis and fragmentation, while Boccioni saw that the decomposition of forms led to a dead end. His return to plastic values included the modeling of volumes and other three-dimensional surfaces. "Most recently," Margherita wrote, "he understood that the very nature of the plastic arts necessarily requires certain unconventional but eternal laws and limitations which, though they can be stretched, cannot be ignored without descending into the arbitrary, the artificial, and the absurd. He had, despite everything, a classical temperament that dreamed of imposing . . . the rule of synthesis and order."[16]

The "classical" temper she admired in Boccioni struck a deeply felt chord in Margherita's own sensibilities. Classicism had been at the core of the aesthetic value system to which she had committed herself since she first had developed a love for art. Even though she and her tutor Fradeletto had disagreed over modern art, they had nevertheless shared an appreciation for the art of ancient Rome and the Italian Renaissance.

Her concern that modernism remain responsive to the principles of traditional aesthetics led to her deep admiration of Boccioni's efforts to reestablish those principles. As early as 1916–1917, she was acutely sensitive to his return to order. After Boccioni's death she began to look to younger artists—"the painters who will make the artistic Italy of tomorrow great"— as his heirs and as the vanguard of a new, modern classicism. "That young generation," Margherita wrote in 1916, "is now on the battlefield":

> They defend with the rifle and the cannon the glory that is to come . . . they will be called Carpi, Carrà, Russolo, Sironi, Notte, Funi, Oppo, Spadini, Martini, and many, many others. Tempered by harsh and basic realities—hunger, death, fear, thirst . . . tomorrow their brushes and palette knives, engraving tools and lithography pencils will be strong enough to cleanse, purify, and sweep away all that is not the true form and expression of a living and substantial reality.[17]

Now that her son had died, the return to order assumed an even greater importance to her. Just as she expected Boccioni's successors to vindicate the painter's death by continuing his revival of classical values, she looked to Italy's armies to restore to her country the power and majesty of ancient Rome. Margherita's contacts with Mussolini grew more frequent. Mussolini's combat experiences and Margherita's loss had made their commitment to the successful conclusion of the war an intensely personal one. By March, Margherita was in correspondence with Mussolini on a regular basis from Il Soldo.[18]

By the spring of 1918, Mussolini was already looking beyond victory. With the example of Lenin's seizure of power in Russia in November 1917, he felt certain that the postwar era held immense possibilities for revolution. He envisioned an "aristocracy of the trenches"—a generation of young, courageous, and disciplined men hardened by combat—whose sacrifices gave them the moral right and the ruthlessness required to create and lead a new Italy. He predicted that after the war, hundreds of thousands of soldiers would return home "conscious of what they had done" and determined to sweep away the old order.

Mussolini insisted on the duty of all Italians to support the men at the front. As a wounded veteran of the trenches, he could speak with the authority of experience. "I have seen them, these soldiers," he told an audience in Rome, "because I have lived with them. . . . I have seen them with their hearts stopped as they awaited from their officers the cry, 'Out of the trenches!' I have seen these sons of Italy and I tell you that they are not soldiers, they are saints and martyrs!" He proclaimed himself their spokesman as early as February 1918, and vowed to stand by them against civilian defeatists.

Before groups of ex-servicemen and wounded soldiers throughout Italy, Mussolini repeated over and over the themes he had made his own: anti-Socialism, anti-Catholicism, and nationalism. Charging that the pacifism of the Socialists and Catholics betrayed the men dying on the battle-fields, he called for a leader who would break the backs of the internal enemy, "punish" and "strike them dead without hesitation." When General Fortunato Marazzi spoke publicly of the useless slaughter at the front, Mussolini angrily asserted the right of the people to lynch him. Against those who wanted "peace at any cost," he invoked the image of countless mothers who would live out their lives knowing that their sons had died for nothing.

Mussolini believed that Caporetto had made most Italians realize the common national bond that tied them to each other. Even the industrial proletariat understood that its fate was tied to the destiny of the nation. The landless peasantry, whose sons provided most of the combat forces, did not yet feel the same sentiments, and would have to be educated. Mussolini demanded an Italian victory that would secure Trieste, the Trentino, and Dalmatia, so that the nation could take its place among the great powers of Europe.[19]

Already there were signs that the Allies had other ideas in mind. In March a director of the London *Times,* Wickham Steed, visited Italy on behalf of the British government. Steed came to Italy to prepare for the Congress of Oppressed Nationalities, designed to bolster support for the Poles, Romanians, Czechs, and Yugoslavs living under Austro-Hungarian rule. If these groups could be encouraged to revolt, they could shatter the Austro-Hungarian Empire and deprive Germany of its major ally. Steed secured Prime Minister Orlando's agreement to support the nationalist aspirations of the Slavs along the Dalmatian coast, who hoped for the formation of a great Yugoslav state. It was a delicate matter, for Slavic desires for independence conflicted with Italian territorial ambitions.

Margherita saw Steed in Milan and she urged Mussolini to speak with him privately before the congress.[20]

Mussolini attended the congress, held in Rome from April 10 to 12, as part of the Italian delegation. Since his release from active duty, Mussolini had allied himself with the Orlando government because of its policy of fighting on to victory. Orlando's Cabinet considered Mussolini useful as a newspaper editor, leading interventionist, and wounded veteran, who could rally leftist support for the war effort. His presence at the Congress would make it more palatable to those Italians who distrusted the southern Slavs. There he reported tongue-in-cheek to Margherita that he had been "Slavisized" into supporting Yugoslav nationalist aspirations. This was a tactical move on his part, for his real goals remained those of an Italian nationalist—to help disrupt the enemy's war effort and bring about the dismemberment of the Austro-Hungarian Empire. Mussolini was, in fact, already thinking in terms of an "imperial" future. Before the congress met, he argued that the oppressed peoples of the Balkans looked to Rome as the ancient center of civilization, and that support for their hopes would enable Italy to create a "vast sphere of political and moral influence" as well as penetrate the region economically.[21]

After the congress, Mussolini remained in Rome to meet secretly with Giovanni Preziosi, a defrocked priest and anti-Semite, and General Cadorna. They seem to have discussed vague plans for a coup and the establishment of a dictatorship, but nothing came of it.

Before Mussolini left for Rome, he had warned his expectant wife not to give birth until he returned. But when he arrived back in Milan on April 22, he discovered that Rachele had given birth to their second son, Bruno. "I told you not to give birth, but you never listen to me!" he shouted at Rachele.[22] Later that summer, Mussolini moved his growing family to a larger apartment on the Foro Buonaparte, across from the huge Sforza Castle in the center of the city. Clearly his personal finances had improved dramatically, but the source of his income remains unclear. Probably he was again receiving money from Italian industrialists and agents of the British and French governments who appreciated his pro-war attitudes.

The letters Mussolini sent Margherita at the time of his Rome trip were written with the possibility in mind that others, including Cesare and government spies, might see them. Later, their written communications took place on two different levels. They sent letters dealing with matters of public or professional concern by regular mail or telegraph, while those of a more intimate nature generally arrived hand-delivered by messengers or friends.

Even the formal letters reveal the subtle evolution of their relationship after Roberto's death. Their concern for each other was evident. While

Mussolini was away in April, Margherita kept him informed about events in Milan, and particularly about any deviation from his views among members of the *Il Popolo d'Italia* staff. By then she had begun regular visits to the newspaper's office. He in turn showed an uncharacteristic tenderness in worrying about her health. When Margherita injured her knee, he joked that her confinement in bed "will allow you to meditate long and deeply about Socrates and all the rest." He also reminded her that he was superstitious about visiting sick people: "I don't promise that I'll come to see you. You know my phobias. But I'm sure that you'll be better soon. One of these days, if it ever happens that I've nothing to do, I will come to your house and we will undertake a discussion about the more subtle curiosities of life."[23]

The long war moved to its climax. After the titanic struggles of late 1917, the Italian Front grew quiet; having knocked the Russians out of the war and temporarily crippled the Italians, the German Army concentrated its storm troops in France. The German General Staff intended to smash the British and French before the arrival of millions of American troops made an Allied victory inevitable. On the first spring day of 1918, the Germans attacked, employing the same infiltration tactics that had proved so successful against the Italians at Caporetto. This time it was the British who fell back in confusion. The Germans poured through the huge gap they had smashed into their enemy's lines. Further German offensives over the next three months forced both the British and French back, ever closer to Paris. But the Americans had been landing in French ports in increasing numbers. The fighting along the Western Front had become a deadly race, with the Germans battling to reach the French capital and the Americans moving into the lines to stop them.

America's entry into the war also provided Italy with desperately needed supplies and loans. The Austrians realized that if they could not defeat the Italians quickly, they would lose the war. In June 1918, the Austrians, encouraged by German successes, unleashed their "Peace Offensive." The very name indicated a need to bolster the flagging morale of the Austro-Hungarian Army.

At 3:00 A.M. on June 15, five thousand Austrian artillery pieces commenced a tremendous bombardment along the entire eighty miles of the Italian lines from the slopes of Monte Grappa to the lagoons of the Adriatic. After six hours of this hammering, Austrian storm troops surged forward, their battle cry: "On to Milan!" In the north, Austrian assault forces seized the Col d'Echele and the Col del Rosso again, despite tenacious Italian resistance. To the south, the Austrians managed to throw pontoon bridges across the Piave and establish a number of bridgeheads on the opposite shore.

The Italians rallied. In the mountains, determined counterattacks regained much of the ground the Austrians had taken. Along the Piave, Italian gunners pounded the enemy handholds across the Piave, and smashed the new bridges with accurate artillery fire. Italian aircraft strafed and bombed along the length of the river, disrupting Austrian attempts to reinforce and resupply. The Austrians were unable to advance beyond their bridgeheads. Rising river waters made the evacuation of the wounded and the landing of fresh troops difficult. After six days, with casualties mounting and breakout impossible, the Austro-Hungarian General Staff accepted their defeat. Over the next two days, the Austrians fell back across the Piave.

The Italian Army had won its first great victory since the capture of Gorizia nearly two years before. Italian morale soared. While the Italians had suffered some 82,000 casualties, the Austro-Hungarians had lost 118,000. More significantly, the Austrians had lost their last chance at victory. The Austrian defeat electrified the Italian people. While the battle raged, Turati himself had risen in Parliament to declare: "While up there they fight, they suffer, they die, our Socialist hearts beat in unison with those of men of all parties . . . pouring out blood and tears, laden with destiny, [our soldiers] confront and surpass history."[24]

Sometime over the summer and fall of 1918, Margherita and Mussolini fell in love. For six years they had shared many intimacies—sexual, emotional, intellectual, political—but until now, their relationship had been based on affection or infatuation, not love. The course their lives had followed until then offers some clues to the strange psychological alchemy that now transformed them. Her feminine grace and refinement, his male roughness and energy, had always excited their passions. Their initial antagonism and a lingering residue of mutual disdain did not diminish their admiration for each other's ideas and courage. Spiritual kinship had developed during the political battles they fought together. Her acquisitiveness offended him, and his crudeness repelled her, so their attraction had cooled several times. But it had always been strong enough to draw them back together.

Since late 1916, Mussolini's physical attraction to Margherita had grown into a deeper longing and a strong emotional need. After Margherita emerged from the worst of her grief for Roberto, she reciprocated Mussolini's feelings. She never fully explained why this did not happen until six years after she had first met him. Once Margherita described herself as drawn to him as much by his weaknesses as by his strengths. She now came to realize that he embodied many elements of genius, yet suffered from numerous flaws. As she later put it, she began to worship Mussolini like a god while fully recognizing that this idol had feet of clay. His political acumen, daring, and charisma, combined with her educated intellect, wealth, and social advantages, made them a formidable team. But it was their wartime experiences that released their love. He had thrown away his position in the Party by supporting intervention. When she finally had chosen to join him, he could offer her none of the advantages that he had been able to provide as editor of *Avanti!*. She had abandoned her carefully constructed world to share his ideals. For the first time in their relationship, she had sacrificed something of real value.

The war wounded each of them, not once but many times. Each had lost close friends. Mussolini's injuries had nearly killed him. Roberto's death had plunged Margherita into the depths of grief. Each needed to find a purpose in all the suffering. After Mussolini had recovered from his wounds, his old revolutionary convictions returned, stronger than ever. He made victory, and the new order that victory could bring to Italy, the aim of his life. As Margherita began to emerge from mourning, she found comfort in this same quest—Roberto had died for a new Italy. Mussolini lifted high the banner that embodied the spirit of her fallen son. He swore vengeance on those defeatists who would make a mockery of Roberto's sacrifice. Mussolini's own suffering and his new purpose granted him a certain nobility in Margherita's mind. The old barriers between them had fallen, brought down by their common experience with grief and pain.

They were both still enjoying the final years of their youth, but they could no longer expect their spouses to satisfy their desires. Cesare carried his fifty-two years heavily, and Roberto's death depressed him terribly. Rachele could never cross the divide that separated her from Mussolini's world. As the fall of 1918 brought first the promise and then the certainty of victory, Margherita and Mussolini shared a ferocious joy in returning to life. They fell in love, passionately and completely.[25]

Their joy increased with signs that the war was moving to a victorious end for Italy. The great Allied victories on the Western Front in July and August 1918 had ended any chance for a German victory. The Allied High Command in Paris pressured Diaz to mount an Italian offensive and drive back the Austrians. But Diaz and Orlando doubted the ability of the Italian Army to sustain such an attack. In late September, however, Allied forces in Greece attacked northward. The Serbs advanced into Austria-Hungary from the south, threatening to conquer the Adriatic coast for the newly emerging nation of Yugoslavia. In order to secure these lands in the Balkans, the Italians had to mount an immediate offensive toward Trieste and the Dalmation coast beyond.

Over the next month, Diaz made plans for an all-out Italian assault. Ferruccio Parri worked out many of the details, though senior officers later claimed credit. Diaz unleashed his great assault up the slopes of Monte Grappa on October 24. Two days of heavy fighting brought no gains but drew Austrian forces away from the line of the Piave. Then, in the early hours of October 26, Diaz launched his armies across the Piave itself. For four days, the enemy fought back with a desperate ferocity, but by the thirtieth resistance slackened noticeably and the Italians surged forward. The Austro-Hungarian Empire had already begun to crack apart as its ethnic nationalities rose in revolution. The Italians tasted victory and pressed their advantage.

They battled their way to Vittorio Veneto, a town just five miles north of Conegliano, the ancestral home of Margherita's paternal forebears. By seizing this key objective, the Italians had driven a wedge between the two halves of the Austro-Hungarian Army. Thereafter, the enemy had no choice but to retreat.

The first days of November witnessed the total collapse of enemy resistance. Thousands of guns, hundreds of thousands of prisoners, fell into Italian hands. The Austrians begged for an armistice. This was granted on November 3 and went into effect the next day. In the meantime, Italian forces reached Trento and drove north for the Brenner Pass. The Italian Navy landed a force of Bersaglieri at Trieste, where Margherita's maternal grandparents had lived. When the fighting ceased on November 4, 1918, Caporetto had been avenged by the Battle of Vittorio Veneto. A week later, the Germans signed an armistice for the Western Front and began their evacuation of France and Belgium. The Great War had ended.[26]

After three and a half years of death and destruction, Italians were delirious with joy. On November 10, Mussolini spoke before a huge crowd at the foot of Milan's monument to its uprising against the Austrians in 1848. Margherita recalled the scene:

> Everywhere in Milan the cry "Victory! Victory!" echoed. People rushed up to one another in the streets, laughing and crying. . . . Twenty times I heard that news and was never tired of hearing it. . . .
>
> These thoughts passed through my mind as I listened to Mussolini, pale, burning, vibrating, as he recalled the memory of the dead at the great celebration of the armistice. . . . Beneath the great granite obelisk, at the foot of the bronze figures, suddenly Mussolini appeared, as strong and firm as those figures themselves. . . . Not the political Chief, still less the demagogue was he in that hour. He was the tribune, but still more the soldier, and because he could answer "Present!" to the call of victory, he could recall to memory in the hearts of those around him those who were absent—those who had fallen, his fellow-combatants.[27]

Mussolini's sister, Edvige, who had come to Milan for the armistice celebrations, was surprised by his clean-cut appearance and his giddy happiness. She guessed that he had fallen in love. For the first time in her memory, he wore a well-cut suit with a clean white collar and a flower in his lapel. He had recently shaved off his mustache. Edvige confirmed her surmise years later, when she read the personal diaries her brother entrusted to her. His entries describing November 1918 offered exuberant contrast to the dark tone of the letters he had written to her from the front in 1916 and 1917. Indeed, as Edvige recalled, the entries revealed that Mussolini had fallen in love with "an intellectual . . . the writer and journalist Margherita S[arfatti]."

> Vela ["Sail"] was the name of the woman in those pages; and such images of the sea, of the sky and of adventure were implied in that name, such a ring of phrases surrounded it!
>
> Benito's love for that woman writer was new and very deep—in my opinion—because it overcame his strongest mental and emotional tendencies, because in that situation he loved even those feminine qualities or defects for which he had always maintained . . . indifference or contempt. Rachele, in her simple way, realized that in Margherita S. lay a special danger and perhaps hated her alone among all the women who created "problems" for her.[28]

Margherita found new strength during this period of personal and public happiness. In October, Ada Negri completed her Orations, dedicated to the memory of Roberto and the "divine children" who had sacrificed themselves for Italy's victory. The moving narrative, composed in the severe language of a Greek tragedy, had a powerful impact on Margherita, and must have induced her to undertake the emotionally wrenching task of publishing her own tribute to her dead son.

In the wake of Vittorio Veneto, she began work on a commemorative volume containing eulogies written by Mussolini, Negri, and D'Annunzio, among others, as well as the letters Roberto had sent to his family from the front. In early December, she asked D'Annunzio for permission to include his letters of condolence in the collection:

> I would consider it a religious act to consecrate the unknown name of the little seventeen-year-old comrade with the great name of the Poet—both heroes through whom our humanity rises and consoles itself. The all-knowing "Ulysses" and the pure child, who had just begun to face the mysterious promise of life—each made their offerings, though unequal, selflessly. The synthesis of their sacrifice is now in Italy and Victory.[29]

Ada Negri's tribute, a much-shortened version of her *Orations,* combined Christian prayer with a kind of pagan mysticism that repeated the same theme:

We cannot weep for him.
We would not be worthy of him if we shed in his memory the
    common little tears of common little people.
He offered himself with full knowledge, virtuously, in the highest and
    clearest certainty of his only duty, of the necessary sacrifice. . . .
His entire being freely sought the Holocaust, an invisible bond with
    the infinite, a logical ascension toward the divine journey. . . .
Let us love him by working.
Let us love him by persevering.
Let us love him by purifying ourselves.

The volume appeared in time for the first anniversary of Roberto's death, privately printed in a limited edition. *Roberto Sarfatti: Le sue lettere e testimonianze di lui* (*Roberto Sarfatti, His Letters and Testaments About Him*) later became a breviary of martyrdom for the interventionists and war veterans who struggled to reshape Italy according to the spirit of the trenches. The final page of the slim volume recorded the proposal for Roberto's *medaglia d'oro*.[30] In a copy presented to Ferdinando Martini, a literary critic and former government minister, Margherita inscribed the following words: "A memory of pain and of pride in torment."[31]

Thereafter, Margherita remained constantly at Mussolini's side, working with him on the staff of *Il Popolo d'Italia* and assuming considerable responsibility for its editorial and managerial policies. Her first signed article for the paper, a review of Negri's *Le solitarie,* had appeared only in September 1917. Some other staff members resented her privileged status. Arturo Rossato, who had written the taunting article about the Sarfattis in 1915, resigned within a year. A subsequent book he wrote about Mussolini omitted any mention of Margherita. She ignored his resentments.[32]

The offices of *Il Popolo d'Italia* were small and cramped, and constantly filled with a stream of veterans and well-wishers. Mussolini's private office—"a very poky little den"—contained a desk, two chairs, and a bookcase. The desk itself held the rare luxury of a telephone, a blotter and inkstand, a revolver and several hand grenades. On the wall behind it hung the banner of the Arditi, a white skull holding a dagger in its teeth, that had been given to Mussolini during the victory celebration. A heap of newspapers littered the floor.[33]

At times, when Mussolini tired of his work, he would engage Margherita and a handful of the staff in debate. In the evenings, writers, artists, and intellectuals—mostly friends of Margherita, like Marinetti, Carrà, the poet Giuseppe Ungaretti, the writer Mario Carli—gathered "in a state of exaltation" to discuss events of the day and plans for the future. Each discussion contributed to the development of Mussolini's ideas. And Margherita supplemented public instruction with private lessons, lending him books of ancient history and modern literature.[34]

Margherita, deeply in love with Mussolini, had never before experienced such intense and happy excitement in which she could combine serious intellectual and political work with personal fulfillment. "We lived, we members of the staff, in a state of fraternal and at the same time Bohemian intimacy that did one's heart good. Four miserable little rooms we had, a wretched little hole of a place, a hovel in one of the lowest streets in an old slum in Milan, and yet what joy, what fervour, what high hopes were ours! And what fun we had to distract and rest us in the midst of all our preoccupation and hard work!"[35]

It was difficult for Margherita not to share the secret of her personal happiness. She seems to have told Ada Negri early on. The staff of Il Popolo d'Italia must have suspected. Eventually, Cesare must have learned. His close political relationship with Mussolini caused some strains, for Cesare continued to consider himself a Socialist even after Margherita and Mussolini were drummed out of the Party. But there were appearances and pride to be preserved on all sides and the two lovers tried to be discreet.

When she could not speak to Mussolini, Margherita confided her private feelings in her poetry, using anonymous interior dialogue to convey her emotions to her unnamed lover—the "well-known face" that was his, the moments of anticipation as she waited for him at secret meeting places, the "silent love" that could not be revealed, and her patience over Mussolini's many infidelities:

> You thought you loved me as a game.
> I smile and suffer: I know.
>
> But I penetrate your soul.
> Like a plague hidden within.
>
> Other women you take, leave, and retake.
> I smile and suffer: I know.
>
> The day will come: you will find that I am inside you,
> In your spirit and flesh, always.
>
> To love you is a long patience.
> I smile and suffer: I know.[36]

Mussolini responded less romantically, more physically. In his private notes to Margherita, he combined the gentleness and the ardor of a passionate romance. "Tonight," he wrote in one, "before you sleep, think of your most devoted savage, who is a bit tired and a bit preoccupied, but all yours, from the surface to the depths. Give me a little of the blood from your lips. Yours, Benito." And in still another: "My love, my thoughts and my heart are with you. We have spent delicious hours together. . . . I love you very much, more than you think. I kiss you with strength, I embrace you with a violent tenderness."[37]

14

Fasci di Combattimento

Battle experience confirmed Mussolini's belief that war would prepare Italy for revolution. He did not think, however, that the revolution would be led by the Socialist party. To his mind the Italian workers had rejected craven appeals from the Socialist leadership to stay out of the war. They had rallied to the nationalist cause. Their labor had produced the weapons that won the victory, and their valor had conquered the Austro-Hungarians in forty-one months of bloody combat. Disgruntled veterans could be won over to a new revolutionary movement under his leadership, Mussolini reasoned.

In mid-November 1918, Mussolini began calling for an assembly of workers and veterans to create the new movement. To gain their support, Mussolini emphasized a program designed to appeal to industrial workers. Foremost among his ideas were an eight-hour workday, a minimum wage, profit sharing, and labor-union participation in drawing up the peace treaties with the defeated enemy states.[1]

To Mussolini's disappointment, his call for a "constitutional convention" of worker veterans drew only a little support and much opposition, even from his friends. Prezzolini summed up the objections: Mussolini was the victim of wishful thinking. His desire to regain control over the Italian working class had blinded Mussolini to their real attitude during the war. The workers had not, for the most part, fought in the trenches. The wartime army was formed mostly of middle-class officers and peasant soldiers. Workers had remained safely behind in the factories, earning good pay. Greed or opposition to the war had motivated them more than patriotism. Facts showed that most workers had remained loyal to the Socialist party leadership and echoed their hostility to the war. It was true that workers had rallied to the defense of the country following the disaster of Caporetto, but that had been a moment of supreme danger.

Reality lay somewhere between Mussolini's fantasy of a working class fired with nationalist ardor and Prezzolini's portrait of a mass of loyal

Socialists. The Italian government had exempted many workers from the draft because they were needed in the armaments factories. Other laborers had escaped the trenches in order to raise crops and livestock to feed the army and the nation. Few of these 600,000 men regretted their escape from the slaughter on the battlefield. Besides, while a soldier earned a miserable fifteen lire a month, a factory worker could expect to take home forty-five lire a week. Farm workers exempted from military service drew much lower pay but the soldiers resented them nonetheless; indeed, they resented anyone who did not fight in the trenches. When the authorities had to use front-line troops to quell labor unrest, they went at the strikers with real gusto. Eventually the government placed armament workers under military discipline, requiring them to wear uniforms and live in barracks. Such measures neither ensured obedience nor placated the soldiers in the trenches. Mussolini was unrealistic to expect to forge a postwar political alliance from these two antithetical groups.[2]

Mussolini published Prezzolini's objections in *Il Popolo d'Italia*. He tried to refute the arguments, but as the weeks passed he ceased his calls for a "constitutional convention" of workers and veterans. Although Mussolini claimed otherwise, no significant support had materialized. By mid-December, he was searching for a new route to power.[3] He kept himself in the public eye by sponsoring a drive to raise funds for a monument for Filippo Corridoni, to which Margherita and Cesare contributed. And in *Il Popolo d'Italia* he announced a subscription for the family of the hero Nazario Sauro; the Sarfattis again gave a generous sum.

Like Cesare Battisti, Sauro had been born an Austrian subject but had fought for Italy in the war. After his submarine ran aground, the Austrians captured all its crew. Sauro was identified, tried, and hanged for treason. Sauro's death in August 1916 made him a symbol of Italian nationalism. Less than two weeks after the armistice, Mussolini raised 81,000 lire for the poverty-stricken Sauro family. He presented the sum to the Sauros in person in their home in the small port city of Capodistria, recently won from the Austrians, in December 1918. On his way there and back, Mussolini also visited newly liberated Trieste and Fiume, at the head of the Adriatic. He delivered a number of patriotic speeches and toured some of the battlefields on which he had fought. He also managed a brief visit to revolutionary Berlin.[4]

Led by groups of militant workers, radical German soldiers and sailors had rebelled in early November 1918, provoking the Kaiser's downfall in favor of a new government that admitted defeat and sought peace. These events sparked Mussolini's interest, since they closely paralleled what he hoped to accomplish in Italy. He wanted to witness these events at first hand. But travel to Germany seemed impossible, since Italian troops had sealed the border with Austria and Allied troops prevented anyone from crossing into Germany from France or Belgium. However, on December 23, the Swiss opened frontiers which had been closed since the outbreak of the war. Mussolini seized his chance.

Exactly how he got to Berlin remains a mystery. He bounced over rutted roads in an open car for four days on his journey to and from Capodistria, finally arriving in Padua on the morning of December 22. From that major rail center, Mussolini probably traveled down the main line to Milan, Zurich, and on to Berlin. He did not stay in Germany for much more than a day, since he was back in Milan by Christmas Day. But the events he witnessed there, put in perspective by his escort and friend, journalist Paolo Monelli, profoundly affected his political thinking.[5]

During the previous week, Germany's capital had been disrupted when a "Congress of Workers and Soldiers Councils," elected by local councils in factories and army units, met in Berlin. Three days later, the congress voted to hold elections for a national constituent assembly to create a new republican government for Germany. Then on December 23, while Mussolini was in Berlin, disgruntled sailors seized the leaders of the provisional government. They demanded a sizable sum as ransom before they released their prisoners, under the threat of attack by loyal army units.[6]

Mussolini arrived in Berlin in high spirits. But his recent travels had exhausted him and he lacked proper winter clothing in a city deprived of heating fuel. He came down with a case of the influenza that was engulfing Europe during the terrible worldwide epidemic of 1918–1919. Whenever he fell ill, Mussolini insisted on drinking milk, which he considered a panacea. Germany remained under blockade by the Allies, and food of every kind was in short supply. Luckily Monelli found Mussolini half a bottle of milk. He must then have helped the feverish Mussolini onto the train back to Milan.[7]

Mussolini recovered soon after his return, but Margherita came down with a more serious case of the same disease. Mussolini worried about her, telephoning frequently and sending an affectionate note. He reassured her that he was continuing to read the books she lent him.[8]

Mussolini wrote nothing about his trip to Berlin. In late January 1919, however, a long article on the German situation appeared in *Il Popolo d'Italia* under Margherita's name. She relied on her considerable knowledge of European history for much of her analysis, but talks with Mussolini were her likely inspiration for the piece. She described Germany as balanced between its militarist, aggressive past and a possibly peaceful and constructive future. Two forces contended for the soul of the nation: the conservative rural population, still loyal to the old order that had plunged

Europe into war in 1914, and the urban working class, inspired by Lenin's recent Bolshevik revolution in Russia. If either gained the upper hand, Germany would represent a threat to her neighbors again. The German middle class, however, stood uncertainly between these contending groups. If it decided to take power into its hands, a very different Germany might develop: one dedicated to cooperation and moderation in concert with the other nations of the Continent.[9] To some extent, the article simply reflected Margherita's hopes for the future. But two themes suggested Mussolini's influence: that the direction Germany took would decide the fate of Europe, and that the middle class could become a decisive political constituency.

Neither idea came easily to Margherita or Mussolini. Roberto's death had transformed Margherita's affection for German culture into hatred. Mussolini's time in Trento had led him to despise the Germans (he considered Austria merely a branch of the German nation) and his wartime service confirmed his feelings. The conclusions Mussolini and Margherita reached about the political role of the middle class were likewise startling, and far more immediately pertinent to his new movement.[10]

Despite their respective expulsions from the Party, both Margherita and Mussolini still considered themselves revolutionary socialists in early 1919. Neither had ever followed orthodox Marxist theory; Margherita's ideology was an outgrowth of her aesthetic beliefs, and Mussolini's was heavily influenced by his readings of Bergson and Nietzsche. At this stage both hoped to seize control of the state not primarily to advance themselves but to better the lot of the poor workers and peasants who comprised the majority of the Italian population.

In the course of the war both lost their faith in the unity of the international working class. Each developed intense feelings of Italian patriotism, even chauvinism. Their wartime losses led to an emotional commitment to the cause for which so many had fought and died: the greatness of Italy. Mussolini struggled to combine the two ideologies, socialism and nationalism. His political education within the Socialist movement had constantly stressed that the two concepts were mutually contradictory. And Mussolini's newest idea was his most heretical yet, that the bourgeoisie was of crucial political importance. As firmly attached as he was to socialism and nationalism separately, he could not reconcile them in his mind.

Margherita found it easier to combine these apparent opposites. She came from a bourgeois family, by her own admission, and knew her class was far from as despicable as Socialist ideology made it out to be. She had never been the extremist that Mussolini had been. She possessed a far more flexible and inventive political imagination. Once drawn to the twin ideals of socialism and nationalism, she seems to have had far less difficulty in creating a synthetic ideology. Then she pulled Mussolini after her, although not without difficulty.

Giuseppe Borgese observed the process. He had known the Sarfatti family well before World War I. After directing the government's Press and Propaganda Bureau in 1917–1918, Borgese took up a professorship at the University of Milan, where he taught German literature, aesthetics, and literary criticism. Starting sometime in late 1918 or early 1919, he began frequenting Margherita's salon. Borgese then became a regular member of the intellectual circles Margherita and Mussolini moved in, and he watched their ideas evolve. As Borgese told the story, Margherita "helped [Mussolini] mix the socialist-nationalist cocktail by which he, rather a zealous bartender than an honest drunkard himself, was later to intoxicate his nation and several others." Nonetheless, Borgese noted a far greater strength of will in Mussolini than in Margherita.[11]

Margherita and Mussolini's next steps followed logically, though tentatively. They had to struggle to translate a half-formed philosophy into a successful movement. Nationalism appealed to the middle class and to proud veterans. Socialism attracted workers and farm laborers and more privileged Italians concerned for the welfare of the working poor. Italy already had strong Socialist and Nationalist parties. The challenge was to win adherents from these well-established organizations as well as attract those dissatisfied with existing parties.

Mussolini was buoyed by his certainty that the war had dealt the old political system severe damage. In their failure to adapt to the new Italian patriotism, Mussolini judged even the leaders of the Socialist party to be reactionary. Socialist calls for an imitation of the Russian Revolution were destined to fail in the face of proud Italian resistance to foreign examples of new political systems. Mussolini believed he embodied postwar Italy's ideas and hopes; once he could determine how best to give them popular expression, he would be recognized as the prophet and the leader of his nation.[12]

Returning veterans were his best potential source of recruits. Of those who had served at the front, some 3.5 million men had survived. By January 1919, 1.4 million had been mustered out, joined by hundreds of thousands more over the following months. Upon release each soldier received the modest sum of 100 lire for his first year of service and 50 more for each successive year. Until limited supplies were exhausted, the government also provided each veteran with a package of clothing and maintained for another three months the subsidy each soldier's family had been receiving. On the average, a returning veteran had three to four months to find employment before he ran through his discharge funds.

Officers fared much better. During the war, the army had commissioned tens of thousands of young men as lieutenants. Their separation pay, also based on length of service, typically ran from 1,000 to 1,500 lire. General Enrico Caviglia, the minister of war, granted former university students the special privilege of being allowed to return to their studies while remaining on the army payroll. Many of these lucky young men rarely attended classes and enjoyed their temporary leisure. But all the 160,000 reserve officers faced an uncertain future.[13]

As 1919 unfolded, it became clear that the Italian economy lay in wreckage. The armaments industry shut down, throwing hundreds of thousands out of work. The war had stimulated a huge surge in imports, blocked exports, and ended emigration for the unemployed. Inter-Allied controls on shipping and raw-material prices ended, as did wartime loans to Italy. The Italians found themselves unable to compete with the far stronger economies of their former Allies. Throughout the spring of 1919, the resulting shortages of coal and wheat in Italy caused serious suffering, while inflation soared. By 1919, the cost of living had risen to four and a half times what it had been in 1913. Returning veterans discovered a country not only unable to reward their heroism but incapable of even restoring the generally hard lot they had endured before the war.[14]

These privations created grave national unrest. The Italian Socialists soon won new followers. On February 17, 1919, the Party organized a huge demonstration in Milan. Tens of thousands marched through the center of the city singing the Socialist anthem "La Bandiera Rossa" ("The Red Flag") and shouting *"Viva Lenin!"* Margherita and Mussolini regarded the parade with a mixture of rage and contempt. Treason seemed to triumph, while those who had fought and suffered for Italy were forgotten.[15]

Throughout the bitter winter months of 1919, a stream of unemployed veterans flowed through the offices of *Il Popolo d'Italia.* Their desperation elicited genuine compassion from Margherita. Mussolini could offer them no work but the word had spread that he would always give them a bit of money and a few words of encouragement. Considering Mussolini's own slender resources, Cesare and Margherita must have helped supply the handouts. When Mussolini and Margherita left the office after work, they often saw the beneficiaries of Mussolini's generosity crowding the local restaurants, with more outside waiting patiently in the rain to get in. Once Mussolini joked that he should have had the sense to negotiate a kickback deal with the restaurant owners, considering the customers he was sending them.[16]

Italian employers initially granted better wages and working conditions to the demanding war veterans they hired. But as the army released more men and unemployment soared, employer resistance stiffened. Labor violence began. In the countryside, peasant veterans began organizing themselves into rural unions to fight for their rights. After the government failed to redeem promises of land for the landless, they seized farms for themselves. By mid-1919 industrial and agricultural strikes, and attendant violence, had reached unprecedented levels.[17]

The government responded by slowing demobilization. It retained some 1.7 million men under arms through the summer of 1919. While many troops remained along the new frontiers, some 300,000 were deployed as public-security forces to deal with strike violence and political demonstrations.[18] Still the situation worsened, especially after the government suffered a series of painful defeats abroad. Italian foreign policy errors and frustrations added to the rage many returning veterans felt, and increased their willingness to seek radical solutions for their country's problems.

The collapse of the German, Austro-Hungarian, Russian, and Turkish empires removed powerful enemies from Italy's frontiers and swept away many obstacles to Italian expansion in the Balkans, the Middle East, and Africa. But the British and French proved as eager as the Italians to extend their influence in the lands adjacent to the eastern Mediterranean and the Red Sea. The Italians faced a new and formidable set of rivals to their interests in these lands.

No sooner had the Austro-Hungarian Empire collapsed than its subject nationalities created a number of new states. The Serbian Army advanced northward into the southern Slav regions of the empire, to create the Kingdom of the Slavs, Croats, and Slovenes later known as Yugoslavia. The Yugoslavs laid claim to many of the areas promised to Italy by the Treaty of London under whose terms Italy had agreed to enter the war in 1915. Before 1918 ended, the real possibility of war between the two countries led the French to send troops to Fiume, to keep apart Italian and Serb forces already in place in the city.

America's new involvement in European and world affairs complicated this situation. President Woodrow Wilson arrived in France in December 1918 to lead the U.S. delegation at the impending peace talks. Wilson refused to accept the Treaty of London and other agreements the Allies had made concerning the division of enemy territory: Since they had been negotiated prior to America's entry into the war, they had never received approval from Washington. Given the material and spiritual exhaustion of Europe that winter, and the combined influence of American resources and idealism, Wilson's words carried tremendous weight.[19]

Since his Fourteen Points speech of January 1918, Wilson had made it clear that he expected a peace settlement based on the principles of liberal democracy, the creation of independent states for national groups, free international trade, and the gradual dismantling of colonial empires. All these concepts reflected American interests and political concepts. He also urged the creation of a League of Nations to promote disarmament, adjudicate international disputes, and prevent the spread of another local dispute into a worldwide catastrophe. In Margherita's biased opinion, Wilson's "ideals and preconceived notions all inclined him to the side of England and France." Certainly the American presence at the Paris Peace Conference placed the Italians at a great disadvantage.[20]

Neither Britain nor France opposed the creation or expansion of nation states from the ruins of the old empires. A Europe of many small, weak countries would give Britain and France even more influence on the Continent. But in order to secure its borders, Italy wanted to annex territory inhabited by Austrians, Slavs, Albanians, and Greeks.[21] The Italians hoped that by gaining these new lands they could acquire the fertile soil and abundant minerals that their own nation and barren possessions in Africa lacked. Renunciation of these promised territories seemed to mean the acceptance of permanent national poverty.[22]

The British and French could accept the official end of their colonial expansion. They already controlled huge empires. They could retain the German and Turkish possessions they had seized during the war with vague promises of granting them independence at some unspecified date. While not as powerful as the American economy, the French and British economies could still prosper under conditions of free international competition. Italy's weaker industries needed tariff barriers to survive. Italian agriculture certainly could not compete with the boundless flood of low-cost American farm products.

Wilson arrived in Italy by train from France on January 2, 1919, and proceeded to Rome. Before the Paris Peace Conference opened later that month, he hoped to swing public opinion in the Allied countries behind his views. But the president was careful not to reveal just how much he expected the Italians to sacrifice in order to achieve harmony with their neighbors.[23]

From Milan, Mussolini greeted Wilson with an inadvertently humorous headline in English: WELCOME TO PRESIDENT WILSON, HONOURED CHIEF OF THE GREAT AMERICAN DEMOCRACY, TO WHICH WE ARE ATTACHED BY TRADITIONAL LIES, STRENGTHENED ON THE BATTLEFIELDS OF EUROPE. This typesetter's error proved prophetic. Mussolini and Margherita were to be disillusioned by Wilson's program for reshaping international relations.[24]

At first, however, Mussolini hailed Wilson as Italy's guarantor of justice in the coming Paris negotiations. When Wilson spoke in Milan on January 6, Mussolini was among those invited to a reception in his honor at the royal palace. Mussolini applauded his calls for a treaty settlement that would bring a durable peace to Europe. To Mussolini this could only mean granting Italy the Italian-inhabited regions of the former Austro-Hungarian Empire, as well as other territories strategically situated to give Italy easily defended frontiers and mastery over the Adriatic Sea. Some of these other territories were not predominantly Italian. But Wilson rejected Italian annexation of areas not inhabited by Italians, insisting that out of the ruins of the fallen empires, national groups be allowed to create states corresponding to national language groups. This principle became known as "national self-determination."

Fiume was overwhelmingly Italian, and so by Wilson's principle of national self-determination, Italy could rightfully annex the city. But if the Italians accepted Wilson's plan they would have to forfeit the eastern shore of the Adriatic, known as Dalmatia, promised them by the Treaty of London. Dalmatia was inhabited by Croatian Yugoslavs, and had been claimed by the fledgling nation. The Italian government refused to renounce its own claim to the territory.

By early 1919, the government came under public pressure to demand both Fiume and Dalmatia. A few Italians, notably Leonida Bissolati, argued against this. Bissolati had resigned from the government in December 1918 over the issue. While supporting the acquisition of Fiume, he argued that Italy stood to gain far more from cooperation with Yugoslavia than from acquiring Dalmatia. By renouncing non-Italian territory in agreement with Wilson's ideas, Bissolati pointed out, Italy could gain the leadership of all the new nations of Eastern Europe that had emerged from the fallen empires. Backed by a league of these states and supported by America, Italy could balance the power of Britain and France, and gain a position of real influence in Europe.

For this basically sensible program, Bissolati and his followers were branded "renouncers" by Italian nationalists. Prominent among his enemies was Mussolini. Despite Bissolati's quiet efforts to aid Mussolini during his time in the trenches, the propaganda opportunity overcame any gratitude Mussolini felt. While Wilson had visited Italy, Bissolati said nothing in public, but when he met the president privately in Rome, he promised Wilson his full support. On the evening of January 11, Bissolati addressed the issue of Italian territorial aims at the La Scala opera house in Milan.[25]

Bissolati entered the hall surrounded by a group of veterans and supporters to face a crowded assembly about evenly divided in sentiment. Most in the audience were also veterans, their gray-green uniforms in somber contrast to the ornate red and gold opera hall, lighted by the huge chandelier suspended from the magnificent molded plaster ceiling.

Bissolati had the chance to speak uninterrupted for only a few minutes.

As soon as he proposed that Italy reject the annexation of Dalmatia, Mussolini, Margherita, and Marinetti, accompanied by a large group of Futurists and staff from *Il Popolo d'Italia,* drowned his words with jeers, whistles, and screeches. As Bissolati struggled to make himself heard over the din, Margherita felt sympathy for her former Party comrade. Although convinced that he was betraying the cause for which Roberto had died, she admired Bissolati's courageous defense of his principles even in the midst of the humiliating cacophony she was helping to make.

Several officers arose to beg Mussolini's followers to respect freedom of speech. A brief silence ensued. When Bissolati returned to his subject, however, the hideous racket was renewed. Momentarily stunned by the barrage of noise, Bissolati ceased his speech. Bissolati's enemies noticed Mussolini, high in the third balcony, and shouted for him to respond. Mussolini declined. After Bissolati succeeded in making a few phrases heard through the uproar, calling for support for his moderate foreign policy, Mussolini jumped to his feet, his face hard and pale with rage. "No! no! no!" he screamed, beating his fists so hard on the red-velvet-covered railing that he raised a cloud of dust. Margherita was thrilled by this display of brute force.

Borgese, who supported Bissolati's ideas, sat near to him on the stage. Suddenly, the two men recognized Mussolini's voice in the chorus of protests, "that unmistakable voice, dishearteningly wooden, peremptorily insistent, like the clacking of castanets." Bissolati turned to those near him and said in a faint voice, "That man—no!" Repeated attempts to silence Mussolini and his companions failed. Bissolati resigned himself to defeat and left the opera house in disgust. The demonstration paralleled a Futurist *serata* but was unprecedented in the political arena. The fragile alliance of the disparate leftists that had supported Italian intervention in World War I had been broken. Crude intolerance had entered the mainstream of Italian politics, threatening the new and fragile democracy.[26]

Margherita had never separated her two roles as art critic and as militant in the Socialist party. She considered her thirst for aesthetic modernism and her Socialist politics both to be forms of an internationalist rebellion against the established order. But just as her Socialism had been moderate, restrained—until she met Mussolini—by her humanist sympathies, so she had reconciled her modernism with the traditions of Renaissance art. Her admiration for the technical skill and iconoclastic views of the Futurists did not lead her to admiration of their extreme abstractionism. She especially disliked Picasso and the Cubists for leading the Futurists to dissect forms into entirely separate pictorial elements.

Margherita viewed the artistic return to order as more than an attempt to restore the elements of aesthetic tradition. For her, it meant a return to the specifically Italian roots of Western art. She was not alone. Carrà recalled that at the end of the war, "I felt an absolute need to reattach myself to our purest traditions," which he found in the work of the fourteenth-century painter Giotto and the Renaissance artist Paolo Uccello. But Margherita went much further, advocating an increasingly strident cultural nationalism. She argued that Italian culture revealed an "innate and atavistic" sense of harmony and balance that stretched back to the monumental architecture of the ancient Romans and the paintings of the High Renaissance masters. Italians, she claimed, "have in their blood long centuries of refined aesthetic tradition."[27]

Early in 1919, Margherita brought out her collected articles on modern art in book form, under the title *La fiaccola accesa* (*The Burning Torch*). Many of the articles had appeared in wartime issues of *Gli avvenimenti*. The book's wide-ranging coverage of contemporary trends confirmed Margherita's reputation as one of Italy's foremost exponents of the avant-garde. The cultural section of *Gli avvenimenti* had been devoted generally to Futurists, but its editor, Umberto Notari, had wanted an open discussion of all trends. As a result, in her articles for the journal, Margherita had touched on all the latest cultural developments.

Margherita also gave her support to two other new cultural journals at this time. She wrote a highly laudatory review of Prampolini's journal of Futurist literature, *Noi* (*We*), which had recently appeared. She initially indicated great admiration for *La Brigata* (*The Brigade*), directed by the twenty-year-old Francesco Meriano. Meriano was a Futurist poet, ardent nationalist, and good friend of Guillaume Apollinaire. With habitual stinginess, Margherita asked Meriano for a free subscription. Her interest in *La Brigata* faded after Meriano refused to publish her poetry."[28]

By 1917, when Margherita encountered the new art movement known as Dada, her concepts about the role of art in politics had become fairly clear. Margherita first encountered Dadaism through Meriano and Prampolini, who championed its cause in Italy. In a Europe made chaotic by war and revolution, Margherita's artistic ideas had grown more conservative. Yet it is doubtful that even her prewar enthusiasm for the avant-garde would have allowed her to greet the bizarre Dada movement with anything but scorn. The Dada movement not only supported pacifist left-wing political views but deliberately set itself against all artistic convention. The Dadaists sought to undermine every traditional basis of culture and social order, even claiming doodling and ready-made commercial objects as art.

Margherita attacked Dadaism as an artistic failure "without meaning or construction" and for its political neutrality in the Allies' life-or-death struggle against the Central Powers. Meriano defended the Dadaists against Margherita, and Prampolini tried without success to convince Margherita to abandon her polemic. On the other hand, fearing Margherita's growing influence in artistic circles, Prampolini also refused to publish the counterattack against her written by the leading Dadaist, Tristan Tzara.

However, Margherita's nationalist sentiments and her rejection of Dadaism did not signify a sweeping renunciation of all modernism. On the contrary, she remained on close terms with Marinetti, Prampolini, and the younger Futurists. She even seems to have visited Picasso during his stay in Rome in the spring of 1917. But while she kept her interest in contemporary developments in international art currents, she increasingly focused her attention on Italy's past artistic glory as the inspiration for its future greatness. Margherita had begun to dream of a second Italian Renaissance that would restore the supremacy of her nation's art and return the center of the art world from France to Italy.

In December 1918 Margherita penned a retrospective essay on Apollinaire. The November death of the French poet and patron of the arts saddened Italian painters such as Carrà and Soffici, for he had been a good friend of the Futurists. He died at thirty-eight of his war wounds. Apollinaire's genius, Margherita argued, lay in his ability to see the continuity between the great culture of the past and the most revolutionary currents of European literature and art—"This classicist, this searcher after things, persons, and manuscripts out of the times that were, this tireless student of the rare volume and the suppressed edition, was also one of the most audacious critics to be found on the extreme edge of modern avant-garde art." And she reminded her readers that Apollinaire had been a war volunteer—"We honor in him a soldier of the good fight, both of the pen and the sword." Apollinaire's achievements as a soldier, classicist, and modernist offered a model for emulation.[29]

A few months after she officially joined the staff of Mussolini's paper, Margherita took over the "Cronache d'Arte" ("Chronicles of Art") section from Arturo Rossato, a weekly column that soon gave her an even more influential voice in Italian cultural affairs. Margherita now began to use *Il Popolo d'Italia* to propagate her artistic ideas.[30]

Her first art review for the new column, on the work of Alberto Martini and Virginia Tomescu, was an important departure from her earlier work. She adopted a more vigorous critical vocabulary—a direct and forceful style, unlike the cautious contorted syntax she had often used to qualify her opinions.

She was also using the vocabulary of the return to order. Thus, she criticized Tomescu for emphasizing color and light in the Impressionist manner rather than "solidity of form," and complained that Martini generally lacked the ability to achieve a "synthesis of plastic values." She declared that painting "is a divinely simple art, executed simply by means of forms, lines, and colored, balanced, and composed masses, but all rendered according to a personal and expressive style" and arrived at intuitively rather than through cold logic. While Mussolini called for discipline and an end to anarchy in political life, Margherita argued for order and a return to Italian roots in cultural life. Art, she declared, required "unity, coordination, hierarchy . . . that great sense of discipline that characterizes Mediterranean art and is the essence of its classic tradition."[31]

Margherita used her art column and her salon as the instruments with which to make herself the arbiter of postwar Italian art. New visitors now joined Marinetti, Negri, Notari, Panzini, and other old friends at her Wednesday evening gatherings. The conductor Arturo Toscanini, the professor Giuseppe Borgese, and the writer Massimo Bontempelli all came regularly, as did the artists Funi, Sironi, Wildt, Dudreville, Tosi, Salietti, and Arturo Martini. She often invited these men to Il Soldo, and introduced them to wealthy collectors such as Piero Preda, Amleto Selvatico, and Federico Gussoni. Because of her patronage she began to think of these artists as *hers,* and she felt responsible for introducing them to the public.[32]

The first artist to whom she gave wide coverage was the sculptor Adolfo Wildt. At fifty-one, Wildt was the oldest of Margherita's favorites. Something of a mystic, his emaciated body, large and protruding black eyes, and taut face seemed to express the same torment that he infused into his sculpture. His extraordinary technical skill in modeling marble had won him recognition in the late 1890s, but in the years before the war he had developed a unique style that combined an austere neoclassical severity with a modernized Gothic anguish. Margherita pronounced Wildt's exhibit at Lino Pesaro's gallery in February 1919 a major triumph. She had reservations about the archaic quality that marked Wildt's work, but admired his ability to possess the marble, as if he were its lustful and domineering lover. A small, simple mask soaring on delicate wings, titled *Victory,* expressive of both the suffering and the triumph of the war, moved her deeply. "He has given us," she wrote, "the reality of a dream: Victory. His Victory; our Victory; Italy's victory." Almost a half-century later, her family would select that same mask as the symbol of her own life.[33]

She renewed her search for a publisher for her poetry. She had written enough verse since 1916 to bring out a book and had by now placed several poems in various journals. Although her work did not excite universal admiration, Margherita was quite proud of her poetry, especially the elegiac poems she had written after Roberto's death. Prezzolini wrote in search of funds to start a new publishing house, and Margherita promised him her help. However, Margherita pointed out that her husband already sat on the board of directors of the Istituto Editoriale Italiano. Lending Prezzolini the money for his new press would create conflict-of-interest problems for Cesare, and Margherita wanted a favor in return. Would Prezzolini agree to publish her poetry, once he had established his new publishing house? Margherita would be glad to send the manuscript for Prezzolini to comment upon. Prezzolini's reply is not available, but Margherita's poetry did not appear in book form until 1921, and then without Prezzolini's help.[34]

In March 1919 she and Mussolini launched a new cultural publication. This was *Ardita,* the monthly literary review of *Il Popolo d'Italia* and something of a successor to their *Utopia* of 1913–1914. The name honored Roberto and the other Arditi veterans who were beginning to gravitate to Mussolini's leadership. When the first issue appeared in mid-March, it included Margherita's poem on Roberto's final departure from Milan, a short story by Massimo Bontempelli, and a range of essays, reviews, and poems by Franco Ciarlantini, Arturo Marpicati, Alessandro Chiavolini, and others. Margherita's name appeared only as the author of articles in the painting and sculpture column, but she had obviously persuaded Mussolini that the journal was needed and clearly determined its content. In his introduction to the first issue, Mussolini rejected the notion of ivory-towered intellectuals isolated from the fray of politics and real life—the same point that Margherita had made repeatedly during the war. *Ardita's* purpose, he announced in a dedicatory preface, was to act as a guide "for those anxious modern spirits caught between the nostalgic worlds that have collapsed and the bold worlds in the making."[35]

> That humanity is good or bad matters little; that it is made up of angels or demons, of saints or beasts matters even less. The essential thing is to live within this humanity, to seize it wherever and however it shows itself: in the streets, in the squares, on the mountains, on the seas, in the cities, in scattered villages, in individuals and in the masses, in the exercise of muscle, in the divine shudder of thought, in the elated passion of all love. *Ardita* wishes this. It is born for this. . . .[36]

More important to their future was Mussolini's decision to hold an organizational meeting for his new political movement on March 23, 1919. Early that month, *Il Popolo d'Italia* began announcing a gathering of the survivors of the interventionist movement that had helped bring Italy into the war.

While Mussolini still longed for support from workers, he had decided to concentrate his attention on recruiting veterans. He enlisted the support of Ferruccio Vecchi, leader of the Milan section of the Arditi Association.

Founded in January 1919, the national association had attracted about one thousand veterans from the elite shock troops of the Italian Army. By the end of the month, Mussolini had formed an alliance with the group, as had Marinetti. Mussolini gave the Arditi free space in his newspaper to announce their meetings, and acquired funds from local industrialists to finance an Arditi Association office in Milan. Mussolini hired a number of unemployed ex-Arditi as guards for his newspaper office and potential street fighters. The Arditi gave Mussolini's movement an aura of patriotism, swagger, and reckless courage.[37]

When Mussolini, Vecchi, and a number of others held a planning session two days before the March 23 meeting, Mussolini explained his purpose. He warned that Bissolati's speech at La Scala had signaled a disastrous split in the interventionist movement. The country had already been divided between the minority who had supported the war and the majority who had opposed it. Now Bissolati's call for "renunciation" of the goals for which the veterans had fought had attracted a considerable following. It appeared that Bissolati intended to lead these interventionists back to the Socialist party. This would leave Mussolini commanding only a small number of veterans and interventionists willing to struggle both for revolution and for the national cause. Those Socialists who still supported the idea of violent revolution had fallen under the spell of Lenin and his Bolsheviks in Russia. Mussolini despised Lenin's Socialism, which he considered too Asiatic. The March 23 meeting, Mussolini insisted, was necessary to reinvigorate the interventionist cause. The interventionists had brought Italy into the war and helped lead it to victory. Now they must begin the next phase of the struggle: not just to bring about a revolution but one with "a Roman and Latin imprint."[38]

March 23, 1919, proved to be a beautiful spring day. That Sunday morning, some 100 to 150 people assembled in the rented hall of an old *palazzo* on the Piazza San Sepolcro to hear Mussolini speak. The small square lay an easy ten minutes' walk from *Il Popolo d'Italia*'s offices and many of the staff attended, including Margherita. Cesare was in Paris on a business trip and it seems that, for the sake of appearances, Margherita asked that her presence not be recorded.[39]

The assembly brought together a varied group of veterans, workers, intellectuals, Futurists, ex-Socialists, syndicalists, and nationalists. There were even two feminists who had joined with Margherita in abandoning the Socialist party for Mussolini: Giselda Brebbia and Regina Terruzzi. The group included other friends and acquaintances of Margherita, such as Marinetti, Achille Funi, Alessandro Chiavolini, Arturo Marpicati, Cesare

Rossi, and Michele Bianchi, as well as those who later would have an important influence on her life, especially Roberto Farinacci.

Ferruccio Vecchi and another former Ardito spoke first, offering the thanks of the veterans to the interventionists. Then Mussolini took his turn. He spoke in general terms but he touched on themes that would define his politics thereafter. He proposed that the new movement dedicate itself to supporting Italy's veterans and the cause for which they had fought. The war had destroyed Germany's ability to threaten the security of the Continent and had earned Italy the right to acquire defensible borders. In particular, Fiume and Dalmatia must be Italian. Italy was a "proletarian nation" oppressed and exploited by rich nations like Britain and France, with their huge colonial empires. Italy too needed a real empire, not just the sandy wastes of Libya, to provide it with natural resources and an outlet for surplus population. An election would be held before the end of the year. The new movement must work to ensure the defeat of all those who had opposed the war or tried to sabotage the war effort. The assembly approved Mussolini's proposals by acclamation.

Next Mussolini described a revolutionary political program that rejected both the old Italian Socialism and the new Russian Bolshevism. He insisted that neither offered Italy any hope of prosperity or national greatness. Instead Mussolini suggested an economic system that put the interests of the nation above those of any class and encouraged cooperation between workers and owners. The war had revealed the incompetence of the present ruling class. It must be replaced by those who had fought and won the war. He advocated a new electoral system—based on voting by every adult, male or female—which would elect a national assembly based on proportional representation. Such a body would abolish the monarchy and establish an Italian republic. He also proposed an idea dear to the syndicalists present: The national assembly would represent the people not through political parties but through "corporations" that would reflect the various industries, economic groupings, and professions of the nation. This would encourage cooperation between workers, managers, and capitalists, rather than class warfare.

Mussolini urged the creation of *Fasci di combattimento*—battle groups— that would fight for the realization of these ideas throughout Italy. Once again, the audience cheered Mussolini's concepts. A discussion followed, dealing with the implementation of the new program. Other ideas were approved, such as confiscation of unjustly accumulated war profits. The members of the new movement finally elected a central executive committee and regional representatives.

Mussolini had deliberately avoided being too precise or detailed in his plans. He had not tried to create a party with a definite ideology but had founded a far looser movement. "We permit ourselves the luxury of being aristocrats and democrats, reactionaries and revolutionaries, legalists and illegalists, according to the circumstances of time, of place, of the ambiance in which we are obliged to live and act," he noted in a description of the meeting. His political movement defined itself through action, creating itself as it struggled to come to power. Thus was Fascism born.[40]

As Margherita later explained, the word *fascism* "is derived from the 'fasces' or bundle of sticks carried by the lictors of ancient Rome as symbols of authority."[41] These bundles of wooden rods were tied around an ax, whose blade protruded through the surrounding staves. The fasces represented the power of the Roman state in the starkest manner: the threat to beat or behead any who refused obedience to the laws of Rome.

The Italian word *fascio* (plural: *fasci*) simply means "bundle," "group," or "association." Italian political groups, particularly on the left, had frequently described themselves as *fasci*. In January 1915, Mussolini had helped organize *Fasci di Azione Rivoluzionario,* hoping to draw the revolutionary left into action groups to support Italian intervention in the war. Since the survivors of these groups helped form the nucleus of his new political movement in 1919, it was natural that they became known in Italy as *fascisti*. Soon, the whole world would know the members of the *Fasci di combattimento* as the Fascists.[42]

Indications of what the Fascists stood for had been revealed that January during the boisterous disruption of Bissolati's speech at La Scala. On April 15 a far more serious demonstration of Fascist tactics occurred. Milan Socialists had proclaimed a general strike, and announced a protest demonstration in the city's central piazza. The Party wished to draw attention to a police killing of one of their officials in a recent labor dispute. As the shops and offices in the center of Milan locked their doors, Margherita hurried to join Mussolini and the staff of *Il Popolo d'Italia,* carrying cigarettes and a thermos of hot coffee to sustain her comrades during the shutdown. After several hours at the barricaded newspaper offices, Margherita left to attend to her family at home. On her way through the deserted streets, she noticed a band of men approaching from the opposite direction. She was uncertain of their identity. As they drew closer, Margherita realized that they were marching in a military column. In front, his face gleaming with pride and his steel helmet stained with blood, strode the group's commander. Behind them came a band of veterans, including Marinetti and Vecchi, brandishing burning torches.

Mussolini and Marinetti had agreed not to interfere with the Socialist demonstration. Nonetheless, Vecchi, Marinetti, and some friends went to watch the political gathering from the nearby Galleria. After a few minutes, they could no longer contain themselves. Forming an assault force of some three hundred veterans and Futurists, forty armed ex-Arditi, and twenty reserve officers, Marinetti and Vecchi led their group back to the piazza in front of the cathedral. The Socialists had begun a parade, led by two boys carrying a portrait of Lenin. The Arditi and reserve officers formed themselves into battle order and without warning launched a combat assault upon the terrified Socialists, firing revolvers and hurling hand grenades. The police moved aside and stood watching, as if encouraging the attack. The unarmed Socialists fled in all directions, pursued by their enraged assailants.

Once they had cleared the piazza, the Arditi spontaneously decided to attack the offices of *Avanti!*. They swept aside a military guard, killing an eighteen-year-old conscript in the process. They shot their way into the building, overcame a spirited defense by the printers, systematically wrecked the presses, and set fire to the building, which soon reduced it to a smoldering ruin. The Arditi then marched undisturbed to the offices of *Il Popolo d'Italia,* passing Margherita on the way, to pay homage to Mussolini and to present him with the charred sign they had removed from the front of the burned building. When she learned what they had done, Margherita felt a thrill of pleasure. She returned with the Arditi, thinking of Roberto, dreaming of revenge and silently praying: "God, I thank you. For our dead, we will make a counterattack."[43]

Mussolini was taken by surprise by the crime, although his newspaper hailed the episode. He seems to have feared government retribution. He blamed the incident on the Socialists, claiming they had fired the first shots.[44]

Vecchi and Marinetti went into hiding. In addition to the young soldier, their attacks had resulted in the murder of three Socialists. To their astonishment, they were contacted by General Caviglia, the minister of war, who offered them safe passage to a meeting with him in Milan. After they arrived, Caviglia told Vecchi and Marinetti that their Arditi had "saved the nation" and set them free. Like many Italian conservatives, the general considered the Socialists to be dangerous subversives, preparing their own Bolshevik revolution for Italy. Despite mass demonstrations of protest by the Socialists, neither the army nor the police took any action against the arsonists and killers.[45]

This officially sanctioned violence marked a terrible change in Italian politics. It also lent a coherence to the recent events in Mussolini's life and offered a guide for future action. Previously a degree of self-restraint had inhibited the use of force in Italian political life. Even the most hostile political groups had rarely gone beyond verbal abuse or fisticuffs when expressing their differences. The government had used gunfire occasionally, as in 1898 or 1914, to suppress strikes or riots. But since King Umberto's murder in 1900, such strong action had been used sparingly and reluctantly.

In April 1919, however, Mussolini's allies introduced the tactics of the battlefield into political life, with the government playing the role of bystander and refusing to punish the clearly identifiable guilty parties. The message was clear to Mussolini. The government feared revolution from the left and would ignore attacks by "patriots" on "subversives." If Mussolini could create an armed force ready to follow his orders, he might be able to defeat the Socialists in the streets rather than at the polls. And if government leaders recoiled from using force against their enemies, then Mussolini could hope to topple them by revolution. This had happened in Russia. He had seen it happen in Germany. Perhaps the same would happen in Italy.[46]

15

Purely, Fiercely Italian

Once Mussolini realized how frightened the government was of a Socialist revolution, he set about trying to raise *fasci* of veterans armed with "war souvenirs" brought home illegally from the battlefield. The offices of *Il Popolo d'Italia* soon became a small arsenal of rifles, pistols, ammunition, and hand grenades contributed by local Arditi and other veterans. Mussolini himself kept a revolver and several grenades on his desk.

One day in early 1919 Margherita came into his office while Mussolini was smoking, a habit he had acquired in the trenches. Once they began talking, Mussolini placed his cigarette down on a receptacle to avoid singeing his wooden desk top. "Does that seem like a proper ashtray?" Margherita asked. Mussolini looked at her with surprise, glanced down at his desk, and then gingerly picked up his cigarette. It had been smoldering on one of the grenades, dangerously near its fuse. Thereafter he was more careful when he smoked at his desk, but he kept the grenades within easy reach. He also began carrying several with him, for rumors circulated in Milan that the Socialists intended to revenge the deaths of their comrades by killing Mussolini. He made sure now there were Arditi always standing guard over the door to *Il Popolo d'Italia*.[1]

Margherita lived happily through the spring, summer, and early fall of 1919. Her regular cultural column in *Il Popolo d'Italia* and occasional pieces in *Ardita* were satisfying outlets for her thoughts on art and society. The day-to-day struggle of assembling and producing Mussolini's newspaper provided challenge and excitement. Advising Mussolini and helping build support for the Milanese *fasci* offered Margherita a fulfilling alternative to her previous labor for the Socialists. Her consuming love for Mussolini was the emotion that bound all her activities together, suffusing them with passion and purpose.

But her relationship with Mussolini still involved considerable conflict. While Margherita's personal interests remained centered on artistic and cultural matters, her involvement with Mussolini meant that politics came increasingly to dominate her existence. She had not abandoned her own commitment to certain political goals. Mussolini's advocacy of voting rights for women at the founding meeting of the Fascist movement strongly suggests her influence, given his own low opinion of women. Probably Mussolini gave in on this point only after strong pressure from Margherita, Regina Terruzzi, and Giselda Brebbia.[2]

But Margherita had surrendered more. Mussolini demanded that she put his needs first in her life, as the price of their love, and she accepted this tyrannical request. The cost grew heavier as his political career gradually made him a national figure. His increasing fame also made their love affair less secret and more embarrassing. While her marriage to Cesare had become little more than a formality, she had no desire to humiliate her husband. Italian moral standards required the appearance of propriety, especially for the sake of Amedeo and Fiammetta.[3]

Cesare seems to have borne no grudge against Mussolini. Perhaps he had extramarital affairs of his own. In any case, he continued to represent Mussolini in legal matters. Furthermore, Cesare wrote to Ada Negri to express his profound admiration for the verses in Il libro di Mara, and his happiness at her literary success. Margherita added her signature to a similar short note several days later. Considering Negri's theme—the joy and anguish of illicit love—it would seem that Cesare felt no great distress at his wife's infidelity.[4]

Margherita and Mussolini nonetheless took care not to be seen together except when working in the company of their newspaper or political colleagues. Margherita left the offices of Il Popolo d'Italia alone, after the paper had been "put to bed" late each evening. After a while, Mussolini would wander off by himself to join her at their usual meeting place near the Sarfatti home on the Corso Venezia. Presumably they would then repair to a hotel or an apartment for their assignations. They continued to meet this way regularly from early 1919 until late 1922, although they spent other times together as well. As he hurried to meet Margherita after work, Mussolini sometimes encountered Cesare Rossi, a reporter for Il Popolo d'Italia and a founding member of the Fasci di combattimento. At first Mussolini avoided Rossi's inquiries about what he was doing in the neighborhood by saying, "I like to walk around in this area." After a while Rossi discovered Mussolini's purpose and made joking references to his affair with Margherita. Mussolini always acted quite flustered, much to Rossi's amusement.[5]

Margherita began using Ardita as a vehicle for publicizing the work of the artists and writers who gathered around her. Dudreville, Salietti, and Bucci drew the magazine's colored covers and black-and-white illustrations, while Negri, Bontempelli, and Margherita herself published new poems, stories, and articles within its pages.[6] The artists drawn to Margherita were uncertain what direction to pursue. Funi, Dudreville, and Sironi clung tenuously to the Futurist label while experimenting both with "Metaphysical" painting and figurative realism. The Metaphysical style, introduced by Giorgio de Chirico and Carlo Carrà toward the end of the war, often used classical statuary and architecture in combination with mannequins and dream imagery. The style had a decisive influence on Surrealism, but had little to do with the "classical" values extolled by Margherita. Indeed, in *Il Popolo d'Italia* she often criticized the Metaphysical painters and emphasized the difference between their "cerebral" theories and her own "intuitive" approach to style.[7]

In March 1919, Funi, Dudreville, and Sironi took part in a big Futurist exhibit orchestrated by Marinetti in Milan. Margherita lent four works from her growing collection to the show—two paintings by Funi, a Sironi portrait of her, and his *Cyclist*.[8] Margherita considered Sironi the most talented of the postwar artists, and their friendship deepened into an intimate relationship. Lean and darkly handsome, the Sardinian painter appeared to her "seductive because of his genuine force of personality hidden carefully beneath complexes of self-doubt." Trained as an architectural engineer, Sironi had studied painting in Rome. Sironi met Severini and Boccioni and frequented the Caffè Aragno, where avant-garde artists and writers gathered.[9]

Margherita may have seen Sironi's cover illustration for *Avanti della Domenica* as early as 1905, but they probably first met only when he moved to Milan late in 1914 or early 1915. He became an official member of the Futurist movement in March 1915, and the next month began doing war illustrations for *Gli Avvenimenti*. His bold drawings of the Prussian military were acclaimed by Boccioni as among the best illustrations of the day. After Italy entered the war, Sironi joined the other Futurists in the Volunteer Cyclist Corps. The theme of his *Cyclist,* painted in 1916 in tempera and collage, came out of that experience. Already it showed Sironi's withdrawal from the dynamism that had once marked his Futurist style: A dark and anonymous figure sits crouched on a bicycle against a background of forbidding buildings whose gaping black windows convey the mysterious, alienated world of the city.

In 1919 Sironi began to paint the melancholy "urban landscapes" for which he would become famous. In some two dozen works, he rendered the drab industrial outskirts of Milan as he tried to come to grips with the urban social problems of postwar Italy. The areas that Boccioni had once painted in dynamic vitality are in Sironi's paintings static and brooding regions where workers live in helpless despair. Apartment houses and factories are stark, anonymous structures, backdrops to beggars, ghostly wanderers, or black, menacing trucks. Margherita, who owned at least one urban landscape, thought them among the most important paintings of the period.[10]

Margherita announced the exhibit in *Il Popolo d'Italia* by pointing out that most of the paintings on display represented a new departure from Futurism. The next month, she wrote an extraordinary, three-part review of the exhibit that was really an announcement of her own aesthetic program. It was clear to Margherita that artists such as Sironi and Funi had little place in a Futurist show. They belonged, instead, to a new artistic movement in the process of evolving, whose origins she examined in a sweeping summary of the history of Western art. In the ancient and medieval worlds, she explained, painting and sculpture had been incorporated into architecture, but the Renaissance had removed both from the architectural context. This had led to the eventual abandonment of volume and three-dimensional appearance that artists call "plastic values."

Following Cézanne's lead, the best modern artists groped toward the restoration of "architectonic" values. Yet Margherita was convinced that they were not fully conscious of the common goal for which they were striving. Too many, she warned, thought of themselves as living in an era of "unrestrained individual liberty"—later she called it more bluntly a "tragic" and "terrible" period of "individual artistic anarchy"—and rejected any suggestion that they should form an artistic movement. "They are wrong. Membership in a 'school' does not automatically mean the loss of artistic personality; those endowed with talent and strong sensibility will always stand out. But it does mean a coordination and a collaboration of effort."

The exhibit gave Margherita an opportunity to publicize Sironi, Funi, and Dudreville. Of the three-dozen painters in the exhibit, Margherita devoted her attention almost exclusively to their work, with only brief mentions of Russolo, Primo Conti, and Ottone Rosai. She believed these men stood at the edge of "a radical revision of artistic values" and presaged the "dawn of a new classical era, one of style, precision and hierarchy."[11]

Margherita's words made perfect sense in the context of Mussolini's political activities. She had in effect urged the formation of a "school" of art. Coming so soon after the founding of the *fasci,* her proposal could hardly have been coincidental. Mussolini's introduction to *Ardita* had called for political commitment from the world of culture, and Margherita and Marinetti had already succeeded in generating more sympathy for Fascism among visual artists than among any other group of the intellectual community. Funi had actually taken part in the San Sepolcro rally, and both Rosai and Conti had sent statements of support. Within a few years she secured Sironi an appointment as political cartoonist for *Il Popolo d'Italia*.[12]

Margherita had concluded that art criticism was no longer enough for her. She wanted to influence the very direction of modern art. Her intimate association with Mussolini played a critical role in expanding her aims, for his own ambition alerted her to the possibilities of shaping the contours of their postwar culture. Just as Mussolini would bring order and grandeur to Italian political life, Margherita determined to restore discipline and greatness to Italian art. Fascism and the artistic "return to order" were in her mind products of the same historical climate. Certainly, given Margherita's convictions concerning the importance of culture in building social cohesion, her goals did not reflect a blind devotion or uncritical admiration for Mussolini. She knew that if a political movement such as Fascism were to remake Italian society, it would need a grounding in a system of cultural values beyond Mussolini's grasp. She wanted to collaborate with him on her own terms.[13]

Matters went poorly for Italy at the Paris Peace Conference in April 1919. President Wilson and the Italian delegation argued over the fate of Fiume and Dalmatia, while the British and French vainly sought to mediate between two irreconcilable positions. Yugoslavia needed a port, Wilson insisted, and the Adriatic coast should be given to the new country on the basis of its predominantly Slavic population. The Italians insisted that Dalmatia be ceded to them, as stipulated in the Treaty of London. They also demanded Fiume on the basis of its Italian-speaking population, although the treaty had not mentioned the city. Neither side would budge. On April 23, Wilson appealed directly to the Italian people to support his position. The president assumed that his popularity among the Italians, demonstrated during his January visit, would allow him to break the intransigent Italian government.

Wilson miscalculated. The vast majority of Italians reacted with rage at this attempt to undermine their government. Even Bissolati rallied to the support of the Italian delegation, which stalked out of the peace conference in indignation. Mussolini and D'Annunzio joined in denouncing Wilson's maneuver and demanding that the Italian government occupy Fiume and Dalmatia by force.[14]

Abandoning his earlier enthusiasm for the president, Mussolini now described Wilson as a vile hypocrite. The president was using the ideal of national self-determination to weaken Italy, while ignoring British and French violations of that principle. What right had the British to suppress

the movements for national liberation in Ireland or Egypt, he demanded?
Why should the French control Tunisia, where the majority of the European population was Italian? Why did Wilson not denounce these examples of injustice? Clearly Wilson had joined the British and French in
attempting to prevent Italy from rising to the rank of a world power.

Mussolini's fury reached such heights that he suggested that Italy might
put aside its bitter grievances toward Germany and join that defeated nation
in overturning the results of World War I. Italy could stir up the peoples
subjected by the British and help overthrow the British Empire, he suggested. Mussolini warned that the conspiracy formed by the Americans,
British, and French against the Italians could lead to a new and terrible war
for control of the world.[15]

The Italian people greeted their delegation with enthusiasm when it
returned from Paris. But Prime Minister Orlando had expected Wilson to
call the Italian delegation back, and capitulate over Fiume and Dalmatia.
Instead the conference proceeded, ignoring Italian interests altogether as it
allotted European and colonial territory. Without the Italians present, the
Allies worked out the details of the treaty with Germany, and they made
it clear that they were prepared to decide the details of the treaties with
Austria and Hungary as well. Without loans and supplies of raw materials
and food from the Allies, the deteriorating Italian economy might completely collapse. Negotiation and cooperation with the Americans, British,
and French offered the only solution. Swallowing their terrible humiliation, Orlando and his advisers returned to Paris on the night of May 5.

Over the following weeks, the angry, cantankerous Italians fought for
every advantage against their increasingly hostile negotiating partners. By
the time the treaties were substantially finished in June, the Italians had
failed to gain any of their ambitious goals. Their hopes for acquiring a large
colonial empire had centered on receiving a protectorate over the independent African nation of Ethiopia, and possession of some of the surrounding
French and British territories. The British and French governments totally
rejected these requests.

Italian claims to Fiume and Dalmatia were made the subject of further
negotiations. Italian failure to gain either of these areas immediately suggested eventual defeat. Orlando and his government could not survive this
debacle. On June 19, a vote of no confidence swept the prime minister and
his Cabinet out of office. Francesco Saverio Nitti became the new prime
minister, with Tommaso Tittoni as his foreign minister.[16]

Nitti ordered Tittoni to resume negotiations in Paris, which dragged
on through the summer. With the main elements of the peace treaties
settled, Wilson sailed for America. Soon the French adopted his stubborn
position on the Fiume issue. Tension between the French and Italian

garrisons in Fiume, joined by the increasingly anti-French civilian population, had been growing for months. On July 6, after a number of aggravating incidents, a mob of Italian sailors and civilians attacked French soldiers in the streets, killing nine of them. In order to keep French government indignation within bounds, Tittoni suggested a commission to determine a better form of rule for Fiume, pending a permanent solution. In late August, the Allies decided to reduce the Italian garrison in the city and turn over policing duties to a mostly British force. The new police force would assume its duties in Fiume on September 12. The possibility that Fiume might be torn from Italian control sent a shock wave through the Italian Army, and the groups led by Mussolini, Marinetti, Vecchi, and D'Annunzio.[17]

For all his anger over Fiume, Mussolini realized the opportunities inherent in the crisis. Not only did it provide his Fascist movement with a highly popular cause, but Orlando and Nitti's mishandling of the negotiations offered further proof of the incapacity of Italian rulers to solve the problems created by the war. Their diplomatic failures reinforced the impression created by their frightened response to the April violence in Milan: The government was growing weak enough to be overthrown. Because of the crisis Mussolini also acquired powerful new allies. Foremost among them was Gabriele D'Annunzio.[18]

Thanks to his demonstrated valor and a talent for dramatic self-promotion, D'Annunzio was Italy's greatest war hero. Fifty-two years old in 1915, D'Annunzio gained a commission in a cavalry regiment through his connections within the government. The cavalry saw little action in a struggle waged among trenches, barbed wire, and machine guns. D'Annunzio persuaded the High Command to set him free from his unit and allow him to serve where and how he saw fit. The High Command decided that with his literary reputation he could lend an air of romance to a struggle notably lacking in both popularity and glamour. Once free to fight as he pleased, D'Annunzio flew bombing raids over Trieste and propaganda demonstrations over Vienna, took part in daring motor-torpedo-boat attacks on the Austro-Hungarian fleet, and assaulted enemy trenches with the Arditi. By the time the war had ended, D'Annunzio had lost an eye in a flying accident and won Italy's highest award for military heroism, the *medaglia d'oro*.[19]

D'Annunzio's highly publicized adventures led many Italians to associate the poet with Italy's victory in the war. He encouraged the associations, and as early as January 1919 had seized the leadership of those demanding Fiume and Dalmatia for Italy. In early June, as a result of the Orlando government's failure to obtain Fiume through negotiations, D'Annunzio published in *Il Popolo d'Italia* a warning that unless the Americans and

European Allies agreed to give Italy the city, he was prepared to lead his followers in an armed takeover.[20]

Margherita had known the poet for about fifteen years. She had come to view D'Annunzio as the embodiment of the ideals for which Robert had died. It may be that D'Annunzio's sympathetic response to Margherita's letters of late 1918 and early 1919 prompted her to suggest that Mussolini solicit the poet's articles for Il Popolo d'Italia. As she grew ever closer to Mussolini, Margherita became more enthusiastic in her support for D'Annunzio's insistence that Italy's victory not be "mutilated." In early June, she expressed her solidarity with the poet in a telegram: SYMBOL OF ITALY, AFTER THE SACRIFICE, THE BLOOD. FOR SOLACE NOW THE HATE. MY DEAD YOUNG SON IS WITH US AND WITH YOU.[21]

Three weeks later, Mussolini and D'Annunzio met for the first time in Rome. Mussolini had gone there to help establish a *fascio* and take part in the inaugural meeting of the National Association of Veterans. Margherita's enthusiastic support for D'Annunzio must have increased Mussolini's interest in linking the new Fascist movement to the poet's popular crusade to gain Fiume. Mussolini was discovering to his dismay that he was failing to attract enough Italian veterans to the Fascists.

In the articles he telephoned to Il Popolo d'Italia, Mussolini claimed that the new Veterans Association and the Fascist movement had substantially similar aims. But privately he told Margherita that he was "troubled and nervous" over the political divisions among the veterans. Many were being attracted by the revolutionary rhetoric of the Socialist party. Others were offering their allegiance to the new Catholic party, the Partito Popolare Italiano, founded in January 1919. Created with the blessing of the Vatican to offer a nonrevolutionary alternative to the Socialists, the Popolari advocated a wide range of reforms to benefit the peasants, workers, and lower middle class. The Popolari also supported the ideas of Wilson, especially the League of Nations. With these alternatives, most veterans felt little attraction to the Fascists. Many saw the Fascists as violent reactionaries, somehow tied to the interests of big business and the landowners.[22]

These doubts were understandable since Mussolini had yet to define the politics of his new movement. In response, Il Popolo d'Italia in June published a program for the Fascist movement based on the resolutions made at the Piazza San Sepolcro the previous March. The program called for reforms for the benefit of the peasants, the workers, and the lower middle classes at the expense of government bureaucracy, big business, the landowners, and the Church.

Mussolini's program was somewhat general, since he did not want to limit his supporters. Despite his hostility to Lenin's Bolsheviks and the Italian Socialists, he continued to view himself as a leftist revolutionary.

This made it impossible for him to seek money or political support from those whose economic interests were being threatened by the Socialists, the Popolari, and the disorganized mobs shouting for revolution. Mussolini had attacked the new government, believing Prime Minister Nitti likely to surrender Italy's claims to Fiume and Dalmatia, but in doing so he had alienated Nitti's followers. He also continued to oppose the Catholic Church and the Liberals. At the same time, his nationalism made him anathema to most leftists, as well as to moderate Italians. And the police watched him with suspicion, for rumors circulated that Mussolini was really a Bolshevik.[23] All these enemies left Mussolini's Fascists with few sources for recruits, and made identification with D'Annunzio all the more important to create a more favorable image.[24]

The summer of 1919 brought an unprecedented wave of labor and social unrest to Italy, especially to the industrial north. Returning veterans had swelled Italian labor unions to unprecedented size, then initiated actions that often led to violent clashes with the police. Rising food costs provoked frequent bread riots. Shops were looted, and assaults made on whomever the angry mobs considered a profiteer or a hoarder. Farm workers formed rural unions. Through intimidation, arson, and the killing of livestock, they imposed their demands for higher wages and better conditions. Socialists took credit (often undeserved) for these events and spoke of the inevitable advent of revolution. The Nitti government refused to intervene, afraid it might provide the spark that would set off a revolutionary explosion. Wide areas fell under de facto rule by the Socialist party. The Socialists considered men in uniform, especially army officers, defenders of the ruling class and singled them out for abuse and even physical assault.[25]

Margherita found the situation almost unbearable. Six years later, she still remembered it with disgust and bitterness:

> The populace had become rude and insulting in its behaviour towards the bourgeoisie, even in the streets and on the trams.
>
> Strikes were perpetual. For a mere nothing work would be brought to a standstill. What work was done was of the most superficial and slovenly character. On the merest pretext appeals would be made "to the solidarity of the workers." The country was in as bad a plight as the towns. Soldiers were spat upon, officers were followed by insulting crowds, simply because they were in uniform. Wound-stripes were torn off the arms of wounded men and medals were trampled underfoot.
>
> Parliament was paralysed and incapable of taking strong action. The Government tried to conciliate the Socialists and win them over. Three separate amnesties were given to all deserters, even to those who had

deserted in the face of the enemy. The attacks on men in uniform were met by a circular, issued by the Minister for War, advising the men not to wear uniform, but to go out in mufti so as to avoid "giving provocation."[26]

She considered escaping from Italy on a wild adventure with D'Annunzio. She spent part of the summer of 1919 at the seaside resort of Bellaria, a few miles up the Adriatic coast from Rimini. The writer Mario Moretti had arranged for Margherita and her children to stay at the vacation home of Giuseppe Brezzi, director of the Ansaldo aircraft company. For some time, D'Annunzio had been planning to lead a spectacular flight from Rome to Tokyo, employing some of the same Ansaldo bombers he had flown in the war. Naturally Brezzi supported the idea enthusiastically, seeing an opportunity to promote sales for Ansaldo at a time when the Italian aircraft industry faced a postwar depression.

Mussolini himself had begun taking flying lessons in July 1919. After a few flights, he had fallen under the spell of flying machines and the romance of the skies. He became determined to acquire a pilot's license; presumably Margherita financed his new hobby. Mussolini's love of flying brought him to the attention of Brezzi, eager for any support the struggling aircraft industry could find. Soon Ansaldo was taking out large ads in *Il Popolo d'Italia,* more to aid Mussolini than to persuade the newspaper's readers to purchase airplanes.

Margherita probably learned of the projected flight to Japan from Brezzi, with whom she had become quite friendly. She wrote to D'Annunzio, begging him to allow her to join the expedition. She had already flown a number of times, probably with Mussolini's flying instructor. Once she reached a height of over 14,000 feet, "the altitude record for a woman passenger," she noted. She was as passionate about flying as Mussolini, even writing articles for the *Gazzetta dell'Aviazione.* She pleaded with D'Annunzio that such an experience would be the final escapade of a rapidly dwindling youth, an adventure that would allow her some surcease from her lingering grief and a tonic for her approaching middle age. "In the meantime, I will train with other flights," she concluded. "I promise you absolute obedience and absolute secrecy. Don't judge me foolhardy or annoying." His reply is unknown.[27]

D'Annunzio's attention also had turned to a developing plot to seize Fiume by force, sponsored by certain circles within the Italian Army. To what extent Mussolini was also privy to these plans remains unclear, but he certainly was involved. At the same time, Mussolini and Marinetti had begun speaking seriously of seizing power through revolution. Mussolini discussed this idea with D'Annunzio in Rome. Apparently Mussolini and

Marinetti considered launching a revolution in northern Italy in response to a successful seizure of Fiume. But the circumstances had to be favorable. Both plans faced serious obstacles, as Mussolini was well aware.[28]

For weeks D'Annunzio could not decide whether to make aviation history or lead the action to seize Fiume. Generals and admirals often called upon the poet at his home in Venice, urging him to undertake the flight to Japan. The Nitti government clearly preferred D'Annunzio out of the country.[29]

Mussolini decided that an attempt at revolution by his followers would be premature. When he learned that D'Annunzio expected a nationalist revolution to follow an armed seizure of Fiume, with or without his personal participation, Mussolini formed an even lower opinion of the poet's political acumen. By itself, the capture of Fiume would not bring down Nitti's government, Mussolini reasoned. But if it served as the signal for a revolutionary uprising, then certainly the Socialists would take it over.[30]

On September 11, 1919, D'Annunzio learned of the imminent arrival of the British police force, which would effectively remove Fiume from Italian control. D'Annunzio decided to forgo the flight to Tokyo and seize control of Fiume. After sending Mussolini last-minute notification, the poet drove into the city about eleven o'clock on September 12, leading a motor column of some two thousand troops. These forces consisted of active-duty Arditi, who joined D'Annunzio in defiance of their orders to stop him, as well as members of the king's own Royal Guards regiment and other soldiers who had deserted to the poet's cause. After D'Annunzio's men entered the city, they received a joyful welcome from the city's inhabitants, who greeted them as saviors.

That evening D'Annunzio initiated a ceremony that he was to repeat hundreds of times in Fiume. At six o'clock, the poet appeared on the balcony of the Governor's Palace to address a crowd of soldiers and citizens in the piazza below. D'Annunzio said the city symbolized all that the Italians had fought and suffered for during the war. He praised the soldiers who had deserted to join him and then unfurled a huge Italian flag, which he had already had consecrated in Rome. Then he reminded his audience of the decision by their municipal council on October 30, 1918, to unite the city with Italy. "Do you confirm your vote of October thirtieth in front of the banner . . . ?" The crowd roared back its approval, with a great shout of "Sì!, sì!" Having gained their approval, D'Annunzio proclaimed the annexation of Fiume to Italy.[31]

D'Annunzio's talents as a playwright, poet, and orator had created a new form of political theater. He addressed the crowd not as a collection of individual citizens but as a single personality with whom he conducted

a dialogue. D'Annunzio had designed a clever facade for personal dictatorship. He appeared to be an all-wise leader capable of reading the hearts of
his people. With an apparent ability to know his followers' minds and
feelings, any necessity for elections or statutory laws disappeared. People
leaving one of their leader's speeches were convinced of a perfect identity
of views between themselves and their ruler. Their mystical sense of communion and participation in their government resolved any doubts about
the strength and wisdom of their leader. On D'Annunzio's political stage,
ruler and ruled appeared to be inseparable. Mussolini later adopted the
poet's methods for his Fascist rallies.[32]

The coup and its results were equally startling to D'Annunzio and
Prime Minister Nitti. D'Annunzio waited up through the night of September 12. He was expecting to hear from Rome about the collapse of the
Nitti government and from Paris about Allied acquiescence to the Italian
annexation of Fiume. Nitti meanwhile suffered a profound shock from the
army's refusal to stop the poet from seizing the city, and even worse, the
defection of some of the elite forces to the poet's cause. For several days,
Nitti was afraid the army would turn against him, and went so far as to call
upon the Socialists and the labor unions to defend the government in the
event of a military revolt.[33]

Nitti's fear proved as unfounded as D'Annunzio's expectations. The
seizure of Fiume did provoke a wave of tremendous enthusiasm within
nationalist circles in Italy. By the end of September more troops, as well as
four naval vessels, defected to Fiume, raising the forces under D'Annunzio's command to about 8,500 men. But D'Annunzio's hope that his
insurrection would spread throughout Italy came to nothing.

D'Annunzio at once accused Mussolini of betrayal. On September 12,
the poet sent a letter to Mussolini demanding to know why Mussolini had
not arrived with Arditi, Futurists, and Fascists, nor sent funds to assist the
insurrection. Mussolini did not reply until September 18. He argued that
conditions in Italy did not favor a revolt by their followers and that such
an attempt might incite the 450,000 workers then on strike to launch a
Bolshevik-style revolution of their own. But Mussolini did promise to
come to Fiume in person to discuss the situation and to raise as much
money as he could for the cause.[34]

A week later, Mussolini proposed by letter that the poet set up a
revolutionary provisional government for Italy, declare the monarchy
abolished, and lead his forces in an invasion of the country. At the same
time, however, Mussolini begged D'Annunzio to take no action until after
he had arrived in Fiume and the two men could confer at length. Mussolini
was stalling. If such a revolt succeeded, it would leave D'Annunzio in
charge of Italy, not Mussolini. If it failed, the best both men could hope for

would be flight into exile, with execution for treason a more likely fate.[35]

After Nitti's initial panic subsided, the prime minister decided that patient negotiations were the only realistic policy. To announce the annexation of Fiume would legitimize D'Annunzio's actions and probably encourage the poet to further adventures, with unpredictable consequences. A formal annexation of the city, however popular in Italy, would infuriate the Allies. Their likely economic retaliations might lead Italy to total collapse and revolution. Orders to dislodge the poet by force might be disobeyed by the army, and might even lead to a general mutiny. Nitti decided to place the city under close military and naval surveillance to prevent the spread of D'Annunzio's control to Dalmatia. Nitti next opened talks through intermediaries both with the Allies and the poet in search of a reasonable compromise. Having regained some control over the situation, the prime minister turned to the nation. On September 29, he dissolved the Chamber of Deputies and announced that Italy's first national postwar elections would be held in November.[36]

The seizure of Fiume, followed quickly by the election campaign, drove virtually every other subject from the pages of *Il Popolo d'Italia.* Margherita's articles on art ceased between early September and early December, although she still had *Ardita* to edit. She devoted most of her energies to assisting Mussolini in his political tasks. He rewarded her efforts with increased displays of affection. At the beginning of the year, Mussolini's letters to her had begun *"Cara Signora e Amica,"* and even in June he had addressed her as *"Cara Amica."* By autumn, his letters began *"Mio Amore."* Whenever she could, Margherita accompanied Mussolini to his speeches both outside Milan and within the city. Other times they met for "delicious hours," as Mussolini described them, near Il Soldo, and far from prying eyes.[37]

On a brilliant day in early October, Margherita accompanied Mussolini and three or four of his staff on a clandestine mission to Venice. Mussolini hoped to find a boat to elude the naval blockade around Fiume and visit D'Annunzio's headquarters. Attempting to lose the plainclothes police who were tailing them, the band sneaked their way through the intricate maze of streets at the heart of the ancient city. Thanks to Margherita's knowledge of the back alleys of Venice, the group managed to elude their pursuers. Margherita found it all delicious fun; the escapade summoned up images for her of Jean Valjean's narrow escapes in *Les Misérables,* and the nocturnal adventures of Casanova in those very same streets. But their success came to naught. Despite offers of assistance from a sympathetic naval officer, Mussolini was unable to reach Fiume that day.[38]

Most of the seven weeks before the election they devoted to hard political campaigning. In August, the Chamber passed a proportional-representation voting law that divided Italy into fifty-four districts, each to elect from five to twenty deputies. So long as a party gained a sufficient percentage of the vote in any district, it could send one or more of its candidates for that district to Parliament. Furthermore, the new law enfranchised all men over twenty-one and any male who had served in the armed forces. This increased the electorate from the 8.6 million of 1913 to over 11 million. Most of the new voters were drawn from the young veterans Mussolini had worked so hard to attract. If Mussolini's followers concentrated their efforts in their strongest districts in Milan, they had good reason to expect to send a few deputies to the Chamber, including Mussolini himself.[39]

Mussolini's hopes increased after the Socialist party underwent another of its periodic internecine battles. At the Bologna congress of October 1919, the revolutionaries seized control of the Party again. They expelled all moderates from leadership positions and announced their support for the "dictatorship of the proletariat" and Lenin's Third Socialist International, established in Moscow earlier that year. They nonetheless proclaimed their enthusiasm for the coming elections, rather than boycotting them as radical Socialist theory demanded. Once again the Italian Socialists revealed that their revolutionary talk was just words. At the same time, they frightened many Italians enough that Mussolini could legitimately hope to win additional votes.[40]

A few days later, the Fascists held their first national congress in Florence. Mussolini had just returned from a flight to Fiume, which enabled him to evade the troops encircling the city. There he delivered to D'Annunzio money raised through an *Il Popolo d'Italia* subscription. The two men discussed plans for a general insurrection but details of the conversation remain unclear. Evidence suggests that Mussolini agreed to the idea in principle but argued that the time was not propitious. It seems that Mussolini was trying to maintain close ties to the nationalist hero, while restraining him from a disastrous action. D'Annunzio's reflected glory might help the Fascists in the coming elections.[41]

In his speech to the Fascist congress, Mussolini reaffirmed his hostility to the monarchy and his desire for an Italian republic. He described the Italian ruling class as exhausted and stressed the need for new men to lead Italy. A more equitable society should be created by heavy taxes on the rich, inheritances, and war profits, he argued. He repeated the need for class cooperation, based on the idea of forming "corporations" of workers, managers, and owners, as advocated by the syndicalists.[42]

Mussolini urged the assembly to approve an electoral alliance of all those on the left who had supported the war. Given the weakness of the Fascists in many areas of Italy, such a coalition with Marinetti's Futurists, his old comrade Pietro Nenni's Republicans, and even reformist Socialists who had supported intervention could greatly improve all their chances of success at the polls. The congress agreed. The other advantage of such an arrangement lay in its camouflage of the confused and confusing identity of Fascism. Thus Mussolini felt he could attract more of "the young who do not yet have political experience and the old who have too much and feel the need of plunging in again, in an atmosphere of freshness and unselfishness."[43]

The other leftist interventionists met Mussolini's appeal for an alliance by the demand that he exclude himself from running for office. He had alienated too many by his vicious attack on Bissolati at La Scala in January. This condition left Mussolini perplexed. After initial consideration, he decided to withdraw as a candidate. Margherita argued against this, but he insisted this was the only correct decision. Overnight, however, he changed his mind and the next day he told her emphatically that his name must head the list of Fascist candidates for the Milan district.

Mussolini's reconsideration left Margherita relieved but bewildered. "Why, you told me yesterday . . ." she began, but he cut her off. Mussolini straightened himself with exaggerated dignity. "Signora, yesterday was yesterday. Very well. But today is today!" Certainly no one could accuse Mussolini of excess rigidity, and Margherita accepted his change of mind with some amusement.[44] Mussolini's decision to stay in the race invalidated the alliance with the other leftists. The Fascists entered the election alone. Even an otherwise likely sympathizer, Prezzolini, refused to support them.[45]

In the end only two notable figures agreed to join Mussolini on the Fascist ticket for the Milan electoral district, Marinetti and Arturo Toscanini. The famed conductor of the La Scala opera orchestra had admired Mussolini's combination of patriotism, antimonarchism, and program of social reforms for some time. Toscanini had already written for *Ardita* and lent his support to Mussolini's election campaign by personal appearances at his speeches and the impressive contribution of 30,000 lire. Marinetti and Toscanini were close friends, and the Futurist had persuaded the conductor to add his name to the list of Fascist candidates. The Sarfattis were also friends of the conductor and had been active in raising funds to aid La Scala. They may also have played a role in gaining Toscanini's assent. The other seventeen Fascist office seekers for the Milan district were all relatively obscure veterans.[46]

The climax of their first electoral campaign, as Margherita described it years later, came on the night of November 10 in the Piazza Belgioioso, a square in the heart of Milan just a few minutes from La Scala. The harsh light of a blazing white flare fired from a Very pistol opened the program.

The flare served to remind the audience of the birth of Fascism in the war and the movement's special ties to veterans. Mussolini and other Fascist candidates delivered speeches from the back of a parked truck. By this public appearance, they had decided to show the Socialists they feared neither death threats nor intimidation. But their use of a motor vehicle as a speaking platform suggested that they were prepared to flee, if necessary.[47]

Margherita remembered that Mussolini "appeared, like one of the ancient tribunes on his rostrum, his figure lit by the light of torches which some of his followers carried. His pose and that of his adherents recalled memories of the war so clearly that it seemed strange to see that the street lights were no longer dimmed for fear of air raids. . . . The very voice of the orator seemed warlike in its clear notes, warm in tone, never strident, but strong and carrying far. In the great piazza not one syllable was missed. By the red flickering light of the torches he looked down on the vast crowd gazing at him wonder-struck."[48]

Mussolini stressed the Fascist idea of organizing Italian society into "corporations," arguing that this concept offered the ideal combination of socialism and nationalism. He rejected charges that his movement represented the interests of the bourgeoisie, stressing the Fascist demands for the heavy taxation of the rich and confiscation of excess war profits.

After a worker questioned Fascist commitment to the working class, Mussolini vowed that he would fight for the workers and against any form of tyranny, either that of the ruling class or that of the Bolsheviks. "We are Italians, we have another mentality, another soul, another past, and if we must make revolution, this revolution can only be profoundly, purely, fiercely Italian." The crowd accompanied Mussolini back to *Il Popolo d'Italia,* where he spoke to them briefly again from the balcony of his office. He thanked them and the veterans of Milan for their support, ending with a salute to D'Annunzio and his men in Fiume.[49] Six days later, the innovative Fascist mixture of revolutionary socialist rhetoric and nationalist violence stood its first test at the polls.

Of the 270,000 votes cast in Milan, the Fascists received 4,795. In the area of their greatest strength, they won not a single seat in Parliament, although one Fascist did manage to gain election from the Genoa area. Nationwide, the November 1919 elections proved to be a triumph for the Socialists and the new Popolari party. The reorganized Catholics increased their seats in the Chamber from 29 to 100. The Socialist party did even better, increasing their deputies from 52 to 156. All the moderate parties, from the Liberals to the Republicans, saw their combined seats sink from 427 to 252. In the 508-seat Italian Parliament, the combined Popolari and Socialist numbers gave them a possible bloc of 256. Had these parties formed an alliance, other reformist parties could have joined them to create

Italy's first leftist government, and one with a firm majority.

But nothing of the sort happened. Under their new "revolutionary" leadership, the Socialists had already decided in October to refuse collaboration with any other party. At the same time, while some Popolari elements wished to form an alliance with the Socialists, many of the Catholics recoiled in horror from the idea of cooperation with atheists. Most Popolari deputies hoped for greater gains in future and wished to remain independent until they could form a government by themselves.

Prime Minister Nitti found the results dumbfounding. He had expected a Liberal victory, in reaction to the violence and confusion of the past year. Consequently he had forsaken the usual election fraud which Giolitti had practiced with such mastery before the war. In fact, he had ordered the police to ignore widespread Socialist violence and threats against the other parties, hoping that this would produce a backlash. But he had failed to reorganize the Liberals into an efficient modern political party, and so was at a terrible disadvantage against the Popolari and the Socialists. The prime minister found himself forced to beg the Popolari for their support in order to remain in office. They agreed, but the inexperience of the many new Catholic deputies made efficient government difficult. The chaos and incoherence of postwar Italian politics only increased.[50]

In his final article of the electoral campaign, Mussolini had described the vote as a referendum on Italy's decision to intervene in World War I, as well as D'Annunzio's seizure of Fiume. Once he learned the results, he could not bring himself to write at all.[51]

The days that followed his electoral defeat proved profoundly depressing. As he later confided to his oldest son, Vittorio, he lost his normally sustaining faith in his abilities and his ideas. He decided that he would never rule Italy and lead his nation to greatness. A terrible sense of isolation, coupled with an inescapable conviction that all his bitter struggles had been for nothing—because of his own miscalculations—plunged him into despair.

The triumph of the Socialists particularly tormented him. He knew that without his leadership, their confused oscillation between revolutionary posturing and ineffective parliamentary maneuvering would get them nowhere. If he had stayed with the Party in 1914 and had held it to the revolutionary course he had charted, he would probably now be the dictator of a revolutionary Italian republic. But the war had convinced him to take another path, to arouse the national feelings of the Italian people and lead them to shake off long centuries of humiliation and degradation. Were his political ideas wrong or was he wrong to think he had a special destiny? Either way, he had only himself to blame for his failure.[52]

When he finally forced himself to write, Mussolini penned a short article claiming that he had never expected great results from the election. The Fascists were great in spirit, he pointed out, not in numbers. They did not have the fifty years of organization of the Socialists, nor the two thousand years of existence enjoyed by the Church. Taken in perspective, his followers had done magnificently. "Our battle continues," he vowed.[53]

That same day, acting on direct orders from Nitti, the police seized Mussolini and Marinetti on weapons charges. Many of the firearms and grenades the Arditi had deposited in the offices of *Il Popolo d'Italia* were hidden elsewhere, for Mussolini had received advance warning of the raid. The Carabinieri and Public Security agents found only twenty pistols, a flare gun, and about one hundred rounds of ammunition.

Margherita was speaking with Mussolini in his private office when the police burst in and arrested him. He put on a gallant front but she knew his nerves were being stretched close to the breaking point. She took over running the newspaper until he was released from jail two days later. In a display of solidarity, she composed a front-page article in which she and the others at the paper declared themselves as guilty as he. After Mussolini regained his freedom, the staff gathered to welcome him back, improvising a celebration in his honor. But the incident clearly had added to Mussolini's depression. Over the next few days, he managed to write a few articles and even to deliver two speeches to his disheartened followers. But Margherita soon persuaded Mussolini to join her on a short two-day vacation in Venice.[54]

Mussolini had been the object of careful attention by the police since the foundation of the Fascist movement, and especially since D'Annunzio's capture of Fiume. Public Security agents followed him everywhere, but Margherita and Mussolini found this no impediment to their enjoyment.[55] Margherita went on ahead, booking them two rooms on the same floor in the splendid Hotel Danieli. It had a commanding view across the San Marco Canal, standing opposite the imposing church of San Giorgio Maggiore. Mussolini arrived at the Venice railroad station in the early hours of November 26, where he was met by Margherita. They took a nocturnal gondola ride to the hotel, remaining there until shortly after noon the following day.

Early the next afternoon, they toured the sights of the Piazza San Marco, stopping to admire the facade of the ornate Byzantine-style cathedral and the recently restored bell tower. They enjoyed a leisurely lunch in the celebrated Restaurant Montin, a favored haunt of D'Annunzio and Eleanora Duse. Afterward, they traveled slowly by gondola down the Grand Canal, past Margherita's childhood home on the Riva del Carbon, to the Ghetto. There they visited furniture and antique shops, though they purchased nothing. They emerged into the waning light and wandered slowly back across the city, Margherita leaning on Mussolini's arm to help support her injured knee. She served as his guide, pointing out the various churches and palaces which Fradeletto had taught her to appreciate. Mussolini would occasionally interrupt her descriptions, saying, "Stop right there! Don't move." He wanted to see the autumn sunlight shining on her golden red hair, which he caressed and kissed gently. Finally twilight approached and they separated; Mussolini arrived back at the Danieli well ahead of Margherita, who returned only after darkness had fallen.

That evening, Mussolini left the hotel first. Margherita joined him half an hour later, under the arches of the nearby Palace of the Doges. They ate a light dinner, went to a play at the Goldoni Theater and got back to the Danieli about midnight. They stayed in until late the next morning. All too soon it was time to return to Milan. Margherita and Mussolini left by train shortly after noon, taking the slower and less expensive local, careful to arrive at the station separately and to sit in different compartments. All the while Public Security kept them under vigilant observation.[56]

While chances to slip away from Milan were rare, Margherita did what else she could to divert Mussolini from his troubles. She arranged entertainments at her home and continued to groom his manners. Slowly and patiently, she weaned him from his habitual recourse to Romagnol curses and obscenities. She continued to guide his reading. After earlier instruction in Marx, Engels, Kropotkin, Proudhon, and Bakunin, Mussolini graduated to her tutorials in the classics. In keeping with his growing rejection of orthodox socialism, Margherita introduced him to Adam Smith, John Stuart Mill, Malthus, and Quesnay. She fed his increasing fascination with nationalism and the history of ancient Rome by introducing him to Machiavelli, whom he now read for the first time, and encouraging him in his studies of the Roman Empire. Margherita also persuaded him to start reading philosophy, especially Aristotle, a knowledge of whom he soon boasted.

But Margherita's most important influence on Mussolini came from the way she shaped his conviction that he was destined for greatness. Using her knowledge of ancient history and her devotion to classical aesthetics, she began to persuade him that he could lead Italy to re-create the empire and civilization of Rome. Hers was not entirely an original vision. The notion that modern Italy was the heir of ancient Rome and would reimpose its rule on the Mediterranean had been prevalent among Italian intellectuals since the Risorgimento. The widely read nationalist poet Giosuè Carducci, whose brother had taught Mussolini, had filled his verse with such images. Margherita encouraged Mussolini to believe that he was the man who could emerge from the Italian people as their new Caesar, rebuild the

Roman Empire, and impose a new cultural order on European civilization, based on the Roman ideals of discipline and order.

In late 1919, neither Margherita nor Mussolini could understand clearly in which political direction such ideas would lead them. Reestablishing the physical territory and the spiritual values of the Roman Empire represented such a radical idea that it could hardly be described as conservative or even reactionary. Margherita and Mussolini were groping toward the creation of a new combination of politics and culture.[57]

There were lighter moments in Margherita's cultural program. Sometime toward the end of 1919, Toscanini discovered the young Czech violinist, Vasa Prihoda, who had been eking out a living playing in a Milan brasserie. After Toscanini mentioned his find to Margherita, she insisted that they arrange a recital for Prihoda at her salon. In early December, the Sarfattis had a piano installed in their apartment to provide accompaniment for the violinist. She invited friends to a private concert. In attendance were Cesare Rossi, Toscanini and his son Walter, Marinetti, Ada Negri, Giuseppe Borgese, Umberto Notari, the writer Massimo Bontempelli, Leonardo Dudreville, and other friends of the Sarfattis. Tucked away among this distinguished company was Mussolini, who squeezed onto a couch at the back of the room between two other guests.

Prihoda played three or four pieces with a rare brilliance. The audience greeted his triumphant debut with an outburst of enthusiastic applause. They also shouted for Margherita to take a bow, in recognition of her part in helping launch what all agreed would be a noteworthy musical career. Then the young violinist excused himself, certain of Toscanini's enthusiastic future support.

Mussolini had no doubt thoroughly enjoyed this brief respite from his worries. His tranquillity ended abruptly when Margherita addressed a demand to her lover: "And now, don't you want to play something for us?"

Dudreville, sitting nearby, could not believe his ears. He knew, as did most present, that Mussolini had a modest ability with the violin, which he sometimes played for relaxation or to put his children to sleep. To follow Prihoda, to play in Toscanini's presence, would make him look completely foolish. Mussolini turned bright red with embarrassment, shaking his head and mumbling desperate excuses. But Margherita would not take no for an answer. She insisted, she pleaded, she cajoled, she teased, she employed every tactic she could muster to force Mussolini to stand up and play. Mussolini could hardly contain his mounting fury. Clenching his teeth, Mussolini whispered angrily to Margherita: "Cut it out, you louse!" All at once it became clear to Margherita, as it already had to those around her, that he was about to explode. She relented, allowing her thoroughly mortified lover to escape.[58]

It is tempting to read the incident as an indication of thinly disguised hostility beneath Margherita's pride in her lover's accomplishments. Certainly their relationship must have contained strong elements of rivalry and resentment. The anecdote also suggests a struggle for dominance, expressed through Margherita's attempts to reshape the object of her affections. Her efforts to educate Mussolini, to change his behavior and appearance, were designed for the superficial goal of making him more acceptable to the polite circles in which she and Cesare moved. Her alterations also betrayed a deeper purpose, as Borgese and Rossi both discerned. Margherita later suggested as much to American journalist Thomas B. Morgan.

While certain that Mussolini could come to power, Margherita was patiently chipping away at his determination to seize power through some form of leftist revolution. The events of the summer and fall of 1919 must have intensified her repugnance at the idea of rule by the lower classes. The life that she and Cesare led, to which she was introducing Mussolini, could hardly survive the violent overthrow of the social order. Even Margherita's enthusiasm for D'Annunzio indicates more than just a desire for an Italian Fiume, or the vindication of Roberto's death. D'Annunzio represented another alternative to leftist revolution.[59]

Perhaps Margherita's visions of a different route to power were no clearer than Mussolini's own ideas in late 1919. But she does seem to have had a very definite idea of what she did not want for Mussolini. She was one of the very few who remained faithful to him after his break with the Socialist party, and was to be one of the few to survive the radical changes that Fascism would undergo. Her support went beyond love or loyalty—it was a product of a deep complicity.

16

Struggle for Power

Few signs of Fascism's imminent primacy appeared during the first ten months of 1920. When the year began, the Fascists counted nationwide a scant 870 members divided into thirty-one small groups. The dismal showing by the Fascists in the November 1919 elections suggested that even these few groups might soon disband. Under these discouraging circumstances, Mussolini and Margherita devoted most of their energies to *Il Popolo d'Italia*.[1]

Mussolini faced problems even at his newspaper. In December two close collaborators, Arturo Rossato and Giovanni Capodivacca, submitted their resignations, pleading severe fatigue. Both had played a major role in putting out both *Il Popolo d'Italia* and *Ardita*. Mussolini pleaded with them to stay on, even offering them paid leave. When they talked the matter over, however, more serious issues arose. The two editors revealed their dislike of Mussolini's despotic management and of his increasing advocacy of violence. The discussion turned ugly and the two editors stormed out.

Rossato and Capodivacca entered a complaint with the Journalist Association for back pay. Mussolini simply didn't have the money, given the perilous state of his newspaper's finances. When he disputed their claims, the two began spreading stories about Mussolini stealing money meant for D'Annunzio. They also spoke frankly of Mussolini's plans to overthrow the government. To Mussolini all this seemed another result of his humiliating defeat at the polls. So long as he appeared to have a bright future, he could count on the loyalty of his followers. Now even his closest subordinates abandoned him.

The Journalist Association rejected the complaint by the two editors, and Mussolini eventually forgave Rossato, rehiring him in the spring of 1920. But Margherita always considered Rossato a traitor and even a government spy. Their mutual dislike dated back to his 1915 article on the Sarfattis' reluctance to support the war. From time to time she reminded Mussolini of how faithful she had been in his darkest hours when others had turned against him and even he had lost faith in his cause.[2]

Bissolati died unexpectedly in early May, and Mussolini published a surprisingly warm tribute to his old adversary. Mussolini went so far as to describe himself as still a Socialist, although of a very different stamp from Bissolati. Mussolini apparently was groping for some way to return himself and his nationalist followers to the mainstream of Italian Socialism.[3]

The eclipse of Mussolini's political activities allowed Margherita to devote more of her time to art and literary criticism. In late April, she persuaded Mussolini, Marinetti, Ugo Ojetti, Umberto Notari, and others to sign a protest letter published in *Il Popolo d'Italia* when it seemed that none of the painters she favored would be shown at the XIIth Venice Biennale. While acknowledging that Fradeletto's successor, Vittorio Pica, had brought the French Post-Impressionists to Venice, she demanded a place for the new Italian painters. If the Biennale had decided at long last to recognize Matisse, she asked, why not Funi or Sironi?[4] But Pica did not prove to be the reactionary she expected. When a number of Italian moderns gained exhibit space, Margherita expressed her delighted surprise. She spent a number of happy days in May at the biennial art exhibit.[5]

In June she managed to escape for several weeks to Sicily. Mussolini's morale must have recovered enough for her to leave his side for a while. Margherita seems to have been interested mainly in taking in the sights of Palermo, and swimming in the warm waters off the northwest coast of the island. But her curiosity led her to lunch with the infamous *mafioso* mayor of Piana dei Greci, Francesco Cuccia. They dined surrounded by his entourage of concubines. The meeting was apparently arranged by their mutual acquaintance, the Socialist deputy Aurelio Drago.

Margherita found the scenery of western Sicily breathtaking, and she felt a modicum of respect for the "men of honor" who had imposed a brutal order on Sicily in the postwar years. But she was dismayed by the oppression of women, and the violence, corruption, and superstition under which the inhabitants of the region lived and died. She recounted with considerable amusement being mistaken for the Virgin Mary during a sunset encounter with the keeper of an isolated lighthouse. Her observations about the island (to which she made subsequent visits) must have been among the factors to shape Mussolini's harsh policies against the Mafia in later years.[6]

In 1920 mainland Italy was experiencing social disruption worse than the black year of 1898. For several months, the government appeared to lose control over the population. Margherita believed the old ruling class was proving its degeneracy by this surrender of authority. She thought the time had come for harder, more vigorous men to rule.[7]

The war, followed by the drastic reduction of Allied economic aid, had produced severe inflation. Between 1913 and 1920, prices rose by 590 percent. Italian wheat production, reduced by bad harvests, labor unrest, and the death of so many peasant soldiers in the war, fell in 1920 to less than three quarters of its prewar level. Bread and pasta became scarce and expensive. Wages failed to keep pace with the rising cost of food; the Nitti government reintroduced rationing and subsidized the cost of bread. Throughout 1919, the government raised the amount of paper currency in circulation by nearly one third. The value of the lira dropped in turn, forcing the Italians to cut their imports of English coal to less than half the minimum requirement for the winter of 1919–1920. Middle-class Italians, their savings already wiped out by inflation, had to shiver through the cold months in unheated city apartments and offices. The government was forced to cut train services drastically, further constricting the economy. The trains that did run were filthy, crowded, and always late.[8]

Serious labor problems added to the nation's troubles. The Socialist and Catholic gains in the November 1919 elections had arisen in part from the huge growth in Italian trade-union membership, now five times the prewar level. The various trade unions, emboldened by their 3.8 million members, launched a comprehensive and debilitating series of strikes in 1920. Italian workers were inspired by the Russian Revolution to seek the creation of a workers' state. They could see no other response to the rising costs of living. Seeking to balance Socialist gains among the urban workers, the Popolari began promoting land seizures and agricultural strikes in the countryside.

Prime Minister Nitti surrendered to the demands of government workers on the railroads and in the post office, and attempted compromise with other strikers. Disruptions of public services particularly infuriated the public, but Nitti's concessions convinced many in the middle class that the government was as blameworthy as the strikers. Whenever food riots broke out, Nitti instructed officials to cooperate with local labor organizations. Together they set up food committees to requisition and distribute supplies, and impose price controls. Many shopkeepers were bankrupted, while their looters went unpunished.[9]

Wartime conscription had reduced police strength. Postwar financial crises prevented the government from adequately rebuilding its security forces. Nitti was often forced to use the army to deal with unruly strikers. Although the army officers had no love for Socialists, the Popolari, or the trade unions, they nonetheless recoiled from assuming the task of maintaining labor peace. The army carried out its orders but acquired leftist hatred for itself and for Nitti in the process.

Nitti had already outraged the officer corps by allowing a parliamentary inquest into the causes of the disaster at Caporetto, and then by announcing

an amnesty for wartime deserters in September 1919. When Nitti's government issued instructions that officers should neither wear their uniforms
nor carry their pistols in public—hoping to avoid even more violence—
army officers were furious at the humiliation, as were Nitti's political
opponents on the right.[10]

Nitti weakened his position still more by attempting to negotiate a
settlement of the Fiume and Dalmatia questions with the Yugoslavs. During the first five months of 1920, Nitti worked toward an agreement that
would acquire Fiume for Italy, while Yugoslavia would receive all but a
few Italian-inhabited enclaves of Dalmatia. From across the Atlantic, Wilson denounced Nitti's proposal as unjust. But the president had already
been politically humiliated in his own country. The U.S. Senate in March
1920 had definitively rejected the Treaty of Versailles and with it American
entry into the League of Nations. Recognizing Wilson's impotence, the
British and the French backed Nitti's proposals for an agreement between
Italy and Yugoslavia. They had already approved the division of Albania
between Italy and Greece.

The international support failed to save Nitti's government. On May
24, the fifth anniversary of Italian intervention in the war, a violent demonstration in Rome demanding all of Dalmatia for Italy was broken up by the
police. One demonstrator and five policemen died in the fighting. On June
4, in an attempt to reduce the soaring budget deficit, Nitti ordered an
increase in the price of bread. Angry protests organized by the Socialists
followed immediately. Recognizing that his attempts to deal with Italy's
problems had alienated both the left and the right, Nitti resigned on June
9. A week later, the Chamber of Deputies recalled the seventy-eight-year-
old Giovanni Giolitti. Even Mussolini offered the new government his
qualified support. Giolitti's strong-arm tactics offered the hope that he
could restore a stable government and prevent a revolution.[11]

The new prime minister made the revival of the Italian economy his
highest priority. But less than two weeks after taking office, Giolitti was
confronted with a totally unexpected challenge. On June 26, a battalion of
Mussolini's old regiment, the 11th Bersaglieri, mutinied in their barracks
in the port of Ancona after receiving orders to embark for Albania. A
number of Socialist and Anarchist agitators had convinced some of the
riflemen that they should resist taking part in an imperialist venture. Widespread insurrection, as well as the ravages of malaria, had driven the Italians
back from the interior of Albania to a few ports along the coast. But Giolitti
followed Nitti in hoping to retain control over those strategic ports, giving
Italy secure control over the mouth of the Adriatic. The revolt by the
Bersaglieri quickly ignited an Anarchist rebellion in Ancona that was not
suppressed until July 1. News of this prompted other uprisings by Socialists

throughout the Marches and the Romagna. An Arditi unit about to sail for Albania revolted on June 29 aboard its troopship in the port of Brindisi. The government was forced to suspend the shipment of any further reinforcements from Italy to Albania, an implicit decision to withdraw all Italian forces from that country.[12]

In early July, the violence spread inland. Right-wing students and local members of the Arditi Association attacked striking trolley workers in Rome. The severity of the fighting reminded many Italians of Red Week in June 1914, but this time Nationalists were as much to blame as Socialists and Anarchists. Giolitti dealt with these outbreaks as he had before the war. While he avoided intervening in peaceful labor disputes, he did not hesitate to employ force to suppress lawlessness and threats to public order. By August, Giolitti had restored a certain degree of calm. At the end of the month, however, he faced a still greater peril.[13]

Nationwide labor troubles had spread to Turin, one of Italy's great industrial centers. In April, virtually the entire working class of Turin went out on strike for ten days to force the industrialists to grant wage concessions and recognize their "factory councils." These were representative bodies of workers elected in each factory, much like the "soviets" that had played a major role in bringing about Russia's Bolshevik revolution. Reformist Socialists felt the councils were dangerously revolutionary. Both the national Socialist labor leadership and the government persuaded the strikers to go back to work. Nonetheless, the factory councils survived, although unrecognized by the factory owners.[14]

Discussions between union leaders and representatives of the industrialists continued through the spring and summer. All the while, the steadily rising cost of living made every passing week harder for the Turin workers to endure. By mid-August the factory owners decided that they would make no wage concessions. As their lawyer put it bluntly: "All discussion is useless. The industrialists will not grant any increase at all. Since the end of the war, they've done nothing but drop their pants. We've had enough. Now we're going to start on you."[15]

The Turin labor unions responded with a slowdown, expecting the drop in production to curtail profits and force the industrialists to come to terms. Over the next two weeks, the slowdown spread throughout Italy's northeastern industrial region. The employers countered with threats of a lockout, despite pleas from Giolitti. Reluctantly he ordered the army to send troops into the cities.

On Monday morning, August 30, two thousand workers of the Alfa Romeo plant in Milan discovered locked factory gates and a contingent of troops guarding the entrances. News of this lockout spread rapidly across Milan, then throughout all the industrial cities of Italy's northeast. Everywhere workers decided to seize control of their factories if other employers followed Alfa Romeo's example. On Tuesday night the industrialists' executive council voted to shut down the factories. Over the next four days, throughout the entire peninsula and in Sicily, half a million Italian laborers occupied their workplaces. The workers ran up the red flag of the Socialists or the black banner of the Anarchists—sometimes the standards flew side by side. Outside the factory gates and on the walls, they posted armed sentries, dubbed "Red Guards," in imitation of the Soviet militia that Lenin had used to topple the Russian government in November 1917.

Giolitti realized the industrial workers were attempting to run the economy on their own, without the help of managers, owners, or the government. If they were to succeed, the next step could be revolution, the overthrow of the monarchy, and the establishment of an Italian Socialist republic. In essence, the workers had decided to prove that they alone could maintain a functioning society.[16]

Giolitti nonetheless ruled out using the police or the army against the strikers. He decided to outwait them, believing their attempts at economic self-sufficiency would fail. He was certain the workers could not run the factories on their own for any length of time. Their failure would discredit those extremists among the workers calling for revolution. On the other hand, Giolitti reasoned, if he ordered the security forces to attack the occupied factories, civil war would surely follow.[17]

He made his case in a sardonic exchange with Giovanni Agnelli, the head of the giant FIAT company in Turin:

GIOLITTI: Only time can solve the problem. Otherwise there is no policy but force.

AGNELLI: Precisely.

GIOLITTI: Perhaps. But let us understand each other. I will not allow the security forces to stay in the streets, defenseless if the Red Guards open fire from above. To drive the workers out of the factories, we need artillery.

AGNELLI: I agree.

GIOLITTI: We are in a position to supply it immediately. At Turin, there is the 7th Mountain Artillery Regiment. I will give the orders at once. At dawn tomorrow, FIAT will be bombarded and liberated from its occupiers.

AGNELLI: No! No!

GIOLITTI: Well then?

AGNELLI: *(no reply)*.[18]

Quite deliberately, Giolitti went on vacation.

As the days passed, news reached the government that the workers were manufacturing weapons in preparation for a revolutionary upheaval. Government inaction created the impression that law and order were collapsing. In Milan, Luigi Albertini, the publisher of the conservative and influential *Corriere della Sera,* thought it best to surrender to the Socialist labor unions and accept the establishment of a republic. After a week of silence, Mussolini came out in favor of the strike, so long as it did not lead to a Bolshevik-style revolution. In private, Mussolini went even further, offering his support to the strike leaders if they attempted a "constructive" revolution.

As supplies of raw materials ran out and new orders were not forthcoming, the factories began grinding to a halt. The strikers, their union leadership, and the Socialist party hierarchy faced the same question: Was the occupation of the factories a tactic in a labor dispute or the preliminary to an assault on the state? As it turned out, the workers were prepared to defend themselves against a government attack, but not to launch a revolutionary insurrection. Once again, the essentially reformist nature of the Italian Left asserted itself.

On September 19, Giolitti summoned the representatives of the strikers and the industrialists to meet him in Rome. Six hours of discussion produced a settlement. The workers received substantial raises and other monetary benefits. Furthermore, the factory owners agreed to legislation that would legalize the factory councils. While it took another week to bring the occupation of the factories to an end, the crisis had passed.[19]

Mussolini hailed the outcome as a victory for the Italian labor movement and for Giolitti but a defeat for what he described as the "Bolshevik plans" of the Socialist party. He pledged his Fascist movement to the defense of the state against any new efforts by the Socialists at revolution.[20]

There were no such attempts. Whatever possibility there had been for a leftist revolution in Italy had passed with the end of the occupation of the factories. The strikers had realized significant economic gains. But any hopes for a takeover of the state, fanned by the extravagant rhetoric of leftist agitators, had been shown to be empty.

The disillusioning failure of the occupation of the factories created new fissures within the Socialist ranks. The old two-way split between reformists and revolutionaries became a three-way division with the emergence of an extreme Communist movement. The Italian Communists followed Lenin's orders and demanded the end to any participation in electoral politics. The Socialists held a congress at Livorno in January 1921 to assess their mistakes in the recent crisis. The Communists demanded that the reformists be ejected from the Party as Lenin's price for Italian Socialist membership in the new Communist International headquartered in Moscow. Even the revolutionary Socialists refused to weaken the Party in this manner. In response the Communists, led by Amadeo Bordiga and Antonio Gramsci, formally left the Party. The left had managed by itself to reduce the possibility of any Marxist revolution. Mussolini soon realized, however, that it was very much in his interest to keep alive the fear of a leftist revolt among the middle and upper classes.[21]

The Fascists gained their first significant successes against the Socialists and Catholics in the countryside. Even with increasing industrialization, Italy remained a primarily agricultural nation in 1919–1920. When demobilization released hundreds of thousands of veterans, most returned to homes in farming country. When land promised by the government was not forthcoming, peasant veterans acted on their own. Those who could used their modest discharge bonuses to buy farms at low prices from intimidated or needy landowners. Those who could not afford the land often took it by force. Groups of peasants usually occupied untilled or grazing land under the leadership of their local priest or a veterans' association. Most of these land seizures took place south of Rome. Early in 1921, there were three and a half million peasant landowners, twice the number of ten years before.

In the fertile and heavily cultivated lands of northern Italy, tenant farming and sharecropping predominated. Postwar unrest centered there around rents, crop prices, and guaranteed tenure. The Socialist farm workers' union demanded higher wages and the hiring of a high minimum number of union workers per hectare. The Socialists enforced their demands during the harvests of 1919 and 1920 with strikes and violence against employers and those peasants who resisted joining the union. Many rural priests supported Catholic strikers from the pulpit. As they did in the cities, the Nitti and Giolitti governments generally sided with the workers.

The agrarian labor struggles reached their most bitter phase in the Po Valley in 1920. The conflict extended beyond disputes over wages and working conditions into a war between the traditional order in the countryside and the new Socialist vision of rural society. In areas where the Socialists enjoyed their greatest strength, the churches stood empty on Sunday. Monday became the Socialist day of rest. Rejecting the saints, Socialist peasants chose "Atheist," "Spartacus," "Lenin," or "Rebellion" as names for their children. Those peasants who refused to join the movement were subjected to ostracism and boycott; their livestock were mutilated and their barns burned. By the fall of 1920, the old landlords seethed with rage against the farm workers' unions. Many victimized peasants bore deep grudges against the Socialists as well.

In October 1920, the Giolitti government gave permanent tenure to peasants who had seized their land. Landlords, and tenants renting enough land to hire workers, came to see the Socialists, the Popolari, and the government alike as enemies. In the local elections of October–November 1920, nearly half the seats in the rural communes were won by Socialists and the Popolari. The landowners saw the balance of power in the countryside slipping permanently out of their hands. Meanwhile poor harvests in 1919 and 1920, made worse by labor disputes, had driven many big farmers to the edge of financial ruin. Even many of the tenant farmers and sharecroppers the Socialists had aided were now terrified by calls for the nationalization of the land. With the government refusing to protect the prewar order in rural areas, there seemed only one source of assistance for the landlords and their new allies—the Fascists.[22]

The Fascists had already established their methods for dealing with the left with the burning of *Avanti!* in April 1919. This was flattering to Mussolini because of his close association with the act, and because it created the impression of bold Fascist defiance at a time of Socialist ascendancy. In truth the real Fascist counteroffensive began only in the summer of 1920. Even then, it took place in Trieste, far from any center of Socialist strength.

In early 1920, the Fascist central committee had appointed Francesco Giunta as head of the Trieste *fascio*. After service as a volunteer officer in World War I, Giunta had followed D'Annunzio in his seizure of Fiume. D'Annunzio then appointed Giunta to direct propaganda for him in Italy. Consequently, Giunta came into close contact with Mussolini.

As part of the territory recently annexed from Austria, Trieste remained under military occupation. The location of this port city on the western edge of Istria made it the logical point of contact between Mussolini's Fascists and D'Annunzio's Fiume legionaries. Since many of the officers of the Trieste garrison sympathized with D'Annunzio and Mussolini, Giunta received their help in creating and arming a number of Fascist squads in the spring of 1920. Each squad came under the command of an active-duty or recently demobilized officer.

While Trieste had a predominantly Italian population, much of Istria was inhabited by Slovenes. Giunta's squads had been formed to aid D'Annunzio in the event that he decided to lead his forces across Istria and into Italy. Giunta and Mussolini had to develop a cover story for the existence of the squads. Giunta assured the army that his men were pledged to defend the Italian character of Trieste and Istria against Slovene separatists and their Bolshevik Italian Socialist allies. However preposterous was the linking of Yugoslav nationalism, Italian Socialism, and Russian Bolshevism, it played successfully to the fears and prejudices of the Trieste army command. Segments of the Slovene working class did harbor strong Socialist sentiments. The leftist political unrest sweeping Italy in 1920, combined with the unhappy Slav population that surrounded Trieste, left army officers in the city feeling besieged.

In July 1920, the hostility between Italians and Yugoslavs over territorial disputes in the Adriatic led to the murder of two Italian naval officers in Spalato. This act gave Giunta an opportunity to order his squads into action. They burned down the headquarters of the Slovene associations in Trieste. When this met with the enthusiastic approval of the local garrison, Giunta ordered his men into the countryside. They first attacked centers of Slav nationalism or Slovene culture. Then they turned against the Socialists in the region, destroying their union and newspaper offices. Army officers did not intervene against the arson, beatings, and murders, but actually applauded Giunta, and offered the loan of trucks and weapons. The Fascists formed labor unions of their own when they had finished crushing their enemies. Some peasants joined willingly; others were coerced.

In late May 1920, at the end of their second national congress, the Fascists nominated a new executive commission to direct the movement's affairs from Milan. While the labor troubles of the summer of 1920 seemed to threaten Italy with a Bolshevik revolution, Mussolini and his lieutenants on the executive commission decided to adopt defensive measures. By August, the focus of the Fascist movement had shifted from helping D'Annunzio launch a nationalist revolution to preventing a Socialist takeover. Giunta's squads served as the Fascist model. The executive commission instructed the local *fasci* to form and train armed squads, relying on demobilized army officers whenever possible. As Mussolini wrote to a follower in early August, size was not important: "Even five members are enough, to start with."[23]

By November, following the victories of the Socialist farm workers' union and the Socialist and Catholic advances in local elections, a climate of desperation and vengeance enveloped the enemies of the left. Industrialists and shopkeepers, farmers and army officers, policemen and office workers, nationalistic students and greedy landowners, all had acquired reasons to hate the Socialists over the previous two years. Many had lost faith in the government's ability to contain the left. Together these groups offered the Fascists sources of money, arms, and recruits. Mussolini sounded the call for action in his November 6 article in *Il Popolo d'Italia* announcing the beginning of "a hard, pitiless, implacable battle" against Socialism. Now it was time for the Fascist squads to strike back.[24]

New Fascist violence began in Bologna. A recent agricultural strike had ended in a Socialist victory and had left great bitterness among the landowners. In early November, a Socialist extremist won the mayoral election. The local *fascio* had been founded by a former Anarchist, Mussolini's close friend Leandro Arpinati, and his old Republican comrade from the Red Week days, Pietro Nenni. The Bologna Fascists gathered reinforcements from nearby *fasci* and swore they would not let the new mayor, Ennio Gnudi, be installed.

On November 21, Gnudi appeared on the balcony of the town hall, the Palazzo d'Accursio. Heavily armed Fascists broke through the police cordon and opened fire at the new mayor. As the crowd in front of the town hall panicked, Socialists on the balcony hurled hand grenades into the piazza, killing nine and wounding dozens of others. The two sides rushed indoors, where the nationalist city councillor and war hero, Giulio Giordani, was shot by a Socialist from the public gallery of the council chamber. Three days later, Mussolini warned his readers that these actions were forcing the Fascists to take up arms against the Socialists.[25]

Many who had previously avoided taking sides felt they no longer had any choice. A young Bolognese lawyer and ex-Alpino captain, Dino Grandi, had long admired Mussolini. As a young journalist, Grandi had witnessed Mussolini's expulsion from the Socialist party in November 1914, and the two had later begun a correspondence. Until November 1920, Grandi had rejected partisan politics, although his fiery nationalism had made him many enemies on the left. The shooting of his friend Giordani, coming a month after Grandi escaped murder at the hands of men who mistook him for a Fascist, changed his mind. Many others joined him. Two days after the Palazzo d'Accursio riot Grandi and a thousand other new Fascists marched through the streets of Bologna to display their increased numbers and their military discipline. Most were young veterans, many others were college students. They had come to the Fascist movement out of their own sense of patriotism and determination to stop "Bolshevism." The great majority of them were middle class and few had any ties to the radical working-class politics Arpinati and Mussolini shared. New recruits such as these fundamentally altered the nature of the Fascist movement.[26]

Twenty-five miles to the northeast of Bologna, similar events were convulsing the Po Valley town of Ferrara. The town's original *fascio*, founded shortly after the inauguration of the Fascist movement, had been little more than a social club for some twenty veterans and students. Besides frequent scuffles with the local Socialists, they had done little more than make noisy demonstrations of their patriotism on public occasions and protect nearby anti-Socialist peasants during boycotts. In the fall of 1920, however, the occupation of the factories and the agricultural strike sent Fascist membership soaring. By late October, the *fascio* reached two hundred members; by December, one thousand.

Italo Balbo, another decorated ex-Alpino officer, had little use for the local Fascists. The Ferrara *fascio* had participated in the violence at the Palazzo d'Accursio and the local Socialists vowed retaliation in kind. In late December 1920, the Ferrara Fascists organized a demonstration in the piazza facing the Castello Estense, the seat of the Socialist town administration. They called in two hundred reinforcements from the *fasci* in Bologna and the surrounding countryside to add to their one hundred participating members. Observing their arrival, Balbo commented with contempt on their slovenly appearance and surly demeanor. The Fascists in turn threatened to make him their first victim.

The Ferrara Socialists organized a protest meeting for the next day to disrupt the Fascist demonstration. When the two sides met before the Castello on the following day, the three hundred Fascists attacked their opponents with clubs and fists. No sooner had the fighting begun than Socialists hidden in the Castello opened fire with rifles. Three Fascists, one Socialist, and an innocent bystander fell dead. The mob fled in all directions.

Until now the violence of the recent labor troubles had been confined to the countryside. The outraged citizens poured out in huge numbers for the funeral and local magnates raised 200,000 lire for the victims' families. Even the local Socialist leaders expressed deep chagrin. The Ferrara Fascists saw their numbers jump to six thousand by February 1921. These new Fascists were hardly the political radicals who had joined Mussolini's movement in 1919. These were solid middle-class citizens, determined to protect the existing social order, not overturn it. And Italo Balbo had become their leader.

Exactly why Balbo changed his mind about the Fascists remains a mystery. At least to some extent he was motivated by practical reasons. To take advantage of their sudden popularity, the Ferrara Fascists wanted a respectable organizer and capable military leader. Balbo offered those requisites. And he needed the job. He demanded a salary of 1,500 lire a month (at a time when a colonel in the army received 977 lire a month, skilled workmen in Milan earned 550 to 700 a month, and a field hand made only 1,500 lire in a year), appointment as the political secretary of the Ferrara *fascio,* and the guarantee of a position in a local bank after the political struggle against the Socialists had been won. Since the local landowners and industrialists were now financing the Fascists, Balbo got what he wanted and took over the *fascio* in January 1921.

Balbo had been offered the leadership of a movement that promised adventure, rapid advancement, and a chance to strike back at the hated Reds. At twenty-four he was older than most members of the Ferrara *fascio.* Fascism seemed to welcome men of many opinions, so long as they loved

Italy, hated the Socialists, and were prepared to crush them by violent means. The contradictions of a movement of big-city radicals and small-town professionals, paid for by wealthy conservatives, were to become apparent later. But for now the growth in Fascist numbers was compelling. From less than 1,000 in January, the *fasci* had leaped upward to 20,600 members by late December 1920. The vast majority had far closer ties to men like Grandi or Balbo than they did to Mussolini.

In late January 1921, Balbo led his squads on their first armed assault against the Socialists in the countryside around Ferrara. Similar attacks were being launched from new Fascist centers in Rovigo, Modena, and Reggio Emilia. Almost everywhere, the police and the army quietly assisted the squads or turned a blind eye to their actions.[27]

The collapse of D'Annunzio's city-state of Fiume also contributed to the transformation of the Fascist movement at the end of 1920. D'Annunzio's legionaries had transformed Fiume into a center of heroic debauchery. Wild sexual excess, public drunkenness, bizarre styles of dress, and the widespread use of cocaine became the norm. The poet's men were, in many cases, reacting to their escape from the horrors of World War I. But their behavior hardly recommended Fiume as an example to the rest of socially conservative Italy. When a group of the city's Capuchin monks demanded the right to marry and hold direct elections for their superiors, and D'Annunzio began to celebrate his own religious holy days, conservative Italian nationalists began to question his leadership.[28]

D'Annunzio expressed considerable sympathy for radical Socialists and even offered to help them seize power in Italy through a revolution in the summer of 1920. He also established contact with Soviet Russia, stressing the common interest of Fiume and Moscow in creating "new social forms." Simultaneously, D'Annunzio promoted the idea of a "League of Fiume" that would lead the struggle for liberation among the oppressed peoples of the world. D'Annunzio issued a constitution in September 1920. It proclaimed Fiume an independent republic—until such time as it would become part of Italy—with a radically new economic and political system. The constitution created "corporations," which would represent the people of Fiume according to their occupations or economic interests. The idea had been advocated for some time by Italian syndicalists. Mussolini had proposed a similar scheme when he had established the Fascist movement in March 1919. However, the constitution departed from Mussolini's ideas by rejecting a strong executive and stressing individual liberty far above the powers of the state. D'Annunzio's followers among conservative nationalists and monarchist army officers were appalled and withdrew their support.

Mussolini remained loyal to D'Annunzio—at least in the public eye. He and Margherita continued to publish articles in support of the poet, but only in the context of Fiume's eventual annexation to Italy. In September, Mussolini secretly promised to help save Italy from its crisis by joining D'Annunzio in a seizure of power. Mussolini would command the armed forces of the revolution in return for agreeing to impose the Fiume Constitution on Italy. In fact, Mussolini agreed only in order to avoid a break with the poet. He wanted to continue to be associated with D'Annunzio's popularity. He had, however, no wish to help D'Annunzio become the leader of an Italian republic, nor did he accept the ultrademocratic concepts of the Fiume Constitution. In mid-October 1920, Mussolini told the poet that no nationalist revolution could be begun earlier than the spring of 1921. Mussolini expected D'Annunzio to be overthrown by then. Treacherously, Mussolini had entered into secret negotiations with Giolitti. He promised to keep his followers in check should Giolitti be forced to attack Fiume. After D'Annunzio's downfall, given the recent improvement in the fortunes of the Fascist movement, Mussolini was hoping to come to power on his own.[29]

On November 12, 1920, the Italians and Yugoslavs signed a treaty at Rapallo settling their territorial disputes in the Adriatic. Italy received all of Istria, as well as the Dalmatian city of Zara and four Dalmatian islands. All the rest of the islands and eastern shore of the Adriatic went to Yugoslavia. Both sides agreed that Fiume would become a Free State, wedged permanently between Italy and Yugoslavia. Giolitti continued to refuse to recognize D'Annunzio's government since the poet now insisted that Fiume must become part of Italy.

D'Annunzio foolishly denounced the Treaty of Rapallo and invaded two nearby islands assigned by the agreement to Yugoslavia. In all these actions, Mussolini publicly supported him. He also criticized the treaty for failing to acquire all of Dalmatia for Italy, though he stressed its positive aspects as well. In private, Mussolini urged D'Annunzio to accept reality. Even from the tone of his newspaper articles, it was fairly easy to detect Mussolini's opinion that Giolitti had negotiated the best agreement possible and that D'Annunzio's days as a head of state were numbered.[30]

Once it was clear that D'Annunzio would not cooperate, and that the Italian land and sea forces marshaled outside Fiume would obey orders, Giolitti ordered General Caviglia to attack the city. On Christmas Eve, Italian troops moved into the outskirts of the city, paused to give the legionaries time to surrender, and then resumed their advance. The battleship *Andrea Doria* signaled the start of the attack by firing a shell through the wall of D'Annunzio's palace, narrowly missing the poet. Then Caviglia's soldiers fought their way into the city. After four days of street fighting, at the cost of fifty-two lives, D'Annunzio's forces surrendered. In early January 1921 thousands of legionaries evacuated the city. Caviglia turned Fiume over to the control of city officials. Two weeks later, D'Annunzio departed for the shores of Lake Garda. There he retreated into daydreams, nursing a bitter grudge against Mussolini but effectively abandoning politics.[31]

Of course, Mussolini denounced the assault on D'Annunzio's city. But he had done nothing concrete to aid the poet. On December 2, in a display of bravado, Mussolini had pledged that if Giolitti ordered an attack on Fiume, he would urge the entire Italian people to revolt. Three weeks later, he did no such thing.[32]

In the last two months of 1920, Mussolini had to accommodate himself to the rapidly altering nature of the Fascist movement. He no longer led a small group of revolutionaries, but a large political movement. His tactics had changed accordingly. In 1913 and 1914, Mussolini had despaired over the possibility of the Socialists coming to power through either revolution or elections. As 1920 turned into 1921, Mussolini began to see a route to power that combined elements of both methods. But it could not involve an open clash with the government. Most Italians still supported their leaders in Rome. Mussolini's squads still could not possibly win an armed confrontation with the forces of the state. Too many of Mussolini's new followers were middle-class patriots who would shrink from an outright assault on the king's government and the army that defended it. To even threaten such an action, Mussolini needed time to discipline and toughen his Fascist squads. Membership in the *fasci* had grown so fast that his control over the movement had become quite shaky by early 1921.[33]

Mussolini's tactics, however clever, cost him the support of many of his original Fascist followers. His old Republican comrade, Pietro Nenni, broke with Mussolini over his adoption of extreme nationalism. In order to fight the Facists, Nenni joined the Socialists in early 1921. Many in the Arditi Association, not to mention D'Annunzio's defeated legionaries, came to see Mussolini as an opportunist. Rumors circulated that Mussolini had accepted a large bribe from Giolitti in return for betraying D'Annunzio. Those who remembered the stories that Mussolini had accepted "French gold" to abandon the Socialist party and to found *Il Popolo d'Italia* in 1914 found these tales quite believable.

But Mussolini gained more than he lost. Many of D'Annunzio's followers had nowhere to go after their expulsion from Fiume. These men not only needed some way to survive, they craved the excitement and sense of purpose they had found in Fiume. In early 1921, the Fascist squads offered both, and Mussolini urged the legionaries to join. By March, the Fascist movement had swollen still further to eighty thousand members. Most of these new Fascists came from the towns of the Po Valley, following the new leaders, like Grandi and Balbo, who had arisen in the previous few months.

Mussolini's prudent political methods were essential to the movement. His tactics helped create a kind of alliance with Giolitti. The prime minister wished to see the Socialists weakened. Because the police and army frequently chose not to interfere, Fascist squads could roam the countryside unimpeded in their campaign of burnings and beatings. Giolitti and his subordinates tolerated Fascist violence only so long as Mussolini forswore revolution and aimed the attacks of his squads exclusively at the prime minister's political opponents. In large cities like Milan, where the local Fascists had a less savory reputation, the police usually took a far stricter line against Fascist misbehavior. In keeping with these attitudes, Mussolini's rhetoric changed appreciably in early 1921. He no longer called for the overthrow of the state. He began to stress the Fascists' role as defenders of traditional Italian values against the barbaric Bolsheviks.[34]

The events of late 1920 and early 1921 threw Margherita's life into turbulence. As the Fascist movement replaced *Il Popolo d'Italia* as Mussolini's main concern, he came to depend on Margherita's help even more. Political activities began to overwhelm her career as an art critic, and even her closest friendships. Ada Negri noted that Margherita's household had became disrupted by the unpredictable demands placed on her by Mussolini. Eighteen-year-old Amedeo joined the Fascist movement in early January 1921. Cesare remained a Socialist, but continued to handle Mussolini's increasingly complicated legal affairs and served as a lawyer for the Fascist Central Committee. Margherita could see Ada now only when her frenetic schedule allowed. Ada was frequently depressed without Margherita's steady companionship and she turned to the Notaris for comfort.[35]

Mussolini repaid the Sarfattis for their devotion as best he could. In late January, he made special preparations for the commemoration of the third anniversary of Roberto's death. He issued strict instructions to the Milan *fascio* to avoid any demonstrations after the ceremony. Mussolini was determined that his unruly followers do nothing violent to upset Margherita and Cesare, nor to desecrate the memory of Roberto.

On the morning of January 30, hundreds of Fascists and Fiume legionaries packed themselves into a meeting hall on the Via Vivaio, just a few blocks from the Sarfatti home on the Corso Venezia. Joining the Sarfattis were Marinetti, the painters Achille Funi and Luigi Russolo, and other friends of the family. After the leader of the Milan Fascists paid homage to Roberto, Mussolini got up to speak.

Mussolini recalled the events of Roberto's short life with fondness and read extracts Margherita had given him from some of her son's letters, as well as the proposed citation for the *medaglia d'oro* that the government had declined to grant posthumously. Then he reminded his audience of Roberto's sacrifice and his lonely grave somewhere far off in the mountains. Three years after his death, Mussolini asked, did they live in an Italy for which the young soldier would have been glad to lay down his life? Yes, he answered, for Italy had acquired secure borders to the north and east. Yes, despite all the domestic humiliations the Italians had suffered, Mussolini insisted that the nation could become worthy of the heroic deaths of Roberto and of many other valiant warriors. But it was for them, the living, to vindicate such losses. They must overcome the forces that still threatened the nation from within, even at the cost of their own lives. The audience saluted Mussolini's peroration with a roar of approval, then filed slowly out of the hall.

Mussolini had taken care not to provoke the gathering with calls for vengeance on the Socialists. Still, his speech had been a self-serving political act as much as it had been a tribute to Roberto. Mussolini had taken the occasion to defend his acceptance of the Treaty of Rapallo. He used Roberto's heroic death to justify Fascist violence. Soon the Fascists would gain other "martyrs" in their battles with the Socialists. But Mussolini had appropriated Roberto—admittedly with his parents' blessing—as the first.

Once outside, the Fascists assumed military formation behind their banners. The police were unable to disband them as they marched, singing patriotic hymns, to the headquarters of the Milan *fascio*. Their parade clearly reflected the influence of D'Annunzio's legionaries, whose uniforms, ceremonies, and war cries the Fascists now adopted. Most carried a cudgel known as the Manganello, which had become notorious as their favorite weapon. Since many of the Fiume legionaries had been Arditi, D'Annunzio's men had taken to wearing similar black uniforms. By early 1921, the Fascists also had adopted black shirts as their particular garb. After that the Fascists, especially their armed squads, became commonly known as the "Blackshirts."

After they disbanded on the afternoon of 30 January, many of the younger Fascists continued to demonstrate. One group of Blackshirts encountered a Socialist and a Communist city official in the Galleria. They tussled with them until the police intervened. Everyone ended up at the police station, where the Fascists were let go with a warning.[36]

By itself the incident had small significance. But it demonstrated how little control Mussolini exercised over the excitable young members of his own Milan *fascio,* and how tolerant the police could be toward Fascist lawlessness. Outside Milan, particularly in the Po Valley, Mussolini enjoyed far less influence over the activities of the new Fascist organizations. There the local police were even more willing to ignore Fascist violence aimed at crushing agrarian Socialism. By April, Mussolini was even urging Arpinati in Bologna and the leaders of the Modena *fascio* to avoid mindless brutality, to use force intelligently and then only when necessary.[37]

While Mussolini could not always rein in his Blackshirts, he was still recognized as the leader of an ever more important political movement. Indeed, his followers referred to him more and more frequently as *il Duce* (the Leader). By May 1921, the *fasci* had expanded to a total of 187,000 members, and Margherita and Mussolini had become certain that he was destined to play a major role in Italian history.[38]

Accordingly, Mussolini decided to resume keeping a regular diary, as he had during his war service. Margherita agreed—or perhaps demanded—to edit it. Mussolini appears to have begun keeping his new diary around the first of the year, for by early June he had written enough to consign it to Ada Negri for temporary safekeeping. In the diary for 1921 and for several years thereafter Mussolini repeatedly and effusively wrote of his love for *Vela,* the name he used to disguise Margherita's identity. On page after page, Margherita wrote her own comments on Mussolini's observations. Other pages were almost entirely in her own handwriting. Even in the sentences penned by Mussolini, whole sections departed radically from his ordinary prose, and were much closer to Margherita's ornate style. There seems little doubt that Margherita dictated these pages or wrote them for Mussolini to copy later.

But the purpose of the diary was not primarily to preserve the story of their love. The volumes held far more than Mussolini's remarks on the personal events of his days. They provided political commentary, detailed pictures of the evolution of his policies, and records of his most confidential conferences. Mussolini and Margherita seem to have conceived of the diary as his testament to the Italian nation and as a unique historical document containing the innermost thoughts and feelings of a man they both expected to change the course of their times. Margherita's extensive editing indicates that they intended the diary to show Mussolini in the best possible light—at least as a political leader, if not as a husband. Perhaps Margherita was inspired by the legendary lost autobiography of the Roman emperor Hadrian. The project was typical of Mussolini's narcissism and Margherita's complete devotion. Mussolini came to treat the diary volumes as his most precious possession. He took great care that his diaries would be safe-guarded but that they would be made public no sooner than fifty years after his death.[39]

Mussolini came perilously close to dying soon after commencing his diary. On March 2, 1921, he suffered serious injuries in an airplane crash at a small airfield northeast of Milan. He was practicing takeoffs and landings under the guidance of the World War I ace Cesare Redaelli when the engine stalled. The plane slipped sideways and fell 130 feet, crushing its left side. Redaelli escaped serious injury and pulled his bloody student from the wreck. Mussolini had serious lacerations on his legs, particularly on the left leg he had injured in the war, and on his left arm.

Mussolini had arrived at the field on a bicycle. Considering its location some thirteen miles from the center of Milan, it seems likely that Margherita had driven him close to the airfield and that he pedaled the rest of the way alone for discretion's sake. Mussolini was quickly delivered to a doctor just a few blocks from Margherita's apartment on the Corso Venezia, strongly suggesting that she had been close to the scene of the accident in her automobile. His injuries were painful but not life-threatening and he telephoned Rachele, then his colleagues at the newspaper, to reassure them. Rachele had that morning warned Mussolini not to go—she had dreamed he would have a flying accident. Perhaps her dream was invented to prevent Mussolini from joining Margherita. Their passion for flying, their periodic excursions in Margherita's car, were typical of activi-ties Rachele could not appreciate. By early 1921, Rachele hated Margherita; she could dismiss Mussolini's other frequent amorous conquests almost as easily as he did himself. Margherita posed a unique threat.[40]

A few days after the accident, Margherita went to see Mussolini at home. She explained to Rachele that she had to discuss *Il Popolo d'Italia* business. It was the only time the two women ever met face-to-face. Mussolini's injuries had brought him home to Rachele for their longest period together since his convalesence in 1917. Margherita's intrusive visit enraged Rachele. Margherita remembered only Mussolini's stoicism and his touchiness over the suggestion that the accident had been due to his inexpertise. But Mussolini's wife still bristled at her own memories forty years later. After Margherita left, Rachele came into the bedroom ostensibly to rearrange the bedclothes and muttered, "It's really true that some people have no shame. I should have thrown her out of the window—it's the least I could have done."[41]

After fifteen days of convalescence, Mussolini grew strong enough to resume writing regular articles for his newspaper. A week later, he was able to get about on crutches and returned to work at *Il Popolo d'Italia*. No sooner had he left his sickbed than he had another close brush with death, this time at the hands of a young Anarchist.

On March 23, 1921, a bomb exploded in the Diana Theater in Milan, killing twenty and wounding dozens more. Margherita was at home, having tea with some friends. A few years later, she described the huge shock of the explosion:

> The cup fell from my hands, the windows rattled and the house rocked as if it would collapse. We ran to the windows. All was deserted. After a moment or two of that deadly stillness which precedes a storm, a crowd of apparent madmen came running down the street, gesticulating, dragging themselves along, in absolute silence, without cries, voiceless, as though they had been struck dumb in the dark abyss from whence they fled. Cries followed later, when—first one by one, then two, then ten at a time—came the terrible procession of cars bearing wounded through the streets of the horror-struck city. A plot of the Communists had filled the pit of the popular theater of Diana with dead and wounded, massacring the audience who were listening to an operetta. Amongst the gilding and bronze and velvet were scattered fragments of flesh, pieces of limbs, mutilated bodies and blood and brains bespattering the whole place.[42]

Despite Margherita's propaganda, the Anarchists were behind the bombing. They were protesting the incarceration of the Anarchist leader, Errico Malatesta. The previous day, a young man had called at Mussolini's home, only to be told by Rachele that he was at work. Mussolini met the visitor, named Biagio Masi, after he came home. Masi asked for employment. Mussolini agreed to help and the two men returned to *Il Popolo d'Italia* together. After they entered Mussolini's office, Masi pulled a revolver out of his pocket and confessed he had been hired to shoot Mussolini. He told Mussolini that the sight of his wife and three children in their humble household had dissuaded him and he begged forgiveness. Mussolini sent Masi to Trieste for protection with Giunta's *fascio* and persuaded the police to drop the matter.[43] Reflecting on his narrow escape from death, Mussolini looked out the window at the first signs of spring and remarked to Margherita: "How beautiful life is. It deserves risking— you have to risk it every now and then—to feel how much it's worth."[44]

The bombing at the Diana did serious damage to the cause of the left, despite the fact that only a few Anarchists had been involved. Five days later, Margherita joined a crowd watching several separate units of the Milan *fasci* march into the cathedral square to take part in the funeral. It was the first public appearance of the Blackshirts in military formation. At their head strode Mussolini, his martial bearing reminding Margherita of some Renaissance *condottiero*. To her it seemed all eyes were drawn to him rather than to the cardinal archbishop of Milan, Achille Ratti, who blessed the coffins from the cathedral steps. She could not take her eyes off her lover, even when the frightening rattle of a descending shutter sent a thrill of panic through the huge gathering. The squads quickly reassured the throng and restored order. Margherita saw this as an omen. Soon, they would do the same for all Italy.[45]

Part Three

THE UNCROWNED
QUEEN OF ITALY

17

The March on Rome

Mussolini had more or less recovered from his airplane crash injuries by the time Giolitti obtained the king's consent to dissolve the Chamber of Deputies on April 7, 1921. Elections for a new Parliament were scheduled for May 15. Giolitti believed that the moment had come for the realization of his prewar dream: a great Liberal-Socialist coalition. He reasoned that the revolutionary Socialists had been discredited by their failures in the fall of 1920, and further weakened by the departure of the Socialist extremists for the new Communist party. Probably the reformist Socialists would now predominate in the Party. After the election, the prime minister expected they would be willing to join with him in governing Italy and continuing the social reform he had begun in the prewar years.

Giolitti needed to produce a comfortable majority of his own deputies in Parliament to ensure his domination of the new Chamber. To that end, he announced the formation of a National Bloc into which he welcomed all the anti-Socialist parties of the right, center, and center left, including the Fascists. Giolitti's ability to manipulate the outcome of elections was unsurpassed, so Mussolini persuaded the Fascists to accept his help.

The electoral alliance gave the Fascist movement even more freedom of action than before, especially in the Po Valley. After all, what policeman, already engaged against the left, would stand in the way of the prime minister's allies? The Blackshirts brutally disrupted meetings of Socialists and Communists, and terrorized their supporters. In the five weeks of the electoral campaign, the losses on both sides amounted to 105 killed and 431 seriously wounded. Mussolini daily grew more confident, insisting that his movement soon would conquer all of Italy. "The final goal of our impetuous march," he announced, "is Rome." On election day, the Fascists got out the vote, and did what they could to prevent the opposition from doing the same. There were forty deaths and seventy serious injuries resulting from violence at the polls.[1]

As a favor, Mussolini endorsed Cesare's candidacy in the Po Valley electoral district of Parma-Piacenza-Modena-Reggio Emilia, an area of particular Fascist strength. Cesare ran as a reformist Socialist, not as a Fascist. Once again he failed to win election, gathering only 3,567 votes. The leading candidate, a Fascist, gained 33,758. Cesare had suffered another humiliating defeat.[2]

Margherita joined Mussolini in rejoicing as the election results came in. Out of the 535 seats in the new Chamber, the Fascists won 35—they had run only 75 candidates. Mussolini was elected, as were Grandi and Giunta. There were others elected who later rose to prominence, including Roberto Farinacci, Giacomo Acerbo, Aldo Finzi, Giuseppe Bottai, and Cesare Maria de Vecchi. Most of the new Fascist deputies were quite young, making Mussolini at thirty-seven the "old man" of their parliamentary group.[3]

Overall, the National Bloc had obtained 275 seats, while the Socialists had fallen to 123. The Catholics of the Popolari party had risen slightly to 108 deputies, and minor party candidates accounted for the other seats. But Giolitti had suffered a major defeat. The core of his Liberal parliamentary support had fallen from 168 to 108 deputies, while the real extremists—the Fascists, the Nationalists (with 10 seats), and the Communists (with 15)— had risen from zero to 60.[4]

Lacking the discipline of a modern political party, the Liberals instead were a loose coalition of factions, grouped around prominent Liberal leaders. The National Bloc soon disintegrated, and so did the Liberals. Even before Parliament reconvened, Mussolini declared himself in opposition to Giolitti. Thereafter different Liberal groups, led respectively by the former prime ministers Salandra, Orlando, and Nitti, revealed their hostility to Giolitti. The Popolari believed that they had cooperated with Giolitti only to receive nothing in return, and remained aloof. Giolitti quickly realized that he could not govern. He resigned in late June 1921. In early July, he was succeeded by his former minister of war, Ivanoe Bonomi.[5]

Mussolini had hoped to make a dramatic arrival by flying down to Rome for the opening of Parliament. But Margherita's friend Giuseppe Brezzi of Ansaldo could not help him obtain an aircraft. Mussolini was forced to make the long journey by train. He found the other deputies' attempts at familiarity insufferable. Thereafter Mussolini had followers, allies, and opponents, but no friends. Mussolini found himself in particular need of Margherita's companionship. By July, he was able to begin making regular round trips between Rome and Milan by air; he traveled so frequently that his exact comings and goings remain unrecorded.[6]

Margherita's travels in 1921 are likewise uncertain. It is clear that she made quick visits to Berlin in April, to see an exhibit featuring modern Italian artists, and to Sicily in June. Her latter absence left Mussolini worried and melancholy because he did not get letters from her. She also went to Vienna in the late fall. The poverty, shabbiness, and disorder of the once vibrant Austrian capital shocked her, although Margherita readily took advantage of the low prices of the objets d'art.[7]

She must have been in Milan for most of her lover's sudden appearances. Certainly she was with him in the city and at Il Soldo in the late summer and early fall. Cesare Rossi remembered that Mussolini had a minor traffic accident in October on his return from one late-night tryst with Margherita. Before a policeman arrived on the scene to settle matters, Mussolini made frenzied efforts to buy off the irate driver of the cart with which he had collided. When Mussolini could not come to Milan, Margherita began to make trips to see him in Rome.[8]

In May 1921, Margherita's only published book of poetry appeared. She had written *I vivi e l'ombra* (*The Living and the Dead*) over the previous five or six years. The free-verse poems depict Margherita's interior life, and describe her feelings about art, women friends, Cesare, Mussolini, and Roberto. One long piece, "The Canto of the Threefold Me" ("Il canto del triplice Io"), offers a disguised portrait of the relationship among Margherita, Ada, and Mussolini. At the end of the volume, twenty-odd poems give voice to her love and grief for her fallen son, the *ombra* (shade or ghost) of the title. His death still haunted her.

Margherita's book received some respectable reviews for its intensity and honesty. Sironi created a dust-jacket illustration for the book, based on an idea of his wife, Matilde. It depicts two mourning women in classical robes comforting each other, confronted by a shadowy figure holding the laurel crown of victory. Even more than its contents, the book's cover portrays the ideals for which Margherita was struggling in 1921.[9]

Margherita's struggles were not confined to art. The first Fascist political successes had led to a major conflict among the new leadership over ideology and strategy. Mussolini nearly lost control over the burgeoning Fascist movement during the second half of 1921. His troubles began with his maiden speech to the Chamber of Deputies on June 21. His general survey of Fascist foreign and domestic policies alarmed many of his followers, both those who had formed the movement with Mussolini in 1919 and the newcomers of recent months. To woo the industrialists, Mussolini attacked any form of collectivization. "We have enough of state socialism!" he shouted. "The real history of capitalism is only beginning now." At the same time, he offered the General Labor Confederation, which had been responsible for the occupation of the factories, an alliance with Fascism—if only it would sever its ties to the Socialist party. Then he praised the Catholic Church. "I affirm here that the Latin and imperial traditions of Rome are represented today by Catholicism . . . the only universal idea

which exists today in Rome is that which radiates from the Vatican." He
suggested a settlement of the fifty-year-old split between Church and State
in Italy, arguing that government aid to Church schools and even to its
missionary efforts was possible. Mussolini concluded by offering to end the
political violence ravaging Italy. If the Socialists agreed to live in peace, he
promised that the Fascists would do the same.[10]

The speech was obviously aimed at gaining the support of as many
groups as possible. Also Mussolini sought to give a new, law-abiding
countenance to his disreputable movement. He had in fact gone so far in
altering course that he sent a wave of alarm through the Fascist ranks. To
his original, radical followers, Mussolini's attack on collectivization and
embrace of Catholicism seemed treasonous. Moreover, he rejected the
syndicalist and corporativist ideals the Fascists had espoused since March
1919. Marinetti and others expressed disgust at Mussolini's pandering to the
Catholics. The Arditi had already lost faith in Mussolini for his betrayal of
D'Annunzio; in July 1921, the Arditi officially broke with Mussolini's
movement, expelling all their Fascist adherents. It was several weeks before
the discontent Mussolini provoked among his followers led to a crisis. In
the meantime, he exacerbated the situation by his political maneuvers.

Bonomi and Mussolini shared a certain amount of respect for each
other, despite their adversarial past. During his tenure as minister of war,
Bonomi had been made aware of the extent to which Fascist lawlessness
was undermining the security of the state. Instances of army cooperation
with Fascist violence particularly worried him. After Bonomi took over the
government, he issued orders to suppress any breaches of the peace.
Bonomi called for some form of agreement between the Fascists and the
Socialists to end the bloodshed.[11]

The advantages of such a pact were made clear to Mussolini by the
events at the town of Sarzana, near La Spezia, on July 21. Acting under
instructions from the new Bonomi government, twelve Carabinieri stood
their ground in the face of an attack by five hundred Blackshirts on
Sarzana's leftist population. After the Carabinieri opened fire, the Fascists
fled in disorder. The people of Sarzana were determined to take revenge
against their tormentors. They pursued the panicked Blackshirts through
the fields, hunting down and killing eighteen, and leaving thirty seriously
wounded.

Mussolini had already entered into negotiations with the Socialists at
Bonomi's urging. He renewed his criticisms of the mindless brutality of the
squads. On August 2, to the surprise of many of his followers, Mussolini
signed a Pact of Pacification with Socialist parliamentary leaders in Rome.
Both sides agreed to cease attacks on each other and to submit any disputes
to arbitration.[12] News of the Pact of Pacification unleashed the resentments

that had been building in Fascist ranks since Mussolini's speech to Parliament in late June. Mussolini immediately found himself under furious assault from both wings of his movement. The greatest threat to his authority was led by Dino Grandi, and seconded by Italo Balbo.[13]

Grandi argued, rather dishonestly, that the killings at Sarzana proved that the left had already rejected Mussolini's call for a truce. For Mussolini to conclude an armistice afterward had been a cowardly surrender. After calling a meeting of dissident Fascists in Bologna, Grandi announced that he did not view Fascism as Mussolini's personal property that Mussolini could do with as he pleased. The movement could do better without him and his reconciliation with the Socialists. The Fascists would come to power by crushing the left, Grandi insisted, not by making deals with them. A few days later, Mussolini responded angrily: "Fascism can do without me? Certainly, but I can also do without Fascism."[14]

Grandi convened a still larger assembly on August 16, representing 544 *fasci*. The Blackshirts supported Grandi's arguments. Fascism, Grandi emphasized, represented a new concept of governing. Grandi rejected the idea that Mussolini had founded the Fascist movement in Milan in March 1919. The night D'Annunzio had marched on Fiume had been the real "baptism of Italian Fascism." At the end of the meeting, the Fascists enthusiastically agreed to Balbo's proposal to offer the leadership of the movement to D'Annunzio. Given the poet's radical economics and fervent nationalism, he seemed the ideal choice to reconcile the two wings of the Fascist movement. The next day, Mussolini resigned from the Fascist Executive Committee. It seemed as if Mussolini was reliving the dark days of his dismissal from the Socialist party in November 1914.[15]

For several months, Mussolini's future remained uncertain. He still had his seat in Parliament and control over *Il Popolo d'Italia*. But if he had hoped to be recalled by desperate Fascists to resume leadership of their movement, his bluff had been called. When Grandi and Balbo visited D'Annunzio to offer him command of the Blackshirts, the poet dismissed them—he said the stars were not propitious. D'Annunzio had probably decided that the Fascists were uncontrollable. Grandi and Balbo continued to demonstrate their independence. On September 10, they occupied Ravenna for three days with three thousand Blackshirts. There the Fascists mercilessly brutalized their opponents. The official occasion for the demonstration was the second anniversary of D'Annunzio's occupation of Fiume, and the six-hundredth anniversary of the death of Dante. In fact, Grandi and Balbo were showing off the numbers they controlled and their fierce commitment to the use of violence.[16]

The movement remained in disarray until the third national congress of *fasci* met in Rome in early November. The unenthusiastic reception accorded the five thousand assembled delegates in the capital helped disabuse Grandi, Balbo, and their followers of their illusions of Fascist power. The Romans treated the Fascists with disdain. The movement had not penetrated that far south. Grandi and Balbo now realized how little support they enjoyed beyond their strongholds in the Po Valley, and why Mussolini's political skills were essential. The two sides began private negotiations to resolve their differences.

Mussolini had already accepted the fact that Fascism could never take over the state by legal means alone, and was ready for compromise. He had considered for some time the idea of transforming the Fascists into an official political party. No longer would it be "Mussolini's movement" but a supposedly depersonalized party run by a central governing body. No longer would one man bear the responsibility (and the blame) for party policy. No longer would the squads run amok, free from party leadership. A party required an articulated program, but Mussolini recoiled from adopting D'Annunzio's Fiume Constitution as the basis for a Fascist platform. He wanted a compromise synthesis of liberal economics and collectivism.[17]

In the midst of the talks, rural Fascists held intimidating marches throughout the city. They swaggered down the Corso, threatening passersby with clubs and knives, and knocking off the hats of men who refused to raise them in obeisance. They invaded the proudly leftist working-class district in Trastevere and staged a provocative demonstration. After the local population resisted and the police intervened, street battles resulted in six dead and nearly two hundred injured. The outraged Roman working class went out on a general strike in protest. All Rome seemed to turn against the Blackshirts. The government feared that angry mobs might attempt to lynch the entire Fascist congress. Mussolini succeeded in calming the situation to some extent, thereby strengthening his hand in the bargaining with Grandi and Balbo. The two young leaders saw even more clearly the limits of their murderous methods and their need for Mussolini's political acumen.

The Fascist congress met in the Augusteo, the ruins of the mausoleum of the Emperor Augustus, which had been rebuilt into a huge concert hall. Insofar as they could be heard, the speeches delivered by Mussolini and Grandi revealed their continuing differences. The continuous uproar produced by the unruly delegates made it almost impossible to follow the speakers. The Fascists amused themselves by covering the walls with graffiti, ripping out the pipes from the theater's organ, and defacing the ornaments on the boxes. In the midst of this vandalism, Mussolini announced his willingness to compromise his old positions and to come to terms with the rural Fascists. After Grandi expressed his own viewpoint, he embraced

Mussolini to the cheers of the Blackshirts. The congress concluded by voting in favor of a formal program and expressed its overwhelming approval for establishing a Fascist party. A few days later, Mussolini formally repudiated the Pact of Pacification.[18]

The extent of Mussolini's victory became clear over the following two months. The establishment of the National Fascist Party and the location of its headquarters in Milan restored Mussolini's position as Duce more firmly than ever. Mussolini could now impose his will far more easily on unruly regional leaders like Grandi and Balbo. He appointed Michele Bianchi—formerly head of the editorial staff of *Il Popolo d'Italia*—secretary general of the Party, further strengthening his position. When the new Party worked out its official program in Florence in late December 1921, Mussolini's ideas generally prevailed.

Fascism had moved to the right of the political spectrum. While many words were devoted to the ideas of syndicalism and corporativism, nationalism and capitalism now took precedence. D'Annunzio's Fiume Constitution was implicitly rejected as the Fascist model. Support for voting rights for women also disappeared, as did the movement's espousal of male-female civil equality.

The armed squads were described as the essence of the party. Violent repression of political opponents was enshrined at the core of Fascism. The Blackshirt units were to be under the firm direction of Party headquarters in Milan. The main point of the new program was that Fascism "aspire[d] to the supreme honor of governing the country." Mussolini had shaped the program to that paramount end. Even the restless twenty-six-year-old Grandi and twenty-five-year-old Balbo reluctantly came to accept this.[19]

Given the leftist revolutionary concepts that had dominated Mussolini's thinking for the previous twenty years, there seems no doubt that he had endorsed these positions for purely opportunistic reasons. His conservative program would enable him to regain control over the Fascists and lead them to conquer the state. What he might attempt after gaining control over the government was another matter. Presumably Margherita rationalized his abandonment of feminist causes in a similar manner.

In a surprisingly candid moment during his address to the Fascist congress in November, Mussolini admitted the conflict between his ideals and his thirst for power. "In me two Mussolinis are in struggle, one which does not love the masses, the individualist, and the other, absolutely disciplined."[20] In fact, the contradictory compromises he worked out with his rivals in late 1921 continued to bedevil Fascism and circumscribe Mussolini's actions for the next twenty-odd years. In November 1921, as in November 1914, Mussolini had cut himself off from his past beliefs, losing almost all of his old associates in the process. The Fascists who surrounded

Mussolini in the winter of 1921–1922 were not the same men with whom Mussolini had founded the movement in the spring of 1919. Margherita was one of the very few people who continued to stand by him. Their continuous personal relationship and political association was unique in Mussolini's life.

Yet his attachment to Margherita had begun to bring him criticism, following the Fascist shift to the right. Margherita had done nothing to restrain her cosmopolitan interests and associations. She invited artists and intellectuals to her salon on the basis of their wit or accomplishments, not for their Fascist sentiments. Outright anti-Fascists were unlikely to accept one of Margherita's invitations. But many people who held Mussolini and his Blackshirt followers in less than the highest regard did frequent her salon, and this upset many Fascists. Margherita's free manner of living also caused unfavorable comment. Mussolini either would not or could not restrain her. But Margherita's circle of acquaintances did help create the useful impression that Mussolini tolerated intelligent dissent. For the moment, the differences between the two lovers proved complementary.[21]

Mussolini and Margherita introduced a new political journal in late January 1922. It succeeded *Ardita;* that name was no longer appropriate, given Mussolini's estrangement from D'Annunzio and the Arditi Association. They named their new publication *Gerarchia: Rivista Politica (Hierarchy: A Political Review)*. The title, which Margherita claimed as hers, reflected the disciplined new structure of Fascism and Mussolini's increasingly antidemocratic pronouncements. Mussolini envisioned *Gerarchia* as the exponent of his views, a publication parallel to *Il Popolo d'Italia,* and not an official journal of the Fascist party. Margherita described her own ambitions for the journal, somewhat disingenuously, as a compendium of cultural criticism, "free of any partisan prejudice," to which the finest minds in Italy would gladly contribute. Together they wrote the foreword to the first edition, stressing the journal's rejection of old concepts and its dedication to fresh ideas for the present and the future.

Although the masthead listed Mussolini as director, Margherita actually ran *Gerarchia,* selecting its staff, soliciting and choosing its articles, and writing many of them herself.[22] She authored so many that she published a large number under the pseudonyms of "El Sereno" or "Cidie." (The latter was a name whose meaning was known only to Mussolini and her.) Mussolini was most likely the author of articles signed "Ausonio," an allusion to a mythological ruler in pre-Roman Italy.[23] *Gerarchia* came to reflect Margherita's tastes far more than Mussolini's, with the majority of its articles devoted to literature, art, science, religious questions, and book reviews rather than politics or international relations. Given Mussolini's shortage of funds, Margherita may have paid the *Gerarchia* contributors out of her own pocket, at least for the initial period of publication. Mussolini retained the final word about political articles and Margherita ensured that only his closest supporters wrote for the journal.[24]

She recruited contributors for *Gerarchia* from her immediate circle of family and friends as well as from the leading Fascist ideologues and government officials. Her son Amedeo, who was to make a career in banking, wrote on international finance. She also published pieces by her childhood friend, the now famous scientist Guglielmo Marconi, and her former tutor, Pietro Orsi. Her consultant on religious matters was Don Brizio Casciola, the controversial priest and spiritual adviser to her father's old acquaintance, Antonio Fogazzaro. The principal graphic artist for *Gerarchia*'s covers was Mario Sironi. His cover illustration for the first issue consisted of a grandiose triumphal arch flanked by two winged victories, an early example of the Fascist identification with the glories of ancient Rome, a propaganda image that Margherita did much to promote.[25]

Mussolini's prescient article "Which Way Is the World Going?" appeared in the second issue of *Gerarchia* in late February. He stated that not only had the worldwide postwar trend toward the left ended but a political shift of historic proportions had begun. The coming decades would see the defeat of liberalism and democracy at the hands of a new authoritarian political philosophy. While Mussolini did not make it explicit, his logic clearly indicated that the twentieth century would be the era of Fascism. He implied that he would lead that transformation. In both its ideas and its language, the article bore all the indications of Margherita's co-authorship.[26]

In Italy the final collapse of the Liberal order had already begun. Bonomi had come under attack from the right for what they characterized as a weak foreign policy toward Britain and France. Unemployment shot up after the collapse of several large industrial firms, including Ansaldo, in late 1921. Matters grew worse following the passage of the Immigration Act of 1921 by the U.S. Congress, which cut down Italian emigration to a trickle. Bonomi responded to the huge increase in jobless young men by an expensive program of public works. This solution was not radical enough to silence the criticisms of the left, yet its expense angered big businessmen. Contributions to the Fascist party from bankers and industrialists increased sharply. Businessmen were reassured by Mussolini's recent conversion to unfettered capitalism.

Bonomi made some attempts to disarm the Fascists after Mussolini disowned the Pact of Pacification. In December 1921, he ordered a crackdown on all armed groups. At the Fascist congress Mussolini had insisted on the complete identity of the Party and the squads partly because he reasoned, correctly as it turned out, that the government would not attempt to outlaw the Fascist party as a whole. As a result, the squads continued about their violent business, albeit under closer supervision from Mussolini.

Bonomi submitted his resignation in mid-February 1922 following the withdrawal of key parliamentary support. His successor was Luigi Facta. He became prime minister because he was a loyal lieutenant of Giolitti, whom many deputies expected to take over in a real crisis. Unfortunately, Facta suffered from a weak character, and the Fascists soon realized they could do as they pleased. In early March, Giunta led one thousand Blackshirts from Trieste in an invasion of Fiume. After driving out the government of the Free State, Giunta announced its annexation to Italy. Three days later Facta was able to organize a countercoup, but he did not have Giunta or his men arrested.[27]

Now that he felt secure again in his control over the Fascist party, Mussolini undertook a visit to central Europe in early March. He wished to broaden his knowledge of foreign affairs in anticipation of coming to power in Italy. He went to Berlin first. Mussolini spent ten days in the German capital, speaking with government figures and giving interviews to a number of journalists, as well as to some exponents of the German right. The Germans made a bad impression on him. While he considered Germany too weak to cause trouble for Europe for the moment, he sensed a widespread desire for revenge for the defeat of 1918. He also noted signs of anti-Semitism and the early manifestations of the Nazi movement. After his return to Italy, Mussolini expressed his concerns in an article in *Gerarchia,* in which Margherita's hand was apparent.[28]

Mussolini cut short his trip when a new crisis threatened the November Fascist accord. Continued disgruntlement over Mussolini's use of conventional politics had flared into a revolt against his authority. Another move to replace him with D'Annunzio, backed by Grandi and Balbo, forced Mussolini to rally his allies and bring his rebellious followers back into line. By early April, he had restored his dominance over the Party, but not enough to resume his foreign travels.[29]

Balbo now directed his restless energies closer to home. Between May and August, Balbo's Blackshirts effectively took control of much of the eastern Po Valley, burning out the Socialists and Popolari with virtually no police or army interference. Many died on both sides. Local authorities either actively cooperated or simply allowed the squads to do as they pleased. The Fascists established labor unions, then lured or coerced the frightened agricultural workers of the Po Valley into joining.

In July, Facta's passivity encouraged other Fascist leaders to imitate Balbo. By the fall, the Fascists had extended their violent rule to every northern Italian city save Turin and Parma, which were leftist strongholds.

The Fascists remained weak only in Rome and to the south. A prolonged parliamentary crisis in July, begun when anti-Fascist deputies tried to find a strong prime minister, led nowhere. Giolitti sabotaged their efforts in the belief that when the situation became truly desperate, Parliament would beg him to return as prime minister to save the nation. Mussolini noted Giolitti's instinct for power and would take masterful advantage of it later.[30]

With its membership left unprotected by police or army, the Socialist party debated what course to take. Internal divisions once again hindered an efficient party response. At a party congress in Rome in October, the revolutionaries expelled the reformists. The disgusted leadership of the General Confederation of Labor declared its independence of both sides. Torn by their own internal disputes, the Communists were unable to operate effectively either.[31]

The Popolari suffered a similar though less drastic fate. The Catholic party leadership could not agree on common action. Some conservatives sympathized with Fascist assaults on the Socialists; others recognized the terrible threat Fascism represented. After Benedict XV died in late January 1922, Cardinal Ratti of Milan was elected his successor, taking the name Pius XI. Mussolini had stood with the crowd in St. Peter's Square awaiting Cardinal Ratti's selection. To some colleagues he expressed his newfound admiration for the political power of the papacy, and his belief in the need for the reconciliation of Church and State in Italy. By means of sympathetic prelates, he informed the new pope of his political ideas and his hostility to the Popolari. In October 1922 the Holy See responded. It informed the Italian bishops that it considered the Popolari no different from other parties. Without the Vatican's sanction and its special protection, the Popolari could not attempt any serious resistance to the Fascists.[32]

Under these circumstances, Mussolini began serious planning to take over the state. At the November 1921 Fascist congress in Rome, some had urged him to take advantage of the presence of so many Blackshirts in Rome and overthrow the government. He wisely refused, for the Fascists were still too disorganized, and the government was still too resolute. But Mussolini saw his time fast approaching.[33] At Mussolini's urging, the Fascist Central Committee appointed a four-man inspectorate, including Italo Balbo, to militarize the armed squads. Balbo soon came to dominate the group, which had drawn up regulations for the squads by February 1922.

Officially renamed the Fascist Militia, the armed forces of the Fascist party continued to be popularly known as the Blackshirts. Their black dress was formalized and made standard. Rumor had it that Margherita designed the new Militia uniforms, although this appears to be untrue. Rank and unit titles were adopted from those of the ancient Roman Army. Legions, cohorts, and centuries were placed under the command of consuls, *seniori,* and centurions. Standards patterned on those of the Roman legions and insignia displaying the *fasces* and Roman eagle were adopted. Officers and men carried daggers, a carryover from the Arditi and the Fiume legionaries.

Most Fascist Militia squads did not measure up to the new regulations. Many Blackshirts remained extremely slovenly in appearance, and were hopelessly unruly. Men who joined the squads were not usually looking to satisfy a longing for formal military order. Balbo and his comrades nonetheless continued to improve the Militia and had made some progress by the fall of 1922.[34]

In July, however, the Blackshirts went on the rampage without orders from either Mussolini or the Central Committee of the Party. Mussolini and Margherita had planned to go to Palermo during the second half of July for a short vacation of swimming and sailing. Instead, Mussolini stayed in Rome. Apparently, Margherita visited him and gave him a beautiful early-nineteenth-century calendar watch, inscribed with his initials and his birth date, on his thirty-ninth birthday. But Mussolini must have pleaded that the pressure of the political crisis enveloping the Facta government required his presence in the capital. Even repeated calls from Cesare Rossi and Arnaldo for Mussolini to return to Milan to deal with the Blackshirt lawlessness went unheeded. In fact, Mussolini had taken off on a romantic fling with another woman. While he and his most recent paramour enjoyed themselves in the Alban Hills south of Rome, the frantic messages from Milan went unanswered.[35]

Finally, on August 12, Mussolini returned to Milan and to Margherita. For several months, she had been pressing him to use the Blackshirts to march on Rome and seize power. Margherita argued that fears of a leftist revolution were fading rapidly, and unless the Fascists acted quickly, the political situation favorable to their cause would end. She saw a growing danger that the government would move to suppress the Fascist Militia. Furthermore, the Party was close to exhausting its funds and Margherita already had lent the Fascist Central Committee one million lire from her personal fortune. As Margherita later told a friend: "That march had to be made, it could not be put off any longer. And I did not want to lose my money, which was not a negligible sum."

Mussolini, who had resisted her advice to make such an irrevocable move, now returned to Milan certain that Margherita was right. He realized that the recent Blackshirt violence had brought matters to a head. The government had lost control over much of northern Italy. Throughout August, September, and October, Mussolini spent much of his time with Margherita, either in her Milan apartment or, to escape the heat, at Il Soldo. There he prepared to take control of Italy.

After the Blackshirts had eliminated or neutralized the other political parties in August 1922, Mussolini could deal as an equal with the Facta government. With the spread of Fascist power and the retreat of official authority, the king and his army had become the final barrier to a Fascist takeover. But the possibility remained that the king might turn to one of Italy's previous prime ministers, or even D'Annunzio, and back him with military force against the Fascists. Therefore Mussolini schemed to keep Facta in power, lest a stronger man take his place, by suggesting the creation of a Liberal–Fascist coalition government. At the same time, Mussolini made similar offers to Salandra, Orlando, Nitti, and Giolitti, to keep them off guard. Finally, he attempted to assure both the king and the army that they had nothing to fear from the Fascists and much to gain from having Mussolini in charge of Italy.

On August 13, Mussolini persuaded the Fascist Central Committee to begin preparations to mobilize the Militia, while he accelerated his political maneuvers. The Blackshirt forces were hardly a match for the army but they could intimidate the government with the threat of insurrection and civil war. Balbo and a small staff received the responsibility for military preparations. Mussolini devoted his energies to the essential political task: eliminating the possibility that anyone besides himself would replace Facta as prime minister. Mussolini confided the complete details of these intricate efforts only to his close adviser, Cesare Rossi, and to Margherita.[36]

On September 19, Mussolini left Milan by car to deliver a major speech at Udine, accompanied by Margherita and a few aides. Assembled there to greet him were thousands of Blackshirts and a number of Fascist leaders. While Mussolini made a particularly long speech, his essential points were few. He emphasized the Fascist intention to govern Italy in the immediate future. He promised to make the nation great and proud again. For the first time, he explicitly renounced his republicanism and promised to respect the monarchy. Clearly, he was addressing his words to the army leadership and King Vittorio Emanuele III.[37]

After reviewing the assembled Blackshirts, Mussolini and his party took the road from Udine east to the Isonzo and then south, passing through the areas Mussolini had fought in during the war. Whenever they came upon a sight familiar to Mussolini, he recounted what he had seen or done there. They enjoyed beautiful late summer weather, but painful memories returned to him. They passed the locations where Mussolini had first entered the trenches, where he had been told of Corridoni's death, and where he had been wounded. When they reached a cemetery, they walked among the graves. News of Mussolini's arrival attracted a small crowd, but he had no wish to speak and remained silent with his thoughts. They ended the day at Aquileia in another war cemetery. Then Margherita took Mussolini to Naples for several days in the sun to pull him out of the despondency their pilgrimage had provoked.[38]

Mussolini continued his fraudulent negotiations with the Liberal leaders and D'Annunzio over the next two weeks. Meanwhile, he perfected his plans at Il Soldo, where he and Margherita discussed the seizure of power. One day Mussolini and Margherita discussed tactics while walking on a hillside trail near the farmhouse, accompanied by thirteen-year-old Fiammetta. When they had finished their conversation, Mussolini left. Margherita and Fiammetta remained outside. "I know what you've been talking about," Fiammetta mischievously informed her mother. "Yes, you two have been talking about a march on Rome."[39]

By October 12, Mussolini realized the moment for action had come. He summoned the leaders of the Militia to a meeting in Milan four days later. Mussolini had learned that Giolitti was preparing to form a government to replace Facta. Stressing the danger presented by Giolitti, Mussolini warned that the old statesman was the only man capable of breaking the Fascist movement. The Blackshirts must forestall him by marching on Rome to take control of the government. The Militia commanders reacted with consternation. They did not consider their forces capable of such an audacious action. Even the impetuous Balbo showed some doubts at first, though he and Bianchi eventually came around to Mussolini's point of view.

With opinion divided, Mussolini revealed crucial information. He had learned that Facta had persuaded Giolitti and D'Annunzio to come to Rome on November 4 for a public reconciliation on the fourth anniversary of Italy's victory over Austria-Hungary. Giolitti would become prime minister, supported by a powerful coalition of anti-Fascist veterans and patriotic groups and backed by his former enemy D'Annunzio. Even this alarming announcement did not win over the frightened Militia commanders.

They did agree that the direction of the Party would be temporarily militarized under four Quadrumvirs—Balbo, Bianchi, the retired Lieutenant General Emilio de Bono, and Cesare Maria de Vecchi, an Arditi war hero with close ties to monarchist circles. The four would perfect their military plans and meet with Mussolini again in a few days in Florence. Then they would travel to Naples, to review a huge assembly of Blackshirts and reconsider Mussolini's plan for a Fascist assault on the state.[40]

Mussolini revealed the depth of his concern to Cesare Rossi after the Militia leaders left:

> If Giolitti returns to power, we're f[ucked]. Remember, he turned the cannon on D'Annunzio at Fiume. We've got to burn our bridges. They

didn't want to understand that. . . . But I've pointed them in the right direction. By the end of the month, we've got to make sure that all our preparations are finished.[41]

◉

As the days passed, Mussolini's arguments for immediate action swung the Militia commanders over to his stratagem. On October 20 and 21 final plans were laid at Il Soldo to seize control of the major cities of Italy, surround Rome with several columns of Blackshirts, and demand that Facta surrender his powers to the Fascists. If Facta refused, the Party would announce the formation of a provisional government, while the Militia would attack Rome and take Italy by force.

The Blackshirt assembly in Naples on October 24 was essentially a mobilization. Nothing better characterizes the weakness of the Facta government than the prime minister's supine acceptance of this challenge to state authority. Following another speech in which Mussolini reiterated the promises and threats he had made in Udine, he and his commanders watched their forces parade before them. Afterward the Blackshirts, many of them southern monarchists, raised a great shout of *"Viva il Re!"* De Vecchi, an ardent monarchist, invited Mussolini to join in. As de Vecchi later remembered the scene:

> I turned to Mussolini, took him by the arm and said to him in a commanding tone, "You too, shout 'Long live the King!' "
> He did not respond.
> I repeated: "Shout 'Long live the King.' "
> He said nothing. I demanded it for the third time and finally he answered me coldly: "No. Stop it."
> "Why?" I asked.
> He shrugged his shoulders and wiped his face with his hand as he often did. Then he looked at the crowd and said: "It's enough that they shout it. . . . Enough and too much!"[42]

Underneath all the compromises, the old revolutionary flame still burned in Mussolini.

The Fascist leadership decided to go forward. All Blackshirt forces would be mobilized on October 27 and military action would commence the following day. Every effort would be made to avoid a clash with the army, but there would be no turning back. Mussolini returned to Milan, where he arrived in the early hours of October 26. One danger had passed. D'Annunzio had decided not to come to Rome for a reconciliation with Giolitti.[43]

Despite the massive military preparations for the "March on Rome," the whole exercise amounted to little. In later years, Mussolini occasionally pretended that the Fascists could have overthrown the government. More often Mussolini admitted the truth. He knew that his forces could not stand up to the army. While the mobilization of the Blackshirts played a very useful role by placing Facta and the king under severe psychological pressure, Mussolini did not really intend to try to start a revolution or attempt a coup d'état. He planned to come to power through political negotiations conducted from Milan.[44]

During the three days that passed from the morning of the twenty-sixth to the morning of the twenty-ninth of October 1922, Mussolini revealed the political mastery he had developed over the previous ten years. A power struggle developed among Facta, Salandra, and Giolitti because of the negotiations Mussolini had conducted with the various Liberal leaders over the preceding weeks. This struggle consumed most of the government's attention until the night of October 27. By then, the Blackshirts had assembled throughout central and northern Italy and had begun to converge on the capital. The army prepared to oppose them but awaited orders from Rome.

The growing possibility of a violent confrontation made Mussolini increasingly nervous. Margherita constantly reassured him but Mussolini's fears became known to his closest advisers. Soon they were repeating the story that Margherita had run out of patience with her worried lover and insisted: "Either you will die or you will march. But I am sure that you will march." But as the date for confrontation approached, Mussolini remained fearful.

Finally realizing the gravity of the situation and the paralysis of his ministers, Vittorio Emanuele III hurried to his capital. After reviewing the situation, the king ordered the army to assume responsibility for public order. Discussions between Facta and the king, as well as a Cabinet meeting early on the twenty-eighth, led to a decision to declare a state of siege and place the country under martial law at noon. Throughout the country, measures taken by the army blocked the Fascists at every turn. The garrison of Rome outnumbered the converging Blackshirt columns, which had been halted well outside the capital. Even the Nationalists rallied to the king and added four thousand of their own party militia to the defense of the state. The ill-armed Fascist Militia, confronted by the machine guns and artillery of the army, did not stand a chance of success. They waited miserably in the rain, warned by their commanders to avoid any confrontation with the troops.[45]

Yet when Facta brought the state-of-siege decree to Vittorio Emanuele for his signature at 9:00 A.M. on October 28, the king refused to sign it. During the night, the king had consulted with his army commanders. They had urged the king not to use force against the Fascists. Mussolini's promises to respect the monarchy had convinced the generals that he had abandoned his revolutionary goals. More important, repeated overtures to the military leadership by various Fascists over the previous months had convinced the High Command that they would benefit considerably from a government headed by Mussolini.[46]

Vittorio Emanuele was a timid man and he seems to have overestimated Fascist strength. He became convinced that if he ordered the army to resist the Blackshirts, a protracted civil war would ensue. He feared that the strain of continued internal strife might split the military. Under those circumstances, the king worried that his popular cousin, Emanuele Filiberto, the Duke of Aosta, might gain enough support to make a successful bid for the throne.

The duke had formed close ties to the Fascists. Mussolini himself had courted the duke, visiting him several times at the Aosta palace at Capodimonte near Naples. Having commanded the Third Army during World War I, the duke also enjoyed great respect among the army's leaders. In October, the duke and his elder son, Amedeo, had gone to Perugia, where Balbo and the other Militia leaders were directing the March on Rome. When Facta asked the king why he refused to sign the state-of-siege decree, Vittorio Emanuele III could only repeat: "It's the Duke of Aosta, it's the Duke of Aosta." After Facta consulted with his Cabinet, he returned to the royal palace and handed the king his resignation.

As he had in the crisis of May 1915, Vittorio Emanuele III turned in desperation to Salandra and begged him to form a government. Giolitti was attempting to reach Rome from Turin. But measures taken by the army had interrupted train service and he could not leave.[47]

Throughout the crisis, Mussolini had maintained the appearance of ostentatious calm. On the evening of October 26, he and Margherita had gone together to the dal Verme theater for the opening night production of Wagner's *Lohengrin*. The next night, he had appeared in a box at the Manzoni Theater with Margherita and Fiammetta to attend a performance of Molnar's *The Swan*. About halfway through the second act, Luigi Freddi, a young member of the editorial staff of *Il Popolo d'Italia,* put his head in the door and gestured to Mussolini. Margherita urged Mussolini to leave but he quietly made a sign for Freddi to be silent and to sit down beside them. Only at the end of the act did Mussolini go into the corridor with Freddi and learn that Farinacci's Blackshirts had begun a premature and bloody attack on the prefecture at Cremona.[48]

The news brought all of Mussolini's fears rushing back. "Let's go to *Il Soldo,*" he suggested to Margherita. "We can cross over to Switzerland for two days in order to see what happens." Margherita said nothing but looked at Mussolini in a rage. Shamed into silence, he returned with Margherita to watch the third act of the play.

After the performance, Mussolini returned to his newspaper office, which had been fortified and was defended by about seventy Blackshirts. The remainder of the Fascist Militia went into action as originally planned, starting at midnight on the night of October 27–28. At sunrise, Mussolini discovered that a large force of police had moved into the area in preparation for an attack on the newspaper. He and Rossi managed to defuse the situation by going outside and talking to the officer in charge of the police. As the morning wore on, news arrived from Rome about Facta's resignation, the king's refusal to proclaim a state of siege, and Salandra's attempt to form a government.

Margherita remained with Mussolini all day on October 28, putting together the next day's edition of Il Popolo d'Italia. All the while, a stream of messengers came and went, bearing news of the Fascist insurrection and carrying Mussolini's orders to his lieutenants. In the midst of this disorder, he and Margherita discussed the composition of a possible Cabinet, which Mussolini began to put together over the telephone.[49]

About 1:30 P.M., Mussolini received a telephone call from Rome relaying Salandra's request to join him in forming a government. Mussolini refused. He decided that he was at the point of complete victory, and simply needed to wait for the king and the politicians to give in. Mussolini returned that evening to the Manzoni, but this time with his wife and his daughter. Rachele must have insisted. News of Mussolini's appearance with Margherita at the theater the night before had spread through Milan. Neither Rachele nor Edda ever forgot the pain Mussolini's prominent appearances with Margherita had caused them. Even forty years later, they found it very difficult to discuss their humiliation in October 1922.

When Mussolini got back to the newspaper from the theater that evening, Margherita confronted him and argued that he should accept Salandra's offer. He would not. Instead Mussolini wrote a short editorial for the next morning's edition demanding full power for the Fascists.[50]

Salandra attempted until the next day to form a viable government without Mussolini. This proved hopeless and the king resigned himself to offering Mussolini the position of prime minister. An intermediary telephoned Mussolini at Il Popolo d'Italia late on the morning of October 29, conveying Vittorio Emanuele III's offer to form a government. Margherita and Mussolini's brother, Arnaldo, expected him to agree immediately. But he declined, despite their entreaties. "Black on white, they've got to send me a telegram," he insisted. Then Mussolini picked up the telephone receiver. "Alright, alright. But I've absolutely got to have a telegram from

Cittadini [the royal aide-de-camp]. As soon as I have the telegram, I'll leave immediately by airplane." The telegram arrived about half an hour later. Mussolini ripped it open, read it, and got up from his desk. In a voice hoarse with emotion, he said to Arnaldo, in their Romagnol dialect, "*Se a i foss'e ba,*" "If only papa were here now."[51]

Mussolini changed his mind and took the slow train to Rome that evening. Either he did not want to seem too eager, or he simply needed a good night's sleep. Mussolini and his staff had been too busy and too exhausted to put out an issue of *Il Popolo d'Italia*. Margherita accompanied Mussolini to the railroad station in an automobile provided by the owners of the *Corriere della Sera*. After traveling all night, Mussolini arrived in the capital late the next morning. About 11:15, wearing the black shirt of the Fascists, Mussolini entered the Quirinal Palace to meet the king. The king formally gave Mussolini permission to try to form a government. Having already put together a Cabinet, Mussolini acted swiftly. That evening, the king accepted Mussolini's choices. About ten in the morning of October 31, Vittorio Emanuele III administered the oath of office to Mussolini and his ministers. The headline of *Il Popolo d'Italia* that morning trumpeted his triumph: MUSSOLINI RECONSECRATES THE ITALY OF VITTORIO VENETO CREATING A GOVERNMENT WORTHY OF ITS CERTAIN DESTINY.[52]

That afternoon, Mussolini allowed his Militia a triumphal march through the capital. Following their victory parade, the new prime minister hurried the Blackshirts out of Rome. Thirteen Fascists and local citizens died in fights before Mussolini's lawless followers left the city by train.

Mussolini and Margherita did not see each other during the first weeks after he became prime minister. He had no time for anything more than the heavy duties of his office. The Cabinet he had formed included only four Fascists, reflecting the reality that the Party still had only thirty-five deputies in the Chamber. He worked hard to prove his competence and to reassure the nation that he would keep the Blackshirts in check.

The new prime minister tried to make a good impression. He worked long hours and impressed the civil service with his enthusiasm and his willingness to heed experience. Salandra, Giolitti, and even Nitti offered their cooperation. Mussolini pleased the Vatican by ordering the crucifix displayed in schools and law courts. In late November, Parliament granted Mussolini's government full powers for a year to carry out fiscal and administrative reforms.[53]

But the threat of violence hovered over everything he did. In his first speech to the Chamber of Deputies, Mussolini announced that he could have turned the halls of Parliament into a barracks for his Blackshirts. The next day, he warned the deputies that they must conform to the new national reality or Parliament would disappear. Many politicians and many more Italians chose to ignore the implications of his words. In the years ahead, they would discover their mistake.[54]

Mussolini had become prime minister at the age of thirty-nine, the youngest in Italian history. He was also the first man of peasant origins to rise to that exalted position. His humble beginnings and the vagaries of his life had made his road to power seem long. Yet only ten years had passed between his rise to national prominence at the Socialist party congress of July 1912 and his appointment as head of the Italian government in October 1922. Along the way, Mussolini had retained very few of his principles; this had cost him almost all of his original friends and companions. The Sarfatti family were virtually alone in their continued personal and political loyalty to Mussolini. Whatever surprising turn Mussolini had taken in his ideas, they had followed. No matter what misfortunes had befallen him, they had supported him. By taking part in the Fascist insurrection of October 1922, the Sarfattis had risked their freedom and their fortune. In recognition of their service, Mussolini bestowed a unique honor on them. Margherita and Cesare, as well as Amedeo and Fiammetta, each received the special Fascist party insignia for those who had taken part in the March on Rome.[55]

Once Mussolini became prime minister, however, their relationship altered fundamentally. Even as head of the Fascist party, Mussolini did not enjoy the authority and prestige he acquired once he took over the Italian government. Before that date, Mussolini had been beholden to the Sarfattis. After October 1922, they became subordinate to him. This proved especially true for Margherita. In a sense both Mussolini and Margherita became the victims of his position, and of their determination that he should retain and expand the power of his office. Eventually both of them paid a heavy price for the fulfillment of their dreams.

18

Novecento Italiano

As she approached her fortieth birthday in 1920, Margherita enjoyed renown as an art critic, author, and advocate of the avant-garde among culturally sophisticated Italians. She was also somewhat notorious for her liaison with the temporarily discredited politician and editor of a minor newspaper, Benito Mussolini.[1] Within three years, Mussolini and Margherita rose to the very height of authority and influence in Italy. By late 1922, once Mussolini had bullied and bluffed his way into the office of prime minister, Margherita acquired the intoxicating opportunity to translate her dreams of aesthetic transformation into reality. She tried to inspire Mussolini to remold Italian culture according to her own vision of modernity.

By late 1919, the Futurists had become disoriented, and Margherita looked for opportunities to help the talented younger artists in the floundering movement. In December Margherita persuaded the industrialists Piero Preda and Amleto Selvatico to support deserving young artists who had fought in the war. She introduced Funi and Arturo Martini to them. From Carlo Ravasi, Margherita rented a villa for the artists' use at Rovenna, near Lake Como. Funi, Martini, and others were soon able to spend months at a stretch working. While at Rovenna, the two visited Il Soldo frequently and Funi painted a haunting portrait of Margherita with a bust of Fiammetta. The portrait showed signs of Funi's Cubist-Futurist technique as well as Metaphysical influences, but by the end of his stay at Rovenna Margherita noted with pleasure that Funi had "purified" himself of Futurism.[2]

In mid-January, Funi joined Sironi, Dudreville, and Russolo in signing an important manifesto titled "Against All Returns in Painting." Drafted by Russolo, the document reflected their belief that Futurism had served its purpose in taking the decomposition of form to its extreme conclusion. The time had come for a new vision that rejected analytical dissection in favor of a "constructive" synthesis. They called for a new style, although they did not define it in detail.[3]

That March the group mounted an exhibit. Margherita convinced a wealthy patron to finance the show, which included Funi, Martini, Dudreville, Sironi, Russolo, Marussig, Carrà, and Anselmo Bucci. Mario Buggelli, a former Futurist writer who had served with the Volunteer Cyclists, improvised a gallery in three basement rooms of a shop on the Via Dante. Margherita seems to have written the preface for the catalog, although a copy has never been found.[4]

Before the opening on March 20, Margherita reached agreement with some of these painters as to how she would present them. Her review in *Il Popolo d'Italia* proclaimed the realization of the goal toward which she had been working:

> We stand . . . at last before a group, a tendency, or, to put it in a single, brutally sincere word, we stand once again before a "school" of art. Let us be clear: because Funi, Carrà, Sironi, Russolo . . . are great artists, the differences between them are great. But the road, the great road that leads toward a single ideal goal . . . seems to have been found.[5]

Margherita's announcement was premature, the group had not yet assumed the form of an organized art movement. But she was convinced that painters such as Funi and Sironi were pioneering an art that reflected Italy's cultural traditions and historic genius. She praised them for their "modern classicity," which went far beyond the blind copying of older styles. Theirs was an art suitable to the spirit of the times. In the preface to the catalog of Funi's first one-man show, she described a painting of a woman that reminded her of the manner of Piero della Francesca and Quattrocento portraiture: "yet, she is also a modern woman of today, not because of how she is dressed or because of her hairdo, but because of her gait, her attitude, the glance, her smile: that indefinable something that bears the stamp of today."[6]

Over the next two years, Margherita turned out a series of reviews to publicize their work. In April 1921, she went to Berlin, where she saw an exhibit of Italian art that included paintings by de Chirico, Morandi, Carrà, and Martini. In her description of the new direction taken by Italian art, she announced her own aesthetic manifesto:

> Italian art must once again become method, order, discipline, must give rise to definite, bodily form, a precise gravity analogous to but also different from that of the ancients, independent of foreign fads and mercantile considerations. Originality and tradition are not contradictory

terms, and by returning to the purest traditions of Giotto, Masaccio, and
Paolo Uccello we do not renounce the uniqueness of our modern times.

Others began to take notice. Reviewing a large and eclectic exhibit at
the Galleria Pesaro that fall, Enrico Somaré agreed that he saw signs of a
new aesthetic unfolding. Conservative critics like Ugo Ojetti reacted more
cautiously.[7]

Some contemporary critics may have been puzzled by Margherita's
energetic defense of the avant-garde at the same time that she insisted on
a return to artistic tradition. Yet her ardor for "modern classicity" was
neither ambivalent nor logically contradictory. It reflected the cultural and
moral values she had carried with her from youth, values that the fear of
the Bolshevik revolution reinforced. Margherita had been taught that art
both mirrored and reinforced the standards of the society in which it was
created. Thus, an orderly society produced orderly art, while, at the same
time, such art encouraged a respect for discipline and control. As Boccioni
had been, Margherita was impelled by the war to reassess the meaning of
art and its relationship to civilization. She embraced with renewed enthusiasm the cultural traditions she had learned as a rebellious girl. In retrospect,
she became convinced that the Futurist and Cubist rebellion against traditional aesthetic values had been "analytical madness."

As she witnessed now the political and social upheaval that beset Italy,
Margherita traced the crisis in art back to the seventeenth century, an age
in which the sober and well-ordered strength of Cinquecento painting
gave way to the artificial Baroque era. Art degenerated as moral values
declined. "How can we judge the art of an age," she asked, "if not as the
expression of its moral habits?" Materialism, religious and secular heresies,
the cult of individualism, all had corroded the cohesiveness of Italy's social
fabric ever since. This was a lesson she recalled from her study of Ruskin's
aesthetics and his history of the decline of Venice. Her solution was to urge
a collective art. Early in 1922, in a review of works by Carrà, Tosi, Funi,
and Soffici, Margherita exhorted the artists to abandon their individual,
"arbitrary" styles and work toward a "collective synthesis."[8]

Margherita preached a return to the stylistic traditions that had made
Italian art great. Massimo Campigli, one of the young artists she gathered
into her fold, agreed: "The painting that follows Cubism and the war is a
work of the spirit, as it is in all periods that give rise to classic painting.
. . . Every element that we discover—and now we must rediscover them
all because they have been lost for almost four centuries—is a conquest that
we should prize and exploit." To Margherita, Funi and Sironi were the
leaders of a crusade that undertook the restoration of order. The task
demanded faith and discipline, but art could not discipline itself in an age

of disorder. "Not only in sculpture," she declared, "not only in painting, has unity been broken. We aspire to restore it, and not in art alone. In reaction to anarchy is born a nostalgia for authority."[9]

One October evening in 1922, shortly before the March on Rome, Margherita attended a meeting at the Galleria Pesaro in Milan of seven of her favorite young artists. These were Anselmo Bucci, Leonardo Dudreville, Achille Funi, Gian Emilio Malerba, Piero Marussig, Ubaldo Oppi, and Mario Sironi—hosted by Lino Pesaro, the gallery's owner.[10] Pesaro's guests gathered to formalize the foundation of the movement Margherita had been calling for.[11]

After the friendship between Pesaro and Margherita had ended, he claimed that the initiative for calling the meeting had been entirely his. Thirty years after, when it was no longer fashionable to be associated with these events, Margherita insisted that it had been her idea. She was probably telling the truth. Although Pesaro's gallery was, along with Mario Buggelli's Bottega di Poesia, one of the few in Italy willing to give Funi, Sironi, and others public exposure, he did not have the breadth of vision to create a new movement. Margherita did, and was at the very time of these discussions assisting Mussolini with his plans for the Fascist seizure of power.[12]

The artists agreed on a fifteen-point plan of action. Pesaro committed gallery space to the painters and agreed to pay for advertising and other expenses. In return he would receive a percentage of all sales. For their part, the artists pledged to each other to exhibit only in group shows, or separately with prior agreement. In time other painters would be invited to join. Margherita became the group's unofficial press agent, charged with generating publicity and reviews.[13]

During a second meeting, the group tried to decide on a name. Anselmo Bucci suggested "The Candelabra," because of the seven artists, but it was rejected. Because both Margherita and Pesaro were Jewish, the name might have provoked adverse public comment. Bucci then proposed to name the group after the century in which they lived and worked—the *Novecento* (Twentieth Century).

The merits of the name were debated for some days. Bucci believed *Novecento* suggested an affinity with some of the greatest periods in the history of Italian art, such as the Quattrocento and Cinquecento. Carlo Carrà attacked the name because it claimed to represent all of twentieth-century art. They decided, therefore, simply to call themselves "Seven Italian Painters." Margherita disagreed, arguing that their art not only fit into the great Italian pictorial tradition, but that the work of the *Novecento* was as expressive of a distinct era in Italian history as the Quattrocento had been. She went ahead and used the name *Novecento Italiano* in all her articles about the new movement, and before long it came into general use.[14]

In early November, several of the painters took part in an exhibit at the Bottega di Poesia. In her review, Margherita noted a collective character in their work of "concreteness and simplicity," a style marked by clearly presented forms and an atmosphere of calm and composure. The critic Enrico Somaré agreed that its images reflected an "intimate and silent world," and that the work on exhibit represented a "collective fact." In announcing the formation of the *Novecento*, Margherita exclaimed that her seven artists were preparing "the future destiny of Italian art."

Margherita inspired the creation of a major new artistic movement at the same time that she and Mussolini presided over the March on Rome. She had united art and politics. The initiation of the *Novecento* and the Fascist seizure of power represented different attempts to reach the same ends: the reimposition of order on Italian society and the restoration of Italy to the center of European civilization. Margherita understood the inspirational power of myth and the need for faith to achieve such goals. The *Novecento* consciously evoked classical principles, just as Fascism deliberately revived the symbols and ceremonies of the Roman Empire. Both encouraged devotion to hierarchy and discipline.

If Margherita's vision were to be realized, whoever enjoyed control over Italian culture would also possess great political influence. As a result, art could not be a matter of indifference to those seeking to gain or hold power. Art would become subject to state control and artistic taste would be considered an expression of political opinion.

For the first two months after Mussolini became prime minister, Margherita lived in a state of passionate happiness. His new position brought Margherita unparalleled influence. Their constant communication by telephone, telegraph, and letter, his deference to her in artistic and literary matters, and their mutual affection allowed Margherita to sway his judgment on a wide range of questions. To keep their missives confidential, they sent them through the Cipher Office of the Ministry of the Interior and usually left them without precise salutations or signatures. Margherita was running *Gerarchia,* writing for *Il Popolo d'Italia,* and managing Mussolini's foreign press service; all these tasks kept her in Milan with her family.[15] Every few weeks she would journey to Rome, where they would try to spend a few uninterrupted hours together.

Their first assignation in Rome set the secret police on alert. Margherita arrived at the Continental, a fashionable hotel near the station, where she stayed to avoid scandal during her visits. Mussolini lived at the more luxurious Grand Hotel, a few blocks from the Continental. After she telephoned him, he sneaked out of his rooms unobserved by either his private secretary or his bodyguards. Going down the service stairs and out the side entrance, he walked alone to Margherita's hotel. Cirillo Tambara, one of Mussolini's chauffeurs, spotted him leaving and called the police authorities, who immediately sent several agents to the Continental disguised as waiters. When Mussolini returned in the early hours of the morning, he found a worried General De Bono, now the chief of police, waiting for him. He promised to be more cautious. News of Mussolini's secret meetings with Margherita reached former prime minister Giolitti, who worried that such escapades made him an easy target for assassins. Michele Bianchi was less concerned. "After all," he commented with a laugh, "the man is not made of wood."[16]

During her visits to Rome, Margherita was constantly in Mussolini's company. At first the two were less than circumspect. Leonid Krasin, Lenin's foreign-trade commissar, arrived from Moscow at the beginning of December to open trade talks with Italy. Much to the chagrin of his Foreign Ministry officials, Mussolini once received Krasin in the bar of the Grand Hotel, with Margherita sitting nearby on a stool. The talks were the first steps toward Italy's recognition of the Soviet Union.[17]

Mussolini left for England on December 10 to attend a reparations conference in London, his first international conference as head of government. There he met British Prime Minister Andrew Bonar Law and French Premier Raymond Poincaré; he also had an audience with King George V at Buckingham Palace. Margherita insisted that he dress properly for the occasion. Remembering the severe influenza he had caught in Berlin in 1919, she bought him a heavy fur coat for the trip, which he was too embarrassed to wear more than a few times.[18] Just before his departure from London, he telegraphed Margherita, asking her to prepare in his absence a detailed report on how the Milanese press treated the conference. This survey was not the first such assignment; when Mussolini became prime minister, he had asked Margherita to scan the newspapers of Milan for comments about him and report by telephone on a regular basis.[19]

On his return from London, Mussolini ordered a special train to take him to Milan, along with Ercole Boratto, another of his chauffeurs, and several secretaries. It was the first time he had visited his family since becoming prime minister. After only a few hours with Rachele and his children, Mussolini instructed Boratto to prepare the car. They drove to an address on the Corso Venezia. While Mussolini went inside, a maid came out to chat with Boratto. She informed the chauffeur that he would no doubt be coming here often, since this was the premier's "real house." The maid, whom Boratto found talkative and imprudent, explained that this was the home of Signora Sarfatti. The next day they all traveled along the curving roads to Il Soldo, where they spent two nights. During the day, Margherita and Mussolini took long drives in the countryside, sometimes accompanied by Boratto and Fiammetta. At night Boratto gossiped in the kitchen with the cook about the two lovers.[20]

Thereafter Margherita made almost weekly visits to Rome. With Rachele still in Milan, Margherita thought she would have Mussolini to herself. However, as his schedule became more demanding, he soon subjected her to a series of humiliations she found unbearable.[21] When she came to Rome over Christmas in 1922, they had an angry quarrel. He had little time for her, for in addition to being prime minister, Mussolini headed the ministries of foreign affairs and the interior.[22]

Margherita returned to Rome for New Year's Day of 1923. Once again his official duties kept them apart for much of the day. She sent Mussolini three emotional letters by messenger, rejoicing in their love and pledging herself completely to him. She wrote that when he left his office in the Palazzo Chigi, she had been standing with the cheering crowd. She was thrilled to see him pass by Trajan's Column, beneath the upraised daggers and Fascist salutes of his Blackshirts. She felt an intense pride in him, but worried that the same crowd that now cried "Hosanna" might some day turn on him and scream "Let him be crucified!"[23] As they drove together down the Appian Way that evening, a shooting star flashed over their heads and seemed to augur their continuing happiness. Margherita could not help but interpret the meteor as an auspicious omen for the start of his first full year as Italy's new ruler. Mussolini, by nature a superstitious man, agreed.[24]

Sometimes he could not see her, and he would not always phone to warn her. In late January, Margherita spent several days in Rome, but Mussolini spared her only a few hours. She waited one day for five hours, as he conducted official business with a stream of visitors. While she suffered the humiliation of Mussolini's neglect, Margherita found their stares embarrassing.[25]

On a few occasions, they were able to escape in his sports car, driving around the suburbs or into the Alban Hills south of the city. At other times, he squeezed a few hours out of his eighteen-hour daily schedule for them to make love. But more often than not, Margherita found herself alone. Sometimes she would write him notes or compose articles at his desk; sometimes she visited the museums of Rome and the Vatican. But if he telephoned unexpectedly and could not find her at his apartment or her hotel, he would get angry. Her disappointment and his possessiveness frequently led to furious argument.[26]

Mussolini wanted complete control over Margherita's life. He insisted that she had to wait patiently for him without question or complaint. He objected to anything that distracted her—her family, her friends, her interest in art, her lectures, her travel plans. When Margherita proposed taking a winter vacation with Amedeo in early 1923 to Tunisia, he forbade her. When she protested, he claimed her desires were worthless compared to his own needs and wishes. He began to find her associations with apolitical or anti-Fascist companions like Giuseppe Borgese unacceptable. He even objected to Cesare having clients outside the Fascist party. He demanded that she sacrifice her entire life to him. Several times, she left him in rage or tears. Afterward she often wept uncontrollably for hours. Sometimes she could not sleep for days.[27]

Invariably, they would reconcile. Although she was furious at the mistreatment, as the days passed, her love generally overcame her anger. She fought the urge to contact him but finally would make the first move with a tearful telephone call or pleading telegram. He frequently would not answer her initial message. After a few days, he would confess his own sleepless agony, beg forgiveness, and promise to make amends. For months the telephone calls, telegrams, letters, and messages they exchanged described the same pattern of anger, guilt, forgiveness, and renewed declarations of love.[28]

Under these circumstances, Margherita found the editing of *Gerarchia* a trial. But she could not abandon the journal. That responsibility forced her to communicate with Mussolini. Because of her knowledge of foreign languages and her journalistic experience, he relied on her to arrange interviews for him with foreign journalists and to plant favorable articles in the American and European press. So many people knew of their connection that Margherita was constantly being approached with requests for favors or private messages for Mussolini. Even when she struggled against it, she could not resist adding a personal note to the formal letters she sent him about these matters. Mussolini would then reply, confessing how much he loved and needed her, and asking for understanding.[29]

During late February and early March 1923, they finally developed an understanding. After another of Mussolini's letters arrived pleading for her forgiveness, she wrote a lengthy, thoughtful reply. "My absurd lover, tyrannical and adored!" she began. She wrote that she had gained enough perspective to see a comical aspect to their predicament. She understood that Mussolini vented his frustrations at the vexations of office in his angry outbursts, which were not really directed at her. Nonetheless his behavior wounded her. She did not recover from their quarrels as easily as he. Still, she believed that he really did depend on her, that fear of losing her had frightened him, that his anger masked his fear. This knowledge gave her the assurance to insist that he respect her rights and her obligations.

Given the reality of her marriage, she informed him, she had no control over Cesare's clients and friends. Had not Cesare proved repeatedly over the years that Mussolini could trust him? In fact, by associating with non-Fascists, Cesare influenced many in/favor/of/Mussolini./And/if/Margherita invited even anti-Fascists to her salon, did he really think that she would be swayed by their opinions? She had a life that extended beyond Mussolini's world and she would not choose her friends and artistic protégés simply on the basis of their politics. If she was to write, if she was to lead a life of dignity, she must have freedom. He had her body and her heart but she must retain control over her mind and her soul. She let him know that his insane jealousy, and his abuse of Cesare, were causing her problems even with Amedeo and Fiammetta.

His behavior, she continued, made her worry about his health. Only severe fatigue and anxiety could explain his actions. She had sacrificed a great deal for Mussolini. She had never once failed to support him, even in his darkest hours of defeat and despair. Did that not prove her boundless love? She, too, wished they could live as man and wife in Rome. But just as his destiny tied him to the capital, her fate chained her to Milan. They must accept that as the price for their love and the fulfillment of their dreams.[30]

Mussolini must have been responsive to Margherita's arguments. She wrote two particularly worshipful articles about him for *Il Popolo d'Italia* in late February and late March to assuage his pride. Margherita had won the struggle, temporarily. She continued to invite whom she pleased to her salon, she resumed her travels (including her postponed trip to Tunisia with Amedeo), her artistic activities expanded even further, and she continued to live with Cesare in Milan.

Tired of the clandestine evening rendezvous, and the constant problems Mussolini had in trying to sneak away from his assistants, she insisted that Mussolini move out of the Grand Hotel and into an apartment, where they could meet easily and privately. She issued him an ultimatum, while simultaneously pleading coyly that either an entire palace or a tiny student attic would do, as long as she could be in his arms behind closed doors.[31]

In March 1923 Mussolini announced that he was taking an apartment in the center of Rome. Margherita had found a large but somewhat dingy apartment for him in the Palazzo Tittoni, located near the Piazza Barberini, the center of Rome's elegant district of expensive shops and luxury hotels. The flat's owner, a wealthy businessman named Baron Alberto Fassini, agreed to rent Mussolini the top floor of his own duplex. Because Mussolini's quarters had no kitchen of their own, his meals were prepared by Fassini's cook and sent upstairs. The bedroom was a gloomy place done in red and black with red carpet. The sitting room contained a piano and a table that held several violins, while the wall bore an enormous Roman eagle with stretched wings. The entire apartment, recalled Paolo Monelli, "was always filled with a strong smell of cheap eau-de-cologne, which Mussolini often used when he had not the time or the inclination to wash."[32]

Margherita also found Mussolini an energetic housekeeper named Cesira Carocci, who had once worked for Gabriele D'Annunzio. Tall and thin, with short-cropped hair, Cesira was a rough and tyrannical woman known affectionately to those close to Mussolini as *la ruffiana*, "the procuress." It was whispered that she helped Mussolini arrange his meetings with female friends. Cesira worshipped the premier, and was unaccustomed to the ways of high society. Her crude wit and country manners caused surprised amusement among his guests. Cesira was also devoted to Margherita, who no doubt wanted to plant a trustworthy confidante close to Mussolini in order to be apprised of his comings and goings.[33]

One afternoon, shortly after Cesira came to the Palazzo Tittoni, she walked into the dining room to serve Mussolini lunch. To her great surprise he was no longer there. A moment later, she heard him moaning and discovered him stretched out across two chairs under the table, holding his stomach and writhing in pain. The incident proved to be the first attack of a recurrent digestive problem that was to plague Mussolini all his life, especially during periods of stress.[34]

Mussolini made little time for relaxation. He shied away from most of the social invitations that began to crowd his calendar, preferring to entertain a handful of guests at home in the evenings. People were anxious to meet the new prime minister—and the famous young lion cub he had been given by an admiring circus owner. Mussolini thought the lion was a wonderful symbol of the aggressive attitudes he wanted to infuse into the country, and he named it Italia. He kept the lion for many months in his apartment and roughhoused with it on the floor of the living room. Italia refused to respect the prime minister's status, frequently dirtying the rugs. Fiammetta, then in her early teens, recalled, "For me and my mother that lion meant only a tremendous stench, such that all the rooms in Via Rasella smelled like a circus." Mussolini was finally persuaded to donate the lion to the Rome zoo, where he continued to visit it.[35]

By 1923, it was an open secret among government officials and high society that Mussolini and Margherita were lovers. Still, it was unwise to speak too openly about the prime minister and his lover. That November, Prezzolini and Giuseppe Ungaretti had too much wine in a Roman trattoria. Ungaretti began to voice obscene comments about the couple a bit too loudly. Prezzolini recovered his wits enough to stifle the drunken poet before the police came for them. Even more widely known was the fact that she played the role of intellectual mentor and cultural adviser to him.

Thomas B. Morgan, an American journalist in Rome who came to know Margherita intimately, put it this way:

> There was an unavoidable suspension when he was called to Rome to head the government but the enormity of the new vista opening before him created such stupendous joy that the forced separation was a minor inconvenience. Both were joyous. He gloried in his power. She, recognized by his lieutenants as *l'ispiratrice,* basked in his reflected glory, satisfied to meditate that she had been a stimulation to a superman and inwardly thinking that he was partly her own creation.[36]

One day, toward the end of her life, Margherita confided to her granddaughter, Magalì: "The only two men I ever loved were your grandfather and Mussolini." Her letters offer vivid evidence of the passion she bore for him. Mussolini's personal reserve, and his sense of dignity, confined his displays of affection toward Margherita to their private moments. Only a few of his hundreds of personal letters to Margherita have come to light, but these few leave no doubt as to his devotion and ardor.[37]

But the disparities in their social origins, educations, incomes, and marriages brought additional strains to their relationship. After Mussolini became prime minister, the complications that arose placed even greater burdens on the ties between them. Mussolini had long depended on Margherita and Cesare's generosity. Because of the chronic financial problems of *Il Popolo d'Italia,* he had to turn to the Sarfattis to entertain his associates and to pay for his flying and fencing lessons and his few luxuries, such as a red four-cylinder Alfa Romeo sports car he acquired in the summer of 1921. Yet Margherita's attachment to money repelled him; whether he also resented being indebted to her is unknown.[38]

Perhaps the most peculiar facet of the relationship between Margherita and Mussolini was its nonexclusive nature. Mussolini was no more faithful to Margherita than he was to Rachele; Margherita heard about many of his affairs from the housekeeper, Cesira. To some extent, Margherita seems to have considered his voracious sexual appetite a sign of health. But when Mussolini flirted with other women in her presence, Margherita would fly into a rage. Sometimes the household help would be attracted by the noise of their arguments. If a servant entered the room, Margherita and Mussolini would continue their quarrel in French.[39]

Margherita was probably not aware of the full extent of Mussolini's sexual adventures. In 1918, at the time when he and Margherita were falling most deeply in love, Mussolini began a relationship with Bianca Veneziana, who bore him a son, Glauco. Their affair lasted for years. In the spring of 1921, while he and Margherita were working side by side on his successful electoral campaign, Mussolini seduced Angela Curti Cucciati, who bore him a daughter, Elena, shortly before the March on Rome. While they parted in late 1922, Mussolini and Angela resumed their affair in 1929. These were just a few of his long-lived sexual relationships, joining others that spanned many years.[40]

Mussolini and Rachele continued to maintain a conjugal relationship. After Bruno was born in April 1918, they had another boy, Romano, in September 1927 and their fifth and last child, a girl, Anna Maria, in September 1929. But Mussolini's infidelities provoked Rachele into taking the railroad stationmaster of Forlì as her lover. Thanks to the Fascist regime's surveillance system, Rachele's letters to the man were intercepted and brought to Mussolini. Mussolini found the matter entertaining and even showed Rachele's letters to his associates. Margherita was astonished by his indecent amusement. When Augusto Turati, then secretary of the Fascist party, learned of Rachele's adultery, he had the stationmaster severely beaten by Blackshirts.[41]

Mussolini exhibited many symptoms of pathological narcissism and megalomania. The psychological weaknesses that Angelica Balabanoff and Leda Rafanelli had observed in him before World War I seem to have been heightened rather than mitigated by his later accomplishments. The need to prove himself grew more insistent with each triumph. Linked to this aspect of his personality was his sense that the rules of ordinary human behavior simply did not apply to him. His profound insecurity may have been his chief motivation in seeking power. It seems to have prevented him from forming close friendships with men. Hence he sought intimacy with women, whom he found less threatening. Even then he resented their efforts to engage him emotionally.[42]

After Mussolini achieved power, his image as a superman attracted large numbers of women. He received a huge volume of mail from feminine admirers. Once his stomach problems forced him to forsake cigarettes, alcohol, and coffee after the spring of 1925, promiscuity became his only release for anxiety and tension. The members of Mussolini's private secretariat selected those letters written by women unknown to him. The letters were then turned over to a police unit to identify correspondents who were not security risks. These women were contacted, and one was escorted into Mussolini's office almost every workday afternoon for a period of nearly twenty years.[43]

Margherita also appears to have had her own love affairs in the twenties and thirties. None of them can be described with certainty. But from gossip and police reports of the time, from hints in her letters, and from what Margherita told her friend Sergio Marzorati in her old age, she seems to have had many. Given the information services available to Mussolini, especially after 1925, he had to have known about Margherita's lovers. But Mussolini did not show any jealousy, a sentiment he appears to have lacked in sexual matters. In fact, among all the different aspects of their relationship, sexual matters seem to have caused them the least friction. Nor, after their initial passion slowly cooled, did sex explain their continuing attraction. The pursuit of power seems to have been the strongest bond between them.[44]

At the end of January 1923, Margherita combined a visit to Mussolini in Rome with a public lecture on modern art before the Circolo di Roma. Although the text of her talk, "On the Sources of Modern Art," has not been recovered, it must have been the first extended discussion of her aesthetic ideas in the context of the *Novecento* movement. Years later she told a journalist that it was one of the two most important speeches she ever made. Her audience, she remembered with pride, "had never till then heard such modern plain speaking." She discussed the themes she was writing about at the time, on the French origins of modern art, including the neoclassicists, the realists, and the Post-Impressionists, and the important role played by the Futurists in modernizing Italian culture. After the "anarchy" and the "deconstruction" of these artistic experiments, came the "return to order," and the new search for synthesis, classical values, and the Italian roots of art.[45]

During initial organizational meetings of the *Novecento*, Margherita deliberately kept politics and Fascism out of the discussions. Not that all of the painters would have objected—Mario Sironi was an official illustrator for *Il Popolo d'Italia* and *Gerarchia* and a convinced Fascist, and Achille Funi had been an early supporter of the *Fasci di Combattimento*. In November, only a few days after Mussolini's appointment as prime minister, a number of painters and writers including Sironi, Funi, and Carrà had signed a statement of homage to Mussolini, who they believed would help Italian artists establish their primacy over the rest of the world.[46]

Once Mussolini came to power, Margherita's hesitations disappeared; she tried to use Mussolini's fame to advance the group. The artists had agreed to hold their first collective exhibition in March 1923. At a meeting planning the exhibit Margherita made a surprising announcement—she had succeeded in persuading Mussolini to open the exhibit. She added that she had promised the prime minister the gift of a special portfolio consisting of sketches by each of the seven artists. Dudreville, deeply angered by the announcement, broke the silence:

DUDREVILLE: And who authorized you to extend such an invitation?

MARGHERITA: No one. It was my own idea. Why? Aren't you pleased?

DUDREVILLE: Not at all. And I'm sorry to have to tell you that I will not contribute a sketch of my own.

MARGHERITA: But why not? That's impossible! How can we present an album that I've already promised with only six sketches and without yours?

DUDREVILLE: I'm sorry, but you can give him a bouquet of flowers or whatever else you think appropriate. In fact, I declare here and now that I will not show my work in this exhibit.[47]

The meeting broke down into a heated argument that carried over into subsequent days. Dudreville suspected that Margherita's purpose was to tie the group to the new Fascist government and to have the *Novecento* become something of an official art for the new Fascist state. He recoiled from both possibilities. Bucci backed him up and threatened to withdraw from the group. Margherita expressed surprise that anyone would not want the obvious advantages of a connection with the prime minister. Everyone eventually agreed on a compromise: The exhibition would go forward, but instead of attending the opening ceremonies, Dudreville and Bucci would seat themselves prominently in a public café. Instead of the portfolio, Margherita would present Mussolini with a bouquet.[48]

Mussolini arrived in Milan late on the night of March 25. At 5:00 P.M. the next evening Margherita greeted him at the Galleria Pesaro, along with a group of city officials and invited guests. Margherita showed Mussolini around the exhibit room, providing a running commentary. Pesaro then introduced Mussolini with a few remarks about the *Novecento:* "Your presence here, in this private art gallery, consecrates an event—that is, the baptism of a vision of beauty—whose influence on our art can only be determined by the great judge of time. . . . What the *Novecento* proposes to do is simple and clear: it wants to create a pure Italian art, inspired by its purest sources and freed from all imported isms and influences. . . . This, excellency, is the vision that animates the *Novecento.*"[49]

Mussolini then delivered a brief speech. Margherita had clearly advised Mussolini on the theme of his speech, for it responded directly to the issues that irked Dudreville and Bucci. Mussolini sent an advance copy to Margherita, who made it available to Pesaro and the others. He proclaimed, "He who governs cannot ignore art or the artist. . . . In a country like Italy, a government uninterested in the arts would be deficient. I declare, however, that the idea of fostering anything resembling a state-sponsored art is far from my mind. The state has only one duty: not to undermine art, but to create humane conditions for artists and to encourage them from the artistic and national points of view. It is important that I say that the government over which I have the honor to preside is a sincere friend of art and of the artist."[50]

Mussolini knew many of the *Novecento* artists, having met most of them at Margherita's salon during and immediately after World War I. But it is unlikely that he understood their aesthetic values or Margherita's efforts to put their work in historical or political context. Walking through the Galleria Pesaro with her, he would have seen no direct connection between the paintings and his own political interests. There were no paintings with obvious political allusions, no portraits of Fascist leaders or Blackshirt squads. Instead, he saw rather conventional images that had been part of the pictorial tradition of Western art for millennia: the nude human figure, portraits (none of famous people), landscapes, and still lifes of everyday objects such as vases and fruit.[51]

At least the paintings Mussolini saw at the *Novecento* exhibit looked familiar in a way that Futurist canvases never did, for the *Novecento* artists deliberately adopted the formal language of traditional Western art. Their concern for volume, three-dimensionality, perspective, and clarity of form necessitated the adoption of precise rules. Gino Severini, the expatriate painter who lived in Paris, wrote a treatise on such rules to explain his own work in 1922. Margherita scolded him for abandoning sentiment and emotion for mathematical laws. Nonetheless she admired the controlled, stable world the *Novecento* created. For Giuseppe Prezzolini, the *Novecento* was "the calm after the storm." Their return to order, after the tumult of Futurism and the nonsense of Dada, was something Mussolini could well appreciate, in politics as in art.[52]

The paintings of Ubaldo Oppi convey the subtle sense of irony that first marked the work of the *Novecento* painters. In the *Portrait of His Wife on a Venetian Background* (1921), Oppi used formal techniques to create an essentially realistic work charged with an otherworldly atmosphere—the introspective gaze of a woman preoccupied by unknown thoughts. Laura Oppi stands at the front of the picture plane, one hand resting on her waist and the other on a balustrade. She is, along with a suspended drapery, motionless and stiff, while a sailboat moves along the Grand Canal in the background. Oppi's lines are hard-edged and his colors appear more like enamel than oil.[53]

During the last few days of March, despite his hectic official schedule in Milan, Margherita also arranged for Mussolini to open the sculptor Medardo Rosso's one-man show. Rosso had been largely ignored by Italian critics, although the Futurists acknowledged the importance of his impressionistic work to the avant-garde. Margherita had long believed in his talent. When Rosso finally returned to Italy from a long sojourn in

Paris, she persuaded Mario Buggelli, director of the Bottega di Poesia, to hold the exhibit.

Rosso's jovial, informal manner appealed to Mussolini and the two men seemed comfortable together. As Rosso showed Mussolini around the exhibit, the sculptor suddenly stopped, put his hand on the prime minister's shoulder, and said: "Tell me, Benito, do you still play the violin? It's good for you, it's good for you—it's more important than politics." Mussolini responded with a hearty laugh. Margherita gave the exhibit a long review in *Il Popolo d'Italia* a few days later. At the end of the same article she appended a brief notice on the *Novecento* show—the first modest salvo in her skillfully orchestrated campaign.[54]

The classical element dominated her critical response and informed Margherita's efforts to develop a coherent aesthetic theory for the movement. But in a commentary on the formation of the *Novecento*, Carrà underscored the lack of an articulated program, pointing out that each of the artists had a different experience and style. Margherita recognized the eclectic nature of the *Novecento*. Yet she noted that the seven artists were moving in common toward an "ideal reconstructive synthesis"—a phrase that became the leitmotif of her own critical thinking about the *Novecento*. The twentieth century, she proclaimed, would become "a century of synthesis." She dubbed the *Novecento* painters "revolutionaries of the modern restoration," for she believed that they would restore classical tradition to Italian art.[55] Some critics were already applying the term "neoclassicists" to them, but Margherita rejected the label as misleading, warning against a slavish copying of antique styles and condemning the "frigid mediocrity" of the late eighteenth and early nineteenth century Neoclassical school. "We do not want to imitate the past," she said. "We claim to be giving birth to new forms."[56]

Margherita maintained that the *Novecentisti* did not repudiate modernism. Rather, the restoration of classical art meant "the art of one's own time," the creation of a "modern classicity." She put the issue most succinctly this way: the *Novecento*, she said, "means an historical vision of the present, capable of transporting the nature of contemporary reality to a higher plane." She argued that every vital epoch of history creates its own original form of beauty. The great artist transforms aspects of everyday reality into eternal, transcendent beauty. Even the most brilliant technician, however, cannot achieve great art if his sense of beauty lacks spirituality. To Margherita beauty was more important than bread, because beauty was the expression of morality. From Ruskin she had derived an abiding faith in art's function as a moral guidepost for society.[57]

Margherita's cultural sensibilities led her to abhor the Fascist kitsch that began to appear after Mussolini came to power, such as the plaster busts of the Duce, the terrible portraits of him by amateur artists, and the commercial advertisements boasting the *Fascio Littorio*. Her articles in the 1920s consistently attacked crass efforts to impose the Fascist imprint on popular culture or the fine arts. In an article written on the first anniversary of the March on Rome, Margherita concluded that apart from Wildt's bust of Mussolini and Sironi's political drawings, Fascism had stimulated the "worst taste" possible. Fascism, she admonished, had to act as a broom, sweeping Italy clean of old mentalities, but the new regime had yet to affect Italian aesthetics. "Style," she said, "is a reflection of the spirit of an age." True art is not the "immediate representation" of events—the formal qualities of art, not its subject matter, reflect the age in which it is created. The real Fascist style, she argued, should be austere, powerful, and direct, like Mussolini's prose—"anti-rhetorical," she called it. Hence, the "style of the classic *Novecento*," she claimed, "is Fascist style." That was as far as she was willing to go in defining what she meant by Fascist art.[58]

Mussolini was more than willing to allow Margherita to shape his views about art. Her ideas were clearly in evidence in his address before a national conference of artistic organizations in May 1924. The concepts of "Italy" and "art" could not, he asserted, be separated: "for centuries art was the very Patria." Every "movement of political restoration," Mussolini proclaimed, had its artistic reflection, and Fascism's role was "to restore style to the Italian people." Mussolini assured his audience that the regime was well aware of the importance of culture and artistic education for the "moral elevation" of the nation. Margherita's own version of the same concept was expressed this way: "The word 'art' is for us Italians another name for the Patria."[59]

In innumerable essays written throughout the 1920s, Margherita groped her way toward a remarkable admission: What she considered "Fascist art" was a product *not* of Fascism but of the spirit of the times. "It may possibly be said," she wrote, "that Fascism and this kind of art spring from a common root." Because of this view, she did not perceive of the *Novecento* as the cultural extension of Fascism, but saw Fascism and the *Novecento* as the products of a similar historical experience. She worked to secure Mussolini's blessing for the *Novecento* as the official art not so much of Fascism but of the twentieth century. To her the movement transcended the narrow confines of a political regime—conceivably the *Novecento* could survive Fascism's demise.[60]

Some contemporaries joined Dudreville and Bucci in suspecting that Margherita's purpose was to put the *Novecento* at the service of Mussolini. In December 1922, when the group began to exhibit at the Galleria Pesaro, she had used the Roman military term *maniple* to describe the group, although she deliberately avoided the more obvious and controversial word *fascio.* When the two renegade painters pressed her to open membership in the *Novecento* to others, Margherita objected with the argument that "in small numbers one governs more effectively and more securely. . . . We must serve as guides and impose a particular line of conduct upon all of Italian painting." These were perhaps superficial similarities to Fascism, but together with Margherita's relationship with Mussolini, the Duce's personal appearance at the 1923 opening, and the blindly ambitious manner in which she promoted the movement, it is no wonder that many contemporaries and later critics claimed to see in the *Novecento* an "official" art.[61]

The first public triumph for the *Novecento* came in 1924, when it received an official invitation to present a group exhibit at the Venice Biennale. The *Novecento* exhibit was the first ever mounted at the Biennale by an organized group.[62] Along with this success came a new crisis. Oppi announced that he would not participate, for he had already been invited to hang a one-man show at the Biennale. His colleagues were outraged by what they considered to be Oppi's perfidy, and in June he resigned from the group. For Margherita, Oppi's treason was especially bitter, since the twenty-five canvases he exhibited were of spectacular quality; also his special invitation had been arranged by Ugo Ojetti, the conservative art critic for *Il Corriere della Sera.* Ojetti understood Margherita's influence with Mussolini, and remained on superficially correct terms with her, but he had come to dislike her. Despite Ojetti's sponsorship, Margherita continued to support Oppi's work and even included him in subsequent *Novecento* exhibits. When a scandal threatened Oppi's reputation a few years later—it was discovered that he had copied his *Reclining Nude* from a photograph—Margherita defended him.

The six remaining artists were given a large room in which to hang almost two dozen works.[63] In February 1924, they met to settle details of their appearance in Venice, and select the person who would write the official catalog description of the *Novecento.* After weighing several possibilities, including Ojetti, and "having considered," recalled Pesaro, "the opportunities of the moment," they selected Margherita. Margherita's role in the development of the group had clearly been so controversial that some of its members doubted the desirability of maintaining their relationship with her. Yet her prestige as a critic, her social and financial contacts, and her association with the government were too powerful a combination to resist.

In her catalog introduction to the Biennale show, Margherita explained that although they at first dropped the name *Novecento,* it had stuck because the artists had remained together as a group and were dedicated to the same broad aesthetic ideas. They especially wanted to advance the notion of "pure visibility." She described each of the six painters in turn, and admitted that all were still preoccupied with polishing the technical language of their art, yet each strove in his own way for the same result: "expressions of humanity and limpid beauty."[64]

Funi's *Maternità* (1921), which Margherita bought, is typical of the *Novecento* paintings exhibited at the Venice Biennale. This beautiful painting contains all the formal language of a Renaissance madonna and child. Funi even retained symbolic conventions such as a vase standing on a classical column and a bowl of fruit. Through the window can be seen a traditional perspectival background landscape, here prominently featuring a modern industrial factory. The mother, smiling at the infant in her arms, represents the ideal of motherhood. Only her contemporary hairstyle marks her as a woman of the moment. The extraordinary large, dark eyes of the child stare out at the viewer. There is a disquieting tension caused by the contradiction between the silent, adoring glance of the mother and the knowing precocity of the child. Funi's modern style creates an ironic contrast with the classically serene aspects of the composition. Margherita asserted *Maternità* was "the most beautiful and complete of Funi's paintings." In a later review, she praised it as "a study of the ancient by assimilation but not imitation, a construction without rhetorical emphasis."[65]

Sironi's unique paintings were also exhibited in Venice. As a committed Fascist, Sironi was engaged in the search for an aesthetic suitable to the socially and politically committed artist. Margherita believed him the most original and talented of the *Novecentisti,* an artist whose paintings were virtually a visual manifesto of her doctrine that a "modern classicism" was best suited to the new era. By the time the *Novecento* had been founded, Sironi's stark urban landscapes (begun in 1919) had given way to a series of portraits executed in a classical manner between 1922 and 1925. During the years immediately following the March on Rome, he exhibited only the latter series.[66]

Two of these works, *L'Allieva* (*The Pupil*) and *L'Architetto* (*The Architect*), were hung at the Venice Biennale. *L'Allieva* shows a seated woman in a studio, against a stark masonry wall and framed by props that include a plaster cast, a vase, and drawing instruments. The contemplative figure combines the classical theme of the muse with a statement about the need for disciplined creativity. While the woman is dressed in black, the man in *L'Architetto* wears an equally stark white gown; he stands surrounded by arches and plinths, with a vase—a reference to pure classical form—also in evidence. The portraits reveal the sense of inner disquiet also seen in the work of Sironi's colleagues, and a darker melancholy enhanced by his somber style.

Sironi conceived of these paintings as emblematic representations of artistic and architectural skills, stressing tradition, craftsmanship, and classical training. His symbols of architecture, and the architectonic quality of his canvases, are no accident—the idea of construction pervaded Fascist rhetoric. In Mussolini's speeches and Margherita's articles, the Romans were described as the great builders of the ancient world. The motif of solid, deliberate construction was part of the "restoration" that Margherita called for in the wake of the "anarchic" destruction wrought by the prewar artistic avant-garde. For Sironi, it was a symbol of Fascism's determination to build a new Italian society.

At the official opening of the Biennale, on April 26, 1924, two events took place that suggested the difficulties that lay ahead for the *Novecento*. While on his way into the Italian pavilion that morning, Dudreville encountered Pesaro and handed him a letter withdrawing from the group. Pesaro convinced him to hold off a few days, until they were able to reassemble in Milan.

A short while later, inside the main hall, Dudreville and Bucci spotted Marinetti. Marinetti appeared red-faced and grim, but Dudreville, preoccupied with the ceremonies that were about to begin, thought little of it. Giovanni Gentile, minister of education and Fascism's most eminent philosopher, was introducing King Vittorio Emanuele III, who was to open the exhibit. Gentile was droning on at length, when suddenly a strident voice shouted through the hall, "Down with backward-looking Venice!"[67]

Many in the audience, including the king, thought that an assassination attempt was being made. It turned out to be Marinetti protesting that once again the Futurists were not represented in the Biennale. Many of the *Novecentisti* had once been Futurists, so their organized rejection of Futurism was particularly galling to Marinetti. He had failed to convince the Duce to make Futurism the official art of Fascism, and he feared that the Futurists would become a marginal group in a regime that favored the *Novecento*.[68] After the incident, Margherita escorted the king through the *Novecento* rooms, bemused by his "courteous indifference."

In her review of the Biennale, "Where Italian Art Is Heading," Margherita expressed sympathy for Marinetti, the leader of the "Futurism that was." While pointing out that she too had once protested the Biennale's exclusion of modern Italian art, she felt Marinetti's gesture was now inappropriate. Futurism had played a legitimate role in modernizing Italian culture, but it was a historical phenomenon, to be respected but surpassed. She claimed the Biennale represented a triumph of the "new Italian art."[69]

Despite the recognition brought to it by the Biennale, the *Novecento* soon collapsed because of internal pressures. At the end of April, a few days after the opening in Venice, Lino Pesaro met with the six painters. He announced that for reasons that he could not divulge, he was withdrawing from the agreement he had made with them. Within a short time Dudreville, Bucci, and Malerba also resigned. The alacrity of the four resignations suggests that Pesaro, Dudreville, Bucci, and Malerba met privately to plan this action because of Dudreville's threatened defection. If so, they apparently decided it was in their best interests to keep the Biennale opening free of scandal, and afterward abandon the group. The fact that the three remaining members—Sironi, Funi, and Marussig—were Margherita's closest supporters in the group suggests that Pesaro's decision had been influenced by his hostile feelings toward her.[70]

News of the resignations was dispiriting to Margherita. From the debates about the future of art that had dominated the Wednesday gatherings at the Sarfatti salon, she had helped to launch a movement quickly and successfully. No sooner had she fulfilled her own obligations to the group than they disbanded. Unfortunately, her own obsessive ambition was the force that drove away the members of the movement as surely as it had once brought them together.

19

A Corpse Between His Feet

Margherita's most important service to Mussolini in the first years of his regime was her work as editor of *Gerarchia. Gerarchia* never became a journal of intellectual debate. *Critica Fascista,* a controversial review directed by Giuseppe Bottai, performed that function for Fascist intellectuals. (Bottai was a brilliant and relatively liberal Fascist who later became minister of corporations and then minister of education.) Margherita's magazine instead presented an "orthodox" Fascism, which essentially reflected Mussolini's ideas of the moment. Because readers recognized *Gerarchia* as the semi-official voice of the Fascist regime, it sold well, reaching a circulation of seventeen thousand by the late 1920s.[1]

For three years Margherita ran *Gerarchia* from Milan; its editorial office was housed in the same building as *Il Popolo d'Italia.* Before Mussolini's departure for Rome in October 1922, they had produced each issue together. Thereafter she obtained his approval for articles every month by phone. Early in 1924, when Mussolini decided that his position as prime minister was incompatible with legal responsibility for the journal, Margherita assumed liability for its content, while his name remained on the masthead as director.

Margherita served Mussolini in other ways, as well. When she finally won Mussolini's grudging permission to travel to Tunisia in the spring of 1923, she promised to study the conditions among the Italians living there and write a book detailing her findings. All this, she assured him, would be useful to the government's foreign policy. Tunisia lay a short distance across the Mediterranean from Sicily. Though it had been technically a part of the Ottoman Empire in the nineteenth century, the French had penetrated the region and in 1881 proclaimed a protectorate over it. The Italian government had its own designs on Tunisia; it protested but did nothing.

There were over 110,000 Italians there, mostly agricultural workers, at the time of Margherita's visit. Italian immigrants were a constant point of friction in relations between France and Italy until 1896, when the two countries worked out a compromise. Italians in Tunisia were permitted to keep their Italian status and establish their own schools and other institutions. In September 1918, when it became clear that Germany had lost World War I and Italian aid was no longer crucial to French survival, France reneged on the 1896 agreement. Thereafter, France did everything it could to force Italian immigrants to abandon their nationality.[2] Mussolini had recently demanded that the French restore Italian autonomy in Tunisia, and was interested in what Margherita's personal perspective on the situation might be.

Accompanied by Amedeo, Margherita left for Tunisia in May of 1923. For two weeks she traveled tirelessly, inspecting schools and living conditions and interviewing members of the Italian community. She visited mosques and climbed through the Punic and Roman ruins. She traveled overnight by rail and camel to the oasis of Tozeur, a place that seemed to her like "the end of the earth." Deep in the Sahara, she came upon the remains of a vast Roman acropolis. "How many years ago were these things made?" asked her Arab guide, who did not know their history. "They were built six hundred years before your Prophet was born," she replied proudly through her interpreter. "Rome made them. I am of that same stock. *Ben Roma* ('Child of Rome')".[3]

That summer she worked at Il Soldo on a pithy account of her exotic voyage. *Tunisiaca* (*Things Tunisian*) proved to be one of her most famous books. Her vivid impressions of the ancient Roman presence in the North African desert, and the fervor with which she presented the Italian position in Tunisia, had a powerful impact on Italian public opinion. While Margherita was writing, Mussolini raised the Tunisian question again with France. He contributed a preface to *Tunisiaca,* which added to the book's success. His pseudonym "Latinus" fooled no one. Margherita had the preface published in *Gerarchia* before the book even appeared in print, in February 1924.[4] The book was one of the first popular works to fuel Fascist ambitions for empire in Africa.[5]

During Margherita's trip to North Africa, Cesare had remained at home in Milan. He was preoccupied with his new duties as president of the Cassa di Risparmio delle Province Lombarde (Lombard Provinces Savings Bank), the largest and most important credit institution in Italy. The king appointed Cesare to the position in July 1923, after Mussolini nominated him. Cesare's Socialist past and lack of banking experience made him an unlikely president. Public reaction was predictably cruel—Filippo Turati repeated a crude joke of the time that Mussolini had managed to stick his penis even into the *Cassa di Risparmio.*[6]

By the time Mussolini had become prime minister, virtually all Italy knew about Margherita and Mussolini; late that year even Margherita's quiet son Amedeo confronted her about the affair. Cesare said nothing.[7] Yet if Margherita's relationship with Mussolini wounded him, he suffered the loss of Roberto even more deeply. The writer Alfredo Panzini remembered a moment that revealed how close to the surface Cesare's pain actually was. On January 5, 1924, while visiting Rome on bank business, Cesare dropped in unexpectedly to see his old friend. After an evening of high-spirited banter and laughter, they left the apartment to go out to dinner. Cesare stopped suddenly in a corner near the door. Panzini had hung some personal mementoes there, including a photograph of Roberto in his army uniform. Cesare looked at the photo, and then read a postcard that the young soldier had sent from the front, and finally the telegram from Ada Negri announcing Roberto's death. Cesare pulled a large white handkerchief out of his pocket and passed it over his eyes. "It was only then that I noticed," recalled Panzini, "that ever since that year 1918, that joyous man had always dressed in black."[8]

Panzini never saw his old friend again. On January 18, while riding in a first-class carriage on the train back to Milan from Rome, Cesare was seized with an excruciating pain in his lower abdomen. Physicians later diagnosed an inoperable appendicitis. Cesare held out for five days, but on January 23 his physical strength and his spirit flagged. "It's over," he murmured. Margherita must have let Mussolini know that the end was near, for he sent Cesare a telegram that evening—"I will never forget those distant days, when it took some courage to defend me." At five in the morning Cesare sank into a coma, and within hours he was dead. Margherita, Amedeo, and Fiammetta, together with Ada Negri and one of Cesare's sisters, were at his bedside.[9]

The news of Cesare's death spread quickly. That afternoon the mayor of Milan called on Margherita, and hundreds of telegrams flooded the apartment from prominent figures in politics, finance, and the arts. On Saturday, January 26, the day of the funeral, cars carrying mourners and flowers lined the entire length of the Corso Venezia. After sunset, the family and a few intimates led a procession by torchlight to the grave site in the Jewish section of the cemetery. His white marble tombstone, designed by Adolfo Wildt, bore a bronze menorah. When Gabriele D'Annunzio heard the news, he sent Margherita a beautiful bracelet of moonstones in memory of his boyhood friend.[10]

At the time of Cesare's death Mussolini was preoccupied with a new election campaign. Throughout 1923, he had been proclaiming his desire for stability in politics. Secretly he planned to extend his authority beyond legal limits, planning to remain in power for thirty years. Two conditions frustrated him: the political constraints imposed on him by a coalition cabinet, and a parliament controlled by his bitterest enemies. Out of 535 seats in the Chamber of Deputies, the Socialists held 156 and the Popolari 100, while his own Fascists had only 35.[11]

Mussolini had proposed a majority electoral bill—called the Acerbo Law, after its official sponsor, Giacomo Acerbo—designed to overcome the paralysis in Parliament. This measure called for the electoral list winning the largest number of popular votes to take two thirds of all the seats in the Chamber. The remaining seats were to be divided proportionally among the other parties. Mussolini's political opponents bitterly opposed the reform. Many of the leading Liberal statesmen, however, gave the Acerbo Law their endorsement. The bill passed the Chamber on July 15, 1923.

In January 1924, two days after Cesare's death, Mussolini dissolved Parliament and ordered elections for April. While careful to appear moderate and reasonable in public, he encouraged his extremist followers to commit acts of violence to intimidate and silence the opposition. In February 1924 Mussolini and other Fascists officials met with Amerigo Dumini. Mussolini had previously sent Dumini and Albino Volpi, both former Blackshirt leaders and professional gangsters, to France to intimidate exiled anti-Fascists. Dumini boasted of having committed twelve murders. Mussolini authorized Dumini to take charge of a Cheka, a secret squad of toughs named after the Soviet secret police, to be used against the opposition.[12] They launched a systematic campaign of coercion against newspaper editors and politicians. Fascist agents ransacked the house of former prime minister Francesco Nitti, who had voted consistently against Mussolini in Parliament. They physically assaulted Socialist deputy Giacomo Matteotti, Turati's thirty-nine-year-old protégé, and the Liberal Giovanni Amendola.[13]

Mussolini had no intention of giving up power, even if he lost the election. "No government in history has ever been based exclusively on popular consensus," he had written in *Gerarchia,* in March 1923, "which is as mutable as the sands of the seashore. . . . Be it known then, once and for all, that Fascism recognizes no idols, worships no fetishes. It has already trampled, and if need be will step quietly once again, over the more or less putrid body of the Goddess Liberty." Margherita defended his use of violence. She believed that "the man who is afire with a great conception is apt to be violent in his attitude towards all opposition. But for this weakness, he would not be strong."[14]

Mussolini selected a list of 350 candidates to run on the Fascist ticket. Vittorio Emanuele Orlando joined the list, the Liberal philosopher Benedetto Croce urged voters to support it, and Giolitti, running on a separate list, helped by refusing to speak against Mussolini. Within a few months all of these men would regret their support for him. Dumini and Volpi unleashed their Cheka against anti-Fascists, and in many districts prevented candidates from even holding meetings. The Fascists injured or killed hundreds of people. Mussolini publicly insisted that he knew nothing of the violence. His strategy worked. The Fascists won 65 percent of the vote, and thus claimed 374 of the seats in the Chamber of Deputies. The opposition held only some 180 seats. The day after the election, Margherita accompanied her victorious and jubilant lover from Milan back to Rome.[15]

Mussolini was determined to restore the country's stability and install Fascism permanently. Only militant anti-Fascists stood in the way. In May, before the new Parliament convened, Mussolini brought the Cheka to Rome in order to intimidate the opposition deputies in the Chamber. Cesare Rossi, his press secretary, financed them from a secret payroll. Their principal target was Giacomo Matteotti, a courageous Socialist deputy who had repeatedly spoken out against Fascist violence.[16]

On May 30, 1924, Matteotti rose in the Chamber of Deputies, now crowded with Fascists, to denounce the election fraud. His efforts to present statistical evidence of government-sponsored violence were shouted down by Fascists. Even Mussolini, unable to contain his temper, interrupted his speeches with intimidating remarks. Rossi ordered all Fascist newspapers to launch attacks against Matteotti. On June 1, Mussolini wrote an unsigned article saying that Matteotti's charges "deserve a more concrete reply."[17] Mussolini commented in anger more than once that opposition leaders needed to be shot in the back. In private, close associates heard him speak of "execution squads" and the need to "get rid" of Matteotti. One of these associates was Giovanni Marinelli, a founding member of the Fascist movement and now the Party's administrative secretary. An accountant by profession, Marinelli was a fanatical Fascist, blindly loyal to the Duce. He interpreted Mussolini's intemperate outbursts as authorization for murder.

As Matteotti left for Parliament on the afternoon of June 10, he was attacked by five men, including Volpi, and forced into a car driven by Dumini. As they drove off, Matteotti put up a terrific struggle. Volpi stabbed him to death, and his body was buried in a ditch on the outskirts of Rome. After dropping his accomplices off in Rome, Dumini drove back to the courtyard of the Ministry of Interior. He left Volpi there to guard the car for the night.

The next morning Dumini moved the car to a garage and attempted to clean up the blood from the rear seat. He delivered Matteotti's briefcase to Marinelli, who rushed immediately to Mussolini's office. Dumini received a sum of cash to be used by the other kidnappers to go into hiding and then took Matteotti's bloodstained passport case to one of the prime minister's private secretaries, Arturo Fasciolo. When he received it from Fasciolo, Mussolini shoved it into his desk drawer.

According to his later testimony, Cesare Rossi first heard about the murder from Fasciolo on the morning of July 11. Immediately guessing the author of the crime, Rossi sought out Marinelli. While Rossi shouted, "Insanity! Insanity!," Marinelli tried to calm the agitated press secretary. "Be careful," warned Marinelli, "that your alarmist tendencies don't put the Duce's head on the block! We'll take care of everything. Just don't lose control of yourself." Rossi tried unsuccessfully to see Mussolini, who was in conference with the French ambassador.[18]

These sordid events came as a surprise to Margherita, who had been traveling in Spain. After Cesare's death, Margherita had had to manage a series of family medical crises. Mussolini voiced concern at the toll these events had on her. "I'm an expert wizard," he told her tenderly, "and you are in a black depression." He suggested she spend some time recuperating in Morocco, where she could relax in the warm climate. As they discussed the possibility, Mussolini had the idea that she could write a series of books of historical and artistic impressions for each region along the coast of North Africa, as she had done for Tunisia.

Always eager to travel, Margherita took Mussolini's advice. She left Italy in May, after the elections, but did not get very far. In Spain she spent some time studying the recently installed military dictatorship of General Miguel Primo de Rivera, and attended a bullfight, but she severely fractured her leg in an accidental fall. She spent several weeks in painful recovery, and returned to Italy on a stretcher, arriving at Genoa on June 12.[19]

The friends who met Margherita and accompanied her to Milan "enveloped me in vague, uncertain, and whispered rumors of strange events. One of the youngest deputies of the Socialist Party, the elegant and talented Giacomo Matteotti, seemed to have disappeared. . . . It was as if the earth had opened up and swallowed him." Margherita had never met Matteotti, but she recalled Cesare had spoken of him with respect. She knew that he had been a determined foe of Fascism.[20]

By the time Margherita returned, Mussolini knew most of the details of the murder. From the first he decided that he had to conceal his own ties to the criminals and provide the public with appropriate scapegoats. When Matteotti's wife reported her husband missing, Mussolini publicly denied any knowledge of his disappearance. On the day Margherita arrived in Genoa, he told Parliament that he suspected foul play, but no evidence of a crime had come to light. Margherita remembered that his statements to the Chamber of Deputies made him appear "weak, confused, and contrite." At the time Mussolini already knew that the abduction car had been found and traced to the killers. That night, public-security agents monitoring a telephone tap recorded a guarded conversation between Rachele and him. He urged her to leave Milan quickly and go to their country place at Carpena, near Forlì. "Just like that, all of a sudden? . . . The weather's not even hot yet," she asked in surprise. "But," he warned, "it may heat up suddenly!"[21]

Margherita must have put through a phone call to Rome after returning home. Mussolini used the German word *spurlos!* meaning "without a trace," as he explained the Matteotti situation. "I can never forget," Margherita confessed decades later, "the tone of admiration, distasteful to me, with which Mussolini said it:—'Spurlos.'" But he swore privately to Margherita that he had known nothing about the plot against Matteotti. "It was," he insisted, "a plot against me, the work of one of my diabolical enemies. . . . I held all of Italy in my hands, with the approval of the entire world. No! The plot against Matteotti was the work of a demon. . . ." He told the Fascist journalist Paolo Orano at the time, "If they have flung a corpse between my feet in order to get me to give up power, they've made a mistake."[22]

What did Margherita know about the murder? More than half a century after the events, members of her family still expressed concern over that question. She suspected that Mussolini was more deeply involved in Matteotti's disappearance than he acknowledged. Initially he admitted only to having contributed to the crime by fostering violence against the opposition. Later he told her more, for in the recollections she wrote after Mussolini was dead, she revealed particulars of the abduction and murder that were not yet part of the public record. "My conviction is," she wrote, "that he was informed of the details of the deed after it was too late to intervene."[23]

But other leading Fascists were certain of Mussolini's guilt. De Bono later told Bottai that he had proof that Mussolini had ordered Matteotti's murder. Bottai himself became convinced that Mussolini had arranged for Matteotti to disappear, but in a manner that would allow the prime minister to disguise his involvement in the crime.

Regardless of her suspicions, Margherita was determined to stand by Mussolini, realizing that their future depended on the outcome. In June she produced an unsigned editorial for *Gerarchia* claiming that the murder was the work of extremist Fascist delinquents, and suggesting that Mussolini would lead Fascism back to a moderate position. Otherwise she kept a low profile, publishing only a few articles during the crisis, editing *Gerarchia,* and making no public appearances. Her decision to remain behind the scenes must have been a deliberate effort to protect herself should Mussolini fall. Her real role in the Matteotti crisis was played out in private, while she kept in contact with Mussolini on a daily basis, urging him to exercise caution and remain calm.[24]

As Mussolini found himself increasingly isolated, he relied heavily on Margherita's advice and comfort. So shaken was Mussolini that he contemplated resigning, and Margherita wondered at times whether he could withstand the pressure. Considering Mussolini's superstitious nature, Margherita encouraged him to consult Dante's *Divine Comedy,* as she herself had begun to do at critical moments in her life. He told one visitor that he had been reading selections from Dante every morning.[25]

Mussolini turned also to other women for support and comfort. In tears he told his troubles to the writer Matilda Serao, who visited him shortly after the murder and brought him a large coral horn she claimed held magic properties. At the end of June he wrote to Ada Negri, asking, "Is there still anyone who will not betray me? I almost don't believe there is." Rachele recalled years later that her husband was fraught with worry and nervous tension during those months. His sister, Edvige, remembered his depression and the excruciating pain caused by his recurring stomach problems. Navarra, his valet, noted that Mussolini's previously crowded outer office was now "like a tomb." Mussolini resented this abandonment so bitterly that he mentioned it in a public speech.[26]

Mussolini suspended Parliament, mobilized the Fascist Militia, and had Dumini arrested. He sent word that Cesare Rossi should submit his resignation as press secretary because Dumini had officially been on his payroll. Rossi finally got to see Mussolini on June 14. "It is," said the prime minister, "a tactical necessity of the moment." Rossi pounded his fist on Mussolini's desk. "This crime began at this desk and you must take the responsibility."[27]

But Mussolini successfully covered his involvement. Chief of Police General Emilio De Bono took personal charge of the official investigation, refusing for a week to turn over the case to the magistrates as required by law. In the meantime important evidence disappeared and some of the Cheka members escaped. Dumini, Marinelli, and Rossi were arrested. But Dumini was held without trial until 1926, and Marinelli and Rossi were let off "for lack of evidence." Rossi then fled to France. As a result of the public outcry, Mussolini dismissed De Bono but otherwise Mussolini made few concessions.[28] The anti-Fascist opposition—Socialists, Popolari, and some Liberals—clamored for his resignation and withdrew from Parliament. Their action deliberately recalled a gesture of popular discontent from 2,400 years before, when the Roman Plebeians had left the city in protest against the Patricians. Only the refusal of the Vatican and Giolitti to support the boycott kept Mussolini in office.[29]

From June 24 to 26, the Senate debated a vote of no confidence in Mussolini's government, but only 21 members voted against him, as opposed to 225 votes in his favor. Since the beginning of the crisis, King Vittorio Emanuele III had respected the continuing conservative support for Mussolini. The Senate vote reinforced his unwillingness to take action.[30]

At the time there was speculation that the king failed to dismiss Mussolini because the murder had kept Matteotti from exposing royal involvement in secret financial corruption. American petroleum interests had been competing for the right to explore for oil in Italy, and the government awarded the concession to the Sinclair Exploration Company. There is evidence to suggest that in order to ensure his compliance, Sinclair Oil secretly transferred a large packet of stocks to the king. Mussolini may have been unaware of Vittorio Emanuele's possible personal interest in the concession. Harold Nicolson of the British Foreign Office believed the Duce suspected some of his Fascist followers were involved. In March, a month before the contract was signed, Mussolini told Sinclair's representative that the agreement would be consummated only after the parliamentary elections.[31]

But Matteotti may have been on the verge of exposing both Mussolini and Vittorio Emanuele's involvement with Sinclair Oil. In a secret account of the murder, written in 1933 and deposited with American attorneys to insure his life, Dumini claimed that Matteotti had been preparing to expose "a certain affair involving oil and stock," possibly involving Mussolini's brother, Arnaldo. The fact that Marinelli ordered Dumini to bring him all the documents in Matteotti's possession—which Dumini later described as "a thick briefcase filled with papers"—lends credence to the idea. Years later, toward the end of World War II, Cesare Rossi told an Allied officer that Mussolini had received a million-dollar bribe from Sinclair.[32]

Meanwhile, trouble had developed within the Fascist party. Opportunists began deserting Mussolini. Roberto Farinacci pressed Mussolini to shoot "a few thousand people" to end the problem. On August 4, Mussolini privately lectured the *squadristi* on the need for obedience to his cautious policies. He assured them that he was capable of any necessary violence—"the cruelty," he called it, "of the surgeon."[33]

The discovery of Matteotti's body on August 16 led to a renewed clamor for Mussolini's dismissal. Emboldened anti-Fascists antagonized the *squadristi;* while *Il Popolo d'Italia* demanded discipline and order, incidents of Fascist violence occurred throughout the country at opposition demonstrations. Mussolini's regime grew still more unstable.

Margherita's greatest concern was that Mussolini would give in to the intransigents and provoke a crisis from which he could not recover. Margherita tried to counter the influence of Farinacci and Costanzo Ciano, an admiral in the Italian Navy and minister of post and telegraph, who daily tried to incite Mussolini to violent action.[34] The following excerpt from a telephone conversation reveals Mussolini's desperate state of mind and her strategy:

MARGHERITA: How are you?

MUSSOLINI: How do you expect me to be, Vela mia!

MARGHERITA: Anything new?

MUSSOLINI: Nothing . . . by now, I'm not surprised at anything, not even the most absurd, the most infamous actions. . . . The thing that upsets me the most is that I don't know what my so-called friends are thinking—they who've betrayed me

MARGHERITA: You'll see, everything will work out; but I beg you to remain calm, not to let your temper run amok. Don't get carried away by your anger.

MUSSOLINI: It's not a question of temper, because I don't hate anyone, I don't hold any rancor! Unfortunately, fate has dealt its card in favor of my enemies, and if I lose the game, which is almost certain, there's not even the possibility of saving face!

MARGHERITA: But you've always shown yourself to be a good player, and you know that many games which seem lost at the start wind up turning themselves around at the end, at the last hand. . . .

MUSSOLINI: Yes, what you say about card games is in a certain way true; but the decision always depends, for the most part, on the ability of the players, and in this case my enemies are good players, and they're supported by those who have betrayed me.

MARGHERITA: You'll take care of them later!

MUSSOLINI: The important thing is to overcome this painful ordeal, something which is a lot more important than me. For now, we must deal with the opposition, whose actions are flanked by the press, which has unleased an all-out, decisive attack. Want to see who my friends are? Here's the proof: even the long lines of adulators and petitioners in my antechamber have come to an end![35]

Although Mussolini had succeeded in preventing the conservative ministers in his Cabinet from resigning, Liberal leaders explored the possibilities of forming a coalition behind a new government. On November 12, when the Chamber of Deputies reopened, Giolitti refused to attend, and a few days later hinted that he had joined the opposition. In the debates on the government's programs that followed, Giolitti joined an increasing number of deputies who voted no, while Orlando abstained. In mid-December, Orlando addressed an appeal to the king from the floor of the Chamber to "take the situation in hand."[36]

By the end of November, rumors circulated wildly that Mussolini was planning to sell out the Fascists in order to stay in office. On December 1, he appointed General Asclepia Gandolfo, a regular army general, commander of the Fascist Militia, but other army generals pressed for the total suppression of the Militia. The resulting tensions prompted some desperate Militia consuls, who regarded Italo Balbo as their leader, to plot a conspiracy to overthrow Mussolini. The impatience of the extremists was further heightened by signals from the royal palace that the king was actually contemplating the formation of a government of "national concentration," with or without Mussolini.[37]

As Mussolini began showing signs of making further concessions to the Liberals and the moderate political forces in Parliament, Farinacci's followers and the Militia consuls joined forces. On December 24 their spokesman, Curzio Malaparte, published a violently worded challenge titled "Fascism Against Mussolini?" He warned Mussolini that his only real base of support lay with the provincial *squadristi* and their call for Fascist revolution. Malaparte denounced the government's arrest of Matteotti's killers as a betrayal of loyal Fascists, and issued an ultimatum: "Either all of us in jail, or none of us." To add to Mussolini's difficulties, on December 27 the anti-Fascist newspaper *Il Mondo* published a memorandum in which Cesare Rossi, now hiding in France, implicated Mussolini in the Matteotti murder. Even Luigi Albertini, the editor of *Il Corriere della Sera,* suggested that Mussolini resign.[38]

Mussolini summoned the consuls of the Fascist Militia to Rome. He hoped to impress on them his determination that they remain under his orders, and at the same time pull them away from their power centers in the provinces. Having reached the limits of their patience, the exasperated *squadristi* decided to confront Mussolini in person.

At noon on December 31, thirty-three Militia consuls stormed into Palazzo Chigi and demanded to see the prime minister. Before Navarra had finished announcing them, they brushed past him and surrounded Mussolini's desk. Surprised and annoyed, Mussolini demanded to know the whereabouts of Tullio Tamburini, one of their most headstrong leaders. In response Aldo Tarabella, a highly decorated war veteran, presented Mussolini with a letter in which Tamburini acknowledged his solidarity with the other consuls. At that very moment, in fact, Tamburini was in Florence directing a force of some 10,000 armed *squadristi* in an all-out assault against anti-Fascists.

Tarabella put the issue to Mussolini squarely: Either he join them in turning themselves in to the judicial authorities as criminals, or lead them in a revolutionary seizure of power. Cautioning the consuls that their behavior was insubordinate, Mussolini pleaded for them to understand the delicacy of his position, arguing that "the corpse flung between [his] feet" had isolated him from everyone. But Tarabella would brook no more compromise. "A corpse cannot stop a revolution!" Mussolini at last promised that he would silence the anti-Fascists once and for all. As the consuls left his office, Mussolini seemed shaken by the confrontation.[39]

But for all his doubts and fears throughout the second half of 1924, Mussolini had never really abandoned his fundamental determination to retain control of the Italian government. When Bottai raised the question of Mussolini's resignation as a way to resolve the Matteotti Crisis, Mussolini replied angrily: "Give up power? Never!" As 1924 turned into 1925, Mussolini decided not only to keep his power but to expand it. Not wanting to give the *squadristi* the impression that he was wavering, Mussolini immediately issued orders that every Fascist deputy attend the next session of Parliament on January 3.

On January 2, he asked the king to sign an undated decree proroguing Parliament. After a personal meeting, Vittorio Emanuele agreed to Mussolini's request. Mussolini's short speech to the Chamber of Deputies stands out as one of the most crucial events of his life. In the space of half an hour, he overcame months of indecision and fear. "I, and I alone," he announced defiantly, "assume the political, moral, and historical responsibility for everything that has happened." Hurling accusations of sedition at the anti-Fascist opposition, he proclaimed that the moment had come to say "Enough! . . . When two elements are engaged in struggle and are irreducible, the solution is force. History has never known any other solution. . . . Italy, my friends, demands peace, tranquility, and constructive calm. We will give it these things, if possible with love, but if necessary with force. You may be sure that within forty-eight hours of this speech, the situation will be clarified in every way."[40]

In the days that followed, public-security forces and bands of *squadristi* shut down all anti-Fascist organizations and confiscated their newspapers. The two Liberal members of the Cabinet resigned. In February, Mussolini appointed Farinacci as Fascist party secretary, and his fanatical followers turned against the leaders of the opposition. Fascist enemies were beaten and arrested, and many, including the Socialists Filippo Turati and Claudio Treves, were forced to flee to France, where they were to die in exile. Anna Kuliscioff had preceded them, having died in December 1925 after a long illness.

Over the next two years, Mussolini suppressed the remaining vestiges of constitutional government and built the foundations for the Fascist regime. After an assassination attempt against him in November 1925, Mussolini pushed through a measure that ended his responsibility to Parliament. Only then did Mussolini allow Dumini to be tried for Matteotti's murder. After a mockery of a trial in early 1926, during which the intransigent Robert Farinacci acted as Dumini's defense counsel, the ringleader of the Cheka received a light sentence and served only two years in prison. Later that year, after three more failed efforts to kill him, Mussolini purged the civil service and replaced elected local officials with appointed men. In November 1926, he instituted a new police law that gave the government far-reaching powers to arrest and confine political "criminals," and deprived the remaining opposition members of Parliament of their seats. Finally in December a "Law for the Defense of the State" imposed the death penalty for attempted assassinations of government officials and the royal family, established a military tribunal to try anti-Fascists, and created a secret police. The personal dictatorship of Benito Mussolini had been born, and for the next seventeen years he remained the undisputed ruler of Italy.[41]

Margherita's views on the Matteotti affair and the crisis that it sparked appear callous and casual. A year later, she described the murder as a "misdeed," one that had implicated people "far too near the Chief himself." While admitting that it had cast an ugly shadow over Fascism, she proffered the excuse that it had been the result of good intentions. "With a party of energetic young men, some of them inclined to violence, the more that is accomplished the more likely is friction to arise, and it is impossible that mistakes will not be made."[42]

Margherita discovered that the pressure of the tumultuous events of early 1925 made Mussolini seriously ill. Shortly afterward, she found him vomiting blood as a result of the aggravated condition of his stomach. In May 1925, when Mussolini decided to visit Gabriele D'Annunzio's villa on Lake Garda, she wrote the poet that Mussolini was suffering from exhaustion and implored him to persuade the prime minister to rest there for a few days.[43]

Yet the crisis brought them together in a way she thought would never be breached. As she looked toward their future, she anticipated sharing the dictatorial power he had seized, and helping to shape it. Still, the turmoil they had lived through together gave Margherita intimate knowledge of the weaknesses of the man she now proclaimed as having "the power and the courage to make history that will become a legend."[44]

20

Dux

In the midst of the Matteotti crisis, Margherita began work on a biography of Mussolini. She had chosen to remain inconspicuous during the crisis, and the book provided an ideal opportunity for concentrated and solitary work. Eventually it appeared in nineteen languages, enhancing Mussolini's image around the world, and bringing Margherita international celebrity. From its initial publication in England in 1925 to its latest reprinting in 1982, the biography linked Mussolini and Margherita in a way that their private relationship could never do. She considered it her greatest literary achievement.

The idea for the book originated with Giuseppe Prezzolini, then living in Paris, who acted as a literary agent on behalf of foreign publishers seeking Italian manuscripts. Sometime in 1924, in response to an English publisher's interest in a biography of Mussolini, Prezzolini suggested that he commission one from a talented writer who knew Mussolini personally. Prezzolini negotiated a deal with Margherita, who agreed to pay him a small percentage of the royalties for arranging the contract. She insisted that Mussolini be allowed to check the proofs and make any corrections he desired.[1]

Mussolini was enthusiastic about the project. He provided Margherita with private papers to supplement her account of the days before she knew him. He helped her locate documents from his hometown, such as his mother's request for a government subsidy for his education, as well as letters he had written during his days in Switzerland. He secured for her the original of an autobiographical sketch he had composed in Forlì prison in 1911 and 1912. She added to these sources quotations from Mussolini's speeches and articles, although not always with complete accuracy. For much of the story, of course, Margherita needed no written documents. And she never claimed to have written an objective account of Mussolini's life. Her point of view was that of a dedicated Fascist.[2]

She began work on the book at Il Soldo in the summer of 1924, and completed it late that winter. Mussolini reviewed it and made a few minor changes in the manuscript. The first edition appeared in September 1925 as *The Life of Benito Mussolini,* bearing as a frontispiece the photograph of a smiling, benevolent Mussolini.

Margherita had the subject of her biography write a short preface, and had his manuscript reproduced in facsimile. While claiming to "detest" biographers, Mussolini nonetheless told his readers that he was resigned to the scrutiny that comes to public figures. He admitted, however, to taking comfort from the fact that "I belong to all—loved by all, hated by all—that I am an essential element in the lives of others: this feeling has on me a kind of intoxicating effect. And then, when one belongs to all, one belongs to none." In his one, indirect, reference to Margherita, he expressed pleasure in the book because it "presents me with a sense of the proportions as regards time and space and events, and without extravagance—despite friendship and community of work and of ideas."[3]

The book sold well in Great Britain and in the United States, and by December had gone into a second printing. Almost immediately Margherita entered into negotiations with the Mondadori publishing house to produce an Italian-language edition, which now she called *Dux,* the Latin form of *Duce.* Margherita issued two prepublication extracts of *Dux,* one in *Gerarchia* and the other in *Il Popolo d'Italia.* The book itself appeared in June 1926, in an elegant, simple blue binding with a gold title. She sent Prezzolini one of the first copies, inscribed with a note of thanks for having suggested the project to her. It was the only occasion on which she ever acknowledged the origin of the book.[4]

The English and Italian editions differed. Margherita and Mussolini could afford to be more frank with foreign readers. With Italy now a dictatorship, they decided to keep certain information from their Italian readers. *The Life* contains photographs of Mussolini's two eldest children, Edda and Vittorio, dressed in Fascist uniforms. The text itself never mentions Rachele. In *Dux,* even the photographs of their children were omitted. The length of *The Life* changed slightly, for its translator had rearranged or merged some chapters and eliminated the occasional passage that would have required detailed explanations for an English reader. Margherita restored these passages for *Dux,* and also brought the political chapters up to date for the Italian edition.[5]

Margherita remained conscious of a sense of propriety, even after Cesare's death. "In Italy," she wrote, "as a rule, women, even revolutionary women, have qualms about their love affairs, or at least are cautious: even when they are most sensually inclined they make some show of modesty and reserve." Margherita edited references to Cesare carefully. In the English edition, she used the phrase "my husband" on several occasions, whereas in the Italian version she referred obscurely to "a person close to me." She excised direct references to Cesare in order to play down the fact that her affair with the prime minister had constituted adultery.[6]

The personal relationship between author and subject imparts a sense of intimacy to the book. Convinced of her own role in shaping Mussolini's mind and character, and mindful of her contributions to the development of Fascism, Margherita thought of the book as a kind of dual biography. She wove her presence subtly into the narrative at every important phase, and recorded her presence at all major events. *The Life of Benito Mussolini* is more a personal memoir than a traditional biography. The reader learns of what Margherita describes as their first meeting, when he had just become editor of *Avanti!* in 1912 and she offered him her resignation, and of the visit she made with Roberto in January 1918 to the office of *Il Popolo d'Italia*.[7]

As Margherita describes general developments and crucial historical events, she mentions her own involvement, revealing to her reader the facts of her own life. When describing Socialism's popularity among the youth of Italy at the turn of the century, she observed, "Even I, a girl of fifteen, living in the seclusion of a family of good standing with clerical and conservative tendencies had embraced Socialism." She explained, too, how she first heard of the outbreak of World War I while sitting in a restaurant with her family, and that news of Mussolini's resignation as editor of *Avanti!* reached her at a session of the Milan city council.[8]

Margherita peppered her story with portraits of the important figures in pre-Fascist Italian public life, especially the Socialist leaders. The reader encounters sharply drawn sketches of Anna Kuliscioff and Filippo Turati, as well as colorful literary figures such as Gabriele D'Annunzio. It is remarkable that in her descriptions of earlier rivals and of Socialists who later became enemies of Fascism, Margherita rarely indulged in personal rancor or political recrimination. She treated her former Socialist comrades with a sense of decorum that other Fascists found grating in the wake of the Matteotti crisis. In a guarded review of *Dux* Ugo Ojetti produced for *Il Corriere della Sera,* he admitted that he found this aspect of the book "courageous."[9]

Margherita made one exception to her otherwise generous policy in describing the fiery Russian exile Angelica Balabanoff. Although she knew that during their days as exiles in Switzerland, Balabanoff and Mussolini had had an affair, Margherita insisted—more out of vanity than propriety—that Balabanoff's relationship with the young Mussolini remained "within the limits of a respectful comradeship." Mussolini edited one detail of Margherita's vindictive portrait of Balabanoff. He crossed out the comment that Balabanoff was bowlegged.[10]

The scathing profile of Balabanoff provides a comic record of Margherita's personal jealousy:

> Ugly as she was, she boasted that she never lacked "partners" . . . for the sake of the aesthetic honor of young socialists, I hope she was exaggerating. . . . She had neither a sense of humor nor, fortunately, a sense of beauty—otherwise, she would have thrown herself down the nearest well. With water she had, in any case, very little familiarity.[11]

In the concluding chapter of *The Life* (but not of *Dux*), Margherita addressed Mussolini directly, explaining with uncharacteristic modesty, "From my post of vantage, bordering the turmoil, in a comparatively quiet backwater, I have noted something of the memorable occurrences of our time." She assured him, however, albeit almost as an afterthought, "The scene, *Signor Presidente,* is dominated by your figure."[12]

Margherita understood that on occasion prudence or good taste suggested that she remove herself from the narrative. This was especially true in the Italian edition, which Rachele and others close to Mussolini would be likely to read. When describing the March on Rome, for example, she claimed in *Dux* that Mussolini surprised her by appearing in her family box at the Manzoni Theater on the evening of October 27. In fact, they had gone there together. She testified in *The Life* as an eyewitness to the shooting star that she and Mussolini had seen on New Year's Day 1923, but the event does not appear at all in *Dux,* for Rachele would no doubt have been considerably upset to learn that her husband had spent the holiday with Margherita instead of his family.[13]

In many ways the book was influenced by her readings of Freud and Joyce. Margherita wrote a psychological biography years before the genre was widely used.[14] She deliberately did not give it a conventional biographical structure, rejecting strict chronological narrative. "The thread of mere chronology," she insisted, "seems a poor thing in the face of a unity so substantial, so indestructible, as the tissue of a man's veins and nerves; one cannot take this tissue to pieces. . . . I shall proceed, therefore, as life has done with him and he with life—by leaps and bounds, by rapid advances and sudden retreats."[15]

Nor was her method of depicting Mussolini conventional. She approached the biography as a modern painter would a portrait. Her purpose was not to offer an exact reproduction of objective reality, but to convey the inner essence of Mussolini's mind and personality as she experienced it: "Connoisseurs of painting know that a good picture is one which imitates with the texture and direction of the stroke of the brush the texture and nature of the thing represented. In the case of a spherical shape, which has consistency and dimensionality, the right brush-stroke has a certain roundness which gives the impression of a plastic body emerging from out of the shade into the light."[16]

In Margherita's account, Mussolini was predestined for greatness. From his humble childhood as the "son of the blacksmith," he rose by sheer force of will above his squalid environment. She revealed aspects of his personal behavior, examined his fears and aspirations, and explored his private motivations with a frankness that only she could get away with. She made no effort to hide the fact that Mussolini was egotistical and arrogant, or that he was inclined by instinct to violence; she told her readers that he feared personal intimacy and deliberately held himself aloof from friends. She asserted that he had a deep disdain for most human beings, that he was strongly antifeminist, and that, in personal relationships as in politics, he was an opportunist.

In revealing these aspects of Mussolini's character, Margherita used these traits to reinforce the image of Mussolini as an uncommon, exceptional man—a strong, ruthless leader who stood apart from ordinary human weakness. Margherita may have been thinking of her own sentiments about Mussolini when she observed, "There is no race more addicted than the Italian to the cult of hero worship." *Dux* was the first step in what became the regime's most enduring and systematic propaganda campaign: to make a myth of Mussolini. When the writer Curzio Malaparte asked Margherita why she had fabricated an event related in *Dux,* she replied with perfect sincerity, "To create the legend."[17]

Part of the popular appeal of Margherita's portrait was the web of contradictions that she said marked Mussolini's personality—a son of the common people who scorned the masses, a Socialist ideologue who became the prophet of a new nationalism, a man of intense earthy passions devoid of material self-interest. The photographs that *Dux* offered were designed to suggest a range of talents beyond the abilities of most men. These included not only his roles as party activist, soldier, newspaper writer, or Fascist Duce, but also as prime minister and world statesman. Margherita was also careful to portray Mussolini as a vigorous and courageous man of action, the master of horses, airplanes, sports cars, and speedboats. He was even shown carousing with Italia, his less than savage beast. Over the next two decades, the media repeated the images first seen in the pages of *Dux* so frequently that they were known to virtually every man, woman, and child in Italy.[18]

The cult of personality to which Margherita contributed sometimes took more subtle forms. With the exception of two passing references, Mussolini is the only Fascist leader mentioned by name in *Dux.* By omitting the role of others in the rise of the Fascist movement, Margherita suggested that only Mussolini was responsible. Moreover, she portrayed the Fascist doctrine and political movement as Mussolini's personal creation.[19]

One aspect of the "legend" Margherita sought to create involved associating Mussolini with Italy's ancient Roman past. Ever since the founding of the first *fascio* in 1919, she had suggested the ideological and propagandistic value of linking Fascism to imperial Rome. She had a vision of Mussolini as the leader who would impose a new order of culture on modern civilization, a culture based on the Roman virtues of discipline and order. Her first article in *Il Popolo d'Italia* following Mussolini's appointment as prime minister stressed the continuity of contemporary Italian culture with that of ancient Rome. Margherita's conception of ancient Rome came not from a close study of the ancient writers, but from late-nineteenth-century Italian literature, especially the works of poet Giosuè Carducci. Some forty years later, while interviewing Margherita, an Italian scholar was struck with the degree to which she was still "diseased with Romanità."[20]

Soon after Mussolini had gained power, he and Margherita had begun to stress *Romanità*—the essence of Roman tradition—as the key element in Fascist cultural policy. Mussolini ordered numerous measures to emphasize his regime's kinship with Rome. Two months after the March on Rome, for instance, Margherita addressed a prearranged public letter to Mussolini advocating that the *fascio* be used on all Italian coinage. The first such coins appeared a year later. In early 1923, Mussolini's government proclaimed the Fascist Militia to be a state security service and, in 1925, a branch of the armed forces. As a result, the Roman insignia and titles of the Militia became official government symbols. In 1925, Mussolini established the Institute of Roman Studies. In December 1926 he made the *fascio* the emblem of the new Italian state. Simultaneously, Mussolini decreed an *Era Fascista* dating from the March on Rome. The Fascist New Year would begin on October 28, designated by a Roman numeral. By the late 1920s, the *fascio* appeared everywhere in Italy, from manhole covers and lampposts to the national coat of arms.[21]

In her biography, Margherita presented Mussolini as the heir to the Caesars, writing that "Benito Mussolini is an archetype of the Italian—he is a Roman from top to toe and to the marrow of his bones. . . . Roman in spirit and appearance, Benito Mussolini is the resurrection of the pure Italic type, which after many centuries flourishes once again." She chose the title of the Italian edition as a tribute to a bust of Mussolini executed by Adolfo Wildt. Wildt had carved *Dux*, a powerful white-marble representation modeled on Roman portrait busts, to depict Mussolini as a new Caesar. The work was executed in 1923 and exhibited the following year at the Venice Biennale. Margherita had secured the commission for Wildt, and praised the bust as the first important work of art inspired by Fascism. She used a photograph of Wildt's sculpture for the Italian frontispiece.[22]

Dux had the effect of depersonalizing Mussolini, removing him from immediate events and placing him in the broad context of Italian history. Margherita's biography helped to legitimize Mussolini's dictatorship, a process that was especially crucial in the wake of the Matteotti crisis.[23] Popular interest in Italy was sparked by the fact that the book's author was generally known as an "intimate friend" of the Duce, and one Party ideologue proclaimed that it was the duty of all Fascists to read *Dux*.[24]

Margherita orchestrated the promotion of *Dux,* arranging discussions and lectures, making sure it was given the widest possible exposure in the Italian press, and using her ties with Mussolini to induce important Fascists to review it in their newspapers. With writers outside the party, Margherita used more subtle methods. At the end of May 1926, just before the book appeared in Italy, she visited her old friend Alfredo Panzini. Besides being a well-known author, Panzini was a regular contributor to *Il Corriere della Sera*. Margherita hinted to Panzini that not only did she want her book reviewed by the paper, she wanted the review written by Ugo Ojetti. Panzini wrote apologetically to Ojetti about Margherita's visit. He understood immediately. Ojetti devoted an entire column to the book in *Il Corriere della Sera,* wondering bitterly in his diary, "Will they be satisfied?"[25]

Soon after the appearance of *Dux,* Margherita was annoyed to discover that she had a new competitor. The journalist Giorgio Pini published his own biography of the Duce, *Mussolini: From the Street to Power.* Pini's book was a short, popular sketch of Mussolini's life, intended for a less literate audience. Pini knew Margherita, who had willingly accepted his articles for *Gerarchia.* Pini even cited Margherita by name several times in his own manuscript, hoping to appease her, and, through his friend Arnaldo Mussolini, sent the proofs to the Duce for approval. Yet as soon as his book had been published, Margherita cut off all communication with Pini. To make matters worse, their publishers competed to have their respective books adopted by the Italian school system. Margherita had the advantage through her close friend Emilio Bodrero, then undersecretary for public instruction. Arnaldo, however, convinced his brother that it would be in bad taste to permit the education ministry to select a biography of Mussolini as required reading in public schools.[26] Nonetheless, *Dux* was still bought by Italian schools.

Even without the school market, *Dux* was an instant best-seller. The price was kept deliberately low. In Italy, five printings sold out before the end of the year, and between 1926 and 1938 Mondadori published seventeen editions. The book proved equally popular abroad. Ultimately the book appeared in eighteen other languages, including Turkish and Japanese—in Japan the book sold some 300,000 copies. *Dux* played a major part in making Mussolini a preeminent international figure in the 1920s, and it did the same for Margherita. The book made her a great deal of money in the process. Prezzolini deeply resented this fact. Margherita refused to recognize his rights to a royalty percentage after the English edition.[27]

While it was enormously successful at the time, later generations of readers have understandably disliked *Dux*. Anti-Fascists ridiculed the book as crude propaganda. Margherita's granddaughter Magalì refers to it as "horrible trash." Margherita never denied that it was an officially sanctioned biography. She deliberately distorted and sanitized aspects of Mussolini's career when she thought it politically advisable. Still, her sins were largely of omission: so completely did she suppress all mention of the violence of the Fascist squads that one foreign reviewer asserted, "The story of Fascism in Italy is the story of an almost bloodless revolution conducted by one essentially sane man of genius."[28]

Margherita revealed remarkably frank details about Mussolini's attitudes toward women. She coyly hinted that while in the Trentino Mussolini had a number of sexual affairs with women of the region. One young woman became enraged when she suspected that he was unfaithful—a woman, Margherita remarked, who "had some right to be jealous"—and burned the manuscript of a history of philosophy that he had written. This woman was probably Ida Dalser, who had borne Mussolini's son Benito. In another instance, Margherita related Mussolini's fight with the jealous fiancé of the landlady with whom he was staying. And, she intimated, "There are today in those regions of Friuli youngsters who will soon be twenty years old" who resembled Mussolini more than typical Friuli natives.[29]

These revelations made reviewers uncomfortable, though they noted that she succeeded in giving a real sense of what Mussolini was like as a human being. Most attributed her psychological insight to her gender, agreeing with Margherita's own assessment that this was "a woman's book," filled with passion and sentiment. Although she told Mussolini, "It is taken up largely with details which you, perhaps, will dismiss as 'gossip,' " she added the disclaimer, "I have read too much of history to disdain gossip."[30]

Why did Margherita, always a shrewd and careful strategist, include these anecdotes? And why did Mussolini permit such scandalous information to remain in the book? Partly, Margherita was coming to public terms with Mussolini in a way that was impossible in their private relationship. Unlike all the other women close to Mussolini, she felt no political or intellectual inferiority to him. The difficulties she had encountered with him gave her sufficient reason to delight in telling what she knew and experienced, even when politics demanded she express her observations "objectively."[31]

Margherita knew her lover viewed women as submissive objects of male sexual pleasure, to be conquered and dominated. She also had to deal with the fact that his views reflected Fascist thinking about women. Still, Margherita struggled to change Mussolini's misogynistic views. By the spring of 1923 Margherita had persuaded him to announce his government's intention to introduce legislation granting Italian women the right to vote. He made this announcement in Rome on May 14 when he addressed the ninth congress of the International Women's Suffrage Alliance. Margherita, dressed in a striking white dress and hat, gave a simultaneous English-language translation of his remarks to the audience, after which Carrie Chapman Catt, the Alliance president, praised Mussolini for his progressive views. In May 1924 Margherita began a campaign to elicit the backing of distinguished political leaders for women's voting rights, hoping, for example, to secure an article by former Prime Minister Orlando for *Gerarchia*.[32]

A year later, the government introduced the legislation in Parliament, and Mussolini endorsed the measure in a speech before the Chamber of Deputies. He argued that industrialization had permanently removed women from the isolation of the home, but he could not resist revealing his true feelings: "A woman's life will always be dominated by love: either for her children or a man. If a woman loves her husband, she will vote for him and for his party. If she doesn't love him, she has already voted against him!" Margherita pressed for the passage of the law in *Gerarchia*. She omitted mentioning that Mussolini had already decided to abolish any kind of voting in local elections.[33]

Over the next decade, as Mussolini adopted increasingly anti-feminist policies toward women, Margherita abandoned any illusions she might have had that her feminism was compatible with Fascism. She wrote occasionally about the regime's social-welfare programs as they affected mothers, and in her travels abroad she was touted as the chief example of a "new Fascist woman." Privately she found herself forced to use against Mussolini the weapons of flattery and manipulation that she had been taught as a girl in a patriarchal society. She had long since recognized the strategic benefits of assuming stereotypically "feminine" roles in order to secure advantage and power: as hostess of a literary and artistic salon, as cultural activist, as "mother of a war hero," and, of course, as mistress to a leader. She knew Mussolini's weaknesses and the depth of his vanity about his sexual prowess. The "feminine indiscretions" noted by reviewers in *Dux* were calculated to stroke his vanity. He delighted in their public retelling.[34]

Margherita also understood that Mussolini's preoccupation with sexual conquest had a certain political power. Mussolini the virile lover, or Mussolini the earthy, bare-chested Duce, were political images as attractive to Italian men as to Italian women. John Carter, an American journalist who reviewed *Dux* in its English edition, perceived the Mussolini myth in this context when he wrote: "Latin races appreciate virility in a statesman far more than do the Anglo-Saxon, whose politicians are expected to have distinguished themselves by their conspicuous chastity at least before seeking elective office. Mussolini's grasp on Italy is susceptible to the analysis of the psychology of sex." In this sense, *Dux* was instrumental in ensuring Mussolini's fascination for the Italian people.[35]

Margherita was proud of the fame it brought her and its subject, and kept a copy of it prominently displayed on a table in her salon. Mussolini approved of the imagery of himself as the new Caesar and Italy's man of destiny. But Margherita's frank portrait of his character also made him uncomfortable. He expressed displeasure privately to his brother and to Giorgio Pini soon after its appearance.[36]

Because he made no public comments disparaging the work until years later, few people had the courage to say anything openly critical of the book. Thus Margherita's old friend Medardo Rosso, the highly acclaimed sculptor whose work she had championed, gave Margherita quite a surprise. In the spring of 1928, word reached her that Rosso had fallen gravely ill. She rushed to see him, bearing the gift of an autographed copy of *Dux*. Despite his weakened condition, the seventy-year-old Rosso greeted her with his usual genial manner. Over the next several days Margherita returned to see Rosso repeatedly, but he never mentioned *Dux*. Finally she asked him point-blank if he liked it. Taking her hands into his affectionately, Rosso responded: "Margherita, Margherita, why don't you write a railway time table, for which there is such a great need? You should write one! You really must!" Drawing back abruptly, Margherita bade her friend good-bye and left. Two days later, on March 31, Rosso died.[37]

21

A New Aspect of Tradition

A short while after Margherita had begun work on *Dux,* Achille Funi brought to Anselmo Bucci and Leonardo Dudreville a new proposal: the reformation of the *Novecento,* this time without Lino Pesaro's support, and with a greatly enlarged membership. Dudreville suspected more than Funi was revealing, and asked bluntly if Margherita was involved. Funi admitted that she was, but added quickly that other talented artists, such as Carlo Carrà, Arturo Tosi, and Alberto Salietti, were interested. Many years later, in an unpublished memoir, Dudreville explained:

> In those days Sarfatti's salon was always very well attended: among many others, Salietti and Tosi were almost never absent. . . . La Sarfatti in that period was a powerful force in artistic circles, and her power, always on the rise, was the magnetic pole toward which the most career-minded of men moved.[1]

More than six months passed before Margherita's new project took concrete shape, for the intervening upheavals following the Matteotti murder occupied her attentions. Throughout the crisis, she continued to lay her plans, and in February 1925—*after* Mussolini proclaimed his dictatorship—the *Novecento Italiano* was reborn.[2]

Unlike the earlier group, this new *Novecento* was a formally structured, highly disciplined organization that Margherita personally directed. By means of her inexhaustible energy, skillful cajolery, and political influence (now greatly expanded as a result of Mussolini's dictatorship), she intended to transform the *Novecento* into a national force. An honorary committee of twenty-two prominent people, headed by Mussolini himself, gave prestige, authority, and financial backing to the movement.[3]

The committee included two highly unlikely members: Marinetti and Ojetti. By the mid-1920s, Marinetti, Ojetti, and Margherita were the most powerful figureheads of the three major artistic currents, all vying for position and recognition among the Fascists. As Margherita's *Novecento* began to assume the aura of an "official" movement, Marinetti's second generation of Futurists acted as a kind of radical "opposition of the left," while Ojetti spoke for the academic classicists, an "opposition of the right." Marinetti and Ojetti reluctantly gave their names to the committee for reasons of political opportunism. Margherita wanted them associated with her group because of her ambition to become the undisputed impresario of Italian artistic culture—a role Ojetti also coveted. Unlike Margherita, Ojetti maintained an unremitting hostility to cultural modernism. In November 1925, he complained to his diary plaintively about Margherita, "Mussolini allows her be the arbiter of everything that has to do with art."[4]

The actual work of organizing the *Novecento* and its exhibitions lay in the hands of an executive committee. The inner core of this group—its "general staff," according to the painter Vincenzo Costantini—included three members of the original *Novecento,* Funi, Marussig, and Sironi, as well as Alberto Salietti, Arturo Tosi, and the sculptor Adolfo Wildt. Salietti was the youngest member at thirty-three and a close friend of Tosi, at fifty-four the oldest of the painters. Both frequented Margherita's salon religiously, and were, according to Dudreville, driven by an insatiable desire for professional success. Salietti's paintings combined some of the qualities of Magic Realism with the archaic folk themes of Carrà's work. Tosi, a master of landscape painting, soon became one of Margherita's favorites. Claiming that his work was in the manner of Cézanne, she began to promote him enthusiastically.[5]

Carlo Carrà had remained aloof from the original group, reviewing the 1923 exhibit in guarded terms. Now Margherita courted him assiduously. She praised his talents in a long essay and induced Mussolini to buy several of his works; finally he agreed to participate. Even Anselmo Bucci, who had broken with the original group over Margherita's high-handed manner, now accepted her personal invitation to join the new movement, graciously acknowledging her role as its "blond and bold godmother."[6]

Throughout the decade and into the early 1930s, Margherita was the dynamo driving the *Novecento*. She wrote letters, called meetings, drafted reviews, and gave public lectures; she traveled incessantly, arranging exhibits, convincing private individuals and government officials to buy *Novecento* paintings, and bolstering the sometimes flagging spirits of its members. The *Novecento* had its headquarters in Milan, where the painters on the committee often met at Margherita's home. Her pride in the movement was immense, and she defended it fiercely against critics who resented her arrogance and her influence. Thirty years later, when the *Novecento* was vilified as the official art of a dictatorial regime, Margherita still defended the group and her central role in its history: "It was I," she wrote proudly, "who brought them together, stimulated them, and held them together."

Margherita planned a series of major exhibits on an annual basis, to encourage public identification of the *Novecento* as a national Italian movement. A detailed list of rules and regulations was drafted. Painting, sculpture, architectural designs, and prints were to be included in the exhibits, but participation was by invitation only. The executive committee retained the right to decide which works would be shown and handled all sales during the shows, taking 15 percent of the price as its fee.[7]

The committee issued a large number of invitations for the first exhibit, scheduled to open in Milan on February 14, 1926, at the Permanente. Some one hundred fourteen artists eventually agreed to take part. Margherita drew up a budget for the show that anticipated some 200,000 lire in receipts and half of that sum in expenses, the difference to be applied toward a second exhibit. She arranged for Mussolini to grant official recognition to the exhibit. She also asked for, and received, an indirect government subsidy in the form of reduced-fare train tickets issued for all Italians traveling to Milan while the show was open. In her formal request to Mussolini she explained that such assistance was justified "in consideration of the great importance that this undertaking (the first of its kind) has assumed throughout the entire nation." Salietti handled all the paperwork and transmitted the necessary documents to Rome. Mussolini must have laughed when he read Salietti's nervous qualification—"I believe," wrote the young painter, "that I have interpreted correctly the instructions given to me by Signora Margherita Sarfatti."[8]

In her preface to the exhibit catalog, Margherita explained the artistic aims of the *Novecento* again as a return to order, a "work of revision and synthesis of analytical elements" which had begun before 1914 but which the war had made a "spiritual necessity." She denied that the *Novecento* intended to compete with the long-established Venice and Rome Biennali, which were international in scope; she claimed that one of its central purposes was to prepare the nation for victory in international competitions by "focusing its strengths." In an unpublished preliminary draft of the *Novecento* program, Margherita's words were even more bellicose, for she spoke of "preparing our forces and militarizing our spirit in the national field" to face foreign competition.[9]

In her desire to stage a major cultural event, Margherita seemed more interested in the number of artists she could attract than in their stylistic cohesiveness. Whereas the original *Novecentisti* shared a core of Magic Realism, this exhibition presented an unwieldy, eclectic combination of artists and styles. She lamely suggested the group shared a modernist idiom, pointing out that the exhibit would take place "within the walls of the most modern and industrious of our cities." She abandoned her notion of a "school" of art; instead, Margherita began to insist that the *Novecento* was successful precisely because of the disparity of its styles and artists.[10]

In 1922, she had found it difficult to put together a group of seven artists, and impossible to keep them together. In 1925, her association with Mussolini's power attracted virtually all of Italy's best artists, including those who had broken with her in the past. Participants in the first exhibition included Carrà, de Chirico, Campigli, Casorati, Virgilio Guidi, Osvaldo Licini, Giorgio Morandi, Cipriano E. Oppo, and Gino Severini. Among the sculptors were Arturo Martini and Adolfo Wildt. The aging Medardo Rosso was given a personal retrospective in a room of his own. Along with Giacomo Balla were the second generation of Futurists, such as Fortunato Depero, Enrico Prampolini, and Luigi Russolo. Carlo Socrate and Primo Sinopico, two artists who were later part of the Roman movement known as the *Scuola Romana,* also participated. Despite tense relations with Margherita, the Tuscan artists Ardengo Soffici, Libero Andreotti, and Antonio Maraini also eventually joined, although Ottone Rosai refused. These men, grouped into the so-called *Strapaese* ("super-country") movement, held strong provincial loyalties. Their spokesmen, the writers Mino Maccari and Curzio Malaparte, were cultural populists who found in the "sober" traditions of rural culture the true wellsprings of Italian civilization. They claimed to despise big cities and bourgeois values, although they did not entirely reject stylistic modernism in their own work. They bitterly resisted the cultural conformity that some Fascists demanded, arguing that their provincial-based values represented the true Fascist revolution. The *Strapaesani* regarded Margherita's *Novecento* as an urban, Milanese phenomenon, and did not want to be openly associated with what many believed was an officially sponsored movement.[11]

Ojetti's resentment of Margherita's growing influence peaked in the fall of 1925, when he suggested to Mussolini that a major exhibition of nineteenth-century Italian art be held in Milan in 1928. Ojetti was stunned when he learned that the Duce had handed the letter over to Margherita, who did not like the idea at all. Margherita responded to Ojetti's request in a letter he said was "throbbing with rhetoric." She told Ojetti that she was planning the *Novecento* exhibit, which she assured him would exclude no movement or style. Be generous, she lectured him, to young artists rather than to dead ones, for a great artistic era was dawning. "A carnival during Lent," he recorded in his diary.[12]

Over the following weeks, Margherita found herself in a growing polemic with Ojetti and the Tuscans, capped by Ojetti's resignation from the honorary committee. Margherita, realizing that the Tuscans were too important to leave out, and not wanting to encourage others to defect, made a special trip to Florence in December to talk with them: Ojetti relented and withdrew his resignation, and in March 1926 Mussolini rewarded him by appointment as interim editor of the *Corriere della Sera*. He and Margherita would clash again.

As a special favor to Margherita, Mussolini agreed to open the *Novecento* exhibit. She heralded the event with articles in *Il Popolo d'Italia*. On the evening of February 13, Margherita escorted him on a preview of the exhibit. The following day Mussolini was greeted officially in the Palazzo della Permanente by the mayor and the honorary committee. Margherita was in a state of high excitement, for it was rare now that the two appeared together in public. Mussolini mounted a low platform to deliver his address, while Margherita seated herself prominently in the front row of the audience.[13]

Holding the typed text of his speech, Mussolini presented the most detailed remarks on art he had ever made in public. Given the topic, the speech was unusually long and knowledgeable. Margherita had written the essential part of it for him, a fact that some in his audience must have suspected.[14]

Mussolini began by confessing his genuine discomfort in speaking of artistic matters. After a rambling introduction concerning the relationship between politics and art, and an explanation of the meaning of the term *Novecento*—not, he said, "a question of mere chronology" but of "artistic direction"—he addressed the issue:

> I have asked myself whether the events that each of us has experienced— War and Fascism—have left their mark on the work exhibited here. An uncouth person would say no, for, with the exception of the Futurist painting *A Noi!,* nothing records or photographs the events we have gone through or reproduces the scenes in which we were either spectators or participants. But, in fact, the sign of events is there. We must just know how to find it. This painting, this sculpture, differs from that which came immediately before in Italy. It has its unmistakable identity. It is clearly the result of severe internal discipline. It is clearly not the product of a facile or mercenary craft, but of an assiduous, sometimes anguished effort. We see the echoes of this Italy that has fought two wars, that has become disdainful of long speeches and of everything that smacks of slovenly democracy, that has in twenty-five years traveled with, caught up to, and even overtaken other peoples: the painting and sculpture shown here is, like the Italy of today, strong in spirit and will. In fact, in the works before us we are struck by these characteristic common elements: decisiveness and precision of line, clarity and richness of color, the solid plasticity of objects and human figures. . . . I believe that many of you who walk through these rooms will understand my view and will find that this first exhibit testifies brilliantly to the secure future of Italian art.

Mussolini's appearance at the opening helped make the launching of the *Novecento Italiano* a newsworthy event and ensure its commercial success—the committee collected almost 300,000 lire in sales. One third of this amount came from public funds. Margherita's ability to secure official purchases for the *Novecento* artists soon became the subject of considerable gossip and criticism.[15]

Margherita's articles about the exhibit provided her an opportunity to explore the nature and aims of the movement. In a lengthy piece published in the inaugural issue of a new magazine titled *Il Novecento Italiano,* she emphasized the primacy that Italy would reassert in the arts during this century. "Art and Italy: greatness of life, greatness of art; they represent for our beloved land a single altar. He who worships the one cannot remain indifferent to the other." Italy's past greatness, she proclaimed, can be reclaimed—"that which once was, can become again."

While she argued that the past can inspire the future, she insisted, "We must be faithful to our own times," to express "the new needs of our spirit in new forms of beauty." This did not mean that beauty must reflect the brutal materialism of the machine, as the Futurists mistakenly believed. "We must listen to the profound voices of our genius, not only as a race but as a culture and a civilization. Limpidity, clarity, humanity, concrete synthesis of the true in beauty: these are the guiding principles of Italy's great art." Those who visited the exhibit would see immediately that the artists were "the militant forces of today. Today—today—today—they belong only to that reality." She ended with a repetition of what had become the *Novecento* credo:

> Precision of line, decisiveness in color; resoluteness of form; deep and sober sentiment unearthed and pared down through meditation, elimination, and study; a yearning for the concrete, the simple, the definite: these are the common characteristics—the family atmosphere—of this generation of artists that aspires to give a physiognomy and an imprint, a collective ideal around which to converge, a line and a style, to art, to life, to the moral, aesthetic, and spiritual needs of our time.[16]

Italian critics did not agree that the *Novecento* represented anything more than an undigested mixture of disparate styles. Carrà wrote a long, desultory preview in the Milanese paper *L'Ambrosiano,* arguing that there had never been any intention of mounting a cohesive exhibition. After all, it had combined avant-garde and traditional works. As a collection designed to demonstrate Italy's new art, he judged it a great success. Other critics expressed less enthusiasm. Corrado Pavolini saw an "acute conflict" between the populist naturalism of Soffici and Tosi, and the neoclassicists such as Sironi and Funi. Ojetti reviewed the show grudgingly and lamented the lack of a clear program.[17]

Perhaps the most serious critical response came from the art historian Lionello Venturi. He wondered, in a broad philosophical vein, why the *Novecento* landscapes seemed more satisfying and successful than the paintings of human figures. He concluded that the figure paintings revealed an attitude of moral indifference, of antagonism, and a lack of hope in the human condition that reflected an Italian civil malaise.[18]

According to Margherita and Mussolini, Fascism was supposed to represent a positive turning point in Italian history and bring improvement to the life of the average Italian. Venturi's sensitive analysis of the *Novecento* canvases indicates that some of the artists were, consciously or not, reflecting the opposite effect of Fascism in their work. Perhaps both the Fascists and the *Novecentisti* called for a return to order because of a loss of faith in man's ability to govern himself, a loss of hope that freedom would bring human happiness.

When she prepared *Dux* for Italian readers, Margherita omitted a fact she had hinted at in the English edition—that in the months after Mussolini became prime minister, she took him on private tours of Rome late at night in his car. They often stopped in St. Peter's Square or some other famous spot, and Margherita improvised lectures on history and culture. Sometimes they went to the Casina Valadier, a haunt of high Roman society at the top of the Pincio Hill. There they dined in seclusion and looked out over the majestic panorama of the city. It was during these tours in 1922 and 1923 that they conceived of remaking the city into the political and spiritual capital of a new Fascist empire.[19]

Their plans called for the restoration of the monuments of imperial Rome and the construction of new buildings designed in a style suitable to the Fascist era. Both approaches reflected their preoccupation with the symbolic power of Roman history. In 1923 the Fascist Grand Council had approved a proposal for placing the administration of Rome under Mussolini's central authority. This move facilitated his plans for the city's development as "a new imperial Rome for the new Italy." Two years later, at the inauguration of the first governor of Rome, Mussolini pointed out that the capital had already begun to change as a result of extensive archaeological excavations of the forums and temples. He demanded that within five years Rome must assume a new appearance: "vast, ordered, powerful, as it was at the time of the first empire of Augustus."[20]

In the years 1923 to 1925, Margherita lauded Armando Brasini as the appropriate architect for Italy's renewal. Brasini's style was eclectic, but he hoped to build grandiose, monumental constructions inspired by ancient Roman architecture. "Seen from afar," explained Margherita, "it seems that we already know his buildings, for they have the appearance and the general physiognomy that is characteristic of our land and of our people." In response to Mussolini's speech, Brasini began to devise a giant new forum involving the clearing of areas from around ancient ruins. Margherita announced, "Rome will become a great capital, a great, singular city of ancient and modern beauty."[21]

The archaeological excavation and urban renewal sponsored by Mussolini provoked considerable controversy, for it meant the destruction of many medieval and baroque neighborhoods. In later years both Fiammetta and Amedeo Sarfatti denied their mother's role in these undertakings. Yet at the time Margherita boasted to Thomas B. Morgan of the United Press that she was a "minister without portfolio." The journalist was so impressed by her "gigantic" aspirations for the excavation of the forum and the preservation of the tomb of Augustus that he titled his article WOMAN REBUILDS OLD ROME: MUSSOLINI LIEUTENANT, SHE PROMOTES PLAN FOR RESTORING THE IMPERIAL CITY.[22] She also backed a proposal for a grand "Imperial" boulevard linking the Colosseum with the Piazza Venezia, where the monument to King Vittorio Emanuele II and the tomb of the unknown soldier were located.[23]

Margherita had some concern for historic sites. She fought against construction speculators to save whatever she saw as an important work of architecture from destruction. In particular, she valued structures reflecting a classical aesthetic, such as Palladio's Loggia at Vicenza and the sixteenth-century piazza of Faenza, both of which she helped preserve from destruction. To Gabriele D'Annunzio, whose support she often enlisted, she told of her "desperate battle" to "protect the old" while "encouraging new forms of beauty." She saw cities as living organisms which needed to grow and change to meet practical problems of traffic control, congestion, affordable housing, and clean water. She called for a program of systematic planning so that issues of beauty and history could be balanced against the requirements of modern existence.[24]

Margherita's interest in architecture had always taken second place to painting and sculpture. Similarly the decorative and industrial arts were not her special study, but when Mussolini's power presented her with opportunities to control the future of these arts, she took them; she realized she would be able to impose a modernist sensibility on all the arts of Fascist Italy. She valued most, following Ruskin, those eras that had such a unified aesthetic style. She wanted to be remembered as the guiding spirit behind a Fascist aesthetic, which she felt could be forced on the country as surely as the government had been.

In 1925 she organized Italian participation in the International Exposition of Modern Decorative and Industrial Arts, which the French government hosted in Paris. The exposition consisted of a series of official French buildings and the pavilions of twenty-one other countries. The French conceived of the fair in highly competitive terms, seeking to reassert their dominance in the production of decorative arts and luxury goods. The planners deliberately emphasized the industrial arts and excluded all forms of folk crafts, putting countries such as Italy at a disadvantage. The exhibition introduced to a large public the new world of modern style, including the application of Art Deco to industrial design.[25]

The Paris exposition was scheduled to take place at the same time as the second International Exhibit of Decorative Arts, hosted by the Italians in Monza, which excluded the industrial arts. Margherita had little to do with the first two Monza fairs beyond securing financial support from Mussolini. The Italian exhibits were organized by region, an arrangement that stressed peasant crafts and folk art. Margherita sarcastically called the Monza exhibit an "ethnographic retrospective" and rejected the application of peasant art to commercially produced decorative objects and furniture.

Margherita appreciated folk art. But her admiration was reserved for peasant craftwork produced according to traditional methods. The Germans, she readily admitted, excelled at precise, high-quality, mechanical reproduction. But she had assumed the elitist attitude that mass-produced items could never be beautiful. Therefore, she glorified the painstaking individual creations of Italian artisans.[26] As a result, Margherita found the work of the Futurist Fortunato Depero displayed at Monza provocative but confusing. Depero's abstract fabric designs and painted panels, "violently torn from any tradition," as Margherita described them, were obviously intended for only the most modern of homes. But Margherita insisted that the principles of modern architecture dictated that decorative objects must be defined by the "severe rhythm of necessity." Since Depero's objects had a purely decorative value, she argued that they made no sense in a modern architectural environment. Margherita's views explain the surprise that awaited her at the Paris exposition.[27]

Italy's participation in the Paris exposition assumed a great importance, for it was the Fascist regime's first international showing after the Matteotti crisis.[28] Although Margherita's involvement in the Italian exhibit in Paris was an extension of her privileged position, she was well suited to the work. As a result of her book on French women in World War I, and her long association with French artists and intellectuals, she was a well-known personality in Paris.

Margherita wielded considerable influence at the Paris fair. She served in six different official capacities. She was president of the Italian jury, and also represented the province of Lombardy on that body. On the international jury, she was vice-president; she also sat on three separate architectural juries, including one on which Mario Sironi served. Clearly Margherita was responsible for Sironi's official presence there. No doubt Margherita also persuaded Mussolini to choose Armando Brasini to design the Italian pavilion. Brasini's structure, a huge, uninspired mausoleum of a building combining Roman and Cinquecento elements, proved to be something of an embarrassment.

The exhibits were only slightly more successful. Margherita managed to exclude from the pavilion the kind of vulgar products she criticized at Monza. But much of the exhibit was unattractively displayed. Individual objects were presented in cases as if in a museum. Two sections were thoughtfully designed, and were more successful. Despite her hesitations regarding Fortunato Depero's contributions to the Monza fair, Margherita allowed Marinetti to plan a Futurist area that included carpets, cushions, painted panels, posters, and book jackets designed by the artists Enrico Prampolini, Giacomo Balla, and Depero. She also included a section featuring products of the Piatti silk mills at Como, including a spectacular series of shawls and fabrics designed by Marcello Nizzoli and others. Adolfo Wildt's bust of Mussolini, first shown at the 1924 Venice Biennale, was again prominently displayed.[29]

Margherita unexpectedly found herself having to defend Italy's disappointing showing. When she first arrived at Brasini's tomblike Italian pavilion, she was taken aback by the Soviet pavilion directly across the street. The audacious design by Konstantin Melnikov was an early example of abstract modernist architecture, in the idiom soon known as "International Style." In homage to the Russian Constructivist artists, Melnikov's two-story building consisted of a severe facade of glass panes broken vertically in the center by a solid wall. The contrast between Brasini's decorative excess and Melnikov's starkly simple structure was unnerving. Margherita's public response to the Soviet building was contradictory: in her preface to the official Italian catalog, intended for visitors at the exposition, she acknowledged Melnikov's design as an "extreme point of the artistic avantgarde." In an article in *Il Popolo d'Italia,* aimed at readers at home, she criticized it as crude, not terribly original, and not at all functional. She pointed out that the objects displayed inside were anything but modern.[30]

Margherita's imagination was more strongly captured by the young Swiss-born architect Charles Édouard Jeanneret, who became known internationally by the pseudonym Le Corbusier. He had designed the revolutionary pavilion for the magazine *L'Esprit Nouveau.* Le Corbusier's architecture employed metals, glass, and reinforced concrete, and was inspired by machine forms in which all unnecessary detail had been eliminated. Two years earlier he had published his articles from *L'Esprit Nouveau* as a book, *Vers une architecture* (*Toward a New Architecture*), a manifesto of simplicity and functionalism, in which he described a house as "a machine to be lived in."

His ideas were not entirely new to Margherita. In 1914, her young friend Antonio Sant'Elia had announced in a manifesto of Futurist architecture that steel, reinforced concrete, and glass were the building materials of the future. Sant'Elia had also condemned the kind of artificial decoration that Brasini favored. Even Le Corbusier's definition of a house as a "machine" had been presaged in Sant'Elia's manifesto. Still, the work of Le Corbusier and Melnikov was revolutionary, and the fact that she had never seen anything like it at home underscored the cultural gap that had separated Italian architecture from progressive international currents since Sant'Elia's death in 1916. She now understood that Brasini's counterfeit historical references were an inadequate tribute to the Fascist revolution.[31]

In analyzing Le Corbusier's work, Margherita set forth the basic tenets of her own architectural ideas. She chided him for what she termed the cold, inhuman qualities of his "rational" approach. The term Rationalism was soon to be generally applied to architectural movements based on the belief that the social, economic, and aesthetic problems of the modern world could be resolved by the application of reason to design.

Margherita acknowledged Le Corbusier as "a man of much genius, of passion, and good faith," but she decried the fact that his "mentality is fanatic, Puritan, and Nordic, of the sort that today we would call . . . Protestant." Her judgment was not entirely negative, for she found in his work a "lyricism" that transcended mathematical rationality. But she expressed concern about those who would take his ideas to the extreme, "those little Le Corbusiers who will certainly follow him, [who will be] totally utilitarian . . . who will place the functional, the rigid, the brutal, the precise, the ordinary above the ornate, the graceful, and the delicate." Despite her hesitations, Margherita acknowledged the "radical and enormous" influence of *Vers une architecture*. Fortunato Depero was similarly convinced. From Paris, he brought copies of Le Corbusier's book to two architectural students in Milan, Luigi Figini and Gino Pollini. One of their colleagues, Carlo Rava, also distributed copies among his friends. Margherita insisted that Le Corbusier's ideas should be studied carefully, without preconceived notions but also without complete surrender to his concepts.

Although Margherita publicly defended Brasini's pavilion, she lost all enthusiasm for it. She praised its "Latin, Roman, and Italian character," stretching all credibility to describe it as having "a boldness of expression that is entirely modern." She admitted that Brasini had allowed "a bit of rhetoric" to impose itself on his otherwise "creative design," but excused the excess as the result of the project's having been conceived and executed in a hurry. Some critics, she noted, would have preferred an Italian pavilion designed by the engineer who had built the FIAT factory in Turin, but she refused to accept the idea that the same angular, unadorned forms used in factory design were also suitable to homes or public buildings. The kind of environment in which people lived, she asserted, was a spiritual question.[32]

Margherita scored a far greater success in Paris than did the Italian pavilion. She worked tirelessly with a tact, intelligence, and cooperative spirit that impressed French officials. During the weeks she spent in Paris, she renewed old friendships, including one with former premier Louis Barthou. Margherita had first met the cultured politician in 1915 when she visited Paris to write her *Milizia femminile in Francia*. Now Barthou hosted an impressive luncheon in Margherita's honor. The Italian ambassador attended, as did French intellectuals and high-ranking government officials. These latter had their own reasons for promoting Italian goodwill: They wanted to secure Mussolini's support for a security pact that guaranteed both the French-German and the Austrian-Italian frontiers.[33]

Ugo Ojetti arrived in Paris for an extended visit during the exposition. Peering skeptically through his monocled right eye, he seemed to like nothing. Ojetti proclaimed the Italian pavilion to be dull and uninspired, and expressed disdain for the many American expatriates flocking to the Left Bank. He reacted negatively to the famous Moulin Rouge—the nudity of an American variety show he thought decadent, and he was not at all taken with the black American musicians and dancers who were becoming the rage across Europe. But Margherita found the African-American dance troupes fascinating. As latently racist as most Europeans of the day, she believed the dancers to have a "natural" sense of rhythm. The young entertainer Josephine Baker had just arrived from New York to star in the variety show *La Revue Nègre*. On the evening of November 7 she performed at a special gala that closed the exposition. Margherita met and took an immediate liking to "la Joséphine." When Baker eventually visited Italy, she stayed at Il Soldo.

Despite the criticisms leveled against Italy's pavilion, Margherita returned home in triumph. In January 1926, the French government awarded her the medal of the Legion of Honor for her work as vice-president of the exposition. She prized the distinction for the rest of her life.[34] Although she still had some doubts, the more Margherita studied Rationalism, the more she became convinced that it was the ideal architecture for the Fascist era. She came to realize that it presented all the elements of classical architecture, yet in a distinctly contemporary guise. She soon found allies to support her view. In January 1926 the critic Roberto Papini, writing in the journal *Architettura e Arti Decorative,* condemned Brasini's "rhetorical passa-

Fondamenta Misericordia, the Venetian canal
in the Old Ghetto where Margherita was
born in 1880, the last child of Amedeo
Grassini and Emma Levi R. S. BROWNING

Margherita Grassini about the age of ten
MAGALI SARFATTI-LARSON

Palazzo Bembo, the stately palace on the
Grand Canal to which the Grassini family
moved in 1894 BRIAN R. SULLIVAN

Margherita Grassini Sarfatti about the time she met Mussolini, ca. 1911–12
E. SOMMARIVA; FIAMMETTA SARFATTI GAETANI

Cesare Sarfatti, the brilliant trial lawyer whom Margherita Grassini married when he was thirty-two and she eighteen, shown here in a portrait by Lino Selvatico, 1901
PRIVATE COLLECTION, ROME

Studio portrait of Margherita and her daughter, Fiammetta, taken in Milan about 1912 E. SOMMARIVA; FIAMMETTA SARFATTI GAETANI

Margherita first encountered the artist Umberto Boccioni at an exhibit in 1908 when she saw a version of his etching *The Mother Knitting*. COURTESY OF LUCA CARRÀ

Boccioni made this sketch of Margherita soon after their first meeting. Her inscription at the bottom reads "1909—Me, done by Boccioni." PRIVATE COLLECTION

Portrait of Margherita's second son, Amedeo, age seven, drawn by Fortunino Matania, 1909 AMEDEO SARFATTI

Margherita's first son, Roberto, was a restless fifteen-year-old when Italy entered World War I. FIAMMETTA SARFATTI GAETANI

Il Soldo, the country villa in Cavallasca, near Lake Como, where Margherita spent her summers, wrote many of her books, and entertained artists and intellectuals
AMEDEO SARFATTI

The poet Ada Negri, ca. 1910. Negri was Margherita's closest friend and "Aunt Ada" to the Sarfatti children.
GIANGUIDO SCALFI

A photograph showing a beautiful and determined Margherita Sarfatti about 1910, taken by the well-known Jewish photographer Mario Nunes Vais
ISTITUTO CENTRALE PER IL CATOLOGO E LA DOCUMENTAZIONE, ROME, NO. F37141

Portrait of Margherita Sarfatti with hat by Mario Sironi, painted during World War I, ca. 1916 PRIVATE COLLECTION, VENICE

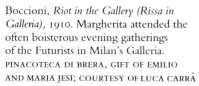

Boccioni, *Riot in the Gallery (Rissa in Galleria)*, 1910. Margherita attended the often boisterous evening gatherings of the Futurists in Milan's Galleria.
PINACOTECA DI BRERA, GIFT OF EMILIO AND MARIA JESI; COURTESY OF LUCA CARRÀ

The Futurist "General Staff," shown here in Paris in 1912. *From left:* Luigi Russolo, Carlo Carrà, F. T. Marinetti, Umberto Boccioni, Gino Severini
COURTESY OF LUCA CARRÀ

A postcard to Margherita during World War I (August 1915) from her Futurist friends in the Volunteer Cyclist Battalion: Carlo Erba, Umberto Boccioni, Anselmo Bucci, Antonio Sant'Elia, Luigi Russolo, and Achille Funi AMEDEO SARFATTI

A youthful Benito Mussolini. *Left:* At age twenty, when he was in Switzerland in order to avoid military service. *Right:* In 1910 he was editor of the Socialist paper *La Lotta di Classe* but had not yet become nationally prominent. WIDE WORLD PHOTOS

Seventeen-year-old Roberto Sarfatti, fired by patriotic fervor and a thirst for action, shown here in his *Alpini* uniform after he enlisted in July 1917 FIAMMETTA SARFATTI GAETANI

Roberto Sarfatti and his older *Alpini* comrades, 1917 FIAMMETTA SARFATTI GAETANI

Mario Sironi, the brooding but brilliant painter, became Margherita's close friend and favorite artist. He is shown here *(right)* in his Milan studio, ca. 1930–33, with the critic Raffaele Carrieri. One of Sironi's *Urban Landscape*s hangs on the wall between them.

Boccioni wrote to Margherita about his last major work, *Portrait of Maestro Busoni (Ritratto di Maestro Busoni),* in 1916. She was among the first to see the painting, which signaled the "return to order" among Italian artists.
GALLERIA NAZIONALE D'ARTE MODERNA DI ROMA

Sironi's *Cyclist (Il ciclista),* 1916, which Margherita owned, marked the painter's break with Futurism.
PRIVATE COLLECTION, ROME

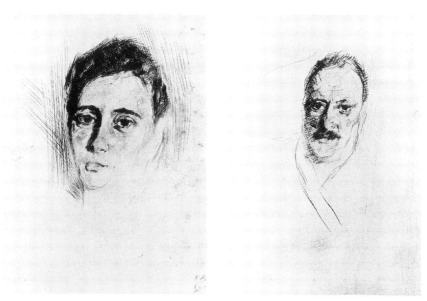

Etchings of grief-stricken Margherita and Cesare Sarfatti by Mario Sironi, done at Il Soldo in 1917 after Roberto's death PRIVATE COLLECTION, ROME

Margherita Sarfatti with head of Fiammetta, by Achille Funi, ca. 1919–20. The painting shows that the artist had abandoned Futurism but was still influenced by the Metaphysical style. PRIVATE COLLECTION, ROME

Oval portrait of Margherita
Sarfatti by Sironi, ca. 1919–22,
when she and Mussolini had
fallen deeply in love PRIVATE
COLLECTION, ROME

Portrait of Margherita Sarfatti
by Sironi, ca. 1919–22 PRIVATE
COLLECTION, VENICE

A humorous sketch of the Sarfatti family and friends at Il Soldo by Achille Funi,
1921. *Clockwise from left:* Margherita, the sculptor Arturo Martini, Cesare, Funi,
and Amedeo; in the center, "A fine boiled capon." PRIVATE COLLECTION, VENICE

Achille Funi, *Motherhood (Maternità)*, 1921. This painting, once part of Margherita's collection, shows how the artist's *Novecento* style combined Renaissance and modern influences.

Ubaldo Oppi, *Portrait of His Wife on a Venetian Background (Ritratto della moglie sullo sfondo di Venezia)*, 1921. Oppi was an early member of Margherita's *Novecento* movement. Like Funi, he employed Renaissance and modern elements in his work. COURTESY OF LUCA CARRÀ

Sironi's painting *The Pupil (L'allieva)*, 1923, on the left, reveals his use of formal classical allusions and a powerfully original style. This work was shown at a special *Novecento* exhibit arranged by Margherita at the 1924 Venice Biennale, along with his *The Architect (L'architetto)*, on the right. BOTH IN PRIVATE COLLECTIONS, ITALY

Gerarchia, Mussolini's Fascist magazine, was edited by Margherita. Here, a 1925 issue with a cover illustration by Sironi shows the Roman theme.

Amedeo Sarfatti, an avid mountain climber, about 1921 AMEDEO SARFATTI

Margherita holding a baby lamb in the countryside near Il Soldo, ca. 1920 GIANGUIDO SCALFI

Margherita in St. Mark's Square, Venice, 1922 GIANGUIDO SCALFI

The Duce (with sash) among his Blackshirts in Naples, October 1922, on the eve of the March on Rome AP/WIDE WORLD PHOTOS

In May 1923, some six months after Mussolini became prime minister, he spoke in Rome before the International Women's Suffrage Alliance. Margherita, in white dress and hat, gave a simultaneous translation of his remarks into English.

Cesare Sarfatti at his desk, shortly before his death in 1924 GIANGUIDO SCALFI

Adolfo Wildt's tomb for Cesare Sarfatti,
Jewish Cemetery, Milan BRIAN R. SULLIVAN

Giacomo Matteotti, the
Socialist deputy whose
murder by Fascist thugs
in the summer of 1924
provoked a political crisis
that almost toppled
Mussolini UPI/BETTMANN

Mussolini visited Gabriele D'Annunzio
at the poet's residence, Il Vittoriale, in
1925. Margherita had written secretly
to D'Annunzio asking him to make
sure Mussolini, who was recuperating
from the tensions of the Matteotti
crisis, got some rest. AP/WIDE WORLD
PHOTOS

Mussolini in 1925 in the apartment on Via Rasella which Margherita had
chosen for him. (From Attilio Tamaro, *Venti anni di storia*. Rome: Tiber, 1953.)

Cesira Carocci, Mussolini's maid, whom Margherita had hired to look after the Duce and to provide her with information about his private activities ISTITUTO LUCE, ROME

Mussolini and his family on the steps of the Villa Torlonia, Rome, about 1929–30. *From left:* Rachele, Anna Maria, Vittorio, Romano, Mussolini, Edda, and Bruno. ISTITUTO LUCE, ROME

The prime minister at his desk in Palazzo Venezia, reading
foreign newspaper clippings, February 1931 WIDE WORLD:
PHOTOGRAPH COURTESY OF THE NATIONAL ARCHIVES

Edda Ciano, Mussolini's favorite daughter, with British diplomat Anthony Eden
(left) and her husband, Galeazzo Ciano, at a reception in Rome, June 1935
INTERNATIONAL NEWS SERVICE

Margherita originally praised architect Armando Brasini's Italian pavilion *(left)* for the 1925 Paris Exposition of Modern Decorative and Industrial Arts, but when she saw Le Corbusier's nearby pavilion for *L'Esprit Nouveau (right)*, she became a champion of architectural modernism.

The modernistic Santa Maria Novella railroad station in Florence, 1932, which Margherita pressed Mussolini to approve, caused great controversy among art critics and Fascist officials. BILDARCHIV FOTO, MARBURG

Dux, Adolfo Wildt's marble bust, ca. 1923–24, portrayed Mussolini as Italy's new Caesar (BETTMANN); his *Margherita Sarfatti,* ca. 1926, was clearly a companion piece. PRIVATE COLLECTION, ROME

An elegant Margherita Sarfatti in Milan at the time she was organizing the 1926 *Novecento* exhibit
E. SOMMARIVA; FIAMMETTA SARFATTI GAETANI

Margherita, in white dress in front row, listens to Mussolini's address at the opening of the *Novecento* exhibit in 1926. L´ILLUSTRAZIONE ITALIANA, FEBRUARY 21, 1926

A pensive Margherita Sarfatti, May 1926
AMEDEO SARFATTI

MARGHERITA SARFATTI - Scrittrice.

ce volante del "Chi è?"

Postcard, October 1929,
showing Margherita and
the motto that came to be
identified with her: "For
Italians the word *Art* is a
second name for *la patria*"
AMEDEO SARFATTI

Portrait of Margherita Sarfatti and
Fiammetta, by the *Scuola Romana* artist
Carlo Socrate, ca. 1929 ANTONIO AND
MARINA FORCHINO, TURIN

On the deck of the *Duilio,* about 1929
FIAMMETTA SARFATTI GAETANI

Nicholas Murray Butler *(white-haired man holding top hat),* president of Columbia University and one of Margherita's American friends, before the Tomb to the Unknown Soldier, Rome, ca. 1929–32 NICHOLAS MURRAY BUTLER COLLECTION, COLUMBIA UNIVERSITY

In 1930, Margherita began writing articles under Mussolini's name for William Randolph Hearst's newspaper chain. She negotiated the deal with Hearst's manager, T. V. Ranck *(left),* and his chief European correspondent, Karl von Wiegand *(right),* who pose here with Hearst's lover, film star Marion Davies. KARL VON WIEGAND COLLECTION, HOOVER INSTITUTION ARCHIVES, STANFORD UNIVERSITY

Society photographer Ghitta Carell did a series of photos of Margherita in her Rome apartment in 1931, including this one of her examining a silver Bible cover. FIAMMETTA SARFATTI GAETANI

Carell also took this shot of Margherita posed beneath Funi's *Maternità*.
FIAMMETTA SARFATTI GAETANI

Margherita at the 1932 Convegno Volta, Rome, with
(*from left*) Fascist intellectual Arturo Marpicati, head of
the Venice Biennale Count Giuseppe Volpi di Misurata,
and former British ambassador Sir Rennel Rodd
L'ILLUSTRAZIONE ITALIANA, NOVEMBER 20, 1932

In 1933, Margherita sailed to Egypt to attend the funeral of her brother Marco.
On board the *Ausonia*, she met Crown Prince Umberto and Princess Maria Josè
LEFT: FIAMMETTA SARFATTI GAETANI RIGHT: FOTO RCS RIZZOLI PERIODICI

Margherita with Captain Lena of the
Conte di Savoia en route to the United
States, 1934 FIAMMETTA SARFATTI GAETANI

The first meeting between Mussolini
and Hitler, Venice, 1934. At left is
journalist Thomas B. Morgan, who
helped Margherita write some of
Mussolini's articles for the American
press. (From Thomas B. Morgan, *Spurs
on the Boot* New York: 1941.)

In Hollywood, 1934, Margherita
visited the MGM studios with Louis
B. Mayer and film star May Robson
ACADEMY OF MOTION PICTURE ARTS
AND SCIENCES, HOLLYWOOD

Margherita with Bernardo Attolico, Italian ambassador to
Berlin, about 1935 FIAMMETTA SARFATTI GAETANI

Roberto Farinacci,
intransigent Fascist leader
whose anti-Semitic and
anti-modernist views
brought Margherita under
attack in the 1930s AP/WIDE
WORLD PHOTOS

American ambassador Breckinridge Long, whose diary records numerous meetings with Margherita, presenting former aviation minister Italo Balbo with the Distinguished Flying Cross, Tripoli, 1936 MRS. ARNOLD WILLCOX

The tomb of Roberto Sarfatti, Col d'Echele, designed by Giuseppe Terragni and completed in 1938
BRIAN R. SULLIVAN

Margherita in Vienna, 1938
AMEDEO SARFATTI

Mussolini and Hitler on the balcony of Palazzo Vecchio, Florence, during the Führer's visit to Italy in May 1938 NATIONAL ARCHIVES

Galeazzo Ciano *(right),* Mussolini's son-in-law and foreign minister, and Dino Alfieri *(center),* minister of popular culture. Alfieri, who had worked in Cesare Sarfatti's law office as a student, tried to lure Margherita back to Italy in 1939. NATIONAL ARCHIVES

Margherita was on a French cruise ship off Norway in August 1939 when Hitler and Stalin signed their Non-Aggression Pact. FIAMMETTA SARFATTI GAETANI

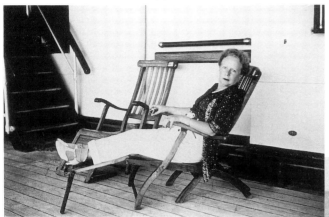

Margherita on board the *Augustus* as
she sailed to exile in South America,
September 1939 FIAMMETTA SARFATTI
GAETANI

On the beach at Montevideo
during World War II MAGALÌ
SARFATTI-LARSON

In an Argentine newspaper, Margherita
saw this photograph of the bodies
of former Fascist Party Secretary
Achille Starace *(left)*, Mussolini *(center)*,
and Clara Petacci hanging in Piazzale
Loreto, Milan, April 29, 1945. AP/WIDE
WORLD PHOTOS

On her return to Italy, an older and thinner Margherita Sarfatti talks with journalists in the garden at Il Soldo, September 7, 1947. FOTO RCS RIZZOLI PERIODICI

In November 1948, Margherita entered into a contract with American plastic surgeon I. Daniel Shorell to sell the letters Mussolini had written to her over the years.

Shorell watched as Margherita consigned the letters to a bank in Rome for safekeeping. FOTO RCS RIZZOLI PERIODICI

In Rome with the painter
Giorgio De Chirico *(center)*,
1949–50 FOTO RCS RIZZOLI
PERIODICI

Left: Margherita at a
restaurant with anti-Fascist
painter and novelist Carlo
Levi *(right)*, January 31, 1949.
Below: At the same function
with actress Anna Magnani,
whose back is to the camera.
FOTO RCS RIZZOLI PERIODICI

Bernard Berenson, famed American
expatriate and connoisseur, with whom
Margherita shared her ideas about art
and life in the years after World War II,
shown here at his Villa I Tatti, 1952
BETTMANN

A corpulent Margherita on the beach at
the Lido, Venice, September 1949 FOTO
RCS RIZZOLI PERIODICI

The grave marker of Margherita
Sarfatti, Cavallasca BRIAN R. SULLIVAN

tism" and advocated Italy's own modern architects.

The editorial director of *Architettura e Arti Decorative* was the architect Marcello Piacentini, whose reputation was rapidly rising. That very year he had built the Hotel Ambasciatori on the fashionable Via Veneto, across from the American embassy. The hotel's multistoried facade suffered from the same overdone, confused mixture of historical styles as had Brasini's Paris pavilion. There were columns, arches, and a Renaissance loggia bearing classical statues at the top. Piacentini was moving toward a cautious style combining the classical and modern idioms. Piacentini manuevered himself close to Margherita over the next several years. This somewhat forced association seems to have aided Piacentini's reputation. His conservative modernism and a talent for compromise secured him numerous government commissions over the next decade and a half. Calculating and ambitious, Piacentini hoped to win the uncontested status of master architect of the Fascist regime. He believed Margherita could help him achieve his goal.[35]

Meanwhile, Milan had become a center of heightened architectural activity, although most architects recognized that professional success depended on the government in Rome. Two quite distinct tendencies began to emerge. Contemporary critics identified one of these as the architectural equivalent to Margherita's *Novecento* movement. Its chief practitioner, Giovanni Muzio, had applied simplified classical motifs to a controversial apartment complex during 1921 and 1922; it was dubbed derisively by critics the *Ca'brutta,* the "ugly house." Margherita thought that many of its decorative elements were artificial, but in spite of her growing admiration for Rationalism, she admired the Roman aspect of the immense archway that led to the entrance courtyard. Because these architects gave classical elements a modern flavor, they appealed to Margherita's aesthetic ideas. Yet she did not feel that the neoclassicists constituted a distinctive group or movement.[36]

The other architectural trend to emerge in Milan was the "Gruppo 7," whose seven members proclaimed themselves Italy's first Rationalists. All were in their twenties when, in December 1926, they published an announcement of a "new spirit" in architecture. Two of their number, Luigi Figini and Gino Pollini, had been among the first in Italy to receive copies of *Vers une architecture* after Depero's return from the Paris exhibition the previous year. A third, Giuseppe Terragni, was especially talented. These young men claimed Gropius, Mies Van Der Rohe, and Le Corbusier as their heroes. The Gruppo 7 defined its mission as the reestablishment of Italy's primacy in architecture. They saw no reason why they could not reconcile their nationalist stance with the international character of the modern style. Their insistence on creating new forms inspired by past traditions put them in direct opposition to the Futurists, who had categorically rejected the past, but the Rationalists considered themselves perfectly in step with Fascism. Their blending of past and future fit perfectly into Margherita's aesthetic. In the spring of 1926, in connection with the opening of the *Novecento* exhibition, she had anticipated that her art movement would give birth to "a new aspect of tradition." A few months later, the Gruppo 7 announced, "We do not want to break with tradition; it is tradition that reforms itself and assumes new aspects."[37]

The members of the Gruppo 7 separated themselves from the neoclassical architects by insisting on a rigid adherence to logic and rationality and a rejection of all decoration that did not derive from function. "The new forms of architecture," they argued, "must receive their aesthetic value only from necessity, only as a result of which . . . will style emerge." Eventually Margherita came around to their position. "Function," she wrote in 1925, "is not beauty. Indeed, beauty begins precisely at that point—not before—where function ends. Function is, however, the trampoline from which beauty springs."[38]

In late 1925 or early 1926, Manlio Morgagni, editor of *La Rivista Illustrata* (an illustrated supplement to *Il Popolo d'Italia*) sponsored competitions for the design of a monumental Terme Littorie (Lictoral Baths) in Rome. and for the interior design of an Italian embassy building. Margherita sat on the jury with Piacentini and others. First prize for the Terme Littorie went to a Venetian architect named Duilio Torres, who soon joined the Rationalist movement despite his essentially classical design. His principal building resembled a basilica, the upper half of which consisted of a series of rounded, terraced levels, each encircled by Roman arches. A secondary prize was awarded to Carlo Enrico Rava, a member of the newly founded Gruppo 7. First prize for the embassy project was given to two neoclassical architects. Neither competition, as Morgagni noted, resulted in architectural "miracles."[39]

More significant was the impact of the third Monza International Exhibition of Decorative Arts in 1927, over which Margherita exerted great influence.[40] Mussolini placed the Monza exhibition under the direct control of the central government. Margherita was appointed to a new organizing committee that also included *Novecentisti* Mario Sironi, Carlo Carrà, and Gio Ponti. The committee gave the Monza fair an entirely new look, eliminating the traditional emphasis on rural crafts and insisting that the Italian pavilions make a "deliberately subversive" modern statement. Margherita declared that the purpose of the exhibition was to "reach the people, to see to it that good taste and modern taste penetrate from above into the widest and deepest strata of the nation." As a result, it was now imperative that Italy learn to manufacture mass-produced objects that were both beautiful and functional so that they could reach the largest number of people.[41] This was an abrupt change from her earlier disdain for industrial goods, probably occasioned by her experience at the Paris exhibition.

Her Paris experience also led her to change the way exhibits were presented. For the first time, the 1927 Monza fair aimed to achieve a collaboration between architects and artists, through the cooperative design of complete room ensembles. Fascism was directly evident in an *Office for a Federal Fascist Party Secretary* by Enrico Del Debbio, containing a marble altar surmounted by a bust of Mussolini by the sculptor Attilio Selva. Another room, dedicated to *Il Popolo d'Italia,* displayed many of Sironi's original drawings and covers, probably from Margherita's private collection. Aesthetically more important, however, were the rooms placed along a "street of shops" created by a group of Piedmontese architects. The "Butcher Shop," a joint project by the painter Felice Casorati and the Rationalist Alberto Sartoris, included a meat counter faced with a bas-relief, while Emilio Sobrero's "Bar" featured a curved, concave marble bar that stood in front of a similarly curved white wall. On the wall, glass shelves set into arched niches bore a series of colored glass bottles. Both displays were of modernized neoclassical designs. Margherita was critical of Gigi Chessa's "Pharmacy," for its dark-wood shelves and ceramic medicine jars she found too reminiscent of an old-fashioned drugstore: her enthusiasm for Rationalism led her to demand a more "antiseptic" environment.[42]

The Monza fair represented the Gruppo 7's first opportunity to introduce its ideas to a wider public. Gino Pollini and Luigi Figini showed plans for a parking garage and a worker *dopolavoro* (afterwork activities) building, while Carlo Enrico Rava and Sebastiano Larco designed a newspaper office and an office building. Giuseppe Terragni first achieved recognition here with designs for a gasworks plant.

Measured in terms of genius, independence of spirit, and strength of conviction, Terragni the architect and Sironi the painter were the most significant creative figures to embrace Fascism. The two men became friends and collaborated on a number of projects. Terragni's relationship with Margherita and her *Novecento* movement was direct, for he was an enthusiastic painter. He met her and Sironi while in Milan. He absorbed their concern for volume, form, and order; in 1929, he even contributed a self-portrait to the second *Novecento* exhibition. Margherita took a strong personal liking to the young Terragni, and over the years used her influence to support his career. When staying at Il Soldo, she frequently visited his studio in nearby Como and often debated details of a particular project with him. She showed the depth of her admiration for Terragni a number of years later when she chose him to design the tomb for her dead son, Roberto.[43]

As the 1927 exhibit closed, Margherita proposed that the fairs be held every three instead of every two years, so as to allow more time for the development of exhibits, and that the site of the fair be moved to Milan, where many more people would visit it. Mussolini approved both suggestions. Mario Sironi played an increasingly crucial role in the fairs. The next two—in 1930 and 1933—saw the the emergence of a Fascist aesthetic of public art under the combined influence of Sironi and the Rationalist architects.[44]

Margherita now saw in Rationalist architecture a bold revolutionary style, perfectly symbolic of the new Italy Fascism was forging. Like the Catholic Church, Fascism turned to architecture—"the most concrete and at the same time the most symbolic of the arts"—to translate its spiritual message into physical images. Of all the various forms of artistic expression, she had come to see architecture as "the most representative of a people and an historical period: architecture, mother of the arts, an art supremely collective, social, and political."[45]

The details of Margherita's role in swaying Mussolini toward Rationalism are uncertain, but evidence indicates that her influence was appreciable. The fate of Brasini is suggestive in this regard. By April of 1928, he had received Mussolini's approval for a project that would have demolished entire sections of the center of Rome in order to "isolate" key monuments and accommodate a grotesque new forum he had designed. But then Mussolini received a memorandum from the head of the Fascist Architects' Union, Alberto Calza Bini (with whom Margherita had served on the jury for the Lictoral Baths), attacking Brasini's project.[46]

At virtually the same moment, the first exhibition of Rationalist architecture opened in Rome. The exhibit included the work of forty-two architects, including the Gruppo 7. Since a large number of the participants were students with no practical experience, most of the displays were projects on paper. Their work was marked by an antidecorative emphasis that excluded classical references such as columns and arches. Luciano Baldessari's contributions consisted of photographs of an exhibition he had put together the previous year for the Como silk fair. Baldessari's design, which Margherita had reviewed enthusiastically, represented a series of futuristic shop windows inside which the visitor stood, thus participating in the "environments" of silks draped against the wall and on odd mannequins designed by the Cubist sculptor Alexander Archipenko.[47]

The Rationalists achieved widespread critical coverage and sparked a broad debate on architectural style. Some critics, including Piacentini and Ojetti, charged that Rationalist architecture was too "international" in spirit and origin to represent Italy's distinctive heritage. Such criticisms were intended to suggest that Rationalism was not an appropriate Fascist style. The Gruppo 7 anticipated such charges. In an early manifesto, Carlo Rava insisted that a Rationalist building would certainly have been more powerfully evocative of Fascist imperialism than Brasini's ridiculous Paris pavilion. "It has clearly been shown," he wrote, "how our movement of rational architecture fits perfectly into the cultural program of Fascism. And this is, we believe, a fact that *is well known*. . . . Some think that so-called traditionalist architecture represents the spirit of an 'imperial' Italy simply because it imitates Roman architecture, rather than creating something new, as that spirit demands." Once Italy put itself at the head of the new European architectural movement, Rava concluded, it would impose upon the entire world an even more powerful form of cultural imperialism.[48]

Mussolini did not personally visit the exhibit, but it was opened by Emilio Bodrero, undersecretary for education and a friend of Margherita's. The show had also been given the official sanction of the Fascist Architects' Union, and Calza Bini was among the exhibitors. Margherita's usual monthly column in *La Rivista Illustrata* was written that April by Roberto Papini, who gave the Rationalists a strong endorsement.[49] Margherita did not directly review the exhibition, writing instead a lengthy article for *Il Popolo d'Italia,* titled simply "Architecture." In this she bitterly assaulted all forms of historical style: "Is it possible," she asked, "that our epoch, unadorned, harsh, and severe, an epoch that is so expressive and distinctive of its own physiognomy, must continue to express itself through imitation and falsification, through camouflage and falsehood? Lies, lies, lies. In statics as in the lesser applied arts, in the industrial and decorative arts, all of which are dependent on and intimately connected to architecture, falsehood is the rule and sincerity the exception." Among the exceptions, however, Margherita noted that some architects were now aspiring toward a more truthful simplicity, that some were beginning to understand that statuary, fake marble, and lion masks were not needed in order to "hold up a roof," and that building design must use space "rationally." By the summer, she had cast off all restraint and declared Rationalism the architecture of the Fascist era.[50]

The deliberately indirect manner in which Margherita endorsed Rationalism, coming just as the Rome exhibition opened, suggests that she had been manipulating events behind the scenes. Mussolini ended by rejecting the same Brasini project that he had approved only months earlier. In desperation Brasini begged Mussolini for another government commission to redeem his stature as the regime's favored architect. Mussolini granted the hapless Brasini some public honors, but he never again received a major commission in Italy.[51] With her successful championing of Rationalist architecture, Margherita had helped change the face of Fascist Italy.

22

Dictator of Culture

By the second half of the 1920s, Margherita's professional life increasingly deprived her of Mussolini's company. She wrote constantly—a weekly column for *Il Popolo d'Italia,* pieces for that paper's monthly illustrated magazine, and numerous articles each month for other publications anxious for her expertise or her insights into Mussolini. She continued to direct and write for *Gerarchia.* Independent publications in this period included, besides *Tunisiaca* and *Dux,* an anthology of her art criticism, *Colori, segni e luci (Color, Line, and Light,* 1925), *Achille Funi,* a monograph (1925), a novel, *Il palazzone (The Mansion,* 1929), a statement of her aesthetic ideas, *Storia della pittura moderna (History of Modern Painting,* 1930), and a collection of her essays on literature, *Segni del meridiano (Signs of the Meridian,* 1931). She also composed poetry and countless letters. When not writing, Margherita took part in committees, went to art exhibits, gave public lectures, and attended to the business of the revived *Novecento Italiano.*

With Mussolini in Rome, Margherita longed to be at his side. As early as 1923, she suggested that he secure Cesare a government appointment in the capital, but Mussolini evidently demurred in order to avoid public gossip.[1] After Cesare's death, and once Mussolini's power was secured following the Matteotti crisis, Margherita began to think about moving to Rome permanently. In the spring of 1926, two months after the *Novecento* exhibit had opened, an incident occurred that reinforced Margherita's thinking. On April 5 Margherita traveled with Mussolini by train from Milan to Rome, where she remained for several days at his apartment on the Via Rasella. The morning of April 6 she prepared a speech he was to deliver to an international convention of surgeons, which included some remarks in English. They spent that night together.[2]

On the morning of April 7, Margherita saw to it that Mussolini dressed properly, and made him take a bowler and an elegant black overcoat. Mussolini's personal valet, Quinto Navarra, arrived at 8:00 A.M. and accompanied him to the Campidoglio for his speech. After his speech, Mussolini stopped momentarily among the cheering crowd. Raising his arm in a Fascist salute, he unintentionally pushed his hat—and his head—back an inch or two, just as a shot rang out a few feet away. Mussolini clutched his face and blood began to pour from his hands. An alert police officer grabbed a pistol from a woman and knocked her to the ground. The would-be assassin was a mentally unbalanced fifty-year-old Anglo-Irish woman named Violet Gibson.

Gibson's shot only nicked the bridge of Mussolini's nose, but he lost a lot of blood, and doctors persuaded him to return to his apartment. Margherita, distraught, rushed to his bedside. Later that afternoon, much to her annoyance, he resumed his regular schedule of appearances, sporting a bandage across his nose.[3]

Margherita was horrified by this second attempt on Mussolini's life. When, on September 11, yet another assassination plot was foiled, Margherita expressed her outrage in an editorial in *Gerarchia*. She argued that Mussolini's life had to be protected at all costs because it belonged not only to Italy but to history itself. To a friend she wrote, "God has protected Italy."[4]

Throughout 1926, as she inaugurated the *Novecento* movement, Margherita made her home in the capital at the Palace Hotel. By the fall, Mussolini agreed to her permanent move to Rome. They felt the need to arrange a subterfuge: She asked Alberto Salietti, secretary for the *Novecento*, to request government authorization to hold a second national exhibition. Mussolini's response had been agreed to in advance—the next exhibition, he instructed Salietti, should have "its natural seat in Rome."[5]

Margherita moved to Rome with Fiammetta, now seventeen. *Gerarchia* continued to be published in Milan. She entrusted the day-to-day operations to Eloisa Errera Foà, a niece of her brother-in-law Paolo Errera. She stayed at Eloisa's house on her frequent visits to Milan.

By 1927, Margherita had found an apartment in Rome at 19 Corso d'Italia, close to the southern edge of the gardens of the Villa Borghese. It was smaller than her apartment in Milan, too small for many of her paintings. Margherita missed her old friends, particularly Ada Negri, as well as Amedeo, who remained in Milan to pursue a career in banking. But she found her new home beautiful, sunny and quiet.[6] She valued her privacy as much as Mussolini did his. When a friend asked why she never spent entire nights with Mussolini, Margherita replied facetiously: "He wears a nightshirt. He would be afraid I'd laugh at him." The truth seems to be that living apart allowed each the freedom to receive private visitors, lovers, and personal friends.[7]

But after Margherita became a widow, their relationship became more domestic. Fiammetta was only eighteen months older than Mussolini's eldest, and he treated her very much as a daughter. The three of them enjoyed a generally relaxed and happy family life together. While Mussolini usually displayed great reserve and little sense of humor, Margherita and Fiammetta teased him out. Both possessed the rare capacity to make him laugh at himself. He could unwind and joke with them good-naturedly, something he did with very few others.[8]

Margherita found it inconvenient to visit him unobserved at his apartment on the Via Rasella and in the winter of 1929 persuaded him to move to more secluded quarters. He left it to Margherita to make the arrangements. She selected the magnificent seventeenth-century Villa Torlonia on the Via Nomentana. The palace had once housed Napoleon's brother Jerome. On occasion Mussolini had used the villa for official receptions. Margherita persuaded Prince Giovanni Torlonia to vacate the premises and offer it to Mussolini for the nominal rent of one lira a year. Margherita visited the villa often, generally alone but sometimes for dinner with her daughter.[9]

In the early spring of 1928, she changed apartments herself, to Via Nicolò Porpora, 21, near the Rome zoo. In this furnished flat she remained only a short time, until she discovered a much larger, more elegant apartment on the exclusive Via Nomentana, diagonally across the street from the Villa Torlonia. It was at this point that she gave up her home in Milan and moved all her possessions, including her art collection, to Rome.[10]

The apartment on the Via Nomentana provided a convenient location for assignations with Mussolini. Thomas Morgan, who knew Margherita well, described the Duce's visits:

> The house when he came must be without visitors of any kind. If you happened to be there when he telephoned that he would take a run over, Margherita got a headache for you, a heartache for him. You were put out somewhat unceremoniously and down the stairs. The servants would look to make sure that you had cleared the hall before his car arrived. He came unseen by anyone. . . . His car did not stop at the front entrance but drove into a courtyard from the side. The car waited in the courtyard until he was ready to return.[11]

Such precautions were taken partly for security reasons, and partly for the sake of propriety. By now most sophisticated Italians knew about the two lovers. Piero Foà, the son of Margherita's Milanese friends, remembers as a university student attending a theatrical satire that poked fun at her relationship with Mussolini. Indeed, the widespread knowledge of her relationship made Margherita the most powerful woman in Italy.

During the three years that followed Margherita's move to Rome, she enjoyed the status of Mussolini's consort. After his seizure of dictatorial powers, Margherita gained an unquestionable authority. When she entered a room, people rose. Even the royal family treated her with respect. The king remained well aware of Mussolini's hostility toward the monarchy. Vittorio Emanuele III hoped that Margherita would alter that attitude, relying on the old ties of loyalty between Italy's Jews and the House of Savoy. In late 1923, Queen Elena appointed Margherita as a lady-in-waiting and a warm friendship developed between them. The queen even turned to Margherita for advice on aiding the charities favored by the royal family. Margherita and Fiammetta were frequent visitors to the Quirinale Palace and attended every royal baptism, wedding, and funeral. Vittorio Emanuele III even gave Mussolini and Margherita unrestricted access to his seaside villa at Castel Porziano on the coast near Rome. There Margherita could swim to exercise her injured knee, while Mussolini indulged his love of speedboating, with Fiammetta his frequent passenger.[12]

One day his hobby almost proved his undoing. Mussolini wanted to take a drive in his motorboat, while Margherita preferred to stay on the beach near the royal villa. Mussolini persuaded Fiammetta to accompany him, along with his chauffeur Ercole Boratto. They headed south to Anzio, some twenty-five miles down the coast. By the time they arrived there, the sun was already setting, and as Mussolini turned back, darkness descended. Some three miles from their destination, the boat's motor ran out of gas. Invisible in the night and too far from shore to be heard, the three found themselves drifting out to sea. Neither man could swim well enough to reach the shore. But Fiammetta was a fine swimmer. They agreed that only she could save them. She unhesitatingly dived overboard and disappeared.

After what seemed to them a very long time, Mussolini and Boratto heard the sound of an approaching motor. A police launch finally spotted them about 10:00 P.M. and took them under tow. Thereafter Mussolini took his boat out only when accompanied by a naval officer.[13] Such emotional incidents as these added to the rich store of shared experiences that tied Margherita and Mussolini together. By the late twenties, Mussolini had spent far more time in the company of Margherita and Fiammetta than he had with his own wife and children. He and Amedeo were not close; Amedeo revered his father. But Mussolini continued to respect Roberto's memory out of a genuine affection for the fallen young man.[14]

In April 1925, on Mussolini's recommendation, the king granted Roberto Sarfatti the *medaglia d'oro* for the heroic actions that had cost him his young life on the Col d'Echele. Although the award might be seen as an act of favoritism, such does not appear to be the case. There is no doubt that Mussolini believed that Roberto had earned "his well-deserved and great glorification." It is unlikely that Vittorio Emanuel III granted the medal under pressure. In matters regarding the honor of the army, the king maintained the highest standards.[15]

The actual presentation ceremony took place in front of the Milan Cathedral, on November 4, 1925, the seventh anniversary of Italy's victory over Austria-Hungary. Dressed in mourning and accompanied by Amedeo, Margherita stood pale and still as the Duke of Bergamo pinned Roberto's *medaglia d'oro* on her black dress. The huge crowd gathered in the cathedral square applauded while the "Roberto Sarfatti" unit of the Milanese Young Fascists rendered honors. Mussolini did not attend the presentation. Rachele's mother, Anna, had died a few days earlier and the family had gathered for the funeral. This was one of the few times that Mussolini had ever placed Rachele's interests above Margherita's. But Mussolini did telegraph his special wishes for the day to Margherita and asked her to remember him to Amedeo and Fiammetta.[16]

The fact that Margherita apparently confined her authority to cultural affairs appeased anti-feminist Fascist leaders. When she tried to influence Mussolini on political questions, she did so privately. She began serving on a variety of government boards and committees. In 1924, she served on the newly created National Theater Council, and in 1925 she worked on the Paris exposition. The following year, Mussolini appointed her, along with his brother, Arnaldo, to a literacy committee. They developed an annual book festival. In 1927 and 1928 she took part in both the Monza exhibition and the Venice Biennale.[17]

She also participated in the Bologna Congress of Fascist Intellectuals, organized in the spring of 1925 under the aegis of the philosopher Giovanni Gentile. The congress was conceived as a response to charges that Fascism was devoid of intellectual respectability. Some 250 intellectuals sent messages of support or attended the conference, among them some of Margherita's closest friends (Ada Negri, Alfredo Panzini, and Carlo Foà), as well as Marinetti, Ojetti, Soffici, Malaparte, and Lionello Venturi. Margherita enjoyed an especially prominent role at Bologna, for she was one of only two dozen people—and the only woman—to make a formal presentation, on the subject "Art and the National Economy."[18]

The congress produced the idea for a *Manifesto of Fascist Intellectuals*. The Fascist manifesto provoked a response ten days later from the venerable philosopher Benedetto Croce, who published *An Answer by Italian Writers, Professors, and Publicists to the Manifesto of Fascist Intellectuals*. Croce proclaimed adherence to political and intellectual freedom rather than to what he called the "new religion" of Fascism. Croce's manifesto was signed originally by 40 others, but over the next few weeks an imposing array of more than 220 intellectuals added their support. Among them were men and women whose presence in the opposition was particularly annoying to Margherita: her childhood tutor Pompeo Molmenti, the writers Sibilla Aleramo, Eugenio Montale, and Corrado Alvaro, the art critic Enrico Somaré, and even her own cousin Giuseppe Levi, a scientist at the University of Turin. Furthermore, the signers included a disproportionately large number of Jews.[19] Croce's determined and courageous action kept the Bologna congress from being a major success.

Since the foundation of Fascism in 1919, Margherita had brought a degree of cultural respectability to a movement that otherwise appeared to be nothing more than a gang of violent, anti-intellectual thugs. Marinetti and Toscanini were the only other early Fascists of cultural prominence, and they were no longer in the mainstream of Fascism. Margherita's extensive network of friends in artistic and literary circles had enabled her to attract a wider range of figures into the Fascist orbit. Her efforts were especially useful in the tumultuous days during and after the Matteotti crisis, when some intellectuals tried to distance themselves from Mussolini.[20]

Margherita's relationship with Giuseppe Prezzolini is illustrative of her efforts to gain the support of intellectuals for Facism. After the March on Rome, Prezzolini recorded in his diary, "I am pleased by my own attitude toward the government, from which I ask nothing and before which I refuse to kneel." Nonetheless, Mussolini approved his appointment as director of the League of Nations Institute for Intellectual Cooperation in 1925.[21] In 1926, a number of vicious attacks on Prezzolini appeared in the Fascist press. Prezzolini's wife wrote to Margherita in an effort to learn who was behind the campaign, and to see if Margherita would intercede. Margherita's response was disingenuous:

> I haven't seen the attacks and don't know anything. . . . But I don't understand why you are surprised at these political attacks, inevitable given the eminent and visible position your husband holds, and given that his political posture is not very clear and is, therefore, open to interpretation. It is difficult these days not to take a stand, and it is only natural that he who does not take a stand must live with the consequences: sometimes good, like the appointment, and sometimes unpleasant. Take both philosophically!

Prezzolini continued to avoid proclaiming support for Mussolini. No doubt he remembered Margherita's cool words years later, when she needed help herself.[22]

Margherita enjoyed more success with other intellectuals. The magazines she edited for Mussolini—*Ardita* and then *Gerarchia*—and the artists and architects she sponsored were part of a personal effort to create a cultural program, one hovering between an avant-garde modernism and the reconstructionist values of the return to order. The inconclusive results of the Bologna congress suggested that the time had come for Fascism to define its cultural policies officially. With the domestic opposition crushed and the basic political instruments of power secured, Mussolini was in a position to do something about these matters.

Mussolini took several institutional initiatives. He launched the *Enciclopedia Italiana* under the direction of Gentile. This work was intended to rival the British and French national encyclopedias and to emphasize Italy's contributions to the world of culture and ideas. Next he signed a decree in 1926 creating the Royal Academy of Italy. It was modeled loosely after the great French Academy founded by Cardinal Richelieu in the seventeenth century, and its purpose was to "promote and coordinate Italian intellectual activity" in the arts and sciences. Its sixty members, chosen ostensibly for their accomplishments, enjoyed a number of privileges, including a handsome monthly stipend and free rail travel. Members also had the right to wear an elaborate dress uniform and be addressed as "Your Excellency." Members of the Royal Academy were required to swear an oath of loyalty to Fascism.[23]

Margherita's role in founding the Royal Academy remains unclear. As early as World War I she had advocated the foundation of an Italian academy, and gossip later had it that the idea originated from conversations in her salon in Milan. The specific suggestion appears to have been made by longstanding Fascist Paolo Orano. Margherita wrote the only article about the announcement to appear in the Italian press, praising the initiative as an important step in the restoration of Italy's spiritual greatness and the diffusion of its culture. She also published an article in *Gerarchia* arguing that the Academy would draw intellectuals out of their ivory towers and into the service of the state.[24]

The opinion was widespread that Margherita had chosen the first members. Although she clearly influenced a number of the initial appointments, many members were chosen for reasons that had little to do with either her influence or their merits. Mussolini seems to have insisted on Marinetti. Physicist Enrico Fermi, playwright Luigi Pirandello, and composer Pietro Mascagni were of international stature. D'Annunzio, Marconi, and Gentile were added later. Among Margherita's favorites were the sculptor Adolfo Wildt, the writer Alfredo Panzini, and the architect Marcello Piacentini. She managed to persuade Mussolini to appoint the writer Massimo Bontempelli and the sculptors Francesco Messina and Romano

Romanelli, although Sironi, whom Mussolini admired but considered too controversial, never received an appointment. Fascist credentials played a part in the selection process, but most appointees were simply men of modest talent who were not politically controversial.[25]

Margherita expected to be made a member, despite her intimate relationship with Mussolini. The rules did not explicitly prohibit women from membership, but public discussion of the issue had left an unstated taboo in force. Years later, in 1940, Ada Negri became the only woman member. Margherita was furious at this particular example of Fascist sexism, especially when she learned that Ugo Ojetti had been nominated. She sought consolation with the writer Giovanni Papini, whose appointment she had failed to secure. She adopted a superior tone in rationalizing her resentment: "It's enough that you are Papini and I, modestly, am M[argherita] S[arfatti], and that they are *Their Excellencies,* and who is better off? . . . The real loser is the Academy."[26]

Margherita's friendship with Negri suffered after her move to Rome. Negri had given Mussolini moral support during the Matteotti crisis, and the three remained close in spirit. After Cesare's death, Negri dedicated a new volume of poems, *I canti dell'isola,* to his memory. Margherita returned the favor by giving her work an emotional review.[27]

In 1926 the relationship changed when Margherita, with Mussolini's full support, launched a campaign to secure for Negri the Nobel Prize for literature. When Negri learned that she was one of two Italian writers—the other being Grazia Deledda—nominated for the prize, she suggested to Margherita that the award be divided between them. While Mussolini applied pressure through diplomatic channels, Margherita traveled to Stockholm, where she visited Crown Prince Gustav Adolf, a patron of the arts, and tried to lobby members of the Swedish Academy of Literature. Word came in December 1926 that Deledda had been awarded the prize. Negri was devastated. She blamed Margherita for not having worked hard enough on her behalf. Margherita bitterly complained that her efforts over the years to advance Negri's career had never been appreciated or reciprocated. The situation worsened when Margherita published an article congratulating Deledda.

A few years later, Margherita told Negri that the prize had been denied her because of her unconventional life-style, but the Nobel committee may simply have balked at the pressure from the Fascists. Margherita joked to Negri that they should end their lovers' quarrel. For a time the old rapport seemed to be restored. Margherita and her children wrote to "Aunt Ada" again as they had in the past, with great affection and humor. But over the following years Margherita and Ada became increasingly estranged.[28]

In the second half of the 1920s, Margherita's personal stature reached its apogee. Known sarcastically within the regime as Mussolini's "Egerian Nymph," she was so influential that many called her the "dictator of culture." Accusations began to circulate that she had created a clique of favored artists and writers who enjoyed special privileges regardless of their talents, and that she used her position to secure lucrative commissions for her followers and kickbacks for herself. Such reports, which led the secret police to open a file on her in 1927, were exaggerated. Still, she did groom the careers of a generation of Italian intellectuals and artists; her salon was one of the most famous and important of such gatherings in Europe.[29]

The old Wednesday evening Milanese salon began to dwindle after Cesare died and Margherita increased the frequency of her visits to Rome. The gap was partially filled by her friends Carlo and Eloisa Foà, whose apartment became a meeting place for the artists of the *Novecento*. Once in Rome, Margherita lost no time in beginning her salon anew. While staying at the Palace Hotel in 1926, she kept a suite of rooms large enough to receive visitors, and there she established a new salon for the artistic and literary personalities of Rome. "When Mussolini became head of state," recalled an American journalist, "Signora Sarfatti attained an immense prestige. She was the universal arbiter of the arts. But the knowing ones said: 'Pay court to Signora Sarfatti. She is the power behind the throne.'" In a self-important gesture, she began to keep a signature album in which distinguished guests would record their visits. Once established in a permanent residence, she started hosting regular gatherings late on Friday afternoons, since Roman society did not keep late-night hours. One visitor remarked, "Even on days when she is not receiving, the chairs in her drawing room still are arranged in a conversational circle. Her study may be an editor's confusion of manuscripts, proof-sheets and unexpected volumes . . . but the salon remains ready for service as a clearing house for artists trying to find themselves in a rapidly changing land and the representatives of the forces which are bringing about the change."[30]

The list of Italian visitors to Margherita's Roman salon included Pirandello, Panzini, Malaparte, and Bontempelli, all writers, the inventor Marconi, the composer Alberto Casella, the actress Marta Abba, and a host of painters: Arturo Tosi, Gino Severini, Scipione, De Pisis, Campigli, Corrado Cagli, Carlo Socrate, and Afro Basaldella. Brasini and Piacentini also visited, as did the sculptors Romano Romanelli, Mirko Basaldella, and Giovanni Prini. (Prini's plaster bust of Amedeo Sarfatti had been shown at the Venice Biennale.) On the walls of the apartment hung hundreds of paintings. Pride of place was given to a stunning white-marble bust by Adolfo Wildt titled *Margherita Sarfatti* (1929). The work evokes a gentler image than *Dux,* the bust of Mussolini first shown in the 1924 Venice Biennale, for which this was clearly the companion piece. Margherita believed its neoclassical serenity to be a distillation of the *Novecento* ideal. *Margherita Sarfatti* was one of Wildt's last major works before his death in March 1931.[31]

The journalist Giovanni Ansaldo described his impression of the setting:

> All the art of the *Novecento* is to be found here, with its insane colors and its cadaver-like heads; to increase the beauty of the collection, there are also pieces of sculpture in the house, protected under glass covers; they are horrible, including the head of a boxer by Romanelli, which I mistook bravely for the head of the Duce. The deity of the place is Funi, who has many pictures in the [exposition], along with his books; in fact, on the shelves of one room are placed two or three thousand volumes of the 'Funi Library,' advertised by innumerable small cards attached to each shelf and compartment. These cards, the brass labels with the name of the artist attached to every painting, the card catalog in the corner, give one the immediate impression of being—and one is—not in the drawing room of a grand dame, but in the apartment of a pretentious bluestocking.[32]

If Ansaldo thought Margherita an intellectual poseur, many found her fascinating and the gatherings stimulating. She was an ideal salon hostess, a lively and brilliant conversationalist. People who knew her then remember an energetic and vital woman, whose intense curiosity tended to draw even the most reclusive guests into the discussion. Margherita may have thought of herself as Italy's Gertrude Stein, of whom she often spoke but apparently never met.[33]

Often relatively unknown intellectuals sought invitations to her salon in the hope of being discovered or adopted as one of her protégés. The case of two writers, Alberto Moravia and Corrado Alvaro, suggests the range of reactions of young intellectuals to the allure of Margherita's salon. In 1929, the twenty-one-year-old author Alberto Pincherle, adopting the name Alberto Moravia, published his first novel, *Gli indifferenti* (*The Indifferent Ones*). A searing portrait of the alienated, morally corrupt lives of the middle class, the book was an immediate success. That July, Giuseppe Borgese hailed it in *Il Corriere della Sera* as an important work.

Margherita's analysis of *Gli indifferenti,* published in September in *Il Popolo d'Italia,* revealed that Moravia's indictment of moral indifference had disturbed her: "In truth it is difficult to find a book more crudely devoid, not of the heroic sense of life, but of every intelligent and healthy attitude." Moravia's view of Italian society ran counter to her belief in the link between moral commitment, order, and social cohesion. She had previously criticized the work of Pirandello for lacking some of these same characteristics. Yet while her review avoided overt praise, she recognized that an author of major importance had been discovered.[34]

The reaction from official quarters was even less favorable, for Moravia's devastating portrait contradicted Fascist claims of the restoration of social values. Mussolini admitted privately that *Gli indifferenti* alerted him to an entire level of unspoken anti-Fascism in Roman society. Moravia later argued that he had never intended to offer a critique of Fascism, but the matter was complicated by the fact that Carlo and Nello Rosselli, two of the major leaders of the anti-Fascist opposition, were his first cousins. Just as *Gli indifferenti* appeared, Carlo Rosselli escaped from imprisonment on the island of Lipari and made his way to France.

Moravia's book was defended by Marinetti and Massimo Bontempelli, and in November 1930 a jury of prominent writers voted it one of the hundred best books of contemporary Italian literature (*Dux* appeared on the same list). Margherita's review, published in Mussolini's official newspaper, no doubt accorded the young author a measure of protection in Fascist circles. In any case, Moravia attended Margherita's salon, at first finding it "crammed full of ambitious painters and members of the Academy of Italy." When he was introduced to Margherita, she greeted him with the comment, "You're a cousin of that pig Carlo Rosselli!" Nevertheless, despite his later denial, Moravia returned again to her salon.[35]

By the time Moravia's novel appeared, Margherita had demonstrated her idea of how a writer should reflect the social values of the Fascist era. That spring she had published her first and only novel, *Il palazzone*. The plot, what she called "a simple and overwhelming love story," was certainly unconventional by Italian standards. The events recounted cover the years from about 1910 to 1922. Fiorella Maggi, a young and intellectually precocious girl of fourteen, encounters Count Raineri Valdeschi while vacationing at the shore with her governess. Taken to his big country house—the *palazzone* of the title—she meets the count's two sons: Sergio, the dashing older son, who has a dominating and aggressive personality, and Manlio, who is sensitive, patient, and more intelligent. Sergio is quite taken with Fiorella. His father, widowed for many years, is also attracted to Fiorella, and in a fit of guilt, he kills himself. At eighteen Fiorella marries Sergio, and the couple eventually have a son, Neri.[36]

Like his father, Neri is hotheaded and self-centered. Fiorella watches him play soldier and fears that one day he will be taken from her by war. When war does come it is the husband and his brother, not the son, who go off to fight. Sergio dies during the last great battle of the conflict and Manlio returns, hardened by his experiences but dedicated to his country. Appalled by the peasant uprisings and postwar civil strife, Manlio joins the Fascist movement as a *squadrista,* exclaiming that Italy "needs a leader." Manlio suddenly confesses his love for Fiorella and carries her away to a squalid hotel room. The widow and her brother-in-law marry, much to the jealous anger of Neri. The book ends as Manlio is about to leave for the March on Rome. Neri, now a teenager and frustrated by not being able to go along, wounds himself while cleaning a gun. In a private talk, Manlio explains his responsibilities to Neri and forges a reconciliation between son and mother. Manlio then joins his column and marches into the distance toward Rome and Italy's "hour of greatness."

Il palazzone is perversely autobiographical. Fiorella is a self-portrait, as the name Margherita chose for her suggests. (*Fiorella* means "little flower," while *Margherita* is the Italian word for "daisy.") The opening scene parallels Margherita's teenage encounter with her mysterious professor and her own sexual awakening. Many years later Amedeo Sarfatti explained that Fiorella's story and Count Raineri's suicide were a play on the suicide of Margherita's sister Lina Vivanti, who fell in love with her son-in-law. One can read Sergio for Cesare, who dies but is revered in memory, while Manlio emerges as a thinly disguised Mussolini. Roberto lives on as Neri, and his jealousy toward Manlio is resolved—as Margherita hoped Amedeo would one day feel reconciled toward Mussolini.[37]

It is difficult to imagine that Fiorella was created by an author who had once been active in the feminist movement. The character is a woman whose personality and life are totally submerged by her men. Fiorella's roles are those of wife, mother, and lover, roles that conformed perfectly to the Fascist perception of women. Unlike Margherita, Fiorella has no professional life of her own. The "love story" aspect of *Il palazzone* is tinged with pornographic episodes and images of male virility and domination, and of female hero-worship. Reviewers agreed that Margherita had written a "feminine" novel.[38]

At about the same time as the publication of *Il palazzone*, Margherita met Corrado Alvaro. Born in Calabria at the southern tip of Italy, Alvaro had fought in World War I as a teenager and then worked as a journalist in Rome. In 1925, while serving as editor of the liberal newspaper *Il Mondo*, he signed Croce's 1925 anti-Fascist manifesto, as a result of which he was denied membership in the Fascist Journalist Union. He had by then published a number of short stories. Sometime in 1929, Alvaro—not in good graces in Fascist circles—met Margherita at the home of a mutual acquaintance. He described the encounter in his diary:

At a certain point my hostess, who had returned from a telephone call, whispered to me, "Look, Margherita Sarfatti is about to arrive." It was clear that I had to leave. While I was moving through the entrance hall, however, the door bell rang and Margherita Sarfatti entered. To my hostess she said, "I would like the opportunity to meet Alvaro." The hostess pointed to me. Signora Sarfatti said to me: "I would like to have the pleasure of seeing you again. I receive visitors every Friday." And she moved on with the air of a general. Signora Sarfatti is feared and courted. Given my circumstance, avoided and held in suspicion, I understand that because of her natural curiosity to meet people and her cultural eclecticism, she offers me a safety anchor, perhaps without knowing it. It's enough for people to see me in her house. No need to explain how or why, and I will have a questionable right, but a right, to circulate, but without coasting too close to the flame. For this is the antechamber of he who commands. This is playing with fire. But I'm on my own.

In his later novel *Tutto è accaduto,* in which Margherita is presented as the character Signora Sofia Pitigliano, Alvaro described the same scene but added a physical description:

A confusion of color, innumerable bracelets on her wrist, a hat that gave her the air of an assassin, and the clear view of a rather protruding stomach, as if for her it was not necessary to take the precautions usually taken by a woman to hide the damage of age. She entered as if she were about to surprise someone, and with a rapacious glance she had immediately taken in all the other women seated in the room.[39]

Despite his political leanings, Alvaro attended Margherita's salon regularly. They became friends—some suggest that they were lovers—and under the cloak of Margherita's protection the Fascist police left him alone.[40]

Margherita's support for Alvaro resulted in the first public recognition of his literary talents. In 1930, the Turin newspaper *La Stampa* established a generous literary prize of 50,000 lire in memory of Edoardo Agnelli, the deceased son of Giovanni Agnelli, owner of the paper as well of the FIAT automobile company. Margherita headed an award committee comprised of *La Stampa*'s editor Curzio Malaparte, Luigi Pirandello, Giuseppe Ungaretti, Ugo Ojetti, Alfredo Panzini, and Camillo Pellizzi. The majority decided to give the prize to Alvaro for his novel of peasant life in his native Calabria, *Gente di Aspromonte (People of Aspromonte)*. Margherita argued that the book would one day be recognized as a masterpiece. The decision was not unanimous, for Panzini objected that Alvaro was an anti-Fascist. Mussolini supported the decision in spite of Alvaro's political attitudes.[41]

Years later Alvaro claimed he never asked Margherita for favors. But he continued to frequent her salon even after making an unpleasant discovery. One evening, while browsing in Margherita's library, he found her personal copy of *People of Aspromonte.* She had scrawled inside the cover "A people dirty, bewildered, and stupid." Nevertheless Alvaro coasted in Margherita's entourage for most of the 1930s, until he decided her friendship was a liability. Some fifty years afterward, Margherita's daughter spoke of Alvaro with great bitterness.[42]

Ada Negri's new book of poetry, *Vespertina,* appeared that same year. Margherita got Mussolini to read the new work, and offered to arrange for Negri to win either the *La Stampa* prize or the so-called Mussolini Prize that had just been instituted by the Royal Academy. Margherita eventually persuaded Negri to choose the latter, presumably so she could save the *La Stampa* prize for Alvaro. She persuaded Panzini, Marinetti, Bontempelli, and other members of the Academy to back Negri. Negri pressed Margherita for a review in *Il Popolo d'Italia,* and it appeared in early 1931. Negri won the prize. It was awarded to her by King Vittorio Emanuele III in a ceremony at the Campidoglio that April.[43]

In the Rome salon Margherita entertained politicians, government officials, military officers, aristocrats, ambassadors, and a host of distinguished foreign guests along with her intellectuals and artists. Among the high-ranking Fascist leaders who occasionally frequented Margherita's salon were Italo Balbo, whom Mussolini had appointed to run the air force in 1926, and Dino Grandi, undersecretary and then minister for foreign affairs (1925–1932). She developed a strong friendship with Giuseppe Bottai, head of the Ministry of Corporations from 1926 to 1932, who had common interests in culture and conversation. Augusto Turati, Fascist party secretary, 1926–1930, and Dino Alfieri came often. Alfieri had been a friend of Cesare Sarfatti and a former Nationalist, who served as Bottai's deputy at the Ministry of Corporations from 1929 to 1932. Balbino Giuliano, an intelligent and cultured man who served as minister of education before his appointment to the Senate, was so close to Margherita that there were rumors of an affair. The secret police reported with consternation on a number of anti-Fascists who were also among Margherita's guests. Rumors circulated that she acted as a spy for Mussolini, reporting on the sentiments expressed by her guests.[44]

Based on the signatures in Margherita's guest books, virtually every distinguished foreign traveler who visited Rome in the late 1920s called at her salon. Among those from France were former premier and foreign minister Louis Barthou, and the authors André Gide, Eugène Marsan, and André Malraux. The writer Colette, Margherita's closest friend from Paris, visited Rome and Il Soldo often during the years between the wars.

Sometime in the 1930s, she and Margherita planned a rustic tour through the Italian countryside together with other French acquaintances. Each member of the party was to be responsible for a particular task. Recalled Fiammetta, "My mother, totally unskilled in manual or domestic labor, was to serve as guide; Colette chose to be the chef, but was very anxious to know whether she could find garlic in Italy, without which she could not, as a good Provençal, possibly cook!"

Margherita's British visitors included many of the expatriates who lived in Italy. Foremost among them was the director and set designer Gordon Craig, who had settled along the Ligurian coast. She found him at once "despotic and adorable," and accompanied him on a tour of the Vatican. Craig felt great sympathy for Margherita and invited her to visit his home near Genoa. She also knew George Bernard Shaw, whom she had visited in London. She spent several days in Venice with him in the summer of 1929, where they discussed D. H. Lawrence's *Lady Chatterley's Lover* while floating in a gondola. During a visit to Rome, Shaw brought Margherita a copy of Somerset Maugham's novel *Cakes and Ale*.[45]

When G. K. Chesterton visited Rome in late 1929, Margherita arranged an audience for him with Mussolini. Both Chesterton and Shaw were apparently pro-Fascist. Chesterton, to his surprise, found Mussolini interviewing him instead of the opposite. During a reception in his honor at the Foreign Press Club, Margherita dogged Chesterton incessantly, seizing every chance to introduce him to other guests and be seen with him. Chesterton's patience finally snapped during a session with photographers, when she pressed herself next to him and he abruptly turned his portly body away. The journalists surrounding them overheard Margherita ask belligerently, "Why are you turning your back on me? Don't you see they're taking photographs?" The secret police reported that Chesterton's reply, expressed to his fellow Englishmen, "was not very flattering to the lady."[46]

The writer and former diplomat Harold Nicolson and the politician Oswald Mosley came to Rome for a firsthand look at Fascism, and met Margherita at a British embassy reception on January 5, 1932, and at subsequent dinners. "A blond questing woman," Nicolson observed, "the daughter of a Venetian Jew who married a Jew in Milan." His somewhat inaccurate comments nevertheless explain why so many foreigners called on her:

> She is at present his [Mussolini's] confidante and must be used by him to bring the gossip of Rome to the Villa Torlonia. She says that Mussolini is the greatest worker ever known: he rides in the morning, then a little fencing, then work, and then after dinner he plays the violin to himself.

Tom [Mosley] asks how much sleep he gets. She answers, 'Always nine hours.' I can see Tom doing sums in his head and concluding that on such a timetable Musso cannot be hard worked at all.

Mosley saw Mussolini on January 7, and was fascinated by the man and by his Fascist program. Mussolini suggested that Mosley call himself a Fascist, and when he got back home he founded the British Union of Fascists. The next year, Mosley came back for a second visit; he paid homage to Margherita at her salon. After he returned to Britain, Mosley began to receive subsidies of 60,000 pounds a year from Mussolini. Dino Grandi, who became ambassador to Britain in 1932, handed over the money. He judged Mosley as no more than a "Marinetti-like politician." Still, he considered supporting the British Fascists to be a good investment.[47]

Of all her foreign guests, Margherita most enjoyed the Americans, partly for what she saw as a natural naïveté, partly because, like many European intellectuals, she was immensely attracted to America's fast-moving, modern image. Josephine Baker, whose sensuous "Banana Dance" was the rage of Europe, came to visit. Mussolini had wanted to keep Baker out of Italy because he thought she embodied the decadent values of American society, but in 1932 Margherita persuaded him to relent. Sinclair Lewis dropped in, as did Ezra Pound, the eccentric poet who resided in Rapallo.[48]

Pound's political views, notorious among fellow Americans and literary colleagues, were based on an odd economic theory Pound believed was reflected in Fascist claims about the Corporate State. Thus he was a great admirer of Mussolini, with whom he had an audience in 1933. He summarized his ideas in a book entitled *Jefferson and/or Mussolini*. He showed Mussolini a draft of some of his new cantos, and the Duce commented, *"Ma questo è divertente"*—"But this is amusing." Pound took as proof of incisive brilliance what Mussolini no doubt meant as a polite dismissal, and Pound susequently included the comment in the opening lines of Canto XLI, from *Eleven New Cantos*:

> "MA QUESTO,"
> said the Boss, "è divertente."
> catching the point before the aesthetes had got
> there;[49]

Margherita seems to have found Pound amusing, and he occasionally gave her advice about poetry. Because he believed that she influenced official policies, Pound also gave her political advice. He tried unsuccessfully to obtain her help in publishing his economic theories: "I can't get my Jefferson/and/or Mussolini published ANYwhere. Communists curse and British Fascists groan (possibly because I can find no points of resemblance between DUX and Mosley. . . .)"

Pound admitted having lifted some passages from *Dux* for the *Eleven New Cantos*. In February 1934 he wrote to Margherita. "Despite your not keeping yr/ promise to send it to me, I read yr 'Dux' and found it a much better book than you had led me to xxpect." Just before his new cantos appeared, he wrote again: "I hope to send you my Cantos 31/41 in a few days. I believe they were published yesterday in New York. If you have patience to read enough of them you will find a few familiar passages, for which my rascally thanks."[50]

While the salon was the setting for the exercise of her power, Margherita was also sought after by ordinary Italians. Countless letters arrived from strangers in needy circumstances. Most were women hoping to find a sympathetic ear from *l'amica del Duce,* the Duce's special friend: a young girl wanting a scholarship for university, a poor laundress asking for a government subsidy, a mother needing her only son at home instead of in the army. Sometimes they were acquaintances who wanted favors, like the Lancia car dealer who got in trouble for using Mussolini's name in a commercial advertisement and asked her for a character reference. Margherita and Fiammetta combed through these requests for one or two that might deserve a positive response. These were sent to Palazzo Venezia for the special attention of Mussolini's private secretary.[51]

Yet throughout the twenties, while Margherita's influence as Mussolini's closest adviser continued to grow, separate developments in religious politics, foreign relations, and Mussolini's family life were coalescing to undermine her position. These can be traced to the period of the bitter quarrel between Margherita and Mussolini that followed his appointment to head the government. On January 20, 1923, Mussolini had held a secret meeting with Cardinal Pietro Gasparri, the papal secretary of state. Their talk hardly resolved the problems that prevented Vatican recognition of the Kingdom of Italy but the discussion began a slow movement in that direction. Thereafter, Pius appointed the Jesuit priest, Pietro Tacchi-Venturi, a good friend of Mussolini's brother, Arnaldo, as his confidential envoy to the prime minister. The Jesuit and Benito Mussolini established a warm relationship. Soon Tachi-Venturi and Margherita became friends, as well.

Although for years Mussolini had been a vociferous atheist, since 1921 he had ceased his attacks and begun a public reconciliation with the Church. In private, Mussolini retained his contempt for religion in general, and for Catholicism in particular. However, Mussolini was willing to go through the motions. On April 2, 1923, Mussolini had his three children baptized as Catholics. His children received the sacraments of communion and confirmation in the summer of 1924. Finally, in December 1925, Mussolini and Rachele underwent a private and very brief Catholic marriage ceremony. Mussolini literally had to drag his anti-clerical wife out of the kitchen and into the presence of the priest.[52]

Mussolini seems to have regarded Judaism as a religion no worse nor better than any other. He considered Jews primarily as a national group, rather than as a religion or a race. As a result, he avoided classic religious anti-Semitism or the pseudo-scientific racist anti-Semitism of the Nazis. Yet Mussolini still accepted crude anti-Semitic clichés regarding the greed of all Jews and their attempts to dominate world money markets. In September 1922, Kurt Ludecke, one of Hitler's henchmen, visited Mussolini in Milan. Ludecke later reported:

> Touching on the issue of international finance, I found [Mussolini's] views paralleled Hitler's. Then, pursuing the subject, I spoke of the Jews. He agreed with my facts, but was evasive about what measures they called for. While he admitted that he watched the Jews carefully, he pointed out that in Italy the Jewish question was not the problem it was in Germany. I did not know at the time that Margherita Sarfatti, his devoted friend and biographer, was a Jewess. . . .[53]

Ludecke came away from this four-hour conversation admiring Mussolini's political skill but disappointed and disgusted that Mussolini had "played in with the Jews." Mussolini believed it unnecessary to adopt special measures against the Italian Jews because he considered most of them patriotic; besides, they were too small a group to threaten the state. Still, he saw Zionism as offering a dangerous alternative to Italian patriotism, and he observed its development with concern.[54]

Margherita had never shared Cesare's great enthusiasm for Zionism or her own Jewish roots, although she did consider Palestine an appropriate refuge for the Jews of Eastern Europe. Nor did she ever expect that Mussolini would be concerned with the loyalty of Italy's Jews. In April 1928, she had a visit from the famous Alma Mahler—lover of Oscar Kokoschka and wife, in succession, of Gustav Mahler, Walter Gropius, and Franz Werfel. Margherita, whom Alma Mahler called the "uncrowned queen of Italy," greeted Mahler while reclining on a chaise in her drawing room, casting a "challenging glance" at her guest. When Mahler asked about the possibility of creating an international Fascist movement, Margherita assured her that such a world order was possible only if Fascist parties in other countries—and here she must have had the Nazis in mind—

followed Mussolini's wisdom in not making an issue of the Jewish question. Margherita's ardent Fascism and the patriotic values she had instilled in Roberto convinced Mussolini of her absolute loyalty as an Italian. But he never forgot that Margherita was a Jew. The possibility that Catholicism would become the national religion left Italian Jews, even nonpracticing ones like Margherita, in an uncomfortable position. In 1928 Margherita converted to Catholicism. In April 1930 Fiammetta also converted, followed in December 1931 by Amedeo.[55]

Margherita's conversion was a practical one, done in the midst of Mussolini's most serious expression of anti-Semitism in the years before the formation of the Berlin-Rome Axis. In early November 1928, the Italian Zionists held a congress in Milan, their first since October 1920. Mussolini had commented with hostility on the 1920 congress. Eight years later, Mussolini was no longer the leader of an obscure political movement but dictator of Italy. Now his opinions carried far more weight.[56]

Some three weeks after the congress, Mussolini published a short, unsigned article, *"Religione o Nazione?"* ("Religion or Nation?") in the Roman newspaper *Popolo di Roma*. The author insisted he did not wish to stir up anti-Semitism "despite the fact that Semites make up almost all the major components of worldwide anti-Fascism." He admitted that the Zionist congress had attracted little attention but pointed out the great danger it represented. The Italian Zionists, he warned, considered themselves not Italians at all, but Jews. Not all Italian Jews were Zionists, the author stressed. But a question had to be posed: "We ask the Italian Jews: are you a religion or are you a Nation? . . . From the answer we will draw the necessary conclusions."[57]

Margherita learned of the publication of the article before leaving for Berlin for surgery on her chronic knee injury. She reacted with alarm. She informed her close friend Carlo Foà of the authorship of the article and asked him to contact Sabatino Lopez, Cesare's successor as president of the Zionist Group of Milan. Sensing that Mussolini was deadly serious about this business, she wrote a powerfully worded letter to Foà:

> What he [Lopez] and others are doing is simply stupid and criminal. He knows that among us in Italy there is no anti-Semitism. But these gentlemen of the Jewish or Zionist Circle, or whatever the hell it's called . . . are doing everything to provoke it.
>
> You know that I speak neither for myself nor for you, because I think totally as one withdrawn from any form of Jewishness, as you are. . . .
>
> What in the world do these people want? . . . I speak as one who foresees a storm gathering over the heads of so many good, brave, innocent and reasonable people—a storm that is the fault of a small handful.

Let them beware of what they are doing. Are they religious? If so, let them practice their cult in peace. But they speak, write, and publish things about *nationality,* about a *separate race,* about *ethnic difference,* in ways that are offensive or at least hostile, to Italy. . . . Let them all go to the devil, but it is not right that they damage through their idiocy so many tens of thousands of good, hardworking and devout citizens. . . .

Beware of what I say. This thing is *very* serious, and the word of warning is not just mine—it comes down by indirect reflection from much higher up, from someone who is much more farseeing than I am, one who looks anxiously upon these people who are stirring up a hurricane that will fall not upon themselves, which wouldn't be so bad, but upon others.

Once in Berlin, she composed an anonymous article that dissociated the Jews of Italy from Zionism. She wrote to Sabatino Lopez, Cesare's successor as president of the Zionist Group of Milan. She begged him to issue a statement affirming the complete loyalty to Italy of Italian Zionists. They must announce, she insisted, that they supported a Jewish refuge in Palestine only for Jews from other countries and completely rejected the creation of an independent Jewish state. But when Margherita telephoned Lopez from Berlin he refused to comply.

Margherita and Carlo Foà arranged for the publication of a number of letters by Fascist Italian Jews in *Popolo di Roma.* Every letter denounced Zionism and proclaimed the loyalty of the overwhelming majority of Italian Jews to both Italy and Fascism. In the second week of December 1928, the leaders of the Italian Zionist movement agreed to send a letter to *Popolo di Roma,* signed by their president, Dante Lattes. Lattes stated that there was no conflict between the patriotism of Italian Jews and Zionism, which he described as a spiritual dedication to the establishment of a Jewish homeland in Palestine.[58]

The letter from Lattes provoked Mussolini to publish another unsigned article in *Popolo di Roma* in mid-December. He rejected Lattes's statement as dishonest. Zionists could not be patriotic Italians and aspire to the creation of a Jewish state in Palestine at the same time. Mussolini warned that Italy contained 80,000 Jews, 20,000 in Rome alone (wildly inflated figures), and that many were Zionists.[59]

On Margherita's orders, Carlo Foà wrote an article for *Gerarchia* in which he refuted the principles of Zionism and argued that it had no place in Italy. Margherita had suggested he stress the fact that after two thousand years' residence in Italy, the Jews had completely intermingled with the rest of the population. For Italian Jews, Rome was their holy city, not Jerusalem.[60] Margherita intended to forward the article to Mussolini. She read

Foà's manuscript in her hospital bed in Berlin, but it was so badly written that Margherita arranged instead for a direct meeting between Foà and Mussolini in early 1929. Foà was to relay the Duce's advice to the Italian Zionists afterward. Fiammetta privately informed Foà that the real purpose of the meeting was for Foà to emerge with the order for the Italian Zionist movement to disband itself. The only politics that Mussolini would tolerate in Italy were Fascist politics.[61]

Much to Foà's and Margherita's surprise, Mussolini acted with graciousness and understanding throughout his conversation with Foà. He praised Foà's contributions to *Gerarchia* and expressed his appreciation of Foà's patriotism and support of the Fascist regime. He assured Foà that there was absolutely no danger of the government undertaking any form of anti-Semitic action. The very idea was barbaric. All Mussolini had wanted to do was to sound a "warning bell" for the benefit of the Italian Zionists. Foà assured the Duce that the Zionists would pay close attention.

A visit by Albert Einstein to Margherita's Berlin clinic added to her relief. Standing beside her bed, he played Margherita a serenade on his violin. Apparently, the physicist had learned of Margherita's efforts to aid the Jews of Italy and had come to offer her his thanks. The two became friends during the years the great scientist remained in Germany.[62]

Mussolini had changed his mind about outlawing Italian Zionism altogether. Apparently he had decided that such an extreme measure would harm his reputation, in view of the blow that he was about to strike against religious freedom in Italy. Just over a month later, in the Church of St. John Lateran in Rome, on February 11, 1929, Mussolini signed the documents known as the Lateran Pact with Cardinal Gasparri. The agreement included the formal recognition of the Kingdom of Italy by the Vatican and Italian recognition of the Vatican as a sovereign state under the rule of the pope, the promise of financial compensation by Italy to the Vatican for the territories seized from the papacy during the Risorgimento, and a concordat regulating Church-State relations. The concordat made Catholicism the official religion in Italy. While separate laws were adopted over the next two years that granted religious toleration to Italian Jews and Protestants, Mussolini had extinguished the religious liberty that had existed in Italy since the founding of the kingdom seventy years earlier.[63]

In the eyes of the Church and of the government, Margherita had become a Catholic upon conversion, as Fiammetta would after her baptism the following year. Neither was affected by the new juridical arrangement. But as the head of government in an officially Catholic state, it no longer sufficed that Mussolini's children had been baptized and that he and Rachele had been married by a priest. The entire Mussolini family must appear to be exemplary Catholics.

About six months after Mussolini signed the Lateran Pact, his eighteen-year-old daughter, Edda, fell in love with the son of Lieutenant Colonel Dante Pacifici of the Italian Army. By the end of 1929, Edda and young Pacifici wanted to marry. Mussolini crushed the young lovers' hopes. The Pacificis were Jews.[64]

This incident helped convince Mussolini to bring his family to Rome. As soon as Margherita had settled him into the Villa Torlonia, Mussolini had Rachele and the children, including the two-month-old Anna Maria, moved from Milan to live with him in Rome.[65] Given all the powers Mussolini commanded as dictator, Mussolini and Margherita may have believed that they could re-create their Milan arrangement in Rome. Indeed, Rachele and the children occupied totally separate quarters in the Villa Torlonia. He explained that he had to have private quarters and a private entrance to the villa because of his official duties. But primarily it allowed Mussolini to receive whom he wished at the villa. Often he had Margherita and Fiammetta to the Villa Torlonia for dinner, playing his violin for them afterward.

The arrival of Mussolini's family in Rome in November 1929 presented Margherita with serious problems. Rachele had Cesira dismissed, and was thereafter the undisputed master of Villa Torlonia.[66] Margherita had lost her principal source of information inside Mussolini's household. The villa had gardens, a tennis court, and a riding track, and required an extensive staff. Mussolini took advantage not only of the opportunities for exercise, but of a pretty young servant as well. To Margherita's consternation, the young woman became a frequent visitor to Castel Porziano. For a time, Mussolini found himself living in a virtual bedroom comedy. Boratto was forced to juggle the entrances and exits of Rachele, Margherita, and the young signorina, while Mussolini kept another of the three women momentarily occupied. Mussolini finally used the excuse of Rachele's jealousy to persuade Margherita not to visit the Villa Torlonia any longer.[67]

In April 1930, Edda married a dashing young diplomat, Count Galeazzo Ciano. The introduction had been arranged by Mussolini's brother, Arnaldo. Young Ciano, son of the World War I naval hero, Admiral Costanzo Ciano, helped Edda forget about young Pacifici. This time Mussolini thoroughly approved the match. Mussolini so admired Admiral Ciano that he had secretly designated him as his successor. Of the son, Mussolini remarked approvingly to Angela Curti Cucciati: "I am pleased because Ciano is a good boy and is extraordinarily intelligent . . . he will go places. Understand, not because of me, on his own abilities."[68]

Margherita herself actually liked Galeazzo, whom she found bright, witty, and basically kind. But she also knew him to be vain, wildly ambitious, and weak. Worse, he was thoroughly dominated by his ruthless and corrupt father.

Edda and Margherita disliked each other intensely. This was probably inevitable, given Margherita's relationship with Mussolini. But Edda also impressed Margherita as spoiled, wild, and vulgar. In the mid-twenties, Mussolini had secretly entrusted supervision of his daughter's education to Margherita. Margherita decided that Edda should attend the prestigious Holy Annunciation boarding school in Florence, where the princesses of the royal family received their educations. But Edda found the strict atmosphere unbearable and fled to complain bitterly to her father. In self-defense, Mussolini revealed that the school had been Margherita's idea. Edda flew into a rage and browbeat her hapless father into agreeing to her release. From then on, Edda and Margherita bore bitter grudges toward each other.

The elaborate prenuptial reception and the marriage ceremony marked the first occasions on which Rachele appeared as a public figure. She acquitted herself well, much to Mussolini's surprise and delight. Obviously Margherita did not attend the wedding. Quite ominously for Margherita, the marriage resulted in an alliance between Rachele and Edda and the Cianos. The mother and daughter made no secret of their hatred of Margherita. After the wedding, the powerful Ciano clan shared their interest in encouraging Margherita's eclipse.

The recognition paid to Margherita in the late 1920s had the effect of reinforcing her worst personality traits. Those who had known her first in Milan, and then at the height of her power in Rome, commented on the fact that she was a changed person. Malicious observers whispered on the decline of her physical beauty. Even Mussolini noted how obvious it was that she dyed her hair. Perhaps more telling were Margherita's insecure comments about her influence with Mussolini and her disdain for Rachele.[69] She grew more haughty and arrogant with those who sought her favors. As Giovanni Ansaldo observed:

> The first thing that strikes one was the tone of the teacher in her voice; more pedagogical than imperious. She is abrupt in her affirmations, peremptory in her judgments; she has not the minimal art of nuance or of shading. She is always having to define or make things more precise. 'If I say so, it must be that I know,' or 'I'm not just babbling,' or else 'On this issue I'm firm.' These and other charming phrases are her oratorical devices. . . . The old habit of being courted and flattered has become second nature to her; she receives homage as if it were her due.[70]

Status inflated Margherita's already ample ego, and often made her seem shallow and tactless. She tended to shroud herself in Mussolini's shadow, making the kind of remarks in public that she had carefully avoided only a few years earlier. One time she was overheard gloating, "The Duce owes a lot to me." If guests were at her home when the doorbell rang, she would excuse herself by saying, "Pardon me if I leave you, but the premier has come to see me." When dining with friends, she would sometimes announce that she had to telephone Mussolini, and then return to the table with the comment, "The Duce loves me so much!"[71]

23

Ghostwriter for the Duce

In the thirteen years between the March on Rome in 1922 and the outbreak of the Ethiopian War in 1935, Mussolini enjoyed a highly favorable image in the foreign press. There were a few journalists and anti-Fascist exiles who had witnessed Blackshirt brutalities and wrote highly critical accounts of Mussolini's dictatorship. Certain liberal or leftist journals and newspapers reminded their readers of the beatings, tortures, imprisonments, and murders by which the Fascist regime had come to power. Their message went largely unheard. Even in Western democracies the majority of news publications depicted Mussolini as a necessary antidote to the chaos that had plagued Italy. He was the man who chased the beggars off the streets, introduced respect for law and order, and saved Italy from Bolshevism.

Mussolini received overwhelmingly positive press coverage in the United States. Conservative, moderate, and even a surprising number of liberal publications found reasons to praise the Duce and his regime. The Duce offered an exciting contrast to the bland personalities of Calvin Coolidge and Herbert Hoover. The "Red Scare" that had afflicted the United States in 1919–1920 also helped his image. Widespread American fear of Communism led to the arrest of thousands and the deportation of hundreds of leftists. The Blackshirt rampage against the Italian left in 1920–1922, and Mussolini's subsequent violence against the Socialist and Communist parties in 1922–1926, won the sympathies of many Americans. Even the rise of organized crime, encouraged by American prohibition laws, made Mussolini's tough anticrime stance attractive in the United States. A surprising number of American journalists visited Italy—among them the prominent muckrakers Ida Tarbell and Lincoln Steffens—and left with very positive impressions.

Representatives of the regime took care to shape the views of the American press. Mussolini's government did not tolerate objective or critical foreign reporting of events in Italy. Foreign journalists who wished to remain in Italy for any length of time had to accept official direction of their reporting. Margherita was often the one doing the directing.[1]

Her special relationship with Mussolini, her long experience as a journalist, and her command of English made Margherita perfect for the task. Despite her knowledge of French and German, she was less able to shape the reporting of European journalists. The influence of European Socialist and Communist parties, the rivalries between Italy and its neighbors, and their far more detailed knowledge of the Fascist dictatorship, made Mussolini seem less heroic to the Europeans.[2] Mussolini had more of an interest in influencing American public opinion. The consequences of World War I had tipped the balance of economic power in favor of the United States. Thus, if the United States proved susceptible to Fascist news manipulation, he had more to gain.

Margherita had begun her cultivation of the American press while she still lived in Milan. But she could not really apply herself to the task until moving to Rome, since the American news agencies and foreign correspondents had their offices there. In the period from 1922 to 1935, the foreign press community in Rome numbered about one hundred twenty, including Italians working for foreign newspapers. Of these, perhaps forty to fifty were genuine correspondents; the rest were police spies or hacks in the pay of the regime. Journalists writing for American newspapers made up a permanent group of about twenty-five. Prominent among them were Salvatore Cortesi of the Associated Press, his son, Arnaldo Cortesi, of *The New York Times,* and Thomas B. Morgan, the head of the Rome bureau of the United Press. While most of their colleagues believed the Cortesis and Morgan to be nothing more than first-rate reporters, all were also agents of the regime. Of the three, Morgan proved the most influential.[3]

By the time Margherita settled in Rome, Morgan had acquired a deserved reputation as the best-informed American reporter in Italy. Born in Wales in 1885 but raised in Ohio, Morgan had arrived in Rome in April 1919 to work under Salvatore Cortesi at the Associated Press bureau. Morgan sneaked into Fiume to interview D'Annunzio, covered the occupation of the factories at first hand, and witnessed the takeover of Trieste by Giunta's Blackshirts. He developed excellent news sources by creating a network of paid informants within the Vatican and the Quirinal Palace. Morgan knew how to keep secrets when necessary, and thus acquired the trust of both the Holy See and the royal family. In 1922, shortly after the coronation of Pius XI, Morgan took over the Rome office of the United Press. There he watched the Fascists straggle into the capital after Vittorio Emanuele III asked Mussolini to form a government.[4]

Morgan's three and a half years in Italy had given him a rather jaundiced attitude toward the Fascists, although he held an even lower opinion of the

Italian left. When he met Mussolini for the first time shortly after the March on Rome, he judged the prime minister to be a boor. Within two years, however, an improbable friendship developed between Morgan and Mussolini. Apparently Margherita brought the two men together.

Although there is no direct evidence that Margherita introduced Morgan to Mussolini, circumstances strongly suggest that she did. Morgan's special contacts with Mussolini began only after Margherita had begun spending more time in Rome. Soon her friends had become acquaintances of his. Morgan became a frequent visitor to Margherita's apartment, and then to Mussolini's own flat on the Via Rasella. The three of them often had dinner together. Morgan even hinted later that he and Margherita had had a clandestine affair, which he did his best to disguise from Mussolini. Margherita was certainly the basis for more than one quarrel between Morgan and his wife.

Probably Margherita sounded Morgan out concerning plans to shape Mussolini's image in the American press, and found him amenable. He might have hoped to develop new contacts to supplement those within the Vatican and the Quirinal. Soon he enjoyed unparalleled access to Mussolini. He also became an informer. By late 1924, as the Matteotti crisis climaxed, other United Press correspondents no longer trusted Morgan with information about anti-Fascist plots. As the years passed, distrust of Morgan spread throughout the entire foreign press community. Yet his influence and his sources placed him at the center of all journalistic activities in Rome. No American reporter could afford to ignore or snub Morgan.

Morgan became the compulsory point of contact for any American, other than those in the diplomatic corps, wishing to meet Mussolini. Few Americans of importance visited Rome without Morgan's offering himself as guide or interpreter. He even began serving as unofficial go-between for Mussolini and the British and American ambassadors. By 1925, the British Foreign Office was seeking copies of Morgan's interviews with Mussolini for insights into the dictator's thinking. Morgan even took it upon himself to send Secretary of Commerce Herbert Hoover an interview in which the dictator praised the American work ethic and the achievements of the U.S. economy.

Morgan made no effort to hide his relationship with Mussolini, although he remained secretive about its precise nature. The most striking feature of his office was the photograph of the Duce that hung behind his desk, inscribed TO TOM MORGAN IN APPRECIATION OF HIS JOURNALISTIC WORK. BENITO MUSSOLINI. Yet Morgan revealed a cynical, even critical, viewpoint about the Fascist regime. Perhaps this reflected Morgan's real thoughts, but it also provided him with a form of camouflage as well as a useful means for drawing out the political opinions of others.[5]

Morgan's position as head of the United Press bureau made him far more useful to Margherita and Mussolini than an ordinary newspaperman. Despite strong American isolationist sentiment during the twenties and thirties, American participation in the Great War and the subsequent rise of the United States to world power had greatly increased American interest in news from Europe. Curiosity intensified after the hundreds of thousands of doughboys who had served in Europe in 1917–1919 returned home. Only the adventurous or well-to-do were able to visit the Continent between the world wars, and journalism provided the vast majority of Americans the news they wanted about Europe.

Marconi had developed the first transatlantic radio communications system before World War I, but the networks inaugurated commercial broadcasting between Europe and North America only in 1938. Regular transatlantic news broadcasts began in the late thirties. Before then newspapers (and to a lesser extent, magazines) remained the ordinary American's major source of information about European affairs. Few American newspaper publishers could afford to station their own correspondents abroad. Consequently, newspaper editors relied on the news services for foreign reporting. Morgan's control over United Press dispatches from Rome allowed him to shape the opinions of millions of American newspaper readers about Fascist Italy. The same was true for Salvatore Cortesi, although he retired as Associated Press bureau chief in 1929.[6]

The possibilities inherent in controlling American news from Italy occurred only gradually to Margherita and Mussolini. Influenced by his years as a professional journalist, Mussolini placed great emphasis on the creation of a favorable image for Fascist Italy. But at first he thought only in terms of influencing the reporting of foreign journalists. Reporters who cooperated with the regime received the free tickets, the letters of introduction, and the invitations they needed to cover important events. The uncooperative did not. Tax exemptions, press junkets, and inexpensive meals at the press club were also provided or denied on a similar basis. An official press card, available only through the Fascist Journalist Union, brought both Italian and foreign newspapermen substantial discounts for theaters and train travel. Foreign correspondents were offered thousands of free words by telegraph—provided the stories were friendly to the regime. Embassies were warned when a foreign reporter was overly critical. Negative stories were intercepted by government censors. If these measures did not curb obstinate journalists, they were expelled from Italy.[7]

There was an important shift in American attitudes toward information after the severe recession of 1920–1922, when the economy burgeoned. From a recession low of $68.7 billion, the gross national product soared to

$98.4 billion in 1929. This nearly 50 percent increase in national output far outpaced a growth in the population of only 16 percent in the 1920–1930 decade. Most Americans enjoyed a significant increase in prosperity in the period from 1922 to 1929.

During the same seven years, the Italian gross national product had also grown, but only from $5.7 billion to $8.5 billion. Mussolini's government was spending an average of 15 percent of the Italian GNP every year, primarily on armaments and on interest on the $3.4 billion in war debts owed to the United States and Britain. From 1922 to 1929, the American government dropped its spending from 7 percent of GNP to only ·3.3 percent of GNP. By Italian standards, the United States was immensely rich, while the average Italian was struggling to survive at an income level Americans had surpassed during Andrew Jackson's presidency.[8]

During the twenties Americans witnessed the flowering of the consumer economy. Urged on by advertising, Americans demanded more leisure-time activities. Motion pictures and national radio networks made entertainment a major American industry. In the face of unprecedented competition for the attention and the income of their readers, newspapers and news magazines were transformed from compilations of news reports to sources of entertainment. At the same time, magazines previously devoted to fiction began featuring reports on international affairs and interviews with foreign leaders.

Soon public figures, whether baseball stars or foreign dictators, seemed of equal interest, and thus of equal importance. Babe Ruth and Mary Pickford got as much newspaper coverage as Calvin Coolidge and Benito Mussolini. Americans became intrigued by Mussolini's political actions, his biography, and the intimate details of his private life. Mussolini had become a celebrity. Margherita noted with amusement that an American tobacco company offered the Duce 300,000 lire to endorse its cigarettes.[9]

The advantages of Mussolini's popularity in the United States became clear in 1925. His propaganda had convinced Americans that his dictatorship was good for Italy and for the world. That November, representatives of Mussolini and Calvin Coolidge agreed to settle Italy's World War I debts on terms highly favorable to Rome. As a result, Italy and Britain quickly reached a similar understanding. In turn, these settlements allowed the Morgan Bank to lend Mussolini's government $100 million. Other American loans, totaling over $140 million, were negotiated over the next two years. All these dollars flowed into the Italian treasury, which doled out lire to the borrowers. This huge amount of hard currency helped pay for Mussolini's public works and armaments programs.

Margherita was impressed by the sales of *The Life of Benito Mussolini* in the United States. The cover price was five dollars, the equivalent of 128 lire at the time. That was ten times the price of the book in Italy. If Americans were willing to pay that much for a collection of legends about Mussolini, why not sell them more?[10]

Because of Morgan's friendship with Mussolini, he had been deluged with requests to approach the dictator to write articles for distribution through the United Press. After he raised the matter, as Morgan remembered it, Mussolini agreed. "Yes, we will do it. My life, no. Everybody knows now that I am the son of a blacksmith. My politics, no. It comes out day by day. Let it be an account of how I spend my time."[11]

According to Morgan, Mussolini supplied him with written material, which the journalist crafted into a series of ten long articles. Once he finished an article, Morgan returned it to Mussolini for editing and approval. Written in the first person, "My Twenty-four Hours" appeared as a United Press exclusive in January 1927. Nothing of the sort had been seen in print before. Mussolini discussed his abstemious diet, his rigorous exercise routine, his sleeping habits, and the details of his fourteen-to-sixteen-hour workday. The dictator confessed his love of danger and his admiration for Theodore Roosevelt. He proclaimed his disdain for women and his contempt for the obese. The overall picture was of a man driven by spartan dedication and bold individuality. The titles of some of the articles express the flavor of the series: "Mussolini Takes Life on Jump," "Setbacks Drive Duce Harder," "Mussolini Cuts Down on Talking," "Duce Monastic in Many Ways," "Mussolini Gives View on Liquor." The series proved a tremendous success and was reissued in book form.[12]

Morgan's account of the origin of the series scarcely rings true. Mussolini did not know English well enough to edit long articles effectively. Margherita did. Both subject matter and style are strongly reminiscent of *The Life of Benito Mussolini*. Morgan never mentioned the matter of payment—Mussolini had at the time no great interest in money, but Margherita did. While friendly with Mussolini, Morgan would hardly have had the effrontery to suggest the idea for the series directly. All this suggests that he collaborated with Margherita, at the very least, and that more probably she inaugurated the entire project.[13]

"My Twenty-four Hours" suggested new commercial and propaganda possibilities in the marketing of Mussolini's writing. In March 1926, the directors of the Houghton Mifflin publishing firm approached Mussolini about writing a book for sale in the United States. Mussolini agreed. The proposed 60,000-word length presented no problem, for he could assign such a relatively short project to Margherita and Morgan. But content offered a real obstacle. Mussolini conceived of the book as propaganda justifying the seizure of power by the Blackshirts. He planned to lay out the philosophy of Fascism and glorify his dictatorial rule. He thought of directing the book specifically at the Italian emigrant community in the United States.[14]

Shortly after negotiations for a publishing contract began, Mussolini approved a radical shift in the regime's policy toward Italian communities overseas. Dino Grandi had become undersecretary for foreign affairs in May 1925, and he persuaded Mussolini to end Fascist party activities among the millions of Italians living abroad. The Party organization *Fasci all'estero* (Fasci Abroad) had directed violent attacks against anti-Fascist exiles. This raised considerable concern within host governments about foreign interference, especially in the United States. Grandi argued that it would be better to cease the attacks in order to maintain the generally positive image Fascist Italy enjoyed abroad. Mussolini shifted control over emigrant policies to the foreign ministry, which he headed himself.[15]

This decision undid much of the justification for the Houghton Mifflin book project. Under the new policy, in his capacity as foreign minister, it no longer made sense for Mussolini to propagandize the Italian-American community openly. Even reshaping the book to direct it more generally toward the American public was problematic. While Mussolini thought of the book as an opportunity to define Fascist ideology, no such definition existed. Any official promulgation of Fascist doctrine was certain to provoke conflict among Mussolini's lieutenants. Despite pretensions of a uniformity of opinion among Fascists, throughout the twenties Mussolini's subordinates advocated many different ideas about what Fascism actually meant.

Under these circumstances, the Houghton Mifflin book project never materialized. Mussolini did not, however, let the chance to propagandize the United States pass, nor did Margherita and Morgan allow the potential profits to slip through their fingers.[16] Mussolini sanctioned another book project. In December 1926, Margherita arranged an interview between Mussolini and S. S. McClure, the aging former editor of *McClure's Magazine,* which had published Steffens's and Tarbell's muckraking articles a generation earlier. McClure had lost control of his magazine to the Hearst organization in early 1925 and was deeply in debt.

McClure left his interview with Mussolini convinced of his "force & charm & kindliness" and placed himself at the Duce's service. The two men agreed that McClure would have a series of articles written, purportedly by Mussolini, describing his rise to power. These were then to be collected and published as an autobiography. Mussolini insisted that Margherita approve each article before publication. When McClure met with Margherita about the project, she demanded $10,000 for her cooperation. McClure agreed.

McClure returned to the United States in late January 1927 and approached George Horace Lorimer, the editor of *The Saturday Evening Post*, about publishing the series. Lorimer accepted, agreeing to pay Mussolini $30,000, Margherita $10,000, and McClure $15,000, in return for exclusive rights to the articles and the subsequent book. Lorimer picked his staff writer Kenneth Roberts to produce the articles. Roberts had already written two flattering series on the rise of Fascism for *The Saturday Evening Post*, and had acquired a number of influential friends in Rome in the process. Among them were Salvatore and Arnaldo Cortesi.

Lorimer made it clear to Roberts that he did not intend to lay out $55,000 unless Mussolini was prepared to give a great deal of time to the project. Roberts did not relish the assignment, particularly after speaking to McClure—he felt the old man was approaching senility. Nonetheless, he sailed to Italy to discuss the project with Margherita. Their meeting was a disaster. Roberts thought Margherita was "a dumpy, hard-voiced, coarse-skinned bleached blonde from North Italy." Margherita rapidly decided that Roberts was a presumptuous fool.

To do a proper job, Roberts insisted that he must conduct several personal interviews with Mussolini. Margherita responded that the Duce was far too busy. She told Roberts that he could compile the series from *The Life of Benito Mussolini,* supplemented by Mussolini's speeches and articles from *Il Popolo d'Italia* and some unpublished material by Arnaldo. Each segment would have to be reviewed, in turn, by McClure, herself, and finally by Mussolini.

Roberts simply snorted in reply. In an icy voice Margherita asked how he would like to proceed. Roberts said that he wanted forty interviews of half an hour's length with Mussolini and that his work required no editing. Margherita was outraged. Consider the matter in reverse, she asked. Could he imagine Margherita, with her less than perfect knowledge of colloquial American English, demanding forty interviews with Calvin Coolidge? Roberts responded that he imagined that the Fascist regime could use all the good publicity it could get in the United States. To have Mussolini's supposed autobiography published in *The Saturday Evening Post* would be worth any amount of trouble. Margherita's furious stare ended their meeting.

McClure attempted to persuade Roberts to work with Margherita as she had insisted. Even McClure's offer of $5,000 did not change Roberts's mind. Roberts wired a full account to Lorimer and took the next ship home.

When Roberts reported to Lorimer, he found the editor conferring with former ambassador Richard Washburn Child. Lorimer had Roberts recount his tale to Child. Child argued that his friendship with Mussolini and Margherita would allow him to succeed where Roberts had failed. A week later, Child sailed to Italy.[17] He got no further with Margherita than Roberts had. But the former ambassador managed to persuade Lorimer to go ahead with the series anyway. By February 1928, Child had cut McClure out of the deal, secured $25,000 from Lorimer for Margherita's cooperation, and accepted her terms for the project. In the end, the articles were written in English by Child and Luigi Barzini, Jr., based on notes supplied by Arnaldo Mussolini and Margherita. They appeared in eight installments in *The Saturday Evening Post,* beginning in May 1928. Scribner's brought them out in book form later that year.

In his introduction to the book, Child insisted that Mussolini had dictated the entire manuscript to him and then had edited the material himself. Less than five years later, Mussolini admitted in print that the whole story was a lie. In any case, Child's wretched prose was an embarrassment to *The Saturday Evening Post,* and the book was published at a loss by Scribner's.[18]

The episode had a noteworthy postscript. McClure returned to New York in early 1928. He agreed to debate Vincenzo Nitti, son of the former Italian prime minister, on the merits of Fascism. One debate took place on March 11, in a theater on West Forty-second Street; before it was over, fights broke out and the police were called. Once he made it outside, a group of Fascist sympathizers hoisted McClure on their shoulders and carried him across Times Square, cheering and singing "Giovinezza." The old man had made a small piece of history that evening, coining the remark that forever epitomized Mussolini's accomplishments: "He made the trains run on time."[19]

Margherita's profits from Mussolini's "autobiography" led to other arrangements. Morgan and she proposed a continuous stream of articles specifically composed for the American audience, ostensibly written by Mussolini and distributed by the United Press. The articles began to appear in American newspapers in late 1927. Margherita and Morgan had conceived of an original form of propaganda. A foreign dictator acquired direct access to the hundreds of papers in the United States (as well as dozens of other countries) served by the United Press. Not only was Mussolini given this privilege gratis, but he and Margherita were richly paid to take it.

Morgan later claimed that he wrote the articles. The articles themselves suggest that they were written by Margherita in Italian on a subject Mussolini approved, then translated by Morgan into English. Finished pieces were reviewed by Mussolini and Margherita before release for publication. Mussolini sometimes changed his mind about the release of an article, requiring the hasty creation of a substitute to meet the deadline. Mussolini once rejected two pieces in a row before approving Margherita and Morgan's third effort. The fees paid by the United Press rewarded even that unusual labor. Morgan received $500 for his troubles, while Margherita and Mussolini split the remaining $1,000 every four weeks. No contract was ever signed. The profits alone ensured compliance. Even by American standards, this was a large amount of money. *The New York Times* was paying many of its reporters only $25 a week at the time. Morgan readily admitted "it was a lucrative undertaking for me."

In Italy, the dollars from the United Press were a small fortune. For example, in payment for feature articles put out by *Il Popolo d'Italia,* Margherita received 300 lire, the equivalent of about $16. This was no small sum by Italian standards. Mussolini's annual salary as prime minister, the highest-paid office in the land, amounted to 32,000 lire. In 1928, the $1,500 that Margherita, Morgan, and Mussolini were splitting every month equalled some 28,500 lire. There is no reason to believe that Margherita or Morgan paid any taxes at all on what they earned from the United Press. Certainly Mussolini didn't.[20] Their articles were well conceived and quite well executed, averaging about fifteen hundred words in length. They blended topics of current interest to Americans with pro-Fascist propaganda. Mussolini addressed his American readers in a direct style calculated to leave the impression that he had shared his private thinking about major questions of the day.

Mussolini tried to flatter and coax the American public into taking the side of the Fascists. He admitted that the United States had assumed the leadership of the world economy. Since the Americans were so generous, he wondered, why not reduce or even forgive Italy's war debts and keep U.S. tariffs on Italian imports low?[21] Everyone knew that the Americans wanted peace and disarmament. So did the Italians, and the Germans seemed to have learned their lesson. But the French and the British didn't seem so reasonable. Shouldn't the United States and Italy coordinate their foreign policies to force the French and British into line?[22]

The articles claimed that dishonest enemies of the regime, especially the Bolsheviks, had spread lies about Fascism. In fact, the Fascists had created a revolutionary new system of democratic government. Mussolini's rule was firm, but just and progressive. He had ended Italy's old quarrel with the pope, made his nation into a technological leader, and instilled a new discipline into the Italian people. While he had no intention of imposing his politics on anyone else, Mussolini suggested there were many features of the Fascist system Americans might want to imitate.[23]

Interspersed with thematic articles were pieces on a variety of topical subjects, such as plans for a European federation, Prohibition, revolution in Afghanistan, and Antarctic exploration. Occasional features stressed Fascism's advantages, or Mussolini's ability to solve any problem.[24]

The remuneration involved was such that Margherita decided to write another book for the American market. She hoped to profit from the Lateran Pact by producing an "autobiographical" novel, officially written by Mussolini, concerning his conversion to Catholicism. It would be titled *Una conversione* (*A Conversion*). An American magazine quoted her précis:

> In this work, which will have a preface by the Jesuit Father Tacchi-Venturi, the Duce will relate the story of the crises through which his conscience passed during the years of his apostolate for both Italy and the Roman Catholic religion. In the story there will appear a woman, Margherita Sarfatti, who loves Il Duce with Platonic affection and is thus loved by him. She will be the Beatrice of the work.[25]

The novel never appeared, probably vetoed by Mussolini. Perhaps Margherita was suffering from excessive self-confidence after publishing *Il palazzone*. Perhaps her articles for the United Press convinced her that Americans would believe anything. In any case, a few months later Margherita found a new source of income.

William Randolph Hearst's journalism empire had been buying from the United Press the rights to print the Mussolini articles for $1,500 apiece. The directors of the Hearst press were not happy with the arrangement, but their representative in Rome, Valerio Pignatelli, could not get near the Duce. Mr. Hearst was an admirer of Mussolini, and insisted on having his articles in the Hearst papers. Despite the expense, the management admitted that the articles were good for circulation.

Karl von Wiegand, the chief European correspondent for the Hearst organization, thought that he could do better than Pignatelli. After receiving permission from Than Vanneman Ranck, who managed the entire Hearst newspaper chain from New York, Wiegand visited Rome in January 1930. He learned what he could about Mussolini's arrangement with Morgan and the United Press. In April Wiegand returned and approached Margherita about acquiring Mussolini's articles for the Hearst press.[26]

Hard bargaining followed between Margherita and Wiegand. She had a decisive advantage. Given how slowly mail traveled by sea, cables or telephone calls between Rome and New York were the only effective means of communication between Wiegand and Ranck. Mussolini's telegraph and telephone intercept service passed on to Margherita transcripts of all their messages.

In the midst of negotiations, Millicent Hearst arrived in Rome. Mrs. Hearst had lost her husband in all but name to film star Marion Davies. But Mrs. Hearst knew all about her husband's business and continued to write occasional pieces for his papers. She easily obtained an interview with

Mussolini. In fact, he even took her for a drive in his Alfa Romeo to the Roman ruins recently excavated at Ostia.

Margherita had already accepted Wiegand's offer of $1,200 per article. While this was less than the United Press had paid, Margherita planned to cut Morgan out of the deal and thus make more money for herself and Mussolini. Mrs. Hearst thought that she would do her husband a favor and secure Mussolini for the Hearst press. During the drive to Ostia, she told him Mr. Hearst would be happy to pay Mussolini $1,500 for every piece. Mussolini passed this piece of information on to Margherita. Wiegand had no choice but to agree to the higher price.

On April 24, Margherita signed a contract guaranteeing that she would deliver twelve articles by Mussolini in 1931 for $1,500 each. On behalf of Mussolini, Margherita agreed to write only on topics approved by the Hearst organization, especially on newsworthy current events. Margherita promised an option on the same arrangement for 1932. Wiegand reluctantly gave Margherita a verbal promise that the Hearst press would accept a few pieces of her own. The Hearst organization expected to make a considerable profit. They were paying no more for the articles than they had when buying them from the United Press, and now they could resell publication rights to other newspapers, more than recovering their costs.[27]

Morgan had no choice but to accept the new arrangement. Margherita had even consulted him during negotiations to ensure that the new contract offered her a deal that was superior to the old agreement with the United Press. But as compensation, Mussolini allowed Morgan to visit Lipari Island, where political prisoners were incarcerated. No journalist had seen the prison before and the trip gave Morgan an exclusive story of a potentially sensational nature. As Pignatelli noted sardonically to Wiegand, "Our poor Tom will not be brave enough to tell everything." Mussolini was quite curious about living conditions on the island. He quizzed Morgan about the prisoners' regimen after the reporter returned. When Morgan described the brutal circumstances the prisoners endured, Mussolini shrugged the stories off. "It is not a hardship," he remarked dryly and turned his back on Morgan.[28]

William Randolph Hearst was not at all bothered by Mussolini's harsh rule over Italy. The two men made natural allies. Hearst detested the League of Nations. He also maintained a solidly anti-British, anti-French, and pro-German editorial line in his newspapers. The Sunday "March of Events" section of the Hearst papers regularly contained a grotesque Francophobe political cartoon from a right-wing German newspaper. These attitudes tallied nicely with Mussolini's own foreign policy. And articles in Hearst's newspapers granted Mussolini direct access to the American people. The Hearst papers enjoyed a Sunday circulation of some 5.7 million in a population of about 124 million in 1931. Given the number of extended families living under the same roof in the Depression years, Margherita's "Mussolini" articles may have been read by as many as one third of adult Americans.

Hearst considered Fascism to be alien to American values. Forced to choose between Bolsheviks and Fascists, however, Hearst readily preferred the latter. A Fascist Italy, he believed, had prevented a Communist Italy. The same could be true for Europe as a whole. Hearst enjoyed a close business relationship with the Rothermere press in Britain and applauded Viscount Rothermere's support for Mussolini, as well as for Oswald Mosley and his British Union of Fascists. As for Mussolini himself, Hearst had long admired him from a distance. He came to appreciate him even more after the two met in Rome in July 1931. So long as Mussolini avoided any statements Hearst considered anti-American, he was delighted to publish the Duce's views on world affairs.[29]

Relations did not proceed as smoothly between Margherita and Ranck. Ranck upset Mussolini and Margherita by referring to them openly in telegrams sent to Rome. The Duce worried that informers or gossips might lurk among the employees of the Italian telegraph system. Margherita instructed Ranck that Mussolini must be referred to as "Albis," and she as "Romis." When Margherita handed over the first article in January 1931, Wiegand, Pignatelli, and Ranck all found the subject and style unprintable. They quickly realized that Morgan must have played a large role in forging the Mussolini articles for the United Press and that Margherita was now trying to do the same on her own. Margherita delivered two articles of her own that Pignatelli and Ranck considered of even poorer quality. Margherita demanded $500 for each, when Wiegand had promised her only $250.

Ranck rejected Margherita's pieces. He made it clear that he would release payments only for articles he considered acceptable and that he wanted prior approval for all topics. At first, Margherita responded with a stubborn refusal to cooperate. Rather quickly, however, she became more accommodating. The money was simply too good for her to jeopardize the arrangement. Even $250 came to the princely sum of 4,800 lire. In turn, the Hearst organization agreed to accept a thirteenth Mussolini article for 1931, increasing by $1,500 the money paid to Margherita and Mussolini.

Margherita gradually learned to write in the far more severe and fact-oriented style of American journalism. Her temper still flared when the Hearst press rejected one of her pieces, but she would calm down and rewrite it until it met with approval. In July, Margherita was away on a trip to London and Paris, and another of her Mussolini articles proved unacceptable. Fiammetta had to rewrite it according to telephoned instructions from her mother. The generous payment was well worth the expensive long-distance telephone calls. A similar problem arose in late September, when Margherita was in Milan and at Il Soldo. Ranck wanted an article already submitted to be postponed and a more topical piece on the British abandonment of the gold standard to take its place. Margherita complied without complaint.

Margherita must have turned to Morgan for help with her writing, at least with the finer points of colloquial American English. During the year she learned to write up to Ranck's standards, until she was able to turn out specially requested articles in a few days.[30]

In order for an article to appear simultaneously in the twenty-eight Hearst newspapers, Ranck needed to receive a copy in New York at least eight days in advance of scheduled publication. When possible, the Hearst office in Rome mailed the article to Ranck. Usually, however, Margherita had an article ready only at the last minute, and it had to be cabled to New York at considerable expense. Afterward the original manuscripts, initialed by Mussolini on every page and signed by him at the end (but extensively edited in Margherita's own hand), were forwarded to Ranck. The articles were always dated the day previous to publication, as if Mussolini had just written them and cabled them immediately to America.

Margherita's own two articles reinforced the impact of her thirteen "Mussolini" articles. Her pieces offered remarkably candid appraisals of Mussolini's character. While superficially flattering, she portrayed Mussolini as he really was in 1931: increasingly isolated, emotionally aloof, and ever more impressed with his sense of superiority over others. As Mussolini claimed a year later: "I cannot have any friends. I have no friends . . . no one exerted any influence upon me. Fundamentally I have always been alone." Margherita also slipped in a little self-advertisement. She represented herself as the one exception to Mussolini's self-imposed isolation, emphasizing her many years of acquaintance with him. She took care to provide intimate details of his office decor and his personal appearance to emphasize her intimacy with the Duce.[31]

The thirteen "Mussolini" articles Margherita wrote in 1931 were much more substantial. Unlike her previous pieces for the United Press, the new articles hammered away at just a few themes, especially the need to address the world economic situation. By early 1931, the severe Depression in the United States following the 1929 Wall Street stock-market crash had spread to Europe. Unemployment figures in Italy had soared from 301,000 in 1929 to 734,000 in 1931 and were heading toward over one million in 1932–1933. The situation was even worse in Germany, where more than 23 percent of the work force were already unemployed and 30 percent were to be without a job by 1932. Hitler and his Nazis were demanding power in order to solve the problem by radical means.[32]

In the 1931 articles, Margherita reiterated the suggestion made in the earlier United Press pieces for a special American-Italian relationship. The articles argued that only the United States, with its gigantic economic potential, could pull the world out of the Depression. Unless the imbalances of wealth between the European states were adjusted, unless the barriers to international trade were lowered, unless Britain and France agreed to massive disarmament and the end of the ruinous arms race, unless the injustices of the Versailles settlement to Italy and Germany were righted, then catastrophe would follow. Europe would either succumb to Bolshevism or explode into another world war. The Fascist corporative state provided the only effective model for the reorganization of the Western economies.

The articles hailed President Hoover's decision to ease the Depression by accepting suspension of Allied war-debt payments to the United States for one year. They asked for a complete end to American isolationism. After all, the recent flight across the Atlantic by a squadron of the Italian Air Force, led by General Balbo, showed that the ocean no longer separated the continents as before. America must support Italian demands for colonies to absorb Italy's expanding population and to acquire the raw materials Italy needed for prosperity. More important than anything else, America and Italy must form a partnership to present "a united front against the menace of the black and yellow peoples."[33]

Given the racist and xenophobic editorial policies of the Hearst press, Margherita's articles probably did not offend many of her American readers. The Japanese invasion of Manchuria, beginning in September 1931, provided a context in which Margherita's calls for white racial solidarity against the yellow hordes would have made some sense to the Hearst readership. But her warnings about the black race must have seemed out of place, except to the most racist of Americans. Few knew that in the summer of 1931 a border war had nearly begun along the ill-defined frontiers of Ethiopia and Italian Somalia. Emperor Haile Selassie had ordered a 12,000-man army to push back Italian-supported guerrillas encroaching on Ethiopian territory. A combination of Italian diplomacy and threats had persuaded the emperor to recall his forces. The full implications of Margherita's racist diatribes did not become clear until the Ethiopian War four years later.[34]

In October, Hearst and his directors were eager to exercise their option to negotiate another contract for 1932. Hearst newspaper sales had been hurt by the Depression, however, and Ranck was struggling to contain expenses under his profligate employer. Ranck tried to get Margherita to deliver twenty-six articles for $1,000 apiece during the coming year. He also vetoed the purchase of any pieces under her own byline. Ranck had persuaded Hearst to purchase only those articles written by the most famous personages. Adolf Hitler, his right-hand man, Hermann Göring, and former president Calvin Coolidge had declined to write. But former British prime minister David Lloyd George, ex-chancellor of the exchequer Winston Churchill, and former French premier Paul Painlevé agreed.[35]

Margherita refused to write so much more for so much less per article. After a month of haggling, the two sides agreed that Margherita would deliver a total of eighteen articles at $1,200 each. This meant an extra $2,100 for the year. But since the lira had fallen in relation to the dollar, the agreement actually provided 41,000 lire more for 1932 than for 1931. Lloyd George, who had once earned $2,000 for an article, was now receiving less than Margherita.

She demanded prompter payment. One of Hearst's bureau chiefs noted that it would be wise to open a credit line with a Rome bank: "Mrs. Sarfatti is very difficult to deal with on money questions particularly when it is time to deliver another article before she has received the money for the previous one. . . . [A credit arrangement] could make the fair lady happier that way and smooth the road for getting important information when the regular channels are closed." Ranck eventually agreed to cable payment directly to the Banca Commerciale, where Amedeo held a subdirectorship. Amedeo ensured that his mother received the best possible rate of exchange and paid no commission.[36]

Even before the first of the new pieces arrived, Ranck wrote to Margherita to tell her how pleased he and Hearst were with the arrangement. A few weeks previously, Ranck had told H. G. Wells, another regular contributor to the Hearst press, about the new contract with Mussolini. "Mussolini," said Wells, "is an extremely able journalist who is doing a wonderful job editing Italy." Ranck asked Margherita to pass the compliment on to the Duce.[37]

For most of 1932, Margherita's second set of articles pleased Hearst and Ranck better than ever. Not only did she and Mussolini prove willing to write on the topics suggested by the Hearst organization, but they offered a number of acceptable ideas of their own. As a result, despite Ranck's cost-cutting suggestion that they buy fewer articles for 1933 or offer a lower price, Hearst insisted on contracting for another eighteen pieces for the coming year. Margherita insisted on again receiving $1,200 per article and Hearst agreed. In 1933, this meant an average of only 17,900 lire for each piece. But the drop in prices caused by the Italian depression gave this much money considerable buying power. Between 1927 and 1932, the purchasing power of the lira in Italy rose by 73 percent. The average Italian worker was earning only about 1,000 lire a month at the time, and even a Cabinet minister in 1932 received only 3,000 to 4,000 lire in monthly salary. In fact, Mussolini and Rachele relied on Hearst's money to pay for their country home in the Romagna. Vittorio Mussolini remembers his mother telling his father: "Benito, you must write an article for America right away. In a week the mortgage payment to the Forlì Savings Bank comes due." Margherita, Hearst, and Mussolini had good reason to be pleased with their new agreement, signed in early November 1932.[38]

As the American presidential elections drew closer, however, aspects of the arrangement began to bother Hearst and Ranck. In late September Mussolini rejected categorically their proposal for an article on his reaction to the failed Geneva Disarmament Conference. He would not discuss in the press what policy Italy might adopt in regard to rearmament. With the Germans growing increasingly restless over the restrictions of the Versailles Treaty, and with the possibility of a new administration to be installed in Washington, Mussolini wanted to keep his options open. He did agree to let Margherita write her own article on the topic. Margherita received only $250, instead of the $500 she expected. She was furious. Were articles under her own name worth only one fifth of those she penned under Mussolini's byline?[39]

She retaliated by arranging for (and presumably profiting from) a number of exclusive interviews with Mussolini. These appeared in various American newspapers, and were sold to the European press, in clear violation of her contract with the Hearst organization. Ranck protested, although he waited until after the contract for 1933 had been signed. Margherita promised that her agreement about exclusivity would "be more carefully observed in the future."[40]

Most annoying to the Hearst press was the changing tenor of the articles. Topics for 1932 had ranged from urging the United States to emulate Mussolini's war on organized crime to advocating an end to Prohibition to warning of the menace posed by the Japanese to "White Civilization." As the Roosevelt-Hoover contest for the White House took over the headlines, Margherita's articles under Mussolini's byline took on a repetitive theme: The world crisis demanded a radical cure.

The articles argued that either the burden of arms spending must be reduced by general disarmament or Germany must be allowed to rearm up to the level of the other great powers. Trade barriers must be lowered, especially the huge 59 percent American tariff. The United States would be wise to copy Fascism to solve its economic problems. The Fascist corporative state had ended class warfare and stifled the threat of Communism by making the government the arbiter in labor disputes. Mussolini's regime had put the unemployed back to work by draining the malarial marshes southwest of Rome. Now the recovered farmland provided a livelihood for tens of thousands of peasants. Shouldn't the United States help its millions of jobless by instituting similar projects?

The arguments were propagandistic, yet Mussolini had been making similar speeches in private, even in confidential statements to the inner leadership of the Fascist party. Mussolini seemed to be taking his own propaganda seriously. After Roosevelt crushed Hoover in an electoral landslide on November 8, 1932, a Mussolini article hailed the results. Roosevelt's victory showed that the people had realized "a complete change was necessary." Hearst was not upset at the praise of the president-elect. After all, he had helped engineer Roosevelt's nomination at the Democratic Convention with the help of their mutual friend Joseph P. Kennedy. But when the final Mussolini article for 1932 arrived in New York on December 16, a special eighteenth piece on his expectations for the coming year, it called for the cancellation of Europe's war debts to the United States.[41]

This proved to be too much for Hearst. He wired Ranck: "I would not print Mussolini's article or any other propaganda for debt cancellation." Apparently Hearst had not been paying very careful attention to the contents of Margherita's previous pieces. Ranck had already retitled her January 24, 1932, article "Europe Can Recuperate Without Help of America," even though Margherita had argued that the United States must forgive the European war debts and seize the leadership in restructuring the world economy. He had changed the title of an article urging Roosevelt's intercession in European economic affairs from "The American Change" to "Depression Is Deepest in U.S., Says Mussolini." Ranck prefaced the article with a totally contradictory short editorial arguing that the calamitous state of the American economy made war-debt cancellation impossible.

Ranck ordered the Hearst representative in Rome to explain to Margherita that they could not publish the article, or any other on debt cancellation. To their surprise, Margherita was accommodating and offered a replacement piece on the place of women in Fascist Italy. Thanks to interception of all telegrams to and from the Hearst office in Rome, Margherita routinely read the organization's internal communications, including Ranck's repeated instructions on the war-debt issue. It seems that Margherita and Mussolini had been testing the limits of Hearst's tolerance.

Mussolini vetoed the subject of women under Fascism. Instead he insisted that she rewrite his forecast for 1933 article. Margherita did this with alacrity. Apparently, Mussolini had offered her the entire payment in return for the rush job. By holding the presses, the Hearst organization managed to squeeze the hastily commissioned piece into its 1933 New

Year's Day editions. The article stressed the severity of the world economic crisis but expressed Mussolini's optimism that the coming year would bring significant improvement.[42]

Two recent developments helped make Mussolini optimistic. In early November, Franklin Delano Roosevelt had been elected president of the United States. And by late December 1932, it seemed only a matter of months before Adolf Hitler and his Nazis came to power in Germany. Mussolini now depended upon these two very different men for a radical transformation of the international scene, and the creation of rich opportunities for himself and Fascist Italy.

Part Four

THE FALL

24

Under Attack

When Mussolini inaugurated the exhibition of the reformed *Novecento* in February 1926 with a speech prepared by Margherita, some observers assumed that her movement was about to receive official sanction. But intransigent Fascists demanded an art that was more directly inspired by Fascism.[1] Indirect criticisms of this sort reached Mussolini's ears, for on October 5, 1926, he made a brief public statement on the topic. "Without art," he proclaimed to an audience in Perugia, "there is no civilization," observing that during the Renaissance, artistic culture had been the only force uniting the politically divided Italians. "Now, on the terrain so well prepared, an art can be reborn that is at once traditionalist and modern. We must create . . . a new art for our times, a Fascist art."[2]

In the fall of 1926, just after the *Novecento* exhibition had closed, Margherita set to work on the next show. Mussolini authorized her to hold the exhibit in 1929 in Rome, in part to provide her with a suitable excuse for making a permanent move to the capital. Thus she was very surprised when he did not agree to preside at the opening, as he had done twice before: "I cannot promise anything as to my possible participation in the opening ceremonies."[3]

Roberto Farinacci, recently dismissed as party secretary but still influential, had begun attacks on Margherita and her artist friends as corrupt international influences in Italian life. Mussolini preferred compromise to clarity, and once he realized that cultural policy was a volatile political question, he decided to take no definite position. With Marinetti pressing in on one side, Ojetti on the other, and Margherita at the center, he felt he had every reason to avoid a precisely defined policy. Instead he proclaimed that Fascism was launching a cultural revolution, and left the specifics of it to be decided by the interested ideologues and intellectuals. One result of his strategy was that he started to withdraw from public association with the *Novecento*.[4]

Taking his cue from Mussolini's Perugia speech, Giuseppe Bottai launched an inquiry into the nature of Fascist art in October 1926 in *Critica Fascista*. Almost two dozen Fascist artists, writers, and critics, from Ardengo Soffici and Gino Severini to Marinetti and Bontempelli, presented their opinions. Not surprisingly, there was no consensus. Some contributors wanted to tolerate all forms and styles of painting because "Fascist art was that produced during the Fascist era," while others demanded a clear, rigid policy of cultural conformity. In summing up, Bottai argued that the only real effect of Fascism on art was to be seen in a "simple tendency . . . toward more solid, ample, and forceful constructions." As Margherita had suggested a number of years earlier, Bottai stressed the need to abandon the propaganda kitsch produced by "Fascist bad taste." Beyond these points, he concluded that the regime should foster free creativity.[5]

Until *Critica Fascista*'s inquiry, Margherita had been able to set the terms for public discussion of art and Fascism through her column in *Il Popolo d'Italia*. She was not pleased that the discourse had been extended. She contributed a separate article for *Critica Fascista* only after the inquiry had ended. In "Art, Fascism, and Anti-Rhetoric," she asserted that Fascism's function was to purge Italian culture of all rhetorical excesses of language and style, just as Mussolini and the Manganello club had purified Italian politics.[6]

The debate Bottai occasioned revealed how many competing groups there were claiming to represent Fascism. Fascist cultural leaders tried to undermine one another's claims, and each became a target of criticism.[7] By 1926, Margherita was forced to admit the existence of centrifugal currents both inside and out of the *Novecento*. She tried to gloss over some differences by creating a category of landscape painters she called *paesisti*, from the Italian word for "country" or "local region." These painters attempted to convey the characteristics and atmosphere of their own regional cultures, by means, Margherita argued, of the overall *Novecento* idiom. The chief artist of this tradition was Arturo Tosi, whose Lombard landscapes recalled a nineteenth-century naturalism. She saw Tosi's work as a synthesis of "the two fundamental and opposing means of creating form on canvas: through line and color—the means of the classicists—or through the play of light and shadow—the means of the naturalists."[8]

Margherita identified two additional regional currents: a *paesisti* school in Tuscany, headed by Ardengo Soffici, and quite a different movement in Rome, led by Carlo Socrate. Contrary to her wishes, Soffici and his fellow Tuscans distinguished their work from the *Novecento,* which they considered foreign and decadent. The Tuscans were bound together by a view of Fascism as the embodiment of the pure and "healthy" values of the Italian peasantry and the rural *squadrismo*. The *Strapaese* ("Supercountry") movement also glorified rural values in contrast to those of modern and corrupt urban civilization. Along with Mino Maccari and Ottone Rosai, Soffici helped to found the Florentine journal *Il Selvaggio (The Wild One),* a mouthpiece for those who began attacking the *Novecento* in the late 1920s. Soffici became increasingly xenophobic and racist in his views over the following decade.[9]

Once Mussolini attacked Zionism as a "foreign" phenomenon, "Jewish" and "foreign" became interchangeable terms in some Fascist camps. When Soffici and Farinacci assaulted the *Novecento* for its "foreign" decadence, they were also making an indirect and anti-Semitic assault on Margherita. Anti-Semitism reached a crescendo about the time of the Concordat between the Fascist regime and the Vatican in late 1928 and early 1929. With Mussolini's apparent desire for all Italians to be or become Catholic, private anti-Semites were emboldened to make public their prejudices. Margherita's conversion to Catholicism was a defensive response to men such as Soffici and Farinacci, but opponents continued to label her and her *Novecento* "Jewish" and "foreign."

Margherita offended Soffici by trying to lure the Florentine writer Raffaello Franchi into serving as a kind of secretary for a *Gruppo Toscano Novecentesco.* Soffici was convinced that Margherita was deliberately keeping the Tuscans out of her exhibits. In June 1927, when Franchi asked that the entire Tuscan contingent be included in the 1929 *Novecento* exhibit, Margherita demanded first that the Tuscan group take a position against *Il Selvaggio* by organizing a *Novecento* exhibit in Florence. Attempts at rapprochement began in 1928, when exhibits were exchanged: The Milanese showed in Florence and the Tuscans in Milan. Yet the gulf between the *Novecento* and the Tuscans remained.[10]

In Rome another group of painters evolved who had in common a lyrical expressionist style. One current of the style centered around three friends: Antonietta Raphael Mafai, Mario Mafai, and Scipione. After a period in London and Paris, Raphael introduced the other two painters to an expressionistic mode noted for its hallucinatory use of color and distorted image. Raphael's studio on the Via Cavour was the center of a circle dubbed the School of Via Cavour by 1929. Another current of the Roman style was represented by artists Corrado Cagli, Giuseppe Capogrossi, and Emanuele Cavalli. Their painting was known as tonalism because of its closely graded hues and vibrant luminosity. That same year, the French critic Waldemar George used the label *Scuola Romana*—the Roman School—in connection with this latter group. Both groups are now known by that name.[11]

Margherita became aware of these groups since she attended cultural events everywhere in the capital in an effort to establish a presence and attract artists into her orbit. In May 1927, she attended the opening of a tonalist exhibit at the Dinesen Hotel showing the work of Capogrossi and Cavalli. Their compatriot Cagli became a regular guest at her salon. She also frequented the famous *Terza Saletta,* "Third Room," of the Caffè Aragno, where Roman artists and literary figures congregated. It was there, as Mario Mafai recalled, that most of the painters of the Roman School first met Margherita, "just arrived fresh from Milan, with a huge load of *Novecento* paintings, ready to conquer the capital."[12]

In April 1927, she arranged an art exhibit at the gallery of an old and distinguished Roman cultural organization, the Società degli Amatori e Cultori di Belle Arti (Society of the Friends and Students of the Fine Arts). She called the show "Ten Artists of the Italian Novecento." Among the ten were Virginio Guidi and Carlo Socrate. Margherita insisted that all were members of the *Novecento,* but frankly admitted that each was moved by individual inspiration. The exhibit was an obvious effort to attract the *Scuola Romana* artists.[13]

Avant-garde artists in Rome had few places in which to show their work. Margherita's efforts in 1928 on behalf of the Paris art dealer Leone Rosenberg, who was hoping to establish a branch of his L'Effort Moderne gallery in Rome, came to nothing. Then the Milanese dealer Pier Maria Bardi opened the Galleria di Roma in the capital to give the Romans an outlet. Margherita bought from him paintings by Guidi and Mario Mafai. La Cometa, financed by the Countess Anna Laetitia "Mimì" Pecci-Blunt, a niece of Pope Leo XIII, became another popular Roman gallery for the artists. La Cometa also became a fashionable center of cultural anti-Fascism. Margherita nonetheless frequented the gallery. Barbara Allason, an ardent anti-Fascist, remembered Margherita appearing there "still very beautiful and elegant; she always arrives in the small piazza in a sumptuous automobile so long that it can hardly turn the corner. She gets out alone, sometimes in furs, sometimes in summer dresses, always in black; around her neck a rope of the most beautiful pearls. I watch her, I admire her, I am a bit envious of her car, but I don't want to speak to her."[14]

In Turin, the industrial capital of Italy, the *Sei di Torino* ("Turin Six") movement emerged in the late 1920s. Like the *Scuola Romana,* the style of the *Sei di Torino* was characterized by a lyrical expressionism devoted to landscapes and still lifes. Its chief proponents, including the painter-novelist Carlo Levi, exhibited together for the first time in 1929. The *Sei di Torino* was more overtly anti-Fascist than the *Scuola Romana.* Many anti-Fascists made their homes in Turin. The group's theoretical mentor was Lionello Venturi, who held the chair in art history at the University of Turin. Venturi had flirted briefly with the Fascists but by the late 1920s had lost faith in them. He was one of fewer than twenty Italian professors who would refuse to swear a loyalty oath to Fascism in 1931; the following year he escaped a police dragnet and made his way to Paris.

Venturi and the *Sei di Torino* rejected the cultural chauvinism that the regime touted, and in declaring themselves apolitical they stood against all efforts to create an art for Fascism. There were some points of agreement between Venturi and Margherita, such as her own recognition of the historical importance of the Impressionists and Cézanne. "From across the seas and across the mountains," she had written, "we have taken and learned much," and she often said that Italians must "absorb everything and copy nothing." For this reason, Ojetti condemned both Venturi and Margherita. Yet her stress on the Mediterranean, Latin roots of Italian art, and her desire to see Italy dominate twentieth-century art, were irreconcilable with Venturi's ideas.

Some critics have argued that the *Scuola Romana* and the *Sei di Torino* courageously pitted themselves against Margherita's *Novecento* in a "resistance" to Fascism. This is an oversimplified interpretation of the cultural scene in Fascist Italy. The "art for art's sake" attitude of the painters in both Rome and Turin opposed the Fascist call for politically engaged art, but it was not conceived as an overt assault against Fascism—after all, four of the six Turin painters took part in the second *Novecento* exhibit in 1929. Besides, the *Novecento* was never proclaimed to be the official Fascist style, and Margherita's attitude toward the Roman and Turin movements was not cast in political terms. What she wanted was to incorporate these and other movements under the *Novecento* umbrella. Autonomous groups weakened the centrality of her position.[15]

As it happened, central organization was imposed by the government, not by Margherita's ambition. Throughout the 1920s, Mussolini had allowed Fascist syndicalists to organize artists and writers into unions. By 1928 these individual unions were consolidated into a Confederation of Professionals and Artists, which eventually contained almost half a million members. The Confederation set policies and standards for work in the arts and professions, bringing them under state control. All artists and writers had to be on an official roster in order to sell their work; a listing on the roster required a Fascist party card and evidence of "good moral and political conduct."[16]

For Margherita's entourage, the Sindacato di Belle Arti ("Union of Fine Arts") was the most important of the Fascist unions. Headed by Cipriano E. Oppo, the Sindacato regulated a system of purchases and commissions and coordinated a vast network of annual regional exhibitions, to be followed by national and international exhibitions. Local juries controlled admission to the regional shows, which were open to all styles and movements. The national exhibit—known as the Quadriennale—was to take place in Rome every four years on the basis of invitations issued through a committee, but was similarly eclectic in the range of the styles it represented.[17]

Oppo was a Roman artist who had come to Fascism from the Nationalist movement. He was also a deputy in Parliament.[18] In late 1927, *La Tribuna,* formerly the organ of the Nationalists, published an article critical of the *Novecento.* Because Margherita had expressed reservations about the artistic unions, she asked the editor whether Oppo was behind the attack. Oppo wrote a disingenuous letter in reply, protesting that he had nothing against the artists of the *Novecento.* He shrewdly placed Margherita and several key *Novecento* painters on the regional committee of the Lombard union exhibit, along with dozens of others, including Farinacci, to neutralize their votes. Knowing Oppo's official status was reinforced by a personal friendship with Mussolini, Margherita moved carefully. When it was clear that their interests were blocked, she warned Mario Sironi, "It's not a good idea to get out [of the union] or to worsen the conflict with it. We already have too many enemies on our backs. If we go up against the corporations, which are now omnipresent and will be for some time to come, we're done for."[19]

Margherita had always had a special interest in the Venice Biennale, but now it too was to be held under the auspices of the government. Fradeletto's exhibit had become the most prestigious art event in the world. For that reason, Margherita had launched the *Novecento* at the 1924 Biennale. *Novecentisti* success in 1926 was marred by Ojetti's accusations that the work was too foreign. Still she felt she might have a special say in the exhibition after Pietro Orsi, another former tutor, was appointed mayor of Venice and president of the Biennale. In order to secure a room for the *Novecento* at the 1928 exhibition, she called on Orsi. The old man decided to try to stay above the fray by appointing both her and Oppo to a committee under a new secretary-general, the sculptor Antonio Maraini. Margherita badgered Orsi about Maraini, for she feared the Florentine sculptor would be difficult to control even though he had taken part in *Novecento* exhibits. She threatened to criticize the Biennale in *Il Popolo d'Italia;* Orsi relented only to the extent of adding Arturo Tosi to the committee. He balanced the selection jury similarly by appointing both Mario Sironi and Ardengo Soffici to it.[20]

Oppo had agreed privately with Maraini to prevent the *Novecento* from participating as a separate group. Margherita blustered but was forced to concede. She turned her efforts to getting as many *Novecento* painters as possible represented, insisting to Sironi, "We must appear in force and in full working order—the *Novecento* for ever."[21]

Separate exhibits were given at the 1928 Biennale to the Futurists and to Ojetti's selection of nineteenth-century Italian painters. Margherita agreed with the importance of these artists as precursors of the *Novecento*, but caviled that better judgment should have been used in selecting the works. She kept up appearances, claiming that the new committee worked with a "cordial unanimity of interests" to produce a "triumph of modern art." In her reviews of the Biennale, she disparaged the polemical tone that was beginning to characterize art criticism, scolding the Tuscans for attacking the *Novecento*. She also experienced several small personal pleasures at Venice, including her collaboration with Marcello Piacentini on an "Art of the Theater" installation and the special exhibit of works by Italian and French painters in France, the "School of Paris."[22]

At the end of the year, Mussolini made the Venice Biennale a state agency run by a committee of five members. One of the five was Ettore Zorzi, a bureaucrat known to be a bitter opponent of the *Novecento*. Margherita never again had a strong voice in the proceedings.[23]

The *Novecento* now had limited prospects. Until the second national exhibition, planned for 1927 but postponed by Mussolini for two years, Margherita had to try to hold the disparate artists together and keep public attention focused on the movement. To accomplish this, she organized a series of small annual shows in Milan, "Fifteen Artists of the Novecento Italiano" in 1927 and "Exhibit of the Seven Painters of the Novecento Italiano" in 1928.[24]

But Margherita continued to worry about the future of the *Novecento*. She escaped to a spa near Padua to relax but could not keep her thoughts from returning to the *Novecento*. To Gabriele D'Annunzio she complained that she was battling alone for modern art, attacked on all sides. Likewise she expressed her concern to Sironi and Tosi:

> In Milan I had the impression that a process of disintegration and crumbling had begun to occur within our group. Please, please, *please resist!* . . . Who can go against us if we are united? . . . Above all, work with courage, faith, and conviction for the triumph of your brilliant genius and of Italian art![25]

In the face of mounting criticism and competition at home, Margherita put her energy into promoting the *Novecento* abroad. From the beginning of 1927 to the end of 1929, almost a dozen exhibitions were launched in Europe, starting in Switzerland and Holland and extending to Germany, France, Czechoslovakia, and Hungary. In the early 1930s, other exhibits were mounted in Scandinavia and South America, and contacts were made for similar shows in Madrid, Tokyo, and New York. The critical success of the exhibit of Italian painters at the Zurich Kunsthaus in March 1927, for which Sironi designed the poster, stimulated the further efforts. Margherita spoke at the opening of the Amsterdam show in November. She then went to Germany, where she lectured at the University of Berlin and arranged an exhibit that eventually traveled from Berlin to Hamburg and Leipzig. When Margherita traveled to Switzerland in 1929, anti-Fascists there threatened to denounce her as a spy and expose details of her personal life, and the police even received reports of an assassination plan.[26]

Margherita managed to obtain government subsidies for the overseas *Novecento* exhibits, arguing they furthered a "cultural imperialism" that spread respect for Italy abroad. The success of the foreign exhibits led Oppo to work to gain government control over future Italian shows sent abroad.[27]

The second national *Novecento* exhibit proved disappointing. At the last moment, she thought Mussolini might not even allow it to be held. When approval finally came in December 1928, she sent a telegram addressed to the "painters' table at the Marchesi Caffè," where the *Novecento* artists usually gathered in Milan, containing the Fascist salute, *A Noi!* ("To Us!"). When the exhibit officially opened in Milan on February 24, 1929, Mussolini was not present—only Party Secretary Augusto Turati showed up, and he did so as a personal favor to Margherita. A telegram arrived from Ojetti saying he could not attend for health reasons.[28]

Margherita had invited some 140 artists to the exhibit, but not everyone accepted. A few of the Romans took part, as did some Tuscans, but all the Futurists refused outright. Since Mussolini did not attend, Margherita took pains to recall in the catalog how in 1926 "the head of government personally inaugurated, with an important speech, an exhibit of young and Fascist artists—a squadron of avant-garde *arditi* in every area of spiritual activity—revolutionaries of the modern restoration in art as in social and political life." Never before had she actually labeled the members of the *Novecento* "Fascist" artists. And she confronted her critics head-on: "The success accorded to the first exhibit of the *Novecento Italiano* by the public, in the press, and by sales, has been underscored by the violent and masked attacks that came . . . from enemies both public and covert."[29]

Press coverage of the exhibit was not effusive. The changing political climate encouraged some to say that the diverse group of artists was united only by the personal ambitions of Margherita Sarfatti. Because Mussolini failed to attend the opening, many assumed that he and Margherita had quarreled. Arturo Martini, who had been friendly with Margherita since World War I and one of the earliest members of her group, formally withdrew from the *Novecento*. From within the movement, the Paris-based militant Mario Tozzi attacked both *Il Selvaggio* and the Lombard *paesisti* for their provincialism: "Just as Fascism has been able to free itself from the slavery of democratic Europe, so must Italian art return to itself and free itself from Franco-European post-impressionism."[30]

The most serious assault against Margherita came in April 1929 in the wake of a talk on the *Novecento* she gave at Fascist party headquarters in Milan. A professional polemicist, Arturo F. Della Porta, published a sharply worded attack against the *Novecento,* which he called an "abortion of life." Della Porta was a right-wing Fascist, a racist, and a rabid xenophobe who stood against all forms of artistic modernism. On the evening of April 23, as the exhibition was about to close, Della Porta attempted to organize a rally against the *Novecento* at the Famiglia Artistica in Milan. When his supporters arrived at the hall, they found the way blocked by police agents, who announced that the meeting had been prohibited by the prefect. Della Porta moved the group to a nearby hotel, where he read telegrams of support from artists and political figures, including one from Roberto Farinacci. Della Porta issued a manifesto that branded the *Novecento* a decadent "artistic current of French and German origin."[31]

That July, the fierce battle that had raged in the press over the *Novecento* finally caused Mussolini to lose his patience. He sent Margherita a bruising, frigidly formal letter denouncing her efforts to advance the *Novecento* by identifying it with Fascism and with his own name. "I disapprove of this most vigorously," he lectured:

> This attempt to make people think that the artistic position of Fascism is represented by your *Novecento* is both futile and a lie. . . . Since you are so shameless in mixing my name as a statesman with your artistic inventions, whatever they are called, you should not be surprised if, quite soon and very explicitly, I make my position and that of Fascism quite clear with regard to the so-called *Novecento,* or what remains of the *Novecento* that once was.

In the wake of Mussolini's threat, Farinacci began publishing Della Porta's articles in his newspaper, *Il Regime Fascista.* Farinacci disagreed with Mussolini's policy of allowing "cultural space" for the diverse artistic currents that existed. Farinacci wanted a simple and easily understood Fascist realist painting. An anti-Semite and an admirer of the Nazis, he identified internationalists, Bolsheviks, and Jews as the principal enemies of the Fascists. No wonder that the first Della Porta article Farinacci published was a vicious condemnation of modern art as the corrupting product of internationalism and Jewish art dealers, as well as of "insane," "drunken" artists like van Gogh, Gauguin, and Cézanne. Della Porta demanded that the regime establish its priorities in artistic matters and that Mussolini create an official state art.[32]

In her own reviews of the show, Margherita repeated arguments that had become part of her standard critical repertoire—that the artists of the *Novecento* were "militants of a revolutionary restoration" in search of a "modern classicity" and motivated by the desire to "sublimate the modern in the eternal." In *Il Popolo d'Italia* she admitted that the *Novecento* was not interested in the "immediate representation of the events of our time"—the Fascist realism some simpleminded people wanted. The *Novecento,* she insisted, offered the only appropriate artists for the Fascist epoch. Margherita went on a speaking tour in southern Italy to gather new adherents.[33]

Further attacks came in the fall, this time from Marinetti. On October 5, 1929, Marinetti opened an exhibit of "Thirty-three Futurists" at Milan's Galleria Pesaro, where the *Novecento* had started. In his introduction to the exhibition, he called the *Novecento* "Futurists of the right" who stubbornly insisted on adherence to plasticity and naïve formalisms. He accused Sironi, Soffici, and Carrà of having abandoned their origins, and criticized Margherita for stealing the language of Futurism to describe her *Novecento* movement. A few weeks later, he delivered a speech contrasting Futurism and the *Novecento* to an overcrowded house on a hot, sweltering evening. Introduced by Innocenzo Cappa, who with Cesare Sarfatti had defended Marinetti at his pornography trial twenty years earlier, Marinetti was in his best form—aggressive, loud, and polemical. He spoke for two and a half hours, tracing the history of Futurism and berating the *Novecento* for wanting to create a monopoly on Italian art. In a later interview Margherita dismissed Marinetti as backward-looking.[34]

As 1929 drew to a close, Alberto Salietti complained to Margherita about the "rabid campaign that has been unleashed against the *Novecento* from all directions." Bewildered by the sudden change in atmosphere, he complained, "There is such confusion in the artistic field that we can no longer understand anything. The Academy tugs from one side, the Sindacati from another, the young from their end and the old from theirs, and everyone pulls at the same time against the *Novecento.*" Margherita could not dismiss the envy and hate that had suddenly been released against her and her friends. What worried her most was the fact that Mussolini allowed it to continue.[35]

The attacks seemed all the more terrible because few in the *Novecento* gave her much help in fighting back. Disgusted by the situation, she thought seriously about closing down the *Novecento* entirely and asked Carlo Foà to survey members of the inner circle. His report was not heartening: Gaspare Gussoni, the gallery owner who hosted the local Milanese exhibits, and Tosi both thought it best to dissolve the *Novecento.* Sironi felt they should exhibit less, work more, and respond to the polemics in the press. Salietti was bitter about the lack of progress in his own career, while Funi "shoots like a machine gun but doesn't know his target." The general feeling was that with Margherita in Rome, it was difficult to hold the group together, and if there were money available they could hire a full-time secretary to organize exhibits and perhaps publish a journal. "Poor *Novecento*," she scrawled across Foà's letter, "if our faith is so low that we need to pay a salary! When things begin to go bad, the fault is always with money instead of with the spirit."[36]

For a time they discussed starting a small review to serve as a private vehicle for responding to their critics. Sironi wanted the journal to be open to a wide group of collaborators—including the Futurists, Ojetti, Lionello Venturi, Maccari, and Oppo—in order to build a united front against the reactionaries. Margherita agreed that there should be "doors open to those close to us and blows against the others," and suggested as the title *Botte da Orbi (Blows of Blind Fury)*. She refused to carry the entire burden. She told Foà:

> You understand that it is not possible to go on like this. We receive blows from all quarters and no one but me tries to do anything. It is a real shame. The others are evangelists who tend to turn the other cheek, but that's not my style. . . . I thought I was dealing with men, not children playing games. . . . I have lived not without usefulness or glory. Now, rather than live a wretched existence, I am firmly of the opinion that it would be much better to close down the *Novecento* and resume our freedom of action. To give our enemies a target by not going on the attack or defending ourselves is dangerous, damaging, and stupid.[37]

Margherita continued to defend modernism, which she said reflected the nature of Fascism itself, in an article written in French and published in Paris. Shortly after this salvo, her new book on art appeared, *Storia della pittura moderna (History of Modern Painting)*, as a further challenge to her enemies. It was a comparative study of modern art as it had developed throughout Europe, with the emphasis on Italy's contributions as part of that general phenomenon and its peculiar "Mediterranean" qualities.

In January 1930, Margherita went to London to see an exhibition of "Italian Art, 1200–1900." The show had been suggested to Mussolini by Mrs. Austin Chamberlain, wife of the British foreign minister. Hailed as the cultural event of the decade, the London show may well have been the first comprehensive international exhibit of the kind major museums so often organize today. At the opening, Margherita entertained British visitors with stories about teaching Mussolini how to wear ties, and other essential social skills. Not having been involved in organizing it, she gave the event a lukewarm review.[38]

She returned to Italy for the 1930 Venice Biennale. No longer on the executive committee, Margherita played only a minor role. She joined a jury that awarded a Fascist party prize for a work of art dealing with a Fascist theme. Despite her distaste for realist propaganda, she helped secure the prize for a member of the *Novecento,* Arnaldo Carpanetti. His painting, *Incipit Novus Ordo (The New Order Begins),* showed Mussolini amid a throng of followers. The canvas was purchased by Party Secretary Augusto Turati for the PNF headquarters in Rome. Turati's successor, Giovanni Giuriati, disliked the painting and moved it to an obscure location. Revealing his continued uncertainty over the issue, Mussolini scolded, "As a Fascist you must be for the *Novecento.*" Giuriati protested that he was against such "horrors and deformations and against the camorra of the *Novecento,*" which he felt discriminated against artists who did not paint in the style. Mussolini replied meekly, "All right, I'll think about it."[39] The secret police reported that people were beginning to talk about Margherita's possible role as an agent of the "Jewish international," and one well-known critic compared the *Novecento* to an underground Masonic organization.[40]

When Mussolini authorized the nationwide Quadriennale as the capstone of the Sindacati's exhibition hierarchy, Margherita was appointed to both its organizing committee and its executive board. She helped arrange rooms for Sironi, Tosi, and other members of the *Novecento* for its inaugural exhibition. After the first Quadriennale opened in January 1931, Oppo persuaded Mussolini to remove her from the committees. The *Novecento* never appeared again in Italy as an organized group. Oppo envisioned his huge exhibit taking the place of Margherita's *Novecento* as the point of reference around which all Italian artists would gravitate.[41]

Margherita attended the opening ceremonies of the Quadriennale, where she easily guessed from Mussolini's speech the arguments Oppo had used against her. Mussolini stressed that Oppo had opened the Quadriennale to artists of all styles and schools. "Otherwise it would be said that the first national exhibition in Rome was an exhibition of a particular group, of a special clique." Police agents reported an incident at the reception following, when Queen Elena pointedly snubbed Margherita. The incident may have been apocryphal. The two women had been friends for some time and years later Margherita spoke warmly of the queen in her memoirs. Nonetheless, the very fact that such rumors were in circulation suggests that Margherita's influence was waning.[42]

In the first of two reviews of the exhibit, published not in *Il Popolo d'Italia* but in an independent review, *Nuova Antologia,* Margherita said Oppo should have been "more audaciously exclusive" in rejecting at least a hundred of the works on display. Her review of the first Quadriennale covered virtually the entire range of Italian painting, from the Lombard and

Tuscan *paesisti* to the *Scuola Romana* and the *Sei di Torino*. It was understandable, if not entirely politic, that she criticized Oppo's achievement, for
he had created an institutional environment in which the *Novecento* was just
one of half a dozen artistic currents.[43]

Margherita concentrated her energies on arranging an upcoming *Novecento* exhibit in Buenos Aires. The exhibit had first been proposed to Soffici
by an Italo-Argentine collector, Juan de Rolleri. Margherita browbeat Sironi and his fellow artists to lend their best work, some two hundred pieces
representing about fifty artists. She contacted Italian diplomatic personnel
and Fascist party officials in Argentina, Uruguay, and Brazil to make local
arrangements, and coordinated a propaganda campaign to exalt her South
American achievements to the public back home.[44]

Margherita sailed from Genoa on board the Italian liner *Conte Verde* on
August 9, arriving in Rio de Janeiro. This first transatlantic voyage inspired
an unpublished book-length series of poems. Once ashore, her first impression was of the "violent exuberance of nature" that made Brazil so different
from the cultivated landscapes of Europe. Her judgment of its people was
shaped by her racism. Even the most cultivated city inhabitants she judged
to be "semi-savage" beneath a veneer of civilization.[45]

She spent two weeks in Brazil. She lectured on modern architecture
and the *Novecento,* and visited the interior districts and coffee plantations.
In Buenos Aires, where a revolution had just taken place, Italian anti-
Fascists greeted her as "the languid star of Benito's harem." She spoke on
"The Sources of Modern Painting" to an audience of more than one
thousand people and was feted by intellectuals and art critics in the Ar-
gentine capital. After Buenos Aires, the exhibit went to Montevideo and
Margherita left for home on September 20.[46]

Travel was apparently an attractive diversion from her professional difficulties and an increasing estrangement from Mussolini. His failure to silence the barrage of criticism against her was directly connected to the
changing nature of their physical relationship. After eighteen years, their
intense passion had diminished. Margherita turned fifty in 1930. She went
often to spas for relief from gout and for mud facials. Never a thin woman,
she now had a marked tendency to put on weight and tried various dieting
drugs to control her appetite. Mussolini abhorred obesity.[47]

Mussolini's family situation also drew him away from Margherita. After
she had given him so much love and sacrifice, Margherita complained to
her seamstress, Mussolini was now spending all his free time with his wife.[48]
In early January 1930 Margherita was the subject of a violent argument
between husband and wife, as a result of which Mussolini finally promised

to end the relationship and retire her from *Il Popolo d'Italia*. Together, Mussolini and Rachele burned a huge pile of Margherita's letters in a fireplace at the Villa Torlonia.[49]

Mussolini tried to follow through with his promise. Margherita discovered a few days later that one of her articles had been published without either a title or her name. Mussolini must have backed down in the face of her wrath, for her articles continued to appear in *Il Popolo d'Italia* in regular fashion throughout January and into February.[50]

On the morning of February 22, when Rachele was at Merano taking the cure with Carolina Ciano, Edda's mother-in-law, she opened her husband's newspaper and saw an article signed "Margherita G. Sarfatti." Rachele grabbed her coat and rushed out, with Carolina Ciano dashing after her. At the post office, she wrote a lengthy—and hotly worded—telegram to Mussolini, but when the clerk saw to whom it was addressed she refused to send it. Rachele wrote another to Arnaldo Mussolini, the editor of *Il Popolo d'Italia*. Mussolini telephoned from Rome that night, protesting his innocence. "I don't know which article of Margherita Sarfatti's you're talking about. All I do know is that I have nothing more to do with her, and I don't want to hear her mentioned again." Rachele seemed satisfied, but warned that she would blow up the editorial offices of the newspaper if another article by Margherita appeared. Contrary to his promises, Margherita was published three more times during the next year in *Il Popolo d'Italia*.[51]

Mussolini did not cut off all contact with Margherita. She had access to his office at Palazzo Venezia, where they saw each other to discuss official business. She continued to act as his intermediary with the foreign press. From time to time she acted as his unofficial agent, especially in dealing with foreigners. And while her role as "dictator of culture" was declining rapidly, Mussolini still listened to her advice on cultural matters, although he now preferred not to make these contacts public.

The enemies of modernism took heart when Margherita's name began appearing only sporadically in the pages of *Il Popolo d'Italia,* and in the months that followed, their campaign resumed with a new urgency. This time they targeted their attacks against Margherita's favorite architects. The previous year, the young Rationalist architects had been given a prominent role in the Triennale exhibit for 1930. That July, Margherita went to Sweden on the invitation of Crown Prince Gustaf Adolf to visit an architectural exhibit. In Stockholm she was impressed by "functionalism," Sweden's version of the international style, and wrote a strong plea for the adoption of Rationalism as Italy's contribution to the universal trend toward modernism. After she returned, she discovered that some forty-six architects had established a formal organization called the Italian Movement for Rationalist Architecture (MIAR). They immediately planned an exhibition of their work in Rome with the approval of the Fascist Architecture Union and the help of art critic Pier Maria Bardi.[52]

Bardi volunteered to host the Rationalists in his new art gallery in the capital, the Galleria di Roma, which was affiliated with the Fascist Fine Arts Union. In connection with the event, Bardi wrote a "Report on Architecture for Mussolini," in which he defined the obstacles he believed impeded modern Italian style. He asked Mussolini to create a state architecture that was as youthful and audacious as Fascism. Bardi persuaded Mussolini to visit the MIAR exhibit on March 30, 1931, the day before its official opening. The Duce was greeted by a large placard bearing his own words calling for "an art of our times." Mussolini did not comment on the centerpiece of the exhibit, called the Panel of Horrors—a large photomontage showing illustrations of public architecture sponsored by the regime, including Piacentini's Hotel Ambasciatori and Brasini's pavilion for the 1925 Paris exposition. As he left the gallery, Mussolini was given a manifesto calling for "a rational architecture" suitable to Fascism.[53]

The Panel of Horrors was the immediate cause of the renewed assault on modernism. The Fascist Architects' Union censored MIAR for the disrespect it had shown to senior architects and threatened to expel its members from the union. Before the opening Piacentini had tried to bribe MIAR with a favorable review in exchange for deleting his work from the Panel of Horrors; now he organized a campaign to discredit the Rationalists. On May 2, he published a viciously anti-Semitic article titled "In Defense of Italian Architecture," calling Rationalism alien to the Italian spirit: "Just as Judaism has played such a major role in Bolshevism, so in the rationalist movement it is the Gropiuses and the Mendelsohns who command the barricades." Margherita must have noted this display of her friend's anti-Semitism with alarm. The Roman members of MIAR wrote a letter asking for Mussolini's support, and Margherita agreed to take it to him. Mussolini failed to respond to this appeal, or to a second letter Margherita delivered to him in late July. By the fall, MIAR was essentially dissolved.[54]

The polemic over modern art and architecture was taken up by the daily press. The controversy even reached into the halls of Parliament, where in May 1931 the traditionalist painter Basilio Cascella called the paintings he had just seen at the Quadriennale "an infection that comes from France." Ojetti added his own reactionary views to the argument, wondering out loud why the regime tolerated the Rationalist antics. Just as summer began, Farinacci published a blistering accusation on June 13 against the presumed monopolistic activities of the foreign *Novecento* exhibits.[55]

A week after this article, Lino Pesaro, the owner of the gallery in which the *Novecento* first made its appearance, contributed to Farinacci's paper a long, detailed account of the origins of the group. He suggested that Margherita had seized control of the movement after others had started it and then tried to use it for her own selfish political ambitions. He charged, too, that she had corrupted the *Novecento* with foreign influences. Pesaro was Jewish, and may have published the article to protect himself. Even Marinetti added his voice to the chorus, although his attitudes toward modernism were far different from Farinacci's reactionary views. One of the first to reply to these attacks was P. M. Bardi, who pointed out that personal rancors and jealousies often hid behind accusations of anti-Fascism.[56]

Throughout the polemic, Mussolini said nothing. He had secretly given Farinacci permission to excoriate the *Novecento* movement. On July 19, unable to hold back any longer, Margherita composed an angry but dignified letter to Farinacci. She explained that she had remained silent up till now because he and his cohorts "speak a language totally different from mine when it comes to art." She therefore assumed that they would not understand anything she had to say about art:

> But there is a language common to everyone, that has to do not with art or aesthetics, but with honesty and morality.
> . . . I do not intend to tolerate the statements and insinuations that your paper spews so abundantly and insistently. I assume that you will find and publish the proof of these statements and insinuations.
> I invite you to make public the documents, or at least to be more specific in the accusations that you make against the *Novecento Italiano* in general and against me in particular. I have the right to demand this.
> I am owed that right, beyond any general and objective reasons, because of my past as an interventionist in 1915, as a Fascist since 1919, as a mother of a decorated volunteer who fell on the battlefield at age seventeen. . . . These things are only too well-known to those who fought in the war and to the Fascists of the first hour for me to have to repeat them.
> I thank you, Mr. Editor, for publishing this letter and for the response that I await with not a little curiosity.

Farinacci published a scornful and chauvinistic reply together with Margherita's letter. He chastised her for hiding behind "a son who died heroically in war and was decorated with a gold medal." Replying only out of a sense of "chivalry," Farinacci presented a litany of supposed charges against the *Novecento*. He ended by saying that he actually liked some of the artists, such as Funi, Sironi, and Soffici—their error was in not reacting against those tendencies within the movement that "prostituted and rendered it ridiculous." He concluded that "Margherita Sarfatti has been guilty, as a woman, of being too weak, and above all in rising up and crying out: 'I am the mother of the Novecento and I alone must answer for it.' "[57]

Margherita and her friends had fought for years against the kind of art that Farinacci demanded. Mario Sironi spoke to Arnaldo Mussolini about the crisis that Farinacci was provoking. As official caricaturist for *Il Popolo d'Italia,* Sironi worked closely with his editor. At Arnaldo's urging, Sironi went to Rome to see Mussolini. Sironi angrily explained to Mussolini that the kind of painting and sculpture men like Farinacci supported was "filling Italy with crap" and that these men suffocated artistic creativity through their insistence on conformity. Mussolini later said that Sironi's plain speaking struck him as a "pronunciamento," similar to the dramatic moment in December 1924 when the leaders of the Fascist Militia confronted him over the Matteotti crisis. Yet the encounter had no lasting impact.[58]

The battle between Margherita and Farinacci slowed by August, although it resurfaced periodically over the next two years. The rest of that summer she spent at Il Soldo. She no longer wrote a weekly column for *Il Popolo d'Italia* or sat on any committees. In the fall she went to Paris to take part in an international jury that awarded the Grand Prix for painting to Arturo Tosi. But when she returned she was unable to stand her inactivity, and she appealed to her friend Augusto Turati for help.

Turati had taken Farinacci's place as Fascist party secretary in 1926, but his role in exposing corruption within the regime—including charges that involved Arnaldo Mussolini—led Mussolini to accept his resignation in September 1930. Turati's poor compensation was the editorship of the Turin daily newspaper *La Stampa;* he offered Margherita a column. The opportunity boosted her morale, although her low status did not stop her from bargaining with Turati over her pay. Margherita's first article in *La Stampa,* printed October 30, 1931, displayed her combative spirit: "Swimming deliberately against the current in order to follow one's own temperament, with ever more conscious and thoughtful courage, is an act of personal honesty and distinction."[59]

In order to put some distance between herself and Mussolini, toward the end of 1931 Margherita left her apartment across from the Villa Torlonia, moving to a large apartment at Via dei Villini, 18, a quiet street located a number of blocks away. This flat was the last she owned in Rome.

After Margherita moved to Via dei Villini, Mussolini cautioned Alfredo Signoretti, Turati's successor as head of *La Stampa,* to "be careful with women, especially those of a certain age who attach themselves and won't let go." Mussolini's impatience with Margherita stemmed partly from his personal discomfort in having to extricate himself from a relationship in which he had lost interest. He had for some time been growing aloof from all human contact. Ugo Ojetti, who saw Mussolini frequently, noted that this pattern of increasingly personal isolation began when "he became convinced of his destiny and his mission." His tendency toward self-reliance and withdrawal became pronounced after the sudden death on December 21 of Arnaldo. Mussolini had been deeply attached to his brother, the only person, besides Margherita, in whom he had shown complete trust. In the years since the seizure of power, Arnaldo had been uniquely able to brake Mussolini's impetuosity.

The regime proved increasingly less tolerant after Arnaldo's death. Two weeks earlier, Mussolini had appointed the stupid and brutal Achille Starace as Party secretary. On Mussolini's orders, Starace imposed ever-greater conformity on Italy throughout the thirties. Margherita's old friend Giuseppe Borgese, whom Arnaldo had protected despite the professor's refusal to swear loyalty to Fascism, became an exile.

Arnaldo's death had quite different implications for Margherita. While she lived in Milan, Arnaldo had supported her cultural initiatives, including the *Novecento*. "Such a terrible loss to all of us," she wrote in English to an American acquaintance, "& especially to me, who has always been great friends with him & worked together with him for many years." Margherita was conspicuously visible at the funeral, and visitors found displays of his photographs and letters at her home. She knew she could ill afford to lose such a valuable and influential ally within the regime.[60]

The results of Mussolini's virtually complete isolation were soon evident in his relationship with Margherita. A few months following Arnaldo's death, Margherita made an appointment to see Mussolini at Palazzo Venezia. She waited for two hours in the antechamber. Finally Quinto Navarra, the dictator's valet, emerged from Mussolini's office. Pained and embarrassed, he informed Margherita that the prime minister would not see her. It was, Navarra recalled, the most distasteful task Mussolini had ever given him.[61]

In March 1932, Margherita went to London again, this time to see an exhibit of French painting organized in answer to the great Italian art show two years earlier. She found the paintings, ranging from the Renaissance to the late nineteenth century, enthralling. The ability to see five centuries of French art all in one place enabled her to trace the development of what she called "classicity" through the Post-Impressionists to the modern Italian painters she preferred. She admired the "wisdom and beauty" of Madame du Pompadour, Louis XV's mistress, in François Boucher's portrait. When she returned to Italy, she attended the opening of the new Biennale. The crown prince of Denmark invited her to a special preview and reception at the Danish pavilion. During the summer, she toured the

Aegean for *La Stampa* on a cruise ship, stopping at Athens, Rhodes, and Crete.[62]

The difficulties she had encountered over the last year and a half had begun to take their toll on Margherita's psyche. She tried alternately to accommodate herself to her reduced status and to rebel against it. She kept a relatively low public profile, staying out of a renewed debate over modern architecture. The regime undertook several Rationalist projects from the summer of 1932 to June 1934: a new railway station in Florence, an exhibit for the tenth anniversary of the Fascist seizure of power, and the Triennale exhibition in Milan. In each case, triumphant Rationalist designs were met with protest from right-wing and conservative Fascists.

News that Mussolini and Margherita's twenty-year affair had ended spread quickly through the upper strata of the regime. Margherita was quite narcissistic. She suffered to discover how many had courted her only for her connections with Mussolini. Nonetheless, some of Margherita's acquaintances made special efforts to display affection or loyalty. For example, while never the bravest of men, Alfredo Panzini nonetheless published a *roman à clef* in mid-1932, in which Margherita was the disguised heroine. Italo Balbo, perhaps only out of his disguised rivalry with Mussolini, continued to seek her favor. Of course, some old friends like Marconi never wavered in their support.

However, a Public Security report—and they are notoriously unreliable—suggested that Margherita may have been betrayed in the spring of 1932 by one closest to her:

Rome 27 June 1932

It has been reported that the daughter of Sarfatti has been on vacation at Lido di Ostia. Several times a week this girl, Fiammetta, has been noticed being taken by motorboat out to sea and then going ashore at Castel Porziano [the royal estate], on the days when the Duce is expected there. The motorboat remains awaiting her for several hours. Then she reboards and it takes her back to the Lido. It has been noticed that on those days the royal villa remains strictly closed to visitors. Lack of discretion has brought these episodes to the attention of the vacationers; especially because one stormy day when Signorina Sarfatti left in pyjamas, it started to rain and she was forced to dismiss the motorboat and put her dress back on at the Lido. At the Lido they speak maliciously about such relations between the Duce and Fiammetta Sarfatti.[63]

Yet despite such rumors and his insults to her self-esteem, Mussolini continued to seek Margherita's counsel. In the spring of 1932, Mussolini had granted interviews to the German journalist Emil Ludwig. Ludwig transformed Mussolini's frank talk into a book. The Italian edition, *Colloqui con Mussolini (Talks with Mussolini),* appeared in July 1932. When Mussolini had reviewed the proofs, he found little to alter. But after he had approved them, he changed his mind. The book revealed Mussolini's cynicism about religion and his hostility toward the Church. Party officials urged its suppression.

When Mussolini discovered that he could do nothing to stop foreign publication, however, he decided only to limit the Italian edition to a small number. Mondadori, the book's Italian publisher, argued that would flatter him. Better a show of tolerance, Mussolini decided, than make *Colloqui* appear forbidden fruit.

This was the type of problem he had always talked over with Margherita. Mussolini decided to speak with her, although he limited this to a telephone call. When they talked, she had already read a copy of the book.

> MARGHERITA: It's exactly in line with the truth; it keeps to what you've always said.
> MUSSOLINI: That's the problem!
> MARGHERITA: But—!
> MUSSOLINI: Some things which can only do you good at one time can prove self-defeating at other times.
> MARGHERITA: Well?
> MUSSOLINI: Well, that's the way it is. We'll see what happens. I'm really annoyed!
> MARGHERITA: Isn't it possible to suppress it?
> MUSSOLINI: You're naïve. But, in Italy at least, only a very few are in circulation, just the first copies, because I've bought almost all of them.
> MARGHERITA: Thank goodness.
> MUSSOLINI: It was the best that I could do.[64]

Mussolini had planned for some time to mount a major exposition to commemorate the first decade of the Fascist revolution—the "Mostra della Rivoluzione Fascista." The exhibit was to be a retrospective of the history of Fascism. He assigned the overall project to the direction of Dino Alfieri, who put together a brilliant and diverse team of architects, painters, and sculptors—Mussolini had ordered Alfieri to make the Mostra "very modern and audacious." The facade was a huge blood-red cube with a severe archway entrance at the center, bearing four seventy-five-foot *fasci* of burnished copper. Giuseppe Terragni, the Futurists Depero and Prampolini, and *Strapaese* artists, all worked on the exhibit. Mario Sironi, working in a severe style inspired by the Soviet architect El Lissitzky, left the most pronounced mark on the interior of the exhibit. The Mostra proved to be a masterpiece of Fascist propaganda. Sironi proclaimed that the building "broke the resistance of the most tenacious opponents of modern art."[65]

Margherita was enthusiastic. She claimed that it was not merely an exhibit of Fascism, but a "demonstration" of its revolutionary impact on culture. Because Mussolini had insisted on an overall modern style, the criticisms directed against the Mostra were limited. Margherita took the opportunity to scold the "highly-placed" persons—Farinacci and his supporters—who had questioned the Mostra's uncompromising modernism.[66]

Margherita had a very personal link to the Mostra della Rivoluzione, for she had provided Alfieri with several personal possessions for the displays. In the room dealing with Italy's victory in World War I, a glass case contained copies of newspapers published for soldiers during the war, including *Gli Avvenimenti,* for which she had taken over Boccioni's art column after his death in 1916. The same case also displayed a series of letters written by young volunteers at the front, in the center of which was placed a photograph of Roberto Sarfatti, together with one of his patriotic letters to Margherita and Cesare.[67]

Margherita naturally expected to receive an invitation to attend the inauguration of the Mostra. When the invitation failed to arrive by the day before the official ceremony, she stormed down to the site on the Via Nazionale, arriving just moments after Mussolini had left following a special preview. She demanded to see Alfieri, who closed his office door and gave orders not to admit her. She was surrounded by a crowd of artists and exhibit personnel. Someone explained to her that Party Secretary Starace had issued explicit orders barring all women from the ceremonies. When she heard that, she began hurling curses at Alfieri for not having the courage to face her. As people tried to calm her, she lost all control and began screaming at the top of her voice. The incident ended only when she was physically escorted out of the building. The next day, precisely ten years after the March on Rome, the last article to bear Margherita's name appeared in *Il Popolo d'Italia.* The article was a survey of the state of the arts under Fascist rule.[68]

In February 1933, the committee appointed to choose the design for the new Florence train-station—including Ojetti, Marinetti, and Piacentini—awarded first prize to a daring plan submitted by the Gruppo Toscano (Tuscan Group), a team of Rationalists headed by Giovanni Michelucci. Their design consisted of a long, low building broken near one end by a cascading band of glass that terraced across the roof of the ticket hall, down one wall, and then over the entrance hall and down again nearly to the ground. The new building would be faced with the same beige stone used to construct the fourteenth-century Church of Santa Maria Novella, which stood opposite. The otherwise stark facade would be subtly broken by the rough texture of the stone and a series of horizontal lines running the length of the structure. The station would be the most daringly modern public building in the country. Yet the Santa Maria Novella Station, as it came to be known, would introduce visitors to the capital of Italian Renaissance art. Naturally, Ojetti voted against the design, although Piacentini, hoping once again to bring the Rationalists under his wing, supported it and swayed the other conservative members.

The press began a fierce debate almost immediately, and the various design plans were taken to Rome, where they were put on public display in Palazzo Venezia. Mussolini kept silent as the polemic raged, but many suspected that he was predisposed toward a Rationalist solution because of the Mostra della Rivoluzione. For her part, Margherita spoke out indirectly, arguing that Italy could not be sealed off from foreign influences and ideas without suffocating.

Just as the Florence station debate was raging, an architectural competition was announced for the national headquarters of the Fascist party, the so-called Palazzo Littorio. The huge building was to be situated on the Via dell'Impero across from the Basilica of Constantine. Architects from each of the major schools and movements submitted more than one hundred designs, but once again the competition ended without immediate resolution.

As a result of all three projects, the Fascist intransigents grew ever more frantic. With the triumph of Rationalism at the Mostra della Rivoluzione, and the formal proposal of the Michelucci project for the Florence station, Farinacci and his associates could not bear the thought that the very headquarters of the Fascist party would also be encased in another example of Mussolini modern. Margherita, who had traveled to Provence that spring, made still another argument in support of Rationalism. In the south of France, she stopped to admire the famous Roman aqueduct at Pont du Gard, which she said convinced her once and for all that Rationalist architecture was spiritually compatible with the best of ancient Rome's achievements—"I see a form of idealism in its harsh austerity that distances itself almost with revulsion from every form of false or frivolous ornamentation."

The arguments over the Michelucci project became so violent that Farinacci and his followers eventually took it to the floor of the Chamber of Deputies, where they joined the issue of modern architecture to their earlier attacks against the *Novecento*. Farinacci shouted charges of Bolshevism and internationalism against the Rationalists. The fury of his attacks may have annoyed even Mussolini, for the story circulated that it was Margherita who actually convinced him to decide in its favor, supposedly by pointing out to him that from the air the railroad-station plan resembled a *fascio*. While the specific nature of her influence is unclear—Mussolini only announced his decision in June 1934, while she was out of the country and her status in the regime had been even further eroded—there is no doubt that she supported the Michelucci design. The Palazzo Littorio proposal did not have such a positive outcome, however, for Party authorities shifted the site of the project over the next two years and the contract was finally awarded to a team of Roman architects who constructed a rather uninteresting building on the northern edge of the city.[69]

In March 1933, Margherita received word that her brother Marco, a businessman with interests in North Africa, had died in Egypt. She and Marco had never been close, and his anti-Fascist sentiments had contributed to their estrangement. Nevertheless, personal regrets, together with the need to get away from Italy, convinced her that she should attend the funeral. At Brindisi on the Adriatic coast, she embarked on a ship headed across the Mediterranean to Alexandria. Once on board, she discovered to her surprise that the ship was also carrying Italian Crown Prince Umberto and Princess Maria Josè, who planned on visiting Egypt incognito. Margherita had met them before on numerous occasions and had been a guest at the prince's residences in Rome and Naples. After she encountered the royal couple at the pyramids and other ancient monuments, the prince invited her to dine with them and to attend a reception at a sumptuous palace along the Nile. The series of articles she wrote about the trip revealed that her excitement at seeing firsthand the great monuments of the ancient world had been diluted by an undertone of bittersweet sadness.

In early May she attended the opening of the fifth Milan Triennale of Modern Decorative Arts, the successor to the Monza fairs she had helped initiate. Margherita was no longer involved in the shows but some prominent *Novecento* artists, including Sironi and Tosi, were. The architectural sections contained the work of twelve major international architects, including Le Corbusier and Konstantin Melnikov (whose pavilions Margherita had encountered at the Paris fair in 1925), as well as Mies Van Der Rohe and Frank Lloyd Wright. Models of brilliantly functionalist houses designed by Italian Rationalists were the centerpieces. Sironi designed some of the most important rooms and conceived of a series of huge decorative murals executed by some thirty major artists, among them Gino Severini, Giorgio de Chirico, Achille Funi, and Carlo Carrà.[70]

While Margherita proclaimed the Triennale a triumph, it provided the target for the last and most violent polemic against the *Novecento*. Farinacci's reactionary critics attacked the "anarchist" foreign designers and the "internationalist" Italian architects, and accused the muralists of creating grotesque "deformations." One called the *Novecento* an anti-Fascist movement tainted by Bolshevik, "plutocratic," Masonic, and Jewish influences. Ojetti joined the chorus with his own more aesthetic disapproval of "Leninist" architecture. Margherita wrote a pointed and scornful response in *La Stampa* directed at Farinacci—without naming him—in which she lectured him on certain fundamental points concerning artistic creativity: that genuine culture cannot be created on orders from above, that the real influence of the times on art manifests itself indirectly, not in a crude and simplistic mirroring of events, and that modern art is not estranged from Fascism. Calling those who demanded Fascist realism "petty bourgeois whiners," she insisted once again that history provides artists only with a certain spirit, not with the material of representation.[71]

Farinacci answered by accusing the *Novecentisti* of anti-Fascism. Margherita fired back with another letter expressing surprise that he thought she had him in mind when she used the expression "petty bourgeois whiners," and asked why, in any case, he had not recognized the supposed anti-Fascist character of the *Novecento* from the beginning when he attended the 1926 show. Farinacci responded by clarifying that while Fascism was Italian, the *Novecento* was inspired by a degenerate strain of German art. He added, "Hitler now thinks like we do" about such degeneracy.[72]

Several *Novecento* artists, including Carrà, Funi, and Sironi, this time helped Margherita defend the movement. Sironi was especially caustic and violent—in an article titled "Enough!" he called the artist and anti-Semite, Sommi Picenardi, "a fat and gilded Freemason," and insisted on the need to study foreign art without copying it. Ojetti, Maraini, Bardi and even Jules Evola, a writer and painter with strong racist views, joined in. The debate began to get out of hand when Farinacci charged that the *Novecento* leaders had pressured government officials into buying their art work.[73]

On June 13, Mussolini's patience with Farinacci snapped and he ordered *Il Regime Fascista* to publish a statement denying that government offices were filled with *Novecento* paintings. In a barb aimed at Margherita, Farinacci spoke of those who belonged to the "race of Shylock." Ignoring the racial slur, Margherita exchanged telegrams with Farinacci during the last week in June; neither was published, for Party Secretary Starace demanded an end to the debate. The polemic ended but Farinacci defended his position to Mussolini privately and complained that the *Novecento* had nothing to do with Fascism. "I'm a complete fool when it comes to art," he wrote to Mussolini, "But are you able to understand anything either?"[74]

Farinacci's incessant attacks had succeeded in damaging the prestige the *Novecento* had held within the regime. The *Novecento* was no longer a cohesive movement. Margherita was unable to launch further exhibits in the 1930s. Most of the leading *Novecento* exponents, including Sironi, were excluded from the next Venice Biennale, and the organization collapsed.

Sironi moved away from easel painting to the kind of murals he had created for the Triennale. In a declaration on mural painting issued in late 1933, he proclaimed it to be the highest form of "social painting." Margherita was uncertain about Sironi's new direction. While she had always applauded the idea of art in an architectural setting, and understood the propaganda value of murals, paintings were for her the superior form.[75]

The fact that Mussolini had allowed Farinacci to attack Margherita personally speaks of the degree to which she had fallen from favor. Toward the end of June 1933, Mussolini expressed his displeasure with her to Antonio Maraini. He had sent the Duce a telegram listing Margherita's name among those who were to serve on the Venice Biennale organizing committee. Maraini was summoned to Palazzo Venezia. Jabbing the telegram on his desk with his finger, Mussolini demanded to know why Margherita had been included in the committee:

> I'm speaking about Signora Sarfatti. Seeing her on all these committees creates the impression that she's named to them because she is my biographer. . . . And then this *Novecento, Novecento*. These horrible figures with such big hands and feet, with eyes in the wrong places, are ridiculous, beyond common sense, outside tradition and Italian art. It's time to stop it, I say, to stop it. And Mario Sironi is an imbecile. His article in *Il Popolo d'Italia* entitled "Enough" is idiotic. Enough! It's not at all enough. By arguing in this way he appears to be an imbecile. . . . Stop it, stop it.

When he returned the next day, Maraini found Mussolini in a calmer mood and ventured to suggest that the entire cultural situation would be improved if only the Duce would make a clear statement about art. "Me?" replied Mussolini rather incredulously. "Nothing doing. It's up to you to deal with the artists. I know what I'm saying. To govern textile, construction, and metal workers is a lot easier than ruling painters."[76]

25

New Deal and New Order

Thirty-two days separated Adolf Hitler's appointment as chancellor of Germany on January 30, 1933, from Franklin Delano Roosevelt's March 4 inauguration as president of the United States. Only eighteen days passed between their deaths in April 1945. During the twelve years in between, Hitler and Roosevelt would wreck the world Margherita had known, reduce the Italian peninsula to a battlefield, and destroy virtually everything that Mussolini had labored to create.

But in 1933, Margherita and Mussolini welcomed the accession of Hitler and Roosevelt to power—although somewhat more warily in the case of the German leader. For several years Mussolini considered himself a mentor to them both, viewing each as a potential junior partner, useful for reaching certain mutual goals. Mussolini clung stubbornly to this illusion for far too long, although he soon realized that an unbridgeable chasm separated Roosevelt's worldview from Hitler's. He could not cooperate with both and would have to choose between them. Margherita would wield major influence in his eventual decision.

Mussolini had paid close attention to the rise of the Nazi movement almost from its inception. Hitler had avidly sought Fascist support even before the March on Rome, as Kurt Ludecke's mission to Mussolini in the fall of 1922 demonstrates. Until 1930, however, Mussolini did not reciprocate. Hitler's Austrian birth prejudiced Mussolini against him. Mussolini was also well aware of Hitler's dreams of expansion, and the Nazi leader's virulent racism left him uneasy. While he harbored a measure of anti-Semitism, Mussolini considered Hitler's racial ideas wildly excessive and his public fulminations against the Jews politically foolish. Despite these concerns, Mussolini established discreet communication with the Nazis in the twenties through personal emissaries. Hermann Göring was Hitler's principal liaison with the Fascists.

The deepening depression brought the Nazis major success in the September 1930 elections. This persuaded Mussolini that Hitler would rule

Germany in four to six years. But Mussolini remained very suspicious about the Nazi leader and rebuffed repeated requests for a meeting.

Shortly after the Nazi successes in the March 1932 German elections, Mussolini met with the Fascist Grand Council. While Farinacci, Starace, Attilio Teruzzi, and Costanzo Ciano supported a Fascist alliance with the Nazis, Mussolini knew that Margherita's friends, including Augusto Turati, Balbino Giuliano, Balbo, and Marconi, feared the consequences if Hitler came to power. Others, including Dino Grandi and Giuseppe Bottai, remained unsure. Mussolini addressed his remarks to the doubters: "There are Fascists who do not approve of Hitler. Why? For my part I think that it must be admitted that he deserves our approval. . . . At the beginning he had scarcely seven followers, or a twentieth part of the number we had at Piazza San Sepolcro in 1919. Today 12 million Germans follow him! You may say that they are extremists, desperadoes . . . but there are also men of standing. . . . A man who succeeds in organizing such imposing masses of people cannot be mediocre . . . he cannot be dismissed as a lucky child of fortune." He discussed what use Hitler might be to Fascist Italy. Mussolini stressed how terrified the French were of Hitler. There was no doubt that Britain would support France, were Germany to take any aggressive action. But Italy would be free to choose between the two sides, selling her support to the highest bidder. Mussolini underscored the finality of that choice. Once made, it would bind Italy to an unalterable course. And once Hitler came to power, the Germans would certainly ignore the arms restrictions imposed on them by the Versailles Treaty:

> It suits us, in one way, that Germany should rearm quickly and efficiently in order to offset France; but on the other hand, so far as we are concerned, we must try to build up ourselves so that we can look Germany in the eyes if and whenever the need arises. . . . Clearly those who have benefited by the peace will not wish to entertain ideas of this kind. But there is no advantage for us in maintaining the peace as it was formulated at Versailles. It is to our interest to set the nations and history on the move. All that is static and anti-historical is contrary to the vital need of the Italian people.[1]

Three months later, Mussolini dismissed Grandi as foreign minister and assumed the post. For the next four years, Mussolini directed Italian diplomacy himself; relations with Germany proved to be his chief concern.

Mussolini's interest in Hitler left Margherita extremely uneasy. Her fears were tempered somewhat by Mussolini's distrust of the Germans. Much of what he knew about Germany and German culture, Margherita had taught him. Her own fears stemmed from her experience of the war.

She had many German friends, but after all, Roberto had died in the face of an Austrian advance at Italy's northern frontier. If the Nazis gained control over Germany, they threatened to revive the danger her son had died to destroy.

Margherita's many visits to Germany had made her uncomfortably familiar with the Nazis. She had met leading officials of the Weimar Republic and had learned about the weakness of German democracy. While Margherita despised representative government, she feared a powerful authoritarian Germany. Margherita worried especially that a Fascist Germany might prove fatally attractive to Mussolini and that a German-Italian alliance would result in subservience for her country.

Sometime in 1925–1926, Margherita had encountered the German author Baron Werner von der Schulenburg at her Milan salon. They discussed the desires of some Germans to annex Austria and the Austrian-inhabited region of northern Italy. Schulenburg convinced her that he was pro-Italian. They quickly developed a friendship.

In 1927, at Margherita's suggestion, Mussolini agreed to create a German-language journal ostensibly devoted to Italian culture. Schulenburg accepted Margherita's offer to become the editor. Entitled *Italien,* the journal used articles and reviews to foster support for Austrian independence and to promote a positive image of the Fascist regime. Margherita wrote for *Italien* frequently.

Starting in late 1929, Schulenburg became a contributor to *Gerarchia.* At Mussolini's urging, he wrote an article under a pseudonym, arguing that Hitler would enjoy more success if he abandoned his strident anti-Semitism. To Schulenburg's surprise, he received a letter from Hitler in early January 1930, thanking him "for the service which [he had] rendered to the National Socialist Party."

Given the nature of *Gerarchia,* Hitler's lieutenants realized that the article had been inspired by Mussolini. Alfred Rosenberg, one of the most vicious Jew-haters among the Nazi leaders, asked Schulenburg to deliver a memorandum to Mussolini on "The Crimes of World Jewry." Rosenberg suggested that Schulenburg give the memo to Margherita to ensure Mussolini's perusal.

With considerable tact, Schulenburg contacted Hitler's deputy, Rudolf Hess, and explained that Margherita was a Jew. Hess reacted with amazement and asked Schulenburg to find another intermediary to deliver the anti-Semitic diatribe to Mussolini. Schulenburg told Hess to find someone else for the task. Thereafter, he attempted to break off contact with the Nazis. Instead, he associated himself with the conservative politician Franz von Papen, to whom he introduced Margherita. For a time, it appears that she hoped that Papen and his fellow conservatives might keep the Nazis from coming to power.

Under these circumstances, Margherita must have been reassured by Mussolini's appointment of Vittorio Cerruti as Italian ambassador to Germany in October 1932. It seemed to signify Mussolini's contempt for Nazi anti-Semitism. Like Margherita, Elisabetta Cerruti was a Jewish convert to Catholicism. By 1932, Margherita had become good friends with the Cerrutis, so she had an excellent source of information about developments in Germany.

Margherita also recognized the advantages a strong Germany offered Italy. The possibility of an Italo-German alliance had frequently arisen in Margherita's conversations with her British and French acquaintances. While Margherita reassured them that this was quite unlikely, she noted the uneasiness that even the possibility of such a coalition created. Clearly that fear could have its uses. It might be manipulated in pursuit of the Roman Empire that Margherita and Mussolini dreamed about.

Efforts toward a Fascist-Nazi understanding were probably behind Margherita's meetings with Hermann Göring. When Göring visited Rome in the spring of 1924, Mussolini rejected his repeated requests for a meeting. When Göring returned in November 1929, Mussolini officially refused to receive him, but Margherita welcomed Hitler's lieutenant to her home on the Via Nomentana. Given the proximity to Mussolini's residence at the Villa Torlonia, it would not be surprising if Mussolini had slipped privately into Margherita's apartment to join in the conversation. After the subsequent improvement in Nazi fortunes, Göring visited Rome again in May 1931 to meet officially with Mussolini. Göring again held talks with Margherita. As Göring told his wife, Margherita still had a *"great, powerful political influence."* This time, when Göring returned to Germany, he carried to Hitler an autographed photograph of Mussolini. Mussolini made such presentations only to those he favored. Hitler immediately returned the present in kind.

Göring returned to Rome in November 1932 to attend the Volta Conference with a Nazi delegation. This time, Mussolini welcomed the Nazis. Göring knew that Margherita was Jewish, and that her relationship with Mussolini had cooled, but he met with her again. He appreciated the considerable influence Margherita still had over Mussolini. What the two of them discussed is unrecorded.[2]

Margherita and Göring shared an admiration for the art of the Italian Renaissance. It was probably she who introduced Göring to her close friend and neighbor in Rome, the art dealer Count Alessandro Contini-Bonacossi. After the Nazis came to power in Germany, Göring acquired the means to assemble a gigantic art collection. Contini became Göring's principal dealer in Italian art.

Contini had avoided Italian service in World War I by managing a fashionable brothel in neutral Rio de Janeiro. He returned to Italy after the war and invested his savings in a small art collection. By enlisting the cooperation of the devious art expert Bernard Berenson and Lord Duveen, a dishonest dealer, Contini soon made a fortune. The three men conspired to buy minor works for low prices, had the paintings "restored" and "authenticated," and then resold them to wealthy foreigners at huge profits. In 1928, Contini was rich enough to buy his title from the royal house. Given her sources of information, Margherita must have known most, if not all, of this story. Perhaps her introduction of Göring to Contini was a subtle act of malice, or perhaps she profited personally.[3]

Because of the dangers inherent in an alliance with a Nazi regime, Mussolini was interested in cultivating a method of counterbalancing German influence in Italy and Europe. He believed the United States, with its enormous economic strength and its detachment from the European situation, could provide the balance. Since the mid-twenties, Margherita and Mussolini had recognized that the Americans and Germans held Fascism and its leader in high esteem. He looked for opportunities to cultivate friendships with Americans. Margherita's journalistic efforts had played a part in creating positive impressions of Fascism in the United States, but her contacts with Americans were limited to those who visited or resided in Italy. Still, with her command of English and her charm, she succeeded in initiating friendships with a number of influential Americans.

Margherita's closest American acquaintance was probably Alexander Kirk. Kirk had come to Rome to become first secretary of the American Embassy in late 1928, after three years as head of the State Department's intelligence agency. Within a year of his arrival, Kirk had become chargé d'affaires of the embassy, its second-highest official. His dispatches, always based on firsthand observation or direct information, were models of the craft of diplomatic reporting. Once familiar with Kirk's cables from Rome, President Roosevelt regarded them as the best he received from any European embassy.

It did not take Kirk long to recognize Margherita's position within the Fascist hierarchy. Kirk cultivated Margherita's friendship. Fiammetta remembered him as being utterly devoted to her mother. Kirk's homosexuality was something of an open secret within the American community in Rome, but that was no hindrance in Margherita's tolerant social circle. Margherita came to prize his discretion and absolute reliability. Kirk was a monthly guest at the Sarfatti table and a regular member of Margherita's salon, while Margherita and Fiammetta accepted frequent invitations to

Kirk's buffet lunches and elegant dinners. As a result of his aquaintance with Margherita, between 1928 and his departure for Moscow in early 1938 Kirk met almost every member of Mussolini's inner circle. He acquired a deep loathing for the Fascists.[4]

Through Kirk, the Cerrutis, and Thomas Morgan, Margherita came to know Anne O'Hare McCormick, one of *The New York Times*'s European correspondents. McCormick's admiration for Mussolini and her unusual access to President Roosevelt made her a natural object of interest to Margherita. But the warm relationship that sprang up between the two women went beyond opportunism and survived harsh future trials. McCormick had known Mussolini since before the March on Rome. She had recognized his political ability at his first appearance in the Chamber of Deputies in the summer of 1921, had gained his trust, and frequently interviewed him.[5]

Another important American friend was the artist George Biddle. Biddle arrived in Italy in the late summer of 1931, shortly after marrying his third wife, Helene Sardeau. The couple spent most of the next fifteen months in a remote village in the Abruzzi, but they occasionally visited Rome. On one two-week stay in the Italian capital, Biddle painted a mural for an exhibit at the International Gallery of Modern Art in Venice that attracted Margherita's attention.

Thereafter when they visited Rome, the Biddles attended Margherita's salon. Because of Biddle's interest in public art Margherita introduced him to Sironi. Besides the artists in Margherita's circle, George Biddle made the acquaintance there of Ezra Pound and André Maurois, the French biographer and novelist. Biddle found Margherita the most fascinating of all—he remembered her vital interest in ideas, in literature, in people, and above all, in art. Margherita expressed admiration for Biddle's paintings, drawings, and lithographs. Biddle tried to get an Italian government commission through Margherita, but to no avail. He later claimed that his espousal of public art had been inspired by Diego Rivera and other Mexican muralists on the far left of the political spectrum. But it seems that Margherita and Sironi played an equal part in generating Biddle's enthusiasm.

Biddle returned to New York in November 1932. In the spring of 1933 he wrote to his Groton prep-school friend Franklin Roosevelt to urge the president to employ out-of-work artists in the decoration of public buildings. The president liked Biddle's suggestion, as did Eleanor Roosevelt. In December 1933, the government signed contracts with the first twenty-five hundred artists under the Federal Art Project of the Works Progress Administration. Margherita had indirectly left her mark on the post offices of America.[6]

An acquaintance with Nicholas Murray Butler, president of Columbia

University, was eventually to provide Margherita with her entrée into American society. Columbia University had an unrivaled reputation in the period before World War II, largely because of Butler's abilities as an administrator, publicist, and fund-raiser. He was also an important figure in the Republican party. Butler had provoked controversy in a speech at the University of Virginia in April 1927 by praising Mussolini for improving the life of the Italian people. At the same time he condemned Fascism for its restriction of individual liberty. To his surprise, Butler received an invitation from Mussolini to come to Rome to discuss his views. Mussolini and his advisers wanted to reinforce Butler's positive opinions. When Butler met with Mussolini late that June, they argued vigorously about the merits of Fascism. Soon Butler was boasting of his friendship with the Duce.[7]

One result of the encounter was Mussolini's enthusiastic support for the Casa Italiana, Columbia's institute for the study of Italian culture, which opened in October 1927. Margherita's old friend Marconi attended the dedication ceremony at the behest of his government. Mussolini's interest in the center increased when his old friend Giuseppe Prezzolini joined its staff in September 1929. Prezzolini subsequently accepted Butler's offer to become its director in March 1930. Mussolini enthusiastically endorsed Butler's choice during their second meeting in Rome that same month. Although Prezzolini had grown disillusioned with Mussolini's regime, the Casa Italiana soon gained the reputation as a showcase of the cultural achievements of the Fascist regime.

During Butler's March 1930 visit to Rome, he and Margherita struck up an acquaintance. After Butler won the 1931 Nobel Peace Prize for his work as head of the Carnegie Endowment for International Peace, he and Margherita began a regular correspondence. Butler declined Margherita's invitation to write for *Gerarchia,* but they often exchanged books, holiday greetings, and family news. Both agreed that in the dreary period of the early thirties, Mussolini alone offered a solution to the world's problems. Mussolini despised Butler's internationalism and pacifism, but he saw how useful it was to have Butler singing his praises.[8]

By late 1932, Mussolini had begun secret contacts with Franklin Delano Roosevelt. The Duce had frequently expressed the opinion that only America possessed the economic power to pull the world out of crisis. After the American election in November 1932, he believed Roosevelt would employ that potential as President Hoover had not. It appears that the critical source of Mussolini's expectations about Roosevelt was a private exchange of messages in the fall of 1932.[9]

Margherita had introduced herself to Fannie Hurst on Easter Sunday, 1930, in Rome. They soon formed a warm friendship. (The novelist seems to have based her description of the salon in her 1942 novel, *The Lonely Parade,* on Margherita's intellectual gatherings.) The relationship proved important for Margherita, since Hurst would become close friends with Franklin and Eleanor Roosevelt in 1932.

In September, Mussolini received Elmer Langworthy, a retired American naval officer and Roosevelt's personal emissary in Europe. Mussolini questioned Langworthy closely about Roosevelt and his programs, and expressed special goodwill to the presidential candidate. On his return to the United States, Langworthy reported to Roosevelt and then wrote to Mussolini on Roosevelt's instructions. Roosevelt left no written record of his communications with Mussolini, but apparently Mussolini expressed the hope that the candidate would adopt public works and corporativist schemes on the Fascist model if elected.[10]

Since his foundation of Fascism, Mussolini had considered reorganizing Italian society by creating official "corporations," to group all owners, managers, and workers in the various economic activities into state-run organizations. These corporations would give the Fascist regime total control over the economy, prevent labor troubles by mandatory mediation, and allow for comprehensive economic planning. The idea had been long advocated by syndicalists and by some Fascists, such as Giuseppe Bottai. Mussolini had established the Ministry of Corporations under Bottai in 1926 to manage the Fascist labor unions. But the spread of the world depression in 1930–1931 inspired Mussolini to proclaim corporativism as the economic dogma of Fascism.

This propaganda gesture helped Mussolini to describe the Fascist Corporate State as the "third way" between the injustices of capitalism and the brutalities of Communism. The idea gained particular popularity in the United States. As the Depression worsened in 1932, many Americans became desperate for a non-Communist alternative to unregulated capitalism. Fascist corporativism seemed to offer the means by which Americans could pull themselves out of economic misery.

The idea was not as absurd as it might sound. One of Mussolini's greatest admirers in the United States, Amedeo Giannini, the powerful head of the Bank of America, had quietly but effectively backed Roosevelt during the electoral campaign. Giannini and his brother, Attilio, visited Italy often and enjoyed close contacts with Mussolini's leading economic advisers. William Randolph Hearst and Joseph Kennedy had played a role in getting Amedeo Giannini to drop his support for Hoover, but so had the banker's conviction that Roosevelt was prepared to adopt some of Mussolini's economic policies, and adapt them to solving America's problems.[11]

Roosevelt's election filled Mussolini with confidence, as if he were sure of a special degree of sympathy and understanding from the new president.

Mussolini went so far as to order Margherita and Thomas Morgan to create two articles for *Gerarchia* suggesting what steps the new president should take on assuming office. In essence, the articles argued that Roosevelt should open American markets to Italian goods, forgive the Italian war debt, and adopt the Fascist economic system. That certainty, together with his conviction of Hitler's imminent rise to power in Germany, seems to have inspired Mussolini to make a most fateful decision. In late November 1932, after considering the matter for months, Mussolini gave his military leaders orders to make preparations for the invasion of Ethiopia.[12]

Meanwhile Margherita made plans to visit the United States. She had been invited by the National Council of Women to head the Italian delegation to the International Conclave of Women Writers scheduled for the Chicago World's Fair in mid-July 1933. Despite Butler's discouragement, she enlisted Ranck's help to try to arrange an American lecture tour for two or three months that spring. The Fascist regime was preparing a great propaganda campaign in the United States, to be opened following Roosevelt's inauguration. Italo Balbo was preparing to lead a squadron of seaplanes on a transatlantic flight to the United States in July at the time of Margherita's visit.

In December 1932, Margherita suggested to Ranck a number of topics for articles for the Hearst press. Apparently she hoped to prepare them beforehand, so that she could visit the United States for several months free of obligations. By early March 1933, Margherita had changed her plans. As Ranck explained, the lecture season in the United States ran from September to March, not at all in keeping with Margherita's schedule. Furthermore, as Butler intimated, the Depression had greatly reduced the lecture-tour audience for all but the biggest names, and Margherita was hardly a celebrity in America. Margherita gave her seat at the Conclave of Women Writers to Maria Luisa Astaldi, and decided to visit America instead in late 1933 or early 1934. On her first trip she planned to make herself known, in preparation for a lecture tour later. Events in Europe may have helped convince her to stay at home. On January 30, 1933, German President Paul von Hindenburg appointed Hitler as chancellor with Franz von Papen as vice-chancellor. Behind a veil of constitutional niceties, the Nazis had finally come to power over Germany.[13]

Through his controlled press, Mussolini welcomed Hitler's success. His attitude was in marked contrast to the reaction of most other European governments. Shortly afterward, violent anti-Semitic acts in Germany, and Nazi pressure on Austria, brought a sharp cooling in Italo-German relations. Mussolini had not expected Hitler to discredit Fascism, or threaten Austria's status as an Italian protectorate. In early April, Hitler sent Göring to Rome to reassure Mussolini and to open talks with the Vatican about a concordat to settle Church-State relations in the new Nazi Germany. In three meetings with Mussolini, Göring insisted that Hitler would strictly respect Austrian independence and adhere to any policy in that regard that Mussolini laid down. In return, Mussolini agreed to help the Germans secretly build a large air force in violation of the Versailles Treaty. For the moment, Italo-German relations improved.[14]

In order to mollify Hitler while keeping him in check, Mussolini elaborated a Four Power Pact by which Britain, France, Italy, and Germany would direct European affairs. In confidential diplomatic discussions Mussolini proposed that the four states agree to maintain peace for ten years, consider the revision of the Versailles settlement, and allow Germany gradually to acquire equality in armaments. Mussolini intended Germany to become strong enough to threaten the British and French—unless Italy came to their aid—yet remain too weak to devour Austria and imperil Mussolini's freedom of action. In Mussolini's mind this freedom included being allowed to carve up Yugoslavia for Italy's benefit and to conquer Ethiopia.

Persuading the other three governments to sign the agreement occupied most of Mussolini's attention throughout the first half of 1933. The pact, dubbed the Patto Mussolini for Italian consumption, was signed in the Palazzo Venezia on July 15. By then French objections to Mussolini's original proposal had reduced the actual agreement to no more than a framework for consultations. Nazi violence in Austria intensified throughout the spring. After meeting with Mussolini and securing his promise of Italian military assistance if necessary, Austrian chancellor Engelbert Dollfuss outlawed the National Socialists altogether in June.[15]

While Mussolini focused on these European events, Margherita's articles for the Hearst press suffered. Many of her pieces were shorter than the agreement for 1933 had stipulated, polemical, dull, and late in arriving. The articles were apparently written in haste, or assembled from the collection of pieces Margherita had prepared in advance of her canceled trip to America. Ranck and Hearst grew increasingly annoyed, since they were paying a great deal of money by Depression standards. They were also angry that Mussolini had resumed granting interviews to other newspapers.

Ranck noted to Hearst that Margherita and Mussolini both had grown insufferably arrogant. Once it became clear the arrangement was endangered, Margherita became more accommodating. In March she attempted to appease Ranck by agreeing to sell some of the Hearst "Senior Statesmen" articles to *Politica Sociale,* a journal that employed Fiammetta as an editor. Presumably this netted Margherita a profit as well. Nonetheless, Ranck remained dissatisfied with the quality of the articles Margherita was sending him.[16]

Mussolini did not want to lose the priceless propaganda vehicle the Hearst articles provided him. If Hearst decided to cancel their agreement, Mussolini knew he would lose access to British, French, and German, as well as American, readers. In order to recoup their costs, the Hearst organization had sold the rights to Mussolini's articles to a number of European newspapers, whose readership ran into the millions. In April 1933, as his preoccupation with gaining agreement to the Four Power Pact mounted, Mussolini realized he needed as much support at home and abroad as he could muster. He decided to devote more time and energy to the articles, since their impact made the labor worthwhile.

This decision proved fortunate for Margherita. Mussolini had taken successive steps to distance himself from her. He had ordered that she was not to be invited to official receptions, as previously. In private, he had made a number of disparaging remarks about Margherita's recent writing. Thus, the Hearst articles represented one of the few links between Mussolini and Margherita at the time.

Previously Mussolini had refused to allow any of the articles to appear in the Italian press. Signed pieces that appeared outside Italy were expressions of Mussolini's personal opinions, not official pronouncements of the Italian government. Admittedly, given Mussolini's dictatorial powers, this was a fine distinction. But foreign governments could not protest the content of an article published abroad, as they could a speech on foreign policy or an official communiqué of the Italian Foreign Ministry. Now Mussolini instructed Margherita to write a certain number of pieces that would be acceptable to Hearst but officially published in Italy as well. Mussolini even seems to have written some of these articles himself, employing Margherita and Morgan's assistance to ensure that they would pass muster with Ranck and Hearst.

The first of these pieces made a sharp attack on French foreign policy. It appeared in the Hearst papers on April 9 and then four days later in *Il Popolo d'Italia*. Ranck placed the article under big headlines on the first page of the Sunday editions, twinned with a rebuttal from former French Premier Herriot. This provided the type of controversy Hearst wanted but the Duce rarely provided.[17]

Mussolini waited three months before releasing another dual-purpose article. First he had an article prepared solely for the Hearst papers in May, as a result of an initial contact between the Mussolini and Roosevelt administrations. In early April, Roosevelt had invited Mussolini to visit the United States to discuss pressing economic and political issues. Of foremost importance were the implications of the Johnson Bill, which, if passed into law, would bar American loans to any government in default on its war-debt repayments. With the severity of the Depression, several European governments, including Mussolini's, had been hinting broadly that they would be unable to continue their payments to the United States.

Mussolini sent in his place his minister of finance, Guido Jung, another Italian Jew who had gained prominence in the Fascist regime. Jung and the team of negotiators who accompanied him made a highly favorable impression on Roosevelt and his advisers. On every issue—disarmament, international economic policy, even the sticky question of war-debts settlement—the Italians and Americans reached easy agreement, or at least congenial disagreement. Jung's detailed exposition of the Duce's domestic programs caused James Warburg, one of Roosevelt's financial advisers, to exclaim that "Mussolini and the President must be brothers!"[18]

On one issue, however, Roosevelt's strong opinions made the Italian finance minister acutely uncomfortable. As Jung later reported to Mussolini:

> The discussion of Germany and of the new direction Germany [is taking] was long and, on my part, I had to adopt considerable tact to deal with the problem. President Roosevelt seemed very worried by the danger which, according to him, the Hitler regime represents for the European peace and for that of the world. . . . President Roosevelt told me that the world situation could not be considered peaceful and satisfactory because Germany would abstain from making war for five years or so, that is, until it would be materially ready to start it.

Roosevelt had received information indicating that Mussolini had begun to fear Hitler as a menace to Italian security and a threat to the positive image of Fascism. The president told Jung that he considered Mussolini to be his only potential partner in preserving world peace. Roosevelt went on to stress the lack of any serious American-Italian disagreements. He said that he considered Italy America's only real friend in Europe and that he intended to support Mussolini any way he could in the Duce's difficult balancing act between France and Germany.[19]

Mussolini's May article dealt with the president's concerns about Hitler. Given the time needed to get the piece to New York prior to its May 21 publication, Margherita and Mussolini must have begun working on the article as soon as Jung reported back. Mussolini chose not to publish it in Italy, probably because he considered its message too strong for the Italian public.

The article—which Ranck titled "Mussolini Calls Rise of Hitlerism an Insurrection of German People"—described Hitler's coming to power as a revolution, backed by the great majority of the German people. The piece made plain Mussolini's full sympathy with the Nazis and likened their methods to those of the Fascist revolution. The article insisted that the excesses of Nazi violence were typical of incidents accompanying any radical realignment of a nation's politics. Just as Mussolini had, Hitler would soon bring such abuses to an end.[20] Mussolini's message to Roosevelt was that Hitler could be trusted. If there was to be the kind of close American-Italian cooperation Roosevelt hoped for, then the president must adopt a more tolerant attitude toward Hitler.

In early July Mussolini and Margherita produced a second article for both Il Popolo d'Italia and the Hearst press. It addressed Roosevelt's political and economic concepts and the first hundred days of his administration. Margherita used Roosevelt's recently published book, Looking Forward, as the basis for the article. Choosing her words carefully to avoid offending American readers, Margherita wrote that the New Deal obviously was inspired by the Fascist corporative state.

The piece continued a familiar propaganda refrain: All the leaders of the world looked to Mussolini and Fascism for inspiration. Now that its outlines had emerged, the New Deal was indeed proving quite similar to Fascism (an observation voiced by Roosevelt's critics in less than complimentary terms). Some passages in Looking Forward calling for long-range government economic planning were suggestive of Fascism. The book also advocated a sharp reduction in tariffs and criticized the League of Nations; Mussolini had long espoused both ideas. Margherita stressed that in his inaugural address, Roosevelt warned that he would demand dictatorial powers, if necessary, to deal with the Depression. Still, his book contained passages criticizing totalitarianism, and insisting on Allied war-debt repayment.[21]

In late July, in parallel articles for Hearst and Il Popolo d'Italia, Margherita replied to Roosevelt's concerns about Hitler. She argued, in Mussolini's name, that all efforts to reach European agreements on trade and disarmament had failed. Only the Four Power Pact held out the promise of real European cooperation. But this would mean revising the Versailles settlement—including the whole question of reparations and war debts—and allowing Germany to rearm. Unless these measures of trust and understanding were extended, a new European war seemed inevitable.[22]

For the rest of the year, the articles followed an alternating pattern. Mussolini would agree to place some pieces in Il Popolo d'Italia as well as in the Hearst press; others were destined only for America. But all hammered away at one theme—Mussolini knew what was best for Europe and the world. Margherita reinforced this message through the widening contacts she established with influential Americans throughout 1933. Her primary target now was Roosevelt's new ambassador to Italy, Breckinridge Long.

Long arrived in Rome in late May 1933. The ambassadorship was his reward for managing Roosevelt's 1932 electoral campaign. Mussolini received him almost immediately to express, in Long's words, "very great personal admiration" for Roosevelt, total confidence in the success of the New Deal, and a strong desire to work as closely as possible with the American government. Long left Mussolini's office in the Palazzo Venezia with a very positive impression of the Duce, which he communicated to Roosevelt that same evening. Two weeks later, the president replied: "There seems no question but that Mussolini is really interested in what we are doing and I am much interested and deeply impressed by what he has accomplished and by his evidenced honest purpose of restoring Italy and seeking to prevent general European trouble."[23]

Very quickly, Long became enamored of Fascist Italy, except for its heavy taxes. Still, Long recognized that Fascist Italy was a dictatorship. He spent much of his time trying to free from jail American tourists who had run afoul of Mussolini's secret police. He soon realized that either the embassy was bugged with listening devices or that his Italian servants were spies. He discovered that censorship and control rendered the Italian press hopelessly unreliable and often uninformative. The lack of any wireless facilities in the embassy and the slowness of the mails from the United States and even from the rest of Europe left him feeling isolated and bereft of timely information.[24]

Margherita became Long's principal source of information about the direction of Mussolini's policies. Alexander Kirk introduced Margherita to the ambassador at a dinner party. They became friends rapidly, in part because they were both in the capital during the first half of August, when most of the local society had left town to escape the ferocious heat of summer. By September, Margherita knew Long well enough to invite him to Fiammetta's wedding, when she married Count Livio Gaetani in October 1933. Margherita made a point of providing Long with the manuscripts of her Hearst articles in advance of publication. Believing them to be written by Mussolini, Long would advise Roosevelt, Secretary of State Cordell Hull, and other American officials of their contents, urging them to read those he considered important. Long accepted most of what Margherita told him at face value.[25]

Two other Americans of note, with whom Margherita quickly established ties, visited Rome in the summer of 1933. The first was the newspaperwoman Marie Mattingly Meloney, known to her friends as "Missy." Two years younger than Margherita, Marie Meloney had become a journalist at the time of the Spanish-American War. Journalism was an unheard-of profession for a woman at the time. In 1900, Missy became the first woman to obtain a seat in the U.S. Senate press gallery, as a correspondent for *The Washington Post*. After moving to New York, she married the author and publisher William Brown Meloney. She left journalism for ten years to raise their son, and to battle tuberculosis, from which she never fully recovered. She returned to her profession in 1914 to edit a number of woman's magazines. Widowed in 1925, Missy took over the editorship of the *New York Herald Tribune Sunday Magazine* the next year.

In the early twenties, Missy gained a measure of fame from her campaign to obtain radium for the research of Marie Curie. After 1930, her reputation spread even more widely as a result of her annual Women's Conference on Current Problems. Soon the conferences, held annually in New York's luxurious Waldorf-Astoria hotel, were attracting more people than could be accommodated and were being broadcast from coast to coast. By the early thirties, Marie Meloney had established a remarkable circle of friends, including the Herbert Hoovers, Nicholas Murray Butler, Sinclair Lewis and Dorothy Thompson, Walter Lippmann, Fannie Hurst, and Alexander Kirk. Despite her staunch Republican politics, Missy was particularly close to her Hudson Valley neighbors Franklin and Eleanor Roosevelt. After March 1933, she was a frequent guest of the president and his wife, at the White House and at Hyde Park.

Missy arrived in Rome late in July 1933, expecting to meet Mussolini, whom she had interviewed twice before. To her extreme annoyance, Mussolini canceled the interview, apparently at the request of the Hearst bureau chief in Rome. Mussolini recognized Missy's importance, and remembered her previous positive assessments of the Fascist regime. He assigned Margherita to smooth things over with the American newspaperwoman. Within a few days, the two women had become warm friends.

When Missy left Rome in early August, she carried autographed photographs of Margherita and Fiammetta, and a copy of *The Life of Benito Mussolini* inscribed: "To 'Missy' Meloney with the expression of my best thanks for her kind, hearty and ready sympathy, which gave me the unexpected pleasure of a sudden 'old' friendship." They decided that Margherita would begin writing occasional articles for the *New York Herald Tribune* and that she would stay with Missy when she came to New York. Despite Margherita's hospitality, Missy was appalled by the militaristic aspects of the Mostra della Rivoluzione. Missy returned from Italy convinced that the Fascists were preparing for war, and that Mussolini and Hitler would eventually march together.[26]

A few days later, Colonel Theodore Roosevelt, Jr., and his wife arrived in Rome on his return from the Philippines, where he had served as Hoover's governor-general. Long invited Margherita to dine with him and the president's cousin at the embassy on the evening of August 2. The Roosevelts and Margherita befriended each other, and Margherita invited them to her home on the Via dei Villini. In the course of the evening, Margherita mentioned her liking for Kipling, also a favorite author of Roosevelt's father. The president had required his son to memorize many of the English author's poems. The younger Roosevelt eventually struck up a friendship with the poet by correspondence. Margherita and Roosevelt began quoting some of Kipling's verses and soon challenged each other to a contest to see who could quote more. To Roosevelt's amused astonishment, Margherita won.

Margherita told Roosevelt of her hopes to visit America and he encouraged her to come. They agreed that the Fascist approach to dealing with the Depression held some lessons for the United States. Roosevelt suggested that Margherita consider a lecture tour of American colleges to describe Mussolini's hopes for the corporate state. As a favor, Margherita arranged for the colonel to meet Mussolini. A few weeks later, Roosevelt visited Kipling at his home in Sussex. Presumably he told the Englishman of his new friend Margherita's extraordinary knowledge of Kipling's poetry.[27]

But for all his fondness for her, Roosevelt had not formed such a high opinion of the Duce. As he wrote to his mother ten days after his interview with Mussolini:

> I had an interesting chat with Mussolini . . . he seems to think now that he is a world prophet. He said in almost so many words that Franklin was his pupil. I told him that he must not judge our people by his and that unless my people had greatly changed they would never consent to a dictatorship. He remained politely unconvinced.[28]

Mussolini remained quite certain that his domestic and foreign policies offered the world the best solutions to its problems. In mid-August, Margherita wrote in a Mussolini article for the Hearst press that liberal democracy was dying. The Depression marked a crisis that only Fascism could solve. Hitler's revolution and Roosevelt's resort to emergency powers were clear signs that the Fascist era of history had begun.

In late September, in a piece published in Italy as well as in America, Margherita described the recent Italian pact with the Soviet Union as a way to bring that state into Mussolini's European Great-Power system. This represented one more step in Mussolini's plan to reorganize Europe along the lines he had been discussing with Roosevelt and Hitler. In fact, as Mussolini privately reassured the Germans, he sought the support of the Soviets only to undermine the Versailles Treaty.

Two months later, the Hearst press printed DUCE PLANS ECONOMIC RULE OF ITALY THROUGH 40 GUILDS in banner headlines across page 1 of its

Sunday editions. Ranck finally had an article from Margherita he considered exciting. To Ranck's great annoyance, the news had appeared in *Il Popolo d'Italia* on Saturday and had been immediately wired to the States by Morgan for the United Press. After explaining the workings of the corporate state, the article predicted the demise of both capitalism and socialism and their eventual replacement by Fascist economics. "I think the Roosevelt experiment will have this epilogue," the piece concluded in its analysis of the Fascist direction in which the New Deal supposedly was headed.[29]

Ranck and Hearst found few of Margherita's other articles very provocative. In some cases, Mussolini suggested good topics, only to withdraw them later for political reasons. The last-minute substitutions proved excruciatingly dull. In late November, Hearst was forced to publish on successive Sundays these two pieces: "Mussolini Works on Farm, Visits Factories to Learn Needs of Italian Masses" and "Prohibition Repeal Shows How Slowly Democracy Moves, Declares Mussolini." Mussolini rejected some topics of obvious interest. He refused Ranck's suggestion for an article on Balbo's mass seaplane flight from Rome to Chicago because he had decided that Balbo was getting far too much publicity already. Mussolini feared him as a rival.[30]

On October 5, Mussolini published a piece on disarmament in *Il Popolo d'Italia;* the piece was intended for the Hearst press, but political developments had led him to jump the Hearst deadline. Hitler had threatened to withdraw from the Geneva Disarmament Conference unless Germany was granted equality in armaments. The article made public Mussolini's diplomatic position: The Nazis could be trusted with an increase in weaponry. He argued that the German economic crisis would keep Hitler's government busy for years. Ranck informed Margherita that he would pay only $250 for the article. Its newsworthiness would be lost by the time it appeared in the Hearst press, as originally scheduled, ten days later. Margherita reluctantly agreed. In fact, Ranck and Hearst decided to kill the piece entirely, since events quickly deprived it of any news interest whatsoever.[31]

By the second week in October, Mussolini was worrying that Hitler would announce a massive rearmament program, regardless of the consequences. Weeks earlier, to compensate for his canceled interview in August, Mussolini had promised to consider speaking by radio to Missy Meloney's third annual Women's Conference on Current Problems on October 12. Margherita also planned to deliver a radio address to the meeting. As the day for the conference approached, Mussolini decided not to speak. The antiwar message of the conference, which was to be reiterated in speeches by Walter Lippmann, Theodore Roosevelt, Jr., and Eleanor Roosevelt, and in concluding remarks by President Roosevelt himself, made Mussolini uneasy. He did not wish to associate himself with an attack on Hitler's policies at this delicate moment.[32]

Soon afterward, Mussolini became annoyed by a New York *Sun* article that described Margherita as the co-author of Fascist ideology. It suggested that she was quietly shaping his policy toward Hitler from behind the scenes: "The beautiful, Titian blonde and Junoesque Signora Sarfatti is a Jewess, and Rome recalls, happily, that there has been no hint of anti-Semitism in the Italian Fascist Regime."[33]

Under the circumstances Margherita scripted her conference address carefully. She planned to repeat her call for the solidarity of "White Civilization," extol Mussolini's Fascism as the answer to the world crisis, and suggest that only through struggle—even war itself—could mankind solve its problems. On October 11, the day before the conference, Mussolini ordered Margherita to cancel her address. Telegraphed protests by Theodore Roosevelt, Jr., and Missy were to no avail. Mussolini had decided that he did not want any connection with potentially anti-German statements. Missy had Margherita's speech read to the conference, and then printed it in the *New York Herald Tribune* the next day; the paper identified Margherita as "Countess Sarfatti."[34]

On October 13, acting on Hitler's instructions, the German ambassador informed Mussolini that Germany would withdraw from the Geneva Disarmament Conference the following day. The news did not alarm Mussolini. He calculated that Hitler's action would revive the Four Power Pact by making that agreement the only means by which Germany could seek equality in armaments.

But Hitler had not told Mussolini the whole story. When the Germans withdrew from the disarmament talks, they left the League of Nations as well. Hitler had revealed his estimation of Italy's real weight in the balance of power. By walking out of the League, Hitler had effectively canceled the Four Power Pact, thus humiliating Mussolini.

It soon occurred to Hitler that he had antagonized Mussolini to such a degree that the Duce might form a united front with the French and British against Germany. Until Germany grew stronger, he preferred to maintain friendly Italo-German relations and to nourish Mussolini's opinion of himself as Hitler's mentor. In early November, Göring traveled to Rome to offer excuses for Hitler's behavior. Göring claimed that Ambassador Cerruti was part of the problem. Göring accused the ambassador of sending false and damaging reports to Rome because of Cerruti's anti-Nazi attitudes. Göring asked for Cerruti's removal and stated that Hitler was prepared to sign a written guarantee of Austrian independence.[35]

On the very first page of *Mein Kampf* Hitler had proclaimed his determination to unite Germany and Austria. As informed observers were noting by the fall of 1933, Hitler was following step by step the plans he had laid down in *Mein Kampf.* Yet in order to form an alliance with Mussolini, Hitler claimed he was prepared to make an exception to his Pan-German dreams. In return for an alliance, he would forgo any claim on the Austrian-inhabited territory of the South Tyrol, which Italy had acquired in 1919. After the creation of an Italo-German coalition, Hitler planned to evacuate those Austrians and settle them elsewhere. But the chancellor's unshakable insistence on annexing the rest of Austria remained the major impediment to a Nazi-Fascist partnership.[36]

Despite Göring's attempt to reassure Mussolini, Hitler's recent actions had offended Mussolini deeply. Hitler decided to have Vice-Chancellor Papen dispatch Schulenburg on a secret diplomatic mission to Rome. Schulenburg was to approach Margherita with Hitler's offer to resolve Italo-German differences.

Hitler and his foreign policy advisers knew of the deterioration of Margherita's relationship with Mussolini. Nonetheless, they considered her better informed than anyone else about Mussolini's thinking, and as a result of her intimate knowledge, the best conduit for Hitler's proposals. Given her Jewishness, her intimacy with the Cerrutis, and her sensitivity in regard to the Austrian question, Margherita's approval might help greatly to win Mussolini's acceptance. Schulenburg was an old friend to Margherita. His aristocratic disdain for Nazi extremism made the baron the likeliest candidate for winning Margherita's sympathies. He had already proved his aptitude for secret diplomacy by previous confidential missions to the Vatican and to the French government.

Schulenburg arrived secretly in Rome on the night of November 17–18. After ensuring that his presence remained unobserved by the foreign press, the envoy arranged to meet Margherita on the afternoon of November 19. Once inside her apartment, the baron laid out Hitler's offer, claiming to have memorized Hitler's actual words:

> If only Mussolini was not letting the present historical opportunity slip by unnoticed. Germany and Italy could reach agreement—in a way and manner to be decided—in order to impose the Fascist idea upon the world. If this agreement were made, Germany would end any propaganda in the South Tyrol; in fact, it would prevent it. It would even cease German pressure on Austria and, for an indefinite period of time, Austrian and German National Socialism would carry on autonomous and independent of each other. I would even stop National Socialist propaganda in Austria.

Hitler matched his offer with a threat. Schulenburg hinted that if Mussolini did not revoke his promise of anti-Nazi military support to

Austria, Hitler would create an alliance with Yugoslavia. Not only would German assistance thwart Mussolini's plans to conquer Yugoslavia, it would create a serious threat to Italy. Hitler had resolved to seize Austria one way or the other. If he did so with Mussolini's acquiesence, the action would be part of a comprehensive Italo-German alliance. If Hitler was forced to grab Austria in the face of Italian opposition, Italy would be exposed to German invasion from the north and from the east, through Yugoslavia.

Schulenburg hoped that Margherita would bring Hitler's proposal directly to Mussolini, but she was afraid to deal directly with such an important issue. Instead she contacted Osvaldo Sebastiani, the deputy director of Mussolini's private secretariat, and arranged for him to meet with Hitler's envoy. After being fully informed by Sebastiani, Mussolini agreed to more formal conversations. The next day, November 20, Schulenburg saw both Alessandro Chiavolini, head of Mussolini's private secretariat, and Baron Pompeo Aloisi, Undersecretary Fulvio Suvich's deputy at the Ministry of Foreign Affairs. Both men expressed concern that the diplomatic feeler had not come through official channels. Perhaps Papen was seeking to replace Göring as Hitler's chief Italian expert by negotiating a spectacular agreement with Mussolini.

Schulenburg assured them he was acting on Hitler's orders. He went on to stress that Hitler wished to expand only toward the east and wanted a comprehensive settlement with Italy to secure his southern flank before proceeding. Mussolini considered the matter for several days and then met with Schulenburg himself. From subsequent events, it is obvious that Mussolini rejected the settlement Hitler wanted.

Hitler flattered and tempted Mussolini by suggesting that an alliance of the two Fascist regimes could dominate Europe and the world. He clearly implied that such a coalition would be led by Mussolini, the founder of European Fascism. Hitler's assignment of Schulenburg to bear his offer held special significance. In his 1929 article in *Gerarchia,* the baron had argued that Fascism and National Socialism were quite different ideologies and that Hitler—in stark contrast to Mussolini—was a narrow-minded demagogue, mired in insane anti-Semitic fantasies. By accepting this assignment, Schulenburg indicated that he had changed his mind about the chancellor and that Mussolini too could trust Hitler.

Hitler's offer did not disguise the fact that he was determined eventually to have the Reich's southern boundary at the Italian frontier. An Italo-German alliance might guarantee Italy's security under such circumstances, but it would force Mussolini to march with Hitler to the end. As Mussolini had revealed to the Fascist Grand Council nineteen months earlier, he knew that he must choose between Germany and France sooner or later.

But French offers of an understanding with Italy continued to attract him.

The European events of late 1933 thrilled Hearst. Not only had the drama helped sell papers, but Hearst had seen the triumph of Hitler, a man whose cause he had championed, and the weakening of the League of Nations. Mussolini seemed of far less interest now, and most of his recent articles had been disappointing. Hearst decided to offer him a smaller contract, or none, for 1934. What he really wanted was a contract with Hitler, whom he was prepared to pay a great deal. A small matter nearly decided the issue. Margherita began demanding $500 for the canceled disarmament article, although she had already agreed to $250. Thoroughly annoyed, Ranck and Hearst were ready to end the arrangement with Mussolini.[37]

In late November, Hearst changed his mind. The possibility of a struggle between Italy and Germany over Austria and Italian demands for a radical reform of the League of Nations intrigued him. Hearst decided to renew Mussolini's contract after all. In return Mussolini offered to write an article on the future of the League of Nations. He and Margherita worked on it up to the very last minute, barely making the deadline for publication on Christmas Eve.[38]

The piece began by arguing that Hitler's actions doomed the League of Nations unless it was drastically reorganized. To ensure smooth functioning, the League had to be restructured for control by a small group of the Great Powers (a suggestion rather like Roosevelt's plan for the United Nations Security Council some twelve years later). As if to please Hearst, Mussolini recognized Italy's obligation to pay its war debts to the United States, but also warned of a new world war if the interrelated problems of debts, disarmament, and international rivalries were not solved. The only answer he could see was Fascism. Roosevelt's National Recovery Administration and Public Works Administration were admirable imitations of Fascism. He concluded: "The world will, within ten years, be either Fascist or Fascistized. I repeat now with great conviction: 1934 will mark a decisive step in this Fascistization of the world."[39]

After reading the piece, Hearst authorized Ranck to offer Mussolini a new contract for 1934 at 16,000 lire per article. Margherita demanded payment in Italian currency to protect herself against Roosevelt's expected devaluation of the dollar, which had been rumored since October. Even with the risk of losing money on an uncertain rate of exchange, Hearst thought Mussolini would be worth the expense. On December 26, 1933, Margherita signed a new contract, agreeing to provide twelve articles for 1934. The next day, Margherita accepted $250 for the disarmament article. With that, the Hearst bureau chief in Rome reported that relations with

Margherita had returned to a cordial plane—although she remained a "most difficult person."[40]

Margherita had good reason to make their dealings as cordial as possible. She had begun preparations for her visit to America, and she hoped to marshal the support of the Hearst press while there. Margherita had requested her passport—issued only for specific trips on a case-by-case basis under the Fascist regime—in early October. She was free to spend considerable time in the United States. Margherita knew that Vito Mussolini, Arnaldo's son, would replace her as managing editor of *Gerarchia* in January 1934. This removed a burden but it also represented a loss to her prestige and another step in her progressive separation from Mussolini.[41]

Her plans were marred at the last minute. Only a week before her departure, on March 11, two young men named Sion Segrè and Mario Levi were intercepted by Fascist police at the border town of Ponte Tresa, where they had been trying to smuggle anti-Fascist literature into Italy from Switzerland. The confiscated propaganda material had been produced by Giustizia e Libertà, an organization headquartered in France and founded by Carlo Rosselli. Segrè was caught but Levi swam to safety.

Two days later, the authorities reported to Mussolini that they had arrested a number of people implicated in the affair, including Mario Levi's brother Gino and his father, Giuseppe. These men, and most of the others eventually implicated, were Jews. Giuseppe Levi was Margherita's cousin. The Fascist press immediately raised cries of conspiracy between Jews and anti-Fascists. Giuseppe Levi was freed for lack of evidence but could not bring himself to ask Margherita for help in securing the release of his son. His wife did go to Rome to try to talk with Margherita, but by then she had already left for the United States.[42]

26

The Pursuit of Happiness

I see in them the effects of that inebriation which America has on everyone, especially on those coming from Italy, the first time that they arrive
here." So Giuseppe Prezzolini wrote of two Italian archaeologists visiting
New York in the spring of 1937. He could just as well have been describing
Margherita on her 1934 tour of the United States. She too became drunk
on America.[1]

Margherita arrived in North America at the age of fifty-three, fluent in
English and already well acquainted with a number of prominent Americans. She had by then read widely in American history, politics, and
literature. Her Fascist outlook colored her impressions of the United States,
so that not everything she saw or heard struck her as marvelous. Nonetheless she returned to Italy with the highest regard for the United States. She
discovered a country whose citizens considered the pursuit of happiness to
be their prerogative; more than a few had apparently really found happiness, even in the midst of a prolonged economic depression. The contrast
with 1934 Europe impressed her deeply.[2]

In three months Margherita traveled down the Atlantic seaboard, over
to Cuba, to the Yucatán, through Mexico to California, and across the
continent to New York. Her stated purpose—to generate publicity for
herself in preparation for a future lecture tour—does not fully explain her
exhaustive itinerary. Why did she feel the need to acquire American dollars
lecturing when she was already a wealthy woman?

Margherita seems to have conceived of her visit as both preparation and
precaution. She faced an increasingly uncertain future in 1934. Deprived of
her intimacy with Mussolini, widowed, and well into middle age, she had
little hope of winning any other powerful man's protection in Fascist Italy.
Roberto Farinacci's racist attacks, reinforced by those of other extremists,
had made clear how much her security depended on Mussolini's continued

benevolence. How safe could any Italian Jew be if the regime were to join with the Nazis? The arrest of her cousin on the eve of her departure underscored the difficulties ahead.

If she could strengthen ties between Roosevelt's America and Mussolini's Italy, she might help to make an Italo-German alliance less likely. Each influential American Margherita met would add to her credibility as an expert on America. In that capacity she could advocate to Mussolini the moderate foreign policy that good Italo-American relations required. Perhaps too she felt that by making herself useful to Mussolini, she might regain his attentions.

However, if Mussolini were to succumb to Hitler's offers of alliance, she knew she would need a means of defense or even an avenue for escape. Margherita and her family might possibly find life under a pro-Nazi Italian government tolerable, but if they were forced to abandon a Europe in flames or under Nazi domination, refuge in America offered them their best hope. In that case, the more powerful American acquaintances she could make and the more dollars she could acquire, the surer she would be of gaining a visa for herself and her children.

Margherita prepared carefully for her trip. Missy Meloney helped generate advance publicity by sending *New York Herald Tribune* reporter Joseph Phillips to interview her in early September 1933. In early October, just before the Women's Conference on Current Problems, the *Herald Tribune Sunday Magazine* published Phillips's flattering profile of Margherita, titled "Italy's Heroine of Fascism." It outlined Margherita's life and lauded her accomplishments as a brilliant hostess, the patron of the *Novecento* movement, the editor of *Gerarchia*, Mussolini's biographer, and one of the founders of Fascism. Mussolini had canceled the Columbus Day radio address with which Margherita was to follow the article a few days later, but Missy published the speech the following day in the *Herald Tribune*. In mid-November, Missy published Margherita's "Women of Fascism," giving it first place in the *Tribune* magazine. Margherita's article defended Mussolini's policy stressing that an Italian woman's primary duty was to be a prolific mother. She argued that the ensuing high birth rate would ensure the growing power of Fascist Italy.

After each article, Nicholas Murray Butler wrote Margherita that he and a good many others had read the pieces with interest. However, he again discouraged Margherita from coming to America, which he said was mired in a spiritual, as well as an economic, depression. He wrote her of his own hopes to visit Italy in March 1934. He made it clear that for him Mussolini represented Europe's last hope for peace. Margherita told Butler that she had passed on his flattery to the Duce, who had expressed his appreciation. Butler's reluctance to receive Margherita in New York crumbled. In turn, Margherita assured Butler that Mussolini would be glad to see him when he came to Rome.[3]

Margherita crafted her early 1934 Mussolini articles for the Hearst press in anticipation of her American visit. Each piece dealt with issues of specific interest to Americans, and encouraged cooperation between Roosevelt and Mussolini. Her January article warned of a possible Russo-Japanese war and a Sino-Japanese alliance sometime in the future. It argued that the West, led by Italy and the United States, must unite against the "Yellow Peril." The article created a diplomatic incident. Believing that the Duce was the author, the Japanese ambassador to Italy delivered an official protest in person to Mussolini in late January. In February, Margherita wrote an admiring assessment of FDR's policies, of course comparing them to Mussolini's views. For March she wrote that Mussolini's corporativism was clearly the model for Roosevelt's National Recovery Act. Her piece praised both as the means by which each nation would escape the Depression.[4]

These articles pleased Ranck and Hearst a good deal more than most of her 1933 efforts. Margherita wanted as much money as possible to finance her long trip to America, and so was very impatient with the slow arrival of her payments from New York. She lied to Ranck, telling him that she would be gone only a month, and that Fiammetta could easily handle getting the April manuscript from Mussolini and into the hands of the Hearst Rome bureau chief.[5]

In mid-March 1934 Nicholas Murray Butler arrived in Rome to enlist Mussolini in the cause of world peace. Butler saw no way to avoid another world war unless international cooperation replaced the economic rivalry that the Depression had sparked. Intensely disappointed that the London Economic Conference of June 1933 had not led to the creation of a world economic organization, Butler began to advocate regional associations as a first step in that direction. He flattered himself into thinking he had inspired Mussolini to reach the economic and political understandings with Austria and Hungary that were to be signed in March 1934. In fact, Mussolini had pressured Chancellor Dollfuss of Austria and Prime Minister Gömbös of Hungary into a coalition to prevent German expansion in Central Europe. Anticipating that Butler's presence would yield him propaganda benefits, Mussolini invited Columbia University's president to be present during the final negotiations. Butler jumped at the chance and sailed to Italy.

Mussolini allowed Butler three interviews. During their second talk on the evening of March 14 in the Palazzo Venezia, Mussolini told Butler what he wanted to hear. "There must be no more wars. Another war would not only ruin Italy, it would destroy civilization."

The Duce also arranged for Butler to meet with Dollfuss and Gömbös. But Margherita did the most to shape Butler's reactions and prompt his remarks to the press. As Butler admitted in a letter to Margherita on the eve of his departure, "No one can give me as accurate and as vivid a picture of the most recent happenings in the political thought and action of Europe." A telegram from Margherita reached Butler after his ship docked in Naples. He visited her late the next afternoon in Rome. The day after, March 12, Butler lunched with her and the Marconis. Six days later, Butler attended a speech Mussolini delivered at the Royal Opera House on the accomplishments of the Fascist regime. Margherita sat beside him to translate. Mussolini extolled Fascism as the wave of the future, and declared ominously that Italy would, in fact, have to expand to the south and the east. On March 21, when Butler left for New York, Margherita sailed with him.[6]

"The moment of departure by sea is a rapture," Margherita wrote. Marconi had come to bid her farewell. After the visitors had gone ashore, she remained topside to wave good-bye. As the huge 51,000-ton *Rex* pulled away from its dock, she gazed once again at the city of Genoa, rising steeply from its harbor up the mountain slopes of the Appenines. The dark smoke from the city's hundreds of factories drifted away into the brilliant blue sky. First the city, then the curving coastline of the Riviera disappeared over the horizon. Margherita found herself alone. She stood silently on the deck, wrapped in a solitude she had craved since sailing back from South America three years earlier. A great longing for the adventures that lay ahead enveloped her.[7]

During the seven days of the cruise, Margherita explored the ship and made the acquaintance of the captain, officers, and sailors. The crew showed immense pride in their ship, just eighteen months in service and the queen of the Italian merchant fleet. The *Rex* had captured the cream of the American tourist traffic because of a transatlantic speed record and luxurious appointments. It had an outdoor swimming pool and a two-deck-high ballroom. The crew kept the *Rex* in superb running order.

Margherita noted with satisfaction that the sailors were as well treated as the ship they manned. From the vestiges of Socialism that she, Mussolini, and other former Marxists had carried over to Fascism, as well as from American-inspired social-engineering concepts, had come the *Dopolavoro* organization. *Dopolavoro* supervised and subsidized the recreational and educational activities of Italian workers. It was an attempt to build enthusiasm for Mussolini's dictatorship, and offset the harsh working conditions imposed by the Fascist regime. Margherita attended a number of concerts and amateur theatricals organized by the *Dopolavoro* on board and found them entertaining.

She spent many hours talking to Butler. They discussed what she should expect after her arrival in America, and what he would say to reporters concerning Mussolini and Fascist Italy. She also conversed with Bishop John Thomas Walsh of Newark, one of three Catholic prelates returning to the United States aboard the *Rex*. The bishop provided Margherita with a mass of information about the status of Italian Americans, based on his knowledge of the thousands in his New Jersey diocese.[8]

On a morning marked by swirling fog and heavy seas, Margherita's ship sailed through the Narrows and into New York Harbor. Bundled in a fur coat against the chill, Margherita came on deck early to watch the skyscrapers of Manhattan emerge from the mist. The gigantic stone towers looked like the architectural fantasies of Sant'Elia's "Cyclopean cities" made real. A number of journalists had come aboard from the pilot boat to interview her. Margherita ignored their questions and stared in silence at the gray, dreamlike city. When she spoke, it was only to ask the reporters to name the enormous buildings that caught her eye.

Recovering her self-possession, Margherita answered questions about her itinerary and her first impressions of New York. She quickly turned the interview to Mussolini and Fascism. She insisted that Rome had become the cultural and political center of the world. It seemed clear to her that President Roosevelt's programs had been inspired by those of Mussolini. "She's giving the Fascist salute," she joked, pointing to the just visible Statue of Liberty in the misty harbor. "It is a very nice greeting upon my first visit to your country."

Elsewhere on the *Rex,* Butler was holding a press conference. He told reporters about his increasing admiration for Mussolini. Parroting Margherita, he said, "Rome again is becoming the capital of the Western world." He issued a written statement Margherita had helped him compose. Butler's handout blamed French stubbornness for encouraging the rise of the Nazis in Germany, and singled out the United States for encouraging a new naval arms race.

Margherita arrived in the United States well prepared and enthusiastically anticipated. Breckinridge Long had written letters of introduction for her to President Roosevelt, Secretary of State Cordell Hull, Undersecretary of State William Phillips, Attorney General Homer Cummings, Senator Key Pittman, Supreme Court Chief Justice Alfred Wheat, Democratic party senior statesman Edward House, and a number of other influential officials. Fascist party organizations along her intended route had prepared, along with the Italian Embassy and its consulates, a wide range of events in her honor. The Hearst press was ready to cover her activities in each of the cities where it controlled newspapers. And while the *Rex* was still steaming across the Atlantic, Missy's *Sunday Magazine* prominently featured an article by Margherita touting Mussolini's corporative state.[9]

Missy came on board to welcome Margherita. She whisked Margherita through immigration and customs, a courtesy provided by Breckinridge Long. After Missy made arrangements for the baggage they sped off in a taxi.[10] Instead of heading straight for Missy's apartment, Margherita wanted to drive uptown to catch a glimpse of Rockefeller Center. By early 1934, many of the buildings in the huge complex had been completed, although six more years would pass before the entire project was finished. The nineteen skyscrapers were already famous as the first coordinated urban development of such size and scope. With an army of 75,000 construction workers and tens of thousands of tenants and daily visitors, Rockefeller Center dwarfed anything that Margherita and Mussolini had planned for the reconstruction of Rome. It was a measure of the wealth of the United States that a complex beyond the resources of the Italian government had been financed, even in the grips of the Depression, by a single American, John D. Rockefeller, Jr.

The center had attracted controversy as well as praise for its starkly modern architecture. Margherita was enthusiastic about the style, and must have approved of the fasces decorating the facade opposite St. Patrick's Cathedral. She lamented the destruction just seven weeks before of Diego Rivera's mural *Man at the Crossroads,* though its political theme offended her Fascist sensibilities. Nelson Rockefeller, a great enthusiast of modern art, had sat beside Rivera on the scaffold the previous spring and watched with growing dismay as the painter created his huge wall painting in the RCA Building lobby. George Biddle had also visited frequently; his leftist leanings made him far more sympathetic toward Rivera's work-in-progress.

Rivera had depicted a representative worker holding in his hands all the power of contemporary science and technology. On one side stood the forces of capitalism ready to seize those resources for the purposes of greed, oppression, and war. Marx, Engels, Lenin, and Trotsky offered a clearly superior alternative from the left. John D. Rockefeller, Jr., decided to accept the mural if Rivera removed the head of Lenin. Rivera refused. Nelson begged Rivera to allow the painting to be removed from the RCA Building lobby and placed in the Rockefeller family's Museum of Modern Art, but Rivera proudly rejected the compromise and returned to Mexico in December.

Many intellectuals and artists, among them George Biddle, rallied to the cause of saving Rivera's work. No acceptable compromise could be found. At midnight on February 10, workmen hammered the masterpiece of propaganda into rubble. In place of Rivera's mural, José Maria Sert was commissioned to paint his mediocre monochrome *American Progress.*[11]

After their quick look at Rockefeller Center, Margherita and Missy drove down Fifth Avenue past the Empire State Building and on to Missy's home just north of Washington Square Park. Margherita spent her first few days in New York there. Late that afternoon, Margherita was visited by Harry Woodburn Chase, the chancellor of nearby New York University, and Antonio Grossardi, the Italian consul general. Grossardi's overt Fascist activities had raised a storm of controversy in New York. Margherita gave a short interview to Missy's friend Arthur S. Draper, the editor of the *Literary Digest,* and received a few other callers, including pro-Fascist Professor Bruno Roselli of Vassar College and editor A. J. Putnam. She ended the day with a long conversation with Grossardi over dinner.

The next morning, accompanied by Missy, Margherita began her inspection of the sights of Manhattan. She conducted a detailed examination of Grand Central Station, modeled on the Baths of Caracalla in Rome. She found the terminal an admirable work of art, and a superbly designed and functioning transportation center. That evening, Margherita dined with the architect Whitney Warren, the man who had designed Grand Central Station some twenty years earlier.[12]

For the remainder of her time in New York, Margherita stayed as planned at the Waldorf-Astoria Hotel on Park Avenue. Some days she devoted to sightseeing, shopping, private conversations, and dinners; some days she gave over to lectures, interviews, receptions, and other more public events. A few weeks later, *Newsweek* described Margherita's seventeen days in and around Manhattan as "Sight-seeing in New York, visiting American friends, dining out each night . . . half a dozen receptions, and perhaps a dozen lectures!" While Margherita sought amusement and self-promotion, she was also a tireless promoter of all things Italian. Even her wardrobe was an advertisement for an Italian friend who had only recently come to prominence in the field of international fashion. Throughout her visit, Margherita dressed entirely in what *Newsweek* characterized as the "simple, startlingly effective clothes" of Elsa Schiaparelli's Paris salon.[13]

Margherita usually pursued her propagandizing, political fact-finding, and intelligence gathering under the guise of fulfilling social obligations, holding press conferences, and attending receptions. She dropped in on Ranck at his office on her third day in New York. She succeeded in charming him, despite their previous difficulties—so much so that he almost forgot to mention that Fiammetta had failed to deliver the latest Mussolini article. It eventually arrived five days late.

Margherita also manipulated Ranck into arranging an interview for yet another article in the Hearst press later that week. She was quoted as describing capitalism as bankrupt and Fascism as the world's only hope. Before leaving his office, Margherita told Ranck of her desire to meet

Hearst and to visit San Simeon, his fabled home in California. Within a day, Ranck had persuaded Hearst to offer Margherita an invitation.[14]

Margherita and Missy spent Easter weekend with Theodore Roosevelt, Jr., and his family at their estate at Oyster Bay on Long Island. She spent two days in the big house filled with hunting trophies and the large and loving Roosevelt family. Adding to the pleasures of her stay was the unseasonably warm weather which brought on the first displays of pale green foliage. On Easter Sunday, Margherita attended high mass at the nearby Italian American church. She was moved to tears by the beauty of the service.

Margherita gathered a wealth of information from Mr. and Mrs. Roosevelt about their cousin, the president of the United States. Margherita returned to Manhattan on Monday knowing more than most Washington diplomats about the sensitive details of Franklin Roosevelt's marriage and extramarital affairs, his quirks and eccentricities, his strengths and weaknesses, and the extent of his paralysis. Eventually Margherita would share all these facts with Mussolini. He would add it to information gathered by a small number of Italian spies who had access to the president's family and friends.[15]

On April 2, after a day touring the city, Margherita went to the RCA Building to give a talk over the National Broadcasting Company radio network. Almost certainly, Marconi had arranged this for Margherita, thanks to his friendship and close professional relationship with David Sarnoff, the president of RCA and the chairman of NBC. To her millions of listeners, Margherita claimed the Fascist revolution had saved Italy from anarchy and class warfare, and restored it to national greatness. She pointedly mentioned her own involvement in those events, describing herself as a "modest but impassioned assistant of our chief, Mussolini." She praised Fascist authoritarianism and elitism as necessary for the undisciplined Italians. Fascist economic and social programs were responsible for leading Italy out of the Depression. She concluded:

> To truly understand Fascism, one must first understand this truth: that it is not a reactionary tyrannical movement or a blind, ferocious hatred of change. On the contrary, it is and intends always to grow into an even more democratic aristocracy, governed not by the people but for the people and for their interests, ruled by a hierarchy which is always open, in which all can join and in which the interests of all have penetrated.

Her canny paraphrase of Abraham Lincoln's words won the congratulations of the many Italian Americans in the studio audience. What pleased her most was the comment of one young woman who loved her blue

Schiaparelli gown: "Ah, Donna Margherita, how wonderful you look tonight! That dress becomes you marvelously."[16]

Margherita returned to the Waldorf for a dinner given in her honor by pro-Fascist Italian Americans. There she met Generoso Pope, the publisher of the largest Italian-language newspaper in the United States, *Il Progresso Italo-Americano,* and Mussolini's major spokesman in America. Also present were Lord Joseph Duveen, the business associate of Bernard Berenson, and Count Alessandro Contini-Bonacossi.[17]

On April 5, Mrs. Hearst gave a luncheon for Margherita at her mansion on Riverside Drive. There Margherita met Dorothy Thompson, Katherine Mayo, a number of other women writers, and Elsa Maxwell, the famous society hostess. Fannie Hurst, Margherita's friend and a frequent contributor to Hearst's *Cosmopolitan,* also attended the gathering.[18]

On the eighth Missy hosted a late-night formal dinner party for Margherita and the Society of American Authors and Editors. Margherita met Fiorello La Guardia, the new mayor of New York; Condé Nast, the publisher of *Vogue* and *Vanity Fair;* Clare Boothe Brokaw, Nast's managing editor at *Vanity Fair* (soon to become Clare Boothe Luce); Sinclair Lewis; the designer Norman Bel Geddes; Roy Howard, chairman of the Scripps-Howard newspaper chain; Nicholas Roosevelt, former U.S. ambassador to Hungary; sculptor Gutzon Borglum (then working on his monument on Mount Rushmore); Brock Pemberton, the theatrical producer; Robert Moses, New York City's all-powerful parks commissioner; the columnist Walter Lippmann; and Roy Chapman Andrews, the adventurous paleontologist famed for his fossil discoveries in the Gobi Desert. Missy had also invited Dorothy Thompson, Fannie Hurst, and a number of other editors, painters, poets, journalists, and authors of lesser note, along with their spouses.[19]

Between engagements Margherita held as many interviews as she could. She varied the subject matter as much as possible, speaking about Mussolini's generous support for the arts and the popularity of American literature in Italy on one occasion, on another extolling the Fascist regime's care for mothers and children.[20]

On April 10, she held a press conference at the Casa Italiana that Prezzolini had arranged with sixteen reporters specializing in foreign affairs. Prezzolini had dreaded the prospect of having to smooth the way for Margherita, with whom he had not gotten on well for many years. He worried about the behavior of the reporters, who he feared would come only to see "Mussolini's lover." To his relief, Margherita proved far more humble than he had expected. He attributed her new demeanor to her fall from Mussolini's favor. The press conference went well, and Prezzolini found himself fondly recalling the Margherita he had known twenty years earlier when she had collaborated with him on *La Voce*.[21]

That evening, Margherita addressed an audience of some seven hundred at a meeting of the World Affairs Institute. Sponsored by the American Women's Association at its West Fifty-seventh Street clubhouse, the event consisted of various speakers presenting their views on the problems facing the major world powers. Earlier that afternoon, Butler had admitted that liberal democracy had fallen into discredit since the onset of the Depression. Both at home and abroad, American ideals of individual freedom were challenged by advocates of Fascism and Communism. Time, he insisted, would prove the superiority of democracy. In the end, liberty would prove more effective than compulsion in solving the world's economic and political problems. Obviously neither Mussolini nor Margherita had been as successful as they had thought in converting Butler to their cause.

During the evening session, Butler served as chairman. After several speakers had discussed the Soviet and British situations, Butler introduced Margherita to the audience. In a speech similar to the one she had given over NBC radio, Margherita described Fascism as the only realistic solution to the world's problems. It was, she thought, an alternative preferable to either the defunct liberal democratic system or the bloody tyranny of Soviet Communism.

She argued that Fascism was essentially Socialism. Mussolini's government was committed to intervention in the social and economic spheres to improve the lives of the weak and disadvantaged. Contrary to what Fascism's critics claimed, it was not a "grim reaction for the benefit of the upper classes. . . . It was rule for the people but not by the people." She insisted that Fascism was superior to democracy: "We Italians no longer believe in the ballot box as some magical device where by putting something into the slot you draw out a box of chocolates." Despite her brazen attack on the American political system, the audience seemed quite impressed. The next day, Butler agreed: "You made a fine address last night and I saw from the audience how splendidly it was received."[22]

Margherita attended yet another banquet in her honor at the Waldorf on April 12, this one sponsored by the Italy America Society and the Royal Italian Orders. This dinner was the major official event on her New York itinerary. Pro-Fascists from the New York area gathered, along with local politicians, financiers, writers, and journalists, this time to hear Butler praise Margherita as a "second Columbus" who had sailed from Genoa to rediscover America. He praised Margherita's accomplishments but also offered his hopes that she would influence Mussolini to continue to guarantee the peace of Europe. In reply, Margherita declared that New York had turned out to be far more beautiful than she had dreamed and thanked everyone for the reception accorded her during her visit. She sat down to prolonged applause.[23]

On April 13, Margherita's last night in New York, she returned to the Casa Italiana to deliver a lecture on the *Novecento*. Margherita surprised many of her listeners by her direct treatment of a rather technical subject, and by her quick wit. She explained the aims of the *Novecento,* admitting there was not yet an official Fascist style. But she held that the collective vision of Fascism had inspired a return to the creation of great public murals, an Italian tradition from the days of Cimabue, Giotto, Rafael, and Tintoretto. She concluded by discussing the art and architecture she had seen in New York. The city's great skyscrapers and the murals that decorated them showed a similar concern with the role of art in inspiring the people. Surely the concrete towers reaching to the heavens were meant to thrill observers with the will to conquer, with a sense of power in action. While no similar gigantic structures existed in Italy, the architecture of the Fascist regime also stressed sharp and audacious vertical lines. This symbolized the aspirations of the Italian people toward an ever higher destiny. In a postscript to her talk Margherita urged a greater artistic and intellectual collaboration between Americans and Italians. Each had much to offer the other, she believed.[24]

Margherita kept a private schedule as extensive as her public one. On April 4, Margherita paid a visit to Edward House. Once Woodrow Wilson's closest adviser, Colonel House was now considered the Democratic party's senior statesmen. He and President Roosevelt frequently talked. When passing through New York, Roosevelt's major ambassadors never failed to give the colonel a report on their mission and solicit his opinion.

In a letter of introduction he had given Margherita to present to House, Breckinridge Long described her as "one of the very intelligent and able women of Italy" and an expert on European politics. In a private letter sent directly to House, Long wrote: "She knows more about what is going on in Italy than most men do. She has been a confidential operator with Mussolini . . . if you are interested in the Fascist movement, she can tell you a great deal in a short time, because she has been a part of it since it began."

In her talk with the colonel, Margherita was careful to commend Long. House passed her compliments along to the ambassador. Once they got down to serious matters, the colonel discovered Margherita to be so informative, and so receptive to his ideas, that a single conversation was insufficient. In another talk a few days later, Colonel House gave her an overview of Franklin Roosevelt's foreign policy.[25]

Two days after her first meeting with House, Margherita paid an evening visit to the Lower East Side offices of *Il Progresso,* accompanied by Consul Grossardi and a small group from the leadership of the pro-Fascist

Italian community in New York. After touring the newspaper's facilities and posing for a number of publicity pictures, Generoso Pope took his guests to dinner in nearby Chinatown. Margherita found the Chinese specialties quite appealing to the eye and judged the first mouthful delicious. As she sampled the assortment of exotic dishes, each successive bite pleased her less. Finally the peculiar flavors and aromas nauseated her. Her foray into Manhattan's Chinatown restaurant left her more convinced than ever of the unbridgeable gap between Occident and Orient.

A visit to Harlem and its nightclubs a few evenings later further reinforced her racial prejudices. While she enjoyed the jazz, her overall impression of African Americans was that they were "passionate" and had "the gift of rhythm" but that they remained "frankly primitive." Multiracial American society left her all the more convinced of the superiority of "White Civilization." She applauded the ways in which American whites kept other races under control. The limited new freedoms accorded African Americans by a sympathetic administration struck her as more than a little dangerous.[26]

Margherita made time for lunch alone with her friend Fannie Hurst at an Italian restaurant in Times Square. By 1934, Fannie Hurst had become close to President and Mrs. Roosevelt. In fact, she had sat at Franklin Roosevelt's right hand as they listened to the returns on the radio the night of his election. Since then, she had been a frequent guest at the White House. Obviously, Margherita must have encouraged Fannie to gossip in return for carefully chosen anecdotes about Mussolini. Margherita also accepted Clare Boothe Brokaw's invitation for an intimate dinner party. "Movie Czar" Will Hays, recently appointed to improve the morality of Hollywood films, took Margherita on her first walk through neon-lit Manhattan at night. He argued a laughing giant of an Irish cop into letting them cross the prohibited intersection of Fifth Avenue and Broadway. Will Hays supported Fascist Italy, and Margherita encouraged his sympathies.

Former New York Governor Al Smith, now president of the Empire State Building Corporation, showed Margherita the city from the top of the world's tallest skyscraper. Together they watched sunset fade into night as the streets below lit up with fifty million lights. She had a thoroughly enjoyable evening as Butler's guest at his house on Morningside Heights, where several Columbia professors amused her by elucidating the differences between the language as spoken in America and in England. Al Smith, like Butler, was a man whose connections made him worth cultivating. When she considered an invitation of little use, as was one from George Biddle to visit his home, Margherita courteously turned it down.[27]

Margherita bade a temporary farewell to Missy and Butler by presenting them with inscribed copies of *Dux*. Missy received yet another autographed photograph. Margherita promised to keep Butler informed of her progress by telegram, before flying to Washington on April 14. Extensive air travel was still quite novel in 1934—one of Missy's friends dubbed Margherita "Signora Seraph."[28]

The day Margherita flew out of the city, *The New York Times* carried two noteworthy stories. The first was a front-page interview Anne O'Hare McCormick had conducted with Mussolini. Mussolini spoke of his continued hope to reduce the level of armaments in Europe despite German departure from the League of Nations and the Geneva Disarmament Conference six months earlier:

> *Il Duce* insists the chief aim of Italian policy is peace.
> "I will peace; I need peace; we must have peace," he declared in clear English, each word like a hammer-stroke. "You say the people look to me to save the peace of Europe. Well, they are right. Italy will never start a war."

McCormick felt Mussolini was the greatest statesman in Europe: "By default of other leadership, Rome rides toward her ancient place—Caput Mundi—and rides with a certain fresh magnificence."[29]

The other story, given far less prominence, concerned the Johnson Act. A year after its introduction in the Congress, under great public pressure (in part orchestrated by the Hearst press), both houses passed the act, and the president signed it into law. The new law forbade any private individual or institution to buy or sell the bonds of any government, or to advance loans to a government, that had defaulted on its war debts to the United States. Roosevelt interpreted the Johnson Act as giving the Italian government two more months to pay before declaring it in default. But Mussolini could not pay the American government the remainder of the annual installment, the equivalent of 146 million lire in gold, before the deadline.

Mussolini had insisted to McCormick that he was devoted to peace at the very moment he was secretly planning his attack on Ethiopia. Costly preparations had consumed funds otherwise available for Italian debt repayment. Mussolini did not take the consequences of defaulting lightly, but he had no intention of delaying the military campaign. From June 15, 1934, he could no longer look to legal American loans to finance his invasion of Haile Selassie's empire.[30]

Official Washington received Margherita as if she were Mussolini's consort. After landing at National Airport, Margherita checked into the Mayflower Hotel, changed into an evening dress, and departed immediately for the Italian Embassy. There Ambassador Augusto Rosso hosted a banquet in her honor. Rosso had invited a number of knowledgeable guests to the dinner, among them the pro-Italian William R. Castle, who had served as undersecretary of state during the last two years of the Hoover administration. Rosso's major purpose was to prepare Margherita for her meeting with Franklin and Eleanor Roosevelt the next afternoon.[31]

The following day, April 15, was a beautiful Sunday, with the cherry trees blossoming along the banks of the Potomac. It amused Margherita to learn that the cherry trees had been a gift from the Japanese emperor to Theodore Roosevelt. They seemed a strangely delicate token of affection between two nations that now seemed to be moving inexorably toward war.

She passed the morning and early afternoon visiting the Capitol Building, the nearby Library of Congress—the idea of collecting every book in print struck her as both marvelous and absurd—and the Lincoln Memorial. The statue of the martyred president brought back memories of Giolitti. To her mind, both men were rustics, rather grudgingly transformed by their genius into political leaders. At four o'clock, she went to the White House. She was treated first to a guided tour of the presidential mansion while the president was out taking a drive around the city.[32]

At 5:00 P.M., once Franklin Roosevelt had settled back into the executive suite, Margherita was ushered in. She entered a sitting room to find President and Eleanor Roosevelt, along with their son James and his wife, awaiting her. Breckinridge Long had written to the president that Margherita was "probably the best-informed woman in Italy," and someone who knew Mussolini's mind intimately. Roosevelt had prepared himself accordingly.

Thinking back on her hour with Franklin Roosevelt, Margherita remembered his geniality most of all. "He played the fascination of his smile like Paganini played his violin," she later noted. Unlike some observers, Margherita did not mistake the president's charm and relaxed wit for an absence of intelligence or willpower. Her talks with Theodore Roosevelt, Jr., had made her acutely aware of Franklin Roosevelt's paralysis and suffering. His evident lack of self-pity and his enormous good humor struck Margherita as proof of the man's tremendous inner strength and confidence. His demeanor offered an instructive contrast with Mussolini's. Despite his far better physical condition, the Duce continued to suffer from frequent bouts of acute anxiety.

Once tea had been served, the president brought the conversation around to Europe, and to Italy in particular. Roosevelt's intimate knowledge of Italian affairs astonished Margherita. Clearly he was not relying on a hasty briefing prior to the meeting. Eleanor's comments about Italy made Margherita bristle. While Margherita did not detail the first lady's remarks in her later account of the meeting, it seems that she made a number of barbed observations about the nature of Fascism and Mussolini's tyranny. To Margherita's great relief, the president gently corrected a few of his wife's facts and moved the talk on to other matters.

Franklin Roosevelt was quite interested in Italo-Austrian relations. To Margherita's surprise, the president revealed a detailed knowledge of the geography of the Italo-Austrian frontier. In answer to her questions, Roosevelt laughingly replied that he had not always been immobile. With a knapsack on his back, he had made an extensive walking tour of the Tyrolean Alps in August 1903, and his memories of that vacation had remained vivid for the last thirty years. The president thought German aggression against Austria was likely. He had studied the matter with care, and relied on Mussolini to defend Italy's small northern neighbor.

Roosevelt mentioned their mutual friend George Biddle and the artist's plans to hire out-of-work artists to decorate government buildings. Margherita voiced her enthusiasm for the project. The president was pleased that government support for art helped the jobless and at the same time improved the quality of life of the average American. But he had more important projects in mind, he said, and launched into a discussion of reforestation, soil conservation, and irrigation.

In regard to the wider question of unemployment, the president was optimistic about the future. He told Margherita that the American domestic market was so enormous that once demand had been stimulated, the American Depression would come to an end. He offered an impressive array of statistics to support his argument. Then he caught himself and smiled. "Watch out," he told Margherita, and quoted Mark Twain's remark about "lies, damned lies and statistics." It was important to remember, he pointed out, that the figures he cited represented real men and women, weighed down under the sorrows brought on by the collapse of the economy.

The time for their talk came to an end. To Margherita's surprise, two Secret Service agents entered the room, helped Roosevelt to his feet, and gave him his crutches. Completely unperturbed, Roosevelt continued his good-byes to Margherita. His smile was as radiant as ever, despite the strain of supporting himself upright.[33]

Margherita left the White House deeply impressed by Roosevelt's personality and his knowledge of foreign affairs. She telegraphed Long immediately to inform the ambassador that she had seen the Roosevelts, and to thank him for arranging their conference. A reporter from *The Washington Post* interviewed her the following day and noted the pleasure she had taken in the meeting. Twenty years afterward the memory was still fresh in her mind.

Three days later she attended one of Roosevelt's weekly press conferences. This reinforced her admiration for the man and the system that had produced him. Once again she noticed his quiet self-confidence, exuberant good humor, and ability to disguise any sign of his affliction. She was intrigued by Roosevelt's voluntary subjection to regular interrogations, and by the journalists' willingness to respect his refusal to answer certain questions and to keep confidential an occasional "off the record" answer. Whatever its faults, the American system had developed an extraordinary blend of freedom and authority, of equality and hierarchy. Even a tea with Alice Roosevelt Longworth (sister of Theodore Roosevelt, Jr.), who provided more scurrilous gossip about the president and his wife, failed to shake Margherita's admiration for Franklin Delano Roosevelt.[34]

Margherita divided her remaining time in Washington, much as she had in New York, among public receptions, dinners, sightseeing, and private conversations. She attended fewer public events in the U.S. capital, devoting more of her hours to talks with government officials. Her main opportunity to meet Washington society came at a reception at the Sulgrave Club on the rainy afternoon of April 16, arranged by the local chapter of the Italy America Society. The Italian Embassy staff assisted members of the society in decorating the club dining room with flowers and candles in the Italian national colors. Margherita arrived at the reception in another Schiaparelli gown, of brown velvet with gold brocade sleeves, and with a small matching hat. For the better part of the next hour, Margherita greeted dozens of notables, assisted by Ambassador Rosso. News of her success in New York had preceded her and she found herself surrounded with a host of curious and attentive Washingtonians.

Margherita's smiling face hid her weariness with these occasions. The obligatory firm American handshakes and endless repetitions of "How-do-you-do" were proving tiresome. In her mind, the "Du-du" ceremony and the formulaic inquiries after her health were absurd. Shortly before five o'clock, Margherita finished with the reception line and delivered her talk on modern Italian art. Then she escaped to her hotel room.[35]

Accompanied by a friend of Missy's, who served as her guide, Margherita spent most of the next day on a relaxing visit to Mount Vernon. George Washington's simple and classically inspired home delighted her, as did the scenery along the Potomac, enhanced by perfect spring weather. Margherita noted with satisfaction the first American president's elitist attitudes and opposition to democracy. She felt these were traditions U.S. leaders would be wise to revive. At the same time, she admired Washington's renunciation of power by refusing to run for a third term as president. By the spring of 1934, Mussolini had been head of the Italian government for eleven and a half years, and he showed no intention of stepping down.[36]

After returning to the capital, Margherita called on Secretary of Labor

Frances Perkins. Perkins was the first American woman Cabinet secretary, indeed the first woman to hold an executive office of such power in any modern government. Margherita knew that the Department of Labor played an important role in Roosevelt's New Deal policies: "Madame Secretary" was far more than a figurehead. Perkins reinforced Margherita's respect by a lucid explanation of the role her department was playing in overcoming the Depression. The demeanor of Perkins's male aides particularly impressed Margherita. Their behavior clearly indicated their respect for Secretary Perkins. How different from the sneers, condescension, and outright hostility Margherita had suffered from Fascist thugs like Farinacci, and even her former colleagues in the Socialist movement.[37]

Margherita spent the evening at the annual meeting of the Daughters of the American Revolution. The ceremonies and protocol of the organization struck her as old-fashioned, but she was envious at the way America's leading politicians courted the assembled women. Margherita recognized that the members of the D.A.R. hardly typified American women. It was precisely the concentration of conservative political power and wealth among the five thousand delegates that affected her. These women had no use for reform, let alone revolutionary politics. They were already confident in the position of authority they held, even though they represented only a tiny minority of the electorate.[38]

Her stay in Washington was too short to do everything that she would have liked. Despite Breckinridge Long's letters of introduction, Margherita failed to see Senator Key Pittman, chairman of the Foreign Relations Committee, or Congressman William Oliver of the Appropriations Committee.[39] She did find time for at least one unplanned meeting, probably arranged by Missy, with William J. Donovan. "Wild Bill" Donovan was a disappointed Republican politician who had managed to build a lucrative international law practice in New York and Washington. Donovan was one of America's greatest heroes from World War I, and was fascinated by the business of intelligence gathering. Despite his party affiliation, he was a close acquaintance of the president.

Donovan was a member of an extraordinary association in New York founded by Roosevelt's friend Vincent Astor, a private intelligence organization known as "The Room." Members included prominent publishers, bankers, lawyers, judges, stockbrokers, and academics. Many had served as intelligence officers in the World War. Theodore Roosevelt, Jr., belonged, as did Roy Chapman Andrews, whom Margherita had met in New York. At least as early as 1933, "The Room" had been supplying Franklin Roosevelt with information outside of official government channels. Margherita and Donovan agreed to stay in contact, but the details of their discussion are unknown.[40]

Margherita concluded her public appointments in Washington on April 18. Undersecretary of State William Phillips and his wife gave a luncheon for Margherita at the State Department, which Frances Perkins attended. Undersecretary Phillips was charmed by Margherita, and was happy to grant her diplomatic privileges for a trip she planned to Havana. She had the same effect at the Italian Embassy as the State Department. Whatever her previous reputation, Margherita was completely amiable to her hosts. Ambassador Rosso extended an unanticipated invitation to a small dinner party he gave for Supreme Court Chief Justice Charles Evans Hughes. The ambassador considered her visit to Washington a complete success.[41]

Details of Margherita's subsequent itinerary in Florida and Cuba are undetermined. She apparently spent several days each at Daytona and Miami Beach, recovering from her strenuous activities in New York and Washington. Thoroughly refreshed, she took a flight across the Straits of Florida to Cuba. She landed in Havana late on the evening of April 23.[42] Her hopes to sample the city's fabled nightlife were disappointed. Starting in the late summer of 1933, the small country had undergone a succession of four bloody revolutions. By early 1934, real power was in the hands of Colonel Fulgencio Batista, but revolutionary violence continued in Havana unabated.

Throughout her brief stay in the city, she heard exploding bombs and volleys of gunfire. By the evening of each day, despite the discomfort of remaining indoors in the tropical heat, the population abandoned the streets to the combatants. Margherita secured an invitation to dinner with Batista through the Italian Embassy. About midday, she received a visit from the colonel's aide-de-camp. Would Donna Sarfatti excuse her host if he served at table that evening with his left hand? It seems that Batista had fallen from his horse that morning and injured his right arm.

Over dinner, Margherita judged Batista to be intelligent and strong-willed—a man of the people who, like Mussolini, had seized control of his country. She learned from him in considerable detail how subordinate his country had become to the United States. Sugar dominated the Cuban economy, and the United States bought all of Cuba's sugar. The next day Margherita learned the truth about his injury. Batista had been wounded by a bomb in an unsuccessful assassination attempt.[43]

From Havana, she flew to the island of Cozumel off the east coast of the Yucatán. From there she visited the recently restored Mayan temples and pyramids at Uxmal and Chichén Itzá. The mysterious, magical Mayan ruins proved a welcome relief from the gunfire of Havana. The reliefs carved into the walls of palaces, ceremonial ball courts, and skull racks portrayed the deaths of sacrificial victims. There was a sacrificial well at

Chichén Itzá, where every year a virgin had been drowned to propitiate the Mayan rain god. Margherita was fascinated by the peculiar horror and beauty of the artifacts. Once again, the vestiges of another society reinforced Margherita's faith in the superiority of "White Civilization." Although they had destroyed the splendid cities of Mexico, the Conquistadores had at least stamped out the rites of human sacrifice. And she was heartened to consider that so few Spanish had overcome so many Indians in their attempt to expand their European domains.[44]

Margherita traveled next to Mexico City, where she stayed for five days. She spent hours in the old Mexican national museum, studying the sculpture, jewelry, and pottery of the Aztecs, Toltecs, Maya, Olmecs, and other indigenous cultures. She walked the cobblestone streets of the colonial center of the city, visiting the cavernous cathedral and the palaces built by Cortés. She traveled outside the capital to admire the gigantic Pyramids of the Sun and the Moon at Teotihuacán, larger even than the Egyptian pyramids she had seen at Giza and Sakkara. She drove 13,000 feet up toward the snow-covered top of the 17,000-foot-high Popocatepetl volcano. From its rim she viewed the breathtaking panorama below her, extending hundreds of miles to the glistening Pacific in the crystal air of that preindustrial time. She drifted slowly by boat along the canals of Xochimilco, past the profusion of flower gardens along the banks. She toured the legendary Shrine of Guadalupe and stood before the miraculous image of the Virgin. She assiduously questioned her guides to gain an understanding of Mexican history. The blood, glory, and passion of the country's past and present enthralled her.[45]

Thirteen years had passed since Margherita had last seen Diego Rivera. Diametrically opposed political positions separated them from the days when they had been friends in prewar Paris and postwar Milan. He continued to be a supporter of Leon Trotsky. But the recent RCA Building mural controversy had piqued Margherita's interest, and during her five days in the Mexican capital she had finally seen some of the famous murals Rivera had painted there since his return to Mexico in 1921.

Rivera painted themes from Mexican history and Indian culture in a bold polemical style, often verging on the grotesque. The Indians were Rivera's heroes or victims, while the Spanish, French, and American invaders of Mexico were the villains and exploiters. His genius infused these images with such passion, clarity, and strength that their artistic truth transcended any historical or political distortions. Rivera had managed a nearly impossible feat of artistic synthesis. His paintings were immediately appealing to uneducated peasants and sophisticated connoisseurs alike.

Margherita was as repelled by Rivera's work as she was attracted to it. She felt that even polemical art should express a positive faith *in* something, not simply an attack on perceived evils. Rivera's capitalists were pigs in human dress, his generals were snarling beasts—she found the vulgar Marxism underlying Rivera's vision unintentionally comic. Yet she could not help being intensely moved by the sweep and grandeur of his creations. And she recognized how much of the artist's work had been inspired by the frescoes of Paolo Uccello and Piero della Francesca.

Years before, Rivera had told her he hated Spain but adored Italy; whatever good the Conquistadores and missionaries had brought Mexico he believed was borrowed from the Italian Renaissance. Rivera's murals paid homage to Aztec and Maya wall painting, but clearly were far more influenced by what he had seen in Italy in 1920 and 1921. How could Margherita fail to admire such a striking tribute to Italian art? What she was seeing in Mexico City made the American public art she had seen almost pathetic in comparison.

After viewing Rivera's work, Margherita could not resist contacting her old friend, whatever their present differences. She left no precise account of their meeting; Rivera did, but he was a notorious liar, and his story seems exaggerated. He claimed that he was awakened by a telephone call in the middle of the night. A local art dealer excitedly told him that a beautiful European woman had just purchased every one of the Rivera paintings in his gallery. She wanted to speak to Rivera before departing. When Margherita came on the line, he immediately recognized her voice:

> Diego, you old fool, I've been thrown over by the Old Man and now even you refuse to speak to your old Parisian friend. I wanted to speak to you, not for personal reasons, but because I have a message from him which I must give you before I leave Mexico. Mussolini instructed me to tell you how much your work is appreciated in Italy, and that anytime you wish to come to Italy, you're welcome. You can paint whatever you like, and everything you need will be at your disposal. He also said this: if you ever feel there's no safe place left in the world for you to plant your feet, you'll always find a haven in Italy.

According to Rivera, he declined politely. He felt Mussolini was far more likely to need a place of refuge than he ever would.[46]

In fact, despite his later denials, Rivera escorted her to galleries and museums. For all his supposed idealism, Rivera had sold himself to the corrupt politicians who had ruled Mexico since the revolution of 1910–1920. He had returned from New York in December 1933 depressed and in poor health. By April 1934, he had been unable to work for several months. Margherita might have tried to enliven Rivera by suggesting he return to Italy. Perhaps she hoped Rivera would share with Sironi his new approaches to political muralism. But Margherita was in no position to make an offer on Mussolini's behalf, as Rivera claimed. And even if she had been, Rivera's recent insulting portrait of Mussolini would have checked her.[47]

While in Manhattan, Rivera had included Mussolini in a panel of his "Portrait of America" series for the New Workers School on West Fourteenth Street. In the background, Rivera depicted the Blackshirts executing some anti-Fascists, administering castor-oil treatments to others, and burning buildings. In the foreground, Pius XI blessed Mussolini as he delivered a speech applauded by Prezzolini, Father Charles Coughlin (the pro-Mussolini "Radio Priest"), and J. P. Morgan. Facing the viewer was Matteotti, about to be stabbed in the back. Most likely Margherita had recently seen this work, or at least knew of it, since it was completed just before her arrival in New York.

Margherita was relieved to leave Mexico City for Los Angeles on May 3. She looked forward to returning to the familiarity and efficiency of the United States. The flight took nearly twelve hours. After taking off, the single-engine plane returned to Mexico City because the pilot had forgotten his cargo of mailbags. These were unceremoniously dumped in the passenger compartment—Margherita carried one in her lap. In flight her sleeve wrapped around the door handle and she nearly opened it by accident. She fantasized about hurtling through space to the gray-brown mountains below. Twice the pilot lost his way. She was more than relieved to have arrived safely.[48]

She found Los Angeles comfortable and entertaining, although she had little chance for rest. On May 4, she visited the Metro-Goldwyn-Mayer Studios for a luncheon in her honor. Louis B. Mayer welcomed her. Mayer had close ties to a number of Margherita's American acquaintances. Mayer and William Randolph Hearst were partners in the motion-picture business, and Hearst's film-star mistress, Marion Davies, had a contract with MGM. Hearst's friend Amedeo Giannini provided financing for MGM through his Bank of America. And now all the Hollywood studio heads made their pictures under the watchful eye of Margherita's new friend Will Hays.[49]

Before lunch, Mayer escorted Margherita through his studios. She looked in on Marion Davies completing work on *Operator 13,* which co-starred Gary Cooper. She watched Maurice Chevalier adjusting his belt and braided kepi one take after another for a few seconds of film in *The Merry Widow.* She observed the same patient attention to detail as Norma Shearer repeated over and over a scene for *The Barretts of Wimpole Street.* She also looked in on William Powell and Myrna Loy as they were filming *The Thin Man.*

Margherita had long been an enthusiastic fan of American pictures and, despite her sophistication, had been slightly in awe of Hollywood movie stars. Now she saw them as professionals hard at work creating an illusion of glamour. Still, Margherita was excited when Mayer introduced her to the film actors after each had finished his or her scene on the set. Their informal Hollywood manners were surprising; she had previously thought of them as a kind of royalty.

Soon it was time for lunch and Mayer brought Margherita to one of the MGM dining rooms. There she was greeted by the Marchese Dalla Rosa, the Italian consul in Los Angeles, Will Hays, Irving Thalberg, Amedeo Giannini, director Frank Capra (fresh from the success of *It Happened One Night*), a group of MGM stars, and a number of prominent local Italian Americans.

In their remarks after lunch, Mayer and Hays stressed their admiration for Mussolini and his Fascist regime. Sicilian-born Capra pointed out the physical similarities between Italy and California, which had attracted many Italians to the state. Giannini praised *The Life of Benito Mussolini* and outlined its contents for the luncheon guests. Margherita told of her love for American films, and her amazement at the size and variety of the United States. She compared the belief in progress shared by Mussolini's Italy and Roosevelt's America. And the United States also had its dictators, she pointed out, comparing Mayer and other studio heads to the Duce. Her informal talk delighted her audience, who stood to applaud her.[50]

Two days later, Margherita was feted at a dinner in Pasadena hosted by Zoe Atkins. Among the guests were Irving Thalberg and his wife, Norma Shearer, Gilbert Roland, the Prince of Thurn and Taxis, and Italian Consul Dalla Rosa. The Italian-American Society of Los Angeles gave Margherita a luncheon the next day at the Biltmore Hotel. Finally, on May 11 at UCLA, Margherita described the similarities between Fascist Corporativism and the New Deal programs to a large gathering of students and faculty:

> Many people believe Fascism to be a sort of hard, grim reactionary movement against the working class. It is nothing of the sort. When Italy was on the verge of Bolshevism . . . Fascism saved us. It is not a capitalistic organization. It is rather a union of people all being inspired by the Government.

During the rest of the week, Margherita relaxed in Hollywood. She decided that Los Angeles was the most modern of any city she had seen, and among the most beautiful. She found the Pacific magnificent and invigorating. After some hesitation and amusement, she also came to appreciate the novel luxury of private swimming pools.

One night, while driving with friends back to Hollywood, Margherita was involved in an automobile collision. She escaped injury, but one of her companions had to be rushed to the hospital by ambulance. What impressed her most was not her narrow escape but the efficiency of the police and their modern communications equipment. The speed with which the police arrived on the scene, summoned medical assistance, and completed a thorough report on the accident surpassed anything she had seen in Italy. It offered one more example of America's technological superiority.

Margherita left Los Angeles for a few days to visit the Grand Canyon and the Petrified Forest. At the Grand Canyon, she gained a sense of the scale of America. When she stood at the edge of the huge chasm carved by the Colorado River, she remembered, "I did not believe that it could be true, at the same time that I looked at it." The immensity of the canyon, the millions of years that had passed in its creation, the ever-changing color of the rock as the desert sun moved across the sky, all filled her with an overpowering sense of human insignificance. Less overwhelming but equally humbling feelings accompanied her visit to the Petrified Forest. In comparison to the variegated array of stone trees, the works of human art seemed vain and transient. She flew back to Los Angeles in a reverie.[51]

Next she flew in Hearst's private plane to his mountaintop complex at San Simeon. Since 1919, Hearst's personal architect, Julia Morgan, had been at work transforming a treeless hill overlooking the Pacific into the grounds for a pleasure palace. By 1934, the summit held three so-called "guest houses," each of palatial dimensions, and La Casa Grande, a monstrous twin-towered assemblage of bits and pieces of castles gathered from across Europe and shipped to Southern California.

On the slopes of La Cuesta Encantada, "The Enchanted Hill," Hearst had planted an amazing variety of trees, bushes, and shrubs. Here and there meadows and beds of brilliant flowers broke the wooded expanse. All these plants had been hauled over the mountains or up from the sea. Up the hill from the coast highway ran Hearst's private road, some six miles long. Beside the road, on a large unfenced portion of the 265,000 acres that surrounded his home, lived large herds of camel, yak, llama, giraffe, gazelle, gnu, zebra, kangaroo, bison, and other exotic species. A private zoo of carnivorous animals stood a quarter mile from the walls of La Casa Grande. Elsewhere on the vast estate, Hearst kept ten thousand head of cattle and several small herds of thoroughbred horses.

To build all this, Hearst had for fifteen years been spending most of his annual $15 million income. Once the Depression had curbed his flow of revenue, the publisher had plunged deeply into debt to continue construction. By 1934, he had borrowed at least $110 million. The gardens and interior of the palaces held even more fabulous riches than the grounds. For fifty years, and over recent decades through Joseph Duveen, Hearst had spent $50 million or more on art acquisitions.

The gardens on La Cuesta Encantada held hundreds of statues, busts, columns, sarcophagi, capitals, and even the facades of entire buildings that had survived from the Roman Empire or medieval Europe. The four residences contained Venetian and stained glass, gold and silver dinnerware, glazed terra-cotta, and a countless profusion of paintings, bronzes, tapestries, enameled reliquaries, Oriental rugs, suits of armor, Greek vases, Etruscan urns, and rare books and manuscripts. Each bedroom was furnished with museum-quality antiques. The common rooms were decorated with richly carved wooden ceilings, huge chandeliers, ornate staircases, and elaborate marble fireplaces carried off from the ruined manors of Europe. Even more art objects lay crated in giant basement crypts or in nearby storehouses.

There were fountains and pools. The indoor swimming pool was eighty feet long and forty feet wide, entirely faced with Murano tile. Pacific saltwater was pumped into it from the ocean below. There was a huge outdoor swimming pool, along with tennis courts, billiard rooms, and a sumptuous movie theater. Hearst gave legendary parties every weekend, to which his private train or airplanes brought his guests from Hollywood. By day, movie stars relaxed in the informal atmosphere, using Hearst's extended sports facilities or adventuring out on luxurious picnics. While Hearst lived a very abstemious existence, he maintained a vast wine cellar, and a kitchen to rival the finest European restaurants. There was a splendid dinner each night at San Simeon, often followed by an advance screening of a motion picture (he showed *Gone with the Wind* to his guests six months before its premiere in December 1939), a costume ball, or some other special entertainment.[52]

After seeing all this, Margherita marveled at the relative simplicity of the private plane that brought her to San Simeon. She wondered why Hearst had not turned it into a flying palace. Everything else about La Cuesta Encantada seemed fantastic. Hearst selected for Margherita a room furnished in Venetian Renaissance style. After settling in, she wandered about the grounds. She amused herself by identifying the provenance of each art object and found herself almost dizzy at the incongruous assemblage.[53]

Margherita's absence from Rome had thrown the schedule for the Mussolini articles into hopeless disarray. Hearst and Ranck once again had considered not renewing the contract at the end of the year. But in early May, Mussolini decided to write an article for the Hearst press personally and ensure its arrival in New York while Margherita was in Los Angeles.

It may have been coincidence or it may have sprung from Mussolini's desire to prevent a painful incident between Hearst and Margherita. In any case, the article arrived on May 9, and was pleasing to both Hearst and Ranck.

In his article, Mussolini declared that the League of Nations efforts at disarmament had failed. He added that Italian efforts to bring about a reconciliation between France and Germany, particularly through the Four Power Pact, had also come to nothing. While he did not say so explicitly, the implications of Mussolini's article were clear. Europe was headed for war; Italy would embark on a major rearmament program and, sooner or later, would have to take sides in the deadly quarrel between France and Germany. The article reflected official policy, and Mussolini ordered it published in *Il Popolo d'Italia* on May 18. Later that month, in a speech before the Chamber of Deputies, Mussolini made his warning about war explicit. These statements certainly were a provocative contrast to the interview he had granted to Anne O'Hare McCormick just a month before.

Hearst instructed Ranck to feature the article on the front page of every Hearst newspaper on Sunday, May 13, under a dire headline. Mussolini delayed Italian publication, giving Hearst an important scoop. Thus, when Hearst came down to lunch with Margherita on the early afternoon of May 12, he was in an excellent mood to meet his guest.[54]

After lunch, Hearst showed Margherita around his estate. First he took her to see his caged animals. She was apprehensive about the consequences of one escaping, but he explained the precautions he had taken. Then he showed her the priceless contents of his library, and a private museum containing his most prized art works.

Later that day, she took advantage of the outdoor pool for a vigorous swim, but it did not lift her deepening sense of oppression. The riotous excess, the anarchy of conflicting artistic styles, the incalculable fortune spent to indulge just one man, overcame her usual tolerance and curiosity. Hearst's creation challenged every notion Margherita had harbored about the limits of private wealth and the obligations of social justice. The lavish dinner that evening in the great hall and the dancing that followed brought her only temporary distractions. That night, the growls and snarls of the big cats pacing in their cages made it difficult for her to sleep.

On Sunday, she borrowed one of the publisher's chauffeured cars to attend mass at a small church near the ocean, and afterward took a long drive along the curving Pacific coast highway. She found the simple coastal towns, the majestic sea, and the rolling green hills a relief after the excesses of San Simeon. On Monday, she left for San Francisco.[55]

The Italian consul, representatives of San Francisco's large Italian colony, and reporters for the local Hearst newspaper met Margherita at the airport. In response to their questions about Mussolini, she told the journalists: "The Premier is today more powerful than ever. He is certain to be a pattern for government leaders during the next several centuries." Then she was ushered off to the Fairmont Hotel, where she wired Butler that she had arrived safely.

Margherita landed in San Francisco in the middle of a violent dock strike that had paralyzed the shipping industry. The contrast between what she had just observed at San Simeon and the misery that drove longshoremen to battle police and the National Guard almost defied description. With every passing day, she was affected more deeply by American extremes of wealth and poverty, of gentility and crime, of urban squalor and natural magnificence. Despite Roosevelt's efforts, it became clear to her that the Depression was far worse in America than it was in Europe.

The scenery and climate in California made it very like Italy, but its social unrest and lawlessness were not so familiar. Every day, the papers of the Hearst press were filled with lurid stories of John Dillinger's robberies and murders, and the criminal exploits of Bonnie Parker and Clyde Barrow, then burning their way across Oklahoma and Texas. On the one hand, Americans deplored lawlessness; on the other, they seemed to render it heroic. Americans worshiped their concept of freedom, yet these same attitudes seemed to render government powerless to act against the individual outlaws and the organized criminal gangs that preyed on American society.

By the time she had arrived in San Francisco, Margherita had decided to record her American adventure in a book. She felt that she could only encompass her experiences in a novel. American reality seemed too wild for any other approach.[56]

Like most visitors, Margherita found San Francisco beautiful, and its perpetual spring climate invigorating. The bridges stretching across the bay to Oakland offered another example of an American triumph over the challenges of nature. A visit to San Francisco's Chinatown did nothing to diminish her racism. Despite their American dress and mannerisms, she felt totally estranged from the Chinese Americans who passed her in the streets. She held a long conversation with the prominent Chinese-born newspaper editor Ng Poon Chew. He mentioned that, in addition to his work for a Ph.D., he had studied the ancient Chinese classics in order to pass the qualifying examinations as a mandarin. To Margherita, this was proof of the man's refusal to abandon his Asian heritage and become a true member of "White Civilization."

She found the soaring grandeur of the rock formations and the trees in Yosemite National Park more to her liking. She journeyed next to Salt

Lake City.[57] Her plane arrived on a clear night, flying over stars reflected in the Great Salt Lake from an unblemished desert sky. Members of the local Italian community brought Margherita to her hotel. The next morning, she attended a concert at the Mormon Tabernacle, and then at a reception she met the governor of Utah and the mayor of Salt Lake City. Afterward she had a long conversation with Anthony Ivins, the second president of the Church of Jesus Christ of Latter-Day Saints. Margherita had known nothing previously of the history and theology of the Mormons. She was fascinated by Ivins's account, as well as by his stories of Mormon missionary work among the Indians. She discovered the Mormons admired Mussolini and Fascism. Italian Consul Fortunato Anselmo had been extraordinarily successful in creating a favorable image of the regime. After only twelve hours she took off on another long flight, heading east to Chicago, fourteen hours away by air.[58]

Both legs of her long aerial journey from the shores of the Pacific to Lake Michigan were far more pleasant than her previous flights. United Airlines had introduced stewardesses only four years earlier, and was the first airline in the world to do so. The youth of the stewardesses, their diminutive size, and their training as nurses was another impressive example of American efficiency. United used the Boeing 247 aircraft in its transcontinental flights. Considered the first modern airliner, and developed from the B-9 bomber, the 247 was fast (155 miles per hour) and fuel-efficient. It cut commercial flight time across the United States by one third, to nineteen and a half hours. The passenger compartments of 247s resembled those of modern airliners. Soundproof, with hot water available for drinks, well-upholstered seats, and an air-circulation system, the 247s brought a unique level of luxury to air travel. All this gave Margherita the picture of a society hurtling into the future on the wings of technology. It seemed like something out of D'Annunzio's poetry or the dreams of the Futurists.[59]

She landed in Chicago late on May 20. The next afternoon, accompanied by the Italian consul, Giuseppe Castruccio, she appeared at a reception in her honor, held by the local chapter of the Italy America Society. After she held forth on Italy's leading role in the arts, a toast was offered to the Duce. A day later, she played guest of honor again at a luncheon held at the headquarters of the Chicago Exposition, then in its second season. Her black crepe dress, another Schiaparelli creation, impressed the Chicago socialites in attendance. Margherita expressed admiration for America and then escaped to view the world's fair, called "A Century of Progress." The strong accent on technology reinforced her sense of the United States as a society dominated by machines.[60]

Margherita had basically fulfilled her obligations in Chicago and was free to tour the city. A visit to the stockyards left her nauseated and horrified. While she appreciated Sullivan and Wright's innovative skyscrapers, and a lengthy visit to the Chicago Art Institute, the city alienated her.

Standing on a moonlit night at a window in a millionaire's apartment, she gazed at the lights of the city reflected in Lake Michigan, and the vivid neon and searchlights of the Chicago Exposition. Her thoughts drifted away from the party she was attending. Her host and his obsession with money, the macabre stockyards, and her sense of America's worship of the machine coalesced in an apocalyptic vision. She saw a Chicago three thousand years hence, a smashed ruin of a great city, destroyed in a war brought on by greed and the monstrous engines of war. The summer before, Italo Balbo had succeeded in leading his squadron of seaplane bombers across the Atlantic to the Chicago Exposition. The feat suggested that no place on earth enjoyed safety from war any longer.[61]

From Chicago she traveled to Buffalo. She flew over Niagara Falls, and later stood beside the falls in sunlight and at night. The sense that America existed on a different scale returned. She had time for hasty visits to Philadelphia and Boston. Both cities evidenced the overwhelming influence of England on America. She could see that Anglo-Saxon attitudes dominated the centers of power and culture. She concluded that Italian Americans would rise to positions of power only by adopting the mentality of the Protestant ruling class. This seemed to be happening naturally. Because of the variety of regional dialects, most Italian immigrants could communicate with each other only in English. Already their children were being assimilated into the Anglo-Saxon mainstream. If the United States was forced to choose sides between Italy and Britain, Margherita had no doubt that it would choose the latter.[62]

She flew back to New York from Boston on the morning of June 2, staying again at the Waldorf. She was exhausted. Since leaving New York seven weeks earlier, she had travelled over ten thousand miles, mostly in small trimotor airliners. She now looked forward to a week's relaxation in New York, and another seven days of leisurely sea travel back to Italy. Her one remaining official obligation was a dinner commemorating Italian entry into World War I. Margherita was to deliver the speech in honor of Italy's war dead.[63]

That evening, Ambassador Rosso, Consul General Grossardi, Margherita, and two thousand others gathered at the West Sixty-second Street Armory. After dining, the audience stood while the band played the national anthems of the victorious Allies. The chorus sang the Fascist anthem, "Giovanezza." Then Rosso addressed the gathering, which included many American, British, French, Belgian, Polish, and American veterans, representatives of local American Legion posts, and a large contingent of Boy Scouts. The ambassador reminded his listeners that Fascism had had its birth in the war, and pointed out how appropriate it was for Margherita to address them on this occasion. After a salute to President Roosevelt and the United States, Rosso called on those present to join him in shouting *"Evviva il Re! Evviva Il Duce! Evviva l'Italia!"* Once the echoes had died in the great hall, Margherita rose to speak.

On her dress, she wore Roberto's *medaglia d'oro*. She told those present that Roberto had not died in vain. Not only had he and the other Italian dead saved their country from German conquest, they had sown the seeds for the Fascist revolution. Now a reborn Italy, the Italy of Mussolini, had proved itself worthy of their supreme sacrifice. She sat down to tumultuous applause.[64]

For her remaining six days in New York, Margherita was free to enjoy herself. Of all the places she had visited in the United States, Manhattan was her favorite. Most of all, she loved walking the streets at night, sensing the immense energy of the city in the rushing cars and the changing traffic lights: "How shall I ever forget, when shall I ever get back to that glitter of bits of mica on the pavements of Fifth Avenue, hard like stars, when the big town roars itself to sleep under the flood of electricity streaming over New York like a stupendous checkerboard of green and red!"[65]

She deliberately avoided Ranck, who was undoubtedly upset about another late Mussolini article. She spent much of her time with Fannie Hurst, lunching with her twice and meeting her for dinner at the Hotel Pierre. The two friends strolled through Central Park one evening. They stopped to watch an outdoor dance arranged by Mayor La Guardia for the visiting sailors of the Atlantic Fleet.

Margherita went to Riverside Park to see the dozens of battleships, aircraft carriers, and cruisers anchored in the Hudson River. It was an imposing display. The U.S. Navy had assembled an unprecedented concentration of warships in the Hudson for an upcoming review by President Roosevelt. The fraction of the American fleet Margherita saw was bigger than Italy's entire navy. She especially noted the aircraft carriers; the Italian fleet had none.

She returned to her favorite Manhattan buildings, and went to see several she had missed two months earlier: the Woolworth Building, the Flatiron Building, and Radio City Music Hall, which Margherita called "the most beautiful, the most refined and comfortable splendor, I have ever seen." She also spent some time with George and Helene Biddle. She saw Missy off to Europe on June 8, after making plans to meet her in Rome. The next day, Margherita boarded the *Conte di Savoia* for her return voyage to Italy.[66]

Ambassador Rosso and representatives of the Italian community saw her off, leaving her cabin overflowing with farewell bouquets. To reporters who had come aboard to interview her, Margherita expressed her appreciation of the United States. "I hope I haven't missed anything, America is so huge. I want to come back and visit again. I did not have enough time to see all that I would like to have seen. But everywhere I found the American people so hospitable. I have had a lovely time."

Margherita had succeeded in creating something of an appetite for her lectures, although she knew now that she had overestimated the size of the American audience for high culture. Certainly she had made an excellent personal impression on almost everyone she met. But too often, she mistook friendliness to her for admiration of Mussolini and Fascism. She had managed to convince some Americans of the benefits of Fascism and the benevolence of the Duce, and she had reinforced the faith of those who already supported him. But some well-informed Americans were sympathetic to her precisely because of her estrangement from Mussolini. They knew that Margherita exaggerated her influence over the Italian dictator.

Sinclair Lewis and his wife, Dorothy Thompson, for example, were pleased to make Margherita's acquaintance. But from close friends George Seldes and Max Ascoli, a Jewish anti-Fascist refugee, they knew of Mussolini's crimes, and so knew something of the extent to which Margherita lied in extolling Fascism. The same was true for Missy, thanks to her warm relationship with Count Carlo Sforza, another Italian exile. Franklin Roosevelt saw in Mussolini a useful bulwark against Hitler, and therefore wished to remain on friendly terms with the Duce. However much he denied it, aspects of Roosevelt's New Deal programs had been inspired by Fascist social and economic programs. But the president abhorred Fascist tyranny, and made that attitude plain to others, if not to Margherita. His wife did make her distaste for Mussolini clear to Margherita. And while Margherita and Mussolini were able to manipulate Nicholas Murray Butler because of his pompous self-importance, he supported Mussolini only insofar as the Duce seemed to serve the cause of peace.[67]

Margherita abandoned plans to write a novel based on her experiences. Instead, she planned a book-length study. Her thoughts on America were already well formed. American racism hardly bothered her, since she had similar biases, but several other aspects of American society repelled her. She had seen disturbing levels of greed, alcoholism, and materialism. The high level of brutality and the crime rate frightened her. As Einstein had warned her she would, she found the degree of American conformity depressing. Her observations confirmed the portrait Sinclair Lewis had painted of his fellows in *Babbitt*. She decided that Americans had made a fundamental mistake in expecting technology to engender human happiness.

But these serious flaws did not alter her basically positive judgment of America. However naïve or foolish they might be, Americans believed in the possibility of human happiness, and had built a nation dedicated to pursuing that elusive goal. Margherita was fascinated and confused to find herself falling under the spell of that dream. She realized that America's vast resources, its gigantic scale, its immense riches—even in the midst of the Depression—might have created the fallacious hope that material advantages could create happiness. But she had come to understand that a belief in the possibility of happiness, which many Europeans had forsaken, and which Fascist ideology disregarded, actually helped make Americans happy.[68]

This seemed particularly true for American women. Compared to their Italian sisters, they had extraordinary freedom. Many had seized opportunities, unparalleled in Margherita's experience, for achievement, self-fulfillment, and love. She knew American women had problems of their own, particularly in the midst of the worst economic crisis in their country's history. Yet she had seen a resilient optimism among them that surprised her. The society women of New York, Washington, and Chicago, the Hollywood actresses, the United Airlines stewardesses, the journalists and writers, all had revived in her the feminist hopes she had harbored since her Socialist days.[69]

Once the great ship had sailed past the Narrows and put out to sea, Margherita began a more pressing piece of writing: a complete report for Mussolini on what she had seen and heard during the previous two months.[70] What could Margherita explain to Mussolini about America that others could not? He had many sources of information about the United States. Rosso was an excellent ambassador, and the same Italian consuls who monitored Margherita's progress across America sent constant reports to the embassy for relay to the Foreign Ministry. Fascist sympathizers such as Generoso Pope, and agents like Contini-Bonacossi, provided other valuable sources of information.[71] But none of these men knew Mussolini at all as well as Margherita did. Despite the end of their love affair, Mussolini trusted no one to the extent that he did Margherita. He was retreating ever deeper into an emotionally isolated megalomania, but Margherita still knew how to get him to heed certain unwelcome truths.

Margherita readily admitted that she had seen only a fraction of the United States. She had largely confined her travels to urban centers of politics, communications, and education on the East and West coasts. She had not witnessed American industrial and agricultural areas. She had caught only a glimpse of the American military apparatus, and had little sense of the day-to-day functioning of the American political system.

Nonetheless, she had conversed with a diverse number of Americans.

She reinforced the value of her conversations by extensive reading about American life. As a result, she had acquired a good sense of the powers that could be placed at the disposal of the American government. She had met Franklin Roosevelt, and had an idea how he wished to use those powers. Finally, she had a notion of the willingness of the American people to apply their resources beyond their own borders.

This question was the crux of her report to Mussolini. To what extent would the United States involve itself in the affairs of Europe? How significant would such intervention be? Shortly after the *Conte di Savoia* entered the Mediterranean, the question took on more than an abstract interest for Margherita. On June 14, Mussolini and Hitler met in Venice to discuss the fate of Austria and, by implication, the question of war and peace in Europe.

27

Alliances Made and Broken

By the time Margherita's ship had docked, Mussolini's meeting with Hitler in Venice had ended. Margherita and Mussolini returned to Rome within a day of each other, on June 17 and 18 respectively. She promptly sent the report of her North American travels to his office. The capital was buzzing with rumors about the disastrous Venice conference. Margherita learned a great deal about what had actually happened from Morgan, the Cerrutis, and others who had been present.

On June 14, Mussolini went by motorboat from the Villa Pisani at Stra down the inland canal and over to the Venice airport. He greeted his guest in German after Hitler hesitatingly stepped off his trimotor Junkers transport into the brilliant morning sunshine. Hitler had tears in his eyes as he met the man he had admired for years. As a special favor to the reporter, Mussolini let Thomas Morgan stand to Hitler's right while the German and Italian national anthems were played. Hitler looked pallid and uncomfortable in his trench coat, awkwardly clutching his hat in both hands. Beside him stood a tanned Mussolini in a well-tailored Fascist Militia uniform, complete with riding boots and a dagger at his belt. Observers noted that even the pudgy Morgan looked more like a dictator than the Führer. Watching from a few feet away with her husband, Elisabetta Cerruti realized that Hitler was deeply embarrassed; it was the first and last time she would ever witness him in such a mood. As the official parties moved toward their boats, Morgan overheard Hitler snarl at the German ambassador: "Why did you not advise me to wear my uniform?"

Mussolini gave Hitler a brief tour of Venice from the Grand Canal, and a glimpse at Italian Navy ships anchored in the lagoon. Then the two parties headed to Stra, where Mussolini insisted on meeting with Hitler alone. Afterward, Galeazzo Ciano announced to the assembled press that the conversation had been quite cordial. But Morgan had been waiting close enough to the gardens where they met to hear Hitler shouting his responses to Mussolini.

Hitler returned to his hotel in Venice, too enraged to even glance at the magnificent Tiepolo murals that adorned the gilded Villa Pisani. Mussolini cleared his head by paying a brief visit to the Nineteenth Biennale, escorted by its president, Count Volpi. That evening, Mussolini and Hitler were scheduled to attend a concert in the Doge's Palace. Both leaders arrived quite late, a sign of their mutual displeasure. The Venetian crowd that had assembled to hail the Duce and catch a glimpse of the Führer had grown impatient and drifted away. Annoyed, Hitler remarked that when Mussolini visited Berlin he would arrange a truly worthy reception. As Mussolini later told Margherita, he looked coldly at Hitler and replied: "That's very possible. I myself am a statesman, not a stage manager."

The next morning, Mussolini deliberately kept Hitler waiting for half an hour on a reviewing stand in Piazza San Marco before arriving for a parade supposedly in the Führer's honor. The ragged marching of the local Fascist Militia left Mussolini in a foul mood, although Hitler tried to act impressed. After that fiasco, Elisabetta Cerruti joined Hitler at his invitation to visit the Biennale. She noted both his evident disgust with the modern Italian painting and sculpture, and his delight at the dull realistic art in the German pavilion. As they departed for lunch and a second meeting with Mussolini, Hitler delivered one of his infamous monologues to Elisabetta, droning on and on about "healthy" and "degenerate" art. This harangue continued through the meal. Mussolini and Hitler sat facing each other, with Elisabetta on the Führer's right. She noticed that Hitler's lecture, combined with the stifling heat, drove Mussolini almost to distraction.

But Hitler had only begun to talk. After lunch, the two dictators left their guests on the clubhouse terrace and sat on a bench some thirty feet away. Mussolini dispensed with an interpreter and relied on his own German. As Elisabetta watched, the two men talked for two hours—or more accurately, Hitler talked, punctuating an almost nonstop monologue with violent arm gestures. After he finally finished and left, Elisabetta saw that Mussolini appeared to be in a daze, his face contorted in a scowl.

During a balcony speech late that afternoon in the Piazza San Marco, Mussolini bluntly reminded the gathered crowd of the terrible damage the Germans and Austro-Hungarians had inflicted on the region in 1917. But he assured his audience that he and Hitler had agreed to preserve an independent Austria as a buffer between their countries. Hitler was listening to an interpreter inside. After prolonged applause, Mussolini made his point even more directly. If necessary, Mussolini emphasized, Italy would use the strength forged by the Fascist regime to defend Austria by force. Mussolini's audience shouted its approval, and began rhythmic chants of *"Duce! Duce! Duce!"* After he disappeared inside, the crowd called him back to the balcony four times to acknowledge their enthusiastic cries of support. Later, Foreign Undersecretary Suvich and Ciano assured reporters that Hitler had guaranteed Austrian sovereignty.

There was a magnificent state banquet and ball that evening at the Hotel Excelsior, and the next morning Mussolini bade Hitler good-bye at the Venice airport. This time Mussolini dressed conservatively in a business suit and a white yachting cap. Perhaps Mussolini's less-than-perfect German had hindered him from understanding Hitler and making himself understood. In any case, he and his advisers came away from Venice certain that they had warned the Germans not to interfere in Austria. But Hitler believed that the Italians had acquiesced to increased Nazi influence over Austria, so long as he made no immediate attempt to annex the country.[1]

Hitler's admiration for Mussolini had increased as a result of their encounter. Mussolini's granite willpower impressed rather than alienated the Führer. Hitler had been touched by Mussolini's simplicity in private conversation, and thrilled by his imperial control of the crowd in the Piazza San Marco. It was a rare opportunity to observe another master of mass hysteria in action. Hitler expressed his deep regard for Mussolini and sincerely offered him friendship. But the Duce returned to Rome filled with loathing for Hitler's fanatical and self-absorbed personality. As he remarked to his advisers, talking to Hitler was like trying to have a conversation with a record player.[2]

Given her concerns about Austrian independence and the developing ties between Germany and Italy, Hitler's diplomatic setback pleased Margherita greatly. She found it particularly delightful that Mussolini had chosen her native city in which to deliver his rebuke to the Nazi. She took malicious pleasure from the story that Mussolini had made an obscene gesture of farewell, once Hitler had turned his back to climb into his airplane, and from hearing that Hitler and his retinue had been plagued by mosquitos at the Villa Pisani.[3]

She had other reasons for satisfaction. Her return from America had been announced on the radio, a sure sign of official favor in a regime that controlled all news reports. And on June 10, while Margherita was crossing the Atlantic, Mussolini had invited Michelucci and his controversial team of architects to the Palazzo Venezia. Mussolini had awarded them the contract to design the Santa Maria Novella railroad station in Florence, at Margherita's urging and against Farinacci's protests. He delivered another rebuke to Farinacci by telling the designers how much it pleased him.[4]

Margherita also learned of an amusing incident involving Marion Davies's portrait at the Biennale. On May 12, the same day that Hearst had received Margherita at San Simeon, Vittorio Emanuele III formally opened the Venice exhibit. Mussolini had clandestinely arranged for a large painting of the publisher's mistress to be hung in the American pavilion. When

Ambassador Long greeted the king inside the American pavilion, the sovereign looked at the portrait and remarked: "I see that portrait arrived." Then he added, "It's a beautiful portrait."

Caught completely off guard, Long was acutely embarrassed by the painting of America's most infamous scarlet woman. But the king, as well as Crown Prince Umberto, seemed amused by the whole episode. Mrs. Gertrude Vanderbilt Whitney, who had sponsored the American pavilion, demanded the immediate removal of Davies's portrait. Acting on Mussolini's orders, Count Volpi refused. Mrs. Whitney then attempted to close the American pavilion. Volpi would not permit this either. By the time Hearst and Davies sailed for Europe on the *Rex* on May 26, the affair had been splashed across the American tabloids.[5]

Thus when Margherita went to see Mussolini in the Palazzo Venezia to deliver her account of her meetings with Roosevelt, Hearst, and other prominent Americans, she had good reason to expect a warm reception. Mussolini had already studied the memorandum, in which Margherita had stressed American economic power and gigantic military potential. She had concluded that American isolationism, while strong, would not block U.S. intervention in a future European war if such a conflict threatened American interests.

Their first topic of conversation was the meeting with Hitler. At first Mussolini denied that Hitler had made a bad impression. He showed great reluctance to admit that he might have made a mistake in favoring the German. But Margherita knew Mussolini too well for him to be able to conceal his feelings from her. Yes, he eventually admitted, Hitler was a visionary, but he lacked Latin subtlety, and the ability to adapt to changing circumstances. Hitler seemed to operate only according to his intuition. He appeared neither willing nor able to listen to Mussolini's point of view. In fact, he had ignored virtually everything that Mussolini said to him.

Hitler had made no mention of Mussolini's German; it was something on which the Duce prided himself. Margherita knew Mussolini had not mastered the language to the degree that he pretended. She guessed that Hitler's silence left Mussolini worried either that he had failed to make himself understood, or that Hitler thought his German was poor, and so had chosen not to compliment it. Mussolini's uncertainty had left him psychologically off-balance during the two days of Hitler's visit.

What had been even more upsetting, Margherita realized, was that the two dictators had antithetical conversational styles. When Mussolini met with a foreign leader, he tended to talk relatively little, asking questions and listening attentively to the answers. Recently his megalomania had made him less tolerant of other viewpoints, but his conversational style had not changed. But to ask Hitler a question was to invite a torrent of unyielding opinions. Margherita saw that even a week later, Mussolini remained frustrated and angry at Hitler's approach to summit diplomacy.

Margherita suspected that Hitler's age—forty-five—also worried Mussolini. Members of the Mussolini family tended to die young. Mussolini's mother had died at forty-six, his father at fifty-six, his brother, Arnaldo, also at forty-six. Mussolini did not expect to live beyond sixty-five and had spoken frequently with Margherita about his intention to retire at sixty. In June 1934, he was about to turn fifty-one, and was increasingly sensitive about his age. His remaining hair had turned white, and Mussolini had begun shaving his scalp to disguise the fact. The idea that he might be dead in ten or fifteen years, while Hitler lived on to dominate Europe, tormented him, Margherita guessed.

Margherita's account of her recent travels triggered Mussolini's suppressed rage. For a short time he listened impatiently to what she had to say about America. Margherita had prepared herself to respond in detail to Mussolini's usual stream of probing questions. Instead Mussolini sat quietly, which made it clear that he did not like what he was hearing.

When she began to describe her conversation with Roosevelt, she emphasized how much the president's intelligence and personality compensated for his paralysis. She described Roosevelt's unusually detailed knowledge of Italy, particularly his understanding of the ways in which the Fascist regime was responding to the Depression. As she began to pass on Roosevelt's admiration for the Duce's economic programs Mussolini cut her off. All this was very nice, he said with obvious irritation, but it really didn't interest him. What mattered in the world now was military force, and in that regard the United States counted for little.

Margherita was taken aback. Mussolini had always impressed her with his astute understanding of what had happened in 1917–1919. He had always appreciated the decisive role American resources had played in the Allied victory. But now he shouted at her: "America does not count!" He angrily insisted that in the next European war, things would go differently. The victors would win quickly. If the United States entered the fighting, it would be too late to matter. This time Europeans were not going to die just to give Roosevelt or some other president the opportunity to rearrange the balance of power according to American interests.

Mussolini abruptly indicated that the interview was at an end. Margherita drove home and threw herself down on the couch in her study. She was filled with bitterness and grief. Mussolini obviously no longer wished to learn anything from her. He had flaunted his indifference to her opinions and stubbornly resisted agreeing with any of her insights into American attitudes.

In fact, Mussolini was deeply curious about the United States. Apparently, after having been humiliated by Hitler, Mussolini needed to humiliate Margherita in turn. He had communicated a painful message: Margherita should not expect to regain any influence over his conduct of international relations. His refusal even to listen to her struck Margherita as a very dangerous development.[6]

Almost immediately, Margherita took to bed with a high fever. An abscessed tooth had flared up so painfully that she could no longer work. There may have been a psychosomatic element to her ailment. By the time she recovered, Margherita faced months of uninterrupted work to meet all her obligations—she had written nothing for publication since leaving for America in March.

Missy had sailed to Europe expecting to visit Margherita in Rome. Margherita had promised to arrange an interview for Missy with Mussolini. From her sickbed, Margherita had Amedeo write to Missy in Paris. He expressed his mother's dishonest regrets that she had been unable to see Mussolini since his conference with Hitler. She offered to set up another meeting sometime soon, and actually managed to arrange one for early July, but Missy had no time to wait and returned to New York. Margherita promised her another interview when next she came to Rome. In fact she begged Missy to return as soon as possible, betraying her own loneliness and depression.[7]

Events beyond the Alps served to restore some of Margherita's influence with Mussolini. Beginning on June 30 and continuing for the next two days, Hitler's SS guards massacred his rivals within the Nazi leadership, as well as a number of others against whom the Führer held a grudge. Many were German conservatives who had helped the Nazis come to power, believing that they could then control them. Papen escaped death on the "Night of Long Knives" only because of Göring's intervention. To his family Mussolini expressed deep revulsion at Hitler's butchery.

A little over three weeks later, on July 25, Austrian Nazis attempted to seize control of Vienna. Although the putsch failed, the Nazis wounded Austrian Chancellor Dollfuss in the attempt and allowed him to bleed to death. The chancellor's wife and children were Mussolini's guests at the time. They had traveled ahead of Dollfuss, who was scheduled to leave later that day to meet Mussolini for a conference. It fell to Mussolini to break the news of Dollfuss's death to his widow.

Margherita was in Venice when she learned of Dollfuss's murder. She had taken a break from her writing to meet with a visiting delegation of the Committee of Intellectual Cooperation. She was sitting on the terrace of the Hotel Excelsior on the Lido, attending the farewell luncheon for the committee members. Looking back years later, it seemed to her the final moment of the spiritual unity of Western civilization. Seated around her were the writers Salvador de Madariaga and Eugenio D'Ors from Spain; her old Socialist comrade from Belgium, Jules Destrée; Le Corbusier and his fellow Frenchman the novelist Jules Romains; the Romanian poet Helen Vacaresco; and one of Missy's friends, James Shotwell, from the history department of Columbia University. The committee had met to discuss the role of governments in protecting art and bringing it to the people. Margherita had extolled George Biddle's Federal Art Project and urged the others to encourage similar programs in their countries.

As the story of Dollfuss's murder passed from table to table, a thrill of fear passed through the group. Margherita saw a friend, Prince Ernst von Starhemberg, the Austrian vice-chancellor, hurrying across the hotel terrace. He had come to the Lido in the lighthearted pursuit of a woman, but now he was rushing to the airport to return to Vienna in a plane provided by Mussolini. Soon the sky over Venice was swarming with squadrons of Italian aircraft, circling to gain altitude and then heading north toward the Brenner Pass.

Obviously Hitler had either ordered the putsch, or had known of it in advance and acquiesced. Considering that Hitler had promised him to respect Austrian independence, the Nazi uprising infuriated Mussolini. Venting his rage to Thomas Morgan, Mussolini called the Germans a nation of pederasts and barbarians. Mussolini rushed four divisions to the Austrian frontier. In response, King Alexander of Yugoslavia, recently aligned with Hitler to counter Mussolini, also concentrated units of his army on the frontier. Suddenly there was a real possibility of war in Central Europe. Over the next few days, however, the Austrian government crushed the Nazis without Italian assistance. Surviving Nazis fled to Germany or across the border to Yugoslavia, where King Alexander gave them refuge.

To statesmen and ordinary people alike, Mussolini emerged a hero. His actions seemed to have stopped Nazi aggression and single-handedly saved the peace. The Duce's popularity in Europe and the United States probably reached an all-time high. But Mussolini burned with a desire for revenge against Hitler.

German President von Hindenburg died on August 2. Hitler absorbed the functions of head of state and supreme commander of the armed forces within his chancellorship. His power in Germany was now absolute. He was forced, however, to adopt a less openly aggressive policy toward Austria. Papen had resigned as vice-chancellor shortly after the Nazi purge in June. In late July, Hitler appointed him emissary to Vienna. Papen was instructed to improve German-Austrian relations, and to prepare the way for a peaceful absorption of the small country into the Third Reich.

Mussolini ordered Cerruti to maintain formally correct relations with the German government. But in August and September, Mussolini wrote for *Il Popolo d'Italia* a series of anonymous articles that attacked the Nazis, particularly for their anti-Semitism, and stressed the differences between the Fascists and the Nazis. Speaking in Bari early that September, Mussolini made his most famous remark against Nazi racism: "Thirty centuries of history allow us to regard with supreme pity certain doctrines from beyond the Alps, upheld by the descendants of people who could not even write in order to pass on records of their own lives, at the very time in which Rome boasted of Caesar, Virgil and Augustus." Mussolini had designed the articles and speeches to prepare the Italian people for a rapprochement with France and to signal to Paris that he was ready to form an alliance against Hitler. If Mussolini had not broken openly with the Germans, it was only in order to extract French acquiescence to his projected takeover of Ethiopia.

By coincidence, in early July Margherita had written a Mussolini article for the Hearst press, arguing that the peace of Central Europe required revision of the Versailles settlement under the guidance of Italy and Britain. She stressed Mussolini's iron determination to defend the Dollfuss regime and warned that the forceful destruction of Austrian independence would lead to a new world war. It appeared in the United States on the Sunday after Dollfuss's murder. Following a number of missed deadlines, two dull articles on crime control and unemployment (probably written by Fiammetta), and a Mussolini veto of an article on the Venice conference, Hearst was pleased to get the kind of topical subject he wanted for his money.

In August, Margherita had written a piece on the dangers the French and British faced by allowing a falling birthrate when the German rate was increasing. The article praised the wisdom of Mussolini's demographic policies and warned that the white race had to unite and reproduce at the maximum rate to face the growing peril represented by the black and yellow races. The article pleased Mussolini, and he had it printed in *Il Popolo d'Italia*.[8]

Over the next twenty-two months, Margherita focused her energies on writing a book about her impressions of America. With Alexander Kirk's encouragement, she wrote it in English. At first she found composing her thoughts in the language difficult, but with hard work and considerable help from Kirk, her written English steadily improved.

As was her custom, she spent much of the late summer and early fall in comfortable seclusion at Il Soldo. There she worked directly on her manuscript. She also wrote about her American experiences for the Hearst press, for Missy's Sunday magazine, and for *La Stampa*. She reused these articles as the basis for chapters in her book. That way she was able to catch up on some of her writing obligations without abandoning the book. Of course, she was paid for the articles, and would be paid again for the book; she had learned by now how to maximize her efforts. In addition to all this work, she put the final touches on a study of the nineteenth-century Milanese painter Daniele Ranzoni.

The heavy workload again resulted in missed deadlines for the Hearst press. Margherita blamed the delays on Mussolini's involvement in the tense international situation. As partial compensation, Margherita negotiated the sale of the Italian rights for a number of Hearst "Senior Statesmen" articles to Renato Trevisani's *Politica Sociale*. Eventually Ranck received a good article that stated bluntly that Mussolini was ordering a major arms buildup to deter the German threat.[9]

Margherita's attention was distracted by family matters that summer. Her first grandchild, a boy christened Roberto, was born to Fiammetta and Livio on August 19. But Margherita received news the same day of her own firstborn. Robert's body had been discovered in the little military cemetery in the village of Stoccareddo, about three miles from where he had fallen on the Col d'Echele. Margherita and Amedeo hurried north to Stoccareddo to identify his remains.[10]

Margherita commissioned Giuseppe Terragni to design a tomb for Roberto, to be built near the peak of the Col d'Echele. His first designs, for a massive tomb faced by a high tower, proved impractical due to the expense and difficulty of transporting materials up the narrow dirt road to the peak. In the end, Terragni and Margherita agreed on a symmetrical T-shaped structure, intersected by stairs leading to an inscribed block on top of the tomb. The monument was unmistakably Rationalist in style, and to Margherita's mind, one worthy of an ancient Roman warrior. Viewed from above, it suggested a body lying upon the ground, its arms outstretched. The structure was to be composed of blocks of granite quarried from the local mountains.[11]

Two months to the day after the identification of Roberto's body, Mondadori printed a second edition of *I vivi e l'ombra*. The reissued poems, many of which were about Roberto, were obviously intended as Margherita's celebration of the discovery of her son's remains. The new version lacked the stunning jacket illustration Sironi had done for the 1921 edition, but Margherita's poems had been set and printed far more elegantly.

Margherita made minor but significant changes from the 1921 edition. She replaced "Il canto del triplice io" with a far shorter version of the same poem, titled "Il canto a tre voci." Anyone with a passing knowledge of Margherita and Mussolini's life in 1918–1921 would have been able to recognize that the earlier poem had concerned the relationship between the two lovers and Ada Negri. The allusions in the new version were far more obscure. Margherita also added "Per Antonio Sant'Elia," which she had written in 1916. She dropped "Letture," which was about how the chivalric tales she had read to young Roberto had inspired him to become a soldier. She anxiously sought Ada Negri's opinion of the new edition. Margherita's mournful reference to having to cut "Il canto del triplice io" hinted that she was jealous of the continuing warm friendship between Ada and Mussolini.[12] The second edition of *I vivi e l'ombra* was hardly noticed.

Even more galling was the fate of the sixteenth edition of *Dux,* which Mondadori brought out in February of 1934. It was badly printed, and so full of typographical errors that the publisher suspended printing after a small run. In September of 1934, Mussolini created the post of undersecretary for the press and propaganda and appointed his son-in-law, Galeazzo Ciano, to fill it. Ciano promptly had *Dux* pulled from circulation. He said that it was unbecoming to show photographs of the peasant home in which Mussolini had been born—in reality, he did not want a new edition of the biography to perpetuate the public link between Mussolini and Margherita. In November, Margherita was humiliated to see the shoddy edition remaindered through newspaper stands.[13]

Galeazzo and Edda Ciano effectively replaced Margherita as Mussolini's closest advisers. Mussolini began assigning Edda the kind of unofficial political and diplomatic tasks he had given to Margherita a few years before. After Galeazzo had returned from diplomatic service in China in June 1933, Mussolini apparently decided to groom the young man to be his successor. Mussolini worried that, given his family's longevity, the transfer of power might have to occur within a decade. Ciano's new position gave him considerable power over Margherita's avenues for publication.[14]

Edda and Margherita were certain to encounter one another, since both moved in the same exalted circles in Roman society. Gossip about the rivalry between them quickly spread among the capital's aristocracy. Hostesses had to choose to invite either Edda or Margherita to dinner, but never both—and as word of Margherita's waning influence with Mussolini spread, her invitations declined. One old princess observed: "Roman society is divided into two parts: one that calls Edda by her first name, and the other that hopes to do so."[15]

In her memoirs, written many years later, Edda refused even to mention Margherita. Mimi Pecci-Blunt, owner of the La Cometa gallery, was one of the few society figures who entertained both Margherita and Edda. "In reality," Edda claimed, Pecci-Blunt "had the only real literary and artistic salon in Italy at that time." Corrado Alvaro, who often escorted Margherita, remembered an amusing evening when Pecci-Blunt had inadvertently invited Margherita and Edda to the same dinner party. When Edda arrived, all the guests, except for Margherita, Alvaro, and Massimo

Bontempelli, immediately surrounded her. Dinner was served at a series of small tables, and those not fortunate enough to sit with Edda Ciano tried not to sit near Margherita. Throughout the evening, the two rivals succeeded in avoiding each other completely, but when Margherita and her two friends tried to make a graceful exit, they came face to face with Edda at the door. Margherita smiled and said, "Good evening, Contessa." Edda uttered a brusque "Good evening." Before Margherita could exit, Edda asked in a deliberately loud voice, "And who is that woman?"[16]

Margherita soon suffered another humiliation. When it came time to renew the contract with Hearst for 1935, Mussolini decided against it, cutting Margherita off from a major source of income. He was willing to write occasional articles, but did not want to be tied to a regular deadline. He does not seem to have aimed this at Margherita; he was simply worried that the articles might be dangerously mistaken for official policy in the inflammatory atmosphere of the time. One 1934 article Mussolini had vetoed, over Hearst's protests, was a piece Margherita had written on the October 9 assassinations of King Alexander of Yugoslavia and French Foreign Minister Louis Barthou in Marseilles. Within a few days of the crime, suspicions had centered on the Duce as the instigator of the murder plot. The matter had become too sensitive for an article on the subject under Mussolini's byline.

The real target of the plot—orchestrated by Galeazzo Ciano—was Alexander. Barthou was apparently killed by accident, as he tried to defend the king against the gunman who shot them both. But Mussolini was almost certainly responsible; the assassination of King Alexander seems to have been a reply to Hitler for the murder of Dollfuss two and a half months earlier. He may also have hoped that Yugoslavia would disintegrate as a result. The Serbs and Croats were already at odds, and Mussolini wanted to march in and pick up the pieces.

After a few tense months, Yugoslav unity was preserved. French diplomats, directed by the new foreign minister, Pierre Laval, put the question of guilt for the murders to rest. They persuaded other European governments that too probing an inquiry would alienate Mussolini. Instead, the French argued, Mussolini should be protected and brought into an anti-German coalition. As a result, official investigations placed the blame solely on the Ustasa Croatian terrorist group. But Barthou's death added to Margherita's depression. He had been an old and dear friend. She must have known or suspected that Mussolini was responsible. Rumors were being whispered everywhere in Italy, and Margherita had her own privileged sources of information.[17]

Her anxiety was noticeable, her status clearly in decline. One observer, Giovanni Ansaldo, spent two days in Margherita's company in early September 1934, as she passed through Genoa to visit Gordon Craig. He was not a disinterested party, since he edited the Ciano family's Livorno newspaper, *Il Telegrafo,* and was secretly an anti-Fascist. Still, his account is in accord with those of others who spoke of her frequent melancholy and listlessness. Ansaldo noted that Margherita ate too much, talked too loudly, and laughed too raucously. For all her airs of the *gran signora,* her greed and parsimony betrayed her pretensions. There was a sign of panic in her behavior.[18]

But beginning in January 1935, Mussolini found he again had need of Margherita's services. He had decided the time was propitious for the Ethiopian invasion he had been planning for years. An intense publicity effort might greatly reduce the international resistance he expected. He knew public opinion was often the decisive force in shaping government policy in the American, British, and French democracies. Margherita's language skills and press contacts were resources Mussolini could not yet afford to lose. Her erudition and charm made her the ideal proponent for what he wanted to portray as a struggle between Western civilization and African savagery. Furthermore, Margherita had cultivated friendships with the leading diplomats in Rome, as well as their wives. In addition to her relationship with Ambassador and Mrs. Breckinridge Long, Margherita was particularly close to Sir Eric Drummond of Britain and to Ambassador Count Charles de Chambrun of France and his new wife, Princess Marie Murat.

Mussolini had already secured from the French a major understanding. Italy and France would cooperate to prevent German expansion. In particular, they would respond with force if Hitler sought to annex Austria or occupy the demilitarized Rhineland. In return Mussolini agreed to end his attempts to subvert Yugoslavia, one of France's allies. And the French offered to settle the colonial claims that the Italians had held against them since the Versailles conference.

What Mussolini wanted was French acquiescence to the Italian control of Ethiopia, and French cooperation in gaining British assent to the same. This final demand left French Premier Pierre Flandin and his government extremely nervous. If Mussolini were to attack Ethiopia, it would represent a direct violation of the League of Nations charter. As a member of the League, Ethiopia would obviously ask for international assistance, particularly from France and Britain. The French had little or no faith in the League of Nations, but Flandin and Laval saw the difficulty of opposing German aggression in Europe while condoning Italian aggression in Africa. Gaining British cooperation would be even more difficult. The French government refused to put any promises in writing and delayed a final agreement until Laval met face-to-face with Mussolini in Rome.

Laval and Mussolini settled matters late on January 7. Exactly what the two men privately agreed to remains controversial and will probably never be precisely known. But almost certainly Laval gave Mussolini the assent of the Flandin government to the Italian conquest of Ethiopia.[19]

Margherita's propaganda efforts began during Laval's visit. She invited to her salon the French journalists who had accompanied Laval to Rome. Most accepted only for a chance to meet the woman who, until recently, had been the Duce's lover. But the gathering still provided Margherita with the opportunity to promote the Italian-French entente. She wrote a special Mussolini article for the Hearst press that appeared on January 27. In it she described the meeting as a reaffirmation of Italian determination to defend Austria against the Nazis. In February, she wrote to Missy and Nicholas Murray Butler that the government had installed radio equipment that would make possible regular broadcasts to American audiences. She asked them to tell their friends that her first talk was scheduled for March 4. Missy was again coming to Rome, and Margherita promised her an interview with Mussolini this time. She even hoped to arrange a Mussolini broadcast to the United States under the auspices of the *Herald Tribune*.

Since August 1934, American diplomats in Europe had warned Roosevelt of Italian plans to attack Ethiopia. In Rome, Breckinridge Long continued for months to interpret the Italian military buildup as intended to protect Austria from Hitler. Roosevelt thought otherwise, and told him so when Long came to Washington over Christmas. Long stuck stubbornly to his opinions; Margherita's influence had done much to shape his erroneous views.

Mussolini sent two army divisions to East Africa in February. By mid-June, Mussolini had called up another eight divisions, including five newly formed from the ranks of the Fascist Militia. Throughout the spring, summer, and fall, hundreds of thousands of Italian troops sailed through the Suez Canal for the Italian colonies of Eritrea and Somalia. Long finally realized that the Italian military had been preparing to invade Ethiopia all along. Now he excused the plan as the necessary price for Italian cooperation with France against Germany.[20]

If European and American public opinion turned decisively against an attack on Ethiopia, Italy faced disaster. What if the British refused to cooperate, and in reaction, the French backed out of the Laval-Mussolini accords? After such lengthy and expensive preparations for war, could Mussolini's regime survive a retreat in the face of British and French threats? The League of Nations charter specified economic sanctions as the punishment for aggressor states. The sanctions, unless undermined by the United States, the greatest economic power outside the League, would be crippling. Italy could suffer economic collapse, defeat in East Africa, and the subsequent dishonor of watching Germany seize Austria. Mussolini, and probably Fascism, would be finished.

But so far his diplomatic maneuvers seemed to be succeeding. Prior to a meeting with Flandin and British Prime Minister Ramsay MacDonald at Stresa, on the shores of Lake Maggiore, from April 11 to 14, Mussolini had expected them to raise the Ethiopian question. Instead, discussions among the three leaders were limited to creating a common front against Germany. In talks among lower-level officials, the Italians warned the British that they did not rule out the use of force against Ethiopia. This crucial fact was not brought to the attention of MacDonald. At the suggestion of Flandin and Laval, British diplomats worded the final communiqué to express the resolve of the three leaders to preserve the peace only "of Europe." Mussolini left the conference convinced that the British had accepted his plans in East Africa.[21]

At first, the Stresa Conference buoyed Margherita's hopes. Italy had joined a firm anti-German coalition. Austrian independence seemed assured. But the Germans made fresh approaches to Mussolini. In May, Hitler publicly denied any intent to annex Austria. Mussolini responded in a speech, stating that only the Austrian question prevented firm German-Italian friendship. Papen asked Schulenburg to see Mussolini and assure him that Hitler intended to move east next, against Poland and the Soviet Union, not south. In turn, fearing the loss of "the German card," should his plans to attack Ethiopia lead to a crisis with Britain and France, Mussolini extended friendly diplomatic feelers to Berlin.

After Schulenburg reached Rome, he first visited Margherita. He revealed his mission but insisted that the Nazi leaders were lying. "Good, I will make your arrival known. But I have to warn you to be ready for failure," Margherita responded. She knew Mussolini deeply distrusted Hitler but also wished to avoid a further deterioration in Italian-German relations.

Margherita could arrange a meeting for Schulenburg with no one higher than Alfieri, then serving as Ciano's deputy. Alfieri proved friendly but insisted that Schulenburg's message from Papen should be sent through formal diplomatic channels, not by a secret emmissary. The truth was that Ciano and Alfieri supported an Italian-German alliance. They feared that if Schulenburg talked with Mussolini, he would reveal what he knew about Hitler's real plans.

Schulenburg returned to Germany only to learn that orders for his arrest had been issued to the Gestapo. Someone had informed the authorities of what he had revealed in Rome. Luckily, Schulenburg managed to escape to Switzerland, where he kept a mountain retreat. Margherita's essay in secret diplomacy had failed.

Margherita offered and Hearst accepted one more Mussolini article in late April. In it Margherita lauded the new Italian-French alliance. But Hearst detested the French and had taken the article only to avoid alienating Mussolini and Margherita. For the same reason, in September, he accepted one of Margherita's own articles on her impressions of American women. Hearst's real feelings are reflected in the numerous pro-Hitler articles he ran in 1935—many written by the anti-Semitic Nazi "philosopher" Alfred Rosenberg—as well as in the attacks on Mussolini he printed, some written by Lloyd George with the publisher's encouragement.[22]

Hearst's editorial policies proved to be more than his star European reporter, Karl von Wiegand, could tolerate. By early 1934, Wiegand had concluded that Hitler would eventually start a war in order to conquer Europe. Taking advantage of contacts within Germany, Wiegand began to gather what information he could and pass it on to American diplomats. Many of his sources were murdered on the "Night of the Long Knives." After Hearst adopted his openly pro-Hitler stance in early 1935, Wiegand went to see William E. Dodd, American ambassador to Germany. He told Dodd what he knew of the links between Hearst and Hitler, and Hearst's deal with Margherita and Mussolini. He also reported a corrupt financial arrangement among Hearst, Mussolini, the Giannini brothers, and Senator William McAdoo of California. Dodd believed that millions of dollars had been transferred from the Bank of America to Mussolini. If these transfers had continued over the past year, they had been in blatant violation of the Johnson Act.

Dodd reported the whole story to Roosevelt. The president found the information disturbing on a personal as well as a political level. McAdoo, President Wilson's secretary of the treasury and son-in-law, had been Roosevelt's friend for nearly a quarter century. The Giannini brothers had been among the very few bankers to support the president. Shortly after meeting with Hitler the previous September, Hearst had broken with Roosevelt. Now the president learned that this "thoroughly dangerous member of society," as he called Hearst, was conspiring with his supposed friends and the enemies of international peace. Roosevelt noted to Dodd that he felt powerless to do anything about it.[23]

Mussolini's ego was inflated after the Stresa conference. Margherita found the effects of his increased self-confidence extremely disturbing when she saw him in late April. She had not spoken to him face-to-face for quite some time. Her announcement of Amedeo's betrothal to Pierangela Daclon apparently gained her an invitation to the Palazzo Venezia. Besides family business, Margherita wanted to talk about arrangements for an Italian art exhibit scheduled to open in Paris in mid-May.

She had been helping to organize the modern section of the exhibit.

She had also fought a losing battle over the selections with Ojetti, who had overall responsibility for what would be displayed. Still, the Paris show was so gigantic that many of her favorites were included. The art exhibit was a token of Mussolini's gratitude to Flandin for their recent accord. Margherita believed the exhibit could also function as propaganda. How could a civilized nation favor the Ethiopians over a people who had produced masterpieces without interruption for seven centuries?[24]

Mussolini revealed to her that he attached hardly any significance to the Paris art show. His confrontation with Hitler, his preparations for war with Ethiopia, and the new respect he had won from the French and British had convinced him that brute force and material power alone really mattered in the world. "A people rise or fall only by the standard of their military victories or defeats," Mussolini told her. Margherita objected. Certainly it was intellectual and spiritual accomplishments that defined the value of a nation. "You're wrong!" Mussolini retorted angrily. "Spiritual values count for nothing. Dante, Leonardo, Galileo, Michelangelo—what have they done for Italy? They've actually lowered our prestige. Other people say: 'Poets! artists!' and then they laugh at the Italians."

Mussolini told Margherita that he was determined to transform the Italians into a warrior race. He had decided that his leadership would be required for another quarter century for this transformation to take place. He could no longer think of retiring in ten years. He was indispensable. Therefore he was taking much better care of his health, making sure to get eight hours of sleep every night, choosing what he ate carefully, and exercising regularly. He had to preserve his strength and vitality to be equal to the enormous task he had set for himself.

Mussolini may have exaggerated his ideas to Margherita, but he was certainly dreaming of molding the Italians into a nation of conquerors. Mussolini and Margherita once had conceived of Fascism as the means by which Italy could reassert its cultural and spiritual primacy. In that sphere, a reinvigorated Italy could aspire to world leadership. But now Mussolini thought in terms of military dominion. Could Italy hope to match the armed forces of France and Britain, let alone Germany? He had convinced himself that it could. Margherita found the man before her totally changed from the Mussolini she had loved.[25]

She was so severely upset by the episode that she spoke of it with others. One of the people to whom she confided her feelings was a French friend, then passing through Rome. The friend recounted the conversation to a French journalist. The reporter felt he could hardly write up the story for publication, but he discussed it with a man who happened to be an informer for the Public Security service. A report of the matter soon lay on Mussolini's desk.

Margherita had recently begun to be sensitive to anything that appeared in print linking her to Mussolini. In January, for example, she wrote an indignant letter to the editor of the Parisian *Journal de la Femme* protesting an article that described her as Mussolini's political adviser and ghostwriter. But she had not taken the same care in her conversations. She was hardly unaware that the Fascist regime had a vast network of informers. She took the telephone off the hook as a precaution before even mentioning Mussolini at home. But she could not resist gossiping about him. In fact, she reveled in recounting his foibles to her friends, and hearing others' accounts of his weaknesses.

Mussolini had received reports about Margherita's indiscreet conversations for years and previously had found them tolerable. But as their relationship cooled he became less forgiving. He had been annoyed by the way she had spoken of him in America. As a result, articles had appeared in the United States describing their old relationship, and illustrated with both their photographs. These particularly upset him. Margherita and her circle had taken to ridiculing Mussolini for his pretensions to omnipotence. They passed stories that he was actually losing power to men like Ciano and Starace. When those tales got back to Mussolini, they injured his touchy pride. But it was Margherita's conversation with her French friend that finally drove Mussolini to retaliate.

In early May, Mussolini ordered Ciano to issue strict instructions to the Italian press to ignore Margherita completely. Her public appearances and her activities were not to be reported. Her name was no longer to appear in any Fascist party publication. Mussolini thought that this would hit Margherita where she was most vulnerable, but she went on gossiping about him anyway. Within a few weeks she began a new round of stories stressing Mussolini's fear of assassination. And Ciano's orders did not prevent respectful—if not terribly positive—reviews of Margherita's biographical study, *Daniele Ranzoni,* from appearing. The book had been issued by the Royal Academy as the first of a series on nineteenth-century Italian artists. There were limits to the Duce's power.[26]

Furthermore, Mussolini did not wish to deprive himself of Margherita's connections. He rejected many of her ideas now, but her access to high circles in Italy and in the European capitals made her a valuable source of intelligence. However he treated her, he expected, and received, her loyalty. He was isolating himself more and more, even from his own leading officials. There were few whom he really trusted. Anne O'Hare McCormick noted that when she was able to see Mussolini for two off-the-record interviews in May and June, a number of Mussolini's lieutenants begged her to convey messages to the Duce. Margherita performed the same service for some, and thus had her supporters.

In fact, despite their recent quarrel, Margherita saw Mussolini after her return from the May opening of the art exhibit in Paris. The show was a huge success. By the time it closed in late July, it had attracted 650,000 visitors. Thanks to Mussolini's personal intervention, all the museums of Italy, the Vatican, Europe, and North America had lent their finest examples of Italian art. Private collectors had also proved remarkably generous with their holdings. Hundreds of paintings, drawings, sculptures, engravings, bronzes, jewels, tapestries, medallions, furniture pieces, and manuscripts offered a sweeping panorama of Italian civilization since the thirteenth century. Virtually every portable masterpiece by Cimabue, Duccio, Giotto, Botticelli, Lippi, Ghirlandaio, Piero di Cosimo, Donatello, Verrocchio, Leonardo, the della Robbias, Michelangelo, Crivelli, Raphael, Cellini, the Bellinis, Giorgione, Tintoretto, Titian, Correggio, Canaletto, Tiepolo, Canova, de Chirico, Boccioni, de Pisis, and, of course, Margherita's *Novecentisti* had been sent to Paris. Ciano, escorted by Marinetti and Bottai, opened the show. The entire French Cabinet, led by President Lebrun and Premier Flandin, greeted them. The hundreds of thousands who followed them were exhilarated and exhausted by the monumental labor of seeing it all.

The nineteenth- and twentieth-century exhibits, housed separately, drew fewer visitors and less admiration than the Renaissance and Baroque sections. Still, Margherita drew great satisfaction from the overwhelming impression of Italian genius and from the considerable attention paid to "her" Futurist and *Novecento* artists.

But Mussolini was much more interested in the political impressions she had gathered in Paris. Margherita confirmed Mussolini's own realization, acquired largely from the foreign press, that public opinion was opposed to his plans for carving out an empire in East Africa. He recognized that if he pushed forward despite British and French resistance, he would run the risk of destroying the anti-German coalition.

Margherita urged him to abandon his dangerous adventure. She could understand, she told him, his attraction to winning military glory in Africa, but the real work of governing often just consisted of sitting behind a desk loaded down with paper. She pointed out that there were plenty of opportunities for other great projects in Italy. "You have enough already to colonize in Apulia, in Sicily, and in Calabria," she argued. "There's much positive work to do here. If you go into Ethiopia, you'll fall into the hands of the Germans and then you'll be lost." Margherita begged him to reconsider. "If we have to pay for the Empire with the ruin of Europe, we will pay too high a price." But Mussolini would not listen to her.[27]

He did what he could to offset growing sympathy for Ethiopia in the Western democracies. His own activities crowned a massive effort by the

new minister of press and propaganda, Ciano, to depict Italian aggression
in the best possible light at home and abroad. Mussolini made himself
available for fourteen lengthy interviews to American, British, and French
journalists between late May and late September 1935. Margherita seems to
have arranged for at least six. Anne O'Hare McCormick saw Mussolini for
the first of the interviews on May 24. Mussolini received two journalists
from the *New York Herald Tribune,* including Missy Meloney, on July 11.
In early August, Thomas Morgan's boss, Edward Keen, United Press
vice-president for Europe, was granted an interview. Representatives of
the Hearst press also were able to question Mussolini for two stories that
summer.[28]

Margherita made several visits to the Palazzo Venezia in June and early
July to ensure that Mussolini would receive Missy. In campaigning for
Missy, Margherita stressed the fact that her Sunday magazine, renamed *This
Week* since February, had a national circulation of five million copies. In
return for all the help, Missy gave Margherita a number of presents, including a particularly stylish bathing suit. July was even hotter than usual in
Rome and the two escaped to the seashore a number of times. Margherita
and Missy enjoyed a busy social schedule in the cooler evenings because of
the presence of an unusually large number of diplomats. The growing crisis
over Ethiopia had forced European ambassadors to remain in the Italian
capital. The two friends spent a good deal of time with Alexander Kirk, the
de Chambruns, and British Ambassador Eric Drummond.

Margherita saw to it that Missy produced a favorable account of her talk
with Mussolini. Margherita wrote Missy's letter of application for the
audience, accompanied her friend to the interview in her limousine, and
even had the chauffeur corroborate Mussolini's assurances that the Italian
people supported him. She encouraged Missy to write an article about the
opportunities for American investment in Ethiopia after it fell under Italian
dominion. And she argued the Italian cause with Kirk, Drummond, and
the de Chambruns. She seems to have had an effect on Drummond. By
mid-July, he was advising his government that it would serve both British
and Italian interests best if Italy received control over Ethiopia.

Beneath her apparent enthusiasm for the Italian cause, there were signs
that Margherita had begun taking precautions in case Mussolini's gamble
led to disaster. She discussed with Missy the possibility of a lengthy return
visit to America, possibly as soon as the spring of 1936, and spoke of some
ideas for screenplays. She knew that Hollywood studios were paying as
much as $30,000 for scripts. Margherita was thinking of a possible refuge
in the United States. But her cultivation of the de Chambruns, and the
transfer of Vittorio Cerruti to Paris as Italian ambassador in June, offers
some evidence that she may have been thinking of France, as well.[29]

But Margherita's major effort to prevent a clash between Italy and Britain was an attempt to halt the invasion of Ethiopia. Her direct methods, arguments with Mussolini, had failed. Instead, she turned to bribery.

She learned that Ciano harbored doubts about the wisdom of his father-in-law's plans. Ciano's worries may have reflected Mussolini's own fears. Perhaps Margherita had heard such stories in May, when she and Ciano had both been in Paris. Or the idea may have been suggested by her friend Ambassador de Chambrun. Whatever stimulated her hopes, she visited London. There, she suggested to British officials that they offer Ciano a block of government-controlled shares in the Suez Canal Company. In return, Ciano would be expected to argue against the Ethiopian adventure and to stifle his pro-Nazi sympathies.

The plan seems clever. An Italian-British war could have damaged or closed the canal. A major stockholder would suffer from such a calamity. Nonetheless, it seems unlikely that Margherita's plan would have worked. The Cianos were corrupt, but Galeazzo dreamed of power, not wealth. He would not remain heir-apparent if he clashed too forcefully with the Duce's will. Furthermore, Mussolini was determined to go forward. Nothing his thirty-two-year-old minister said would deter him. In any case, the British refused to consider the idea. Meanwhile, Mussolini moved toward war.

Throughout most of July, Mussolini believed that the British would offer no more than diplomatic protests if he invaded Ethiopia. But in late July and early August, the attitude of the British government changed. Mussolini's propaganda campaign had gained him little sympathy with the British public. The overwhelming majority of British voters expected their government to support the League. In addition to this pressure, Cabinet thinking changed about the implications of the Italian conquest of Ethiopia. Unless they stopped Mussolini in Africa, how could the British and French persuade the other countries of Europe to join them in halting Hitler?

After consultations with Laval, who had become French premier in June, the British joined the French in persuading the Italians to meet in Paris from August 14 to 18 to work out a peaceful settlement of the East African crisis. Reluctantly backed by the French, who had suggested far more generous proposals, the British offered the Italians extensive economic concessions in Ethiopia. On Mussolini's instructions, the Italian representatives rejected the settlement. The Duce wanted war.

In response to this impasse, the British Cabinet held emergency meetings on August 21–22. It ordered units of the Royal Navy's Home Fleet to concentrate at Gibraltar, and the Mediterranean Fleet to leave its vulnerable base at Malta and deploy to Alexandria. The two fleets were in position to blockade the Italians in the Mediterranean. Rumors circulated that the British might shut the Suez Canal, cutting off Mussolini's forces in East Africa. Trapped in Rome by the crisis, sweltering in the terrible heat of August, Mussolini displayed increasing signs of anxiety. Adding to his discomfiture, Mussolini came under unexpected pressure from Roosevelt.[30]

During the crisis, a serious stomach-ulcer attack had confined Breckinridge Long to a clinic in Austria and kept him there until early September. In Long's absence, Alexander Kirk kept the president informed of developments in Italy. As a result, Roosevelt finally began receiving accurate information about Mussolini's intention to attack Ethiopia, the support he was receiving from Laval, and the efforts of some British diplomats to prevent Italian aggression. There was little that Roosevelt could do in a formal capacity. The isolationist majority in Congress planned to block any legislation that might give the president power to take action against Italy in the dispute. By the end of August, Roosevelt realized that he could act only in secret.[31]

Meanwhile, Roosevelt received Karl von Wiegand at the White House on the late afternoon of July 18. When Wiegand entered the White House, he expected to meet a broken cripple. Instead he met a vibrant, utterly charming man, filled with "such absolute 'joy of life.' " To his amazement, the cynical reporter found himself falling under the spell of the man. By the time he left the White House, he had agreed to serve Roosevelt as a confidential agent. He bore a personal letter from Roosevelt to Mussolini.

Before Wiegand arrived in Rome a month later, Mussolini received another letter from Roosevelt, delivered to him by Kirk on August 19. The letter begged Mussolini to resolve the Italian-Ethiopian crisis "without resort to armed conflict." Mussolini replied in an uncharacteristically angry manner, warning Kirk that if other countries tried to stop Italy by blocking the Suez Canal, he would respond with war. Three days later, Wiegand delivered Roosevelt's other message to Mussolini. After reading it, Mussolini told Wiegand that he would conquer Ethiopia whatever any country did to try to stop him. Mussolini insisted to Wiegand that "he could destroy Malta in half an hour and deal drastically with the Mediterranean Fleet."[32]

No trace of the letter that Wiegand delivered to Mussolini can be found. From subsequent statements by Roosevelt, as well as from Mussolini's apparently irrational retort to Kirk, it appears that Roosevelt had secretly urged the British to shut the Suez Canal and had so informed Mussolini. Mussolini almost certainly knew this already. Italian Army Intelligence was routinely reading coded American, British, and French diplomatic messages, and was burglarizing Ambassador Drummond's safe as well.

From these same sources, Mussolini knew that the British Admiralty felt woefully unprepared for war. The entrance of the main units of the Royal Navy into the Mediterranean was largely a bluff. It seemed unlikely that the British would really risk war by blocking the Suez Canal. Roosevelt had unwittingly antagonized Mussolini to no purpose. In Mussolini's eyes, the president had revealed himself as a hypocrite and an enemy. In public, Roosevelt called for a peaceful resolution of the crisis, but in secret, he urged the British to take a step that was tantamount to war. From this moment on, Mussolini's antagonism toward Roosevelt grew.[33]

Two minor incidents aggravated Mussolini's hostility toward Americans. Neither Margherita nor Mussolini could enlist Nicholas Murray Butler's support for the cause of Italian expansion. In July, following a trip to Europe, Butler had expressed considerable sympathy for Italy's plight as a poor, overcrowded nation, deprived of the resources of the colonial empires enjoyed by Britain and France. But Butler was appalled when he realized Mussolini meant to conquer Ethiopia by force of arms. For all his admiration of Mussolini, the Nobel Peace Prize winner could not countenance aggression. Through an intermediary, Butler informed Mussolini that his resort to war to settle an international grievance represented an act of anachronistic barbarism. The ardor of the president of Columbia University for the Duce had finally cooled.[34]

In July, the directors of the United Press had discovered that Thomas Morgan was a secret member of the Fascist party. Morgan's parroting of the official Italian line on the crisis with Ethiopia during the spring and the summer of 1935 had brought UP Vice-President Edward Keen to investigate matters in Rome. Keen soon learned enough about Morgan's shabby politics, corruption, laziness, and sordid sex life to convince him that the reporter should be dismissed. But first he used Morgan to arrange an interview with Mussolini. Then Keen told Morgan what he knew and forced his resignation to avoid paying the reporter a severance settlement.

Morgan complained bitterly to Mussolini. Cut off without a salary, with a wife, two sons, and several girlfriends to support, Morgan found himself in considerable financial difficulty. Mussolini agreed to help Morgan in a lawsuit against the UP. Even Ambassador Long expressed his sympathy after he returned to Rome, and offered Morgan a loan. In the meantime, Morgan scraped by with a number of free-lance assignments, and by serving as an Italian propagandist. In the summer of 1936, the UP settled with Morgan for $4,878, and he left Rome for New York. Keen never made public what he knew. Morgan escaped being branded as a Fascist agent, and began a new career in America as an author. He maintained his credentials as a journalist, occasionally working for Hearst's International News Service and Henry Luce's *Time* and *Life*.

With the possible exception of Richard Washburn Child, Morgan had been the American closest to Mussolini for the previous ten years. Added to Mussolini's problems with Roosevelt and Butler, the whole episode reinforced Mussolini's growing convictions about American hypocrisy, puritanism, and anti-Italian prejudice.[35]

With Morgan gone, Margherita's influence with Americans such as Ambassador Long, and her connections through Anne O'Hare McCormick and Missy Meloney to *The New York Times* and *Herald Tribune,* made her especially valuable to Mussolini. U.S. government policy and American public opinion were to become crucial factors in the struggle that began in late August. Despite appearances, the conflict proved to be more diplomatic and economic than military.

A secret exchange of messages between Rome and London indicated that each side wished to avoid war with the other. Given the Royal Navy's concerns about the state of its readiness, the British did not want to risk war with Italy without firm guarantees of French support. These Laval refused to give. As a result, the British government promised Mussolini to keep the Suez Canal open, and to seek only economic, not military, sanctions through the League. In turn, Mussolini offered assurances that he would confine the conflict to East Africa, and maintain his vigilance against Germany in Europe. Fascist propaganda portrayed Mussolini as having faced down the powerful British Empire in order to secure for his people the great riches of Ethiopia. Patriotic support for the Duce soared.[36]

Following Missy's departure from Rome, Margherita had spent most of the remaining summer and the early fall at Il Soldo. Fiammetta's husband, Livio, was mobilized with one of the new Fascist Militia divisions, and sailed in September for Eritrea. Fiammetta, pregnant for the second time, and little Roberto kept Margherita company. Margherita and her family had escaped the summer heat on their hillside outside Cavallasca for many years. But Il Soldo lay conveniently close to the Swiss border. She may have been preparing to flee abroad in the event of a European war. Breckinridge Long, who returned to Rome in early September, had sent his wife and daughter to Como for the same reason.

But the immediate danger of a clash between Italy and Britain seemed to have diminished by late September. Margherita could not resist seeing the spectacle of Mussolini's mobilization announcement in Rome. She returned to the capital sometime shortly before October 2.[37]

28

The Second Roman Empire

On the evening of October 2, Margherita watched quietly while the group around her pressed forward at the window of the Palazzo delle Assicurazioni Generali. After millions across Italy had assembled to listen by broadcast, Mussolini stepped onto his balcony to speak to a huge crowd in the Piazza Venezia. Looking across the great, torch-lit square, packed with thousands of black-shirted Fascist Militia, Margherita had trouble distinguishing his features. But his harsh, metallic voice boomed clearly through the loudspeakers.

That night, Mussolini delivered one of his finest speeches. The crowd interrupted him repeatedly with shouts of approval. He demanded, had not the Allies guaranteed Italy fitting rewards for the nearly 700,000 dead it had suffered in the Great War? Then, had they not robbed Italy of its well-deserved colonial prizes at the peace table? Now, after twenty years of broken promises, Mussolini was ready to seize what was rightfully Italian. He swore that he would be victorious in East Africa, and maintain the peace in Europe. The Italians had no quarrel with the British and French, but they were determined to defend their honor and their rights.

Mussolini warned his people that they were about to face a great test. But in this "historic moment" they would prove themselves worthy of their glorious past and their heroic Fascist present. It was "against this people of heroes, of saints, of poets, of artists, of explorers, of colonizers, of immigrants" that the League dared to speak of sanctions. Would they show their mettle to the world? Mussolini looked down at the great crowd and waited for its reply.

The tens of thousands gathered beneath his balcony let forth a great shout of support and then broke into repeated chants of *"Duce! Duce! Duce!"* Watching from across the piazza, Margherita laughed bitterly to herself. "The hypocrite!" she thought. After arguing the previous May that the Italian cultural heritage had no practical value, Mussolini cynically invoked it to whip his listeners into a frenzy.

Turning to her companion, Renato Trevisani, she said quietly: "It is the beginning of the end." "Why do you say that?" asked Trevisani, taken aback by her remark. "Do you think we are going to lose this war in Africa?" "No, Renato," she replied, "I say it because, unfortunately, we will win, and he will lose his head!" Restless and gloomy, Margherita repeated the phrase over and over again that night. Shortly afterward she returned to Il Soldo.[1]

The next morning, Mussolini's forces invaded Ethiopia from the north and south. Italian bombers struck deep into Haile Selassie's empire. Two of the planes were piloted by Mussolini's sons Vittorio and Bruno and one by his son-in-law, Galeazzo Ciano.

Within two weeks, the League imposed an arms and credit embargo on Italy. In the United States, neutrality legislation and the provisions of the Johnson Act duplicated the effects of the embargo. The League considered shutting down all trade with Italy, but U.S. cooperation was considered crucial for the success of further sanctions. As a result, they postponed a decision about banning iron, steel, coal, and oil exports to Italy until the American position became clear.

The invasion of Ethiopia placed Margherita's relations with her American friends under severe strain. Three times that late summer and early fall, Margherita wrote to Missy asking for help in arranging another visit to the United States. She received no reply. It seems that the only American who responded to her letters was Ezra Pound. He suggested that Margherita use Kipling's "The White Man's Burden" as the basis of an article pointing out the hypocrisy of British opposition to the Ethiopian War. Her reply indicated scant enthusiasm.

In mid-October, Margherita, Fiammetta, and little Roberto returned to Rome for Amedeo's wedding on the twenty-sixth. Mussolini did not attend the ceremony, but he invited Amedeo and Pierangela to visit him in the Palazzo Venezia, to express his personal congratulations. Mussolini was kind to the young couple, and put them at their ease. Despite the strain between himself and Margherita, Mussolini had fond memories of Amedeo stretching back twenty years. When the young couple expressed their anxiety about the future, Mussolini assured them that Italy would win its war with Ethiopia and its struggle with Britain. Pierangela asked bluntly how Italy could deal with an economic blockade imposed by most of Italy's trading partners. Mussolini was annoyed by her question and brought the interview to an abrupt conclusion.[2]

In fact, Mussolini was quite worried about the progress of his invasion of Ethiopia. His supreme commander in East Africa, General Emilio De Bono, was advancing far too slowly in the north. Meanwhile, Prime Minister Stanley Baldwin had scheduled a general election in Britain for

November 14. The prime minister had campaigned on a platform of complete support for the League. Mussolini expected Baldwin's reelection, followed by firm British backing for the economic sanctions. De Bono had to seize a significant chunk of Ethiopian territory quickly. Otherwise, if the Italian war effort was perceived as slackening, the League might decide to apply the coup de grâce of an oil boycott. But logistical problems and difficult terrain had slowed De Bono's invasion to a crawl. He had yet to win a significant victory. The Ethiopians had melted away before the Italian advance, refusing to give battle until their main armies had assembled.

On October 31, Long attended ceremonies marking the inauguration of the new campus of the University of Rome. Under the leadership of Piacentini, a team of architects had designed and directed the construction of the university city over the previous three years. The architecture was varied but most buildings were Rationalist in conception. In the Great Hall, Mario Sironi had painted a huge mural representing Italy standing defiantly before a huge *fascio* and an arch of triumph, while a winged victory soared overhead. Margherita found the predominantly orange-brown stucco and travertine university buildings to her taste. She took pride in the degree to which the campus reflected her influence on official architecture.

Mussolini, his ministers, and the entire university faculty appeared at the opening in the uniforms of the armed services or the Fascist Militia. The Duce took the occasion to remind those present of the links between ancient and modern Rome, of how at that moment, Italian troops represented the vanguard of civilization in Africa. Mussolini raged against the League for daring to oppose his civilizing mission by imposing sanctions. He swore that the Italian people would never surrender to pressure. Mussolini used such intemperate language that his speech was heavily edited for diplomatic reasons before publication in *Il Popolo d'Italia*.

Long was not sure if Mussolini actually felt the anger he displayed during his oration. Still, the ambassador worried that Mussolini might be close to some rash action, and he feared the consequences. Hoping to forestall this, Long asked Margherita to meet with him at the American Embassy on November 3. But before she met with Long, Margherita saw Mussolini.[3]

On November 2, the League ordered trade sanctions against Italy to commence on the eighteenth. Since they were not members, neither the United States nor Germany was affected by the order. Brazil and Switzerland, as well as the Italian client states of Albania, Austria, and Hungary, refused to comply.

When Margherita came to see Long, she acted extremely anxious. She told Long that Mussolini was convinced that Britain was using the League to destroy Italy. The British, she said, regarded the Italian attempt to conquer Ethiopia as the first step in an Italian attack on their empire. This was untrue, she insisted, but Mussolini would never surrender to British threats. He would sooner fight them. A war with Britain would inevitably spread, and would destroy European civilization. As a result, the Germans would seize Austria, and Hitler would become master of the continent. Margherita begged Long to request Roosevelt's intervention to arbitrate the dispute. She added that after her conversation with the president in April 1934, she knew how much Roosevelt listened to Long's advice.

Long told her that it was politically impossible for Roosevelt to act. Congress had tied his hands. But Long promised that he was always ready to send a personal message from Mussolini to the president. He remarked on Mussolini's behavior two days earlier. Was it true, he inquired, that Mussolini was as inflamed as he appeared? Margherita replied that the Duce was under enormous strain; she had never seen him lose control in public to the degree that he had during his speech at the University of Rome. Long begged her to tell Mussolini how dangerous such public displays could be in a time of crisis. She promised to convey the warning.

Margherita also indicated that she had been in touch with Vatican officials. She argued that it was unfair and illegal for sanctions to be imposed on the Holy See, but that would be the consequence of the League's decision. She hinted strongly that Pius XI stood behind Mussolini. She also expressed her opinion that democratic electoral politics were driving Baldwin toward a confrontation with Mussolini he would otherwise have avoided. Long assured her this was not the case. He had little admiration for the British, and considered their opposition to the Italian campaign in East Africa to be inspired by selfishness and unreasonable fear. Nonetheless, the ambassador believed that after Baldwin's probable reelection, the prime minister would do his utmost to settle matters with Italy peacefully. Stressing that he was speaking only for himself, Long suggested to Margherita that Mussolini contact the British government and reassure them about his intentions. One way to defuse the Mediterranean crisis would be to calm British fears about threats to their empire and their communications network in the Mediterranean.[4]

It is unlikely that Margherita had suggested Roosevelt's mediation on her own initiative. Not only had she seen Mussolini just before her conversation with Long, but she reported back to the Duce immediately afterward. Given Roosevelt's aggressive messages in late August, how could Mussolini have expected the president to try to settle the crisis between Italy and Britain in an impartial manner? Mussolini's real object must have been to avoid an American oil embargo.

League trade sanctions did not threaten Italy's immediate future. Mussolini had stockpiled enough raw materials to endure a fairly long economic siege. He used the threat of sanctions to depict Italy as the victim of Western "plutocracy" and whip up patriotic fervor for the war against Ethiopia. The sanctions also made it easy for Mussolini to impose comprehensive state controls over the economy. Under ordinary circumstances, the measures would have been highly unpopular, but he considered economic controls essential in order to wage further wars of conquest.

An oil boycott would have had far more serious repercussions. Available storage facilities could hold no more than three or four months' worth of fuel. Anticipating a petroleum ban by the League, Mussolini had ordered his government to begin purchasing as much oil as possible from American companies, rather than from Italy's usual European suppliers, in mid-1935. This diminished the threat of League oil sanctions, but left Italy vulnerable to a possible American oil embargo.

This seems to explain Margherita's proposal to Long. Had Roosevelt agreed to arbitrate the dispute, he could hardly have asked Congress to cut off or reduce the flow of American oil to Italy. Such an action would completely undercut any attempt to settle the crisis. Perhaps Long understood Margherita's ploy, but more likely he simply rejected her suggestion for domestic political reasons. Long was not a professional diplomat, but a politician who had been rewarded for managing Roosevelt's 1932 campaign.[5]

Still the American ambassador had supplied Margherita with a useful suggestion: that Mussolini approach the British and offer them a general agreement on the security of their communications through the Mediterranean and Red seas. After Margherita's report to him, the Duce contacted British Ambassador Drummond and initiated a series of conversations on the subject. An accord would reduce British support for the League and Ethiopia, refocus British and French attention on the German threat, and allow Italy to do the same.

Mussolini's talks with Drummond achieved nothing, but they did help delay decisive British action on oil sanctions. When Margherita dined with Long on November 29, she repeated her view that a League petroleum boycott would lead to war between Italy and Britain. But she thanked Long for helping to initiate the Drummond-Mussolini conversations. Long assured Margherita that she had no reason to worry. The ambassador was convinced that Mussolini was going to overawe the British and win his war in Africa.

Throughout November, the Italian ambassadors in London and Paris conferred with British and French officials about a comprehensive settlement of the Ethiopian War. On December 7–8, British Foreign Secretary

Sir Samuel Hoare met Laval in Paris and agreed on the final details of the plan. Italy would receive relatively small pieces of Ethiopia to annex to Eritrea and Somalia. The remainder of Ethiopia would remain formally independent, but most of it would become a zone for exclusive Italian economic exploitation. The plan was to remain secret until Mussolini accepted it. Then it would be submitted to the League for *pro forma* approval and imposed on Haile Selassie.

Unfortunately for Hoare and Laval, the plan was leaked to the press almost immediately. The outrage of the British and French public, and a justified sense of betrayal at League headquarters, effectively doomed the plan. And even before the scheme collapsed, Mussolini indicated that the plan did not offer Italy enough. Hoare was forced to resign as foreign secretary. Laval hung on as French premier for a few weeks, but his prestige had suffered a mortal blow and he resigned in late January. The Ethiopian War and the Mediterranean crisis were only going to be ended on the battlefields of East Africa.[6]

Meanwhile, Mussolini replaced the slow-moving De Bono with Italy's foremost soldier, Marshal Pietro Badoglio. Badoglio arrived at his East African headquarters on November 28 and immediately set to untangling the supply and communications mess left behind by De Bono. Despite Mussolini's pleas that the diplomatic situation required decisive military action, Badoglio maintained his position on the ground while he straightened out his rear area.

On December 15, as the Hoare-Laval plan was collapsing, Ethiopian forces smashed into Badoglio's right flank. This attack marked the start of a great Ethiopian counteroffensive. Over the next three weeks, the Italians were driven back across their entire northern front.

The collapse of efforts to settle the war by negotiations, followed by the Ethiopian counterattack, plunged Margherita into gloom. In early November, she had received an angry visit from a Fascist Militia officer. He had a number of postcards signed with Margherita's name, and he demanded to know if they were genuine. The cards were addressed to various Italian and foreign officials and contained obscene remarks about Mussolini. A monthlong investigation revealed the cards to be forgeries and the Militia officer was disciplined for his unauthorized actions. Margherita received profuse apologies from the authorities for the affair. But she and Fiammetta found the incident very disturbing. It underscored how easily their lives could be destroyed at Mussolini's whim.[7]

Other aspects of her personal life were more pleasant. Newlyweds Amedeo and Pierangela were very happy. Fiammetta was bearing up well to her separation from Livio and her pregnancy. Livio had recently sent news from northern Ethiopia that he was safe. Margherita's work on her book on America was proceeding smoothly. Ada Negri sent her a new book of poems, *Il Dono,* and Margherita took genuine pleasure in her friend's verse. But her favorites among Ada's new poems were the saddest. Beyond the circle of her family and friends, Margherita saw reason to fear what was happening in Italy.

Of course, Margherita appeared to support the war enthusiastically. Writing to Missy shortly after the Hoare-Laval plan had been revealed, Margherita stressed her approval of their friend Walter Lippmann's advice that Roosevelt keep America out of the growing crisis in Europe. She hoped that the Hoare-Laval plan would be acceptable to all parties. And she expressed her admiration for the patriotism and self-sacrifice she was witnessing among her people. Ten days later, she expressed similar sentiments to Butler and begged his understanding of the Italian position.

The sanctions had inspired Mussolini to launch one of his most successful domestic propaganda campaigns. He called on the Italian people to save and sacrifice in any way they could. Most Italians responded with touching generosity. In particular, a genuinely spontaneous movement arose for the contribution of precious metal to the state treasury. Vittorio Emanuele III donated gold bullion, Gabriele D'Annunzio his military decorations, church congregations their votive offerings, and the Jewish community of Rome the gold menorah from its synagogue. Even anti-Fascists, like Benedetto Croce and Luigi Albertini, willingly handed over medallions and jewelry. Most Italian women had only one small piece of gold or silver to offer. In a countrywide ceremony on December 18, the wives, mothers, and widows of Italy—from Queen Elena on down—exchanged their wedding rings for new rings of iron.

As the "Day of the Ring" approached, Ada Negri published a poem summoning all the women of Italy, among whom "not one was deaf to the bell toll," to sacrifice their gold to the fatherland. Margherita was not ready to do that. She acquired a special handbag that concealed a small strongbox. She put her entire horde of gold coins into it. She urged a friend to take similar precautions. If Mussolini continued in the direction he was going, Margherita warned, Italy would be ruined, and the gold might buy a ticket out of the country.

But "The Day of the Ring" was entirely symbolic. None of the rings or other objects was ever melted down. Mussolini still held them in his personal possession in April 1945. The conquest of Ethiopia was not in danger of faltering over a lack of gold, only of petroleum.

When the Ethiopians attacked Badoglio's forces, Margherita shared her fears with Ada. Fiammetta had become very frightened for Livio. The propaganda organs of the regime had made it sickeningly clear what the Ethiopians did to wounded and captured Italians. Margherita worried that

Amedeo might soon be called up for military service. She remarked, "I've had enough of these 'historic hours,' thanks. I'd like a few ordinary years, no?" It was a dark Christmas season, Italy's worst since the days after Caporetto.[8]

The fighting in northern Ethiopia had taken a far more serious turn than censorship permitted most Italians to know. On December 22, after a week of ferocious enemy assaults, Mussolini ordered Badoglio to employ Italy's secret weapon: poison gas. Within hours, Italian bombers were dropping canisters filled with mustard gas on the advancing Ethiopian columns. Even with horrible burns inflicted on thousands of advancing soldiers, the surviving Ethiopians pressed their attacks. The confidence of the Italian High Command began to crack.

Galeazzo Ciano, pleading medical problems, had sailed from Eritrea when the Ethiopian counteroffensive appeared imminent. To Mussolini, Ciano described the military situation as hopeless and urged his father-in-law to seek some kind of understanding with Hitler. He argued that this was the only way for Italy to break out of its diplomatic isolation and find a way to negotiate a reasonable settlement of the conflict. As rumors about the real situation in East Africa spread, the lira, then officially pegged at twelve to the dollar, plunged to eighteen to the dollar on the black market. Rich Italians began transferring their funds abroad illegally. Others, such as Alberto Moravia, left the country. Exempted from military service by an adolescent bout with tuberculosis, the novelist sailed to New York and sought out Prezzolini at the Casa Italiana.[9]

Between the precarious stalemate in Ethiopia, the menace of oil sanctions, and a contracting economy, Mussolini found himself in an increasingly desperate position. All he could do was to stall and bluff while he hoped for a military victory in East Africa to rescue him. When Roosevelt delivered his State of the Union message on January 3, 1936, he strongly condemned "nations which are dominated by the twin spirits of autocracy and aggression" and which attempted to solve problems by reverting "to the old belief in the law of the sword." Roosevelt submitted new neutrality legislation to Congress. The bill proposed giving the president the authority to ban oil and metal exports to any nation, should he decide such action could bring a war to an end.

Mussolini had no doubt about the intended target of Roosevelt's initiative. He ordered the press to respond with an angry rejection of American interference in Italian domestic politics. Faced with the abandonment of U.S. neutrality, Mussolini took Ciano's advice. On January 7, 1936, Mussolini called the German ambassador to his office. The Duce informed him that the Italian-French agreements had effectively been voided. There was a strong possibility of war with Britain. In return for assistance from Hitler,

Mussolini indicated his willingness to abandon his defense of Austria.[10]

In the second week of January, military events brought Mussolini some grounds for hope. In northern Ethiopia, continuing gas attacks and tenacious Italian resistance finally brought the counteroffensive against Badoglio's forces to a halt. The immediate danger of the collapse of the Italian campaign was past. And on the southern front, starting on January 12, General Rodolfo Graziani, commander of Italian forces based in Somalia, launched a major offensive. In a week, Graziani's bombers, motorized infantry, and artillery destroyed one of the two main Ethiopian armies in the south.

Beginning in late December, Mussolini had rushed three more divisions to Eritrea. He ordered Badoglio to renew the Italian advance in the north. He wanted to convince the American Congress that Italy was winning the war in Ethiopia, so that it would be a senseless provocation to give the president oil-embargo powers. If the danger of a petroleum ban passed, Mussolini could bring overwhelming force to bear against Haile Selassie.

Badoglio escaped catastrophe by the barest margin in the major offensive he began on January 19. The marshal's men had advanced too confidently; one Italian division was cut off and surrounded. The Ethiopians poured all their reserves into the gap this created. By the evening of January 22, Badoglio was in despair—his only apparent option was to order a general retreat. To do so meant abandoning huge supplies of ammunition to the enemy. Without those munitions, Badoglio could not defend Eritrea. The Ethiopians would flood into the colony, and any Italians who survived the rout would be driven into the Red Sea.

Nonetheless, Badoglio ordered a withdrawal. He saw no alternative. Fortunately for him and for Mussolini's regime, the marshal's staff refused to obey. They simply could not bring themselves to set a massacre in motion. They argued strenuously with their commander until he reversed his order. At daybreak, Italian bombers took off with their deadly loads of poison chemicals. For twelve hours, they dropped mustard gas on the advancing Ethiopians. On the ground, the Italian forces fought grimly to hold their positions. A day and another night of bloodshed followed. Finally, on January 24, the Ethiopians fell back.

Ciano's Propaganda Ministry managed to keep the truth about this near-disaster from the Italian people, as well as from the European and American public. Even the various European intelligence services did not have a clear picture of what had happened. Mussolini's propaganda machine trumpeted Badoglio's failed offensive as a great victory.[11] American advisers were duped into believing an Italian victory was imminent; they informed the president that oil sanctions would not deter but only antagonize Mussolini. The Duce was prepared to continue fighting, even if it meant the ruin of Europe, before he surrendered to pressure.

Influential Italian-Americans, notably Generoso Pope and the Giannini brothers, urged Roosevelt not to apply economic pressure on Italy. Breckinridge Long also advised the president against the sanctions. Margherita had persuaded Long that Mussolini was the hero of the crisis, leading his embattled nation against a British Empire too jealous to grant the Italians even a small piece of Africa. He secretly lobbied against Roosevelt's bill together with Key Pittman, chairman of the Senate Foreign Relations Committee.

Walter Lippmann worried that banning petroleum exports was hardly a neutral act. Giving the president the power to take such an aggressive action on his own initiative set a dangerous precedent for the future. By the first days of February, Roosevelt abandoned his bill. He recognized that he would be unable to get congressional approval for the sanctions.

Mussolini experienced tremendous relief when he realized the president's proposal had been defeated. Anne O'Hare McCormick saw him for an interview on February 4, and noticed he seemed to be free of the terrible strain of the previous two months. He made no secret of the fact that the reason for his calm was the impending withdrawal of Roosevelt's neutrality bill.[12]

Mussolini still needed a military victory to bring the Ethiopian War to a successful conclusion. Recognizing what was at stake for both of them and for Italy, Badoglio promised him one. This time, the marshal delivered. After three new divisions and masses of artillery were moved to the front, the Italian forces on the northern front began a large offensive by ground and air on February 10. The Italians smashed through the Ethiopian mountain defenses that had blocked their southward advance. Badoglio had the fleeing enemy bombed. By the time he called off the aerial bombardment on February 19, thousands of Ethiopians had fallen.

On February 27, Badoglio launched another offensive against one of the two remaining Ethiopian armies in the north. In a two-pronged attack, Badoglio sought to encircle and annihilate his opponents. Thanks to superior mobility, many Ethiopians escaped the trap. But they could not outrun the Italian bombers. In ferocious gas attacks lasting until March 6, Badoglio's air forces pursued and slaughtered the retreating Ethiopian warriors.

Badoglio turned his attention to the last of the Ethiopian armies, arrayed on his extreme right flank. The marshal attempted another encircling maneuver. Once again, the Ethiopians broke out and fell back. By now the Italian air force had perfected its gas tactics. This time, rather than preparing bombs, Italian ground crews had rigged up spray devices on the aircraft. Anticipating the enemy's line of retreat, Italian bombers saturated all river crossings and roads with mustard gas. As the Ethiopians blundered their way south, many fell victim to lingering pools of the noxious chemicals. The survivors reached the Takaze River on the morning of March 3. One hundred twenty Italian bombers were circling overhead. Ciano piloted one; Farinacci flew in another as an observer. Encouraged by Badoglio's victories, Ciano had returned to Africa in mid-February, accompanied by Farinacci.

As the Ethiopian soldiers began wading across the river, they were blanketed in phosgene, chlorine, and mustard gas. Through this deadly haze, the Italian bombardiers rained eighty tons of high explosive. Other bombers dropped incendiary bombs to set fire to the woods on either riverbank. Those desperate men who made it across the river and through the burning forest on the other side encountered a vast area saturated with mustard gas. The soldiers were forced to flee through the chemicals barefooted, under continuous strafing and bombing. By the evening of March 4, Badoglio had wiped out the last of the northern Ethiopian armies. All that lay between him and Addis Ababa was Haile Selassie's select army, formed around the Imperial Guard.[13]

Hitler had been observing these events carefully. The crisis brought on by the Italian invasion of Ethiopia had greatly weakened the anti-German front. Since the summer of 1935, Mussolini had defied the League, disregarded French pleas, withstood British threats, frustrated Roosevelt's political maneuvers, and gone on to smash the Ethiopians on the battlefield. Hitler's admiration for Mussolini soared, while his contempt for the Western democracies increased.

Hitler decided to take advantage of the moment to reintroduce German Army units into the demilitarized Rhineland in defiance of the Versailles Treaty. British forces were concentrated in the Mediterranean, the Middle East, and East Africa in response to Mussolini's campaign. Hitler believed that the French would be too frightened to act against him, despite the return of the German threat to their Rhineland borders.

In late February, the German ambassador received Mussolini's assurance that he would cause no trouble if Hitler moved German troops into the Rhineland. Hitler feared that if he waited too long, Mussolini would complete his conquest of Ethiopia and reconstitute the anti-German front in return for an end to sanctions. Hitler occupied the Rhineland on March 7. At the same time, he announced his willingness to rejoin the League of Nations. The offer frightened Mussolini. He thought Hitler was seeking to prevent a strong Western response to the reoccupation by offering to join in League sanctions against Italy.

As Hitler had predicted, the French refused to act against him without

British support, and the British were too overextended to offer any. The possibility of League sanctions against Germany was discussed. But Hitler's offer to rejoin the League muddied the issue hopelessly. In the end, the French and British only issued diplomatic protests, which Hitler ignored.

After a few days, Mussolini realized that Hitler's League offer had been nothing but a clever ploy. Germany would never return to Geneva. The advantages of having British attention shifted from East Africa to Western Europe became obvious. For all practical purposes, the German remilitarization of the Rhineland had ended any lingering threat of oil sanctions or the closing of the Suez Canal. If Badoglio and Graziani could destroy the last of Haile Selassie's armies, all of Ethiopia could be brought under the dominion of Rome. Mussolini could deal with the problem of Germany and Austria after settling matters in Africa.

Badoglio's victories in February had relieved Margherita's immediate anxieties. She put aside her plans to flee the country. The plans had been a source of considerable tension, since Fiammetta was scheduled to give birth in mid-March. But Margherita's underlying fear of a division of Europe into rival British-French and Italo-German camps returned, even before the Rhineland crisis. After she and Anne O'Hare McCormick had tea with Long on February 23, Margherita stayed behind to have another lengthy talk with the American ambassador.

She indicated her continuing unhappiness over the failure of the Hoare-Laval plan and the subsequent worsening of Italian relations with the Western democracies. Margherita told Long a preposterous story about how the entire Italian submarine force had surfaced in the vicinity of the British Mediterranean Fleet in September, then raised and lowered their ensigns in salute. However fictitious the tale, she made the point that the Italians sought no quarrel with the British, but expected respect for their new military might and Great Power status. The problem lay in British disdain for Italian demands for "a place in the sun."

Margherita worried that British stubbornness and French acquiescence to the British lead were driving Mussolini into an alliance with Hitler. Long agreed that British insistence on placing Italy under League sanctions had only strengthened Mussolini's hold over the Italian people. Margherita expressed her appreciation for Long's help in preventing American participation in an oil boycott. This had saved Europe from a war. But even the mere threat of a boycott had left the Duce in a mood for revenge against the democracies.

Margherita encouraged Long to consider an American remedy to Italy's estrangement from the West. If there was a way to resolve the war-debt question, then Italy could escape the restrictions of the Johnson Act and float new loans in the United States. American money could be used to develop Italy's new empire in Ethiopia. And unlike loans from the British and French, there would be no political strings attached. Italy could escape being forced to choose sides in Europe. American assistance might provide a way to keep Italy from falling into the German orbit, and Mussolini could devote his energies to exploiting his East African conquests. Long found Margherita's arguments exciting.[14]

No longer concerned about access to the Swiss frontier, Margherita left Il Soldo to give lectures in Naples and Sardinia in late February and early March. She took Fiammetta with her for company and for a brief vacation. Because of this both of them missed a ceremony honoring Ada's poetic achievements organized by the Milan city government. Margherita made up for the slight by advocating that *La Stampa* award Ada its Berardelli Prize for her latest book of poetry.

No sooner had she relaxed, however, than Hitler's remilitarization of the Rhineland renewed Margherita's worries. She believed that Hitler, encouraged by the supine French reaction, would probably make his next move against one of France's allies in Central or Eastern Europe. She agreed to give a series of lectures in Vienna and Budapest in early April on Fascism and modern art, despite the refusal of Dino Alfieri, Ciano's deputy at the Ministry of Press and Propaganda, to subsidize her trip or grant it any official recognition. She wanted to learn what she could from Papen and other friends in Austria and Hungary about Hitler's intentions in that region.

Before she left, Fiammetta gave birth to a girl on March 17, who was named Margherita in her grandmother's honor. No reply came back from Livio in response to telegrams announcing the arrival of his daughter. Fiammetta acted bravely, but the news of the recent heavy fighting prompted real fears for her husband's safety. Margherita contacted Mussolini and begged for his personal intervention. Even the highest priority messages from the Duce brought no information for several days. Finally Livio was located, and they learned that he was quite safe. Adding to this good news, Amedeo and Pierangela informed the family that they were expecting their first child.

Margherita often escaped from her fears by busying herself with her book on America. While Livio's fate was in doubt, she finished the final pages. She felt considerable pride in having written it in English. Still, she delivered the handwritten manuscript to Alexander Kirk with some trepidation. To her relief, he read it quickly and thought it excellent. "You positively have a style of your own as a very original English writer," he told her. Margherita promptly sent five chapters to Missy and asked for her help in finding an American publisher.

But she had not heard from Missy in some time. Margherita wondered whether their differences over the Ethiopian War had come between them. Italians felt such gratitude, she wrote, for the American refusal to join in sanctions against them. That had saved Europe, possibly the world, from a terrible war. The attitudes of enlightened Americans, such as their friends Walter Lippmann and Sinclair Lewis, had been very helpful. Margherita didn't even mind Lewis's anti-Fascist attitudes in his new novel, *It Can't Happen Here*. After all, no one was saying the Americans should become Fascists against their will. To show that there were no hard feelings on her part, she had written Lewis to thank him for the personally inscribed copy of the novel he had sent her.[15]

Just before her departure for Austria, Margherita telephoned Long and asked the ambassador and his wife to accompany her to the opera. But it was really only an excuse to talk, and when Long declined the invitation, they agreed to meet instead for tea. Long told her that he had discussed his plan for war-debt settlement and Ethiopian investment with Suvich, but he doubted that the foreign undersecretary understood the importance of the ideas. Margherita suggested that she speak directly to Mussolini. The ambassador readily agreed, so long as she did not antagonize Suvich. The project that Margherita had suggested to Long would be presented to Mussolini as the ambassador's own proposal. A few days later, Margherita left for Vienna.

Throughout March, Badoglio had been advancing cautiously southward in anticipation of a clash with Haile Selassie's personal army. The marshal prepared a motorized column for a rapid descent on Addis Ababa following the expected defeat of the emperor's force. On the southern front, Graziani concentrated his army before the enemy defenses stretched across the Ogaden desert. The general intended to smash his way through and then dash northwest toward the Ethiopian capital.

To Badoglio's surprise, Haile Selassie struck first, mounting a surprise attack at dawn of March 31. Italian firepower overwhelmed the Ethiopians' heroic assaults. The two exhausted armies faced each other across the battlefield for several days. Finally Haile Selassie ordered his forces to withdraw after sunset on April 3. Despite the danger of air attack, the Ethiopians continued their retreat by daylight, fearing an Italian encirclement if they halted. When they reached Lake Ashangi, the Ethiopians split into two columns to move south along both sides of the water.

Wave after wave of bombers swept down on the retreating columns, strafing, gassing, and dropping high explosive. Among the pilots and aircrew taking part in the gruesome slaughter were Ciano, Farinacci, and Mussolini's two sons. The air attacks continued for over ten hours, ceasing only with sunset. Wounded Ethiopians crawled to the edge of the lake to drink, but the Italians had dumped mustard gas into the water. The men died in terrible agony.

Badoglio ordered relentless chemical attacks for ten more days. The entire region was soaked in mustard gas. The slaughter plunged Haile Selassie into a depressed shock for over a week. When he recovered his equilibrium, he resumed his march south to Addis Ababa, returning in late April.

Meanwhile, Starace, the Fascist party secretary, had recently come to the war in search of glory. Badoglio ordered him to lead another motorized force to the west. The party secretary was to occupy the region around Lake Tana, an area vital to British interests since the lake is the source of the Blue Nile. Starace encountered virtually no resistance and reached his objective in early May. The party secretary decided that a dose of terror would guarantee the obedience of the peaceful inhabitants of the area. He ordered mass executions. At first, Starace shot his victims in the heart. But he soon decided that his prisoners suffered too little. Thereafter he fired point-blank into their genitals. But fate provided a small compensation for these atrocities. While fishing with hand grenades in a lake near his bomber-squadron base, Roberto Farinacci blew his right hand off. The grenade had exploded prematurely.

Goaded to emulate Badoglio's successes, Graziani launched his own offensive across the Ogaden on April 14. The last southern Ethiopian army offered desperate resistance, but after two weeks of pounding by Italian artillery and bombers, and constant gas attacks, the Ethiopian defenses crumbled. With this defeat, and British refusal to come to his aid, Haile Selassie decided that further resistance was useless. The emperor abandoned his capital on May 2 and left for exile in England. Three days later, Badoglio entered Addis Ababa at the head of his truck column. On May 9, advance units from the armies of Badoglio and Graziani linked up to the east of the Ethiopian capital.[16]

Margherita arrived in Vienna while the great battle north of Lake Ashangi raged. Her lectures, delivered in fluent German, were quite successful. She stressed Fascist Italian encouragement of modern trends in culture, and contrasted it with Hitler and Goebbels's intolerance of what they defined as decadent art. Her talks received excellent publicity in the Vienna and Budapest papers, but what she learned there left her very frightened.

Her conversations with Papen, Starhemberg, and other officials, diplomats, and cultural figures indicated that Italian influence in Austria and Hungary was crumbling, while German power in those countries was surging. The trend was particularly evident in Austria. Mussolini was withdrawing his subsidies for Starhemberg's staunchly anti-Nazi militia. Papen had begun talks to lift the ban on Nazi activities in Austria. The pro-Nazi wing of the Austrian labor movement was engaging in increasingly violent anti-Semitic demonstrations, with little interference from the police. To avoid offending Mussolini, Hitler was delaying the seizure of Austria for the moment. Instead he was preparing to move against Czechoslovakia. After he had absorbed France's democratic ally, Hitler would consider what to do with Austria.[17]

While Margherita was lecturing in Vienna and Budapest, Hitler sent his minister of justice, Hans Frank, to deliver lectures in Rome. But Frank's more important mission was to deliver Hitler's personal message to Mussolini. On April 4, Frank assured the Duce that Hitler was filled with admiration for the ongoing Italian conquest of Ethiopia. Surely Mussolini could see that British hostility and French treachery during the war proved the need for a partnership between Italy and Germany. Mussolini made no precise commitment but indicated his strong support for Hitler's march into the Rhineland. He also suggested that Hitler could do more to remove barriers to better relations with Italy by moderating Nazi attacks on the Catholic Church in Germany. Frank hoped that after Ciano returned from Africa, he would accept Hitler's invitation to attend the 1936 Olympic Games. Frank's trip to Rome was the first in a series of visits by high-ranking Fascists and Nazis to one another's countries over that spring, summer, and fall.[18]

There was very little that Margherita could do to offset the rapprochement between Berlin and Rome. When she visited Long on April 16, she learned that the American ambassador was leaving for America to have an ulcer treated. He was unlikely to return. Roosevelt had asked Long to manage his 1936 presidential campaign. Margherita and Long spoke for quite some time; she left certain that he would be a permanent friend to Fascist Italy.

The ambassador's last-minute attempt to arrange an Italo-American understanding came to nothing. When he saw Mussolini for a farewell visit on April 20, the Duce showed great interest in arranging a war-debt settlement and obtaining new loans from the United States. But Long was too sick to pursue the matter adequately. He left Rome three days later, and the chance for a comprehensive understanding between Roosevelt and Mussolini began to fade.

Mussolini's feelings toward Hitler may not have warmed, but his appreciation of German power and Western timidity had been sharpened by recent events. Despite the threat Nazi Germany posed to Austrian independence and Italian security, Hitler's offer of an Italo-German alliance against Bolshevik Russia and the democratic West had become more attractive to

Mussolini by the spring of 1936. In 1934 and 1935, Mussolini had stressed the differences between Fascism and National Socialism. After mid-1936, he came to see the ideologies as Italian and German versions of the same ideas.[19]

Mussolini was also interested in the project that Margherita and Long had conceived for American loans and investments in Ethiopia. In early May 1936, Mussolini explained his plans and hopes for Italian East Africa to one of his advisers. He wanted "to organize an Ethiopian force of one million soldiers, to create 50 air bases, a metallurgical industry, so that Ethiopia would find on its soil everything needed for its military development. Then we could carry out that juncture with Libya and free ourselves from the slavery to the Suez Canal." In other words, Mussolini intended to develop his new African empire in preparation for war with Britain.

The United States would never cooperate knowingly with such a venture. Nor would the Roosevelt administration offer Italy any special agreement on war debts without some spectacular gesture in return. But what could Mussolini offer, except a firm commitment to the Western camp? This he was no longer willing to make. He believed that he had defended the West against Nazi Germany in July 1934, only to be betrayed the following year over Ethiopia.[20]

Mussolini was not again going to sacrifice what he saw as Fascist Italy's interests for the benefit of the "plutocratic democracies." A chasm had opened up between Mussolini and the Western allies. Given Margherita's friendships and associations, her possessions and her love of wealth, her Jewish origins and her antagonism toward the Nazis, it was increasingly clear to Mussolini on what side of that divide she stood.

Nonetheless, Mussolini invited Margherita to join a select group who would listen to his proclamation of Empire from his office in the Palazzo Venezia. He was pleased by all she had done, despite her doubts and fears, to bring about his triumph. Thus, while all Italy awaited word of Badoglio's arrival in Addis Ababa, Margherita remained in Rome. In late April and early May she carried on negotiations with Frank Gervasi, Hearst's new Italian bureau chief, about the possibility of a new series of Mussolini articles for the American publisher. She also secretly gave the French ambassador a detailed account of what she had observed in Vienna and Budapest. Margherita warned de Chambrun that German influence in Central Europe was overwhelming. And she was able to spend some time with Bernard Berenson when the art expert visited Rome in late April.[21]

A week later, after Badoglio's troops had occupied the Ethiopian capital, Mussolini announced the victorious conclusion of the war to a vast throng assembled in the Piazza Venezia. On May 7, he delivered another address to more than one hundred thousand women of Rome, to thank them and all the women of Italy for their special sacrifices during the conquest of Ethiopia. Two nights later, Mussolini gave the greatest oration of his career: "The Proclamation of the Empire."

Another gigantic crowd began gathering in the center of Rome before sunset on May 9. By nine-thirty that spring night, hundreds of thousands had packed the piazza and the adjacent streets so tightly that women fainted in the crush. Floodlights illuminated the white bulk of the Vittorio Emanuele II Monument, glittering with the bayonets of the massed troops drawn up on its steps. Every window around the square shone with brilliant light. Searchlights played ceaselessly over the mob. All eyes were fastened on the Palazzo Venezia, its battlements aglow with torches.

Shortly before ten, cheered lustily by the crowd, the members of the Fascist Grand Council and the Council of Ministers arrived. The mood soared from excitement to exultation. A dozen brass bands competed with stirring renditions of patriotic tunes. The throng locked arms and sang, swaying back and forth. Between songs, Fascist party claques orchestrated rhythmic chants of *"Duce! Duce! Duce!"* Loudspeakers amplified the sound across the great plaza.

As the moment approached, the shutters of the great windows to the dictator's office in the Palazzo Venezia swung open. Shortly before ten-thirty, to the blare of trumpets, Mussolini strode proudly onto his balcony above the square. From the mob beneath there arose a great roar. With half-closed eyelids, Mussolini looked sternly down on the upturned faces, his chin thrust out and his head tilted back in his usual imperious manner.

The Duce gestured for silence. Once the bedlam had ceased, he leaned forward, seized the stone balustrade with his hands and began speaking. Through the harsh tones of his voice coursed a palpable current of emotion.

His speech was short. The multitude could not contain its passion. After a few sentences, they screamed their approval. Again and again came the responses from tens of thousands of throats, as Mussolini struggled to make himself heard. He had chosen his words to incite his audience to frenzy. He proclaimed that Italy had conquered and annexed its own great empire in Ethiopia, that King Vittorio Emanuele III had assumed the title of emperor, that the door on Italy's past failures had been closed forever, and that the way to a glorious future had been forced open. Mussolini finished with a peroration of fevered inspiration, his own feelings overwhelming any traces of restraint:

> The Italian People have created the Empire with their blood. They will enrich it with their labor and they will defend it against anyone with their arms.

In this supreme certainty, raise high, legionaries, your standards, your
swords and your hearts to salute, after fifteen centuries, the reappearance
of the Empire on the fateful hills of Rome.
Will you be worthy?

The enormous crowd collectively screamed its answer. "Yes!" Mussolini stared down sternly.

This cry is like a sacred oath, which binds you before God and before men
for life and for death!
Blackshirts! Legionaries!
Salute the king!

For a brief moment there was silence. Then the crowd broke into wild
shouts of jubilation. They had just witnessed the formal creation of the
Fascist Roman Empire.[22]

His face flushed from his effort and the excitement, Mussolini stepped
back into his office. Gathered before him were his leading officials,
and Margherita. Mussolini received their congratulations for his brilliant
speech. But he was in a foul mood. He muttered angrily, in a voice loud
enough for at least one of his officials to hear, that it was outrageous he had
to share credit for the triumph with the king. It was only he, Mussolini,
who deserved the title just conferred on him by the Fascist Grand Council:
"Founder of the Empire." But Mussolini's temper quickly cooled as he was
recalled repeatedly to the balcony to acknowledge the acclaim from the
celebrating masses below. Soon his face was aglow from joy and pride.

Although pleased to have been invited to witness such an important
event, Margherita found the occasion rather ridiculous. Overrunning Ethiopia was hardly equivalent to Scipio's defeat of Hannibal or Caesar's
conquest of Gaul. "We have been a little kingdom, now we're just a little
empire," she murmured sarcastically. The roars of the crowd continued to
shake the windows. Finally, Mussolini stepped inside after his last salute and
the doors to the balcony were shut behind him.

In an adjoining room, the diplomatic representatives of the nations that
had not adhered to the League sanctions had been invited to listen to
Mussolini's speech. They were brought into his office to present their
compliments. About fifty diplomats walked to the center of the room
where the Duce was standing. Long had returned to America, and Kirk had
been unwilling to attend the celebration. The senior American representatives present were the army and navy attachés. They stood to the rear,
behind the ambassadors and other senior diplomats, as befitted their relatively low status.

To their astonishment, Mussolini ignored the other diplomats and pushed his way to the two attachés. He shook the hand of each officer cordially. Then he spoke appreciatively of Breckinridge Long. Mussolini stressed that Long had understood the Italian people and had appreciated the difficult situation they had faced for the last eight months. He expressed his special thanks to the Americans for everything their ambassador had done to help Italy conquer Ethiopia.

A month later, while he was recuperating from a stomach-ulcer operation at the Mayo Clinic, Long received a letter from Margherita. She expressed Mussolini's personal thanks to the ambassador. "I am sure you will have rejoiced in seeing your prophecies of our victory so well fulfilled," she added. The victory became complete on July 15. That day, recognizing their futility, the League of Nations lifted the sanctions it had imposed on Italy. Without an American oil boycott, the other sanctions had done nothing but enrage Mussolini and unite his nation behind him. Long had been instrumental in preventing effective sanctions from saving Ethiopia. And Margherita, despite her doubts about Mussolini's foreign policy, had done her part for Fascist Italy too.[23]

29

The End of Illusions

Frank Gervasi was fascinated by Margherita. She was old enough to be his mother, but the twenty-eight-year-old Hearst reporter found her disturbingly attractive when they met for the first time in February 1936. Gervasi knew enough about art and literature to realize that the modern paintings and signed first editions in Margherita's Roman home were worth a fortune. He wanted to ask her permission to examine them closely, but didn't want to interrupt her cynical digs at Mussolini, or her hilariously malicious comments about Hitler.

However, they also had business to discuss. Hearst knew, regardless of his annoyance with Mussolini the previous year, that the Ethiopian War had made the Duce newsworthy. The publisher wanted a new contract and was willing to pay fifteen hundred dollars an article. Margherita promised Gervasi to raise the question with Mussolini. Over the next three months, she avoided giving Gervasi a definite answer. Margherita did obtain Mussolini's agreement for her to ghostwrite a new series of newspaper pieces, but she opened up the bidding to Missy's *Herald Tribune* and the United Press.

By mid-May 1936, Gervasi learned that both the UP and the *Herald Tribune* had made final offers of $1,675 an article. Gervasi offered Margherita $1,750. She said that Mussolini would probably find $21,000 a year satisfactory. On May 23, Margherita signed a preliminary agreement for a minimum of twelve articles to be delivered between the middle of that year and mid-1937. After working out the details of the contract, Margherita secured Gervasi's tentative acceptance of Mussolini's right to write for other foreign publications as well. Hearst grudgingly agreed to this, and the document was ready for signature by the end of the month. But Margherita had left Rome before the papers were ready, traveling first to Milan to attend the king's opening of the triennial exhibit of decorative and applied industrial art, and then to Venice for Vittorio Emanuele III's inauguration of the twentieth Biennale. After frantic but discreet inquiries, to avoid alerting UP and *Herald Tribune* reporters that they still had time to improve their offers, Gervasi located her in Venice. He rushed north to meet her at the Hotel Daniele.

Margherita was in a good mood. She was still marveling over *The Triumph of Italy,* Sironi's monumental mosaic commemorating the Ethiopian victory, and Martini's sculpture, *The Hero Subdues the Lion of Judah.* She had just seen both pieces in Milan. She found the Biennale less interesting, thanks to the encroachment of the propagandistic art favored by Farinacci. Still, enough of her artists were represented to satisfy her. She assured Gervasi that the contract would be signed soon. Some of Mussolini's officials were causing certain difficulties and delaying matters. They must proceed quietly and patiently, she told him.

Gervasi returned to Rome. More than a week passed and he heard nothing from Margherita. Finally she telephoned to tell him the deal was off. She was very sorry but there was nothing to be done. The six-year collaboration with the Hearst press had abruptly come to an end. Gervasi never did learn why Mussolini decided to reject Hearst's offer. He could only guess that it had something to do with the Italo-German rapprochement that was beginning that spring and summer.

He was partially right. Galeazzo and Edda Ciano had blocked the deal, believing that it would hinder the achievement of the Nazi-Fascist alliance they hoped for.[1] Edda had been captivated by Hitler, and charmed by Joseph and Magda Goebbels, during her visit to Berlin on June 8–10, 1936. When she returned, Mussolini appointed her husband Italian foreign minister, and his heir apparent. The Cianos, who now had the power to injure Margherita, must have seen Mussolini's continuing relationship with a Jew as an affront to the Nazis.

Mussolini began meeting with Galeazzo daily to coordinate foreign policy. By the fall of 1936, the pro-German turn in Italian diplomacy was obvious. The gossips in Roman society interpreted this as proof that Edda had eliminated Margherita from her father's life. Edda had brought the ghostwriting to an end, but it was Claretta Petacci, whose existence was unknown to all but a handful of Mussolini's closest advisers, who finally eclipsed Margherita.[2]

Mussolini had known the attractive twenty-four-year-old Claretta since a chance encounter on the highway in the spring of 1932. Mussolini found Claretta so charming that he began to invite her to visit him occasionally in the Palazzo Venezia. They were no more than friends; Claretta married a young air force officer in 1934.

After the death of Arnaldo, and the end of his intimacy with Margherita, Mussolini had no real friendships. The events of 1935–1936 had added a terrible strain to his emotional isolation. The multiple crises of the

Ethiopian War were followed by news that his youngest child, Anna Maria, had been stricken with polio. For some time in May and June 1936, her death seemed likely. Once her survival was no longer in doubt, Mussolini lived through weeks of anxiety at the possibility of her paralysis, at last finding out that Anna Maria would walk again. Meanwhile, Claretta's marriage had collapsed. Shortly afterward, she and Mussolini began an affair.

Claretta was deeply infatuated with Mussolini. He returned her passion with deep affection, but was no more faithful to her than he had been to Margherita. Mussolini continued at least one steady physical relationship with another old lover, Angela Curti Cucciati. He maintained his practice of receiving different women on afternoons in his office and during his travels in Italy. But his relationship with Claretta became regular enough to cause Margherita considerable jealousy.

Claretta had little political influence on Mussolini. He made it clear to her that she should not think of replacing Margherita in that regard. "You don't want to play the *Presidentessa,* do you?" he asked her sarcastically. "There's already been one woman who broke my balls and I don't mean to take that from another." When Mussolini referred to Margherita, even when it was with disgust, it inflamed Claretta's jealousy. Mussolini's frequent allusions to his old relationship were a painful reminder that she would never subdue him the way Margherita had. Claretta could not approach Margherita's intellectual level. She could only get her way with Mussolini by weeping or whining, which almost always softened his heart or wore down his will.

Despite her frivolity, Claretta proved a valuable, if unwitting, ally of the Cianos. She provided Mussolini with daily companionship after he gave her an apartment in the Palazzo Venezia. She made him feel young again. He had turned fifty-three in July 1936 and felt a growing dread of old age and death. Claretta mitigated his fears, and as a result, she became very precious to him.

Equally important, however, in causing the final break between Margherita and Mussolini were foreign policy developments in the late spring and summer of 1936. When Mussolini appointed the pro-German Ciano foreign minister, he also decided to send the anti-German Suvich to Washington as ambassador. This might have seemed an indication on Mussolini's part that he desired closer relations with Roosevelt. But in truth, he had already completely rejected Suvich's policies. Before Suvich presented his credentials in Washington, the revolution in Italian-German relations had begun. On July 11, Germany and Austria signed a series of agreements. The Germans promised to respect Austrian independence. The Austrians agreed to coordinate their foreign policy with the Germans. In effect, Italian protection of Austria had come to an end. Hitler's promise to observe Austrian sovereignty was no more reliable than any of his other promises. But for the time being, he decided to do nothing to Austria that would antagonize the Italians.

Nine days later, the Spanish Civil War began as the result of popular resistance to a failed military coup. The rebel generals continued their attempt to seize power, and both sides appealed for outside help. Within weeks, the French and Soviets were providing weapons and technicians to the Spanish Republic, and the Comintern encouraged anti-Fascist volunteers to join them. Many anti-Fascist Italian exiles living in France did so, organized by Carlo Roselli. The fact that the French premier of the moment, Léon Blum, and Roselli were both Jews made a deep and unfortunate impression on Mussolini.

The Italians and Germans began sending arms and advisers to the Nationalist rebels. By the late summer of 1936, the growing scale of their efforts in Spain prompted Mussolini and Hitler to coordinate their military aid. Their new cooperation was cemented during Ciano's visit to Germany in late October. Hitler bluntly informed Ciano that Germany would be ready for a new European war as early as the fall of 1939. A few days after Ciano's return, Mussolini described the limited alliance between Berlin and Rome as "an axis around which all the European states could collaborate." Thus did the Axis get its name.[3]

Margherita could do little to hinder the strengthening of Italo-German ties, and the consequent decline of her political, professional, and social position. On July 1, accompanied by Fiammetta and Livio, Margherita attended the unveiling of a bust of Roberto at the Milan Fascist party headquarters. The local Party section was named in honor of her son. Margherita might once have used the occasion to write of the patriotism of Italian Jews, and to suggest the need to resist German expansionism. But Alfieri's Ministry of Press and Propaganda continued the ban Ciano had imposed when he had headed that organization. Now that the Hearst connection had ended, Margherita was cut off from publishing anything overtly political. She was limited to writing general appeals to Italian nationalism within the confines of her articles on art.

Even outside Italy, her freedom of action had been curtailed. Margherita's support for the Ethiopian War had damaged her relations with her American connections. Margherita's American friends did not reject her personally. They all wrote with sincerity that *America* was an excellent book. Alexander Kirk genuinely thanked Margherita for the sympathy she showed him after his mother died. Missy likewise appreciated Margherita's concern when she suffered another bout with tuberculosis. Fannie Hurst, a good liberal Democrat, still wanted to see Margherita when she visited Italy.

But her politics were no longer tolerable in America. At first gently, then more bluntly, Missy, Nicholas Murray Butler, Theodore Roosevelt, Jr., and Breckinridge Long each suggested that neither a lecture tour of the United States nor the publication of her book on America would be advisable under present circumstances. By late 1936, Fascist Italy was perceived by many Americans as an aggressor nation led by a megalomaniac.

Margherita had always argued that Mussolini was a reasonable man and not the brutal tyrant the anti-Fascist press depicted. But in less than a year between the fall of 1935 and the late summer of 1936, Mussolini had invaded Ethiopia, allied with Hitler, and intervened in the Spanish war. Since 1922, Margherita had proclaimed herself a moderate Fascist. Now many of her friends were finding that to be a contradiction in terms. Whether a person considered it to be a cause for shame or pride, by 1936 "Fascism" had become synonymous with aggression, fanaticism, and racism.

In Italy, Margherita feared that her Jewish heritage was making her similarly unacceptable to her Fascist friends. Again on a personal level, she was not yet estranged from them. She could fondly remind Alfieri of the days before World War I, when she and Cesare were Socialists, he was a Nationalist, and all were good friends. She could tell anti-Fascist jokes to Bottai and provoke the minister's unrestrained laughter. In his calmer moments, even Mussolini could be reminded of his many debts to Margherita and the Sarfatti family.[4]

On a political level, however, the world was dividing into two armed camps. It was obvious which side Mussolini preferred to join. If he did make a firm alliance with Hitler, Mussolini was likely to adopt some sort of official policy of anti-Semitism. Then she would be forced to flee Italy because of a tradition she had repudiated.

Margherita chose to believe that Mussolini had made no firm decision. She blamed Mussolini's flirtation with pro-Nazi sentiments on his advisers, including Edda and Galeazzo Ciano, Farinacci, and Starace. Her attitude begged the question of why Mussolini had chosen these advisers. She simply believed that Mussolini was susceptible to strong opinions; she assured herself that she could regain her privileged position, and then talk him into a sensible foreign policy. But he was no longer her pupil.

In September 1936, the first signs of officially sanctioned anti-Semitism appeared in Italy as attacks published in Farinacci's newspaper, *Il Regime Fascista*. These articles were encouraged by Alfieri on Mussolini's orders, in advance of Ciano's visit to Hitler. The articles did not cease after Ciano returned. Instead, attacks on the Jews grew stronger and more frequent through the winter and spring of 1936–1937. On the last day of 1936, an anonymous anti-Semitic article by Mussolini appeared in *Il Popolo d'Italia*. He inquired: Who was to blame for hatred of the Jews? The Jews themselves, he answered, because of their pushiness, their refusal to assimilate, and their lust for power.[5]

By February, Mussolini had shipped nearly 50,000 troops and 250 aircraft to Spain. This army was concentrated on the Castilian Plateau by early March. Its orders were to capture Madrid. On March 10, Mussolini sailed to Libya for a theatrical inspection of his North African colony. The retinue that accompanied his triumphal progress included Alfieri, Bontempelli, Ojetti, and Marinetti. In Tripoli a week later, Mussolini mounted a horse and brandished "The Sword of Islam," symbolic of his dream to drive the British and French from the Arab world and bring it under Italian rule. Mussolini was hoping the Spanish war would end during his visit to Africa. The Duce wanted to announce the fall of Madrid from the Roman ruins at Cyrene, Sabratha, or Leptis Magna as one more victory in his re-creation of the Roman empire.

But the Italian advance on Madrid was broken by the Republicans on March 18. The poorly trained Fascist Militia panicked when waves of heavy Soviet tanks lumbered forward, followed by the crack infantry of the International Brigades. By sunset, the Blackshirts were fleeing in disorder. The Republican attack was halted by regular Italian Army troops the next day, but the Fascists continued their cowardly retreat.

In a miniature but bitter civil war, the anti-Fascist Italian exiles of the Garibaldi Battalion threw themselves against the positions of the Italian Army's Littorio Division. The Littorio troops fought stubbornly for three days. Late on March 22, the Republicans called off their attacks. The losses suffered by Mussolini's forces still remain undetermined: At least 2,700 were killed, wounded, or taken prisoner. Republican losses were more than twice as high. But the International Brigades and their Soviet tanks had saved Madrid. The bloody clash became known as the Battle of Guadalajara.

After walking over the battlefield a few days later, Ernest Hemingway trumpeted the Republican victory as one that would "take its place in military history with the other decisive battles of the world." Lloyd George gleefully pronounced it "the Italian skeedaddle." Even some Germans snickered behind their Italian allies' backs at the "Spanish Caporetto." A year later, Ciano still remembered it as "the worst day of my life"—the day he learned the Blackshirts had been routed. Fascist boasts of military prowess had been exposed as bluster.[6]

Guadalajara presented a major blow to Mussolini's prestige. Before the battle, Mussolini had told an American reporter: "Next fall I am going to invite Hitler to come into Austria and make Austria German." Mussolini knew that Hitler would take Austria with or without his invitation. But he had expected to have control of the Mediterranean before having the Germans at the Brenner Pass. If Italian troops had been able to capture Madrid and win the war in the spring of 1937, Mussolini would have had a grateful ally in Nationalist Spain. He would have brought his divisions home and strengthened his defenses in the Alps and the Mediterranean, then waited to see whether the Germans or the British and French offered the better terms for an alliance. Now his forces were revealed as being too weak to stand up even to the Spanish Republicans and their Communist allies.

After Guadalajara, Mussolini felt bound to retain a military commitment in Spain until a total victory had been achieved. All the while, Germany would grow stronger, Italy relatively weaker. The Ethiopian War had depleted the Italian Army and Air Force, and drained the Italian treasury. The government was meeting its financial obligations by huge deficit spending, borrowing at usurious interest rates, and printing billions of lire in paper money. In return for cooperation in Spain and elsewhere, Mussolini might persuade Hitler to delay the *Anschluss* for six months or so. This might give him time to win some victories in Spain, and restore some of his prestige in Italian and foreign eyes. Still, Mussolini feared German power, Italian weakness, and the logical consequences of the Axis.[7]

Mussolini had no one to blame but himself, but he found it easier to blame the Jews. Had not the traitorous Jew, Carlo Roselli, been instrumental in recruiting anti-Fascist Italians to fight in Spain? Carlo Roselli had documented Guadalajara in humiliating detail in his newspaper, *Giustizia e Libertà*. Acting on orders from Mussolini, Ciano organized the murder of Roselli. By unhappy coincidence, Nello was visiting his brother at the time. They were knifed to death by French Fascist thugs in early June.

The Communists, the Socialists, and the Liberals had proclaimed the Spanish Civil War to be a crusade against the spread of Fascism. The Nazis explained this all quite simply: Bolshevism, Marxism, Liberalism, and democracy all were Jewish conspiracies. Mussolini had begun to believe that the most vociferous anti-Fascists in America, Britain, France, and elsewhere were Jews. Mussolini had only a small step to take from concluding that Jews were the enemies of Fascism to the Nazi position that the Jews were the enemies of mankind.

For the moment, Mussolini was not ready to make that step. An official anti-Semitic policy would entail a final break with the West. During a visit Generoso Pope made to Rome in June, Mussolini instructed the publisher to issue a categorical denial of Fascist anti-Semitism on his return to America. Mussolini wanted to keep his options open. He had recently received diplomatic overtures from Roosevelt, and from the new British prime minister, Neville Chamberlain. At the same time, Mussolini was making preparations for an official tour of Germany in the fall of 1937. The creation of the Axis had made it incumbent upon Mussolini to reciprocate Hitler's visit to Venice of June 1934.[8]

By the spring of 1937, Mussolini was very close to believing that all Jews were members of a separate race, incapable of patriotism or loyalty to their native land. If that conviction took hold, Margherita was in a hopeless position. As long as he continued to explore the offers coming from Washington and London, Mussolini valued Margherita's foreign contacts. But her affiliations helped reinforce his suspicion that Italian Jews were allied with the interests of the West and would do everything they could to prevent closer ties between Italy and Germany. Thus the Jews of Italy— Margherita among them—would not accept unconditionally whatever path Mussolini chose. In other words, they were all potential traitors.

In early April 1937, Margherita began pestering Alfieri for official permission to make an Armistice Day broadcast to the United States that November. After several insistent letters from her, Alfieri referred the matter to Mussolini. In May, Margherita learned from the minister that "a Higher review" had decided that the international situation was too uncertain to know what Italo-American relations would be six months hence. Any permission to broadcast would have to wait upon events.

Margherita had received definite news from Butler and Prezzolini that there was no chance for her book on America to be published in the United States. She took her rejections with good grace. She had already translated *L'America, ricerca della felicità* (*America, the Pursuit of Happiness*) into Italian, and had a contract for it with Mondadori. Several excerpts had been published in journals. The book received excellent reviews after it appeared in early June, even from those journalists who had little love for Margherita. It became a best-seller. Margherita had Mondadori send a copy to every one of her friends, including those who could not read Italian.[9]

Even in its Italian version, *L'America* retained the spare and succinct style of American journalistic prose. The style had come to dominate American literature since World War I. Perhaps Margherita had imitated it because she hoped *L'America* would be a major success in the United States, or perhaps she had acquired it during her years of writing for the Hearst press. But this was the first extended work in which she stated her opinions clearly, overcoming her more usual impressionistic style. Her voice had grown more assured as her personal circumstances became more uncertain.

L'America did not present an entirely favorable picture of the United States. Margherita expressed her horror at the gangsterism, drunkenness, high unemployment, hedonism, greed, and blind worship of technology that blighted the country. Many opinions she expressed reflected her Fascist biases, or were calculated to appeal to the Party leadership. Thus she extolled American racism. She also wrote that American isolationism and fear of war would prevent Roosevelt or his successors from intervening in European affairs, in direct contrast to what she had said to Mussolini immediately after returning from America. Nonetheless, Margherita's account of her travels around the United States, Cuba, and Mexico betrayed her awe of the riches and beauty of the continent, and a considerable admiration for the American people and their government.

America had reawakened in Margherita the dreams of her youth, dreams she had abandoned in the service of Mussolini's regime. Those abandoned visions informed her response to America. Seeing the relative power and freedom of American women reminded Margherita of her abandoned commitment to feminism. The colossal achievements of American technology were the fantasies of her old Futurist friends made real; once she had cheered their efforts to transform Italy into just such a modern state. America provoked a desperate longing for something she had once hoped to create, first through Socialism, then through Fascism. What she had experienced in America was the practical reality of pursuing personal fulfillment. Human happiness was apparently possible in America; it no longer seemed to be so in Mussolini's Italy. America, not the Duce's Fascist Italy, was the real land of the future.[10]

Most likely, Mussolini read *L'America* in the late summer of 1937. This perhaps explains the savage comments Ciano recorded early that September:

> The *Duce* hurled abuse at America, country of Niggers and Jews, the disintegrating elements of civilization. He wants to write a book: *Europe in the Year 2000*. The races which will play an important role will be the Italians, the Germans, the Russians and the Japanese. The other peoples will be destroyed by the acid of Jewish corruption. They even refuse to have children because that costs pain. They don't know that pain is the only creative element in the life of peoples. And also in that of men.[11]

Roosevelt's diplomatic initiatives also helped generate Mussolini's anti-American rage. The president had proposed a face-to-face meeting with Mussolini to the Italian ambassador in late July, and in a personal letter he addressed to the Duce. He repeated his offer when he and Eleanor received Vittorio Mussolini at the White House in October, during the young man's three-week visit to Hollywood, New York, and Washington.

Roosevelt was so eager to confer with Mussolini that he proposed overcoming the problem of a location by meeting on a ship somewhere in the mid-Atlantic.

Mussolini had come to view Roosevelt as a dictator, not a democratic leader, who was doing everything he could to drag his isolationist nation into a new war in Europe. He knew that if they met, the president would attempt to weaken the growing ties between Rome and Berlin, either by bribes or threats. By the end of 1937, Mussolini regarded Roosevelt as a man who was using the huge wealth of the United States to corrupt and ensnare his victims, hypocritically forcing his ideals on others, as Wilson had done, while trying to impose an American dominion over the world. This idea of the American president's motivations tallied neatly with Mussolini's growing anti-Semitic fantasies. He had come to believe that Roosevelt and the Jews were in league against him and Fascism in a monstrous capitalist plot.[12]

In retrospect it seems that Margherita should by now have made plans to quit the country for good. But she was receiving very mixed signals from the Fascist regime. During the summer of 1937, there was an increase in Jew-baiting in the controlled press prior to Mussolini's visit to Germany. At the same time Margherita was rewarded with official favors. After appointment to a government board to prepare her nation's pavilion at the Paris International Exposition, Margherita took part in designing the Italian exhibit and was present at its opening in July. As a reward for this service (and as a sign that Mussolini did not yet wish to cut his ties to America), Margherita received official permission to make her Armistice Day broadcast to the United States in November.

Margherita was also made a member of a commission to select the recipient of a poetry prize, to be awarded in Mussolini's own name. But she accused the winner, Fanny Dini, of plagiarizing her verses from *I vivi e l'ombra*. Apparently to get her to drop her objections, Ciano promised to ensure that Margherita would get a passport to go to America for a lecture tour. Rumors spread that she was under Alfieri's special protection on Mussolini's orders.[13]

After much effort, she had written out a series of talks on art and culture, and had made a contract with the Colston Leigh agency to deliver them in America in the winter and spring of 1939. She was looking forward to seeing Missy again, now too sick with tuberculosis to travel, and to visiting the New York World's Fair.

Yet Margherita was taking various precautions to protect herself. She drew as close as possible to the royal family. The House of Savoy and the Jews of Italy had forged a close alliance during the Risorgimento, and had retained special bonds of mutual loyalty ever since. Despite his decision to avoid public disagreement with Mussolini, Vittorio Emanuele III indirectly made plain his disapproval of the outbursts of official anti-Semitism. Margherita took heart from this. As she noted in a letter to Bernard Berenson, she had made a special point of professing her monarchism by journeying to Naples in early June 1937 for the Royal Historic Carousel. This pageant, performed in the Naples soccer stadium, commemorated seven hundred years of the royal house by an elaborate re-creation of the history of the Savoy family. Various members of the royal family dressed in the costumes of their illustrious ancestors and rode in parade before the king, Crown Prince Umberto and Crown Princess Maria José, and the Duchess of Aosta. Afterward, a huge reception was held in the magnificent royal palace at Caserta.

Margherita lost a dear friend and a loyal protector when Marconi died in late July. The inventor had been the head of the Royal Academy, and a member of the Fascist Grand Council since 1932. Although Mussolini had valued Marconi's friendship and political advice, he appointed the more malleable D'Annunzio as his new president of the Academy. Marconi's demise removed one more obstacle in the Duce's path toward unquestioned anti-Semitism and anti-Western hostility.

Following Marconi's funeral, Margherita left Rome for Il Soldo in early August. She made a brief visit to Venice to study the city's Tintorettos, as a recent letter from Bernard Berenson had inspired her to do. She also traveled extensively in the Italian Swiss canton of Ticino, just across the border from Il Soldo, and visited Lucerne. Was she considering Switzerland as a place of exile? Or was she checking routes for a quick escape across the frontier?

Both motives are likely, and from later events it seems that she carried out a third task at this time. At some point Margherita smuggled abroad the hundreds of letters Mussolini had written her over the years, together with other sensitive documents concerning their relationship. During this trip, she may have deposited them in a Swiss bank for safekeeping.

On September 23, the day before Mussolini left for his official visit to Nazi Germany, Margherita sent a telegram to D'Annunzio. She reminded the poet of his role in forcing Italian intervention in the Great War, of his heroic exploits against the Austrians, and of his dedication to the safety of Italy's northern borders. Margherita was hoping to keep D'Annunzio from adding his symbolically crucial support to the idea of an Italo-German alliance.[14]

Unfortunately for Margherita, Mussolini's five-day visit to Germany made a deep and favorable impression on him. Hitler and Goebbels had devoted great energy and expense to ensuring that the Duce and his large entourage would be overwhelmed by visions of military power and national discipline wherever they went. In addition to banquets and ceremonies, Mussolini saw army and air force maneuvers and the Krupp cannon factory in Essen. On his last evening, Mussolini addressed a huge crowd assembled at the main sports stadium in Berlin. A sudden downpour soaked him and his text—and his captive audience—but Mussolini managed to struggle through his speech in German. He concluded with an image of the German and Italian people united, forming "a daunting, always growing mass of one hundred fifteen million souls . . . united in a single unbreakable decision." He typically neglected to specify what that decision was.

During his return to Rome by train, Mussolini made one brief stop, at the railroad station at Verona. There to greet him was Gabriele D'Annunzio. Mussolini stepped down from his train and embraced the old man. The living symbol of Italy's victory in the Great War had given his approval to the Axis. Then the Duce climbed back into his compartment and the poet returned to his home high above Lake Garda. D'Annunzio had performed his last service for Mussolini.

Mussolini seemed intoxicated by what he had seen and experienced. Even to Rachele and Edda, he went on at length about the unbelievable might of the Third Reich. The German government announced that Hitler would pay a return visit to Italy in the spring of 1938. After Margherita heard of his new infatuation with Nazi Germany, she managed to gain one of her increasingly rare audiences with Mussolini. As she told Amedeo, she was determined to "talk some sense" into Mussolini, to "calm him down." Exactly what passed between the two remains unknown but the conversation became heated. When Margherita returned home she lamented bitterly to Fiammetta: "God, how he's changed, he's really another person. I am a writer, I sense it even in his style that he is completely changed."[15]

During his visit to Germany, Mussolini had inquired in detail about Nazi policies toward the Jews. To his hosts, Mussolini claimed that the small number of Jews in Italy presented him with no problems. He even admitted that he found Hitler's fanatic hatred of the Jews an embarrassment. Nonetheless, his own anti-Semitism had developed into something far more insidious than his old stereotypical notions about Jewish greed. Official Fascist anti-Semitic pronouncements did not cease after Mussolini's return from Germany. On the contrary, Mussolini directed Farinacci to keep up his attacks on the Jews. None of this was due to any pressure from the Nazis.

Sometime during this period Mussolini retrieved his diaries from his sister Edvige, to whom he had given them for safekeeping. Edvige's children had studied the volumes with fascination, and remembered many passages in detail. A few days later, Mussolini had the diaries returned to

Edvige. When Edvige's children again examined the volumes they noticed pages had been torn out from some of the books. In other places, whole sections had been smeared or heavily inked over. All passages referring to "Vela," and the sections actually written in Margherita's own hand, had been removed or rendered illegible.

When the children brought this to Edvige's attention, she went to speak to her brother at once. She wanted to make sure he knew about the deletions and would not hold her responsible. He reacted with embarrassment. Mussolini admitted that he had altered his diaries, but tried to make light of the whole business. Edvige noticed a certain weariness and tension in his voice, so she immediately dropped the matter.

Mussolini had erased any mention of Margherita from the most intimate record of his life. There is no doubt that he was thinking far beyond the politics of the moment. Along with the diaries, Mussolini had consigned a letter to Edvige stating that they must not be made public for at least fifty years after his death. He was determined that history would not record just how passionately he had loved a Jew, and how much she had guided his early career.[16]

Of course, Margherita did not know what Mussolini had done. The last months of 1937 brought signs rather that she had actually risen a step in his esteem. On Armistice Day, her promised broadcast to America went on the air over CBS, forming part of an international peace appeal organized by Butler's Carnegie Endowment for International Peace. A month later, Margherita learned that *L'America* had received the Galante Prize, a literary award established by the Bompiani publishing firm. As Margherita confessed to Ada, she had never heard of the prize. She was disappointed to learn from Alfieri that there was no cash award attached. Nonetheless, the congratulatory telegrams and bouquets she received really pleased Margherita. It was a taste of her former celebrity. Neither of these favors would have come to her if Mussolini had disapproved.

Despite these hints of official favor, Margherita remained fearful of the consequences of Mussolini's policies. Since the summer of 1937, Chamberlain and Mussolini had been in secret contact through confidential agents. The British prime minister was attempting to discover what reward Mussolini would demand for good behavior. If the price was right, Chamberlain was prepared to pay. Mussolini made things very difficult for Chamberlain throughout the second half of 1937. He wished to emphasize that his friendship came at a very high cost.

In late August, Mussolini had ordered Italian submarines to sink British, French, Soviet, and other merchant ships carrying military supplies to the Spanish Republic. These piratical attacks led to a serious crisis that was settled by an international conference. Mussolini raised British and French tempers again by adhering to the Anti-Comintern Pact in early November. Formed by Germany and Japan in November 1936, the pact was officially directed against international Communism. However, Mussolini understood the agreement to be the basis for a secret understanding aimed against the British, French, and Americans, and had thus hesitated to join. But once he did join, the pact effectively expanded the Axis to a three-member anti-Western coalition.

In mid-November, angry at the ambassador's attempts to improve Italo-French relations, Mussolini withdrew Cerruti from Paris. He had lost all respect for the anti-German diplomat and his wife, that "Jewish actress from Hungary," as he had begun to refer to her. Back in Rome Vittorio Cerruti argued with Mussolini over the direction of Italian foreign policy, and Mussolini brought his diplomatic career to an abrupt end. Then, in early December, Mussolini withdrew Italy from the League of Nations.

Margherita did the little she could to improve Italian relations with France and Britain. Ten days after Cerruti's final meeting with Mussolini, she published an article in *La Stampa,* ostensibly on the recent exhibit of masterpieces of French art in Paris. She stressed the common Latin heritage of Italy and France, and their profound cultural differences with Germany. Margherita must have known from the Cerrutis that there was no chance of a sudden improvement in the relations between Paris and Rome. Her only hope lay in the ongoing contacts between Chamberlain and Mussolini.

In November, leaks of the previously secret talks had forced Chamberlain to admit in Parliament that he and Mussolini were communicating. Chamberlain's foreign minister, Anthony Eden, opposed appeasement on principle, and correctly feared Chamberlain was prepared to recognize the Italian conquest of Ethiopia. Some Fascists saw improved relations with Britain as a setback to war against the Western democracies. Eden and Farinacci, bitter opponents otherwise, both attempted to derail any possible agreement between Chamberlain and Mussolini. Through their supporters, a bitter war of words broke out in the Italian and British press in December 1937.[17]

Meanwhile, German pressure on Austria had increased. Only a rapprochement between Britain and Italy would give Mussolini the ability to deter Hitler and preserve Austrian independence. While Mussolini had formed a partnership with Hitler, that did not mean that he wanted the Germans at his northern border. He knew an *Anschluss* was the price he would eventually have to pay for continued cooperation with Germany. But many Fascist leaders harbored fierce anti-German feelings, including Grandi, Balbo, and Bottai. For them, and for the king, an agreement between Rome and London offered some prospect of loosening the growing ties with the Germans.

In late December 1937, Ivy Chamberlain, the widowed sister-in-law of the British prime minister, visited Rome. She came to assure Mussolini that Neville Chamberlain greatly desired an understanding. On the evening of December 22, Mrs. Chamberlain visited Margherita, who had also invited the Cerrutis. Undoubtedly, they discussed ways to end the rift between their two countries. A week later, Margherita went to see Sir William McClure, the press officer for the British embassy in Rome. McClure had held the post since June 1921. He and Margherita knew each other well. Exactly what passed between the two remains uncertain, but it seems likely that they discussed what could be done to put an end to the polemics in the British and Italian press. She may deserve some small part of the credit for the resumption of the talks a few weeks later.

When they resumed, Eden prevented the smooth progress of the negotiations. Chamberlain slowly outmaneuvered his foreign secretary over the next few weeks, finally forcing Eden's resignation on February 21. But time was running out. Nine days earlier, Hitler had summoned the Austrian chancellor; he browbeat Schuschnigg into accepting an agreement sharply limiting the small country's independence. Once in effect, the accord would probably lead to the annexation of Austria in a matter of months.

Chamberlain and his advisers expected that Hitler's scheduled visit to Italy in May would prevent any move against Austria for three or four months. In the meantime, they had a good chance of preventing the *Anschluss* through a comprehensive understanding with Mussolini. Mussolini was hopeful that the German absorption of Austria might be delayed until after a Nationalist victory in Spain. A triumph of Italian arms and foreign policy would greatly strengthen Italy's security south of the Alps, and do much to soften the shock of having the Germans at the Brenner Pass.

But Hitler decided the moment had arrived to settle the Austrian question. Hurried consultation with Rome gained him Mussolini's reluctant agreement. The French government begged the Italians to stand up to the Germans. But as Ciano noted, too much hostility had been built up between them since 1935 to allow common action. Mussolini was convinced that if a single Italian soldier were to cross the Brenner frontier, the Austrians would join the Germans in joint resistance. He might have been right. When the German Army invaded Austria, to Hitler's surprise, most Austrians welcomed the takeover. On March 14, Hitler annexed Austria by decree.

Himmler and the vanguard of the SS and Gestapo had already arrived in Vienna. Egged on by their new overlords and by returning Austrian Nazis, Viennese mobs went on a vicious anti-Semitic rampage. Many Jews were beaten and murdered in the streets while their homes or shops were ransacked. Over the next few weeks, the Nazis made over 75,000 arrests, dispatching their wretched victims to the concentration camps.

When Margherita went to see Ciano on March 22 to protest these atrocities, the horror brought tears to the foreign minister's eyes. In response, Ciano promised Margherita to ask Hitler to secure Sigmund Freud's safe passage out of Vienna. Ciano was true to his word and Freud, already suffering from terminal cancer, was allowed to leave for London to die in peace. Few Austrian Jews were so fortunate.[18]

The *Anschluss* was only one of the blows to Margherita's peace of mind in the winter and spring of 1938. In January and February, rumors circulated that she and the architect Vittorio Ballio Morpurgo, also a Jew, had made huge profits from real-estate speculation in the reconstructed neighborhood around the tomb of Augustus and the nearby Augustan monument, the Ara Pacis. In 1934, to celebrate the coming two-thousandth anniversary of the birth of the first Roman emperor, Mussolini had ordered the buildings adjacent to the emperor's burial place cleared. Over the next four years, the Augustan tomb and sacrificial altar were beautifully restored, and a piazza was formed by a hollow square of new office buildings. Stories spread that Mussolini intended the complex as his burial site. Margherita and Morpurgo were reported to head a Jewish cabal controlling all of the construction in the area. The stories suggest slanders launched by her enemies or by anti-Semites, perhaps on Mussolini's orders.

When Margherita saw Ciano in mid-February to get Mussolini's formal approval for her passport to America, she expressed her deep concern about the rising tide of anti-Semitism in Italy. The foreign minister assured her that he deplored these excesses, and told Margherita that in a few days the Foreign Ministry would issue an anonymous announcement, written by Mussolini himself, denying that there were any plans to institute an official anti-Semitic policy in Italy.

The statement, issued on February 16, gave Margherita cause for alarm, not comfort. While denying plans to deprive Italian Jews of their rights, the pronouncement insisted that "the currents of world anti-Fascism are regularly headed by Jewish elements" and the Jews of Italy would not be allowed influence "disproportionate to . . . the numerical importance of their community."

The bulletin soured Margherita's mood. A few days later, she attended a dinner party at Bernard Berenson's villa outside Florence and got into an angry quarrel with other guests. She wrote a charming letter of apology to

Berenson, and he sent her an art book as a sign that all was forgiven, but their friendship suffered. Over the next few weeks, Margherita lost two friends. In early March, D'Annunzio died. Despite the scene at the Verona railroad station, Margherita harbored deep affection for the writer. Mussolini surprised Ciano by his own genuine grief at D'Annunzio's death. Later that month, Alexander Kirk left Rome for a government appointment in Moscow. Margherita never saw him again.

The next month was happier. In early April, she was presented with the Galante Prize at a banquet in Milan. A week later, she was further buoyed by the signing of the "Easter Accords" between Italy and Britain. Although it was too late to save Austria, Mussolini and Chamberlain had finally managed to resolve their differences, at least temporarily. Under the accords, the Italians agreed to reduce their garrison in Libya, and gradually to withdraw their forces from Spain. They also promised, despite signs of a probable Nationalist victory, not to seek any Spanish territory as reward for Italian aid. In turn, the British formally recognized Italian claims to Ethiopia. Roosevelt believed that Chamberlain had made a deal with "a gangster."

Margherita considered the agreements a peace treaty between Italy and Britain. She looked forward to a radical change in Mussolini's foreign policy. But this was wishful thinking, as she saw three weeks later when Hitler toured Italy.[19]

Accompanied by a large retinue, Hitler arrived in Rome by train on the evening of May 3. Protocol required Vittorio Emanuele III to greet the Führer, as one head of state receiving another. Forced into the background at the Rome railroad station, and whenever the king was present during Hitler's visit, Mussolini displayed visible irritation. Custom even prevented Mussolini from sharing the royal carriage with Vittorio Emanuele III and Hitler. The Duce retreated to his office in the Palazzo Venezia after the welcoming ceremonies.

Mussolini had ordered extensive preparations for Hitler's visit. To the king's great annoyance, the Duce even had the Italian Army adopt the goose step (renamed the "Roman step" to placate his generals). Mussolini himself supervised the units practicing the new march. Rome, Naples, and Florence had been cleaned, and large areas of the capital were transformed by decoration.

The king and the Führer rode through the streets together, hailed by a crowd of 300,000. On the way to the Quirinal Palace the official procession passed through the square below Mussolini's balcony. High above the piazza, Mussolini and his two older sons, Vittorio and Bruno, watched the stately horse-drawn cortege move toward them. Directly opposite across the square stood Crown Prince Umberto and Crown Princess Maria José.

They were joined by the royal princesses and other members of the House of Savoy. With them were their special guests, Margherita and Fiammetta.

The procession passed slowly down the Via dell'Impero. Floodlights illuminated the ancient monuments on either side in brilliant contrast to the night sky. Huge white pylons lined the avenue; some were topped with scarlet flames, and some with colorful banners—the green, red, and white of Italy, the purple and gold of Rome, and the crimson banner with the white circle and the black swastika of Nazi Germany. Within each arch of the Colosseum a burning flare silhouetted a steel-helmeted Blackshirt grasping a rifle with fixed bayonet.

When the king and the Führer moved beneath her window, Margherita could not bear to watch. Overcome with anxiety, she and Fiammetta had been hovering about the buffet table, gorging themselves on the hors d'oeuvres. Margherita had also been drinking heavily: eight, or even ten, small glasses of whiskey, according to some witnesses. The mother and daughter made such a spectacle of themselves that their behavior caused more comment than the sight of Hitler passing by with the king. Margherita may have felt some sense of security because of Prince Umberto's invitation to spend that fateful evening with him, but she and Fiammetta knew that Hitler's visit to Rome left their lives poised on the brink of disaster.[20]

The first night in the Quirinal, at one o'clock in the morning, Hitler demanded the services of a woman. Absolute consternation reigned until it was explained that Hitler only wanted a maid to turn down his bedcovers. Still, the king thought he was a "degenerate."

No significant agreements were reached during Hitler's week in Italy. Ceremonies, parades, banquets, and military displays in and around Rome—and a magnificent naval review in the Bay of Naples—filled the five days. Mussolini was amused to see that Hitler wore rouge to disguise his pallor. On May 9, the two dictators left the king behind and escaped for what both looked forward to as the high point of the visit, a day together in Florence.

To Mussolini's disgust, however, Hitler insisted on dragging him through the Uffizi Gallery. While the Nazi studied the great paintings of the Italian Renaissance with evident delight, the Duce suffered excruciating boredom. Years later, Bottai remembered Mussolini's suffering with amusement. But when an exuberant Florentine crowd cheered the two dictators as they stood on the balcony of the Palazzo Vecchio, Mussolini's happiness was evident. Here was proof that he was winning his people over to the difficult idea of an alliance with Germany.

Nonetheless, whenever Hitler's foreign minister, Joachim von Ribbentrop, pressed the offer of a political-military pact, Ciano rebuffed him. The

Duce believed that more time was needed to prepare the Italian people for such a step. The real import of Hitler's visit was apparent at Micchelucci's magnificent railroad station, when Mussolini bade his guest farewell. Both men were moved at the moment of their separation. As Hitler prepared to board his train, Mussolini grasped his hand and said: "From now on nothing can separate us any more." Hitler's eyes filled with tears.[21]

It hardly mattered to Margherita whether or not Mussolini and Hitler had made a formal alliance. The whole atmosphere surrounding the Führer's visit to Italy, the implications of the *Anschluss* for the future of Italo-German relations, and Mussolini's public insistence five days after Hitler's departure on the indissoluble links between the Fascist and Nazi revolutions, all pointed in the same direction. Mussolini intended to align Italy closely to Germany. Given the policies of the Third Reich, that meant that some form of racial anti-Semitism would be imposed on Margherita's homeland. She began making serious preparations to leave Italy on short notice.

On May 13, Margherita left Rome for Istanbul. Before departing, she left a message for the foreign minister thanking him for his positive reaction to *L'America* and asking his help in getting her book awarded the Viareggio Prize. These seem actions calculated to disguise her preparations for fleeing Italy. A month later, Margherita visited Paris. Ostensibly she was there to lecture at a conference at the Louvre on da Vinci and other painters of the Lombard School. But she also spent time arranging for a possible move. Alfieri ordered an agent to monitor the conference.

Shortly afterward, Margherita returned to Rome. Her travels had raised Mussolini's suspicions. He ordered her placed under careful surveillance. A Venetian relative learned about the order. While at Abano for a mud cure, Margherita received a postcard from Venice. Among the usual commonplaces were these words, written in English to escape the postal censors: "Look out, you are watched."

On July 14 "The Manifesto of the Race" was published in the Roman newspaper *Giornale d'Italia*. Eleven days later, Fascist party headquarters published with approval the names of the supposed authors. Mussolini was actually the principal author of the ten pseudoscientific propositions. In essence, the manifesto declared that Italians were Aryans and that Jews were neither one nor the other. In order to protect the racial superiority of the "Italian race," marriage or sexual intercourse with Jews must be prohibited. In his diary, Goebbels exulted that the proclamation was "a great triumph for us." On July 28, Pope Pius XI branded the manifesto a "disgraceful imitation" of Nazi racism.

But there was no public protest from the king or the other members of the House of Savoy. Vittorio Emanuele III was too cautious to confront

Mussolini over the issue of anti-Semitism. The king's anti-clerical attitudes made it impossible for him to take sides with the papacy against his own head of government. Perhaps the royal silence, more than anything else, convinced Margherita that she could not expect any special protection, and that her best option was to flee Italy.

Prince Umberto had closer ties to Margherita than did his father. But the heir to the throne could not act effectively without his father's consent, which was not forthcoming. Furthermore, the prince knew that while the Fascists were unlikely to move against the throne while Vittorio Emanuele III was alive, guarantees for his own succession were another matter. Mussolini kept a dossier on the crown prince's homosexual love affairs. If these facts were made known, even staunch monarchists were unlikely to support him. Umberto kept silent.

In late July, Margherita told acquaintances she was going to Il Soldo. In fact, she slipped over the Swiss border and returned to Paris. From the French capital, she wrote Missy to ask for help in getting work as a screenwriter. She also requested that Missy ask Theodore Roosevelt, Jr., to look for an American publisher for L'America. She wondered if Missy could use weekly or biweekly columns about life in Paris. She knew everyone who was anyone in the city, she wrote; she was good friends with celebrities such as Somerset Maugham and Coco Chanel. She thought that she could write the series under the pseudonym of "Perdida" ("The Lost One").[22]

Mussolini began to display extraordinary sensitivity over any mention of his old relationship with Margherita. Paul Cremona, the Rome correspondent for The Christian Science Monitor, remarked to a group of journalists that Mussolini could not take any more anti-Semitic steps beyond issuing the manifesto. After all, Cremona remarked, Mussolini had not so long ago taken money from Jews. In the old days, his mistress had practically supported him. When an agent informed him of the journalist's words, Mussolini ordered Ciano to expel him from Italy at once. Mussolini told Ciano that if Cremona had not been a British subject and a foreign correspondent, he would have had the journalist hauled before the Special Tribunal for the Defense of the State. No amount of pleading by the American or British ambassadors could save Cremona from expulsion. After that object lesson, there was little speculation in the American press about Margherita's fate. No major news organization wanted to risk having its Rome correspondent deported.[23]

To a large extent, Margherita deserved the blame for her own downfall. She had played a major role in developing Fascism and establishing Mussolini's dictatorship. It was she who had introduced Mussolini to the racist theories of Gobineau, the ideas that had been leading him toward racial anti-Semitism since the early 1930s. But at least she had considerable warning about the evolution of Mussolini's thinking. And she possessed the resources to go into a comfortable exile. For most of the Jews of Italy, "The Manifesto of the Race" came as a sudden shock. Many had taken comfort from Mussolini's previous condemnations of anti-Semitism. Margherita melodramatically wrote to Missy that summer begging for assistance: "Help me out of this hell for Heaven's sake!" Most Italian Jews had neither the means nor the friends to help them go abroad. At the time, Vittorio Mussolini passed a request on to his father from a Jewish friend asking what he should do. The Duce replied that a wise Jew should leave not only Italy but Europe.[24]

Throughout the late summer and early fall of 1938, certain obligations and hopes kept Margherita at Il Soldo. She had made preparations to live comfortably in Paris, but it was no easy thing for her, at the age of fifty-eight, to break her ties to her country. For one thing, she had to bid a final farewell to Roberto.

Margherita had been following the progress of construction on Roberto's tomb with mounting anxiety, even making an inquiry about it from Istanbul in May. Work was finally completed in August, and Roberto's casket was prepared for transfer to Terragni's monument on the Col d'Echele. Vittorio Emanuele III insisted on attending the ceremony: Roberto had been awarded Italy's highest medal for valor in the king's name. It was a gesture of protest against the racial manifesto, if only a small one. Under the circumstances, Alfieri had issued instructions that the event would not be covered by the press.

Angered by the royal acquiesence to official anti-Semitism, Amedeo refused to attend. Margherita arrived escorted by Livio, Fiammetta, Terragni, and their mutual friend from Como, Luigi Zuccoli. Awaiting the Sarfatti family on the mountain slope above Stoccaredo were the king, his military aides, local army and civil authorities, and an honor guard formed by a company of Alpini from Roberto's old regiment. The entombment was simple and moving. So were the words that Margherita had ordered carved upon the block of stone surmounting the monument:

ROBERTO SARFATTI

VOLUNTEER AT SEVENTEEN

MEDAGLIA D'ORO

CORPORAL OF THE 6TH ALPINI

FELL HERE

RECLAIMING THIS EARTH

FOR ITALY

VENICE 5-10-1900 COLLE D'ECHELE 1-28-1918

At the end of the ceremony, the Alpini presented arms and fired a final salute under the warm summer sun. Afterward family and guests descended to a mountain hut where a simple meal had been prepared.

Margherita had been holding her feelings inside for months since Roberto's body had been discovered. After she sat down, she could eat only a little. Then she began to weep. Once her tears started to flow, they would not stop. She laid her head down on the table and cried herself to sleep. A few minutes passed. A mountain storm blew overhead, and a loud thunderclap awoke Margherita with a start. She looked around in confusion. Her family led her away and took her back to Il Soldo.[25]

There Margherita pondered her choices. She was well informed enough to know that "The Manifesto of the Race" was a prelude to further expressions of Mussolini's anti-Semitism. On August 30, *Il Popolo d'Italia* initiated a series of articles attacking the presence and the influence of Jews in the professions. Jews were described as lacking any spiritual values, and as incapable and unworthy of holding positions of influence in a Fascist state.

Either Margherita was going to remain in her homeland and endure life as a pariah, or she was going to have to leave for good. She leaned toward the second alternative. But she knew she was under careful surveillance now, and feared the consequences if she were caught attempting to flee the country illegally. Perhaps her recent trip through Switzerland had warned the authorities to place the frontier guards on special alert for her.

As she had done for a decade now, Margherita consulted her volume of Dante. She took down the familiar volume from its shelf and inserted her right thumb within its pages. Her finger had fallen on a *terzina* from Canto XXXII of the *Purgatorio*:

> If I could portray how sank to slumber
> the pitiless eyes, hearing of Syrinx,
> the eyes whose long vigil cost so dear

To her this was a clear answer. The "pitiless eyes" of Mussolini's police system would be closed when she crossed the frontier. Margherita knew that she was free to go. Still she lingered in Italy.

She did launch a small campaign of intimidation and self-protection. In mid-September, rumors surfaced in Switzerland that Margherita was planning to publish a second biography of Mussolini outside Italy. This time, she would reveal the whole truth about him and their relationship. A month later, new stories began to circulate. Margherita, it was said, had placed sensitive documents about Mussolini in safekeeping abroad. She intended to publish them, and was in contact with anti-Fascist exiles, like

Gaetano Salvemini at Harvard University, who would help her. Similar rumors were heard in Berne, Lausanne, and Paris throughout the autumn of 1938.

Mussolini acted unconcerned. In mid-September he remarked to his minister of finance, Paolo Thaon di Revel, how prescient he had been to free himself from Margherita. He also mentioned how he had forced Farinacci to dismiss his Jewish secretary and lover, Jole Foà. Farinacci had resisted Mussolini's demands, using the excuse that he couldn't just throw the woman out on the street after she had worked for him for ten years. Mussolini answered Farinacci's objections by handing him 50,000 lire. He told Farinacci to give that to Foà and then to fire her.

A few days later, the Duce unveiled the restored Ara Pacis near the Augusteo. Mussolini spent a few moments alone with Bottai afterward, and he told Bottai something already well known:

> Even I have had a Jewish lover: Sarfatti. Intelligent, Fascist, the mother of a real hero. But, five years ago, foreseeing that the Jewish problem would become a major concern, I took steps to free myself from her. I had her dismissed from *Il Popolo d'Italia* and from her editorship at *Gerarchia* . . . with regular severance pay, you understand.

Then he told Bottai of a discussion he had once had with Margherita about the symbolic significance of the crucifix, and of his complete surprise to see from a photograph of Terragni's tomb for Roberto that it bore no cross. This was a sign of the invincibly stubborn character of the Jewish race, Mussolini commented.[26]

In September a European war nearly broke out. Following the seizure of Austria, the Nazi press began accusing the Prague government of monstrous violations of the rights of the Germans of the Sudetenland. Meanwhile Hitler ordered his generals to prepare plans to conquer Czechoslovakia. By early September, following an unsuccessful Nazi-inspired revolt by thousands of Sudeten Germans, a German invasion appeared imminent. Hitler had kept Mussolini ignorant of his intentions, so the crisis caught him by surprise. To Mussolini's complete shock, the British and French threatened war if the Germans attacked Czechoslovakia. After their supine response to the conquests of Ethiopia and Austria, and Chamberlain's appeasement of Italy through the "Easter Accords," Mussolini had dismissed the Western democracies as decadent and cowardly.

Then Chamberlain made two flights to Germany. Both times, the British prime minister offered Hitler major concessions over Czechoslovakia in return for a peaceful resolution of the crisis. Both times, Hitler demanded more than Chamberlain could deliver. On September 26, Hitler screamed out a speech so filled with rage and insults against the government in Prague that it seemed he had gone insane. That same day, the Spanish Nationalists announced that in case of conflict, they would remain neutral. Mussolini had been betrayed again. His troops in Spain would be cut off if hostilities broke out.

Mussolini longed to join Hitler in a decisive struggle with the West, but the Ethiopian and Spanish wars had exhausted the Italian armed forces. A limited Italian mobilization proved chaotic, and revealed crippling shortages of arms, ammunition, and equipment. Meanwhile, Vittorio Emanuele III and Marshal Badoglio secretly conspired to overthrow Mussolini in case of war. They felt that Mussolini was leading Italy to ruin.

Almost paralyzed with anxiety, Mussolini advised Hitler to seek a negotiated settlement. His caution surprised and disappointed Hitler, who decided to halt his war preparations for the moment. Seizing the delay, Chamberlain appealed to Mussolini to arrange a diplomatic conference. Mussolini urged Hitler to accept and he reluctantly agreed to a meeting to be held on September 29 in Munich.

At first, Margherita had hoped that the crisis might prove her salvation. She had close connections to the royal house, but her isolation at Il Soldo makes it unlikely that she knew of the plot to topple Mussolini. She simply wished for a war that would lead to Hitler's destruction. That in turn would either bring about Mussolini's downfall or at least end his blind infatuation with the Nazis. The sudden reversal in the events during the last days of September left her confused. Should she abandon her plans to flee or should she press forward with her preparations? Once again, she consulted Dante.

This time she opened the book to the following passage from Canto XIX of the *Paradiso:*

> There shall be seen, among the deeds of Alberto,
> that which will soon set the pen in motion,
> by which the Kingdom of Prague shall be made a desert.

"Alberto" was rather close to "Adolfo," she believed. He was about to get a written agreement that would destroy the land ruled from Prague. Now Margherita knew that Hitler would win what he wanted through a negotiated settlement. She resumed preparations to leave.

Margherita's expectations were fulfilled at the Munich Conference. Prodded effectively by Mussolini, and without any consultation with the Czech government, Chamberlain and French Premier Édouard Daladier agreed to German annexation of the Sudetenland. Hitler announced that he had satisfied all his territorial ambitions in Europe. Over the next five weeks, Poland and Hungary received smaller pieces of the rest of Czecho-slovakia. Nazi Germany had become the most powerful state in Europe without firing a shot.[27]

Mussolini returned home to a victor's welcome. But the frenzied reception along his rail route annoyed him. He wanted his people cheering for war, not hailing peace. A week later, he convened the Fascist Grand Council to discuss what measures to take against the Jews. Mussolini claimed to have been an anti-Semite since the age of twenty-five. He blamed the Jews for what little anti-Fascist opposition remained in Italy. The Jews were behind the small anti-Nazi demonstrations during Hitler's visit, Mussolini said. Now he would pay them back.

During a break in the discussions, Ciano's father-in-law boasted: "Now anti-Semitism has been injected into the blood of the Italians. It will continue all by itself to circulate and develop." Only Balbo, De Bono, and President of the Senate Luigi Federzoni argued against the laws that were proposed. Bottai surprised Ciano by insisting that the Jews be crushed. Margherita had misjudged another old friend.

On October 6, the Grand Council secretly adopted Mussolini's proposals to place Italy's Jews under the types of restrictions and prohibitions the Nazis had imposed on the Jews of Germany and Austria. To prepare the public for their promulgation, Mussolini ordered Alfieri to orchestrate a newspaper and radio propaganda campaign. For over a month, Italians were subjected to ceaseless attacks on the Jews. They were advised not to have any pity for them, yet bizarrely were assured that "to discriminate was not to persecute."

Mussolini's domestic intelligence network reported that most people were repelled by the propaganda. This public reaction of disgust and pity intensified in early November, after the Nazis launched the murderous attack on German Jews known as *Kristallnacht*. Cardinal Ildefonso Schuster of Milan was particularly outspoken in his criticism of Fascist anti-Semitism.

However, nothing could sway Mussolini from his course. Tacchi-Venturi, the Jesuit priest who had married Mussolini and Rachele and baptized their children, pleaded with the Duce to show mercy on the Jews. Edvige begged her brother to relent, and reminded him of his former love for Margherita. Mussolini agreed that any notion of Italian racial purity was nonsense and that there was no Jewish peril. It was all a matter of politics, to please his new German partners. But whether Mussolini was no more than an opportunistic hypocrite or a genuine anti-Semite made little difference to the tens of thousands of Italian Jews. What counted were his actions—and those were brutal.

Almost unnoticed amid this anti-Semitic onslaught, the regime had also promulgated laws sharply curtailing the rights of women to work outside the home or to engage in the professions. It was as if, having struck at Margherita's influence in one way, through his anti-Semitic decrees, Mussolini had decided to erase another form of her influence. Mussolini was determined to confine the women of Italy to the roles of wives and mothers.

As the mother of one of Italy's foremost war heroes, Margherita was expected in Rome for the ceremonies marking the twentieth anniversary of Italy's victory in 1918 on November 4. She wanted to go, but Fiammetta and Livio persuaded her that she would only humiliate herself if she took part.[28]

Over the next few days, Margherita finally decided that she must flee Italy. Confirmation came on November 10 with the public announcement of the Grand Council's decision to discriminate against the Jews of Italy. The next day, Amedeo was dismissed from his position at the Banca Commerciale in Turin. Six days later, a series of decrees laid down the major prohibitions and restrictions. For Margherita and her family the most relevant decrees were those that barred Jews from the professions and government service, forbade them to contract mixed marriages, and prohibited them from employing non-Jews. Those Jews, such as Margherita, who had performed special service to the country or to the regime were exempted from the harshest provisions of the new laws. On November 21, as if by afterthought, Jews were expelled from the Fascist party.

Meanwhile, Margherita had summoned Amedeo to Il Soldo and gave him a large sum of money. He was to buy diamonds—far easier to conceal or transport than cash. Then she sent Amedeo to Rome, to live with Pierangela and their daughter Magalì in her apartment on the Via dei Villini. Amedeo had to settle their affairs, and planned to leave Italy with his family later.

Acting on the advice of his supervisor at his former bank, Amedeo wrote to Mussolini shortly afterward, officially requesting permission to seek another banking job in Uruguay. He mentioned a letter Mussolini had written to him after Cesare's death. Mussolini had urged Amedeo to come to him for help at any time, and to think of him as a protector in place of Cesare. The Duce kept his word. Amedeo was left unmolested as he packed the family possessions and prepared to leave Italy.

Margherita had placed her most precious jewels, her strings of pearls, a certain amount of money, a few drawings by her favorite modern artists, and some clothes into two suitcases. She still had the passport Ciano had given her to go to America. That would allow her to travel abroad legally. Until the last, she had continued to hope to remain in Italy yet escape the humiliations of the anti-Semitic decrees. But these illusions collapsed when

Cardinal Schuster refused to intercede for her with Mussolini. Mussolini was well aware of her plight from information supplied by his police chief, Arturo Bocchini. Mussolini seems to have ordered Bocchini to give Margherita free passage.

On November 14, Margherita's chauffeur drove her north from Il Soldo to Pedrinate, where she passed through the Italian customs post without her bags being searched or any questions asked. The car passed the Swiss frontier and rolled on to the railroad station at Chiasso. Once the train arrived, Margherita's chauffeur helped her aboard.[29]

Lake Como Area

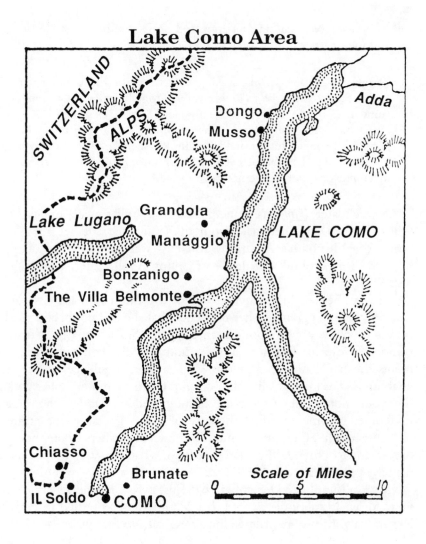

30

Purged Ghost

When the *New York Mirror* appeared on December 31, 1938, it carried the following item under a Paris byline:

> Margherita Sarfatti, titian-haired Jewess who was the guiding star of Premier Mussolini's rise to power, arrived tonight under mysterious circumstances apparently linked to Italy's anti-Semitic campaign. . . .
>
> "I have not been exiled," she told [Hearst's] International News Service. "I could return to Italy tonight. Please make it clear in anything you write that I have not been exiled. I am going to stay here on an indefinite visit, but I have not been exiled."

A week later, *Time* magazine published a similar piece, titled "Purged Ghost," which explained that Margherita's influence, and her role as ghost-writer for Mussolini's American articles, "waned when her old friend decided to pal around with Jew-tormenting Adolf Hitler, whom she detests."[1]

In Margherita's brief interview with the International News Service (the only one she granted), her insistence that she had not been exiled was meant to convey an important message to Mussolini. She had spread rumors, before leaving her native country, of the compromising documents she had in her possession. With a discreet silence she hoped to establish that as long as Mussolini did not try to harm her or her children, she would not reveal his secrets. Fiammetta and her family, who remained in Rome, became in effect the hostages who guaranteed Margherita's circumspection. She refused American newspaper offers to buy her memoirs, saying to a friend, "I cannot give them what they would of course ask, namely, politics and scandal."[2]

It wasn't until late December 1938, just before her news service interview, that Mussolini discovered that Margherita had settled in Paris after leaving Italy. Mussolini ordered inquiries made, to find where and how she was living, what people she saw, and what kind of public comments she made about him or Italy. Some police agents still didn't realize that Margherita had left Italy. For a time they thought she had gone to the mountain resort of Cortina d'Ampezzo. As late as February 1939, an agent in Rome reported that he had cleverly tricked Margherita's secretary into arranging a meeting with her, only to be told by his superiors that perhaps he should consult *Time* magazine.[3]

As Mussolini's agents discovered, the press accounts of Margherita's "exile" were incorrect about the date of her arrival in Paris. She had been there since late November, arriving by train at the Gare de l'Est station. An old friend, the novelist Francis Carco, met her with a bouquet of flowers. She took rooms at the first-class Hotel Lotti, located on the Rue de Castiglione near the Tuileries gardens, and remained there until mid-May of the following year. She then moved to the Hotel St. James, one of the best hotels in Paris, on the exclusive Rue Saint-Honoré.[4]

Among her first visitors were Colette, Marie de Chambrun, and Jean Cocteau. Considering the circumstances, her stay in Paris proved rather pleasant. She had many dinner companions, and opportunities to attend the theater and visit galleries. She became friends with the film actress Corinne Luchaire and her husband, Jean, whose father Margherita had known since World War I. She spent much time with Cocteau, the celebrated homosexual writer and set designer. One evening at the theater they encountered a well-known intellectual, who snubbed them both. Only a few days earlier the same man had been very friendly to them. When Margherita asked Cocteau for an explanation, he said that the man was with his wife, who was jealous. "Of whom?" inquired Margherita. "Of me—I was his first!"[5]

The pleasures of Paris could not, however, obscure the fact that her life was in disarray. She did not expect to return to Italy in the immediate future. As she had told the newspaper reporter, her plans were to remain in Paris for an "indefinite" period. She was looking to start a new life outside of Europe, preferably in America. She anticipated that the European situation would only get worse. While she waited for her son Amedeo and his family to join her, she began writing letters asking help from her American friends. Among the first was this to Nicholas Murray Butler:

> It is a sad & heartbroken Margherita who addresses you from the despair of her soul. But first of all, promise to keep this letter of mine, & what it contains, as a confidential, strictly confidential secret. Much harm could befall me, & even worse than me, my children, if it came to be made anyhow public. You know what happened to us! I am a Catholic, & so are both my children, both married to Catholics, & fathers & mothers of

Catholic children. But I myself as well as my husband, are of Jewish descent, therefore both my children & myself are considered Jews, that most heinous (so it seems to be) sin of today, being searched in us, in such a measure, that my son's glorious death, as a hero, at 17 years of age in the War, & my husband's & mine own & my other son's fascist & Italian faith & works during all our lives, account to nothing. I am not permitted to print any articles in Italian papers or reviews, & am not permitted to have even one single servant. . . . I do not know . . . what will happen to my moneys, houses, estates, etc etc.

Under these circumstances, I came to Paris, & am writing to you from here, addressing you an appeal as from soul to soul. S.O.S.! If you do care for pity, & justice, & humanity, & for me, let me come to America, find some job for me.[6]

Over the following weeks, she wrote repeatedly to Butler and to Missy Meloney, hoping that they could arrange a teaching position for her at a university. "It is rather grim humour," she told Missy, that her books, once prefaced by Mussolini himself, would soon be burned in Italy "like in the Middle Ages."

Since I am in Paris, amidst human people, away from the pressure & the poison of falsehood & ruthlessness, I begin to breathe more freely, & to take a broader historic view, if not a cheerful one, at least a hopelessly cheerful one, of a very hopeless, cheerless & altogether monstrous situation . . . [yet] I cannot & will not face the music of going against, so to say, my own breed—fascism. However degenerate from what it used & had to be, I still feel towards it like towards a much-beloved, erring & sinful son! And besides, eternal Italy, my country = right or wrong = is lurking with its eternal beauty besides & back of that now hideously grinning mask!

When Butler suggested that perhaps some of her property and income could be salvaged if she returned to Italy, she replied, "The whole feeling of being crushed under an inferiority treatment is such that I do not feel I could bear it. . . . No, as long as I hold pen & have the power & strength to earn a bit of bread abroad, even if it should be scanty (a very good thing for my figure) I cannot & will not submit to such indignities in my own land."[7]

Despite her complaints to others, Margherita suffered no shortage of funds. She spent money freely in Paris, on hotel accommodations, entertainment, and restaurants. She did worry about her lack of regular income. She tried to raise cash by selling some of the original lithographs she had taken out of Italy with her, including a Cézanne, a Renoir, an Ensor, and the complete set of Toulouse-Lautrec's *Elles,* which she had purchased on her honeymoon in Paris in 1898. Missy approached Abby Aldrich Rockefeller on Margherita's behalf, but the works in question were already part of the Rockefeller collection.[8]

Margherita wrote to Missy and Butler that she needed money, and proposed, if she could get an advance, to write a book for an American publisher on Maria Theresa of Austria, Isabella of Spain, Cesare Borgia, or even on the image of the madonna in Italian art. She applied for a U.S. visa at the American consulate in Paris, pleading that Amedeo and his family also wanted desperately to come to America—"I look towards America as all have done, all the persecuted of all times, as towards 'God's own land,' the heir & only hope of the White Civilization now, I am afraid, doomed to die out in Europe! We are travelling fast towards ruin."[9]

Butler wrote, "After all that you yourself have done for the intellectual life of Italy and its people and for their guidance and inspiration in politics, in letters and in art, the facts which you state fill me with horror." After writing unsuccessfully to the presidents of a number of Ivy League colleges, he asked Giuseppe Prezzolini whether he could find a place for Margherita at Columbia's Casa Italiana. Prezzolini vetoed the idea, arguing that it was "better to save a Jew who is of real value and is poor." As a result, Butler reported to Margherita that it was difficult to find Americans sympathetic to anyone who had been officially connected to Fascist Italy or Nazi Germany, and that "the outlook here was quite hopeless at present." He continued to assure Margherita that he was doing everything he could.[10]

Mussolini ordered his men not to keep Margherita under regular surveillance. If Margherita felt that assassins were stalking her, he worried, she would rush to publish his letters. Reports about her activities were sent to Rome only occasionally. One suggested that she had attempted to contact, but had been rebuffed by, Emilio Lussu and Alberto Cianca, two leading anti-Fascists in exile in Paris. Some anti-Fascists thought she had been sent to Paris to spy on them. Anti-Fascists in New York City, better informed than Mussolini's agents, learned that Margherita was attempting to reach the United States. They declared they had no use for her there, either as a refugee or as a turncoat. However, in January 1939, Paul Levi, the anti-Fascist editor of *Aux Écoutes,* published a series of critical articles on Mussolini that included a sympathetic portrait of Margherita. She was presented as the center of opposition to the Duce's pro-German policies.[11]

Margherita made it a point to stay away from anyone who might be considered politically controversial back in Italy. She did see Carlo Levi, but because he was a painter, not because he was an anti-Fascist. Similarly she visited the artist Corrado Cagli only because he was a Jewish refugee. At a party at the studio of Vincenzo Tallone, son of the famous Italian

painter Cesare Tallone, an informant reported that although political figures were in attendance, Margherita talked only about art and the high cost
of living, and studiously avoided any discussion of Italian affairs.[12]

Margherita did try to connect with other Italian "exiles" who were
victims of persecution. Although she had long ignored her Jewish roots, she
thought her victimization might generate more sympathy with the Americans. Otherwise she continued to protest her complete loyalty to Fascism
and to Italy. "I wish to make it quite clear," she told Butler, who she feared
might view her plight as the result of a lovers' quarrel, "that what has
happened to me is not the consequence of any particular personal or
peculiar animosity or special measure taken against me or mine, but the
result of the general laws newly promulgated against all & every person of
Jewish ancestry. I am not particularly or personally a special target." Subsequent letters to others prove that she really did believe she had been
particularly targeted for persecution.[13]

Margherita made a number of approaches to exiled Jews in Paris. She
also frequently saw Alma Mahler, who was a refugee from Nazi persecution. Mahler held a salon in her hotel room that was attended by Jewish
artists and intellectuals. "When I first met her," Mahler recorded in her
diary, "she was the uncrowned queen of Italy. Now she is the crowned
pauper of the exiles. As always, she is bold and spirited—but filled with
much bitterness. Her deep love affair with Mussolini has become a boundless hatred. She visits us often, and her great energy animates all the
emigrants." Margherita wrote an autobiographical article for *Le Temps* in
which she described her family's Jewish roots. She published in *L'Univers
Israélite* an article on the Jewish painter Amedeo Modigliani, who had lived
and worked in Paris for many years. Many Italian Jewish refugees in Paris
also stayed at the Hotel Lotti, including the family of Tullia Zevi. Although
a young girl at the time, Zevi remembers the arrival of Margherita, "around
whom there immediately formed a vacuum," and recalls seeing her in the
hotel dining room, "this woman sitting alone at a table, having made
unsuccessful attempts to approach us in the name of a common Jewish
background."[14]

The social engagements and cultural events began to wear on Margherita. Few wrote from Italy except for her family—Carrà sent a support-
ive card, but she was wounded to have received nothing from Ada Negri.
Visiting her in Paris, Elisabetta Cerruti found Margherita depressed. For the
first time in four decades, she had no deadlines to meet and little to do.
Margherita told Elisabetta of her bitterness at having been betrayed by
Mussolini: "He is not," she said, "the same Mussolini I knew for so many
years." To others who asked why she was in Paris, she claimed to be
researching a book. She did publish a number of articles on art in a Swiss

newspaper, and gave lectures at the Louvre on Leonardo da Vinci and on the Venetian school of painting.[15]

Margherita's spirits were lifted by Amedeo's arrival in early March of 1939. Amedeo brought with him the thirty-six diamonds he had purchased with his mother's money. His wife, Pierangela, and their young daughter, Magalì, remained temporarily in Rome. Pierangela was not Jewish, so she had stayed behind for a time in order to arrange for the packing and shipment of a number of paintings—including works by de Chirico, Utrillo, and Tosi—which Margherita believed could be sold easily should the need for cash arise. When Pierangela encountered difficulty with regulations concerning the export of art works, Education Minister Giuseppe Bottai secured permission for her to take them out of the country. Amedeo booked passage on a ship bound for Montevideo, Uruguay, where he was to start a new job at the Banca Francese e Italiana dell'America Latina. The position had been quietly arranged for him by Raffaele Mattioli, president of the Banca Commerciale Italiana. On March 27, just after Hitler's armies occupied what remained of the Czechoslovak state, Amedeo sailed from Cannes. Pierangela and Magalì reached Montevideo several months later.[16]

After seeing Amedeo off at Cannes, Margherita joined Sacha Guitry, the flamboyant actor, playwright, and film director, for a week at Nice, enjoying the sea and the crush of international tourists. From her room at the Hôtel Impérator, Margherita wrote again to Butler as well as to Breckinridge Long, who was now in charge of visa requests for the State Department. She explained to Long that she had left Italy with a valid passport but needed a job in the United States. "I am pretty well off in Italy," she lamented, "but as you probably know, no Italian can get anything of his moneys outside the frontiers. Therefore, I live a simple life . . . through my royalties in foreign papers etc, & also I had the chance of winning at the French Lotterie a nice little morsel." Long turned to Bernard Baruch for advice, and checked with several people in a position to provide her employment, but concluded that her Fascist past made her too controversial. Long cabled her to see Anne O'Hare McCormick of *The New York Times,* who was then in Paris. Long eventually told her that there were no prospects for her in America, and hence little chance for a visa.[17]

As they were leaving Nice, the spendthrift Guitry announced that he could not get back to Paris with the francs he had in his pocket. They stopped off in the casino at Monte Carlo, where he proceeded to win enough to allow them to stay a few more days.[18]

While Margherita and Guitry were in Monte Carlo, Hitler demanded the cession of Danzig from the Polish government. Britain and France reacted stiffly, issuing a joint guarantee of assistance to Poland in the event of German aggression. Taking advantage of their preoccupation with Poland and the end of the Spanish Civil War a few days earlier, Mussolini bombarded the coastal towns of Albania and landed an Italian army on April 7. He rapidly overran the small Balkan country. Five days later, Vittorio Emanuele III wore the Albanian crown.

Joachim von Ribbentrop arrived in Milan on May 5 for diplomatic talks with Ciano. French newspapers reported that the Milanese had greeted the German foreign minister icily. Piqued by this slight to his prestige, Mussolini unexpectedly telephoned his son-in-law with instructions to conclude a political and military alliance with Germany. The resulting alliance, which Mussolini dubbed the "Pact of Steel," provided for immediate military assistance if either party became involved in "warlike complications" with another power. The agreement also called for immediate consultation on issues affecting common interests, and for joint military and economic commissions. Mussolini may have been looking for some control over Hitler's ability to declare war on his own, but in fact the pact gave the German dictator the impetus to move against Poland.[19]

The Pact of Steel was signed in Berlin on May 22. The same day, Fascist agents reported that Fiammetta had shipped three large trunks of dresses, shoes, furs, and other personal effects to her mother in Paris. Clearly Margherita had no intention of coming back to Italy anytime soon. Mussolini read the report, and decided that he wanted Margherita back in Italy. He ordered Dino Alfieri, minister of popular culture, to lure her home.[20]

Alfieri had already been receiving secret reports on Margherita's activities from Amedeo Landini, Italian consul in Paris. Landini reported she frequently expressed bitterness over Italy's anti-Semitic laws, and had a deep antipathy for Nazi Germany, which she blamed for having pushed Italy into a racist policy. Alfieri invited Livio Gaetani to his office for a private conversation. He suggested that Livio and Fiammetta go to Paris and persuade Margherita to come home. Livio replied that he could not promise to give his mother-in-law that advice.

The next day, Fiammetta went to see Alfieri. The conversation was tense:

FIAMMETTA: Livio told me that the *Duce* wants us to go to Paris. . . .

ALFIERI: No, I never mentioned the *Duce!* This was my idea.

FIAMMETTA: Oh, Livio must have been mistaken. In any case, we'll go to Paris, but not to advise my mother to come back. Why would she want to—so that the racial laws can prevent her from having a maid, owning a radio, or publishing?

ALFIERI: Well, you know, her absence may create a very bad impression. . . .

Fiammetta and Livio did visit Margherita in Paris. She was convinced that a return to Italy would bring humiliation and continual persecution. "Tell them that I'm not coming back. But remember that if you should read in the newspapers that I killed myself as a result of depression, or because I miss my home, or some such story, don't believe it: it means that they did me in!"[21]

Angry that her family had been involved, Margherita composed a stern letter to Alfieri, which she asked the new Italian ambassador, Raffaele Guariglia, to transmit to Rome by diplomatic pouch. She scolded Alfieri for sending private messengers:

> If the *Duce* or the government of my country have something to communicate to me, I insist that it be done directly and personally, in an explicit and responsible way. . . . I can understand, Excellency, that you are worried . . . about my returning home, since it was you who first provoked my legitimate indignation, having prohibited the newspapers from publishing my articles. . . . No pretext excused it then, and no legislative actions can ever legally justify this measure, which bears clear signs of private, special, and personal persecution against me.

She suggested that if he wanted to make up for his mistake, she would be happy to accept an official overseas mission, perhaps to the United States.[22]

Alfieri responded with an obvious ploy. He offered her exactly the mission she suggested, but said that she should come to Rome to talk over the details in person so as to avoid the French censors, as well as to clear up previous "equivocations and misunderstandings." "Excellency and dear minister," Margherita answered. "At some point you will explain in person what you call the 'equivocations and misunderstandings,' but in any case these belong to the past and the future is more interesting." Regretfully, she apologized, she could not possibly stop the research she was doing in the Bibliothèque Nationale in order to come to Rome. She pointed out that if Alfieri was worried about keeping their correspondence confidential, they could use the diplomatic pouch. When Alfieri showed him Margherita's letter, Mussolini muttered, "The crafty bitch."[23]

In mid-August, Margherita took passage aboard a French cruise ship bound for the Norwegian fjords. On August 21, Berlin radio announced that Germany and the Soviet Union were about to sign a nonaggression pact, which included a provision for neutrality by one side if the other was attacked by a third power. It also involved a secret protocol in which Hitler and Stalin agreed to carve up Poland in the event of war.

The news surprised Mussolini as much as it did the rest of Europe. He warned Hitler that it was too soon for a general war, and that Italy was not prepared to fight the Western powers, who would no doubt come to Poland's defense. Margherita guessed that war was imminent, and that she could find herself trapped in the midst of a German invasion. She rushed back to Paris and telegraphed Alfieri urgently about her overseas mission. On August 24, the day Britain and Poland signed a pact of mutual assistance, Alfieri replied that "The situation is such that I think you should come to Italy." Two days later, Ambassador Guariglia wired Alfieri that Margherita wished to leave France immediately for Lisbon. She had requested an authorized passport that would allow her to cross through Spain to Portugal. Margherita's request reached Mussolini's desk. If he granted it, he knew she would not come back to Italy. He scrawled "Yes/M" in the margin of Guariglia's telegram.[24]

Unaware of Mussolini's personal intervention, Margherita packed her trunks and made her way to Barcelona, and then across Spain to Lisbon. In the sudden international crisis, the Portuguese capital had become a major port of embarkation for thousands of Europeans. To her dismay, Margherita found herself stranded in Lisbon with little hope of getting a place on one of the overbooked ships that crowded the harbor. Rather than face the uncertainty of waiting alone in Lisbon, Margherita retraced her route to Barcelona, where she had friends. Their news was grim: At dawn on September 1, Germany had invaded Poland. The following day, Mussolini proclaimed Italian neutrality. On September 3 Britain and France declared war on Germany.

In Barcelona, Margherita called upon Carlo Bossi, an old family friend and a career diplomat then serving as Italian consul general in the Catalan capital. Also serving in Madrid was Massimo Gaetani d'Aragona, a relative of Fiammetta's husband and secretary at the embassy. Bossi informed her that an Italian ship, the *Augustus,* was about to stop overnight at Barcelona en route to South America, and that he could arrange passage for her. It was somewhat risky, for once on board Margherita would come technically under Italian authority, but there seemed little choice. The day the *Augustus* was due to depart, Bossi lunched with Margherita and then accompanied her onto the ship. Bossi told the captain that as consul general he was officially placing Margherita in his care, and charging him with personal responsibility for her safety.[25]

The voyage across the Atlantic gave Margherita time to reflect on the more intimate aspects of the almost sixty years of her life, as well as on the public stature and power that she had known. As the ship put more and more distance between her and her past, she grew pensive. On board, a photographer caught her in an informal moment as she reclined on a deck chair in white slacks and matching heels, a cigarette in her hand, her hair cut short and still blond. Her relaxed pose fails to hide the impact of recent events, for she appears to have lost weight, her face is taut with tension, and her tightly drawn lips cannot manage a smile. Her eyes betray her real emotions—a look of bewilderment has replaced the usual determination.

Margherita reached Uruguay in mid-September. Although she lent Amedeo the money to buy a house in Montevideo, she insisted on maintaining an independent life apart from her family. Almost immediately, she took a suite of rooms at the Hotel Nogaró in downtown Montevideo. As soon as she was settled she wrote to Butler, asking him again to find her a job in South America or the United States. By then, Poland had fallen to German and Russian armies, while the French settled in along the Maginot Line during the "Phony War." She told him, "I am very much afraid Europe is doomed. . . . It is up to America to save what is to be saved, and not only mechanics and technique of what I call 'The White Civilization.' . . . You must be the new Noah's Ark of this new Deluge. Do you think I could publish in some review or newspaper an essay of mine on this mission of America?" Butler assured her he would do what he could to find her something in South America. Eventually he put her in contact with Cupertino del Campo of Buenos Aires, president of the North American-Argentine Cultural Institute, with the idea of arranging a lecture series for her in Argentina.[26]

Communication with family and friends back home was relatively easy while Italy remained at peace. In December, a letter arrived from Ada Negri, who protested that she had not written sooner because she had not known the address. After a two-year silence, Margherita was bitter. She replied with a short, sarcastic note. When Negri wrote again in March, she protested her friend's harsh reaction but offered assurances of her friendship. This time Margherita was slightly warmer, but could not resist telling Negri how much the long silence had surprised and pained her. The two occasionally exchanged letters over the next several years, but Margherita never got over having been abandoned by her old friend.[27]

Margherita soon adjusted to her new surroundings. She found Montevideo rather small—"a quiet backwater"—but life was pleasant. During her first months there, she studied Spanish, and by March 1940 she was fluent, and writing articles for the local press. That spring, she moved to the more comfortable Parque Hotel, overlooking the boulevard that skirted the beach. There she was famous for exercising every morning at 7:00 A.M. and returning in the afternoon for a long and vigorous swim. Once she swam so far out from shore that Amedeo sent lifeguards to bring her back.[28]

From a distance, Margherita watched events in Europe unfold. She was saddened by the death and destruction the spreading war would bring. The prospect of Italy's joining the war was especially distressing because of the possible danger facing Fiammetta and her family. In April 1940, Hitler overran Denmark and Norway, and on May 10 the Nazis turned against the Low Countries and France. By the end of the month, the Germans had driven deep into northern France. On June 4 the British completed a miraculous withdrawal from the beaches of Dunkirk. With the Germans free to attack the French lines across the entire arc from Sedan to Abbeville, Margherita knew their victory was imminent. She guessed that Mussolini would not resist the temptation to join in. On June 10, he declared war on Britain and France. The same day she wrote to Butler:

> Time flies, and it brings with it, alas! always new sorrows and troubles to this foolish and criminal mankind. It would be so simple and fine to live in peace and goodwill under God's blessed sun and breeze trying to improve our minds and the standard of life, but Europe thinks of nothing but killing and having her best youth killed, her people famished and barbarised. Where are we going? I cannot but tremble. Do you still believe in an all-powerful and man-loving God? Methinks he lets the devil get the upper most.[29]

Although safe from direct harm, Margherita still wanted to go to the United States. Her request for an American visa was finally granted in June, although it was valid only until October. Amedeo and Pierangela recalled that "someone—possibly in the American government—stopped it." Butler's correspondence contains no mention of the matter, but there is evidence that FBI director J. Edgar Hoover wrote to the Immigration and Naturalization Service, and to Adolf Berle of the State Department, requesting further information about Margherita's travel plans and the possible date of her arrival. Federal agents kept U.S. ports under surveillance but reported no sign of her entry into the country.[30]

Instead Margherita went to Buenos Aires at the end of August, where she met Butler's contact, Cupertino del Campo. He angered her by asking that she give a free lecture. She protested to Butler, "I am no longer, alas! a slip of a girl who is delighted at any occasion to have some few pupils listening to her, and perhaps also of getting her name in the papers. . . . Life and men are funny things, when they are no worse than funny!" The trip was occasioned by an invitation from a local book club to give a lecture on the Italian historical novel. Clemente Pellegrini, the club's president, escorted Margherita around Buenos Aires and introduced her to many of the city's prominent journalists and writers. Her arrival in the Argentine capital caused something of a stir in the local press. Stories about her lamented the "ingratitude" of the Fascist regime toward the woman who had been so important to its success.

Public notoriety made her uncomfortable; one incident especially outraged her. On the evening of August 27, a journalist from *Noticias Gráficas* interviewed Margherita at the Hotel Continental. The newspaper appeared a few hours later. The interview quoted her as having commiserated with the Italian people, who had been led astray by a Mussolini who had lost his balance. Horrified that Mussolini would think she had broken her silence, she quickly wrote a formal letter to the paper denying that she had made the statements. She sent a copy to Baron Serena di Lapigio, an official in the Italian embassy. Serena reported the matter to Rome, assuring his superiors that Margherita was doubtless an innocent victim of the sensation-mongering press. Actually she had made statements similar to those quoted by the reporter, but only in private conversation.[31]

Margherita had already visited Buenos Aires to preside at the *Novecento* exhibit of 1930. In the city's Italian community, which Mussolini's diplomatic envoys had bombarded with Fascist propaganda for years, her name was familiar as the author of *Dux*. It had been published in Spanish translation in June 1940. At her lecture on September 5 Margherita was introduced by Victoria Ocampo, a prominent writer who hosted the most important cultural salon in the country. Ocampo was a woman of decidedly anti-Fascist sympathies. She was a prolific writer as much at home in Paris and Rome as in Buenos Aires. Despite Margherita's Fascist past, Ocampo and other left-wing intellectuals welcomed her into their circle of writers and artists. The friendly reception she received convinced Margherita that she should live at least part of the time in Buenos Aires, which she found more interesting than Montevideo. Buenos Aires was a cosmopolitan capital of two and a half million people, mainly of European origin, including a large number of Italians. High culture, from music and theater to literature and art, took its inspiration chiefly from Europe, and especially from Paris. Margherita decided to divide the seasons between the two cities, spending winters in Argentina, when the social season was at its height, and summers in Uruguay.[32]

Margherita socialized with the modernist author Jorge Luis Borges, the writer Julio Pairò, Jorge Romero Brest, who edited an art journal, José Luis Romero, a historian at the University of Buenos Aires, and the Chilean poet Gabriela Mistral. She also renewed an old friendship with the painter Emilio Pettoruti, whom she had known in Italy. Among the prominent social and political figures she came to know was Don Manuel José Guiraldes, former intendant of Buenos Aires, whose obituary Margherita published in Montevideo's *El Diario* in 1941. Cecilio Materazzo, son of a wealthy Brazilian industrialist, enlisted her advice when purchasing paintings for a museum of modern art he founded in Sâo Paolo. Margherita was not the only Italian Jewish exile living in the Argentine capital—there were the former diplomat Paolo Vita-Finzi, her Venetian friend Edgardo Morpurgo, once director of the Assicurazioni Generali company, the industrialist Gino Olivetti, and scores of others. But Margherita preferred for the most part to socialize with Argentines.[33]

Margherita wrote occasionally in Buenos Aires for Elvio Botana's sensationalist newspaper *Crítica,* and for *La Prensa.* In Montevideo she published criticism and travel articles in *La Mañana.* Over the next several years, she busied herself with a number of books. "I am writing in Spanish," she informed Butler, "which by now I know pretty well and am able to write easily and fluently a book on Giorgione, the painter, one on Titian and one on Vasari, the art critic of the XVI century, and have finished a book on Casanova, the Venetian delightful Don Juan and memoirist." After the appearance of *Dux* in Argentina in the summer of 1940, a Brazilian publisher put out a Portuguese edition (despite the wishes of the Italian authorities) in Rio de Janeiro. Alessandro Pavolini, the new minister of popular culture in Rome, sent orders to the pro-Fascist newspapers in Rio de Janeiro that reviews should focus on Mussolini, and should avoid any mention of Margherita.[34]

Margherita studiously avoided any involvement in the struggles taking place abroad between Italian Fascists and anti-Fascists. She also tried to avoid involvement in the political affairs of her host countries, although in Argentina she socialized often with Vice-President Ramón S. Castillo and his circle. She sent Butler a detailed account of her observations on the Argentine political situation. Castillo had served under President Robert M. Ortiz, who favored a formal alliance with the Allies. In 1942, Castillo took over the reins of government and declared Argentina neutral instead. On June 4, 1943, a coup toppled Castillo from power. Among the military officers who took over the government was Colonel Juan Perón. Perón eventually became vice-president, and in 1946 began a decade-long rule as dictator of Argentina, aided by his wife Eva.[35]

Margherita was naturally preoccupied with events in Europe. She studied the course of the war closely through the newspapers. Mail to and from Italy became irregular at best, and there was scant news from Fiammetta, who had given birth to a third child in 1940. In October 1941, Pierangela and Amedeo had a baby boy, whom they named Roberto. When Margherita finally heard from Fiammetta later that same month, she was distressed to learn that the war had produced critical shortages of food and medicine in Italy. She wrote immediately to Butler, begging him to try to get essential supplies delivered to Fiammetta. "Everything is all wrong in the world!" she exclaimed to her American friend. "What do you hold of the future? Will the Devil triumph?" Five weeks later, on December 7, 1941, Japan surprised American forces with an attack on Pearl Harbor.

Three days later, Mussolini and Hitler declared war against the United States. Obviously, Butler was unable to get supplies to Rome. Letters to and from Fiammetta were thereafter transmitted through Vatican channels via Lisbon, thanks to the help of Father Tacchi-Venturi.[36]

Margherita's moods swung between optimism for the eventual outcome of the war and a black depression. She hoped to see the Axis defeated. Mussolini's invasion of Greece in the fall of 1940 resulted in a military debacle that Hitler had to reverse with German troops. In North Africa the British dealt Italian forces powerful blows, until they were reinforced by General Rommel's Afrika Korps. After the German Army was repulsed before Moscow, Hitler assumed supreme command himself on December 19, 1941. As Margherita wrote to Butler the next day, this gave her some grounds for hope:

> I am rather elated by the present pieces of good news, and hopeful of Mr. A.[dolf] H.[itler's] move to direct command: when man believes himself all-knowing besides all-powerful, he generally stumbles blindly. As to the Russians flying in the face of all their time-honored traditions by turning unexpectedly into such efficiently killing soldiers, I will quote a short sentence, knowing you prefer it rightly to a long pompous speech in a nut-shell—: New Gods unused to worship are thirstier of blood than the old ones. . . .[37]

Margherita's analysis was cogent; throughout the spring and summer of 1942, Hitler overextended his armies in Russia, leading to the disaster at Stalingrad that fall.

In the spring of 1942, Margherita's name was once again linked publicly with the Duce. *Time* magazine carried a small article titled "Et Tu, Benito," about Mussolini's love affairs, including those with "the brilliant exiled Jewess, Margherita Sarfatti" and the French journalist Magda Fontanges. "Last week," the article continued with considerable exaggeration, "she would scarcely have recognized her onetime lover. In his private study at the Palazzo Venezia, Mussolini no longer entertains visitors. In deep gloom he sits alone, reading Dante and Virgil, while his people faint on the streets from hunger."[38]

Mussolini's war effort deteriorated as Italy suffered from an acute shortage of vital war matériel, while repeated promises from Hitler for German supplies went unfulfilled. The Führer's tendency to assume the role of superior angered Mussolini, who had once enjoyed the status of senior statesman among Fascist nations.

In November 1942, the Axis suffered a triple defeat. The British smashed through the German-Italian lines at El Alamein, a few days later

American and British forces landed in Morocco and Algeria, and two weeks after that, the Red Army launched its counteroffensive at Stalingrad.

Later that month, the Philadelphia *Evening Bulletin* published a lengthy biographical sketch of Margherita with a title that must have pleased her: "She Could Tell Mussolini 'I Told You So': Il Duce's Biographer, Now in Exile, Warned Him of Doom." The reporter, Inez Robb, announced that Margherita, "an aging refugee in a second rate hotel," had been living in Buenos Aires:

> But even the privilege and the solace of crying, 'I told you so' at Mussolini as he and Fascism stand on the brink of disaster is denied Signora Sarfatti as long as her daughter, Fiammetta, remains a virtual hostage within fascist Italy. . . . Once the most powerful woman in Italy and among the most brilliant in Europe, Signora Sarfatti repeatedly warned Mussolini that Hitler would engulf him and Fascism to their eventual destruction.[39]

In January 1943, Roosevelt, Churchill, and other Allied leaders met at Casablanca for the first of a series of wartime conferences. They discussed, among other things, the imposition of a policy of "unconditional surrender" on the Axis powers, and made plans for the first invasion of Europe. Although the Americans insisted on the importance of a cross-Channel invasion of France, Roosevelt agreed with Churchill that they should first invade Sicily. With a foothold in the Mediterranean, they might trigger the overthrow of Mussolini. That March a major strike led by Communists had halted industrial production in Turin and Milan. The Fascist regime's support systems had begun to disintegrate in the face of military disaster. Many industrialists, and a group of military officers led by Marshal Badoglio, had already begun to explore possibilities for a separate peace with the Allies. After the Sicilian invasion was launched on July 10, 1943, a group of important Fascist leaders, headed by Dino Grandi, began to plot to remove Mussolini from power and engineer the withdrawal of Italy from the war.

Mussolini was dispirited and frequently ill. He played into the hands of the conspirators when he called a special session of the Fascist Grand Council for the evening of July 24. The Duce had just returned from a disastrous meeting with Hitler at Feltre, where his military advisers had wanted him to announce that Italy could not continue the war effort. Instead, he allowed Hitler to convince him that victory was still possible. Grandi had secured the support of Giuseppe Bottai, De Bono, Luigi Federzoni, and even Galeazzo Ciano. After Mussolini had failed to stand up to Hitler, they agreed that the only way to save themselves was to remove the Duce. They planned to introduce a motion of no confidence in Mussolini's leadership. In the days before the meeting, Grandi made contact with King Vittorio Emanuele III, to whom he wanted to restore full military and political power.

Certain of the king's support, Mussolini ignored the information he received that dissidents within the Grand Council might attempt a coup. Grandi worried needlessly about Mussolini's reaction, and arrived at the Palazzo Venezia that evening armed with grenades. Instead of taking decisive action, Mussolini opened the session with a lame defense of the German alliance and his conduct of the war. After he finished speaking, Grandi, Bottai, and Ciano each denounced the Axis alliance, while Farinacci and others defended Mussolini and the Germans. Well after midnight, the vote was taken. Grandi's motion won by a majority of 19 to 7, with one member abstaining. Mussolini wrote that when he left Palazzo Venezia at 3:00 A.M., "there was in the gray early morning air the feeling of inevitability that is created by the turning wheel of fate, of which men are often the unwitting cogs."

Once the king learned of the Grand Council's decision, he mobilized army and police units in the capital. The next day, when Mussolini went to see the king, the Carabinieri arrested him. Vittorio Emanuele dismissed him as prime minister and replaced him with Marshal Badoglio, who immediately assured the Germans that "the war continues."[40]

The next day, an Associated Press journalist in Buenos Aires asked Margherita to comment on the momentous news. She publicly expressed her satisfaction and relief. Her statement was carried by American newspapers: "I do hope the Italians will immediately go in for peace and have confidence in the Allies. The sooner Italy gets out of the war—not only unpopular but unnatural to its closest and highest traditions—the better. If the Allies show leniency and moderation toward Italy, it will have a profound effect on the morale of the German people."

In the days following, Fiammetta cabled Margherita that she and the family were safe. But in August, after hearing of the Allied bombings over Italy, Margherita wrote to Butler:

Events are galloping fast. I hoped better things a month ago to-day, when Mussolini fell at last. But things are difficult, & I feel Badoglio is not up to his position, which to be fair, is extremely delicate. However he does not seem to manage it at all. Italy longs for peace. . . . Mankind is all together a great mistake on God's part, or whatever it is, evolution or the devil, who is responsible for it.[41]

Early in 1943, the U.S. embassy in Montevideo, worried that she might be engaged in espionage activities, asked J. Edgar Hoover for information on Margherita's background. In August, the well-known columnist West-brook Pegler, whose opinion of all Italians was tainted by prejudice, read her comments about Mussolini's fall. In answer he wrote a venomous article for the *Washington Daily News* about a visit he had once made to Margherita's salon in Rome. He recalled her as a "moist and sloppy object . . . pink-haired and portly," who "gurgled like a hot-water bottle as she shifted on her couch." Pegler accused Margherita of having been a "sordid, arrogant grafter" and wrote, "If we ever go thru with our threats to destroy not only Fascism but those who were blood-guilty of Fascism, Sarfatti, by any fair process, should be put against a wall, for she was one of the lowest and meanest of the whole greedy crew." The FBI filed a report on Pegler's observations and supplied a copy of the article to the embassy in Monte-video.[42]

All this was unknown to Margherita. Freed from the silence she had been forced to maintain for the last five years, she moved quickly to profit from her changed circumstances with the kind of book people had long expected her to write. She intended to call it *My Fault: Mussolini as I Knew Him*. She had begun to work on the book before July 25, for in August she told Butler that she had completed six chapters, which she had written directly in English. She struck a deal with an American newspaper group—undoubtedly the Hearst chain—to publish the chapters as a series of articles. "I have left off Spanish & art, & have gone for English & politics or chronicles, if you prefer, or *Memoirs."* The Didier publishing house, which had a branch office in Buenos Aires, made her an offer for the book rights. She asked for advice. Butler contacted Columbia University Press and Scribner's, and both expressed interest in the project.[43]

On September 8, after nearly two months of secret negotiations, a separate armistice was announced between the Badoglio government and the Allies. At the same time, the Americans and British landed in southern Italy. Hitler had suspected that the Italians were planning to switch sides. He immediately ordered his forces to seize the northern three quarters of the peninsula. Margherita somehow obtained information—perhaps from within the Italian exile community—that an Allied invasion of Italy was impending. She sent Fiammetta a telegram warning of the impending danger. To avoid the censors, the telegram contained only three words, *"Raddopiate porco reggio,"* which meant in effect that "the fattened pig was ready for slaughter." Margherita frequently used the humorous old dialect phrase in informal conversation, and was sure Fiammetta would understand her warning. The police intercepted the telegram, suspecting a plot against the king, and questioned Fiammetta about it the next day. Instead of "reggio," meaning a pig of the Reggio Emilia region, the telegraph company had typed "regio," which made the phrase translate roughly into "kill the royal pig."[44]

Vittorio Emanuele had already abandoned Rome in the early hours of September 9, along with Badoglio, the Cabinet and the general staff. The king fled south to the safety of Allied lines and established his government in Brindisi. Meanwhile, the Germans placed the rest of Italy under brutal occupation.

Originally imprisoned on the island of Ponza, Mussolini had been moved to a location atop the Gran Sasso, a mountain in the Abruzzi. On September 12, a daring German commando raid swept down and rescued the Duce, flying him to Munich, where he was reunited with Rachele and his children. On September 18, Mussolini announced over Munich radio the formation of a new Fascist regime, which he called the Italian Social Republic. Fascism, he proclaimed, had been betrayed by a conspiracy involving the king, the conservative establishment, and a gang of traitors. The "true" Fascists (such as Farinacci and Pavolini) had followed Mussolini north. Despite the terror and violence that the new regime encouraged, some of the most prestigious cultural figures of the former regime— including Marinetti, Gentile, Negri, Ojetti, and Sironi—remained loyal to the Duce.

Supported by the devoted Claretta Petacci, the shadow of his former swaggering self, Mussolini returned to Italy to the Villa Feltrinelli at Gargnano on Lake Garda. Informally known as the Republic of Salò, after the town on the lake where the Foreign Ministry and the Ministry of Popular Culture had their headquarters, the resurrected Fascist regime was only a puppet republic in Hitler's crumbling empire. Mussolini was under constant guard by the Nazi SS, and helplessly allowed the Germans to control most aspects of life in the Salò Republic.

Along with the fanatical republican Fascists, Hitler demanded vengeance against those who had turned against the regime. Grandi and Bottai managed to escape, but some of the other conspirators, including Ciano, were not so fortunate. With incredible naïveté, Edda had arranged for her husband to escape to Germany, expecting that her father would forgive him for her sake. Once back in Italy, Ciano and five other "traitors" were imprisoned in Verona. In January, a special tribunal condemned Ciano, De Bono, and Marinelli to death, along with two other prisoners. Despite Edda's desperate pleading, the condemned men were executed by firing squad. The deaths of De Bono and Marinelli removed the two men who knew the most about Mussolini's part in the murder of Matteotti.

The rapidly unfolding events terrified Margherita. Her fears for Fiammetta were renewed with the Nazi occupation of Rome. She wrote to

Scribner's in late September that she could not possibly go forward with *My Fault* under the changed circumstances, asking that they keep the entire matter confidential in view of the fact that she had "precious hostages in Italy." Margherita also wrote Father Tacchi-Venturi, begging him to secure refuge for her family in the Vatican, but he never answered her letter. "Perhaps," speculated Fiammetta, "because we weren't important enough," but more likely because the Sarfatti family had been too compromised with Fascism. With no avenue of escape possible, Fiammetta and Livio Gaetani made what arrangements they could. Margherita's old friend Renato Trevisani, who had police connections, offered to help. They agreed that should he receive advance notice of an arrest, he would send word and the family would go immediately to the nearby home of Trevisani's secretary, Signora Bisi.

On September 25, 1943, SS chief Heinrich Himmler alerted his commander in Rome, Major Herbert Kappler, that the city's Jews were to be deported to Germany and liquidated. Kappler first extorted an enormous quantity of gold from the Jewish community. Then, before dawn on Saturday, October 16, the SS security police descended on the old Jewish ghetto of Rome. Breaking methodically into the apartments in the district, they rounded up men, women, and children and herded them into trucks. As similar raids began elsewhere in the city, a police official sent word that Fiammetta "should visit Signora Bisi." Fiammetta and Livio made their way carefully along the Via Lima with their three children, barely avoiding two truckloads of German troops. From there, the family was forced to separate. With the help of an anti-Fascist friend, Dr. Biocca, Fiammetta went into a clinic disguised as a patient, while her children were placed in Catholic orphanages under assumed names. Livio was not Jewish, but he remained hidden. Altogether the Germans rounded up 1,259 people that day, and eventually had them transported to Auschwitz.[45]

For the next eight months, Margherita had no word from Fiammetta. She pleaded with Butler to use his influence to obtain some information about her daughter and grandchildren. "Events," she lamented, "have taken such a tragic unforeseen turn, and are taking us with them in their turmoil at such a maddening pace. . . . Unhappily, as always, the rivers of blood and suffering are the innocent ones." After the Allies liberated Rome on June 4, 1944 (two days before the invasion of Normandy), Margherita saw the event in a newsreel and wrote to Fiammetta, from whom she finally received an answer months later. In the hope of getting assistance to them, Butler asked U.S. Ambassador William Dawson in Montevideo to cooperate with Margherita, although Dawson refused even to acknowledge the recommendation. Breckinridge Long later sent a similar request to the new American representative in Rome, Alexander Kirk, but he showed no more than a perfunctory politeness in dealing with the daughter of his old friend. Eventually medicines reached Fiammetta from the United States through Piero Foà, the son of Margherita's old friends Carlo and Isa.

Other members of Margherita's family were not as fortunate, for among the victims of the Italian Holocaust were her sister Nella and brother-in-law Paolo Errera. In 1942, the couple had formally renounced Judaism, although they had been unwilling to be baptized. In December 1943, they managed to avoid the roundup of Venetian Jews conducted by the Fascist Republican National Guard. Sometime the next year, the German SS arrested the Erreras as they sat drinking coffee in the garden of their villa in Mirano, outside Venice. They were taken to the internment camp at Fossoli, and from there were sent to Auschwitz; they perished in the train en route.[46]

By the time Margherita had reestablished contact with Fiammetta, the war had reached its climax. In mid-March 1945, the Western allies crossed the Rhine. The Russians were some thirty miles from Berlin. In Italy, the Allies and the anti-Fascist partisans steadily pushed back the shrinking confines of the Salò Republic. On April 27, Margherita wrote to Breckinridge Long expressing her admiration for Franklin Roosevelt, who had died on the twelfth just a few weeks short of victory. She mentioned to Long that she had completed the manuscript of *My Fault*.[47]

As Margherita was finishing her memoir, Mussolini gave orders for the transfer of his headquarters from Lake Garda to Milan. He returned to the city where he and Margherita had first met as Socialists, and from which they had launched the Fascist movement. The Germans warned Mussolini that he might find himself trapped in Milan, and urged him instead to move to a location near the Brenner Pass.

As the Allies and the partisans closed in, Mussolini remained in Milan until April 25, among a diminishing number of loyal followers. Some advised him to flee to Switzerland and Spain. From South America came a letter from Francesca Lavagnini, with whom he had had a relationship between 1938 and 1940, saying that she had arranged a refuge for him in Argentina. All these options he strenuously rejected, declaring that he would rather die on Italian soil. He believed that he could negotiate safe passage from the Socialist members of the Committee of National Liberation (CLN), the partisan high command.

By April 23, Bologna, Genoa, and Parma had fallen; in Milan the partisans were assuming control. Two days later, Mussolini saw Cardinal Schuster, who agreed to preside at a meeting between Mussolini and representatives of the CLN. The talks collapsed when the CLN announced that it would accept nothing short of unconditional surrender. Mussolini was further taken aback when he learned that General Karl Wolff, the

German SS commander in Italy, had secretly negotiated a surrender agreement with the Allies. "They have always treated us like slaves," Mussolini bitterly exclaimed of the Germans, "and now they have betrayed us."[48]

Mussolini left Milan on April 25 and moved up the western shore of Lake Como, with the object of reaching the mountains of Valtelline, some forty miles beyond Il Soldo. The Italians, including Mussolini's son Vittorio, his nephew Vito, and Claretta Petacci, traveled with a retreating German troop unit heading for the Austrian border. In the column was a truck filled with documents from government ministries and Mussolini's secret files. The truck disappeared en route, and the fate of most of its cargo remains a mystery. One important box, covered in zinc, did turn up in partisan hands. Among its contents were folders on the murder of Giacomo Matteotti, the trial of Galeazzo Ciano, various military and diplomatic documents, and a file labeled "Sarfatti, Margherita." This last contained, among other items, an old letter from Margherita asking for an audience, across which Mussolini had scrawled in blue pencil a large "No."[49]

The next day, while they stopped in Como, Milan was liberated. Before moving on farther north, Mussolini wrote a sentimental farewell letter to Rachele: "I ask your forgiveness for all the trouble I have unconsciously caused you. But you know that you are the only woman I have ever really loved."[50]

After a night at Menaggio, the column left at 3:00 A.M. on April 27. It headed for the village of Grandola, some ten miles from the Swiss border, and then to Musso at the northern end of the lake. At Musso a partisan force halted the column. For six hours the group remained stalled until the partisans announced that no Italians would be permitted to go forward and that a search would be conducted at Dongo, the next town. By now listless and compliant, Mussolini agreed to the German commandant's request that he put on a German overcoat and helmet and hide in a truck among the soldiers. When the column reached Dongo that afternoon, Mussolini was nonetheless immediately discovered and taken prisoner. The partisans confiscated Mussolini's diaries and the other personal papers and official documents that he was carrying. The diaries have never been recovered.

In Milan, the CLN was alerted to Mussolini's capture. Most members weren't sure what action to take, except the Communists, who were determined that Mussolini should not be saved by the Allies. The partisans moved their prisoner into the mountains. Mussolini appeared to be calm and unconcerned about his safety. He asked only that his guard, known by his underground name Pedro, convey his love to Claretta Petacci, who was being held at Dongo. Petacci persuaded Pedro to allow her to join Mussolini, who in the meantime was being moved again, this time south to a villa near Brunate, located two miles from Como on the other side of the lake. Petacci caught up with Mussolini back at Dongo, and they made the journey in separate cars in a cold rain. Some four miles from Como, the partisans heard firing from Allied guns. They headed to the village of Bonzanigo, where they knew a farmer who would hide them. In the heavy rain at three in the morning, the party struggled up a hillside to the farm.

Mussolini and Petacci, both exhausted, slept in the rustic farmhouse. In Milan the CLN had decided their fate. One of its Communist members, Walter Audisio—known as Colonel Valerio—was empowered to bring Mussolini back to Milan, but leaders of the Communist party had secretly ordered him killed. At Dongo, he encountered difficulties from the local partisans, who wanted to have the honor of bringing in Mussolini themselves. Audisio finally explained that his orders were to shoot Mussolini. He obtained a list of their Italian prisoners and arbitrarily marked fifteen other names for execution.

A group of men made their way to Bonzanigo, arriving at the farmhouse at 4:00 P.M., Audisio announcing that they had come to rescue Mussolini. The exact events that followed remain unclear. Mussolini was probably shot as he lay asleep, but in any case, his bullet-ridden body was later found, together with that of Petacci, about a mile down the road, at the gate of the lakeside Villa Belmonte, just outside the village of Giulino di Mezzagra. It was April 28, 1945. Benito Mussolini had lived not quite sixty-two years.

The next day, the two bodies were taken by truck to the Piazzale Loreto in Milan, where they were strung up by their ankles on a steel girder at a filling station. Beneath them were piled the bodies of Pavolini, Starace, and other Fascist leaders. Farinacci had been executed by a partisan firing squad the day before. When Margherita heard the news in Buenos Aires, she opened her old edition of *The Divine Comedy*. The book fell open to Canto XXVIII of the *Inferno*. Her Dante had never spoken with more accuracy:

> "And death destroyed your kind";
> and having heaped despair upon grief,
> he departed as one mad with misery.[51]

An Allied victory was proclaimed in Europe on May 8.

Margherita had begun *My Fault* before September 1943 as a means of raising money. In the final version of *Mussolini as I Knew Him*, Margherita explored her own historical responsibility. She emphatically declared that her fault was not in keeping silent after she left Italy, or in refusing to join the anti-Fascist opposition; she felt no need to apologize for putting the welfare of her family above politics. Rather, her responsibility lay first in having believed in Fascism, and second in having written *Dux*. She dropped "My Fault" from the title because she believed that by writing the piece she had expiated her sins.

She wanted the new work to replace the glorified portrait she had painted in *Dux* twenty years earlier with an image of the real man. The Mussolini she had known was no figure of destiny who by sheer force of will overcame all obstacles, but simply a man whose thirst for power was so strong that it blinded him to his own limitations. She told how his increasingly inflated ego had led him to confuse the welfare of the Italian people with his personal status, and how because of his hubris he had lost sight of the original goals of the Fascist movement. The real Mussolini, she revealed, was an insecure man who had feared the competition of comrades like Balbo and Grandi. She dismissed him as a man without culture or original intellect. By the 1930s, he was no longer a man she admired.

Margherita claimed that Mussolini had not been a charismatic leader, but a passive figure shaped entirely by the desires of other people. Thus she implied her own complicity, and the complicity of the nation. The idea might have been compelling had she chosen to develop it; instead, she tried to settle old grudges as she explored his susceptibility to others. Mussolini's decline began, she explained, as a result of the vulgar influence of Rachele and his corrupting daughter Edda. In international politics Mussolini had allowed himself to be carried away by the evil genius of Hitler. Margherita claimed that Claretta Petacci had been an avaricious parasite who served as a spy for the Nazis. As a woman, she wrote, she felt pity and repulsion when looking at the photograph of Petacci's body at Piazzale Loreto, but as an Italian she could not forget how Petacci had contributed to the suffering of her people.

Margherita lost her nerve, and abandoned her earlier effort to publish *Mussolini as I Knew Him* in the United States. She would have made a considerable amount of money there, but her confessions would have had too wide an audience for her comfort. Instead she sold the rights to Elvio Botana, who issued the work in the Spanish-language paper *Crítica* in fourteen installments in June and July 1945. Botana announced that Margherita had finally broken her silence with sensational revelations. In truth, the most important revelations were those she made, or failed to make, about herself. The newspaper series drew little attention.[52]

In Buenos Aires, the anti-Fascist paper *L'Italia del Popolo* launched a series of bitter articles—titled sarcastically "A 'Lady' Walking the Sidewalks of South America"—attacking her sudden decision to reveal the truth. "Didn't she know all this before," asked the paper, "or did she learn it in Montevideo?" No other notice, beyond a brief mention in an American paper a year later, ever appeared. Years later, Fiammetta and Amedeo both said that they had never seen *Mussolini as I Knew Him*. Having published the memoir, Margherita refused to look back again on that aspect of her past.[53]

Margherita instead turned to the future. At first, she planned to make a permanent life for herself and her family in the Western Hemisphere. She wanted Fiammetta to join her and Amedeo in South America. She tried to secure jobs for her son-in-law, Livio, in Brazil, Argentina, and even in North Carolina, but eventually the idea was abandoned.[54]

She began to think about the possibility of going back to Italy. She did not expect that her return would be greeted with enthusiasm. The Fascist dictatorship, of course, had died along with Mussolini. The forces that had led the resistance against Fascism—the Action Party, the Socialists, the Communists, and the recently formed Christian Democrats—dominated the provisional government. Italy's new political leaders were men who had lived in exile or fought in the underground, and they controlled a constituent assembly that had been elected to draw up a democratic constitution. The CLN had forced Badoglio to resign as prime minister in June 1944, and replaced him with the former Socialist Ivanoe Bonomi.

A year later, just as *Mussolini as I Knew Him* began to appear in South America, the anti-Fascist leader Ferruccio Parri took office as prime minister. Margherita had known Parri since he was a young army officer in World War I, when they had corresponded about artistic theories. When Hearst's International News Service asked her to comment on developments in Italy, she declared that Parri might be the "new man" that the country needed, adding that his profound knowledge of art had created an excellent impression when they had first met. Parri's efforts to institute democratic reforms were too radical for the more conservative parties, and not radical enough for the Communists and Socialists. He stepped down after five months in office and was replaced by the more conservative Christian Democrat Alcide De Gasperi.[55]

Political upheavals continued in 1946. In June, the Italian people voted to abolish the monarchy. King Vittorio Emanuele III had remained a passive partner for twenty years to the Fascist regime, and his abandonment of Rome in 1943 had undermined whatever popular support remained for him. Vittorio Emanuele's abdication in favor of his son Umberto on the eve of the plebiscite had not saved the monarchy. Umberto reigned for less than a month.

Another unexpected development made Margherita hesitate about returning to Italy. During his brief ministry, Parri had appointed Socialist leader Pietro Nenni head of a commission to purge Fascism from Italian political life, and to confiscate wealth acquired through Fascist connections. Margherita's wealth mainly had been inherited, but she felt her Fascist past put her assets at risk. This fear ended only when De Gasperi issued a political amnesty that put an end to the purge.

Margherita discussed the possibility of returning to Italy in June 1946, when she visited her old friends Carlo and Isa Foà in São Paulo, Brazil, where they had been living since 1939. Their son Piero remembers her as heavily made up, with a peroxide-blond hairdo. When he introduced his new bride, Margherita congratulated him on having had the courage to marry a Jew. Apparently, Margherita was warned that anti-Semitism had become rooted everywhere, even in Italy.[56]

In February 1947, the Italian situation improved when Italy officially signed peace treaties with the Allies, freeing its soil from Allied occupation. As Italy began to create a stable democracy and rebuild its economy, Margherita finally decided that it was time to go home.[57]

31

Home Again

An Argentine Airlines airliner brought Margherita Sarfatti to Rome's Ciampino airport on July 18, 1947. She made her way carefully down the steps of the boarding ladder, carrying packages in each arm. Amedeo and Fiammetta waited at the visitors' area on the field, and to them she appeared to carry her sixty-seven years lightly, despite the long and tiring flight from Buenos Aires. The bright Roman sun highlighted her curled hair, dyed a copper-blond. She peered anxiously into the crowd. When she spotted Fiammetta, whom she had not seen since 1939, she rushed forward, dropping both packages to the ground as she embraced her daughter.[1]

Margherita's apartment at Via dei Villini had been rented for years, so she stayed at Fiammetta's flat on Via Lima, crowded with her four children. Margherita found her first days back in Rome alternately exhilarating and alienating. The summer heat felt unbearable, and she had her pocketbook picked while riding on a bus. After little more than a week she insisted on going to Il Soldo. At Il Soldo she hoped to find the tranquility she needed to adjust to her new circumstances, and to decide her future—before leaving Buenos Aires, she had bought a round-trip ticket valid for one year.[2]

Il Soldo was not the haven Margherita expected. Soon after she arrived, she fell and broke her left foot, which was set in a cast for weeks. The entire family, including the grandchildren's nannies, descended on the normally quiet spot. Fiammetta's husband, Livio, came, together with their four children: thirteen-year-old Roberto and his sisters Sancia, Ippolita, and Margherita. The last was still a baby, who spent most of her day in a playpen under the cypress trees Mario Sironi had once painted. Amedeo left his two children—eleven-year-old Magalì and her brother, Roberto ("Bobby"), who had been born in Uruguay in 1941—and then returned to Rome, where Pierangela was looking after her ailing mother. The romping and yelling of the grandchildren annoyed Margherita, who was no more doting a grandmother than she had been a conscientious mother. Magalì recalls with amusement that her grandmother could not abide children until they had matured enough to sustain an intelligent conversation. "That fatal summer," as Margherita jokingly referred to it, she generally remained in her own room, taking her meals alone or with the adults, and refusing to allow anyone to use her private bathroom.[3]

News of Margherita's arrival in Rome had been kept from the press, but journalists soon learned of her return. In August they converged on Il Soldo. When the reporters were told that Margherita was not available, they offered candy to the grandchildren, who led them astray in the woods instead of to their grandmother. Margherita finally realized, however, that only by granting an interview would she be able to get rid of the journalists permanently.

On the appointed day Fiammetta, surrounded by the children, led a number of journalists into the garden. After a rather long wait, Margherita appeared, using a cane and leaning heavily on Fiammetta's arm. She hobbled to a seat and propped her left leg up on a chair. For her first public appearance in postwar Italy, she wore an understated rust-colored dress and a white sweater. She confined her flamboyance to a flashing ruby on her little finger, and matching red nail polish and lipstick. "Only as she seated herself with some difficulty, impeded by her plastered foot," remarked one journalist, "did the weight of her years show for a moment on her face."

Margherita covered her legs with a shawl, lighted a cigarette, and showed the reporters a copy of her most recent book, *Espejo de la pintura actual,* a Spanish-language version of her history of modern painting just published in Buenos Aires. She tried to steer the conversation away from what they wanted to hear about, focusing instead on her work in South America. When they finally asked her about Mussolini's visits to Il Soldo years earlier, she grew defensive, using phrases that were evasive and obviously prepared. "Yes, I had a friendship with him," she said, "I believed in him as long as his policies were coherent, until, let's say, the Ethiopian war. But then no longer."

When it began to rain, the group moved inside to the dining room. The reporters were struck by the contrast between the soberly furnished country house and the modern paintings on the walls—works by Marussig, Funi, and Tosi, and two portraits of Margherita by Sironi. When asked what she thought about postwar Italy, she expressed cautious optimism. To a question about her own political sentiments, she replied that in her youth she had been an ardent Socialist. She would not say which of the current Socialist groups she preferred. "All my life I have been involved in politics, but now I want to stay out of it." About Italian literature she claimed not to know much, but in the weeks since her arrival, she had been impressed by Curzio Malaparte's *Kaputt,* a novel about the devastating economic and social collapse of Italy. Moravia's *La Romana,* about a prostitute and her lovers, she found disappointing. With a sardonic smile she pretended to be surprised that so many of the journalists who had once worked for the Fascist press were still writing. She ended the interview by saying that perhaps one day she would write her memoirs.[4]

In September, before returning to Rome, Margherita went to Venice. She stayed at the Palazzo del Mare hotel, since it was still warm enough to swim at the Lido. She visited a Tintoretto exhibition and a film festival. On the night of September 13, as she was leaving the Doge's Palace after one of the movies, she recognized Pietro Nenni in the crowd. Despite his staunch anti-Fascist sentiments, and his work as head of the defascistization program, Margherita judged him to be a humane man and had no hesitation in approaching him. They chatted cordially for a few minutes. That night, Nenni recorded the encounter in his diary, noting that Margherita was "still blond, corpulent, and expansive. She told me that she was writing her memoirs. They should be interesting."[5]

The next day, Margherita wrote a letter to Bernard Berenson, who had lived undisturbed throughout the war at his Villa I Tatti outside Florence. Berenson proposed that they meet somewhere for a reunion. In her best effort at colloquial English, she wrote, "Your letter has been the gladdest tiding I have had for a week of Sundays." Thereafter, they shared a cynical view of life and the trials of advancing age, but it was primarily their common interest in art that brought them together:

> Have you seen the Tintoretto exhibition here at St. Rocco? You must not miss it. I know, or believed I did, my Tintoretto, my own personal Tintoretto, born (?) or at least lived & died in my self-same parish, by heart. Well, not at all, that terrible man took me entirely by surprise. It has been quite a new thunderbolt of a revelation. . . .
>
> The whole world is all a mess. So let us enjoy whatever we can, as long as the *parva sapientia* or immense foolishness, madness & wickedness of human beings will permit us. Next time, an atomic bomb will settle the question. Life is a damned foolishness, but I like it despite all, & we have no other choice to pick out. . . .
>
> P.S. I wonder if you really know how world-wide your name & fame has spread. If you do realise it you are wonderful not to have grown awfully conceited. Nobody, in South America, says: *"mai sentito nominare* [I've never heard the name] of BB."[6]

Back in Rome, Margherita did not return to her apartment at Via dei Villini. The place held too many memories for her, and furthermore was much too large for the less active social life she now led. She took up residence in hotels, where she did not have to worry about the requirements of daily life. She stayed for some months at the Hotel Majestic, and in late 1948 moved permanently to the Hotel Ambasciatori, designed by Piacentini in the 1920s and situated on the fashionable Via Veneto, directly across from the American Embassy. There she had a two-room apartment. She had breakfast and one meal a day in the hotel restaurant. Every Sunday afternoon she joined Fiammetta for lunch. The rooms were large enough to entertain a few friends at a time, and the location allowed her to walk or take a bus to art galleries, theaters, and restaurants.[7]

That fall she went to her old hotel at Abano, outside Padua, to take the mud baths, as she had done regularly in past years. In Padua, she visited the Scrovegni Chapel to see Giotto's famous cycle of frescoes. She explained to Berenson—calling him "Great, charming & altogether uncomparable BB, & when I say 'altogether' I mean the man & the friend no less than the writer"—that when she discovered that scaffolding had been erected in front of the frescoes, she simply climbed up a ladder and onto them in order to have a better view.

Margherita thought about going back to South America after being snubbed by a number of people from whom she expected some measure of compassion. Some refused even to acknowledge her on the street, let alone in more intimate settings. The political culture of the country was charged with a militant anti-Fascist spirit. Most of the surviving personalities of the regime, such as Dino Grandi and Giuseppe Bottai, remained abroad or led quiet, retiring lives. But Margherita was not just another important Fascist. For many years she had been Mussolini's intimate associate, and had been courted and flattered by politicians, diplomats, intellectuals, and artists. In the current atmosphere, most of those who had once frequented her salon and sought favors from her felt they would be compromised by public association with her. She expected no sympathy from those who had resisted the regime, but she was surprised to be shunned by those who had been supporters. As she put it to Berenson, "They are afraid somebody could remember what I did to help them!"[8]

Margherita witnessed the full impact of the anti-Fascist climate in June 1948 when she visited the first postwar Venice Biennale. The Biennale that year was a retrospective dedicated to international modernism, with special shows on French Impressionism, on the Italian Metaphysical painters led by Giorgio de Chirico and Giorgio Morandi, and on German Expressionism. Peggy Guggenheim, the wealthy American patron, had lent her private collection of modern art, including works by Jackson Pollock, Robert Motherwell, and Clifford Still. The new secretary-general, Rodolfo Pallucchini, portrayed the Biennale as an effort to inform the newly liberated Italian people about the international artistic heritage that Fascism had denied them any knowledge of for twenty years.[9]

Margherita found Pallucchini's claim absurd, for no one had done more than she to acknowledge Italy's debt to European modernism, nor had anyone tried harder to fight against the xenophobic Fascists like Farinacci who had wanted to cut Italy off from the rest of European culture. Moreover, the Italian commission included the artists Carlo Carrà and Felice Casorati, as well as de Chirico and Morandi, all of whom had exhibited their work in her *Novecento* shows in the 1930s. De Chirico admitted that the Biennale distorted the truth about the artistic situation in Italy under Fascism:

> Efforts were made to spread the legend that fascism, like Nazism, had forced our artists to paint for a long time in a conventional manner and [forbade them] to go along with 'liberty in art,' linking them to the 'glorious' Paris school. . . . But for the sake of truth it must be said that the fascists never forbade people to paint as they wished. The majority of the fascist hierarchy were in fact modernists enamoured of Paris.[10]

An incident that occurred at the Biennale wounded Margherita deeply. One day, she joined a group of people trying to get on a bus to visit one of the pavilions. She was recognized by a Communist official, who pushed her off the line and shouted, "There's no room for you here."[11]

De Chirico was one former acquaintance—he had never been a close friend—who had little interest in acknowledging Margherita after the war. They came face-to-face for the first time in years one afternoon near the Via Veneto, on a narrow side street. De Chirico feigned a look of surprise, and in a sarcastic tone said to her, "Well, well, it is *la Sarfatti!*" She replied matter-of-factly, "Good day, maestro." "So," he stuttered in the face of her unexpected nonchalance, "go ahead, say what you have to say," as if consenting to an audience. She replied, "I've already said it—good day," and pushed past him.[12]

Carrà and Sironi were among the few who remained in touch with Margherita after the war. But she missed the kind of intimate friendship she had shared with Ada Negri, who had died in January 1945. And of course she missed being at the center of attention. She was rarely invited to receptions or dinner parties, and her acquaintances in the European diplomatic corps were all either retired or stationed elsewhere. From 1953 to 1957, the American ambassador was Clare Boothe Luce. She had given a dinner party for Margherita in New York in 1934, but claimed not to remember.[13]

Not all anti-Fascists snubbed Margherita. Some, like the writer and painter Carlo Levi and the celebrated actress Anna Magnani, recognized the moderating role she had played in cultural life under Fascism, and were even willing to be photographed with her. She visited with the writer Giovanni Papini, with whom she discussed a publishing project, and remained on good terms with the novelists Giovanni Comisso, Massimo Bontempelli, and Aldo Palazzeschi. But life now was mainly limited to her family and a small circle of friends, including George and Helene Biddle, the New York art dealer Xavier Fourcade, and Berenson. As the days passed, she grew more comfortable with the idea of remaining in Italy.[14]

In the first years after her return, Margherita was worried by the state of the Italian economy, and was obsessed by the fear that her income would not be sufficient. Her concerns were typical of an aging person, but in her case totally without foundation. Although she no longer derived a regular income from her writing, she had rents from inherited property holdings in Venice, Rome, and elsewhere, and during the nine years in South America she had not found it necessary to sell the thirty-six diamonds she had taken with her into exile. Margherita had always been inexplicably concerned about money. Mussolini had noted her stinginess with astonishment when they first knew each other, and her family found her concern for money amusing and exasperating. "Grandmother would often take people to lunch or dinner," recalled Magalì Sarfatti-Larson, "but generally to cheap restaurants."[15]

The war and its attendant economic devastation had produced a severe inflationary cycle. In 1946, wholesale prices were more than twenty-five times higher than they had been when Margherita had left Italy in 1938. By the spring of 1947, some wholesale prices had risen to fifty times their prewar levels, and in September they went even higher. "Scared to death" by the inflation, said her daughter-in-law, Pierangela, Margherita began to sell paintings from her collection—which had also remained intact—"left and right." She even negotiated with Peggy Guggenheim, who wanted to buy Boccioni's *Antigrazioso* (1912), but Margherita demanded too high a price. Livio finally persuaded her to stop selling her art.[16]

It was in the context of her concern over money that the supposed sale of the Mussolini letters took place. The story of this venal affair began one morning in early March 1948. Margherita was crossing the Via Veneto in front of Doney's Caffè. She heard her name called out by a short, stocky man with a round face and a pencil mustache. He introduced himself as Guido Orlando, a naturalized Italian American who had made an international reputation as the "king of publicity" for his slick promotion schemes. "He was," recalled Art Buchwald, who knew him in Paris, "a very delightful scalawag who never took more than he needed."[17]

Margherita had seen his name often in the press in recent days. Two months earlier, a new Constitution creating the Italian republic had been adopted, and national elections had been called. Orlando had been sent to

Italy by Howard Hughes, to escape a subpoena from a Senate committee investigating corruption in wartime defense contracts. Hughes had used Orlando to entertain President Roosevelt's son Elliott, apparently hoping to obtain aircraft contracts as a result. It seems that Hughes used his connections with the newly founded Central Intelligence Agency to find employment for Orlando in Rome. Orlando was placed in charge of anti-Communist publicity for the April 1948 elections. The De Gasperi government was battling the Italian Communist party for control of Italy. Among other gimmicks, Orlando had the influential American publisher Generoso Pope ask his Italian-American readers to urge their relatives in Italy to vote against the Communists.

Orlando believed there was money to be had in the story of Margherita's relationship with Mussolini. Over lunch at the Majestic Hotel, which Orlando bought, Margherita conned the con man, telling him that she was broke and had had to sell her jewels in order to buy passage home from Argentina. Orlando promised to make her money, and to put her back in the spotlight with a sensational magazine series. She mentioned that she still had about a hundred of the letters Mussolini had written to her but that she did not want to publish them. In any case, she added, "they're in a safe-deposit box in a bank in Paris and I can't get a passport visa to pick them up." Orlando, doubly excited, said he could arrange a passport for her. After four days of negotiations—"she was," Orlando later wrote, "a very tough dame"—they agreed to sign a contract: Margherita would go to Paris at Orlando's expense and retrieve Mussolini's letters. Orlando would select the letters that had historical importance, excluding any of a strictly personal nature, and within ninety days would make a formal financial offer based on the eventual use of the letters for articles or a book to be written by Margherita. The expenses for the trip to Paris constituted the legal basis for Orlando's option on the publication of the letters. Margherita retained ultimate control—none of the letters could be published without her authorization.[18]

Once the Italian elections were over on April 18 (the Christian Democrats won 304 seats in the Chamber of Deputies to the Communists' 183), Orlando flew to New York and met with Tom Beck, publisher of *Collier's* magazine. Beck said he would pay as much as $100,000 for the right to publish the letters, provided they were as important as Orlando said they were. Beck was unwilling to commit himself to anything without at least seeing copies. Then Margherita—persuaded by her daughter, who feared the publicity would soil her husband's illustrious family name—backed out of the deal.

Orlando kept in contact with Margherita until he could conceive another approach:

This is just to let you know there is no hard feeling between us . . . even though you made it impossible for me to close an outstanding deal for you and make a lot of money for both of us. Anyway, you are in my will and if I should die soon, which I will as I am getting old, you will get a share of my dollar and a half fortune so that it will remind you, when you get to be as old as I am, that you once had an ardent admirer in America.

Margherita did not bother to answer the letter.[19]

Orlando brought Vincent Giordano, the Rome correspondent for the *Progresso Italo-Americano,* into the deal to keep Beck interested. Orlando knew he could lose money if, after having committed himself to pay Margherita, he could not sell the rights for as much as he hoped. He decided to find a middleman willing to put up the front money. In the fall, Orlando found him in one of his publicity clients, Dr. I. Daniel Shorell, a wealthy New York plastic surgeon who numbered the Duchess of Windsor among his clients. Orlando convinced Shorell that he would become world famous if he bought Margherita's letters, and told him that Beck was willing to pay $100,000 for the right to publish them. He also contacted Ken McCormick of Doubleday & Company about the possibility of a book based on the letters, and McCormick gave Orlando a letter of introduction to someone in Paris who could verify their authenticity.[20]

With the various pieces of his campaign in place, Orlando wrote to Margherita, asking that she meet Giordano to discuss a new transaction. Margherita sent back a canny letter:

Dear Guido, of course I will be very pleased to see yr friend Mr. V. Giordani [*sic*] about whom I have heard a lot of good things, and I believe I also met him in New York. I am now in the country, staying in my villa near Como but am returning soon to Rome. Meanwhile I telegraphed that Mr. Giordano should contact my daughter & eventually let me hear about him through her channel.

Equally of course I am not grudging you or bearing you any ill will. On the contrary, I consider you a most interesting sample of human flora & am glad to have had such a good opportunity to meet you: the American hustle & bustle & rush of dynamic business-making on the complex of an emotional, temperamental Latin & romantic southern Italian. The result is of course somehow confusing and sometimes more apparently than substantially American. However, I hope this time it will prove to be really & truly efficient & result in facts—hard, positive cash & especially fame & the rest!

Apologizing for not having answered Orlando's first letter, she quipped, "Thanks so much for the bequest of 1 (one) dollar on your last will & testament. Being burdened with a family I cannot return the compliment on equal terms, but I will inscribe you for 1 (one) lira—if it will not be atomized before that, & if the heavy duties on heirlooms will permit such mad generosity."[21]

Giordano met Margherita at the end of October and explained that Shorell was interested in buying the letters. Once she agreed to go to Paris to get them, Orlando extracted a written agreement from Shorell for a round-trip flight from Rome to New York for himself, and the sum of $1,000 to defray the cost of Margherita's Paris trip. Shorell stipulated that if he did purchase the letters, he would take 60 percent of the net profits derived from their publication.[22]

When Margherita returned from Paris in early November, she brought with her a bundle of some 1,272 letters, written over the years from 1917 to 1935. Once in Rome, Orlando consulted the magazine publisher Aldo Garzanti to get an idea of the commercial value of the letters, but Margherita told him furiously, "I don't need you or anyone to sell these letters in Italy. I don't want them published here—they're much too personal!" Fiammetta also intervened, objecting that publication of the letters and the story of her mother's romance with Mussolini would injure her father's memory. Orlando calmed them down, assuring them that he had no intention of publishing the material in Italy. "Why a plastic surgeon?" Margherita asked. "Why not a publisher like Mr. Hearst—or Mr. Luce?" He assured her that Shorell had contacts with the right people, and she agreed to meet him. Shorell flew to Rome and Orlando briefed him on how best to flatter Margherita.[23]

Between November 20 and 24, a series of four separate contracts was signed. The most important of these stipulated that Shorell would be Margherita's "exclusive agent" with regard to the letters. Shorell received a three-year option which provided that *if* he sold the publication rights, he would pay Margherita and Orlando each 10 percent of the price. If Shorell had not sold the letters in America within one year, he would pay her $5,000 (to be deducted from her 10 percent), and an additional $5,000 each year for the life of the option while they remained unsold. It was further stipulated, on Margherita's insistence, that the letters would not be published in Italy. Margherita gave Shorell two of Mussolini's letters to take with him.[24]

Until an eventual sale could be arranged, the letters were to be kept in a vault at the Banca Nazionale del Lavoro. They were to be released to Shorell only with Margherita's approval. All the parties gathered at the bank for the formal consignment of the letters. Dressed in a dark suit and matching hat, Margherita appeared unusually subdued. When a photographer arranged by Orlando entered the meeting room, Margherita balked, for she wanted no publicity. Orlando assured her the photographs were only to provide a record of the transaction. Appropriate forms were filled out and signed, and when the large package, wrapped in paper and bound in cord and wax seals, was about to be turned over to the bank director, Orlando asked Margherita to kiss the bundle. When she objected, Orlando explained that it was in order "to leave the print of your lipstick so we can be sure no one tampers with it."

Orlando had every intention of leaking the story, and using the photographs as part of a campaign to generate public interest in the letters. One reporter who learned of the transaction asked her if it was true that she had sold Mussolini's love letters. "No," she insisted, with the specific terms of the agreement in mind, "I have not sold anything. I have spoken to several Americans but we only talked about a possible lecture tour for me. I have not given anything to anyone. We also talked about a book of memoirs that I may write, but this is something yet to be arranged, if at all."[25]

The "king of publicity" now went to work. Orlando and Shorell left Rome by plane, carrying a leather briefcase in which they claimed to have the letters. At the Rome airport, Orlando let it "slip" that they had purchased the letters for $120,000. In Paris, he asked the French police for bodyguards, claiming that Italian Fascists had threatened to kill them and steal the letters. In London, he asked the same of Scotland Yard, declaring that the letters were worth half a million pounds. When they reached New York, reporters met the plane and soon Italian and American newspapers were carrying Orlando's almost completely false story.

Orlando explained all this to Shorell as an effort to jack up the value of the letters to potential buyers, but the real purpose was to convince Shorell that he had pulled off a tremendous deal. Shorell had already turned down an offer of £20,000 from a London publisher for the English rights. When Orlando repeatedly asked Shorell to buy him out, the hapless doctor may have begun to suspect something was amiss. Orlando threatened to sue Shorell, who finally paid the publicist $18,000 for his interest in the letters. When Shorell demanded $250,000 from *Collier's* for the publication rights, Tom Beck turned him down. He had no more success with other publishers, for the two samples Margherita had given him were intimate notes of little historical interest. Margherita had refused to provide copies of the many other letters that revealed the full extent of her involvement with Mussolini.[26]

The letters were never published. Fiammetta Gaetani admitted years later that the doctor never came into their actual possession. Margherita collected $15,000 from Shorell, and eventually recovered the letters from the bank once the doctor's option had expired. When she and Orlando encountered each other in Venice that same year, she told him testily, "Orlando, you made more money out of those letters than I did—and I had to be Mussolini's mistress for nineteen years to get them!" He sent a story about their encounter to Igor Cassini ("Cholly Knickerbocker"), who published it in Hearst's *New York Journal-American*. When the item was picked up by the Italian press, Margherita was furious and refused to speak to him again, although they saw each other almost daily when Orlando stayed at the Hotel Ambasciatori.

The only aspect of the affair that Margherita regretted was not being able to go on the lecture tour of the United States that had been part of the arrangement. "I was going to America," she told Berenson with less than total accuracy, "for a tour of lectures, radio etc, but then some very nasty publicity campaign was put out about my journey, & so I thought & still do think it was & is perhaps better to wait a bit until those utterly false news have blown & faded away, & to start anew, from the real point of view of a lecturing tour etc & not of scandal mongering." Another opportunity came in 1949, when James Soby and Alfred Barr of the Museum of Modern Art in New York mounted the first important exhibit of twentieth-century Italian art since before the war. By then she had reversed her opinion about the desirability of sending paintings overseas for shows—"I am furious," she told Berenson, "at this modern habit of sending the works of art on every occasion on dangerous errands abroad." Still Margherita lent the MoMA two paintings in her collection, Felice Casorati's *Room in an Inn* (ca. 1929) and Luigi Russolo's *The Fog* (1912). She had hoped that Soby might arrange a visa and perhaps pay her fare so that she could visit New York, but the American government did not welcome the former Fascist. She never returned to the United States.[27]

By the end of 1948, Margherita's fears that inflation would wipe out her assets disappeared. The De Gasperi government adopted policies that brought stability to Italy's economy. Together with family pressures, and her own reluctance to publicize the details of her affair with Mussolini, her financial security eliminated any desire she may have had to sell or publish the letters. By late 1952, when the Hearst organization expressed an interest in them, she rejected the idea completely. She did tell Colonel Peter Borrè, an American acquaintance, that she was thinking about writing a book based on the letters. But she decided there was every reason not to dwell on her relationship with Mussolini, on her personal contributions to the rise and philosophy of Fascism, or on what she considered Mussolini's grotesque betrayal of her loyalty. After her return to Italy, she never spoke about these matters publicly or wrote about them for publication.[28]

Margherita discussed Mussolini and Fascism only with her closest friends, and then only reluctantly. On the other hand, when George Biddle in 1951 asked her point blank about the cause of Mussolini's downfall, he recorded this conversation in his diary:

MS: It is because he remained too long in power. The sense of power destroys everyone. It destroyed Roosevelt, too.

GB: If at the end of his life Roosevelt made mistakes, it was due to ill health, not a complete moral disintegration. From the beginning Mussolini was corrupt.

MS: No. All men are alike. Power corrupts them.

GB: Is Churchill corrupt? And he has had power for a generation.

MS: Ah, but he has had the fortune to have been in and out of office.

GB: And Lincoln?

MS: He was shot in time. It would have been the same thing with him too.

A few days later, Biddle returned to the subject, asking her about the relationship with Mussolini. "I first met him," she explained erroneously, "in 1909. Both I and my husband were socialists of the reform or Fabian party. Mussolini had been well-known in the revolutionary section of the Socialist party since as early as 1905. He had spent years in prison where he read St. Simon and Proudhon. But he was not a man of culture, as we are." When asked to describe the early Fascist movement, she gave what had by then become a standard line among former Fascists: "It was not a socialist movement but a social movement, one of reform; and from the beginning anti-communist but not anti-democratic. It was directed against the lawless chaos that was sweeping over Italy."

Perhaps Margherita thought to settle some old scores, for she added:

But I will tell you two or three things that are not generally known, but which to me are—how do you say it in English? "Straws in the wind." Mussolini's wife was an ignorant brutal peasant. She had an affair with a railroad station master and her daughter also had an affair at Forlì. His wife wrote letters to her lover and he showed them about. This came to the knowledge of Turati, the Secretary of the Party. He had the lover "bastonato" [beaten]. One should not show such letters about. And Mussolini had his wife and Edda recalled to Rome. Now his wife was a violent, brutal, uneducated peasant. She had sufficient power to have had Turati "demissionner." And Starace took his place. Turati had been an honest, liberal and educated man. Starace was not even a condottiere. But he was brave and had many war decorations. He was from Lecce. But stupid and vulgar. That was one of the tragic things that happened to fascism. . . . I had great influence on Mussolini, but I never attempted to tell him what to do. Everyone influenced him of course. It is so with all dictators. But the last things that made me draw away were Hitler and Spain and the war in Africa. I said to him: "Spain has nothing to do with Italy. Africa has nothing to do with Italy. Keep your eyes on our own country. Here there is much to do." However, there was never an open rupture. It was a gradual separation. A "refroidissement."

These conversations took place in late December 1951, while Margherita toured Puglia and the Adriatic coast with Biddle and Helene. The Americans enjoyed Margherita's company but in private Biddle's judgment of her was severe:

This woman is the tragic example of how dictatorship can corrupt. She is an unusual woman. For Italy a unique and remarkable woman. She speaks English, French, German, Spanish, and Italian; has published books, lectured on art in German cultural centers; been a newspaper editor; an influence in national politics. Yet her mind and morals have become so vitiated by her long association with a vile movement, her thinking is so emotional and prejudiced, that with all her really vast learning one can hardly ever trust a word she says. . . . This unhappy woman can only think, reason, act, in terms of prejudice, hurt vanity and a frustrated drive for power.[29]

When the Biddles saw Margherita for the first time since the mid-1930s, on the eve of their trip, they were nonplussed. "She has trouble walking from a broken knee and at times seems quite deaf. She is a little bald, unkempt and her obviously dyed, curly hair looked as if it were seldom washed and never brushed. But what struck me most in this once gay, vital and dominating woman was the frightened look in her eyes, a little bewildered, a little pleading, the look of an old woman." Later that evening, as they dined and talked, "her old self showed itself, an interest in people, events and ideas." During their tour of the Adriatic coast, they saw the best and worst aspects of Margherita's personality. She immediately assumed the role of guide; her knowledge of Italy's art, monuments, and people was fascinating, but she constantly disputed what guidebooks or official guides at the sites told them, and argued fiercely with hotel proprietors and waiters wherever they went. Biddle saw that despite "her high-blood-pressure violence and insistence that she is always right," she also had a "human warmth, for which one forgives her occasional prejudices, assertiveness, and intellectual arrogance. And also, what I love, tremendous spiritual vitality and a great curiosity about ideas and people."

The cold, damp weather bothered Margherita's leg but she refused to slow down or complain. In Bari, Biddle recorded the following:

We drove into the narrow, crowded streets of the old town as Margherita
is too lame to walk. Her ankle is badly swollen and she had it swathed with
bandages or probably soiled handkerchiefs. She wears two pairs of socks,
an old homespun coat on top of her fur coat, a white woolen shawl and
a rayon cape. Newspapers tucked into her bosom for further protection
against the damp air and a pair of red woolen gloves . . .[30]

In February, when the Biddles announced that they were going up to
I Tatti to visit Berenson, Margherita spoke of her friendship with the aging
connoisseur and asked Biddle to convey her love. Berenson's reaction took
Biddle by surprise: "He remarked distastefully that she had gone quite to
pieces. 'She is quite filthy. I am sure she never washes.'" Yet when
Margherita visited I Tatti later that year, Berenson wrote in his diary:
"Have been good friends with Margherita Sarfatti for years, but only
yesterday could I get her to talk about Mussolini and Fascism. We agreed
about events, occurrences, all that happened. She denied none, but when
we came to discuss how and why, we seldom agreed about the how, and
never about the why."[31]

Of course her memories of Fascism were problematic for Margherita,
but she had always felt looking back was a waste of time, and preferred to
live in the present. In the fall of 1952, when she began at last to write a book
of reminiscences, she decided that she would not compose a "memoir."
When the book—titled *Acqua passata* (*Water Under the Bridge*)—appeared
in 1955, those who expected scandal and gossip were disappointed. *Acqua
passata* was less about her own life than it was about the people she had
known. The only really autobiographical sections in the book were the
opening chapters, in which she spoke wistfully about her Venetian childhood and her family, especially her maternal grandmother and her father.
She hid occasional insights into her personal life in carefully crafted phrases
and subordinate clauses, as she had done in *Dux*. Readers were surprised
to find the word *Fascism* only once in the entire book, and no mention at
all of Benito Mussolini, although she carried the story into 1934, ending
with her visit to the Roosevelt White House. She also avoided dealing with
the painful memories of Roberto's death, or her treatment of Cesare.[32]

At times, she experienced bouts of loneliness and depression. She
confessed once to Berenson:

Personally what distresses me more than anything, is the brutal blindness
of men & their (or, rather, our) steady, untiring, constant & strenuous
research of unhappiness. It is perhaps the only permanent fixture in
human history. Which I sum up crudely in 3 basic elements: conservation,
i.e. eating; reproduction, i.e. . . . kissing; destruction, i.e. killing. Well,

then why should I feel depressed? But philosophy never helped over a toothache.

This was a refrain that she repeated to other friends. She remarked to Helene Biddle:

> As long as there are men on earth, I am afraid we must accept the brutal eventuality of war. . . . My personal philosophy and experience have taught me that there are in animal nature, man included, & even his mate, woman, no more than three absolute fundamental instincts: 1) conservation, 2) propagation, & 3) destruction.

Margherita believed that human beings could control their base instincts only by accepting the inhibitions imposed on them by civilization—"better not to search too deeply in our subconscious under-world, peopled with monsters and snakes, better to stifle them through want of air & light in the dark!"[33]

Her pessimism stemmed as much from her contemplative reaction to the events of the 1950s as from her Fascist past. The "fall of the British Empire" was a symbolic loss:

> of the hegemony of Europe & the prestige of Europe & also of the Inevitable White peoples with it. *Untergang des Abendlandes,* Spengler was alas only too right. Something may, let us hope, be saved by America, only the grosser & not the finer part of the heirloom of centuries, as Rome saved some part of the Greek heirloom, in a less refined, coarser & more robust & vital way. And the Communists are the 5th column, as the Christians were in Rome for the barbarians, though these were idolaters.[34]

The Italian political scene, which she saw as caught between the perils of left and right extremism, offered her little hope. Communism she rejected as only another totalitarian system. "I made that mistake once," she told her granddaughter Magali. On the other hand, during national elections in the 1950s, she was more worried about a resurgence of Fascism than about a Communist victory.[35]

Margherita's philosophical despair was brought on by a rapidly changing world in which she could find little meaning or comfort. As the pace of modern life accelerated, most people, she believed, rejected the basic values of Western culture and lost their bearings. Classical rules and a sense of discipline had been smashed along with the atom. She cast the dilemma of modern life as a struggle between the "German" concept of *werden*—the constant struggle to become something else—and the "Latin" notion of *essere*—the acceptance of things as they are. Postwar society, she felt, put too much emphasis on the future and too little on the present. Once while walking in the country near Il Soldo with Magalì, Margherita encountered a Gypsy who wanted to predict her future. She refused, but offered to tell the Gypsy's fortune instead.[36]

Margherita argued that the latest fashionable artists had abandoned discipline as they moved toward the pure abstraction she deplored. "Aestheticism," she told Helene Biddle, "is no friend, but a dangerous lure for art. See where it has led us, to abstract dots & lines." She rejected abstract painting as merely decorative, and incomprehensible to the traditional art-loving public. In 1952, she complained to Berenson, "Venice Biennale simply awful . . . The *mobiles* of Calder are nasty playthings for snobs, not even precious in their make-up." After 1947, she had no outlets for expressing her opinions regularly, although she wrote occasionally for magazines such as *Scena Illustrata* and *Il Giornale di Roma,* and published travel pieces for *L'Elefante* and *Como.* Most of her views were aired in private letters.[37]

Margherita continued to consider the Italian artists of the interwar period who had belonged to the *Novecento Italiano* to be the best that modernism had produced. She put Mario Sironi at the top of a list that included Carrà, de Pisis, Severini, Casorati, de Chirico, and Morandi. In the 1950s she visited Sironi's studio in Milan with Magalì. They found drawings and canvases strewn across the floor, and she bought one of his postwar works. At the Galerie Michel in Paris she purchased Toulouse-Lautrec's *Elles* print series, which she regretted having sold in South America. Otherwise she added little of importance to her collection after the war.[38]

Margherita remained indomitable and energetic despite her foreboding thoughts. In the midst of a dreary and cold winter, she could exclaim, "The sun is shining & the sky is blue & life is wonderful in via Veneto by noon, all the people sitting & sipping coffee in *plein* air!" And in her last letter to Berenson, written at the age of seventy-seven, Margherita tried to perk up the flagging spirits of her ninety-two-year-old friend: "Of course, who has been *really* young in blood & soul & heart, & not only in chronological years, finds it hard (like you & me, if I may make bold to compare myself to you) to accept this body of to-day, no more untiring, & fresh, & beautifully fine & strong, as it used to be! C'est la vie—cette chienne de vie, so fine notwithstanding! Heart up!"[39]

Throughout the 1950s, Margherita spent the seasons in different locales. From late October until July she lived in Rome, summers she passed at Il Soldo (with a week or so of bathing at the Lido), and once a year she visited Paris. Amedeo and his family lived there from 1950 to 1956.

Margherita loved Paris, where a number of old friends still lived, including Colette, who died in 1954, and the famous art historian André Chastel. When in the French capital, Margherita spent her time in museums, art exhibits, restaurants, and at the theater. "Nothing like overdoing it in Paris," she shrugged, "which might, but would not, have tired me out. But it did not, because I am never tired when I am amused & happy."

Tita Brown-Castellanos, who had grown up in Montevideo and was a friend of Amedeo's daughter, Magalì, recalled an amusing incident that took place on one Paris trip. Tita and her mother were staying at the Hotel St. James on the fashionable Rue Saint-Honoré. They were shocked to see a slip, a bra, a bottle of milk, and some sausages hanging on the terrace they shared with the room directly across from theirs. "Imagine," said Tita's mother indignantly, "what kind of people must be staying here these days!" That afternoon Margherita took Magalì and Tita to the Louvre, and in the evening all three visitors dined at Amedeo's house. They shared a taxi back to the hotel with Margherita, who was also staying at the St. James. Tita and her mother discovered that it was her room that opened on to the terrace.[40]

Margherita was always ready to visit new places, although as she grew older she disliked traveling alone. In 1956, she decided to see the Far East, where she had never been, "before the iron curtain shuts and blots it out!" Because of her age—she was seventy-six at the time—her family was not enthusiastic about the idea. Even though she could not tempt any of her friends to go with her, she packed her bags and booked passage in May on a cruise that was going across the Mediterranean to Syria and Israel and then through the Suez Canal to India, Ceylon, Malaya, Hong Kong and continuing on to Japan. On board she met Prince Christian De Rosemberg, nephew of the king of Denmark, and the two became good friends. In Hong Kong, the prince bought her a set of brightly colored Chinese lanterns. She discovered a beautiful figure of the Buddha in a flea market. When she returned to Italy, she hung the lanterns at Il Soldo and greeted her guests in exquisite silk jackets that she had had made in Hong Kong.[41]

The journey to Asia was Margherita's last overseas adventure. After Amedeo's family returned to Buenos Aires in 1956, her trips to Paris became less frequent. Her life was increasingly contained within the narrower limits of Rome and Il Soldo. Her writing for publication had virtually ceased, beyond a few pleasant travel articles for *Como*, a local magazine published near Il Soldo. In June 1958, she published a lengthy pamphlet bearing the title *L'amore svalutato (Undervalued Love)*, a philosophical excursion into the nature of life in the modern age. She had been working on it for the past four years. Originally she wanted to call the work *Supersonic Love*, because, as she explained to Berenson, "I mean to prove that rapidity, this modern Goddess, is not only a material, but also a moral factor of our lives & customs, & that it takes away a part of the best of love, where prefaces are often as important as the book." Her basic point was that men and women no longer took enough time or interest in the traditional rituals of lovemaking. Margherita saw the pamphlet as a summation of her philosophy of human existence, but it was a disjointed and loosely structured work.[42]

As Margherita grew older, her weight became more pronounced, and she tended to take less care with her appearance. Her friends and family noticed that she overdressed and wore heavy makeup, which she rarely bothered to retouch when it smeared. George Biddle's startled reaction to her physical appearance was typical—although she sometimes bathed twice a day, she was so unkempt that she seemed dirty. In 1960, just as she turned eighty, her increasingly careless physical appearance became the source of public embarrassment in the midst of a family tragedy: the death of Roberto, Fiammetta's oldest child. Named after Margherita's firstborn son, Roberto Gaetani was his grandmother's favorite. He was a good-looking young man with a law degree who shared the monarchist sympathies of the other young nobles with whom he socialized. From birth, however, he had suffered from epileptic seizures. One evening that spring, twenty-six-year-old Robert stepped out onto a terrace to smoke a cigarette and fell to his death. Whether the tragedy was the result of an accident or suicide is unclear, but it deeply affected Margherita. At the funeral, with her lips painted a brazenly bright red and her pale face and white hair, she looked, said one observer, like an "aged, painted up whore." A relative quickly moved her away from the casket and back into the car.[43]

Margherita remained more or less a recluse in her apartment at the Ambasciatori during the winter of 1960–1961. As the weather grew milder in the spring of 1961, she ventured forth for a few public appearances in Rome. She attended a talk by the American historian H. Stuart Hughes. Hughes was lecturing at the offices of the Einaudi publishers, which had just issued the Italian edition of his book, *Consciousness and Society*. After the lecture, a woman Hughes remembered as "elderly and rather unattractive," began to harangue him. A group of well-wishers surrounding him withdrew with him to another part of the room. Later Hughes asked the name of the woman, and someone exclaimed that it was *"La Sarfatti!"*[44]

In April, Margherita's granddaughter Magalì visited. Her family had recently settled again in Paris after several years in Buenos Aires. Magalì held a special place in Margherita's affections. Margherita looked upon her as a girl whose mind and morals she could help shape. She recommended books to the girl, read poetry to her, and nurtured and admired her intelligence. Margherita shared her private thoughts with her granddaughter more openly than with most people. She advised her against promiscuity, not on any bourgeois moral grounds but because she believed that men used women for their own selfish pleasure. When Magalì turned seventeen, Margherita lectured her that "a person who enjoys the dual privilege of intelligence and culture owes an obligation for such a favor of fate to treat others less fortunate with kindness, generosity, and indulgence." When Magalì expressed her displeasure at having to go back to Buenos Aires, Margherita explained that people had to find joy and happiness not in their physical surroundings but within themselves.[45]

Magalì found her grandmother "still in very good shape" despite the fact that she had just turned eighty-one. A few minutes past midnight on April 8—her birthday—Margherita opened her well-worn copy of Dante. Her finger fell on a *terzina* from Canto XXV of the *Purgatorio*:

> When Lachesis has no more thread
> the soul is loosed from the flesh, and in potency
> carries with it both the human and the divine

So she would die soon. Margherita consulted her Dante again about the manner of her passing. This time the volume fell open to reveal a phrase from Chapter IV of the *Convivio:* "Like a ripe apple easily and without violence is taken from its branch." She penned a note beside the passage in the *Purgatorio:* "Plucked like a ripe apple from its branch. Aristotle speaks without sadness of the death that lies within old age. It is clear that I will not see the next April 8, 1962. But thanks to God it says that I will not suffer. Amen. So be it." Margherita told no one of her fateful augury.

A short while later, Margherita took Magalì on a whirlwind tour of Rome, visiting churches, museums, monuments, and the opera. Magalì remembers that whenever they entered a gallery, the owner and the artists—most of whom were too young to have known Margherita before the war—were extremely deferential to her. At the Palazzo Venezia, where Mussolini had kept his offices during the Fascist regime, they saw an exhibit of the new work of Gino Severini, which Margherita did not at all like. "Gino," she muttered to herself, "these things you're doing, they're so ugly!" Yet when they ran into Severini's daughter, Margherita assured her how important her father's work had been to the development of modern painting.[46]

Shortly after Magalì left Rome Margherita went to Il Soldo. There she received the journalist Marcello Staglieno, who found her a "pleasant woman of great learning and good manners, wearing a hair net, which gave her very white hair a blue cast, and a small gold ring on her left pinky: a gift, the only one she ever received, from 'him.' "[47]

That fall, she returned briefly to Rome, where she granted an interview to Renzo De Felice, an Italian historian who had recently begun a study of Mussolini and the Fascist regime. They met in her rooms at the Ambasciatori Hotel on a bleak, chilly evening, and talked for hours. Margherita did not offer to show the young scholar any of her papers and provided no revelations. She did give him some insight into her influence on Fascist cultural policy by speaking at length about classicism, which had been one of the guideposts of her art criticism during the years of the regime. De Felice recounted an odd incident that occurred that night. Toward the end of their conversation, Margherita rose from her chair and walked over to the window, which framed a full moon suspended against the darkened sky. Making her way back to her guest, she placed a gnarled hand on his shoulder. "Come, professor, come," she coaxed. As they reached the window, Margherita pointed up at the yellow moon and cried, "Lucifer!"[48]

On the evening of Saturday, October 28, 1961—thirty-nine years to the day after Benito Mussolini's March on Rome—Margherita Sarfatti picked up the telephone in her study at Il Soldo and called Carla Porta Musa, a friend from Cavallasca who edited the magazine *Como*. Only a few days earlier they had traveled together by automobile to Mantua to see an exhibit of paintings of the fifteenth-century artist Andrea Mantegna. "I expect you tomorrow," Margherita insisted. "Tomorrow, understand? Don't betray me. Come. I leave Monday and want to say good-bye."

Musa arrived at Il Soldo at four o'clock on Sunday, a glorious fall afternoon bathed in golden sunlight. These days the villa was quiet, undisturbed by the laughter of children, the animated shouts of artists, or the political debates that had once accompanied Mussolini's visits. Now and then Margherita entertained foreign visitors there, as well as friends from Cavallasca, but Il Soldo had become the tranquil summer house of an old woman whose mind was filled with memories.

Entering the living room, Musa called out. "You've arrived!" came Margherita's voice from the study. "How wonderful!" Margherita entered carrying an handful of light green pages on which she had just finished an article titled "But Is It a Discovery?" She read the piece to her friend; it was a short, wry essay recounting her "stupendous discovery" of the relationship between what people of various countries drink and their sense of humor. The understated British sense of humor, for example, reflected the two national beverages of England, whiskey and tea. When Margherita had finished reading, Musa assured her that she had made a real discovery. Smiling happily, she stood up and offered her guest a choice of whiskey or tea.

The two friends passed a pleasant evening. Musa commented on the joys of writing. "You're talking to the right person!" observed Margherita. "Since the age of fifteen I've done nothing else but write, read, and learn." In the study where decades past she had spent a summer working across the desk from Ada Negri and where she had written *Dux,* Musa found a vase of fresh flowers standing before a photograph of Roberto. Suddenly pensive, Margherita made a confession: "I will die regretting that I never remarried."

Darkness fell. As Margherita walked Musa to her car, she observed that the hydrangea grown at Il Soldo were of a distinctive color found nowhere else.

"Ciao, Margherita."

"Ciao, Carla," replied Margherita, embracing her friend. "When will you come to Rome?"

"In January or February."

"Try to come sooner."

Margherita spent that evening helping her maid pack her bags and filling envelopes with money to pay her local bills. After supper, she played a few rounds of solitaire and retired around midnight, perhaps wondering, as she had once put it to Bernard Berenson, "Why is night always worse for pains? And why do most people decease between 1/2-night and before dawn?"

The next morning, October 30, 1961, at eight-thirty, the maid came into Margherita's bedroom and opened the shutters, calling her name. There was no response.[49]

Against a wall of the small cemetery in Cavallasca, there stands today a severe marble plinth, designed by the sculptor Emilio Greco. A hydrangea bush grows in front of the marker, across which is chiseled in primitive letters the name MARGHERITA SARFATTI and beneath that "A 1880 Ω 1961." A haunting mask of a female face in profile gazes westward toward Il Soldo, which lies against the green hills in the distance. The mask, taken from a sculpture by Adolfo Wildt, which Margherita had purchased in 1919, is an allegorical portrait of "Victory."

THE FAMILY OF MARGHERITA SARFATTI

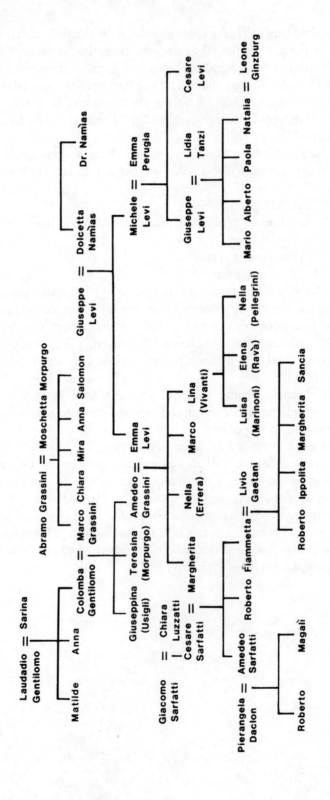

Notes

ABBREVIATIONS USED IN NOTES

ACDEC	Archivio Centro di Documentazione Ebraica Contemporanea, Milan
ACS	Archivio Centrale dello Stato, Rome
AFM	Archivio Francesco Meriano, Fondazione Primo Conti, Fiesole
AGP	Archivio Giovanni Papini, Fondazione Primo Conti, Fiesole
AmSP	Amedeo Sarfatti Papers, Cortina d'Ampezzo
AOMP, NYPL/NYTA	Anne O'Hare McCormick Papers, New York Public Library/*New York Times* Archives
APC	Archivio Primo Conti, Fondazione Primo Conti, Fiesole
ASACB	Archivio Storico d'Arte Contemporanea della Biennale, Venice
AS/CMM	Agenzia Stefani/Carte Manlio Morgagni
ASMAE	Archivio Storico Ministero Affari Esteri, Rome
ASP	Aglae Sironi Papers, Rome
AVI, AG	Archivio del Vittoriale degli Italiani, Archivio Generale, Lake Garda
b.	busta (bundle)
BBP	Bernard Berenson Papers, Villa I Tatti, Florence
BLP	Breckinridge Long Papers, Library of Congress
BP	George Biddle Papers, Library of Congress
BRS	Brian R. Sullivan
CAHJP, PAGM	Central Archives for the History of the Jewish People, Jerusalem, Private Archive of the Grassini-Morpurgo Family
CCCP	Carrie Chapman Catt Papers, Library of Congress
CCD	Carte Cornelio Di.Marzio
CCP	Carlo Carrà Papers
CEB	Carte Emilio Bodrero
CEP	Carnegie Endowment Papers, Butler Library, Columbia University
CFM	Carte Ferdinando Martini
CFP	Carte Ferruccio Parri
CIA	Central Intelligence Agency
COM	Carte Oddino Morgari
CP	Andrea Costa Papers, Biblioteca Comunale, Imola
CPC	Casellario Politico Centrale
CSSA	Charles Scribner's Sons Archives, General Files, Princeton University Library
CZA, IZP	Central Zionist Archives, Jerusalem, Israel Zangwill Papers
DBFP	*Documents on British Foreign Policy,* followed by series, volume, and document number

DCP	Charles and Marie de Chambrun Papers, Paris
DDF	*Documents diplomatiques français,* followed by series, volume, and document number
DDI	*I documenti diplomatici italiani,* followed by series, volume, and document number
DGFP	*Documents on German Foreign Policy,* followed by series, volume, and document number
DGP	Dino Grandi Papers, Georgetown University
DTP	Dorothy Thompson Papers, Syracuse University
ECP	E. D. Coblentz Papers, Bancroft Library, University of California at Berkeley
EGCP	Edward Gordon Craig Papers, Humanities Research Center, University of Texas, Austin
EMHP	E. M. House Papers, Sterling Library, Yale University.
EPP	Ezra Pound Papers, Yale University
ERP	Eleanor Roosevelt Papers, Hyde Park, New York
f.	fascicolo (folder)
FAO, ACGV	Fondo Angiolo Orvieto, Archivio Contemporaneo del Gabinetto Vieusseux, Florence
FBI	Federal Bureau of Investigation, Washington, D.C.
FDRP	Franklin D. Roosevelt Papers, Hyde Park, New York
FHP	Fannie Hurst Papers, Brandeis University
FOR, ACGV	Fondo Ottone Rosai, Archivio Contemporaneo del Gabinetto Vieusseux, Florence
FP	Piero Foà Papers, Detroit
FPP	Frances Perkins Papers, Butler Library, Columbia University
FRUS	*Papers Relating to the Foreign Relations of the United States*
FSGP	Fiammetta Sarfatti Gaetani Papers, Rome
FTM	Filippo T. Marinetti Papers, Beinecke Library, Yale University
GBP	Giuseppe Bottai Papers, Rome
GFP	Guglielmo Ferrero Papers, Butler Library, Columbia University
GGSP	Grace Gallatin Seton Papers, Schlesinger Library, Radcliffe College
GHLP	George Horace Lorimer Papers, Historical Society of Pennsylvania, Philadelphia
GOP	Guido Orlando Papers, Motion Picture Academy Archives, Hollywood, California
GSP	Gianguido Scalfi Papers, Milan
HGP	Hermann Göring Papers, U.S. Army Military History Institute, Carlisle, Pennsylvania
HHP	Herbert Hoover Papers, West Branch, Iowa
HMP	Houghton Mifflin Papers, Houghton Library, Harvard University
HNP	Harold Nicholson Papers, Balliol College, Oxford
HPFP	Henry Prather Fletcher Papers, Library of Congress
HSTP	Harry S. Truman Papers, Independence, Missouri
IBP	Italo Balbo Papers, Rome
IDSP	I. Daniel Shorell Papers, New York City
JPMP	J. P. Moffat Papers, Houghton Library, Harvard University
KAJP	Kenyon A. Joyce Papers, U.S. Army Military History Institute, Carlisle, Pennsylvania
KP	Keller Papers, Sterling Library, Yale University
KRP	Kenneth Roberts Papers, Dartmouth College
KWP	Karl von Wiegand Papers, Hoover Institution, Stanford University
LKF	Laura K. Fleming
MCP	Ministero della Cultura Popolare
MFB	Military Field Branch, National Archives, Suitland, Maryland

MGS	Margherita Grassini Sarfatti
MI-DPP	Ministero dell'Interno, Divisione Polizia Politica
MMMP	Marie Mattingly Meloney Papers, Butler Library, Columbia University
MoMA	Museum of Modern Art, New York
MP	Margherita Manili Papers, Rome
MSLP	Magalì Sarfatti-Larson Papers
MWC	Mahler-Werfel Collection, Special Collections, Van Pelt Library, University of Pennsylvania
NA	National Archives, Washington
NDP	Norman Davis Papers, Library of Congress
NMBP	Nicholas Murray Butler Papers, Butler Library, Columbia University
OF	[President's] Official File
OHP	Oral History Project, Butler Library, Columbia University
OO	*Opera Omnia di Benito Mussolini,* Edoardo and Duilio Susmel, eds., 37 vols. (Florence, 1952)
OOA	*Opera Omnia di Benito Mussolini, Appendici,* Edoardo and Duilio Susmel, eds., 7 vols. (Rome, 1978–81)
OSS	Office of Strategic Services
PCM	Presidenza del Consiglio dei Ministri
PP	Giuseppe Prezzolini Papers, Biblioteca Cantonale, Lugano
PPF	President's Personal File
PPYP	Prince Paul of Yugoslavia Papers, Butler Library, Columbia University
PRO, FO	Foreign Office, Public Record Office, London
PSF	President's Secretary's File
PVC	Philip V. Cannistraro
RDP	Richard Dunlop Papers, U.S. Army Military History Institute, Carlisle, Pennsylvania
RDS	Records of the Department of State, National Archives
RG	record group
RKP	Roberto Klinger Papers, Rome
RP	Annie Russell Papers, New York Public Library
RWCP	Richard Washburn Child Papers, Library of Congress
RWHP	Roy W. Howard Papers, Library of Congress
SBP	Sol Bloom Papers, New York Public Library
sf.	sottofascicolo (sub-folder)
SHKF	Samuel H. Kress Foundation, New York City
SPD, CR/CO	Segretaria Particolare del Duce, Carteggio Riservato/Carteggio Ordinario
Spingarn Report	Report of Major Stephen J. Spingarn, 305th Counter Intelligence Detachment, U.S. Fifth Army, on Count Contini-Bonacossi, to Assistant Chief of Intelligence, G-2 (Counter Intelligence), December 20, 1944
SSMP	S. S. McClure Papers, Lilly Library, University of Indiana at Bloomington
T/K	*Filippo Turati e Anna Kuliscioff Carteggio,* Alessandro Schiavi and Franco Pedone, eds., 7 vols. (Turin, 1977)
TLP	Thomas Lamont Papers, Baker Library, Harvard University
TRJP	Theodore Roosevelt, Jr., Papers, Library of Congress
TVRP	T. V. Ranck Papers, Sterling Library, Yale University
UCG	Udienze del Capo del Governo
UKP	Umberto Klinger Papers, Rome
USE	Stato Maggiore Esercito. Ufficio storico.
VEOP	Vittorio E. Orlando Papers
VMDP	Vera Micheles Dean Papers, Schlesinger Library, Radcliffe College
WEDP	William E. Dodd Papers, Library of Congress
WLP	Walter Lippmann Papers, Sterling Library, Yale University
WPD	William Phillips Diary, Houghton Library, Harvard University

WRCD   William R. Castle Diary, Houghton Library, Harvard University
WRCP   William R. Castle Papers, Herbert Hoover Library, West Branch, Iowa

Mussolini: Como lo conocí, followed by the relevant number of the fourteen installments published
     in 1945 by MGS in *Crítica* (Buenos Aires), as follows:
     I   "El diablo dijo: 'Sí,' y le dio el poder que no supo conservar," June 18
     II "El Duce sentia terror por la vejez y odiaba a todo posible sucesor," June 19
     III "Hasta Lenin creyó en el Duce como en el hombre de la revolución," June 20
     IV " 'Han matado a Matteotti para hundir al fascismo'—dio el Duce," June 21
     V "La familia del Duce entra en escena; Italia se une al eje," June 22
     VI "El hogar del Duce, Doña Raquel y otras cosas por el estilo," June 23
     VII "El hogar y las mujeres en la vida del Duce; por qué se casó Edda," June 25
     VIII "Claretta Petacci, ultimo amor del Duce, fué una espía de los Nazis," June 26
     IX "El Duce fué un hombre huraño y sin amigos, que huyó de la multitud," June 27
     X "La tragedia del Conde Ciano, el títere que quiso ser hombre," June 28
     XI "Al principio, el Duce se burlaba de Hitler y le daba consejos," June 29
     XII "Hitler le contagió su error más funesto: desdeñar a Estados Unidos," June 30
     XIII "A cambio de Austria, Hitler dejó al Duce apoderse de Etiopía," July 2
     XIV "Mi culpa y mi fuga—por Qué callé—Mussolini traicionó la revolución," July 3

CHAPTER I: IN THE GARDEN

1 Emilio Pardo, *Luci ed ombre* (Venice, 1965), 15–7.
2 MGS, *Acqua passata* (Rocca San Casciano, 1955), 5–14, 165; Giuseppe Bassi, "Emma
  Levi-Grassini," *Il Corriere Israelitico* (Trieste), August 31, 1900, 93; comments by Magalì
  Sarfatti-Larson before the American Historical Association, December 29, 1986; MGS,
  "Decadimento," in *I vivi e l'ombra* (Verona, 1934), 25, and "Il fanciullo cattivo," ibid.,
  57–8.
3 Judith, "She Is the Comrade of Il Duce," *The American Hebrew,* October 24, 1929, 600; MGS
  to Mussolini, n.d. but 1923, GSP.
4 Judith, "She Is the Comrade of Il Duce," 600.
5 MGS, *Casanova contro Don Giovanni* (Verona, 1950), 15–6; MGS, *L'amore svalutato* (Rome,
  1958), 9–10; MGS to George and Helene Biddle, February 2, 1958, BP.
6 "Judith," "She Is the Comrade of Il Duce"; interview with Fiammetta Sarfatti Gaetani, July
  10, 1985; interview with Magalì Sarfatti-Larson, September 28, 1985; I. Giordani and S.
  Taylor, eds., *Who's Who in Italy, 1957–1958* (Milan, 1958), 863; MGS, *Acqua passata,* 15–6.
7 Natalia Ginzburg, *Lessico famigliare* (Turin, 1963), 27; MGS, *Acqua passata,* 15–23; interview
  with Magalì Sarfatti-Larson, June 16, 1986.
8 MGS, *Acqua passata,* 58–61; Degna Paresce Marconi, *Marconi, mio padre* (Milan, 1967), 12–3.
9 Interview with Amedeo Sarfatti, May 24, 1985; Federico Luzzatto, "La comunità ebraica di
  Conegliano Veneto ed i suoi monumenti," *La Rassegna Mensile di Israel,* XXII, 4 (April
  1956), 182; Cecil Roth, *The History of the Jews of Italy* (Philadelphia, 1946), 373.
10 Interview with Amedeo Sarfatti, May 24, 1985; Attilio Milano, *Storia degli ebrei in Italia*
  (Turin, 1963), 276–85, 309–22; Cecil Roth, *Venice* (Philadelphia, 1930); Riccardo Calimani,
  The Ghetto of Venice (New York, 1987).
11 Luzzatto, "La comunità ebraica"; Amedeo Sarfatti to PVC, October 1985; MGS, *Segni,
  colori, e luci* (Bologna, 1925), 72–4; interview with Amedeo and Pierangela Sarfatti, May 24,
  1985.
12 Sergio Marzorati, *Margherita Sarfatti: Saggio biografico* (Como, 1990), 11.
13 Roth, *History,* 336, 456; idem, *Venice,* 156, 269; Milano, *Storia,* 133; Luzzatto, "La comunità
  ebraica," 184; interview with Amedeo and Pierangela Sarfatti, May 24, 1985. The history
  of the Grassini family is described in the "Famiglia Grassini/Albero Genealogico," CAHJP,
  P/62, PAGM, b. 18-V, and in the catalog entry entitled "Genealogia dei Grassini di

Conegliano," CAHJP, P/62, PAGM, b. 1-a; Brian Pullan, *The Jews of Europe and the Inquisition of Venice, 1550–1670* (Totowa, N.J.: Barnes & Noble, 1983), 149.

14 MGS, "Menues légendes pontificales," *Le Temps* (Paris), February 25, 1939.

15 Marco Grassini's activities during the unification struggle and his subsequent career are described in Luzzatto, "La comunità ebraica," and in Pio Baruffi, *Alla cara memoria dell'Avvocato Cav. Marco Grassini* (Venice, 1885), in CAHJP, P/62, PAGM, b. 45. In 1876, the king elevated Marco to the rank of Officer of the Crown of Italy.

16 Interviews with Amedeo and Pierangela Sarfatti, May 24, 1985, and with Magalì Sarfatti-Larson, December 31, 1985; Amedeo Sarfatti to PVC, January 1986; Fiammetta Sarfatti Gaetani to PVC, July 28, 1985; Baruffi, *Alla cara memoria*.

17 Catalog entry entitled "Genealogia dei Grassini di Conegliano," CAHJP, P/62, PAGM, b. 1-a; interview with Amedeo and Pierangela Sarfatti, May 24, 1985; interview with Fiammetta Sarfatti Gaetani, July 9, 1985; MGS, *Acqua passata*, 8; Giuseppe Bassi, "Emma Levi-Grassini."

18 "I funerali del Cav. Uff. A. Grassini," *Gazzetta di Venezia*, September 2, 1908.

19 Luzzatto, "La comunità ebraica," 184; MGS, *Acqua passata*, 45; interview with Fiammetta Sarfatti Gaetani, July 9, 1985.

20 MGS, *Acqua passata*, 17, 21; interview with Fiammetta Sarfatti Gaetani, May 13, 1985; Calimani, *The Ghetto of Venice*, 258.

21 On the politics of Venice in this period, see Emilio Franzina, *Venezia* (Rome-Bari, 1986), 132–40.

22 Francamaria Trapani, "Fu mia madre a convincerlo: 'Benito sposa la tua Rachele,' " *Gente*, September 17, 1982, 48; Ginzburg, *Lessico famigliare*, 15; Marzorati, *Margherita Sarfatti*, 58.

23 John Ruskin, *The Stones of Venice*, III (London, 1908; originally published in 1853), 255; Giulio Lorenzetti, *Venice and Its Lagoon* (Rome, 1961), 467; Amedeo Sarfatti to PVC, October 1985; MGS, in L. M. Personè, ed., *Il primo passo: Confessioni di scrittori contemporanei* (Florence, 1930), 269; "I funerali del Cav. Uff. A. Grassini"; MGS, *Acqua passata*, 5.

CHAPTER 2: WIDE VISTAS OF THOUGHT

1 "Judith," "She Is the Comrade of Il Duce," 600; Trapani, "Fu mia madre," Part II, 50; MGS, *Acqua passata*, 58.

2 MGS, *Acqua passata*, 103.

3 MGS to Bernard Berenson, June 9, 1937, BBP; Fiammetta Sarfatti Gaetani to PVC, July 5, 1987; Ester Coen, "Una vita difficile: La Sarfatti fra arte e fascismo," *Art Dossier* (January 1987), 23.

4 MGS, *Acqua passata*, 39–40.

5 On Italian women see Donna Gabaccia, "In the Shadows of the Periphery: Italian Women in the Nineteenth Century," in Marilyn J. Boxer and Jean H. Quataert, eds., *Connecting Spheres: Women in the Western World, 1500 to the Present* (New York, 1987), 166–76.

6 MGS, *Acqua passata*, 39; Trapani, "Fu mia madre," Part II, 50; interview with Amedeo Sarfatti, May 24, 1985, and Magalì Sarfatti-Larson, December 11, 1986; *Chi è? Dizionario degli italiani d'oggi*, 4th ed. (Rome, 1940), 684–5.

7 Franzini, *Venezia*, 137–38. See also Alberto Malatesta, *Ministri, deputati, senatori dal 1848 al 1922* (Milan, 1940); *Enciclopedia italiana*, XV (Milan, 1932), 831; Edoardo Savino, ed., *La nazione operante* (Milan, 1928), 123; Teodoro Rovito, *Letterati e giornalisti italiani contemporanei*, 2nd ed. (Naples, 1922), 174; Antonio Gramsci, "Antonio Fradeletto," in *Quaderni del carcere*, III (Turin, 1975), 2242–3.

8 Antonio Fradeletto, "La volontà come forza sociale," "Malattie d'arte," "La letteratura e la vita," and "La psicologia della letteratura italiana," all in his *Conferenze* (Milan, 1911); "Margherita Sarfatti," typescript of biographical sketch, in ECP, f. TS Italy, SW, CG56.

9 "Judith," "She Is the Comrade of Il Duce," 600; MGS to Bernard Berenson, July 14, [1952], BBP.

10 Lawrence Alloway, *The Venice Biennale, 1895–1968* (New York, 1968), 32–3, 49; Franzina, *Venezia,* 430–41; Fradeletto, "La letteratura e la vita," 105.

11 Sarfatti's annotated copy of Dante's works, *Le opere di Dante* (Florence, 1921), is preserved in the FSGP, Rome.

12 "Judith," "She Is the Comrade of Il Duce"; MGS to Bernard Berenson, December 9, 1955, BBP; MGS, "La passione morale negli scrittori inglesi," *Gerarchia* (February 1922), 65–9; interview with Fiammetta Sarfatti Gaetani, May 16, 1985; MGS, *Acqua passata,* 103–4, 114–5, 139; interview with Amedeo Sarfatti, October 1985; Personè, *Il primo passo,* 267–73; MGS to Bernard Berenson, October 9, 1951, BBP.

   In 1898, Sarfatti translated Shaw's play *Candida* into Italian, although it was never published.

13 MGS, "Menues légendes pontificales"; MGS, *Acqua passata,* 25–37, 42–54; Alloway, *The Venice Biennale,* 46; Franzina, *Venezia,* 435–6; MGS, "Questione di pudore o questione di estetica?," *Gazzetta di Venezia,* August 14, 1903.

14 On the decline of Italian Jewish identity in this period, see Mario Toscano, "The Cultural Revival of Italian Hebraism at the Beginning of the Twentieth Century," paper delivered at the conference on "Italy and the Jews," New York, December 11, 1986 (typescript in authors' possession), and idem, "The Jews in Italy from the Risorgimento to the Republic," in Vivian B. Mann, ed., *Gardens and Ghettos: The Art of Jewish Life in Italy* (Berkeley, 1989), 27–30; Marzorati, *Margherita Sarfatti,* 28–9.

15 MGS, *Acqua passata,* 41–2; MGS, "Scrittori stranieri: Israele Zangwill," *Nuova Antologia* (September 16, 1926), 245–8; MGS to Bernard Berenson, January 6, 1948, BBP; Israel Zangwill, "Chad Gadya," in *Dreamers of the Ghetto* (London, 1898), 454, 457–8; on Zangwill see Maurice Wohlgelernter, *Israel Zangwill* (New York, 1964); Elsie B. Adams, *Israel Zangwill* (New York, 1971).

CHAPTER 3: THE RED VIRGIN

1 Corinne Lowe, "The Woman Behind Mussolini," *Pictorial Review* (September 1934), 4; Bianca Veneziana, *Storia italiana d'amore* (Milan, 1977), 29.

2 The professor may have been Eugenio Tanzi, who was distantly related to Sarfatti. On Tanzi see ACS, *Ministero della Pubblica Istruzione, Personale Universitario,* 2nd Versamento, f. "Tanzi, Eugenio"; Alfredo Angiolini and Eugenio Ciacchi, *Socialismo e socialisti in Italia* (Florence, 1919), 236.

3 Ermanno Usigli, the husband of Amedeo Grassini's sister Giuseppina, had published a pamphlet entitled *Il socialismo e la Bibbia* in Venice in 1863. Luzzatto, "La comunità ebraica," 184.

4 Margherita later described her reaction to the plight of the peasant girl as her first encounter with the Marxist concept of *Schandenemporung,* or "shameful indignation." See note 5.

5 MGS, *Acqua passata,* 7–8; Lowe, *Il primo passo,* 267–73; interview with Magalì Sarfatti-Larson, June 16, 1986; Personè, "The Woman Behind Mussolini," 4; MGS, *Dux* (Milan, 1926), 116.

6 On Costa see *Il movimento operaio italiano: Dizionario biografico,* II (Rome, 1977), 109–20; on Kuliscioff see Beverly Tanner Springer, "Anna Kuliscioff," in Jane Slaughter and Robert Kern, eds., *European Women on the Left* (Westport, 1981), 13–27.

7 On the early development of Italian Socialism see Richard Hostetter, *The Italian Socialist Movement,* I, *Origins (1860–1882)* (Princeton, 1958); Nunzio Pernicone, "The Italian Labor Movement," in E. R. Tannenbaum and E. P. Noether, eds., *Modern Italy* (New York, 1974), 197–230; Gastone Manacorda, *Il movimento operaio italiano attraverso i suoi congressi, 1853–1892* (Rome, 1963); Leo Valiani, *Questioni di storia del socialismo* (Turin, 1975), 3–80.

8 Spencer Di Scala, *Dilemmas of Italian Socialism: The Politics of Filippo Turati* (Amherst, 1980); Paolo Pillitteri, *Anna Kuliscioff: Una biografia politica* (Venice, 1986); Nino Valeri, *Turati e la Kuliscioff* (Florence, 1974).

9 MGS, *Acqua passata*, 67–8. On Crispi's repressive policies see Christopher Seton-Watson, *Italy from Liberalism to Fascism, 1870–1925* (London, 1967), 129–176.

10 Personè, *Il primo passo*, 267, 270.

11 "Judith," "She Is the Comrade of Il Duce," 600; Ruskin, *The Stones of Venice*, II, 149. The best treatment of Ruskin's social criticism is still John A. Hobson, *John Ruskin, Social Reformer* (Boston, 1898).

12 MGS, "Proletariato e patria," *Avanti!*, December 23, 1914; MGS, "La passione morale negli scrittori inglesi," *Gerarchia*, February 1922, 65–9.

CHAPTER 4: A SOCIALIST MARRIAGE

1 Interviews with Fiammetta Sarfatti Gaetani, July 10, 1985, and Magalì Sarfatti-Larson, June 16, 1986.

2 *The Jewish Encyclopedia*, XII (New York, 1906), 637; *The Universal Jewish Encyclopedia*, IX, (New York, 1943), 370; *Encyclopaedia Judaica*, XIV (Jerusalem, 1971), 878–79; Amedeo Sarfatti to PVC, January 1986.

3 ACS, CPC, no. 60867, "Sarfatti, Cesare," report dated February 1, 1900; interview with Magalì Sarfatti-Larson, June 16, 1986; Trapani, "Fu mia madre," Part II, 52.

4 MGS, *Acqua passata*, 13, 57; interview with Magalì Sarfatti-Larson, June 16, 1986.

5 Interviews with Amedeo Sarfatti, May 24, 1985, and Magalì Sarfatti-Larson, September 28, 1985, and June 16, 1986.

6 Amedeo Sarfatti to PVC, July 16, 1986; "Stato civile," *Gazzetta di Venezia*, May 31, 1898; Bianca Riccio, "Margherita la regina," *La Repubblica Mercurio*, April 29, 1989, 3; interview with Magalì Sarfatti-Larson, September 28, 1985; Ambroise Vollard, *Recollections of a Picture Dealer* (New York, 1978), 65–102; Richard W. Murphy, *The World of Cézanne, 1839–1906* (New York, 1968), 174; MGS, "Un mercante di quadri," *La Stampa*, February 7, 1938.

7 James R. Mellow, *Charmed Circle: Gertrude Stein and Company* (New York, 1974), 5; MGS to Bernard Berenson, June 14, 1951, BBP; P. Huisman and M. G. Dortu, *Lautrec by Lautrec* (New York, 1964), 96–7, 120–43; comments by Magalì Sarfatti-Larson before the American Historical Association, December 29, 1986.

8 "La morte di Cesare Sarfatti," *Il Popolo d'Italia*, January 25, 1924; *Il movimento operaio italiano*, V (Rome, 1980), 59; Martin Clark, *Modern Italy, 1871–1982* (London, 1984), 130.

9 Angiolini and Ciacchi, *Socialismo e socialisti*, 313, 380; Gabriele De Rosa, *Storia del movimento cattolico in Italia*, I (Bari, 1966), 176–79; MGS, "Menues légendes pontificales."

10 Seton-Watson, *Italy from Liberalism*, 176–92.

11 *Il movimento operaio italiano*, I, 532–4; III, 566–70; Letterio Briguglio, "Caratteri del movimento operaio a Venezia dopo l'unità," *Miscellanea in onore di Roberto Cessi*, 3 (Rome, 1958), 355–79. On the Events of May and the subsequent government reaction see Umberto Levra, *Il colpo di stato della borghesia* (Milan, 1975).

12 Cesare Sarfatti to Andrea Costa, November 29, 1899, CP, no. 2494; *Il movimento operaio italiano*, III, 626–29; ESMOI, *Bibliografia del socialismo e del movimento operaio italiano*, I, *Periodici* (Rome-Turin, 1956), 827–8.

13 ACS, CPC, no. 60867, "Sarfatti, Cesare," report of February 1, 1900.

14 ACS, CPC, no. 60867, "Sarfatti, Cesare," prefect reports of February 13, March 13, June 4, 1900; *Statistiche delle elezioni generali politiche* (Rome, 1901).

15 Bassi, "Emma Levi-Grassini."

16 The ideological currents within the Socialist party are discussed in Luigi Cortesi, *Il socialismo italiano tra riforme e rivoluzione, 1892–1921* (Bari, 1969); Enzo Santarelli, *La revisione del marxismo in Italia* (Milan, 1977); Gaetano Arfè, *Storia del socialismo italiano, 1892–1926* (Turin, 1965); Stefano Caretti et al., *Storia del partito socialista italiano, 1892–1976* (Florence, 1977).

17 ACS, CPC, no. 60867, "Sarfatti, Cesare," reports of February 1, September 25, November 14, 1900; Franco Pedone, ed., *Il partito socialista italiano nei suoi congressi*, I (Milan, 1959), 122–3; Angiolini and Ciacchi, *Socialismo e socialisti*, 404.

18 Cortesi, *Il socialismo italiano*, 125–8; Pedone, *Il partito socialista*, I, 123; Israel Zangwill, *Le suffragiste militanti*, trans. Margherita G. Sarfatti (Florence, 1914); Franca Pieroni Bortolotti, *Alle origini del movimento femminile in Italia, 1848–1892* (Turin, 1963), 186, 232–51, 194; idem, *Socialismo e questione femminile in Italia, 1892–1922* (Milan, 1974), 37–40 and passim; *La Rassegna Femminile* (Florence), February 23, 1902.

19 *Il Secolo Nuovo*, April 18, June 22, July 13 and 20, August 3, 10, 31, and September 14, 21, and 28, 1901. See also *Unione Femminile*, May 1901.

20 Ugo Ojetti, "Diritti e doveri del critico d'arte moderna," *Nuova Antologia*, Series IV, XCI (December 16, 1901); Pedone, *Il partito socialista italiano*, I, 121, 170–1; Cosimo Ceccuti and Marcello Vannucci, eds., *Immagini nelle parole: Ugo Ojetti* (Milan, 1978), 105–17.

21 MGS to Gabriele D'Annunzio, n.d. but 1919, August 5, 1928, October 7, 1933, AVI, AG, LVIII, 3; MGS, "La fiaccola sotto il moggio," *Avanti della Domenica*, undated clipping (1905), GBP; MGS, *Acqua passata*, 8, 104–5.

22 Amedeo Sarfatti to PVC, October 17, 1986; interviews with Magalì Sarfatti-Larson, September 28, 1985, and December 11, 1986.

23 Interview with Magalì Sarfatti-Larson, December 11, 1986.

24 Seton-Watson, *Italy from Liberalism*, 192–7.

CHAPTER 5: THREE OR FOUR *PRIME DONNE*

1 Marinetti is quoted in Mario De Micheli, "Preface," in Zeno Birolli, ed., *Umberto Boccioni: Gli scritti editi e inediti* (Milan, 1971), vii–viii; Filippo T. Marinetti, *La grande Milano tradizionale e futurista* (Verona, 1969), 3–4; Boccioni diary, July 12, 1907, in *Umberto Boccioni: Gli scritti*, 249.

2 MGS, *Acqua passata*, 67.

3 MGS, *Acqua passata*, 71–2, 75, 78–9; idem, *The Life of Benito Mussolini* (London, 1925), 170–1; idem, *Dux* (Milan, 1926), 129–30; Kuliscioff to Turati, December 9, 1910, T/K, III, Part 2, 303.

4 Kuliscioff to Turati, May 26, 1908, T/K, II, Part 2, 901; Maria Giudice, "Piccole curiosità non del tutto inutile da sapersi," in Angelica Balabanoff, *Il traditore Mussolini* (Milan, 1945), 119.

5 MGS, *Acqua passata*, 74–5, 79; *Il movimento operaio italiano*, III, 19; Di Scala, *Dilemmas*, 9; Virgilio Brocchi, *Luce di grandi anime* (Verona, 1956), 143–91; Antonio Graziadei, *Memorie di trent'anni* (Rome, 1950), 41; Marinetti, *La grande Milano*, 50–1; Pieroni Bortolotti, *Socialismo e questione femminile*, 98–9.

6 Pieroni Bortolotti, *Socialismo e questione femminile*, passim; *Movimento operaio italiano*, III, 257–60, IV, 305–6.

7 *Movimento operaio italiano*, III, 228–30; MGS, *Acqua passata*, 81.

8 ESMOI, *Bibliografia del socialismo*, I, 82–3, II, 744–5, 878; Olga Molinari, *La Stampa periodica romana dal 1900 al 1926*, I (Rome, 1977), 87–8; *Gazzetta degli Artisti*, June 20, July 4, 11, 25, August 1, 8, 12, 29, September 13, 30, 1903; *Patria*, April 6, May 2, 16, 23, June 6, 13, July 3, August 2, 9, 1903; Maria Mimita Lamberti, in *Storia dell'arte italiana*, Part II, Vol. 3 (Turin, 1982), 109–110; Kuliscioff to Turati, June 1, 1909, T/K, II, Part 2, 1112; "Bibliografia degli scritti di Margherita Sarfatti sull'arte," MP.

9 Notari's other lawyers represented a range of political currents—two deputies, the Socialist Agostino Berenini and the liberal Carlo Fabbri, the republican Innocenzo Cappa, and the monarchist Ezio Molesini. Marinetti testified as one of several literary experts. MGS, "Questione di pudore o questione di estetica?," *Gazzetta di Venezia*, August 14, 1903; Walter Vaccari, *Vita e tumulti di F. T. Marinetti* (Milan, 1959), 116–28; Cesare Sarfatti, *I processi al futurismo per oltraggio di pudore: Arringhe* (Milan, 1910), 103.

10 Di Scala, *Dilemmas*, 75–85; Cortesi, *Il socialismo italiano*, 170; ACS, CPC, "Sarfatti, Cesare," no. 60867, report of April 28, 1904.

11 MGS, *The Life*, 114–15, and *Dux*, 77; Angelica Balabanoff, *My Life as a Rebel* (New York, 1938), 62; Nancy G. Eshelman, "Forging a Socialist Women's Movement: Angelica Balabanoff in Switzerland," in Betty Boyd Caroli, R. F. Harney, and L. F. Tomasi, eds., *The*

Italian Immigrant Woman in North America (Toronto, 1978), 45–7; Jane Slaughter, "Humanism versus Feminism in the Socialist Movement: The Life of Angelica Balabanoff," in Slaughter and Kern, *European Women on the Left*, 181–2; Ronald Florence, *Marx's Daughters* (New York, 1975), 161–9; "La Balabanoff," *Corriere della Sera*, November 26, 1965.

12 MGS, *Acqua passata*, 80–1.

13 Kuliscioff to Turati, February 24, 1907, T/K, II, Part 1, 498–99; Cesare Sarfatti to Andrea Costa, February 9, 1907, CP, no. 3739; ACS, CPC, no. 60867, "Sarfatti, Cesare," reports dated July 10, 1907, and July 27, 1908.

   Margherita's first article in *Avanti!* (Rome) was entitled "Incoraggiamenti al gusto artistico," August 27, 1902; another was published as "Naseide . . . Di che lacrime grandi e di che sangue," May 11, 1904. The first regular contribution appeared on February 16, 1908. Anna Nozzoli, "Margherita Sarfatti, organizzatrice di cultura," in Marina Addis Saba, ed., *La corporazione delle donne: Ricerche e studi sui modelli femminili nel ventennio* (Florence, 1988), 233–4.

14 Alloway, *The Venice Biennale*, 46; Franzina, *Venezia*, 435–6; MGS, "Questione di pudore o questione di estetica?"; *Acqua passata*, 25–37.

15 MGS, *Acqua passata*, 45–52; idem, "Menues légendes pontificales"; Luzzato, "La comunità ebraica," 186; Amedeo Sarfatti, unpublished memoir, 5, AmSP; Marzorati, *Margherita Sarfatti*, 75–81; Arturo Carlo Jemolo, *Chiesa e stato in Italia negli ultimi cento anni* (Turin, 1948), 514–19; *Dizionario biografico degli italiani*, Vol. 21, 284.

16 Interview with Magalì Sarfatti-Larson, May 18, 1988; "VI convegno sionistico italiano," *Corriere Israelitico* (February 29, 1908), 320.

17 Roth, *The History*, 520; Edgardo Morpurgo to Felice Ravenna, November 19, 1903, CZA, A353/46; "Le riunioni del Gruppo Sionistico Milanese," *L'Idea Sionistica* (November 1903), 142–3; "Il Gruppo Sionistico Milanese," *Corriere Israelitico* (December 31, 1903), 210; Marzorati, *Margherita Sarfatti*, 79, 83; Barbara W. Tuchman, *Bible and Sword: England and Palestine from the Bronze Age to Balfour* (New York, 1968), 225–8, 281–309.

18 "Quarto convegno sionistico italiano," *Corriere Israelitico* (March 31, 1904), 298–301.

19 Felice Ravenna to Federico Iarach, January 17, 1906, ACDEC, Fondo Leone e Felice Ravenna, b. 13, f. 2; Felice Ravenna, "La conferenza di Bruxelles," February 19, 1906, ibid.; "Gruppo Sionistico Milanese," *Corriere Israelitico* (January 31, 1906), 268; "La conferenza panebraica di Bruxelles," and Cesare Sarfatti, "Dopo la conferenza di Bruxelles," ibid., February 26, 1906; Jewish Territorial Organization petition, CZA, A36/44; Umberto Nahon, "La polemica antisionista del *Popolo di Roma*," in D. Carpi, A. Milano, and U. Nahon, eds., *Scritti in memoria di Enzo Sereni* (Milan-Jerusalem, 1970), 225, note; Michele Sarfatti to PVC, January 21, 1987.

20 Angelo Sullam to Felice Ravenna, December 6, 1906, CZA, A353/46; "Elezioni alla fraterna israelitica," *Gazzettino di Venezia*, December 3, 1906.

21 MGS, "Le nuove leggi sull'ordinamento della famiglia," *La difesa delle Lavoratrici*, March 8, 1914; "Quel che pensa dell'instruzione sessuale una mamma," *La Voce*, February 10, 1910; Marzorati, *Margherita Sarfatti*, 14–5, 52–3, 56, 93–4, 119–20.

22 Nino Podenzani, *Il libro di Ada Negri* (Milan, 1969), 135.

23 Interviews with Fiammetta Sarfatti Gaetani, May 16, 1985, Magalì Sarfatti-Larson, September 28, 1985, and December 4, 1986, and Pierangela Sarfatti, October 1985; MGS, "Germogli," *I vivi e l'ombra*, 18.

24 Interviews with Amedeo Sarfatti, October 1985, and Magalì Sarfatti-Larson, September 28, 1985, June 16, 1986, and May 12, 1987; Amedeo Sarfatti to PVC, January 1986.

25 MGS, "Menues légendes pontificales."

26 "Il Cav. Uff. Amedeo Grassini," *Gazzetta di Venezia*, August 30, 1908; "Per la morte del Cav. Uff. Amedeo Grassini," ibid., August 31, 1908; "I funerali del Cav. Uff. A. Grassini," ibid., September 2, 1908; "Trigesimo," *Corriere Israelitico* (Trieste), September 30, 1908.

27 Francamaria Trapani, "Dovette fuggire dall'Italia, e per lei Mussolini non mosse un dito," *Gente*, September 24, 1982, 66; Henry James, *William Wetmore Story and His Friends*, II (Boston, 1903), 330–1.

28 Ministero dell'Industria, Commercio e Lavoro, *Statistiche delle elezioni generali politiche* (Rome, 1909); Kuliscioff to Turati, February 18, 1911, T/K, Vol. III, Part 2, 411. Cesare ran as a candidate from Oleggio, near the city of Novara.

29 Kuliscioff to Turati, December 9, 1912, T/K, III, 789; Alfredo Panzini, *Roberto Sarfatti* (Piacenza, 1924), 14; Fiammetta Sarfatti Gaetani to PVC, August 7, 1986; MGS, *Acqua passata*, 98.

30 MGS to Bernard Berenson, June 4, 1951, BBP; interviews with Fiammetta Sarfatti Gaetani, July 9, 1985, and Magalì Sarfatti-Larson, September 28, 1985; Fiammetta Sarfatti Gaetani to PVC, August 7, 1986.

CHAPTER 6: PRIMITIVES OF A NEW SENSIBILITY

1 Sarfatti's account of the exhibit, related in *Acqua passata*, 93, does not date the meeting with Boccioni. In July 1908 Boccioni first showed an etching titled *La madre con l'uncinetto*, but executed and showed a number of other etchings on the same theme over the years. Sarfatti had already begun to write for *Avanti!*. It is likely, however, that the Permanente exhibit she described was the "Exhibit of Lombard Artists" that opened on April 10, 1909, since she remembered him wearing a sweater, which he would not have done in the middle of the summer. Moreover, the "Mouzik" sweater she mentioned was undoubtedly one of the articles of clothing Boccioni had brought back from a recent visit to Russia. See *Boccioni a Milano* (Milan, 1982), 320; Ester Coen, *Umberto Boccioni* (New York, 1988), xxii.

2 Sarfatti's letter, dated December 13, 1909, is cited in Maria Mimita Lamberti, "La stagione di Ca' Pesaro e le Biennali," in *Venezia: Gli anni di Ca'Pesaro, 1908–1920* (Milan, 1987), 49–50.

3 *Gazzetta degli Artisti*, June 20, July 4, 11, 25, August 1, 8, 12, 29, September 13, 30, 1903; *Patria*, April 6, May 2, 16, 23, June 6, 9, 13, 29, July 3, August 2, 9, 1903; Maria Mimita Lamberti, in *Storia dell'arte italiana*, Part II, Vol. 3 (Turin, 1982), 109–110; Giuseppe Giacosa, Pompeo Molmenti, and Ugo Ojetti, "Relazione della giuria per conferimento dei premi ai migliori studi critici sulla Va Esposizione Internazionale d'Arte di Venezia," February 7, 1904, ASACB, Va Esposizione Internazionale d'Arte di Venezia, 1903, b. 2. On Sarfatti's early connections with Fradeletto and the Biennale, see Sileno Salvagnini, "Margherita Sarfatti: Una vita nella tormenta," *Arte*, September 1991, 81, 84.

4 Kuliscioff to Turati, June 1, 1909, T/K, II, Part 2, 1112; ESMOI, *Bibliografia del socialismo*, II, 878; "Bibliografia degli scritti di Margherita Sarfatti sull'arte," MP.

5 The best treatment of the antipositivist revolt remains H. Stuart Hughes, *Consciousness and Society: The Reorientation of European Social Thought* (New York, 1958).

6 MGS, *The Life*, 156, and *Dux*, 116; MGS, *Storia della pittura moderna* (Rome, 1930), 95–6; MGS, *Segni del meridiano* (Naples, 1931), 3–4, 53–62; Walter L. Adamson, "Modernism and Fascism: The Politics of Culture in Italy, 1903–1922," *The American Historical Review*, April 1990, 365, 370–1.

7 See the anthologies titled *La Voce (1908–1914)*, ed. Angelo Romano (Turin, 1960), and *La Voce, 1908–1916*, ed. Giansiro Ferrata (Rome, 1961); Giovanni Papini, "L'Italia risponde," *La Voce*, December 20, 1908, 2; Emilio Gentile, "Fascism As Political Religion," *Journal of Contemporary History*, May–June 1991, 232.

8 Nozzoli, "Margherita Sarfatti," 240–8; Sarfatti's correspondence with the Orvieto brothers is in the FAO, ACGV, f. "Margherita Sarfatti."

9 MGS to Prezzolini, January 14, March 20, 1909, October 10, December 2, 1910, June 6, July 24, 1911, February 6, February 10, March 11, 1912, August 24, 1913, PP; Cesare Sarfatti to Prezzolini, November 2, 1910, PP; Giuseppe Prezzolini, *Il Tempo della Voce* (Milan-Florence, 1960), 206–07; Sarfatti's coverage of the Ninth Biennale appeared in *Avanti!*, May 9, 30, July 18, 27, 28, August 1, 1909.

10 Marianne W. Martin, *Futurist Art and Theory, 1909–1915* (New York, 1978), 8–9; Severino Pagani, *La pittura lombarda della scapigliatura* (Milan, 1955); MGS, *Daniele Ranzoni* (Rome, 1935), and *Segni, colori, e luci*, 81–91.

11 Martin, *Futurist Art and Theory*, 9–13; *Gazzetta di Venezia*, January 17, 1904, *Avanti della Domenica*, May 7, June 18, 1905, *L'Adriatico*, September 5, 1905, September 23, 1906, *Il Tempo*, July 20, September 2, 1906; MGS, *Le opere di Gaetano Previati dell'associazione nazionale fra mutilati ed invalidi di guerra* (Milan, 1927), 12; Rossana Bossaglia, *Il "Novecento italiano"* (Milan, 1979), 210; MGS, "Le esposizioni alla famiglia artistica," *Avanti!,* January 1, 1914. Margherita's coverage of the Sixth Biennale appeared in *L'Adriatico*, May–July 1905.

12 MGS to Bernard Berenson, July 24, 1952, BBP.

13 MGS, "Fernand Khnopff," *Il Rinascimento* (Milan), April 1906, 57–66. On her criticism see also S. Ludovici, ed., *Storici, teorici e critici delle arti figurative*, Series IV (Rome, 1942), 326.

14 First Futurist Manifesto, published February 20, 1909, quoted from Luciano De Maria, ed., *Marinetti e il futurismo* (Milan, 1981), 5–8; for "Contro Venezia passatista" see ibid., 26–30; MGS, *Acqua passata*, 99–100; Amedeo Sarfatti, unpublished memoir, 9, AmSP.

15 Quoted in James Joll, *Three Intellectuals in Politics* (New York, 1965), 141.

16 MGS, *Acqua passata*, 97; MGS, *Storia della pittura moderna*, 95–6; F. T. Marinetti, "Contro l'amore e il parlamentarismo," now in De Maria, *Marinetti e il futurismo*, 42–6; Maria Antonietta Macciocchi, *La donna nera: Consenso femminile e fascismo* (Milan, 1976), 145–54; Denise Detragiache, "Il fascismo femminile da San Sepolcro all'affare Matteotti," *Storia Contemporanea*, XIV, 2 (April 1983), 215.

17 MGS, *Acqua passata*, 88; Carlo Carrà, *La mia vita* (Milan, 1981; originally published in 1942), 14–57; Birolli, *Umberto Boccioni: Gli scritti*, 276–7; Enrico Crispolti, *Storia e critica del futurismo* (Rome-Bari, 1986), 8; Catalogue of *Arte e socialità in Italia dal realismo al simbolismo, 1865–1915* (Milan, June–September 1979); ESMOI, *Bibliografia del socialismo*, I, 82.

18 The two manifestos of Futurist painters are in De Maria, *Marinetti e il futurismo*, 20–5. On Futurism see also Claudia Salaris, *Storia del futurismo* (Rome, 1985); M. Drudi Gambillo and T. Fiori, *Archivi del futurismo*, 2 vols. (Rome, 1958–62); Maurizio Calvesi, *Il futurismo*, 3 vols. (Milan, 1967); Marjorie Perloff, *The Futurist Movement: Avant-Garde, Avant Guerre, and the Language of Rupture* (Chicago, 1986); MGS, *Acqua passata*, 97.

19 Luigi Freddi, *Il cinema*, I (Rome, 1949), 149–50. On the Mafarka trial see Vaccari, *Vita e tumulti di F. T. Marinetti*, 239–46; Marinetti, *La grande Milano*, 102–3; idem, "Guerra sola igiene del mondo" (1915), in *Teoria e invenzione futurista*, ed. Luciano De Maria (Milan, 1983), 240–1; idem, "Processo di Mafarka il futurista," ibid., 586–7; Emilio R. Papa, *Fascismo e cultura* (Padova, 1974), 53–4; Cesare Rossi, *Personaggi di ieri e di oggi* (Milan, 1960), 183–8; Marinetti to Francesco B. Pratella, September 28, 1910, in Giovanni Lugaresi, ed., *Lettere ruggenti a F. Balilla Pratella* (Milan, 1969), 15.

20 The text of Cesare Sarfatti's speech is in *I processi al futurismo per oltraggio al pudore*, 88–115, republished in the appendix of Marinetti's *Distruzione* (Milan, 1920), 321–45; Palazzeschi to Marinetti, January 1911, in *Carteggio Marinetti–Aldo Palazzeschi* (Milan, 1978), 34.

21 "Judith," "She Is the Comrade of Il Duce," 657; Ardengo Soffici, "Risposta ai futuristi," *La Voce*, May 19, 1910; MGS to Prezzolini, May 23, 1910, PP, "Margherita G. Sarfatti" folder; Lamberti, in *Storia dell'arte italiana*, Part II, Vol. 3, 127–35.

22 MGS, "L'esposizione intima alla famiglia artistica," *Avanti!*, December 13, 1911; Boccioni to Vico Baer, March 15, 1912, in Birolli, *Umberto Boccioni: Gli scritti*, 272, and the original in MoMA, Special Collections, Boccioni Letters.

23 Conversation between Emily Braun and Lydia Winston Malbin as related to authors; Maurizio Calvesi and Ester Coen, *Boccioni: L'opera completa* (Milan, 1982), 229, 244, 260, 304, 416, 551; Gianfranco Bruno, ed., *L'opera completa di Boccioni* (Milan, 1969), 102; Guido Ballo, *Boccioni: La vita e l'opera* (Milan, 1964), illustrations 251–58; Coen, *Umberto Boccioni*, 83; Amedeo Sarfatti, unpublished memoir, 8, AmSP; Carla Porta Musa, "Il Soldo e Margherita Sarfatti," *Il Foglietto* (Foggia), February 7, 1957; interview with Amedeo Sarfatti, May 24, 1985; Alberto Longatti, "Cavallasca, ritrovo di 'stelle,'" in Beniamino Fargnoli, ed., *Cavallasca* (Como, n.d.), 126.

24 Carrà, *La mia vita*, 82; Bruno, *L'opera completa di Boccioni*, 100–1; Calvesi and Coen, *Boccioni*, 302–3; interview with Amedeo Sarfatti, October 1985; memo, Alfred H. Barr to Bernard

Karpel, October 16, 1958, MoMA, Museum Collections, "Boccioni—General"; Coen, *Umberto Boccioni*, 186.

25 Emilio Settimelli, *Edda contro Benito* (Rome, 1952), 81–2.

26 Interviews with Fiammetta Sarfatti Gaetani, May 13, 1985, Amedeo Sarfatti, October 1985, and Magalì Sarfatti-Larson, June 16, 1986; Fiammetta Sarfatti Gaetani to PVC, August 7, 1986; Panzini, *Roberto Sarfatti*, 8–9; Podenzani, *Il libro di Ada Negri*, 135; Luigi Maria Personè, *Le belle statuine* (Florence, 1930), 288–91.

27 MGS, *Acqua passata*, 99; interviews with Amedeo and Pierangela Sarfatti, October 1985; Podenzani, *Il libro di Ada Negri*, 138.

28 Interviews with Fiammetta Sarfatti Gaetani, May 16, 1985, and Pierangela Sarfatti, May 24, 1985; Carrà, *La mia vita*, 144; Pieroni Bortolotti, *Socialismo e questione femminile*, 98–9; Victoria de Grazia, "Il fascino del priapo," 149–52; MGS, *The Life*, 170–1.

29 Ada Negri, "Sacra infanzia: A Ersilia Maino," in *Maternità*, in *Poesie* (Verona, 1948), 347. The two best treatments of Negri's life are Podenzani, *Il libro di Ada Negri*, and Salvatore Comes, *Ada Negri da un tempo all'altro* (Verona, 1970).

30 Podenzani, *Il libro di Ada Negri*, 135–6, 139–40; Ada Negri, "A Margherita Sarfatti," dedication to *Le solitarie* (Milan, 1917); see also Negri's poem "Fiammetta vestita di verde," in *Poesie*, 938–9, and "La gioia," ibid., 372; Carla Porta Musa, "Il Soldo e Margherita Sarfatti," *Il Foglietto* (Foggia), February 7, 1957.

The description of the often stormy relationship between Margherita and Negri is based on Margherita's letters to the poet in GSP.

CHAPTER 7: A WONDERFUL LEAN YOUNG MAN

1 MGS, *Dux*, 129–32; *Avanti!*, September 30, 1911.

2 Prezzolini, "A Tripoli," *La Voce*, October 5, 1911.

3 Prezzolini, "Perchè non si deve andare a Tripoli," *La Voce*, August 17, 1911, 1; idem, "L'illusione tripolina," *La Voce*, May 11, 1911; Luigi Albertini, *Venti anni di vita politica*, 5 vols. (Bologna, 1950–53), I, Part 2, 116–7, 123–4; Maurice Simon, ed., *Speeches, Articles and Letters of Israel Zangwill* (London, 1937), 292–308; Joseph Leftwich, *Israel Zangwill* (New York, 1957), 216; Stuart A. Cohen, *English Zionists and British Jews: The Communal Politics of Anglo-Jewry, 1895–1920* (Princeton, 1982), 85–7, 101–3; Seton-Watson, *Italy from Liberalism*, 364–5.

4 MGS, *Acqua passata*, 72; Di Scala, *Dilemmas*, 77–8, 107, 121–4; Seton-Watson, *Italy from Liberalism*, 237–83.

5 MGS, *The Life*, 170–2; idem, *Acqua passata*, 73, 82.

6 MGS to Prezzolini, February 6, 1912, PP; Maurizio Degl'Innocenti, *Il socialismo italiano e la guerra di Libia* (Rome, 1976), 224–5; Fausto Torrefranco, "In Germania," *La Voce*, January 18, 1912; MGS, "L'utopia pacifista," January 20, 1912, "Lezioni di gentilezza," February 4, 1912, "Passa la civiltà . . . ," April 7, 1912, "Madri dolorosi," July 7, 1912, all in *La Difesa delle Lavoratrici*.

7 *Avanti!*, October 18, 1911; Giuseppe Mammarella, *Riformisti e rivoluzionari nel Partito Socialista Italiano 1900–1912* (Florence, 1968), 315–24; Luigi Cortesi, *Le origini del PCI* (Bari, 1972), 18–21.

8 Di Scala, *Dilemmas*, 131–2.

9 Renzo De Felice, *Mussolini il rivoluzionario* (Turin, 1965), 1–9; MGS, *The Life*, 20–1, 35.

10 MGS, *The Life*, 57, 77–81, 105, 232; idem, *Dux*, 39–40, 46, 73, 91–2, 203; Luigi Preti, *Mussolini giovane* (Milan, 1982), 10–11.

11 De Felice, *Mussolini il rivoluzionario*, 22–25; Ivone Kirkpatrick, *Mussolini: A Study in Power* (New York, 1964), 29–37; MGS, *The Life*, 82–92, 98–114.

12 Balabanoff, *Il traditore Mussolini*, 24.

13 Balabanoff, *Il traditore Mussolini*, 24–32; idem, *My Life as a Rebel*, 42–52; idem, *Errinerungen und Erlebnisse* (Berlin, 1927), 76–7; MGS, *The Life*, 32–3, 114–5; Leda Rafanelli, *Una donna*

e Mussolini (Milan, 1975), 52; De Felice, *Mussolini il rivoluzionario*, 25–7; Preti, *Mussolini giovane*, 13.

14 MGS to Mussolini, July 15, 1922, GSP; MGS, *The Life*, 29; Quinto Navarra, *Memorie del cameriere di Mussolini* (Milan, 1972), 223; Hugh Baillie, *High Tension* (New York, 1959), 95; *The Empire at Bay: The Leo Amery Diaries, 1929–1945*, eds. John Barnes and David Nicholson (London, 1989), 503.

For visual evidence of Mussolini's eyes, see Renzo De Felice and Luigi Goglia, *Mussolini: Il mito* (Bari, 1983), photographs nos. 14–6, 20, 27–9.

Frank Fox, *Italy To-Day* (New York, 1927), 89; Navarra, *Memorie*, 223; Giuseppe Bottai, *Diario, 1944–1948*, ed. Giordano Bruno Guerri, (Milan, 1988), 214, 316; MGS, "Benito Mussolini Predicted: 'I Shall Make My Mark on This Epoch, For I Have the Will and the Desire,'" *New York American*, March 15, 1931.

15 Eshelman, "Forging a Socialist Women's Movement," 58–65; Balabanoff, *My Life as a Rebel*, 51; Graziadei, *Memorie*, 116–17; Bottai, *Diario, 1944–1948*, 316; NMBP, MGS to Butler, n.d. but June–July 1935, letter beginning "How very kind . . ."

16 Balabanoff, *My Life as a Rebel*, 45–7.

17 Preti, *Mussolini giovane*, 12; MGS, *The Life*, 47, 60–1, 101–2, 141–3; Balabanoff, *My Life as a Rebel*, 46; De Felice, *Mussolini il rivoluzionario*, 37–8; Indro Montanelli, *L'Italia in camicia nera* (Milan, 1976), 21.

18 Eshelman, "Forging a Socialist Women's Movement," 55; Balabanoff, *My Life as a Rebel*, 43–5, 47, 49; idem, *Il traditore*, 30–4; idem, *Errinerungen*, 76–7; Preti, *Mussolini giovane*, 13.

19 Preti, *Mussolini giovane*, 22–4; Denis Mack Smith, *Mussolini* (New York, 1983), 9; Giorgio Pini and Duilio Susmel, *Mussolini: L'uomo e l'opera*, 4 vols. (Florence, 1953–55), I, 94.

20 Kirkpatrick, *Mussolini*, 39–40, Mack Smith, *Mussolini*, 9–13; De Felice, *Mussolini il rivoluzionario*, 46–61.

21 Seton-Watson, *Italy from Liberalism*, 284–306, 325–38, 342–65.

22 Gaetano Arfè, "Cesare Battisti," *Dizionario biografico degli italiani*, Vol. 7, 265–9.

23 MGS, *Dux*, 97–8; idem, *The Life*, 146; Antonio Spinosa, *I figli del duce* (Milan, 1983), 23; De Felice, *Mussolini il rivoluzionario*, 62–75; Mack Smith, *Mussolini*, 13–23; OO, II, 5–252.

24 De Felice, *Mussolini il rivoluzionario*, 79–82, 94.

25 Cortesi, *Il socialismo italiano*, 350–1; De Felice, *Mussolini il rivoluzionario*, 84–9; MGS, *The Life*, 162; OO, III, 5–207; OO, IV, 5–99, 113–228; OO, XXXV, 13–19; Gaudens Megaro, *Mussolini in the Making* (New York, 1967), 187; Ernst Nolte, *Faschismus in seiner Epoche* (Munich, 1963), 204.

26 De Felice, *Mussolini il rivoluzionario*, 76–8; OO, II, 53–6, 146, 265, 269; OO, XXXIII, 151–213.

27 De Felice, *Mussolini il rivoluzionario*, 75–6; OO, XXXIII, 4–147.

28 De Felice, *Mussolini il rivoluzionario*, 83, 95, 100.

29 De Felice, *Mussolini il rivoluzionario*, 95–6; Cortesi, *Il socialismo italiano*, 350–2; Michele Terzaghi, *Fascismo e massoneria* (Milan, 1950), 11–12; OO, III, 256–8.

30 MGS, *Dux*, 137; BP, Diary entry for December 29, 1951; De Felice and Goglia, *Mussolini: Il mito*, photographs nos. 19, 20, 22, 33.

31 MGS, *The Life*, 172–3; Di Scala, *Dilemmas*, 135–7; OO, IV, 102–3; De Felice, *Mussolini il rivoluzionario*, 105–9.

32 OO, IV, 74; De Felice, *Mussolini il rivoluzionario*, 96–110; Cortesi, *Il socialismo italiano*, 421–3.

33 OO, IV, 123; De Felice, *Mussolini il rivoluzionario*, 110–25; Cortesi, *Il socialismo italiano*, 373–81; Di Scala, *Dilemmas*, 137–43; Seton-Watson, *Italy from Liberalism*, 372–3.

34 Di Scala, *Dilemmas*, 117–9; MGS, "Il suffragio amministrativo femminile: Prima e adesso," *Gerarchia*, May 1925, 291–2; Cortesi, *Il socialismo italiano*, 344, 397; Springer, "Anna Kuliscioff," 22.

35 ESMOI, I, 256–57; MGS, *Acqua passata*, 81; MGS, "L'utopia pacifista," January 20, 1912, "Lezioni di gentilezza," February 4, 1912, "Passa la civiltà . . . ," April 7, 1912, "Madri dolorosi," July 7, 1912, all in *La Difesa delle Lavoratrici*; MGS to Prezzolini, letters numbered 12 and 13, n.d. [but 1912], May 30, 1912, PP; Birolli, *Umberto Boccioni: Gli scritti*, 273.

36 De Felice, *Mussolini il rivoluzionario*, 125; Degl'Innocenti, *Il socialismo*, 224–5.

37 OO, IV, 161–70.

38 MGS, *Dux*, 137–8; idem, *The Life*, 176; Francamaria Trapani, "Mia madre Margherita Sarfatti, Pa grande passione di Mussolini," *Gente*, September 10, 1982, 42; Cortesi, *Il socialismo italiano*, 509; OO, IV, 292–3.

39 De Felice, *Mussolini il rivoluzionario*, 125–36; Di Scala, *Dilemmas*, 143–6; Cortesi, *Il socialismo italiano*, 522–9, 545–8; Eshelman, "Forging a Socialist Women's Movement," 66; MGS, *The Life*, 176–7; Balabanoff, *My Life as a Rebel*, 98–100; idem, *Il traditore Mussolini*, 69–80; Kirkpatrick, *Mussolini*, 52–3.

40 De Felice, *Mussolini il rivoluzionario*, 136–40.

41 MGS, "Echi del presente e voci della 'Città Futura,' " September 22, 1912, "Voce della 'Città Futura,' " October 6, 1912, both in *La Difesa delle Lavoratrici*; idem, *Acqua passata*, 81; Springer, "Anna Kuliscioff," 18; T/K, III, Part 1, 781. Sarfatti's translation of the memoirs of Adelaide Popp continued to appear in *La Difesa delle Lavoratrici* until January 1913.

42 MGS, *Dux*, 138; Pini and Susmel, *Mussolini*, I, 193; De Felice and Goglia, *Mussolini: Il mito*, photographs nos. 24, 27; Cesare Rossi, *Mussolini com'era* (Rome, 1947), 239–40.

It remains unclear when Sarfatti first met Mussolini. In her memoirs of Mussolini written in the mid-1940s, *Mussolini: Como lo conocí*, she claims variously to have heard of him in September-October 1911 and that their "friendship" dated from that time. However, in December 1951, she told her friends George and Helene Biddle that she met Mussolini in 1909. Elsewhere, she claims to have encountered him in Milan in November-December 1912. MGS, *Mussolini: Como lo conocí*, I and VII; BP, diary entry for December 29, 1951; MGS, *Dux*, 138; Pini and Susmel, *Mussolini*, I, 193.

43 MGS, *Dux*, 144; idem, *The Life*, 177; idem, *Mussolini: Como lo conocí*, I; George Seldes, "Dictators' Day Off," *Saturday Evening Post*, August 18, 1934, 68.

44 T/K, III, Part 1, 781, 789, 796–7, 799; MGS, *Dux*, 144.

45 MGS, *Dux*, 144; Marzorati, *Margherita Sarfatti*, 51.

46 Corrado Alvaro, *Quasi una vita: Giornale di uno scrittore*, 2d ed. (Milan-Rome, 1951), 111.

CHAPTER 8: THE NEGATION OF SOCIALISM

1 MGS, *The Life*, 176–7; idem, *Mussolini: Como lo conocí*, I, VI, and IX.

2 OO, V, 52–69; De Felice, *Mussolini il rivoluzionario*, 145–6; Preti, *Mussolini giovane*, 139–40; Gherardo Bozzetti, *Mussolini direttore dell'Avanti!* (Milan, 1979), 97–9.

3 OO, V, 143; De Felice, *Mussolini il rivoluzionario*, 146–68; Preti, *Mussolini giovane*, 140–9; Cortesi, *Il socialismo italiano*, 61–4.

4 MGS, *Mussolini: Como lo conocí*, V; idem, "Benito Mussolini Predicted: 'I Shall Make My Mark,' " *New York American*, March 15, 1931; Edda Ciano, *La mia testimonianza* (Milan, 1975), 31–2; Thomas B. Morgan, *Spurs on the Boot*, 112, 114; Guido Orlando, *Confessions of a Scoundrel*, 73. Rafanelli, *Una donna*, 7–20, 49–53.

5 MGS to Prezzolini, May 2, 1913, PP; Constance Rover, *Women's Suffrage and Party Politics in Britain, 1866–1914* (London, 1967), 121–97; Andrew Rosen, *Rise Up, Women!* (London, 1974), 79–224; Edith Zangwill to Annie Russell, May 3, 1909, August 9, 1909, August 13, 1909, December 8, 1910, August 12, 1911, February 4, 1914, RP; "The Government and the Suffragettes," *The Manchester Guardian*, April 30, 1913.

6 MGS, "Le suffragiste inglesi," *La Voce*, October 2, 1913; MGS to Prezzolini, September 20, 1913, letter no. 22, n.d. (but 1913), PP.

7 Gino Severini, *La vita di un pittore* (Milan, 1965), 145, 181–2.

8 MGS to Prezzolini, May 2, 1913, June 15, 1913, PP; Vincenzo Cardarelli, "Charles Péguy," *La Voce*, September 7, 1911; Giuseppe Prezzolini, *Diario, 1900–1941* (Milan, 1978), 90, 131; Charles Péguy, "La tapisserie de Sainte Genevieve e de Jeanne d'Arc," *La Voce*, November 21, 1912; Hans A. Schmitt, *Charles Péguy: The Decline of an Idealist* (Baton Rouge, 1967); F. C. St. Aubyn, *Charles Péguy* (Boston, 1977).

9   "Canudo, Ricciotto," in *Dizionario biografico degli italiani*, Vol. 18, 346–9; Ardengo Soffici, *Fine di un mondo*, IV (Florence, 1955), 405; Lolo de la Torriente, *Memoria y razón de Diego Rivera*, I (Mexico City, 1959), 340. Rivera does not give a date for his first meeting with Sarfatti, but it must have been sometime between November 1909 and June 1910, during his first lengthy stay in Paris. On Rivera in Paris see Bertram D. Wolfe, *The Fabulous Life of Diego Rivera* (New York, 1984), 64–75.

10 Diego Rivera with Gladys March, *My Art, My Life: An Autobiography* (New York, 1960), 220; de la Torriente, *Memoria y razón*, 340; Claudia Salaris, "Saint Point, Valentine de," in *Futurismo e futurismi* (Milan, 1986), 562.

11 Interview with Magalì Sarfatti-Larson, June 16, 1986; Marzorati, *Margherita Sarfatti*, 107.

12 Salaris, "Saint-Point, Valentine de," and "Women, Futurist," *Futurismo e futurismi*, 602–3, italics in original; Germano Celant, "Love and Sexuality," ibid., 503–4; Caroline Tisdall and Angelo Bozzolla, *Futurism* (London, 1977), 153–63.

13 "Why New York Must Become the New Paris," *The New York Times*, February 4, 1917; *Montjoie!* (February 10, 1913), 1.

14 MGS to Prezzolini, June 3, 1913, July 4, 1913, July 31, 1913, August 5, 1913, August 24, 1913, September 20, 1913, letter no. 22, PP; "Il voto alle donne," *La Voce*, June 26, 1913; F. Agnoletti, "Il voto alle donne," *La Voce*, August 14, 1913.

15 De Felice, *Mussolini il rivoluzionario*, 169; Preti, *Mussolini giovane*, 149–57; Seton-Watson, *Italy from Liberalism*, 378–9, 396–403; Cortesi, *Il socialismo italiano*, 64–6; Bozzetti, *Mussolini direttore*, 100–10.

16 MGS to Prezzolini, July 4, 1913, PP; Cortesi, *Il socialismo italiano*, 57.

17 Anita Pensotti, *Rachele* (Milan, 1983), 23; Balabanoff, *Il traditore Mussolini*, 142–6; Bozzetti, *Mussolini direttore*, 115–16; Preti, *Mussolini giovane*, 157–8; Vahdah Jeanne Bordeux, *Benito Mussolini: The Man* (London, 1927), 94–5. Sarfatti was almost certainly Bordeux's source for her information on Balabanoff.

18 De Felice, *Mussolini il rivoluzionario*, 172–6; OO, V, 235–351; Preti, *Mussolini giovane*, 158–70; Seton-Watson, *Italy from Liberalism*, 385–8.

19 MGS, "Le scuole nell'Agro di Roma," *La Voce*, August 21, 1913; idem, "Le suffragiste inglesi."

20 "Corrispondenze da Como," *La Difesa delle Lavoratrici*, November 2, 1913; MGS, "Perchè le donne han bisogno del voto," *La Difesa delle Lavoratrici*, November 16, 1913.

CHAPTER 9: RED WEEK

1   De Felice, *Mussolini il rivoluzionario*, 171; "Judith," "She Is the Comrade of Il Duce," 600; *Statistiche delle elezioni generali politiche* (Rome, 1913); *Atti Parlamentari. Camera dei Deputati. Legislatura XXIV. Sessione 1913–14. Documenti. Disegni di legge e relazione*, Doc. V, n. 21; ibid., *la Sessione. Discussioni*, 4140–44; "Un impegno scritto dell'on. Sarfatti," *Corriere della Sera*, November 4, 1913; "Il caso singolare di Oleggio," *Corriere della Sera*, November 5, 1913; "L'on. Sarfatti dismissionario," *Avanti!*, November 6, 1913; "Le organizzazione socialiste del collegio di Oleggio e l'elezione dell'on. Sarfatti," *Avanti!*, November 18, 1913; ACS, CPC, no. 60867, "Sarfatti, Cesare," prefect report of November 8, 1913.

2   Panzini, *Roberto Sarfatti*, 6–9; interview with Amedeo Sarfatti, October 1985; MGS, *Dux*, 76–7; Balabanoff, *My Life as a Rebel*, 55–6.

3   Rafanelli, *Una donna*, 108–11, 120; Renzo De Felice, "Presentazione," *Utopia* (reprint, Milan, 1973), ix; Michel Trebitsch, "Six lettres de Mussolini à Jean-Richard Bloch (1913–1914)," *Revue d'histoire moderne et contemporaine*, April–June 1987, 313; MGS, *The Life*, 187–9; idem, "Le esposizioni alla famiglia artistica," *Avanti!*, January 1, 1914; "Fiori, pittura e donne," *Avanti!*, March 22, 1914; "La mostra della sezione artistica al lyceum femminile," *Avanti!*, March 25, 1914; "Sua maestà l'onore!" *Avanti!*, June 4, 1914; "I pittori delle 'nuove tendenze' alla famiglia artistica di Milano," *Avanti!*, June 17, 1914; "Clericalismo vecchio e nuovo," *Utopia*, January 30, 1914; "Confronti," *Utopia*, March 15–30, 1914; Mussolini, unsigned comment on "Sua maestà l'onore!," *Avanti!*, June 4, 1914.

4 Giudice, "Piccole curiosità," 115.

5 Seton-Watson, *Italy from Liberalism,* 390–2.

6 OO, VI, 35–6; ACS, COM, b. 11, f. 22, sf. 17, "Cesare Sarfatti"; Morgari to Sarfatti, February (?), 1914; Sarfatti to Morgari, February 9, 1914; Sarfatti to Morgari, March 2, 1914; Sarfatti to Morgari, March 11, 1914; *Atti Parlamentari. Camera dei Deputati. Legislatura XXIV. Sessione 1913–14. Documenti. Disegni di legge e relazione,* Doc. V, n. 21; ibid., *1a Sessione. Discussioni. Tornata del 13 giugno 1914,* 4144.

7 Pini and Susmel, *Mussolini,* I, 220–2; OO, VI, 142–5; MGS, *The Life,* 181–3; idem, *Dux,* 142–4; Rafanelli, *Una donna,* 122–4; Francesco Bonavita, *Mussolini svelato* (Milan, 1924), 146–7; Luigi Lotti, *La settimana rossa* (Florence, 1972), 54; De Felice, *Mussolini il rivoluzionario,* 180.

8 Emilio Gentile, *Mussolini e La Voce* (Florence, 1976), 18.

9 De Felice, *Mussolini il rivoluzionario,* 181; "Judith," "She Is the Comrade of Il Duce," 600; Mussolini interview with Andrea Rovesz of November 17, 1925, reported in PRO, FO 371/10785 75511.

10 De Felice, *Mussolini il rivoluzionario,* 175–6, 189; Cortesi, *Il socialismo italiano,* 549; Clark, *Modern Italy,* 51–4, 166; Seton-Watson, *Italy from Liberalism,* 284; Lucio Ceva, *Le forze armate* (Turin, 1981), 98, 119–20.

11 De Felice, *Mussolini il rivoluzionario,* 188–95; Cortesi, *Il socialismo italiano,* 559–610; MGS to Prezzolini, July 4, 1913, PP; Pedone, *Il partito socialista,* II, 242–3, 247–8; MGS, *The Life,* 177–8.

12 Lotti, *La settimana rossa,* 61–241; Cesare Rossi, *Mussolini com'era* (Rome, 1947), 59–60; *Chi è?* (Rome, 1940), 13.

13 Lotti, *La settimana rossa,* 242–70; OO, VI, 227–9; De Felice, *Mussolini il rivoluzionario,* 206–20; MGS, *The Life,* 190–2.

14 Giuseppe Prezzolini, "An Aristocracy of Brigands," in Adrian Lyttelton, ed., *Italian Fascism* (New York, 1973), 126; Seton-Watson, *Italy from Liberalism,* 395; Clark, *Modern Italy,* 180.

15 *Atti Parlamentari, Camera dei Deputati. Legislatura XXIV. Sessione 1913–14. Documenti. Disegni di legge e relazione,* Doc. V, n. 21; ibid., *1a Sessione. Discussioni. Tornata del 13 giugno 1914,* 4144; "Il processo Sarfatti 'Perseveranza,' " *Avanti!,* July 2, 1914.

16 "Il processo Sarfatti 'Perseveranza,' " *Avanti!,* July 2, 1914; *Atti parlamentari.* ibid., *Tornata del giugno 1914,* 4144, 4151, 4158; Balabanoff, *My Life as a Rebel,* 56; OO, VI, 176; Seton-Watson, *Italy from Liberalism,* 395; "I candidati socialisti," *Avanti!,* June 14, 1914; *Avanti!,* June 16, 1914; *Statistiche delle elezioni generali politiche* (Rome, 1914).

17 Rafanelli, *Una donna,* 149; MGS, *The Life,* 191.

18 MGS, "Confronti," *Utopia;* idem, "Perchè le donne han bisogno del voto," November 16, 1913; "Racconto di Natale," January 4, 1914; "I cani . . . e le altre bestie," February 15, 1914; "Le nuove leggi sull' ordinamento della famiglia," March 8, 1914, all in *La Difesa delle Lavoratrici.*

19 Sergio Panunzio, "Il lato teorico e il lato pratico del socialismo," *Utopia,* May 15–30, 1914, 205; De Felice, *Mussolini il rivoluzionario,* 195–7, 217–18.

CHAPTER 10: NEUTRALISTS OR NOT?

1 The other painters represented in the exhibit were Adriana Bisi Fabbri (Boccioni's cousin), Alma Fidora, Marcello Nizzoli, and the sculptor Giovanni Possamai. Crispolti, *Storia e critica,* 130–62; Salaris, *Storia del futurismo,* 61–2; P. Thea et al., *Nuove tendenze: Milano e l'altro futurismo* (Milan, 1980), and the accompanying volume of *Documenti* by the same title.

 Shortly after the exhibit, Funi, Dudreville, and Erba all made formal requests to join the Futurist movement.

2 Crispolti, *Storia e critica,* 23, 131–4, 144–5; Giulio Arata's review, originally in *Pagine d'Arte,* August 30, 1914, is now republished in *Nuove tendenze: Milano e l'altro futurismo. Documenti,* 37–9.

3 MGS, *La fiaccola accesa* (Milan, 1919), 218; idem, *Achille Funi* (Milan, 1925), 13–15.

4 MGS, "I pittori delle 'nuove tendenze' alla famiglia artistica di Milano," *Avanti!*, June 17, 1914.

5 Sarfatti had written her last article for Kuliscioff's *La Difesa delle Lavoratrici* and in early June wrote an appeal on behalf of the thousands of Russian political prisoners "buried alive" in the frozen wastes of Siberia. MGS, "Dal sepolcro dei vivi," June 9, 1914, and "I pittori delle nuove tendenze," June 17, 1914, both in *Avanti!*.

6 MGS, *Dux*, 151–2.

7 MGS, *Dux*, 152–3; De Felice, *Mussolini il rivoluzionario*, 221–6; Leo Valiani, *Il partito socialista italiano nel periodo della neutralità, 1914–1915* (Milan, 1963), 8–9; OO, VI, 286–7.

8 MGS, *Dux*, 157–8; idem, *The Life*, 194; Harvey Goldberg, *The Life of Jean Jaurès* (Madison, Wis., 1962), 442, 464–72; Carrà, *La mia vita*, 121; Pini and Susmel, *Mussolini*, I, 236; Cesare Sarfatti's eulogy of Jaurès is in *Avanti!*, August 11, 1914; Marzorati, *Margherita Sarfatti*, 84.

9 Valiani, *Il partito socialista*, 23, 56, 58, 67–8; De Felice, *Mussolini il rivoluzionario*, 227; Pini and Susmel, *Mussolini*, I, 221; Carlo Pinzani, *Jaurès, l'Internazionale e la guerra* (Bari, 1970), 105–6, 117–20; Brunello Vigezzi, *L'Italia di fronte alla prima guerra mondiale*, I, *L'Italia neutrale* (Naples, 1966).

10 De Felice, *Mussolini il rivoluzionario*, 233–9, 242–3; Orietta Lupo, "I sindacalisti rivoluzionari nel 1914," *Rivista storica del socialismo*, Vol. X, 43–82; Valiani, *Il partito socialista*, 48–54.

11 "Note di guerra," OO, VI, 321–5; MGS, *Dux*, 153.
   Mussolini and Margherita may also have had in mind Marinetti's denunciation of the *Tango* as "a sentimental, decadent, paralytic romanticism" and *Parsifal*'s "dehumanizing" self-denial. See Marinetti's circular, "Down with the Tango and Parsifal," January 11, 1914, in De Maria, *Marinetti e il futurismo*, 138–40. A year earlier, Gino Severini had also executed a number of paintings entitled *Argentine Tango*.

12 Edvige Mussolini, *Mio fratello Benito* (Florence, 1957), 163–4, 230–1; Giuseppe A. Borgese, *Goliath: The March of Fascism* (New York, 1938), 195–6.

13 Ada Negri, *Orazioni* (Milan, 1918), 136; Amedeo Sarfatti to PVC, October 17, 1986; MGS, "L'utopia pacifista," January 20, 1912, and "Madri dolorose," July 7, 1912, in *La Difesa delle Lavoratrici*.

14 Amedeo Sarfatti to PVC, October 17, 1986; *Avanti!*, August 4, 1914; MGS, *The Life*, 211; *La Voce*, August 28, 1914; *Avanti!*, August 30, 1914; MGS, *Acqua passata*, 88; MGS, *La milizia femminile in Francia* (Milan, 1915), 67.

15 James L. Stokesbury, *A Short History of World War I* (New York, 1981), 51–6.

16 Cesare Rossi, *Trentatrè vicende mussoliniane* (Milan, 1958), 83; MGS, *The Life*, 196–7; idem, *Dux*, 159–60; Valiani, *Il partito socialista*, 40; De Felice, *Mussolini il rivoluzionario*, 243–5, 257; OO, VI, 354–8; Margherita's motion was reported in "Alla sezione socialista," *Avanti!*, September 10, 1914; Pini and Susmel, *Mussolini*, I, 246.

17 Boccioni's letters of September 15, 19, 22, 1914, in Birolli, *Umberto Boccioni: Gli scritti*, 375–7; Crispolti, *Storia e critica*, 178–81; De Felice, *Mussolini*, 249; on the attitudes of Italian artists and intellectuals toward the war, see Ugo Leonzio, ed., *La grande guerra vista dagli artisti* (Rome, n.d.), and Luisa Mangoni, *L'interventismo della cultura* (Rome-Bari, 1974).

18 De Felice, *Mussolini il rivoluzionario*, 258–80; Valiani, *Il partito socialista*, 41–53; Pini and Susmel, *Mussolini*, I, 249; Rafanelli, *Una donna*, 272–80.

19 "Dalla neutralità assoluta alla neutralità attiva ed operante," *Avanti!*, October 18, 1914, reprinted in OO, VI, 393–403; Marzorati, *Margherita Sarfatti*, 62–3, 85.

20 "Il convegno di ieri per gli orti semi-gratuiti," *Avanti!*, October 21, 1914; MGS, *Relazione morale e finanziaria del comitato "Pro Orti Operai," gestione 1916* (Milan 1917), 7–10; interview with Fiammetta Sarfatti Gaetani, May 16, 1985; MGS, *Dux*, 162; idem, *The Life*, 201; Pini and Susmel, *Mussolini*, I, 254–5.

21 "L'assemblea della sezione socialista," *Avanti!*, October 22, 1914; OO, VI, 417–18; Pini and Susmel, *Mussolini*, I, 255; Luigi Rossi, *Uomini che ho conosciuto: Mussolini* (Rome, 1982), 61–2.

22 Pini and Susmel, *Mussolini*, I, 135, 250, 262, 270; De Felice, *Mussolini il rivoluzionario*, 276, 731–2; Alfredo Pieroni, "Il figlio segreto di Mussolini," *La Settimana Incom*, January 7, 14, 21, 28, 1950.

23 MGS, *Dux*, 163; idem, *The Life*, 203; De Felice, *Mussolini il rivoluzionario*, 271–8, 286–8, 300–3; Pini and Susmel, *Mussolini*, I, 264–70; Mario Girardon, *The Key to Mussolini's Secret* (New York, 1937); William A. Renzi, "Mussolini's Sources of Financial Support, 1914–1915," *History: The Journal of the Historical Association* (June 1971); idem, *In the Shadow of the Sword: Italy's Neutrality and Entrance into the War, 1914–1915* (New York, 1987), 139–40; Kirkpatrick (*Mussolini*, 63) believes Margherita's explanation "implausible."
   Angelica Balabanoff later spread the story that Margherita bore major responsibility for converting Mussolini into an interventionist. However, the sequence of events shows clearly that it was Mussolini who influenced Margherita in favor of war, although only with difficulty. Marzorati, *Margherita Sarfatti*, 110–11.

24 "Un discorso dell'On. Destrée," *Il Popolo d'Italia*, November 27, 1914; Luigi Gasparotto, *Diario di un deputato: Cinquant'anni di vita politica italiana* (Milan, 1945), 70; Federazione degli Avvocati Belgi, *Appello agli avvocati italiani di Giulio Destrée* (Milan, 1915). On Destrée and the propaganda campaign in Italy, see the works by Jules Destrée, *Souvenirs des temps de guerre*, ed. Michel Dumoulin (Louvain, 1980), and *Un belga in Italia avanti la guerra* (Milan, 1915); Julien Luchaire, *Confession d'un français moyen*, 2 vols. (Florence, 1965); Yvon De Begnac, *Taccuini mussoliniani*, ed. Francesco Perfetti (Bologna, 1990), 31.

25 "Benito Mussolini espulso dal partito!," *Il Popolo d'Italia*, November 25, 1914; Pini and Susmel, *Mussolini*, I, 266–8; De Felice, *Mussolini il rivoluzionario*, 278–9; Lucio Ceva to BRS, February 15, 1990; MGS, *Dux*, 164; idem, *The Life*, 205.

26 MGS, "Proletariato e patria," *Avanti!*, December 23, 1914.
   Margherita's carefully chosen words were simply synonyms for those used by Mussolini—whereas he had called for a neutrality that was "attiva" and "operante," she insisted on one that was "fattiva" and "operosa."

27 Maria Rygier's articles appeared the next year in book form as *Sulla soglia di un'epoca: La nostra patria* (Rome, 1915); MGS, "Patria e proletariatio," *Il Popolo d'Italia*, January 13, 1915; Valiani, *Il partito socialista*, 67–8; "Solenne plebiscito intorno alla bara di Luigi Maino," January 11, 1915, and "Le solenne commemorazione di Luigi Maino," January 12, 1915, *Avanti!*; "Il giury per il caso Mussolini," *Il Popolo d'Italia*, January 16, 1915; *Dux*, 163; Valera, *Mussolini*, 22–3; "Relazione della commissione d'inchiesta sul caso Mussolini," *Avanti!*, February 27, 1915, reprinted in OO, VII, 475–80; De Felice, *Mussolini il rivoluzionario*, 273–5.

28 MGS, *La milizia*, 15–18, 49, 97–8.

29 MGS, *La milizia*, 102, 81–2, 42–55.

30 MGS, *La milizia*, 30, 55, 45–8.

31 Severini, *La vita*, 181–2.

32 Arros [Arturo Rossato], "Sfoglia la margherita . . ." *Il Popolo d'Italia*, March 26, 1915.

33 Lido Caiani, "A Parigi durante la guerra (Nostra intervista con Margherita G. Sarfatti)," *Il Lavoro* (Genoa), April 1, 1915.

34 MGS, *Acqua passata*, 82; Pini and Susmel, *Mussolini*, I, 284–5.

35 "La donna e la guerra," *Il Popolo d'Italia*, April 2, 1915; MGS, *La milizia*, 85–7.

36 "L'avv. Cesare Sarfatti è per la guerra," *Il Popolo d'Italia*, May 19, 1915.

37 Seton-Watson, *Italy from Liberalism*, 440–9.

38 Alberto Malatesta, *I socialisti italiani durante la guerra* (Milan, 1926), 111–12.

39 MGS, *La milizia*, 104; "Cronachetta bibliografica," *Il Marzocco*, August 29, 1915, 4; Michela De Giorgio, "Dalla donna nuova alla donna della nuova Italia," in Diego Leoni and Camillo Zadra, eds., *La Grande Guerra* (Bologna, 1986), 315–17.

40 MGS, *La milizia*, 68; Luchaire, *Confession*, II, 27, 40; Louis Barthou, *L'effort italien* (Paris, 1916); idem, *The Effort of the French Women* (Paris, 1918); Octave Aubert, *Louis Barthou* (Paris, 1935), 95, 177; MGS to Prezzolini, May 26, 1910, PP; Emile Vandervelde, *Souvenirs d'un militant socialiste* (Paris, 1939), 135.

41 GFP, "Margherita Sarfatti" folder, MGS to Ferrero, July 12, 1915; MGS, *Acqua passata*, 105–6; Destrée, *Souvenirs*, 212; "Conferenza di Emile Vandervelde," *Avanti!*, July 21, 1915; Pini and Susmel, *Mussolini*, I, 290.

42 MGS, *Dux*, 189–90; idem, *Acqua passata*, 83.
43 Giovanni Ansaldo diary (courtesy of Renzo De Felice), entry for September 7, 1934.

CHAPTER 11: ORDER, COUNTERORDER, DISORDER

1 OO, VII, 417, VI, 410, VII, 77, 79, 172, 204, 292.
2 Seton-Watson, *Italy from Liberalism*, 451; Prezzolini, *Diario, 1900–1941*, 162–3.
3 Boccioni et al. to MGS, July 9, 1915, AmSP; "Entusiastiche manifestazioni cittadine per la partenza dei volontari ciclisti," *Corriere della Sera*, July 22, 1915; Crispolti, *Storia e critica*, 180; Salaris, *Storia del futurismo*, 81; Tisdall and Bozzolla, *Futurism*, 178.
4 De Felice, *Mussolini il rivoluzionario*, 319–21.
5 De Felice, *Mussolini il rivoluzionario*, 321–2; OO, XXXVIII, 87.
6 Pini and Susmel, *Mussolini*, I, 295–6; OO, XXXIV, 11–13.
7 Gianni Rocca, *Cadorna* (Milan, 1985), 69–96; Ceva, *Le forze armate*, 112–3, 119–22, 157; James E. Edmonds and H. R. Davies, *Military Operations, Italy, 1915–1919* (London, 1949), 9–13; Emilio Faldella, *La grande guerra* (Milan, 1978), 130.
8 OO, XXXVIII, v–vi, 15–16; Pini and Susmel, *Mussolini*, I, 296, 318; Osvaldo Roncalini and Fernando Gori, *I Bersaglieri nella storia* (Rome, 1971), 310; Monelli, *Mussolini piccolo borghese*, 400, n. 23.
9 Ministero della Guerra, Comando del Corpo di Stato Maggiore, Ufficio Storico, *Riassunti storici dei corpi e comandi nella guerra 1915–1918*, Vol. 9, *Bersaglieri* (Rome, 1929), 402–3; OO, XXXIV, 17–49, XXXVIII, 89–90.
10 MGS, *Dux*, 181; OO, XXXIV, 41; *Dizionario biografico degli italiani*, vol. 29, 531; Faldella, *La grande guerra*, 130.
11 OO, VIII, 227, XXXIV, 26–8, 32–3, XXXVIII, 88, 90, 96; Pini and Susmel, *Mussolini*, I, 298–300; De Felice, *Mussolini il rivoluzionario*, 320.
12 OO, VIII, 296, XXXIV, 46–9; De Felice, *Mussolini il rivoluzionario*, 320; Pini and Susmel, *Mussolini*, I, 303.
13 OO, XXXIV, 48–50; Pini and Susmel, *Mussolini*, I, 304.
14 Pini and Susmel, *Mussolini*, I, 303–4; Spinosa, *I figli del duce*, 23–5; De Felice, *Mussolini il rivoluzionario*, 731–2; BP, diary entry for December 29, 1951; Trapani, "Fu mia madre," 50; Faldella, *La grande guerra*, 130; Mario Fusti Carofiglia, *Vita di Mussolini e storia del fascismo* (Turin, 1950), 69; Rachele Mussolini, *Mussolini privato* (Milan, 1980), 81–2.
15 Pini and Susmel, *Mussolini*, I, 304–5; Carofiglio, *Vita di Mussolini*, 69; Spinosa, *I figli del duce*, 26–7; Rossi, *Trentatrè vicende*, 34–5.
    For the pathetic story of the life of Benito Albino, see Pieroni, "Il figlio segreto di Mussolini."
16 OO, VIII, 206–25, XXXIV, v.
17 "Un'educatrice inglese," October 17, 1915, "La feroce esecuzione di Miss Cavell," October 23, 1915, and "Una commemorazione di Miss Cavell," November 22, 1915, all in *Avanti!*; Ada Negri, "Saluto a Miss Cavell," *Il Secolo*, December 25, 1915.
18 "Miss Cavell commemorata al Conservatorio," *Il Popolo d'Italia*, December 30, 1915.
19 Mary Iacovella, "Margherita Sarfatti: A Modern Woman," *Atlantica* (April 1934), 125; "Margherita Grassini-Sarfatti," United Press Association release, May 22, 1939, Philadelphia *Inquirer* morgue files; Panzini, *Roberto Sarfatti*, 16.
    Shortly after Margherita's speech, Antonio Gramsci published a criticism of those who were using Cavell's death to justify patriotism. See "La commemorazione di Miss Cavell," January 17, 1916, in Antonio Gramsci, *Scritti giovanili, 1914–1918* (Turin, 1958), 17–20.
20 Pini and Susmel, *Mussolini*, I, 307–8.
21 OO, XXXIV, 61–3; MGS, *Dux*, 98–9; Pini and Susmel, *Mussolini*, I, 310.
22 Ministero della Guerra, *Bersaglieri*, 33–4; OO, XXXIV, 63–76; Pini and Susmel, *Mussolini*, I, 310–12; MGS, *Dux*, 177.
23 OO, XXXIV, 69–70.

24 OO, XXXIV, 77–8.

25 OO, XXXIV, 78–80; Pini and Susmel, *Mussolini*, I, 313; Faldella, *La grande guerra*, 171–5; Rocca, *Cadorna*, 121–3.

26 OO, VIII, 234–8, 304–5; Seton-Watson, *Italy from Liberalism*, 458–9.

27 OO, XXXVIII, 92–3.

28 Rocca, *Cadorna*, 136–47; Ceva, *Le forze armate*, 125, 133–5; Pini and Susmel, *Mussolini*, I, 314.

29 *Dizionario biografico degli italiani*, Vol. 7, 270; OO, VIII, 239; Pini and Susmel, *Mussolini*, I, 315.

30 Ministero della Guerra, *Bersaglieri*, 36; OO, VIII, 305–7; Pini and Susmel, *Mussolini*, I, 314–5; Rocca, *Cadorna*, 148; Ceva, *Le forze armate*, 125.

31 Seton-Watson, *Italy from Liberalism*, 458–9; Ceva, *Le forze armate*, 126–7; Faldella, *La grande guerra*, 228–48.

32 "L'orgoglio italiano," in Ettore Camesasca and Claudia Gian Ferrari, eds., *Mario Sironi: Scritti editi e inediti* (Milan, 1980), 9–11. The manifesto was signed by Marinetti, Boccioni, Sironi, Russolo, Sant'Elia, and Piatti.

33 Crispolti, *Storia e critica*, 21, 182; Salaris, *Storia del futurismo*, 82; Boccioni to F. Balilla Pratella, June 16, 1916; Birolli, *Umberto Boccioni: Gli scritti*, 388–9; Boccioni to MGS, June 17, 1916, AmSP.

34 "Very Confidential Résumé on the Italian Royal Family," NA, RG 226, Entry 125, b. 42, f. 534; Boccioni to Baer, July 15, 1916, MoMA, Special Collections, "Vico Baer" file.

35 Boccioni to MGS, June 17, 1916, AmSP.; Boccioni to Baer, July 15, 1916, MoMA, Special Collections, "Vico Baer" file, but quoted incorrectly in Birolli, *Umberto Boccioni: Gli scritti*, 388–9, in reference to the visit of Sarfatti, Sironi, and Russolo.

36 Kenneth E. Silver, *Esprit de Corps: The Art of the Parisian Avant-Garde and the First World War, 1914–1925* (Princeton, N.J., 1989), 63–73; Rossana Bossaglia, "Caratteri e sviluppo di Novecento," in *Mostra del Novecento Italiano (1923–1933)* (Milan, 1983), 19; idem, "The Iconography of the Italian Novecento in the European Context," *The Journal of Decorative and Propaganda Arts* (Winter 1987), 56; Piero Pacini, *Gino Severini: Disegni e incisioni* (Florence, 1977), 14–15.

37 Prezzolini, *Diario, 1900–1941*, 216; Carrà to Soffici, September (1?), 1916, Soffici to Carrà, September 18, 1916, and February 16, 1917, in Massimo Carrà and Vittorio Fagone, eds., *Carlo Carrà–Ardengo Soffici: Lettere 1913–1929* (Milan, 1983), 99–101, 103–4.

38 Birolli, *Umberto Boccioni: Gli scritti*, 391; Salaris, *Storia del futurismo*, 82; Mangoni, *L'interventismo*, 30; Lamberti, *Storia dell'arte italiana*, 163; Paolo Fossati, *Valori plastici, 1919–1922* (Turin, 1981), 10–12; Guido Balla, "Boccioni a Milano," in *Boccioni a Milano* (Milan, 1982), 70–2.

39 Boccioni to MGS, August 16, 1916, Russolo to MGS, August 2 and 22, 1916, AmSP; MGS, "Umberto Boccioni," *Vita d'Arte*, March-April, 1917, 41; idem, *Acqua passata*, 97; Fiammetta Sarfatti Gaetani to PVC, July 5, 1987.

40 Russolo to MGS, August 22, 1916, AmSP; MGS, "L'opera di Umberto Boccioni," *Gli Avvenimenti*, September 24, 1916; idem, "L'inaugurazione della mostra Umberto Boccioni," and "La mostra postuma delle opere di Umberto Boccioni," both in *Gli Avvenimenti*, January 1917; idem, "Umberto Boccioni," *Vita d'Arte*, March-April 1917.

41 MGS, "Artisti morti in guerra," *Il Popolo d'Italia*, November 12, 1920; idem, "Per Antonio Sant'Elia, Architetto," *I vivi e l'ombra*, (1934), 67; idem, "Antonio di Sant'Elia," *Il Popolo d'Italia*, October 4, 1930; Claudio Maneri, "Antonio Sant'Elia," *Architecture and Urbanism*, February 1978.

42 MGS, "Sant'Elia e la sua opera," *Gli Avvenimenti*, October 29–November 5, 1916, reprodotto in MGS, *La fiaccola accesa*, 236–52; interview with Magalì Sarfatti-Larson, September 28, 1985.

43 Pini and Susmel, *Mussolini*, I, 315.

44 De Felice, *Mussolini il rivoluzionario*, 323–4; OO, VIII, 350–2; Roncolini and Gori, *I Bersaglieri*, 353; Prezzolini, *Diario, 1900–1941*, 343.

45 Pini and Susmel, *Mussolini*, I, 316, 449.
46 Pini and Susmel, *Mussolini*, I, 316–8; OO, XXXIV, 81.
47 *Roberto Sarfatti: Le sue lettere e testimonianze di lui* (Milan, 1919), 16; MGS, "Trieste," *I vive e l'ombra* (1934), 59–61; Marzorati, *Margherita Sarfatti*, 94.
48 OO, XXXIV, 104.
49 OO, XXXVIII, 93–5.
50 OO, VIII, 248–52, XXXIV, 97–8; Pini and Susmel, *Mussolini*, I, 317–18, 323; De Felice, *Mussolini il rivoluzionario*, 327; Carofiglio, *Vita di Mussolini*, 69.
51 OO, XXXIV, 82–100, XXXVIII, 99–101; Pini and Susmel, I, *Mussolini*, 318–21.
52 OO, XXXIV, 101; MGS, *The Life*, 223.
53 OO, XXXIV, 102–6.
54 Antonio Gramsci, *Letteratura e vita nazionale* (Turin, 1950), 149; OO, VIII, 248–52.
55 OO, XXXIV, 107.
56 Pini and Susmel, *Mussolini*, I, 322.
57 OO, XXXIV, 108–11, XXXVIII, 94, 98, 100, 102.
58 MGS, *Dux*, 182–3.
59 MGS, *Dux*, 183.
60 Ministero della Guerra, *Bersaglieri*, 37; OO, XXXIV, 112; Pini and Susmel, *Mussolini*, I, 323–4; De Felice, *Mussolini il rivoluzionario*, 667; MGS, *Dux*, 183–4.
61 OO, VIII, 367; MGS, *Dux*, 185.
62 Pini and Susmel, *Mussolini*, I, 325; MGS, *Dux*, 185; Renzo De Felice, *Mussolini il fascista. I. La conquista del potere* (Turin, 1966), 310.
63 OO, XXXIV, 112–3; MGS, *Dux*, 185.
64 Pini and Susmel, *Mussolini*, I, 326–7.
65 MGS, *The Life*, 232; Rachele Mussolini, *My Life with Mussolini* (London, 1959), 61; Ceva, *Le forze armate*, 127–8.
66 Pini and Susmel, *Mussolini*, I, 327–8; OO, VIII, 280–8; De Felice, *Mussolini il rivoluzionario*, 353, 667; Edvige Mussolini, *Mio fratello Benito*, 80.

CHAPTER 12: ROBERTO SARFATTI, ALPINO

1 *Roberto Sarfatti: Le sue lettere e testimonianze di lui* (Milan, 1919), 25–6.
2 Ada Negri, in *Roberto Sarfatti: Le sue lettere*, 7, and *Orazioni*, 125–7; Panzini, *Roberto Sarfatti*, 16; MGS, *Dux*, 174; idem, *I vivi e l'ombra* (1934), "I reali di Francia," 155–6. The stories Margherita read to Roberto during his illness were from *I reali di Francia*, a popular version of Andrea da Barberino's *Chansons de Geste*.
3 Negri, *Orazioni*, 122–3; Panzini, *Roberto Sarfatti*, 12.
4 MGS, *Acqua passata*, 90; Negri, *Orazioni*, 123, 130, 141; Panzini, *Roberto Sarfatti*, 12–13.
5 Negri, *Orazioni*, 124, 146; Panzini, *Roberto Sarfatti*, 8–9, 13.
6 Interviews with Magalì Sarfatti-Larson, December 11, 1986, and May 12, 1987; recollections of Elena Vivanti Ravà to Magalì Sarfatti-Larson, as told to PVC, June 16, 1986; Negri, *Orazioni*, 138; Marzorati, *Margherita Sarfatti*, 84.
7 Negri, *Orazioni*, 131.
8 Panzini, *Roberto Sarfatti*, 9, 14–15; Negri, *Orazioni*, 123, 131; Negri in *Roberto Sarfatti: Le sue lettere*, 7.
9 Panzini, *Roberto Sarfatti*, 14.
10 Negri, *Orazioni*, 132–3; Panzini, *Roberto Sarfatti*, 16, 33, and in *Roberto Sarfatti: Le sue lettere*, 16.
11 *Roberto Sarfatti: Le sue lettere*, 25–6.
12 "Entusiastiche manifestioni cittadine per la partenza dei volontari ciclisti," *Corriere della Sera*, July 22, 1915.
13 OO, X, 305.
14 Negri, *Orazioni*, 137–8; Panzini, *Roberto Sarfatti*, 25, 29–31; Negri in *Roberto Sarfatti: Le sue lettere*, 8; Jean Jacques [Ottavio Dinale], "Gli adolescenti che muoiono per la Patria," *Il*

Popolo d'Italia, February 7, 1918; Gaetano Carolei, *Le medaglie d'oro al valor militare 1918* (Rome, 1968), 28.

15 Panzini, *Roberto Sarfatti*, 30–1; Negri, *Orazioni*, 139; Faldella, *La grande guerra*, 167–9.

16 Negri, *Orazioni*, 139; *Roberto Sarfatti: Le sue lettere*, 27–8.

17 Panzini, *Roberto Sarfatti*, 34–5; *Roberto Sarfatti: Le sue lettere*, 18, 28–9; Negri, *Orazioni*, 140–6.

18 Negri, *Orazioni*, 147–8.

19 Emilio Faldella, *Storia delle truppe alpine, 1872–1972*, 3 vols. (Milan, 1972), I, 31–4, 38–48, 151–74.

20 Faldella, *Storia delle truppe*, II, 662–720; Gianni Pieropan, *Ortigara 1917* (Milan, 1975); Ceva, *Le forze armate*, 129; Rocca, *Cadorna*, 195.

21 Carolei, *Le medaglie d'oro al valor militare*, 28; "L'eroica morte. Episodi e ricordi," *Il Popolo d'Italia*, February 7, 1918; *Roberto Sarfatti: Le sue lettere*, 29–32.

22 Amedeo Sarfatti to PVC, August 29, 1986; Claudia Gian Ferrari, ed., *Sironi, 1885–1961* (Milan, 1985), 187; S. Bartolini, *Mario Sironi: L'opera incisa* (Reggio Emilia, 1976), illustrations IV–VII; Podenzani, *Il libro di Ada Negri*, 139–40; Ada Negri, "A Margherita Sarfatti," in *Le solitarie* (Milan, 1917); idem, *Poesie*, 938–9; MGS, "Un libro d'amore: 'Le Solitairie' di Ada Negri," *Il Popolo d'Italia*, September 4, 1917.

23 Seton-Watson, *Italy from Liberalism*, 469–73: OO, IX, 176.

24 OO, IX, 116–42; Ceva, *Le forze armate*, 130.

25 Ceva, *Le forze armate*, 133–43; Seton-Watson, *Italy from Liberalism*, 477–80.

26 Seton-Watson, *Italy from Liberalism*, 473–7.

27 Piero Melograni, *Storia politica della grande guerra, 1915–1918* (Bari, 1969), 435.

28 Melograni, *Storia politica*, 423–33, 459–60; Ceva, *Le forze armate*, 140; Seton-Watson, *Italy from Liberalism*, 482–5; OO, X, 13.

29 Ceva, *Le forze armate*, 138–43.

30 Ceva, *Le forze armate*, 143–4; Seton-Watson, *Italy from Liberalism*, 482; Piero Pieri, *L'Italia nella prima guerra mondiale* (Turin, 1968), 171–3; Piero Meldini, "La sventurata Margherita: Panzini e la Sarfatti," in Ennio Grassi, ed., *Alfredo Panzini nella cultura letteraria italian fra '800 e '900* (Rimini, 1985), 367.

31 *Roberto Sarfatti: Le sue lettere*, 35–6; "Sarfatti, Roberto," *Enciclopedia italiano*, XXX, 870; Panzini, *Roberto Sarfatti*, 36.

32 Panzini, *Roberto Sarfatti*, 37–40; Negri, *Orazioni*, 151–2.

33 *Roberto Sarfatti: Le sue lettere*, 37–40; Roberto Sarfatti to Ada Negri, November 13, 1917, GSP; Faldella, *Storia delle truppe*, II, 829.

34 *Roberto Sarfatti: Le sue lettere*, 40, 58; Ministero della Guerra, Comando del Corpo di Stato Maggiore, Ufficio Storico, *Riassunti storici dei corpi e comandi nella guerra 1915–1918*, Vol. 10, Part 2, *Alpini: reggimenti-battaglioni* (Rome, 1931), 812–13; Faldella, *Storia delle truppe*, II, 829–32.

35 *Roberto Sarfatti: Le sue lettere*, 45.

36 Faldella, *Storia delle truppe*, II, 871–5; *Roberto Sarfatti: Le sue lettere*, 41.

37 "Arditi," in Philip V. Cannistraro, ed., *Historical Dictionary of Fascist Italy* (Westport, Conn., 1982), 34–5; Giorgio Rochat, *Gli Arditi della grande guerra* (Milan, 1981), 29–63.

38 Ministero della Guerra, *Alpini*, 813; Faldella, *Storia delle truppe*, II, 875–6; *Roberto Sarfatti: Le sue lettere*, 45; Ceva, *Le forze armate*, 134, 167: Melograni, *Storia politica*, 445–8.

39 *Roberto Sarfatti: Le sue lettere*, 45–54; Roberto Sarfatti to Ada Negri, December 14, 1917, GSP; Negri, *Orazioni*, 152–4.

40 *Roberto Sarfatti: Le sue lettere*, 56.

41 *Roberto Sarfatti: Le sue lettere*, 55–8; Panzini, *Roberto Sarfatti*, 7–8; Negri, *Orazioni*, 156–7.

42 *Roberto Sarfatti: Le sue lettere*, 47, 49, 54, 58; Negri, *Orazioni*, 157–60; Panzini, *Roberto Sarfatti*, 43–4. Roberto's return home that January 1918 offered the inspiration for Negri's poem "Ritorno per il dolce natale," in her *Canti dell'isola* (Milan, 1925).

43 MGS, *Dux*, 195; Melograni, *Storia politica*, 480–4; OO, X, 305.

44 MGS, *I vivi e l'ombra* (1934), "La Tradotta," 128–31, "La Partenza," 133; Negri, *Orazioni*, 160–1.

45 *Roberto Sarfatti: Le sue lettere,* 59; Negri, *Orazioni,* 161.

46 Ministero della Guerra, *Alpini,* 814–15; Faldella, *Storia delle truppe,* II, 898–903; Pompilio Schiarini, *L'armata del Trentino (1915–1919)* (Milan, 1926), 321–2; Aldo Valori, *La guerra italo-austriaca, 1915–1918* (Bologna, 1925), 433–4; Carolei, *Le medaglie d'oro al valor militare,* 28; "Italia eroica: Gli adolescenti che muoiono per la Patria. Roberto Sarfatti," *Il Popolo d'Italia,* February 7, 1918; "La vibrante commemorazione di Roberto Sarfatti a Milano," *Il Popolo d'Italia,* January 2, 1921; "Grande manifestazioni e riti austeri a Milano. L'esaltazione di Roberto Sarfatti," *Il Popolo d'Italia,* November 5, 1925; Negri, *Orazioni,* 161–4; Lucio Ceva, "La battaglia dei '3 monti,' " *Storia e Dossier,* January 1989.

47 MGS, "L'annuncio," *I vivi el'ombra* (1934), 137; *Roberto Sarfatti: Le sue lettere,* 60; Negri, *Orazioni,* 164.

CHAPTER 13: ITALY AND VICTORY

1 "Roberto Sarfatti," OO, X, 305–6; Jean Jacques [Ottavio Dinale], "L'eroica morte," *Il Popolo d'Italia,* February 7, 1918; Pini and Susmel, *Mussolini,* I, 348.

2 Panzini, *Roberto Sarfatti,* 7; Podenzani, *Il libro di Ada Negri,* 145; Antonio Fradeletto, *La gioventù italiana e la guerra* (Milan, 1917); Kulischioff to Turati, February 8, 1918, T/K, IV, II, 844.

3 MGS to Mussolini, February 12, 1918, OO, X, 447, published in *Il Popolo d'Italia* on February 14, 1918.

4 MGS to D'Annunzio, n.d. (but February–March 1918), letters beginning "Signore ed amico" and "Mio nobile amico," AVI, AG, LVIII, 3.

5 MGS, "Sepolta viva," *I vivi e l'ombra* (1934), 142–3.

6 MGS to D'Annunzio, January 3, 1922, AVI, AG, LVIII, 3.

7 MGS, "Il re del creato (Kipling)," *Gerarchia,* March 1922, 132.

8 MGS, "San Silvestro," *I vivi e l'ombra* (1934), 164.

9 Negri, "Offerta di primavera," "Mater," and "Gli zoccoletti rosa," in *Poesie,* 918, 920–1, 924; idem, *Orazioni;* Podenzani, *Il libro di Ada Negri,* 145–6; Giuseppe Villaroel, *Gente di ieri e di oggi* (Rocca San Casciano, 1954), 64.

10 MGS, *La fiaccola accesa,* 46–8; idem, "Artisti morti in guerra," *Il Popolo d'Italia,* November 12, 1920; idem, *Achille Funi,* 15; Francesco Perfetti, *Il dibattito sul fascismo* (Rome, 1984), 74–5; Crispolti, *Storia e critica,* 21; Severini as quoted in Lamberti, in *Storia dell'arte italiana,* 163; Jean Clair, "Données d'un problème," in *Les realismes, 1919–1939* (Paris, 1980), 8–15; Adriano Tilgher, "L'estetica dell'attivismo," in *Ricognizioni* (Rome, 1924), 132–5; Jean Cocteau, *Le retour à l'ordre* (Paris, 1917).

11 Linda Nochlin, "Return to Order," *Art in America,* 69 (September 1981), 76–9; Denys Sutton, "Order and Enigma: Italian Art of the 1920s," *Apollo* (December 1980), 408–9; Paolo Fossati, "Pittura e scultura fra le due guerre," in *Storia dell'arte italiana,* 178–9.

12 MGS to Ferruccio Parri, April 6, 1917, ACS, CFP, b. 2, f. 21.

13 Extracts from Parri's letter, originally in *Gli Avvenimenti,* are in *Fiaccola accesa,* 141–2; on Pure Visibility in Italian art theory at the time, see Emily Braun, *Mario Sironi, 1919–1945: Art and Politics in Fascist Italy,* Ph.D. dissertation, Institute of Fine Arts, 1991, Chapter 3.

14 MGS, *Fiaccola accesa,* 143–7.

15 MGS, *Fiaccola accesa,* 80, 193–4; idem, "Umberto Boccioni," *Rassegna d'Arte Antica e Moderna,* II (1917), 41–8; idem, "Fiori, pittura e donne," *Avanti!,* March 22, 1914; idem, "Renoir," December 16, 1919, and "La lezione di Cézanne," May 30, 1920, both in *Il Popolo d'Italia;* idem, *Storia della pittura moderna,* 28–39; Clair, "Données d'un problème," 8–9; Crispolti, *Storia e critica,* 147, 153; Lamberti, in *Storia dell'arte italiana,* 164; John Rewald, *Cézanne: A Biography* (New York, 1986), 225–37.

16 MGS, *Fiaccola accesa,* 193–7, 200–1, 205–6; idem, "Umberto Boccioni," 41–8; idem, *Storia della pittura moderna,* 28–39; Carrà, *La mia vita,* 126–7.

17 MGS, *Fiaccola accesa,* 54–5.

18 Mussolini to MGS, April 1, 1918, OO, X, 109–10.
19 "Trincerocrazia," December 15, 1917, 140–42; "Una politica," February 23, 1918, 342; "I motivi dei pacifondai ad ogni costo," speech of March 3, 1918, 365; "Patria e Terra," November 16, 1917, 55–7; "L'Italia è immortale," speech of February 24, 1918, 344–9, all in OO, X. On Mussolini's political views in this period, see De Felice, *Mussolini il rivoluzionario,* 391–418, and Pini and Susmel, *Mussolini,* I, 329–365.
20 Mussolini to MGS, April 1, 1918, OO, X, 109–10; Rene Albrecht-Carrie, *Italy at the Paris Peace Conference* (New York, 1938), 44–5; Henry Wickham Steed, *Through Thirty Years, 1892–1922,* II (Garden City, N.Y., 1924), 208–11.
21 Mussolini to MGS, April 10–12(?), 1918, OO, X, 110; "L'adunata di Roma," April 7, 1918, OO, X, 433–5; De Felice, *Mussolini il rivoluzionario,* 382–3, 401.
22 Pini and Susmel, *Mussolini,* I, 353–4; De Felice, *Mussolini il rivoluzionario,* 400; Spinosa, *I figli del duce,* 27–8; Rachele Mussolini, *Mussolini: An Intimate Biography* (New York, 1974), 28–9.
23 Mussolini to MGS, April 10–12 (?) and mid-April, 1918, OOA, II, 110–11, January 14, 1919, OOA, II, 114–15; Renzo De Felice, "Prefazione"; Gentile, *Mussolini e "La Voce,"* ix.
24 Pieri, *L'Italia nella prima guerra mondiale,* 186–192; Ceva, *Le forze armate,* 146–7.
25 Panzini, *Roberto Sarfatti,* 6–9; MGS to Nicholas Murray Butler, n.d. (but c. December 20, 1938), NMBP; Edvige Mussolini, *Mio fratello Benito,* 164; Alvaro, *Quasi una vita,* 111; BP, diary entry for December 29, 1951; Marzorati, *Margherita Sarfatti,* 93.
26 Pieri, *L'Italia nella prima guerra mondiale,* 195–204; Ceva, *Le forze armate,* 146, 150–2; idem, "La grande guerra nel Veneto: Scrittori e memorialisti," *La Cultura* (no. 1, 1988), 123–24; Ferruccio Parri, *Scritti 1915–1975* (Milan, 1976), 13; George Macauley Trevelyan, *Manin and the Venetian Revolution of 1848* (London, 1923), 170, n. 1.
27 MGS, *The Life,* 248–9; idem, *Dux,* 195–6.
28 Edvige Mussolini, *Mio fratello Benito,* 163–4; Rachele Mussolini, *Mussolini: An Intimate Biography,* 81; Trapani, "Fu mia madre," II, 50; Kirkpatrick, *Mussolini,* 75; Pini and Susmel, *Mussolini,* I, 365.
29 MGS to D'Annunzio, December 7, 1918, AVI, AG, LVIII, 3.
30 MGS, *Dux,* 199; AVI, AG, LVIII, 3, MGS to D'Annunzio, December 7, 1918; *Roberto Sarfatti: Le sue lettere.*
31 Negri, in *Roberto Sarfatti: Le sue lettere,* 8–9; presentation copy, with inscription to Ferdinando Martini, in the Biblioteca di Storia Moderna e Contemporanea, Rome, "Miscellanea," C-10-17.
32 MGS, *The Life,* 256; idem, *Dux,* 199; Podenzani, *Il libro di Ada Negri,* 152; Edvige Mussolini, *Mio fratello Benito,* 163; OO, XIV, 303–6; De Felice, *Mussolini il rivoluzionario,* 583–5; MGS, "Un libro d'amore: 'Le solitarie,' " *Il Popolo d'Italia,* September 4, 1917; Arturo Rossato, *Mussolini* (Milan, 1919).
33 MGS, *The Life,* 40–7; idem, *Dux,* 202–13.
34 Carrà, *La mia vita,* 149–50; Mussolini to MGS, January 14, 1919, OOA, II, 114–15.
35 MGS, *The Life,* 40; idem, *Dux,* 202.
36 Amedeo Sarfatti to PVC, October 17, 1986; "La paziente," in *I vivi e l'ombra* (1934), 106; also "Ballata segreta," "L'attesa," and "Il silenzioso amore," ibid., 84–5, 88–9, 90.
37 Mussolini to MGS, undated letters (but 1919), IDSP, New York.

CHAPTER 14: FASCI DI COMBATTIMENTO

1 OO, XII, 3–8; Prezzolini, *Diario, 1900–1941,* 282.
2 Ceva, *Le forze armate,* 135–6, 175–9.
3 OO, XII, 9–16, 20–1, 27–8, 52–5; Prezzolini, *Diario, 1900–1941,* 301.
4 *Il Popolo d'Italia,* December 14, 1918; "Per il monumento a Filippo Corridoni," ibid., December 16, 1918; Carlo Pignatti Morano, *La vita di Nazario Sauro* (Milan, 1922); Pini and Susmel, *Mussolini,* I, 372–6.
5 MGS, *Mussolini: Como lo conocí,* XI; Pini and Susmel, *Mussolini,* I, 372–6; OO, XII, 80, 84.

6 Hajo Holborn, *A History of Modern Germany, 1840–1945* (New York, 1969), 524–5.

7 MGS, *Mussolini: Como lo conocí*, XI; Holborn, *History of Modern Germany*, 519. In her 1945 memoir of Mussolini, Sarfatti clearly confused some details of Mussolini's 1922 visit to Germany with his trip to Berlin in 1918.

In his articles on his March 1922 visit to Germany, Mussolini hinted at his earlier trip by remarking how much Berlin had changed. See OO, XII, 94.

8 OOA, XXXVIII, 114–15; Podenzani, *Il libro di Ada Negri*, 152.

9 MGS, "Raffronti," *Il Popolo d'Italia*, January 23, 1919.

10 MGS, *Mussolini: Como lo conocí*, XI; OO, XII, 152, 203–5, 212–13, 220–1.

11 Borgese, *Goliath*, 195–6; Eva Kuhn Amendola, *Vita con Giovanni Amendola* (Florence, 1960), 276; "Borgese, Giuseppe Antonio," in Cannistraro, *Historical Dictionary of Fascist Italy*, 86–7; Fernando Mezzetti, *Borgese e il fascismo* (Palermo, 1978), 20–5.

12 Ivon De Begnac, *Palazzo Venezia: Storia di un regime* (Rome, 1950), 157–8; OO, XIII, 67–9.

13 Ceva, *Le forze armate*, 165–6; Giorgio Rochat, *L'esercito italiano da Vittorio Veneto a Mussolini (1919–1925)* (Bari, 1967), 30–2; Michael Ledeen, *The First Duce: D'Annunzio at Fiume* (Baltimore, 1977), 39.

14 Seton-Watson, *Italy from Liberalism*, 519–20; De Felice, *Mussolini il rivoluzionario*, 434.

15 MGS, *Dux*, 215; OO, XII, 231–3.

16 MGS, *Dux*, 199–201; idem, *The Life*, 256–7; "Calipso," *Vita segreta di Mussolini* (Rome, 1944), 22.

17 Seton-Watson, *Italy from Liberalism*, 519–22.

18 Ledeen, *The First Duce*, 41.

19 FRUS, 1919, *The Paris Peace Conference*, 5 vols. (Washington, 1942), I, 487–8.

20 MGS, *The Life*, 252.

21 Sidney Sonnino, *Diario, 1916–1922* (Bari, 1972), 314–20; DDI, Sixth Series, II, nos. 196, 208, 373, 456, 684, 787.

22 Sonnino, *Diario*, 319; DDI, Sixth Series, II, nos. 132, 142, 147, 155, 176, 196, 197, 834, 920, 942.

23 DDI, 6, II, no. 83.

24 *Il Popolo d'Italia*, January 3, 1919; MGS, *Dux*, 208.

25 OO, XII, 19, 22–6, 33–4, 44, 60, 63, 72–7, 82–4, 88–90, 102–23, 125–30; Seton-Watson, *Italy from Liberalism*, 505–9; Prezzolini, *Diario, 1900–1941*, 343; FRUS, 1919, I, 470–4; Mezzetti, *Borgese e il fascismo*, 26.

26 "Il discorso di Bissolati alla Scala," *Il Corriere della Sera*, January 12, 1919; "Bissolati Backs Wilson's Policy," *New York Times*, January 14, 1919; MGS, *Dux*, 198; Pini and Susmel, *Mussolini*, I, 379–80; OO, XII, 137–40; Seton-Watson, *Italy from Liberalism*, 509; Borgese, *Goliath*, 143; De Felice, *Mussolini il rivoluzionario*, 484–8; Mezzetti, *Borgese e il fascismo*, 25–6.

27 Carrà, *La mia vita*, 140; idem, "Parlata su Giotto," *La Voce* (March 31, 1916), and ibid., "Uccello costruttore" (September 30, 1916); idem, *Giotto* (London, 1925); MGS, *Fiaccola accesa*, 155; Mangoni, *L'interventismo della cultura*, 30, 36–7.

28 MGS, *Fiaccola accesa*, 9; *Archivi del futurismo*, II, 352; Notari to Francesco Cangiullo, February 4, 1915, ibid., 351–2; Salaris, *Storia del futurismo*, 105; Giovani Lista, *De Chirico et l'avant-garde* (Lausanne, 1983), 87, 197; MGS, "Noi, raccolta internazionale d'arte d'avanguardia," *Gli Avvenimenti*, August 1917, 5–12; Carlo Ernesto Meriano, "Appunti per servire alla storia di Francesco Meriano," in *Arte e vita: Quaderni della Fondazione Primo Conti* (Milan, 1982), 9–18; MGS to Meriano, May 9 and November 28, 1917, AFM, "Margherita Sarfatti"; Clemente Rebora to Mario Novaro, January 8, 1917, and to Meriano, January 13, 20, March 1, 1917, in Margherita Marchione, ed., *Clemente Rebora: Lettere*, I (Rome, 1976), 309, 311–12, 316; Prampolini to Bino Sanminiatelli, October 1, 1917, *Archivi del futurismo*, II, 56; Prampolini to Tzara, March 17 and August 4, 1917, in Lista, *De Chirico et l'avant-garde*, 200–4; Meriano to Tzara, August 7, 1917, ibid., 107–08; MGS, "Le tre Venezie," *Pagine d'Arte* (April 1917), 86–8; idem, "Esposizioni e polemiche," *Il Popolo d'Italia*, February 2, 1922; idem, "Qualche pittori straniero a Roma," *Il Popolo d'Italia*, March 7, 1924; idem,

Fiaccola accesa, 185, 199 (emphasis added); idem, "Umberto Boccioni," 41, 46; idem, "Pittura e scultura," *Ardita* (July 1919), 317; idem, "L'Esposizione lombarda d'arte decorativa," *Il Popolo d'Italia,* September 8, 1919.

29 Carrà to Soffici, December 18, 1918, in Carrà and Fagone, eds., *Carlo Carrà–Ardengo Soffici: Lettere,* 123; MGS, "Un critico di avanguardia: Guillaume Apollinaire," *Il Popolo d'Italia,* December 31, 1918.

30 Rossato left the staff of *Il Popolo d'Italia* in December 1919 after a disagreement with Mussolini. De Felice, *Mussolini il rivoluzionario,* 583–4.

31 MGS, "Le esposizioni Tomescu e Martini a Milano," *Il Popolo d'Italia,* January 28, 1919. On Sarfatti's earlier relationship with Martini, see Bossaglia, *Il "Novecento Italiano,"* 210.

32 Amedeo Sarfatti to PVC, October 1985; Gian Ferrari, *Sironi: 1885–1961,* 188; Giovanni Comisso, ed., *Arturo Martini: Le Lettere, 1909–1947* (Florence, 1967), 48; Sironi to Paolo Buzzi, April 3, 1920, Camesasca and Gian Ferrari, *Mario Sironi: Scritti,* 18, 428; Raffaele De Grada, "Achille Funi," *Arte* (January 1987), 42; Enzo Dematte, ed., *Trecento lettere di Giovanni Comisso a Maria e Natale Mazzola, 1925–1968* (Treviso, 1972), 136–7; *Mostra del Novecento Italiano,* 321; Leonardo Dudreville, "Manoscritto autografo," in Bossaglia, *Il "Novecento Italiano,"* 68, 73, 80; Rossi, *Mussolini com'era,* 213–14.

33 MGS, "Adolfo Wildt e l'esposizioni alla Galleria Pesaro," *Il Popolo d'Italia,* February 10, 1919; G. M. Ciampelli, "Adolfo Wildt," *Ardita* (March 15, 1919), 21–7; MGS, "Delle scuole del marmo," *Il Popolo d'Italia,* March 10, 1921.

34 *Clemente Rebora: Lettere,* I, 309, 311, 312, 316; PP, MGS to Prezzolini, n.d. but probably February 1919; Prezzolini, *Diario, 1900–1941,* 311–13.

35 Mussolini, "Preludio," *Ardita,* March 15, 1919, now in OO, XII, 299–300; MGS, *La fiaccola accesa,* 48–9, 59; Nozzoli, "Margherita Sarfatti," 249–52; Giuseppe Ungaretti, "Così mi sono legato al duce," *Storia Illustrata,* March 1986.

36 OO, XII, 299; *Il Popolo d'Italia,* February 9, 1919; ibid., March 14, 1919; Enzo Santarelli, *Storia del fascismo,* 3 vols. (Rome, 1973), I, 98.

37 Giorgio Rochat, *Gli Arditi della grande guerra: Origini, battaglie e miti* (Milan, 1981), 113–17.

38 OO, XII, 314–7; Adrian Lyttelton, *The Seizure of Power: Fascism in Italy, 1919–1929* (New York, 1973), 52.

39 MGS, "Marzo 1919," *Gerarchia* (March 1932); idem, *The Life,* 258; "Sansepolcristi," in Cannistraro, *Historical Dictionary of Fascist Italy,* 485; Monelli, *Mussolini piccolo borghese,* 401, n. 24; Pini and Susmel, *Mussolini,* I, 389; PP, MGS to Prezzolini, n.d. but probably February 1919; ACS, CPC, f. 60867, "Sarfatti, Cesare," Pesce to minister of the interior, June 19, 1919; OO, XVI, 478.

No one kept a careful record of those present at the founding of the Fascist movement. Only later did that question assume importance for Fascists and, later yet, for historians.

Sarfatti's name does not appear on any list of those in attendance at the meeting, who came to be known as the "Sansepolcristi." Given the prestige later attached to those who attended, it seems contradictory that Sarfatti did not insist on her name being included in the official roster when the definitive list was eventually created. However, in her March 1932 article, Sarfatti states that she was present. By that time, she had acquired many powerful enemies, including indisputable Sansepolcristi, and had slipped from Mussolini's favor. Since no one disputed her claim, made in the semi-official Fascist party journal, it seems certain that it was true.

40 "Fasci d'azione fra interventisti," *Corriere della Sera,* March 24, 1919; OO, XII, 321–7; Pini and Susmel, *Mussolini,* I, 389–94 [quote, p. 393].

41 MGS, *The Life,* 265.

42 "Fasci di Azione Rivoluzionario," "Fasci di Combattimento," and "Fascio Littorio" in Cannistraro, *Historical Dictionary of Fascist Italy,* 200–2, 205. For a comprehensive history of the first three and a half years of Fascism, see Emilio Gentile, *Storia del Partito Fascista, 1919–1922: Movimento e milizia* (Rome-Bari, 1989).

43 MGS, *Dux,* 220–1.

44 OO, XIII, 60–6.

45 F. T. Marinetti, "Benito Mussolini" in Antonio Beltramelli, *L'uomo nuovo (Benito Mussolini)* (Milan, 1923), viii–xi; Rochat, *Gli Arditi*, 116; De Felice, *Mussolini il rivoluzionario*, 519–21.
46 De Felice, *Mussolini il rivoluzionario*, 484; Mack Smith, *Mussolini*, 36.

CHAPTER 15: PURELY, FIERCELY ITALIAN

1 MGS, *Dux*, 203; Mack Smith, *Mussolini*, 36; De Felice and Goglia, *Mussolini. Il mito*, 150, photograph no. 105; De Felice, *Mussolini il rivoluzionario*, 521; Vittorio Mussolini, *Vita con mio padre* (Verona, 1957), 29.
2 Regina Terruzzi, "Il voto alle donne," *Il Popolo d'Italia*, March 17, 1919; Denise Detragiache, "Du socialisme au fascisme naissant: Formation et itineraire de Regina Terruzzi," in Rita Thalmann, ed., *Femmes et fascismes* (Paris, 1986), 55–8; idem, "Il fascismo femminile da San Sepolcro all'affare Matteotti (1919–1925)," *Storia Contemporanea*, April 1983, 213–4; Pieroni Bortolotti, *Socialismo e questione femminile in Italia*, 14.
3 GSP, MGS to Mussolini, January 21, 1923; ibid., MGS to Mussolini, n.d. but early 1923, beginning "adorato, adorato mio adorato . . ."; ibid., MGS to Mussolini, n.d. but early 1923, beginning "ore 2 del mattino mercoledì"; Borgese, *Goliath*, 196.
4 Balabanoff, *My Life as a Rebel*, 55–6; OO, XIII, 100, 376, 378; Podenzani, *Il libro di Ada Negri*, 152–4; GSP, Cesare Sarfatti to Ada Negri, July 10, 14, 19, 1919.
5 IDSP, Mussolini to MGS, letter 12 of 1919 beginning "Amore! domani alle 17 ti attendo . . ."; Rossi, *Trentatrè vicende*, 28, 54.
6 Sarfatti's poems appeared in the March and June 1919 issues of *Ardita*, her articles in April, June, and July of the same year; Gian Ferrari, *Mario Sironi, 1885–1961*, 188; Lyttelton, *The Seizure of Power*, 387, 391; Mangoni, *L'interventismo della cultura*, 31.
7 Fernando Tempesti, *Arte dell'Italia fascista* (Milan, 1976), 16–24; Mangoni, *L'interventismo della cultura*, 29–39; Fossati, "Pittura e scultura," 187–99; Bossaglia, *Il "Novecento Italiano,"* 9–10; MGS, "Le esposizioni Tomescu e Martini," *Il Popolo d'Italia*, January 25, 1919; idem, "Adolfo Wildt e l'esposizione alla Galleria Pesaro," *Il Popolo d'Italia*, February 10, 1919; Fiammetta Sarfatti Gaetani to PVC, July 5, 1987; MGS, "Dedalo, valori plastici e altre riviste d'arte," *Il Popolo d'Italia*, November 30, 1920. On the Metaphysical school, see Renato Barilli and Franco Solmi, eds., *La metafisicia: Gli anni venti*, 2 vols. (Bologna, 1980).
8 Galleria Centrale d'Arte, *Grande Esposizione Nazionale Futurista* (Milan, 1919), 17, 21; MGS, *Achille Funi*, plate 1, *Famiglia a Tavola* (1915).
  Exactly which Sironi portrait of Margherita was in the show is unclear, but it may well have been the 1915 portrait now reproduced in *Mostra del Novecento Italiano*, 21. Interestingly enough, Funi and Dudreville showed several of the same paintings they had hung in the 1914 New Tendencies exhibit.
9 MGS, *Acqua passata*, 94–5. The information on Sironi in this and the following paragraph is taken largely from Emily Braun, "Illustrations of Propaganda: The Political Drawings of Mario Sironi," *The Journal of Propaganda Arts* (Winter 1987), 84–107, and idem, *Mario Sironi, 1919–1945*, Chapter 2, "The Urban Landscapes."
10 *Mostra del Novecento Italiano*, 401.
11 MGS, "A proposito dell'esposizione futurista," March 25, 1919; "L'esposizione futurista a Milano. I. Di alcuni principi generali," April 4, 1919, "L'esposizione futurista a Milano: Di alcuni pittori," April 11, 1919, and "L'esposizione futurista a Milano: Terzo ed ultimo articolo," April 13, 1919, all in *Il Popolo d'Italia*; idem, "Renoir," *Ardita*, June 1919, 254; idem, "Pittura e scultura," *Ardita*, July 1919, 317.
12 Lyttelton, *The Seizure of Power*, 384; Giorgio De Chirico, *Storia della rivoluzione fascista* (Florence, 1929), I, 100, 238; Pini and Susmel, I, *Mussolini*, 391; Braun, "The Political Drawings," 90; Fabio Benzi and Andrea Sironi, *Sironi illustratore* (Rome, 1988), 48–51. Sironi's first drawings for the paper appeared in August 1921.
13 Bossaglia, *Il "Novecento Italiano,"* 11.
14 Seton-Watson, *Italy from Liberalism*, 528–30.

15 OO, XIII, 57–9, 70–2, 75–6, 80–9, 93–4, 98–9, 101–3.
16 Seton-Watson, *Italy from Liberalism*, 532–6.
17 Seton-Watson, *Italy from Liberalism*, 536–40; Ledeen, *The First Duce*, 34.
18 De Felice, *Mussolini il rivoluzionario*, 529–33.
19 Ledeen, *The First Duce*, 1–12.
20 Ledeen, *The First Duce*, 14–15; Renzo De Felice and Emilio Marrano, eds., *Carteggio D'Annunzio-Mussolini (1919–1938)* (Milan, 1971), 6, 386; Paolo Alatri, *Gabriele D'Annunzio* (Turin, 1983), 415.
21 AVI, AG, LVIII, 3, MGS to D'Annunzio, June 2, 1919; De Felice and Marrano, *Carteggio*, ix–x; OOA, XXXVIII, 114–17; Ledeen, *The First Duce*, 14.
22 IDSP, Mussolini to MGS, letter 1 of 1919, n.d. but c. June 24, 1919; OO, XIII, 3, 201–3, 207–9, 214, 218–20; Seton-Watson, *Italy from Liberalism*, 512–5.
23 Filippo T. Marinetti, *Taccuini, 1915–21* (Bologna, 1987), 427.
24 OO, XIII, 198–200, 204–6, 210–12, 221–2.
25 Seton-Watson, *Italy from Liberalism*, 520–4.
26 MGS, *The Life*, 268–9.
27 Sergio Marzorati, "Margherita Sarfatti e Gabriele D'Annunzio, 30 anni d'amicizia," *La Provincia*, December 17, 1988; Attilio Longoni, *Fascismo ed aviazione: Gli aviatori nella rivoluzione fascista* (Milan, 1931), 84, 86; Guido Mattioli, *Mussolini aviatore e la sua opera per l'aviazione* (Rome, 1935), 33–60; *Il Popolo d'Italia*, April 6, 1920, 6; AFM, MGS to Meriano, August 23, 1919; OO, XIII, 303, 335–7; OO, XIV, 480–1; D'Avanzo, *Ali e poltrone*, 56–7, 60–1; Giorgio Apostolo, *Guida agli aeroplani d'Italia dalle origini a oggi* (Verona, 1981), 46; Oscar Marchi and Vittorio Zardo, *Aeronautica militare museo storico catologo: Velivoli* (Bologna, 1980), 35–7; *Almanacco aeronautico 1930* (Milan, 1930), 211.
28 Ledeen, *The First Duce*, 48–55, 86; Marinetti, *Taccuini*, 427; OO, XIII, 475.
29 Ledeen, *The First Duce*, 55–6.
30 De Felice and Marrano, *Carteggio*, x–xi; De Felice *Mussolini il rivoluzionario*, 562–3.
31 Ledeen, *The First Duce*, 65–71, 86.
32 Ledeen, *The First Duce*, 71.
33 Ledeen, *The First Duce*, 72–6.
34 Ledeen, *The First Duce*, 86; OO, XIII, 475.
35 OO, XIII, 475–6; De Felice, *Mussolini il rivoluzionario*, 562–3; Ledeen, *The First Duce*, 87.
36 OO, XIII, 362–4; OO, XIV, 6–14, 17–34; Seton-Watson, *Italy from Liberalism*, 540–2, 547; Ledeen, *The First Duce*, 73–81.
37 MGS, "L'Esposizione lombarda d'arte decorativa," *Il Popolo d'Italia*, September 8, 1919; MGS, "La mostra Belloni," *Il Popolo d'Italia*, December 8, 1919; OOA, XXXVIII, 114; IDSP, Mussolini to MGS, n.d. but marked "3 autunno 1919"; MGS, *The Life*, 270–1.
38 MGS, *Dux*, 224–5.
39 IDSP, Mussolini to MGS, n.d. but marked "3 autunno 1919"; Seton-Watson, *Italy from Liberalism*, 547–8; OO, XIII, 221–2, 230–3, 264–6.
40 Seton-Watson, *Italy from Liberalism*, 548.
41 Ledeen, *The First Duce*, 87; OO, XIV, 50–1, 56–8, 476; Enzo Santarelli, *Storia del fascismo*, 3 vols. (Rome, 1973), I, 139–40.
42 De Felice, ed., *Autobiografia del fascismo: Antologia di testi fascisti, 1919–1945* (Bergamo, 1978), 26–7; Santarelli, *Storia*, I, 141–2; OO, XIV, 51–4.
43 OO, XIII, 248–55, 279–81, 301–2, 304; OO, XIV, 6–7, 41–8, 55, 59–60 [quote, 60]; Santarelli, *Storia*, 140.
44 MGS, *The Life*, 102–3.
45 De Felice *Mussolini il rivoluzionario*, 539–43; Santarelli, *Storia*, I, 94–5, 141; OO, XIV, 71, 88, 487–92; Prezzolini, *Diario 1900–1941*, 319–20.
46 OO, XIV, 72, 486–7; F. T. Marinetti, "Toscanini," *Il Popolo d'Italia*, October 29, 1919; Harvey Sachs, *Toscanini* (London, 1978), 139–40, 154; James Joll, *Three Intellectuals in Politics* (New York, 1960), 172; Santarelli, *Storia*, I, 98; Rossi, *Mussolini com'era*, 212; conversation with Prof. Marion Miller, December 29, 1986.

47 OO, XIV, 126.
48 MGS, *The Life,* 271.
49 OO, XIV, 122–5.
50 Seton-Watson, *Italy from Liberalism,* 549–51; Santarelli, *Storia,* I, 146–9; Serge Noiret, "Riforme elettorali e crisi dello stato liberale: La 'proporzionale' 1918–1919," *Italia Contemporanea,* March 1989, 50–1; D. A. Binchy, *Church and State in Fascist Italy* (London, 1941), 67–8.
51 OO, XIV, 134–7.
52 Vittorio Mussolini, *Vita con mio padre,* 22.
53 OO, XIV, 136–7.
54 MGS, *The Life,* 273–4; OO, XIV, 138–56, 492–8; De Felice, *Mussolini il rivoluzionario,* 574; "Duce Not As Hard As He's Painted, Says Biographer," *Chicago Daily Times,* May 22, 1934.
55 De Felice, *Mussolini il rivoluzionario,* 462, 574; OO, XIV, 513; MGS, *The Life,* 270.
56 ACS, Ministero Interno, DGPS, Divisione Affari Generali e Riservati (1903–1949). b. 3, A 5, "Agitazione pro Fiume e Dalmatia," "Relazione circa la sorveglianza su Benito Mussolini," Venice, November 27, 1919; GSP, MGS to Mussolini, January 21, 1923.
57 Ottavio Dinale, *Quarant'anni di colloqui con lui* (Milan, 1953), 97; Thomas B. Morgan, *Spurs on the Boot: Italy Under Her Masters* (New York, 1941), 135–7; Marzorati, *Margherita Sarfatti,* 94–5; "Nemo" [James Vincent Murphy], "Mussolini Is Out for Lunch," *The Star,* February 10, 1941; idem, "She Dreamed of a New Empire," ibid., February 13, 1941; Mariella Rigotti Colin, "L'idée de Rome et l'idéologie impérialiste dans l'Italie libérale de 1870 a 1900," *Guerres Mondiales et Conflits Contemporains,* January 1991, 7–8; Borgese, *Goliath,* 88–92; Romke Visser, "Fascist Doctrine and the Cult of *Romanità,*" *Journal of Contemporary History,* January 1992, 7–8.
58 Guido Podrecca, "Conversando con Vasa Prihoda: Il grande interprete di Paganini," *Il Popolo d'Italia,* January 20, 1920; Bossaglia, *Il "Novecento Italiano",* 80–1; Rossi, *Mussolini com'era,* 212–3; De Felice and Goglia, *Mussolini: Il Mito,* photograph no. 33; Marzorati, *Margherita Sarfatti,* 99, 166.
59 Borgese, *Goliath,* 195–6; Rossi, *Mussolini com'era,* 213; Morgan, *Spurs on the Boot,* 135–7; "Nemo," "Mussolini Is Out for Lunch.,"

CHAPTER 16: STRUGGLE FOR POWER

1 De Felice, *Mussolini il rivoluzionario,* 510, 512–13.
2 Pini and Susmel, *Mussolini,* II, 54, 60–1, 82–3, 94; OO, XIV, 303–6; OOA, XXXVIII, 123; De Felice, *Mussolini il fascista,* I, 228–9, 583–5; De Begnac, *Taccuini mussoliniani,* 31, 36, 58–9; GSP, MGS to Mussolini, n.d. but early 1923, letter beginning, "Adorato adorato mio adorato . . ."
3 OO, XIV, 436–8.
4 MGS, "Uno scandalo: La Galleria d'Arte Moderna al Castello," *Il Popolo d'Italia,* February 3, 1919; idem, "L'avanguardia artistica italiana e gli inviti alle Biennale di Venezia," ibid., February 29, 1920; idem, "Inaugurandosi la XII Biennale di Venezia," ibid., May 12, 1920; idem, "Premi non assegnati," ibid., July 2, 1920; Carrà to Soffici, February 23, 1920, and Soffici to Carrà, February 25, 1920, in Carrà and Fagone, *Carlo Carrà–Ardengo Soffici,* 133–4.
5 MGS, "L'avanguardia artistica italiana e gli inviti alle Biennali di Venezia," *Il Popolo d'Italia,* February 29, 1920; idem, "Dopo gli inviti all'avanguardia francese, si reclamano inviti per l'avangardia italiana a Venezia," ibid., April 25, 1920; idem, "Inaugurandosi la XIIa Biennale di Venezia," ibid., May 12, 1920; idem, "L'Esposizione di Venezia: La lezione di Cézanne," ibid., May 30, 1920.
  Throughout 1920, nearly forty articles by Sarfatti appeared in *Il Popolo d'Italia,* the great majority devoted to art or art criticism, the rest to literary criticism or book reviews. Two articles notable for their intertwining of art and nationalism appeared in the second half of the year: "Il monumento al fante: L'esito del concorso," August 30, 1920, in which she discussed her reactions to projects for the huge ossuary for the Italian war dead to be erected at San

Michele, and "Artisti morti in guerra," November 12, 1920, her tribute to Boccioni,
Sant'Elia and Carlo Erba.

6 MGS, *Acqua passata*, 55–7; Christopher Duggan, *Fascism and the Mafia* (New Haven, Conn.,
   1989), 103; "Mailed Fist Ends Terrorism in Sicily Within Nine Months," *New York American*, April 4, 1926.
   Sarfatti does not give a precise date in her memoirs for her visit to Sicily in 1920.
   However, given the gaps between the appearances of her articles in *Il Popolo d'Italia*, the
   political events of 1920 and the Sicilian weather, the period June 8–22 seems to have been
   the time of her trip. Another clue comes from the fact that she returned to the island at the
   same time in 1921.

7 MGS, "Una voltura," *Gerarchia*, May 1922, 253.

8 De Felice, *Mussolini il rivoluzionario*, 434; Paolo Spriano, *The Occupation of the Factories: Italy
   1920* (London, 1975), 42–3; Seton-Watson, *Italy from Liberalism*, 551; Clark, *Modern Italy*, 206.

9 Spriano, *The Occupation*, 25–7; Seton-Watson, *Italy from Liberalism*, 551–3; Clark, *Modern
   Italy*, 206–7.

10 Rochat, *L'esercito italiano*, 75–128; Mario Piazzesi, *Diario di uno squadrista toscano, 1919–1922*
    (Rome, 1980), 49.

11 Seton-Watson, *Italy from Liberalism*, 553–61; OO, XV, 30–2.

12 Vincenzo Gallinari, *L'esercito italiano nel prima dopoguerra, 1918–1920* (Rome, 1980), 177–9;
    Mario Montanari, *Le truppe italiane in Albania (Anni 1914–20 e 1939)* (Rome, 1978), 223; OO,
    XV, 28–9, 33–7, 62–74; Spriano, *The Occupation*, 47.

13 Seton-Watson, *Italy from Liberalism*, 563.

14 Spriano, *The Occupation*, 27–45; Seton-Watson, *Italy from Liberalism*, 563–4; Clark, *Modern
    Italy*, 207–8.

15 Spriano, *The Occupation*, 45–6.

16 Spriano, *The Occupation*, 52–61.

17 Giovanni Giolitti, *Memorie della mia vita*, 2 vols. (Milan, 1922), II, 598.

18 Alfredo Frassati, *Giolitti* (Florence, 1959), 30.

19 Clark, *Modern Italy*, 208; Spriano, *The Occupation*, 69–80, 96–106, 188–93; Seton-Watson,
    Italy from Liberalism, 564–5; OO, XV, 178–94, 206–8, 211–13, 224–5; Pini and Susmel,
    Mussolini, II, 76.

20 OO, XV, 231–3.

21 OO, XVI, 115–21, 124–7. On the foundation of the Italian Communist party, see Paolo
    Spriano, *Storia del partito communista italiano*, 5 vols. (Turin, 1967–75), I.

22 Clark, *Modern Italy*, 209–10, 215; Seton-Watson, *Italy from Liberalism*, 566–7; Paul Corner,
    Fascism in Ferrara, 1915–1925 (London, 1975), 81.

23 Lyttelton, *The Seizure of Power*, 52–4; Ferdinando Gora, *L'impresa di Fiume*, 2 vols. (Milan,
    1975), I, 230, II, 147; Seton-Watson, *Italy from Liberalism*, 570–1; OO, XIV, 471; OO, XV,
    157, 197–8, 226–8; OOA, XXXVIII, 124.

24 Martin Clark, *The Failure of Revolution in Italy, 1919–1920* (Reading, 1973); Seton-Watson,
    Italy from Liberalism, 566–7, 570; OO, XV, 300.

25 Seton-Watson, *Italy from Liberalism*, 571; Dino Grandi, *Il mio paese: Ricordi autobiografici*
    (Bologna, 1985), 112; Santarelli, *Storia*, I, 227–8; OO, XVI, 27–8. The details of this
    notorious incident remain controversial.

26 Anthony L. Cardozo, *Agrarian Elites and Italian Fascism: The Province of Bologna, 1901–1926*
    (Princeton, 1982), 329–31; Gianfranco Bianchi, *Dino Grandi racconta l'inevitabile "Asse"*
    (Milan, 1984), 28; Grandi, *Il mio paese*, 70–5, 110–5, 119–21; OOA, XXXVIII, 112.

27 Giordano Bruno Guerri, *Italo Balbo* (Milan, 1984), 57–71; Giorgio Rochat, *Italo Balbo*
    (Turin, 1986), 39–45; Claudio G. Segrè, *Italo Balbo: A Fascist Life* (Berkeley, 1987), 37–47;
    Spriano, *The Occupation*, 41, 106, 141; OO, XVI, 202; Lyttelton, *The Seizure of Power*, 436–7;
    De Felice, *Mussolini il fascista*, I, 5.

28 Ledeen, *The First Duce*, 102–4, 147–50.

29 Ledeen, *The First Duce*, 162–94; Odon Por, *Fascism* (New York, 1923), i–xxi; De Felice,
    Mussolini il rivoluzionario, 634–43; OO, XV, 55–6, 75, 78–9, 103–4, 126–7, 131–2, 150–1,

158–61, 172–4, 195–6, 199–201, 209–10, 234–5, 255, 259, 279–80; Olga Majolo Molinari, *La stampa periodica romana dal 1900 al 1926*, 2 vols. (Rome, 1977), I, 314–5; Seton-Watson, *Italy from Liberalism*, 570.

30 OO, XV, 306–8; OO, XVI, 5–24, 32–43, 47–8, 50–3, 61–2, 66–80, 449.

31 Gerra, *L'impresa*, 275–307; Ferdinando Cordova, *Arditi e legionari dannunziani* (Padua, 1968), 114–15; Seton-Watson, *Italy from Liberalism*, 581–2.

32 OO, XVI, 39, 81–9; Seton-Watson, *Italy from Liberalism*, 586.

33 OO, XVI, 11, 75, 155–7; De Felice, *Mussolini il rivoluzionario*, 651–6.

34 Giuseppe Tamburrano, *Pietro Nenni* (Bari, 1986), 61, 72–3; Cordova, *Arditi*, 115–17; Pini and Susmel, *Mussolini*, II, 87–9, 93–5; Lyttelton, *The Seizure of Power*, 40, 48–9; De Felice, *Mussolini il rivoluzionario*, 607; Seton-Watson, *Italy from Liberalism*, 586–7; OO, XVI, 96–7, 101–3, 124–5, 129, 131.

35 Podenzani, *Il libro di Ada Negri*, 155–6, 160; NA, T586, roll 23, frame 438; NMBP, MGS to Butler, n.d. but mid-December 1938; ACS, Mostra della Rivoluzione Fascista, b. 44, f. 114, sf. 99, "Sarfati [*sic*], avv. Cesare," Marinelli to Cesare Sarfatti, May 23, 1921.

36 OOA, XXXVIII, 128; Pini and Susmel, *Mussolini*, II, 104; "La vibrante commemorazione di Roberto Sarfatti a Milano," *Il Popolo d'Italia*, February 1, 1921; T/K, V, 630.

37 OO, XVI, 453; OOA, XXXVIII, 128; Pini and Susmel, *Mussolini*, II, 103–4.

38 De Felice, *Mussolini il rivoluzionario*, 607.

39 Edvige Mussolini, *Mio fratello Benito*, 163–4, 229–31 [quote, 164]; Comes, *Ada Negri*, 117–8; OOA, XXXVII, vi–xiii; Duilio Susmel, "Verità e romanzo giallo sui diari di Mussolini," *Tempo*, July 9, 1960, 22–3; Bernard W. Henderson, *The Life and Principate of the Emperor Hadrian, A.D. 76–138* (London, 1923), 274.

According to Susmel, the opening passage of Mussolini's diary may have read: "The year 1921 appears bearing great hopes but also great bitterness. In the silence of this final night [of the year], I hear the story of all the years past, eager, today as yesterday, to live, to struggle, to conquer . . ." (Susmel, "Verità," 22–3). Authentic or not, this reads more like Margherita's prose than Mussolini's.

40 OO, XVI, 464–6; Pini and Susmel, *Mussolini*, II, 105; Mattioli, *Mussolini aviatore*, 61–6.

41 Edvige Mussolini, *Mio fratello Benito*, 164; Marcello Staglieno, "Margherita Sarfatti, la ninfa Egeria del Duce," *Il Giornale*, July 28, 1987; MGS, *The Life*, 275; idem, *Dux*, 233; Rachele Mussolini, *Benito il mio uomo*, (Milan, 1958), 68–9 [quote]; idem, *Mussolini privato*, (Milan, 1980), 80, 83–4.

42 MGS, *The Life*, 283.

43 Pini and Susmel, *Mussolini*, II, 107–9; OO, XVI, 214–226; Seton-Watson, *Italy from Liberalism*, 563.

44 MGS, *Dux*, 233.

45 MGS, *The Life*, 283–4; Pini and Susmel, *Mussolini*, II, 109.

CHAPTER 17: THE MARCH ON ROME

1 Seton-Watson, *Italy from Liberalism*, 585–8; OO, XVI, 272–3; 317, 476.

2 OO, XVI, 478; *Statistiche delle elezioni generali politiche* (Rome, 1921).

3 *Il Popolo d'Italia*, May 19, 1921; "L'elenco dei deputati fascisti," ibid., May 20, 1921; OO, XVI, 349–55; MGS, *The Life*, 284–5.

4 Seton-Watson, *Italy from Liberalism*, 588–9; De Felice, *Mussolini il fascista*, I, 92.

5 Seton-Watson, *Italy from Liberalism*, 590–1; OO, XVI, 358–62, 377–9; ibid., XVII, 5–16.

6 Mattioli, *Mussolini aviatore*, 81–4; Pini and Susmel, *Mussolini*, II, 123–4; Comes, *Ada Negri*, 117; OO, XVI, 3.

7 Giuseppe Villaroel, "Margherita Sarfatti," *Giornale dell'Isola*, July 4, 1921; Mussolini to Negri, July 1921, OOA, II, 131; MGS, "Venti giorni attraverso la civiltà della Sicilia," *Secolo XX*, December 1, 1921; idem, "Lettere da Berlino: Un'affermazione d'arte italiana," *Il Popolo d'Italia*, April 30, 1921; idem, *Acqua passata*, 204–13; Comes, *Ada Negri*, 117.

8 *Clemente Rebora: Lettere,* I, 411; Arnaldo Frateili, *Dall'Aragno al Rosati: Ricordi di vita letteraria* (Milan, 1963), 182; ACS, CFM, b. 20, f. 33, sf. "Sarfatti," MGS to Martini, October 20, 1921; Staglieno, "Margherita Sarfatti"; Rossi, *Trentatrè vicende,* 54; Dino Mattoli, *Mezzo secolo di strada* (Perugia, 1953), 111.

9 MGS, *I vivi e l'ombra* (Milan, 1921); MGS to Meriano, May 27, 1921, AFM; E. Farietti, *"I vivi e l'ombra* di Margherita Sarfatti," *La Parola e il Libro,* January 1922, 22; Arturo Marpicati, *Saggi di letteratura* (Florence, 1933), 389–93; Benzi and Sironi, *Sironi illustratore,* 219.

10 OO, XVI, 431–46. Sarfatti may have collaborated directly on writing Mussolini's speech for the Chamber. Her mark on it is unmistakable. She had introduced Mussolini to the writings of the Manchester School of economists, whose ideas Mussolini clearly had adopted in his defense of capitalism. The quotes Mussolini used in his speech from Carducci and the Latin playwright Terence also indicate her influence. In the foreign-policy sections of his address, Mussolini's strong anti-German tone and his description of the advance of Germanic culture over the Alps reflected one of Sarfatti's deepest concerns.

Two other passages also suggest her role in shaping the text indirectly. After describing the situation in Palestine and asking whether Zionism was incompatible with Italian nationalism, Mussolini stressed his antipathy to anti-Semitism and added: "I recognize the sacrifice of blood given by the Italian Jews in the war has been large and generous . . ." (ibid., 439).

Further on, when analyzing the domestic policies of the Popolari, Mussolini noted: "I am not, when you come down to it, an advocate of divorce, because I believe that problems of a sentimental nature cannot be resolved with juridical formulas. But I beg the Popolari to consider if it is just that the rich can divorce by going to Hungary, while ordinary poor devils are forced sometimes to carry their chains all their lives" (ibid., 443).

11 Seton-Watson, *Italy from Liberalism,* 592; Cordova, *Arditi,* 70.

12 OO, XVI, 39, 42; Gaetano Salvemini, *The Fascist Dictatorship in Italy* (London, 1928), 80; Pietro Nenni, *Storia di quattro anni* (Rome, 1946), 147–9; De Felice, *Mussolini il fascista,* I, 753–5.

13 Seton-Watson, *Italy from Liberalism,* 592–3; Pini and Susmel, *Mussolini,* II, 129; OO, XVI, 67–70, 73–5, 79–83; De Felice, *Mussolini il fascista,* I, 753–5.

14 For a detailed history of Fascism from June 1921 to March 1922, see De Felice, *Mussolini il fascista,* I, 100–201.

15 Grandi, *Il mio paese,* 144–6; OO, XVII, 91.

16 Grandi, *Il mio paese,* 146–8; OO, XVII, 103–5.

17 Guerri, *Italo Balbo,* 90–1, 96–7; Segrè, *Italo Balbo,* 62–5; OO, XVII, 206–7, 211–2.

18 De Felice, *Mussolini il fascista,* I, 183–9; OO, XVII, 216–24, 229–35, 241; Lilian T. Mowrer, *Journalist's Wife* (New York, 1937), 93–4.

19 OO, XVII, 271–2, 319–20, 334–50; Segrè, *Italo Balbo,* 68–72; MGS, *The Life,* 46; Grandi, *Il mio paese,* 155; Seton-Watson, *Italy from Liberalism,* 594–6; Detragiache, "Il fascismo femminile."

20 OO, XVII, 221.

21 Bottai, *Diario, 1944–1948,* 544–5; Enrico Franchi, "Mercoledì sera: Casa Sarfatti," *Corriere Adriatico,* July 8, 1926.

22 Mussolini to Sarfatti, January 9(?), 1924, OO, XX, 343; Mussolini, "Breve preludio," *Gerarchia* (January 1922), 1–2, now in OO, XVIII, 19–20; Georges Roux, *Mussolini* (Paris, 1960), 97; De Felice, *Mussolini il fascista,* I, 228; MGS, *The Life,* 289; idem, *Dux,* 255.

23 Fiammetta Sarfatti Gaetani to PVC, November 4, 1987. Sarfatti used El Sereno in *Avanti!* as early as 1908. See Nozzoli, "Margherita Sarfatti, Organizzatrice di cultura," 234.

24 Roux, *Mussolini,* 97; OO, XVIII, 19–20; MGS, *Acqua passata,* 35; interview with Dr. Piero Foà, July 27, 1987; ACS, CFM, b. 20, f. 33, sf. "Sarfatti," MGS to Martini, January 5, 1922; Rossana Bossaglia to PVC, August 6, 1987; De Felice, *Mussolini il fascista,* I, 188, 228–9. Three of Sarfatti's first four articles under her own name for *Gerarchia* were devoted to English literature: "La passione morale negli scrittori inglesi," February 1922; "Il re del creato (Kipling)," March 1922; "Lo spirito che nega (Shaw)," June 1922. The other article,

"Una voltura," May 1922, was a review of her friend Alfredo Panzini's latest novel, *Il padrone sono me.*

25 MGS, *Acqua passata,* 35–6; Emily Braun, "Illustrations of Propaganda," 100.

26 OO, XVII, 66–72. The article is clearly the genesis of many of the ideas and arguments in "The Doctrine of Fascism," the official credo of the Fascist party that appeared over Mussolini's name in 1932.

27 Seton-Watson, *Italy from Liberalism,* 596–8, 601–6; De Felice, *Mussolini il fascista,* I, 202–8.

28 Pini and Susmel, *Mussolini,* II, 169–74; De Felice, *Mussolini il fascista,* I, 233–9; OO, XVIII, 90–106, 119–24. The *Gerarchia* article, "Maschere e volto della Germania" (March 1922), took its title from the concluding lines of Sarfatti's January 23, 1919, *Il Popolo d'Italia* article on Germany, "Raffronti."

29 De Felice, *Mussolini il fascista,* I, 195–201.

30 De Felice, *Mussolini il fascista,* I, 263–81; Cardozo, *Agrarian Elites,* 336–9.

31 Seton-Watson, *Italy from Liberalism,* 606–11; Segrè, *Italo Balbo,* 79–89; Guerri, *Italo Balbo,* 109–22; Grandi, *Il mio paese,* 161–4.

32 Seton-Watson, *Italy from Liberalism,* 611–2; Carlo Alberto Biggini, *Storia inedita della conciliazione* (Milan, 1942), 63–5; OO, XVIII, 221, 252–3, 318–20, 331; De Felice, *Mussolini il fascista,* I, 260–2; "Il Vaticano e il Partito Popolare," *Il Popolo d'Italia,* October 20, 1922.

33 Pini and Susmel, *Mussolini,* II, 151–2.

34 Segrè, *Italo Balbo,* 71–3, 95–7; Grandi, *Il mio paese,* 161; Fiammetta Sarfatti Gaetani to PVC, November 27, 1985; NA, Microfilm record group M1446, roll 9, frames 1180, 1182.

35 Trapani, "Mia madre Margherita Sarfatti," 40; Ercole Boratto, "Esercizi spirituali per la 'marcia su Roma,' " *Giornale del Mattino,* March 29, 1946; Marzorati, *Margherita Sarfatti,* 97, 123 (MGS quote).

36 De Felice, *Mussolini il fascista,* I, 281–320.

37 OO, XVIII, 411–21; De Felice, *Mussolini il fascista,* I, 333–5.

38 MGS, *The Life,* 225–30; Pini and Susmel, *Mussolini,* II, 209.

39 Boratto, "Esercizi spirituali"; Trapani, "Mia madre Margherita Sarfatti."

40 De Felice, *Mussolini il fascista,* I, 335–45; OO, XVIII, 581–2; Segrè, *Italo Balbo,* 98–100; Cesare Maria De Vecchi, *Il quadrumviro scomodo: Il vero Mussolini nelle memorie del piu monarchico dei fascisti* (Milan, 1983), 65–7.

41 Marzorati, *Margherita Sarfatti,* 125; Rossi, *Mussolini com'era,* 113.

42 De Vecchi, *Il quadrumviro scomodo,* 71.

43 De Felice, *Mussolini il fascista,* I, 344–7; OO, XVIII, 299–300, 453–60; Pini and Susmel, *Mussolini,* II, 219–32; Seton-Watson, *Italy from Liberalism,* 622–3.

44 De Begnac, *Palazzo Venezia,* 208; De Felice, *Mussolini il fascista,* I, 306 n. 3.

45 Piazzesi, *Diario,* 245–7; Werner von der Schulenburg, "Um Benito Mussolini," 6, unpublished typescript, Biblioteca Comunale di Como; NA, M1446, roll 9, frames 1181–3. For the most thorough account of the March on Rome, see Antonio Repaci, *La marcia su Roma,* 2 vols. (Rome, 1963).

46 Rochat, *L'esercito italiano,* 399–408; Emilio De Bono, "L'esercito così come è oggi," *Il Popolo d'Italia,* September 14, 1922.

47 Giovanni Artieri, *Cronaca del regno d'Italia,* 2 vols. (Milan, 1978), II, 254–5; De Felice, *Mussolini il fascista,* I, 354–70; Seton-Watson, *Italy from Liberalism,* 623–7; KAJP, memoirs, Chapter XXI, "King Victor Emmanuel III," 327. Margherita may have accompanied Mussolini on some of his trips to Capodimonte. She hinted at close ties with Elena, the Duchess of Aosta, in 1922. See her article of December 1, 1922, in *Il Popolo d'Italia,* "Nostalgie d'Africa."

48 "Il 'Lohengrin' al Dal Verme" and " 'Il Cigno' di Franz Molnar," *Il Popolo d'Italia,* October 25, 1922; Rossi, *Trentatrè vicende,* 365; L. Kemechey, *Il Duce: The Life and Work of Benito Mussolini* (New York, 1930), 170; Monelli, *Mussolini piccolo borghese,* 132; Gaspare Giudice, *Benito Mussolini* (Turin, 1971), 371; MGS, *Dux,* 275; Staglieno, "Margherita Sarfatti."

49 Marzorati, *Margherita Sarfatti,* 126; MGS, *Dux,* 277–81.

50 De Felice, *Mussolini il fascista*, I, 372–4; OO, XVIII, 464; Richard Collier, *Duce! The Rise and Fall of Benito Mussolini* (London, 1971), 27–8; Gian Franco Vené, *La lunga notte del 28 ottobre 1922* (Milan, 1972), 286; Anita Pensotti, *Rachele: settant'anni con Mussolini nel bene e nel male* (Milan, 1983), 40–1; idem, *Rachele*, 39; Staglieno, "Margherita Sarfatti."

51 KAJP, memoirs, folder for chapters XX and XXI, 327; Staglieno, "Margherita Sarfatti"; De Felice, *Mussolini il fascista*, I, 374.

52 MGS, *Dux*, 281; De Felice, *Mussolini il fascista*, I, 374–87; Pini and Susmel, *Mussolini*, II, 249–56; *Il Popolo d'Italia*, October 31, 1922.

53 Seton-Watson, *Italy from Liberalism*, 629–32.

54 OO, XIX, 17, 27; Seton-Watson, *Italy from Liberalism*, 631.

55 NA, Microfilm record group T586, roll 23, frames 438–9; Italo Balbo to Umberto Klinger, January 16, 1926, UKP; Marzorati, *Margherita Sarfatti*, 95; Schulenburg, "Um Benito Mussolini," 5.

CHAPTER 18: NOVECENTO ITALIANO

1 Rebora, *Lettere*, I, 394; Roux, *Mussolini*, 85.

2 Crispolti, *Storia e critica del futurismo*, 149–50. On the origins of the December 1919 survey, which was actually Marinetti's summary of the currents displayed at the Futurist exhibit that March, see Galleria Centrale d'Arte, *Grande Esposizione Nazionale Futurista, cit.*, 6; *Mostra del Novecento Italiano*, 321–2; MGS, *Achille Funi*, 16; Marzorati, *Margherita Sarfatti*, 65; Comisso, *Arturo Martini: Lettere*, 48–52, 503; Amedeo Sarfatti, unpublished memoir, 18–19, AmSP.

3 Emily Braun, *Mario Sironi*, Chapter 4, "Sironi and the Novecento," n. 89. The manifesto, "Contro tutti i ritorni in pittura: Manifesto futurista," January 11, 1920, is now in Camesasca and Gian Ferrari, *Mario Sironi: Scritti*, 13–7.

4 MGS, *Espejo de la pintura actual* (Buenos Aires, 1947), 151; Achille Funi, "Il Novecento," *MG* (March 10, 1971), now in Bossaglia, *Il "Novecento Italiano,"* 78; see also MGS, *Storia della pittura moderna*, 125; idem, "Il Novecento Italiano (sunto)," ms (n.d.), FP; Amedeo Sarfatti, unpublished memoir, 1, AmSP; Comisso, *Arturo Martini: Lettere*, 48–52, 503; Raffaele De Grada, "La critica del Novecento," in *Mostra del Novecento Italiano*, 48; Dematte, 136–7; Vincenzo Costantini, *Pittura italiana contemporanea* (Milan, 1934), 243; Crispolti, *Storia e critica del futurismo*, 116, 150; Bossaglia, *Il "Novecento Italiano,"* 9, 11–12; Camesasca and Gian Ferrari, *Mario Sironi: Scritti*, 428; Gian Ferrari, *Sironi*, 186, 188.

5 MGS, "La nuova Galleria d'Arte," *Il Popolo d'Italia*, April 3, 1920; idem, "Considerazioni sulla pittura a proposito dell'Esposizione 'Arte,'" *Il Convegno*, III (1920), 69–74. The "Contro tutti i ritorni" manifesto, cit., bears strong resemblance to sections of this review and to Sarfatti's "La Mostra Funi," *Il Popolo d'Italia*, October 27, 1920. The other artists in the exhibit were Aldo Carpi, S. Penagini, Vincenzo Costantini (Sironi's brother-in-law), Ada Van der Schalk, Gigiotti Zanini, Leto Livi, Ugo Piatti, and Emilio Pettoruti.

6 MGS, *Achille Funi*, 16; idem, "La Mostra Funi." On Sarfatti's concept of "modern classicity" see Elena Pontiggia, "Il miraggio della classicità: Cenni sulla poetica del Novecento," *Italia anni trenta: Opere dalle collezioni d'arte del commune di Milano* (Milan, 1989), 23–36.

7 MGS, "Lettere da Berlino: Un'affermazione d'arte italiana," *Il Popolo d'Italia*, April 30, 1921; idem, *Acqua passata*, 207–8; Enrico Somarè, "Arte italiana contemporanea," *Il Primato* (November 1921), 52–60; Bossaglia, *Il "Novecento Italiano,"* 12.

8 MGS, "Il Seicento," *Valori Plastici* (April 1921), 95–6. The article was written as a response to the debate on the seventeenth century opened by Giorgio De Chirico; Mangoni, *L'interventismo della cultura*, 38–9, 86; MGS, "Bottega di poesia e altre esposizioni," *Il Popolo d'Italia*, January 13, 1922.

9 Massimo Campigli to MGS, June 16, 1922, AmSP; MGS, "La pittura italiana alla XIII Biennale internazionale," *Il Popolo d'Italia*, May 4, 1922; idem, "Teorie," ibid., September 8, 1922; Bossaglia, *Il "Novecento Italiano,"* 12–13.

10 Bossaglia, Il "Novecento Italiano," 7–9; idem, "Caratteri e sviluppo di Novecento," in *Mostra del Novecento Italiano*, 23–4; Anselmo Bucci to Ugo Nebbia, n.d., in Ugo Nebbia,

La pittura del Novecento, 2nd ed. (Milan, 1946), 184–6; Tempesti, *Arte dell'Italia fascista,* 59–60; Costantini, *Pittura italiana contemporanea,* 243.

11 MGS, *Storia della pittura moderna,* 123–5; Raffaele De Grada, "La critica del Novecento," in *Mostra del Novecento Italiano,* 48; autobiographical manuscript by Leonardo Dudreville, in Bossaglia, *Il "Novecento Italiano,"* 65–6; MGS, "Il Novecento Italiano (sunto)," ms (n.d.), FP.

12 Bossaglia, "Caratteri e sviluppo di Novecento," 23; Lino Pesaro, "Luci ed ombre del '900," *Il Regime Fascista,* June 19, 1931, now in Bossaglia, *Il "Novecento Italiano,"* 123; MGS, "Il movimento artistico del Novecento Italiano," *Scena Illustrata* (January 1953), 14; interview with Fiammetta Sarfatti Gaetani, May 16, 1985.

13 Dudreville manuscript, 66–7; Funi, "Il Novecento," 78–9; Pesaro, "Luci ed ombre," 123–4.

14 Bucci to Nebbia, cit.; Dudreville manuscript, 66; Pesaro, "Luci ed ombre," 125; Carlo Carrà, "Il Novecento alla ribalta," *L'Ambrosiano,* December 18, 1922.

The concept of the *Novecento* as a cultural movement may not have been entirely original with the Italians. As early as 1906, Eugenio d'Ors, a young Spanish intellectual from Barcelona, had coined the term *Noucentisme* to describe a cultural movement of his own that preached a return to Mediterranean traditions and a simplified classicism in art. As Sarfatti was to do in Italy, d'Ors rejected the "anarchy" of artistic modernism and insisted on a return to order. In later years, Sarfatti and d'Ors became friends, and she probably visited him during her trip to Spain in 1924. Whether she knew him earlier is unknown, although she must have been familiar with his ideas. Before World War I, d'Ors and other Catalans spent considerable time in Paris, which Sarfatti also visited often. Moreover, Bucci, who suggested the name for the Italian group, had lived in Paris from 1906 to 1914, when d'Ors was there. Francesc Fontbona, "The Art of *Noucentisme,*" in Michael Raeburn, ed., *Homage to Barcelona: The City and Its Art, 1888–1936* (London, 1986), 169–81; Alan Yates, "Catalan Literature Between Modernisme and Noucentisme," ibid., 253–63; Bossaglia, *Il "Novecento Italiano,"* 213; Robert S. Lubar, "Cubism, Classicism, and Ideology," in Elizabeth Cowling and Jennifer Mundy, eds., *On Classic Ground: Picasso, Léger, de Chirico and the New Classicism, 1910–1930* (London, 1990), 309–21.

15 MGS to Mussolini, letter headed "Ore 2 del mattino, Mercoledì," n.d. but January 1923, GSP.

16 Rossi, *Mussolini com'era,* 132–3, 140–2; Collier, *Duce!,* 71; Mattoli, *Mezzo secolo di strada,* 111; Pini and Susmel, *Mussolini,* II, 279.

17 "Krassin a colloquio con Mussolini," December 4, 1922, OO, XIX, 424–5; Roy MacGregor-Hastie, *The Day of the Lion: The Life and Death of Fascist Italy, 1922–1945* (New York, 1963), 137; Giorgio Petracchi, *La Russia rivoluzionaria nella politica italiana, 1917/25* (Rome-Bari, 1982), 232.

18 MGS, *Mussolini: Como lo conocí,* XI.

19 Mussolini to Sarfatti, December 11, 1922, OO, XXXV, 272–3; Trapani, "Mia madre Margherita Sarfatti," I, 45.

20 Ercole Boratto, "Esercizi spirituali."

21 Only some of the letters Margherita sent to Mussolini in January and February 1923 can be dated. These mention events that occurred during Margherita's visits to Rome and Mussolini's to Milan during that period. While Mussolini's movements can be dated with precision, Margherita's cannot. As a result, the exact sequence of events described in the letters cannot be established.

22 MGS to Mussolini, n.d., beginning "Ore 2 del mattino, Mercoledì", GSP; Rossi, *Mussolini com'era,* 191–2.

23 MGS to Mussolini, three letters, January 1, 1923, GSP; Armando Ravaglioli, *Roma la capitale: Immagini di cento anni,* 2 vols. (Rome, 1971), II, 35; Pini and Susmel, *Mussolini,* II, 287.

24 MGS to Mussolini, letter headed "Ore 2 del mattino, Mercoledì," n.d. but January 1923, GSP; MGS, *Life,* 317; Navarra, *Memorie* (Milan, 1972), 73.

25 Boratto, "Un'enciclica non vale una telefonata," *Giornale del Mattino,* April 3, 1946; GSP; MGS to Mussolini, January 27, 28, 30, 1923.

26 MGS to Mussolini, January 28, 30, 1923, and letters, n.d., beginning "Caro, caro, adorato, mio infinitamente adorato" and "Caro adorato, se vuoi, io sola vengo a prenderti," GSP.

27 MGS to Mussolini, n.d., letters beginning "Adorato adorato mio adorato," "Illustre Presidente, sarebbe mia intensione di ricarmi," "Amore mio, ma come fai," GSP; Amedeo Sarfatti to PVC, March 17, 1989.

28 MGS to Mussolini, 23 letters, telegrams, and notes, January-February 1923, GSP. These messages indicate that Margherita sent even more missives to Mussolini and refer to his many replies. Numerous telephone calls are also mentioned. Some undated envelopes contain more than one letter, giving some indication of their sequence.

29 GSP, unnamed Milan city councilor to MGS, January 25, 1923; Stanford Griffith to MGS, January 30, 1923; MGS to Mussolini, January 30 [?], 1923; MGS to Mussolini, n.d. but late February 1923; MGS to Mussolini, n.d., letters beginning "Illustre presidente, sarebbe mia intensione di ricarmi," "Adorato adorato mio adorato," "Amore caro, grande adorato e disperante."

30 MGS to Mussolini, February 24, 1923, GSP.

31 MGS to Mussolini, n.d. but early 1923, four-page letter in blue and black ink addressed "Amore mio," GSP.

32 Collier, *Duce!*, 71; Morgan, *Spurs on the Boot*, 137; Rossi, *Mussolini com'era*, 143; Navarra, *Memorie*, 25–6; Paolo Monelli, *Mussolini: The Intimate Life of a Demagogue* (New York, 1954), 98–9.

33 Mussolini, *Benito il mio uomo*, 97; Ugo Guspini, *L'orecchio del regime: Le intercettazioni telefoniche al tempo del fascismo* (Milan, 1973), 69–70; Carofiglio, *Vita di Mussolini*, 148; Monelli, *Mussolini*, 98–9; Morgan, *Spurs on the Boot*, 100–1; Novara, *Memorie*, 25–6; Kirkpatrick, *Mussolini*, 168.

34 Carofiglio, *Vita di Mussolini*, 147–8; Monelli, *Mussolini*, 99.

35 Trapani, "Fu mia madre," II, 50; Carofiglio, *Vita di Mussolini*, 148–49; Navarra, *Memorie*, 29; MGS, *Dux*, 304; MGS, *The Life*, 342.

36 Prezzolini, *Diario, 1900–1941*, 378–9; Morgan, *Spurs on the Boot*, 137.

37 Interview with Magalì Sarfatti-Larson, May 12, 1987; Balabanoff, *My Life as a Rebel*, 55–6; ACS, MI-DPP, f. "Sarfatti, Margherita," report of April 26, 1930; GSP, passim; FP, passim; Amerigo Montemaggiori, *Dizionario della dottrina fascista* (Turin, 1934), 479–80; U[go] S[tille], "La Sarfatti ha venduto le lettere di Mussolini," *Corriere d'Informazione*, December 3, 1948; Guido Orlando as told to Sam Merwin, *Confessions of a Scoundrel* (Philadelphia, 1954), 72; IDSP, passim.

38 Calipso, *Vita segreta di Mussolini* (Rome, 1944), 22; Galeazzo Ciano, *Diario, 1937–1943* (Milan, 1980), 161; Pini and Susmel, *Mussolini*, II, 110; Collier, *Duce!*, 76; Boratto, "Avventure di lestofanti," *Giornale del Mattino*, March 28, 1946; Trapani, "Mia madre Margherita Sarfatti," September 10, 1982, 42, 45; MGS to Mussolini, January 28, 1923, GSP.

39 Carofiglia, *Vita di Mussolini*, 148; MGS, "Lo spirito che nega (Shaw)," *Gerarchia*, June 1922, 317; Boratto, "Liquidazione dell'amica matura," *Giornale del Mattino*, March 31, 1946.

40 Veneziana, *Storia italiana d'amore*; Angela Curti Cucciati, "Un'amica di Mussolini racconta," *Oggi*, November 10, 1949; Spinosa, *I figli del duce*, 11, 213; Navarra, *Memorie*, 209–19. His biographer, Duilio Susmel, counted 169 women as Mussolini's lovers. Giordano Bruno Guerri, *Galeazzo Ciano, una vita, 1903–1944* (Milan, 1979), 69.

41 Curti Cucciati, "Un'amica di Mussolini," *Oggi*, November 17, 1949; BP, diary entry for December 29, 1951; MGS to Sironi, July 11, 1930, FP; Boratto, "Liquidazione dell'amica matura"; ACS, MI-DPP, f. "Sarfatti, Margherita," report of December 31, 1929.

   Turati was secretary of the Fascist party from March 1926 to December 1930. It should be mentioned that Biddle followed his account of Sarfatti's story about Rachele by adding, "One can hardly ever trust a word [Sarfatti] says." Nonetheless, the story rings true for reasons that follow.

42 Curti Cucciati, "Un'amica di Mussolini," November 10, 1949.

43 Navarra, *Memorie*, 209–15; Renzo De Felice, *Mussolini il duce*, I.: *Gli anni del consenso, 1929–1936* (Turin, 1974), 20.

44 Simonetta Fiori, "Quando Dux entrò nella sua vita," *La Repubblica Mercurio*, April 29, 1989; interview with Frank Gervasi, May 5, 1986; Navarra, *Memorie*, 219; Calipso, *Vita segreta*, 22; ACS, MI-DPP, f. "Sarfatti, Margherita," reports of April 11, 1930, November 31, 1931, June 28, 1933, and February 26, 1934; Marzorati, *Margherita Sarfatti*, 14–15, 52, 173–4.

45 Sarfatti mentions the speech in an interview, "Judith," "She Is the Comrade of Il Duce," 657; MGS to Mussolini, four-page letter on blue paper, n.d. but January 1923, GSP; "Una conferenza di Margherita Sarfatti," *La Donna* (February 1923), 35; "Una conferenza di Margherita Sarfatti," *La Tribuna*, January 24, 1923; "Margherita Sarfatti al Circolo Roma," *Il Giornale d'Italia*, January 26, 1923; "Una conferenza di Margherita Sarfatti al Circolo di Roma," *Il Popolo d'Italia*, January 26, 1923. In 1930 Sarfatti gave a speech with the same title, "Alle fonti della pittura moderna: La bella conferenza tenuta de Margherita Sarfatti," *Il Mattino d'Italia* (Buenos Aires), September 17, 1930.

46 "Un omaggio a Mussolini di poeti, romanzieri e pittori," November 3, 1922, in Camesasca and Gian Ferrari, *Mario Sironi: Scritti*, 20.

47 Camesasca and Gian Ferarri, *Mario Sironi: Scritti*, 67–8.

48 Camesasca and Gian Ferarri, *Mario Sironi: Scritti*, 68.

49 Pesaro, "Luci ed ombre," 125–6.

50 "Alla mostra del Novecento," March 26, 1923, OO, XIX, 187–88; Bianca Riccio, "La Sarfatti, Mussolini e il Novecento," *La Repubblica Mercurio*, April 29, 1989.

51 Bossaglia, "Caratteri e sviluppo di Novecento," 30–1.

52 Gino Severini, *Du cubisme au classicisme* (Paris, 1922); MGS, "Teorie," *Il Popolo d'Italia*, September 8, 1922; Tempesti, *Arte dell'Italia fascista*, 43–4; Carlo Carrà's review of Severini's book is in *L'Esame* (June 1922), 212–18.; Ugo Nebbia, "Sul movimento pittorico contemporaneo (1913–1924)," *Emporium* (March 1924), 185, 188; "Novecento," *Enciclopedia italiana*, XXIV (Rome 1934), 994; Giuseppe Prezzolini, *La cultura italiana*, 2nd ed. (Milan, 1930), 420.

53 Claudia Gian Ferrari, ed., *Ubaldo Oppi* (Milan, 1989), 10.

54 "Alla mostra del Novecento," *Il Popolo d'Italia*, March 27, 1923; Francesco Messina, "Ricordo di Medardo Rosso: Dì un pù, Benito!" *Il Mondo*, undated clipping in authors' possession; Nino Barbantini, *Medardo Rosso* (Venice, 1950), 68; MGS, "Medardo Rosso," *Il Popolo d'Italia*, March 30, 1923; idem, *Segni colori, e luci*, 104–118.

55 Carrà, "Il Novecento alla ribalta;" MGS, "Medardo Rosso," *Il Popolo d'Italia*, March 30, 1923; idem, "L'ottocento et le novecento," *L'Amour de l'art* (May 1935), 190.

56 MGS, "Del Novecento," *L'almanacco degli artisti* (Rome, 1930), 74; idem, "Alcune considerazioni intorno alla Prima Mostra del Novecento Italiano," preface to the first issue of *Il Novecento Italiano* (Spring 1926), 2; idem, *Storia della pittura moderna*, 126, 136; idem, "La Seconda Mostra del Novecento a Milano," *Rivista Illustrata del Popolo d'Italia* (April 1929), 39; idem, "Classicismo e Novecento," *Problemi d'arte attuale* (1929), 120; idem, "Il Novecento Italiano (sunto)."

57 MGS, letter of invitation to artists, October 22, 1928, in catalog, *IIa mostra del "Novecento Italiano"* (Milan, 1929); idem, "La pittura alla IIa mostra del Novecento Italiano," *Il Popolo d'Italia*, March 2, 1929; idem, "Dove va l'arte italiana," *Rivista Illustrata del Popolo d'Italia* (April 1924), 46; idem, "La classicità all'esposizione francese di Londra," *La Stampa*, March 12, 1932; idem, "Lettre d'Italie: ottocento et novecento," *Formes* (January 1930), 28; Emily Braun, "Political Rhetoric and Poetic Irony: The Uses of Classicism in the Art of Fascist Italy," in Cowling and Mundy, *On Classic Ground*, 345–58; MGS, *Storia della pittura moderna*, 131, 139; idem, "La mostra dei sette alla Galleria di Milano," *Il Popolo d'Italia*, April 13, 1928; Piero Bargellini, *L'arte del Novecento* (Florence, 1970), 74; MGS to Bernard Berenson, July 14, [1952], BBP.

58 MGS, "Anno 1923," in *Segni, colori, e luci*, 5–8; idem, "Nei dodici mesi dall'avvento: L'arte," *Il Popolo d'Italia*, October 26, 1923; idem, "La seconda mostra del Novecento Italiano," cit., 41; MGS as quoted in Joseph B. Phillips, "Italy's Heroine of Fascism," *New York Herald Tribune, Sunday Magazine*, October 8, 1933; MGS, "Arte, fascismo e antiretorica," *Critica Fascista* (March 1, 1927), 82–4, later reprinted in her *Segni del meridiano* (Naples, 1931),

97–109; idem, "L'arte e il fascismo," in Giuseppe Pomba, ed., *La civiltà fascista* (Turin, 1928), 218, reprinted in *Il Popolo d'Italia,* February 10, 1928.

59 MGS to Mussolini, eight-page letter, n.d. but January 1923, GSP; "Per le associazioni artistiche," May 20, 1924, OO, XX, 275–6; Sarfatti's phrase appeared first in her article "Alcune considerazioni intorno alla prima mostra del Novecento Italiano," in *Il Novecento Italiano* (Spring 1926), 1, and later in her preface to the catalog, *Dieci artisti del Novecento Italiano* (Rome, 1927), 30. See also *L'almanacco degli artisti* (Rome, 1930), 48, for a facsimile of Sarfatti's autograph of that inscription.

60 MGS, "L'arte e il fascismo," 217; see also "Famous Author Sees Fascist Art in the Making," *Il Progresso Italo-Americano* (New York), August 25, 1929; MGS, "Arte e costume fascista," *Politica sociale* (1929), 203–7; idem, "Il fascismo nell'arte," *La Stampa,* May 18, 1933, and "Fascism and Art," *Atlantica* (January 15, 1937), 5, 21.

61 Dudreville manuscript, in Bossaglia, *Il "Novecento Italiano,"* 67; Camesasca and Gian Ferrari, "Note biografiche," in *Mario Sironi: Scritti,* 189; Bossaglia, *Il "Novecento Italiano,"* 55; Mario De Micheli, *Le circostanze dell'arte* (Genoa, 1987), 152; Corrado Maltese, *Storia dell'arte in Italia, 1785–1943* (Turin, 1960), 335.

62 *Chi è? Dizionario degli italiani d'oggi* (Rome, 1940), 684; *Catalogo della XIII esposizione internationale d'arte della Città di Venezia* (Milan, 1922), 3.

63 Gian Ferrari, *Ubaldo Oppi,* 10; MGS, "Artisti nuovi: Ubaldo Oppi," *Rivista Illustrata del Popolo d'Italia* (November-December 1924); idem, "Daguerre non ne ha colpa," *Il Popolo d'Italia,* April 16, 1926; Pesaro, "Luci ed ombre," 129; Bossaglia, *Il "Novecento Italiano,"* 17–18; Fagiolo dell'Arco, *Realismo magico,* 19–20, 289, 339.

64 Pesaro, "Luci ed ombre," 129–30; MGS, "Mostra dei sei pittori del '900," *Catalogo della XIV esposizione internazionale d'arte della Città di Venezia* (Milan, 1924), 76–8, now also in Bossaglia, *Il "Novecento Italiano,"* 84–5.

65 MGS, *Achille Funi,* 17; idem, "La pittura italiana alla XIII Biennale internazionale," *Il Popolo d'Italia,* May 4, 1922; idem, "Le arti plastiche," *Almanacco enciclopedico del Popolo d'Italia, 1923* (Milan, 1923), 328; *On Classic Ground,* 107–8.

66 This and the subsequent discussion of Sironi's work is based on the important work of Emily Braun, *Mario Sironi, 1919–1945,* Chapter 4. See also Bossaglia, *Il "Novecento Italiano,"* 18; *Mostra del Novecento Italiano,* 24; MGS, *Segni, colori, e luci,* 136.

67 The two episodes are recounted in the Dudreville manuscript, in Bossaglia, *Il "Novecento Italiano,"* 72, 86–7.

68 Fossati, *Pittura e scultura fra le due querre,* Part Two, III, *Storia dell'arte italiana,* 175–6; Crispolti, *Storia e critica del futurismo,* 230–4; Salaris, *Storia del futurismo,* 172–7; MGS, *Acqua passata,* 173–4.

69 MGS, "Dove va l'arte d'Italia," 46; idem, "Primavera d'arte a Venezia: Alcuni artisti italiani alla XIV Biennale," *Il Popolo d'Italia,* April 25, 1924.

70 Pesaro, "Luci ed ombre," 130–1; Dudreville manuscript, in Bossaglia, *Il "Novecento Italiano,"* 72.

CHAPTER 19: A CORPSE BETWEEN HIS FEET

1 De Felice, *Mussolini il fascista,* I, 228; Renato Bertacchini, *Le riviste del Novecento* (Florence, 1980), 141–42; De Begnac, *Palazzo Venezia,* 235; Arnaldo Mussolini to Mussolini, May 10, 1927, in Duilio Susmel, ed., *Carteggio Arnaldo-Benito Mussolini* (Florence, 1954), 83.

2 Gaetano Salvemini, *Prelude to World War II* (New York, 1954), 86–95; Cesare Tumedei, *La questione tunisina e l'Italia* (Bologna, 1922).

3 Amedeo Sarfatti to PVC, March 17, 1987; MGS, *Tunisiaca* (Milan, 1924), 63–4.

4 The original manuscript of Mussolini's preface to *Tunisiaca* is in ACS, *Carte della Cassetta di Zinco,* "Autografi del Duce," b. 7, f. 6.5.2; Latinus, "Italia e Tunisia," *Gerarchia* (February 1924), 71–4, now in OO, XXXV, 76–85. Other segments of *Tunisiaca* were published separately: "Qualche aspetto della terra d'Africa," *Il Popolo d'Italia,* July 13, 1923, and "Ancora il problema di Tunisia," *Gerarchia* (September 1923).

5 Cassels, *Mussolini's Early Diplomacy*, 201–6; Romano Rainero, *La rivendicazione fascista sulla Tunisia* (Milan, 1978), 126–37; Antonio Pirazzoli, "Tunisiaca," *Il Popolo d'Italia*, March 5, 1924; F. D'Amato, "Margherita Sarfatti: Tunisiaca," *La Nuova Politica Liberale* (December 1924), 354–6; Tommaso Tittoni, "Tunisia, Tripolitania e l'Italia," *Nuova Antologia* (April 1, 1924).

6 "L'on. Marcora lascia la Cassa di Risparmio," *Il Corriere della Sera*, July 12, 1923; Filippo Turati to Anna Kuliscioff, July 22, 1923, T/K, VI, 148; Michele Sarfatti to PVC, January 21, 1987; Barbariccia [Carlo Tresca], "Presentiamo Margherita Sarfatti," *Il Martello*, April 28, 1934; "La donna contaminata dal fascismo," *Risorgimento* (Buenos Aires), December 28, 1930.

7 Balabanoff, *My Life as a Rebel*, 56; MGS to Mussolini, n.d. but January 1923, GSP, letter beginning "Il giorno di Mercoledì."

8 Panzini, *Roberto Sarfatti*, 6.

9 "La morte di Cesare Sarfatti," *Il Popolo d'Italia*, January 25, 1924; "La morte dell'avv. Sarfatti," *Il Corriere della Sera*, January 25, 1924; "Necrologio," *L'Illustrazione Italiana*, February 3, 1924.

10 "I funerali dell'avv. Sarfatti," *Il Corriere della Sera*, January 27, 1924; MGS, *Acqua passata*, 104; MGS to D'Annunzio, n.d. but early 1924, letter addressed "Maestro e amico," AVDI, AG, LVIII, 3. The following year, Ada Negri dedicated her collection of poems entitled *I canti dell'isola* to Cesare and Roberto Sarfatti. The sculptor Adolfo Wildt executed a death mask of Cesare in 1927; see *Arte moderna in Italia, 1915–1935* (Florence, 1967), 149, number 726, "L'avvocato Sarfatti."

11 De Felice, *Mussolini il fascista*, I, 388–517; Carleton Beals, *Rome or Death: The Story of Fascism* (London, 1923), 310.

12 On the Cheka and Dumini's role, see "Il Memoriale Dumini," *Il Ponte*, XLII (March-April 1986), 76–93.

13 On the election and Mussolini's policies, see De Felice, *Mussolini il fascista*, I, 518–618.

14 Benito Mussolini, "Forza a consenso," *Gerarchia*, March 1923, 801–3, now in OO, XIX, 195–6; MGS, *Dux*, 291; idem, *The Life*, 327–29.

15 MGS, *Dux*, 299.

16 In 1945, while under Allied arrest, Rossi took responsibility for forming the Cheka, which he said occurred on Marinelli's orders in May 1924, the date when it came under his direction in Rome. See "Cesare Rossi si dichiara estraneo al rapimento e all'assassinio di Matteotti," *Italia del Popolo*, July 18, 1945; Dumini testimony, January 24, 1947; Rossi, *Il delitto Matteotti*, 246; De Felice, *Mussolini il fascista*, I, 619, states that the Cheka was created after April 1924.

17 On the Matteotti murder, see Giuseppe Rossini, *Il delitto Matteotti tra il Viminale e l'Aventino* (Bologna, 1966); Lyttelton, *The Seizure of Power*, 239; Mussolini, "Sobrero," in OO, XX, 303; Salvemini, *The Fascist Dictatorship in Italy*, 248.

18 "Il Memoriale Dumini," 84–8; Rossi, *Il delitto Matteotti*, 51–2; "Cesare Rossi si dichiara estraneo al rapimento e all'assassinio di Matteotti."

19 Upon her return to Italy, Sarfatti wrote two long articles on her impressions of Spain. See MGS, "Cinema Spagna," *Gerarchia*, October 1924, 614–23, and "Film di Spagna numero due," *Gerarchia*, December 1924, 725–34; idem, *Dux*, 164.

20 MGS, *Mussolini: Como lo conocí*, IV.

21 Guspini, *L'orecchio*, 46.

22 Sarfatti's recollections are in *Mussolini: Como lo conocí*, IV; Paolo Orano's meeting with Mussolini, in mid-June, is described in his *Mussolini da vicino* (Rome, 1935), 78–86.

23 Interview with Magalì Sarfatti-Larson, June 16, 1986; MGS, *Mussolini: Como lo conocí*, IV.

24 MGS, "L'inevitabile bivio," *Gerarchia*, June 1924, 333–6.

25 Monelli, *Mussolini*, 107; MGS, *Dux*, 299; Orano, *Mussolini da vicino*, 94–102; Pini and Susmel, *Mussolini*, II, 408.

26 Monelli, *Mussolini*, 108; Mussolini to Negri, June 26, 1924, GSP; MGS, *Mussolini: Como lo conocí*, IV; idem, *Dux*, 265; Rachele Mussolini, *Benito il mio uomo*, 72; Edvige Mussolini,

Mio fratello Benito, 117; Navarra, *Memorie,* 32; De Felice, *Mussolini il fascista,* I, 672; MGS, *The Life,* 275.

27 Rossi, *Il delitto Matteotti,* 62–3; Mauro Canali, ed., "La contabilità di Cesare Rossi," *Storia Contemporanea,* XIX (August 1988), 739.

28 De Felice, *Mussolini il fascista,* I, 669.

29 De Felice, *Mussolini il fascista,* I, 623–4.

30 De Felice, *Mussolini il fascista,* I, 652; Lyttelton, *The Seizure of Power,* 243.

31 See the documents in RDS "Italy. Internal Affairs, 1940–1944," 865.00/2212 1/2; "Belgium, 1923–25," Box 1, WRCP, HHP; PRO, FO, 371/10789, 75449, "Alleged British intervention to ensure cancellation of Sinclair oil concession in Italy," March 27, 1925; "Odor di petrolio e di casa Savoia," *Corriere della Sera,* December 21, 1988.

32 "Il Memoriale Dumini," 82, 86, 89; De Felice, *Mussolini il fascista,* I, 625–6; Marcello Staglieno, "Fu uno sporco affare di petrolio," *Storia Illustrata* (November 1984), 54–61; Renzo De Felice, "Capire il delitto Matteotti," *ibid.* (April 1985), 48–9; Franco Scalzo, *"Indagine per un delitto,"* ibid. (January 1986), 132–40; Claudia Damiani, *Mussolini e gli Stati Uniti, 1922–1935* (Bologna, 1980), 38–43; Matteo Pizzigallo, *Alle origini della politica petrolifera italiana* (Varese, 1981), 133–5; George Seldes, *Sawdust Caesar: The Untold Story of Mussolini and Fascism* (New York and London, 1935), 147, 221; Norman Lewis, *Naples '44* (New York, 1978), 91; James and Patience Barnes, *James V. Murphy, Translator and Interpreter of Fascist Europe* (New York, 1987), 24; Antonio G. Casanova, *Matteotti: Una vita per il socialismo* (Milan, 1974), 256; Matteo Matteotti, *Quei vent'anni: Dal fascismo all'Italia che cambia* (Milan, 1985), 205–8.

33 Cited in De Felice, *Mussolini il fascista,* I, 671.

34 MGS, *Mussolini: Como lo conocí,* X.

35 Guspini, *Orecchio,* 48–9.

36 De Felice, *Mussolini il fascista,* I, 662–70.

37 Lyttelton, *The Seizure of Power,* 260–3; De Felice, *Mussolini il fascista,* I, 696–9.

38 Rossi's memorandum is reprinted in Rossi, *Il delitto Matteotti,* 115–62; De Felice, *Mussolini il fascista,* I, 712; Pini and Susmel, *Mussolini,* II, 406.

39 On the meeting between the consuls and Mussolini, see De Felice, *Mussolini il fascista,* I, 714–15; Pini and Susmel, *Mussolini,* II, 407–8.

40 On the events of December 31–January 3, see De Felice, *Mussolini il fascista,* I, 711–22; Pini e Susmel, *Mussolini,* II, 407–8. Mussolini's speech of January 3, 1925, is in OO, XXI, 235–41. In January, Sarfatti published an article in *Gerarchia* by a regular contributor who argued that "the Matteotti kidnapping, with all its consequences, belonged *morally, politically, and historically* to fascism." See Alfredo Felici, "Politica interna," *Gerarchia,* January 1925, 63; Rossi, *Il delitto Matteotti,* 74.

41 On the establishment of the Fascist dictatorship, see De Felice, *Mussolini il fascista,* II, *L'organizzazione dello stato fascista* (Turin, 1968); Alberto Aquarone, *L'organizzazione dello stato totalitario* (Turin, 1965); Lyttelton, *The Seizure of Power,* esp. 269–307.

42 MGS, *Dux,* 264–5, 298; idem, *The Life,* 338; idem, *Dux,* 251–298; idem, *The Life,* 338.

43 MGS to Gabriele D'Annunzio, n.d. but May 1925, AVI, AG; Boratto, "Esercizi spirituali"; *Giornale del Mattino,* March 29, 1946; Sergio Marzorati, "Dal dolore alla sete d'avventura," *La Provincia,* December 17, 1988; OO, XXI, 337.

44 MGS, *Mussolini: Como lo conocí,* IV; idem, *Dux,* 298; idem, *The Life,* 339.

CHAPTER 20: DUX

1 MGS, *Dux,* 9–10; Giuseppe Prezzolini, *L'Italiano inutile: Memorie letterarie di Francia, Italia e America* (Milan, 1953), 201; idem, *Intervista sulla destra,* ed. Claudio Quarantotto (Rome, n.d.), 110; Trapani, "Mia madre Margherita Sarfatti," I, 45, II, 54; Giorgio Pillon, "Quando il Duce amava Margherita," *Il Borghese,* February 21, 1982, 496; Giovanni Ansaldo, diary entry for September 7, 1934, published as "Il pesante guidizio di Giovanni Ansaldo," *Il Giornale,* July

28, 1987; Luisa Passerini, *Mussolini immaginario: Storia di un biografia, 1915–1939* (Bari, 1991), 20, 50–1, 95.

2 On the Forlì prison notebook see MGS, *Dux*, 15, and *The Life*, 30, 64; De Begnac, *Palazzo Venezia*, 18. The notebook is now published as "La mia vita dal 29 luglio 1883 al 23 novembre 1911" in OO, XXXIII, x, 219–69. In May 1962, the notebooks were sold at Christie's in London; see Edward Lazare, ed., *American Book Prices Current, 1962, Part I* (New York, 1963), 749.

3 Trapani, "Fu mia madre," 54; Mussolini, "Preface," in MGS, *The Life*, 9–10.

4 Trapani, "Fu mia madre," 54; MGS, "Mussolini e le voci di Roma," *Gerarchia* (April 1926), 217–21; another section of *Dux* appeared in *Il Popolo d'Italia* on June 11, 1926; Nicola Tranfaglia, Paolo Murialdi, and Massimo Legnani, *La stampa italiana nell'età fascista* (Rome-Bari, 1980), 55; Prezzolini to MGS, June 28, 1926, in Margherita Marchione, ed., *Prezzolini: Un secolo di attività* (Milan, 1982), 24.

5 On page 284 of *Dux*, Sarfatti speaks of the Fascist laws passed in the winter of 1926. She therefore added to the original manuscript before it was published in Italian. See also Keighley Snowden, "Benito Mussolini," *The Bookman*, February 1926.

6 MGS, *The Life*, 115, 176, 181; idem, *Dux*, 137–8, 142.

7 MGS, *The Life*, 177, 243–4; idem, *Dux*, 144, 194–6.

8 MGS, *The Life*, 155; idem, *Dux*, 116, Sarfatti made the personal reference to her Socialist youth more oblique; on World War I, see *Dux*, 151; on Mussolini's resignation, see *The Life*, 201, and *Dux*, 162.

9 Luigi Tonelli, "Margherita Sarfatti," in *Alla ricerca della personalità: Seconda serie* (Catania, 1929), 250; Ugo Ojetti, "Mussolini," *Corriere della Sera*, July 4, 1926.

10 MGS, *Dux*, 78, *The Life*, 116; Prezzolini, *Intervista sulla destra*, 111.

11 MGS, *Dux*, 76–8.

12 MGS, *The Life*, 346.

13 MGS, *The Life*, 92–93, 307, 317; idem, *Dux*, 65–6, 275, 285.

14 Piero Meldini, "La sventurata Margherita: Panzini e la Sarfatti," in Ennio Grassi, ed., *Alfredo Panzini* (Rimini, 1985), 367; Giuseppe Bottai's review of *Dux* appeared in July 1926 in the Rome newspaper *Giornale d'Italia*; Panzini's appeared in *La Tribuna*, June 12, 1926. See Stanis Ruinas, *Scrittrici e scribacchine d'oggi* (Rome, 1930), 103–4; Arturo Marpicati, "*Dux* di Margherita Sarfatti," in *Saggi di letteratura* (Florence, 1933), 394–5; "Mussolini: From Socialist to Fascist," *The Times* (London), October 2, 1925; Nicola Tranfaglia, "Il Duce e Margherita," *La Repubblica*, August 3, 1982; Nozzoli, "Margherita Sarfatti, organizzatrice di cultura," 268–9.

15 "The Mind of Mussolini," *The Times Literary Supplement*, October 8, 1925, 6; Guido Cantini, "L'unità del pensiero di Mussolini in un libro biografico," *La Fiera Letteraria*, July 18, 1926; Gigliola De Donato and Vannas Gazzola Stacchini, *I Best Sellers del Ventennio* (Rome, 1991), 319–20.

16 MGS, *The Life*, 56–7.

17 MGS as quoted in John Carter, "Mussolini, Master of Italy," *The New York Times Book Review*, February 7, 1926; MGS to Mussolini, n.d. but January 1923, GSP; MGS, "Atti de fede," *Il Popolo d'Italia*, February 23, 1923; idem, "Mussolini al fronte," *Il Popolo d'Italia*, March 23, 1923; Passerini, *Mussolini immaginario*, 45–6, 56–7, 107; Curzio Malaparte, *Battibecco, 1953–1957* (Florence, 1967), 112–13.

Malaparte's memory of the conversation with Sarfatti was faulty. He claimed that Sarfatti described Mussolini's triumphant trip to Rome in October 1922 as having been on horseback. But, in fact, the event as described in *Dux*, 281–2, was accurate—Mussolini traveled by train.

18 On the propaganda images of Mussolini see Dino Biondi, *La fabbrica del Duce* (Florence, 1973); Philip V. Cannistraro, *La fabbrica del consenso* (Rome-Bari, 1975); De Felice and Goglia, *Mussolini: Il mito*; MGS, "Duce Glimpsed Greatness Thirty Years Ago, His Biographer Reveals," *New York American*, March 15, 1931; Nicola Tranfaglia, "Il Duce e Margherita," *La Repubblica*, August 3, 1982.

19 The only two Fascist leaders mentioned in *Dux* were Michele Bianchi and Emilio De Bono.

20 MGS, "Sosta innanzi alla mètope di Selinunte," July 28, 1922, "Dalla selce al Colosseo," November 3, 1922, "Nell'annuale della fondazione di Roma la costruttrice," April 20, 1923, "L'arte di Roma," July 6, 1923, "Qualche aspetto della terra d'Africa," July 7, 1923, "Il Museo dell'Impero," April 29, 1927, all in *Il Popolo d'Italia*; idem, "Pompei risorta," *Dedalo* (April 1924), 663 and passim; Renzo De Felice, *Intervista sul fascismo*, ed. Michael Ledeen (Rome-Bari, 1975), 12; Nemo [James Vincent Murphy], "Mussolini Is Out to Lunch," *The Star* (London), February 10, 1941.

21 MGS, "L'arte e il fascismo," in Giuseppe Pomba, ed., *La civiltà fascista* (Turin, 1928), 215; Morgan, *Spurs on the Boot*, 136. On *Romanità* see Emily Braun, "Political Rhetoric and Poetic Irony: The Uses of Classicism in the Art of Fascist Italy," in Cowling and Mundy, *On Classic Ground*, 345–358; Dino Cofrancesco, "Appunti per un'analisi del mito romano nell'ideologia fascista," *Storia Contemporanea* (June 1980), 383–412; "Il fascio romano simbolo dello stato sulle nuove monete," *Il Giornale d'Italia*, December 29, 1922; Chester L. Krause and Clifford Mischler, *Standard Catalog of World Gold Coins*, 2nd ed. (Iola, Wis., 1987), 427–8; Luigi Salvatorelli and Giovanni Mira, *Storia dell'Italia nel periodo fascista* (Turin, 1957), 385; Ricciotti Lazzero, *Il Partito Nazionale Fascista* (Milan, 1985), 36–43; "Araldica," *Enciclopedia italiana*, III, 941.

22 MGS, *The Life*, 20, *Dux*, 10; MGS, "Nei dodici mesi dopo dall'avvento: L'arte," *Popolo d'Italia*, October 26, 1923; Paola Mola, "Wildt classico, gotico e barocco," in *Adolfo Wildt, 1868–1931* (Milan, 1989), 23. Wildt also did a bronze version of the bust. See Paola Mola, "Adolfo Wildt," in *Mostra del Novecento Italiano (1923–1933)*, 435.

23 Alberto Cecchi, *"Dux di Margherita Sarfatti,"* *Critica Fascista*, July 1, 1926, 243–4; Gian Piero Brunetta, *Storia del cinema italiano, 1895–1945* (Rome, 1979), 375; Tranfaglia, "Il Duce e Margherita"; Passerini, *Mussolini immaginario*, 45–6.

24 Marpicati, *"Dux di Margherita Sarfatti,"* 398.

25 Giuseppe Brunati, "Margherita Sarfatti e la biografia del Duce," *Rivista Illustrata del Popolo d'Italia* (July 1926), 28; Sarfatti's letters to Bottai concerning *Dux*, dated October and November 1925, and February 1926, are in GBP, f. "Sarfatti, Margherita"; Cecchi, *"Dux di Margherita Sarfatti"*; Glauco Licata, *Storia del Corriere della Sera* (Milan, 1976), 189, 220; MGS to Ada Negri, n.d. but 1926, on *Gerarchia* stationery, GSP; Ugo Ojetti, "Mussolini," *Il Corriere della Sera*, July 4, 1926, and *I taccuini*, 222.

26 Giorgio Pini, *Filo diretto con Palazzo Venezia*, 2nd ed. (Milan, 1967), 33, 37; idem, *Benito Mussolini: La sua vita fino ad oggi dalla strada al potere* (Bologna, 1926), 88–90, 124; Arnaldo to Benito Mussolini, December 1, 1926, in Duilio Susmel, ed., *Carteggio Arnaldo-Benito Mussolini* (Florence, 1954), 59. Pini's title was the one that Mussolini had wanted to give to an autobiography that he never wrote. Passerini, *Mussolini immaginario*, 43.

27 John Bond, *Mussolini: The Wild Man of Europe* (Washington, D.C., 1929), 37; Valentino Bompiani, *Vita privata* (Verona, 1973), 47; Prezzolini to MGS, June 28, 1926, "Sarfatti, Margherita," PP; Marchione, *Prezzolini*, 24–5; Pillon, "Quando il Duce amava Margherita,"495; MGS to Cornelio Di Marzio, September 11, 1926, ACS, CCD, Scatola 8, "Sarfatti"; Carla Porta Musa, "Il Soldo e Margherita Sarfatti," *Il Foglietto* (Foggia), February 7, 1957; Lowe, "The Woman Behind Mussolini," 31; Prezzolini, *L'italiano inutile*, 201; Renzo De Felice, *Mussolini il fascista II*, 371; idem, *Mussolini il duce I. Gli anni del consenso, 1929–1936* (Turin, 1974), 577.

28 Interview with Magalì Sarfatti-Larson, June 16, 1986; Gaetano Salvemini, "Mussolini poliglotta," in *Scritti sul fascismo*, III (Milan, 1974), 386–97; "Mussolini: From Socialist to Fascist," *The Times*, October 2, 1925 (quote); "The Mind of Mussolini," *The Times Literary Supplement*, October 8, 1925; see also John Carter, "Mussolini, Master of Italy: A New Picture Emerges From His Authorized Biography," *The New York Times Book Review*, February 7, 1926; Luigi Albertini, *Venti anni di vita politica: Parte Seconda*, I (Bologna, 1951), 372–3; Tranfaglia, "Il Duce e Margherita"; "The Life of Benito Mussolini," *Punch*, October 21, 1925.

29 MGS, *The Life*, 138, 149; idem, *Dux*, 98; Bond, *Mussolini*, 31–40.

30 "Dux," *L'Illustrazione Italiana*, July 1926, 464; Tonelli, *Alla ricerca della personalità*, 251; Cecchi, *"Dux di Margherita Sarfatti*," 244; "Mussolini: From Socialist to Fascist"; Ruinas, *Scrittrici e scribacchine d'oggi*, 102; MGS, *The Life*, 346; "The Life of Benito Mussolini," *American Political Science Review* (May 1926), 462.

31 Sapori, *L'arte e il Duce*, 139; Marpicati, *"Dux di Margherita Sarfatti*," 395.

32 Alexander De Grand, "Women Under Italian Fascism," *The Historical Journal*, 19, 4 (1976), 952–3; De Felice, *Mussolini il rivoluzionario*, 744; Detragiache, "Il fascismo femminile da San Sepolcro all'affare Matteotti," 211–251; Maria Antonietta Macciocchi, *La donna nera: Consenso femminile e fascismo* (Milan, 1976), 29–47; MGS to V. E. Orlando, May 2, 1924, and cover letter from Alfredo Felici, in ACS, VEOP, b. 11, f. "Sarfatti."

   For Margherita and Mussolini's commitment to female suffrage in 1922–23, see Elisabetta Mondello, *La nuova italiana: La donna nella stampa e nella cultura del ventennio* (Rome, 1987), 70–1; Carrie Chapman Catt, "Diary of Trip to Europe and South America, 1922–23," 18–21, CCCP, reel 2; "Al congresso dell'alleanza internazionale pro suffragio femminile," OO, XIX, 215–6; "Mussolini to Give the Vote to Women," *The New York Times*, May 15, 1923; "Italian Suffragette Raps U.S. Meddlers," *Chicago Daily News*, May 18, 1923; "Suffragettes March to Italian Premier," *The New York Times*, May 20, 1923; "Gift of Vote to Italy's Women Expected to Win France Over," *The New York Times*, May 20, 1923; "Mrs. Catt Predicts Suffrage in Europe," *The New York Times*, June 2, 1923; "Mussolini Approves Bill Giving Women Suffrage in Italian Municipal Elections," *The New York Times*, June 4, 1923; "Peter Carter Says:," *Washington Herald*, April 17, 1934; Anne O'Hare McCormick, "The Women March on Mussolini," *The New York Times Magazine*, June 17, 1923; Pieroni Bortolotti, *Femminismo e partiti politici*, 181–93; Victoria de Grazia, *How Fascism Ruled Women: Italy, 1922–1945* (Berkeley, 1992), 30–5.

33 Mussolini, "La donna e il voto," May 15, 1925, OO, XXI, 304; MGS, "Il suffragio amministrativo femminile: Prima e adesso," *Gerarchia*, May 1925, 290–2. See also Mariapia Bigaran, "Il voto alle donne in Italia dal 1912 al fascismo," *Rivista di Storia Contemporanea*, April 1987, 240–65.

34 Passerini, *Mussolini immaginario*, 50–1, 95, 161; OO, XXII, 363–7, 388–9; Donald Meyer, *Sex and Power: The Rise of Women in America, Russia, Sweden, and Italy* (Middletown, Conn., 1987), 28–30; de Grazia, *How Fascism Ruled Women*, 36–41, 147–8, 247–8; Augusto Turati, *A Revolution and Its Leader* (London, 1930), 160–83; MGS, "Women of Fascism," *New York Herald*, November 12, 1933, 4, 22; idem, *Dux*, 12, and *The Life*, 24–5; Victoria de Grazia, "Il fascino del priapo: Margherita Sarfatti, biografa del duce," *Memoria*, June 1982, 152–3.

35 Carter, "Mussolini, Master of Italy."

36 "L'exilée," *Aux Écoutes* (Paris), January 7, 1939, 9; Pini, *Filo diretto*, 38; Trapani, "Fu mia madre," 54; Simonetta Fiori, "Quando Dux entrò nella sua vita," *La Repubblica Mercurio*, April 29, 1989, 4; Salvemini, "Mussolini poligotta," 388; Indro Montanelli and Mario Cervi, *Milano ventesimo secolo* (Milan, 1991), 97.

37 Messina, "Ricordo di Medardo Rosso: Dì un pù, Benito!"; idem, *Poveri giorni: Frammenti autobiografici, incontri e ricordi* (Milan, 1974), 324–5. Despite his criticism, Sarfatti wrote a highly favorable essay on Rosso after his death. See MGS, "Medardo Rosso," *Il Popolo d'Italia*, April 3, 1928.

CHAPTER 21: A NEW ASPECT OF TRADITION

1 Dudreville manuscript, in Bossaglia, *Il "Novecento Italiano,"* 73–4.

2 This dating is based on the fact that responses received to Sarfatti's invitation were dated in early March. See the list of letters in the *Archivi del Novecento* held by Claudia Gian Ferrari, in Bossaglia, *Il "Novecento Italiano,"* 165–6.

3 "Lettera circolare," in Bossaglia, *Il "Novecento Italiano,"* 89. Among the members of the committee were Education Minister Pietro Fedele, industrialists Stefano Benni, Piero Preda, Giuseppe De Capitani d'Arzago, Mario Crespi, and Giovanni Treccani, as well as Ada Negri, Umberto Notari, and the composer Ildebrando Pizzetti.

4 The concept of "left" and "right" opposition to the *Novecento* is raised by Maltese, *Storia dell'arte in Italia*, 334–6. In *Twentieth-Century Italian Art* (New York, 1949), 27, however, James Thrall Soby and Alfred H. Barr, Jr., see the *Novecento* as "deliberately reactionary."

Cosimo Ceccuti and Marcello Vannucci, *Immagini nelle parole: Ugo Ojetti* (Milan, 1978), 177–83; "Ojetti, Ugo," *Enciclopedia biografica e bibliografica italiana*, Series IV (Rome, 1942), 264–6; Edoardo Savino, *La nazione operante* (Milan, 1934), 191–2; Ojetti, *I taccuini, 1914–1943*, 204, entry for November 4, 1925.

5 *Mostra del Novecento Italiano*, 385–6, 418–19; Bossaglia, *Il "Novecento Italiano,"* 232–4, 238–40; Dudreville manuscript, 73; MGS, "Bottega di poesia e altre esposizioni," *Il Popolo d'Italia*, January 13, 1922; idem, "Arturo Tosi," *Il Popolo d'Italia*, December 21, 1923; idem, "Il Natale e l'arte a Milano," *Rivista Illustrata del Popolo d'Italia* (January 1924), 37–9; idem, "Arturo Tosi alla Mostra di Roma," *Il Popolo d'Italia*, February 22, 1931; idem, "Il Tosi delle nature morte," *La Stampa*, February 25, 1938; idem, *Segni, colori, e luci*, 119–25.

The other members of the executive committee were Luigi Mangiagalli, mayor of Milan, the industrialist senator Borletti, Giulio Brusadelli, the wealthy gallery owner Gaspare Gussoni, and Enrico Varenna.

6 "Una conferenza di Margherita Sarfatti," *Il Corriere Padano* (Ferrara), January 19, 1926; Costantini, *Pittura italiana contemporanea*, 246; interview with Piero Foà, July 26, 1987; Carlo and Eloisa Foà guest book, entry dated April 5, 1928, FP; MGS, "Il movimento artistico del Novecento Italiano," 14; Bucci to Sarfatti, April 3, 1925, in Bossaglia, *Il "Novecento Italiano,"* 93.

7 Bossaglia, *Il "Novecento Italiano,"* 20; "Regolamento dell'Esposizione," ibid., 90–2; Costantini, *Pittura italiana contemporanea*, 244.

8 There is a minor dispute over the actual number of artists invited. In the preface to the exhibit catalog, Sarfatti indicated that 130 artists had been invited and 110 had accepted; a list in the *Archivi del Novecento*, in Bossaglia, *Il "Novecento Italiano,"* 200–3, contains 137 names and 114 acceptances, while the list of sales in ibid., 204–8, has 111 names.

MGS, "Preventivo finanziario per la prima mostra del Novecento Italiano," ACS, PCM (1928–30), f. 14/1/2690, 1926; MGS to Mussolini, November 28, 1925, and Salietti to Mussolini, November 28, 1925, ibid.

9 The published version of Sarfatti's statement, which appeared both in the letter of invitation to artists and in her catalog preface, spoke of "chiarendo sopratutto le posizioni" (see "Lettera circolare," May 18, 1925, in Bossaglia, *Il "Novecento Italiano,"* 90, and 95–6); the unpublished version, which speaks of the need to "preparare le forze e agguerrire gli spiriti," is in "Riassunto del programma," ACS, PCM (1928–30), f. 14/1/2690, 1926.

10 Camesasca, *Mario Sironi*, 22; "Riassunto del programma," cit.; "Lettera circolare," in Bossaglia, *Il "Novecento Italiano,"* 90; Massimo Carrà, "Neoumanesimo arcaismo primitivismo," in *L'arte moderna* (Milan, 1967), IX, 162–3; Costantini, *Pittura italiana contemporanea*, 245; Pesaro, "Luci ed ombre," 131; MGS, "Del Novecento," in *L'almanacco degli artisti*, 74, 79; idem, "Il movimento artistico del Novecento Italiano," 14; idem, preface to catalog, *Dieci artisti del Novecento Italiano*, 29–30; Maltese, *Storia dell'arte in Italia*, 342, argues that the indecisive character of the Novecento allowed for the emergence within it of talented artists who, although members of the movement, were not closely attached to it.

11 MGS, "Carlo Dalmazzo Carrà," *Rivista Illustrata del Popolo d'Italia* (May 1925), 39–44; Soffici to Carrà, July 7, 1925, and Carrà to Soffici, July 15, 1925, in Carrà and Fagone, *Carlo Carrà–Ardengo Soffici: Lettere*, 162–4.

12 Ojetti, *I taccuini*, 204–5; Bossaglia, *Il "Novecento Italiano,"* 21–2, 166–7.

13 MGS, untitled article of January 5, 1926; "Alcune considerazioni . . . alla mostra del Novecento," February 12, 1926, both in *Il Popolo d'Italia*; "La mostra del Novecento Italiano inaugurata a Milano dall'on. Mussolini," *Il Popolo d'Italia*, February 16, 1926; OO, XXII, 82, note; photograph, "La mostra dell'900 inaugurata da Benito Mussolini," *L'Illustrazione Italiana*, February 21, 1926, 231.

14 That Sarfatti wrote portions of the speech is clear from both an internal and an external examination of the document. There is, for example, a decided difference between the first

half of the speech, obviously written by Mussolini, and the analysis of the *Novecento* in the second half, which bears the unmistakable hand of Sarfatti. The technical vocabulary in the latter section, with which Mussolini was simply unfamiliar, was lifted virtually intact from Sarfatti, who often repeated her own words in her articles and books. Finally, unlike most of Mussolini's speeches from the period, an original handwritten manuscript of this one does not exist—only a typed version bearing corrections. See ACS, *Carte della Cassetta di Zinco, Autografi del Duce*, b. 7. See also Bossaglia, 22; Tempesti, *Arte dell'Italia fascista*, 66, 121–22; Fossati, *Pittura e scultura*, 213, note; Camesasca, *Mario Sironi*, XIV. The full text of the speech is now in OO, XXII, 82–4.

15 "Elenco opere vendute alla mostra del Novecento," in Bossaglia, *Il "Novecento Italiano,"* 204–8.

16 MGS, "Alcune considerazioni intorno alla prima mostra del Novecento Italiano," 1–4. See also her "Alla prima mostra del Novecento Italiano," *Rivista Illustrata del Popolo d'Italia* (March 1926) and her "Alcuni problemi e alcuni pittori alla mostra del Novecento," *Il Popolo d'Italia*, March 12, 1926.

17 Carlo Carrà, "Il vernissage della mostra del Novecento Italiano," *L'Ambrosiano*, February 12, 1926; Corrado Pavolini, "La mostra del Novecento Italiano," *La Stirpe*, February 26, 1926, 81–5; Emilio Cecchi, "La prima mostra del 1900 italiano," *La Fiera Letteraria*, February 21 and March 14, 1926; Bossaglia, *Il "Novecento Italiano,"* 25; Raffaele De Grada, "La critica del Novecento," 43–51; "Novecento," in Alfredo Panzini, *Dizionario moderno delle parole che non si trovano negli altri dizionari*, 6th ed. (Milan, 1931), 455.

18 Lionello Venturi, "Un problema della mostra del Novecento Italiano," *Pretesti di critica* (Milan, 1929), 191–6; Maltese, *Storia dell'arte in Italia*, 336–7.

19 MGS, *The Life*, 158; idem, *Dux*, 118, 262, 264; Fiammetta Sarfatti Gaetani to PVC, October 6, 1986; Boratto, "Liquidazione dell'amica matura."

20 PNF, *Il Gran Consiglio nei primi cinque anni dell'era fascista* (Rome, 1927), 28–9; "La nuova Roma," December 31, 1925, OO, XXII, 47–8; Ellen Ruth Shapiro, *Building Under Mussolini*, unpublished Ph.D. dissertation, Yale University, December 1985, Vol. I, 153–88; MGS, "Nei dodici mesi dall'avvento: L'arte," *Il Popolo d'Italia*, October 26, 1923.

21 MGS, "Nell'annuale della fondazione di Roma la costruttrice," *Il Popolo d'Italia*, April 20, 1923, later amplified and republished in idem, *Segni, colori, e luci*, 227–47; Antonio Cederna, *Mussolini urbanista: Lo sventramento di Roma negli anni del consenso* (Rome-Bari, 1980), xvii–xviii, 56–7; MGS, "L'arte e il fascismo," cit., 218; Giorgio Ciucci, *Gli architetti e il fascismo* (Turin, 1989), 88–9; "Brasini, Armando," *Dizionario biografico degli italiani*, 14 (Rome, 1972), 65.

22 Ercole Boratto, "Liquidazione dell'amica matura"; Carofiglio, *Vita di Mussolini*, 174; "Woman Rebuilds Old Rome," *New York World Telegram*, February 6, 1926; MGS, *Dux*, 262, 264.

23 Amedeo Sarfatti to PVC, December 17, 1986; Fiammetta Sarfatti Gaetani to PVC, February 22, 1987; "Woman Rebuilds Old Rome," *New York World Telegram*, February 6, 1926; "Fascism and Women," *The Times*, May 18, 1929, 11; Spiro Kostof, "The Emperor and the Duce: The Planning of Piazzale Augusto Imperatore in Rome," in Henry A. Millon and Linda Nochlin, eds., *Art and Architecture in the Service of Politics* (Cambridge, Mass., 1978), 270–325; Cederna, *Mussolini urbanista*, xxii–iii; MGS, *Acqua passata*, 108–9. Mussolini moved his office to the Palazzo Venezia in 1929.

24 MGS, "I monumenti e la vita," *Il Popolo d'Italia*, July 16, 1926; idem, "In tema di sventramenti e di conservazioni," in *Veneto* (Padua) and *Avvenire d'Italia* (Bologna), July 17, 1926; idem, "Criteri di applicazione per i piani regolatori," *Il Popolo d'Italia*, August 12, 1927; MGS to Gabriele D'Annunzio, June 21, 1928, AVI, AG; Marzorati, *Margherita Sarfatti*, 47–8.

25 Silver, *Esprit de Corps*, 362–70; Giulia Veronesi, *Into the Twenties: Style and Design, 1909–1929* (London, 1968), 206, 219; Fernando Tempesti, *Arte dell'Italia fascista* (Milan, 1976), 186–7.

26 MGS, "Le arti industriali e l'arte," in *La fiaccola accesa*, 152–62, originally in *Gli Avvenimenti* (October 1916), 15–22.

27 MGS, "L'esposizione lombarda d'arte decorativa," September 8, 1919; idem, "Giocatoli e ricami," July 12, 1920; idem, "Le ceramiche della Cascella," April 26, 1921; idem, "Arte decorativa o decorazione industriale?, October 6, 1922; idem, "Una mostra di stoffi," November 17, 1922; idem, "Fatti e commenti: La corporazione sindacale delle arti decorativi," December 15, 1922; idem, "La mostra degli scialli," February 6, 1925, all in *Il Popolo d'Italia;* Rosamaria Giuliani, "Margherita Sarfatti: L'arte applicata e l'architettura," in *La cultura italiana negli anni '30–'45* (Naples, 1984), 857–8.

   [Guido Marangoni] to MGS, January 25, 1923, GSP; Tempesti, *Arte dell'Italia fascista,* 86; OO, XIX, 190, note; MGS, "Arte decorativa a Monza," May 19, 1923; idem, "Alla Villa di Monza," June 8, 1923; idem, "A Monza giornata delle vernici," May 15, 1925; idem, "Ancora a Monza," May 22, 1925; idem, "Artigianato o industrialismo nella decorazione," October 2, 1925, all in *Il Popolo d'Italia; Catalogo, Seconda Mostra Internazionale delle Arti Decorative* (Milan, 1925), xlvii–xlviii. On the Monza exhibits, see Agnoldomenico Pica, *Storia della Triennale di Milano* (Milan, 1957) and Anty Pansera, *Storia e cronaca della Triennale* (Milan, n.d.); Vittorio Magnago Lampugnani, "Architecture, Painting and the Decorative Arts in Italy, 1923–1940, from the First Biennale to the Seventh Triennale," in Pontus Hulten and Germano Celant, eds., *Arte italiana: Presenze 1900–1945* (Milan, 1989), 69–70.

28 Sapori, *L'arte e il duce,* 254–5.

29 *L'Italia all esposizione internazionale di arti decorative e industriale moderne* (Paris, 1925), xiii–xvi; Ojetti, *I taccuini,* 120; Veronesi, *Into the Twenties,* 224–5; Tempesti, *Arte dell'Italia fascista,* 87; Silver, *Esprit de Corps,* 371; MGS, "La mostra degli scialli," February 6, 1925, and "Sua divinità la donna all'Esposizione di Parigi," September 25, 1925, both in *Il Popolo d'Italia.*

30 Veronesi, *Into the Twenties,* 224, 312–14; Maltese, *Storia dell'arte in Italia,* 404; MGS, "Alcune architetture alla Esposizione di Parigi," *Il Popolo d'Italia,* September 18, 1925.

31 Antonio Sant'Elia, "L'architettura futurista," July 11, 1914, now in Gambillo and Fiori, *Archivi del futurismo,* I, 81–5; MGS, "Le arti decorative italiane a Parigi," in *L'Italia alla esposizione internazionale,* 57; idem, "Arti decorative, ovvero: L'oggetto corre dietro alla propria ombra," *Nuova Antologia* (July 1, 1936), 58–9; idem, "Nell'annuale della fondazione di Roma la costruttrice"; idem, "Antonio Sant'Elia, architetto comasco," *Como* (Autumn 1959), 32–4.

32 MGS, "Alcune architetture alla Esposizione di Parigi," September 8, 1925, *Il Popolo d'Italia;* idem, "La mostra delle arti decorative a Parigi," *Rivista Illustrata del Popolo d'Italia* (October 1925); idem, "Le arti decorative italiane a Parigi," 57–9; Bossaglia, *Il "Novecento Italiano,"* 29; Rossana Bossaglia, "Margherita Sarfatti, critica d'arte," in A. Gigli Marchetti and N. Torcellan, eds., *Donna lombarda, 1860–1945* (Milan, 1992), 403.

33 Louis Barthou, *L'Effort italien* (Paris, 1916), and idem, *The Effort of the French Women* (Paris, 1918); MGS, *Acqua passata,* 107; Alan Cassels, *Mussolini's Early Diplomacy,* (Princeton, N.J., 1970), 277; Ojetti, *I taccuini,* 193; MGS to Gabriele D'Annunzio, August 7, 1925, AVI, AG; Marzorati, *Margherita Sarfatti,* 143–4.

34 *Légion d'Honneur. Annuaire Officiel* (Paris, 1929), 2363; Carla Porta Musa, "Il Soldo e Margherita Sarfatti," *Il Foglietto* (Foggia), February 7, 1957; "Sarfatti, Margherita," *The Universal Jewish Encyclopedia,* IX (New York, 1943), 370.

35 Roberto Papini, "Le arti a Parigi nel 1925," *Architettura e arti decorative* (January 1926); Carlo Cresti, *Architettura e fascismo* (Florence, 1986), 149; Maltese, *Storia dell'arte in Italia,* 405; Giorgio Ciucci, *Gli architetti e il fascismo* (Turin, 1989), 81–2; Gaetano Minnucci, "L'Architettura all'Esposizione di Parigi," *Ingegneria* (August 1925), 276–83.

36 Ciucci, *Gli architetti e il fascismo,* 62–9; Cesare De Seta, *La cultura architettonica in Italia tra le due guerre* (Bari, 1972), 124–7; Vittorio Gregotti, "Milano e la cultura architettonica tra le due guerre," in Silvia Danesi and Luciano Patetta, eds., *Il razionalismo e l'architettura in Italia durante il fascismo* (Venice, 1976), 16–18; Maltese, *Storia dell'arte in Italia,* 403–4; MGS, "Nell'annuale della fondazione di Roma la costruttrice," *Il Popolo d'Italia,* April 20, 1923, republished with revisions in idem, *Segni, colori e luci,* 232; idem, "Mailands neues Denkmal," *Italien* (April 1929), 220–3; Richard A. Etlin, *Modernism in Italian Architecture, 1890–1940* (Cambridge, Mass., 1991), 165–224.

37 The Gruppo 7's first statement appeared as an article titled "Architettura," in *Rassegna Italiana* (December 1926), followed over the next few months by three others, now reprinted in Michele Cennamo, ed., *Materiali per l'analisi dell'architettura moderna: La prima esposizione italiana di architettura razionale* (Naples, 1973), 37–90; De Seta, *La cultura architettonica*, 141, 185–96; idem, *L'Architettura del Novecento* (Turin, 1981), 54–7; Ciucci, *Gli architetti e il fascismo*, 69–76; Silvia Danesi, "Aporie dell'architettura italiana in periodo fascista—Mediterraneità e purismo," in *Il razionalismo e l'architettura*, 21–24; Dennis Doordan, *Building Modern Italy: Italian Architecture, 1914–1936* (Princeton, N.J., 1988), 47; MGS, "Alcune considerazioni intorno alla prima mostra del Novecento Italiano," *Il Novecento Italiano* (Spring 1926), 4; Etlin, *Modernism in Italian Architecture*, 225–35.

38 It was at this point that the term "Rational" began to come into general use in Italy. Although Sartoris and Rava claimed to have introduced the term in 1926, Margherita had used it a year earlier. Ciucci, *Gli architetti e il fascismo*, 69–70, n. 1; MGS, "Razionalismi ed estetismi," *Il Popolo d'Italia*, October 9, 1925; idem, "Arti decorative, ovvero," 59 (quote); Laura Malvano, *Fascismo e politica dell'imagine* (Turin, 1988), 160.

39 Roberto Papini, "Due concorsi accademici," *Architettura e arti decorative* (December 1926), 161–91; "L'esito dei consorsi per le terme littorie e per l'arredamento di un'ambasciata indetti dalla nostra rivista," *Rivista Illustrata del Popolo d'Italia* (January 1927), 33–5; Cresti, *Architettura e fascismo*, 99–100.

40 MGS, "Artigianato o industrialismo," *Il Popolo d'Italia*, October 2, 1925.

41 Pica, *Storia della Triennale*, 18, 20, 80; Pansera, *Storia e cronaca*, 27; Tempesti, *Arte dell'Italia fascista*, 87–9; Lampugnani, "Architettura, pittura e arte decorativa," 70; MGS, "Le mostre di Monza e Como," *Rivista Illustrata del Popolo d'Italia* (September 1927), 34; idem, "Monza 1927," *Il Popolo d'Italia*, June 3, 1927.

42 MGS, "Monza 1927," June 3, 1927, and "La esposizione delle arti decorative," October 28, 1927, both in *Il Popolo d'Italia*; Giulio Rosso, "Alcune affermazioni del Gruppo 7 di Milano," *L'architettura italiana* (September 1927), now in Cennamo, *Materiali . . . La prima esposizione*, 75–6.

43 Doordan, *Building Modern Italy*, 52–3; Tempesti, *Arte dell'Italia fascista*, 89; De Seta, *L'architettura del Novecento*, 54–6; idem, *La cultura architettonica*, 197; Ciucci, *Gli architetti e il fascismo*, 73–5; *Mostra del Novecento Italiano (1923–1933)*, 416–17; "Elenco degli artisti invitati alla mostra 1929," ACS, PCM (1928–29), f. 14/1/2690, 1928; Luciano Caramel, "Abstract Art in Italy in the Thirties," in Emily Braun, ed., *Italian Art in the 20th Century: Painting and Sculpture, 1900–1988* (Munich and London, 1989), 188; Gruppo 7, "Impreparazione, incomprensione, pregiudizi," *Rassegna Italiana* (March 1927), now in Cennamo, *Materiali . . . La prima esposizione*, 59; Enrico Crispolti, "La politica culturale del fascismo, le avanguardie e il problema del futurismo," in Renzo De Felice, ed., *Futurismo, cultura e politica* (Turin, 1988), 271–2; Zuccoli, *Quindici anni*, 37.

44 MGS, "La esposizione delle arti decorative," *Il Popolo d'Italia*, October 28, 1927; *Catalogo Ufficiale della IVa Esposizione Triennale Internazionale delle Arti Decorative ed Industriali Moderne* (Milan, 1930), 3.

45 MGS, "Architettura," *Il Popolo d'Italia*, March 2, 1931; Emily Braun, interview with Alberto Sartoris, November 25, 1986, Cassoney-Ville, Switzerland.

46 Cederna, *Mussolini urbanista*, 56–7; Ciucci, *Gli architetti e il fascismo*, 82, 89–91.

47 MGS, "Le mostre di Monza e Como," 39; Doordan, *Building Modern Italy*, 70–1. On the exhibition, see especially Cennamo, *Materiali . . . La prima esposizione*.

48 Diane Ghirardo, "Italian Architects and Fascist Politics: An Evaluation of the Rationalists' Role in Regime Building," *Journal of the Society of Architectural Historians*, May 1988, 115; Carlo E. Rava, "Dell'europeismo in architettura," *Rassegna Italiana* (February 1928), now in Cennamo, *Materiali . . . La prima esposizione*, 77–84; the principal reviews of the exhibit are in ibid., 121–214; Ugo Ojetti, open letter to Mussolini, January 1929, reprinted in *Venti lettere* (Milan, 1931), 5–6.

49 Adalberto Libera, "La mia esperienza di architetto," in *La Casa* (1959), cited in Cennamo, *Materiali . . . La prima esposizione*, 94; Carlo Belli, "Origini e sviluppi del Gruppo 7," ibid.,

95; Roberto Papini, "Architettura razionale," *La Rivista Illustrata del Popolo d'Italia*, ibid., 196–8.

50 MGS, "Architettura"; idem, "Architettura moderna," *La Lettura* (July 1931), 588–97.

51 Cederna, *Mussolini urbanista*, 57. On Brasini's later career see Luca Brasini, ed., *L'opera architettonica e urbanistica di Armando Brasini* (Rome, 1979).

CHAPTER 22: DICTATOR OF CULTURE

1 MGS to Mussolini, "Lettera n. 3 sabato," n.d. but early 1923, GSP.

2 OO, XXII, 105, note; Richard Collin, *La donna che sparò a Mussolini* (Milan, 1985), 62–3; Guspini, *L'orecchio del regime*, 70; De Felice, *Mussolini il fascista*, II, 200–1.

3 "Al settimo congresso di chirugia," April 7, 1926, in OO, XXII, 105–6; Collin, *La donna*, 63–8, 71; Navarra, *Memorie*, 37–9; OOA, XXXX, 48, 50.

4 [MGS], "L'attentato," *Gerarchia* (September 1926), 541; MGS to Cornelio Di Marzio, September 11, 1926, ACS, CCD, Scatola 8, "Sarfatti."

5 Bossaglia, *Il "Novecento Italiano*," 20; Mussolini to Salietti, September 18, 1926, ibid., 99.

6 The chronology of Sarfatti's residences in Rome that follows has been reconstructed from a variety of sources, including her letters to and from a number of correspondents. GSP, MGS to Negri, n.d. but early 1924; Comes, *Ada Negri*, 120; Trapani, "Fu mia madre," 50; Ludovico Toeplitz, *Il banchiere* (Milan, 1963), 161; Marzorati, *Margherita Sarfatti*, 62.

7 Pini and Susmel, *Mussolini*, II, 429; Piero Foà to BRS, May 30, 1987; interview with Piero Foà, July 26, 1987. Roth, *History of the Jews of Italy*, 510, wrote that it was Carlo Foà who acted as secretary to *Gerarchia*, but Piero Foà has corrected that error; MacGregor-Hastie, *The Day of the Lion*, 148; Boratto, "Liquidazione dell'amica matura"; Enrico Franchi, "Mercoledì sera: Casa Sarfatti," *Corriere Adriatico*, July 8, 1926; Trapani, "Fu mia madre," 52.

8 Rossi, *Trentatrè vicende mussoliniane*, 366; Trapani, "Mia madre Margherita Sarfatti," *Gente*, September 10, 1987, 45.

9 Boratto, "Liquidazione dell'amica matura"; Trapani, "Mia madre Margherita Sarfatti," *Gente*, September 10, 1982, 47; Guspini, *L'orecchio del regime*, 71–2; Charlotte Aillaud, "Prince Giovanni Torlonia," *Architectural Digest* (January 1990), 60.

10 MGS to Ada Negri, n.d. but early 1927, GSP; Fiammetta Sarfatti Gaetani to PVC, August 7, 1986; Comes, *Ada Negri*, 120; Trapani, "Mia madre Margherita Sarfatti," *Gente*, September 17, 1982, 45, 50; Staglieno, "Margherita Sarfatti"; Morgan, *Spurs on the Boot*, 137–9.

11 Morgan, *Spurs on the Boot*, 138; police report of December 20, 1931, ACS, MI-DPP, "Sarfatti, Margherita."

12 Trapani, "Mia madre Margherita Sarfatti," 43; idem, "Fu mia madre," 50, 52, 54; OO, XXXV, 272–3; OOA, XXXVIII, 529, and XXXIX, 48–50, 437; conversation with Roberto Lopez, February 19, 1985; ACS, MI-DPP, f. "Sarfatti, Margherita," reports of September 1, 1928, October 19, 1929, March 3, 1930, January 11, 1931, February 21, 1932, June 27, 1932; Boratto, "Collazione per due a Castel Porziano," *Giornale del Mattino*, April 2, 1946; Pieroni Bortolotti, *Femminismo e partiti politici in Italia*, 198; Marzorati, *Margherita Sarfatti*, 58; De Felice, *Mussolini il fascista*, I, 310–5; idem, *Mussolini il duce*, I, 276–87; idem, *Mussolini il duce*, II. *Lo stato totalitario, 1936–1940* (Turin, 1981), 16–9.

13 Boratto, "Collazione per due a Castel Porziano."

14 Interview with Amedeo Sarfatti, May 24, 1985.

15 Faldella, *Storia delle truppe*, II, 667; OOA, XXXIX, 546.

16 "Grandiose manifestazioni e riti austeri a Milano," *Il Popolo d'Italia*, November 5, 1925; Pini and Susmel, *Mussolini*, III, 9: OOA, XXXIX, 546.

A few weeks earlier, on October 15, 1925, Mussolini had signed an order conferring a postumous *medaglia d'oro* on Filippo Corridoni, who had helped the under-age Roberto join the army in 1915. Ivon De Begnac, *L'arcangelo sindacalista (Filippo Corridoni)* (Verona, 1943), appendix, lxviii.

17 Emanuela Scarpellini, *Organizzazione teatrale e politica del teatro nell'Italia fascista* (Florence, 1989), 34; "Per la battaglia del libro," *Il Giornale d'Italia*, July 1, 1926; de Grazia, "Il fascino del priapo," 149, 152, 154; Maramotti, "Margherita Sarfatti," 105; interview with Piero Foà, July 26, 1987.

18 Papa, *Fascismo e cultura*, 159–6; Tempesti, *Arte dell'Italia fascista*, 72; De Begnac, *Taccuini mussoliniani*, 290; Alberto Asor Rosa, *Storia d'Italia*, IV, 2, *La Cultura* (Turin, 1975), 1464–70.

19 Papa, *Fascismo e cultura*, 186–94, 211–17; Cannistraro, *La fabbrica del consenso*, 22–4.

20 Arcangelo Leone de Castris, *Egemonia e fascismo: Il problema degli intellettuali negli anni trenta* (Bologna, 1981), 90; Mario Isnenghi, *Intellettuali militanti e intellettuali funzionari: Appunti sulla cultura fascista* (Turin, 1979), esp. 3–27.

21 Mussolini to MGS, December 11, 1922, OO, XXXV, 272–3; Trapani, "Mia madre Margherita Sarfatti," 45.

22 MGS to Dolores Prezzolini, April 6, 1926, and G. Prezzolini to MGS, April 14 and June 28, 1926, PP.

23 Gabriele Turi, "Ideologia e cultura del fascismo: L'enciclopedia italiana," in *Il fascismo e il consenso degli intellettuali* (Bologna, 1980), 13–150; Marinella Ferrarotto, *L'Accademia d'Italia: Intellettuali e potere durante il fascismo* (Naples, 1977).

24 MGS, *La fiaccola accesa*, 166; de Grazia, "Il fascino del priapo," 149; MGS, "Promesse e azioni: L'Accademia d'Italia," *Il Popolo d'Italia*, January 15, 1926; idem, "La sede dell'Accademia," *Rivista Illustrata del Popolo d'Italia* (March 1927), 38–47; Ferrarotto, *L'Accademia d'Italia*, 28, 39; Arturo Marpicati, "Tommaso Tittoni, presidente della Reale Accademia d'Italia," in *Saggi di letteratura* (Florence, 1933), 414–39; Silvio Longhi, "Funzioni politiche dell'Accademia d'Italia," *Gerarchia* (March 1926), 150–3.

25 Police reports of October 19, 1929, and February 8, 1938, ACS, MI-DPP, "Sarfatti, Margherita"; Ermanno Amicucci, *I 600 giorni di Mussolini* (Rome, 1948), 196; Ojetti, *I taccuini, 1914–1943*, 344; De Begnac, *Taccuini mussoliniani*, 348, 590. For a complete list of members, see Ferrarotto, *L'Accademia d'Italia*, 118–54; Smith, *Mussolini*, 133.

26 "Referendum sull'opportunità di ammettere le donne nell'Accademia d'Italia," *Il Tevere*, January 14 and February 6, 1926, cited in Ferrarotto, *L'Accademia d'Italia*, 39, n. 3; De Begnac, *Taccuini mussoliniani*, 305; Ojetti, *I taccuini*, 343; MGS to Giovanni Papini, October 17, 1930, and March 21, 1934, AGP.

By the time the opening ceremonies had taken place, Sarfatti's opinion about the Academy had become more negative. For the occasion she wrote a guardedly skeptical article in which she posed the rhetorical question, "Can an academy not be academic?" She concluded that only people of genius, not an institution or a government, can create an artistic revival or force culture to flourish. The article caught the attention of Fascist officials. MGS, "Può un'Accademia non essere accademica?," *Politica sociale* (1929), 671–6. A copy of the article is found in ACS, MCP, b. 28, f. 147, "Reale Accademia d'Italia."

27 Ada Negri to Mussolini, June 19, 1924, ACS, SPD/CR, f. 209R, "Negri, Ada"; MGS to Negri, telegram, January 19, 1925, GSP; Ada Negri, *I canti dell'isola* (Milan, 1924), dedication; MGS, "I canti dell'isola," *Il Popolo d'Italia*, January 2, 1925.

28 MGS to Negri, December 12, 16, 21, 23, 1927, postcard from Tirana, Albania, n.d. (but July 1928), and letter of July 9, 1930, GSP; MGS, " 'Le strade' di Ada Negri," *Il Popolo d'Italia*, December 31, 1926, later republished as "Ada Negri" in idem, *Segni del meridiano*, 35–41; idem, "Premio Nobel," *Il Popolo d'Italia*, December 16, 1927, later republished as "Grazia Deledda" in *Segni del meridiano*, 43–51; "Appunto per il Duce," November 4, 1944, ACS, SPD/CR, f. 209R; Podenzani, *Il libro di Ada Negri*, 180, 195; Renzo De Felice to PVC, June 24, 1988.

29 See, for example, Arnaldo Geraldini, "Si è spenta Margherita Sarfatti," *Il Corriere della Sera*, October 31, 1961; "Margherita Sarfatti, la ninfa Egeria del Duce," *Il Giornale*, July 28, 1987; Carlo Emilio Gadda, *Quer pasticciaccio brutto de via Merulana* (Milan, 1957), 58; Magalì Sarfatti-Larson interview with Pierangela Sarfatti, October 1985; police reports of September 7, 1927, October 26, 1931, and June 18, 1934, ACS, MI-DPP, "Sarfatti, Margherita."

30 Enrico Franchi, "Mercoledì sera: Casa Sarfatti"; interview with Dr. Piero Foà, July 26. 1987; "Nemo," "She Dreamed of a New Empire"; Sarfatti guest book for 1926–31, FSGP; Joseph B. Phillips, "Italy's Heroine of Fascism," *New York Herald Tribune Sunday Magazine*, October 8, 1933.

31 MGS to Adolfo Wildt, August 6, 1930, cited in Paolo Mola, ed., *Wildt* (Milan, 1988), 109; *Enciclopedia italiana*, XXXV (Rome, 1937), 748; "La morte dell'academico Adolfo Wildt," *Il Corriere della Sera*, March 13, 1931; "Il cordoglio della nazione per la morte immatura di Adolfo Wildt," *Il Popolo d'Italia*, March 13, 1931; Francesco Grossi, *Battaglie sindacali* (Rome, 1988), 32–3.

32 MGS to Carlo Carrà, March 22 and December 4, 1928, CCP; Magalì Sarfatti-Larson interview with Amedeo and Pierangela Sarfatti, October 1985; interview with Fiammetta Sarfatti Gaetani, May 20, 1985; Sarfatti guest books, 1926–31, 1932–38, FSGP; MGS, "Arte e artisti," *Il Popolo d'Italia*, January 8, 1926; Coen, "La Sarfatti fra arte e fascismo," 20; Seymour Berkson to T. V. Ranck, November 19, 1932, TVRP; Giovanni Ansaldo, *Diario*, entry for June 20, 1935 (made available by Renzo De Felice).

33 Interviews with Fiammetta Sarfatti Gaetani, May 13 and 16, 1985, with Amedeo and Pierangela Sarfatti, May 24, 1985, and with Tita Brown-Castellanos, December 9, 1986.

34 MGS, "Alcuni scrittori," *Il Popolo d'Italia*, September 9, 1927; idem, "Scrittori nuovi," *Il Popolo d'Italia*, June 8, 1928, republished as "Italienische Schriftsteller unserer Zeit," *Italien* (February 1929), 89–101; idem, "Gli indifferenti," *Il Popolo d'Italia*, September 25, 1929; idem, "Gli indifferenti," *Italien* (April 1930), 197–201; idem, "La passione morale negli scrittori inglesi," *Gerarchia* (February 1922), 65–9; idem, "Problemi pirandelliani," *Il Popolo d'Italia*, March 13, 1924, republished as "Pirandello-Probleme," in *Italien*, April 1928, 205–10; Enrico Falqui, *Novecento letterario*, 10th Series (Florence, 1969), 262–7; Robert De Traz, "Quelques jours à Milan," *La Revue Hebdomadaire* (January 10, 1925), 136; Nozzoli, "Margherita Sarfatti, organizzatrice di cultura," 268–70.

35 "I cento libri più belli della letteratura contemporanea," *La Fiera Letteraria*, November 2, 1930; De Begnac, *Taccuini mussoliniani*, 483–4; Moravia signatures for 1932 and 1933, Sarfatti guest books, 1926–31, 1932–38, FSGP; Gregory Alegi to BRS, November 18, 1991; Alain Elkann and Alberto Moravia, *Vita di Moravia* (Milan, 1990), 50, 63.

36 MGS, "Dalla noticina bibliografica dell'editore," n.d. but attached to a letter to Giovanni Prezzolini dated April 8, 1929, PP; *Il palazzone* (Milan, 1929) was published by Mondadori; Margherita also published a short extract from the novel as ". . . E colloqui diplomatici" in *Nuova Antologia* (April 16, 1929), 436–40.

37 Interviews with Fiammetta Sarfatti Gaetani, May 20, 1985, and with Magalì Sarfatti-Larson, September 28, 1985, and between Magalì Sarfatti-Larson and Amedeo Sarfatti, October 1985.

38 Goffredo Bellonci, "Il palazzone," *La Fiera Letteraria*, June 23, 1929; Alfredo Coen, "Margherita Sarfatti: Il palazzone," *Bibliografia Fascista*, November 1929, 51–2; Fanfulla, "Notizie bibliografiche," *Minerva*, July 1, 1929; Alfredo Panzini, "Un romanzo di Margherita Sarfatti," *Il Corriere della Sera*, May 26, 1929; "Some Italian Novels," *The Times Literary Supplement*, November 28, 1929; de Grazia, "Il fascino del priapo," 153–4; Maramotti, "Margherita Sarfatti: Appunti per una storia della letteratura femminile nel periodo fascista," 101–12; Antonio Gramsci, *Letteratura e vita nazionale* (Rome, 1971), 187.

39 Alfredo Signoretti, *La stampa in camicia nera* (Rome, 1968), 25; Alvaro, *Quasi una vita*, 58; idem, *Tutto è accaduto* (Milan, 1961), 102, 105; Armando Balduino, *Corrado Alvaro* (Milan, 1972), 143–4.

40 Luigi Reina, *Esperienze novecentesche* (Naples, 1979), 97–8; idem, "Società e cultura degli anni trenta nel diario di Alvaro," in *La cultura italiana negli anni '30–'45*, I (Naples, 1984), 612.

41 Reina, *Esperienze novecentesche*, 98; Signoretti, *La Stampa in camicia nera*, 10, 83; MGS to Manlio Morgagni, n.d. but April 1931, ACS, AS/CMM, b. 47, f. 822, "Sarfatti, Margherita"; Sarfatti guest book, 1926–31, entry for April 23, 1931, FSGP; Trapani, "Mia madre Margherita Sarfatti," 40; De Begnac, *Taccuini mussoliniani*, 321–2; Marzorati, *Margherita Sarfatti*, 137.

The Agnelli Prize committee also included Arturo Farinelli, Luigi Federzoni, Francesco Chiesa, and Raffaele Calzini.

42 Alvaro, *Quasi una vita*, 123; Reina, *Esperienze novecentesche*, 100; Trapani, "Mia madre Margherita Sarfatti," 40–1; interview with Fiammetta Sarfatti Gaetani, May 20, 1985; Luigi M. Personè, "Nel salotto della Sarfatti," *La Nazione*, September 18, 1989; De Felice, *Mussolini il duce*, I, 108.

43 MGS to Ada Negri, December 26, 31, 1930, January 6, April 31, 1931, GSP; MGS, "Ada Negri," *Il Popolo d'Italia*, February 1, 1931; NA, T586, reel 1093, frames 068758–63.

44 Personè, "Nel salotto della Sarfatti"; interviews with Fiammetta Sarfatti Gaetani, May 16, 20, 1985; Sarfatti guest books, 1926–31, 1932–38, FSGP; Magalì Sarfatti-Larson interview with Amedeo and Pierangela Sarfatti, October 1985; MGS, "Entusiasmo italico, rigidezza romana," *Gerarchia* (February 1931), 159–61; Italo Balbo to MGS, August 2 and October 24, 1932, IBP; Italo Balbo to Umberto Klinger, January 16, 1926, RKP; Guerri, *Italo Balbo*, 208; Fiori, "Quando Dux entrò nella sua vita"; MGS to Giuseppe Bottai, n.d. (but 1921), May 29, 1923, October 21, 1925, February 5, 1926, and n.d. (but 1933), GBP; Giuseppe Bottai, *Diario, 1935–1944* (Milan, 1982), 111–12; Morgan, *Spurs on the Boot*, 138; police reports of June 2, 1928, May 12, December 31, 1929, November 30, 1931, ACS, MI-DPP, "Sarfatti, Margherita."

45 Gordon Craig's letters to Sarfatti, together with his comments on her in his *Day-book*, are in the EGCP; MGS, "Lo spirito che nega (Shaw)," *Gerarchia* (June 1922), 317–23; idem, *Acqua passata*, 133–4, 137–53; Dan H. Laurence to PVC, October 5, 1985; Arnold Silver, *Bernard Shaw, the Darker Side* (Stanford, 1982), 38; *The Diary of Beatrice Webb, IV, 1924–43, "The Wheel of Life"* (Cambridge, Mass., 1985), 131–2, 135, 334; Marzorati, *Margherita Sarfatti*, 109.

46 De Begnac, *Taccuini mussoliniani*, 396; police report of December 12, 1929, ACS, MI-DPP, "Sarfatti, Margherita"; MGS, "How Mussolini Interviews Interviewers in His Monumental Workroom in Rome," *New York American*, June 28, 1931; Maisie Ward, *Gilbert Keith Chesterton* (New York, 1943), 578–81; G. K. Chesterton, *The Resurrection of Rome* (London, 1930), 225–91, 345–6; Michael Ffinch [sic], *G. K. Chesterton* (New York, 1986), 334.

47 Harold Nicolson, *Diaries and Letters, 1930–1964*, ed. Stanley Olson (London, 1980), 35–6; Oswald Mosley, *My Life* (London, 1968), 358–64; Robert Skidelsky, *Oswald Mosley* (London, 1975), 284–5; Sarfatti guest book, 1932–38, FSGP; HNP, diary, entries for January 5–9, 1932; "Mussolini and Mosley: The Mystery Payments," *The Times* (London), October 30, 1981; Nicholas Mosley, *Beyond the Pale* (London, 1983), 43; DDI, Series 7, XIII, no. 615.

48 Dominique Fernandez, *Il mito dell'America negli intellettuali italiani* (Caltanissetta-Rome, 1969), 7–82; Bryan Hammond and Patrick O'Connor, *Josephine Baker* (London, 1988), 90, 98, 145; OO, XXIII, 233.

49 Biddle diary, entry for December 27, 1951, BP, Box 6; Forrest Read, *'76: One World and the Cantos of Ezra Pound* (Chapel Hill, N.C., 1981), 221–3; Noel Stock, *The Life of Ezra Pound* (New York, 1970), 306–7; Ezra Pound, *Eleven New Cantos, XXXI–XLI* (New York, 1934), 52; Niccolò Zapponi, *L'Italia di Ezra Pound* (Rome, 1976); Robert Casillo, *The Genealogy of Demons: Anti-Semitism, Fascism, and the Myths of Ezra Pound* (Evanston, 1988).

50 C. David Heymann, *Ezra Pound: The Last Rower* (New York, 1976), 147; MGS to Ezra Pound, September 5, 18, 1935, July 1936, and Pound to MGS, February 25 and October 8 (?), 1934, EPP; Tim Redman, *Ezra Pound and Italian Fascism* (New York, 1991), 72, 95–8, 122–52; Humphrey Carpenter, *A Serious Character: The Life of Ezra Pound* (London-Boston, 1988). Pound's Canto XLI contains several allusions to *Dux*, although this seems to have escaped Pound's critics and commentators. See Pound, *Eleven New Cantos*, 54; MGS, *Dux*, 184–7; Carroll F. Terrell, *A Companion to the Cantos of Ezra Pound*, I (Berkeley, 1980), 166–8.

51 Many of the letters sent to Mussolini's secretary are in ACS, SPD/CO, in the following folders bearing Sarfatti's name: 509.663/1, 528.925, 529.071, 529.816, 536.418, 540.135, 541.701, 549.404.

52 De Felice, *Mussolini il fascista*, I, 494–8; PRO, FO, 371/12948, Russell to Chamberlain,

March 2, 1928; De Begnac, *Taccuini mussoliniani*, 591; Sarfatti guest book, 1926–31; interviews with Fiammetta Sarfatti Gaetani, July 9 and 10, 1985; D. A. Binchy, *Church and State in Fascist Italy* (London, 1941), 104–6; Mack Smith, *Mussolini*, 159; Pini and Susmel, *Mussolini*, II, 301; Vittorio Mussolini, *Vita con il mio padre*, 31; Pensotti, *Rachele*, 43; Ercole Boratto, "Un'enciclica non vale una telefonata," *Giornale del Mattino*, April 3, 1946.

53 Kurt G. W. Ludecke, *I Knew Hitler: The Story of a Nazi Who Escaped The Blood Purge* (New York, 1937), 69.

54 WRCD, vol. 5, January–June 1924, 51, entry for February 8, 1924; PRO, FO 371/8993, Graham to Curzon, January 5, 1923; Raffaele Guariglia, *Ricordi (1922–1946)* (Naples, 1949), 181–2. For Mussolini's early views on anti-Semitism, Italian Jews, and Zionism, see Meir Michaelis, *Mussolini and the Jews: German-Italian Relations and the Jewish Question in Italy, 1922–1945* (Oxford, 1978), 10–30; OO, XIII, 168–70; OO, XV, 269–71; OO, XVI, 438–9; OO, XVII, 30; OO, XVIII, 279–81.

55 Alma Mahler diary, 222, entry for April 5 [?], 1928, MWC; Alma Mahler-Werfel, *Mein Leben* (Frankfurt, 1960), 191, has a slightly different account; Karen Monson, *Alma Mahler: Muse to Genius* (London, 1984), 227. Marzorati, *Margherita Sarfatti*, 140, relates that Sarfatti told him Mahler had brought with her a written statement signed by important intellectuals warning abour Nazi attitudes toward Germany's Jews, and that Sarfatti gave it to Mussolini, but Mahler's diary makes no mention of this document.

ACS, MI-DPP, reports of October 29, 1928, March 14, 1929, March 16, 1930; Bottai, *Diario, 1935–1944*, 134; NA T586, roll 23, frames 438–9; interview with Amedeo Sarfatti, May 24, 1985; interview with Fiammetta Sarfatti Gaetani, July 9–10, 1985; interview with Piero Foà, July 27, 1987; Marzorati, *Margherita Sarfatti*, 14, 86–9.

56 OO, XV, 270–1; Nahon, "La polemica antisionista," 217–8.

57 Nahon, "La polemica antisionista," 221–3, 225.

58 MGS to Carlo Foà, n.d. but November 30–December 3, 1928, beginning "Caro Amico"; idem, December 4, 1928; MGS to Isa Foà, n.d., beginning "Cara Isa, vedi con Carlo e consultati . . ."; Amedeo Sarfatti to Foà, December 5, 1928, all in FP; GSP, MGS to Negri, December 3, 1928; Nahon, "La polemica antisionista," 225–45.

59 Nahon, "La polemica antisionista," 245–49. Given the difficulty in arriving at a satisfactory definition of whether or not an individual is a Jew, it is unclear how many Italian Jews there were in 1928. However, at the time of the adoption of anti-Semitic legislation in Italy in 1938, there seem to have been about 47,000 Italian citizens who either practiced Judaism or could be identified as having been born to two ethnically Jewish parents. See Eitan Franco Sabatello, "Aspetti economici ed ecologici dell'ebraismo romano prima, durante e dopo le leggi razziali (1928–65)," 256–7, in Carpi, Milano, and Nahon, *Scritti in memoria di Enzo Sereni*.

60 Amedeo Sarfatti to Carlo Foà, December 5, 1928, FP.

61 Fiammetta Sarfatti to Carlo Foà, n.d. but late December 1928, FP.

62 MGS to Carlo Foà, December 4, 1928, MGS to Isa Foà, December 17, 1928, FP; Nahon, "La polemica antisionista," 251–3; interview with Piero Foà, July 27, 1987; Michaelis, *Mussolini and the Jews*, 30–1; Marzorati, *Margherita Sarfatti*, 144–5; "Einstein Distracted by Public Curiosity, Seeks Hiding Place," *The New York Times*, February 4, 1929; MGS, *Acqua passata*, 213–9.

63 For an analysis of the negotiations for and the contents of the Lateran Pact, see De Felice, *Mussolini il fascista*, II, 382–436.

64 Edvige Mussolini, *Mio fratello Benito*, 122–3; Michaelis, *Mussolini and the Jews*, 33–4; *Annuario militare del regno d'Italia: Anno 1929 (VII)*, I, Part 1a (Rome, 1929), 626.

65 ACS, MI-DPP, f. "Sarfatti, Margherita," reports of June 2 and 15, 1928; Boratto, "Liquidazione dell'amica matura"; De Felice, *Mussolini il fascista*, II, 19; Trapani, "Mia madre Margherita Sarfatti," 47; NMBP, Butler to MGS, December 14, 1931.

66 Pini and Susmel, *Mussolini*, III, 183.

67 Trapani, "Mia madre Margherita Sarfatti," 52; Boratto, "Liquidazione dell'amica matura" and "Collazione per due a Castel Porziano"; Pini and Susmel, *Mussolini*, III, 183.

68 Pini and Susmel, III, *Mussolini,* 192–3; De Felice, *Mussolini il fascista,* II, 349 n.3; idem, *Mussolini il duce,* I, 301; Curti Cucciati, "Un' amica di Mussolini racconta," November 17, 1949, 14.

69 MGS, *Mussolini: Como lo conocí,* X; Lucio Ceva and Andrea Curami, *Industria bellica, anni trenta: Commesse militari, l'Ansaldo ed altri* (Milan, 1992), 12–23, 53–4, 62–3, 111–3; Ciano, *Diario, 1937–1943,* 312–7; "Nemo," "She Dreamed of a New Empire"; idem, "Mussolini's Evil Genius," *The Star* (London), February 14, 1941; Antonio Spinosa, *Mussolini: Il fascino di un dittatore* (Milan, 1989), 195; Pensotti, *Rachele,* 53–4; Boratto, "Liquidazione dell'amica matura"; MacGregor-Hastie, *The Day of the Lion,* 149; ACS, MI-DPP, f. "Sarfatti, Margherita,"reports of May 12 and October 19, 1929,April 26 and August 11, 1930, January 26, 1931; Giuseppe Villaroel, "Margherita Sarfatti, l'irriducibile," *Il Giornale d'Italia,* March 10, 1950.

70 Personè, "Nel salotto della Sarfatti"; Lowe, "The Woman Behind Mussolini," 31; Giovanni Ansaldo, *Diario,* entry for September 7, 1934, in "Il pesante giudizio di Giovanni Ansaldo," *Il Giornale,* July 28, 1987.

71 Police reports of October 19, 1929, and July 22, 1931, ACS, MI-DPP, "Sarfatti, Margherita"; interview with Piero Foà, July 26, 1987.

CHAPTER 23: GHOSTWRITER FOR THE DUCE

1 On the image of Fascist Italy in the United States and its creation in Rome, see John P. Diggins, *Mussolini and Fascism: The View from America* (Princeton, N.J., 1972), 22–73, 204–39; Morrell Heald, *Transatlantic Vistas: American Journalists in Europe, 1900–1940* (Kent, Ohio, 1989), 85–7, 116–8; David Darrah, *Hail Caesar!* (Boston, 1936). Much can also be gleaned from Seldes, *Sawdust Caesar.*

For the reactions of Steffens (1924–25) and Tarbell (1926) to Fascism, see Ida M. Tarbell, *All in the Day's Work: An Autobiography* (New York, 1939), 378–84; Lincoln Steffens, *The Autobiography of Lincoln Steffens* (New York, 1958), 808–18, 824–32; idem, *The Letters of Lincoln Steffens,* 2 vols. (New York, 1938), II, 668, 681–2.

2 For examples of the limits to Sarfatti's ability to manipulate the European press, see Robert De Traz, "Quelques jours à Milan," 136–8. Despite her best efforts in an interview during the Matteotti Crisis, she failed to convince De Traz that the youth of Italy stood completely behind Mussolini.

3 GSP, MGS to Mussolini, January 30, [?] 1923; Darrah, *Hail Caesar!,* 40–1; Thomas B. Morgan, *The Listening Post: Eighteen Years on Vatican Hill* (New York, 1944), 27; George Seldes to BRS, February 15, 1987; idem, *Even the Gods Can't Change History* (Secaucus, N.J., 1976), 61; ACS, MI-DPP, f. "Morgan, Thomas B.," report of July 21, 1935.

4 "Thomas B. Morgan Dies at 87. Author Led U.P. Rome Bureau," *The New York Times,* July 11, 1972; Robert W. Desmond, *Crisis and Conflict: World News Reporting Between Two World Wars, 1920–1940* (Iowa City, 1982), 121, 238; Joe Alex Morris, *Deadline Every Minute: The Story of the United Press* (Garden City, N.Y., 1957), 140–2, 157; Baillie, *High Tension,* 71–2; Morgan, *The Listening Post,* 14–5, 18, 21; idem, *Spurs on the Boot,* 1–62, 144, 155; ACS, MI-DPP, f. "Morgan, Thomas B.," report of July 15, 1933.

5 Morgan, *Spurs on the Boot,* 59, 82–5, 91–113, 134–43, 242; idem, *The Listening Post,* 149–50; idem, *Italian Physical Culture Demonstration* (New York, 1932); interview with Frank Gervasi, May 5, 1986; ACS, MI-DPP, f. "Morgan, Thomas B.," reports of August 6, 1930, February 10, 1932, July 15, 1933; conversation with Edward A. Morgan, February 23, 1985; Robert W. Desmond, *Tides of War: World News Reporting, 1940–1945* (Iowa City, 1982), 151; Gaetano Salvemini, *Prelude to World War II* (Garden City, N.Y., 1954), 158, n. 5; TVRP, Wiegand to Ranck, January 31 and February 26, 1930; RWHP, Howard to Bickel, November 6, 1924; PRO, FO 371/11383, CX 702, McCann to Willert, January 14, 1926; Diggins, *Mussolini and Fascism,* 53 n. 21, 56–7; Jo Davidson, *Between Sittings: An Informal Autobiography* (New York, 1951), 226; Reynolds Packard, *Rome Was My Beat* (Secaucus, N.J., 1975), 15 (quote).

6 Morris, *Deadline Every Minute*, 118–44: Morgan, *The Listening Post*, 24; Seldes, *Even the Gods Can't Change History*, 57–66; Alice G. Marquis, *Hopes and Ashes: The Birth of Modern Times, 1929–1939* (New York, 1986), 43–6.

7 Darrah, *Hail Caesar!*, 38–62; Seldes, *Even the Gods Can't Change History*, 59–64.

8 Harry N. Scheiber, Harold G. Vatter, and Harold Underwood Faulkner, *American Economic History* (New York, 1976), 333–5; Gilbert C. Fite and Jim E. Reese, *An Economic History of the United States* (Boston, 1973), 498; W. W. Rostow, *The World Economy: History and Prospect* (Austin, 1978), 210; B. R. Mitchell, *European Historical Statistics, 1750–1970* (London, 1978), 378, 413; Seton-Watson, *Italy from Liberalism*, 488, n. 2; Morgan, *Spurs on the Boot*, 337; Paul Kennedy, *The Rise and Fall of the Great Powers: Economic Change and Military Conflict from 1500 to 2000* (New York, 1987), 293.

9 For an example of how this transformation of American culture affected one magazine, see Jan Cohn, *Creating America: George Horace Lorimer and "The Saturday Evening Post"* (Pittsburgh, 1989).

On the cigarette endorsement offer, see MGS, "Il fascismo visto dall'estero," *Gerarchia*, June 1929, 440.

10 *Combined Annual Reports of the World War Foreign Debt Commission* (Washington, D.C., 1927), 222–6; Ron Chernow, *The House of Morgan: An American Banking Dynasty and the Rise of Modern Finance* (New York, 1990), 277–84; Diggins, *Mussolini and Fascism*, 270–6; HPFP, box 13, Fletcher to Kellogg, April 30, 1927; TLP, box 85-13, Butler to Lamont, February 10, 1934; Shepard B. Clough, *The Economic History of Modern Italy* (New York, 1964), 228; John Carter, "Mussolini, Master of Italy: A New Picture Emerges from His Authorized Biography," *The New York Times Book Review*, February 7, 1926; Curzio Malaparte, *Battibecco, 1953–1957* (Florence, 1967), 113.

11 Morgan, *Spurs on the Boot*, 95.

12 Morgan, *Spurs on the Boot*, 96; Pini and Susmel, *Mussolini*, III, 116; *My Twenty-four Hours: Mussolini, His Principles, His Methods and His Moods as Told by Himself* (Montreal, 1927).

Some idea of the demand for the articles can be ascertained from the fact that they appeared in two New York papers simultaneously, *The New York Sun* and *The New York Herald*, January 5–15, 1927. In Italy, they appeared at the same time in *La Stampa*.

13 Mussolini clearly had a total command of French but some historians have cast doubts on his command of German and English. In fact, he seems to have been able to read, speak, and understand both languages fairly well by the early thirties, after he had taken lessons. A number of diplomats and journalists record long conversations with Mussolini in either English or German. But he certainly lacked the ability to edit texts in those languages, while Margherita was able to do so. Margherita described Mussolini as having "studied and made himself a master of French and German and learned some Spanish and English." MGS, "How Mussolini Interviews Interviewers."

On Mussolini's knowledge of English and German, see Salvemini, "Mussolini poliglotta," 386–97, and Mack Smith, *Mussolini*, 8, 10, 114, 183, 246, 274–5, 289, for highly negative (and erroneous) opinions. For the contrary, see WLP, box 91, folder 1569, memorandum of conversation with Mussolini, June 9, 1931; KP, box 41, folder 1141, memorandum of conversation with Mussolini, n.d. [1930–31?]; "The Reminiscences of Chester C. Davis," OHP, 463; "The Reminiscences of William Phillips," OHP, 113; NA, State Dept. Records, Reports Prepared by Psychological Warfare Branch on Material Discovered in Archives of Ministry of Culture (Italian) 1922–44, box 4, report 61, 3; Tarbell, *All in the Day's Work*, 383; Emil Ludwig, *Talks with Mussolini* (Boston, 1933), 26; Franz von Papen, *Memoirs* (New York, 1953), 279; Baillie, *High Tension*, 96; Barnes and Nicholson, *The Empire at Bay*, 502; Fox, *Italy To-Day*, 90; "Virginia Cowles Sees Duce As Dapper Nietzsche Superman," *New York American*, November 17, 1935; Hector Bolitho, *Older People* (New York, 1935), 194; Charles H. Sherrill, *My Story Book* (privately printed, 1937), 208; Miller, *I Found No Peace*, 133; Isaac F. Marcosson, *Before I Forget. A Pilgrimage to the Past* (New York, 1959), 374.

14 HMP, Scaife to Mussolini, March 12, 1926, Scaife to Paulucci [sic], April 29, 1926, Scaife to Mussolini, May 19, 1926.

15 Philip V. Cannistraro and Gianfausto Rosoli, "Fascist Emigration Policies in the 1920s: An Interpretative Framework," *International Migration Review,* 13 (1979); PVC, "Fasci all'estero," *Historical Dictionary of Fascist Italy,* 197–8.

16 HMP, de Martino to Scaife, June 17, 1926.

Despite the attempt to include every interview with Mussolini in the OO and OOA, the compilation is far from complete. An idea of the many interviews with Mussolini that appeared in American newspapers in the late twenties can be gathered from the following: " 'Why I'll No Longer Let Women Teach in the Schools of Italy'—Mussolini," *New York American,* January 9, 1927; " 'What My Bachelor Tax Is Doing for Women of Italy'—Mussolini," *New York American,* May 15, 1927; "Mussolini Tells—'How the Solitude of Greatness Bars Me from the Fun I Crave,' " *New York American,* September 5, 1927; "Mussolini—'Why I Intend to Put Adulterers in Prison,' " *New York American,* November 13, 1927.

17 Peter Lyon, *Success Story: The Life and Times of S. S. McClure* (New York, 1963), 399–401; "McClure Praises Fascism," *The New York Times,* January 26, 1927; John Tebbel, *George Horace Lorimer and "The Saturday Evening Post"* (Garden City, N.Y., 1948), 151–4 (quote, 152); Kenneth Roberts, *I Wanted to Write* (Garden City, N.Y., 1949), 153–4, 170, 176–80; SSMP, box 9, Burton to Fletcher, July 9, 1926, S. S. McClure to Hattie McClure, December 19 and 21, 1926, Costain to McClure, February 24, 1927; KRP, box 14, folder 2 [sic]; GHLP, Adelaide W. Neall scrapbook, 221, Roberts to Neall, January 2, 1942.

18 SSMP, McClure to Luiggi, September 11, 1927, S. S. McClure to Hattie McClure, November 3, 1927, Child to McClure, March 15, 1928; RWCP, box 1, Child to father, October 15, 1927 (quote), box 2, Child to father, November 23, 1927; GHLP, Adelaide W. Neall scrapbook; Benito Mussolini, *La mia vita,* ed. Silvio Bertoldi (Milan, 1983), 5–12; CSSA, author files, box 106, reports on Mussolini autobiography; Diggins, *Mussolini and Fascism,* 27–8; Cohn, *Creating America,* 184–5; Lyon, *Success Story,* 401; *My Autobiography by Benito Mussolini,* with a Foreword by Richard Washburn Child (New York, 1928), ix–x.

In 1928, Sarfatti assisted Charles Sherrill, an influential writer, diplomat, and Republican, to write another highly complimentary study of Mussolini: *Bismarck and Mussolini* (New York, 1931), 151; see also idem, *Kamal Roosevelt Mussolini* (Bologna, 1936), 98; idem, *My Story Book,* 208, 244.

19 Lyon, *Success Story,* 401–2; "Mussolini Debate Turns into Clash," *The New York Times,* March 12, 1928.

20 Morgan, *Spurs on the Boot,* 139; Herbert L. Matthews, *The Education of a Correspondent* (New York, 1946), 5; "Karl A. Bickel, 90, Led News Service," *The New York Times,* December 12, 1972; TVRP, Ranck to Knox, December 10, 1928; ibid., Wiegand to Ranck, December 26, 1929; ibid., Stansbury to Ranck, April 10, 1930; ibid., Wiegand to Ranck, n.d. but April 10/11, 1930; ACS, AS/CMM, b. 47, f. 822 (1925–37), MGS to Morgagni, April 11, 1926; ibid., Morgagni to MGS, n.d. but April 1926.

In the passage from his memoirs cited, Morgan describes the arrangement as being with the Hearst press. However, the later agreement with the Hearst press was rather different. It seems clear that Morgan actually describes the contract he negotiated with the United Press. He did not know the details of the arrangement between Sarfatti and the Hearst press. Apparently, Morgan did not wish to admit he defrauded his former employer by selling them articles under false pretenses. Furthermore, Morgan claims that Mussolini took none of the money. This may be what Sarfatti told Morgan, but Vittorio Mussolini's memoirs and Mussolini's later remarks to Karl von Wiegand indicate that Mussolini did take money for his articles from the American press.

21 "United States Is Now Economic and Moral Leader of the World," November 4, 1928; "Reparations Settlement Would Aid Europe's Ills," January 6, 1929; "Mussolini Tells Why Europe Fears Tariff," July 21, 1929; "Foresees Limited Tariff Pacts in Europe; Thinks

Geneva Plan Impractical," March 2, 1930. All these and subsequent articles cited are as printed in the *New York American*.

22 " 'Duty of America Is to Defend National Heritage,' Says Duce," December 2, 1928; "Peace Progress Is Hampered by Rival Interests," April 30, 1929; "Stresemann a Giant Figure in European Rebirth—Mussolini," October 6, 1929; "Germany Has Succeeded Already in Overcoming Versailles Restrictions," February 2, 1930; "Woe to Any Nation That Tries to Embroil Italy in Conflict, Warns Duce," November 9, 1930.

23 "Fascism Wrote a Bloody and Magnificent Page in History, Says Duce," October 24, 1927; " 'Papal Treaty Is Not Only a Blessing for Italy but for Whole World,' Says Duce," March 3, 1929; "Representation by Districts Is Ended," March 31, 1929; "Mussolini Sees Future of Flying in Rapid and Amazing Airplane Development," May 26, 1929; "Fascism in Italy Stays Aloof from Foreign Movements," September 28, 1930.

24 "Amanullah's Reforms and Reign Wrecked on Rock of Religious Tradition," February 3, 1929; "Why I Am for Temperance Rather Than Prohibition," May 25, 1930; "Conflicts of National Aims Vital Obstacle to Such a Union, Says Duce," June 22, 1930; "Antarctic Claims by U.S. Raise New Sovereignty Issue," July 20, 1930.

25 "Judith," "She Is the Comrade of Il Duce," *The American Hebrew*, 600.

26 TVRP, Wiegand to Ranck, December 26, 1929; Ranck to Wiegand, January 18, 1930; Wiegand to Ranck, January 31, 1931; Wiegand to Ranck, February 1, 1930; Ranck to Wiegand, February 17, 1930; Wiegand to Ranck, February 26, 1930; Wiegand to Ranck, April 7, 1930.

27 TVRP, Ranck to Wiegand, April 9, 1930; Wiegand to Ranck, n.d. but April 10/11, 1930; Hearst to Ranck, April 12, 1930; memo by Ranck, April 12, 1930; Stansbury to Ranck, April 16, 1930; Wiegand to Ranck, April 17, 1930; Wiegand to Ranck, April 18, 1930; Ranck to Wiegand, April 18, 1930; Wiegand to Ranck, April 20, 1930; Wiegand to Ranck, April 23, 1930; contract between MGS and *New York American* of April 24, 1930; Wiegand to Ranck, April 30, 1930; Pignatelli to Ranck, December 4, 1930; Connolly to Ranck, January 7, 1931; memorandum, January 8, 1931; Ranck to White, February 20, 1931; Sarfatti guest book, 1926–33, signatures for April 1930; "Millicent Hearst Describes Her Chat with Mussolini," *New York American*, May 11, 1930.

28 TVRP, Pignatelli to Wiegand, April 26, 1930; Morgan, *Spurs on the Boot*, 230–4.

29 NA, T586, reel 426, frames 13045–52, 13058–9, 13069, 13072, 13074; W. A. Swanberg, *Citizen Hearst: A Biography of William Randolph Hearst* (New York, 1961), 430; Ferdinand Lundberg, *Imperial Hearst: A Social Biography* (New York, 1936), 308; Oliver Carlson and Ernest Sutherland Bates, *Hearst, Lord of San Simeon* (New York, 1937), 302–3; De Felice, *Mussolini il duce*, I, 591–2, n. 1; A.J.P. Taylor, *Beaverbrook* (New York, 1972), 329–30; TVRP, Wiegand to Ranck, August 2, 1931; PRO, FO 371/17588, "U.S. Personalities, 1934—Hearst, William Randolph"; EDCP, part 1, box 3, Hearst to Coblentz, September 13, 1934; ibid., part 1, box 4, Hearst to Coblentz, July 20, 1936; ibid., Hearst to Gervasi, August 31, 1936.

30 TVRP, Pignatelli to Ranck, December 4, 1930; Ranck to Hearst, Hearst to Ranck, December 27, 1930; Pignatelli to Ranck, January 9, 1931; Ranck to Wiegand, January 10, 1931; Wiegand to Ranck (2), Ranck to Wiegand, January 12, 1931; Wiegand to Ranck, January 14, 1931; Pignatelli to Ranck, January 30, 1931; Ranck to Pignatelli, Pignatelli to Ranck, February 7, 1931; Pignatelli to Ranck, February 9, 1931; Ranck to Miller, February 11, 1931; Pignatelli to Ranck, February 26, 1931; Pignatelli to Ranck, March 2, 1931; Pignatelli to Ranck, March 10, 1931; Ranck to MGS, March 28, 1931; Pignatelli to Ranck, April 8, 1931; Pignatelli to Ranck, April 13, 1931; Stansbury to Ranck, June 15, 1931; Ranck to Clark, July 1, 1931; Clark to Ranck, July 2, 1931; Clark to Ranck, July 3, 1931; Ranck to MGS, July 24, 1931; Ranck to Emanuel, September 21, 1931; Emanuel to Ranck, Ranck to Emanuel, September 22, 1931; Emanuel to Ranck, September 23, 1931; Emanuel to Ranck (2), Ranck to Emanuel (2), September 24, 1931; Ranck to Hearst, October 17, 1931; West to Ranck (2), October 20, 1931.

Morgan, *Spurs on the Boot*, 139; interview with Fiammetta Sarfatti Gaetani, May 13, 1985.

31 MGS, "Benito Mussolini Predicted: 'I Shall Make My Mark This Epoch, For I Have the Will and the Desire,' " March 15, 1931; idem, "How Mussolini Interviews Interviewers in His Monumental Workroom in Rome," June 28, 1931; Ludwig, *Talks with Mussolini* (quote), 222–3.

In June 1931, Sarfatti placed another article in an American journal. *The International Digest: A Monthly Review of Foreign Affairs* published her "Fascism and Individualism," an abridgment of "Individualismo e fascismo," which had appeared in *Gerarchia* in March. In her article, she defended the Fascist regime's restrictions on individual liberties, including its infringement of freedom of the press, by extolling collective cooperation and discipline.

32 Holborn, *A History of Modern Germany 1840–1945*, 677–88.

33 "Historic Feat Gives New Significance to Italy's Air Progress," January 25, 1931; "Prompt Action Necessary; Geneva Parley Should Be Held at Once, Not in 1932," February 22, 1931; "Italian-French Naval Agreement Assures Peace in Europe and World Until 1936," March 22, 1931; "Mussolini Sees Italy as Key to Customs Union," April 19, 1931; "Mussolini Sees Danger to Civilization in Over-Rapid Industrial Development," May 17, 1931; "Italy's Balance of Power Insures Justice to Austro-German Union, Hints Mussolini," June 14, 1931 (quote on "black and yellow races"); "Debt Plan Promises World Trade Revival—Mussolini," July 12, 1931; "World Must Disarm and Make Peace or Face Economic Ruin," August 9, 1931; "Mussolini Sees Relief from Unemployment as a New Responsibility of Governments," September 6, 1931; "Nine Years of Fascism Have Forged New and Stronger Italy, Asserts Mussolini," November 1, 1931; "Mussolini Declares Italy Is Prepared to Extend Holiday on Armaments," November 22, 1931; "World Is in Economic 'State of War' Says Mussolini"; Asks Tariff Disarmament," December 27, 1931.

34 Guido Corni, *Somalia italiana* (Milan, 1937), 34–7; Angelo Del Boca, *Gli italiani in Africa orientale*, 3 vols., Vol. II, *La conquista dell'impero* (Bari, 1979), 209–13.

35 Interview with Doris Ranck Rend, August 1, 1985; Swanberg, *Citizen Hearst*, 363–4; TVRP, Ranck to Hearst, Hearst to Ranck, Ranck to Emanuel, October 17, 1931; "SCHEDULE OF ARTICLES FOR MARCH OF EVENTS BY FAMOUS STATESMEN," n.d. (but late 1931); Ranck to Barry, Ranck to White, November 24, 1931; Flick to Ranck, December 21, 1931; Flick to Ranck, December 22, 1931; Hearst to White, December 23, 1931; Ranck to MGS, January 21, 1932.

36 TVRP, Salmon to Ranck, October 21, 1931; memorandum, October 23, 1931; Salmon to Ranck, October 30, 1931; memorandum, October 30, 1931; Salmon to Ranck, November 3, 1931; Hearst to Ranck, November 9, 1931; Ranck to Salmon, November 13, 1931; Ranck to Hearst, November 17, 1931, and October 23, 1933; contract between MGS and *New York American* of November 26, 1931; Salmon to Stansbury, November 27, 1931 (quote); Ranck to Salmon, January 20, 1932; Berkson to Ranck, March 2, 1934.

37 TVRP, Ranck to MGS, December 15, 1931.

38 TVRP, Salmon to Ranck, February 27, 1932; Ranck to Hearst, August 2, 1932; Ranck to Willicombe, October 13, 1932; Hearst to Ranck, October 14, 1932; Ranck to Salmon, October 17 and 20, 1932; Ranck to White, October 17 and 26, 1932; White to Ranck, October 19, 28, and 30, 1932; Ranck to Emanuel, October 22, 1932; Emanuel to Ranck, October 24, 1932; Salmon to White, November 12, 1932; agreement between MGS and *New York American*, witnessed by Amedeo Sarfatti, n.d. but November 11 or 12, 1932; NA, MFB, Record Group 331, reel 476-A, Extract No. 11, "Address by Mussolini to the Fascist Grand Council—7 April 1932," 15; Ludwig, *Talks with Mussolini*, 109; Vittorio Mussolini, *Vita con mio padre*, 83 (quote); idem, *Mussolini e gli uomini nel suo tempo* (Rome, 1977), 59.

39 TVRP, Salmon to Ranck (via London), September 29, 1932; Emanuel to Ranck, October 21 and 24, 1932; Ranck to Emanuel, October 22, 1932.

40 TVRP, Ranck to Berkson, November 7, 1932; Berkson to Ranck, November 26, and December 8 (quote), 1932; Fredericka Blankner, "War—An Authorized Interview with Mussolini," *New York Herald Tribune Sunday Magazine,* October 16, 1932; "War!—By Mussolini," *Sunday Dispatch* (London), October 30, 1932.

41 TVRP, Ranck to Berkson, November 4 and 8, 1932; Berkson to Ranck, December 5, 1932,

with manuscript entitled "The Safety of the Ship"; Ranck to Hearst, December 16, 1932; Michael R. Beschloss, *Kennedy and Roosevelt: The Uneasy Alliance* (New York, 1980), 69–73; David E. Kaskoff, *Joseph P. Kennedy: A Life and Times* (Englewood Cliffs, N.J., 1974), 44–5; Richard J. Whalen, *The Founding Father: The Story of Joseph P. Kennedy* (New York, 1964), 121–5; "Address by Mussolini to the Fascist Grand Council—7 April 1932," 1–15.

"Europe Can Recuperate Without Help of America," January 24, 1932; "World Trade Balance Must Be Restored to Aid Prosperity Revival, Says Mussolini," February 14, 1932; "Mussolini Sees Government Speeded Up by 'Lame Duck' Amendment to Constitution," March 6, 1932; "Mussolini Warns of Danger from Far East Unless Disunity Among White Races Ends," March 27, 1932; " 'Europe Must Unite to Avert an Economic Collapse of Danube Nations'—Mussolini," April 17, 1932; "Mussolini Tells How Italy Is Employing War Veterans on Vast Governmental Works," May 8, 1932; "Mussolini Sees Weapons of Aggression as Keynote of Disarmament Problem," May 29, 1932; "Nations Must Loosen Economic Barriers to Restore Prosperity," June 19, 1932; "Mussolini Warns of Danger to Civilization in Lack of Decision at Geneva Conference," July 10, 1932; "Mussolini Cites Italy's Cabinet Shift as a Proof of Fascist Efficiency," July 31, 1932; "Sick World Must Have Help of U.S., Avers Mussolini," August 21, 1932; "Germany Is Justified in Demanding Equality of Armaments—Mussolini," September 11, 1932; "Fascist State Limits Useless Liberty, Upholds Religion, Declares Mussolini," October 16, 1932; "Highest-Placed Criminals Must Be Mercilessly Suppressed, Says Mussolini," October 23, 1932; "Fascism Has Unified Italy for New Era of Progress, Declares Mussolini," November 13, 1932; "Depression Is Deepest in U.S., Says Mussolini," December 4, 1932 (quote); "Mussolini Urges Legalizing of Wine to Solve Temperance Problem in U.S.," December 25, 1932.

42 TVRP, Hearst to Ranck, December 16, 1932; Ranck to Hearst, December 17 and 26, 1932; Ranck to Berkson, December 17, 26, 28, 1932; Ranck to Hillman, December 18, 22, and 24, 1932; Wrigley to Ranck, December 24, 1932; Berkson to Ranck, December 27, 1932; NA, T586, reel 426, frames 013067–8; "Mussolini Sees Signs of Recovery with 1933 as the Decisive Year," January 1, 1933.

CHAPTER 24: UNDER ATTACK

1 MGS, "Promesse e azioni: L'Accademia d'Italia," *Il Popolo d'Italia*, January 15, 1926; Ojetti, *I taccuini*, 204; Guido De Luca, "La battaglia per la cultura," *Critica Fascista* (August 15, 1926), 305–6.
2 "Arte e civiltà," October 5, 1926, OO, XXII, 230.
3 Mussolini to Alberto Salietti, May 17, 1928, reproduced in Bossaglia, *Il "Novecento Italiano"*, 104.
4 Enrico Crispolti, "La politica culturale del fascismo, le avanguardie e il problema del futurismo," in Renzo De Felice, ed., *Futurismo, cultura e politica* (Turin, 1988), 247–79.
5 The responses to the inquiry were published in *Critica Fascista* over a four-month period starting on October 15, 1926, and concluding with Bottai's "Resultanze dell'inchiesta sull'arte fascista" on February 15, 1927. See also Fossati, *Pittura e scultura fra le due guerre*, 186; Manlio Morgagni, "Il Raduno degli artisti di tutte le arti," *La Rivista Illustrata del Popolo d'Italia* (August 1927), 5–6; Giuseppe Bottai, *La politica delle art: Scritti, 1918–1943*, ed. Alessandro Masi (Rome, 1992), 71–83.
6 MGS, "Arte, fascismo e antiretorica," *Critica Fascista* (March 1, 1927), 82–4; she had made similar points in "Nei dodici mesi dall'avvento: L'arte," *Il Popolo d'Italia*, October 26, 1923, in "Problemi dello stile moderno," *Gerarchia* (August 1925), 500–4, in "Questioni di parole," *Il Popolo d'Italia*, December 28, 1930, and in "Lingua e fascismo," *Il Giornale d'Italia*, January 3, 1931; Albertina Vittoria, *Le riviste del duce: Politica e cultura del regime* (Turin, 1983), 74–8.
7 Fossati, *Pittura e scultura fra le due guerre*, 231; Vito Zagarrio, "Il fascismo e la politica delle arti," *Studi Storici* (Spring 1976), 247–50.
8 MGS, "Alcuni problemi e alcuni pittori alla mostra del Novecento," *Il Popolo d'Italia*, March

12, 1926; idem, "Alla prima mostra del Novecento Italiano," *Rivista Illustrata del Popolo d'Italia* (March 1926), 32–6; Braun, *Mario Sironi: Art and Politics in Italy, 1922–1945,* Chapter 4.

9 Bossaglia, *Il "Novecento Italiano,"* 21–2; Joan M. Lukach, "Giorgio Morandi and Modernism in Italy Between the Wars," in Braun, *Italian Art in the 20th Century,* 160–1; Giorgio Luti, *Cronache letterarie tra le due guerre* (Bari, 1966), 143–66; Maltese, *Storia dell'arte in Italia,* 337–42; Luciano Troisio, ed., *Strapaese e stracittà* (Treviso, 1975); Fossati, *Pittura e scultura fra le due guerre,* 208–11; Tempesti, *Arte dell'Italia fascista,* 97–105.

10 Ardengo Soffici to Carlo Carrà, January 9, 1926, and April 28, 1927, and Carrà to Soffici, May 3, 1927, in Carrà and Fagone, *Carlo Carrà–Ardengo Soffici,* 180–81; Camesasca, *Mario Sironi: Scritti,* 35; MGS, "Spunti polemici," *Il Popolo d'Italia,* April 15, 1927; idem, "Tranquillo Cremona und das Heroische XIX. Jahrhundert," *Italien* (September 1929), 433–8; Rossana Bossaglia, "Caratteri e sviluppo di Novecento," in *Mostra del Novecento Italiano,* 25–6; idem, *Il "Novecento Italiano,"* 27–8; Hulten and Celant, *Arte italiana,* 667.

11 Emily Braun, "The Scuola Romana: Fact or Fiction?," *Art in America* (March 1988), 129–36; idem, exhibition catalog, *Scuola romana: Artisti tra le due guerre* (Milan, 1988), 209–14; Pia Vivarelli, "Personalities and Styles in the Figurative Art of the Thirties," in Braun, *Italian Art in the 20th Century,* 184–5.

12 *Scuola romana: Artisti tra le due guerre,* 237; Magali Sarfatti-Larson interview with Amedeo and Pierangela Sarfatti, October 1985; Giovanni Audoli and Vittorio Sgarbi, *I "Volti" della Scuola Romana* (Turin, 1987); Frateili, *Dall'Aragno al Rosati,* 8 and ff.; Mafai as quoted in Duilio Morosini, *L'arte degli anni difficili (1928–1944)* (Rome, 1985), 70.

13 MGS, "Alla Biennale di Roma: La bellezza che ritorna," *Il Popolo d'Italia,* December 7, 1923; idem, preface to *Dieci artisti del "Novecento Italiano"* (Rome, 1927), 26–9; idem, "Dieci artisti del Novecento Italiano," *Rivista Italiana del Popolo d'Italia* (March 1927), 44–8; Enrico Aeberli to MGS, November 2, 1929, ASP; Fabio Benzi, "Villa Strohl-Fern tra Caffè Aragno, valori plastici e Novecento," in Lucia Stefanelli Torossi, ed., *Gli Artisti di Villa Strohl-Fern tra Sinbolismo e Novecento* (Rome, 1983), 17–18.

14 Morosini, *L'arte degli anni difficili,* 65–6, 86; Edda Ciano, *La mia testimonianza* (Milan, 1975), 94–5; see the correspondence between Gino Severini and Leonce Rosenberg in 1928, edited by Ester Coen in "Un carteggio con Rosenberg," and published in Maurizio Fagiolo, Ester Coen, and Gina Severini, eds., *Gino Severini entre les deux guerres* (Rome, 1980), 92–100; *Scuola Romana,* 302, 306; Riccio, "La Sarfatti, Mussolini e il novecento," 5; Barbara Allason, *Memorie di un'antifascista, 1919–1940* (Rome-Florence-Milan, 1946), 212–13.

15 Cited in Nozzoli, "Margherita Sarfatti," 260; MGS, preface to the first issue of *Il Novecento Italiano* (1926), 1; Braun, "The Scuola Romana: Fact or Fiction?," 131–5; Vivarelli, "Personalities and Styles in the Figurative Art of the Thirties," 182–3; Alessandra Borgogelli, "La reazione contro il Novecento," in *Annitrenta* (Milan, 1982), 105–37; Enotrio Mastroleonardo, "Pittura italiana contemporanea," *Idea* (January 1960), 42; Camesasca, *Mario Sironi: Scritti,* 51; Tempesti, *Arte dell'Italia fascista,* 111–17; Maltese, *Storia dell'arte,* 365; Fossati, *Pittura e scultura fra le due guerre,* 219–24; Cesare De Seta, *La cultura architettonica in Italia tra le due guerre* (Bari, 1972), 154–5.

16 Cannistraro, *La fabbrica del consenso,* 30–8; Ferdinando Coscera, *Le professionali e le arti nello stato fascista* (Rome, 1941).

17 Fossati, *Pittura e scultura fra le due guerre,* 230–3; Sapori, *L'arte e il Duce,* 169–83; C. E. Oppo, "L'ordine delle esposizioni," *Politica Sociale,* January–February 1929, 144–6.

18 Fabio Benzi, "Materiali inediti dall'archivio di Cipriano Efisio Oppo," *Bollettino d'Arte* (May–August, 1986), 169–71; C. E. Oppo, "Lo stato e gli artisti," *La Politica Sociale,* September–October 1929, 789–92; Fossati, *Pittura e scultura fra le due guerre,* 233; Oppo's articles have been published as *Mostri figuri e paesaggi* (Turin, 1930) and *Forme e colori nel mondo* (Lanciano, 1938).

19 Nozzoli, "Margherita Sarfatti," 258; MGS, "Artisti, bottegai e governo," *Il Popolo d'Italia,* April 17, 1925; C. E. Oppo to MGS, October 22, 1927, in Benzi, "Materiali inediti," 172; Bossaglia, *Il "Novecento Italiano,"* 105–8; MGS to Mario Sironi, June 5, 1929, and MGS to [Tosi], n.d., ASP.

20 MGS to Fradeletto, May 3, 1927, reproduced in Sileno Salvagnini, "Margherita Sarfatti, una vita nella tormenta," *Arte*, n. 221 (September 1991), 87; idem, "L'avanguardia arriva dal nord," ibid., n. 222 (October 1991), 95; MGS, "Alla XV Biennale di Venezia," *Rivista Illustrata del Popolo d'Italia* (June 1926), 44–9; MGS to Sironi, addressed "Caro Amico," n.d. (but late 1926/early 1927), ASP; XVI Esposizione Internazionale d'Arte, *Catalogo, 1928* (Venice, 1928), 3; Pascale Budillon-Puma, "Les Biennales de Venise pendant l'époque fasciste: Leurs rapports avec le pouvoir (1928–1942)," in *Aspects de la culture italienne sous le fascisme* (Grenoble, 1982), 32–3.

21 Antonio Maraini to Oppo, June 26, 1927, in Benzi, "Materiali inediti," 173; MGS to Sironi, addressed to "Caro amico, come state," n.d. (but early 1927), ASP; Bossaglia, *Il "Novecento Italiano"*, 30–1.

22 Hulten and Celant, *Arte italiana*, 666; MGS, "Scultori e pittori d'oggi a Venezia," *Nuova Antologia* (October 16, 1928), 465–9; idem, "Architettura, teatro e mostra dell'ottocento a Venezia," ibid. (July 1, 1928), 56–61; idem, "La XVI Biennale," May 3, and "Posizioni e problemi," May 19, 1928, both in *Il Popolo d'Italia*; idem, "La XVI Biennale di Venezia," *Rivista Illustrata del Popolo d'Italia* (June 1928), 38–48.

23 Budillon-Puma, "Les Biennales," 32; Malvano, *Fascismo e politica dell'immagine*, 46, n. 40; Hulten and Celant, *Arte italiana*, 686.

24 MGS, preface to catalog, *Quindici artisti del Novecento Italiano* (Milan, February 1927), 7–8; idem, "La mostra dei sette alla Galleria di Milano," *Il Popolo d'Italia*, April 13, 1928; Hulten and Celant, *Arte italiana*, 662, 667; Bossaglia, *Il "Novecento Italiano"*, 99–101.

25 MGS to Sironi, February 3, 1928, ASP; MGS to Arturo Tosi, February 5, 1928, reproduced in Bossaglia, *Il "Novecento Italiano"*, 103–4; MGS to D'Annunzio, June 21, 1928, AVI, AG.

26 MGS, "Esposizioni," *Il Popolo d'Italia*, April 1, 1927; idem, "Der Novecento," *Italien* (December 1927), 19–26; idem, "L'attività del Novecento per il 1927," *Il Popolo d'Italia*, February 18, 1927; "Una conferenza di Margh. Sarfatti all'Aja," *Il Corriere della Sera*, November 20, 1927; "Margherita Sarfatti parla a Berlino," *Il Corriere della Sera*, November 30, 1927; Camesasca and Gian Ferrari, "Note biografiche," 193; Emily Braun, "Die Gestaltung eines kollektiven Willens," in Jürgen Harten and Jochen Poetter, eds., *Sironi (1885–1961)* (Cologne, 1989), 40–1; Hulten and Celant, *Arte italiana*, 662–78; Bossaglia, *Il "Novecento Italiano"*, 35; Sapori, *L'arte e il Duce*, 258–9; Marzorati, *Margherita Sarfatti*, 159–60.

27 MGS, "Vita e trasmigrazione delle opera d'arte," *Il Popolo d'Italia*, October 14, 1920; Roberto Forges Davanzati, "Cultura e politica estera nazionale," *Gerarchia* (April 1925), 226–31; Tempesti, *Arte dell'Italia fascista*, 75–6; Ojetti, *I taccuini*, 249; C. E. Oppo, "L'ordine delle esposizioni," *Politica Sociale*, January–February 1929, 146.

28 Pages from Foà guest book dated April 5, 1928, "Casa Carlisi," FP; Sironi to Tosi, August 14, 1927; Camesasca, *Mario Sironi: Scritti*, 275; Mussolini to Salietti, May 17, 1928, in Bossaglia, *Il "Novecento Italiano"*, 104 and 30; details of the arrangements for the exhibit have been reconstructed from the correspondence listed by Claudia Gian Ferrari in Bossaglia, *Il "Novecento Italiano"*, 172–5.

29 "Elenco degli artisti invitati alla Mostra 1929 Anno VII," ACS, PCM (1928–30), f. 14/1/2690, 1928; Soffici to Carrà, April 5, 1929, in *Carlo Carrà–Ardengo Soffici: Lettere*, 189; Maltese, *Storia dell'arte in Italia*, 334; Sarfatti's catalog preface, in *Catalogo della II mostra del Novecento Italiano* (Milan, 1929), and reproduced in Bossaglia, *Il "Novecento Italiano"*, 110, was taken virtually unchanged from the text of the official invitation sent to artists by the executive committee, a copy of which is in APC.

30 Police reports dated March 14 and May 12, 1929, ACS, MI-DPP, "Sarfatti, Margherita"; Umberto Fracchia, "Mascagni contro il Novecento," *Politica Sociale*, September–October 1929, 677–8; Maltese, *Storia dell'arte in Italia*, 352; Mario Tozzi, "Per un'arte italiana," *La Fiera Letteraria*, February 3, 1929.

31 A. F. Della Porta, *Polemica sul '900* (Milan, 1930), 13–15, 40–51; Vittorio Fagone, "Arte, politica e propaganda," in *Annitrenta* (Milan, 1982), 45; Bossaglia, *Il "Novecento Italiano"*, 34.

32 Mussolini to MGS, July 9, 1929, published in Salvagnini, "Mussolini le intimò: 'Smetta di confondere Novecento con fascismo,'" *Arte* (November 1991); A. F. Della Porta, "Arte

italiana e arte straniera," *Il Regime Fascista*, July 20, 1929, reproduced in *Polemica sul 900*, 63–6; Enrico Crispolti, *Il mito della macchina e altri temi del futurismo* (Trapani, 1969), 610.

33 Carlo Carrà, "La seconda mostra del '900," *L'Ambrosiano*, March 2, 1929; Vincenzo Costantini, "La II mostra del Novecento Italiano," I (March 3, 1929) and II (March 17, 1929), *La Fiera Letteraria;* MGS, "La pittura alla II mostra del Novecento Italiano," *Il Popolo d'Italia*, March 2, 1929; idem, "La seconda mostra del Novecento a Milano," *Rivista Illustrata del Popolo d'Italia* (April 1929), 39–46; idem, "Arte e costume fascista," *Il Popolo d'Italia*, July 10, 1929, reprinted in *Politica Sociale*, March–April 1929, 203–7; a response by A. F. Della Porta to Sarfatti's article was published as "Costume fascista e arte italiana" in July 18, 1929, in *Giornale degli Artisti*, and republished in his *Polemica sul 900*, 57–61; Alberto Salietti to MGS, December 20, 1929, in Bossaglia, *Il "Novecento Italiano,"* 116; MGS to Berenson, September 19, 1953, BBP.

34 F. T. Marinetti, preface to *Trentatrè futuristi* (Milan, 1929), 5–12; Hulten and Celant, *Arte italiana*, 671; Marinetti, "Il futurismo e il Novecento," in *Futurismo e Novecentismo* (Milan, 1930), 9–29; "Marinetti e il Novecento," October 19, 1929, and "La Conferenza di F. T. Marinetti sul Futurismo e Novecentismo," *Il Popolo d'Italia*, October 19, 1929; "Un'intervista polemica di Margherita Sarfatti: Il passatismo di F. T. Marinetti," *Il Mattino* (Naples), December 7–8, 1929; MGS to Emilio Bodrero, October 5, 1930, ACS, CEB, b. 35, f. 97, sf. 211.

35 Alberto Salietti to MGS, December 20, 1929, reproduced in Bossaglia, *Il "Novecento Italiano,"* 116–17.

36 Carlo Foà to MGS, bearing Sarfatti's marginal comments, January 23, 1930, FP.

37 MGS, manuscript, "Programma per il giornale," n.d. (but January 1930), and MGS to Foà, January 30, 1930, FP.

38 MGS, "Lettre d'Italie: Ottocento e Novecento," *Formes* (January 1930), 26–8; idem, *Storia della pittura moderna*, esp. 94–147; Franco Ciarlantini, "La storia della pittura moderna," *Augustea* (April 15, 1930), 221–2; *Italian Art: An Illustrated Souvenir of the Exhibition of Italian Art at the Burlington House, London* (London, 1930); MGS, "La pittura italiana a Londra," *Rivista Illustrate del Popolo d'Italia* (April 1930), 36–41; "518,000 Saw Italian Art at the London Exhibition," *The New York Times*, March 21, 1930; police report, April 26, 1930, ACS, MI-DPP, "Sarfatti, Margherita"; Ojetti, *I taccuini*, 314–15.

39 Malvano, *Fascismo e politica dell'immagine*, 46, n. 40; Ojetti, *I taccuini*, 417–18.

40 Police reports of March 3 and 18, 1930, ACS, MI-DPP, "Sarfatti, Margherita"; Corrado Pavolini, "Arte e rivoluzione," *Politica Sociale*, July–August 1930, 629–30; MGS to Sironi, July 11, 1930, ASP.

41 MGS to Sironi, May 28, 1930, ASP; *Prima Quadriennale d'arte nazionale, 1931* (Rome, 1931); Benzi, "Materiali inediti," 172 and n. 8; Rossana Bossaglia, "L'ultimo Novecento," in *Annitrenta*, 80; Antonello Trombadori, introduction to *Gli artisti di Villa Strohl-Fern*, 6.

42 OO, XXIV, "Agli artisti della Quadriennale," January 3, 1931, 331–2; police report of January 11, 1931, ACS, MI-DPP, "Sarfatti, Margherita."

43 MGS, "Gli scultori italiani al convegno di Roma," (January 16, 1931), 225–31, and "I pittori alla Quadriennale," (February 16, 1931), 488–98, both in *Nuova Antologia*.

44 Soffici to Carrà, April 5, 1929, and Carrà to Soffici, April 8, 1929, *Lettere Carrà-Soffici*, 189–90; MGS to Sironi, May 28, 1930, ASP; Bossaglia, *Il "Novecento Italiano,"* 118–20.

45 Sarfatti's impressions of the lands and people she encountered are in MGS, "Vita di bordo," November 1, 1930, and "Paesaggi e spiriti del Brasile," November 13, 1930, both in *Il Popolo d'Italia;* idem, "La povertà delle terre ricche," *Gerarchia* (December 1930), 1016–23; idem, "Terra do Brazil," *Nuova Antologia* (June 16, 1931), 436–58.

46 "Margherita Sarfatti in Argentina," August 10, 1930, "Margherita Sarfatti a São Paolo," September 6, 1930, and "Il Novecento Italiano a Buenos Aires," September 16, 1930, all in *Il Corriere della Sera;* MGS, "Il Novecento Italiano a Buenos Aires," *Poligono* (June-August 1930), 437, 464; idem, "Bilancio della mostra del '900 a Buenos Aires," October 24, 1930, and "La mostra a Buenos Aires del Novecento Italiano," October 30, 1930, both in *Il Popolo d'Italia;* "Il Novecento Italiano a Buenos Aires," August 21, 1930, and "Alle fonti della

pittura moderna: La bella conferenza tenuta da Margherita Sarfatti agli Amigos del Arte,"
September 17, 1930, both in *Il Mattino* (Buenos Aires); Alberto Spaini, "Margherita Sarfatti,
il Novecento e la mostra di Buenos Aires," *La Fiera Letteraria*, November 9, 1930; Vincenzo
Caputo, *I poeti d'Italia in trenta secoli* (Milan, 1962), 375; Marzorati, *Margherita Sarfatti*, 204.

Sarfatti's second collection of poems, which she called *Il canzoniere del mare*, has never
been published. She seems to have added to the series during her stay in Uruguay in the
1940s.

For the anti-Fascist attacks against Sarfatti, see "La fascista Margherita Sarfatti contro
l'Argentina," December 2, 1930, and "Fascismo, merce di esportazione?," December 13,
1930, both in *Risorgimento* (Buenos Aires).

47 Boratto, "Liquidazione dell'amica matura"; MacGregor-Hastie, *The Day of the Lion*, 149;
ACS, MI-DPP, f. "Sarfatti, Margherita," reports of May 12 and October 19, 1929, April 26
and August 11, 1930; Giuseppe Villaroel, "Margherita Sarfatti l'irriducibile," *Il Giornale
d'Italia*, March 10, 1950; MGS to Ada Negri, n.d. but 1931, GSP; Navarra, *Memorie*, 99.

48 Police report of August 11, 1930, ACS, MI-DPP, "Sarfatti, Margherita"; Pini and Susmel,
Mussolini, III, 192–3; De Felice, *Mussolini il fascista*, II, 349, n. 3; idem, *Mussolini il duce*, I
(Turin, 1974), 301; Giordano Bruno Guerri, *Galeazzo Ciano: Una vita, 1903–1944* (Milan,
1979), 53–72; Curti Cucciati, "Un'amica di Mussolini racconta," November 17, 1949, 14.

49 Rachele Mussolini, *Mussolini: An Intimate Biography*, 82; idem, *Benito il mio uomo*, 69, 70.

50 MGS to Manlio Morgagni, January 6, 1931, ACS, AS/CMM, b. 47, f. 822, "Sarfatti,
Margherita."

51 MGS, "Arturo Tosi alla mostra di Roma," *Il Popolo d'Italia*, February 22, 1931; Rachele
Mussolini, *Mussolini: An Intimate Biography* (New York, 1974), 82–3; idem, *Benito il mio
uomo*, 70–1; Duilio Susmel, *Vita sbagliata di Galeazzo Ciano* (Milan, 1962), 42.

52 For the 1930 Triennale, Sarfatti was a member, along with Ojetti, of the international jury,
not of the organizing committee. See *Catalogo ufficiale della IV esposizione triennale internazionale delle arti decorative ed industriali moderne* (Milan, May-October 1930), 1–8; MGS,
"Stoccolma e il funzionalismo," *Il Popolo d'Italia*, August 5, 1930; idem, *Acqua passata*, 159;
MGS to Ada Negri, July 9, 1930, GSP; Doordan, *Building Modern Italy*, 75–6.

53 Doordan, *Building Modern Italy*, 77, 90; Sapori, *L'arte e il Duce*, 194; Ciucci, *Gli architetti e
il fascismo*, 99–107.

54 Marcello Piacentini, "Difesa dell'architettura italiana," *Il Giornale d'Italia*, May 2, 1931,
reprinted in Michele Cennamo, ed., *Materiali per l'analisi dell'architettura moderna: Il MIAR*
(Naples, 1976), 285–9; the letters delivered by Sarfatti to Mussolini, dated May 20 and July
27, 1931, are in idem, *Materiali*, 448–50, 457–8; Doordan, *Building Modern Italy*, 91–93; De
Seta, *La cultura architettonica*, 196–7; Marcello Piacentini, *Architettura d'oggi* (Rome, 1930).

55 *Atti Parlamentari, Camera dei Deputati*, XXVIII Legislatura, 1st Session, May 15, 1931,
4694–4702, and May 19, 1931, 4752–62; "Difesa dell'arte moderna," *L'Italia Letteraria*, May
24, 1931; Ugo Ojetti, "Dell'architettura razionale," *Dedalo* (March 1931), 951–2; De Seta,
La cultura architettonica, 170, 196; G. Sommi Picenardi, "Il Novecento e le esposizioni
all'estero," *Il Regime Fascista*, June 13, 1931 (Sommi Picenardi also collaborated with Giovanni Preziosi's anti-Semitic journal *La Vita Italiana*); Bossaglia, *Il "Novecento Italiano,"* 43;
Camesasca, *Mario Sironi: Scritti*, 103.

56 The details of these polemics are recounted in Bossaglia, *Il "Novecento Italiano,"* 42–6, with
some of the articles reproduced in her appendix.

57 Roberto Farinacci to Mussolini, June 25, 1933, NA, T-586, reel 448, frames 026368–75;
Farinacci, "Su l'arte del Novecento: La polemica è chiusa," *Il Regime Fascista*, July 23, 1931,
reprinted in Bossaglia, *Il "Novecento Italiano,"* 138–9.

58 De Begnac, *Taccuini mussoliniani*, 426–7.

59 Marzorati, *Margherita Sarfatti*, 160; Bossaglia, *Il "Novecento Italiano,"* 241; police report of
November 6, 1931, ACS, MI-DPP, "Sarfatti, Margherita"; Fiammetta Sarfatti Gaetani to
PVC, November 4, 1987; MGS, "Casorati o dell'ironia," *La Stampa*, October 30, 1931;
Alfredo Signoretti, *La Stampa in camicia nera* (Rome, 1968), 34–5.

Another factor which may have contributed to the growing estrangement between

Margherita and Mussolini in late 1931 was the troubles of the Banca Commerciale. Giuseppe Toeplitz, the director of the bank, had built Italian industry with long-term loans, as Mussolini desired. But the depression left the bank with short-term debts. Mussolini feared the possible collapse of the entire economy and placed much of the blame on Toeplitz. In November, Mussolini separated the banking and credit activities of the bank, placing the latter under a new state agency, the Istituto Mobiliare Italiano. Mussolini eventually forced Toeplitz to resign from the bank in 1933.

The Sarfatti and the Toeplitz families were old friends; Amedeo held a position with the Banca Commerciale. But since all were Jews, Mussolini probably made some unpleasant connections, heavily tinged with anti-Semitism. Mussolini may have destroyed Toeplitz's career in 1933 only as a friendly gesture to Hitler, but he himself may have already begun to believe certain myths about the "International Jewish Financial Conspiracy." See De Felice, *Mussolini il duce*, I, 169–71; Toeplitz, *Il banchiere*, 183–96; "Industry," in Cannistraro, *Historical Dictionary*, 276–8; "Italian Bank Plans Increased Activity," November 5, 1931; "Shake-Up in Italian Bank," March 9, 1933; "Giuseppe Toeplitz, Financier, Is Dead," January 30, 1938, all in *The New York Times*.

60 Morgan, *Spurs on the Boot*, 140; ACS, MI-DPP, f. "Sarfatti, Margherita," reports of December 20, 1931, and June 28, 1932; Signoretti, *La Stampa*, 17; Ojetti, *I taccuini*, 249–50; MGS to T. V. Ranck, December 29, 1931, TVRP; MGS, "Per Arnaldo Mussolini," *Gerarchia* (December 1932), 1; John T. Whitaker, *We Cannot Escape History* (New York, 1943), 62–3; De Felice, *Mussolini il duce*, II, 274–5; Mezzetti, *Borgese e il fascismo*, 11, 18, 33–40.

61 De Felice, *Mussolini il Duce*, I, 300–303; Navarra, *Memorie*, 100; Staglieno, "Margherita Sarfatti," *Il Giornale*, July 28, 1987; MGS quoted in Amerigo Montemaggiori, ed., *Dizionario della dottrina fascista* (Turin, 1934), 479–80.

62 MGS, "La classicità all'esposizione francese di Londra," March 12; "La tecnica nell'arte francese," March 18; "I primitivi francesi," March 23; "Alcuni ritratti," April 6; "Watteau o l'evasione," April 7; "L'insegnamento di David," April 19; "Alcuni lignaggi," April 27; "Dopo l'impressionismo," May 10, 1932, all in *La Stampa;* idem, "Cinque secoli di pittura francese," *Nuova Antologia* (May 1, 1932), 41–51; idem, "L'odierna grande manifestazione d'arte a Venezia," April 28, 1932, and "Alcune mostre individuali a Venezia," May 18, 1932, both in *Il Popolo d'Italia;* idem, "Creta," September 23; "Il Labirinto," September 28; "Tirinto, il focolare," October 5; "Micene," October 13; "Colloquio con Pennosco," October 19; "La difesa di una regina," November 1; "La morea," November 6; "L'isola medioevale," November 16; "Rodi," November 25, 1932, all in *La Stampa*.

63 Morgan, *Spurs on the Boot*, 141–2; Meldini, "La sventurata Margherita," 37–3; IBP, Balbo to MGS, August 2, 1932; Marzorati, *Margherita Sarfatti*, 32–3; MGS, *Acqua passata*, 65–6; ACS, MI-DPP, f. "Sarfatti, Margherita," report of June 27, 1932.

64 De Felice, *Mussolini il duce*, I, 45–7; De Begnac, *Taccuini mussoliniani*, 486–7; Guspini, *L'orecchio del regime*, 102 (MGS-Mussolini conversation).

65 Dino Alfieri and Luigi Freddi, *Mostra della rivoluzione fascista* (Bergamo, 1932), 8–9; Emily Braun, *Mario Sironi*, Chapter 4; Doordan, *Building Fascist Italy*, 131–4; Mario Sironi, "L'architettura della rivoluzione," *Il Popolo d'Italia*, November 18, 1932, now in Camesasca, *Mario Sironi: Scritti*, 132–5.

For the origins and history of the Mostra della Rivoluzione, see Jeffrey T. Schnapp, "Epic Demonstrations: Fascist Modernity and the 1932 Exhibition of the Fascist Revolution" in Richard J. Goslan, ed., *Fascism, Aesthetics and Culture* (Hoover, N.H., 1992).

66 MGS, "Architettura, arte e simbolo alla mostra del fascismo," *Rivista Illustrata del Popolo d'Italia* (November 1932), 1–17; idem, "The Fascist Exhibition at Rome," *Formes* (January 1933), 355; idem, "Dimostrazioni e moniti," *La Stampa*, December 22, 1932.

67 Alfieri and Freddi, *Mostra della rivoluzione*, 108.

68 Police report, November 5, 1932, ACS, MI-DPP, "Sarfatti, Margherita"; Giovanni Ansaldo, diary entry for April 1933, as quoted in Indro Montanelli and Marcello Staglieno, *Leo Longanesi* (Milan, 1984), 212–14; MGS, "Le arti plastiche nel Decennale," *Il Popolo d'Italia*, October 28, 1932.

In the preceding month, Sarfatti had already begun to receive hints that her contributions were no longer welcomed by the editor of the *Rivista Illustrata del Popolo d'Italia*. See Manlio Morgagni to MGS, September 3, 1932, ACS, AS/CMM; Libero Andreotti, *Art and Politics in Fascist Italy: The Exhibition of the Fascist Revolution (1932)*, Ph. D. dissertation, Massachusetts Institute of Technology, 1989, Appendix 4, 468.

69 On the Florence station see Doordan, *Building Modern Italy*, 102–5, 109, 134–7; Ciucci, *Gli architetti e il fascismo*, 134–7; Etlin, *Modernism in Italian Architecture*, 297–310, 486–7; Nicolò De Luigi, "Il concorso e la polemica per la stazione di Firenze," *La Casa*, n. 6 (1959); MGS, "L'architetto Perret," *La Stampa*, September 13, 1932; idem, "Architettura razionale," *La Stampa*, March 17, 1933; *Atti Parlamentari, Camera dei Deputati, Discussione*, May 26, 1934, 330–9; Tempesti, *Arte dell'Italia fascista*, 158–9; Marco Palla, *Firenze nel regime fascista (1929–1934)* (Florence, 1978), 341–2, 3553–61; Giovanni K. Koenig, *Architettura in Toscana, 1931–1968* (Turin, 1968), 19–25; MGS, "Agli architetti italiani: Per il Palazzo Littorio," *La Stampa*, June 23, 1934.

70 Seymour Berkson to T. V. Ranck, April 15, 1933, TVRP; interviews with Fiammetta Sarfatti Gaetani, May 20, 1985, and with Magalì Sarfatti-Larson, June 16, 1986; MGS, *Acqua passata*, 187–8; idem, "L'Egitto," June 6, "Gside e Osiride," June 13, "Le tombe in Egitto," June 29, "Una regina di tremila anni fa," July 8, "Sempre quelle vecchie piramidi," July 20, 1933, all in *La Stampa*; Triennale di Milano, *Catalogo ufficiale* (Milan, 1933), 9–11, 75; Braun, *Mario Sironi*, Chapter 5.

71 MGS, "Triennale e pittura murale a Milano," *Rivista Illustrata del Popolo d'Italia* (June 1933), 31–9; Anty Pansera, *Storia e cronaca della Triennale* (Milan, 1978), 41–3; Bossaglia, *Il "Novecento Italiano,"* 48–50; U. Alfassio Grimaldi and Gherardo Bozzetti, *Farinacci il più fascista* (Milan, 1972), 139–41; G. Sommi Picenardi, "Triennale contro Roma," *Il Regime Fascista*, May 11, 1933; Giuseppe Carlo Marino, *L'autarchia della cultura: Intelletuali e fascismo negli anni trenta* (Rome, 1983), 104; MGS, "Il fascismo nell'arte," *La Stampa*, May 18, 1933.

72 Roberto Farinacci, "Ma no!," *Il Regime Fascista*, May 24, 1933; "Una lettera di Margherita Sarfatti," *Il Regime Fascista*, May 27, 1933, reproduced in Bossagla, *Il "Novecento Italiano,"* 145–7.

73 Achille Funi, "Le origini del '900," *Il Corriere della Sera*, June 2, 1933; Carlo Carrà, "La pittura murale della Triennale e i soliti denigratori," *L'Ambrosiano*, June 1, 1933; Arnaldo Carpanetti, "Fronte unico," *Il Lavoro Fascista*, June 18, 1933; Mario Sironi, "Basta!," *Il Popolo d'Italia*, May 31, 1933, and "Tanto peggio," June 3, 1933, now in Camesasca, *Mario Sironi: Scritti*, 142–54, and in Bossaglia, *Il "Novecento Italiano,"* 142–8; Roberto Farinacci, "Ma che Basta!," June 1, and Jules Evola, "Novecento e classicismo fascista," June 2, 1933, both in *Regime Fascista*; Crispolti, *Il mito della macchina*, 606–10.

74 Roberto Farinacci, "Fronte, corbezzoli! unico," *Il Regime Fascista*, June 20, 1933; ACS, SPD/CR, b. 41, f. 242/R, "Farinacci, R.," sf. 10, "Polemica sull'arte del Novecento"; bibliography, "Polemica Sarfatti/Farinacci 1933," MP; for Mussolini's and Starace's orders see Cannistraro, *La fabbrica del consenso*, 63–4 and notes 114 and 115; Farinacci to Mussolini, June 25, 1933, NA, T586/448, frames 026368–75; Mussolini to Prefect of Cremona, June 13, 1933, and Farinacci to Mussolini, December 6, 1933, both cited in Zagarrio, "Il fascismo e la politica delle arti," 256.

75 Braun, *Mario Sironi, 1922–1945: Art and Politics in Fascist Italy*, Chapter 5; Bossaglia, *Il "Novecento Italiano,"* 52–5, 155–64; Camesasca, *Mario Sironi: Scritti*, 155–7, 172–5; Malvano, *Fascismo e politica dell'imagine*, 175–84.

76 Ojetti, *I taccuini*, 413–14.

CHAPTER 25: NEW DEAL AND NEW ORDER

1 De Felice, *Mussolini il fascista*, I, 234–5; idem, *Mussolini il duce*, I, 339–64, 418–34; Jens Petersen, *Hitler e Mussolini: La difficilie alleanza* (Bari, 1975), 16–20, 24–50; Ludwig, *Talks with Mussolini*, 70–1, 84–5; MacGregor Knox, "Il fascismo e la politica estera italiana," in Richard J. B. Bosworth and Sergio Romano, eds., *La politica estera italiana (1860–1985)* (Bologna, 1991),

306; MGS, *Mussolini: Como lo conocí*, XI; "Fascism in Italy Stays Aloof from Foreign Movements," *New York American*, September 28, 1930; "Address by Mussolini to the Fascist Grand Council—7 April 1932," 11–13, 18–19.

2 Marzorati, *Margherita Sarfatti*, 144–5; "Stresemann a Giant Figure in European Rebirth—Mussolini," *New York American*, October 6, 1929; Schulenburg, "Um Benito Mussolini," 5–7, 17–8, 23–5; "Geert von Schwochau" [Werner von der Schulenburg], "La Germania e Hitler," *Gerarchia*, December 1929; Schulenburg, "Le ripercussioni del patto a quattro," *Gerarchia*, June 1933; MGS, *Mussolini: Como lo conocí*, XI, XII, XIII.

 The Sarfatti articles in *Italien: Monatsschrift fur Kultur, Kunst und Literatur* were: "Der Novecento," December 1927; "Pirandello-Probleme," April 1928; "Italienische Schriftsteller unserer Zeit," February 1929; "Die zweite Novecento-Ausstellung," June 1929; "Tranquillo Cremona und das heroische XIX. Jahrhundert," September 1929; "Faschistische Kunst und faschistische Sitten," October 1929; "Panzini, der Huter der Scholle," December 1929; "Francesco Chiesa," February 1930; "Eine Venezianerin des achtzehnten Jahrhunderts," March 1930; "Gli indifferenti," April 1930.

 "Hitler's Letter and Photograph to Mussolini, 8 June 1931," *Cesare Barbieri Courier* (1980); Carin Göring to mother, May 30, 1931, HGP, box 2, 106; *Hitler: Memoirs of a Confidant*, Henry Ashby Turner, Jr., ed. (New Haven, Conn., 1985), 134–5; David Irving, *Göring, a Biography* (New York, 1989), 68–82, 99–100; interview with Fiammetta Sarfatti Gaetani, May 20, 1985; Sarfatti guest books, 1926–31, 1932–38; "Il convegno 'Volta' in Campidoglio," *L'Illustrazione Italiana*, November 20, 1932; *Trial of the Major War Criminals Before the International Military Tribunal: Proceedings*, XI, (Nuremberg, 1947), 454; ACS, MI-DPP, f. "Sarfatti, Margherita," report of November 24, 1933. Elisabetta Cerruti, *Ambassador's Wife* (London, 1951), 118–92, 225–6, 249; Petersen, *Hitler e Mussolini*, 42, 107–8; MGS, "Il fascismo visto dall'estero."

3 Colin Simpson, *Artful Partners: Bernard Berenson and Joseph Duveen* (New York, 1986), 232–5, 256–8; Giuseppe Bottai, *Diario, 1935–1944* (Milan, 1982), 466; Raoul Bertini Frassoni, *Provvedimenti nobiliari dei re d'Italia* (Rome, 1968), 49; "Continis Give a Dinner," *The New York Times*, June 12, 1929; Spingarn report, CIA to BRS, June 11, 1987; SHKF, Contini-Bonacossi to Kress, August 14, 1945; ibid, "Contini Bills. Receipted Bills"; Bernard Berenson, *Sunset and Twilight: From the Diaries of 1947–1958*, Nicky Mariano, ed. (New York, 1963), 283; Irving, *Göring*, 381.

4 VMDP, box 1, folder 5, "Diary Rome Oct. 1929," entry for October 11, 1929; Noel F. Busch, "Ambassador Kirk," *Life*, August 13, 1945; "Kirk, Alexander Comstock," Anna Rothe, ed., *Current Biography: Who's News and Why 1945* (New York, 1946), 323–5; interview with Fiammetta Sarfatti Gaetani, May 20, 1985; interview with Frank Gervasi, May 5, 1985; Eleanor Lansing Dulles to BRS, January 20, 1987; OHP, reminiscences of Eleanor Lansing Dulles, 369; Jefferson Patterson, *Diplomatic Duty and Diversion* (Cambridge, Mass., 1956), 21–2, 247–9; George F. Kennan, *Memoirs, 1925–1950* (Boston, 1967), 112–5, 119–20; Charles E. Bohlen, *Witness to History, 1929–1969* (New York, 1973), 56–65; Rhodri Jeffreys-Jones, *American Espionage from Secret Service to CIA* (New York, 1977), 158–9; Ray Bearse and Anthony Read, *Conspirator: The Untold Story of Tyler Kent* (New York, 1991), 48; FDRP, OF 447, Breckinridge Long, 1933–45, Long to Howe, November 24, 1933; ibid, PPF, 6240, Roosevelt to Phillips, July 3, 1935; ibid, PPF, 4180, "Alexander C. Kirk"; PRO, FO 371, 27461, Egyptian 1941, Egypt and Sudan, Heads of Mission Report, August 15, 1941, "Alexander C. Kirk."

5 Cerruti, *Ambassador's Wife*, 243; Julia Edwards, *Women of the World: The Great Foreign Correspondents* (Boston, 1988), 75–9; Meyer Berger, *The Story of "The New York Times," 1851–1951* (New York, 1951), 326–7; AOMP/NYPL, Morgan to McCormick, n.d. but summer 1937; Kirk to McCormick, January 7 and March 2, 1938; MGS to McCormick, May 22, 1939; Bromfield to McCormick, June 13, 1939.

6 BP, MGS to Biddle, n.d. but 1932/33; MGS to Biddle, April 5, 1934; MGS to Biddle, January 17, 1935, and Barbantini to Biddle, August 12 and 15, 1932 [?], box 13, folder B; Diary, entries for December 21 and 27, 1951; George Biddle, *An American Artist's Story* (Boston, 1939),

58–9, 252–6, 261–87, 302–5; "Artists to Adorn Nation's Buildings," *The New York Times,* December 12, 1933; Carpenter, *A Serious Character,* 489; EPP, Pound to MGS, February 25, 1934.

7 MGS, "Il fascismo visto dall'estero," 440; ASMAE, UCG, 1923–29, "Butler, Nicholas Murray," Caetani to Mussolini, June 14, 1927; Nicholas Murray Butler, *Across the Busy Years: Recollections and Reflections,* Vol. II (New York, 1940), 153–60.

8 ASMAE, UCG, 1923–29, "Butler, Nicholas Murray," Butler to Fletcher, October 13, 1927, Robbins to Mussolini, November 15, 1927; Prezzolini, *Diario, 1900–1941,* 431, 436–55; Albert Marrin, *Nicholas Murray Butler* (Boston, 1976), 180–3; NMBP, MGS to Butler, June 1, 1930; Butler to MGS, June 12, 1930; MGS to Butler, December 1930; Butler to MGS, December 14, 1930; MGS to Butler, January 25, 1932; Butler to MGS, February 8, 1932; Isa Foà to Butler, August 7, 1932; Fackenthal to MGS, September 27, 1932; Butler to MGS, January 3, 1933; MGS to Butler, April 29, 1933; Butler to MGS, May 1, 1933; ACS, SPD, CO, UCG, f. 107461, "Butler, Nicholas Murray," passim; Nicholas Murray Butler, *Between Two Worlds: Interpretations of the Age in Which We Live: Essays and Addresses* (New York, 1934), 9, 386.

Officials in the American embassy in Rome had information that Butler was a secret member of the Fascist party. Other Americans on the list included Richard Washburn Child and the financier Otto Kahn, another enthusiastic supporter of Mussolini. SBP, box 61, folder D, enclosure in Dominian to Bloom, January 26, 1929.

9 FDRP, OF, 233, "Italy, Gov't. of, 1933–36," Langworthy to Mussolini, December 9, 1932; Grossardi to Langworthy, February 23, 1933; Langworthy to Roosevelt, March 21, 1933; Blankner, "War," 2.

The sections of this and the next two chapters devoted to the relations between Mussolini and Roosevelt, 1932–36, are drawn from BRS, "Roosevelt, Mussolini e la guerra d'Etiopia: Una lezione sulla diplomazia americana," *Storia Contemporanea,* February 1988.

10 Fannie Hurst, *Anatomy of Me: A Wanderer in Search of Herself* (Garden City, N.Y., 1958), 291–3, 303–9, 319–22; Mary Rose Shaugnessy, *Myths About Love and Women: The Fiction of Fannie Hurst* (New York, 1980); FDRL, PPF 926, "Hurst, Fannie"; ERP, 100, Personal Letters, boxes 1266, 1303, 1343, 1385.

11 Herman Finer, *Mussolini's Italy,* (London, 1935), 492–534; Marquis and Bessie Rowland James, *Biography of a Bank: The Story of Bank of America N.T. & S.A.* (New York, 1954), 339, 359–61, 370–3; Julian Dana, *A. P. Giannini, Giant in the West* (New York, 1947), 133, 144, 164–8, 232; Diggins, *Mussolini and Fascism,* 83, 415, n. 32; Gian Giacomo Migone, *Gli Stati uniti e il fascismo: Alle orgini dell'egemonia americana in Italia* (Milan, 1980), 355; Gerald D. Nash to BRS, August 11, 1989; Gaetano Salvemini, *Italian Fascist Activities in the United States,* ed. Philip V. Cannistraro (New York, 1977), 115–6.

12 Thomas B. Morgan, "L'influenza del movimento mussoliniano negli Stati Uniti," *Gerarchia,* October 1932; idem, "Mutamento della politica americana," *Gerarchia,* November 1932; Arthur A. Ekirch, Jr., *Ideologies and Utopias: The Impact of the New Deal on American Thought* (Chicago, 1969), 66–70; Giorgio Rochat, *Militari e politici nella preparazione della campagna d'Etiopia: Studio e documenti, 1932–1936* (Milan, 1971), 26–33; Franco Fucci, *Emilio De Bono, il maresciallo fucilato* (Milan, 1989), 185–7.

13 GGSP, box 12, folder 187V; TVRP, Berkson to Ranck, December 13, 1932, January 11, February 25, and March 2, 1933; Seton to Feakins, December 20, 1932; Ranck to Berkson, December 28, 1932, and February 9, 1933; Jones to Ranck, February 3, 1933; Giovanna Bosi Maramotti, "Margherita Sarfatti: Appunti per una storia della letteratura femminile nel periodo fascista," in Bruno Bandini, ed., *Il pensiero reazionario: La politica e la cultura dei fascismi* (Ravenna, 1982), 106.

14 De Felice, *Mussolini il duce,* I, 437–43; Nicholas Roosevelt, *A Front Row Seat* (Norman, Okla., 1953), 215–6; Irving, *Göring,* 122–3; Sergio Pelagalli, "Il generale Pietro Gazzera al ministero della guerra (1928–1933)," *Storia Contemporanea,* October 1989, 1046–9; DDI, 7th Series, vol. XIII, nos. 67, 76, 91, 219, 298, 339, 343, 400, 406, 504; MGS, *Mussolini: Como lo conocí,* XIII.

15 De Felice, *Mussolini il duce*, I, 443–76; Petersen, *Hitler e Mussolini*, 111–68; Konrad Jarausch, *The Four Power Pact* (Madison, Wis., 1965); Giancarlo Giardana, *Il patto a quattro nella politica estera di Mussolini* (Correggio, 1976); Esmonde M. Robertson, *Mussolini as Empire-Builder: Europe and Africa, 1932–36* (New York, 1977), 22–58; DBFP, Second Series, V, no. 44.

16 "Mussolini Sees Monument Destruction by Jugo-Slavia an Insult to Italy," January 15, 1933; "Machine Must Be Servant of Man, Not His Master, Declares Mussolini," February 5, 1933; "Economic Parley Must Act, Not Talk, Says Duce; Sees World Back to Gold," March 5, 1933; " 'Women Unfit for Politics,' Says Duce," March 19, 1933; "Duce Insists on Treaty Change," April 9, 1933; "Statemen Must Rule the Masses, Not Consult Them, Says Mussolini," April 30, 1933; "Mussolini Calls Rise of Hitlerism an Instrument of German People," May 21, 1933; "Must Make Country Alluring as City or It Will Fail, Declares Premier," June 10, 1933.

   TVRP, Ranck to Berkson, January 3, February 16, 18, 23, March 12, 15, May 31, June 5, 1933; Berkson to Ranck, February 16, 18, 20, 21, 1933; Ranck to Hearst, February 17, 18, 20, 23, March 13, 1933; Hearst to Ranck, February 19, 20, March 14, 1933.

   In 1933–34, Margherita managed to place nine Hearst press articles by Lloyd George, former German Foreign Minister Julius Curtius, and German Vice-Chancellor Franz von Papen in *Politica Sociale*.

17 Interviews with Fiammetta Sarfatti Gaetani, May 20, 1985, and with Magalì Sarfatti-Larson, June 16, 1986; MGS, *Acqua passata*, 187–8; Montanelli and Staglieno, *Leo Longanesi*, 213–4; TVRP, Berkson to Ranck, March 2, 1933; Berkson to Ranck, April 5, 1933; Ranck to Berkson, May 31, 1933; Ranck to MGS, November 27, 1933.

   Hereafter, the Italian titles of those Hearst articles that also appeared in *Il Popolo d'Italia* will be placed in brackets with their date of publication, following their English-language equivalent. "Must Revise Treaty—Il Duce," 9 April 1933 ["Piccola intesa e pace europea," April 13, 1933]; OO, XXV, 221–4.

18 DDI, 7th Series, vol. XIII, no. 547; FDRP, PSF, Roosevelt to Mussolini, May 14, 1933; Damiani, *Mussolini e gli Stati Uniti*, 212–3, 220–1; Migone, *Gli Stati Uniti e il fascismo*, 293–7, 301; OHP, James P. Warburg Diary, 637–59 (quote, 647).

19 NDP, box 57, Davis to Roosevelt, April 13, 1933; DDI, 7th Series, vol. XIII, no. 539.

20 "Mussolini Calls Rise of Hitlerism an Insurrection of German People," May 21, 1933.

21 "Roosevelt System Moves in Atmosphere Similar to That of Fascism—Mussolini," July 2, 1933 ["Roosevelt e il sistema," July 7, 1933]; OO, XXVI, 22–4; Franklin D. Roosevelt, *Looking Forward* (New York, 1933), 9, 13, 30–1, 39–51, 55–68, 125–36, 144, 249, 254–5, 268; De Felice, *Mussolini il duce*, I, 167, 438, 541–2; Nathan Miller, *FDR: An Intimate History* (New York, 1983), 330; Diggins, *Mussolini and Fascism*, 164–6.

22 "Put Embargo on Parleys or Prestige of Nations Will Fail, Says Mussolini," July 23, 1933 ["Dopo Londra," July 29, 1933].

23 BLP, box 105, Long to Roosevelt, June 1, 1933; Roosevelt to Long, June 15, 1933.

24 OHP, reminiscences of Marion Dickerman, 73–4; EMHP, box 71, folder 2369, Long to House, June 9, November 2, 1933; FDRP, OF 447, Breckinridge Long 1933–45, Long to Roosevelt, October 13, 1933; Henry L. Feingold, *The Politics of Rescue: The Roosevelt Administration and the Holocaust, (1938–1945)* (New Brunswick, N.J., 1970), 133–4.

25 *Day Before Yesterday: The Reminiscences of Mrs. Theodore Roosevelt, Jr.* (New York, 1959), 364; BLP, box 106, invitation to the wedding of Livio Gaetani and Fiammetta Sarfatti; box 163, memorandum of telephone conversation between Long and Hull, November 7, 1933; box 105, Long to Roosevelt, December 8, 1933; box 111, Long to MGS, March 1, 1934; ACS, MI-DPP, f. "Sarfatti, Margherita," report of October 13, 1933; Edoardo Savino, *La nazione operante* (Novara, 1937), 402.

26 "Mrs. William Brown Meloney, Director of 'This Week,' Dies," *New York Herald Tribune*, June 24, 1943; "Mrs. W. B. Meloney, Noted Editor, Dies," *The New York Times*, June 24, 1943; Ishbel Ross, *Ladies of the Press: The Story of Women in Journalism by an Insider* (New York, 1936), 141; Rosalynd Pflaum, *Grand Obsession: Marie Curie and Her World* (New York, 1989), 217–28; Richard Kluger, *The Paper: The Life and Death of the "New York Herald*

Tribune" (New York, 1986), 286, 293–4; MGS, *The Life,* inscribed by MGS to "Missy" Meloney, August 2, 1933, Rare Book Collection, Butler Library, Columbia University; FDRP, OF 447, Breckinridge Long, 1933–45, Long to Howe, July 21, 1933; MMMP, box 3, autographed photographs of Mussolini, Margherita, and Fiammetta Sarfatti; box 36, "Manuscripts . . . Mrs. W. B. Meloney," manuscript dated "Jan 16th 1928"; MGS to Meloney, September 10, 1933; Long to Meloney, October 12, 1933; HHP, Post-Presidential Individual, "Meloney, Mrs. Wm. Brown," box 434, Meloney to Reid, August 29, 1933; MMMP, box 3, autographed photographs of Mussolini, Margherita, and Fiammetta Sarfatti.

27 BLP, box 105, Long to Franklin Roosevelt, August 2, 1933; *Day Before Yesterday,* 364; Sarfatti guest book, 1932–36; "14 Roosevelts Meet on Liner as Tourists of 2 Clans Return," *New York Herald Tribune,* September 8, 1933; TRJP, T. Roosevelt, Jr., to Kipling, August 20, 1933; MGS to T. Roosevelt, Jr., November 29, 1933, T. Roosevelt, Jr., to MGS, January 8, 1934; "Liberty Gives Signora Sarfatti 'Fascist Salute,' " *New York Herald Tribune,* March 29, 1934.

28 TRJP, container 20, T. Roosevelt, Jr., to mother, August 13, 1933.

29 "Mussolini Sees the World Entering a New Era of Fascist Civilization," August 13, 1933; "Mussolini Sees New Italo-Soviet Pact Hastening End of Russia's Isolation," September 24, 1933 ["Italia e Russia," September 30, 1933]; "Duce Plans Economic Rule of Italy Through 40 Guilds," November 5, 1933; OO, XXVI, 22–4, 36–8, 61–3; DGFP, C, II, no. 104; TVRP, Ranck to MGS, November 27, 1933.

30 "Mussolini Works on Farm," November 19, 1933; "Prohibition Repeal," November 26, 1933; "Italy's Gigantic Increase," December 17, 1933; TVRP, Ranck to Berkson, June 5, 17, 22, August 28, 31, September 1, October 4, November 3, 27, 1933; Berkson to Ranck, June 4, 22, August 5, 22, 23, 24, 28, 29, 30, 31, September 1, October 4, 5, 7, 9, 1933; Ranck to Hearst, October 9, 1933; Hearst to Ranck, October 9, 1933.

31 "Disarmo e Ginevra," *Il Popolo d'Italia,* October 5, 1933; OO, XXVI, 70–2; DBFP, Second Series, V, nos. 383, 393, 395, 405, 424, 431; TVRP, Berkson to Ranck, three, October 4, 1933; Ranck to Berkson, October 3, 1933.

32 DBFP, Second Series, V, no. 444; MMMP, MGS to Meloney, September 10, 1933; "President to Talk to Women Here," *The New York Times,* October 8, 1933.

33 "Who's News Today," *New York Sun,* September 30, 1933.

34 MMMP, Roosevelt to Caetani, October 11, 1933; Long to Meloney, October 12, 1933; Caetani to Roosevelt, October 15, 1933; Hensey to Shephard, October 15, 1933; Shephard to Hensey, October 31, 1933; "Today on the Radio," *The New York Times,* October 12, 1933; "Ban on War Urged by Mrs. Roosevelt," *The New York Times,* October 13, 1933; "Countess Sarfatti Sends Appeal to Youth from Historic Italy," *New York Herald Tribune,* October 13, 1933.

35 Robertson, *Mussolini as Empire-Builder,* 57–63; Gerhard L. Weinberg, *The Foreign Policy of Hitler's Germany: Diplomatic Revolution in Europe, 1933–36* (Chicago, 1970), 96, 165–7; Baron [Pompeo] Aloisi, *Journal (25 Juillet 1932–14 Juin 1936)* (Paris, 1957), 160; DDI, 7th Series, vol. XIV, no. 284; DGFP, C, II, no. 28.

36 Adolf Hitler, *Mein Kampf* (New York, 1941), 3, 902–3, 908, 911–6; Weinberg, *The Foreign Policy of Hitler's Germany,* 3, 16–18, 166–7; De Felice, *Mussolini il duce,* I, 412, n.4, 448, 470, n.1, 472, n.2.

37 TVRP, Hearst to Ranck, October 9, 21, 23, December 19, 1933; Ranck to Hearst, October 11, 23, November 23, December 1, 1933; Flick to Ranck, December 19, 1933; Emanuel to Ranck, October 21, 22, 24, 1933; Ranck to Emanuel, October 22, 1933; Hillman to Ranck, October 24, 1933; Ranck to Berkson, October 23, November 3, 27, 1933; Berkson to Ranck, November 16, 21, 1933; MGS to Ranck, November 14, 1933; Ranck to MGS, November 27, 1933.

38 TVRP, Hearst to Ranck, November 24, 1933; Ranck to Willicombe, December 17, 1933; Berkson to Ranck, December 20, 1933; Ranck to Berkson, December 21, 22, 1933.

39 DBFP, Second Series, V, nos. 457, 476; TVRP, Ranck to Hearst, December 19, 1933;

Hearst to Ranck, December 19, 1933; Flick to Ranck, December 19, 1933; "Big States Should Have Stable Understanding, Says Duce," December 23, 1933; OO, XXV, 148.

40 TVRP, Ranck to Hearst, December 18, 1933; Hearst to Ranck, December 22, 1933; Ranck to Berkson, December 25, 1933; Berkson to Ranck, December 16, 26, 27 (quote), 28, 1933; FDRP, OF 447, Breckinridge Long, 1933–45, Long to Roosevelt, October 13, 1933.

Sarfatti's demand for payment in lire proved wise. The American dollar was devalued by 41 percent on January 31, 1934.

41 ASMAE, Fondo Interno, I, 11/10 (1933), MGS request for passport to United States; NMBP, MGS to Butler, November 29, 1933; TVRP, Berkson to Ranck, February 24, 1934; ACS, MI-DPP, f. "Sarfatti, Margherita," report of April 23, 1934.

Margherita's last article in *Gerarchia*, a tribute to Arnaldo Mussolini on the first anniversary of his death ("Per Arnaldo Mussolini"), had appeared in December 1932.

42 Police reports in ACS, MI-DGPS, PS-G1, b. 280, f. 1, Torino; De Felice, *Storia degli ebrei italiani sotto il fascismo*, 145–8; Ginzburg, *Lessico famigliare*, 101–12; Alexander Stille, *Benevolence and Betrayal: Five Italian Jewish Families Under Fascism* (New York, 1991), 49–56.

CHAPTER 26: THE PURSUIT OF HAPPINESS

1 Prezzolini, *Diario, 1900–1941*, 567; MGS, *L'America, ricerca della felicità* (Milan, 1937), 7, 24–5, 36–7, 42, 51–60, 97, 100, 102, 109–10.

2 MGS, *L'America*, 75, 86–7, 152–5, 163–6, 171–2, 176–81, 202, 281–3, 293.

3 MMMP, MGS to Meloney, September 10, 1933; Joseph B. Phillips, "Italy's Heroine of Fascism," *New York Herald Tribune Sunday Magazine*, October 8, 1933; MGS, "Women of Fascism," ibid., November 12, 1933; NMBP, Butler to MGS, October 9, 16, November 10, 13, December 8, 26, 1933, MGS to Butler, [late] October, November 29, 1933.

4 "Mussolini Sees U.S. Involved As Russia and Japan Face Hostilities in the Far East," January 14, 1934 ["Estremo Oriente," January 17, 1933], OO, XXVI, 153–6; "Mussolini Sees Roosevelt Inspired by Spirit of the American Pioneer," February 11, 1934; "U.S. Abandons Individual Enterprise, Adopts State Control, Says Mussolini," March 11, 1934; "Japan Chides Mussolini on 'Yellow Peril' Remark," *The New York Times*, January 20, 1934; DDI, 7th Series, vol. XIV, no. 617.

5 TVRP, Ranck to Berkson, January 2, 3, 4, 6, 10, 20, 25, February 3, 1934; Berkson to Ranck, January 2, 3, 4, 6, 8, 9, 10, 19, 25, February 2, 24, 1934; Ranck to Hearst, January 8, 1934; Hearst to Ranck, January 8, 1934; Ranck to Kilgallen, February 26, March 2, 3, 15, 1934; Kilgallen to Ranck, March 15, 1934.

6 Butler, *Across the Busy Years*, II, 163–5 (quote by Mussolini, 165); "Dr. Nicholas Murray Butler, Sir Campbell Stuart writes" *The Times* (London), December 9, 1947; De Felice, *Mussolini il duce*, I, 484–6; NMBP, box 2, "Itinerary and Diary notations for European trips: 1923, 1926, 1927, 1930, 1931, 1934," entries for March 11, 12, 14 and 18, 1934; ibid., Butler to MGS, March 2, 1934 (quote); MGS to Butler, March 10, 1934; MGS to Butler, letter beginning "Mr. and Mrs. Marconi are lunching with me today," n.d. but March 12, 1934; "Dr. Butler Chats an Hour with Premier Mussolini," *The New York Times*, March 15, 1934; OO, XXVI, 185–93; "Dr. Butler Asks Regional Pacts to Avert War," *New York Herald Tribune*, March 29, 1934.

7 MGS, *L'America*, 1 (quote), 6; AGP, MGS to Papini, March 21, 1934; "L'illustre scrittrice Margherita Sarfatti giungendo a New York ci parla dell'Italia rinnovata dal Duce," *Il Progresso Italo-Americano*, March 29, 1934; Alberto Spaini, "Margherita Sarfatti, il Novecento e la mostra di Buenos Aires," *La Fiera Letteraria*, November 9, 1930.

8 Tom Hughes, *The Blue Riband of the Atlantic* (New York, 1973), 149–51, 177; NMBP, Butler to MGS, April 17, 1934; MGS to Butler, September 22, 1934; "Shipping and Mails," *The New York Times*, March 22, 1934; "L'illustre scrittrice Margherita Sarfatti giungendo a New York ci parla dell'Italia rinnovata dal Duce," *Il Progresso Italo-Americano*, March 29, 1934.

9 BLP, box 111, Long to MGS, March 1, 1934; MGS to Long, March 21, 1934; MMMP, MGS to Meloney, March 4, 1934; "Mrs. Hearst Entertains," *New York Journal*, April 6, 1934;

Theodore Roosevelt, Jr., to Meloney, March 29, 1934; NMBP, Prezzolini to Butler, April 3, 1934; PP, MGS to Prezzolini, November 29, 1933; BP, MGS to Biddle, April 5, 1934; Prezzolini, *Diario, 1900–1941*, 518; "Margherita Sarfatti giunge stamane a N.Y. con il 'Rex,' " *Il Progresso Italo-Americano*, March 28, 1934; *Italy America Monthly*, March 15, 1934, 9; FDRP, OF, 233 A, "Italy-Misc., 1934," Roosevelt to Dunn, March 21, 1934; RDS, ADT 611.65241/135, Memorandum of April 18, 1934; ibid., H/D 033.6511/63, "Memorandum Of Conversation with the Italian Ambassador," April 19, 1934; TVRP, Ranck to MGS, April 1, 1934; BRS conversations with Taylor Coffman, February 1986; Diego Rivera, *My Art, My Life* (New York, 1960), 220–1; MGS, *L'America*, 81–2, 249–50; MGS, "Italy's New Economic Rule," *New York Herald Tribune Sunday Magazine*, March 25, 1934; "Lo stato corporativo in un articolo di M. Sarfatti," *Il Progresso Italo-Americano*, March 12, 1934.

10 "L'illustre scrittrice Margherita Sarfatti giungendo a New York ci parla dell'Italia rinnovata dal Duce," *Il Progresso Italo-Americano*, March 29, 1934; Mary Iacovella, "Margherita Sarfatti: A Modern Woman," *Atlantica*, April 1934, 125; "Liberty Gives Signora Sarfatti 'Fascist Salute,' " *New York Herald Tribune*, March 29, 1934 (MGS quote); "Duce's Biographer Here, Hails Liberty as Fellow Fascist," *New York American*, March 29, 1934; "Liberty? She's Fascist, Says Duce's Boswell," *New York Journal*, March 29, 1934; "Butler Asks Regional Pacts to Avert War," *New York Herald Tribune*, March 29, 1934 (Butler quote); "Dr. Butler Assails Vote of Congress," *The New York Times*, March 29, 1934; MGS, *L'America*, 7, 36; RDS, ADT 611.65241/136, Memorandum of April 18, 1934.

11 "Liberty Gives Signora Sarfatti 'Fascist Salute,' " *New York Herald Tribune*, March 29, 1934; *The WPA Guide to New York City* (New York, 1982), 333–41; Victoria Newhouse, *Wallace K. Harrison, Architect* (New York, 1989); Marquis, *Hopes and Ashes*, 159–62; William Zinsser, "An Icon Among American Places," *Center*, July–August 1992, 6; *Diego Rivera: A Retrospective*, (New York, 1986), 85–9, 294–7, 302–4; Biddle, *An American Artist's Story*, 263; MGS, *L'America*, 39–40, 184, 249–50.

12 "Liberty Gives Signora Sarfatti 'Fascist Salute,' " *New York Herald Tribune*, March 29, 1934; "Margherita Sarfatti in giro per New York e primi discorsi," *Il Progresso Italo-Americano*, March 30, 1934; MGS, *L'America*, 17; "They Stand Out from the Crowd," *The Literary Digest*, April 14, 1934; ACS, MI-DPP, f. "Sarfatti, Margherita," report of April 26, 1934; "Presentiamo Margherita Sarfatti: L'agente del cuore di Mussolini è venuta a fare propaganda in America," *Il Martello* (New York), April 28, 1934; ACS, MI, DGPS, Div. AGR, Cat. F4, b. 57, f. "Il Martello," 2.

13 "Signora Sarfatti: Il Duce's Aide, Oracle of Italy's Art," *News-week*, April 28, 1934; "Schiaparelli, Elsa," *Current Biography: Who's News and Why 1940* (New York, 1940), 719–20.

14 TVRP, Ranck to Hearst, March 30, 1934; Hearst to Ranck, March 31, 1934; Ranck to MGS, April 1, 1934; Mitchell to Emanuel, April 1, 1934; Ranck to Emanuel, April 3, 1934; Emanuel to Ranck, April 3, 1934; MGS to Ranck, April 6, 1934; Ranck to MGS, April 9, 1934; interview with Doris Ranck Rend, August 1, 1985; "Fascism Holds Salvation of World, Says Mme. Sarfatti," *New York American*, April 4, 1934; "Youth Is Seizing New Leadership Throughout World, Says Mussolini," *New York American*, April 8, 1934.

15 MMMP, MGS to Meloney, Easter 1937; MGS, *Acqua passata*, 228–30; idem, *L'America*, 108; Spingarn Report, CIA to BRS, June 11, 1987; interview with Magalì Sarfatti-Larson, September 28, 1985.

Another of Mussolini's informants about Franklin Roosevelt's private life was Margherita's close friend, the well-connected Count Alessandro Contini-Bonacossi.

16 Recorded Sound Reference Center, NBC Personality Index, "Sarfatti, Margherita—The Italian Revolution," 7:45–8:00 P.M., April 2, 1934; "Essenza, finalità e metodi del fascismo illustrati al radio da Margherita Sarfatti," *Il Progresso Italo-Americano*, April 5, 1934; Carl Dreher, *Sarnoff, an American Success* (New York, 1977), 217; Kenneth Bilby, *The General: David Sarnoff and the Rise of the Communications Industry* (New York, 1986), 24–6, 30, 48–50, 101–3, 109, 111–2; Corinne Lowe, "The Woman Behind Mussolini," *Pictorial Review*, September 1934, 31.

17 "Un pranzo a Margh. Sarfatti," *Il Progresso Italo-Americano*, April 5, 1934.
18 "Luncheon for Author," *The New York Times*, April 6, 1934; "Mrs. Hearst Entertains," *New York Journal*, April 6, 1934; NMBP, Prezzolini to Butler, April 3, 1934; Prezzolini, *Diario, 1900–1941*, 518.
19 "Italian Writer Greeted," *The New York Times*, April 9, 1934; ERP, series 100, box 1309, Meloney to E. Roosevelt, March 28, 1934; E. Roosevelt to Meloney, March 30, 1934; MMMP, La Guardia to Meloney, March 29, 1934; Finley to Meloney, April 9, 1934; MGS to Meloney, December 14, 1935, March 25, 1936; FHP, appointment book 1934, entry for April 8, 1934; MGS, *L'America*, 50; Alex Heard, "Mount Rushmore: The Real Story," *The New Republic*, July 15 and 22, 1991.
20 "Says Fascism Fosters Arts," *New York Sun*, April 4, 1934; Iacovella, "Margherita Sarfatti."
21 Prezzolini, *Diario, 1900–1941*, 518; PP, MGS to Prezzolini, November 29, 1933; Casa Italiana guest book, entry for April 10, 1934.
22 "Dr. Butler Finds Liberty in Peril," *The New York Times*, April 11, 1934 ("grim reaction" quote); Lowe, "The Woman Behind Mussolini," 31 ("box of chocolates" quote); NMBP, Butler to MGS, April 10, 11, 1934; MMMP, MGS to Meloney, July 4, 1937.
23 TLP, Orlando Garabelli to Lamont, March 26, 1934; Lamont to Orlando Garabelli, March 27, 1934; "Mme. Sarfatti Honored. Dr. Butler Hails Italian Author as a 'Second Columbus,' " *The New York Times*, August 13, 1934; "Un altro banchetto a Margherita Sarfatti dall'Italy America Society," *Il Progresso Italo-Americano*, April 13, 1934; *Italy America Monthly*, May 15, 1934,
24 "La conferenza della Signora M. Sarfatti alla Casa Italiana," *Il Progresso Italo-Americano*, April 14, 1934; "La pittura italiana del 1900 nella conferenza di M. Sarfatti," *Il Progresso Italo-Americano*, April 15, 1934.
25 EMHP, box 71, folder 2369, Long to House, March 1 and 2, 1934; House to Long, April 5, 1934.
26 "Margherita Sarfatti visitò ieri gli uffici del 'Progresso,' " *Il Progresso Italo-Americano*, April 7, 1934; MGS, *L'America*, 10–1, 162, 166, 227, 292.
    A photograph of Margherita's visit to the *Il Progresso* offices appeared in that newspaper in Section III, page 1, of April 15, 1934.
27 FHP, appointment book 1934, entry for April 10, 1934; BBP, MGS to Berenson, March 6, 1953; Clare Boothe Luce to BRS, November 10, 1986; MGS, *L'America*, 8, 24–5, 27–37, 131; *The Memoirs of Will H. Hays* (New York, 1955), 424–5, 449, 465, 513, 516–7; Hurst, *Anatomy of Me*, 319–22; BP, MGS to Biddle, April 5, 1934.
28 NMBP, Butler to MGS, April 11, 17, 1934; MGS to Butler, April 15, 1934; Meloney to Butler, April 16, 1934; MMMP, Butler to Meloney, April 17, 1934; Finley to Meloney, April 9, 1934 (quote); box 31, photograph of MGS inscribed: "To Missy, with my love and so many thanks for being her dear, darling self. New York, April 3rd 1934 XII, Margherita G. Sarfatti."
29 "Mussolini Willing to Guarantee Enforcement of an Arms Treaty," *The New York Times*, April 14, 1934.
30 "President Signs the Johnson Bill," *The New York Times*, April 14, 1934; "Il Johnson Bill firmato ieri dal Pres. Roosevelt," *Il Progresso Italo-Americano*, April 14, 1934; RDS, 800.51 W 89 Italy/245, Memorandum of Conversation with the Italian Ambassador, May 10, 1934; 800.51 W 89 Italy/246, Hull to Long, May 11, 1934; 800.51 W 89 Italy/255, Hull to Long, June 15, 1934; Rochat, *Militari e politici*, 47–51, 313–20
31 "L'illustre scrittrice Margherita Sarfatti giungendo a New York ci parla dell'Italia rinnovata dal Duce," *Il Progresso Italo-Americano*, March 29, 1934; NMBP, Butler to MGS, April 17, 1934; WRCD, vol. 24, entry for April 15, 1934; FDRP, OF 233 A, "Italy—Misc., 1934," Roosevelt to Dunn, March 21, 1934; ERP, series 170, box 2549, Dunn to Scheider, April 12, 1934; "Italy's Women Free, Says Donna Sarfatti," *Washington Herald*, April 14, 1934; "Signora Sarfatti, Duce Biographer, Is in Washington," *Washington Herald*, April 15, 1934.
32 "Notes of Capital Society. Noted Italian Visitor," *The Washington Times*, April 14, 1934;

"150,000 See Cherry Buds; Autos Block Roads to City," *Washington Post,* April 16, 1934; MGS, *L'America,* 75–9; idem, *Acqua passata,* 223; "Roosevelt Leaves Desk for Hour in the Country," *The New York Times,* April 16, 1934.

33 FDRP, OF 233 A, "Italy—Misc., 1934," Long to Roosevelt, February 28, 1934; Long to Howe, February 28, 1934; White House Usher's Diary, 1934, entry for April 15; President's Appointment Diaries, 1934, entry for April 15; President's Diaries and Itineraries, 1934, entry for April 15; MGS, *Acqua passata,* 223–30 (quote, 223); idem, *L'America,* 185; "Aristocracy Responding to Large Family Drive Announces Italian Woman Leader Visiting Here," *The Washington Post,* April 17, 1934;   Ted Morgan, *FDR: A Biography* (New York, 1985), 85.

34 BLP, box 111, MGS to Long, April 15, 1934; "Aristocracy Responding to Large Family Drive Announces Italian Woman Leader Visiting Here," *The Washington Post,* April 17, 1934; MGS, *Acqua passata,* 221, 228, 230; idem, *L'America,* 187; *Complete Presidential Press Conferences of Franklin D. Roosevelt,* vols. 3–4, 1934 (New York, 1972), vol. 3, 278–83.

35 "Looking On with Helen Essary," *The Washington Times,* April 16, 1934; "Reception at Sulgrave Club for Eminent Italian," *The Washington Times,* April 17, 1934; "Peter Carter Says:," *Washington Herald,* April 17, 1934; "Italy-America Party Honors Donna Sarfatti," *The Washington Post,* April 17, 1934; "Capitol Fetes Italian Author," *New York World Telegram,* April 18, 1934 (quote); *Italy America Monthly,* May 15, 1934, 22; MGS, *L'America,* 127–8.

36 MGS, *L'America,* 61–7, 203–4; idem, "The Heart of America," *This Week,* February 17, 1935.

37 MGS, *L'America,* 209–10; FPP, box 65, Desk Calendars—II, 1933–39, calendar for 1934, entry for April 17, 1934.

38 MGS, *L'America,* 205–7; "D.A.R. Meeting to Draw 4,000 Delegates Here," *The Washington Post,* April 15, 1934.

39 BLP, box 110, Long to Pittman, March 1, 1934; Long to Oliver, March 1, 1934; Pittman to Long, April 24, 1934.

Pittman wrote Long informing him that Margherita had agreed to return to Washington and have dinner with the senator and his wife, and that they had extended an invitation for May 9. It seems highly unlikely that Margherita had made any such promise. More likely, the seriously alcoholic Pittman had become confused.

40 Until recently, Missy's only child, William Brown Meloney, Jr., had worked for Donovan in his Wall Street law office. Richard Dunlop to BRS, April 29, 1986; RDP, Dunlop to Kermit Roosevelt, April 6, 1981; Jeffrey M. Dorwart, "The Roosevelt-Astor Espionage Ring," *New York History,* Vol. LXII (1981), no. 3; Anthony Cave Brown, *"C": The Secret Life of Sir Stewart Graham Menzies, Spymaster to Winston Churchill* (New York, 1987), 123–4; Phillip Knightley, *The Second Oldest Profession: Spies and Spying in the Twentieth Century* (New York, 1987), 211–4.

41 WPD, entry for April 18, 1934; FPP, box 65, Desk Calendars—II, 1933–39, entry for April 18, 1934; "Embassy Tea Honors Italian Guest Author," *The Washington Post,* April 19, 1934; RDS, ADT 611.65241/135, Memorandum of April 18, 1934; H/D 033.6511/63, Memorandum of Conversation with the Italian Ambassador, April 19, 1934; *Italy America Monthly,* May 15, 1934, 22.

42 TVRP, MGS to Ranck, April 17, 1934; Ranck to Italian Consulate, Los Angeles, April 18, 1934; MGS, *L'America,* 91–2; NMBP, MGS to Butler, April 23, 1934.

43 MGS, *L'America,* 243–6; Hugh Thomas, *Cuba, or The Pursuit of Freedom* (London, 1971), 626–95.

44 MGS, *L'America,* 96, 251–2, 268; NMBP, MGS to Butler, April 26, 1934; GSP, MGS to Negri, April 26, 1934; R.E.G. Davies, *Airlines of the United States Since 1914* (London, 1972), 217.

45 MGS, *L'America,* 97, 119, 247–70; NMBP, MGS to Butler, April 27, May 3, 1934; MMMP, MGS to Meloney, April 29, 1934; BLP, MGS to Long, May 3, 1934.

46 Rivera, *My Art, My Life,* 221.

47 De Micheli, *Le circostanze dell'arte,* 158–9; Kandell, *La Capital,* 450; *Diego Rivera,* 89, 298–30; Emily Braun conversation with Mrs. Ruth Davidoff, October 1991.

48 MGS, *L'America,* 97, 220–2; NMBP, MGS to Butler, 3 May 1934; Davies, *Airlines of Latin America Since 1919,* 10.

49 TVRP, Willicombe to Ranck, 24 April 1934; "Italian Writer Welcomed," *Los Angeles Times,* May 5, 1934; Swanberg, *Citizen Hearst,* 377, 387, 410–2, 442–3, 450; Ken Murray, *The Golden Days of San Simeon* (Garden City, N.Y.; 1971), 24; Greg Mitchell, *The Campaign of the Century: Upton Sinclair's Race for Governor of California and the Birth of Media Politics* (New York, 1992), 297, 322, 381–2, 454, 479.

50 MGS, *L'America,* 100–2; Fred Lawrence Guiles, *Marion Davies: A Biography* (New York, 1972), 270–3; "Italian Writer Welcomed," *Los Angeles Times,* May 5, 1934; "Mussolini Biographer Luncheon Guest at MGM," *The Hollywood Reporter,* May 5, 1934; "Honor Guest from Italy," *Los Angeles Examiner,* May 5, 1934.

Frank Capra greatly admired Mussolini. Those feelings were reciprocated, for Mussolini (and Hitler) enjoyed Capra films. Capra's 1930s comedies reveal a Fascist sensibility, rather than a liberal or socialist attitude, as is commonly supposed.

Sarfatti's meeting with Capra seems to have inspired an unexpected proposal. Apparently his enthusiasm for *The Life of Benito Mussolini* led Margherita to believe that Capra wanted to make a film biography of Mussolini. In the fall of 1935, Mussolini notified Columbia Pictures that he was willing to invest $1 million in a picture based on his life to be directed by Capra. This led to serious discussions in Rome but the outbreak of the Ethiopian War and second thoughts by studio head Harry Cohn halted the project. See Joseph McBride, *Frank Capra: The Catastrophe of Success* (New York, 1992), 241–2, 253–7, 334; William L. Shirer, *Berlin Diary: The Journal of a Foreign Correspondent, 1934–1941* (New York, 1941), 587–8.

51 "Mrs. Hugo Rumbold to Fete Donna Margherita Sarfatti at Smart Dinner Sunday," May 4, 1934; "Luncheon Honors Italian Writer," May 8, 1934; "Mussolini Aid [sic] Talks at U.C.L.A.," May 12, 1934 (all *Los Angeles Examiner*); MGS, *L'America,* 51–2, 56–60, 97–101, 103, 181 (quote, 60); NMBP, MGS to Butler, May 8, 1934; conversations with Taylor Coffman, February 1986; Davies, *Airlines of the United States Since 1914,* 168.

52 Swanberg, *Citizen Hearst,* 288–9, 362–4, 413–7, 450, 452–62, 466; Murray, *The Golden Days of San Simeon,* passim; Armand Hammer with Neil Lyndon, *Hammer* (New York, 1983), 232–44; Adela Rogers St. Johns, *The Honeycomb* (Garden City, N. Y., 1969), 129–30, 137–40.

53 MGS, *L'America,* 103–4.

54 TVRP, Ranck to Emanuel, April 23, May 5, 1934; Forte to Ranck, April 26, May 1, May 7, 1934; Emanuel to Ranck, April 28, 1934; Ranck to Forte, April 30, 1934; Ranck to Hearst, May 2, 9, 1934; Hearst to Ranck, May 2, 1934; Willicombe to Ranck, May 9, 1934; "Mussolini Warns the World of Arms Race and New War; Says Europe's Fate Is at Stake," *New York American,* May 13, 1934; OO, XXVI, 224–6, 258–9; De Felice, *Mussolini il duce,* I, 493–4.

55 MGS, *L'America,* 102–9.

56 "Aide of Italy's Leader," *The San Francisco Examiner,* May 9, 1934; "Mme. Sarfatti, Mussolini Aide, on Visit Here," *The San Francisco Examiner,* May 15, 1934 (quote); "2 More Unions Aid Striking Dockmen; Line Halts Sailings," ibid.; NMBP, MGS to Butler, May 15, 1934; MGS, *L'America,* 163–4, 166–72, 177–82.

57 MGS, *L'America,* 52, 54–6, 79–80, 109–20; Laverne Mau Dicker, *The Chinese in San Francisco: A Pictorial History* (New York, 1979), 93; "Chinese Editor Leader in Americanizing Race Here," *The New York Times,* March 11, 1923 [sic].

58 MGS, *L'America,* 81–5; "Italian Women Getting New Deal, Says Friend of Mussolini on Visit to S.L.," *The Deseret News,* May 21, 1934; "Italian Writer, Consul Hear Choir," *The Salt Lake Tribune,* May 21, 1934.

59 MGS, *L'America*, 211–2, 290; Davies, *Airlines of the United States Since 1914*, 168, 180–3; Carl Solberg, *Conquest of the Skies: A History of Commercial Aviation in America* (Boston, 1979), 152–3, 211–7.

60 NMBP, MGS to Butler, May 21, 1934; "Pleasant Meeting of Italy America Society," *Chicago Daily Tribune*, May 22, 1934; " 'the social wirl' . . . Margherita Sarfatti Honored at Tea," *Chicago Herald and Examiner*, May 22, 1934; "Luncheon at Fair Today" and "Guest of Honor at Tea," *Chicago Daily News*, May 22, 1934; " 'the social wirl' . . . Rosalina Miller Missed by Friends," *Chicago Herald and Examiner*, May 23, 1934; "Italy America Society of Chicago," *Italy America Monthly*, June 15, 1934; MGS, *L'America*, 284–5.

61 "Duce Not as Hard as He's Painted, Says Biographer," *Chicago Daily News*, May 22, 1934; MGS, *L'America*, 32, 34–5, 85–90.

62 MGS, *L'America*, 7, 11–2, 25, 52–4, 68–75, 124–5, 136–43, 200–1, 273–5, 281.

63 NMBP, MGS to Butler, June 1, 1934; TVRP, Ranck to MGS, June 12, 1934; "Il Regio Ambasciatore Rosso alla festa dei combattenti," *Il Progresso Italo-Americano*, June 2, 1934.

64 "Margherita Sarfatti esalta l'eroismo dei fanti d'Italia," *Il Progresso Italo-Americano*, June 3, 1934; "Alla commemorazione degli ex-combattenti italiani," *Il Progresso Italo-Americano*, June 4, 1934.

65 MGS, "The Heart of America."; idem, *L'America*, 8.

66 MMMP, Hurst to Meloney, June 3, 1934; FHP, appointment book 1934, entries for June 2, 4, and 7, 1934; TVRP, Ranck to MGS, June 12, 1934; ERP, Series 100, Box 1309, Meloney to Eleanor Roosevelt, June 5, 1934; BP, MGS to Biddle, January 17, 1935; "President Reviews Great Naval Pageant; 81 Warships, 185 Planes Sweep Up the Bay, Thrilling City Throngs with Might of Fleet," *The New York Times*, June 1, 1934; "125,000 Board the Fleet, While As Many More Fail; 2 Drown, 38 Prostrated," *The New York Times*, June 4, 1934; *The WPA Guide to New York City*, 204–5, 246–7; MGS, *L'America*, 19, 24, 33, 35, 39–42 (quote, 39).

67 MGS, *L'America*, 124, 208; Lowe, "The Woman Behind Mussolini," 31; Prezzolini, *Diario, 1900–1941*, 518; MMMP, Lewis to Meloney, June 27, 1934; DTP, Series I, Box 2, Ascoli to Thompson, June 21, 1934; Series III, Box 5, Seldes to Thompson, n.d.; MMMP, Sforza to Meloney, May 24, 1934; Carmen Harder, *Do We Want Fascism?* (New York, 1934); "Roosevelt Replies to Critics in Book," *The New York Times*, March 29, 1934; Franklin D. Roosevelt, *On Our Way* (New York, 1934), ix.

68 MGS, *L'America*, 152–65, 176–7, 180–1, 201–3, 282–3, 292–3; MGS, *Acqua passata*, 213.

69 MGS, *L'America*, 40, 133, 189–200, 203–4, 209–15; Pieroni Bortolotti, *Femminismo e partiti politici in Italia*, 382–3.

70 "Signora Sarfatti Sails," *The New York Times*, June 10, 1934; "Personal Intelligence," *New York Herald Tribune*, June 10, 1934; "Donna Margherita Sarfatti parte, lodando l'America," *Il Progresso Italo-Americano*, June 10, 1934; "Signora Sarfatti, Duce Aide, Sails for Home Lauding U.S.," *New York American*, June 10, 1934 (quote); interview with Magalì Sarfatti-Larson, September 28, 1985.

71 A selection of such reports can be seen in the relevant volumes of the DDI, Seventh Series.

CHAPTER 27: ALLIANCES MADE AND BROKEN

1 Morgan, *Spurs on the Boot*, 289–92; Cerruti, *Ambassador's Wife*, 146–50; Darrah, *Hail Caesar!*, 249–59; OO, XXVI, 263–5; Petersen, *Hitler e Mussolini*, 311–3; Henry M. and Robin K. Adams, *Rebel Patriot: A Biography of Franz von Papen* (Santa Barbara, 1987), 246–7, 250–3; Alloway, *The Venice Biennale*, illustrations 6, 7; MGS, *Mussolini: Como lo conocí*, XII (quote); RWHP, container 95, Howard to Morgan, July 10, 1934; "Hitler Leaves; Duce Promises to Visit Berlin," United Press dispatch, *International Herald Tribune*, June 17, 1934; DDI, Seventh Series, vol. XV, no. 411.

While Sarfatti had been in the United States, an important Mussolini article had appeared in both the Hearst press and *Il Popolo d'Italia*. The article stated that Europe faced a crucial question: Either all the major powers could disarm and hope to lure Germany back into the

League of Nations or a new arms race would begin. Mussolini argued that German rearmament would make another world war likely. Despite her previous authorship of such dualpurpose articles, it seems unlikely that Sarfatti could have written this one. Probably Mussolini himself wrote it and Thomas Morgan translated it into English. Despite the import of the piece, Mussolini did not rush it into print. For once, he respected the Hearst deadline. See "Re-Armament," *New York American*, May 13, 1934 ["Verso il riarmo," May 18, 1934]; OO, XXVI, 224–6; TVRP, Forte to Ranck, May 1, 1934, Ranck to Hearst, Willicombe to Ranck, May 9, 1934; De Felice, *Mussolini il duce*, I, 493–4.

2 De Felice, *Mussolini il duce*, I, 494–7; Weinberg, *The Foreign Policy of Hitler's Germany*, 100–1; Petersen, *Hitler e Mussolini*, 312–23; Vittorio Mussolini, *Mussolini e gli uomini nel suo tempo*, 132–3; Pietro Badoglio, *Italy in the Second World War: Memories and Documents* (Westport, Conn., 1976), 2; De Vecchi, *Il quadrumviro scomodo*, 226; *Between Hitler and Mussolini: Memoirs of Ernst Rudiger Prince Stahremberg* (New York, 1942), 147–8; DDI, Seventh Series, vol. XV, nos. 419, 429.

3 TVRP, Ranck to Chaplin, June 17, 1934; OO, XXVI, 265; MGS, *Mussolini: Como lo conocí*, XII; idem, "Settecento veneto," *La Stampa*, December 7, 1934.

4 ACS, MI-DPP, f. "Sarfatti, Margherita," report of June 18, 1934; Giuseppe Basadonna, *Mussolini e le opera napoletane del ventennio* (Naples, 1980), 12–3; Koenig, *Architettura in Toscana*, 34–5; Arrigo Petacco, *Pavolini: L'ultima raffica di Salò* (Milan, 1982), 49–50; Cresti, *Architettura e fascismo*, 283.

5 "Italian King Opens Venice Art Exposition," *Los Angeles Examiner*, May 13, 1934; RDS, FP 865.607M/15, Long to Hull, May 14, 1934; 865.607M/16, Long to Welles, June 23, 1934; 865.607M/17, Long to Hull, July 13, 1934; Fred Lawrence Guiles, *Marion Davies* (New York, 1972), 274–5; Alloway, *The Venice Biennale*, 112–3; "U.S. Is Definitely on Road to Recovery, Says W. R. Hearst As He Sails for Europe," *New York American*, May 27, 1934.

6 MGS, *Mussolini: Como lo conocí*, XII; PVC interview with Magalí Sarfatti-Larson, September 28, 1985; "Il pesante giudizio di Giovanni Ansaldo"; Morgan, *Spurs on the Boot*, 267; ACS, MI-DPP, f. "Sarfatti, Margherita," report of April 25, 1935.
   That Mussolini retained great interest in conditions in the United States and in Roosevelt's policies is clear from his intensive grilling of Ambassador Rosso on those subjects during an interview in the Palazzo Venezia some weeks later. JPMP, Vol. 23, memorandum of September 14, 1934.

7 MMMP, Amedeo Sarfatti to Meloney, June 25, 1934; MGS to Meloney, July 3, 1934; MGS to Meloney, n.d. (but July 1934); GSP, MGS to Negri, August 5, 1934.

8 De Felice, *Mussolini il duce*, I, 496–513; Weinberg, *The Foreign Policy of Hitler's Germany*, 102–7, 195–6; Petersen, *Hitler e Mussolini*, 323–7; Adams, *Rebel Patriot*, 255; Edvige Mussolini, *Mio fratello Benito*, 147; Vittorio Mussolini, *Mussolini e gli uomini nel suo tempo*, 133; Morgan, *Spurs on the Boot*, 293, 333; AVI, AG, LV, 3, MGS to D'Annunzio, July 21, 1934; MGS, *Mussolini: Como lo conocí*, XIII; *Between Hitler and Mussolini*, 149; "Dr. Shotwell Sails Tomorrow," *The New York Times*, June 28, 1934; James T. Shotwell, "The League's C.I.C. Breaks New Ground," *The New York Times*, September 2, 1934; Gottfried-Karl Kindermann, *Hitler's Defeat in Austria, 1933–1934: Europe's First Containment of Nazi Expansionism* (Boulder, Colo., 1988), 99–103, 116–7; Darrah, *Hail Caesar!*, 262; DBFP, Second Series, vol. 6, 530–3; DGFP, C, col. 3, no. 137; OO, XXVI, 298, 309–10, 315–28 (quote, 319).
   TVRP, Ranck to Chaplin, June 17, 1934; Forte to Ranck, June 20, 1934; Ranck to Forte, June 22, 1934; Ranck to Chaplin, June 26, 1934; Chaplin to Ranck, June 28, 1934; Chaplin to Ranck, July 2, 1934; Ranck to Chaplin, July 4, 1934; Hillman to Ranck, August 18, 1934; Ranck to Hillman, August 19, 1934; " 'Italy Curbed Crime When It Throttled Local Politicians,' Declares Mussolini," *New York American*, June 3, 1934; "Mussolini Sees 40-Hour Week Solving World-Wide Unemployment Problem," *New York American*, July 15, 1934; "Austria Must Be Kept Independent to Prevent European War—Mussolini," *New York American*, July 28, 1934; "Mussolini Warns Falling Birthrate Is Leading White Race to Disaster," *New York American*, August 26, 1934 ["La razza bianca muore?"]; OO, XXVI, 312–5.

9 "Noted Italian Author Visits America, Finds Our 'Continent' Big, but Helpless," *New York American*, October 7, 1934; "Italian Author Finds America Saved White Civilization," *New York American*, October 14, 1934; "Orizzonti aerodinamici," *La Stampa*, November 16, 1934; "L'americano come lo si parla," *Nuova Antologia*, December 1, 1934; "The Heart of America," *This Week, New York Herald Tribune*, February 17, 1935; BLP, box 111, MGS to Long, August 2, 1934; NMBP, MGS to Butler, September 22, 1934; MMMP, MGS to Meloney, August 8, 15, 1934, January 17, 1935, March 25, 1936; TVRP, Berkson to Ranck, August 29, 1934; Ranck to Chaplin, September 9, 15, 22, 26, October 3, 1934; Chaplin to Ranck, September 14, 19, 22, October 2, 9, 1934; Ranck to MGS, October 8, 1934; receipt for 16,000 lire signed by MGS, October 10, 1934; receipt for 16,000 lire signed by Amedeo Sarfatti, November 3, 1934; "Italy Glories in Militarism, Says Mussolini; 'Pacifists the Worst Enemies of Peace,' " *New York American*, September 30, 1934; "Mussolini Envisions World on Threshold of an Advanced and Better Civilization," *New York American*, October 28, 1934.

In 1934, *Politica Sociale* printed articles by Lloyd George: "La politica estera nel discorso di Mussolini" (January-February), "La pace fra i popoli e l'eccidio die Marsiglia" (September-October), "Discordia nel pacifico" (November-December), and by Göring: "La Germania e il disarmo" (May-June). Another Lloyd George article appeared early in 1935: "America e Inghilterra di fronte alla ricostruzione" (January-February).

10 GSP, MGS to Negri, August 5, 1934; Livio and Fiammetta Gaetani to Negri, August 20, 1934; "L'identificazione della salma della Medaglia d'oro Sarfatti," *Corriere della Sera*, August 21, 1934; MMMP, MGS to Meloney, September 9, 12, 1934.

11 Thomas L. Schumacher, *Terragni e il Danteum, 1938* (Rome, 1983), 82–6; idem, *Surface and Symbol*, 59, 70, 126–31; Luigi Zuccoli, *Quindici anni di vita e di lavoro con l'amico e maestro architetto Giuseppe Terragni* (Como, n.d.), 37; observations of BRS and LKF, Col d'Echele, May 26, 1986.

12 MGS, *I vivi e l'ombra* (1934); GSP, MGS to Negri, n.d. but late 1934; NA, T586, reel 1093, frames 068769–78.

In early March 1934, Mussolini had sent Negri a gift of 25,000 lire. NA, ibid., frame 068775.

13 MI-DPP, f. "Sarfatti, Margherita," reports of May 19, November 9, 1934.

14 De Felice, *Mussolini il duce*, I, 186, 804–5; MGS, *Mussolini: Como lo conocí*, X; Edda Ciano, *La mia testimonianza*, 119–20; "Countess Ciano," *The Times* (London), June 18, 1934, photograph, 18; *L'Illustrazione Italiana*, June 24, 1934, photograph, 953.

15 Guerri, *Galeazzo Ciano*, 79–107; Susmel, *Vita sbagliata di Galeazzo Ciano*, 58–9; interview with Amedeo and Pierangela Sarfatti, May 24, 1985; police reports of September 30, 1936 and January 30, 1937, ACS, MI-DPP, "Sarfatti, Margherita"; "Nemo," "She Dreamed of a New Empire"; Alvaro, *Quasi una vita*, 162.

16 Edda Ciano, *La mia testimonianza*, 94; Alvaro, *Quasi una vita*, 108; "Il pesante giudizio di Giovanni Ansaldo," *Il Giornale*, July 28, 1987.

17 TVRP, Ranck to Chaplin, October 9, 13, November 1, 1934; Chaplin to Ranck, October 9, 11, 13, 15, 1934; Darrah, *Hail Caesar!*, 269–71; DBFP, Second Series, vol. 12, nos. 15, 112, 135; ibid., series 1A, vol. 2, no. 385; DGFP, C, vol. 3, nos. 381, 459, 462; DDF, series 1, vol. 7, nos. 462, 465, 466, 468, 471, 493, 504, 528, 531; ibid., vol. 8, nos. 130, 168, 320; Aloisi, *Journal*, 213, 215, 221, 224–6; MI-DPP, 1927–1944, no. 84, "Attentato e morte del Re Alessandro di Yugoslavia, 1932–34"; PRO, FO 371, R6295, British Legation, Bucharest, to Simon, November 8, 1934; ibid., 18456, Simon to Cowan, November 26, 1934; Clara Conti, *Servizio Segreto* (Rome, 1945), 9–11, 15–7, 20–4, 46–80, 127, 138, 165; *Il processo Roatta*, Clara Conti, ed. (Rome, 1945), 10–1, 19, 30, 42, 45–7, 55, 62, 102, 137, 183, 194; Peter II of Yugoslavia, *A King's Heritage* (New York, 1954), 42–7; Vladeta Milicevic, *A King Dies in Marseilles: The Crime and Its Background* (Bad Godesberg, 1959), 52–85; Neil Balfour and Sally Mackay, *Paul of Yugoslavia* (London, 1980), 97–9, 105–6.

The most damning evidence for Mussolini's direct responsibility for the murders is contained in the PPYP, box 5, Diary, entries for December 12, 1934, May 17, 1935.

18 "Il pesante giudizio di Giovanni Ansaldo"; S. Renzo de Pasquale, *Dietro la maschera!* (San Remo, 1945), 98–100; MI-DPP, f. "Sarfatti, Margherita," report of December 31, 1934.

19 De Felice, *Mussolini il duce,* I, 519–33; Rainero, *La rivendicazione fascista sulla Tunisia;* Galeazzo Ciano, *Diario, 1937–1943,* 227, 472; DDF, series 2, vol. XV, no. 220; DDI, Seventh Series, vol XVI, nos. 391, 399.

20 Genevieve Tabouis, *They Called Me Cassandra* (New York, 1942), 230; Brice Harris, Jr., *The United States and the Italo-Ethiopian Crisis* (Palo Alto, Calif., 1964), 31; EMHP, Long to House, August 17, 1934; Rochat, *Militari e politici,* 135, 147, 151; USE, *L'esercito italiano tra la 1a e la 2a guerra mondiale, novembre 1918–giugno 1940* (Rome, 1954), 232; BLP, box 114, MGS to Long, January 1, 1935; Long to Roosevelt, February 8, 15, 1935.

21 NA, T120, reel 6059, frames E447588–94; DBFP, Second Series, vol. XII, no. 722, especially note 43; Robertson, *Mussolini as Empire-Builder,* 130–1; De Felice, *Mussolini il duce,* I, 661–2.

22 Petersen, *Hitler e Mussolini,* 358–67; Schulenburg, *"Um Benito Mussolini,"* 27–30; TVRP, Willicombe to Ranck, March 18, July 1, 1935; Ranck to Willicombe, March 20, April 25, 26, 1935; Ranck to Hearst, April 24, June 13, 14, 30, 1935; Hearst to Ranck, April 26, 27, June 14, 1935; Ranck to Hillman, September 29, 1935; "Pact of Rome Ends Long Controversy Between Italy and France, Says Duce," May 5, 1935; MGS, "Scratch an American Flapper, You'll Find a Pioneer, Says Italian Novelist," September 29, 1935.

A sampling of Hearst's pro-Hitler and anti-Mussolini articles that appeared in the Hearst press for the first nine months of 1935 included: "Now Is the Turn of Other Nations to Meet Germany's Desire for Peace—Rosenberg," February 24, 1935; "George Bernard Shaw Says: 'Germany Should Be Permitted to Arm to the Hilt!,' " March 24, 1935; "Britain's 'White Book' Is an Insult to the German People, Says Rosenberg," March 24, 1935; "Lloyd George Says: Danger of War Lies with Allies Not Germany," April 7, 1935; "Reich's Re-armament Marks English-French Decline—Ferrero," April 28, 1935; "Franco-Soviet Treaty Threatens World with Communism—Rosenberg," May 19, 1935; " 'Nobody in Germany Wants War,' Says Hitler," May 19, 1935; "Hitler Opens Doors to New Path of Peace—Lloyd George," May 26, 1935; "Reich's Re-armament Only Guarantee of Peace in Europe, Says Mackensen," June 30, 1935; "Lloyd George Calls Duce's African Aims 'Buccaneering,' " September 15, 1935.

On March 3, 1935, the Hearst newspapers ran an editorial that stated: "In Italy the Fascist Government has suppressed all freedom of thought and expression, has drilled and dragooned all independent industry and all prosperity out of the country, and has utterly impoverished the people in order to gratify the Government's imperial ambition, and to maintain a nation in arms." These charges were substantially true. But it would have been hard to find any of these facts in a Hearst newspaper over the previous ten years.

Page 3 of the April 14, 1935, "March of Events" section of the Hearst papers displayed a map showing Germans "under foreign rule." These areas included Alsace-Lorraine, all of Czechoslovakia, and all of northeastern Italy.

23 RDS, GRC 862.20/676, Long to Hull, March 14, 1934; KWP, box 1, biographical outline, 10; WEDP, container 48, Dodd to Wiegand, February 15, 1935; Wiegand to Dodd, February 27, 1935; FDRP, PSF, "Germany—Dodd 1933–35," Dodd to Roosevelt, March 20, 1935; Roosevelt to Dodd, April 16, 1935 (quote); Dodd to Roosevelt, June 27, 1935; Dodd to Moore, August 31, 1936; FDRP, PPF, 308, Roosevelt to McAdoo, March 16, 1938; "NRA Accomplice of Communist Party in Breeding Revolt Here, Says Tinkham," *New York American,* June 2, 1935; "Coffin Finds New Deal Policies Realization of Karl Marx Program," *New York American,* August 11, 1935; "Who Will Defeat Mr. Roosevelt? Asks Mr. Hearst," *New York American,* October 6, 1935.

It seems certain that Soviet intelligence learned of this whole affair. Martha Dodd, the ambassador's daughter, who handled his most sensitive correspondence, was a Soviet agent. Herbert Romerstein and Stanislav Levchenko, *The KGB Against the "Main Enemy": How the Soviet Intelligence Service Operates Against the United States* (Lexington, Mass., 1989), 188; "Martha Dodd Stern Is Dead at 82; Author and an Accused Soviet Spy," *The New York Times,* August 29, 1990.

24 "Austria Must Exist as an Independent German State in Europe, Asserts Duce," *New York American,* January 27, 1935; MMMP, MGS to Meloney, January 17, February 19, March 31, 1935; NMBP, MGS to Butler, February 19, 1935; Butler to MGS, March 23, 1935; "World's Greatest Exhibition of Italian Art Opened in Paris," *The New York Herald,* (Paris) May 16, 1935; Martin Fuchs, *Showdown in Vienna: The Death of Austria* (New York, 1939), 140.

Margherita's struggles with Ojetti over modern art that winter and spring are reflected in the following *La Stampa* articles: "Confessioni alla Quadriennale," February 21, 1935; "In margine alla Quadriennale—Cerecchini o il balletto," February 27, 1935; "Scultori," March 23, 1935; "Disegni a Roma," April 20, 1935; "Ritratto e composizione," October 5, 1935.

25 ACS, MI-DPP, f. "Sarfatti, Margherita," report of April 25, 1935; GSP, MGS to Negri, April 26, 1935; MGS, *Mussolini: Como lo conocí,* XIII (spiritual values quote); ACS, SPD, CR, b. 46, f. 242R, "Starace," Starace to Mussolini, September 14, 1934; ibid., Starace to Mussolini, January 5, 1935; ACS, Ministero dell'Africa Italiana, b. 9, Commissione suprema di difesa, Segretaria generale, verbale della XII sessione, February 1935, la seduta V—Cultura e discipline militari negli istituti civili di istruzione, 20.

26 ACS, MCP, b. 170, f. 4, MGS to editor of the *Journal de la Femme,* January 24, 1935; ACS, MI-DPP, f. "Sarfatti, Margherita," reports of April 25, May 13, June 15, 1935; Magalì Sarfatti-Larson interview with Amedeo Sarfatti, October 1985; GSP, MGS to Negri, n.d. but June–July 1935; MGS, *Daniele Ranzoni* (Rome, 1935); Enzo Borelli, "Margherita Sarfatti, *Daniele Ranzoni,*" *Leonardo,* August 1935.

A note at the end of *Daniele Ranzoni* states: "After the editing of the present volume (1933) which, for technical editorial reasons, has been licensed for the public only in May 1935 . . ." Ibid., 177. One suspects the hand of Ciano in the delay.

27 AOMP/NYTA, Markel to Sulzberger, June 17, 1935; ibid, microfilm, "James, Edwin L.," reel 69, McCormick to James, May 31, 1935; MMMP, MGS to Meloney, n.d. but May 1935; "World's Greatest Exhibition of Italian Art Opened in Paris," *New York Herald,* May 16, 1935; "Visitors from All Parts of World Coming to See Exhibit in Paris," *The New York Times,* May 17, 1935; "Primitive to Surrealist: The Long Range of Italian Art Revealed in Two Huge Paris Exhibitions," *The New York Times,* July 21, 1935; "Italian Art Exhibition Drew 650,000 in Paris," *The New York Times,* July 23, 1935; Schulenburg, *"Um Benito Mussolini,"* 36 ("You have enough already"); Giovanni Ansaldo diary (courtesy of Prof. Renzo De Felice), entry for June 2 (?) 1935 ("If we have to pay").

28 De Felice, *Mussolini il duce,* I, 622–3, 663 n.1; RDS, 811.91265/34, Kirk to Hull, August 24, 1935.

29 RDS, 865.002 Mussolini/170, Hull to Meloney, June 15, 1935; MMMP, MGS to Meloney, May (?), June 22, n.d. but July-August, August 13, September 5, n.d. but early October, 1935; ibid., letter by MGS beginning: "Duce, Being a great lover of Italy"; ibid., Meloney to Grazzi, August 27, 1935; ibid., Drummond to Meloney, September 24, 1935; OOA, XVIV, 121–4; DBFP, Second Series, vol. 14, no. 366; Marquis, *Hopes and Ashes,* 74.

30 Marzorati, *Margherita Sarfatti,* 172, 198; MGS, *Mussolini: Como lo conocí,* X; Bottai, *Diario, 1935–1944,* 60–1, 89–90; idem, *Diario, 1944–1948,* 277; Fuchs, *Showdown in Vienna,* 140; Hugh J. Schonfield, *The Suez Canal* (London, 1939), 111; idem, *The Suez Canal in World Affairs* (London, 1952), 90; Robertson, *Mussolini as Empire-Builder,* 148–51, 156–66; Renato Mori, *Mussolini e la conquista dell'Etiopia* (Florence, 1978), 57–64, 78–9.

31 BLP, diary 1935–36, entries for August 6, 18, 26, 28, September 2, 4, 1935; FDRP, PPF, 6240, Roosevelt to Phillips, July 3, 1935; FDRP, OF, 652, "Hugh R. Wilson, 1933–44," Wilson to Roosevelt, August 13, 1935, Roosevelt to Wilson, August 26, 1935; FRUS, 1935, vol. I, 610–3, 616–8, 623; DBFP, Second Series, vol. 14, nos. 404, 438, 439, 441, 448, 453, 460; Robert Dallek, *Franklin D. Roosevelt and American Foreign Policy, 1932–1945* (New York, 1981), 104–8.

32 FDRP, White House Usher's Log, entry for July 18, 1935; KWP, box 9, Wiegand to Drummond Hay, July 30, 1935 ("joy of life" quote); FRUS, 1935, vol. I, 742 ("armed

conflict" quote); NA, T-586, roll 426, frames 013076, 013083-4; PRO, FO 371/19130-75649, Kelly to Foreign Office, August 29, 1935 ("destroy Malta" quote).

33 FRUS, *The Conference at Cairo and Teheran 1943* (Washington, 1961), 530–1; *The Secret Diary of Harold C. Ickes*, II: *The Inside Struggle, 1936–1939* (New York, 1954), 84; FDRP, PSF, "Italy—William Phillips, 1935–40," Phillips to Roosevelt, October 6, 1938; David Dilks, "Flashes of Intelligence: The Foreign Office, the SIS and Security Before the Second World War," in Christopher Andrew and David Dilks, eds. *The Missing Dimension: Governments and Intelligence Services in the Twentieth Century* (London, 1984), 106–11; De Felice, *Mussolini il duce*, I, 674, 679–80; idem, *Mussolini l'alleato*, I: *L'Italia in guerra, 1940–1943* (Turin, 1990), 1286.

34 NMBP, Butler to MGS, May 22, 1935, MGS to Butler,n.d. but June-July 1935, Butler to MGS, January 13, 1936; "Dr. Butler on Italy and Abyssinia," *Italy America Monthly*, July 1935, 5; Butler, *Across the Busy Years*, II, 165–80; CEP, box 136, Butler to Hull, September 24, 1935, Hull to Butler, October 3, 1935.

35 ACS, MI-DPP, f. "Morgan, Thomas B.," reports of July 21, September 10, 20, 1935, May 14, 1936; RDS, 811.91265/34, Kirk to Hull, August 24, 1935, 811.91265/36, Tittmann to State Dept., October 16, 1935; RWHP, container 106, Keen to Howard, August 9, 1935, Howard to Keen, August 25, 1935; ibid., container 105, Baillie to Keen, October 15, 1935; ibid., container 117, Brown to Howard, February 15, 27, 1936; "Fourth Estate. MORGAN: United Press Reporter Finds the Duce's Courts Kind," *Newsweek*, August 29, 1936; BLP, box 133, Morgan to Long, March 27, 1940; Overseas Press Club of America, *Deadline Delayed* (New York, 1947), 200; "Thomas B. Morgan Dies at 87; Author Led U.P. Rome Bureau," *The New York Times*, July 11, 1972.

36 De Felice, *Mussolini il duce*, I, 621–43, 679–86, 693–4; DBFP, Second Series, vol. 14, nos. 575, 579, 589, 599, 604, 630; Robertson, *Mussolini as Empire-Builder*, 176–81.

37 MMMP, MGS to Meloney, August 13, September 5, n.d. (but early October), 1935; BLP, diary 1935–36, entries for September 12, 20, 21, 23, 24, 27, 1935.

CHAPTER 28: THE SECOND ROMAN EMPIRE

1 "Italy Will Fight, Mussolini Asserts," *The New York Times*, October 3, 1935; Augusto Simonini, *Il linguaggio di Mussolini* (Milan, 1978), 70–7 (Mussolini quote, 77); MGS, *Mussolini: Como lo conocí*, XIII ("hypocrite" quote); Trapani, "Mia madre Margherita Sarfatti," III, 58 ("beginning of the end" quote).

Mussolini's speeches were always reedited for publication in *Il Popolo d'Italia*. This is the source for most texts in OO. But recordings are available of some speeches as actually delivered. Simonini prints the authentic text of the Mobilization speech.

2 MMMP, MGS to Meloney, August 13, September 5, n.d. (but early October), December 3, 14, 1935; EPP, MGS to Pound, September 5, 18, 1935; Redman, *Ezra Pound and Fascism*, 164–8; Magalì Sarfatti-Larson interviews with Amedeo Sarfatti, June 25, September 28, 1985.

3 BLP, diary 1935–36, entries for October 31, November 3, 1935; OO, XXVII, 177–8; MGS, "La città universitaria di Roma," *Nuova Antologia*, November 16, 1935; Bossaglia, "Margherita Sarfatti critica d'arte," 403–4; "L'Ateneo Romano conferisce la laurea 'honoris causa' a S.M. il Re," *L'Illustrazione Italiana*, November 10, 1935, 899; MGS, "Lo spirito della nuova casa," *Almanacco della donna italiana 1936 XIV* (Florence, 1937), 38.

4 BLP, diary 1935–36, entry for November 3, 1935; PRO, FO 371/20424, R3494, Sargent to Lindsay, June 16, 1936; RDS, 765.84/2421, Long to Hull, November 8, 1935; OO, XXVII, 179; Baer, *Test Case*, 25–6.

5 BLP, diary 1935–36, entry for November 29, 1935; De Felice, *Mussolini il duce*, I, 695–705; Baer, *Test Case*, 164–70; Boca, *La conquista dell'impero*, 464–70; Max Gallo, *Mussolini's Italy* (New York, 1973), 433; DBFP, Second Series, vol. 15, nos. 268, 270.

6 Baer, *Test Case*, 121–55; De Felice, *Mussolini il duce*, I, 714–24; OO, XXVII, 201–6.

7 MI-DPP, f. "Sarfatti, Margherita," reports of November 7, 8, December 3, 4, 7, 10, 1935.

8 GSP, MGS to Negri, November 26, December 22, 1935 (MGS quote), n.d. but December 1935–January 1936; MMMP, MGS to Meloney, December 14, 1935; Walter Lippmann, "Today and Tomorrow: The Breathing Spell," *New York Herald* (Paris), December 14, 1935; NMBP, MGS to Butler, Christmas 1935; Del Boca, *La conquista dell'impero,* 469 (Negri quote); MI-DPP, f. "Sarfatti, Margherita," report of December 16, 1935.

9 Del Boca, *La conquista dell'impero,* 487–94; "Ciano Reported on Way Home," *The New York Times,* December 16, 1935; Guerri, *Galeazzo Ciano,* 133–4; BLP, diary 1935–36, entry for November 27, 1935; Alberto Moravia and Giuseppe Prezzolini, *Lettere* (Milan, 1982), 9–22; Elkann and Moravia, *Vita di Moravia,* 73–9.

10 Brian R. Sullivan, " 'A Highly Commendable Action': William J. Donovan's Intelligence Mission for Mussolini and Roosevelt, December 1935–February 1935, and Its Consequences," *Intelligence and National Security,* July 1991, 343–55; U.S. Department of State, *Peace and War, United States Policy 1931–1941* (Washington, 1943), 305–6; Baer, *Test Case,* 201–3; BLP, diary 1935–36; entries for January 4–6, 1936; Alberto Pirelli, *Taccuini 1922/1943* (Bologna, 1984), 152; DGFP, C, vol. 4, nos. 480, 485, 498.

11 Del Boca, *La conquista dell'impero,* 510–34; USE, *L'esercito italiano,* 232; Baer, *Test Case,* 176, 199, 203–5; Sullivan, "A Highly Commendable Action"; RDS, 765.84/3445, Long to Hull, January 14, 1936; Pedro A. del Valle, *Semper Fidelis* (Hawthorne, Calif., 1976), 80–92; HSTL, PSF, Hoover to Vaughan, "Major General Pedro del Valle," February 20, 1946; BLP, diary 1935–36, entry for February 3, 1936.

12 Diggins, *Mussolini and Fascism,* 289–92, 302–5; Dallek, *Franklin D. Roosevelt and American Foreign Policy,* 117–21; Baer, *Test Case,* 205; "Most Britons Want No Part in African Row, Giannini Declares After Stay in England," *The New York Times,* September 3, 1935; "America Has No Interests in British Africa," *New York American,* December 7, 1935; Walter Lippmann, "Today and Tomorrow: Bad Law from a Hard Case," *New York Herald Tribune,* December 17, 1935; FDRP, OF, 547-A, "Memo for Mac," A. P. Giannini to MacIntyre, November 25, 1935; MacIntyre to Giannini, December 3, 1935; NMBP, Butler to MGS, January 13, 1936; BLP, diary 1935–36, entries for January 2, February 4, 10, 13, 1936; ibid., box 105, Long to Roosevelt, December 6, 1935; Key Pittman Papers, Library of Congress, box 45, Long to Pittman, February 19, 1936; EMHP, Long to House, February 19, 1936; PRO, FO, 20410, enclosure in Drummond dispatch no. 209 (266/29/36) of February 14, 1936 (quote). 371/20424, R3494, Sargent to Lindsay, June 16, 1936; ibid., R4106, Lindsay to Moley, June 30, 1936; FDRP, PPF 434, "Breckinridge Long," Long to Early, September 22, 1936; Anne O'Hare McCormick, "Mussolini Declares Events Favor Italy," *The New York Times,* February 16, 1935.

13 Del Boca, *La conquista dell'impero,* 549–600; Guerri, *Galeazzo Ciano,* 138.

14 BLP, diary 1935–36, entries for February 23, 28, March 28, 1936; interview with Frank Gervasi, May 5, 1986; MMMP, MGS to Meloney, March 25, 1936.

15 GSP, MGS to Negri, n.d. but mid-February 1936, Fiammetta Sarfatti Gaetani to Negri, February 26, 1936; Comes, *Ada Negri,* 148; MI-DPP, f. "Sarfatti, Margherita," report of March 18, 1936; MMMP, MGS to Meloney, March 25, 1936 (two letters: Kirk quote in one beginning "Dearest Darling, here are 2 copies . . ."); ACS, MCP, b. 9, f. 127, "Sarfatti, Margherita," Alfieri to MGS, March 27, 1936, Luciano to Alfieri, April 1, 1936.

In February–March 1936, Alexander Kirk and Missy Meloney appear to have agreed that she should approach Roosevelt with their suggestion for a joint American-Vatican diplomatic proposal to bring the Ethiopian War to a negotiated end. They also seem to have hoped for the establishment of formal diplomatic relations between the United States and the Holy See. Given her close ties to the Vatican, as well as to Kirk and Missy, it is possible that Sarfatti may have played a role in this project. In any case, nothing came of it. MMMP, Kirk to Meloney, March 15, 1936.

16 Del Boca, *La conquista dell'impero,* 606–705; Bottai, *Diario, 1935–1944,* 102–3.

17 BLP, diary 1935–36, entry for March 28, 1936; MMMP, MGS to Meloney, March 25, 1936; Max Altdorfer, "Begegnung mit Margherita G. Sarfatti," *Bund ab Blatt,* March 29, 1936;

MGS, "Kampf um die neue Kunst Italiens," *Neues Wiener Journal,* April 3, 1936; "Vortrag Margherita Sarfatti," *Neue Freie Presse,* April 4, 1936; "Margherita Sarfatti am Vortragspult," *Neues Wiener Journal,* April 4, 1936; "Margherita Sarfatti," *Wiener Zeitung,* April 5, 1936; "Der Lebensstil des neuen Italien," *Rechtpost,* April 5, 1936; "Wiener Brief," *Steyrer Zeitung,* April 7, 1936; "Wiener Brief," *Kirchdorfer Zeitung,* April 7, 1936; Weinberg, *The Foreign Policy of Hitler's Germany,* 265–9; DDF, series 2, vol. 2, no. 272, p. 430, n. 1.

18 Weinberg, *The Foreign Policy of Hitler's Germany,* 266–7; Aloisi, *Journal,* 366; DGFP, C, vol. 5, no. 255; Filippo Anfuso, *Roma Berlino Salò (1936–1945)* (Milan, 1950), 18–9.

19 BLP, diary 1935–36, entries for March 10, 14, April 16, 20, 23, 1936; ibid., box 117, MGS to Long, June 15, 1936, Long to MGS, June 26, 1936; De Begnac, *Taccuini mussoliniani,* 221, 549, 564–5, 609–14, 617–9; De Felice, *Mussolini l'alleato,* I, 1285.

20 Aloisi, *Journal,* 382 (quote); FDRP, OF, 233, "Italy, Gov't. of, 1933–36," Phillips to Roosevelt, June 3, 1936; De Begnac, *Taccuini mussoliniani,* 526, 550–1; BLP, diary 1935–36, entry for April 20, 1936.

21 Marzorati, *Margherita Sarfatti,* 151; TVRP, Ranck to Hearst, March 8, May 19, 1936, Hearst to Ranck, May 19, 1936; interview with Frank Gervasi, May 5, 1986; DDF, series 2, vol. 2, no. 272; Dario Biocca, ed., *A Matter of Passion: Letters of Bernard Berenson and Clotilde Margieri* (Berkeley, 1989), 172–3.

22 OO, XXVII, 264–9 (quote, 269); "Italy Annexes Ethiopia: King Becomes Emperor and Badoglio Viceroy," *The New York Times,* May 10, 1936.

23 Luigi Federzoni, *Italia di ieri per la storia di domani* (Verona, 1967), 233; Elena Canino, *Clotilde tra due guerra* (Milan, 1956), 372–3; OO, XXVII, 267; Marzorati, *Margherita Sarfatti,* 151; BLP, box 117, McNair to Long, August 25, 1936; ibid., MGS to Long, June 15, 1936 (quote).

CHAPTER 29: THE END OF ILLUSIONS

1 Interview with Frank Gervasi, May 5, 1936; TVRP, Hearst to Ranck, May 19, 21, 23, June 6, 1936, Ranck to Hearst, May 19, 21, 22, 23, 27, June 6, 1936, Willicombe to Ranck, May 27, 28, 1936; MGS, "Arti decorative, ovvero: L'oggetto corre dietro alla propria ombra," *Nuova Antologia,* July 1, 1936; idem, "Onestà delle arti applicate," *La Stampa,* July 4, 1936; ECP, part 1, box 4, Hearst to Coblentz, July 20, 1936, Hearst to Gervasi, August 31, 1936; NA, T586, reel 426, frame 013044.

In mid-June, through intermediaries, Haile Selassie offered Hearst a 20,000-word account of the Ethiopian War. Ranck thought the story "gripping," particularly the emperor's firsthand account of the Italian use of poison gas. Hearst turned it down. He argued that there would be "little if any interest and no circulation in [the] series." TVRP, Ranck to Hearst, June 18, 1936.

2 Edda Ciano, *La mia testimonianza,* 122–5; *Die Tagebucher von Joseph Goebbels* (Munich, 1987), part 1, vol. 2, 621–3, 637; De Felice, *Mussolini il duce,* I, 804–8; idem, *Mussolini il duce,* II, 12–3, 274–83; "Anna Maria Mussolini gravemente inferma," *Corriere della Sera,* June 30, 1936; Prezzolini, *Diario, 1900–1941,* 555; Navarra, *Memorie,* 218–9, 224–47; Monelli, *Mussolini piccolo borghese,* 230–1, 312 ("presidentessa" quote); Curti Cucciati, "Un'amica di Mussolini racconta," *Oggi,* November 24, 1949, 18; MI-DPP, f. "Sarfatti, Margherita," report of September 30, 1936.

3 Weinberg, *The Foreign Policy of Hitler's Germany,* 266–74, 331–7; OHP, The Reminiscences of William Phillips, 113; WPD, entries for April 18, 1934, October 6, 1936; interview with Frank Gervasi, May 5, 1936; John F. Coverdale, *Italian Intervention in the Spanish Civil War* (Princeton, 1975), 66–126; Prezzolini, *Diario, 1900–1941,* 574; Primo Levi, *If Not Now, When?* (New York, 1985), 5; De Felice, *Mussolini il duce,* II, 344–75; OO, XXVIII, 69–70 (quote).

4 "Un busto a Roberto Sarfatti," *Corriere della Sera,* June 30, 1936; "Il busto a Sarfatti inaugurato dall'on. Manaresi," *Corriere della Sera,* July 2, 1936; EPP, MGS to Pound, July (?) 1936; MGS, "Ville e poesia," *La Stampa,* September 11, 1936; idem, "L'architettura e le altre arti," *La Stampa,* November 3, 1936; idem, "La nostra architettura e il nostro tempo," *La Stampa,*

November 28, 1936; idem, "A tu per tu con Michelangelo," *La Stampa,* December 19, 1936; idem, "Fascism and Art," *Atlantica* (New York), January 15, 1937; MMMP, MGS to Meloney, September 1, n.d. but November–December, n.d. but late, 1936, February 6, 1937; ibid., Hurst to Meloney, February 16, 1937; CEP, box 127, MGS to Butler, December 24, 1936, Butler to MGS, January 9, 1937; NMBP, MGS to Butler, n.d. but mid-February 1937, Butler to MGS, February 25, 26, 1937; ACS, MCP, b. 9, f. 127, "Sarfatti, M.," Luciano to MGS, September 25, 1936; FDRP, OF, 233, "Italy, Govt. of, 1933–36," MGS to Roosevelt, November 7, 1936; "Mrs. James A. Kirk," *The New York Times,* November 24, 1936; De Begnac, *Taccuini mussoliniani,* 45, 423, 632; Bottai, *Diario, 1935–1944,* 112.

5 Magalì Sarfatti-Larson interview with Amedeo Sarfatti, October 1985; MI-DPP, f. "Sarfatti, Margherita," reports of January 27, 30, 1937; "Italy's Jews: Loyal Groups Wonder at Mussolini's Attitude Following Nazi Accord," *The Literary Digest,* February 6, 1937; Frank Gervasi, *The Violent Decade* (New York, 1989), 82–3; NA, M1221, OSS, Research and Analysis Reports, report 1213, 3; Meir Michaelis, "Fascist Policy Toward Italian Jews: Tolerance and Persecution," in Ivo Herzer, Klaus Voigt, and James Burgwyn, eds., *The Italian Refuge: Rescue of Jews During the Holocaust* (Washington, 1989), 46–51; idem, *Mussolini and the Jews,* 107–38; OO, XXVIII, 98.

6 Coverdale, *Italian Intervention in the Spanish Civil War,* 175–7, 225–51 (Hemingway quote, 250); OO, XXVIII, 140–53; Whitaker, *We Cannot Escape History,* 54; Ciano, *Diario, 1937–1943,* 115; De Felice, *Mussolini il duce,* II, 404–5.

7 Coverdale, *Italian Intervention in the Spanish Civil War,* 263–75, 392–5; De Felice, *Mussolini il duce,* II, 405–14; Whitaker, *We Cannot Escape History,* 55–7 (quote, 55); OO, XXVIII, 32; Giuseppe Maione, "I costi delle imprese coloniali" in Angelo Del Boca, ed., *Le guerre coloniali del fascismo* (Bari, 1991), 413–7.

8 Gaetano Salvemini, *Carlo and Nello Roselli: A Memoir* (London, 1937), 57–66; Lucio Ceva, "Aspetti politici dell'azione di Carlo Roselli in Spagna," *Atti del convegno di studi nel venticinquesimo anniversario della fondazione della Domus Mazziniana, 1952–1977* (Pisa, 1978); De Felice, *Mussolini il duce,* II, 415, 419–23, 445–6; Michaelis, *Mussolini and the Jews,* 90–3, 100–3, 135–8; "Generoso Pope Returns," *The New York Times,* June 25, 1937.

9 ACS, MCP, b. 9, f. 127, "Sarfatti, M.," note by Luciano, April 2, 1937, Alfieri to Mussolini, April 19, 1937, MGS to Alfieri, April 22, 1937, Alfieri to MGS, May 3, June 8, 1937; NMBP, Prezzolini to MGS, April 19, 1937, Prezzolini to Butler, April 20, May 12, 1937, Butler to Prezzolini, April 21, May 14, 1937; PP, MGS to Prezzolini, n.d. but April–May, June 4, 1937; MMMP, MGS to Meloney, July 4, 1937; MGS, "West o Europa" *Nuova antologia,* February 1, 1937; MGS, "Il gratticielo," *Architettura,* June 1937; ACS, AS/CMM, b. 47, f. 822 (1925–37), MGS to Morgagni, August 16, 1937; Allason, *Memorie di un antifascista,* 213.

10 MGS, *L'America,* 7, 10–2, 152–65, 176–81, 189–200, 210–5, 227, 236–8, 275, 290; Giuseppe Massara, *Viaggiatori in America (1860–1970)* (Rome, 1976), 154–9.

11 Ciano, *Diario, 1937–1943,* 34.

12 De Felice, *Mussolini il duce,* II, 446–7, 911–3; Vittorio Mussolini, *Vita con mio padre,* 79–85; idem, *Mussolini e gli uomini nel suo tempo,* 51–3; "President Greets Mussolini's Son," *The New York Times,* October 12, 1937; FDRP, OF, 233, "Italy, Gov't of, 1937–43," Roosevelt to Hull, August 26, 1937; TLP, box 191, folder 13, "Memorandum of Interview with Duce April 16th 1937," 1; William R. Rock, *Chamberlain and Roosevelt: British Foreign Policy and the United States* (Columbus, 1988), 26–50; OO, XXVIII, 186–7, 223–4; De Begnac, *Taccuini mussoliniani,* 614, 618–9; Bottai, *Diario, 1935–1944,* 120; Ciano, *Diario, 1937–1943,* 40; Pirelli, *Taccuini,* 200 (enemy quote).

13 MMMP, MGS to Meloney, July 4, August 1, n.d. (but September), n.d. (but September–October), October 31, November 30, 1937; Ciano, *Diario, 1937–1943,* 34, 98; MI-DPP, f. "Sarfatti, Margherita," report of August 14, 1937.

14 BBP, MGS to Berenson, June 7, 1937; "Le glorie sabaude nella visione del Carosello di Napoli," *L'Illustrazione Italiana,* June 13, 1937; OO, XXVIII, 193, 197, 245; Michaelis, *Mussolini and the Jews,* 130, 153; Denis Mack Smith, *Italy and Its Monarchy* (New Haven, 1989), 276; OO, XXIX, 30–1; De Begnac, *Taccuini mussoliniani,* 304–5, 322, 324–5, 338;

MMMP, MGS to Meloney, August 1, 1937; MGS "Aria lombarda nel Canton Ticino," *La Stampa,* September 8, 1937; "Intorno al Tintoretto," *La Stampa,* October 26, 1937; "Colonia italiana di Lucerne," *Vaterland,* December 1, 1937; MI-DPP, f. "Sarfatti, Margherita,"report of October 10, 1938; AVI, AG, LVIII, 3,MGS to D'Annunzio, September 23, 1937.

15 OO, 245–53 (Mussolini quote, 253); *Die Tagebucher von Joseph Goebbels,* part I, vol. 3, 280–5; Massimo Magistrati, *L'Italia a Berlin* (Milan, 1956), 65–71; "D'Annunzio on Hand at Verona," *The New York Times,* October 1, 1937; "Hitler's Return Visit Planned," *The New York Times,* October 1, 1937; Rachele Mussolini, *Mussolini: An Intimate Biography,* 141–2; Edda Ciano, *La mia testimonianza,* 142; Vittorio Mussolini, *Vita con mio padre,* 85; Magalì Sarfatti-Larson interview with Amedeo Sarfatti, October 1985; Trapani, "Dovette fuggire dall'Italia," 60 (MGS quote about Mussolini).

16 Michaelis, *Mussolini and the Jews,* 138–40; Rosetta Ricci Crisolini, Maria Teresa Baccherini, Giuseppina Romanini, and Paolo Mancini, "Alcune verità e un poco di logica a proposito dei diari," in Edvige Mussolini, *Mio fratello Benito,* 229–31.

17 "Today on the Radio," *The New York Times,* November 11, 1937; *A Résumé of CBS Broadcasting Activities During 1937* (New York, 1938); 11; Emilio Radius, "Il Premio Letterario Galante 1937 è stato assegnato a Margherita Sarfatti," *Almanacco letterario Bompiani 1938-XVI* (Milan, 1937), xlvii; GSP, MGS to Negri, n.d. but c. December 10, 1937; ACS, MCP, b.9, f. 127, "Sarfatti, Margherita," Alfieri to MGS, December 10, 12, 1937; Rock, *Chamberlain and Roosevelt,* 51–79; Coverdale, *Italian Intervention in the Spanish Civil War,* 306–16; DGFP, series D, vol. I, no. 2, p. 4 ("Jewish actress" quote); OO, XXIX, 32–4; "Mr. Chamberlain and Signor Mussolini," *The Times* (London), November 4, 1937; "Italian Press Annoyed," *The Times,* December 22, 1937; "Italian Press and Britain," *The Times,* December 24, 1937; "British Warn Italy Anew to Halt Propaganda; Laborite Cites Press Orders to Harass Eden," *The New York Times,* December 24, 1937; Sarfatti guest book, 1932–38; Alan Cassels, "Deux empires face à face: la chimère d'un rapprochement anglo-italien (1936–1940)," in *Guerres mondiales e conflits contemporains* (January 1991), 77; David Carlton, *Anthony Eden* (London, 1981), 107–18; De Felice, *Mussolini il duce,* II, 423–53; Ciano, *Diario, 1937–43,* 29–82; DGP, reel 6, frames 20–49; ibid., reel 7, frames 1–52.

18 DGP, reel 6, frames 24, 52–148; Ciano, *Diario, 1937–1943,* 42, 67–8, 82, 95–6, 103–4, 108, 110–3, 116, 149–50; Bottai, *Diario, 1935–1944,* 123–4; MGS, "Passeggiata fra alcuni capolavori," *La Stampa,* November 27, 1937; *Index to the Correspondence of the Foreign Office for the Year 1937* (London, 1969), 26; AOMP, NYTA, McCormick to Sulzberger, March 1, 1938; Holborn, *A History of Modern Germany,* 775–7; De Felice, *Mussolini il duce,* II, 453–61, 467–75; MGS, *Mussolini: Como lo conocí,* X.

While not stated explicitly, the passage in Ciano's diary for March 22, 1938, combined with the section of Margherita's memoirs cited above, makes it clear when she pleaded for Freud's release. It was Mussolini's response to Freud's plight that seems to have saved him. In 1933, Freud had sent a gift to Mussolini, via another of Mussolini's ghostwriters, Giovacchino Forzano. This was an inscribed copy of the book he had written with Albert Einstein, *Why War?.* Freud had written: "With the devoted greeting of an old man, who recognizes the cultural hero in the ruler." Forzano also intervened with Mussolini on Freud's behalf. See Nozzoli, "Margherita Sarfatti," 268–9; De Begnac, *Taccuini mussoliniani,* 392, 646; Peter Gay, *Freud: A Life for Our Time* (New York, 1988), 448, n. 1; Michael Molnar, ed., *The Diary of Sigmund Freud, 1929–1939. A Record of the Final Decade* (New York, 1992), 148, 231.

19 Romke Visser, "Fascist Doctrine and the Cult of the *Romanità,*" *Journal of Contemporary History* (January 1992), 15; OO, XVI, 367–8; Kostof, "The Emperor and the Duce"; MI-DPP, f. "Sarfatti, Margherita," reports of February 8, April 10, 1938; Ciano, *Diario, 1937–1943,* 98, 106–8; Gianfranco Bianchi, *Perchè e come cadde il fascismo: 25 luglio crollo di un regime* (Milan, 1972), 53; OO, XXIX, 494–5; BBP, (late) February 1938; AOMP/NYPL, Kirk to McCormick, March 22, May 28, June 7, 1938; Rock, *Chamberlain and Roosevelt,* 85–6, 95–6 ("gangster" quote, 86); MMMP, MGS to Meloney, Easter 1938; DGP, reel 7, frames 165–8; De Felice, *Mussolini il duce,* II, 461–6.

20 "Mussolini Greets Hitler in a Resplendent Rome; 300,000 Applaud Visitor," *The New York Times*, May 4, 1938; Ciano, *Diario, 1937–1943*, 91, 132–3; Vittorio Mussolini, *Mussolini e gli uomini nel suo tempo*, 73; MI-DPP, f. "Sarfatti, Margherita," report of May 5, 1938; Trapani, "Dovette fuggire dall'Italia," 60; interview with Fiammetta Sarfatti Gaetani, may 16, 1985; BRS personal observations.

21 OO, XXIX, 94–8; Ciano, *Diario, 1937–1943*, 132–4 ("degenerate" quote, Mussolini quote, 134); Bottai, *Diario, 1944–1948*, 510; De Felice, *Mussolini il duce*, II, 479–83; Gervasi, *The Violent Decade*, 120–3; *L'Illustrazione Italiana*, May 15, 1938, photograph, 805.

22 Guerri, *Galeazzo Ciano*, 51, n. 29; ACS, MCP, b. 9, f. 127. "Sarfatti, Margherita," Landini to Luciano, June 14, 1938, Tudisco to Luciano, March 11, 1939; Marzorati, *Margherita Sarfatti*, 184 (English quote); MMMP, MGS to Meloney, July 30, 1938; Michaelis, *Mussolini and the Jews*, 152–3 (Pius XI quote, 152); Bottai, *Diario, 1935–1944*, 136; *Die Tagebucher von Joseph Goebbels*, part I, vol. 3, 482; Vittorio Mussolini, *Mussolini e gli uomini nel suo tempo*, 34; idem, *Vita con mio padre*, 92; NA, M1221, OSS, Research and Analysis Reports, report 2080, 3–4; De Felice, *Mussolini il duce*. II, 14–42, 313–6, 491–2, 866–77.

23 Ciano, *Diario, 1937–1943*, 161; NA, RDS, 811.91265/48, Phillips to Hull, July 26, 1938; Lemuel F. Parton, "Who's News Today: Mussolini's Former Jewish Friend Out of It," *New York Sun*, August 4, 1938; idem, "Who's News Today: Margherita Sarfatti Said Il Duce Was Foe of Tyranny," *New York Sun*, September 3, 1938; G. A. Borgese, "The Rise and Decline of Mussolini," *Life*, October 3, 1938, 43, 62.

24 MGS, "Gobineau," *Nuova Antologia*, September 1, 1922; De Felice, *Mussolini il duce*, II, 287, n. 73; Laura Fermi, *Atoms in the Family: My Life with Enrico Fermi* (Chicago, 1954), 118–20; MMMP, Meloney speech of October 25, 1938 quoting MGS; Vittorio Mussolini, *Mussolini e gli uomini nel suo tempo*, 134.

25 Interview with Fiammetta Sarfatti Gaetani, May 16, 1985; Zuccoli, *Quindici anni*, 36–7; BRS personal observations.

26 Tranfaglia, Murialdi, Legnani, *La stampa italiana nell'età fascista*, 206; Marzorati, *Margherita Sarfatti*, 183–4; Dante Alighieri, *The Divine Comedy*, translated, with a commentary by Charles S. Singleton, *Purgatorio*, 1: *Italian Text and Translation* (Princeton, 1973), 354–5 [translation transposed]; MI-DPP, f. "Sarfatti, Margherita," reports of September 16, October 10, 1938; Bottai, *Diario, 1935–1944*, 134; Pini, *Filo diretto con Palazzo Venezia*, 223.

27 Holborn, *A History of Modern Germany*, 779–82; Ciano, *Diario, 1937–1943*, 160, 166–89; Williamson Murray, *The Change in the European Balance of Power: The Path to Ruin* (Princeton, 1984), 195–215; Donatella Bolech Cecchi, "Un colpo di stato antifascista di Maria Josè nel settembre 1938?," *Il Politico*, December 1979; *The Divine Comedy*, idem, *Paradiso*, 1:Italian Text and Translation (Princeton, 1975), 216–7; Marzorati, *Margherita Sarfatti*, 184; De Felice, *Mussolini il duce*, II, 507–32.

Sarfatti may not have known of the royal plot against Mussolini prior to the Munich conference. But she seems to have been aware of deep dissatisfaction within the House of Savoy and elements of the Italian Army leadership over Mussolini's acquiescence to the *Anschluss*. Sarfatti had been visited by Crown Princess Maria Josè and Marshal Rodolfo Graziani on March 28. (Graziani was disaffected at the time, believing that he had been dismissed unfairly as Viceroy of Ethiopia by Mussolini.) What the three discussed that day is unknown, but the meeting suggests part of a conspiracy. Graziani, his wife and daughter were frequent visitors to Margherita's house throughout 1938. Sarfatti guest book, 1936–38; ACS, *Carte Graziani*, Graziani to Duke of Aosta, December 31, 1937, Mussolini to Duke of Aosta, January 1, 1938; Ciano, *Diario, 1937–43*, 105; Alessandro Cova, *Graziani: Un generale per il regime* (Rome, 1987), 193–202.

28 Ciano, *Diario, 1937–1943*, 189, 193 (Mussolini quote, 193); Bottai, *Diario, 1935–1944*, 135–7; Tranfaglia, Murialdi, and Legnani, *La stampa italiana nell'età fascista*, 206–9 (quote, 207); De Felice, *Mussolini il duce*, II, 494–500, 914–7; Guspini, *L'orecchio del regime*, 156–7; Edvige Mussolini, *Mio fratello Benito*, 175; *Le leggi e i decreti reali secondo l'ordine della inserzione nella Gazzetta ufficiale: Anno 1938–XVI* (Rome, 1939), 1261; De Grazia, *How Fascism Ruled*

Women, 166; De Felice, *Mussolini il duce.* II, 78–82; GSP, MGS to Negri, November 18, 1938.

Bottai's anti-Semitic outburst at the Grand Council meeting seems to have been both self-protection and a means of advancing his career. Hitler was convinced that Bottai was a Jew. As a result, the Führer had delayed the signing of an Italian-German cultural agreement that meant a great deal to both Mussolini and Bottai. In late November 1938, however, Hitler relented and the agreement was concluded. See DGFP, series D, vol. IV, no. 402; Jens Petersen, "L'accordo culturale fra l'Italia e la Germania del 23 novembre 1938," in K. D. Bracher and Leo Valiani, eds., *Fascismo e nazionalsocialismo* (Bologna, 1986).

29 Stille, *Benevolence and Betrayal,* 77; *Le leggi,* 1377–9; De Felice, *Mussolini il duce.* II, 498; Marzorati, *Margherita Sarfatti,* 89, 187–8; Tranfaglia, Murialdi, and Legnani, *La stampa italiana nell'età fascista,* 208, n. 39; Mario Missori, *Gerarchie e statuti del P.N.F.* (Rome, 1986), 413; Staglieno, "Margherita Sarfatti"; Trapani, "Dovette fuggire dall'Italia," 60; interview with Fiammetta Sarfatti Gaetani, July 10, 1985; MGS, *Mussolini: Como lo conocí,* XIV.

CHAPTER 30: PURGED GHOST

1 Merrill Mueller, "Duce's Non-Aryan Aide Denies She's in Exile," *New York Mirror,* December 31, 1938; "Purged Ghost," *Time,* January 9, 1939.

2 Police reports dated September 16, October 10, 1938, and January 30, 1939, ACS, MI-DPP, "Sarfatti, Margherita"; MGS to Nicholas Murray Butler, letter received January 27, 1939, NMBP; Fiammetta Sarfatti Gaetani to PVC, November 27, 1985.

3 Police reports of December 28 and 29, 1938, January 6, 1939; letters of inquiry to four agents dated January 17–18, 1939; reports dated January 20, 23, 25, 26, 29, 1939; police chief Arturo Bocchini to questura of Milan, January 22, 1939, all in ACS, MI-DPP, "Sarfatti, Margherita"; ACS, MCP, b. 9, f. 127, "Sarfatti, Margherita," memo of January 9, 1939.

4 Sarfatti's letters to friends such as Nicholas Murray Butler and Marie Mattingly Meloney, written on Hotel Lotti stationary, begin on November 28, 1938; in a letter to Butler dated March 29, 1939, she gave her permanent address as the Hotel St. James, but continued to receive mail and packages at the Lotti until mid-May 1939. See also ACS, MCP, b. 9, f. 127, "Sarfatti, Margherita," memo dated May 20, 1939.

5 Marzorati, *Margherita Sarfatti,* 198–201.

6 MGS to Butler, November 28, 1938, NMBP.

7 MGS to Butler, received January 27, 1939, NMBP.

8 MGS to Gertrude Smith (Meloney's secretary), December 22, 1938, Meloney to Butler, January 30, 1939, Abby Rockefeller to Meloney, February 1, 1939, NMBP.

9 MGS to Butler, n.d. (but approximately December 20, 1938), n.d. (but January 1939), and letter received January 27, 1939, NMBP.

10 MGS to Meloney, December [?] and 20, 1938, MMMP; Butler to MGS, December 12, 1938, NMBP; Butler to Ada Louise Comstock and other college presidents, December 13, 1938, CEP, box 127, 34481; Prezzolini, *Diario, 1900–1941,* 616, entry for January 12, 1939; Butler to MGS, December 30, 1938, January 13, 16, 27, and April 11, 1939, NMBP.

11 Police reports dated February 3, 20, May 11, July 11, October 14, 1939; memos to police agent dated January 26 and February 14, 1939; two reports dated December 28, together with an open letter by anti-Fascists in New York, all in ACS, MI-DPP, "Sarfatti, Margherita;" "L'exilée," *Aux Ecoutes,* January 7, 1939, 9.

12 Marzorati, *Margherita Sarfatti,* 190; police reports dated January 18 and February 24, 1939, ACS, MI-DPP, "Sarfatti, Margherita."

13 MGS to Butler, n.d. (but approximately December 20, 1938), NMBP.

14 Police reports dated January 22, 30, February 28, 1939, ACS, MI-DPP, "Sarfatti, Margherita"; Alma Mahler, Diary, entry for January 24, 1939, MWC; Mahler-Werfel, *Mein Leben,* 286–7; Monson, *Alma Mahler,* 259; MGS, "Menues Légendes Pontificales"; idem,

"Amedeo Modigliani," *L'Univers Israélite* (Paris), June 23, 1939; Tullia Zevi, "L'emigrazione razziale," in Antonio Varsori, ed., *L'Antifascismo italiano negli Stati Uniti durante la seconda guerra mondiale* (Rome, 1984), 77–8.

15 Marzorati, *Margherita Sarfatti,* 161, 188; Fiammetta Sarfatti to Negri, March 13, [1939], GSP; Cerruti, *Ambassador's Wife,* 225–6; MGS, "F. Chiesa," February 1, "Leonardo," April 24, "Una passeggiata dentro un quadro," May 25; "Quattrocento anni fa," June 10; "L'universalità dell'arte," July 25; "Il gran vecchio Tiziano," August 22, 1939, all in *Il Corriere del Ticino;* report dated June 14, 1939, ACS, MCP, b. 9, f. 127, "Sarfatti, Margherita;" MGS to McCormick, May 22, 1939, AOMP, NYPL, box 1; MGS to Butler, July 3, 1939, and Butler to MGS, July 11, 1939, NMBP.

16 Interview with Amedeo and Pierangela Sarfatti, May 24, 1985; Paolo Vita-Finzi, *Giorni lontani: Appunti e ricordi* (Bologna, 1989), 397.

17 MGS to Breckinridge Long, March 28, 1939, BLP, box 128; Long to MGS, telegram and letter, both April 11, 1939, and letter of May 15, 1939, BLP, box 128; diary, 1935–36, entries for April 11, 26, 1939, BLP, box 4; Feingold, *The Politics of Rescue,* 137–8; MGS to Butler, March 29, 1939, NMBP; ACS, MCP, b. 9, f. 127, "Sarfatti, Margherita," memo dated March 11, 1939.

18 Marzorati, *Margherita Sarfatti,* 188, 199.

19 De Felice, *Mussolini il duce,* II, 618–25; Mario Toscano, *The Origins of the Pact of Steel* (Baltimore, 1967), 307–70; Elizabeth Wiskemann, *The Rome-Berlin Axis* (New York, 1949), 130–50; Brian R. Sullivan, "The Impatient Cat: Assessments of Military Power in Fascist Italy, 1936–1940," in Williamson Murray and Allan R. Millett, eds., *Calculations: Net Assessment and the Coming of World War II* (New York, 1992), 112–13.

20 ACS, MCP, b. 9, f. 127, "Sarfatti, Margherita," memo dated May 22, 1939.

21 Amedeo Landini to Celso Luciano, November 7, 1939, report 15A, document 62, Documents found in the Ministry of Popular Culture, Rome, NA; Trapani, "Dovette fuggire dall'Italia," 65; Marzorati, *Margherita Sarfatti,* 190–1; police report dated November 29, 1939, ACS, MI-DPP, "Sarfatti, Margherita."

22 ACS, MCP, b. 9, f. 127, "Sarfatti, Margherita," MGS to Alfieri, with cover letter from Guariglia dated June 9, 1939.

23 ACS, MCP, b. 9, f. 127, "Sarfatti, Margherita," Alfieri to MGS, June 14, 1939, and MGS to Alfieri, June 22, 1939; Alfieri recorded Mussolini's comment—"questa nicchia"—as a marginal notation on the latter on July 2.

24 ACS, MCP, b. 9, f. 127, "Sarfatti, Margherita," Alfieri to MGS (copy), August 24, 1939, Guariglia to Foreign Ministry, August 26, 1939 (with Mussolini's marginal notation of approval), and Alfieri to Guariglia, August 27, 1939; Trapani, "Dovette fuggire dall'Italia," 65.

25 Interview with Fiammetta Sarfatti Gaetani, May 16, 1985; Trapani, "Dovette fuggire dall'-Italia," 65; Marzorati, *Margherita Sarfatti,* 201.

26 Interviews with Amedeo and Pierangela Sarfatti, May 24, 1985, between Magalì Sarfatti-Larson and Amedeo and Pierangela Sarfatti, October 1985, and with Magalì Sarfatti-Larson, December 11, 1986; MGS to Butler, October 25 and December 1, 1939, and Butler to MGS, November 15, 1939, NMBP.

27 MGS to Negri, December 20, 1939, and March 8, 1940, GSP.

28 MGS to Negri, March 8, 1940, GSP; Philip C. Jessup to Butler, August 13, 1941, NMBP, "Jessup, Philip C."; Orlando and Merwin, *Confessions of a Scoundrel,* 69; interview with Magalì Sarfatti-Larson, December 11, 1986.

29 MGS to Butler, June 10, 1940, NMBP.

30 MGS to Long, letter received May 29, 1939, letter dated May 22, 1939, letter dated July 24, 1940, BLP, box 128; memorandum dated June 28, 1940, RDS, RG59, 1940–1944, file n. 811.111, "Sarfatti, Margherita"; MGS to Butler, June 10, 1940, NMBP; interview with Amedeo and Pierangela Sarfatti, May 24, 1985; FBI, file n. 100-4579-1, "Sarfatti, Margherita,"memos dated October 30, November 1, November 22, December 2, 1940, Hoover to Berle, November 2, 1940.

31 MGS to Butler, September 26, 1940, NMBP; report from Serena di Lapigio dated October 2, 1940, together with MGS to Serena, August 28, 1940, and MGS to director of *Noticias,* August 28, 1940, in ACS, MCP, b. 9, f. 127, "Sarfatti, Margherita."

32 MGS, *Mussolini: El hombre y el duce,* trans. Luis Horno Liria and Carlos Alvarez Pena, intro. by Ernesto Giménez Caballero (Buenos Aires, 1940); Mario C. Nascimbene, "Storia della collettività italiana in Argentina," in *La popolazione di origine italiana in Argentina* (Turin, 1987), 448–55; Victoria Ocampo, *Autobiografia* (Buenos Aires, 1984); Diego A. De Santillán, *Gran enciclopedia argentina,* VI (Buenos Aires, 1960), 21; MGS to Butler, August 12, 1941, NMBP; Serena di Lapigio to Alfieri, October 2, 1940, ACS, MCP, b. 9, f. 127, "Sarfatti, Margherita"; interview with Amedeo and Pierangela Sarfatti, May 24, 1985; interview with Magalì Sarfatti-Larson, June 16, 1986.

33 Interviews with Fiammetta Gaetani d'Aragona, May 13, 1985, Amedeo and Pierangela Sarfatti, May 24, 1985, and Magalì Sarfatti-Larson, June 16, 1986; oral reminiscences of José Luis Romero, recorded July 12, 1971, OHP, Argentina Project; MGS to Butler, August 31, 1942, NMBP; MGS, "Retonos criollos," *El Diario,* November 27, 1941, reprinted in *Bulletin of the Pan American Union* (December 1942), 690; interview with Magalì Sarfatti-Larson, May 2, 1991; MGS, *Así veo yo el Uruguay* (Montevideo, 1941); Mario Gastaldi and Carmen Scano, *Dizionario delle scrittrici italiane contemporanee* (Milan, 1957), 178; Marzorati, *Margherita Sarfatti,* 202–3; Vita-Finzi, *Giorni lontani,* 396–7.

34 Interviews with Fiammetta Gaetani d'Aragona, May 13, 1985, and Amedeo and Pierangela Sarfatti, May 24, 1985; MGS to Butler, March 30, 1943, NMBP; MGS, *Casanova; Amores de juventud* (Buenos Aires, 1943); idem., *Giorgione, el pintor misterio* (Buenos Aires, 1944); idem, *Tiziano, o de la fè en la vida* (Buenos Aires, 1945); idem, *Espejo de la pintura actual* (Buenos Aires, 1947); idem, *Vasari y sus tiempos* (Buenos Aires, 1947); Giuseppe Valentini to Pavolini, November 7, 1940, and Pavolini to Valentini (telegram), ACS, MCP, b. 9, f. 127, "Sarfatti, Margherita."

35 MGS to Butler, June 12, 1942, NMBP; Joseph S. Tulchin, "The Origins of Misunderstanding: United States-Argentine Relations, 1900–1940," in Guido di Tella and D. Cameron Watt, eds., *Argentina Between the Great Powers, 1939–1946* (Pittsburgh, 1990), 49–50; Nicholas Fraser and Marysa Navarro, *Eva Perón* (New York, 1980), esp. 28–87.

36 MGS to Negri, November 6, 1941, GSP; MGS to Butler, October 30, 1941, Butler to MGS, January 2, 1942, NMBP; Fiammetta Sarfatti Gaetani to Ada Negri, March 13, [1942], GSP; J. Edgar Hoover to Department of State, February 9, 1943, FBI, file n. 100-4579-1, "Sarfatti, Margherita;" interview with Amedeo and Pierangela Sarfatti, May 24, 1985.

37 MGS to Butler, December 20, 1941, NMBP

38 "Et Tu, Benito," *Time,* March 16, 1942.

39 Inez Robb, "She Could Tell Mussolini 'I Told You So,' " *Evening Bulletin,* November 26, 1942.

40 Benito Mussolini, *The Fall of Mussolini: His Own Story,* trans. Frances Frenaye (Westport, 1975), 66. On the events preceding, during, and immediately after the Grand Council meeting, see F. W. Deakin, *The Brutal Friendship: Mussolini, Hitler and the Fall of Italian Fascism* (New York, 1962); Renzo De Felice, *Mussolini l'alleato, 1940–1945,* I, esp. 959–1410; Bianchi, *Perchè e come cadde il fascismo;* Dino Grandi, *25 luglio. Quarant'anni dopo,* ed. Renzo De Felice (Bologna, 1983).

41 "Margherita Sarfatti Pleased," *The New York Times,* July 27, 1943; "Pleased Il Duce Is Out," *New York Journal American,* July 27, 1943; MGS to Butler, August 25, 1943, NMBP.

42 J. Edgar Hoover to U.S. embassy, Montevideo, February 9, 1943, and memorandum of May 6, 1943; Westbrook Pegler, "Fair Enough," *Washington Daily News,* August 24, 1943; memorandum of October 29, 1943, "Margherita G. De [sic] Sarfatti, Argentina Espionage," and Hoover to U.S. embassy, November 4, 1943, all in FBI, file n. 100-4579-1, "Sarfatti, Margherita."

43 MGS to Butler, August 25, and Butler to MGS, September 10, 1943; Butler to Charles G. Proffitt, September 10, and Proffitt to Butler, September 16, 1943, "Proffitt, Charles G."; Butler to Scribner's, September 10, Charles Scribner's Sons to Butler, September 14,

"Scribner's Sons" (folder 4), all in NMBP; Charles Scribner's Sons to MGS, September 14, 1943, CSSA, General Files (Perkins/Wheelock), box 24.

44 Interview with Pierangela Sarfatti, October 12, 1989.

45 MGS to Charles Scribner's Sons, September 24, 1943, and Scribner's Sons to MGS, October 19, 1943, CSSA, General Files (Perkins/Wheelock), box 24; Trapani, "Dovette fuggire dall'Italia," 66; Marzorati, *Margherita Sarfatti*, 89; interview with Pierangela Sarfatti, October 12, 1989; Susan Zuccotti, *The Italians and the Holocaust: Persecution, Rescue, Survival* (New York, 1987), 101–138.

46 MGS to Butler, October 26, 1943, and Butler to MGS, November 8, 1943, NMBP; MGS to Fiammetta Sarfatti Gaetani, July 1944 and January 25, 1945, both quoted in Marzorati, *Margherita Sarfatti*, 205–6; Alexander Kirk to Breckinridge Long, January 10, 1945, BLP, box 158; Naval Intelligence report, August 8, 1944, FBI, file n. 100-4579-1, "Sarfatti, Margherita"; interview with Fiammetta Sarfatti Gaetani, May 16, 1985; Marzorati, *Margherita Sarfatti*, 21, 24; interview with Piero Foà, July 27, 1987.

47 MGS to Long, April 27, 1945, BLP, box 128.

48 Pini and Susmel, *Mussolini*, IV, 487; Mussolini quoted in Kirkpatrick, *Mussolini*, 659.

49 Gianfranco Bianchi and Fernando Mezzetti, *Mussolini: Aprile '45: L'Epilogo* (Milan, 1979), 154.

50 Mussolini to Rachele Mussolini, April 26, 1945, oo, XXXII, 213.

51 *Le Opere di Dante* (Florence, 1921), seen during interview with Fiammetta Sarfatti Gaetani, May 16, 1985. In the margin, she added in her own hand a Latin quotation about the end of mad dictators; see also Marzorati, *Margherita Sarfatti*, 184.

52 "Los artículos de Margherita Sarfatti son un fiel reflejo de la vida de Mussolini," *Crítica*, June 17, 1945. The articles themselves, titled "Mussolini: Como lo conocí," appeared June 18, July 3, 1945; see also "Current Notes on the Argentine Press," June 27, 1945, RDS, RG59, 835.911/6-2745.

53 Albano Corneli, "Una 'signora' a spasso per i marcia piedi di Sudamerica," appeared in *L'Italia del Popolo* on June 27, July 8, 14, 29, and August 5, 10, 1945; New York *Journal American*, July 22, 1946.

54 Alexander Kirk to Breckinridge Long, January 10, 1945, BLP, box 158; MGS to Butler, June 18 and September 11, 1946, and Butler to MGS, September 24, 1946, CEP, box 127; Marzorati, *Margherita Sarfatti*, 207.

55 "Margherita Sarfatti in cerca dell' 'uomo nuovo,'" *Ricostruzione*, June 15, 1945.

56 Interview with Piero Foà, July 27, 1987.

57 MGS to Charles and Marie de Chambrun, March 6, 1947, DCP.

CHAPTER 31: HOME AGAIN

1 Enrico Roda, "L'uomo in bombetta non visita più Margherita," *Oggi*, September 7, 1947, 9; Magalì Sarfatti-Larson interview with Amedeo Sarfatti, October 1985.

2 Interviews with Magalì Sarfatti-Larson, May 21, 1990, and May 2, 1991; Roda, "L'uomo in bombetta non visita più Margherita," 10.

3 Roda, "L'uomo in bombetta non visita più Margherita," 9–10; interviews with Magalì Sarfatti-Larson, September 28, 1985, May 21, 1990, and May 2, 1991.

4 Interview with Magalì Sarfatti-Larson, September 28, 1985; Roda, "L'uomo in bombetta non visita più Margherita," 9–10.

5 Pietro Nenni, *Tempo di guerra fredda: Diari, 1943–1956*, ed. G. Nenni and D. Zucàro (Milan, 1981), 383–4.

6 MGS to Bernard Berenson, September 14, 1947, BBP.

7 Interviews with Fiammetta Sarfatti Gaetani, July 10 and October 7, 1985, and with Magalì Sarfatti-Larson, May 2, 1991.

8 MGS to Bernard Berenson, January 6, 1948, BBP; Marcello Staglieno, Margherita Sarfatti ; interviews with Fiammetta Sarfatti Gaetani, July 10, 1985, and with Amedeo and Pierangela Sarfatti, May 24, 1985; MGS to Berenson, July 20, 1951, BBP.

9 Marcia E. Vetrocq, "National Style and the Agenda for Abstract Painting in Post-war Italy," *Art History* (December 1989), 454–5; Giorgio De Marchis, "L'arte in Italia dopo la seconda guerra mondiale," in Zeri, *Storia dell'arte italiana*, Part II, Vol. 3, 567–71.

10 *The Memoirs of Giorgio de Chirico,* trans. Margaret Crosland (London, 1971), 184–5.

11 Interview with Magalì Sarfatti-Larson, September 28, 1985; Marzorati, *Margherita Sarfatti,* 162, recounts a similar incident in the 1950s.

12 Interview with Fiammetta Sarfatti Gaetani, July 10, 1985.

13 Interview with Fiammetta Sarfatti Gaetani, July 10, 1985; MGS to Berenson, March 6, 1953, BBP.

14 See photographs of MGS with Levi, Bontempelli, and Magnani, dated January 31, 1949; Giovanni Papini, *Scritti postumi,* II: *Pagine di diario e di appunti* (Verona, 1968), 568; MGS to Papini, October 26, 1948, AGP; "Il romanziere Aldo Palazzeschi insieme a Margherita Sarfatti," *Oggi,* February 17, 1949; Giovanni Comisso to Lino Mazzolà, May 19, 1947, in Comisso, *Trecento lettere,* 130; Sarfatti's correspondence with Biddle is in BP; Fourcade's correspondence with her is in MSLP.

15 Interview with Magalì Sarfatti-Larson, June 16, 1986.

16 Clough, *The Economic History of Modern Italy,* 283, 291–7; interview with Pierangela Sarfatti, October 12, 1989.

17 Art Buchwald to BRS, November 5, 1986; on Orlando's career see Dotson Rader, "Guido Orlando: Cosa Sua," *Esquire* (January 1971), 135–37, 169, 171, 173–4; David Shaw, "Pace Setter in the Publicity Game," *Los Angeles Times,* March 22, 1972; Alfonso A. Narvaez, "Guido Orlando, 80, Press Agent Who Devised Outlandish Stunts," *The New York Times,* May 28, 1988; Burt A. Folkart, "Legendary Publicist Guido Orlando, 80," *Los Angeles Times,* May 26, 1988.

18 Eightieth Congress, First Session, *Hearings before a Special Committee Investigating the National Defense Program,* part 40, *Aircraft Contracts (Hughes Aircraft Co. and Kaiser-Hughes Corp.)* (Washington, 1947), 24070; "Summoned by Inquiry Counsel," *New York Sun,* August 2, 1947; "Says Birdwell, Ex-Aide of Hughes, Ruled Elliott," *New York Mirror,* August 4, 1947; HSTP, PSF, National Security Council Meetings, Box 23, Minutes of the 7th Meeting of the National Security Council, March 11, 1948. Orlando has left four versions of the meeting with Sarfatti and their negotiations, each presenting slightly different details: Guido Orlando, *Le faiseur de gloires,* trans. Michel Chrestien (Paris, 1953), 186–7; Orlando and Merwin, *Confessions of a Scoundrel,* 68–70; Ronald Handyside, *Never Sleep with a Client* (London, 1964), 73–4; unpublished typescript by Guido Orlando and Jack Matcha, *"Trouble Shooter in Paradise,"* 149–50, GOP.

A copy of the contract between Orlando and Sarfatti, dated March 8, 1948, is in GOP.

19 Guido Orlando to MGS, May 12, 1948, GOP.

20 Thomas H. Beck to Vincent Giordano, August 25, 1948, GOP.

Who's Who in America, 1954–55 (Chicago, 1955), 2437; "Report Duchess of Windsor Plans Plastic Operation Here," *New York World Telegram,* July 31, 1940; "Lupescu's Face Lifted in Mexico by N.Y. Doctor," *New York Herald Tribune,* March 29, 1944; Orlando and Merwin, *Confessions of a Scoundrel,* 70–71; Handyside, *Never Sleep with a Client,* 74–5; Orlando and Matcha, *"Trouble Shooter,"* 151.

Ken McCormick to Stuart Gilbert, November 7, 1948, GOP.

21 MGS to Guido Orlando, October 19, 1948, GOP.

22 Letter of agreement signed by I. Daniel Shorell, New York City, November 8, 1948, GOP.

23 Orlando and Merwin, *Confessions of a Scoundrel,* 70–1; Handyside, *Never Sleep with a Client,* 74–5; Orlando and Matcha, *Trouble Shooter,* 151.

24 Letter of agreement signed by I. Daniel Shorell, December 16, 1948; Orlando and Merwin, *Confessions of a Scoundrel,* 72; Handyside, *Never Sleep with a Client,* 75; Orlando and Matcha, "Trouble Shooter," 151–2; Orlando, *Le faiseur de gloires,* 1989.

25 Orlando and Merwin, *Confessions of a Scoundrel,* 72; Handyside, *Never Sleep with a Client,* 75–6; Orlando and Matcha, "Trouble Shooter," 152; Renzo Trionfera, "Margherita e Benito: Bacia le lettere di Mussolini e le vende all'America," *L'Europeo,* December 12, 1948.

26 "Una borsa che vale un miliardo contiene lettere di Mussolini portate in aereo a Londra," *Il Corriere della Sera,* November 28, 1948; "Cholly Knickerbocker Observes," *New York Journal American,* December 1, 1948; "La Sarfatti vende in America le lettere d'amore di Mussolini," *Il Nuovo Corriere* (Florence), December 3, 1948; "La Sarfatti ha venduto le lettere di Mussolini," *Corriere d'Informazione,* December 3, 1948; "L'ultimo bacio," *Vie Nuove* (Rome), December 12, 1948; "Letters from Benito," *New York Herald Tribune,* February 27, 1949.

 Letter of agreement signed by I. Daniel Shorell, December 16, 1948, GOP; Orlando and Merwin, *Confessions of a Scoundrel,* 73; Handyside, *Never Sleep with a Client,* 77; Orlando and Matcha, "Trouble Shooter," 153.

27 Fiammetta Sarfatti Gaetani to PVC, September 24, 1986; Orlando and Merwin, *Confessions of a Scoundrel,* 73; Handyside, *Never Sleep with a Client,* 77; Orlando and Matcha, *Trouble Shooter,* 153; Cholly Knickerbocker, "Smart Set," *New York Journal American,* April 26, 1953; Vittorio Foschini, "La Sarfatti non saluta il 're della pubblicità,' " *La Notte* (Milan), May 21, 1953; MGS to Bernard Berenson, January 10, 1949, and January 6, 1954, BBP; MGS to James T. Soby, July 21, 1949, MoMA, Soby Papers, File 22B; Soby and Barr, Jr., *Twentieth-Century Italian Art,* 128, 134; interview with Fiammetta Sarfatti Gaetani, May 16, 1985.

28 Igor Cassini to Guido Orlando, December 3, 1952, GOP; interview with Frank Gervasi, May 5, 1986.

29 Biddle diary, entries for December 27 and 29, 1951, BP.

30 Biddle diary, entries for December 21–31, 1951, BP.

31 Biddle diary, entry for February 7, 1952, BP; MGS to Berenson, March 12, 1952, BBP; Berenson, *Sunset and Twilight,* entry for November 11, 1952, 283.

32 MGS to Berenson, October 7, 1952, BBP; MGS to George and Helene Biddle, December 21, 1954, BP; MGS, *Acqua passata.*

33 MGS to Berenson, December 1, 1950, BBP; MGS to Helene Biddle, June 26, 1956, BP; MGS to Berenson, March 30, 1957, BBP.

34 MGS to Berenson, April 5, 1951, and October 9, 1951, BBP.

35 Interview with Magalì Sarfatti-Larson, June 16, 1986; Biddle diary, entry for May 25, 1952, BP.

36 MGS, unpublished manuscript titled "Divenire o essere?," n.d. but mid-1950s, author's possession; idem, *Acqua passata,* 208; idem, *Casanova contro Don Giovanni* (Verona, 1950), 136–7; interview with Magalì Sarfatti-Larson, June 16, 1986.

37 Interview with Magalì Sarfatti-Larson, May 2, 1991; MGS to Helene Biddle, June 26, 1956, BP; MGS, "Valori plastici o decorazione?," clipping from unknown newspaper attached to letter dated Ferragosto 1952 to Berenson, BBP; idem, "Il divorzio tra le arti e il pubblico," *Giornale di Roma,* October 12, 1957; MGS to Berenson, July 28, 1952, BBP; see also MGS to the Biddles, February 2, 1958, BP, and to Berenson, October 29, 1951, and July 24, 1957, BBP. Sarfatti wrote for *Scena Illustrata* from January 1951 to June 1953.

38 Biddle diary, entry for March 17, 1952, BP; MGS, "Il movimento artistico del Novecento Italiano," *Scena Illustrata* (January 1953), 14–15; interview with Magalì Sarfatti-Larson, May 31, 1991.

39 MGS to Helene Biddle, January 18, 1953, BP; MGS to Berenson, August 14, 1957, BBP.

40 Interview with Magalì Sarfatti-Larson, May 2, 1991; MGS to Berenson, Ferragosto [August 1], 1952, BBP; telephone interview with Tita Brown-Castellanos, December 9, 1986.

41 MGS to George and Helene Biddle, January 24 and June 26, 1956, BP; MGS to Berenson, February 9, 1956, BBP; MGS to Berenson, undated letter beginning "Darling: have not heard from you for ever so long," BBP; Marzorati, *Margherita Sarfatti,* 214; Carla Porta Musa, "Il Soldo e Margherita Sarfatti," *Il Foglietto,* February 7, 1957.

42 MGS, "Vacanze e affresco: E chi dice meglio?," *Como* (Winter 1958), 27–9; idem, "Antonio Sant'Elia: Architetto comasco," *Como* (Fall 1959), 32–4; interview with Magalì Sarfatti-Larson, September 28, 1985; interview with Dr. Piero Foà, July 26, 1987; MGS to Berenson, September 23, 1954, BBP; Musa, "Il Soldo e Margherita Sarfatti"; MGS, *L'amore svalutato* (Rome, 1958); MGS to Xavier Fourcade, July 29, 1960, MSLP.

43 Interviews with Magalì Sarfatti-Larson, June 16, 1986, and May 2, 1991; MGS to Xavier

Fourcade, n.d. but spring 1960, headed "Cher Xavier" and written on Hotel Ambasciatori stationery, MSLP; Gregory Alegi to BRS, April 8, 1991.

44 Peter Selz to Umberto Appolonio, July 17, 1960, and attached list of paintings from Appolonio, in MoMA, "1961 Futurist Exhibit," General Correspondence; Marcia E. Vetrocq to PVC, September 24, 1990; H. Stuart Hughes to BRS, September 5, 1986.

45 MGS to Magalì Sarfatti-Larson, April 10, 1953, and January 15, 1961, MSLP; interviews with Magalì Sarfatti-Larson, September 28, 1985, and June 16, 1986.

46 Interviews with Magalì Sarfatti-Larson, June 16, 1986, and May 31, 1991; Marzorati, *Margherita Sarfatti*, 219–20; *The Divine Comedy*, Singleton, ed., *Purgatorio*, 272–3; Dante Alighieri, *Il Convivio*, G. Busnelli and G. Vandelli, eds. (Florence, 1964), Part II, 352; MGS as quoted in Carla Porta Musa, "L'ultimo giorno di Margherita Sarfatti," *Como* (Spring 1962), 67.

47 Staglieno, "Margherita Sarfatti."

48 De Felice, *Intervista sul fascismo*, 12; interview with Renzo De Felice, October 6, 1985.

49 MGS, "Andrea Mantegna a Mantova," *Como* (Spring 1962), 37–41; idem, "Ma sono scoperte?," published in *Como* (Winter 1961), 50–1; MGS to Berenson, May 25, 1953, BBP; Musa, "L'ultimo giorno di Margherita Sarfatti," now also in idem, *Itinerari e incontri* (Como, 1982).

Select Bibliography

The most important source used in writing this biography was the large body of published work written by Margherita Sarfatti herself. In addition to her books, which are cited below, Sarfatti wrote thousands of articles for scores of newspapers and journals, both Italian and foreign. Many of them are cited in the notes.

The following bibliography lists the major published works upon which this biography is based. For archival sources or additional information on a particular subject, readers should consult the relevant notes.

ALVARO, CORRADO. *Quasi una vita: Giornale di uno scrittore*. Milan, 1951.
"A Parigi durante la guerra (Nostra intervista con Margherita G. Sarfatti)." *Il Lavoro* (April 1, 1915).
BARUFFI, PIO. *Alla cara memoria dell'Avvocato Cav. Marco Grassini*. Venice, 1885.
BASSI, GIUSEPPE. "Emma Levi-Grassini." *Il Corriere Israelitico* (Trieste) (August 31, 1900).
BENZI, FABIO, AND ANDREA SIRONI. *Sironi illustratore*. Rome, 1988.
BORATTO, ERCOLE. "Parla Boratto, autista di Mussolini." *Giornale del Mattino* (March 25–April 11, 1946).
   Articles cited:
   "Avventure di lestofanti." March 28, 1946.
   "Esercizi spirituali per la marcia su Roma." March 29, 1946.
   "Liquidazione dell'amica matura." March 31, 1946.
   "Collazione per due a Castel Porziano." April 2, 1946.
   "Un'enciclia non vale una telefonata." April 3, 1946.
BORGESE, GIUSEPPE A. *Goliath: The March of Fascism*. New York, 1937.
BOSI MARAMOTTI, GIOVANNA. "Margherita Sarfatti: Appunti per una storia della letteratura femminile nel periodo fascista," in Bruno Bandini, ed. *Il pensiero reazionario: La politica e la cultura dei fascismi*. Ravenna, 1982.
BOSSAGLIA, ROSSANA. *Il Novecento Italiano*. Milan, 1979.
———. "Margherita Sarfatti, critica d'arte," in A. Gigli Marchetti and N. Torcellan, eds. *Donna lombarda, 1860–1945*. Milan, 1992.
BOTTAI, GIUSEPPE. *Diario, 1935–1944*. Milan, 1982.
———. *Diario, 1944–1948*. Milan, 1988.
BRAUN, EMILY. *Mario Sironi, 1919–1945: Art and Politics in Fascist Italy*. Ph.D. dissertation, Institute of Fine Arts, 1991.
CANNISTRARO, PHILIP V. *La fabbrica del consenso: Fascismo e mass media*. Rome-Bari, 1975.
———. ed. *Historical Dictionary of Fascist Italy*. Westport, Conn. 1982.
CALVESI, MAURIZIO, AND ESTER COEN. *Boccioni: L'opera completa*. Milan, 1982.
CARRÀ, MASSIMO, AND VITTORIO FAGONE, eds. *Carlo Carrà–Ardengo Soffici: Lettere, 1913–1929*. Milan, 1983.

CIANO, GALEAZZO. *Diario, 1937–1943.* Milan, 1980.

CIUCCI, GIORGIO. *Gli architetti e il fascismo.* Turin, 1989.

COEN, ESTER. "Una vita difficile: La Sarfatti fra arte e fascismo." *Art Dossier* (January 1987).

CURTI CUCCIATI, ANGELA. "Un'amica di Mussolini racconta." *Oggi* (November 10, 17, and 24, 1947).

DE BEGNAC, YVON. *Taccuini mussoliniani.* Bologna, 1990.

DE FELICE, RENZO. *Mussolini il rivoluzionario, 1883–1920.* Turin, 1965.

————. *Mussolini il fascista,* I: *La conquista del potere, 1921–1925.* Turin, 1966.

————. *Mussolini il fascista,* II: *L'organizzazione dello stato fascista, 1925–1929.* Turin, 1968.

————. *Mussolini il duce,* I: *Gli anni del consenso, 1929–1936.* Turin, 1974.

————. *Mussolini il duce,* II: *Lo stato totalitario, 1936–1940.* Turin, 1981.

————. *Mussolini l'alleato, I: L'Italia in guerra, 1940–43.* Turin, 1990.

————. *Storia degli ebrei italiani sotto il fascismo,* 4th ed. Turin, 1988.

DE GRAZIA, VICTORIA. "Il fascino del priapo: Margherita Sarfatti, biografa del duce." *Memoria* (June 1982).

DELLA PORTA, A.F. *Polemica sul "Novecento."* Milan, 1930.

DE MICHELI, MARIO. *Le circostanze dell'arte.* Genoa, 1987.

DE SETA, CESARE. *La cultura architettonica in Italia tra le due guerre.* 2 vols. Rome-Bari, 1978.

ETLIN, RICHARD A. *Modernism in Italian Architecture, 1890–1940.* Cambridge, Mass., 1991.

FRANCHI, ENRICO. "Mercoledì sera: Casa Sarfatti." *Corriere Adriatico* (July 8, 1926).

GINZBURG, NATALIA. *Lessico famigliare.* Turin, 1963.

GIULIANI, ROSAMARIA. "Margherita Sarfatti: L'arte applicata e l'architettura," in *La cultura italiana negli anni '30–'45 (Omaggio ad Alfonso Gatto).* Tomo II. Naples, 1984.

GUSPINI, UGO. *L'orecchio del regime: Le intercettazioni telefoniche al tempo del fascismo.* Milan, 1973.

"Judith." "She Is the Comrade of Il Duce." *The American Hebrew* (October 4, 1929).

LEDEEN, MICHAEL L. *The First Duce: D'Annunzio at Fiume.* Baltimore, 1977.

LOWE, CORINNE. "The Woman Behind Mussolini." *Pictorial Review* (September 1934).

LYTTELTON, ADRIAN. *The Seizure of Power: Fascism in Italy, 1919–1929.* New York, 1973.

MAHLER-WERFEL, ALMA. *Mein Leben.* Frankfurt, 1960.

MARPICATI, ARTURO. *Saggi di letteratura.* Florence, 1933.

MARZORATI, SERGIO. *Margherita Sarfatti: Saggio biografico.* Como, 1990.

MASSARA, GIUSEPPE. *Viaggiatori italiani in America (1860–1970).* Rome, 1976.

MELDINI, PIERO. "La sventurata Margherita: Panzini e la Sarfatti," in Ennio Grassi, ed. *Alfredo Panzini nella cultura letteraria italiana fra '800 e '900.* Rimini, 1985.

MICHAELIS, MEIR. *Mussolini and the Jews: German-Italian Relations and the Jewish Question in Italy, 1922–1945.* Oxford, 1978.

MORGAN, THOMAS B. *Spurs on the Boot: Italy Under Her Masters.* New York, 1941.

[MORGAN, THOMAS B.]. "Woman Rebuilds Old Rome." *New York World Telegram* (February 6, 1926).

MUSSOLINI, EDVIGE. *Mio fratello Benito,* ed. Rosetta Ricci Crisolini. Florence, 1957.

MUSSOLINI, RACHELE. *Benito il mio uomo.* Milan, 1958.

————. *Mussolini: An Intimate Biography.* New York, 1974.

MUSSOLINI, VITTORIO. *Mussolini e gli uomini nel suo tempo.* Rome, 1977.

NAHON, UMBERTO. "La polemica antisionista del *Popolo di Roma* nel 1928," in D. Carpi, A. Milano, and U. Nahon, eds., *Scritti in memoria di Enzo Sereni: Saggi sull'ebraismo romana.* Jerusalem, 1970.

NAVARRA, QUINTO. *Memorie del cameriere di Mussolini.* Milan, 1972.

NEGRI, ADA. *Orazioni.* Milan, 1918.

————. *Poesie.* Verona, 1948.

"NEMO" [JAMES VINCENT MURPHY]. "Italy Revelations." *The Star* (February 10–22, 1941). Articles cited:

"Mussolini is [sic] Out for Lunch." February 10, 1941.

"She Dreamed of a New Empire." February 13, 1941.

"Mussolini's Evil Genius." February 14, 1941.

NOZZOLI, ANNA. "Margherita Sarfatti, organizzatrice di cultura: *Il Popolo d'Italia,*" in Marina Addis Saba, ed. *La corporazione delle donne: Ricerche e studi sui modelli femminili nel ventennio fascista.* Florence, 1988.

OJETTI, UGO. *I taccuini, 1914–1943.* Florence, 1954.

ORLANDO, GUIDO. *Confessions of a Scoundrel.* As told to Sam Merwin. Philadelphia, 1954.

PERFETTI, FRANCESCO. "Arte e fascismo tra 'Novecento' e 'Novecento Italiano.'" *Storia contemporanea* (April 1981).

PERSONÈ, LUIGI MARIA. *Le belle statuine.* Florence, 1930.

———, ed. *Il primo passo: Confessioni di scrittori contemporanei.* Florence, 1930.

———. "Nel salotto della Sarfatti." *La Nazione* (September 18, 1989).

PHILLIPS, JOSEPH B. "Italy's Heroine of Fascism." *New York Herald Tribune Sunday Magazine* (October 8, 1933).

PIERONI BORTOLOTTI, FRANCA. *Femminismo e partiti politici in Italia, 1919–1926.* Rome, 1978.

———. *Socialismo e questione femminile in Italia, 1892–1922.* Milan, 1974.

PIGATO, G. B. "Margherita Sarfatti come la conobbi io." *Como* (Winter 1961).

PINI, GIORGIO, AND DULIO SUSMEL. *Mussolini l'uomo e l'opera.* 4 vols. Florence, 1953–55.

PODENZANI, NINO. *Il libro di Ada Negri.* Milan, 1969.

PONTIGGIA, ELENA. "Il miraggio della classicità: Cenni sulla poetica del Novecento," in *Italia anni trenta: Opere dalle collezioni d'arte del comune di Milano.* Milan, 1989.

PORTA MUSA, CARLA. "Il Soldo e Margherita Sarfatti." *Il Foglietto* (February 7, 1957).

———. "L'ultimo giorno di Margherita Sarfatti." *Como* (Spring 1962).

PREZZOLINI, GIUSEPPE. *Diario, 1900–1941.* Milan, 1978.

RAFANELLI, LEDA. *Una donna e Mussolini.* Milan, 1946.

RICCIO, BIANCA. "Margherita 'la regina.'" *La Repubblica Mercurio* (April 29, 1984).

Roberto Sarfatti. Le sue lettere e testimonianze di lui. Milan, 1919.

ROBERTS, KENNETH. *I Wanted to Write.* Garden City, N.Y.; 1949.

ROSSI, CESARE. *Mussolini com'era.* Rome, 1947.

SALVAGNINI, SILENO. "L'avanguardia arriva dal Nord." *Arte* (September 1991).

———. "Margherita Sarfatti: Una vita nella tormenta." *Arte* (October 1991).

———. "Mussolini le intimò: 'Smetto di confondere Novecento con fascismo.'" *Arte* (November 1991).

SARFATTI, MARGHERITA GRASSINI. *Achille Funi.* Milan, 1925.

———. *Acqua passata.* Rocca San Casciano, 1955.

———. *L'America, ricerca della felicità.* Milan, 1937.

———. *L'amore svalutato.* Rome, 1958.

———. *Así veo yo el Uruguay.* Montevideo, 1941.

———. *Casanova: Amores de juventud.* Buenos Aires, 1943.

———. *Casanova contro Don Giovanni.* Verona, 1950.

———. *Daniele Ranzoni.* Rome, 1935.

———. *Dux.* Milan, 1926.

———. *Espejo de la pintura actual.* Buenos Aires, 1947.

———. *La fiaccola accesa.* Milan, 1919.

———. *Giorgione, el pintor misterio.* Buenos Aires, 1944.

———. *Jules Laforgue.* Milan, 1917.

———. *The Life of Benito Mussolini.* London, 1925.

———. *La milizia femminile in Francia.* Milan, 1915.

———. "Mussolini: Como lo conocí." *Crítica* (June 18–July 3, 1945).

———. *Il palazzone.* Milan, 1929.

———. *Segni, colori, e luci.* Bologna, 1925.

———. *Segni del meridiano.* Naples, 1931.

———. *Storia della pittura moderna.* Rome, 1930.

———. *Tiziano, o de la fè en la vida.* Buenos Aires, 1944.

———. *Tunisiaca.* Milan, 1924.

———. *Vasari y sus tiempos.* Buenos Aires, 1947.

———. *I vivi e l'ombra.* 1st edition, Milan, 1921; 2nd edition, Milan, 1934.

SCHIAVI, ALESSANDRO, AND FRANCO PEDONE. *Filippo Turati e Anna Kuliscioff: Carteggio.* 7 vol. Turin, 1977.

SCHULENBURG, WERNER VON DER. "Um Benito Mussolini." Unpublished typescript in Biblioteca Comunale di Como, Italy.

SETON-WATSON, CHRISTOPHER. *Italy from Liberalism to Fascism, 1870–1925.* London, 1967.

"Si è spenta Margherita Sarfatti, biografa di Benito Mussolini." *Corriere della Sera* (October 31, 1961).

"Signora Sarfatti: Il Duce's Aide, Oracle of Italy's Art." *Newsweek* (April 28, 1934).

STAGLIENO, MARCELLO. "Margherita Sarfatti, la ninfa Egeria del Duce." *Il Giornale* (July 28, 1987).

SUSMEL, DUILIO, ED. *Carteggio Arnaldo–Benito Mussolini.* Florence, 1954.

SUSMEL, EDOARDO AND DUILIO, EDS. *Opera omnia di Benito Mussolini.* Florence, 1952.

———. *Opera omnia di Benito Mussolini: Appendici.* Florence, 1978–81.

TEMPESTI, FERNANDO. *Arte dell'Italia fascista.* Milan, 1976.

TONELLI, LUIGI. *Alla ricerca della personalità.* Catania, 1929.

TRAPANI, FRANCAMARIA. "Mia madre Margherita Sarfatti, la grande passione di Mussolini." *Gente* (September 10, 1982).

———. "Fu mia madre a convincerlo: 'Benito, sposa la tua Rachele." *Gente* (September 17, 1982).

———. "Dovette fuggire dall'Italia, e per lei Mussolini non mosse un dito." *Gente* (September 24, 1982).

TRIONFERA, RENZO. "Margherita e Benito: Bacia le lettere di Mussolini e le vende all'America." *L'Europeo* (December 12, 1948).

VILLAROEL, GIUSEPPE. "Margherita Sarfatti." *Giornale dell'Isola* (July 4, 1921).

———. "Margherita Sarfatti, l'irriducibile." *Il Giornale d'Italia* (March 10, 1950).

VITA-FINZI, PAOLO. *Giorni lontani: Appunti e ricordi.* Bologna, 1989.